The Soka Gakkai

Dictionary of Buddhism

The Soka Gakkai

DICTIONARY OF BUDDHISM

The English Buddhist Dictionary Committee

[redacted]

MOTILAL BANARSIDASS PUBLISHERS
PRIVATE LIMITED • DELHI

First Indian Edition: Delhi, **2009**
Earlier Published in 2002 by Soka Gakkai
32, Shinanomachi, Shinjuku-ku, Tokyo 160-8583, Japan

ISBN: 978-81-208-3334-0

MOTILAL BANARSIDASS
41 U.A. Bungalow Road, Jawahar Nagar, Delhi 110 007
8 Mahalaxmi Chamber, 22 Bhulabhai Desai Road, Mumbai 400 026
203 Royapettah High Road, Mylapore, Chennai 600 004
236, 9th Main III Block, Jayanagar, Bangalore 560 011
Sanas Plaza, 1302 Baji Rao Road, Pune 411 002
8 Camac Street, Kolkata 700 017
Ashok Rajpath, Patna 800 004
Chowk, Varanasi 221 001

[redacted]

PRINTED IN INDIA

BY JAINENDRA PRAKASH JAIN AT SHRI JAINENDRA PRESS,
A-45 NARAINA, PHASE-I, NEW DELHI 110 028
AND PUBLISHED BY NARENDRA PRAKASH JAIN FOR
MOTILAL BANARSIDASS PUBLISHERS PRIVATE LIMITED,
BUNGALOW ROAD, DELHI 110 007

Contents

Foreword

Fifty years ago, in 1952, the Soka Gakkai published the *Nichiren Daishonin gosho zenshū* (The Complete Works of Nichiren Daishonin). The publication project was initiated and supervised by Jōsei Toda, the second president of the Soka Gakkai. On the fiftieth anniversary of that important event, it is my pleasure to witness the publication of a new English dictionary of Buddhist terms, *The Soka Gakkai Dictionary of Buddhism*.

Since the publication of the Soka Gakkai edition of Nichiren's writings, their translation into various languages has been progressing steadily. In the fall of 1999, the Soka Gakkai published *The Writings of Nichiren Daishonin,* which contains English translations of fully half the writings in the Japanese edition, and those translations have been enthusiastically welcomed by persons interested in Nichiren Buddhism.

The members of the Soka Gakkai practice Nichiren Buddhism, which is based on the Lotus Sutra, a text embodying the essence of Mahayana Buddhism. Nichiren Buddhism has inherited the idea expressed in the sutra that all people are capable of achieving Buddhahood, and the great vow of the Buddha to enable all people to do so. The aim of Nichiren Buddhism is to realize that great vow in our present age, the Latter Day of the Law.

This new dictionary focuses largely on Nichiren Buddhism. But it is my conviction that by studying Nichiren Buddhism, one can familiarize oneself with the core of Mahayana Buddhist thought, which expresses the central teaching of the Buddha aimed at enabling everyone to attain enlightenment.

The Buddhist idea that everyone possesses the Buddha nature, or the potential for enlightenment, expresses a spirit of profound respect for human beings and leads naturally to a philosophy that deeply treasures life. This in turn can provide a spiritual and philosophical basis for dealing with such modern global issues as the protection of human rights, the preservation of the environment, and the attainment of world peace. In this sense, I believe it is extremely important to understand such Buddhist concepts and consider them in terms of their modern significance.

Mahayana Buddhism originated in India, and in the long process of its transmission to new lands with different cultures, it has evolved into a world religion. We are able to discern the beginnings of Mahayana within the Buddhism of India, but it began to flower and bear fruit in earnest as it encountered and spread among different cultures.

Within this universal religion called Mahayana Buddhism there are some ideas that appear to be contrasting or contradictory. The Lotus Sutra, however, sets forth principles that resolve and integrate those apparent contradictions. In addition, it contains a living system of thought and a spiritual tradition that clearly transmit the essence of Buddhism.

For example, regarding the method or way to achieve enlightenment, Buddhist tradition speaks of two contrasting approaches: the power of self and the power of another. The school of Buddhism known as Pure Land attributes salvation to the power of another, that is, to the saving grace of Amida Buddha, while Zen Buddhism advocates salvation through the power of self, or the discipline of seated meditation.

Each of those views offers a partial perspective and, taken by itself, may be considered biased or one-sided. Through the unifying principle expressed in the Lotus Sutra, however, those contrasting views are integrated and resolved, giving rise to the concept of the fusion of self and other. In short, salvation or enlightenment in Buddhism is best achieved by bringing forth the powers of the Buddha and the Law (the power of another) through the power of one's own faith and practice (the power of self).

In another example, from a psychological perspective, earthly desires, which Buddhism regards as the cause of suffering, stand in stark contrast to *bodhi,* or the enlightenment of the Buddha. That is why early Buddhism taught that enlightenment can only be gained by extinguishing earthly desires.

Mahayana Buddhism, however, ultimately views enlightenment and desire as inseparable, in a relationship described as "two but not two." It treats them as mutually inclusive aspects of the same reality. Though one may speak of desires and illusions, they originate from the essential nature of life itself, or the Dharma nature, and in that sense are no different from enlightenment.

The Great Teacher T'ien-t'ai, in his work *Great Concentration and Insight,* states: "Ignorance or illusions are in themselves enlightenment to the essential nature of phenomena. But due to the influence of delusions enlightenment changes into ignorance." This expresses the principle of non-duality described in the phrase "earthly desires are none other than enlightenment." The meaning of this principle is that, though one does not extinguish one's desires and illusions, by developing the wisdom of enlightenment, one is no longer tormented by them; that is, desires and illusions cease to function as negative influences in one's life.

The resolution of contending viewpoints in the above examples also suggests that, when we view things from the perspective of Buddhist wisdom, it is possible to transform the division and contention of today's world into harmony and cooperation.

Naturally, human beings themselves are essential to this process. This is because the various contradictions we see in society and the world ultimately boil down to contradictions within the human being. Buddhism aims to shed light on and thoroughly examine the complex inner realm of the human being and thereby provide a broad and comprehensive overview of life itself.

When we assess things from this holistic perspective, it becomes evident that even life and death are actually "not two"; that is, they are one in their essential nature.

How do we keep ourselves at peace with and transcend the problem of death, our unavoidable destiny as human beings? In a speech I delivered in 1993 at Harvard University, I spoke of the Mahayana Buddhist view of life and death, and its aim "to enable us to know a deep and abiding joy in death as well as life."

Once we are born into the world, none of us can escape death. To address and resolve the problems and suffering associated with life and death, living and dying, is perhaps the most important problem facing humanity in the twenty-first century.

Buddhism elucidates the essential equality present on the level of life itself. It enables people to make the most of their unique natures and qualities, just as "cherry, plum, peach, and apricot" blossoms, to cite a familiar Buddhist metaphor, each display unique color and fragrance. The aim of Buddhism is to enable people to bring forth and display the innate and enduring power of life itself, to remain unbent and unbowed by any hardship or opposition, and to fully enjoy a condition of absolute happiness—enduring happiness that emerges from within and is not dependent on externals. It is a philosophy of life reformation by which one can completely transform tragedy, even death, into profound joy based on an eternal view of life.

Buddhism places strong emphasis on the human heart and mind. We can summarize its message as follows: If people's hearts and minds change, everything changes. It is the perspective of Buddhism that both conflict and peace arise from the human mind. Mind, however, is not limited to mere process of thought.

An early Buddhist text known as the *Dhammapada* reads: "Hard it is to train the mind, which goes where it likes and does what it wants. But a trained mind brings health and happiness." And the same text states: "For hatred can never put an end to hatred; love alone can. This is an unalterable law" (*Dhammapada*, 3.35 and 1.5, trans. by Eknath Easwaran, Penguin Books, 1987).

The famous opening line of the Preamble to the UNESCO Constitution reads, "Since wars begin in the minds of men, it is in the minds of men that the defenses of peace must be constructed." In other words, only when human beings achieve real peace of mind can world peace be possible.

The fundamental goal of Buddhism is to enable people to build a "fortress of peace and happiness" within their hearts and minds. It is from here that the real path to world peace begins.

Buddhism enables everyone to achieve inner peace, which is inseparable from world peace, through a transformation of life, that most fundamental of changes that occurs through Buddhist practice. Global peace will, therefore, be realized if this principle and its practical application are shared among people.

A Buddhist writing states, "The Law does not spread by itself. Because the people spread it, both the people and the Law are respectworthy" (*Gosho zenshū*, p. 856).

If the Buddha, having awakened to the Dharma, or Law of life, had not endeavored to teach it to others, his enlightenment would have been incomplete. Moreover, even though the Buddha himself expounded this Law, without others to spread it, it would not have benefited the people.

We of the Soka Gakkai earnestly hope our publication of English works, such as the translation of Nichiren's writings and this dictionary, may serve to make the wisdom of Buddhism accessible to more people, enabling them to find a way to true happiness and thereby contributing to the realization of a peaceful world. If, by encountering this dictionary, many people are able to deepen their understanding of and appreciation for Buddhist philosophy, I will be deeply gratified.

Finally, I want to extend my heartfelt appreciation to those who have assisted with the preparation and editing of this dictionary.

Daisaku Ikeda
President, Soka Gakkai International

Preface

As of the publication of *The Soka Gakkai Dictionary of Buddhism,* there are virtually no other English-language dictionaries of Buddhist terms in print in which so many entries are given in their English translation. It is thus the editors' hope that this volume may contribute substantially to the information available to English-speaking students of Buddhism.

This dictionary is a completely revised and dramatically expanded version of *A Dictionary of Buddhist Terms and Concepts* (1983) published by the Nichiren Shoshu International Center (NSIC). The present new dictionary is a byproduct of nearly three decades of translation work aimed at making the writings of Nichiren, the thirteenth-century Japanese founder of a Buddhist tradition that has gained worldwide popularity, accessible to readers of English.

The translation of Nichiren's writings has been carried on by the Soka Gakkai to promote worldwide understanding of Nichiren's teachings and of Buddhism in general. Nichiren wrote prolifically, offering detailed explanations of Buddhist philosophy based on the Lotus Sutra, as well as direct encouragement to practitioners. His writings range from short letters to major treatises. Nichiren was thoroughly familiar with the extensive body of Buddhist literature available in Japan in the thirteenth century. To illustrate his points and support his arguments, he referred in his writings to concepts found not only in the Lotus Sutra, but in the Buddhist tradition as a whole.

We hope this volume will shed light on the many references to Buddhist terms, concepts, traditions, scriptures, and commentaries, and historical events, persons, and places that appear in Nichiren's writings. It should also be noted that the dictionary is not limited to ideas and concepts directly related to Nichiren or the Lotus Sutra. The editors have tried to include as many entries as possible that would be of interest to students of Buddhism in general.

Of course, a single dictionary cannot cover the entire history and philosophical development of Buddhism, which spread from India, the country of its origin, southward to Sri Lanka and to Southeast Asia, and northeast to Central Asia, China, Tibet, Korea, and Japan, and today is regarded as a major world religion. Any treatment of Buddhism is bound to take on a certain perspective. Buddhist scholarship in the West has tended to focus on the teachings and traditions of the Pali canon, that is, the scriptures of the Theravāda, or Southern, Buddhist tradition. Zen, a tradition that attaches great importance to meditation, often symbolizes Buddhism as a whole to those in the West, and many have studied Buddhism from its unique perspective.

Nichiren and his contemporaries in Japan had access to the body of teachings that arose as Buddhism spread from India northeast, particularly to China, and later Korea and Japan. Much of the reference material drawn upon in the compilation of this dictionary is in the Japanese language, though Chinese, English, and Sanskrit sources were also consulted. The Buddhist history and works of Southeast Asian countries, which each possess a rich and long Buddhist tradition, are not covered in any detail here. Nor are those of Korea or Tibet, though an entry on Tibetan Buddhism is included. Language references in this dictionary accordingly are limited to Sanskrit, Pali, Chinese, and Japanese.

The dictionary contains more than 2,700 entries, including cross references. Most entries appear as the English translation of a term or concept. The titles of most Buddhist scriptures appear in English, too, while biographical and geographical names are in their original languages, except when the original-language name is unknown or when persons assumed different names in the countries where they went to live.

Non-English words are romanized for the reader's convenience. The Chinese-character rendering provided for almost every entry appears in brackets following the entry. Sanskrit and Pali words are romanized as they are pronounced; diacritical marks are omitted in the text, but are shown in the appendixes. The names of Buddhas and bodhisattvas are in most cases given in English, with their original names in parentheses, to convey the meaning those names represent.

English translations of the same Buddhist term often differ. For example, the Sanskrit *pancha-skandha* is variously rendered as the five components (of life), five aggregates, or five *skandhas*. The Japanese word *bompu* is translated as ordinary persons, common mortals, or worldlings. Though all possible translations are not listed as entries, you will find many of them referenced under related entries. For those who read Japanese, a cross-referenced list of Japanese terms and names refers to their equivalents in English and/or their original language.

This dictionary should be especially useful for the readers of Nichiren's works as they appear in the volume *The Writings of Nichiren Daishonin,* published in 1999 by the Soka Gakkai. The dictionary lists as entries Buddhist terms as they appear in that work. As mentioned above, the dictionary also includes terms and subjects not found in Nichiren's writings, but that students of Buddhism in general may find interesting and instructive.

We recommend that you read "Guide to the Dictionary" to make the most of this reference work as you travel through the world of Buddhism.

The English Buddhist Dictionary Committee

Guide to the Dictionary

Buddhist terms

Any established field of human thought, belief, or endeavor has a list of specialized terms and concepts that convey specific meaning within that field. Buddhism, too, has developed its own vocabulary to convey in precise form its unique ideas, concepts, and beliefs. The earliest Buddhist terms were set down in writing in the Indic languages of Sanskrit and Pali, and many more were formulated later, as Buddhism spread to China and Japan. Buddhism has more recently taken its place as a global religion, and much effort has been made to translate those terms into other languages.

It is our conviction that Buddhist study should not merely be the province of academic specialists, but an integral part of a living religion; it should provide a foundation for the faith and practice of Buddhists, and impart to anyone interested an understanding of the humane principles of Buddhist philosophy. For this reason, we have for some time adhered to an editorial policy of translating Buddhist terms into English wherever possible, so that the concepts they express may be more readily assimilated and applied by English-speaking students of Buddhism. The reader will therefore find that the majority of Buddhist term entries in this dictionary are given in English.

There are, however, a few groups of exceptions. The first are those words of Indic origin, such as karma, nirvana, or bodhisattva, which have no precise English equivalents. Some of these words have already become a part of the English language, and appear in standard English dictionaries. Many more of these terms, even though used frequently in Buddhist scriptures, have yet to be assimilated into English. Another group comprises Japanese terms and expressions that were not translated for lack of good English equivalents and because of their familiarity to practitioners of Nichiren Buddhism. These include such terms as ***daimoku, gongyō, shōju,*** and ***shakubuku,*** which have been listed as they are, in Japanese pronunciation.

All the entry items appear in roman type, except for the titles of Buddhist documents other than sutras, such as treatises and commentaries, which are italicized throughout. Terms in a language other than English (those not found in a standard English dictionary) are italicized in the body of a definition. Moreover, most are identified as Sanskrit (Skt), Pali, or Japanese (Jpn) in parentheses, but when the language is evident in the context, it is not explicitly indicated. How to locate specific entries is explained later in this Guide.

Proper names

The names of actual historical figures are given in the language of their country of origin, except in cases where they have moved from one country to another and their original names are not known, or where they have become so closely identified with their adopted country that their original names are rarely used (e.g., Ganjin). The names of historical figures in India are generally given in their Sanskrit, rather than Pali, form. Chinese names are romanized according to the Wade-Giles system, with the alternate pinyin romanization given in parentheses following the name entry. Japanese and Chinese personal names appear with the family name first and the given name second, except for modern Japanese persons, in which case the given name comes first.

Most of the names of the Buddhas, bodhisattvas, deities, and mythical personages are translated into English, following the example of the Central Asian monk Kumārajīva (344–413) who, when translating Sanskrit Buddhist sutras into Chinese, rendered the meaning of such names into Chinese. For instance, a Buddha named Prabhūtaratna appears as the Buddha Many Treasures, and the bodhisattva Sadāparibhūta, as the bodhisattva Never Disparaging. Sanskrit equivalents, where known, appear in parentheses following a name entry. The names of most Buddhist schools are also rendered in English. In the cases of proper names where the meaning of the Chinese original is unclear, or where the Sanskrit original is unknown, the name is presented in romanized Japanese (e.g., the kings Sen'yo and Dammira). Persons with the same name in romanized form are listed as separate definitions within the same entry.

Titles of sutras, treatises, commentaries, and other works are given mostly in English. Except for those of sutras, titles of works are italicized (e.g., *Great Concentration and Insight*). Sanskrit and Chinese equivalents, where applicable, appear in parentheses following a title entry. The titles of sutras that retain their Sanskrit names, such as the Susiddhikara Sutra, appear in romanized Sanskrit. Longer titles of works may appear in shortened form in the body of a definition.

Names of historical places are in the language of the country where they are located. Names of places appearing only in the sutras or other writings are given either in Sanskrit (e.g., Jambudvīpa, Mount Sumeru) or in English (Heat-Free Lake, Snow Mountains).

Romanization

Sanskrit and Pali words are romanized according to pronunciation, with macrons indicating long vowels; the elaborate diacritical marks required by strict Indology are not used in the body of the dictionary itself. For reference, readers may consult the list of Sanskrit and Pali Words (Appendix A), which shows all diacritical marks.

Chinese words, with a few exceptions, are romanized according to the traditional Wade-Giles system. The newer pinyin system equivalents, designated by the letters PY, appear in parentheses following Chinese name or place entries. Readers may also refer to the list of Chinese Proper Names (Appendix B), which gives the pinyin equivalents. Tibetan personal names are romanized according to pronunciation.

Japanese words are romanized according to the modified Hepburn system. The Japanese syllable ending *"n"* when it appears before *b, m,* or *p* is rendered *m,* as it is pronounced (e.g., *sambō* [three treasures], *hommon* [essential teaching], *jūjō-kampō* [ten meditations]), except when separated from these letters by a hyphen (Jōken-bō). Long vowels are indicated by macrons on all words, with the exception of well-known place names (Kyoto, Tokyo) and a few frequently used Buddhist words (Nam-myoho-renge-kyo, Myoho-renge-kyo; though the components of these include macrons, as in *myōhō, myō, hō,* and *kyō*). In Japanese words and expressions, hyphens are sometimes used to set off syllables in order to highlight their meaning or pronunciation. In proper nouns, a hyphen appears before the ending terms *kyō* (sutra), *ji* (temple), *shū* (school), *koku* (country), etc. (e.g., Hoke-kyō, Tōdai-ji, Shingon-shū), except when they are inseparable in terms of pronunciation (Daijikkyō).

Chinese characters

The Chinese or Japanese characters for each entry are given in brackets, and their reading in romanized Japanese appears in parentheses immediately following the entry word. In a few cases, for reasons of style or convention, the entry word and its accompanying Japanese form may differ slightly. For example, the entry "Ajātashatru" is followed by the character reading "Ajase-ō" (meaning "King Ajātashatru"; the Japanese ending "ō" in this case means "king"), because the title of king, by convention, usually appears together with the name in Chinese and Japanese texts.

Locating entries

Entry titles are listed in alphabetical order. If you know the exact wording of a particular entry, you can look it up directly. The alphabetization is letter by letter, not word by word.

Few Japanese terms appear as entries; if you know the Japanese for a particular name or term but are not sure about the English, please consult the list of Terms and Names in Japanese (Appendix J) to find how it is listed as an entry. Romanized Japanese equivalents of virtually all entries in the dictionary, as well as terms that appear in the body of the definitions, are listed in alphabetical order in that appendix, followed by Chinese characters in parentheses and the corresponding entry. For example:

Agon-gyō (阿含経): Āgama sutras
gojū-no-sōtai (五重の相対): fivefold comparison
Tendai (天台): T'ien-t'ai

Similarly, if you know a Sanskrit or Pali term but cannot find it as an entry, you may refer to the list of Sanskrit and Pali Terms and Names (Appendix F). For example:

cintāmani	wish-granting jewel (如意宝珠)
Sadāparibhūta	Never Disparaging (常不軽菩薩)

Buddhist terms appearing without explanation in the body of a definition generally also are listed as independent entries, but are not highlighted in the text.

Names, places, and terms are listed exactly as they appear in *The Writings of Nichiren Daishonin* in almost all cases. In the few cases where they differ, a cross reference is included.

Other information

Ages of Chinese and Japanese individuals are given according to the traditional way of reckoning in these countries, in which a child is regarded as one year old at birth and a year is added to his or her age with the passing of each New Year's Day.

Concerning dates, in pre-modern times, Japan and China recorded dates in terms of a lunar calendar. Thus, the date of Nichiren's birth is the sixteenth day of the second lunar month of 1222, which corresponds to April 6, 1222, in the Gregorian, or solar, calendar.

References to specific chapters of the Lotus Sutra are based on the Lotus

Sutra of the Wonderful Law, the twenty-eight-chapter Chinese translation by Kumārajīva. The quotations from the Lotus Sutra are based primarily on the English translation by Dr. Burton Watson (*The Lotus Sutra:* Columbia University Press, New York, 1993). In addition, in citing Nichiren's words, we have used *The Writings of Nichiren Daishonin,* published in 1999 by the Soka Gakkai. For the convenience of the reader, the numbers in parentheses following the quotations indicate the page numbers therein.

Certain entries serve both as brief explanations on general subjects and as cross references to the same subjects treated at greater length and in greater depth elsewhere.

Concerning denominations above one million, this dictionary uses the American system, i.e., 1,000 millions is a billion.

Regarding assignment of birth and death dates, nothing at all is specified for Shakyamuni's contemporaries, since scholarly opinion is invariably widely divided.

In accordance with recent developments in American English usage, instead of the era identifiers B.C. (before Christ) and A.D. (anno Domini), the abbreviations B.C.E. (before the Common Era) and C.E. (Common Era) are employed in the dictionary.

List of Abbreviations

b.	born
B.C.E.	before the Common Era
c.	circa
C.E.	Common Era
Chin	Chinese (Wade-Giles)
d.	died
Jpn	Japanese
Kor	Korean
n.d.	no dates
PY	pinyin
r.	reign
Skt	Sanskrit
WG	Wade-Giles

Dictionary of Buddhism

A

Ābhāsvara Heaven [光音天] (Skt; Jpn Kō'on-ten): One of the eighteen heavens in the world of form. *See* Light Sound Heaven.

abhidharma [阿毘達磨] (Skt; Pali *abhidhamma;* Jpn *abidatsuma*): Doctrinal treatise and commentary. One of the three divisions of the Buddhist canon, the other two being sutras and *vinaya* (rules of monastic discipline). *Dharma* means the Law or the Buddha's teachings, and *abhi* literally means to, toward, or upon. *Abhidharma* means "upon the Law" and refers to commentaries on the Law, that is, doctrinal studies of the Buddha's teachings, or the sutras. Between the fourth and the first centuries B.C.E., schisms arose repeatedly within the Buddhist Order, resulting in the formation of twenty schools. Many of those schools worked out their own doctrinal systematizations of the sutras, and these were included in the *abhidharma.*

The Sarvāstivāda school, the most influential of the Hinayana schools, produced a number of *abhidharma* works. Among these, *The Treatise on the Source of Wisdom,* written by Kātyāyanīputra in the second century B.C.E., contributed greatly to the development of Sarvāstivāda thought and formed the basis for further studies. Some two hundred years later, a voluminous commentary on *The Treatise on the Source of Wisdom* called *The Great Commentary on the Abhidharma* was completed. *The Dharma Analysis Treasury,* by Vasubandhu (fourth or fifth century), is often regarded as the pinnacle of *abhidharma* literature because it explains the contents of the above two works, reexamines traditional Sarvāstivāda doctrines, and cites the studies of a number of other schools; it is therefore an invaluable reference for the study of the *abhidharma* in general. Very few Sanskrit *abhidharma* manuscripts are extant; most are known through their Chinese translations. The present Theravāda school of Southern Buddhism has a collection of seven Pali works that comprise the *abhidharma* of this school.

Abhidharmakosha [阿毘達磨俱舍論] (Skt; Jpn *Abidatsuma-kusha-ron*): See *Dharma Analysis Treasury, The.*

Abhidharma school [毘曇宗] (Skt; Chin P'i-t'an-tsung; Jpn Bidon-shū): Also known as the P'i-t'an school. One of the so-called thirteen schools of Chinese Buddhism, the Abhidharma school prospered in northern China during the Northern and Southern Dynasties period (439–589). It based its teachings on *abhidharma* works such as

Dharmashrī's *Heart of the Abhidharma* and Dharmatrāta's *Supplement to "The Heart of the Abhidharma."* Hence the name of the Abhidharma school. P'i-t'an is the Chinese transliteration of *abhidharma*. The Sanskrit term *abhidharma* means doctrinal commentary, one of the three divisions of the Buddhist canon, the other two being sutras and *vinaya* (rules of monastic discipline). The twenty Hinayana schools in India, particularly the Sarvāstivāda, produced *abhidharma* works. During the Northern and Southern Dynasties period in China, they were regarded as essential references on Buddhist doctrine. Later in the seventh century, when Hsüan-tsang translated *The Dharma Analysis Treasury, The Great Commentary on the Abhidharma,* and other *abhidharma* works into Chinese, the Dharma Analysis Treasury (Chü-she) school absorbed the rapidly declining Abhidharma school.

Abhirati [阿比羅提] (Skt; Jpn Ahiradai): Also, Land of Joy. The land of the Buddha Akshobhya in the east. This land is described in the Land of Akshobhya Buddha Sutra. *See also* Akshobhya.

abhisheka [灌頂] (Skt; Jpn *kanjō*): A ceremony commonly performed in Esoteric Buddhism to invest the recipient with a certain status. *See* ceremony of anointment.

absolute myō [絶待妙] (Jpn *zetsudai-myō*): One of two contrasting perspectives that demonstrate the profundity of the Lotus Sutra. See *myō*.

Abutsu-bō [阿仏房] (d. 1279): Also known as Abutsu-bō Nittoku. A lay follower of Nichiren who lived in the province of Sado, an island in the Sea of Japan. His secular name was Endō Tamemori. Tradition has it that Abutsu-bō was once a samurai who served the Retired Emperor Juntoku in Kyoto and accompanied him to Sado Island when Juntoku was banished there after an abortive attempt by the imperial court to overthrow the Kamakura shogunate in what is known as the Jōkyū Disturbance of 1221. According to recent studies, however, it seems more probable that he was actually a native of Sado. When Nichiren was exiled to Sado in late 1271, Abutsu-bō, an ardent Pure Land believer, visited him at Tsukahara to confront him in debate. Bested in debate by Nichiren, who refuted the Pure Land teachings, Abutsu-bō converted to Nichiren's teachings together with his wife, the lay nun Sennichi. The couple sincerely assisted Nichiren during his exile, supplying him with food and other necessities for more than two years until he was pardoned and left the island in 1274. After Nichiren went to live at the foot of Mount Minobu, Abutsu-bō, despite his advanced age, made at least three journeys to visit him with offerings. Abutsu-bō is said to have died on the twenty-first day of the third month, 1279, at age ninety-one. In 1279 his son, Tōkurō Moritsuna, traveled to Minobu with Abutsu-bō's ashes and there laid them to rest. Moritsuna continued to uphold Nichiren's teachings, and his grandson, known by his priestly name Nyojaku Nichiman, went as a child to Fuji where he became a disciple of Nikkō, Nichiren's immediate successor.

Accumulated Great Treasures Sutra [大宝積経] (Chin *Ta-pao-chi-ching;* Jpn *Daihōshaku-kyō*): Also known as the Accumulated Treasures Sutra. A compilation of 49 smaller sutras into a single work comprising 77 chapters in 120 volumes. Under the aegis of the imperial court of the T'ang dynasty in China, Bodhiruchi began the translation and compilation of the sutra in 705 and completed it in 713. It contains numerous teachings included in a variety of Mahayana sutras. Among the 49 smaller sutras from which he compiled this sutra, Bodhiruchi translated 26 himself. The remaining 23 had been translated by Kumārajīva, Dharmaraksha (the Dharmaraksha known as the "Bodhisattva of Tun-huang"), and others.

Accumulated Treasures Sutra [宝積経] (Jpn *Hōshaku-kyō*): *See* Accumulated Great Treasures Sutra.

Achala [不動明王] (Skt; Jpn Fudō-myō'ō): The wisdom king Immovable, regarded as the head of the five great wisdom kings. *See* Immovable.

āchārya [阿闍梨] (Skt; Jpn *ajari*): An honorific title meaning teacher, conferred upon a virtuous monk who guides the conduct of disciples and serves as their example. In Japan, *ajari* was a rank in the priesthood, and the term was also used to designate an official post.

acquired enlightenment [始覚] (Jpn *shikaku*): *See* inherent enlightenment.

ādāna-consciousness [阿陀那識] (Skt *ādāna-vijnāna;* Jpn *adana-shiki*): Another name for *ālaya*-consciousness in the Consciousness-Only doctrine. *Ādāna*-consciousness was interpreted in China as "maintaining-consciousness" because it maintains the life and body of a sentient being. See also *ālaya*-consciousness.

administrator of priests [僧正] (Jpn *sōjō*): An official post within the Buddhist clergy in China and Japan. In Japan, the system of supervision of the clergy, with the administrator of priests as the highest post, was established in 624 by the imperial court. Kanroku (Kor Kwallŭk), a priest from the Korean state of Paekche, was appointed the first administrator of priests. In selecting the administrator, the Buddhist community recommended a priest it recognized as being virtuous to the imperial court, which then made the appointment. Later this system for supervising priests became a formality, losing its original significance. This and related titles came to be bestowed on priests simply to honor them. In 1872 the

Meiji government abolished this system, but individual Buddhist schools still privately adhere to it and appoint priests of their own schools to positions similar to the administrator of priests.

Afterword to the Lotus Sutra Translation, The [法華翻経後記] (Chin *Fa-hua-fan-ching-hou-chi;* Jpn *Hokke-hongyō-kōki*): A short account of Kumārajīva's translation of the Lotus Sutra into Chinese and of his work the Lotus Sutra of the Wonderful Law. It was written by the Chinese priest Seng-chao (384–414), one of Kumārajīva's major disciples. This document describes why the Lotus Sutra of the Wonderful Law, or the version translated by Kumārajīva, consists of twenty-eight chapters including the "Devadatta" chapter, while the Lotus Sutra of the Correct Law, Dharmaraksha's version translated prior to Kumārajīva's, consists of twenty-seven chapters. *The Afterword to the Lotus Sutra Translation* is included within *The Lotus Sutra and Its Traditions,* an eighth-century work by Seng-hsiang.

agada [阿伽陀] (Skt, Pali; Jpn *akada*): A medicine in ancient India, believed to be most effective in curing disease. *Agada* is also a common noun for medicine. The beginning *a* of *agada* means not, non-, or without, and *gada* means disease or sickness.

Āgama [阿含] (Skt, Pali; Jpn Agon): "Teachings handed down by tradition." In Buddhism, Āgama was originally a generic term for Shakyamuni's teachings. After the rise of Mahayana, however, it came exclusively to mean the Hinayana teachings and scriptures. The only surviving Āgama scriptures are a Pali version in five sections and a Chinese version in four sections (called the four Āgama sutras). The Pali Āgamas constitute the sutra section of the Pali canon and were set down in writing around the first century B.C.E. Theravāda Buddhism has handed them down in their entirety. *See also* Āgama sutras; five Āgamas; four Āgama sutras.

Āgama period [阿含時] (Skt, Pali; Jpn Agon-ji): The period of the Āgama or Hinayana sutras. The second of the five periods, a classification of Shakyamuni's teachings by T'ien-t'ai. *See* five periods.

Āgama sutras [阿含経] (Skt, Pali; Jpn *Agon-gyō*): A group of sutras containing Shakyamuni's earlier teachings, which Mahayanists later categorized as Hinayana. Āgama means "teachings handed down by tradition." The Chinese Āgama sutras comprise four groups, each containing a number of sutras. The four groups, or the four Āgama sutras, as they are commonly known, are the Long Āgama Sutra, the Medium-Length Āgama Sutra, the Miscellaneous Āgama Sutra, and the Increasing by One Āgama Sutra. Theravāda Buddhism bases itself on the five Āgamas of the Pali canon, which are similar in composition to the four Chinese Āgama sutras. The five Āgamas are *Dīgha-nikāya* (long sutras), *Majjhima-nikāya* (medium-length sutras), *Samyutta-nikāya* (sutras on related topics), *Anguttara-nikāya* (sutras of numerical doctrines), and *Khuddaka-nikāya* (minor sutras). *Nikāya* means group or collection. The first four correspond respectively to the Chinese Long Āgama, Medium-Length Āgama, Miscellaneous Āgama, and Increasing by One Āgama sutras. *See also* five Āgamas; four Āgama sutras.

Agastya [阿竭多仙] (Skt; Jpn Akada-sen): The ascetic Agastya. An Indian ascetic who practiced the Brahmanistic teachings. According to the Nirvana Sutra, he used his supernatural powers to pour the water of the entire Ganges River into his ear and keep it there for twelve years.

age of conflict [闘諍堅固] (Jpn *tōjō-kengo*): *See* age of quarrels and disputes.

age of quarrels and disputes [闘諍堅固] (Jpn *tōjō-kengo*): Also, age of conflict. The last of the five five-hundred-year periods following Shakyamuni's death, which are described in the Great Collection Sutra. It corresponds to the beginning of the Latter Day of the Law. In the Great Collection Sutra, Shakyamuni Buddha speaks to Bodhisattva Moon Storehouse about the first four of the five five-hundred-year periods following his death, and then says that, in the next five hundred years, quarrels and disputes will arise among the followers of his teachings, and that the pure Law will be obscured and lost.

Agnidatta [阿耆達多・阿耆達・阿耆多] (Skt; Jpn Agidatta, Agitatsu, or Agita): Also known as Ajita. A Brahman who lived during the time of Shakyamuni. Agnidatta was a wealthy householder who lived in a district named Vairanjā in Kosala, India. He respected Shakyamuni and invited him to stay at his home for three months. Shakyamuni went to Agnidatta's mansion with his five hundred monk-disciples, but Agnidatta was so completely absorbed in the pursuit of pleasure that he forgot about his invitation and had the gate shut for three months. It was a time of famine, and Shakyamuni's disciples walked about begging for alms, but in vain. Finally, a horse groom offered oats meant as horse fodder to Shakyamuni and his disciples, who survived on this alone for a period of three months. In *The Treatise on the Great Perfection of Wisdom,* this incident is listed as one of the nine great ordeals that Shakyamuni underwent. The Buddha's Preaching Life Sutra and the above treatise describe Agnidatta as a Brahman, while *The Ten Divisions of Monastic Rules* indicates that he was the ruler of Vairanjā and an adherent of Brahmanism.

ahimsā [アヒンサー] (Skt, Pali; Jpn *ahinsā*): The underlying principle of Indian religions and philosophies. *Ahimsā* means non-injury, nonkilling, or nonviolence toward any living being; it is the negation of *himsā,* which means killing. Non-killing, or the preservation of life, is a fundamental ethic in Buddhism as well, ranking first among the five precepts. Based on the principle of *ahimsā*, Buddhists and Jainas opposed the Brahmans and their ritual killing of domestic animals. A ritual called the life-liberating practice, conducted in China and Japan, was an expression of this commitment to avoid killing. In this ceremony, living things such as fish and birds were released into the wild. Jainism is particularly strict in observing the non-killing of any living being and regards this practice as a means of attaining emancipation. In the early twentieth century, Mahatma Gandhi of India developed his idea of *satyāgraha* (devotion to truth) and its application to nonviolent resistance based on *ahimsā*.

Aizen [愛染] (Jpn): The wisdom king Craving-Filled (Aizen-myō'ō). *See* Craving-Filled.

Ajātashatru [阿闍世王] (Skt; Pali Ajātasattu; Jpn Ajase-ō): A king of Magadha in India in the time of Shakyamuni Buddha. Incited by Devadatta, he gained the throne by killing his father, King Bimbisāra, a follower of Shakyamuni. He also made attempts on the lives of the Buddha and his disciples by releasing a drunken elephant upon them. Ajātashatru warred with King Prasenajit of Kosala over the domain of Kāshī, but later made peace with Kosala. During the reign of Prasenajit's son, Virūdhaka, however, Ajātashatru conquered Kosala. Under Ajātashatru's reign, Magadha became the most powerful kingdom in India. Later he converted to Buddhism out of remorse for his evil acts and supported the First Buddhist Council in its compilation of Shakyamuni's teachings undertaken the year following Shakyamuni's death.

According to one account, because King Bimbisāra's wife, Vaidehī, had borne him no heir, he consulted a diviner. The diviner told him of a hermit living in the mountains who would be reborn as Bimbisāra's son after he died. Bimbisāra was so impatient for the birth of his heir that he had the hermit killed. Shortly after, Vaidehī conceived, and the diviner foretold that the child would become the king's enemy. Fearing his son, the king dropped him from atop a tower, but Ajātashatru survived with only a broken finger. Hence he was also called Broken Finger. It is said that he was persuaded to rebel against his father by Devadatta, who revealed to him the story of his birth. After killing his father, however, Ajātashatru came to regret his conduct deeply. Tormented by guilt, he broke out in virulent sores on the fifteenth day of the second month of his fiftieth year, and it was predicted that he would die on the seventh day of the third month. At the advice of his physician and minister Jīvaka, he sought out Shakyamuni, who responded by teaching him the doctrines of the Nirvana Sutra. Ajātashatru was thereby able to eradicate his evil karma and prolong his life. Concerning the Sanskrit name Ajātashatru, *ajāta* means unborn, and *shatru* means enemy. Chinese translations of Buddhist scriptures interpret Ajātashatru as "Enemy before Birth" or "Unborn Enemy." The Sanskrit name is also translated as "Victor over Enemies," i.e., one who has no born enemies.

Ajita (Skt) (1) [阿逸多] (Jpn Aitta): Another name for Bodhisattva Maitreya. Ajita means invincible.

(2) [阿逸多] (Jpn Aitta): A follower of Shakyamuni whose story appears in the Nirvana Sutra, where the great physician Jīvaka relates it to assure Ajātashatru that his grave offenses can be eradicated. When Ajātashatru broke out in virulent sores and repented for having killed his father, Jīvaka advised him to seek the teachings of Shakyamuni and told him the following story: Ajita, who lived in Vārānasī, had an incestuous relationship with his mother and killed his father. When his mother had relations with another man, he killed his mother as well. He also killed an arhat. He then went to Jetavana Monastery in Shrāvastī and sought admission to the Buddhist Order. Knowing that he had committed three of the five cardinal sins, the monks refused him. In anger, he burned down many of the monastery buildings and then went to Rājagriha to meet Shakyamuni and seek entry into the Order. Shakyamuni granted him admission and expounded teachings to eradicate his serious offenses and arouse in him the aspiration for supreme enlightenment.

(3) [阿耆多] (Jpn Agita): Also known as Agnidatta. *See* Agnidatta.

Ajita Kesakambala [阿耆多翅舎欽婆羅] (Pali; Jpn Agita-shishakimbara): An influential non-Buddhist thinker during Shakyamuni's time. *See* six non-Buddhist teachers.

Ajitavatī [阿恃多伐底河] (Skt; Jpn Ajitabattei-ga): Also known as Airavatī, Ajiravatī, or Achiravatī. A river flowing through Kushinagara in India. According to *The Record of the Western Regions,* the Chinese priest Hsüan-tsang's record of his travels through Central Asia and India in the seventh century, the Ajitavatī River is where Shakyamuni Buddha entered nirvana. Therefore the river is generally believed to be identical with the Hiranyavatī River, which is where Shakyamuni died in a grove of sal trees near its west bank.

Ājīvika school [アージービカ派・邪命外道] (Skt, Pali; Jpn Ājībika-ha or Jamyō-gedō): A religious school in ancient India during Shakyamuni's time. The Ājīvika school is said to have been as prosperous and influential as Buddhism and Jainism. It continued to flourish until the Maurya dynasty that began in the late fourth century B.C.E., and then it gradually declined. Ājīvika was a name used disparagingly by Buddhists to mean one who performs religious practice in order to earn a living. The

Sanskrit word *ājīva* means livelihood. In the Chinese translations of Buddhist scriptures, Ājīvika is rendered as "the school of false livelihood." Makkhali Gosāla, one of the six non-Buddhist teachers, was well known as the leader of the Ājīvika school. The doctrine of this school is known only from descriptions found in Buddhist and Jain texts. The school held a completely deterministic and fatalistic view of the nature of existence, asserting that all events are predetermined by fate, and that the will and actions of human beings are totally ineffective in altering the course of their transmigration. Nevertheless, the followers of this school practiced asceticism as Jain followers did. The school existed in southern India until the fourteenth century.

Ājnāta Kaundinya [阿若憍陳如] (Skt; Pali Annā Kondanna; Jpn Anya-kyōjinnyo): Also known as Kaundinya. One of the five ascetics who heard Shakyamuni Buddha's first sermon and thereupon converted to his teachings. He was born to a Brahman family of Kapilavastu in northern India. When Shakyamuni renounced the secular world, Kaundinya and four other men accompanied him at the order of Shakyamuni's father, King Shuddhodana, and practiced austerities together with him. When Shakyamuni discarded his ascetic practice, however, they abandoned him and left for Deer Park. After Shakyamuni attained enlightenment, Kaundinya and the others again encountered the Buddha at Deer Park and embraced his teachings. The "Five Hundred Disciples" (eighth) chapter of the Lotus Sutra predicts that he will become a Buddha named Universal Brightness. *See also* five ascetics.

Akanishtha Heaven [阿迦尼吒天・色究竟天] (Skt; Jpn Akanita-ten or Shikikukyō-ten): Also, Summit of Being Heaven. The highest of the eighteen heavens of the world of form. The living beings in this heaven are said to possess a pure body, free from all desires, suffering, and illness. The world of form is the middle division of the threefold world.

ākāsha [虚空・空] (Skt; Jpn *kokū* or *kū*): Space. One of the five elements or six elements. *Ākāsha* indicates the physical space where dharmas, or things and phenomena, exist. It is characterized as unhindered and without obstacles.

Ākāshagarbha [虚空蔵菩薩] (Skt; Jpn Kokūzō-bosatsu): The bodhisattva Space Treasury. A bodhisattva whose wisdom and good fortune are said to be as vast and boundless as the universe. *See* Space Treasury.

Ākāshānantya Realm [空無辺処] (Skt; Jpn Kūmuhen-jo): The first and the lowest of the four realms of the world of formlessness. *See* Realm of Boundless Empty Space.

Ākimchanya Realm [無所有処] (Skt; Jpn Mushou-sho): The third of the four realms of the world of formlessness. *See* Realm of Nothingness.

Akimoto Tarō Hyōe-no-jō [秋元太郎兵衛尉] (d. 1291): A lay follower of Nichiren who lived in Imba District of Shimōsa Province, Japan. Akimoto is believed to have converted to Nichiren's teachings in 1260 when Nichiren, having narrowly escaped an attack in Kamakura that came to be called the Matsubagayatsu Persecution, went to Shimōsa and stayed at the residence of Toki Jōnin, one of his leading followers, for nearly half a year. Akimoto was on friendly terms with Soya Kyōshin and Ōta Jōmyō who lived in the same area and took faith around the same time. It is said that he was a relative of Toki Jōnin. Akimoto died on the seventeenth day of the ninth month, 1291, and his house later became Shūhon-ji temple. He was the recipient of *Letter to Akimoto* and other letters from Nichiren.

Akshobhya [阿閦仏] (Skt; Jpn Ashuku-butsu): A Buddha said to be lord of the Land of Joy (Skt Abhirati) located in the east. Akshobhya means immovable; hence this Buddha is also known by the name Immovable. According to the Land of Akshobhya Buddha Sutra, Akshobhya Buddha carried out his bodhisattva practice under the Buddha Large Eyes and attained enlightenment, completely freeing himself from all animosity and earthly desires, and now preaches in the Land of Joy. According to the "Parable of the Phantom City" (seventh) chapter of the Lotus Sutra, Wisdom Accumulated, the first of the sixteen sons of Great Universal Wisdom Excellence Buddha, following his father, practiced the Lotus Sutra and attained enlightenment as Akshobhya Buddha. The Nirvana Sutra describes King Possessor of Virtue and the monk Realization of Virtue as having been born together in the land of Akshobhya Buddha. Akshobhya Buddha, who is said to dwell in the east, appears in many Mahayana sutras along with Amida Buddha of the west.

Ālāra Kālāma [阿羅邏迦藍] (Pali; Skt Ārāda Kālāma; Jpn Arara-karan): A hermit-sage and master of yogic meditation who lived near Rājagriha (Vaishālī, according to another account) in ancient India. He is said to have mastered the meditation on the Realm of Nothingness. He was the first teacher under whom Shakyamuni studied and practiced after renouncing the secular world. Shakyamuni quickly mastered the same meditation but, unable to gain the enlightenment he had sought, left Ālāra Kālāma.

ālaya-consciousness [阿頼耶識] (Skt *ālaya-vijnāna;* Jpn *araya-shiki*): Also, storehouse consciousness, never-perishing consciousness, or maintaining-consciousness (*ādāna*-consciousness). According to the Consciousness-Only school, the eighth and deepest of the eight consciousnesses; *ālaya* means abode, dwelling, or receptacle, and *vijnāna* means discernment. Located below the realms of conscious awareness, it is called the storehouse consciousness, because all karma created in the present and previous lifetimes is stored there. It is also called the never-perishing consciousness, because the karmic seeds preserved there continue even after death, and the maintaining-consciousness, because it maintains the life and body of a sentient being. The *ālaya*-consciousness is regarded as that which undergoes the cycle of birth and death, and determines the nature of individual existence. All the actions and experiences of life that occur through the first seven consciousnesses, such as sight, hearing, touch, and mind, are accumulated as karma in this *ālaya*-consciousness, which in turn exerts an influence on the workings of these seven. The Consciousness-Only school, which postulates the existence of the eight consciousnesses, holds that all phenomena arise from the *ālaya*-consciousness and that the *ālaya*-consciousness is the only reality.

alms bowl [鉢] (Skt *pātra;* Pali *patta;* Jpn *hachi* or *hatsu*): A begging bowl used by monks. *Pātra* means a bowl, vessel, receptacle, alms bowl, dish, plate, or utensil. According to monastic rules, a monk was permitted to possess three different robes and one begging bowl. This bowl was used as receptacle for food at mealtime, or for alms received during the practice of begging. Monastic discipline prescribed that alms bowls be either iron or earthenware. *See also* three robes.

almsgiving [布施] (Skt, Pali *dāna;* Jpn *fuse*): Also, offering. (1) One of the six *pāramitās,* or six kinds of practices required of bodhisattvas. The "Devadatta" (twelfth) chapter of the Lotus Sutra describes Shakyamuni in a past existence as the ruler of a kingdom who, in order to fulfill the six *pāramitās,* diligently distributed alms, never stinting in heart no matter how precious were the goods he gave away. He did not begrudge, the sutra says, even his own life.

(2) The offering of alms to others, including the Buddha and the Buddhist Order. Among the various kinds of almsgiving, two are best known. They are the offering of goods and the offering of the Law; the former means to offer food, robes, and other goods, and the latter means to share or explain the Buddha's teachings. There is also a concept of three kinds of almsgiving, which consists of the two just mentioned and the offering of fearlessness. The offering of fearlessness means to inspire courage and remove fear.

amala-consciousness [阿摩羅識] (Skt *amala-vijnāna;* Jpn *amara-shiki*): Also, free-of-defilement consciousness or pure consciousness. The ninth and deepest of the nine consciousnesses. *Amala* means pure or undefiled, and *vijnāna* means discernment. The eight consciousnesses set forth in the Consciousness-Only doctrine consist of the six consciousnesses (discernment by eyes, ears, nose, tongue, body, and mind), the *mano*-consciousness, and the *ālaya*-consciousness. To these the Summary of the Mahayana (Chin She-lun; Jpn Shōron) school founded by Paramārtha (499–569), the Flower Garland (Hua-yen; Kegon) school founded by Tu-shun (557–640), and the T'ien-t'ai (Jpn Tendai) school added a ninth consciousness, which is defined as the basis of all of life's functions. While the eighth, or *ālaya*-consciousness contains karmic impurities, the *amala*-consciousness is pure, free from all defilement, and corresponds to the Buddha nature. *See also* nine consciousnesses.

Ambapālī [菴婆羅女] (Pali; Skt Āmrapālī; Jpn Ambara-nyo): A courtesan in Vaishālī, India, who, upon hearing the teachings from Shakyamuni Buddha, donated her forest of mango trees to the Buddhist Order. Chinese versions of Buddhist scriptures refer to this forest of mango trees as Ambapālī Garden. Legend has it that Ambapālī was born from a mango tree. *Amba* means mango tree. According to another legend, she was left in a forest of mango trees after birth and was found and raised by the forest's caretaker. According to yet another legend, she was the mother of the skilled physician Jīvaka. It is said that, at age eighty, Shakyamuni left Rājāgriha to set forth on his last journey. He proceeded northward across the Ganges to Vaishālī where he and his disciples stayed in Ambapālī's mango-tree forest. It was then that she heard the Buddha preach and joyfully invited him and his disciples to a meal at her home.

Ambapālī Garden [菴沒羅園・菴羅園] (Pali; Jpn Ammora-on or Anra-on): Also known as Āmrapālī Garden or Āmra Garden. The garden of mango trees on the outskirts of the city of Vaishālī in India offered to Shakyamuni Buddha and his followers by Ambapālī (Skt Āmrapālī), a courtesan in Vaishālī. *Amba* means mango tree. *See also* Ambapālī.

Amida [阿弥陀] (Jpn; Skt Amitāyus or Amitābha): The Buddha of the Pure Land of Perfect Bliss in the west. Amida is the Japanese transliteration of the first half of both Amitāyus and Amitābha, names referring to the same Buddha that appear in Sanskrit texts and are rendered in Chinese as the Buddha Infinite Life (or the Buddha of Infinite Life) and the Buddha Infinite Light (or the Buddha of Infinite Light) respectively. The Sanskrit word *amita* means infinite. Amitāyus is a compound of this word with *āyus,* which means life, and Amitābha with *ābha,* which means light. According to the Buddha Infinite Life Sutra, immeasurable *kalpas* ago, a certain king, delighted with the preaching of a Buddha named World Freedom King (Skt Lokeshvararāja), renounced the throne to follow him. He took the name Dharma Treasury (Dharmākara) and began to practice bodhisattva austerities under the guidance of the Buddha. After examining an infinite number of Buddha lands and pondering for five *kalpas,* the bodhisattva Dharma Treasury made forty-eight vows in which he pledged to create his own Buddha land upon attaining enlightenment, a land that would combine the most outstanding features of all those he had examined. In the eighteenth vow, he pledged to bring all sentient beings who placed their hopes of salvation with him (Shan-tao, a patriarch of the Chinese Pure Land school, interpreted this to mean calling upon the name of Amida Buddha) to this Buddha land, which he named Perfect Bliss (Sukhāvatī), except those who had committed the five cardinal sins and those who had slandered the correct teaching. Dharma Treasury completed his practice and became the Buddha Amida. His pure land was established in a part of the universe located "a hundred thousand million Buddha lands to the west" of this *sahā* world. Belief in Amida Buddha spread from India to China. After its introduction to Japan, Hōnen (1133–1212) was responsible for popularizing it there and establishing the Pure Land (Jōdo) school. *See also* Nembutsu; Pure Land school.

Amida Sutra [阿弥陀経] (Skt *Sukhāvatīvyūha;* Chin *O-mi-t'o-ching;* Jpn *Amida-kyō*): One of the three basic scriptures of the Pure Land school, the others being the Buddha Infinite Life Sutra and the Meditation on the Buddha Infinite Life Sutra. The Amida Sutra is a translation of what is known as the smaller *Sukhāvatīvyūha,* rendered into Chinese by Kumārajīva in 402. Two other Chinese translations were made by Gunabhadra in 455 and by Hsüan-tsang in 650, but Gunabhadra's version is not extant. Kumārajīva's version, titled Amida Sutra, consists of one volume. Written in the form of a discourse delivered by Shakyamuni to Shāriputra and others at Jetavana Monastery, it describes the blessings associated with Amida Buddha and his Pure Land of Perfect Bliss in the west, and asserts that one can attain rebirth in this land by relying solely on Amida. Subsequently the Buddhas in the six directions are described as bearing witness to the truth of this teaching of Shakyamuni.

Amitābha [阿弥陀仏・無量光仏] (Skt; Jpn Amida-butsu or Muryōkō-butsu): The Buddha Infinite Light or the Buddha of Infinite Light. The Sanskrit name of Amida Buddha, the Buddha of the Pure Land of Perfect Bliss in the west. *See* Amida.

Amitāyus [阿弥陀仏・無量寿仏] (Skt; Jpn Amida-butsu or Muryōju-butsu): The Buddha Infinite Life or the Buddha of Infinite Life. The Sanskrit name of Amida Buddha, the Buddha of the Pure Land of Perfect Bliss in the west. *See* Amida.

Amoghavajra [不空] (Skt; Jpn Fukū): An Indian monk who went to China to disseminate Esoteric Buddhism and became known in China as Pu-k'ung. *See* Pu-k'ung.

Āmrapālī [菴婆羅女] (Skt; Jpn Ambara-nyo): Ambapālī in Pali. A courtesan in Vaishālī, India. *See* Ambapālī.

Āmrapālī Garden [菴沒羅園・菴羅園] (Skt; Jpn Ammora-on or Anra-on): Also known as Ambapālī Garden. *See* Ambapālī Garden.

amrita [甘露] (Skt; Pali *amata;* Jpn *kanro*): A legendary, ambrosia-like liquid. In ancient India, it was regarded as the sweet-tasting beverage of the gods. In China, it was thought to rain down from heaven when the world became peaceful. *Amrita* is said to remove sufferings and give immortality. The word *amrita* means immortality and is often translated as sweet dew.

Amritodana [甘露飯王] (Skt; Pali Amitodana; Jpn Kanrobonnō): A younger brother of Shakyamuni's father, King Shuddhodana. Amritodana's father was Simhahanu, the king of the Shākya tribe, who had four sons and one daughter. The eldest son was Shuddhodana, and Amritodana was the youngest son. According to one account, Amritodana was the father of Ānanda and Devadatta, and according to another, he was the father of Aniruddha and Mahānāma.

anāgāmin [阿那含・不還] (Skt, Pali; Jpn *anagon* or *fugen*): The stage of the non-returner, the third of the four stages of Hinayana enlightenment. *See* non-returner.

Ānanda [阿難] (Skt, Pali; Jpn Anan): One of Shakyamuni's ten major disciples. He was a cousin of Shakyamuni Buddha. His father is regarded as either Dronodana, Amritodana, or Shuklodana, each of whom was Shakyamuni's uncle. Ānanda is also known as the younger brother of Devadatta. He accompanied Shakyamuni Buddha as his personal attendant for many years and thus heard more of his teachings than any other disciple. He was known, therefore, as foremost in hearing the Buddha's teachings. In addition, he is said to have possessed an excellent memory, which allowed him to play a central role in compiling Shakyamuni Buddha's teachings at the First Buddhist Council shortly after the Buddha's death. He helped Mahāprajāpatī, Shakyamuni's aunt and foster mother, enter the Buddhist Order. When she wished to renounce secular life and be admitted to the Buddhist Order, Shakyamuni refused her request. Ānanda reminded Shakyamuni that the Buddha was deeply indebted to her, his foster mother, and implored him to comply with her earnest request. Shakyamuni finally listened to their entreaty, and Mahāprajāpatī became the first nun admitted to the Buddhist Order. Ānanda is regarded as the second of the Buddha's twenty-three or twenty-four successors (Mahākāshyapa was the first). He belongs to the last of the three groups of voice-hearers who understood the Buddha's teachings on hearing about their own relationship with Shakyamuni in the distant past, as described in the "Parable of the Phantom City" (seventh) chapter of the Lotus Sutra. The "Prophecies" (ninth) chapter predicts his future enlightenment as the Buddha Mountain Sea Wisdom Unrestricted Power King. *See also* three groups of voice-hearers.

ananta [無辺・無量] (Skt, Pali; Jpn *muhen* or *muryō*): Endless, eternal, boundless, limitless, infinite, or innumerable. Anantachāritra (Jpn Muhengyō) is the name of one of the four bodhisattvas who appear in the "Emerging from the Earth" (fifteenth) chapter of the Lotus Sutra as the leaders of the Bodhisattvas of the Earth. Bodhisattva Anantachāritra is translated as Bodhisattva Boundless Practices. *Chāritra* means action, conduct, or good conduct. The "Introduction" (first) chapter of the Lotus Sutra refers to Anantamati, one of eight princes the Buddha Sun Moon Bright had fathered as a king before leaving secular life. Anantamati is translated as Immeasurable Intention. *Mati* means intention, resolution, or mind. *Ananta-nirdesha-pratishthāna* is the type of *samādhi,* or meditation, that Shakyamuni Buddha entered into before preaching the Lotus Sutra, according to the "Introduction" chapter of the sutra. *Ananta-nirdesha-pratishthāna* is interpreted in Kumārajīva's Chinese version of the Lotus Sutra as the *samādhi* of the origin of immeasurable meanings. *Nirdesha* means description, elucidation, or explanation, and *pratishthāna* means basis, foundation, dwelling, or support.

Anāthapindada [給孤独] (Skt; Pali Anāthapindika; Jpn Gikkodoku): Another name of Sudatta, a wealthy merchant of Shrāvastī in Kosala, India, who, with the assistance of Prince Jetri, built Jetavana Monastery as an offering to Shakyamuni Buddha. *See* Sudatta.

Anavatapta [阿耨達竜王] (Skt; Jpn Anokudatsu-ryūō): A dragon said to live in Anavatapta Lake, or Heat-Free Lake, north of the Snow Mountains. Anavatapta is one of the eight great dragon kings who joined those assembled to hear the Lotus Sutra, as described in the "Introduction" (first) chapter of the sutra. According to the Long Āgama Sutra, although dragons are tormented by fiery heat, stripped of their jeweled clothing by fierce winds, and afraid of *garuda* birds that prey on them, the dragon king Anavatapta is free from all these distresses. For this reason this dragon is called Anavatapta, which means free from or not afflicted by heat. Anavatapta is also the name of the lake where the dragon king Anavatapta is said to dwell. *See also* dragon deity; eight great dragon kings.

Anavatapta Lake [阿耨池・阿耨達池・無熱池] (Skt; Jpn Anokuchi, Anokudatchi, or Munetchi): Heat-Free Lake. A lake said to give rise to the four rivers that nurture the soil in the four quarters of Jambudvīpa. Anavatapta means heat-free or not afflicted by heat. According to

The Great Commentary on the Abhidharma and *The Dharma Analysis Treasury*, this lake lies north of the Snow Mountains and south of Mount Fragrant, and according to *The Treatise on the Great Perfection of Wisdom*, it lies within the Snow Mountains. *The Great Commentary on the Abhidharma* defines the lake's circumference as eight hundred *ri* (one *ri* is about 0.45 kilometers), and *The Dharma Analysis Treasury* as two hundred *yojanas* (one *yojana* is about 7 kilometers). Anavatapta Lake is bounded by shores of gold, silver, emerald, and crystal, and inhabited by a dragon king named Anavatapta. The clear, cool water is said to originate from the mouth of this dragon king and flow out from the four sides of the lake into four rivers: the Gangā River, Sindhu River, Vakshu River, and Shītā River. These rivers flow respectively eastward, southward, westward, and northward, supplying water to the land of Jambudvīpa.

An Fa-ch'in [安法欽] (n.d.) (PY An Faqin; Jpn An-hōkin): A priest from Parthia in western Asia who was active in China as a translator from the late third through the early fourth century. He went to Lo-yang in China from his native Parthia, where he translated five Sanskrit Buddhist scriptures into Chinese, including *The Story of King Ashoka*. "An" in his name refers to An-hsi, the Chinese name for Parthia, a state that stretched from northwest India to Persia.

Anga [鴦伽国] (Skt, Pali; Jpn Ōga-koku): One of the sixteen great states in India in Shakyamuni's time. Anga was located in the lower Ganges Valley and was the easternmost of the sixteen states. Its capital was Champā, which is thought to have been at the site of present-day Bhagalpur in northeastern India, just south of the Ganges River. Bounded on the west by the Magadha kingdom, Anga later fell under its rule.

anger [瞋恚・瞋] (Skt *dvesha;* Pali *dosa;* Jpn *shinni* or *shin*): In Buddhism, one of the three poisons, or three sources of vice and suffering, the other two being greed and foolishness. In Buddhism, anger refers particularly to malice born of hatred and is regarded as a great obstacle to Buddhist practice. It is seen as preventing one's heart from turning to goodness and as destroying the good roots of benefit accumulated through Buddhist practice. T'ien-t'ai (538–597) says in *The Words and Phrases of the Lotus Sutra,* "Because anger increases in intensity, armed strife occurs." Buddhism emphasizes the practice of compassion and forbearance. See also *dvesha.*

Angulimāla [央掘摩羅] (Pali; Skt Angulimālya; Jpn Ōkutsumara): A follower of Shakyamuni in Shrāvasti, India. In Buddhist scriptures, he is often referred to as an example of the conversion of a heinous man to Buddhism. Angulimāla means necklace of fingers, a name said to derive from a necklace he wore made of the severed fingers of those he had murdered. According to the Sutra on the Wise and the Foolish, he originally studied under a teacher of Brahmanism in Shrāvastī.

When Angulimāla spurned the advances of his teacher's wife, she was angered and slandered him to her husband, saying that he had made advances to her. Enraged, the teacher told Angulimāla falsely that, if he killed a thousand people (a hundred according to another account) and cut off one finger from each of them, he could be reborn in the Brahma Heaven. Obeying his teacher, he killed and continued to kill. When he was about to kill his mother to make his thousandth victim, he met Shakyamuni Buddha. He tried to kill Shakyamuni, but was instead instructed and converted by the Buddha. Repenting of his evil deeds, he devoted himself to Buddhist practice. According to the Increasing by One Āgama Sutra, upon seeing Angulimāla, however, people heaped abuse on him and injured him with stones and swords because of his past atrocious deeds. Shakyamuni taught him to endure these attacks and make amends for his offenses. Angulimāla persisted in his Buddhist practice, as instructed by the Buddha.

Anguttara-nikāya [増支部] (Pali; Jpn Zōshi-bu): A collection of sutras of numerical doctrines. *See* five Āgamas.

Aniruddha [阿那律] (Skt; Pali Anuruddha; Jpn Anaritsu): A cousin of Shakyamuni Buddha and one of his ten major disciples. Either Amritodana or Dronodana is regarded as his father, each of whom was a younger brother of King Shuddhodana, the father of Shakyamuni. Aniruddha is known as foremost in divine insight among the Buddha's disciples. According to the Increasing by One Āgama Sutra, he once fell asleep while the Buddha was preaching at Jetavana Monastery in Shrāvastī, the capital of the Kosala kingdom, and was severely reprimanded. He vowed never to sleep in front of the Buddha. From that night on he did not sleep at all, and this damaged his eyesight. Shakyamuni admonished him to sleep, but he never broke his vow. He eventually went blind as a consequence of sleep deprivation, but simultaneously obtained divine insight, or extraordinary powers of discernment. The "Five Hundred Disciples" (eighth) chapter of the Lotus Sutra predicts that he will become a Buddha named Universal Brightness.

An'ne [安慧] (794–868): The fourth chief priest of Enryaku-ji, the head temple of the Tendai school on Mount Hiei in Japan. As a child, he studied under Kōchi, a priest of Ono-dera temple in Shimotsuke Province. At age thirteen, he became a disciple of Dengyō, and after Dengyō's death, he studied under Jikaku, the third chief priest of Enryaku-ji, and in 827 he passed an official examination administered by that temple concerning the Mahāvairochana Sutra. In 844 he was appointed as a lecturer for Dewa Province in northern Japan and there propagated the Tendai teachings. In 864, when Jikaku died, he became the chief priest of Enryaku-ji. He authored *A Clarification of the Meaning of the Lotus Sutra* and *The Doctrine of Attaining Buddhahood in One's Present Form.*

Annen [安然] (b. 841): A priest of the Tendai school in Japan. He is noted as having helped establish the doctrine and practice of Tendai Esotericism. Born in Ōmi Province, he is said to have been a relative of Dengyō. He studied the exoteric and esoteric teachings under Jikaku, the third chief priest of Enryaku-ji temple on Mount Hiei, from whom he received the bodhisattva precepts in 859. After the death of Jikaku, he continued his studies under Henjō, a senior disciple of Jikaku. In 884 he became a chief instructor of Gangyō-ji temple, following Henjō, and later founded a temple called Godai-in on Mount Hiei, where he devoted himself to writing. Hence he was called the Preceptor Godai-in or the Reverend Godai-in. Annen authored more than one hundred works dealing with the exoteric and the esoteric teachings and Siddham, a medieval Sanskrit orthography. They include *Questions and Answers about the Teaching and the Time, The Treatise on the Meaning of the Mind Aspiring for Enlightenment, An Extensive Commentary on the Universally Bestowed Bodhisattva Precepts, The Storehouse of Siddham,* and *Different Views on the Teaching and the Time.* The first two works are regarded as major textbooks of Tendai Esotericism.

annihilating consciousness and reducing the body to ashes [灰身滅智] (Jpn *keshin-metchi*): A Hinayana doctrine asserting that one can attain nirvana only upon extinguishing one's body and mind. *See* reducing the body to ashes and annihilating consciousness.

Annotations on "Great Concentration and Insight," The [止観輔行伝弘決] (Chin *Chih-kuan-fu-hsing-chuan-hung-chüeh;* Jpn *Shikan-bugyō-den-guketsu*): A detailed commentary in ten volumes by Miao-lo (711–782) on *Great Concentration and Insight,* one of T'ien-t'ai's three major works. After T'ien-t'ai's death, a number of differing interpretations of *Great Concentration and Insight* began to appear both within and outside of the T'ien-t'ai school. Miao-lo wrote *The Annotations on "Great Concentration and Insight"* to refute mistaken interpretations and clarify the correct doctrines of the T'ien-t'ai school.

Annotations on the Flower Garland Sutra, The [華厳経疏] (Chin *Hua-yen-ching-shu;* Jpn *Kegongyō-sho*): An exposition of the eighty-volume version of the Flower Garland Sutra written by Ch'eng-kuan (738–839), the fourth patriarch of the Flower Garland (Hua-yen) school in China. It is based on a commentary on the sutra by Fa-tsang, Ch'eng-kuan's teacher and the third patriarch of the school. Ch'eng-kuan later expanded this work and wrote a much longer one titled *The Meaning of the Flower Garland Sutra Based on an Earlier Commentary,* which is considered a major reference work in the study of this sutra along with Fa-tsang's *Delving into the Profundity of the Flower Garland Sutra.*

Annotations on the Mahāvairochana Sutra, The [大日経疏] (Chin *Ta-jih-ching-shu;* Jpn *Dainichikyō-sho*): A compilation by I-hsing (683–727) of the lectures Shan-wu-wei (Skt Shubhakarasimha) gave on the Mahāvairochana Sutra. After Shan-wu-wei translated the Mahāvairochana Sutra into Chinese in 725, he lectured on this sutra to his disciple I-hsing, who in turn recorded the teacher's lectures. After I-hsing's death, Chih-yen and Wen-ku revised the commentary and titled their work *The Commentary on the Meaning of the Mahāvairochana Sutra.* In Japan, *The Annotations on the Mahāvairochana Sutra,* which was brought to Japan by Kōbō, became the textbook of True Word (Jpn Shingon) Esotericism, while *The Commentary on the Meaning of the Mahāvairochana Sutra,* which was brought by Jikaku and Chishō of the Japanese Tendai school, became the textbook of Tendai Esotericism.

Annotations on the Meaning of the Lotus Sutra, The [法華義疏] (1) (Chin *Fa-hua-i-shu;* Jpn *Hokke-gisho*): A twelve-volume work by Chi-tsang (549–623) of China who systematized the doctrines of the Three Treatises (San-lun) school. Chi-tsang highly esteemed the Lotus Sutra and wrote several commentaries on it. *The Treatise on the Profundity of the Lotus Sutra* is another of his major works. In *The Annotations on the Meaning of the Lotus Sutra,* he supports his views with quotations from various sutras, treatises, and commentaries, and with interpretations of the Lotus Sutra put forth by other scholars. For this reason, this work is valued for the study of not only Chi-tsang's but also other Chinese scholars' views on the Lotus Sutra.

(2) (Jpn *Hokke-gisho*): A four-volume work attributed to Prince Shōtoku (574–622), the second son of Emperor Yōmei of Japan. This work is one of the three commentaries attributed to Prince Shōtoku, the other two being commentaries on the Shrīmālā and Vimalakīrti sutras. Though based on Fa-yün's *Meaning of the Lotus Sutra,* it includes original opinions and interpretations regarding the Lotus Sutra of the Wonderful Law, or Kumārajīva's translation of the sutra. The existence of such an in-depth work in the very early stage of Japanese Buddhism deserves attention. The original text is extant.

Annotations on "The Profound Meaning of the Lotus Sutra," The [法華玄義釈籤] (Chin *Fa-hua-hsüan-i-shih-ch'ien;* Jpn *Hokke-gengi-shakusen*): A detailed commentary in ten volumes by Miao-lo (711–782) on

The Profound Meaning of the Lotus Sutra, one of T'ien-t'ai's three major works. It is Miao-lo's compilation of his lectures and his answers to questions on *The Profound Meaning of the Lotus Sutra.* In this writing, Miao-lo clarifies T'ien-t'ai's teachings in terms of both theory and practice, and establishes the principle of "ten non-dualities" or "ten onenesses." In the tradition of T'ien-t'ai, he reiterates the supremacy of the Lotus Sutra, refuting the views of the Flower Garland (Chin Hua-yen) and Dharma Characteristics (Fa-hsiang) schools that flourished in his time.

Annotations on "The Treatise on the Middle Way," The [中観論疏] (Chin *Chung-kuan-lun-shu;* Jpn *Chūganron-sho*): A commentary by Chi-tsang (549–623) on Nāgārjuna's *Treatise on the Middle Way.* Chi-tsang systematized the doctrines of the Three Treatises (San-lun) school in China. This work was widely studied in China and Japan, and many subcommentaries on it were produced. It is regarded as one of the fundamental works of the Three Treatises school.

Annotations on "The Words and Phrases of the Lotus Sutra," The [法華文句記] (Chin *Fa-hua-wen-chü-chi;* Jpn *Hokke-mongu-ki*): A ten-volume commentary by Miao-lo (711–782) on *The Words and Phrases of the Lotus Sutra,* one of T'ien-t'ai's three major works. It clarifies the meaning of T'ien-t'ai's teachings on the whole text of the Lotus Sutra and refutes interpretations of the sutra advanced by the Flower Garland (Chin Hua-yen), Three Treatises (San-lun), and Dharma Characteristics (Fa-hsiang) schools. Miao-lo also addresses the controversy over the position of the "Entrustment" chapter in the Lotus Sutra, that is, whether it comes after the "Supernatural Powers" (twenty-first) chapter or at the end of the sutra. He upholds Kumārajīva's view that placed the "Entrustment" chapter after the "Supernatural Powers" chapter, refuting the opposing view set forth by Tz'u-en and Hsüan-tsang.

anointment ceremony [灌頂] (Jpn *kanjō*): *See* ceremony of anointment.

Anraku [安楽]: Also known as Junsai. A disciple of Hōnen, the founder of the Pure Land (Jōdo) school in Japan. *See* Junsai.

An Shih-kao [安世高] (n.d.) (PY An Shigao; Jpn An-seikō): A priest from Parthia in western Asia who was active in China as a translator in the latter part of the second century. Born the crown prince of Parthia, he renounced secular life and studied Buddhism. After traveling through several kingdoms to propagate Buddhist teachings, he went to Lo-yang in China in 148, where he translated thirty-four Buddhist scriptures from Sanskrit into Chinese over a period of twenty-some years. "An" in his name is an abbreviation of An-hsi, the Chinese name for Parthia.

Anthology of the Propagation of Light, The [弘明集] (Chin *Hung-*

ming-chi; Jpn *Gumyō-shū*): A collection of essays on Buddhism compiled by Seng-yu (445–518) of China. It records the conflicts that arose between Buddhism and the indigenous Chinese philosophies of Confucianism and Taoism during the first five hundred years following the introduction of Buddhism to China during the reign of Emperor Ming (r. 57–75). Along with Seng-yu's *Collection of Records concerning the Tripitaka,* it is considered a valuable reference work for the study of the history of Chinese Buddhism.

Anti-Lokāyata school [逆路伽耶陀] (Skt; Jpn Gyakurokayada): A non-Buddhist school in ancient India that is thought to have arisen in opposition to the Lokāyata school. Both schools existed in Shakyamuni's time. The Lokāyata school, also known as the Chārvāka school, argued that people are made of earth, water, fire, and wind, and that they have neither a previous life nor a next life. Followers of the school obeyed the conventions and trends of the world, including public opinion, and expounded a materialist and hedonistic doctrine. In Shakyamuni's time, Ajita Kesakambala, one of the six non-Buddhist teachers, expounded such a doctrine. The Anti-Lokāyata school taught that one should oppose the conventions of the world and tried to refute the Lokāyata followers. The "Peaceful Practices" (fourteenth) chapter of the Lotus Sutra reads, "They [bodhisattvas] should not associate closely with non-Buddhists, Brahmans, or Jains, or with those who compose works of secular literature or books extolling the heretics, nor should they be closely associated with Lokāyatas or Anti-Lokāyatas."

Anuruddha [阿那律] (Pali; Jpn Anaritsu): Aniruddha in Sanskrit. One of the ten major disciples of Shakyamuni. *See* Aniruddha.

anuttara [阿耨多羅・無上] (Skt, Pali; Jpn *anokutara* or *mujō*): Unsurpassed, unexcelled, supreme, highest, peerless, or incomparably excellent. *Anuttara* is a component of various Buddhist terms. *Anuttara-samyak-sambodhi* means the supreme and perfect enlightenment of a Buddha. *Anuttara-dharma-chakra* means the wheel of the unsurpassed Law. *Anuttara* is also one of the ten honorable titles of a Buddha and in this context is rendered as "unexcelled worthy." This title signifies that a Buddha stands supreme among all living beings.

anuttara-samyak-sambodhi [阿耨多羅三藐三菩提・無上正等正覚] (Skt; Jpn *anokutara-sammyaku-sambodai* or *mujō-shōtō-shōgaku*): Supreme perfect enlightenment, the unsurpassed enlightenment of a Buddha. *Anuttara* means supreme, highest, incomparable, unsurpassed, or peerless. *Samyak* means right, correct, true, accurate, complete, or perfect, and *sambodhi* means enlightenment. The expression *samyak-sambodhi* by itself is also used to mean perfect enlightenment. *Bodhi* and *sambodhi* also mean wisdom or perfect wisdom. In this sense, *anuttara-samyak-sambodhi* means supreme perfect wisdom.

Aparagodānīya [瞿耶尼・牛貨洲・西牛貨洲] (Skt; Jpn Kuyani, Goke-shū, or Sai-goke-shū): Also known as Godānīya. One of the four continents surrounding Mount Sumeru, according to the ancient Indian worldview. The Sanskrit *apara* means west. *The Dharma Analysis Treasury* indicates that it is a continent located to the west of Mount Sumeru, in the sea between the outermost of the seven concentric gold mountain ranges and the iron mountain range that constitutes the outermost borders of the world. This iron mountain range is known as the Iron Encircling Mountains. *The Dharma Analysis Treasury* describes Aparagodānīya as circular, 2,500 *yojanas* in diameter, while the Long Āgama Sutra describes it as semicircular.

aranya [阿蘭若・阿練若・空閑] (Skt; Jpn *arannya, arennya,* or *kūgen*): A secluded place of retirement for Buddhist practice. To concentrate on their Buddhist practice, monks lived in a quiet place such as a forest, with few distractions and far from human habitation. *Aranya* means forest, wilderness, or a foreign or distant land. In the Chinese version of Buddhist scriptures, *aranya* is interpreted as "a deserted and quiet place," "an empty and silent place," etc.

arhat [阿羅漢] (Skt; Jpn *arakan*): One who has attained the highest of the four stages that voice-hearers aim to achieve through the practice of Hinayana teachings, that is, the highest stage of Hinayana enlightenment. *Arhat* means one worthy of respect. In Chinese Buddhist scriptures, it is interpreted in several ways: one worthy of offerings; one who has nothing more to learn, meaning that an arhat has completed his learning and practice; destroyer of bandits, meaning that an arhat has repelled the "bandits" that are the illusions of thought and desire; and a person of "no rebirth," because an arhat has freed himself from transmigration in the six paths. Of these, the "one worthy of offerings" is among the ten honorable titles of a Buddha, thus indicating that arhat was originally synonymous with Buddha. With the rise of Mahayana Buddhism, the term *arhat* came to refer exclusively to the sages of Hinayana Buddhism.

Arida [阿利吒] : Also known as Arita. The name of Aniruddha, one of Shakyamuni's ten major disciples, in a previous lifetime. The story appears in the Storehouse of Various Treasures Sutra and elsewhere. Ninety-one *kalpas* ago, there lived a wealthy man who had two sons, Rida and Arida (Jpn; their original Sanskrit names are unknown). On his deathbed, he admonished them not to divide his property between them but to live together. This they did, following their father's advice, and they respected and helped each other. Later, when the younger brother, Arida, married, his wife complained to him that he acted like a servant to his elder brother, Rida. She persuaded him to divide his father's wealth with his brother and to live independently.

Arida and his wife were satisfied but in time squandered their portion of the wealth and asked Rida for more. Rida complied, but Arida lost all his wealth again, eventually repeating this cycle six times. When Rida fulfilled his younger brother's request a seventh time, he admonished him against wasteful living. From then on, Arida and his wife lived frugally until finally they amassed a fortune. The elder brother, Rida, then happened to become destitute and came to Arida for money, but he was refused. Disappointed, he renounced the secular world and eventually became a *pratyekabuddha*.

Meanwhile, Arida again lost his fortune and eked out a living selling firewood. One day, he saw a *pratyekabuddha* in the city with an empty alms bowl. Arida, not knowing that the mendicant was his brother, offered him a meal of millet, which he had managed to obtain by selling firewood. Then one day while collecting wood, he came across a hare and struck it dead with his staff. The hare changed into a dead person, who folded his arms about Arida's neck and would not loosen his hold. When Arida returned home, the corpse released its hold and changed into a statue of gold. Upon separating the golden head from the statue, Arida saw it regenerate itself. When he broke off its hands and feet, they were also restored. In this way, he again accumulated wealth.

After his death, he was reborn as the deity Shakra and then as a wheel-turning king. During the following ninety-one *kalpas,* he repeated this cycle of birth and death, finally being reborn as a member of the Shākya clan. Aniruddha related this story to reveal that, as a reward for offering a meal to a *pratyekabuddha* in a prior existence, he had been able to repeat a wonderful cycle of birth and death and was not lacking for food and drink in his present life as a monk.

arjaka [阿梨樹] (Skt; Jpn *ari-ju*): A tree that grows in India and other tropical areas. It is said that when a branch of this tree falls to the ground it splits into seven pieces. When the ten demon daughters in the "Dhāranī" (twenty-sixth) chapter of the Lotus Sutra pledge to protect the sutra's votaries, they are quoted as saying, "If there are those who fail to heed our spells and trouble and disrupt the preachers of the Law, their heads will split into seven pieces like the branches of the *arjaka* tree."

armor of perseverance [忍辱の鎧] (Jpn *ninniku-no-yoroi*): Also, armor of forbearance. A metaphor for the spiritual endurance with which one withstands insult or persecution. The armor of perseverance is also that which protects one against evils and hindrances. The "Encouraging Devotion" (thirteenth) chapter of the Lotus Sutra says: "In a muddied *kalpa,* in an evil age there will be many things to fear. Evil demons will take possession of others and through them curse, revile, and heap shame on us. But we, reverently trusting in the Buddha, will put on the armor of perseverance. In order to preach this sutra we will bear these difficult things."

arrogance [慢] (Skt, Pali *māna;* Jpn *man*): In Buddhism, a function of the mind that obstructs Buddhist practice and the way to enlightenment. Arrogance means to hold oneself to be higher than and to look down upon others, and therefore hinders correct judgment. Buddhism discerned the functions and pitfalls of an arrogant mind, and various Buddhist writings define seven, eight, and nine types of arrogance. A number of figures representing arrogance appear throughout the Buddhist scriptures as well, such as the five thousand arrogant persons in the Lotus Sutra and the Great Arrogant Brahman in *The Record of the Western Regions.* Expressions such as "the banner of arrogance" and "the banner of pride" are also found in Buddhist writings. *See also* five thousand arrogant persons; Great Arrogant Brahman; nine types of arrogance.

ārūpya-dhātu [無色界] (Skt; Jpn *mushiki-kai*): The world of formlessness, the highest level of the threefold world. *See* world of formlessness.

Āryadeva [提婆・聖提婆] (n.d.) (Skt; Jpn Daiba or Shōdaiba): Also known as Kānadeva. A scholar of the Mādhyamika school in southern India during the third century and the successor of Nāgārjuna. Born to a Brahman family, he studied the doctrine of non-substantiality under Nāgārjuna. One source regards him as a prince of Sri Lanka. According to *The Biography of Āryadeva,* he offered one eye to the god Maheshvara at the latter's request. Because he had only one eye (the Sanskrit *kāna* means one-eyed), he was also called Kānadeva. He traveled throughout India to instruct the people. After he defeated non-Buddhist teachers in a religious debate at Pātaliputra, he was killed by one of their disciples. According to the above biography, Āryadeva displayed compassion even during his last moments, telling his assailant about the Buddhist teaching in order to save him. He wrote *The One-Hundred-Verse Treatise, The Four-Hundred-Verse Treatise,* and *The One-Hundred-Word Treatise. The One-Hundred-Verse Treatise* is one of the three works on which the Three Treatises (Chin San-lun; Jpn Sanron) school was founded. Āryadeva is regarded as the fourteenth of Shakyamuni's twenty-three, or the fifteenth of his twenty-four, successors. He transferred the Buddha's teachings he had received from Nāgārjuna to Rāhulabhadra.

Āryasimha [師子尊者] (n.d.) (Skt; Jpn Shishi-sonja): Also known as the Venerable Āryasimha. The last of Shakyamuni Buddha's twenty-three or twenty-four successors, who lived in central India during the sixth century. *A History of the Buddha's Successors* states that, when Āryasimha was propagating Buddhism in Kashmir in ancient India, King Mirakutsu (also known as Dammira, both names are Japanese transliterations; the original Sanskrit is unknown), who was hostile to Buddhism, destroyed many Buddhist temples and stupas, and murdered a number of monks. Āryasimha was among those beheaded by the king. When he was beheaded, the text states, milk instead of blood flowed from his neck. According to *The Record of the Lineage of the Buddha and the Patriarchs*, at the moment of the execution, the king's arm, still holding the sword, fell to the ground, and he died seven days later. Āryasimha is often cited as the epitome of willingness to give up one's life for the sake of the Law.

asamkhya [阿僧祇] (Skt; Jpn *asōgi*): Innumerable. Also, *asamkhyeya*. A numerical unit of ancient India used to indicate an exceedingly large number. One source has it equal to 10^{59}, while another describes it as 10^{51}.

Asanga [無著] (n.d.) (Skt; Jpn Mujaku): A scholar of the Consciousness-Only doctrine in India who is thought to have lived in the fourth or fifth century. Born to a Brahman family at Purushapura in Gandhara, northern India, he contributed greatly to the systematization of the Consciousness-Only doctrine. Vasubandhu was his younger brother. According to *The Record of the Western Regions*, Asanga became a monk of the Mahīshāsaka school of Hinayana, but according to Paramārtha's *Biography of the Dharma Teacher Vasubandhu*, he belonged to the Sarvāstivāda school. In either case, he later converted to the Mahayana teachings and succeeded in persuading Vasubandhu to do the same. *The Biography of the Dharma Teacher Vasubandhu* describes how Asanga, dissatisfied with the Hinayana view of non-substantiality, used his supernatural powers to ascend to the Tushita Heaven and there received the Mahayana doctrine of non-substantiality from Bodhisattva Maitreya. This is probably a mythicizing of his actually having studied the doctrine under a teacher named Maitreya, a contemporary historical figure. Asanga's works include *A Collection of Mahayana Treatises, The Summary of the Mahayana, The Treatise on the Diamond Wisdom Sutra,* and *The Accordance with "The Treatise on the Middle Way."*

Ashoka [阿育王] (r. c. 268–232 B.C.E.) (Skt; Jpn Aiku-ō): The third ruler of the Indian Maurya dynasty and the first king to unify India. He was the grandson of Chandragupta, the founder of the Maurya dynasty, and the son of the second king, Bindusāra. Ashoka began as a tyrant but later converted to Buddhism and governed compassionately in accordance with Buddhist ideals. He is said to have put to death his ninety-nine half brothers upon ascending the throne. In 259 B.C.E., nine years after becoming king, he conquered the kingdom of Kalinga, where he is reputed to have killed about 100,000 people and imprisoned 150,000.

Though Ashoka had converted to Buddhism two years earlier, seeing the tragedy his forces had brought upon the conquered populace of Kalinga awakened him to his own cruelty and led him to become a devout Buddhist. He renounced conquest by force, adopted "conquest by Dharma" (principles of right life), and thereby established a peaceful reign. Proclaiming a policy of public works, he founded hospitals for people and animals and, along major trade routes, planted trees, dug wells, and built resthouses and other facilities. Every five years he dispatched officials to outlying areas to ascertain the people's condition. He sent Buddhist missionaries to southern India, Kashmir, Gandhara, and Sri Lanka, and even as far away as Syria, Egypt, and Macedonia. To Sri Lanka he sent his son Mahendra and his daughter Samghamitrā, who spread Buddhism there, while to Kashmir and Gandhara he sent a Buddhist monk named Madhyāntika.

Though devoted to the spread of Buddhism, he did not enforce Buddhism as a state religion, but protected the religious freedom of the Jains, Brahmans, Ājīvikas, and others. The Third Buddhist Council for compiling the Buddha's teachings was held at the Mauryan capital, Pātaliputra, under Ashoka's patronage. His achievements and views are recorded not only in Buddhist scriptures but also in the many edicts inscribed on rock surfaces and pillars that have been discovered.

ashoka tree [阿輸迦樹・無憂樹] (Skt; Jpn *ashuka-ju* or *muu-ju*): Also, *asoka* tree or sorrowless tree. A tall leguminous tree that produces beautiful orange- or scarlet-colored blossoms. It is found in India, Sri Lanka, and other tropical countries, and used as timber. The Sanskrit word *ashoka* is translated in Chinese as "free from distress," and thus the *ashoka* tree is often referred to as the sorrowless tree. Tradition has it that, when Māyā, Shakyamuni's mother, reached for a branch of this tree to pick its blossoms in the grove at Lumbinī, she gave birth to her son. For this reason, in Buddhism the *ashoka* tree is considered sacred, along with the *bodhi* tree under which Shakyamuni attained enlightenment, and the sal tree representing his entrance into nirvana. Shakyamuni died in a grove of sal trees.

Ashvaghosha [馬鳴] (n.d.) (Skt; Jpn Memyō): A Mahayana scholar and poet from Shrāvastī in India who lived from the first through the second century. According to another account, he was from Shāketa in India. *Ashva* means horse, and *ghosha*, cry or sound. Originally a follower and scholar of Brahmanism, he converted to Buddhism. He was reputed to be an outstanding poet, an excellent composer of music, and an author of literary works. Ashvaghosha disseminated the *kāvya* (court epic) style of Sanskrit poetry and led many people to Shakyamuni Buddha's teachings through his skills in music and literature. According to tradition, when *Rāshtrapāla,* a Buddhist drama he wrote, was staged, five hundred princes immediately renounced secular life to become Buddhist monks. He propagated Buddhism in northern India under the patronage of King Kanishka. He wrote epics such as *Buddhacharita* and *Saundarananda. Buddhacharita* recounts the Buddha's life and is considered a masterpiece of Indian literature. *Saundarananda* is the story of Nanda, a cousin of the Buddha, who severed his relationship with his beloved and beautiful wife and became a monk. *The Awakening of Faith in the Mahayana* is attributed to Ashvaghosha, who is regarded as the eleventh of Shakyamuni's twenty-three, or the twelfth of his twenty-four, successors. Some accounts, however, attribute it to another person of the same name or to others.

Ashvajit [阿説示] (Skt; Pali Assaji; Jpn Asetsuji): One of the five ascetics who were Shakyamuni's first converts. While begging for alms in Rājagriha in India after his conversion, he happened to encounter Shāriputra, who, impressed with Ashvajit's bearing and integrity, decided to embrace Shakyamuni's teachings. *See also* five ascetics.

Asita (1) [阿私仙人] (Skt; Jpn Ashi-sennin): A seer mentioned in the "Devadatta" (twelfth) chapter of the Lotus Sutra and referred to as a former incarnation of Devadatta. According to this chapter, when Shakyamuni was a king in a past existence, he renounced the throne to seek the Law. At that time, a seer named Asita came to the retired king and said: "I have a great-vehicle text called the Sutra of the Lotus of the Wonderful Law. If you will never disobey me, I will expound it for you." Overjoyed, the former king served the seer, carrying firewood, drawing water, and making a couch of his own body for the seer to sleep on. One thousand years passed, and the king finally received instruction in the Lotus Sutra from the seer. In the "Devadatta" chapter, having related this story, Shakyamuni identifies the king with himself, and the seer with Devadatta. Moreover, he says that Devadatta acted as a "good friend" to him, or one who leads other people to the correct teaching, and that he was thus able to attain enlightenment. He then predicts that Devadatta will become a Buddha named Heavenly King. Kumārajīva's Chinese translation of the Lotus Sutra carries the name of this seer, but his name does not appear in the extant versions of the Sanskrit text.

(2) [阿私陀] (Skt, Pali; Jpn Ashida): A seer of Kapilavastu, the kingdom of the Shākyas, in northern India. According to the Causality of Past and Present Sutra, when Shakyamuni was born, his father, King

Shuddhodana, asked Asita to examine his newborn child's physiognomy. Asita, perceiving in the child the thirty-two features of a great man, foretold that, if the boy remained in the secular world, he would become a wheel-turning king by the age of twenty-nine; but if he renounced secular life, which was more probable, he would achieve supreme wisdom and become a Buddha. Asita lamented that, since he himself was already ninety years old, he would die before the prince attained enlightenment and therefore be unable to hear the Buddha's teaching.

aspiration for enlightenment [菩提心] (Skt, Pali *bodhi-chitta;* Jpn *bodai-shin*): Also, desire for *bodhi* or aspiration for the way. "Aspiration for enlightenment" is the mind or spirit to seek *bodhi,* or enlightenment, or to pursue the Buddha wisdom. *Bodhi* of the Sanskrit word *bodhi-chitta* means enlightenment, and *chitta* means thought, intention, aim, wish, longing, or mind. *Bodhi-chitta* is also called *anuttara-samyak-sambodhi-chitta,* which means the aspiration for supreme perfect enlightenment. In Mahayana Buddhism, to arouse aspiration for enlightenment is regarded as the basis and starting point of Buddhist practice. Bodhisattvas arouse the aspiration for enlightenment and pronounce the four universal vows: to save all living beings, to eradicate all earthly desires, to master all the Buddhist teachings, and to attain the supreme enlightenment.

Aspiration for the Law [楽法梵志] (Jpn Gyōbō-bonji): The name of Shakyamuni in a past existence when he practiced bodhisattva austerities. The story appears in *The Treatise on the Great Perfection of Wisdom.* The ascetic named Aspiration for the Law had been seeking the Law in every corner of the land, but had not yet met a Buddha. A devil disguised as a Brahman appeared to him and said that he would teach him one verse of a Buddhist teaching if the ascetic was ready to transcribe it using his skin as paper, one of his bones as a pen, and his blood as ink. When the ascetic gladly complied and prepared to write down the Buddhist teaching, the devil vanished. Instead, in response to his seeking mind, a Buddha appeared and taught him a profound teaching. As a result, he attained the stage of bodhisattva practice in which one realizes that nothing is born and nothing dies.

āsrava [漏] (Skt; Jpn *ro*): Outflows, or earthly desires. *See* outflows.

Asuka-dera [飛鳥寺]: Another name for Gangō-ji temple. The temple was built at Nara in Japan in 596. *See* Gangō-ji.

asura [阿修羅] (Skt, Pali; Jpn *ashura*): A type of demon in Indian mythology. Contentious and belligerent, *asuras* fight continually with the gods. Buddhist scriptures often regard *asuras* as enemies of the gods, especially of Shakra, or Indra. *Asuras* are one of the eight kinds of non-human beings. The world of *asuras* is counted as one of the six paths, or the six lower states of existence among the Ten Worlds. *See also* Ten Worlds.

atimuktaka [阿提目多伽] (Skt; Jpn *adaimokutaka*): A plant that appears in Buddhist scriptures. It reaches more than ten meters in height, and its flowers are light crimson. Perfumed oil produced from the seeds of *atimuktaka* was used as an offering to the Buddha. The "Distinctions in Benefits" (seventeenth) chapter of the Lotus Sutra states, "Constantly burning fragrant oil extracted from *sumanā, champaka,* or *atimuktaka* flowers, if he offers alms such as these he will gain immeasurable merits." See also *champaka* tree; *sumanā.*

Atsuhara Persecution [熱原の法難] (Jpn Atsuhara-no-hōnan): A series of threats and acts of violence against followers of Nichiren in Atsuhara Village, in Fuji District of Suruga Province, Japan, over a period of three years, beginning in earnest in 1278. Around 1275, after Nichiren had taken up residence at Mount Minobu, propagation efforts in the Fuji area began under the leadership of Nichiren's disciple Nikkō. At Ryūsen-ji, a temple of the Tendai school in Atsuhara, Nikkō converted several of the younger priests, who in turn converted a number of local farmers.

Alarmed at the defection of priests and lay supporters, Gyōchi, a lay priest and a member of the ruling Hōjō clan who acted as the deputy chief priest of the temple, demanded that the priests Nisshū, Nichiben, and Nichizen, who had converted and been renamed, discard their belief in Nichiren's teachings. When they refused, Gyōchi ordered them to leave the temple. Nichizen returned to his home, but the other two remained and redoubled their propagation efforts. Having failed to shake the conviction of those priests, Gyōchi turned his attention to the lay believers. He enticed the samurai Ōta Chikamasa and Nagasaki Tokitsuna as well as other followers of Nichiren to renounce their faith and join forces with him in intimidating Nichiren's believers among the peasantry. In the fourth month of 1279, Shirō, a lay follower of Nichiren, was attacked and wounded during an archery contest at a local shrine, and in the eighth month another believer named Yashirō was beheaded. Gyōchi's group tried to attribute the offenses to Nichiren's followers, including Nisshū and Nichiben.

On the twenty-first day of the ninth month, twenty farmers, all believers, were helping to harvest the rice crop from Nisshū's private fields when they were arrested for allegedly stealing rice from the fields of Ryūsen-ji. During the arrest the farmers resisted, and Daishin-bō was thrown from his horse and died. Ōta Chikamasa and Nagasaki Tokitsuna who joined the attack also lost their lives. Gyōchi filed charges with the Kamakura shogunate against the arrested believers, and their case was presided over by Hei no Saemon, the deputy chief of the Office of Military and Police Affairs. Ignoring a joint petition from Nisshū and others, drafted on their behalf by Nichiren and Nikkō, the officer had them imprisoned and tortured at his private residence, urging them to recant. Not one of them yielded. Eventually he had three of them executed—the brothers Jinshirō, Yagorō, and Yarokurō. The date of their execution was the fifteenth day of the tenth month (the eighth day of the fourth month, 1280, according to another account). The other seventeen were banished from Atsuhara. This incident marked the first time that official persecution of this magnitude had been directly leveled at Nichiren's followers rather than Nichiren himself. It is believed that their steadfast faith in the face of this persecution inspired Nichiren to inscribe the Dai-Gohonzon, the great mandala he later transferred to Nikkō, his successor, which he intended as the object of devotion for the enlightenment of humankind.

attaining Buddhahood in one's present form [即身成仏] (Jpn *soku-shin-jōbutsu*): *See* attainment of Buddhahood.

attaining Buddhahood in this lifetime [一生成仏] (Jpn *isshō-jōbutsu*): *See* attainment of Buddhahood.

attainment of Buddhahood [成仏] (Jpn *jōbutsu*): To become a Buddha. Several principles concerning the attainment of Buddhahood or enlightenment have been expounded on the basis of the sutras: (1) Attaining Buddhahood in one's present form. This means to attain Buddhahood just as one is, without discarding the body of an ordinary person. Also referred to as attaining Buddhahood as an ordinary person, this principle was formulated by the T'ien-t'ai school on the basis of the Lotus Sutra. According to many of the teachings other than the Lotus Sutra, one can attain Buddhahood only after having discarded the body of an ordinary person that gives rise to earthly desires and illusions.

In contrast, the Lotus Sutra teaches that one can attain Buddhahood in one's present form, or as an ordinary person. This principle is often illustrated by the example of the dragon king's daughter who, according to the "Devadatta" (twelfth) chapter, attained Buddhahood in a single moment without changing her dragon form. The concept of attaining Buddhahood in one's present form contrasts with that of attaining Buddhahood through transformation of sex and character. The latter means, for example, that a woman must be reborn as a man in order to attain enlightenment.

(2) Attaining Buddhahood in this lifetime or in a single lifetime. This concept contradicts the idea that one must carry out austere practices over a period of many *kalpas* in order to attain Buddhahood. This con-

cept is essentially the same as attaining Buddhahood in one's present form.

Other principles concern the attainment of Buddhahood by certain categories of people and derive from the Lotus Sutra per se: (1) Attainment of Buddhahood by persons of the two vehicles. In the first half of the Lotus Sutra, persons of the two vehicles—voice-hearers and cause-awakened ones—receive a prophecy from Shakyamuni Buddha that they will attain Buddhahood in future ages. This prophecy refutes the view of the provisional Mahayana teachings, which deny persons of the two vehicles the attainment of Buddhahood, for they seek only personal salvation and do not strive to save others. The Lotus Sutra says that they will practice the bodhisattva way and attain Buddhahood.

(2) Attainment of Buddhahood by women. In the first half of the sutra, the dragon king's daughter attains Buddhahood, and Yashodharā, Mahāprajāpatī, and other women receive Shakyamuni's prophecy of their future enlightenment. Almost all sutras deny women the capacity for attaining Buddhahood and insist that they must be reborn as men in order to attain enlightenment. The Lotus Sutra, however, teaches that both women and men are equally endowed with the potential for Buddhahood, based on the teaching of the true aspect of all phenomena.

(3) Attainment of Buddhahood by evil persons. Even those who oppose and slander the correct teaching of Buddhism, such as *icchantikas,* or persons of incorrigible disbelief, can attain Buddhahood through a reverse relationship. That is, because they establish a connection with the correct teaching by opposing it, though they receive the negative effect, eventually they profess faith in it and attain Buddhahood. In the Lotus Sutra, this idea is illustrated by the examples of Devadatta and those who ridiculed and attacked Bodhisattva Never Disparaging. *See also* Buddhahood.

attainment of Buddhahood by evil persons [悪人成仏] (Jpn *akunin-jōbutsu*): *See* attainment of Buddhahood.

attainment of Buddhahood by persons of the two vehicles [二乗作仏] (Jpn *nijō-sabutsu*): *See* attainment of Buddhahood.

attainment of Buddhahood by women [女人成仏] (Jpn *nyonin-jōbutsu*): *See* attainment of Buddhahood.

attainment of Buddhahood in the remote past [久遠実成] (Jpn *kuon-jitsujō*): Shakyamuni's original attainment of enlightenment in the inconceivably remote past as related in the "Life Span" (sixteenth) chapter of the essential teaching (latter fourteen chapters) of the Lotus Sutra. In this chapter, Shakyamuni discloses that he actually attained enlightenment in the distant past. He then illustrates in rather awe-inspiring detail the cosmic proportions of the time that has elapsed since then, the magnitude of which is abbreviated as "numberless major world system dust particle *kalpas*." Nothing Shakyamuni had taught until this point challenged people's basic assumption that he had attained enlightenment in his present lifetime after sitting in meditation under the *bodhi* tree near Gayā, India. This is the assumption upheld in the theoretical teaching (first fourteen chapters) of the Lotus Sutra and in the other sutras. Through this revelation in the "Life Span" chapter, however, Shakyamuni demolishes the belief that he attained enlightenment for the first time in his present lifetime. The "Life Span" chapter says: "In all the worlds the heavenly and human beings and *asuras* all believe that the present Shakyamuni Buddha, after leaving the palace of the Shākyas, seated himself in the place of meditation not far from the city of Gayā and there attained supreme perfect enlightenment. But good men, it has been immeasurable, boundless hundreds, thousands, ten thousands, millions of *nayutas* of *kalpas* since I in fact attained Buddhahood."

Auspicious [吉祥天] (Skt Shrīmahādevī or Mahāshrī; Jpn Kichijō-ten): Originally a goddess of Indian mythology named Lakshmī, later incorporated into Buddhism. Auspicious is known as the goddess of fortune and beauty, and is said to bestow fortune and benefit on living beings. In Japan, prayers for peace and agricultural fertility were offered to the goddess. Some sources regard her as a daughter of the Mother of Demon Children and the wife of Vaishravana, one of the four heavenly kings.

avadāna [阿波陀那] (Skt; Jpn *abadana*): One of the twelve divisions of the Buddhist teachings. It refers to those parts of the sutras relating parables, allegories, or stories that help the understanding of the doctrines. *Avadāna* also indicates the stories of the previous lives of Shakyamuni's monk-disciples and lay followers.

avaivartika [阿毘跋致] (Skt; Jpn *abibatchi*): The stage of non-regression in Buddhist practice. The other Sanskrit equivalents are *avivartika* and *avinivartanīya*. When one reaches this stage, one is certain to persist in Buddhist practice. *See* stage of non-regression.

Avalokitasvara [観世音菩薩] (Skt; Jpn Kanzeon-bosatsu): The bodhisattva Perceiver of the World's Sounds. According to the "Perceiver of the World's Sounds" (twenty-fifth) chapter of the Lotus Sutra, this bodhisattva is called Perceiver of the World's Sounds because he perceives the sounds and voices of those who are suffering and compassionately releases them from that suffering. *See* Perceiver of the World's Sounds.

Avalokiteshvara [観自在菩薩・観世音菩薩] (Skt; Jpn Kanjizai-bosatsu or Kanzeon-bosatsu): The bodhisattva Freely Perceiving. Another name for Avalokitasvara, or the bodhisattva Perceiver of the World's Sounds. *See* Perceiver of the World's Sounds.

Avanti [阿槃提国] (Skt, Pali; Jpn Ahandai-koku): An ancient kingdom of west-central India. In Shakyamuni Buddha's time, Avanti was one of the sixteen great states, and Ujjayinī was its capital. From the time of King Pradyota in the sixth century B.C.E., Avanti prospered as a powerful kingdom and rival to the kingdom of Magadha. King Pradyota was a contemporary of Bimbisāra, the king of Magadha, and his son Ajātashatru. Mahākātyāyana, one of Shakyamuni Buddha's ten major disciples, was a native of Avanti. According to one account, Utpalavarnā, a nun in Shakyamuni's Order, was also a native of Avanti.

Avatamsaka Sutra [華厳経] (Skt; Jpn *Kegon-gyō*): *See* Flower Garland Sutra.

Avīchi hell [阿鼻地獄] (Skt, Pali; Jpn Abi-jigoku): Also, hell of incessant suffering. The most terrible of the eight hot hells. The Avīchi hell is located at the lowest level of the world of desire; it is often referred to as the great citadel of the Avīchi hell because it is surrounded by seven solid iron walls that make it impossible for its inhabitants to escape. The Sanskrit word *avīchi* was rendered into Chinese as "incessant," indicating that in this hell pain and suffering continue without interruption. "The flames of the Avīchi hell" is an expression often used to refer to the sufferings of this hell, whose dwellers are consumed in flames. According to *The Dharma Analysis Treasury*, the Avīchi hell is located twenty thousand *yojanas* beneath the ground, and its depth is twenty thousand *yojanas*. Accordingly, the bottom of this hell is located forty thousand *yojanas* beneath the ground. The hell measures up to eighty thousand *yojanas* in length and width. *The Treatise on the Great Perfection of Wisdom* says that one who commits any of the five cardinal sins or slanders the correct teaching is destined to be reborn in the Avīchi hell.

avivartika [阿毘跋致] (Skt; Jpn *abibatchi*): The stage of non-regression in Buddhist practice. One who reaches this stage never backslides, always advancing toward attaining Buddhahood. *See* stage of non-regression.

Awakening of Faith [起信論] (Jpn *Kishin-ron*): See *Awakening of Faith in the Mahayana, The.*

Awakening of Faith in the Mahayana, The [大乗起信論] (Chin *Ta-ch'eng-ch'i-hsin-lun;* Jpn *Daijō-kishin-ron*): Abbreviated as *Awakening of Faith.* A work traditionally attributed to Ashvaghosha, a Mahayana scholar who lived from the first through the second century, though opinions on this differ. There are two Chinese translations of this work, the first done in 550 by Paramārtha, who had gone from India to China, and the second around 700 by Shikshānanda, a monk from Khotan in Central Asia. Paramārtha's version has been the more popular. *Awakening of Faith* sets forth the fundamental doctrines of Mahayana Buddhism and attempts to awaken people to faith in it. It specifically takes up the concept of *tathatā,* literally thusness or suchness, meaning the true aspect of reality. It was widely studied in China and Japan, and in China several commentaries on it were written.

Awa Province [安房国] (Jpn Awa-no-kuni): Also known as Bōshū. The old name for the southern part of what is now Chiba Prefecture (adjacent to Tokyo) on the main island of Japan. In 1222 Nichiren was born in this province in a fishing village called Kominato on the Pacific Ocean. Seichō-ji temple, where Nichiren first chanted Nam-myoho-renge-kyo and publicly proclaimed his teaching, and Komatsubara, where the steward of Tōjō Village, Tōjō Kagenobu, and his warriors attacked him, are located in this province.

Awesome Sound King [威音王仏] (Skt Bhīshma-garjita-svara-rāja; Jpn Ionnō-butsu): A Buddha mentioned in the "Never Disparaging" (twentieth) chapter of the Lotus Sutra. According to this chapter, in the remote past a Buddha named Awesome Sound King appeared and expounded the four noble truths for persons seeking to become voice-hearers, the teaching of the twelve-linked chain of causation for persons seeking to become *pratyekabuddhas,* and the teaching of the six *pāramitās* for bodhisattvas, so that they could gain their respective benefits. After the death of this Buddha, Buddhas bearing the same name, Awesome Sound King, appeared one after the other, numbering "twenty thousand million" in all.

Bodhisattva Never Disparaging appeared during the Middle Day of the Law after the death of the original Awesome Sound King Buddha. He bowed to any and all people he happened to meet, showing respect for their inherent Buddha nature. Arrogant and conceited, however, they ridiculed, vilified, stoned, and beat the bodhisattva with staves. This Buddha also expounded a Lotus Sutra. The chapter reads: "When this monk [Never Disparaging] was on the point of death, he heard up in the sky fully twenty thousand, ten thousand, a million verses of the Lotus Sutra that had previously been preached by the Buddha Awesome Sound King, and he was able to accept and uphold them all. Immediately he gained ... purity of the faculties ... Having gained this purity of the six faculties [eyes, ears, nose, tongue, body, and mind], his life span was increased by two hundred ten thousand million *nayutas* of years, and he went about widely preaching the Lotus Sutra for people."

Ayodhyā [阿踰闍] (Skt; Jpn Ayuja): A city in ancient India. Ayodhyā is thought to have been at the site of present-day Oudh in northeastern Uttar Pradesh, a northern state of India, though there are differing views. It was the capital of the kingdom of Kosala, but later, from the sixth century through the fifth century B.C.E., during Shakyamuni's time, Shrāvastī became the capital. A prevailing view identifies Ayodhyā with Shāketa, where Shakyamuni often went to preach. Ayodhyā was a center for the activities of Asanga and Vasubandhu, who lived during the fourth or fifth century C.E. It is well known as the birthplace of Rāma, a hero of the Indian epic *Rāmāyana*. In the seventh century, Hsüan-tsang traveled from China to India and authored *The Record of the Western Regions*, an account of his travels. In this work, he noted that Ayodhyā was rich in crops and fruit, and that there were approximately three thousand monks studying Mahayana and Hinayana Buddhism at more than one hundred monasteries there.

B

Bāladitya [幻日王] (n.d.) (Skt; Jpn Gennichi-ō): A king of Magadha in India said to have lived around the sixth century. A devout Buddhist, the king erected a temple at Nālandā Monastery, and monks from throughout India assembled to celebrate its completion. According to *The Record of the Western Regions*, Mihirakula, the ruler of the neighboring kingdom of Cheka (also known as Takka), opposed Buddhism and attempted to conquer Bāladitya. When Mihirakula attacked Magadha, the people united against him and took him prisoner. Bāladitya intended to put Mihirakula to death, but released him instead, moved by his own mother's plea that he act compassionately. After wandering through various countries, Mihirakula conquered Kashmir and Gandhara, where he destroyed Buddhist temples and monasteries. Soon after, Mihirakula died. It was said that upon his death dark clouds gathered, a strong wind blew, and the earth quaked violently, and these were interpreted by Buddhist sages as signs that Mihirakula had fallen into the hell of incessant suffering and would for a long time transmigrate through the evil paths of existence.

Bālin [婆稚阿修羅王] (Skt; Jpn Bachiashura-ō): One of the four *asura* kings who attended the ceremony of the Lotus Sutra depicted in the sutra. The *asura* king Balin appears in the sutra's "Introduction" (first) chapter. The chapter reads, "There were four *asura* kings, the *asura* king Balin, the *asura* king Kharaskandha, the *asura* king Vemachitrin, and the *asura* king Rāhu, each with several hundreds of thousands of followers." The Sanskrit word *balin* means strong, mighty, or powerful.

Bamboo Grove Monastery [竹林精舎] (Skt Venuvana-vihāra; Jpn

Chikurin-shōja): Also known as Venuvana Monastery. A monastery situated in the northern part of Rājagriha in Magadha, India. It was built by King Bimbisāra as an offering to Shakyamuni Buddha. According to one account, it was Kalandaka, a wealthy man in Rājagriha, who built the monastery and donated it to the Buddha. According to another account, Kalandaka offered his bamboo grove, and Bimbisāra built a monastery there. Bamboo Grove Monastery and Jetavana Monastery in Shrāvastī were the two major centers of Shakyamuni's propagation activities. The Chinese, Japanese, and English names are all literal translations of the Sanskrit, Venuvana-vihāra: *venu* and *vana* mean bamboo and grove, respectively, and *vihāra* means monastery.

Bamboo Staff school [竹杖外道] (Jpn Chikujō-gedō): A reference to any of several different groups of Brahmans in Shakyamuni's time whose members are said to have carried staves. The members of one such group are known to have killed Shakyamuni's disciple Maudgalyāyana. According to *The Monastic Rules on Various Matters,* Maudgalyāyana came across some Brahmans of the Bamboo Staff school who engaged him in discussion, whereupon he refuted their teacher. Enraged, they beat him to death with their staves. A Brahman of another Bamboo Staff school is known as the one who attempted to measure Shakyamuni Buddha's height with his bamboo staff, but discovered that his staff was too short to take the measurement.

before and after Sado [佐前佐後] (Jpn *sazen-sago*): A reference to the teachings and writings of Nichiren before, and those after, the Tatsunokuchi Persecution and his subsequent exile to Sado, an island in the Sea of Japan. The Tatsunokuchi Persecution took place on the twelfth day of the ninth month, 1271, and his exile lasted two and a half years from the tenth month of 1271 through the third month of 1274. Before Tatsunokuchi, Nichiren spread the invocation, or daimoku, of Nam-myoho-renge-kyo, but did not mention anything about the object of devotion known as the Gohonzon or the Three Great Secret Laws. After Tatsunokuchi, however, he revealed the object of devotion in terms of both the Person and the Law. He implicitly revealed the former, i.e., his identity as the Buddha of the Latter Day of the Law, in *The Opening of the Eyes,* and the latter, i.e., the object of devotion in his teachings, in *The Object of Devotion for Observing the Mind,* works he completed during his exile. He referred to the Three Great Secret Laws as "the three important matters of the 'Life Span' chapter of the essential teaching" of the Lotus Sutra in his letter of 1272 titled *Earthly Desires Are Enlightenment.* That is his earliest reference to the Three Great Secret Laws in his extant writings. He inscribed the Dai-Gohonzon, the object of devotion he identified as his life's purpose, at Minobu, Kai Province, on the twelfth day of the tenth month, 1279. In his *Letter to Misawa,* Nichiren compares his earlier teachings to the pre-Lotus Sutra teachings, which Shakyamuni preached as an expedient means to lead his disciples to the Lotus Sutra. Concerning his later, true teaching, Nichiren says in the same letter, "I secretly conveyed my teaching to my disciples from the province of Sado. . . . only this great teaching will spread throughout the entire land of Jambudvīpa" (896). Nichiren identified "this great teaching" with the Three Great Secret Laws that he revealed only after Tatsunokuchi.

begging bowl [鉢] (Jpn *hachi* or *hatsu*): *See* alms bowl.

beings of the two worlds and the eight groups [二界八番] (Jpn *nikaihachiban*): The beings that assembled to listen to the preaching of the Lotus Sutra. They are listed in the "Introduction" (first) chapter of the sutra. They are beings that reside in the two worlds—the world of desire and the world of form. The eight groups are a further division of the beings of the two worlds. They are (1) the gods of the world of desire, (2) the gods of the world of form, (3) dragon kings and their followers, (4) *kimnara* kings and their followers, (5) *gandharva* kings and their followers, (6) *asura* kings and their followers, (7) *garuda* kings and their followers, and (8) the king of the human world (i.e., Ajātashatru) and his followers.

"Belief and Understanding" chapter [信解品] (Jpn *Shinge-hon*): The fourth chapter of the Lotus Sutra. In this chapter, the four great voice-hearers, having heard the parable of the three carts and the burning house that Shakyamuni related in the "Simile and Parable" (third) chapter, now rejoice in their understanding of its meaning. They understand that Shakyamuni's true intention is to reveal the one Buddha vehicle that leads all people to Buddhahood. The four great voice-hearers are Mahākāshyapa, Kātyāyana, Maudgalyāyana, and Subhūti. To display their understanding of the meaning of the parable, they relate a parable of their own creation, the parable of the wealthy man and his poor son. In relating it, the four voice-hearers identify the wealthy man in the parable with the Buddha, and the poor son with themselves. Just as the poor son did not recognize his wealthy father and was content with lowly employment, so they did not realize that they were children of the Buddha entitled to attain the same state of Buddhahood; thus they were satisfied with inferior teachings. The Buddha, perceiving their limited aspirations, led them gradually through provisional teachings to the one Buddha vehicle. He was just like the wealthy man who allowed his son to engage in lowly employment, gradually helping him develop confidence and ability, and finally declared him to be his heir, transferring all his wealth to him. After relating the parable, the four voice-hearers state that they have received the greatest treasure of Buddhahood without earnestly seeking it. *See also* parable of the wealthy man and his poor son.

Benchō [弁長] (1162–1238): Also known as Ben'a or Shōkō. The second patriarch of the Japanese Pure Land (Jōdo) school and founder of the Chinzei branch of that school. At first, he studied the Tendai doctrine at Enryaku-ji temple on Mount Hiei. In 1190 he returned to his home in Chikuzen Province. There the death of his younger brother awoke him to the uncertainty of life, and he became interested in the idea of rebirth in the Pure Land. In 1197 Benchō went to Kyoto, where he met Hōnen, the founder of the Pure Land school, and became his disciple. Thereafter he returned home, but went again to Kyoto in 1199 to continue his study under Hōnen. In 1204 he went to propagate the Pure Land teaching in his home area of Chikuzen and in Chikugo, Higo, and other provinces. He is said to have built forty-eight temples. He wrote several treatises including *The Doctrine of "The Nembutsu Chosen above All"* and *The Essentials of the Pure Land Doctrine*. Ryōchū, the third patriarch of the school, was his most famous disciple.

benefit [功徳] (Skt *guna* or *punya;* Jpn *kudoku*): Also, merit, virtue, or blessing. In Buddhism, (1) meritorious acts or Buddhist practice that produce beneficial reward in this or future existences; and (2) benefit gained as a result of such good deeds or Buddhist practice. The Buddhist view of the law of causality holds that benefits accompany meritorious deeds. Deeds recognized as bringing about benefits differ among Buddhist schools. In general, however, religious deeds such as building monasteries or temples, erecting stupas, making images of the Buddha, transcribing sutras, and the practice of prayer have been considered throughout the history of Buddhism as major sources of benefit.

The "Expedient Means" (second) chapter of the Lotus Sutra reads, "If there are those who hear the Law, then not a one will fail to attain Buddhahood." The "Perceiver of the World's Sounds" (twenty-fifth) chapter of the sutra describes the beneficent power possessed by the bodhisattva Perceiver of the World's Sounds to save the practitioners of the Lotus Sutra from all kinds of crises. The Immeasurable Meanings Sutra explains ten inconceivable benefits, the fourth of which, for instance, it describes as follows: "If living beings are able to hear this sutra, though they hear only one recitation, one verse, or just one line, they will be filled with brave and stalwart thoughts. Though they have not yet saved themselves, they will be able to save others." The sutras describe the various meritorious deeds and practices Shakyamuni carried out in his past existences and the benefits he consequently enjoyed in his life in India.

In his *Object of Devotion for Observing the Mind,* Nichiren (1222–1282) states: "Shakyamuni's practices and the virtues he consequently attained are all contained within the five characters of Myoho-renge-kyo. If we believe in these five characters, we will naturally be granted the same benefits as he was" (365). Nichiren also states in *The Record of the Orally Transmitted Teachings:* "Benefit means the reward of purification of the six sense organs [eyes, ears, nose, tongue, body, and mind]. . . ." Nichiren thus associates benefit with the purification of the mind and other human faculties that results from Buddhist practice, specifically from the practice of chanting Nam-myoho-renge-kyo.

benefiting oneself and benefiting others [自利利他・自益益他・自利利人・自行化他] (Jpn *jiri-rita, jiyaku-yakuta, jiri-rinin,* or *jigyō-keta*): Also, practice for oneself and practice for others. An ideal of Mahayana bodhisattvas. Bodhisattvas are those who seek enlightenment for themselves and at the same time strive to instruct others, leading them to enlightenment. "Benefiting oneself" means to devote oneself to the Buddhist way and thereby accomplish personal growth and gain. Ultimately, it means to strive to attain enlightenment. "Benefiting others" means to bring benefit and eventually enlightenment to others. These two kinds of practice are mutually supportive. That is, practice for self-benefit leads to benefiting others, while practice for benefiting others leads to self-development and self-benefit.

"Benefits of Responding with Joy" chapter [随喜功徳品] (Jpn *Zuiki-kudoku-hon*): Abbreviated as the "Responding with Joy" chapter. The eighteenth chapter of the Lotus Sutra, which describes the benefits of rejoicing upon hearing Shakyamuni Buddha reveal his original attainment of enlightenment in the "Life Span" (sixteenth) chapter. The "Distinctions in Benefits" (seventeenth) chapter deals with the four stages of faith and the five stages of practice. The "Responding with Joy" chapter further explains the first of the five stages of practice, i.e., rejoicing on hearing the Lotus Sutra. This chapter begins with Bodhisattva Maitreya's question to Shakyamuni Buddha: "After the World-Honored One has passed into extinction, if those who hear this sutra are able to respond with joy, what amount of blessings will they acquire?" To reply, the Buddha relates the principle of continual propagation to the fiftieth person. Suppose, he says, a person responds with joy upon hearing the Lotus Sutra after Shakyamuni's death and preaches it to a second person, who in turn preaches it to a third, and so on, until a fiftieth person hears the sutra. Shakyamuni explains that the benefit this fiftieth person receives by rejoicing upon hearing the sutra is immeasurable; all the more so is that obtained by the first to hear it.

"Benefits of the Teacher of the Law" chapter [法師功徳品] (Jpn *Hosshi-kudoku-hon*): The nineteenth chapter of the Lotus Sutra. In this chapter, Shakyamuni Buddha addresses Bodhisattva Constant Exertion. It begins with Shakyamuni's statement that, by carrying out the five practices of embracing, reading, reciting, expounding, and transcribing the Lotus Sutra, one can purify one's six sense organs—the eyes, ears, nose, tongue, body, and mind. The chapter then elaborates on the benefits and powers pertaining to each of the purified sense organs. The "Teacher of the Law" in the chapter title indicates one who practices the Lotus Sutra oneself and preaches it to others.

benevolent gods [善神] (Jpn *zenjin*): *See* heavenly gods and benevolent deities.

Benevolent Kings Sutra [仁王経] (Chin *Jen-wang-ching;* Jpn *Ninnō-kyō*): Also known as the Benevolent Kings Wisdom Sutra. The full title is the Benevolent Kings Perfection of Wisdom Sutra. Translated into Chinese by Kumārajīva in the early fifth century, the sutra, regarded as the concluding sutra of the Wisdom sutras, consists of a discourse between Shakyamuni Buddha and Prasenajit, the king of Kosala. It enumerates seven disasters that will occur when the correct teaching perishes. It then stresses that the only way to avoid these disasters and ensure the protection and prosperity of the nation is to uphold the teaching of the perfection of wisdom. In China, Korea, and Japan, the Benevolent Kings Sutra was revered widely as a sutra for the protection of the nation. In Japan, the sutra was one of the three scriptures believed to protect the nation, the other two being the Lotus Sutra and the Golden Light Sutra. There is another Chinese translation of the Benevolent Kings Sutra done by Pu-k'ung in 765, which is used mainly by the Japanese True Word (Shingon) school.

Bennen [弁円]: Also known as Enni, a priest of the Rinzai school of Zen in Japan. *See* Enni.

Benten [弁天] (Jpn): Also known as Benzai-ten. The goddess Eloquence, one of the seven beneficent deities. *See* Eloquence.

Benzai-ten [弁才天] (Jpn): Also known as Benten. The goddess Eloquence, one of the seven beneficent deities. *See* Eloquence.

"Bestowal of Prophecy" chapter [授記品] (Jpn *Juki-hon*): The sixth chapter of the Lotus Sutra. The "prophecy" in the title means that made by Shakyamuni Buddha as to when, where, and under what names his disciples will become Buddhas. In this chapter, Shakyamuni prophesies that the four great voice-hearers—Mahākāshyapa, Maudgalyāyana, Subhūti, and Kātyāyana—will all attain enlightenment. In the theoretical teaching (first half) of the Lotus Sutra, Shakyamuni declares that the goal of Buddhist practice is the one vehicle of Buddhahood, not any of the three vehicles, i.e., voice-hearers, cause-awakened ones, and bodhisattvas. This principle is called "replacement of the three vehicles with the one vehicle." Shakyamuni explains this principle in three ways: (1) with the doctrine of the true aspect of all phenomena in the "Expedient Means" (second) chapter; (2) with the parable of the three carts and the burning house in the "Simile and Parable" (third) chapter; and (3) by clarifying his past relationship with his disciples in the "Parable of the Phantom City" (seventh) chapter. He employs these three explanations to enable the three groups of voice-hearer disciples—those of superior capacity, intermediate capacity, and inferior capacity, respectively—to understand the principle of the one vehicle teaching.

The "Bestowal of Prophecy" chapter predicts the enlightenment of those of intermediate capacity who realized the Buddha's true intention through the parable of the three carts and the burning house. In it, Shakyamuni first prophesies that Mahākāshyapa will attain Buddhahood in the future as Light Bright Buddha. Then he predicts that Subhūti, Kātyāyana, and Maudgalyāyana will also attain enlightenment and bear the names Rare Form Buddha, Jāmbūnada Gold Light Buddha, and Tamālapattra Sandalwood Fragrance Buddha, respectively. He concludes this chapter by proclaiming that he will next reveal the relationship between himself and his disciples in a previous existence.

Bestower of Fearlessness [施無畏者] (Skt *abhayam-dada;* Jpn *semui-sha*): A title of Bodhisattva Perceiver of the World's Sounds. The "Perceiver of the World's Sounds" (twenty-fifth) chapter of the Lotus Sutra reads: "This bodhisattva and mahāsattva Perceiver of the World's Sounds can bestow fearlessness on those who are in fearful, pressing, or difficult circumstances. That is why in this *sahā* world everyone calls him Bestower of Fearlessness." The Sanskrit word *abhayam-dada* means one who gives fearlessness or safety.

Bhadrapāla [跋陀婆羅] (Skt; Jpn Baddabara): The name of several figures appearing in various sutras: (1) In the Accumulated Treasures Sutra, the son of a wealthy man who went to Shakyamuni Buddha to seek the answers to questions that troubled him.

(2) In the Upholder of the Age Sutra, a bodhisattva who vowed to protect and propagate the Law in the age after Shakyamuni Buddha's

death when the Buddha's teachings would perish. For this he was praised highly by Shakyamuni, who prophesied that he would enjoy immeasurable benefits.

(3) One of the eighty thousand bodhisattvas described in the "Introduction" (first) chapter of the Lotus Sutra as attending the assembly on Eagle Peak where Shakyamuni preached the sutra. In the "Never Disparaging" (twentieth) chapter of the Lotus Sutra, Bhadrapāla is identified with one of those who slandered Bodhisattva Never Disparaging and as a result fell into the Avīchi hell. After undergoing great suffering there for a thousand *kalpas* and paying for his offenses, he once more encountered Bodhisattva Never Disparaging and accepted his teaching.

Bhadraruchi [賢愛論師] (n.d.) (Skt; Jpn Ken'ai-ronji): A Mahayana Buddhist scholar of western India. According to *The Record of the Western Regions,* Hsüan-tsang's record of his travels through Central Asia and India during the seventh century, he bested a Brahman called the Great Arrogant Brahman in a debate in Mālava, an ancient kingdom in India. The Great Arrogant Brahman was extremely learned and had more than one thousand disciples. He made four statues—one each of the gods Maheshvara, Vishnu, and Nārāyana, and one of the Buddha—and used them as the pillars of his preaching platform, asserting that his wisdom far surpassed that of these four. Hearing this, Bhadraruchi challenged him to debate and won. Thereupon the king of Mālava realized that he had been deceived by the Brahman into believing his teaching and sentenced him to death. Bhadraruchi petitioned the king to let the Brahman live, and he was spared. Nevertheless, the Brahman bore a grudge against Bhadraruchi, slandering him and the Mahayana teachings, and for this reason he is said to have fallen into hell alive.

Bhadrika [跋提・跋提梨迦] (Skt; Jpn Batsudai or Batsudairika): One of the five ascetics to whom Shakyamuni Buddha preached his first sermon after attaining enlightenment and whom he thereby converted. *See also* five ascetics.

bhagavat [世尊] (Skt, Pali; Jpn *seson*): One of the ten honorable titles of a Buddha. *Bhagavat* means possessing fortune, venerable, or holy. It is also applied to the names of deities. In Buddhism, it is used as an epithet for a Buddha and is often translated as "blessed one." In the Chinese versions of Buddhist scriptures, *bhagavat* is rendered as World-Honored One, indicating one who is revered as the most venerable in the world.

bhaishajya [薬] (Skt; Jpn *yaku* or *kusuri*): Curativeness, medicine, or remedy. The word *bhaishajya* is a component of the names of many Buddhas and bodhisattvas found in Buddhist scriptures. For example,

Bhaishajyarāja, or Medicine King, is a bodhisattva said to possess the power to cure all physical and mental illnesses. The word *rāja* means king. Bhaishajyasamudgata, or Medicine Superior, is also a bodhisattva of healing. His name means one who has come forth from medicine. *Samudgata* means appeared, risen up, or come forth. Bhaishajyaguru, or Medicine Master, is also known as the Buddha of Healing, the Buddha of Medicine, and by similar names. *Guru* means a teacher, a master, or a venerable person.

Bhaishajyaguru [薬師如来] (Skt; Jpn Yakushi-nyorai): The Thus Come One (or Buddha) Medicine Master. *See* Medicine Master.

Bhāvaviveka [清弁] (c. 490–570) (Skt; Jpn Shōben): Also known as Bhavya. An Indian Buddhist scholar of Mādhyamika philosophy. He is the founder of the Svātantrika school, one of the two schools of Mādhyamika, the other being the Prāsangika school led by his contemporary, Buddhapālita. Born to the royal family in Magadha, India, Bhāvaviveka studied the Mahayana sutras and Nāgārjuna's works under Samgharakshita, a Mādhyamika scholar. Later, he wrote *The Treatise on the Lamp of Wisdom* (Skt *Prajnā-pradīpa*), a commentary on Nāgārjuna's *Verses on the Middle Way (Madhyamaka-kārikā),* in which he criticized Buddhapālita's method of demonstrating the truth of non-substantiality. As a result, the Mādhyamika school split into two. To demonstrate the truth of non-substantiality, Bhāvaviveka adopted Dignāga's method of Buddhist logic. He wrote *The Heart of the Middle Way (Madhyamaka-hridaya)* in which he criticized the doctrine of the Vijnānavāda, or Consciousness-Only, school. Dharmapāla of the Consciousness-Only school retorted Bhāvaviveka's criticisms. Bhāvaviveka took the position that all phenomena are interdependent and have no independent existence of their own, or are non-substantial in nature. Dharmapāla asserted that phenomena arise from consciousness *(vijnāna),* which is the only reality. (The Sanskrit words *mādhyamika* and *madhyamaka* both mean intermediate or middle.)

bhikshu [比丘] (Skt; Pali *bhikkhu;* Jpn *biku*): A Buddhist monk. In the strict sense, a fully ordained monk who has renounced the secular world and observes the entire set of commandments, or two hundred and fifty precepts according to *The Fourfold Rules of Discipline,* set forth for monks. The term *bhikshu* means one who begs, particularly for alms, and generally one who devotes oneself to Buddhist practice and subsists entirely on alms received from laypersons through the practice of alms-begging. A nun is called *bhikshunī.* With the development of the community of monks and the establishment of a system of monastic rules, *bhikshu* came to refer to only those men who had gained admission into the Buddhist

Order by going through an established ordination ceremony. They were permitted to own only three robes, all made of cast-off rags, and one begging bowl. Thus equipped, they carried out their practice of religious mendicancy. Monks still in their teenage years were not recognized as *bhikshu*. In the early period of Buddhism, *bhikshus* lived alone in forests and other quiet locations, devoting themselves to meditation and other practices. Later they gathered with other Buddhists to form a community. *See also* two hundred and fifty precepts.

bhikshunī [比丘尼] (Skt; Pali *bhikkhunī;* Jpn *bikuni*): A Buddhist nun. *Bhikshunī* is a female believer of Buddhism who has renounced secular life and been accepted into the Buddhist Order on the condition that she observe monastic rules. According to traditional accounts, Mahāprajāpatī, Shakyamuni's foster-mother, was the first woman to be admitted by Shakyamuni into the Order and thus become a nun. Nuns are often said to have observed five hundred precepts, though the actual number of precepts was smaller. *The Fourfold Rules of Discipline* lists 348 precepts for nuns. A *bhikshunī* was required, in all matters, to respect and seek guidance from a *bhikshu*, or monk, as represented by the formulation of the eight precepts of reverence. In Japan, Zenshin is known as the first *bhikshunī;* she renounced secular life along with two other women in 584. In the early seventh century, the number of Buddhist nuns in Japan was more than five hundred. *See also* eight precepts of reverence; five hundred precepts.

Bimbisāra [頻婆娑羅王] (Skt, Pali; Jpn Bimbashara-ō): A king of Magadha, one of the most powerful kingdoms in India. He was the father of Ajātashatru and a devout follower of Shakyamuni. Tradition has it that, when Shakyamuni first left his home to seek enlightenment, he arrived in Rājagriha, the capital of Magadha, where his noble bearing attracted the attention of King Bimbisāra who offered him riches and the command of his armies. Shakyamuni refused, explaining that he sought nothing but enlightenment. Bimbisāra then requested that Shakyamuni teach him the truth he was seeking once he found it. After Shakyamuni attained enlightenment, he did in fact return to Magadha, and Bimbisāra became his follower. Bimbisāra donated Bamboo Grove Monastery to the Buddhist Order and is said to have built a flight of stone steps to the top of Eagle Peak near Rājagriha where Shakyamuni often taught. According to *On the Destruction of the Order,* Bimbisāra's son Ajātashatru, at the urging of Devadatta, imprisoned Bimbisāra and ascended the throne. When Ajātashatru later fell seriously ill, Bimbisāra felt deep pity for him. Realizing this, Ajātashatru regretted his actions and sent his men to release Bimbisāra. Bimbisāra took his own life, however, thinking that they were coming to torture him. According to another account, Ajātashatru had King Bimbisāra killed or starved him to death in prison; and still another says that Bimbisāra discovered Ajātashatru's conspiracy beforehand and, seeing how eager his son was to reign, abdicated voluntarily.

Biographies of Eminent Priests, The [高僧伝] (Jpn *Kōsō-den*): See *Liang Dynasty Biographies of Eminent Priests, The.*

Biographies of Eminent Priests of the Great T'ang Dynasty Who Sought the Law in the Western Regions, The [大唐西域求法高僧伝] (Chin *Ta-t'ang-hsi-yü-ch'iu-fa-kao-seng-chuan;* Jpn *Daitō-saiiki-guhō-kōsō-den*): Also known as *The Biographies of Eminent Priests Who Sought the Law in the Western Regions* and *The Biographies of Eminent Priests Who Sought the Law.* A collection of biographies of sixty priests of the T'ang dynasty in China who journeyed to Central Asia or India in the seventh century in search of Buddhist scriptures and teachings. This work, completed by the Chinese pilgrim I-ching in 691 before his return to China, also contains the record of his own travels in India and other southern countries. Because of his reverence for Fa-hsien and Hsüan-tsang, who had journeyed to India in search of the Buddha's teachings in the fifth and seventh centuries, respectively, I-ching left Canton in 671 and journeyed to India by sea. In 695 he returned to Lo-yang with numerous Sanskrit scriptures. I-ching's work is highly esteemed because of descriptions it contains of the religions and circumstances of India and the other countries south of China.

Biographies of Eminent Priests Who Sought the Law, The [求法高僧伝] (Jpn *Guhō-kōsō-den*): See *Biographies of Eminent Priests of the Great T'ang Dynasty Who Sought the Law in the Western Regions, The.*

Biography of the Tripitaka Master of Ta-tz'u-en-ssu Temple, The [大慈恩寺三蔵法師伝] (Chin *Ta-tz'u-en-ssu-san-tsang-fa-shih-chuan;* Jpn *Daijionji-sanzō-hosshi-den*): A ten-volume biography of Hsüan-tsang (602–664), the patriarch of Ta-tz'u-en-ssu temple, completed in 688. It was written by Hui-li (b. 615) and revised by Yen-ts'ung. According to another account, the first five volumes are attributed to Hui-li, and the latter five volumes, to Yen-ts'ung. Its full title is *The Biography of the Tripitaka Master of Ta-tz'u-en-ssu Temple of the Great T'ang Dynasty.* The first five volumes contain the record of Hsüan-tsang's travels in Central Asia and India. The latter five recount his translation of Buddhist scriptures and the lectures he gave after his return to Ch'ang-an in China in 645. Together with *The Record of the Western Regions* by Hsüan-tsang himself, this work is valued as an important reference in the study of Central Asia and India of that period.

Bishamon-ten [毘沙門天] (Jpn): Also known as Vaishravana or

Hearer of Many Teachings. One of the four heavenly kings. *See* Vaishravana.

Bodh Gaya [仏陀伽耶] (Jpn Buddagaya): *See* Buddhagayā.

bodhi [菩提] (Skt, Pali; Jpn *bodai*): Enlightenment, enlightened wisdom, or perfect wisdom, as described in Buddhism. It is rendered in Chinese scriptures as awakening, enlightenment, wisdom, or the way. Buddhism describes three kinds of *bodhi:* the *bodhi* of a voice-hearer, the *bodhi* of a cause-awakened one, and the *bodhi* of a Buddha. The *bodhi* of a Buddha, or the *bodhi* that a Buddha has attained, is the highest; hence it is called *anuttara-samyak-sambodhi,* or supreme perfect enlightenment. A Mahayana practitioner who seeks this supreme enlightenment is called a bodhisattva. A bodhisattva is a *sattva* (being) who strives for *bodhi.* Mahayana Buddhism states emphatically that one should first arouse the mind to seek, or the aspiration for, *bodhi* and then strive to achieve the goal of *bodhi,* or Buddhahood, through bodhisattva practice.

Bodhidharma [菩提達磨] (n.d.) (Skt; Jpn Bodaidaruma): The founder of Chinese Zen, or Ch'an, Buddhism. Biographical information concerning him is scanty and contradictory, and it is difficult to distinguish fact from legend. He is said to have been a prince of a kingdom in southern India. He studied Mahayana and eventually devoted himself to the practice of meditation. Thereafter he traveled through several countries and went to China by sea. There he was welcomed by Emperor Wu of the Liang dynasty (502–557) and preached the Zen doctrine in Chien-k'ang, the capital city. However, since his teaching was not accepted, he retired to Shao-lin-ssu temple on Mount Sung, where he is said to have meditated facing a wall for nine years, thus awakening to the profound truth of Zen. His successor was Hui-k'o. Some sources put the year of Bodhidharma's death at 528, and others at 536. He is said to have lived to be 150.

Bodhiruchi (Skt) (1) [菩提流支] (d. 527) (Jpn Bodairushi): The founder of the Chinese Ti-lun, or Treatise on the Ten Stages Sutra, school. A native of northern India, in 508 he went to Lo-yang in China where he translated thirty-nine Buddhist texts into Chinese including *The Treatise on the Ten Stages Sutra, The Treatise on the Lotus Sutra,* the Diamond Wisdom Sutra, and the Lankāvatāra Sutra. He is also regarded as a patriarch of the Pure Land school because he presented T'an-luan with a copy of the Meditation on the Buddha Infinite Life Sutra and because he translated *The Treatise on the Pure Land,* a commentary by Vasubandhu on the Buddha Infinite Life Sutra.

(2) [菩提流志] (d. 727) (Jpn Bodairushi): A translator of Buddhist scriptures who went from India to Ch'ang-an in China in 693. Born

to a Brahman family in southern India, he first studied Brahmanism and later converted to Buddhism. In China, he stayed at Fo-shou-chi-ssu temple in Lo-yang, where he engaged in the translation of Buddhist scriptures. Together with I-ching and others, Bodhiruchi assisted Shikshānanda, a monk from Khotan in Central Asia, in translating the Flower Garland Sutra into Chinese, and in 699 the eighty-volume Chinese translation was completed. This version is noted as one of the three Chinese translations of the Flower Garland Sutra. Bodhiruchi also selected forty-nine Chinese sutras, some of which were his translations, and compiled them as the 120-volume Accumulated Great Treasures Sutra. He translated a total of fifty-three scriptures.

bodhisattva [菩薩] (Skt; Jpn *bosatsu*): One who aspires to enlightenment, or Buddhahood. *Bodhi* means enlightenment, and *sattva,* a living being. In Hinayana Buddhism, the term is used almost exclusively to indicate Shakyamuni Buddha in his previous lifetimes. The *Jātaka,* or "birth stories" (which recount his past existences), often refer to him as "the bodhisattva." After the rise of Mahayana, *bodhisattva* came to mean anyone who aspires to enlightenment and carries out altruistic practice. Mahayana practitioners used it to refer to themselves, thus expressing the conviction that they would one day attain Buddhahood. In contrast with the Hinayana ideal embodied by the voice-hearers and cause-awakened ones who direct their efforts solely toward personal salvation, Mahayana sets forth the ideal of the bodhisattva who seeks enlightenment both for self and others, even postponing one's entry into nirvana in order to lead others to that goal. The predominant characteristic of a bodhisattva is therefore compassion.

According to Mahayana tradition, upon embarking on their practice of the six *pāramitās,* bodhisattvas make four universal vows: (1) to save innumerable living beings, (2) to eradicate countless earthly desires, (3) to master immeasurable Buddhist teachings, and (4) to attain the supreme enlightenment. The six *pāramitās* are (1) almsgiving, (2) keeping the precepts, (3) forbearance, (4) assiduousness, (5) meditation, and (6) the obtaining of wisdom. Some sutras divide bodhisattva practice into fifty-two stages, ranging from initial resolution to the attainment of enlightenment. Bodhisattva practice was generally thought to require successive lifetimes spanning many *kalpas* to complete. From the standpoint of the Lotus Sutra, which recognizes that one can attain Buddhahood in one's present form, the bodhisattva practice can be completed in a single lifetime.

In Japan, the title bodhisattva was occasionally given to eminent priests by the imperial court, or by their followers as an epithet of respect. It also was applied to deities. When Buddhism was introduced to Japan, deities of the Japanese pantheon were regarded as afflicted with an assortment of flaws, delusions, and vices. Later, their status was raised when they were identified with bodhisattvas due to the syncretism of Buddhism and Shintoism. Great Bodhisattva Hachiman is an example of this.

In terms of the concept of the Ten Worlds, the world of bodhisattvas constitutes the ninth of the Ten Worlds, describing a state characterized by compassion in which one seeks enlightenment both for oneself and others. In this state, one finds satisfaction in devoting oneself to relieving the suffering of others and leading them to happiness, even if it costs one one's life. *See also* fifty-two stages of bodhisattva practice.

bodhisattva-mahāsattva [菩薩摩訶薩] (Skt; Jpn *bosatsu-makasatsu*): An honorific title for bodhisattvas. *Mahāsattva* means a great being, implying one who has a great aspiration. *See also* mahāsattva.

"Bodhisattva Never Disparaging" chapter [常不軽菩薩品] (Jpn *Jō-fukyō-bosatsu-hon*): Abbreviated as the "Never Disparaging" chapter. The twentieth chapter of the Lotus Sutra, in which Shakyamuni illustrates, with the story of Bodhisattva Never Disparaging, both the benefit of embracing and practicing the Lotus Sutra and the gravity of retribution for slandering its votaries. The chapter describes this bodhisattva as having lived in the Middle Day of the Law after the death of a Buddha named Awesome Sound King, at a time when arrogant monks held great authority and power. Never Disparaging venerated all people, repeating the phrase "I have profound reverence for you, I would never dare treat you with disparagement or arrogance. Why? Because you are all practicing the bodhisattva way and are certain to attain Buddhahood."

Monks, nuns, laymen, and laywomen mocked him and attacked him with staves and stones. Bodhisattva Never Disparaging, however, persevered in his practice and achieved purification of his six senses through the benefit of the Lotus Sutra. When the arrogant clerics and laypersons who had treated Never Disparaging with ridicule and contempt heard his preaching and saw that he had purified his senses, they all took faith in him and became his followers. But due to their past offenses of treating him with animosity, they did not encounter a Buddha, hear of the Law, or see the community of monks for two hundred million *kalpas*. For a thousand *kalpas*, they underwent great suffering in the Avīchi hell. After they had finished paying for their offenses, they again encountered Bodhisattva Never Disparaging and received instruction from him in attaining supreme perfect enlightenment.

This story illustrates the principle of attaining enlightenment through a reverse relationship, or the connection established with the correct teaching through rejecting or slandering it. It illustrates the great power of the Lotus Sutra to save even those who oppose or slander it. Shakyamuni identifies Bodhisattva Never Disparaging as himself in a past existence and reveals that those who disparaged him are present in the assembly of the Lotus Sutra on Eagle Peak. Shakyamuni further states that these people are now at the stage of practice where they will never regress in their pursuit of supreme perfect enlightenment. He then urges that the Lotus Sutra be single-mindedly embraced and propagated after his death.

"Bodhisattva Perceiver of the World's Sounds" chapter [観世音菩薩品・観音品] (Jpn *Kanzeon-bosatsu-bon* or *Kannon-bon*): The abbreviated title of the twenty-fifth chapter of the Lotus Sutra. Also "Perceiver of the World's Sounds" chapter. *See* "Universal Gateway of the Bodhisattva Perceiver of the World's Sounds" chapter.

Bodhisattva Practice Jeweled Necklace Sutra [菩薩瓔珞本業経] (Chin *P'u-sa-ying-lo-pen-yeh-ching;* Jpn *Bosatsu-yōraku-hongō-kyō*): Also known as the Jeweled Necklace Sutra. A sutra that focuses on bodhisattva practice and its stages. According to tradition, Chu Fo-nien translated it into Chinese between 376 and 378. Recent research suggests, however, that this sutra was produced in China sometime in the fifth or sixth century. It expounds the process by which a bodhisattva becomes a Buddha and sets forth fifty-two stages of bodhisattva practice—ten stages of faith, ten stages of security, ten stages of practice, ten stages of devotion, ten stages of development, the stage of near-perfect enlightenment, and the stage of perfect enlightenment. This sutra also addresses the Mahayana, or bodhisattva, precepts. Because of its description of bodhisattva practice, bodhisattva stages, and bodhisattva precepts, this work greatly influenced Buddhism in China and Japan.

Bodhisattvas of the Earth [地涌の菩薩] (Jpn *jiyu-no-bosatsu*): An innumerable host of bodhisattvas who emerge from beneath the earth and to whom Shakyamuni Buddha entrusts the propagation of the Mystic Law, or the essence of the Lotus Sutra, in the Latter Day of the Law. They are described in the "Emerging from the Earth" (fifteenth) chapter of the Lotus Sutra, the first chapter of the sutra's essential teaching (latter fourteen chapters). In this chapter, countless bodhisattvas from other worlds ask for permission to propagate the sutra in the *sahā* world after the Buddha's death, but Shakyamuni refuses, saying that bodhisattvas who will carry out that task already exist in the *sahā* world. At this point the earth trembles and splits open, and from within it emerges a host of bodhisattvas equal in number to the sands of sixty thousand Ganges

Rivers, each with his own retinue of followers. Their bodies are golden and they possess the thirty-two features that characterize a Buddha. They are led by four bodhisattvas—Superior Practices, Boundless Practices, Pure Practices, Firmly Established Practices—and Superior Practices is the leader of them all. In the "Supernatural Powers" (twenty-first) chapter, Shakyamuni transfers the essence of the Lotus Sutra to the Bodhisattvas of the Earth, entrusting them with the mission of propagating it after his death, specifically, in the Latter Day of the Law.

As the person who first revealed the Mystic Law, or Nam-myoho-renge-kyo, which he described as the essence of the Lotus Sutra, and began its propagation in the Latter Day, Nichiren (1222–1282) identified himself with Bodhisattva Superior Practices, the leader of the Bodhisattvas of the Earth. He also regarded his followers who embrace and propagate the teaching of the Mystic Law as the Bodhisattvas of the Earth. In this connection, Nichiren states in his work *The True Aspect of All Phenomena:* "There should be no discrimination among those who propagate the five characters of Myoho-renge-kyo in the Latter Day of the Law, be they men or women. Were they not Bodhisattvas of the Earth, they could not chant the daimoku. At first only Nichiren chanted Nam-myoho-renge-kyo, but then two, three, and a hundred followed, chanting and teaching others. Propagation will unfold this way in the future as well. Does this not signify 'emerging from the earth'?" (385). *See also* bodhisattvas of the essential teaching.

bodhisattvas of the essential teaching [本化の菩薩] (Jpn *honge-no-bosatsu*): Bodhisattvas taught by the true Buddha, i.e., the Buddha whose true identity is revealed in the essential teaching (latter fourteen chapters) of the Lotus Sutra. In this teaching, Shakyamuni reveals his true identity as the Buddha who attained enlightenment at a time commonly known as numberless major world system dust particle *kalpas* in the past. The disciples whom he had taught in this capacity since the time of his original attainment of enlightenment are the bodhisattvas of the essential teaching. They are also known as the Bodhisattvas of the Earth, and are first described in the "Emerging from the Earth" (fifteenth) chapter of the Lotus Sutra, the first chapter of the essential teaching. Shakyamuni entrusts them with the mission of propagating the Mystic Law, or the essence of the sutra, in the Latter Day of the Law. In the pre-Lotus Sutra teachings and in the theoretical teaching (first fourteen chapters) of the Lotus Sutra, Shakyamuni assumes a transient identity—that of the Buddha who had attained enlightenment for the first time in India after sitting in meditation under the *bodhi* tree. The bodhisattvas whom

Shakyamuni taught in this capacity, such as Manjushrī and Universal Worthy, are the bodhisattvas of the theoretical teaching. *See also* Bodhisattvas of the Earth.

bodhisattvas of the theoretical teaching [迹化の菩薩] (Jpn *shakke-no-bosatsu*): Bodhisattvas who are followers of a provisional Buddha. They include the bodhisattvas Manjushrī, Universal Worthy, Perceiver of the World's Sounds, and Medicine King. A provisional Buddha is a Buddha who, in order to save people, assumes a transient identity that accords with the people's capacity, without revealing his true identity. In the pre-Lotus Sutra teachings and in the theoretical teaching (first fourteen chapters) of the Lotus Sutra, Shakyamuni did not reveal his true identity, i.e., he did not reveal himself as a Buddha who had attained enlightenment in the remote past, but assumed the provisional status of a Buddha who had first attained enlightenment in that lifetime in India. The bodhisattvas whom he taught in this capacity are the bodhisattvas of the theoretical teaching.

This term is used in contrast with the bodhisattvas of the essential teaching, who are the Bodhisattvas of the Earth, or followers of the Buddha who has revealed his original enlightenment and true identity in the essential teaching (latter fourteen chapters) of the Lotus Sutra. According to Nichiren, the bodhisattvas of the theoretical teaching are said to appear in the Former Day and Middle Day of the Law and spread provisional Mahayana or the theoretical teaching of the Lotus Sutra. They are contrasted with the Bodhisattvas of the Earth who appear in the Latter Day of the Law and devote themselves to spreading the Mystic Law, or the essence of the Lotus Sutra.

"Bodhisattva Universal Worthy" chapter [普賢菩薩品] (Jpn *Fugen-bosatsu-hon*): The abbreviated title of the twenty-eighth and last chapter of the Lotus Sutra. Also "Universal Worthy" chapter. *See* "Encouragements of the Bodhisattva Universal Worthy" chapter.

"Bodhisattva Wonderful Sound" chapter [妙音菩薩品] (Jpn *Myō'on-bosatsu-hon*): Abbreviated as the "Wonderful Sound" chapter. The twenty-fourth chapter of the Lotus Sutra. It describes a bodhisattva named Wonderful Sound who possesses the faculty of assuming at will any of thirty-four forms in order to propagate the Lotus Sutra. At the beginning of the chapter, Shakyamuni emits a beam of light from the knob of flesh on top of his head and another beam from the tuft of white hair between his eyebrows, illuminating innumerable Buddha lands to the east, beyond which is a land called Adorned with Pure Light. In this land dwells the Buddha Pure Flower Constellation King Wisdom, who is attended by Bodhisattva Wonderful Sound. The beam of light emanating from Shakyamuni Buddha fully illuminates this land as well. At that time, Wonderful Sound announces to the Buddha Pure Flower Constellation King Wisdom that he will go to the *sahā* world to make offerings to Shakyamuni Buddha. After first causing eighty-four thousand jeweled lotus blossoms to appear magically on Eagle Peak, he arrives with a retinue of eighty-four thousand bodhisattvas.

Bodhisattva Flower Virtue asks Shakyamuni Buddha about what causes Bodhisattva Wonderful Sound has created in order to acquire his supernatural powers. Shakyamuni replies that in the remote past Wonderful Sound served a Buddha named Cloud Thunder Sound King for twelve thousand years, employing one hundred thousand kinds of musical instruments to provide an offering to the Buddha and presenting to him eighty-four thousand alms bowls made of the seven kinds of treasures. As a result of this devotion, he acquired his supernatural abilities. He is said to have the power to appear as a god, a human being, a dragon, a demon, or in other forms in order to preach the Lotus Sutra. Shakyamuni describes thirty-four forms that Bodhisattva Wonderful Sound assumes in order to save the people. After making offerings to Shakyamuni Buddha, Wonderful Sound returns to his original land.

bodhi tree [菩提樹] (Skt, Pali; Jpn *bodai-ju*): Also, *bo* tree. The pipal tree (also spelled the peepul tree) at Buddhagayā, India, under which Shakyamuni Buddha attained enlightenment. In Sanskrit this variety of tree was called *pippala* or *ashvattha*. It is a tall evergreen belonging to the mulberry family that reaches thirty meters in height. Its leaves are heart-shaped with an elongated, pointed end. Because Shakyamuni attained enlightenment under this tree, Buddhists came to regard it as sacred and refer to it as the *bodhi* (enlightenment) tree. In early Buddhist sculptures, the *bodhi* tree was used in carvings depicting the events of Shakyamuni Buddha's life to symbolize Shakyamuni and his enlightenment. At that time, no representation of the Buddha himself was made in the carvings. The Buddha was depicted symbolically as the *bodhi* tree, and his teachings as the wheel of the Law.

body of the Law [法身] (Jpn *hosshin*): One of the three Buddha bodies. *See* Dharma body.

Bonten [梵天] (Jpn): The heavenly king Brahmā. A leading Buddhist god. *See* Brahmā.

Born from the Crown of the Head [頂生王・曼陀多王] (Skt Mūrdhagata or Māndhātri; Jpn Chōshō-ō or Mandata-ō): A king who appears in many sutras, some of which describe him as a previous incarnation of Shakyamuni Buddha. Descriptions of him differ slightly among sutras. Born from the top of King Uposatha's head, he ruled Jambudvīpa, one of the four continents surrounding Mount Sumeru, by justice rather than force and brought ease and comfort to the people. He went on to rule the other three continents and later ascended to the Heaven of the Thirty-three Gods on the summit of Mount Sumeru. He was welcomed there by Shakra, the lord of this heaven, who seated him by his side in the Hall of the Good Law. He was outstanding in appearance, power, and authority, no less so than the lord Shakra. He conceived a desire to drive Shakra from the Heaven of the Thirty-three Gods, however, and become its ruler. As a result, he eventually fell to the ground of Jambudvīpa. He became gravely ill, and when his life came to an end, he told his retainers that, though he ruled the four continents and obtained all kinds of pleasures, these things failed to satisfy him.

bo tree [菩提樹] (Jpn *bodai-ju*): See *bodhi* tree.

Boundless Practices [無辺行菩薩] (Skt Anantachāritra; Jpn Muhengyō-bosatsu): One of the four leaders of the Bodhisattvas of the Earth. In the "Emerging from the Earth" (fifteenth) chapter of the Lotus Sutra, Bodhisattva Boundless Practices appears from beneath the earth together with the other Bodhisattvas of the Earth. The chapter reads: "Among these bodhisattvas were four leaders. The first was called Superior Practices, the second was called Boundless Practices, the third was called Pure Practices, and the fourth was called Firmly Established Practices." According to Tao-hsien's *Supplement to "The Words and Phrases of the Lotus Sutra,"* of the four virtues of the Buddha's life—true self, eternity, purity, and happiness—that these four bodhisattvas represent, Boundless Practices represents eternity.

"bowed in obeisance and departed" [作礼而去] (Jpn *sarai-niko*): An expression used to conclude many sutras. For example, the Lotus Sutra ends with the following words: "When the Buddha preached this sutra, Universal Worthy and the other bodhisattvas, Shāriputra and the other voice-hearers, along with the heavenly beings, dragons, human and non-human beings—the entire membership of the great assembly were all filled with great joy. Accepting and upholding the words of the Buddha, they bowed in obeisance and departed." This expression represents the respect and gratitude the listeners show to the Buddha, who has preached his teachings to instruct and enlighten them.

Brahmā [梵天] (Skt, Pali; Jpn Bonten): Also, Mahābrahmā, the great heavenly king Brahmā, or the heavenly king Brahmā. A god said to live in the first and lowest of the four meditation heavens in the world of form above Mount Sumeru and who rules over the *sahā* world. In Indian mythology, he was regarded as the personification of the fundamental universal principle (Brahman), and he was incorporated into Buddhism as one of the two major tutelary gods, the other being Shakra, known also as Indra.

Brahmā Excellent Thought Sutra [思益経] (Chin *Ssu-i-ching;* Jpn *Shiyaku-kyō*): *See* Questions of Brahmā Excellent Thought Sutra.

Brahma Heaven [梵天] (Skt, Pali; Jpn Bon-ten): The first and lowest of the four meditation heavens in the world of form above Mount Sumeru. The Brahma Heaven comprises three realms or levels. They are, in an ascending order, the Heaven of Brahmā's Retinue, the Heaven of Brahmā's Aide, and the Heaven of Great Brahmā. The Heaven of Brahmā's Retinue is located 1,280,000 *yojanas* above the Heaven of Freely Enjoying Things Conjured by Others, the highest heaven in the world of desire. The Heaven of Brahmā's Aide is located 2,560,000 *yojanas* above the Heaven of Brahmā's Retinue, and the Heaven of Great Brahmā, 5,120,000 *yojanas* above the Heaven of Brahmā's Aide.

Brahman [婆羅門] (Skt, Pali *brāhmana;* Jpn *baramon*): Also, Brahmin. A member of the priestly class, the highest of the four castes in ancient India. The other three were the Kshatriya, the military or ruling class; the Vaishya, or class of peasants, merchants, and artisans; and the Shūdra, or slave class. The Brahmans retained exclusive rights over the administration of religious matters such as instruction on the Vedas and performance of rites and rituals. Since Brahmanism held that the accumulation of merit and the gods' beneficence depended upon the correct performance of rituals, this right invested the Brahmans with tremendous social authority. Their ascendancy over the other castes was secured in the later Vedic period, from around 1000 B.C.E. through 500 B.C.E. During this period, an agricultural society developed in the Ganges Valley, and rituals assumed great importance. The Brahmans formed a detailed system of rites and held sole claim over their administration. By the time of Shakyamuni, however, a flourishing of commerce and industry was under way, and many cities had appeared. As powerful monarchic states were formed, the Kshatriya and Vaishya classes rose in social standing, and the authority of the Brahmans declined proportionately.

Brahmā Net Sutra [梵網経] (Chin *Fan-wang-ching;* Jpn *Bommō-kyō*): Also known as the Bodhisattva Precepts Sutra. A sutra regarded as fundamental among scriptures elucidating Mahayana bodhisattva precepts. Translated into Chinese in the early fifth century by Kumārajīva, the Brahmā Net Sutra consists of two volumes. The first volume expounds forty stages of bodhisattva practice that are classified into four groups: (1) ten initial stages, (2) ten steps in the nourishment of perfection, (3) ten diamond steps of firmness, and (4) ten stages of development. The second volume sets forth the ten major precepts and the forty-eight minor precepts. This sutra was highly valued in China and Japan because it describes the precepts for Mahayana bodhisattvas, and many commentaries were written on it. In Japan, Dengyō (767–822), the founder of the Japanese Tendai school, used this sutra to replace the Hinayana precepts observed by the six schools of Nara with Mahayana precepts at ordination.

brahma practice [梵行] (Skt *brahma-charyā* or *brahma-charya;* Jpn *bon-gyō*): Pure practice, or Buddhist practices of a pure nature. Brahma practice refers specifically to the practice of observing precepts, and especially to observing the precept of eliminating one's sexual desires. Monks were required to observe the discipline of celibacy and refrain from all sexual relationships and acts. Brahma practice refers to such a way of life, but in a broader sense, it refers to those practices aimed at freeing oneself from all earthly desires.

brahma sound [梵音声] (Skt; Jpn *bonnonjō*): The voice of a Buddha. *See* pure and far-reaching voice.

branch teaching [枝末法輪・枝末教] (Jpn *shimatsu-hōrin* or *shimatsu-kyō*): (1) One component of the "thrice turned wheel of the Law," a division of Shakyamuni's lifetime teachings into three categories set forth by Chi-tsang (549–623) of the Three Treatises (San-lun) school in China. *See* thrice turned wheel of the Law.

(2) The term used by Fa-tsang (643–712), the third patriarch of the Flower Garland (Hua-yen) school in China, in reference to all sutras except the Flower Garland Sutra, including the Lotus Sutra. Fa-tsang called the Flower Garland Sutra the root teaching.

breath-counting meditation [数息観] (Skt *ānāpāna-smriti* or *ānāpāna-samādhi;* Jpn *susoku-kan*): Also, counting-of-breath meditation. One of the five meditations. A method of quieting the mind by counting one's breaths. This meditative practice prepares one to enter *samādhi,* a high level of serene meditative contemplation. The Sanskrit word *ānāpāna* means breath or breathing. *Smriti* means mindfulness, awareness, memory, or remembrance, and *samādhi* means concentration, contemplation, or meditation.

Brief History of Japan, A [扶桑略記] (Jpn *Fusō-ryakki*): A work of Japanese history centering on Buddhism. It covers the period from the reign of the legendary Emperor Jimmu through Emperor Horikawa (r. 1086–1107). Written in chronological order by Kōen (d. 1169), a priest of the Japanese Tendai school, it contains biographies of priests, histories of temples, and stories related to Buddhism. The author, Kōen, is also known as a teacher of Hōnen, the founder of the Pure Land (Jōdo) school in Japan.

Buddha [仏] (Skt, Pali; Jpn *hotoke* or *butsu*): One enlightened to the eternal and ultimate truth that is the reality of all things, and who leads others to attain the same enlightenment. In India, the word *buddha* was originally a common noun meaning awakened one or enlightened one, referring to those who attained any kind of religious awakening. In Buddhism, it refers to one who has become awakened to the ultimate truth of all phenomena. In this context, the term *Buddha* at first was applied exclusively to Shakyamuni. Later, however, with the development of Buddha as an ideal, numerous Buddhas appeared in Mahayana scriptures. These include such Buddhas as Amida and Medicine Master. Expressions such as "the Buddhas of the ten directions" and "the Buddhas of the three existences" communicate the idea that Buddhas, or the potential for enlightenment they represent, are omnipresent. The state of perfect enlightenment sought in Buddhism is called Buddhahood.

Various definitions of Buddha are set forth in Buddhist teachings. In Hinayana teachings, it means one who has entered the state of nirvana, in which both body and mind are extinguished. Mahayana teachings generally maintain that one becomes a Buddha only after innumerable *kalpas* of austere and meritorious practices, by eradicating illusions and earthly desires and acquiring the thirty-two features of a Buddha. The Lotus Sutra views Buddha as one who manifests the three virtues of sovereign, teacher, and parent, who is enlightened to the true aspect of all phenomena, and who teaches it to people to save them from suffering. The Buddhism of Nichiren, which is based on the Lotus Sutra and regards it as Shakyamuni's most profound teaching, recognizes the potential of every person to become a Buddha.

Buddha-beholding meditation [般舟三昧] (Jpn *hanju-zammai*): *See* meditation to behold the Buddhas.

Buddhabhadra [仏陀跋陀羅] (359–429) (Skt; Jpn Buddabaddara): A monk of northern India who was active as a translator in China. He entered the monkhood in his youth and received instruction in the teachings on meditation in Kashmir. In 408 (406 according to another account) he went to Ch'ang-an in China and propagated the teachings. He assisted Kumārajīva in the translation of Buddhist scriptures, but later he went south, where he was welcomed by Hui-yüan at Mount Lu and lectured on the doctrine of meditation at Hui-yüan's request. Later he lived at Tao-ch'ang-ssu temple in Chien-k'ang and there translated a number of Buddhist scriptures into Chinese. Together with Fa-hsien, he translated *The Great Canon of Monastic Rules* and the six-volume Mahāparinirvāna Sutra. He also translated the sixty-volume version of the Flower Garland Sutra. In total, he is said to have translated 13 works in 125 volumes (some sources say 15 works in 117 volumes), contributing greatly to the development of Chinese Buddhism.

Buddhacharita [仏所行讃] (Skt; Jpn *Busshogyō-san*): See *Praising the Buddha's Deeds.*

Buddha eye [仏眼] (Jpn *butsu-gen*): The supreme perceptive faculty possessed by a Buddha. One of the five types of vision. A Buddha is said to perceive the true nature of all things and phenomena, transcending limitations of time and space. The Nirvana Sutra says, "Those who study the teachings of the great vehicle, though they have the eyes of ordinary beings, are said to have the eyes of the Buddha."

Buddha Eye [仏眼] (Skt Buddhalochanā; Jpn Butsugen): Also known as the Honored One Buddha Eye or Buddha Eye Buddha Mother. A Buddha described in Esoteric Buddhism and believed to be Mahāvairochana Buddha in a different form. Buddha Eye is a personification of the Buddha's supreme wisdom, viewed as the source or "mother" of all Buddhas and bodhisattvas; hence the name Buddha Eye Buddha Mother. Buddha Eye appears on the Womb Realm mandala, a mandala of the True Word (Jpn Shingon) school. The ceremony of Buddha Eye, an esoteric ritual, employed a mandala with Buddha Eye seated in the center as an object of devotion, to which prayers were offered to bring an end to calamities and misfortune.

Buddhagayā [仏陀伽耶] (Skt, Pali; Jpn Buddagaya): The place where Shakyamuni attained enlightenment under the *bodhi* tree. Today it is called Bodh Gaya or Buddh Gaya. Located about ten kilometers south of Gaya in the state of Bihar, northeastern India, Bodh Gaya is one of the four sacred sites connected with Shakyamuni; the other three are Lumbinī, his birthplace; Deer Park, where he gave his first sermon; and Kushinagara, near the site of his death, or entry into nirvana. Bodh Gaya is located west of the Lilaja River, or the Nairanjanā River, in which Shakyamuni immersed himself after having renounced ascetic practices. In Bodh Gaya stands a massive pyramid-shaped Buddhist monument known as the Mahābodhi temple, which measures about fifty meters high. Its origins are assigned to a simple shrine built by King Ashoka to mark the location of *bodhi* tree. It was rebuilt and enlarged in the sixth century C.E.

Buddhaghosa [仏音] (n.d.) (Pali; Jpn Button): A Buddhist scholar of India in the fifth century. Born to a Brahman family near Buddhagayā, he became learned in the Vedas. Later the Buddhist monk Revata converted him to Buddhism. In order to study commentaries on the three divisions of the Buddhist canon, he went to Sri Lanka and lived in a monastery called Abhayagiri-vihāra. Later he moved to another monastery, Mahāvihāra, and there studied the Pali canon and Sinhalese Buddhist commentaries. Buddhaghosa translated these Sinhalese commentaries into Pali, and also wrote a number of commentaries on the three divisions of the Buddhist canon. The *Visuddhimagga* ("The Way of Purification"), a compendium of Buddhist doctrine he wrote in Pali, served to systematize the doctrines of Theravāda.

Buddhahood [仏界] (Jpn *bukkai*): The state of awakening that a Buddha has attained. The ultimate goal of Buddhist practice and the highest of the Ten Worlds. The word *enlightenment* is often used synonymously with Buddhahood. Buddhahood is regarded as a state of perfect freedom, in which one is awakened to the eternal and ultimate truth that is the reality of all things. This supreme state of life is characterized by boundless wisdom and infinite compassion. The Lotus Sutra reveals that Buddhahood is a potential in the lives of all beings. *See also* attainment of Buddhahood.

Buddha Infinite Life Sutra [無量寿経] (Skt *Sukhāvatīvyūha;* Chin *Wu-liang-shou-ching;* Jpn *Muryōju-kyō*): One of the three basic scriptures of the Pure Land school, the other two being the Amida Sutra and the Meditation on the Buddha Infinite Life Sutra. The Buddha Infinite Life Sutra is also called the Two-Volumed Sutra because it alone among the three consists of two volumes. It relates how a bodhisattva named Dharma Treasury (Skt Dharmākara) made forty-eight vows and, on fulfilling them, achieved enlightenment as the Buddha Infinite Life, or Amida (Skt Amitāyus). The sutra describes this Buddha's pure land, known as Perfect Bliss, located "a hundred thousand million Buddha lands to the west," and explains that one can be reborn there after death if one has faith in Amida. Twelve Chinese versions of this sutra are said to have existed, but only five are extant, of which the Buddha Infinite Life Sutra, translated by the Indian monk Samghavarman in 252, is the most popular.

Buddhajīva [仏陀什] (n.d.) (Skt; Jpn Buddajū): A monk of the Mahīshāsaka school in Kashmir, ancient India, during the fifth century. He became a disciple of a monk of the Mahīshāsaka school and studied that school's *vinaya,* or monastic rules of discipline. He went to China in 423 and translated *The Fivefold Rules of Discipline,* the *vinaya* text of the Mahīshāsaka school, at Lung-kuang-ssu temple in Chien-k'ang along with Tao-sheng and Hui-yen, disciples of Kumārajīva. *The Fivefold Rules of Discipline* is a translation of the Sanskrit text that Fa-hsien, the noted Chinese Buddhist pilgrim, brought from Sri Lanka to China in the early fifth century.

Buddha land [仏国土] (Skt *buddha-kshetra;* Jpn *bukkoku-do*): Also, pure land, Land of Tranquil Light, or Land of Eternally Tranquil Light.

In Buddhism, a land where a Buddha dwells after having vowed to save living beings, completed his own practice, and attained enlightenment. The Sanskrit word *kshetra* means land. According to the Sarvāstivāda school, a major Hinayana school, the *sahā* world, or the world in which Shakyamuni Buddha appeared, is the only Buddha land. In contrast, Mahayana Buddhism makes reference to numerous Buddhas and their lands; it describes, for instance, Akshobhya Buddha's Land of Joy located in the east, Amida Buddha's Land of Perfect Bliss in the west, and Medicine Master Buddha's Pure Emerald World in the east.

Mahayana Buddhism developed the concept of the three bodies of a Buddha: the Dharma body, the reward body, and the manifested body. It was taught that each Buddha possesses one of these three bodies—hence the Buddha of the Dharma body, the Buddha of the reward body, and the Buddha of the manifested body—and that each Buddha has his own Buddha land. The Pure Land teachings regard the Land of Perfect Bliss as the land where Amida, the Buddha of the reward body, was reborn as a reward for his many *kalpas* of Buddhist practice. Because of the Buddhist view that the land or environment is an element of one's entire being, however, the term *Buddha land* also refers to the enlightened state or absolute happiness that Buddhas enjoy, and does not necessarily indicate a paradise or pure land removed from the real world.

Buddhamitra [仏陀密多] (n.d.) (Skt; Jpn Buddamitta): A monk of northern India, and the eighth of Shakyamuni's twenty-three, or the ninth of his twenty-four, successors. He studied under Buddhananda, his predecessor among the Buddha's successors, converted people by skillful means, and defeated a number of Brahmanists in debate. The king of his country, however, was strongly attached to Brahmanism and tried to rid the kingdom of all Buddhist influences. Determined to overcome the king's prejudice, Buddhamitra, bearing a red flag, is said to have walked back and forth in front of the palace for twelve years. Finally the king, moved by his resolve, allowed him to debate with a Brahmanist teacher in the king's presence. Buddhamitra refuted his opponent and thus converted the king to Buddhism. On another occasion, he refuted an ascetic who was slandering the Buddha, and converted the man and his five hundred followers to Buddhism, an accomplishment for which he became widely known.

Buddha Mother [仏母] (Jpn Butsumo): A Buddha described in Esoteric Buddhism and believed to be Mahāvairochana Buddha in a different form. *See* Buddha Eye.

Buddhananda [仏陀難提] (Skt; Jpn Buddanandai): Also known as Buddhanandiya or Buddhanandi. A monk of Kāmarūpa in northern

India, and the seventh of Shakyamuni's twenty-three, or the eighth of his twenty-four, successors. He was converted to Buddhism by Mikkaka, his predecessor among the Buddha's successors, and is said to have immediately attained the state of arhat. He excelled in preaching and propagated the Hinayana teachings.

Buddha nature [仏性] (Skt *buddha-dhātu* or *buddha-gotra;* Jpn *busshō*): The internal cause or potential for attaining Buddhahood. The Sanskrit word *dhātu* means root, base, foundation, ground, or cause, and *gotra* means family, lineage, basis, source, cause, or seed. Mahayana Buddhism generally holds that all people possess the innate Buddha nature, though its existence is obscured by illusions and evil karma. The Nirvana Sutra is especially famous for the phrase "All living beings alike possess the Buddha nature."

The history of Buddhism has witnessed doctrinal arguments concerning the Buddha nature, especially with regard to whether all people possess it. The Dharma Characteristics (Chin Fa-hsiang; Jpn Hossō) school, for instance, teaches the doctrine of the five natures, which classifies all people into five groups by their inborn capacities: those destined to be bodhisattvas, those destined as cause-awakened ones, those destined as voice-hearers, an indeterminate group, and those who can neither become bodhisattvas nor attain the enlightenment of voice-hearers or cause-awakened ones. Of these, only those destined to be bodhisattvas and some among the indeterminate group can attain Buddhahood. In contrast, the T'ien-t'ai (Chin; Jpn Tendai) school, which is based on the Lotus Sutra, holds that all people are endowed with the three inherent potentials of the Buddha nature—the innate Buddha nature, the wisdom to perceive it, and the deeds to develop it—and therefore can attain enlightenment.

Buddha of absolute freedom [自受用身] (Jpn *jijuyūshin*): *See* Buddha of limitless joy.

Buddha of beginningless time [久遠元初の自受用身] (Jpn *kuonganjo-no-jijuyūshin*): Also, eternal Buddha, original Buddha, or true Buddha. The Buddha who has been eternally endowed with the three bodies—the Dharma body, the reward body, and the manifested body, thereby embodying the eternal Law or the ultimate truth of life and the universe. This term appears in Nichiren's (1222–1282) writing given to his successor Nikkō. Titled *On the Mystic Principle of the True Cause,* it refers to "the Mystic Law, uncreated and eternal, of the Buddha of beginningless time," and states that the Mystic Law lies in the depths of the "Life Span" (sixteenth) chapter of the essential teaching of the Lotus Sutra. Nichikan (1665–1726), the twenty-sixth chief priest of Taiseki-ji temple, identified Nichiren as that Buddha, based on the fact that Nichiren was the first to spread the Mystic Law. According to Nichiren, the Japanese term *jijuyūshin* literally means the "body that is freely received and used." The Buddha of beginningless time is also called the Buddha of limitless joy—indicating the Buddha who freely derives boundless joy from the Law while enjoying absolute freedom, and who directly expounds the Law that he realized within his own life. In the "Life Span" chapter, Shakyamuni revealed his attainment of Buddhahood numberless major world system dust particle *kalpas* in the past. No matter how far in the past, however, it occurred at a fixed point in time and therefore is not eternal. Moreover, he did not clarify the Law or cause that enabled him to attain enlightenment at that time.

In contrast, the Buddha of beginningless time is eternal and also represents eternal life endowed with both the nine worlds and Buddhahood. In *The Opening of the Eyes,* Nichiren states: "This is the doctrine of original cause and original effect. It reveals that the nine worlds are all present in beginningless Buddhahood and that Buddhahood is inherent in the beginningless nine worlds. This is the true mutual possession of the Ten Worlds, the true hundred worlds and thousand factors, the true three thousand realms in a single moment of life" (235). Here "original cause" refers to the "beginningless nine worlds," and "original effect" to "beginningless Buddhahood." What Nichiren defined as "the true three thousand realms in a single moment of life" is the original state of life. To manifest this state of life is the attainment of Buddhahood for all people. Nichiren established the practice that enables everyone to achieve this by inscribing the Gohonzon, or the object of devotion that embodies this original state of life, and prescribing the invocation of Nam-myoho-renge-kyo. *See also* Buddha of limitless joy; true Buddha.

Buddha of beneficence [他受用身] (Jpn *tajuyūshin*): Also, body of beneficence. One of the four bodies of a Buddha. These four bodies correspond to the three bodies. They are (1) the self-nature body, which corresponds to the Dharma body; (2) the body of self-enjoyment, which corresponds to the reward body; (3) the body of beneficence, which also corresponds to the reward body; and (4) the transformation body, which is similar to the manifested body. A Buddha of beneficence is one who responds to the people's desire and benefits them through the various teachings that they hope to hear. This concept of Buddha is contrasted with that of a Buddha of self-enjoyment, who enjoys enlightenment attained as a result of past meritorious acts, such as Shakyamuni when he attained enlightenment under the *bodhi* tree. *See also* Buddha of limitless joy; Buddha of self-enjoyment.

Buddha of Healing [薬師如来] (Jpn Yakushi-nyorai): Also known as the Buddha Medicine Master. *See* Medicine Master.

Buddha of Infinite Life [無量寿仏] (Jpn Muryōju-butsu): Also known as the Buddha Amida. *See* Amida.

Buddha of Infinite Light [無量光仏] (Jpn Muryōkō-butsu): Also known as the Buddha Amida. *See* Amida.

Buddha of limitless joy [自受用身] (Jpn *jijuyūshin*): Buddha of limitless joy is broader in meaning than Buddha of self-enjoyment, which is another translation of *jijuyūshin*. (1) T'ien-t'ai (538–597) identified the Buddha of limitless joy with the Buddha revealed in the essential teaching (latter half) of the Lotus Sutra, whom he defined as the Buddha originally endowed with the three bodies—the Dharma body, the reward body, and the manifested body. Here, these three bodies are regarded as the three integral aspects of a single Buddha, i.e., the fundamental truth or Law to which he is enlightened (the Dharma body), the wisdom to realize it (the reward body), and the merciful actions to help people attain Buddhahood (the manifested body). *See also* Buddha of beginningless time.

(2) Dengyō (767–822), the founder of the Japanese Tendai school, is quoted in Nichiren's *Real Aspect of the Gohonzon* as having stated, "A single moment of life comprising the three thousand realms is itself the Buddha of limitless joy; this Buddha has forsaken august appearances" (832). Dengyō identified the true identity of the Buddha of limitless joy as a single moment of life in which all three thousand realms exist. This is Dengyō's description of the same Buddha T'ien-t'ai mentioned.

(3) Nichiren (1222–1282) identified the doctrine of three thousand realms in a single moment of life as the Law of Nam-myoho-renge-kyo that he realized within his own life. In other words, Nichiren established two concepts of three thousand realms in a single moment of life; one is T'ien-t'ai's and the other, his own. In his *Treatment of Illness*, Nichiren writes: "There are two ways of perceiving the three thousand realms in a single moment of life. One is theoretical, and the other, actual. What T'ien-t'ai and Dengyō practiced was theoretical, but what I practice now is actual. Because what I practice is superior, the difficulties attending it are that much greater. The doctrine of T'ien-t'ai and Dengyō was the three thousand realms in a single moment of life of the theoretical teaching, while mine is that of the essential teaching. These two are as different as heaven is from earth" (1114–115). T'ien-t'ai established the doctrine of three thousand realms in a single moment of life based on "the true aspect of all phenomena," the phrase from the "Expedient Means" (second) chapter of the Lotus Sutra.

On the other hand, Nichiren states in *The Opening of the Eyes:* "The doctrine of three thousand realms in a single moment of life is found in only one place, hidden in the depths of the 'Life Span' chapter of the essential teaching of the Lotus Sutra. Nāgārjuna and Vasubandhu were aware of it but did not bring it forth into the light. T'ien-t'ai Chih-che alone embraced it and kept it ever in mind" (224). Obviously what T'ien-t'ai embraced and kept ever in mind does not refer to the doctrine of three thousand realms in a single moment of life that he expounded publicly. Nichiren regarded it as Nam-myoho-renge-kyo.

Nichikan (1665–1726), the twenty-sixth chief priest of Taiseki-ji temple, who is known for his commentaries on Nichiren's writings, interpreted Nichiren's teaching, saying that the Buddha of the essential teaching is not the eternal Buddha but the Buddha who attained enlightenment at a fixed point in time. From this viewpoint, the Buddha of the essential teaching is not eternally endowed with the three bodies, but is rather the Buddha who advanced to the state of limitless joy through the bodhisattva way, thereby acquiring the three bodies. In contrast, Nichikan stated that the Buddha who embodies eternal life endowed with all of the Ten Worlds and the Law of Nam-myoho-renge-kyo whereby all Buddhas attained enlightenment, is originally endowed with the three bodies since time without beginning, and that that Buddha is what Nichiren called the Buddha of beginningless time. Nichikan concluded that Nichiren embodied that Buddha. *See also* Buddha of beginningless time; Buddha of self-enjoyment.

Buddha of Medicine [薬師如来] (Jpn Yakushi-nyorai): Also known as the Buddha Medicine Master. *See* Medicine Master.

Buddha of self-enjoyment [自受用身] (Jpn *jijuyūshin*): One of the four bodies of a Buddha. These four bodies correspond to the three bodies. They are (1) the self-nature body, which corresponds to the Dharma body; (2) the body of self-enjoyment, which corresponds to the reward body; (3) the body of beneficence, which also corresponds to the reward body; and (4) the transformation body, which is similar to the manifested body. A Buddha of self-enjoyment is one who enjoys the benefits of enlightenment he attained as a result of his past meritorious achievements, such as Shakyamuni when he attained enlightenment under the *bodhi* tree. This concept of Buddha is contrasted with that of a Buddha of beneficence who responds to the people's desire and benefits them through the various teachings that they hope to hear. *See also* Buddha of limitless joy.

Buddha of the Dharma body [法身・法身仏] (Jpn *hosshin* or *hosshin-butsu*): *See* Dharma body.

Buddha of the inferior manifested body [劣応身] (Jpn *retsu-ōjin*): Also, inferior manifested body. *See* superior manifested body.

Buddha of the manifested body [応身・応身仏] (Jpn *ōjin* or *ōjin-butsu*): *See* manifested body.

Buddha of the reward body [報身・報身仏] (Jpn *hōshin* or *hōshin-butsu*): *See* reward body.

Buddha of the superior manifested body [勝応身] (Jpn *shō-ōjin*): Also, superior manifested body. *See* superior manifested body.

Buddhapālita [仏護] (c. 470–540) (Skt; Jpn Butsugo): The founder of the Prāsangika school of Mādhyamika philosophy in India. In the sixth century, Buddhapālita and his contemporary, Bhāvaviveka, wrote commentaries on Nāgārjuna's *Verses on the Middle Way* (Skt *Madhyamaka-kārikā*). Differences in their approach and explanation of the truth of non-substantiality resulted in the division of the Mādhyamika school into the Prāsangika school led by Buddhapālita and the Svātantrika school led by Bhāvaviveka. The Prāsangika school was continued by Chandrakīrti. The Sanskrit original of Buddhapālita's commentary on *Verses on the Middle Way* is not extant, but a Tibetan translation exists. *See also* Bhāvaviveka.

Buddhashānta [仏陀扇多] (n.d.) (Skt; Jpn Buddasenta): A monk of northern India who, in the early sixth century, went to China and engaged in the translation of Buddhist scriptures into Chinese. Among his translations are the Lion Roar of the Thus Come One Sutra, the Silver-Colored Woman Sutra, and *The Summary of the Mahayana*. He is also said to have assisted with the translation of *The Treatise on the Ten Stages Sutra*.

Buddha-shāsana [仏教] (Skt; Pali Buddha-sāsana; Jpn Bukkyō): The Buddha's teachings or Buddhism. *Shāsana* means teaching or doctrine.

Buddhasimha [師子覚] (n.d.) (Skt; Jpn Shishikaku): An Indian monk who lived in the fifth century. A disciple of Asanga, he wrote a commentary on Asanga's *Collection of Mahayana Treatises*.

Buddha's Legacy Teachings Sutra [仏遺教経] (Jpn *Butsu-yuikyō-gyō*): *See* Legacy Teachings Sutra.

Buddhas' Names Sutra [仏名経] (Chin *Fo-ming-ching*; Jpn *Butsumyō-kyō*): A work translated into Chinese around 520 by Bodhiruchi, founder of the Treatise on the Ten Stages Sutra (Chin Ti-lun) school. This sutra lists the names of 11,093 Buddhas and bodhisattvas and describes their blessings. There are several sutras of this kind, such as the Names of Three Thousand Buddhas Sutra. They were used in a ceremony that gained popularity in China around the fifth or sixth century, in which the names of the Buddhas of past, present, and future were recited to expiate past offenses. In Japan, it is thought that the earliest such ceremony was held in 774. In the early ninth century, this ceremony came to be observed in the imperial palace and in provincial temples over a period of three days, beginning on the fifteenth day (later, the nineteenth day) of the twelfth month. Later the period was shortened to one night.

Buddha's relics [仏舎利] (Jpn *busshari*): The Buddha's cremated remains. Shakyamuni Buddha's ashes are said to have been divided into eight portions and enshrined in eight countries in stupas built for them. In 1898 relics were discovered at Piprahwa (also spelled Piprava), on the northern border of India, and inscriptions on their receptacle identified them as those of Shakyamuni Buddha. Scholars today believe them to be one of the original eight divisions of Shakyamuni's remains, the portion that had been enshrined in Kapilavastu (present-day Piprahwa).

According to tradition, King Ashoka erected eighty-four thousand stupas to house the Buddha's relics. The practice of revering the Buddha's relics spread to Central Asia, China, and Japan; in these areas the Buddha's relics consisted of no more than a few small particles. Later some people came to believe that such grains or particles of the Buddha's relics would appear in response to one's sincere devotion to the Buddha's teachings. In China, the first stupa dedicated to the Buddha's relics is believed to have been erected in the third century, and, from the fourth century on, stupas came to be erected at various locations.

Veneration of the Buddha's relics flourished particularly during the T'ang (618–907) and the Sung (960–1279) dynasties. In Japan, following the introduction of Buddhism in the sixth century, faith in the Buddha's relics spread, influenced by the tradition established earlier in India, China, and Korea. Particles of the supposed relics, which were brought at first from Paekche and Silla on the Korean Peninsula and then from China, were housed in pagodas. The Chinese priest Chien-chen, known as Ganjin in Japan, and Japanese priests who went to China to study Buddhism brought such relics to Japan. Ceremonies dedicated to the Buddha's relics were observed at temples, and a great number of small pagodas were produced.

From a doctrinal viewpoint, two kinds of relics are set forth: the Buddha's physical remains and the teachings that he expounded. The former are called the relics of the physical body, while the latter are called the relics of the Dharma body. In the Lotus Sutra, Shakyamuni Buddha calls for the enshrinement of the sutra rather than his relics. The "Teacher of the Law" (tenth) chapter of the sutra says: "In any place whatsoever where this sutra is preached, where it is read, where it is recited, where it is copied, or where a roll of it exists, in all such places there should be erected towers made of the seven kinds of gems, and they should be made very high and broad and well adorned. There is no need to enshrine the relics of the Buddha there. Why? Because in such towers the entire body of the Thus Come One is already present."

Buddha's Successors Sutra [付法蔵経] (Jpn *Fuhōzō-kyō*): See *History of the Buddha's Successors, A.*

Buddha Treasury Sutra [仏蔵経] (Chin *Fo-tsang-ching;* Jpn *Butsuzō-kyō*): A sutra translated into Chinese in 405 by Kumārajīva. A Tibetan translation also exists. The sutra takes the form of a discourse between Shakyamuni and Shāriputra held on Eagle Peak near Rājagriha, the capital of Magadha. It maintains that all phenomena are without birth or extinction, and that to perceive this truth of phenomena means to behold the Buddha. It also says that monks who preach from an impure motive, i.e., to gain profit and support, suffer the retribution of falling into hell. The sutra goes on to refer to the time following the passing of the Buddha Great Adornment in the far remote past.

One hundred years after Great Adornment's death, his followers split into five schools, led by the monks Universal Practice, Shore of Suffering, Sawata, Shōko, and Batsunanda, respectively. Among these five leaders, only Universal Practice correctly upheld the Buddha's teaching. The four other leaders held erroneous views and, along with their followers, cursed Universal Practice. For this reason, these four monks and their followers fell into hell. In the following section, Shakyamuni Buddha speaks of his past existences, saying that, although he practiced under various Buddhas in order to gain enlightenment, he was not given a prophecy of enlightenment by these Buddhas because of his attachment to making distinctions among phenomena and his ignorance about the truth of non-substantiality.

Buddha vehicle [仏乗] (Jpn *butsujō*): The teaching that leads all people to Buddhahood. *See* one vehicle.

Buddha wisdom [仏智] (Jpn *butchi*): The supreme wisdom of a Buddha that penetrates the true aspect of all phenomena. The "Expedient Means" (second) chapter of the Lotus Sutra states: "The wisdom of the Buddhas is infinitely profound and immeasurable. The door to this wisdom is difficult to understand and difficult to enter. Not one of the voice-hearers or *pratyekabuddhas* is able to comprehend it." The "Simile and Parable" (third) chapter of the sutra explains that even Shāriputra, who was known as foremost in wisdom among all Shakyamuni's disciples, could attain enlightenment only by taking faith in the Buddha's teachings. That is, it attributes Shāriputra's enlightenment not to his wisdom but to his faith. The Lotus Sutra makes clear that all human beings have Buddha wisdom as a potential, and that only faith in the sutra can bring it forth. Concerning the relationship between faith and wisdom, Nichiren (1222–1282) set forth the principle of substituting faith for wisdom in *On the Four Stages of Faith and the Five Stages of Practice*. Here, wisdom indicates the Buddha wisdom that is beyond ordinary understanding. This principle means that through faith one can gain the Buddha wisdom and attain enlightenment.

Buddhayashas [仏陀耶舎] (n.d.) (Skt; Jpn Buddayasha): An Indian monk and a translator of Buddhist scriptures into Chinese. Born in Kashmir in ancient India, he went to Ch'ang-an in China in 408 at Kumārajīva's invitation and assisted him in his translation work. The Chinese translations of *The Fourfold Rules of Discipline* and the Long Āgama Sutra are attributed to Buddhayashas. He returned to Kashmir in 412, and it is said that from there he sent his translation of the Space Treasury Sutra to China.

Buddh Gaya [仏陀伽耶] (Jpn Buddagaya): *See* Buddhagayā.

Buddhism of sowing [下種仏法] (Jpn *geshu-buppō*): The Buddhism that plants the seeds of Buddhahood, or the cause for attaining Buddhahood, in people's lives. In Nichiren's teachings, the Buddhism of sowing indicates the Buddhism of Nichiren, in contrast with that of Shakyamuni, which is called the Buddhism of the harvest. The Buddhism of the harvest is that which can lead to enlightenment only those who received the seeds of Buddhahood by practicing the Buddha's teaching in previous lifetimes. In contrast, the Buddhism of sowing implants the seeds of Buddhahood, or Nam-myoho-renge-kyo, in the lives of those who had no connection with the Buddha's teaching in their past existences, i.e., the people of the Latter Day of the Law. *See also* sowing, maturing, and harvesting; teacher of the true cause.

Buddhism of the harvest [脱益仏法] (Jpn *datchaku-buppō*): The Buddhism directed toward the salvation of those who received the seeds of Buddhahood in their lives through the practice of Buddhism in their past existences. The process by which the Buddha leads people to enlightenment may be divided into three stages called sowing, maturing, and harvesting. This process is described in the Lotus Sutra.

Shakyamuni first planted the seeds of enlightenment in the lives of his disciples at the time of his original enlightenment numberless major world system dust particle *kalpas* in the past, as expounded in the "Life Span" (sixteenth) chapter, and then nurtured the seeds through his preaching as the sixteenth son of the Buddha Great Universal Wisdom Excellence at a time major world system dust particle *kalpas* in the past, as related in the "Parable of the Phantom City" (seventh) chapter. He continued nourishing the seeds in his lifetime in India through the provisional teachings he expounded during the forty-two years after his enlightenment under the *bodhi* tree as well as through the theoretical teaching (first fourteen chapters) of the Lotus Sutra. Finally he brought his disciples to full enlightenment with the essential teaching (latter fourteen chapters) of the sutra, particularly the "Life Span" chapter. Therefore the essential teaching of the Lotus Sutra is called the Buddhism of the harvest.

In contrast, Nichiren's teaching is called the Buddhism of sowing because it implants the seeds of Buddhahood, i.e., Nam-myoho-renge-kyo, in the lives of the people of the Latter Day of the Law, who had not received the seeds in the past. *See also* Buddhism of sowing.

Buddhist Councils [結集] (Skt *samgīti;* Jpn *ketsujū*): Assemblies of monks held after Shakyamuni Buddha's death to compile and confirm the Buddha's teachings so as to ensure their accurate preservation and transmission. It is said that four such councils were held during the four hundred years following the Buddha's death. The Sanskrit *samgīti* means singing or reciting in unison. This reflects the method by which the Buddha's teachings were passed from one generation to the next during that period, that is, by memorization and recitation, rather than by written record.

(1) The First Buddhist Council was convened shortly after Shakyamuni's death with the support of King Ajātashatru in the Cave of the Seven Leaves near Rājagriha in Magadha, India. About five hundred monks (one thousand according to another account) participated under the leadership of Mahākāshyapa. It is said that Ānanda recited the sutras and Upāli recited the *vinaya,* or monastic rules of discipline. The others confirmed the correctness of their recitation and then recited the teachings again in unison, thus establishing a definitive version.

(2) The Second Buddhist Council was held about one hundred years after the first council, when seven hundred monks led by Yasa gathered in Vaishālī, India. It is therefore known also as the Gathering of Seven Hundred Monks. At that time, the monks of the Vriji tribe in Vaishālī were advocating a more liberal interpretation of the precepts, a move that disturbed many of the older, more conservative monks. The council headed by Yasa rejected that interpretation, but controversy over this issue eventually led to the first schism in the Buddhist Order. (Tradition in Kashmir holds that it was disagreement over the five teachings of Mahādeva that provoked the schism.) *See also* ten unlawful revisions.

(3) The Third Buddhist Council was held with the support of King

Ashoka at Pātaliputra in India some one hundred years after the second council. One thousand monks under Moggaliputta Tissa assembled to clear up confusion and correct misinterpretations in the Buddha's teachings. It is said that at this assembly the *abhidharma* works, or commentaries and treatises, were compiled and incorporated into one of the three divisions of the Buddhist canon.

(4) The Fourth Buddhist Council was held in Kashmir under the patronage of King Kanishka about two hundred years after the third council. Five hundred monks led by Vasumitra revised the canon and established a definitive version. *The Great Commentary on the Abhidharma* is attributed to this council.

Accounts of these Buddhist Councils in Northern Buddhism differ slightly from those in Southern Buddhism.

Buddhist gods [諸天善神] (Jpn *shoten-zenjin*): *See* heavenly gods and benevolent deities.

burning house [火宅] (Jpn *kataku*): A simile for the threefold world where people continually undergo transmigration in a state of delusion and suffering. This simile is derived from the "Simile and Parable" (third) chapter of the Lotus Sutra where the parable of the three carts and the burning house is related. The chapter states, "There is no safety in the threefold world; it is like a burning house, replete with a multitude of sufferings, truly to be feared, constantly beset with the griefs and pains of birth, old age, sickness and death, which are like fires raging fiercely and without cease." *See also* parable of the three carts and the burning house.

Burning Torch [燃燈仏] (Skt, Pali Dīpamkara; Jpn Nentō-butsu): Also known as Fixed Light. A Buddha to whom Shakyamuni, when practicing as a bodhisattva named Learned Youth in a previous existence, once offered flowers. It is said that, when Learned Youth tossed five lotus blossoms toward the Buddha Burning Torch as an offering, they remained afloat in the air. When Bodhisattva Learned Youth spread his deerskin cloak and his own hair over marshy ground for the Buddha to walk upon, Burning Torch predicted that Learned Youth would become a Buddha in the future.

The Buddha Burning Torch is described in several texts. *The Treatise on the Great Perfection of Wisdom* refers to him as Burning Torch, and the Sutra of the Buddha's Marvelous Deeds in Previous Lifetimes, as Fixed Light. According to the "Introduction" (first) chapter of the Lotus Sutra, the Buddha Burning Torch was one of the eight sons of a Buddha named Sun Moon Bright. He practiced the Lotus Sutra under his father's disciple, Bodhisattva Wonderfully Bright, and attained enlightenment.

C

calamity of invasion from foreign lands [他国侵逼難] (Jpn *takoku-shimpitsu-nan*): Also, foreign invasion. One of the seven disasters described in the Medicine Master Sutra. In *On Establishing the Correct Teaching for the Peace of the Land,* written in 1260, Nichiren predicted that this and the calamity of revolt within one's own domain would occur if the rulers of Japan failed to accept the correct teaching. His prediction of foreign invasion was realized in the form of invasions by the Mongol Empire in 1274 and in 1281. *See also* seven disasters.

calamity of revolt within one's own domain [自界叛逆難] (Jpn *jikai-hongyaku-nan*): Also, internal strife. One of the seven disasters described in the Medicine Master Sutra. In *On Establishing the Correct Teaching for the Peace of the Land,* written in 1260, Nichiren predicted that this and the calamity of invasion from foreign lands would occur if the rulers of Japan failed to accept the correct teaching. His prediction of internal strife was realized when a revolt took place within the ruling Hōjō clan. In the second month of 1272, Hōjō Tokisuke revolted against his younger half brother, the regent Hōjō Tokimune, in an attempt to seize power. *See also* seven disasters.

Calm and Bright [安明] (Jpn Ammyō): Another name for Mount Sumeru. *See* Sumeru, Mount.

casting off the transient and revealing the true [発迹顕本] (Jpn *hos-shaku-kempon*): The revealing of a Buddha's true status as a Buddha, and the setting aside of that Buddha's provisional or transient identity. In the "Life Span" (sixteenth) chapter of the Lotus Sutra, Shakyamuni declares: "In all the worlds the heavenly and human beings and *asuras* all believe that the present Shakyamuni Buddha, after leaving the palace of the Shākyas, seated himself in the place of meditation not far from the city of Gayā and there attained supreme perfect enlightenment. But good men, it has been immeasurable, boundless hundreds, thousands, ten thousands, millions of *nayutas* of *kalpas* since I in fact attained Buddhahood." Through this statement, he discards his provisional identity as the Buddha who first attained enlightenment under the *bodhi* tree in India and reveals his original enlightenment, or the enlightenment he attained numberless major world system dust particle *kalpas* in the past.

This concept has also been applied to Nichiren (1222–1282), who wrote in *The Opening of the Eyes:* "On the twelfth day of the ninth month of last year [1271], between the hours of the rat and the ox [11:00 P.M. to 3:00 A.M.], this person named Nichiren was beheaded. It is his soul that has come to this island of Sado and, in the second month of the following year, snowbound, is writing this to send to his close disciples" (269). Nichikan (1665–1726), the twenty-sixth chief priest of Taiseki-ji temple, who is known for his commentaries on Nichiren's writings, interpreted this passage on two levels: First, the phrase "this person named Nichiren was beheaded" corresponds to the passage from the Lotus Sutra that reads, "[Ignorant people] will attack us with swords and staves"; and "his soul that has come to this island of Sado" corresponds to the Lotus Sutra passage "again and again we will be banished." This, Nichikan said, shows that Nichiren is the votary of the Lotus Sutra who lives in the spirit expressed in the sutra to "care nothing for our bodies or lives but are anxious only for the unsurpassed way."

Second, Nichikan attributed a deeper significance to these passages, citing another passage from Nichiren's writing *Persecution by Sword and Staff* that reads, "All the Buddhas of the past, present, and future attain enlightenment during the hours of the ox and the tiger [1:00 to 5:00 A.M.]" (965), and compares this with the above passage from *The Opening of the Eyes.* "The hours of the rat and the ox" indicates the time Nichiren as an ordinary person died; hence the phrase "this person named Nichiren was beheaded." Because the "hour of the tiger" is the time immediately following Nichiren's attempted execution, Nichikan interprets this to indicate the time Nichiren as the Buddha was born; hence the phrase "It is his soul that has come to this island of Sado." In identifying Nichiren as the Buddha of the Latter Day of the Law, Nichikan also referred to a passage from Nichiren's *Reply to Kyō'ō* that reads, "I, Nichiren, have inscribed my life in *sumi* ink, so believe in the Gohonzon with your whole heart. The Buddha's will is the Lotus Sutra, but the soul of Nichiren is nothing other than Nam-myoho-renge-kyo" (412).

Catalog of Buddhist Scriptures, The [内典録] (Jpn *Naiten-roku*): See *Great T'ang Dynasty Catalog of Buddhist Scriptures, The.*

Causality of Past and Present Sutra [過去現在因果経] (Chin *Kuo-ch'ü-hsien-tsai-yin-kuo-ching;* Jpn *Kako-genzai-inga-kyō*): Also known as the Causality Sutra. A sutra translated from Sanskrit into Chinese in the mid-fifth century by Gunabhadra, a monk from central India. It is set in Jetavana Monastery in Shrāvastī, India, and takes the form of an account by Shakyamuni Buddha of his own past. He tells of his practice in a past existence as a seer named Good Wisdom, explaining that he obtained the supreme wisdom in this life as a result of performing bodhisattva austerities in the past. The sutra then describes his passage through the eight phases of a Buddha's existence, or successive phases manifested by a Buddha for the purpose of saving all people. Its literary merit makes the sutra outstanding among the biographies of the Buddha translated into Chinese. This sutra became popular in China and Japan, and in Japan was published with illustrations. *See also* eight phases of a Buddha's existence.

cause and effect [因果] (Jpn *inga*): (1) Buddhism expounds the law of cause and effect that operates in life, ranging over past, present, and future existences. This causality underlies the doctrine of karma. From this viewpoint, causes formed in the past are manifested as effects in the present. Causes formed in the present will be manifested as effects in the future. Buddhism emphasizes the causes one creates and accumulates in the present, because these will determine one's future.

(2) From the viewpoint of Buddhist practice, cause represents the bodhisattva practice for attaining Buddhahood and effect represents the benefit of Buddhahood. Based on the doctrine that the ordinary person and the Buddha are essentially the same, it is taught that cause (the nine worlds, or practice) and effect (Buddhahood, or the result of practice) are non-dual and simultaneous. Nichiren (1222–1282) wrote, "Shakyamuni's practices and the virtues he consequently attained are all contained within the five characters of Myoho-renge-kyo. If we believe in these five characters, we will naturally be granted the same benefits as he was" (365).

(3) From the viewpoint that, among the Ten Worlds, cause represents the nine worlds and effect represents Buddhahood, Nichiren refers to two kinds of teachings: those that view things from the standpoint of "cause to effect" (Jpn *jūin-shika*) and those that approach things from the standpoint of "effect to cause" *(jūka-kōin)*. The former indicates Shakyamuni's teaching, by which ordinary persons carry out Buddhist practice (cause) aiming at the goal of Buddhahood (effect). In contrast, the latter indicates Nichiren's teaching, in which ordinary persons manifest their innate Buddhahood (effect) through faith and practice, and then, based on Buddhahood, go out among the people of the nine worlds (cause) to lead them to Buddhahood.

cause-awakened one [縁覚] (Skt *pratyekabuddha;* Jpn *engaku*): Also, self-awakened one. One who perceives the twelve-linked chain of causation, or the truth of causal relationship. Cause-awakened one also means those who, in an age when there is no Buddha, realize on their own the truth of impermanence by observing natural phenomena. Because their awakening is self-gained, cause-awakened ones are also called self-awakened ones. Together with voice-hearers, they constitute the persons of the two vehicles. Unlike bodhisattvas, they seek their own emancipation without thought of preaching for and instructing others.

The Sanskrit term *pratyekabuddha* means "independently enlightened one" or "individually enlightened one." In the early Chinese translations of Buddhist scriptures, it was rendered cause-awakened one, which implies one enlightened through perceiving causal relationship. *The Treatise on the Meaning of the Mahayana,* written by Hui-yüan (523–592), describes *pratyekabuddha* as one who perceives the twelve-linked chain of causation or who awakens to the truth by observing natural phenomena such as the scattering of blossoms or the falling of leaves. Later the term was rendered as self-awakened one. In *The Words and Phrases of the Lotus Sutra,* T'ien-t'ai (538–597) distinguishes these two types of *pratyekabuddha*—cause-awakened ones and self-awakened ones. Mahayana, which upholds practice to benefit others, referred to the vehicle of *pratyekabuddha,* or the teaching that leads one to the state of *pratyekabuddha,* as Hinayana (Lesser Vehicle), because it concerns only one's own salvation. The realm of cause-awakened ones is also viewed as a condition of life, in which one perceives the transience of life in the six paths and strives to free oneself from the six paths by seeking eternal truth through one's own effort. This realm or state constitutes the eighth of the Ten Worlds and is sometimes called the world of realization. *See also* Ten Worlds.

Cave of the Seven Leaves [七葉窟] (Skt Saptaparna-guhā; Jpn Shichiyō-kutsu): The site where the First Buddhist Council for the compilation of Shakyamuni Buddha's teachings was held shortly after his death with the support of Ajātashatru, the king of Magadha in India. According to Buddhist tradition, it was located halfway down a hill near Rājagriha in Magadha. Some accounts identify the Cave of the Seven Leaves as Pippalī Cave. *See also* Pippalī Cave.

Cave of the Thousand Buddhas [千仏洞] (Jpn Sembutsu-dō): Also known as the Mo-kao Caves. The Buddhist caves at Tun-huang in northwestern Kansu Province, China. *See* Mo-kao Caves.

Ceremony in the Air [虚空会] (Jpn *kokū-e*): The second of the three assemblies described in the Lotus Sutra, in which the entire gathering is suspended in space above the ground. The two other assemblies take place on Eagle Peak. The Ceremony in the Air is depicted from the latter half of the "Treasure Tower" (eleventh) chapter through the "Entrustment" (twenty-second) chapter of the sutra. In the "Treasure Tower" chapter, the treasure tower of the Buddha Many Treasures emerges from beneath the earth and is suspended in midair. Shakyamuni, after summoning the Buddhas who are his emanations from the ten directions, stations himself in midair, opens the treasure tower, and enters it, taking a seat beside the Buddha Many Treasures. Then, using his transcendental powers, he lifts the entire assembly into space so that they are at the same level. This begins the Ceremony in the Air. The "Treasure Tower" chapter ends with Shakyamuni urging the audience to propagate the sutra in the evil age after his death. In the "Encouraging Devotion" (thirteenth) chapter, the innumerable bodhisattvas attending vow to fulfill the Buddha's will even if they must endure persecution by the so-called three powerful enemies.

In the "Emerging from the Earth" (fifteenth) chapter, the bodhisattvas of the other worlds make the same vow, but the Buddha refuses to entrust the mission to them. At that moment the Bodhisattvas of the Earth make their appearance; this marks the beginning of the essential teaching of the sutra. In the "Life Span" (sixteenth) chapter, Shakyamuni reveals his original enlightenment—the enlightenment that he attained numberless major world system dust particle *kalpas* in the past. In the "Supernatural Powers" (twenty-first) chapter, Shakyamuni transfers the essence of the sutra specifically to the Bodhisattvas of the Earth led by Bodhisattva Superior Practices, entrusting them with its propagation in the Latter Day of the Law. In the "Entrustment" chapter, he transfers the sutra to all the bodhisattvas present. Then Shakyamuni's emanations return to their lands, the treasure tower reverts to its former position, and the Ceremony in the Air comes to an end. The heart of this ceremony consists of the revelation of Shakyamuni Buddha's original enlightenment and the transfer of the essence of the sutra to the Bodhisattvas of the Earth.

Nichiren (1222–1282) states that the object of devotion he revealed as the Gohonzon is the perfect embodiment of the Law, which is the essence of the Lotus Sutra, and that it is also a representation of the Ceremony in the Air. *The Real Aspect of the Gohonzon* reads, "This Gohonzon was revealed . . . in eight chapters [of the Lotus Sutra], from the 'Emerging from the Earth' chapter through the 'Entrustment' chapter" (831). It also reads, "Without exception, all these Buddhas, bodhisattvas, great sages [attending the Ceremony in the Air] . . . dwell in this Gohonzon" (832). The fact that the ceremony takes place in the air signifies that it transcends the framework of time and space.

ceremony of anointment [灌頂] (Skt *abhisheka;* Jpn *kanjō*): Also, anointment ceremony. A ceremony commonly performed in Esoteric Buddhism to invest the recipient with a certain status. The ceremony is said to have derived from the ancient Indian practice of pouring water on the heads of rulers when they ascended the throne. In Esoteric Buddhism, there are three kinds of anointment ceremonies, the respective purposes of which are (1) to establish a relationship between the individual and the Buddha, (2) to confer the status of practitioner of Esoteric Buddhism, and (3) to invest a person with the rank of *āchārya,* qualifying him to teach the esoteric doctrine.

ceremony of reciting the Buddhas' names [仏名会] (Jpn *butsumyō-e*): *See* Buddhas' Names Sutra.

chakra [輪宝・輪] (Skt; Jpn *rimbō* or *rin*): Also, *chakra* treasure or wheel treasure. One of the seven treasures that a wheel-turning king (Skt *chakravarti-rāja*) is said to possess. A wheel-turning king was a wise and benevolent ruler, an ideal king in Indian mythology. The Sanskrit word *chakra* means the wheel of a carriage. The seven treasures of a wheel-turning king are a *chakra,* elephants, horses, jewels, jewel-like women, excellent ministers of financial affairs, and generals. A *chakra,* or wheel, is of four kinds: gold, silver, copper, and iron.

A wheel-turning king possesses one or another of these four kinds of wheels, an indication of his rank. Turning his *chakra,* a wheel-turning king advances without hindrance, overthrows his enemies, establishes peace, and rules with justice and benevolence wherever he goes. In Buddhism, a *chakra* is regarded as a symbol of the Buddha's teachings, which vanquish earthly desires and illusions. The word *dharma-chakra,* or the wheel of the Law, is often used to describe the teachings. The Buddha's preaching is expressed as "the turning of the wheel of the Law." In the history of Buddhism, before images of the Buddha appeared, the Buddha was depicted in carvings symbolically as a wheel, a *bodhi* tree, and other images. A *chakra* was originally a wheel- or disk-shaped weapon in ancient India that was hurled as a missile at enemies.

Chakravāda [鉄囲山・鉄輪囲山] (Skt; Jpn Tetchi-sen or Tetsurin'i-sen): The Iron Encircling Mountains. The mountain range that, according to the ancient Indian worldview, forms the circular periphery of the world. Located at the center of the world, Mount Sumeru is surrounded by eight concentric mountain ranges, which are separated by eight concentric seas. The Chakravāda are the eighth and outermost of these mountain ranges and are made of iron, while the other seven are made of gold. *See* Iron Encircling Mountains.

Chakravāda-parvata [鉄囲山・鉄輪囲山] (Skt; Jpn Tetchi-sen or Tetsurin'i-sen): Also known as Chakravāda or the Iron Encircling Mountains. *See* Chakravāda; Iron Encircling Mountains.

chakravartin [転輪聖王] (Skt; Jpn *tenrin-jō'ō*): Also, *chakravarti-rāja.* Wheel-turning king or wheel-turning sage king. Ideal rulers in Indian mythology. The Sanskrit word *chakra* means wheel, and *vartin,* one who turns. The *chakravartin* indicates one who, turning a wheel bestowed by heaven, advances anywhere at will to establish peace and rule the world with justice rather than with force. See also *chakra;* wheel-turning king.

Champā [瞻波] (Skt, Pali; Jpn Sempa): The capital of Anga, one of the sixteen great states in India of Shakyamuni's time, bordered on the west by the Magadha kingdom. Champā was one of the six great cities in India, the others being Shrāvastī, Shāketa, Vaishālī, Vārānasī, and Rājagriha. It is believed to have been at the site of present-day Bhagalpur in northeastern India or its vicinity, just south of the Ganges River. Shakyamuni Buddha visited Champā several times to preach. According to *The Record of the Western Regions,* Hsüan-tsang's record of his travels through Central Asia and India during the seventh century, when he visited Champā, he saw dozens of monasteries, though many were in disrepair; he reported that about two hundred monks were studying the Hinayana doctrines in those monasteries.

champaka tree [瞻蔔樹] (Skt, Pali; Jpn *sempuku-ju*): A large tree with fragrant yellow flowers native to India. *Champaka* flowers and their fragrance are often mentioned in Buddhist scriptures.

Chandaka [車匿] (Skt; Pali Channa; Jpn Shanoku): A servant of Shakyamuni before he renounced secular life. The night Shakyamuni, as Prince Siddhārtha, left the palace of Kapilavastu to embark on a religious life, Chandaka accompanied him, holding his horse, Kanthaka, by the bridle. It is said that, when Shakyamuni had gone some distance to the south, he cut his hair and handed over his crown and a bright jewel in his topknot to Chandaka, whom he sent back to Kapilavastu with the message that he would not return until he had fulfilled his objective. After Shakyamuni attained enlightenment, Chandaka became his disciple. Being arrogant by nature, however, he had trouble getting along with the other monks. After Shakyamuni's death, Chandaka followed Ānanda, one of the Buddha's ten major disciples, and attained the state of arhat.

chandāla [旃陀羅] (Skt, Pali; Jpn *sendara*): A class of untouchables, below the lowest of the four castes in the ancient Indian caste system. People in this class handled corpses, butchered animals, and carried out other tasks associated with death or the killing of living things. The Māyā Sutra mentions a *chandāla* who drives sheep or oxen to the slaughterhouse. Nichiren (1222–1282) declared himself to be a member of the *chandāla* class because he was born to a fisherman's family. In his letter *Banishment to Sado,* Nichiren says, "Nichiren is the son of a *chandāla* family who lived near the sea in Tōjō in Awa Province, in the remote countryside of the eastern part of Japan" (202). In his *Letter from Sado,* he also described himself as one "who in this life was born poor and lowly to a *chandāla* family" (303). Through such statements Nichiren implied that even someone from the lowest rung of society, such as himself, can attain supreme enlightenment; hence, his teaching is meant particularly for those without wealth or status.

Chandrakīrti (Skt) (1) [月称] (c. 600–650) (Jpn Gesshō): A scholar of the Mādhyamika school in India. In the early sixth century, Buddhapālita and Bhāvaviveka wrote commentaries on Nāgārjuna's *Verses on the Middle Way* (Skt *Madhyamaka-kārikā*). The differences in their approach and explanation of the truth of non-substantiality resulted in the division of the Mādhyamika school into the Prāsangika school led by Buddhapālita and the Svātantrika school led by Bhāvaviveka. Chandrakīrti inherited the doctrine of Buddhapālita and criticized the doctrine of Bhāvaviveka, thus completing the doctrine of the Prāsangika school. For this reason, he is regarded as the effective founder of the Prāsangika school. He asserted that the truth of non-substantiality is beyond the reach of logical demonstration and is attainable only by practice. The most important of his works is the *Prasannapadā* ("The Clear Worded"), which is the only extant Sanskrit commentary on *Verses on the Middle Way*. Knowledge of the original Sanskrit text of *Madhyamaka-kārikā* is available only through the *Prasannapadā*, the translation and study of which have therefore been carried out with great care and interest. Chandrakīrti also wrote commentaries on Nāgārjuna's other works and on Āryadeva's *Four-Hundred-Verse Treatise*. His original work is *Entering the Middle Way (Madhyamakāvatāra)*. These works are extant in their Tibetan translations.

(2) [月称大臣] (Jpn Gasshō-daijin): Also known as Chandrayashas. A minister who served Ajātashatru, the king of Magadha in India. He is mentioned in the Nirvana Sutra. The king was suffering from virulent sores all over his body because of his offense of killing his father, Bimbisāra, a patron of Shakyamuni Buddha. His six ministers appeared in succession before him, each exhorting him to consult a different one of the six non-Buddhist teachers for a remedy. Chandrakīrti was the first of these ministers to address the king. He urged Ajātashatru to see Pūrana, the non-Buddhist teacher known for his denial that there is a causal relationship between one's deeds and what one experiences as a result. *See also* six ministers.

Chandraprabha (Skt) (1) [月光大臣] (Jpn Gakkō-daijin): A minister of Bimbisāra, king of Magadha in ancient India. He also served as a minister to Ajātashatru, a son of Bimbisāra, after Ajātashatru's ascent to the throne. When Ajātashatru killed his father to usurp the throne and further attempted to kill his mother, Vaidehī, Chandraprabha, along with Jīvaka, dissuaded Ajātashatru from slaying her.

(2) [月光菩薩] (Jpn Gakkō-bosatsu): The bodhisattva Moonlight. *See* Moonlight.

Chandrayashas [月称大臣] (Skt; Jpn Gasshō-daijin): Also known as Chandrakīrti. A minister who served Ajātashatru, the king of Magadha in India, during Shakyamuni's time. *See* Chandrakīrti (2).

Chang-an [章安] (561–632) (PY Zhang'an; Jpn Shōan): Also known as Kuan-ting or the Great Teacher Chang-an. The second patriarch of the T'ien-t'ai school in China. *The Biographies of the Nine Patriarchs of the T'ien-t'ai School,* which regards Nāgārjuna as the original founder of the school, counts him as the fifth patriarch. Chang-an is the name of his birthplace. In 583 he became a disciple of T'ien-t'ai and learned from him the doctrine and meditational practices of the school. For the next fifteen years, he recorded and compiled T'ien-t'ai's lectures, including his so-called three major works, *The Words and Phrases of the Lotus Sutra, The Profound Meaning of the Lotus Sutra,* and *Great Concentration and Insight.* After T'ien-t'ai's death he devoted himself to sustaining and developing the T'ien-t'ai community and wrote a biography of his teacher titled *The Biography of the Great Teacher T'ien-t'ai Chih-che of the Sui Dynasty. The One Hundred Records of the Great Teacher T'ien-t'ai* is his compilation of his teacher's letters and important documents concerning the T'ien-t'ai school. He also wrote *The Profound Meaning of the Nirvana Sutra, The Annotations on the Nirvana Sutra, The Annotations on "The Treatise on the Observation of the Mind,"* and other works.

changing poison into medicine [変毒為薬] (Jpn *hendoku-iyaku*): The principle that earthly desires and suffering can be transformed into benefit and enlightenment by virtue of the power of the Law. This phrase is found in a passage from Nāgārjuna's *Treatise on the Great Perfection of Wisdom,* which mentions "a great physician who can change poison into medicine." In this passage, Nāgārjuna compares the Lotus Sutra to a "great physician" because the sutra opens the possibility of attaining Buddhahood to persons of the two vehicles, or voice-hearers and cause-awakened ones, who in other teachings were condemned as having scorched the seeds of Buddhahood. T'ien-t'ai (538–597) says in *The Profound Meaning of the Lotus Sutra:* "That persons of the two vehicles were given the prophecy of their enlightenment in this [Lotus] sutra means that it can change poison into medicine." This phrase is often cited to show that any problem or suffering can be transformed eventually into the greatest happiness and fulfillment in life.

Chan-jan [湛然] (PY Zhanran; Jpn Tannen): Also known as Miao lo. The sixth patriarch of the T'ien-t'ai school in China. *See* Miao-lo.

Ch'an school [禅宗] (PY Chanzong; Jpn Zen-shū): *See* Zen school.

Ch'en Chen [陳鍼] (n.d.) (PY Chen Zhen; Jpn Chinshin): A military officer of the Liang dynasty (502–557) in China and the elder brother of the Buddhist teacher T'ien-t'ai. In 555 the two brothers lost both parents. According to *The Biography of the Great Teacher T'ien-t'ai Chih-che of the Sui Dynasty* by Chang-an, T'ien-t'ai's successor, T'ien-t'ai begged his brother Ch'en Chen to permit him to renounce secular life and become a priest. Unwilling to part from his only brother, Ch'en Chen tried to dissuade him from entering the priesthood. T'ien-t'ai's determination was firm, however, and Ch'en Chen eventually accepted his younger brother's wish. According to *The Record of the Lineage of the Buddha and the Patriarchs,* Ch'en Chen was told by a seer named Chang-kuo that he would die in one month, but he prolonged his life fifteen years by practicing T'ien-t'ai's teaching of concentration and insight.

Ch'eng-kuan [澄観] (738–839) (PY Chengguan; Jpn Chōkan): Also known as the Teacher of the Nation Ch'ing-liang. The fourth patriarch of the Flower Garland (Hua-yen) school in China. At age eleven, he renounced secular life and began studying Mahayana Buddhism. In 775 he practiced the T'ien-t'ai meditation under Miao-lo and later studied the doctrines of various schools under their teachers. He became fascinated with the Flower Garland teaching and lectured on the Flower Garland Sutra at Ta-hua-yen-ssu temple on Mount Wu-t'ai. He produced a number of commentaries on the sutra, including *The Annotations on the Flower Garland Sutra.* Because of his contribution to the propagation of the Flower Garland doctrine, the emperor granted him the title Teacher of the Nation Ch'ing-liang. Ch'ing-liang is another name for Mount Wu-t'ai.

Ch'eng-shih school [成実宗] (PY Chengshizong; Jpn Jōjitsu-shū): *See* Establishment of Truth school.

Chen-yüan Era Catalog of the Buddhist Canon, The [貞元釈教録・貞元入蔵録] (Chin *Chen-yüan-shih-chiao-lu* or *Chen-yüan-ju-tsang-lu;* Jpn *Jōgen-shakkyō-roku* or *Jōgen-nyūzō-roku*): Also known as the Chen-yüan era catalog. An index of Chinese Buddhist scriptures compiled by Yüan-chao. Completed in 800, the sixteenth year of the Chen-yüan era, during the reign of Emperor Te-tsung, this catalog lists 2,417 works in 7,388 volumes written or translated by 187 persons during the 734 years from C.E. 67, when Buddhism is said to have been first introduced to China, until 800. The scriptures are listed in chronological order of completion along with a brief biography of the writer or translator, and notations include multiple translations of the same work, alternate titles, whether the text is extant, and so forth. This catalog is based on *The K'ai-yüan Era Catalog of the Buddhist Canon* compiled in 730.

Chia-hsiang [嘉祥] (PY Jiaxiang; Jpn Kajō): Another name for Chi-tsang. A systematizer of the doctrines of the Three Treatises (San-lun) school in China. *See* Chi-tsang.

Chief Wise [賢首菩薩] (Jpn Genju-bosatsu): A bodhisattva who appears in the Flower Garland Sutra. In the chapter of the sutra that bears his name, Bodhisattva Chief Wise, replying to Bodhisattva Manjushrī's wish, speaks about the benefits of belief and those of a mind that aspires for enlightenment. In this context, he says, "Faith is the basis of the way and the mother of blessings."

Chien-chen [鑑真] (PY Jianzhen; Jpn Ganjin): A naturalized Japanese priest from China who founded the Precepts (Ritsu) school. Known in Japan as Ganjin. *See* Ganjin.

Chih-che [智者] (PY Zhizhe; Jpn Chisha): "Person of wisdom." An honorific title given in 591 to the Great Teacher T'ien-t'ai by Prince Kuang of the Sui dynasty in China (who later became Yang-ti, the second emperor of that dynasty). T'ien-t'ai was also called the Great Teacher Chih-che and the Great Teacher T'ien-t'ai Chih-che. *See also* T'ien-t'ai.

Chih-ch'ien [支謙] (n.d.) (PY Zhiqian; Jpn Shiken): A translator of Buddhist scriptures in China during the third century. His family was from the Great Yüeh-chih kingdom in Central Asia. A layperson well versed in six languages, he studied Buddhism under Chih-liang, a disciple of Lokakshema. Later, to avoid the danger of war, he fled south to the kingdom of Wu where he was welcomed and esteemed by the king Sun Ch'üan, and became a teacher to the royal prince. During the thirty years from 223 to 253, he translated into Chinese a number of scriptures including the Vimalakīrti Sutra, the Words of Truth Sutra, and the Sutra of the Buddha's Marvelous Deeds in Previous Lifetimes, thus contributing to the propagation of Buddhism in China. As to the number of sutras he translated, different accounts claim 27, 36, 49, 88, and 129.

Chih-chou [智周] (678–733) (PY Zhizhou; Jpn Chishū): The third patriarch of the Dharma Characteristics (Fa-hsiang) school in China. At age twenty-three, he became a disciple of Hui-chao and mastered the doctrines of that school. He lived at Pao-ch'eng-ssu temple in P'u-yang and wrote a number of treatises. Chih-chou taught the Consciousness-Only doctrine to the Japanese priests Chihō, Chiran, and Chiyū, who came to China in 703, and to Gembō, who came in 717.

Chih-i [智顗] (PY Zhiyi; Jpn Chigi): Also known as T'ien-t'ai. The founder of the T'ien-t'ai school in China. *See* T'ien-t'ai.

Chih-li [知礼] (960–1028) (PY Zhili; Jpn Chirei): A priest of China, noted as a restorer of the T'ien-t'ai school. Also known as Ssu-ming Chih-li after his birthplace, Ssu-ming. At age twenty, he studied the T'ien-t'ai doctrines under I-t'ung. By that time, the T'ien-t'ai school had already split into two lineages: that of I-chi and that of Chih-yin. Chih-li, with Tsun-shih, succeeded to the lineage of I-chi and called their group the Mountain (Chin Shan-chia; Jpn Sange) school to show that it was within the orthodox stream of the school of Mount T'ien-t'ai where the founder T'ien-t'ai had lived. Chih-li wrote several commentaries including *The Essentials of "The Ten Onenesses"* and *The Annotations on "The Profound Meaning of the Perceiver of the World's Sounds Chapter."*

Chihō [智鳳] (n.d.) (Jpn; Kor Chipong): A priest of the Dharma Characteristics (Chin Fa-hsiang; Jpn Hossō) school. Born in Silla, a state on the Korean Peninsula, he went to Japan while young and became known as Chihō. In 703, together with Japanese priests Chiran and Chiyū, he traveled to China and studied the Dharma Characteristics doctrine under Chih-chou. After returning to Japan, he settled at Gangō-ji temple and propagated the Consciousness-Only doctrine. This is regarded as the third transmission of the Dharma Characteristics teachings to Japan.

Chih-tsang [智藏] (458–522) (PY Zhizang; Jpn Chizō): A priest of China, also known as K'ai-shan because he lived at K'ai-shan-ssu temple. Chih-tsang entered the priesthood at age sixteen and studied under various eminent priests such as Seng-jou and Hui-tz'u. Emperor Wu of the Liang dynasty respected him and donated K'ai-shan-ssu temple to him. There he lectured on *The Treatise on the Establishment of Truth,* the Wisdom sutras, and other scriptures, and wrote a number of commentaries. Chih-tsang is considered one of the three great Dharma teachers of the Liang dynasty, the other two being Fa-yün and Seng-min.

Chih-tu [智度] (n.d.) (PY Zhidu; Jpn Chido): A priest of the T'ien-t'ai school in China. A disciple of Miao-lo (711–782), he is known as the author of *The Supplement to the Meanings of the Commentaries on the Lotus Sutra.* Because he lived at Tung-ch'un, this work is also called *Tung-ch'un.*

Chih-wei [智威] (d. 680) (PY Zhiwei; Jpn Chii): The third patriarch of the T'ien-t'ai school in China. Chih-wei entered the priesthood at Kuo-ch'ing-ssu temple on Mount T'ien-t'ai and studied the T'ien-t'ai doctrine under Chang-an, T'ien-t'ai's immediate successor. Later he lived on Mount Lien-tan and taught large numbers of disciples, and it is said that his lectures attracted as many as seven hundred listeners.

Chih-yen (1) [智厳] (n.d.) (PY Zhiyan; Jpn Chigon): A Chinese priest who was active as a translator from the fourth through the fifth century. Chih-yen went to Kashmir to seek Buddhist scriptures and study Buddhist doctrines. He returned to Ch'ang-an with Buddhabhadra and translated fourteen sutras. Later he went again to India, where he died.

(2) [智儼] (602–668) (PY Zhiyan; Jpn Chigon): The second patriarch of the Flower Garland (Hua-yen) school in China. At age twelve, he became a disciple of Tu-shun, the founder of the school. He first studied various Hinayana and Mahayana texts such as *The Summary of the Mahayana, The Fourfold Rules of Discipline, The Treatise on the Establishment of Truth,* and the Nirvana Sutra, but later devoted himself solely to the study of the Flower Garland Sutra and the Flower Garland doctrines. In his later years, he lived at Yün-hua-ssu temple in Ch'ang-an, where he propagated the Flower Garland doctrines. His disciple Fa-tsang is known as the systematizer of the Flower Garland doctrine.

Chih-yüan [志遠] (768–844) (PY Zhiyuan; Jpn Shi'on): A priest of the T'ien-t'ai school in China. At Mount Wu-t'ai he studied the T'ien-t'ai doctrine and practiced the Lotus meditation, a meditation based on the Lotus Sutra. Jikaku, later the third chief priest of the Japanese Tendai school, traveled to China in 838, and in 840 he studied the T'ien-t'ai doctrine under Chih-yüan at Mount Wu-t'ai.

children of the Buddha [仏子] (Jpn *busshi*): The Buddha's disciples; those who believe in and practice Buddhism. In Buddhist scriptures, this term also applies particularly to bodhisattvas, and generally to all living beings. This is because all beings possess the Buddha nature and are therefore potential Buddhas; moreover, the Buddha regards all beings with compassion, as if they are his children. For instance, in the "Simile and Parable" (third) chapter of the Lotus Sutra, Shakyamuni says: "This threefold world is all my domain, and the living beings in it are all my children. Now this place is beset by many pains and trials. I am the only person who can rescue and protect others." In Buddhist scriptures, where "children of the Buddha" refers to the Buddha's disciples such as Shāriputra, it is often translated as "sons of the Buddha."

Chinchā [旃遮・旃遮女] (Skt, Pali; Jpn Sensha or Sensha-nyo): Also known as Chinchāmānavikā (*mānavikā* means girl or daughter). A woman who defamed Shakyamuni. *The Treatise on the Great Perfection of Wisdom* tells the story of Chinchā who tied a tub to her belly under her robe and publicly declared that she was pregnant by Shakyamuni. Five hundred Brahmans joined her in condemning him. Shakyamuni remained calm and tranquil, however, and did not change his expression. This served to expose her lie. According to the Sutra of Verses, the god Shakra, assuming the form of a rat, crept under her robe and gnawed through the string that held the tub in place. It dropped to the ground, revealing her fraud. Then the earth split open and Chinchā fell into hell alive. The slander of Chinchā is counted as one of the nine great ordeals that Shakyamuni underwent.

Chinchāmānavikā [旃遮・旃遮女] (Skt, Pali; Jpn Sensha or Sensha-nyo): *See* Chinchā.

Ching-hsi [荊渓] (PY Jingxi; Jpn Keikei): Also known as Miao-lo, the sixth patriarch of the T'ien-t'ai school in China, in the tradition that counts T'ien-t'ai as the first. *See* Miao-lo.

Ch'ing-liang [清涼国師] (PY Qingliang; Jpn Shōryō-kokushi): The Teacher of the Nation Ch'ing-liang, the honorific name for Ch'eng-kuan. *See* Ch'eng-kuan.

Ch'ing-liang, Mount [清涼山] (PY Qingliang-shan; Jpn Shōryō-zan): Another name for Mount Wu-t'ai in China. *See* Wu-t'ai, Mount.

Ch'ing-lung-ssu [青竜寺] (PY Qinglongsi; Jpn Seiryū-ji): A temple in Ch'ang-an, China. It was built by Emperor Wen of the Sui dynasty (581–618) and was originally named Ling-kan-ssu. In 711, the name was changed to Ch'ing-lung-ssu. Kōbō, the founder of the Japanese True Word (Shingon) school, studied Esoteric Buddhism under Hui-kuo at this temple. In the middle of the ninth century Jikaku and Chishō of the Japanese Tendai school also studied Esoteric Buddhism respectively under I-chen and Fa-ch'üan at the same temple.

Ching-te Era Record of the Transmission of the Lamp, The [景徳伝燈録] (Jpn *Keitoku-dentō-roku*): See *Transmission of the Lamp, The.*

Chin-kang-chih [金剛智] (671–741) (PY Jingangzhi; Skt Vajrabodhi; Jpn Kongōchi): An Indian monk who went to China to disseminate Esoteric Buddhism. Chin-kang-chih is his Chinese name. Born in southern India (or central India according to some sources), he entered Nālandā Monastery at age ten and formally received the precepts at twenty. He studied the monastic disciplines of Hinayana and Mahayana, as well as *The Treatise on the Lamp of Wisdom, The One-Hundred-Verse Treatise, The Treatise on the Twelve Gates,* and other treatises. At thirty-one, he became a disciple of Nāgabodhi, who initiated him into the study of the esoteric scriptures. In 720 Chin-kang-chih went to Lo-yang in China, where he won the patronage of Emperor Hsüan-tsung and translated into Chinese several esoteric scriptures, including the Diamond Crown Sutra. The True Word (Jpn Shingon) school regards him as the fifth patriarch in the lineage of Esoteric Buddhism. His disciple Pu-k'ung (Skt Amoghavajra) succeeded him.

Chishō [智証] (814–891): Also known as Enchin or the Great Teacher Chishō. The fifth chief priest of Enryaku-ji, the head temple of the Tendai school on Mount Hiei in Japan. He was born in Sanuki Province and was a nephew of Kōbō, the founder of the Japanese True Word (Shingon) school. He practiced under Gishin, the first chief priest of Enryaku-ji temple, and studied both the exoteric and esoteric teachings. In 853 he went to China, where he visited various places to study. He learned the T'ien-t'ai practice of concentration and insight and studied the treatises of the T'ien-t'ai school under Wu-wai at Mount T'ien-t'ai. He also learned the esoteric doctrines of the Womb Realm mandala and the Diamond Realm mandala from Fa-ch'üan at Ch'ing-lung-ssu temple. After returning to Japan in 858, he lived on Mount Hiei and contributed to the development of Tendai Esotericism. In 868 he became the chief priest of Enryaku-ji. He also erected a hall at Onjō-ji temple for performing the esoteric ceremony of anointment. His works include *The Commentary on "The Treatise on the Lotus Sutra," A Collection of Orally Transmitted Teachings,* and *The Essentials of the Mahāvairochana Sutra.* About one hundred years after his death, priests in his lineage broke away from Mount Hiei and established the Temple (Jimon) school based at Onjō-ji temple. *See also* Temple school.

Chitatsu [智達] (n.d.): A priest of the Dharma Characteristics (Hossō) school in Japan. In 658, together with Chitsū, he journeyed to China and studied the doctrine of the Dharma Characteristics school under Hsüan-tsang and his disciple Tz'u-en. They brought the doctrine back with them. Earlier, Dōshō of Gangō-ji temple in Nara went to China in 653 and studied under Hsüan-tsang. On his return he spread the Dharma Characteristics teaching at Gangō-ji. Thus Chitatsu and Chitsū are regarded together as the second to propagate the doctrine of this school in Japan. After his return, Chitatsu lived at Gangō-ji temple and disseminated the Dharma Characteristics doctrine.

Chi-tsang [吉蔵] (549–623) (PY Jizang; Jpn Kichizō): A systematizer of the doctrines of the Three Treatises (San-lun) school in China. Also known as Chia-hsiang because he lived at Chia-hsiang-ssu temple. His father's family went to China from Parthia. Born in Chin-ling, Chi-tsang became a disciple of Fa-lang at Hsing-huang-ssu temple before his teens and studied the three treatises—*The Treatise on the Middle Way, The Treatise on the Twelve Gates,* and *The One-Hundred-Verse Treatise.* Later he went to live at Chia-hsiang-ssu and, devoting himself to the study of the three treatises, completed the theoretical foundation of the Three Treatises school. For this reason he is often regarded as the founder of the school. He was also versed in other scriptures such as the Lotus and Nirvana sutras. In 597 he corresponded with T'ien-t'ai concerning the Lotus Sutra. At the beginning of the seventh century, he carried out the practice of transcribing the Lotus Sutra two thousand times. His works include *The Profound Meaning of the Three Treatises, The Treatise on the Profundity of the Mahayana,* and *The Treatise on the Profundity of the Lotus Sutra.*

Chitsū [智通] (n.d.): A priest of the Dharma Characteristics (Hossō) school in Japan. In 658, together with Chitatsu, he went to China and studied the doctrine of the Dharma Characteristics school under Hsüan-tsang and his disciple Tz'u-en. They brought the doctrine back to Japan. This is known as the second transmission of the doctrine to Japan, following that of Dōshō, who went to China in 653 and studied under Hsüan-tsang. Chitsū built Kannon-ji temple in Yamato Province to spread the Dharma Characteristics doctrine. In 672 he was appointed administrator of priests.

Chizō [智蔵] (n.d.) (Jpn; Chin Chih-tsang): A priest of the Three Treatises (Chin San-lun; Jpn Sanron) school. Born in China, he went to Japan in the seventh century, was naturalized, and studied the Three Treatises doctrines under Ekan (Kor Hyekwan) of Gangō-ji temple. (Ekan was a disciple of Chi-tsang who systematized its doctrines and is regarded as the first patriarch of the school.) Thereafter Chizō went to China where he furthered his study of the Three Treatises doctrines under Chi-tsang. On his return Chizō taught the Three Treatises doctrines at Hōryū-ji temple. The doctrines of the Three Treatises school were transmitted to Japan on three occasions, and the transmission by Chizō is regarded as the second. The first was the transmission by his teacher, Ekan, in 625. The third was by Chizō's disciple, Dōji, who went to China in 702 and returned to Japan in 718. When the imperial court ordered the transcription of the entire collection of Buddhist scriptures, Chizō was appointed the supervisor, and as a reward for his contribution, he was appointed administrator of priests in 673. Dōji, Chikō, and Raikō are known as his disciples. *See also* Three Treatises school.

Chōgen [重源] (1121–1206): Also known as Shunjō-bō. A Japanese priest noted as a restorer of Tōdai-ji temple and as a disseminator of the Pure Land teachings. He learned the esoteric teachings at Daigo-ji temple and received instruction in the Pure Land teachings from Hōnen, the founder of the Pure Land (Jōdo) school in Japan. In 1167 Chōgen traveled to China to study, and there he encountered Eisai, a Japanese priest who came to China in 1168. That year Chōgen returned to Japan together with Eisai, who would later found the Rinzai school of Zen. In 1181, on the recommendation of Hōnen, Chōgen was appointed to restore Tōdai-ji temple, which had been burned by the Taira clan the previous year. He devoted himself to raising funds to repair the great image of Vairochana Buddha housed at the temple and for the repair and reconstruction of the temple's buildings. He completed the restoration with strong support from the Retired Emperor Goshirakawa, the shogun Minamoto no Yoritomo, and other authorities. Thereafter he practiced the Pure Land teachings and erected many Pure Land temples. It is said that he made three journeys to China.

Chōnen [奝然] (d. 1016): A priest of Tōdai-ji temple in Nara, Japan. A native of Kyoto, he studied at Tōdai-ji temple where he learned the doctrine of the Three Treatises (Sanron) school from Kanri, and the doctrine of the True Word (Shingon) school from Gengō. In 983 Chōnen journeyed to China where he was welcomed by the emperor and made pilgrimages to Mount Wu-t'ai and elsewhere. He also had an image of Shakyamuni Buddha sculpted after the Buddha image enshrined at K'ai-yüan-ssu temple. In China, it was believed that the K'ai-yüan-ssu image had been sculpted in Shakyamuni's time by order of King Udayana of Kaushāmbī in India. In 987 Chōnen returned to Japan with his reproduction of this Buddha image and numerous Buddhist scriptures. In 989 he became the superintendent of Tōdai-ji temple. After his death, the Buddha image he brought from China was enshrined at Seiryō-ji temple in Kyoto, where worship of it became popular because it was believed to be the image transmitted directly from India to China, and then to Japan.

Chōsai [長西] (1184–1266): Also known as Kakumyō. A priest of the Japanese Pure Land (Jōdo) school and founder of that school's Kuhon-ji branch. Born in Sanuki Province, he became a disciple of the school's founder, Hōnen, at age nineteen. After Hōnen's death, he became a disciple of Shōkū, the founder of the Seizan branch of the Pure Land school. He furthered his studies, learning the meditation of the Tendai school from Shunjō and Zen doctrines from Dōgen. Later he lived at Kuhon-ji temple in Kyoto and maintained that, in addition to the Nembutsu, or chanting of Amida Buddha's name, other practices could help one achieve rebirth in the Pure Land. As a result, he departed from Hōnen's doctrine that only the Nembutsu enables one to be reborn in Amida's paradise, and that all the other practices should be abandoned. He wrote *The Doctrine of the Original Vow in the Nembutsu*. Kakushin and Rien were his disciples.

Chūdapanthaka [周利槃特] (Skt; Pali Chūlapanthaka; Jpn Shurihandoku): The younger of two brothers who were followers of Shakyamuni Buddha. The Sanskrit word *chūda* means small, and *panthaka*, produced on the way. The elder brother, Mahāpanthaka (*mahā* meaning great), was clever, but Chūdapanthaka was slow by nature. According to one account, they were the sons of a Brahman living in Shrāvastī. When Mahāpanthaka was born, the Brahman, praying for his son's health and longevity, had him placed by the side of a main road so that a passing religious practitioner blessed him. When Chūdapanthaka was born, he gave the same instructions to the maidservant, but she put the baby by the side of an alley. According to another account, the daughter of a wealthy man had relations with a servant and ran away with him. Later she became pregnant and wanted to return home. On her way home, she bore a son, Mahāpanthaka, on the roadside. Later she gave birth to her second son, Chūdapanthaka, again on the roadside.

Chūdapanthaka was instructed in the Buddha's teachings by his brother who had renounced secular life and attained the state of arhat. Consequently, Chūdapanthaka also renounced secular life and became a monk. According to the Increasing by One Āgama Sutra, Shakyamuni attempted to have Chūdapanthaka memorize and recite the words "sweeping broom" in order for him to realize that the sweeping of dust signifies expiating defilements in life. Chūdapanthaka could not memorize these two words, however. Whenever he tried to say the phrase, he forgot either "sweeping" or "broom." He finally understood the true intent of the Buddha's instruction, however, awakening to the way to expiate defilements, and became an arhat.

The Stories of the Words of Truth Sutra states that Chūdapanthaka was so dull-witted that, though instructed by five hundred arhats for three years, he was unable to learn even a single verse of the Buddhist teachings. Taking pity on him, the Buddha gave him a verse to learn, which states that, by guarding one's speech, governing one's mind, and not committing any wrong deeds, one will surely attain liberation, and explained its meaning to Chūdapanthaka. Finally Chūdapanthaka attained an awakening and reached the state of arhat. According to still another account, Chūdapanthaka was taught a single verse of the teachings by his brother. Because he was unable to memorize it even in the span of four months, the brother considered Chūdapanthaka too inept to learn the Buddha's teachings and decided to have him return to secular life, expelling him from the monastery. At that time, Shakyamuni offered instructions to Chūdapanthaka, who earnestly followed them until he attained the state of arhat.

Chu Fa-lan [竺法蘭] (n.d.) (PY Zhu Falan; Jpn Jiku-hōran): A monk of central India said to have been the first to introduce Buddhism to China. Chu Fa-lan is his Chinese name. According to Chinese tradition, he traveled from India to Lo-yang in China with another Indian monk, Kāshyapa Mātanga, in C.E. 67 at the invitation of Emperor Ming of the Later Han dynasty. Because they arrived in China with white horses laden with Buddhist scriptures, Buddhism was referred to as the "teaching brought by white horses." He lived at Pai-ma-ssu (White Horse Temple) in the suburbs of Lo-yang and there translated five sutras into Chinese, including the Sutra of Forty-two Sections. Of the five sutras, this is the only one extant, but it is considered to have been produced in China. The Sanskrit name for Chu Fa-lan is uncertain, although scholars assume it to have been Dharmaratna, Dharmaraksha, or Dharmāranya.

Chu Fo-nien [竺仏念] (n.d.) (PY Zhu Fonian; Jpn Jiku-butsunen): A Chinese priest who was active as a translator from the latter part of the fourth century through the early fifth century. A native of Liang-chou, Chu Fo-nien assisted Samghabhūti and Dharmanandi in the Chinese translation of Buddhist scriptures in Ch'ang-an. Dharmanandi and Chu Fo-nien produced the Chinese version of the Increasing by One Āgama Sutra and the Medium-Length Āgama Sutra. Later, Chu Fo-nien by himself produced Chinese translations of several other scriptures including the Sutra of Verses and the Jeweled Necklace Sutra. He was widely admired for his excellent translations. He is said to have recited from memory many sutras and to have also been versed in non-Buddhist scriptures.

Chūlapanthaka [周利槃特] (Pali; Skt Chūdapanthaka; Jpn Shuri-handoku): The younger of two brothers who were followers of Shakyamuni Buddha. The elder brother, Mahāpanthaka, was clever, but Chūlapanthaka was slow by nature. *See* Chūdapanthaka.

Chunda [純陀] (Skt, Pali; Jpn Junda): A blacksmith in Pāvā Village in northern India who offered Shakyamuni Buddha his last meal before his death. According to the Long Āgama Sutra, when Shakyamuni was visiting Pāvā Village on the day before he entered nirvana, Chunda heard him preach the teachings. Moved and delighted, Chunda invited the Buddha and his monks to his home and had a special meal prepared for them. After leaving Chunda's house, the Buddha proceeded to Kushinagara, where he died in a grove of sal trees.

Chü-she school [倶舎宗] (PY Jushezong; Jpn Kusha-shū): *See* Dharma Analysis Treasury school.

Chu Tao-sheng [竺道生] (PY Zhu Daosheng; Jpn Jiku-dōshō): Also known as Tao-sheng. One of the major disciples of Kumārajīva in China. *See* Tao-sheng.

Chūzan [仲算] (n.d.): A priest of the Dharma Characteristics (Hossō) school in Japan. He studied under Kūsei at Kōfuku-ji temple and excelled in debate. In 963, when Emperor Murakami summoned learned priests from various schools for religious debate, Chūzan challenged the priests of the Tendai school, but the debate ended in a draw. For his performance, however, Chuzan received a reward from the imperial court and enhanced the prestige of the Dharma Characteristics school. In 969 Chūzan went to Kumano, a mountainous area that was regarded as a sacred site, Kii Province, and lectured there on the Heart Sutra near the Nachi Falls. Some sources regard his dates as 935–976, and others as 899–969.

City of Fragrances [衆香城 · 香城] (Skt Gandhavatī; Jpn Shukō-jō or Kō-jō): A city mentioned in the Wisdom sutras where Bodhisattva Dharmodgata lived and preached on the perfection of wisdom. According to the Larger Wisdom Sutra, when Ever Wailing (Skt Sadāprarudita) was seeking the teaching of the perfection of wisdom, he heard of Bodhisattva Dharmodgata who was preaching on it in the City of Fragrances, five hundred *yojanas* to the east. On the way, Ever Wailing, poor and having nothing to offer the bodhisattva for his sermon, expressed a desire to sell his body in a marketplace to obtain money. Thereupon the god Shakra assumed the form of a Brahman and appeared to Ever Wailing in order to test his resolve to seek the Law. Shakra told him that he wanted a human heart, blood, and marrow to perform a ritual. Overjoyed, Ever Wailing cut his flesh and broke open his bones to sell his blood and marrow. Seeing this, the daughter of a wealthy householder stopped him, volunteering to provide any offerings. *See also* Ever Wailing.

Clarification of Doctrine, A [顕宗論] (Chin *Hsien-tsung-lun;* Jpn *Kenshū-ron*): A forty-volume work written by Samghabhadra (fourth or fifth century) of the Sarvāstivāda school in India and translated into Chinese in the mid-seventh century by Hsüan-tsang. Along with *The Treatise on Accordance with the Correct Doctrine,* which is also Samghabhadra's work, this work attempts to refute Vasubandhu's critical argument in his *Dharma Analysis Treasury* on the Sarvāstivāda doctrine and describe the orthodox doctrine of the Sarvāstivāda school.

Clarification of the Precepts, A [顕戒論] (Jpn *Kenkai-ron*): A work written in 820 (819 according to another account) by Dengyō, the founder of the Japanese Tendai school, and submitted to the imperial court. This work clarifies the significance of the Mahayana precepts of perfect and immediate enlightenment and stresses the necessity of building an ordination platform for administering these precepts. In 819 Dengyō petitioned the throne for permission to build a Mahayana ordination platform on Mount Hiei, pointing out that the ordination platform in Nara initiated priests only in the Hinayana precepts. At that time he faced strong opposition by Gomyō and other eminent priests of the six schools of Nara. *A Clarification of the Precepts* was written to refute their arguments. *See also* Mahayana ordination platform.

Clarification of the Schools Based on T'ien-t'ai's Doctrine, A [依憑天台集] (Jpn *Ehyō-tendai-shū* or *Ebyō-tendai-shū*): A work written in 813 by Dengyō, the founder of the Japanese Tendai school. It shows how the

Buddhist teachers and scholars in China based their thought on T'ien-t'ai's doctrines and, on this basis, refutes the errors of the True Word (Chin Chen-yen; Jpn Shingon), Flower Garland (Hua-yen; Kegon), Three Treatises (San-lun; Sanron), Dharma Characteristics (Fa-hsiang; Hossō), and other schools. Thus it asserts the superiority of the T'ien-t'ai teaching over the doctrines of the other schools. In 816 Dengyō wrote the preface to this work, in which he stated: "The True Word school of Buddhism that has recently been brought to Japan deliberately obscures how its transmission was falsified in its recording [by I-hsing, who was deceived by Shan-wu-wei], while the Flower Garland school that was introduced earlier attempts to disguise the fact that it was influenced by the doctrines of T'ien-t'ai. The Three Treatises school, which is so infatuated with the concept of emptiness, has forgotten Chia-hsiang's humiliation, and conceals the fact that he was completely won over to the T'ien-t'ai teachings by Chang-an. The Dharma Characteristics school, which clings to the concept of being, denies that its leader Chih-chou was converted to the teachings of the T'ien-t'ai school, and that Liang-pi used those teachings in interpreting the Benevolent Kings Sutra. . . . Now with all due circumspection I have written *A Clarification of the Schools Based on T'ien-t'ai's Doctrine* in one volume to present to wise men of later times who share my convictions."

Clear and Cool, Mount [清涼山] (Chin Ch'ing-liang; Jpn Shōryō-zan): The abode of the bodhisattva Manjushrī, according to the Flower Garland Sutra. It later came to be identified with Mount Ch'ing-liang in China, whose name is written with the same characters meaning "clear and cool." Mount Ch'ing-liang is also known as Mount Wu-t'ai. *See also* Wu-t'ai, Mount.

clear cool pond [清涼池] (Jpn *shōryō-chi*): Also, clear cool lake. A pond or lake said to remove sufferings caused by earthly desires. According to *The Treatise on the Great Perfection of Wisdom,* when someone who is greatly afflicted enters a clear cool pond, that person is relieved of sufferings. The "Medicine King" (twenty-third) chapter of the Lotus Sutra says, "This sutra can bring great benefits to all living beings and fulfill their desires, as a clear cool pond can satisfy all those who are thirsty." A clear cool pond is often likened to nirvana, or the realm that is free of afflictions.

clothes of patched rags [糞掃衣・納衣] (Skt *pāmsu-kūla;* Jpn *funzōe* or *nōe*): Also, clothes of cast-off rags, robe of rags, etc. A monk's garment. In India, monks collected discarded pieces of dirty rags, and washed and sewed them together to make a garment.

Cloud Thunder Sound Constellation King Flower Wisdom [雲雷音宿

王華智仏] (Skt Jaladhara-garjita-ghosha-susvara-nakshatra-rāja-samkusumitābhijnā; Jpn Unraion-shukuōkechi-butsu): The Buddha who appears in the "King Wonderful Adornment" (twenty-seventh) chapter of the Lotus Sutra. According to this chapter, he gave instruction to King Wonderful Adornment, who was the father of Pure Storehouse and Pure Eye. *See also* "Former Affairs of King Wonderful Adornment" chapter.

Cloud Thunder Sound King [雲雷音王仏] (Skt Megha-dundubhi-svara-rāja; Jpn Unraionnō-butsu): The Buddha who appears in the "Wonderful Sound" (twenty-fourth) chapter of the Lotus Sutra. This chapter says that in the remote past Bodhisattva Wonderful Sound served the Buddha Cloud Thunder Sound King. One view identifies this Buddha with the Buddha Cloud Thunder Sound Constellation King Flower Wisdom, who appears in the "King Wonderful Adornment" (twenty-seventh) chapter of the Lotus Sutra.

cold-suffering bird [寒苦鳥] (Jpn *kanku-chō*): A legendary bird said to live in the Snow Mountains. This bird, tortured during the night by the cold, determines to build a nest in the morning. When day breaks, however, it instead sleeps away the hours in the warm sunlight and forgets about building its nest. When night falls, the bird suffers again. Thus it continues to be tortured by the cold throughout its life. The cold-suffering bird often appears in Buddhist works in reference to the tendency of ordinary beings to easily forget their resolve to seek Buddhism and to live vainly and shortsightedly without making efforts toward their enlightenment.

Collected Essays on the World of Peace and Delight, The [安楽集] (Chin *An-lo-chi;* Jpn *Anraku-shū*): A work by Tao-ch'o (562–645), a patriarch of the Pure Land school in China. The "World of Peace and Delight" in the title is another name for the Pure Land of Perfect Bliss created by Amida Buddha. In this work, Tao-ch'o divides all of Shakyamuni's teachings into two categories—Sacred Way teachings and Pure Land teachings—based on the Meditation on the Buddha Infinite Life Sutra. He asserts that the people of the Latter Day of the Law should embrace only the Pure Land teachings and rely solely upon Amida Buddha in order to be reborn in his Pure Land of Perfect Bliss in the west. Referring to the difficult-to-practice way and the easy-to-practice way set forth in Nāgārjuna's *Commentary on the Ten Stages Sutra,* he identifies the difficult-to-practice way with the Sacred Way teachings, and the easy-to-practice way with the Pure Land teachings. Thus Tao-ch'o urges people to abandon the difficult-to-practice way, or the Sacred Way teachings that teach the attainment of Buddhahood in this world through one's own power, and embrace the easy-to-practice way, or the Pure Land teachings that lead one to rebirth in the Pure Land of Perfect Bliss simply through recitation of the name of, and reliance upon, Amida Buddha. This work formed the basis of Shan-tao's *Commentary on the Meditation on the Buddha Infinite Life Sutra.* Hōnen, the founder of the Pure Land (Jōdo) school in Japan, used *The Collected Essays on the World of Peace and Delight* and Shan-tao's commentary as major references in writing his *Nembutsu Chosen above All.*

Collection of Orally Transmitted Teachings, A [授決集] (Jpn *Juketsu-shū*): A work by Chishō (814–891), the fifth chief priest of Enryaku-ji temple on Mount Hiei, the headquarters of the Japanese Tendai school. It records the oral teachings he received during his stay in China from Liang-hsü of Ch'an-lin-ssu temple on Mount T'ien-t'ai. The Temple (Jpn Jimon) school, a branch of the Tendai school, reveres this work as a foundational scripture.

Collection of Records concerning the Tripitaka, A [出三蔵記集] (Chin *Ch'u-san-tsang-chi-chi;* Jpn *Shutsu-sanzō-kishū*): The oldest extant catalog of Chinese translations of the Buddhist canon, compiled by Seng-yu (445–518). It lists Chinese translations of sutras, texts of the rules of monastic discipline, Buddhist commentaries, and other works produced during the period from the Later Han dynasty (25–220) to the Liang dynasty (502–557). This work also includes prefaces to the translations as well as the biographies of thirty-two translators. This collection is one of the most important reference works in the study of Chinese Buddhism and the history of the Chinese translation of Buddhist scriptures. Since it was compiled on the basis of Tao-an's *Comprehensive Catalog of Sutras,* which is no longer extant, it also sheds light on the contents of Tao-an's work.

combining, excluding, corresponding, and including [兼但対帯] (Jpn *ken-tan-tai-tai*): A concept propounded by T'ien-t'ai (538–597) in *The Profound Meaning of the Lotus Sutra* that categorizes the various provisional sutras and differentiates between them and the Lotus Sutra. These four categories show the relationship between the first four of the five periods and the four teachings of doctrine. The five periods are T'ien-t'ai's classification of Shakyamuni's teachings according to the order in which he believed they had been expounded. They are the Flower Garland period, the Āgama period, the Correct and Equal period, the Wisdom period, and the Lotus and Nirvana period.

The four teachings of doctrine are T'ien-t'ai's classification of Shakyamuni Buddha's teachings according to their content. They are the Tripitaka teaching, the connecting teaching, the specific teaching, and the perfect teaching. T'ien-t'ai explained that during the Flower Garland period, the specific teaching, a higher level of Mahayana, was combined (hence *combining*) with the perfect teaching. During the Āgama period, only the Tripitaka, or Hinayana, teaching was expounded, and the connecting teaching, or introductory Mahayana, the specific teaching, and the perfect teaching were excluded *(excluding)*. In the Correct and Equal period, all four teachings were taught in a manner corresponding to the people's capacity *(corresponding)*, while during the Wisdom period, the connecting and specific teachings were included in the perfect teaching *(including)*. In contrast with the provisional doctrines preached during these periods, which either excluded the perfect teaching or mixed it with other teachings, the Lotus Sutra contains only the perfect teaching; hence it is referred to as the pure and perfect teaching. *See also* five periods; four teachings of doctrine.

Commentary on the Mahayana Treatise, The [釈摩訶衍論] (Chin *Shih-mo-ho-yen-lun;* Jpn *Shaku-makaen-ron*): A commentary on *The Awakening of Faith in the Mahayana* attributed to Nāgārjuna (c. 150–250) and translated into Chinese by Fa-t'i-mo-to in the fourth or fifth century. Kōbō (774–835), the founder of the Japanese True Word (Shingon) school, regarded it as an exposition of Esoteric Buddhism and used it to criticize the Lotus Sutra. Contemporary scholars view this commentary as having been produced in China.

Commentary on the Meaning of the Mahāvairochana Sutra, The [大日経義釈] (Chin *Ta-jih-ching-i-shih;* Jpn *Dainichikyō-gishaku*): A revision, by Chih-yen and Wen-ku, disciples of I-hsing (683–727), of *The Annotations on the Mahāvairochana Sutra,* a compilation by I-hsing of Shan-wu-wei's lectures on the Mahāvairochana Sutra. In Japan, the esoteric tradition within the Tendai school uses this commentary, while the esoteric True Word (Shingon) school instead relies on *The Annotations on the Mahāvairochana Sutra.* See also *Annotations on the Mahāvairochana Sutra, The.*

Commentary on the Meditation on the Buddha Infinite Life Sutra, The [観無量寿経疏] (Chin *Kuan-wu-liang-shou-ching-shu;* Jpn *Kammuryōju-kyō-sho*): A work by Shan-tao (613–681), a patriarch of the Chinese Pure Land school. Shan-tao set forth an original interpretation of the Meditation on the Buddha Infinite Life Sutra, asserting that the primary practice for attaining rebirth in Amida's Pure Land is Nembutsu, recitation of the name of Amida Buddha. Among the many commentaries on the Meditation on the Buddha Infinite Life Sutra, this is the best known; it moved Hōnen to dedicate himself to the exclusive practice of the Nembutsu and establish the Pure Land (Jōdo) school in Japan.

Commentary on the Ten Stages Sutra, The [十住毘婆沙論] (Chin *Shih-*

chu-p'i-p'o-sha-lun; Jpn *Jūjū-bibasha-ron*): A commentary on the "Ten Stages" chapter of the Flower Garland Sutra. This chapter by itself is also known as Ten Stages Sutra. Kumārajīva translated the commentary, which is attributed to Nāgārjuna, into Chinese around 405. Only the Chinese version is extant. "Ten stages" refers to the ten stages that lead to enlightenment. *The Commentary on the Ten Stages Sutra,* or more precisely Kumārajīva's Chinese version, consists of thirty-five chapters devoted to only the first two of the ten stages. The ninth chapter of this commentary, titled "Easy Practice," discusses two ways of Buddhist practice—the difficult-to-practice way and the easy-to-practice way. The Pure Land school employed these categories and interpreted the easy-to-practice way as the practice of calling upon the name of Amida Buddha. The "Easy Practice" chapter is therefore valued highly by the Pure Land school.

Commentary on "The Treatise on Rebirth in the Pure Land," The [往生論註] (Jpn *Ōjōron-chū*): See *Commentary on "The Treatise on the Pure Land," The.*

Commentary on "The Treatise on the Pure Land," The [浄土論註] (Chin *Ching-t'u-lun-chu;* Jpn *Jōdoron-chū*): Also known as *The Commentary on "The Treatise on Rebirth in the Pure Land."* A commentary by T'an-luan (476–542) of China on Vasubandhu's *Treatise on the Pure Land,* which is itself a commentary on the Buddha Infinite Life Sutra. *The Commentary on "The Treatise on the Pure Land"* consists of two volumes. The first volume comments on the verse section of Vasubandhu's treatise, and the second, on the prose section. This work explains the practices for attaining rebirth in the Pure Land of Amida Buddha and exhorts the practitioner to discard the difficult-to-practice way and follow the easy-to-practice way by relying solely upon Amida Buddha's mercy. This idea of reliance on Amida's grace has been emphasized in the Japanese Pure Land school.

comparative classification [教判・教相判釈] (Jpn *kyōhan* or *kyōsō-hanjaku*): Also, doctrinal classification. The classification of sutras and their teachings. The vast array of sutras and their teachings were in effect introduced in a random manner from India to China and translated into Chinese. Buddhist scholars made an earnest attempt to evaluate them in terms of their relative profundity, the style of presentation, and the order in which they were believed to have been expounded. Thus they attempted to organize Buddhist scriptures into coherent systems of comparative classification, and numerous such systems arose. These differed among the Buddhist schools, with each school holding that its own doctrine and fundamental scripture represented the Buddha's supreme teaching, or true intent, in its own system of comparative classification. For instance, the T'ien-t'ai school set forth a comparative classification known as the five periods and eight teachings and ranked the Lotus Sutra highest, while the Flower Garland (Chin Hua-yen) school set forth the five teachings and ten doctrines to rank the Flower Garland Sutra highest. Ten schools known as the three schools of southern China and seven schools of northern China set forth their own systems of comparative classification of sutras.

comparative myō [相待妙] (Jpn *sōdai-myō*): One of two contrasting perspectives that demonstrate the profundity of the Lotus Sutra. See *myō*.

Comparison of Exoteric and Esoteric Buddhism, A [弁顕密二教論・二教論] (Jpn *Ben-kemmitsu-nikyō-ron* or *Nikyō-ron*): A work by Kōbō (774–835), the founder of the Japanese True Word (Shingon) school. In this work, Kōbō compares the esoteric teachings with the exoteric teachings and asserts that the former are superior. Kōbō designates the teachings of the Flower Garland (Kegon), Tendai, Dharma Characteristics (Hossō), Three Treatises (Sanron), and other Japanese schools as the exoteric teachings, and the teachings of the True Word school as the esoteric teachings. He asserts that only through the esoteric teachings can one attain Buddhahood in one's present form, and that the esoteric teachings can save all people, even those who cannot be saved by the exoteric teachings. This work also outlines the ten stages of the mind.

compassion [悲・慈悲] (Skt, Pali *karunā;* Jpn *hi* or *jihi*): In Buddhism, altruistic action that seeks to relieve living beings from their sufferings and give ease and delight to them. An outstanding characteristic of bodhisattvas is a mind of pity and compassion that seeks to save others even at the risk of their own lives. A Buddha is revered as one who shares in the torments of all living beings and strives to release all beings from suffering and bring them happiness. The Nirvana Sutra says, "The varied sufferings of all living beings—all these the Thus Come One himself undergoes as his own sufferings."

Compassionate Honored One [慈尊] (Jpn Jison): An epithet for Bodhisattva Maitreya. *See* Maitreya (1).

Compassionate One [慈氏] (Jpn Jishi): An epithet for Bodhisattva Maitreya. *See* Maitreya (1).

Compassionate White Lotus Flower Sutra [悲華経] (Skt *Karunā-pundarīka-sūtra;* Chin *Pei-hua-ching;* Jpn *Hike-kyō*): A sutra translated into Chinese by Dharmaraksha (385–433). The sutra says that Shakyamuni, out of his immeasurable compassion, was born not in a pure land but in the troubled *sahā* world to save the people. Therefore he is compared to the most beautiful of all flowers, the white lotus flower, described in the sutra as a symbol of great compassion, and the other Buddhas in their respective pure lands are compared to lesser flowers. Both the Sanskrit text and its Tibetan translation are also extant.

complete precepts [具足戒] (Jpn *gusoku-kai*): Also, comprehensive precepts, full commandments, or complete commandments. The complete set of rules of monastic discipline for the monk (Skt *bhikshu*) and for the nun *(bhikshunī)*. The total number of rules or commandments for monks is 250, and those for nuns, 348 (in many Buddhist scriptures stated as 500 indicating a large number). The Buddhist ordination rite in which a novice vows to observe the complete precepts as a monk or nun is called *upasampadā* in Sanskrit and Pali. Before this point, there are levels of precept observance: A lay practitioner vows to observe the five precepts, and a novice who has renounced secular life and entered monastic life must observe the ten precepts. A novice who vows to observe the complete precepts is ordained as a full-fledged monk or nun. In the ordination ceremony, the candidate takes an oath to observe the complete precepts in the presence of ten monks known as the "three leaders and seven witnesses." The three leaders are (1) a preceptor (also called teacher of discipline), or a monk who administers the precepts to the candidate; (2) a monk who acts as a chairperson, reciting words that describe the intent of the ceremony; and (3) a monk who examines whether the applicant is qualified for admission. The candidate is required to be twenty years of age or over, with no disease, and no faults that would prevent admission into the monkhood. He or she is also required to have undergone the instruction and training needed by a novice.

Complete Works of the Fuji School, The [富士宗学全集] (Jpn *Fuji-shūgaku-zenshū*): A work compiled by Nichikō (1867–1957), the fifty-ninth chief priest of Taiseki-ji, the head temple of Nichiren Shōshū, formerly known as the Fuji school, in Japan. It was published in 1938. The work comprises more than 170 documents originating within both Nichiren Shōshū and various other Nichiren schools. Major works from *The Complete Works of the Fuji School* were selected by Nichikō and published as *The Essential Works of the Fuji School.*

comprehensive precepts [具足戒] (Jpn *gusoku-kai*): *See* complete precepts.

concentration and insight [止観] (Jpn *shikan*): The entire system of meditation set forth by T'ien-t'ai (538–597) in *Great Concentration and Insight,* the ultimate goal of which is to perceive "the region of the unfathomable," that is, the unification of the three truths within one's mind or the three thousand realms in a single moment of life. "Concentration" means focusing one's mind on one point without any distractions, and "insight" means seeing all things as they are, or perception that penetrates the ultimate reality, or true aspect, of all phenomena.

concise replacement of the three vehicles with the one vehicle [略開三顕一] (Jpn *ryakkaisan-ken'ichi*): *See* replacement of the three vehicles with the one vehicle.

connecting teaching [通教] (Jpn *tsū-gyō*): One of the four teachings of doctrine, a classification of Shakyamuni's teachings set forth by T'ien-t'ai (538–597). The connecting teaching corresponds to introductory Mahayana. It is so called because it forms a link between the Tripitaka teaching (Hinayana) and the specific teaching (a higher level of Mahayana). Like the Tripitaka teaching, the connecting teaching involves casting off attachment to the threefold world. On the other hand, like the specific teaching, the connecting teaching denies the view of the Tripitaka teaching that nothing, when analyzed thoroughly and reduced to its constituents, can be found in any of its components, and that hence all things exist as mere concepts and are without substance. Thus this view equates non-substantiality with nothingness. In contrast, the connecting teaching sets forth the view that all things, just as they are, are without substance and they arise and disappear only by virtue of dependent origination. Whereas the Tripitaka teaching is addressed to voice-hearers and cause-awakened ones and the specific teaching to bodhisattvas, the connecting teaching is addressed to all of them.

Conqueror of the Threefold World [降三世明王] (Skt Trailokyavijaya; Jpn Gōsanze-myō'ō): The wisdom king Conqueror of the Threefold World. One of the five great wisdom kings. The wisdom kings are a group of deities revered in Esoteric Buddhism as the conqueror of all obstacles. The other four of the five great wisdom kings are Immovable, Kundalī, Great Awesome Virtue, and Diamond Yaksha. Conqueror of the Threefold World is regarded as either a conqueror of the three poisons of greed, anger, and foolishness, or as a conqueror of the god Maheshvara, the lord of the threefold world. *See also* five great wisdom kings.

Consciousness-Only school [唯識派] (Skt Vijnānavāda; Jpn Yuishiki-ha): Also known as the Yogāchāra school, one of the two major Mahayana schools in India, the other being the Mādhyamika school. Maitreya, who is thought to have lived around 270–350 (350–430 according to another account), is often regarded as the founder of the Consciousness-Only school. He is attributed with composing *The Treatise on the Stages of Yoga Practice,* which explains the Consciousness-Only doctrine, and passing it on to Asanga. Thereafter the Consciousness-Only doctrine was further developed by Asanga and by Vasubandhu in the first half of the fifth century. This school upholds the concept that all phenomena arise from the *vijnāna,* or consciousness, and that the basis of all functions of consciousness is the *ālaya*-consciousness. The Consciousness-Only doctrine was a major subject of Buddhist studies in Nālandā Monastery. Dharmapāla and his disciple Shīlabhadra further developed the doctrine in the latter half of the sixth century. Shīlabhadra taught the Consciousness-Only doctrine to Hsüan-tsang, who brought it back to China. Gunamati and his disciple Sthiramati were also well-known scholars of the Consciousness-Only doctrine. The Dharma Characteristics (Chin Fa-hsiang; Jpn Hossō) school in both China and Japan carried on the philosophy of the Consciousness-Only school.

conspicuous benefit [顕益] (Jpn *ken'yaku*): Benefit that appears in clearly recognizable form. The term is used in contrast with inconspicuous benefit, or benefit that accumulates over a period of time and is not immediately recognizable. *The Teaching, Practice, and Proof,* a work by Nichiren (1222–1282), states: "Those who obtained benefit during the Former and Middle Days of the Law received 'conspicuous' benefit, because the relationship they formed with the Lotus Sutra during the lifetime of the Buddha had finally matured. On the other hand, those born today in the Latter Day of the Law receive the seeds of Buddhahood for the first time, and their benefit is therefore 'inconspicuous'" (474). This passage explains conspicuous benefit as the benefit of the Buddhism of the harvest (Shakyamuni's teachings), and inconspicuous benefit as that of the Buddhism of sowing (Nichiren's teachings).

Constellation Kalpa [星宿劫] (Jpn Shōshuku-kō): One of the three *kalpas*—the past Glorious Kalpa, the present Wise Kalpa, and the future Constellation Kalpa. The major *kalpa* following the present one. According to *The Record of the Three Thousand Buddhas of the Three Kalpas,* in this Constellation Kalpa a thousand Buddhas will appear in succession, the first being the Buddha Sunlight and the last being the Buddha Sumeru Appearance. According to *The Record of the Lineage of the Buddha and the Patriarchs,* the Constellation Kalpa is so called because the Buddhas who will appear in this *kalpa* are as numerous as the constellations in the heavens.

Constellation King Flower [宿王華] (Skt Nakshatra-rāja-samkusumitābhijna; Jpn Shukuōke): The bodhisattva who, in the "Medicine King" (twenty-third) chapter of the Lotus Sutra, asks Shakyamuni Buddha: "World-Honored One, how does the bodhisattva Medicine King come and go in the *sahā* world?" In reply, Shakyamuni reveals that a previous incarnation of Bodhisattva Medicine King was a bodhisattva named Gladly Seen by All Living Beings, who learned the Lotus Sutra from the Buddha Sun Moon Pure Bright Virtue and in gratitude made offerings to this Buddha and to the sutra. Shakyamuni says to Constellation King Flower, "After I have passed into extinction, in the last five-hundred-year period you must spread it abroad widely throughout Jambudvīpa and never allow it to be cut off." The Buddha orders him to guard and protect the sutra with his transcendental powers because it provides good medicine for the ills of the people of the entire world.

Contemplation on the Mind-Ground Sutra [心地観経] (Chin *Hsin-ti-kuan-ching;* Jpn *Shinjikan-gyō*): A sutra translated by the Indian monk Prajnā, who went to China in 781. The eighth and last volume says that the states attained by Buddhas, bodhisattvas, cause-awakened ones, voice-hearers with nothing further to learn (arhat), and voice-hearers still in the process of learning—all originate from the minds of ordinary people. Thus it compares the mind to the ground, which produces grain. The sutra also defines the four debts of gratitude—those owed to one's parents, to all living beings, to one's sovereign, and to the three treasures of Buddhism—and extols the benefit of observing the mind in a quiet and remote place.

contentment while desiring little [少欲知足] (Jpn *shōyoku-chisoku*): *See* little desire and contentment with a little gain.

continual propagation to the fiftieth person [五十展転] (Jpn *gojū-ten-den*): A principle described in the "Benefits of Responding with Joy" (eighteenth) chapter of the Lotus Sutra. This chapter describes the benefits of rejoicing upon hearing the Lotus Sutra. Suppose, the sutra says, that, after Shakyamuni Buddha's death, a person were to hear the Lotus Sutra and rejoice, then preach it to a second person, who also rejoices and in turn preaches it to a third, and so on, until a fiftieth person hears the sutra. The benefit this person receives by hearing the sutra and responding with joy, even fifty times removed from the first, would be immeasurable. Shakyamuni states that this benefit is far greater than that gained by a person who gives objects of amusement, gold, silver, other precious gems, carriages, palaces, and the like to all the beings in "four hundred ten thousand million *asamkhya* worlds," doing this for eighty years, and goes on to lead these beings to arhatship.

Continued Biographies of Eminent Priests, The [続高僧伝] (Chin *Hsü-kao-seng-chuan;* Jpn *Zoku-kōsō-den*): Also known as *The T'ang Dynasty Biographies of Eminent Priests.* A thirty-volume work compiled in 645 by Tao-hsüan in China. It is a continuation of *The Liang Dynasty Biographies of Eminent Priests* (completed in 519) and states in its preface that it contains a collection of the biographies of five hundred prominent priests of the period from 502, the beginning of the Liang dynasty, to 645, the nineteenth year of the Chen-kuan era of the T'ang dynasty.

Correct and Equal period [方等時] (Jpn Hōdō-ji): The period of the introductory Mahayana sutras. The third of the five periods, a classification of Shakyamuni's teachings by T'ien-t'ai. *See* five periods.

correct and equal sutras [方等経] (Jpn *hōdō-kyō*): Also, Vaipulya sutras. Another term for Mahayana sutras, or great vehicle sutras. In the Chinese Buddhist scriptures, the correct and equal sutras are often referred to as "the correct and equal sutras of the great vehicle" or other similar titles. The expression "the correct and equal sutras" is differentiated from "the Correct and Equal sutras," the sutras that were expounded during the Correct and Equal period, the third of the five periods formulated by T'ien-t'ai (538–597).

Correct and Equal sutras [方等経] (Jpn Hōdō-kyō): Also, sutras of the Correct and Equal period. A generic term for the sutras that were expounded during the Correct and Equal period, the third of the five periods into which T'ien-t'ai (538–597) divided Shakyamuni's teachings. According to T'ien-t'ai's classification, these are lower provisional Mahayana sutras, in which Shakyamuni refuted his disciples' attachment to Hinayana and led them toward the higher teachings. Representative among them are the Shrīmālā Sutra, the Revelation of the Profound Secrets Sutra, the Golden Light Sutra, the Vimalakīrti Sutra, the three Pure Land sutras, and the three basic sutras of Esoteric Buddhism: the Mahāvairochana, Diamond Crown, and Susiddhikara sutras.

Correct Law, age of the [正法] (Jpn *shōbō*): Also, Former Day of the Law. The first of three periods following Shakyamuni's death. *See* Former Day of the Law; three periods.

Correct Views [善見城] (Skt Sudarshana; Jpn Zenken-jō): Also known as Joyful to See or Good to See. The abode of the god Shakra located in the center of the Heaven of the Thirty-three Gods on the peak of Mount Sumeru. This palace is described in detail in *The Great Commentary on the Abhidharma*, *The Dharma Analysis Treasury*, and other Buddhist texts. Each of the palace's four sides measures twenty-five hundred *yojanas* and its height one-and-a-half *yojanas*. The grounds of the palace are made of gold and are adorned with a hundred kinds of jewels. A gate is placed every ten *yojanas* around the palace; there are a thousand gates in all, each of which is guarded by five hundred *yakshas*. Within the palace grounds, there is a building called Superior Palace, and to the southwest there is the Hall of the Good Law.

Counterfeit Law, age of the [像法] (Jpn *zōbō*): Also, Middle Day of the Law. The second of the three consecutive periods following Shakyamuni's death. *See* Middle Day of the Law; three periods.

countless kalpas of practice [歴劫修行] (Jpn *ryakkō-shugyō*): Also, *kalpas* of practice or many *kalpas* of practice. Practice toward enlightenment over a period of countless *kalpas* (one *kalpa* being approximately sixteen million years according to one account). In the pre-Lotus Sutra teachings, enlightenment, or Buddhahood, was thought to require countless *kalpas* of practice to attain. It was maintained that practitioners of Buddhism, as represented by bodhisattvas, had to practice lifetime after lifetime for countless *kalpas* to attain Buddhahood. This idea contrasts with that of attaining Buddhahood in this lifetime or in a single lifetime. Those who aspired for enlightenment were required to carry out the six *pāramitās* and other bodhisattva practices over innumerable *kalpas*. When they had fulfilled the six *pāramitās,* they approached enlightenment but had not yet reached it. The Immeasurable Meanings Sutra, which serves as the prologue to the Lotus Sutra, says: "If there are living beings who are able to hear this sutra, they will gain great profit. Why? Because if they can practice it, then without fail they will quickly gain unsurpassed enlightenment. As for those living beings who are unable to hear it, one should know that they will lose great profit, for though immeasurable, boundless, inconceivable *asamkhya kalpas* may pass, they will in the end fail to gain unsurpassed enlightenment. Why? Because they will not know about the great direct way to enlightenment, but will travel perilous byways beset by numerous hindrances and trials."

Nichiren (1222–1282) states in *The Object of Devotion for Observing the Mind:* "Shakyamuni's practices and the virtues he consequently attained are all contained within the five characters of Myoho-renge-kyo. If we believe in these five characters, we will naturally be granted the same benefits as he was" (365). In the Latter Day of the Law, "the five characters of Myoho-renge-kyo"—which is the essence of the Lotus Sutra and which Nichiren embodied as the object of devotion—is the teaching that enables people to attain Buddhahood in this lifetime.

Craving-Filled [愛染明王] (Skt Rāgarāja; Jpn Aizen-myō'ō): The wisdom king Craving-Filled. A Buddhist deity who is said to purify earthly desires and free people from the illusions and sufferings caused by earthly desires. Craving-Filled belongs to a group of deities, called the wisdom kings, who are said to destroy all obstacles. *Rāga* in his Sanskrit name means passion, love, affection, and desire; and to be dyed or saturated, as with emotion, desire, or love; *rāja* means king. In Esoteric Buddhism, his true identity is regarded as Vajrasattva. Craving-Filled appears on the Diamond Realm mandala and is depicted with three eyes, six arms, and a furious face. He holds a bow and arrows in his hands. On the Gohonzon, the object of devotion inscribed by Nichiren (1222–1282), his name appears on the left as one faces it, and symbolizes the principle that earthly desires are enlightenment. *See also* earthly desires are enlightenment.

D

Daian-ji [大安寺]: A temple of the True Word (Shingon) school in Nara, Japan. One of the seven major temples of Nara. Its origin can be traced back to Kumagori-dera, a temple built by Prince Shōtoku in 617. This temple was relocated and its name changed several times. Finally in 710 it was moved to Nara and in 729 renamed Daian-ji. From the late seventh through the early eighth century, it was designated a national seat of prayer. Eminent priests such as Shinjō (Kor Simsang), who came from Silla on the Korean Peninsula to found the Flower Garland (Kegon) school in Japan, and Dōji, third patriarch of the Three Treatises (Sanron) school, lived there. Kōbō, founder of the True Word school, was at one time appointed the temple's superintendent, after which it became affiliated with the True Word school.

Daigaku Saburō [大学三郎]: A follower of Nichiren in Japan, whose full name was Hiki Daigaku Saburō Yoshimoto. *See* Hiki Yoshimoto.

Dai-Gohonzon [大御本尊] (Jpn): The object of devotion that Nichiren inscribed at Minobu, Japan, on the twelfth day of the tenth month in 1279, and which he referred to as the purpose of his advent. "Dai-Gohonzon" literally means the great object of devotion.

In *On Persecutions Befalling the Sage,* written on the first day of the same month, Nichiren states: "Now, in the second year of Kōan (1279), cyclical sign *tsuchinoto-u,* it has been twenty-seven years since I first proclaimed this teaching at Seichō-ji temple. It was at the hour of the horse [noon] on the twenty-eighth day of the fourth month in the fifth year of Kenchō (1253), cyclical sign *mizunoto-ushi,* on the southern side of the image hall in the Shobutsu-bō of Seichō-ji temple . . . The Buddha fulfilled the purpose of his advent in a little over forty years, the Great Teacher T'ien-t'ai took about thirty years, and the Great Teacher Dengyō, some twenty years. I have spoken repeatedly of the indescribable persecutions they suffered during those years. For me it took twenty-seven years, and the great persecutions I faced during this period are well known to you all" (996).

The Dai-Gohonzon was entrusted to Nikkō, and then to Nichimoku, and preserved at Taiseki-ji temple. *Matters to Be Observed after Nikkō's Death,* a document of entrustment from Nikkō to Nichimoku, reads: "As for the Dai-Gohonzon of the second year of Kōan [1279] that was entrusted to my person, I bestow it on Nichimoku."

Nichiren inscribed the Dai-Gohonzon during the time of the Atsuhara Persecution. Twenty farmers were arrested and pressured with threats to disavow their belief in Nichiren's teachings, but all refused to do so. Three were then beheaded. It is said that Nichiren inscribed the Dai-Gohonzon in response to the sincere and courageous faith of these ordinary believers. *See also* Gohonzon; Three Great Secret Laws.

Daiitoku [大威徳] (Jpn): The wisdom king Great Awesome Virtue (Daiitoku-myō'ō). *See* Great Awesome Virtue.

Daikoku [大黒] (Jpn; Skt Mahākāla): Also known as Daikoku-ten. A god of wealth and good fortune and one of the seven beneficent deities worshiped in Japan. This deity was originally the god of darkness and god of battle in Indian mythology. In his Sanskrit name Mahākāla, *mahā* means great, and *kāla,* black. The Japanese name Daikoku-ten means the great black god, and he was usually painted as a black figure with a furious expression. I-ching (635–713) says in *The Record of Southern Countries,* a record of his travels in India, that an image of Mahākāla was installed in the kitchens of the temples in India, and that it carried a bag of gold in its hand, indicating the power to bestow good fortune. Daikoku was introduced in this form to China and Japan, where he became an object of popular belief, evolving from a kitchen deity to the god of rice and rice fields. In the Edo period (1600–1867) in Japan, Daikoku was depicted in painting and sculpture with a happy expression and widely worshiped, together with Ebisu, who is also a god of wealth and one of the seven beneficent deities.

daimoku [題目] (Jpn): (1) The title of a sutra, in particular the title of the Lotus Sutra of the Wonderful Law (Chin *Miao-fa-lien-hua-ching;* Jpn *Myoho-renge-kyo*). The title of a sutra represents the essence of the sutra. Miao-lo (711–782) says in *The Annotations on "The Words and Phrases of the Lotus Sutra,"* "When for the sake of brevity one mentions only the daimoku, or title, the entire sutra is by implication included therein."

(2) The invocation of Nam-myoho-renge-kyo in Nichiren's teachings. One of his Three Great Secret Laws. *See also* daimoku of the essential teaching.

daimoku of the essential teaching [本門の題目] (Jpn *hommon-no-daimoku*): The invocation of Nam-myoho-renge-kyo; more precisely, the practice of chanting Nam-myoho-renge-kyo with belief in the object of devotion of the essential teaching. Here, "essential teaching" refers to the teaching of Nam-myoho-renge-kyo, not to the essential teaching defined as the latter half of the Lotus Sutra. The daimoku of the essential teaching is one of the Three Great Secret Laws set forth by Nichiren

(1222–1282). There are two aspects of daimoku: the daimoku of faith and the daimoku of practice. In his *Letter to Hōren,* Nichiren writes, "If you try to practice the teachings of the [Lotus] sutra without faith, it would be like trying to enter a jeweled mountain without hands [to pick up its treasures]" (511). Thus the daimoku of the essential teaching requires both faith and practice. *See also* Three Great Secret Laws.

Dainichi [大日] (Jpn): (1) The Thus Come One (or Buddha) Mahāvairochana (Dainichi-nyorai). *See* Mahāvairochana.

(2) Also known as Dainichi Nōnin or Nōnin. A priest who spread the Zen teachings in Japan during the twelfth century. *See* Nōnin.

Daishin [大進] (n.d.): A Japanese priest, commonly known as Āchārya Daishin (Daishin-ajari). A priest and disciple of Nichiren. Born in Shimōsa Province, he is believed to have been a relative of the Soya family. He and Nisshō, later one of the six senior priests designated by Nichiren, taught and guided the believers in Kamakura while Nichiren was in exile on Sado Island. From a letter Nichiren wrote to Soya Dōsō, a son of the lay priest Soya, it appears that Daishin died before the eighth month of 1279. He is thought to have been a different person from Daishin-bō, who lived in the Fuji area and later betrayed Nichiren.

Daishin-bō [大進房] (d. 1279): A priest who lived in the Fuji area in Japan during the time of Nichiren and was at one time Nichiren's disciple. Gyōchi, the deputy chief priest of Ryūsen-ji temple, persuaded him to abandon his faith in Nichiren's teaching and join in harassing Nikkō and other Nichiren's followers in the area. Daishin-bō was in the group that rode to arrest twenty of the peasant-believers in Atsuhara on the twenty-first day of the ninth month, 1279, on false charges of stealing rice crop. The peasants resisted, and in the melee he was thrown from his horse and died.

Daishonin [大聖人] (Jpn): Literally, "great sage." This honorific title is applied to Nichiren to show reverence for him as the Buddha who appeared in the Latter Day of the Law.

Dammira [檀弥羅] (n.d.): Also known as Dammiri or Mirakutsu. A king of Kashmir in ancient India. In *A History of the Buddha's Successors,* he appears under the name Mirakutsu. He had no reverence for Buddhism and destroyed Buddhist temples and stupas in his kingdom, killing many monks including Āryasimha, the last of Shakyamuni's twenty-three or twenty-four successors. It is written that, when the king beheaded Āryasimha, milk, rather than blood, flowed from the wound. According to *The Record of the Lineage of the Buddha and the Patriarchs,* the king's arm fell, still holding the sword, to the ground, and seven days later, he died. The names Dammira, Dammiri, and Mirakutsu are Japanese reading of the Chinese names, which derive from the Sanskrit. The original Sanskrit names are unknown.

Dammiri [檀弥利・檀弥栗]: *See* Dammira.

dāna [布施] (Skt, Pali; Jpn *fuse*): *See* almsgiving.

dāna-pati [檀那・檀越] (Skt, Pali; Jpn *danna* or *dan'otsu*): An almsgiver, or a person who offers alms to others including the Buddha and Buddhist Order. *Dāna* means to donate and also gift, and *pati* means master, lord, or owner. In Japan, a lay believer who regularly makes offerings to a priest or a temple is called *danna,* which derives from the Sanskrit word *dāna,* or almsgiving, and his family is called *danka* (donating family).

Dandaka, Mount [檀特山] (Skt; Jpn Dandoku-sen): Also known as Mount Dandaloka. A mountain said to be located in Gandhara, India. Dandaka was believed to be the mountain where Shakyamuni carried out austerities after he renounced the secular world. It is also known as the place where Sudāna, Shakyamuni as a prince in a former life, went into retreat and carried out austerities. The Chinese priest Hsüan-tsang mentions visiting Mount Dandaka in *The Record of the Western Regions,* the record of his travels through Central Asia and India in the seventh century. According to his notes about his travels through Gandhara at that time, a stupa built by King Ashoka still stood on the mountain where, he said, the prince Sudāna had lived in seclusion. *See also* Sudāna.

Danna [檀那]: Also known as Kakuun. The founder of the Danna school, a branch of the Tendai school in Japan. He was popularly called the Supervisor of Priests Danna and the Administrator of Priests Danna. *See* Kakuun.

Danna school [檀那流] (Jpn Danna-ryū): A branch of the Japanese Tendai school that traces its lineage from Kakuun (953–1007). Kakuun was a major disciple of Ryōgen, the eighteenth chief priest of Enryaku-ji, the head temple of the Tendai school on Mount Hiei. Because he lived in Danna-in temple on Mount Hiei, Kakuun was also called Danna. The line of Genshin (942–1017), another disciple of Ryōgen, was called the Eshin school. (Genshin was also called Eshin after the temple Eshin-in on Mount Hiei, where he lived.) The Danna school attached greater importance to doctrinal studies, while the Eshin school emphasized the practice of meditation.

According to tradition, the origin of these two schools dates back to Dengyō's journey to China in 804. In China, Dengyō studied different interpretations of T'ien-t'ai Buddhism under Tao-sui and Hsing-man. After his return to Japan, he transferred both of these teachings to his successors, and they were transmitted through the lineage of chief priests of Enryaku-ji. Ryōgen transferred both teachings to Genshin, emphasizing Tao-sui's, but transferred only Hsing-man's teachings to Kakuun. This is said to have been the origin of the schism between the Eshin and Danna schools. In reality, however, it is not known how Tao-sui's teachings differed from those of Hsing-man, nor is the difference between Genshin's and Kakuun's interpretations entirely clear. Later the Danna school split further into four branches.

Dashabala Kāshyapa [十力迦葉] (Skt; Pali Dasabala Kassapa; Jpn Jūriki-kashō): One of the five ascetics who practiced austerities with Shakyamuni before he attained enlightenment and who later became one of his first disciples. *See also* five ascetics.

Decadent Law, age of the [末法] (Jpn *mappō*): Also, Latter Day of the Law. The last of the three consecutive periods following Shakyamuni's death. *See* Latter Day of the Law; three periods.

decayed seeds [敗種] (Jpn *haishu*): In Mahayana scriptures, persons of the two vehicles—voice-hearers and cause-awakened ones—are often compared to decayed or rotten seeds that will never sprout, implying that they are incapable of attaining Buddhahood. *See also* rotten seeds; two vehicles.

Decline of the Law Sutra [法滅尽経] (Chin *Fa-mieh-chin-ching;* Jpn *Hōmetsujin-kyō*): A very short sutra that describes how Shakyamuni's teaching will disappear after his death. The translator of this sutra into Chinese is unknown. It says that, in the latter age, the devil will appear in the form of Buddhist monks and carry out slanderous acts against the Law. According to the Decline of the Law Sutra, Shakyamuni Buddha preached this sutra to Ānanda three months before his death. The sutra reads: "After I have entered nirvana, in the troubled times when the five cardinal sins prevail, the way of the devil will flourish. The devil will appear in the form of Buddhist monks and attempt to confuse and destroy my teachings. . . . Those who do evil will become as numerous as the sands of the ocean, while the good will be extremely few, perhaps no more than one or two persons."

Deer Feet [鹿足王] (Jpn Rokusoku-ō): The king Deer Feet. Also known as Spotted Feet. *See* Spotted Feet; Universal Brightness (1).

Deer Park [鹿野苑] (Skt Mrigadāva; Pali Migadāya; Jpn Rokuya-on): A park in Vārānasī in India, the site of present-day Sarnath. Deer Park was also known as Rishipatana (Skt; Pali Isipatana), or Sage Ascetics-Gathering. Here Shakyamuni delivered his first sermon. The Sanskrit word *mriga* of Mrigadāva means deer, and *dāva* means forest. *Rishi* of Rishipatana means sage, saint, ascetic, or hermit, and *patana* means gathering, falling, or descending. According to the Miscellaneous Āgama Sutra, after his awakening under the *bodhi* tree, the Buddha went to Deer Park where he delivered his first sermon on the four noble truths and converted the five ascetics. Hsüan-tsang's *Record of the Western Regions* explains the origin of the name Deer Park. According to this work, the lord of Vārānasī once hunted and killed many deer on this land. The deer population was presided over by a deer king, who implored the lord to stop the unnecessary killing and in turn promised that each day he would give the lord the number of deer that he required. One day the deer king was faced with the necessity of sending a pregnant doe. Rather than sacrifice her with her unborn fawn, the deer king went to the lord to offer his own flesh instead. The lord was so moved by the deer king's compassion that he gave him the land. Hence it was named Deer Park. Vārānasī prospered until the Muslim invasion in the thirteenth century. Stupas and monasteries were built in this area, where Buddhist believers came to visit. In modern times, ruins have been discovered here, including one of King Ashoka's stone pillars topped by a sculpture of a lion.

Deer Park period [鹿苑時] (Jpn Rokuon-ji): Also called the Āgama period. The second of the five periods, a classification of Shakyamuni's teachings by T'ien-t'ai. *See* five periods.

Delving into the Profundity of the Flower Garland Sutra [華厳経探玄記] (Chin *Hua-yen-ching-t'an-hsüan-chi;* Jpn *Kegongyō-tangen-ki*): A commentary on the sixty-volume Flower Garland Sutra by Fa-tsang (643–712), the third patriarch of the Flower Garland (Hua-yen) school in China, who systematized the school's doctrines. It consists of ten chapters in twenty volumes. The first volume explains in nine chapters the sutra's background, its position among the Buddhist teachings, its core doctrines, title, the history of its translations, the school's classification of the Buddhist teachings, etc. The other volumes, which together comprise the last or tenth chapter, interpret the text of the entire sutra, citing various sutras and commentaries. This commentary is considered a major reference work in the study of the Flower Garland Sutra along with Ch'eng-kuan's two commentaries on the eighty-volume Flower Garland Sutra, *The Annotations on the Flower Garland Sutra* and *The Meaning of the Flower Garland Sutra Based on an Earlier Commentary.*

demon [悪鬼・鬼] (Jpn *akki* or *ki*): Also, evil demon, evil spirit, or simply spirit. Evil beings who torment people. Indian mythology and Buddhist scriptures mention various kinds of demons, such as *rākshasa, yaksha,* and *kumbhānda.* The "Encouraging Devotion" (thirteenth) chapter of the Lotus Sutra, for example, states: "In a muddied *kalpa,* in an evil age there will be many things to fear. Evil demons will take possession of others and through them curse, revile, and heap shame on us. But we, reverently trusting in the Buddha, will put on the armor of perseverance. In order to preach this sutra we will bear these difficult things." Demon also means negative functions or influences that deprive people of happiness or vitality, and obstruct correct judgment. In contrast with the function of gods that protect people's welfare, demons indicate forces in the environment that act to prevent or destroy human happiness. In *Great Concentration and Insight,* T'ien-t'ai (538–597) regarded attack by demons as one of the six causes of illness.

Demon Eloquence [鬼弁婆羅門] (n.d.) (Jpn Kiben-baramon): A Brahman who lived in India during the second century, who is mentioned in *The Record of the Western Regions* by Hsüan-tsang. According to that work, Demon Eloquence was revered widely as a sage because of his eloquence, though this quality was bestowed by a demon he worshiped. He often conducted debates from behind a curtain, and no scholar could surpass or refute him. One day Ashvaghosha, who was well versed in the Buddhist teachings, confronted him in debate and argued him into silence. Ashvaghosha then lifted the curtain, revealing the demon.

Dengyō [伝教] (767–822): Also known as Saichō. The founder of the Tendai school in Japan. His posthumous honorific name and title are the Great Teacher Dengyō. At age twelve, he entered the Buddhist priesthood and studied under Gyōhyō at a provincial temple in Ōmi Province. In 785 he attended the ceremony for receiving the entire set of Hinayana precepts at Tōdai-ji temple in Nara, and in the seventh month of the same year he went to Mount Hiei where he built a small retreat. There he studied Buddhist scriptures and treatises, especially those of the T'ien-t'ai school.

In 788 he built a small temple on the mountain and named it Hieisan-ji (Temple of Mount Hiei). (After Dengyō's death, Emperor Saga renamed it Enryaku-ji in 823.) In 802, at age thirty-six, Dengyō was invited to Kyoto by the brothers and court nobles Wake no Hiroyo and Wake no Matsuna to lecture at their family temple, Takao-dera. There he expounded T'ien-t'ai's three major works to eminent priests representing the seven major temples of Nara. This event catapulted Dengyō to prominence, winning him the support of Emperor Kammu, and greatly enhanced the prestige of the T'ien-t'ai doctrine.

In 804, accompanied by his disciple Gishin who acted as interpreter, Dengyō went to China. After making a pilgrimage to Mount T'ien-t'ai, the center of the T'ien-t'ai school, they stayed in the province of T'ai-chou, where the center was located. There Dengyō received the essentials of T'ien-t'ai Buddhism from Miao-lo's disciple Tao-sui and then from Hsing-man, another disciple of Miao-lo. He also received the bodhisattva precepts, or those of perfect and immediate enlightenment, from Tao-sui, the Zen teachings from Hsiao-jan, and the anointment of Esoteric Buddhism from Shun-hsiao. In 805 he returned to Japan and the next year established the Tendai school. In those days, all Buddhist priests were ordained exclusively in the Hinayana precepts. Dengyō wished to ordain his disciples with Mahayana precepts and made continual efforts to obtain imperial permission for the building of a Mahayana ordination center on Mount Hiei in the face of determined opposition from the older schools of Nara. Permission was finally granted a week after Dengyō's death in 822, and in 827 his successor Gishin completed the ordination center.

After his return to Japan, in addition to this project, Dengyō concentrated his efforts on refuting the doctrines of the older Buddhist schools. In particular, his ongoing debate with Tokuitsu, a priest of the Dharma Characteristics (Hossō) school, is well known. That debate began in the early Kōnin era (810–824). Tokuitsu asserted that the one vehicle teaching of the Lotus Sutra was a provisional teaching that Shakyamuni Buddha expounded in accordance with the people's capacity, while the three vehicle teachings were true teachings, and that there are some people who are without the potential to attain Buddhahood. In opposition to this assertion, Dengyō maintained that all people have the Buddha nature, and that the one vehicle of Buddhahood expounded in the Lotus Sutra is the true teaching.

Among Dengyō's major disciples were Gishin, Enchō, Kōjō, Jikaku, Chishō, and Ninchū. His works include *The Outstanding Principles of the Lotus Sutra, A Clarification of the Precepts, An Essay on the Protection of the Nation,* and *The Regulations for Students of the Mountain School.*

dependent origination [縁起・因縁] (Skt *pratītya-samutpāda;* Pali *paticcha-samuppāda;* Jpn *engi* or *innen*): Also, dependent causation or conditioned co-arising. A Buddhist doctrine expressing the interdependence of all things. It teaches that no beings or phenomena exist on their own; they exist or occur because of their relationship with other beings and phenomena. Everything in the world comes into existence in response to causes and conditions. That is, nothing can exist independent of other things or arise in isolation. The doctrine of the twelve-linked chain of causation is a well-known illustration of this idea. *See also* twelve-linked chain of causation.

desiring little and knowing satisfaction [少欲知足] (Jpn *shōyoku-chisoku*): A virtue that monks should possess, as described in Buddhist scriptures. *See* little desire and contentment with a little gain.

determinate groups [決定性] (Jpn *ketsujō-shō*): Those predestined by nature to be voice-hearers, cause-awakened ones, or bodhisattvas. The determinate groups correspond to three of the five natures, a doctrine set forth by the Dharma Characteristics (Chin Fa-hsiang; Jpn Hossō) school dividing human beings into five groups according to their inborn religious capacity. The other two are (1) an indeterminate group, which has two or all of the natures of the determinate group, and (2) those without the nature of Buddhahood or the enlightenment of voice-hearers or cause-awakened ones. Those predestined to be voice-hearers, those predestined to be cause-awakened ones, and those predestined to be bodhisattvas are called the determinate groups because the state of awakening they will achieve is predetermined. The term most often applies to those predestined to become persons of the two vehicles, i.e., voice-hearers and cause-awakened ones, and who therefore cannot attain Buddhahood. *See also* five natures.

deva [天] (Skt, Pali; Jpn *ten*): A god, deity, or heavenly being. *See also* heavenly gods and benevolent deities.

Devadatta [提婆達多] (Skt, Pali; Jpn Daibadatta): A cousin of Shakyamuni who, after Shakyamuni's enlightenment, first followed him as a disciple but later became his enemy. Devadatta was a younger brother of Ānanda (an elder brother according to another account). His father was Dronodana (or Amritodana). In Buddhist scriptures, he is described as a man of utmost evil who tried to kill Shakyamuni Buddha and disrupt his Order. When both were young, before Shakyamuni embarked on a religious life, Devadatta is said to have beaten to death a white elephant that had been given to him by Shakyamuni. Devadatta was also a rival for the hand of Yashodharā, whom Shakyamuni eventually married. Later Devadatta renounced secular life and became one of Shakyamuni's disciples.

In his arrogance, however, he grew jealous of Shakyamuni and sought to usurp the Buddha's position. He fomented a schism in the Buddhist Order, luring away a number of monks. He also goaded Ajātashatru, prince of Magadha, into overthrowing his father, Bimbisāra, a patron of Shakyamuni, and ascending the throne in his stead. With the new king supporting him, Devadatta made several attempts on Shakyamuni's life and caused a schism in his Order. As a result of his misdeeds, Devadatta is said to have fallen into hell alive. In the "Devadatta" (twelfth) chapter of the Lotus Sutra, however, Shakyamuni reveals that in some past existence he himself had learned the Lotus Sutra from a seer named Asita, and that this seer was Devadatta. He also predicts that Devadatta will attain enlightenment in the future as a Buddha named Heavenly King.

Nichiren (1222–1282) takes this prediction to illustrate the principle that even evil persons have the potential for enlightenment.

"Devadatta" chapter [提婆達多品] (Jpn *Daibadatta-hon*): The twelfth chapter of the Lotus Sutra. It teaches that both women and evil persons are capable of attaining Buddhahood, something generally denied in the provisional, or pre-Lotus Sutra, teachings, as well as the principle of attaining enlightenment in one's present form without completing many *kalpas* of practice. In the first half of the chapter, Shakyamuni discloses that in a past life he was a king who renounced his throne to seek the truth. For one thousand years, he served a seer named Asita, who in turn taught him the Lotus Sutra. This seer, he explains, is none other than Devadatta. He then prophesies that, in the distant future, Devadatta will attain enlightenment as a Buddha called Heavenly King. Devadatta had tried on several occasions to kill Shakyamuni and foment disunity within the Buddhist Order and is said to have fallen into hell alive. The prediction of his future enlightenment indicates that even the most depraved person has the potential to become a Buddha.

At this point in the "Devadatta" chapter, a bodhisattva named Wisdom Accumulated is about to return to his original land when Shakyamuni urges him to stay a while and listen to the discourse of Bodhisattva Manjushrī. Manjushrī relates how he has preached the Lotus Sutra in the palace of a dragon king and converted innumerable beings, and Wisdom Accumulated asks him if there is anyone there who applies the sutra in practice and gains Buddhahood quickly. Manjushrī replies that the eight-year-old daughter of the dragon king has attained the stage of non-regression and is capable of readily achieving the supreme Buddha wisdom. Wisdom Accumulated and Shāriputra both challenge this; Wisdom Accumulated on the grounds that Buddhahood requires the practice of austerities spanning many *kalpas*, and Shāriputra for the same reason and also because women are said to possess the five obstacles and to be incapable of attaining enlightenment. By now the dragon king's daughter has appeared in front of them. After presenting a jewel to Shakyamuni Buddha, she at once transforms herself into a male and instantaneously perfects the bodhisattva practice. Acquiring the thirty-two features and eighty characteristics of a Buddha, she appears in a land to the south called Spotless World, where she preaches the Lotus Sutra to all beings in the ten directions. Her attainment of Buddhahood shows not only that women can reach enlightenment but also—because she attained enlightenment while remaining a dragon—that one can become a Buddha in one's present form.

The enlightenment of evil people, represented by Devadatta, and that of women, represented by the dragon king's daughter, illustrate the universal possibility of Buddhahood that the sutra teaches. In Kumārajīva's translation of the Lotus Sutra, the "Devadatta" chapter is an independent chapter, but in both the Lotus Sutra of the Correct Law by Dharmaraksha and the Supplemented Lotus Sutra of the Wonderful Law by Jnānagupta and Dharmagupta, it is included as part of the preceding chapter, "Treasure Tower." Thus these two versions of the Lotus Sutra each consist of only twenty-seven chapters. *See also* dragon king's daughter.

devil [魔] (Skt, Pali *māra;* Jpn *ma*): A personification of evil. The Sanskrit word *māra* also means killing, death, pestilence, or obstacle, and in China it was translated as "robber of life." In Buddhist scriptures, Māra is the name of a devil king who rules over numerous devils who are his retinue. He is described as the great evil enemy of Shakyamuni Buddha and his teachings. When Shakyamuni entered into meditation under the *bodhi* tree, Māra attempted to prevent him from attaining enlightenment but failed. After Shakyamuni's enlightenment, he also tried to induce the Buddha to abandon his intent to preach. Māra is identified with the devil king of the sixth heaven. The sixth heaven is the highest heaven in the world of desire, or the Heaven of Freely Enjoying Things Conjured by Others, and its ruler delights in manipulating others to submit to his will. In Buddhism, devils indicate those functions that block or hinder people's effort to complete their Buddhist practice.

devil king [魔王] (Jpn *maō*): *See* devil king of the sixth heaven; Heaven of Freely Enjoying Things Conjured by Others.

devil king of the sixth heaven [第六天の魔王] (Jpn *dairokuten-no-maō*): Also, devil king or heavenly devil. The king of devils, who dwells in the highest or the sixth heaven of the world of desire. He is also named Freely Enjoying Things Conjured by Others, the king who makes free use of the fruits of others' efforts for his own pleasure. Served by innumerable minions, he obstructs Buddhist practice and delights in sapping the life force of other beings. One of the four devils. *See also* devil; four devils; Heaven of Freely Enjoying Things Conjured by Others.

Dhammapada [法句経] (Pali; Jpn *Hokku-kyō*): The second text in the *Khuddaka-nikāya* (minor sutras) of the *Sutta Pitaka* (Basket of Discourse). *Dhammapada* means words of truth. The *Dhammapada,* which contains 423 stanzas in 26 chapters, is an anthology of religious and ethical sayings, used in the countries of Theravāda Buddhism such as Sri Lanka. The Chinese title is *Fa-chü-ching,* which means Words of Truth Sutra.

There are numerous translations, including the English version by Max Müller and the German version by Karl Eugen Neumann. *See also* Words of Truth Sutra.

dhāranī [陀羅尼] (Skt; Jpn *darani*): A formula said to protect those who recite it and to benefit them by virtue of its mysterious power. The word *dhāranī* literally means to preserve and uphold [the Buddha's teachings in one's heart]. *Dhāranī* is rendered in Chinese Buddhist scriptures as "all-retaining" or "able to retain." One who upholds and recites a *dhāranī* is believed not only to remember all of the Buddha's teachings and never to forget them, but also to deflect evil influences. *Dhāranīs* are recited in Sanskrit, and some have no known meaning. They are especially valued in Esoteric Buddhism.

"Dhāranī" chapter [陀羅尼品] (Jpn *Darani-hon*): The twenty-sixth chapter of the Lotus Sutra. In this chapter, the bodhisattvas Medicine King and Brave Donor, the heavenly gods such as Vaishravana and Upholder of the Nation, the ten demon daughters, and the Mother of Demon Children recite *dhāranīs* with which to protect those who uphold and propagate the Lotus Sutra. *Dhāranīs* are mystic formulas that are said to protect those who recite them. The ten demon daughters and the Mother of Demon Children, after chanting their *dhāranīs,* say, "If there are those who fail to heed our spells and trouble and disrupt the preachers of the Law, their heads will split into seven pieces like the branches of the *arjaka* tree." Shakyamuni then describes the great benefit the daughters will receive for protecting the votaries of the sutra.

dharma [法] (Skt; Pali *dhamma;* Jpn *hō*): A term fundamental to Buddhism, *dharma* derives from the root *dhri,* which means to preserve, maintain, keep, or uphold. It has a wide variety of meanings, including law, truth, doctrine, the Buddha's teaching, decree, observance, conduct, duty, virtue, morality, religion, justice, nature, quality, character, characteristic, essence, elements of existence, or phenomena.

Some of the more common usages are: (1) (Often capitalized) The Law, or ultimate truth. For example, Kumārajīva translated *saddharma,* the Sanskrit word that literally means Correct Law, as Wonderful Law or Mystic Law, indicating the unfathomable truth or Law that governs all phenomena. (2) The teaching of the Buddha that reveals the Law. *Dharma* of *abhidharma* means the Buddha's doctrine, or the sutras. (3) (Often plural) Manifestations of the Law, i.e., phenomena, things, facts, or existences. The word *phenomena* in "the true aspect of all phenomena" is the translation of *dharmas.* (4) The elements of existence, which, according to the Hinayana schools, are the most basic constituents of the individual and his or her reality. (5) Norms of conduct leading to the accumulation of good karma.

The word *dharma* is a component of the names of many Indian Buddhist monks, including Dharmagupta, Dharmaraksha, Dharmamitra, Dharmapāla, Dharmayashas, Dharmakāla, and Bodhidharma.

Dharma Analysis Treasury, The [阿毘達磨俱舍論] (Skt *Abhidharmakosha-bhāshya* or *Abhidharmakosha-shāstra;* Chin *A-p'i-ta-mo-chü-she-lun;* Jpn *Abidatsuma-kusha-ron*): Also known as *Abhidharmakosha.* An exhaustive study of the Sarvāstivāda *abhidharma,* written by Vasubandhu (fourth or fifth century) and translated into Chinese in 651 by Hsüan-tsang. A Sanskrit manuscript is extant. There is another Chinese translation, done by Paramārtha in 564, as well as a Tibetan translation. As a systematic explanation of Buddhist ideas and concepts, *The Dharma Analysis Treasury* includes a comprehensive discussion of Buddhist themes organized in nine chapters: (1) "Elements" (or dharmas), (2) "Sense Organs," (3) "Realms," (4) "Actions," (5) "Earthly Desires," (6) "Stages of Worthies and Sages," (7) "Wisdom," (8) "Meditation," and (9) "Refutation of the Idea of the Self."

The first two chapters are a categorization of the dharmas, or elements of existence, and their functions. The third through the fifth chapter elaborate on the realms of delusion. Among these, the third chapter describes the Buddhist view of the universe, including the concept of transmigration within the realms of delusion. The fourth chapter outlines the actions that cause one to fall into the realms of delusion. The fifth chapter explains that earthly desires and illusions produce actions that in turn bring about suffering in the realms of delusion. Here, earthly desires are divided into two categories: fundamental and derivative. The following three chapters, from the sixth to the eighth, clarify the way to enlightenment. The sixth chapter explains the stages through which voice-hearers advance toward the level of arhat. The seventh chapter deals with the wisdom that leads one to enlightenment. Two kinds of wisdom are defined: wisdom that continues to be bound by earthly desires and wisdom that is free from earthly desires. The eighth chapter discusses the practice of meditation that brings forth wisdom that is untainted by earthly desires. The ninth and last chapter discusses the doctrine of non-self, refuting the idea of the self.

This work is primarily a critical analysis of *The Great Commentary on the Abhidharma,* the principal text of the Sarvāstivāda school, one of the major early Indian schools of Buddhism. In *The Dharma Analysis Treasury,* Vasubandhu, originally a Sarvāstivādin, reexamined traditional

Sarvāstivāda teachings from a broader standpoint, drawing on the interpretations of several schools, most notably those of the Sautrāntikas. In response, Samghabhadra wrote *The Treatise on Accordance with the Correct Doctrine* to refute the ideas of *The Dharma Analysis Treasury* and exalt the traditional Sarvāstivāda doctrine. *The Dharma Analysis Treasury* itself contains an excellent and thorough exposition on Sarvāstivāda doctrine and forms a unified doctrinal system, and has been regarded as a textbook of the Sarvāstivāda school. A pinnacle of doctrinal study, *The Dharma Analysis Treasury* greatly influenced people's understanding of Buddhism in later ages and was studied widely in India, China, and Japan. Consequently, a number of commentaries on it were produced, and the Dharma Analysis Treasury (Chin Chü-she; Jpn Kusha) school was founded in China based on this work. The school was brought to Japan and became known as one of the six schools of Nara.

Dharma Analysis Treasury school [倶舎宗] (Chin Chü-she-tsung; Jpn Kusha-shū): A school based on *The Dharma Analysis Treasury* of Vasubandhu. This work was translated into Chinese, once by Paramārtha in 564 and again by Hsüan-tsang in 651. After Paramārtha completed his translation, the Dharma Analysis Treasury school, which was based on this treatise, came into being in China. It enjoyed a brief existence during the T'ang dynasty (618–907). The Dharma Analysis Treasury system was brought to Japan along with the Dharma Characteristics (Chin Fa-hsiang; Jpn Hossō) school and was widely studied during the Nara period (710–794). The Dharma Analysis Treasury school was counted as one of the six schools of Nara, but it never became fully independent. Its doctrine teaches that the self has no independent existence but the dharmas are real, and that past, present, and future have independent existences. It also classifies all things and phenomena into seventy-five dharmas in five categories. See also *Dharma Analysis Treasury, The.*

Dharma body [法身] (Skt *dharma-kāya;* Jpn *hosshin*): Also, body of the Law. The *dharma* of *dharma-kāya* means Law, and *kāya,* body. One of the three bodies—the Dharma body, the reward body, and the manifested body. The Dharma body means the essence of Buddhahood, the ultimate truth or Law, and the true nature of the Buddha's life. It also means a Buddha per se, whose body is the Law itself. A Buddha of this kind is referred to as the Buddha of the Dharma body or the Buddha in his body of the Law. *See also* three bodies.

dharma-chakra [法輪] (Skt; Jpn *hōrin*): The wheel of the Law, meaning the Buddha's teachings. *See* wheel of the Law.

Dharma Characteristics school [法相宗] (Chin Fa-hsiang-tsung; Jpn Hossō-shū): A school that aims to clarify the ultimate reality by analyzing and classifying the aspects and characteristics of things and phenomena. The basic scriptures of the school comprise six sutras and eleven treatises, including the Revelation of the Profound Secrets Sutra, *The Treatise on the Establishment of the Consciousness-Only Doctrine,* and *The Treatise on the Stages of Yoga Practice.* The Dharma Characteristics doctrine classifies all phenomena into five categories, which are further subdivided into one hundred dharmas, or elements of existence. It maintains that all phenomena arise from the *ālaya*-consciousness, and that nothing can exist without the *ālaya*-consciousness. The doctrines of this school derive from the teachings of the Consciousness-Only school of Maitreya, Asanga, and Vasubandhu, which was introduced to China by Paramārtha and Hsüan-tsang. In the first half of the seventh century, Hsüan-tsang journeyed to India and brought back *The Treatise on the Establishment of the Consciousness-Only Doctrine,* which he translated into Chinese with the aid of his disciple Tz'u-en. Based on its teachings, Tz'u-en founded the Dharma Characteristics school. His teachings were transmitted to Hui-chao and then to Chih-chou. The school prospered during the T'ang dynasty (618–907) but later declined. Its teachings were introduced to Japan on four occasions: by Dōshō, who went to China in 653 and studied under Hsüan-tsang; by Chitsū and Chitatsu, who made the journey in 658 and also studied under Hsüan-tsang and Tz'u-en; by Chihō, Chiran, and Chiyū, who went in 703 and received the teachings from Chih-chou; and by Gembō, who went in 716 and also studied under Chih-chou. Dōshō's line, based at Gangō-ji temple, is called "the transmission of the Southern Temple," while Gembō's, based at Kōfuku-ji, is called "the transmission of the Northern Temple." *See also* Consciousness-Only school.

Dharma eye [法眼] (Jpn *hōgen*): (1) One of the five types of vision. A bodhisattva is said to perceive the nature of all Buddhist teachings with the Dharma eye in order to save the people. The Dharma eye also indicates a bodhisattva's clear perception of all phenomena.

(2) An official rank within the priesthood. Such official ranks changed over time, the rank of the Dharma eye having been established in Japan in 864. While initially it defined a function or level of responsibility, later, as with other such ranks, it became a formality, conferred only as an honorific title.

Dharmagupta (Skt) (1) [達摩笈多] (d. 619) (Jpn Darumagyūta): A native of Lāra in southern India. He became a monk at age twenty-three and later traveled through various kingdoms in Central Asia to pursue study of the sutras. He went to Ch'ang-an in China in 590, where he lived at Ta-hsing-shan-ssu temple and engaged in the translation of Buddhist scriptures. Together with Jnānagupta, he produced a Chinese version of the Lotus Sutra titled the Supplemented Lotus Sutra of the Wonderful Law.

(2) [達摩掬多] (n.d.) (Jpn Darumakikuta): A monk of Nālandā Monastery in India at the end of the sixth century. He was the teacher of Shan-wu-wei (Skt Shubhakarasimha). *The Sung Dynasty Biographies of Eminent Priests* says that he looked like a man of forty when he was in reality eight hundred. He is said to have transferred Esoteric Buddhism to Shan-wu-wei and instructed the latter to propagate it in China, aiding him through his supernatural powers. One view identifies Dharmagupta with Nāgabodhi. Another holds that he is an imaginary figure, in view of the mysterious legends surrounding him.

Dharmagupta school [法蔵部・曇無徳部] (Skt; Jpn Hōzō-bu or Dommutoku-bu): Also known as the Dharmaguptaka school. One of the twenty Hinayana schools of ancient India. According to *The Doctrines of the Different Schools,* during the third one-hundred-year period after Shakyamuni Buddha's death, the Dharmagupta school branched out from the Mahīshāsaka school, which had derived from the Sarvāstivāda school. *The Fourfold Rules of Discipline,* a text of the *vinaya* (rules of monastic discipline), belongs to the Dharmagupta school. This text had a great influence on Chinese Buddhism. According to *The Doctrines of the Different Schools,* the Dharmagupta school attached greater importance to making offerings to the Buddha himself than to the Buddhist Order. It asserted that the building of stupas would result in great reward. Although the school is within the lineage of the Sthaviravāda (Pali Theravāda) school, its ideas are similar to those of another, more progressive and flexible lineage, the Mahāsamghika school and its branches. It is said that the Long Āgama Sutra, one of the four Āgama sutras, was preserved and transmitted by the Dharmagupta school.

Dharmakāla [曇摩迦羅・曇柯迦羅] (n.d.) (Skt; Jpn Dommakara or Donkakara): A monk from central India in the third century. He was well versed in the Vedas and other branches of learning. At age twenty-five, he listened to a Buddhist monk preaching *The Heart of the Abhidharma* by Dharmashrī and, realizing the law of causality, converted to Buddhism. He earnestly studied Buddhist scriptures relating to the rules of monastic discipline. Later he went to Lo-yang in China where, in the middle of the third century, he translated *The Basic Rules of Discipline* at Pai-ma-ssu temple. This work is said to be the first text introduced into China that defined the precepts for Buddhist monks. He outlined the rules of Buddhist rituals and regulations for monks, and performed the first ordination ceremony for administering Buddhist precepts in China.

Dharmākara [法蔵比丘] (Skt; Jpn Hōzō-biku): A bodhisattva described in the Buddha Infinite Life Sutra who is identified as Amida Buddha before he became a Buddha and was still engaged in bodhisattva practice. *See* Dharma Treasury.

dharma-kāya [法身] (Skt; Jpn *hosshin*): The Dharma body, one of the three bodies of a Buddha. *See* Dharma body.

Dharma King [法王] (Skt *dharma-rāja;* Jpn *hō'ō*): Also, king of the Law. A Buddha. In Buddhist scriptures, Shakyamuni Buddha is often called the Dharma King, and he also calls himself the Dharma King. For example, in the "Simile and Parable" (third) chapter of the Lotus Sutra, Shakyamuni says, "I am the Dharma King, free to do as I will with the Law. To bring peace and safety to living beings—that is the reason I appear in the world."

Dharma master [法師] (Jpn *hosshi*): *See* Dharma teacher.

Dharmamitra [曇摩蜜多・曇無蜜多] (356–442) (Skt; Jpn Dommamitta or Dommumitta): A monk from Kashmir in ancient India who translated Buddhist sutras into Chinese. He entered the Buddhist Order while young and traveled through various kingdoms to pursue study of the sutras. He dedicated himself to the practice of meditation and, passing through Kucha and Tun-huang, went to China in 424, where he exhorted people to practice meditation. In 433 he went to Chien-k'ang, the capital of the Liu Sung dynasty, and in 435 founded Ting-lin-shang-ssu temple, where he lived. He converted the empress and crown prince of the Liu Sung dynasty. His works include *The Secret Essentials of Meditation* and Chinese translations of the Universal Worthy Sutra and the Meditation on Bodhisattva Space Treasury Sutra.

Dharma nature [法性] (Jpn *hosshō*): The unchanging nature inherent in all things and phenomena. *See* essential nature of phenomena.

Dharmapāla [護法] (530–561) (Skt; Jpn Gohō): An Indian scholar of the Consciousness-Only school. One of the ten great scholars of the school, he contributed greatly to establishing its theoretical basis. Born in southern India, he became a monk on the eve of his planned marriage. He studied both Hinayana and Mahayana, and while still young, he became a chief instructor of Nālandā Monastery and produced many excellent disciples. Hsüan-tsang, who journeyed to India in the seventh century, studied Dharmapāla's doctrine under Dharmapāla's disciple Shīlabhadra and brought it back to China. Dharmapāla wrote *The Treatise on the Establishment of the Consciousness-Only Doctrine,* a commentary on Vasubandhu's *Thirty-Stanza Treatise on the Consciousness-Only Doctrine.*

In this commentary he cites the different interpretations of Vasubandhu's treatise by the other nine great scholars of that school and emphasizes the correctness of his own interpretation.

Dharmaraksha (Skt) (1) [竺法護] (n.d.) (Jpn Jiku-hōgo): A monk from Tun-huang who went to China during the Western Chin dynasty (265–316). Considered the most significant translator of Buddhist scriptures into Chinese prior to Kumārajīva, his translations played an important role in the development of Chinese Buddhism. According to one account, he lived from 239 through 316 (from c. 233 through c. 310, according to another account). Descended from the Yüeh-chih, a nomadic people of Central Asia, his ancestors settled and continued to live in Tun-huang, an oasis town in Central Asia, for successive generations. Therefore Dharmaraksha was also called the Bodhisattva of the Yüeh-chih or Bodhisattva of Tun-huang. Among his works is the oldest extant Chinese translation of the Lotus Sutra, titled the Lotus Sutra of the Correct Law. He became a monk at age eight. Apparently gifted with intelligence and wisdom, he extensively studied the Buddhist scriptures. In his early thirties, he traveled with his teacher to the kingdoms of Central Asia in search of Mahayana sutras. During India's Kushan dynasty, Mahayana Buddhism was flourishing and its scriptures were still being compiled. During his travels in Central Asia, Dharmaraksha is said to have mastered thirty-six languages spoken in the region and brought to Ch'ang-an and Lo-yang in China a large number of Buddhist scriptures written in Sanskrit and in the languages of Central Asia.

At that time, only a few Mahayana sutras existed in China. Thereafter, for more than forty years until 308, he devoted himself to translation work with his assistants Nieh Ch'eng-yüan and Nieh Tao-chen, who were father and son. He is said to have translated more than 150 scriptures, including the Wisdom, Vimalakīrti, Buddha Infinite Life, Multitudinous Graceful Actions, and Flower Garland sutras. The sutras he translated, such as the Lotus Sutra of the Correct Law and the Vimalakīrti Sutra, have greatly influenced the development of Buddhist thought through the ages.

(2) [曇無讖] (385–433) (Jpn Dommushin or Dommusen): A monk from central India and a translator of Buddhist scriptures into Chinese. As a youth, he became a monk and studied the Hinayana teachings. When he read a manuscript of the Nirvana Sutra, he was so moved that he converted to Mahayana. It is said that at age twenty he memorized a large number of scriptures, and that, gifted with supernatural powers, he was favored highly by his ruler. But he soon left India, bringing with him the beginning sections of the Nirvana Sutra and other Sanskrit Buddhist

scriptures. Traveling eastward to Central Asia, he passed through Kucha and then Tun-huang, and in 412 he reached Ku-tsang, the capital of Liang-chou.

There he received special favor from the ruler Chü-ch'ü Meng-hsün of the Northern Liang kingdom and later served him as royal advisor. He was requested by the ruler to translate the Buddhist scriptures he brought with him, but Dharmaraksha was not yet versed in Chinese. Therefore he first devoted himself to the study of Chinese, and then began to translate the scriptures. In order to translate the entire Nirvana Sutra, he returned to his homeland to obtain the remaining portions of the Sanskrit manuscript and finally completed the Chinese translation of the Nirvana Sutra titled the Mahāparinirvāna Sutra (Chin *Ta-pan-nieh-p'an-ching*), or the so-called northern version consisting of forty volumes. His other translations include the Great Collection Sutra, the Golden Light Sutra, the Compassionate White Lotus Flower Sutra, the Upholding the Bodhisattva Stage Sutra, the Great Cloud Sutra, and the Precepts for Laymen Sutra. Then he set out again on a journey westward to seek another Sanskrit version of the Nirvana Sutra, but was murdered along the way. The ruler Meng-hsün, suspecting that Dharmaraksha was moving to the rival Northern Wei kingdom, had sent an agent to assassinate him. He had feared his gifted advisor, whom he believed had supernatural powers, would end up supporting his enemies.

Dharmaruchi [曇摩流支] (n.d.) (Skt; Jpn Dommarushi): A fifth-century monk from Central Asia. In 405 he went to Ch'ang-an in China. He completed the Chinese translation of *The Ten Divisions of Monastic Rules* with Kumārajīva. Kumārajīva and Punyatāra earlier had begun to translate this work from Sanskrit into Chinese, but due to Punyatāra's death the translation had been suspended. Upon the request of the priest Hui-yüan and the ruler Yao Hsing of the Later Ch'in dynasty, Dharmaruchi, who was well versed in rules of monastic discipline, completed the translation with Kumārajīva. Later aspiring to disseminate the rules of monastic discipline to areas where they were still unknown, he embarked on a journey. His life after that is not known.

Dharma seal [法印] (Jpn *hōin*): (1) (Skt *dharma-uddāna*) Also, seal of the Law. A standard for judging whether a certain doctrine is Buddhist; also, basic principles applied to this standard. In this context, "seal" indicates a doctrine's reliability, authenticity, and universality. Three Dharma seals are generally known. The first is that all things are impermanent. The second is that nothing has an independent existence of its own. The third is that nirvana, or enlightenment, is tranquil and quiet. According to another tradition, the doctrine that all existence is suffering replaces the third or is added to the above three. With the addition of this doctrine, the three Dharma seals become the four Dharma seals. Later on, Mahayana Buddhists in China regarded the three Dharma seals as the Dharma seals of Hinayana, asserting that there is only one Dharma seal in Mahayana, the Dharma seal of the ultimate reality, of the true aspect of all phenomena.

(2) In Japan, an official rank among priests. The ranks of the Dharma seal, Dharma eye, and Dharma bridge were established in 864 in Japan. These positions were given to the three classes of priests supervising all other priests and nuns. The three classes were, in descending order of rank: administrator of priests (Jpn *sōjō*), which corresponded to the rank of Dharma seal; supervisor of priests *(sōzu)*, to the rank of Dharma eye; and discipline master *(risshi)*, to the rank of Dharma bridge. Later, however, these titles became formalities and lost their original significance. Eventually Dharma seal became simply a title of honor. Later the title was also given to Confucianists, sculptors of Buddhist statues, physicians, and artists.

Dharma teacher [法師] (Jpn *hosshi*): Also, Dharma master, teacher of the Law, or preacher of the Dharma. A Buddhist practitioner who is well versed in Buddhist teachings and who preaches them to and serves as a role model for other people by purifying himself through Buddhist practice. "Dharma Teacher" was an honorific title referring to such a priest. The "Teacher of the Law" (tenth) chapter of the Lotus Sutra defines one who carries out the five practices of the Lotus Sutra—to embrace, read, recite, expound, and copy it—as a teacher of the Law.

Dharma Treasury [法蔵比丘] (Skt Dharmākara; Jpn Hōzō-biku): A bodhisattva described in the Buddha-Infinite Life Sutra who is engaged in bodhisattva practice prior to his becoming a Buddha named Amida. According to the sutra, Dharma Treasury was originally a king but renounced the throne and began his Buddhist practice under a Buddha called World Freedom King (Skt Lokeshvararāja). He took the name Dharma Treasury and, as a bodhisattva, made forty-eight vows concerning the type of pure land he would create after attaining enlightenment. In the eighteenth vow, he pledged to bring all sentient beings who placed their hopes of salvation with him to this Buddha land, which he named Perfect Bliss (Sukhāvatī). Excepted were those who had committed the five cardinal sins and those who had slandered the correct teaching. *See also* Amida.

Dharma-wheel [法輪] (Jpn *hōrin*): The Buddha's teachings. *See* wheel of the Law.

Dharma Wisdom [法慧菩薩] (Jpn Hōe-bosatsu): One of the four great bodhisattvas appearing in the Flower Garland Sutra, the other three being Forest of Merits, Diamond Banner, and Diamond Storehouse. The preaching of the Flower Garland Sutra is described as occurring in eight successive assemblies in seven different locations, beginning at the place of Shakyamuni Buddha's enlightenment and then shifting to various heavens. At the third assembly, held in the Heaven of the Thirty-three Gods, the bodhisattva Dharma Wisdom expounds the doctrine of the ten stages of security, the eleventh through the twentieth of the fifty-two stages of bodhisattva practice.

Dharmayashas [曇摩耶舎] (n.d.) (Skt; Jpn Dommayasha): A monk from Kashmir in ancient India who traveled to China, where he translated Buddhist scriptures into Chinese. He studied Buddhism under Punyatāra and was well versed in the Buddhist sutras and rules of monastic discipline. At about age thirty, he embarked on a series of journeys to other countries and visited China in the Lung-an era (397–401) of the Eastern Chin dynasty. In the early fifth century, he stayed in the city of Ch'ang-an and translated *The Treatise on Shāriputra's Abhidharma*. There he widely disseminated the practice of meditation and later traveled west to Central Asia.

Dharmodgata [曇無竭菩薩] (Skt; Jpn Dommukatsu-bosatsu): Also known as Dharma Emerged or Dharma Arisen. A bodhisattva described in the Wisdom sutras. According to the Larger Wisdom Sutra, Bodhisattva Dharmodgata lived in his palace in the City of Fragrances (Skt Gandhavatī). While satisfying the five desires and being accompanied by sixty-eight thousand women, he preached the doctrine of the perfection of wisdom three times a day. The people in the city held him in high esteem and presented him with offerings. Those who listened to his sermon and embraced it were saved from falling into the evil paths of existence. From Dharmodgata, Bodhisattva Ever Wailing learned the teaching of the perfection of wisdom, mastered six million types of meditation, and finally attained supreme wisdom. In the Wisdom sutras, Bodhisattva Dharmodgata is described as a "good friend" who leads Bodhisattva Ever Wailing to enlightenment in lifetime after lifetime.

dhātu [界] (Skt, Pali; Jpn *kai*): Realm, world, element, root, base, cause, or relics. The word *dhātu* is a component of various Sanskrit Buddhist terms: *kāma-dhātu* (world of desire), *rūpa-dhātu* (world of form), *ārūpya-dhātu* (world of formlessness), *tri-sāhasra-mahā-sāhasra-loka-dhātu* (major world system), *buddha-dhātu* (Buddha nature), *dhātu-garbha* (a sanctuary for enshrining ashes, or a sanctuary that houses ashes regarded as the Buddha; here *dhātu* means relics or ashes), *dharma-dhātu* (Dharma realm, which means both the phenomenal world and the world of the truth), etc.

Dhritaka [提多迦] (n.d.) (Skt; Jpn Daitaka): Also known as Dhītika. A monk of Mathurā, India. He is regarded as the fifth of Shakyamuni Buddha's twenty-three, or the sixth of his twenty-four, successors, who received the Buddha's teachings from Upagupta. According to *The Record of the Lineage of the Buddha and the Patriarchs,* once when Upagupta was visiting a wealthy man in Mathurā, the man promised that if he had a son in the future he would make the child Upagupta's disciple. Dhritaka was born to the wealthy man and later renounced the secular world to become a disciple of Upagupta, thereby fulfilling his father's promise. He devoted himself to Buddhist practice, mastered the six transcendental powers, and became an arhat. Before Upagupta died, he transferred the Buddha's teachings to Dhritaka. Dhritaka thereafter propagated the Buddha's teachings until he entrusted them to Mikkaka.

Dhritarāshtra [持国天] (Skt; Jpn Jikoku-ten): The heavenly king Upholder of the Nation. One of the four heavenly kings. *See* Upholder of the Nation.

dhūta practice [頭陀・頭陀行] (Skt, Pali; Jpn *zuda* or *zuda-gyō*): A discipline or ascetic practice to purify one's body and mind and remove one's desire for food, clothing, and shelter. The Sanskrit word *dhūta* means "shaken off," "removed," or "abandoned." In Buddhism, it indicates shaking off the dust and defilement of desires. Buddhism sets forth twelve disciplines to obtain release from ties to food, clothing, and dwelling. They are known as the twelvefold *dhūta* practice or twelve *dhūtas.* Among Shakyamuni's ten major disciples, Mahākāshyapa was known as foremost in *dhūta,* or ascetic, practice. In the "Treasure Tower" (eleventh) chapter of the Lotus Sutra, Shakyamuni says: "This sutra is hard to uphold; if one can uphold it even for a short while I will surely rejoice and so will the other Buddhas. A person who can do this wins the admiration of the Buddhas. . . . This is what is called observing the precepts and practicing *dhūta.*" The Twelvefold Dhūta Practice Sutra, a Chinese translation by Gunabhadra (394–468), gives a detailed explanation of the twelvefold *dhūta* practice. *See also* twelvefold *dhūta* practice.

dhyāna [禅・禅定] (Skt; Jpn *zen* or *zenjō*): *See* meditation.

Diamond Banner [金剛幢菩薩] (Jpn Kongōdō-bosatsu): One of the four great bodhisattvas appearing in the Flower Garland Sutra, the other three being Dharma Wisdom, Forest of Merits, and Diamond Storehouse. The preaching of the Flower Garland Sutra is described as occurring in eight successive assemblies in seven different locations, beginning at the place of Shakyamuni Buddha's enlightenment and then shifting to various heavens. At the fifth assembly, held in the Tushita Heaven, the bodhisattva Diamond Banner expounds the doctrine of the ten stages of devotion, or the thirty-first through the fortieth of the fifty-two stages of bodhisattva practice.

Diamond Crown Sutra [金剛頂経] (Skt *Sarvatathāgata-tattvasamgraha;* Chin *Chin-kang-ting-ching;* Jpn *Kongōchō-kyō*): Also known as the Vajrashekhara Sutra. One of the three basic scriptures of Esoteric Buddhism, the other two being the Mahāvairochana and Susiddhikara sutras. There are three Chinese versions translated by Indian monks: (1) A three-volume sutra, translated in 743 by Pu-k'ung (Skt Amoghavajra), which is the most popular and the one usually referred to by the title "Diamond Crown Sutra"; (2) a four-volume sutra, translated by Chin-kang-chih (Vajrabodhi) in the early eighth century; and (3) a thirty-volume sutra, translated by Dānapāla in 1015. The content of Dānapāla's version is closest to that of the extant Sanskrit manuscript. In contrast with the Mahāvairochana Sutra, which reveals the teaching of the Womb Realm—the basis for the Womb Realm mandala—this sutra explains the teaching of the Diamond Realm, on which the Diamond Realm mandala is based.

Diamond-like Perfection of Wisdom Sutra [金剛般若波羅蜜経] (Skt *Vajracchedikā-prajnāpāramitā;* Chin *Chin-kang-pan-jo-po-lo-mi-ching;* Jpn *Kongō-hannya-haramitsu-kyō*): Also known as the Diamond Wisdom Sutra, the Diamond Sutra, or the Vajracchedikā Sutra. A sutra translated into Chinese by Kumārajīva in the early fifth century. There are several Chinese versions, but Kumārajīva's version is the oldest and most widely used. The sutra is set in Jetavana Monastery in Shrāvastī, India, and records Shakyamuni's discourse to Subhūti on the constant flux of all phenomena and the doctrine of non-substantiality. It teaches that one should rely upon one's innate Buddha wisdom, which is as solid, sharp, and brilliant as a diamond. This sutra is held in high esteem by the Zen school. The Sanskrit manuscript and a Tibetan translation also exist.

diamond-pounder [金剛杵] (Skt *vajra;* Jpn *kongō-sho*): Originally a kind of weapon used in ancient India. It is so called because of its legendary hardness—it was thought capable of destroying any other weapon, as a diamond is impervious to all other materials. In the rituals of Esoteric Buddhism, the diamond-pounder symbolizes the firm resolve to attain enlightenment, which can destroy all illusions. This diamond-pounder, or *vajra,* usually made of iron or copper, is slender in shape with pointed ends. There are usually three types: a single-armed, a three-pronged, and a five-pronged diamond-pounder. Among these, the three-pronged pounder represents the three mysteries, and the five-pronged pounder, the five kinds of wisdom possessed by the one Buddha Mahāvairochana or by five Buddhas, respectively.

diamond precept [金剛宝器戒] (Jpn *kongō-hōki-kai*): The precept that, like a diamond chalice, is impossible to break. *See* precept of the diamond chalice.

Diamond Realm [金剛界] (Skt *vajradhātu;* Jpn *kongō-kai*): Also, Diamond World. A realm described in the Diamond Crown Sutra. The Sanskrit word *vajra* means diamond, which symbolizes hardness, indestructibility, or purity, and *dhātu* means realm. The term is contrasted with the Womb Realm described in the Mahāvairochana Sutra. The Diamond Realm represents the wisdom of Mahāvairochana Buddha, while the Womb Realm represents the fundamental truth that is identical with Mahāvairochana Buddha. Mahāvairochana's wisdom is compared to the hardness and purity of a diamond because it can crush all earthly desires and illusions. The Diamond Realm is represented graphically in Esoteric Buddhism by the Diamond Realm mandala.

Diamond Realm mandala [金剛界曼荼羅] (Jpn *kongōkai-mandara*): Also, Diamond World mandala. One of the two mandalas of Esoteric Buddhism, the other being the Womb Realm mandala. Based on the Diamond Crown Sutra, this mandala depicts the Diamond Realm that represents the wisdom of Mahāvairochana Buddha. In contrast, the Womb Realm mandala, based on the Mahāvairochana Sutra, represents the fundamental principle of the universe, or the Dharma body of Mahāvairochana, perceived by this wisdom. The Diamond Realm mandala and the Womb Realm mandala are placed at the center of the esoteric rituals of the True Word (Jpn Shingon) school. The Diamond Realm mandala is composed of nine square sections or assemblies; in these squares Mahāvairochana and other Buddhas, bodhisattvas, and gods are depicted, with Mahāvairochana in the central square.

Diamond Scalpel, The [金剛錍・金剛錍論] (Chin *Chin-kang-pei;* Jpn *Kongōbei* or *Kongōbei-ron*): A work by Miao-lo (711–782) designed to clarify the supremacy of T'ien-t'ai's teaching and restore the T'ien-t'ai school by refuting the doctrines of the Flower Garland (Hua-yen), Dharma Characteristics (Fa-hsiang), and Zen (Ch'an) schools that prospered after T'ien-t'ai. The title derives from a passage in the "Nature of the Thus Come One" chapter of the Chinese version of the Mahāparinirvāna Sutra, and symbolizes the power to remove the delusions of living beings. In this treatise, in question-and-answer form, Miao-lo upholds the doctrine of the Buddha nature inherent in insentient beings, denying the Flower Garland position that insentient things do not possess the Buddha nature.

This work reads: "A plant, a tree, a pebble, a speck of dust—each has the Buddha nature, and each is endowed with cause and effect and with the function to manifest and the wisdom to realize its Buddha nature." It also rejects the Dharma Characteristics doctrine that certain categories of people are by nature forever incapable of attaining Buddhahood and reiterates the teaching of the Lotus Sutra that Buddhahood is accessible to all.

Diamond Storehouse [金剛蔵菩薩] (Skt Vajragarbha; Jpn Kongōzō-bosatsu): One of the four great bodhisattvas appearing in the Flower Garland Sutra, the other three being Dharma Wisdom, Forest of Merits, and Diamond Banner. The preaching of the Flower Garland Sutra is described as occurring in eight successive assemblies in seven different locations, beginning at the place of Shakyamuni Buddha's enlightenment and then shifting to various heavens. At the sixth assembly, held in the Heaven of Freely Enjoying Things Conjured by Others, the bodhisattva Diamond Storehouse expounds the doctrine of the ten stages of development, or the forty-first through the fiftieth of the fifty-two stages of bodhisattva practice.

Diamond Sutra [金剛経] (Jpn *Kongō-kyō*): *See* Diamond-like Perfection of Wisdom Sutra.

Diamond Wisdom Sutra [金剛般若経] (Jpn *Kongō-hannya-kyō*): *See* Diamond-like Perfection of Wisdom Sutra.

Diamond World [金剛界] (Jpn *kongō-kai*): *See* Diamond Realm.

Diamond World mandala [金剛界曼荼羅] (Jpn *kongōkai-mandara*): *See* Diamond Realm mandala.

Dictionary of the Pronunciation and Meaning of Buddhist Terms, A [翻訳名義集] (Chin *Fan-i-ming-i-chi;* Jpn *Hon'yaku-myōgi-shū*): A dictionary of the Chinese transliterations and definitions of Sanskrit Buddhist terms completed in 1143 by Fa-yün. He is said to have spent some twenty years compiling the text. This Sanskrit-Chinese Buddhist dictionary contains some 2,040 entries in sixty-four sections and was considered an indispensable reference work for translators.

difficult-to-practice way [難行道] (Jpn *nangyō-dō*): One of the two ways of Buddhist practice mentioned in Nāgārjuna's *Commentary on the Ten Stages Sutra,* the other being the easy-to-practice way. The difficult-to-practice way refers to the exertion of strenuous effort in austere practices for many *kalpas* in order to attain enlightenment. It means the attainment of enlightenment through one's own power. In contrast, the easy-to-practice way means to call upon the names of Buddhas, relying upon their power of salvation to attain enlightenment. The Pure Land (Jōdo) school interprets the difficult-to-practice way as the practice of any sutra other than the three basic sutras of that school (the Amida, Buddha Infinite Life, and Meditation on the Buddha Infinite Life sutras), and the easy-to-practice way as that of calling upon the name of Amida Buddha, relying solely on his power of salvation to attain enlightenment.

Dīgha-nikāya [長部] (Pali; Jpn Chō-bu): A collection of long sutras, one of the five Āgamas. *See* five Āgamas.

Dignāga [陳那] (n.d.) (Skt; Jpn Jinna): An Indian scholar of the Consciousness-Only school who lived from the fifth through the sixth century. Also a scholar of Buddhist logic. Born to a Brahman family in southern India, he studied both Hinayana and Mahayana Buddhism. He further developed the ideas of Vasubandhu and established a branch of the Consciousness-Only school that regarded the images stored in the *ālaya*-consciousness as real rather than non-substantial. This teaching was inherited by Asvabhāva, Dharmapāla, Shīlabhadra, and Hsüan-tsang. Hsüan-tsang laid the foundation for the Dharma Characteristics (Fa-hsiang) school in China. Dignāga also contributed to the development of Buddhist logic, advancing a new form of deductive reasoning. His works include *The Treatise on the Objects of Cognition, The Treatise on Systems of Cognition,* and *The Treatise on the Correct Principles of Logic.*

dīpa [灯明] (Skt, Pali; Jpn *tōmyō*): A lamp, light, or lantern. A lamp was regarded as an important offering to the Buddha. After the time of Shakyamuni, lamps were offered before Buddhist stupas, images of the Buddha, and sutra scrolls. The offering of *dīpa* was believed to be a meritorious deed that brought benefit to the donor. The Sutra on the Wise and the Foolish tells the story of a poor woman who wished to offer an oil lamp to Shakyamuni Buddha. She went out begging, but could gain only one coin. With that coin, she obtained a single oil lamp and offered it to the Buddha. That night, though all the lamps offered by kings and other people went out, her lamp alone continued to burn throughout the night.

This story is also found in the Prophecy of Buddhahood for King Ajātashatru Sutra, though it differs somewhat in its details. In either version, it is widely known as "The Poor Woman's Lamp." Buddhist sutras mention lamps with various kinds of oil. The Lotus Sutra, for example, refers to lamps of *champaka* oil, lamps of *sumanā* oil, lamps of *pātala* oil, lamps of *vārshika* oil, lamps of *navamālikā* oil, and lamps of *utpala* oil. These Sanskrit names indicate the trees and flowers that produce the oil. In Buddhism, the lamp is compared to wisdom, the "light" of which dispels the darkness associated with ignorance. The Lotus Sutra compares Shakyamuni Buddha to a bright lamp of wisdom. The lamp of Dharma or the Law means the Buddha's teachings. The *Mahāparinibbāna-suttanta,* the Pali version of the Nirvana Sutra, says that one should be one's own lamp, and that one should take the truth as one's own lamp.

Dīpamkara [燃燈仏] (Skt, Pali; Jpn Nentō-butsu): A Buddha who bestowed a prophecy of enlightenment on Shakyamuni when the latter was a bodhisattva in a past existence. *See* Burning Torch.

Dīpavamsa [島史] (Pali; Jpn *Tōshi*): "The History of the Island." The Pali word *dīpa* means island, and *vamsa* means tradition or history. This is the oldest extant historical record of Sri Lanka, written in Pali verse. It was compiled during the period from the late fourth through the early fifth century, and is generally attributed to multiple authors. This record consists of twenty-two sections and describes the birth of Buddhism, the introduction of Buddhism into Sri Lanka, the successive rulers of Sri Lanka, and the Buddhist history of the country, beginning with the time of Shakyamuni Buddha and ending with that of the king Mahāsena who reigned from the late third through the early fourth century. It is valued as a reference for the study of the early history of India and Sri Lanka and the development of Buddhism in Sri Lanka.

direct pointing to the human mind [直指人心] (Jpn *jikishi-ninshin*): Also expressed as "directly pointing to the human mind." A common saying of the Zen school, attributed to Bodhidharma, the first patriarch of Chinese Zen (Ch'an), that represents the school's essential doctrine. It is the first part of a two-phrase saying, the second part of which is the phrase "perceiving one's true nature and attaining Buddhahood." A four-phrase saying, in which those two phrases are combined with another two, reads, "[The Zen teaching represents] a separate transmission outside the sutras, independent of words or writing; it points directly to the human mind, and enables one to perceive one's true nature and attain Buddhahood." When each phrase is quoted independently, the translation often differs slightly. This describes the teaching of the Zen school that enlightenment is not achieved through scriptural or doctrinal study, but by directly beholding and penetrating the true nature of the mind through seated meditation *(zazen).* In this way, the school says, one realizes that the true nature of one's mind is the Buddha nature and thereby attains enlightenment.

"discard, close, ignore, and abandon" [捨閉閣抛] (Jpn *sha-hei-kaku-hō*): The assertion of Hōnen (1133–1212), the founder of the Japanese Pure Land (Jōdo) school, that one should discard, close, ignore, and abandon all teachings and practices other than those relating to Amida Buddha and his Pure Land, and that one should rely entirely on the Nembutsu, that is, chant only the name of the Buddha Amida. Hōnen set this forth in his work *The Nembutsu Chosen above All,* though he did not use these four words in this particular form. He asserted that the practice of the Lotus Sutra and the various other sutras belongs to the category of sundry practices, while the practice of the Pure Land teachings belongs to the category of correct practices, and hence that the former should be discarded, closed, ignored, and abandoned.

For instance, in the concluding passage of *The Nembutsu Chosen above All,* Hōnen states: "If one wishes to escape quickly from the sufferings of birth and death, one should confront these two superior teachings and then proceed to put aside the teachings of the Sacred Way and choose those of the Pure Land. And if one wishes to follow the teachings of the Pure Land, one should confront the correct and sundry practices and then proceed to abandon all of the sundry and devote one's entire attention to the correct."

In his treatise *On Establishing the Correct Teaching for the Peace of the Land,* Nichiren criticizes Hōnen for encouraging people to abandon the Lotus Sutra in particular, saying: "In doing so, he [Hōnen] turns his back on the passage in the three Pure Land sutras, the sutras of his own school, which contains Amida's vow to save the people 'excepting only those who commit the five cardinal sins and those who slander the correct teaching.' More fundamentally, he shows that he fails to understand the warning contained in the second volume of the Lotus Sutra, the heart and core of the entire body of teachings the Buddha expounded in the five periods of his preaching life, which reads, 'If a person fails to have faith but instead slanders this [Lotus] sutra . . . When his life comes to an end he will enter the Avīchi hell'" (14). Nichiren used the four-word phrase "discard, close, ignore, and abandon" to summarize Hōnen's assertions about all Buddhist teachings other than those of Pure Land. *See also* eighteenth vow.

discarding the provisional and revealing the true [開権顕実] (Jpn *kaigon-kenjitsu*): A doctrine set forth in the Lotus Sutra. *See* opening the provisional and revealing the true.

discipline master [律師] (Jpn *risshi*): Also, *vinaya* master. A priest who is proficient in the Buddhist rules of discipline and excels in observing them. "Discipline Master" was also an official rank among the priesthood. A priest was appointed as a discipline master by the government to act as an official instructor of priests and nuns. In Japan, the three official ranks of administrator of priests *(sōjō),* supervisor of priests *(sōzu),* and Dharma magistrate *(hōzu),* in descending order of rank, were created in 624. In 683 the office of Dharma magistrate was replaced with that of discipline master, and later other official ranks were added. Discipline master was also used simply as an honorific title.

"Distinctions in Benefits" chapter [分別功德品] (Jpn *Fumbetsu-kudoku-hon*): The seventeenth chapter of the Lotus Sutra. In the "Life Span" (sixteenth) chapter, Shakyamuni Buddha tells of the inconceivable length of time that has passed since his original attainment of enlightenment, and the subsequent chapter, "Distinctions in Benefits," says that all who heard the Buddha's preaching concerning his original enlightenment, specifically, concerning his boundless life span as a Buddha, have gained incalculable benefit. The benefits they gained differ among them in terms of profundity, however; hence the chapter's title. The chapter begins by revealing various kinds of enlightenment and benefit that have been obtained by those listening to the Buddha preach on his boundless life span.

When the entire Lotus Sutra is analyzed according to the three divisions known as preparation, revelation, and transmission, the teaching of revelation constitutes the main part, beginning with the "Expedient Means" (second) chapter and ending with the first half of the "Distinctions in Benefits" chapter; the teaching of transmission—that of encouraging the future propagation of the Lotus Sutra—begins with the second half of the "Distinctions in Benefits" chapter. This latter half of the chapter expounds the unfathomable benefits of embracing and practicing the sutra after the Buddha's death. On the basis of this content, T'ien-t'ai (538–597) formulated the concept of four stages of faith and five stages of practice explained in *The Words and Phrases of the Lotus Sutra*.

Divākara [地婆訶羅] (612 or 613–687) (Skt; Jpn Jibakara): Also known by the Chinese name Jih-chao. A monk of central India who went to China around 676 and engaged in the translation of Buddhist texts at T'ai-yüan-ssu and Hung-fu-ssu temples in Ch'ang-an. He produced the Chinese translations of eighteen texts in thirty-four volumes. They include the "Entering the Dharma Realm" chapter of the Flower Garland Sutra, the Secret Solemnity Sutra, the Clarification of Consciousness Sutra, and the Correct and Vast Great Adornment Sutra. Fa-tsang (643–712), the third patriarch of the Chinese Flower Garland (Hua-yen) school, used Divākara's translation of the "Entering the Dharma Realm" chapter to supplement a deficiency in the old translation.

Divergent Concepts in the Sutras and Vinaya Texts [経律異相] (Chin *Ching-lü-i-hsiang;* Jpn *Kyōritsu-isō*): An explanation of Buddhist concepts written by Seng-min (467–527) at the command of Emperor Wu of the Liang dynasty in China and then revised and enlarged by Pao-ch'ang and other scholars. A Buddhist dictionary, this work was completed in 516 and consists of fifty volumes. It is divided broadly into twenty-one sections addressing themes such as heaven, earth, Buddhas, bodhisattvas, voice-hearers, laymen, laywomen, demons, and hells. For example, the section on "heaven" explains the twenty-eight heavens of the threefold world and includes related stories. The section on "earth" describes Mount Sumeru and the four continents surrounding it, as well as the mountains, rivers and seas, plants and trees, and the monasteries of Jambudvīpa; it also introduces related stories. Thus, this work includes numerous stories from the sutras and *vinaya* texts (scriptures on the rules of monastic discipline). Moreover, because some of the quoted sutras are no longer extant, this work is regarded as a valuable reference for the study of Buddhism. It is generally said that *Tales of Times Now Past* and other collections of Buddhist stories compiled in Japan are based on this work and other similar works, rather than on the sutras themselves.

doctrinal classification [教判・教相判釈] (Jpn *kyōhan* or *kyōsō-hanjaku*): The classification of sutras and their teachings. *See* comparative classification.

doctrine of many-time recitation [多念義] (Jpn *tanen-gi*): Also, doctrine of many callings. A doctrine of the Pure Land (Jōdo) school set forth by Ryūkan (1148–1227), a disciple of Hōnen, the founder of the Japanese Pure Land school. It states that, to attain rebirth in the Pure Land, the practitioner should continue to recite the name of Amida Buddha as many times as possible until the moment of death. This doctrine was in opposition to that of one-time recitation, which asserts that even one recitation with single-minded faith in Amida's grace is sufficient to attain rebirth in the Pure Land.

doctrine of one-time recitation [一念義] (Jpn *ichinen-gi*): Also, doctrine of one calling. A teaching of the Pure Land (Jōdo) school propounded by Kōsai (1163–1247), a disciple of Hōnen, the founder of the school. It states that, with sincere faith, a single recitation of the Nembutsu, or the name of the Buddha Amida, is sufficient to ensure rebirth in the Pure Land, though subsequent recitations may be performed as an expression of gratitude. This stood in opposition to the doctrine of many-time recitation expounded by Ryūkan, another disciple of Hōnen, which maintains that each recitation deepens one's devotion to Amida, and one should therefore recite the Nembutsu continually until the moment of death in order to be reborn in the Pure Land.

Doctrines of the Different Schools, The [異部宗輪論] (Skt *Samaya-bhedoparachana-chakra;* Chin *I-pu-tsung-lun-lun;* Jpn *Ibushūrin-ron*): A one-volume work by Vasumitra, translated into Chinese in 662 by Hsüan-tsang. The Sanskrit original is not extant, but a Tibetan translation exists. As for the Chinese translation, two more versions are extant: *The Dif-*

ferent Tenets of the Schools by Paramārtha and *The Eighteen Schools* by Kumārajīva. *The Doctrines of the Different Schools* elaborates on the various Hinayana schools created as a result of schisms in the Buddhist Order that began one hundred years after Shakyamuni's death. Written from the viewpoint of the Sarvāstivāda school, one of the major Hinayana schools, this treatise describes details of the schisms and the doctrines of the various schools. It is valued as a reference for the study of the Hinayana schools in India.

Document for Entrusting Minobu-san, The [身延山付嘱書] (Jpn *Minobu-san-fuzoku-sho*): One of the two transfer documents by Nichiren specifying the transmission of his teachings to Nikkō. See *Ikegami Transfer Document, The.*

Document for Entrusting the Law that Nichiren Propagated throughout His Life, The [日蓮一期弘法付嘱書] (Jpn *Nichiren-ichigo-guhō-fuzoku-sho*): One of the two transfer documents by Nichiren specifying the transmission of his teachings to Nikkō. See *Minobu Transfer Document, The.*

Dōgen [道元] (1200–1253): The founder of the Japanese Sōtō school of Zen. His father was Kuga Michichika, a minister of the imperial court in Kyoto. Having lost both parents at an early age, Dōgen entered the priesthood in 1213 at Enryaku-ji, the head temple of the Tendai school on Mount Hiei. Doubtful of the Tendai view of inherent enlightenment, however, and of the undisciplined atmosphere at Hiei, in 1217 he went to Kennin-ji temple in Kyoto where he studied the Zen teachings under Myōzen, a disciple of Eisai. In 1223 Dōgen went to China with Myōzen to further his studies. After journeying from one temple to another in search of a worthy teacher, he studied Zen (Ch'an) under Ju-ching at Mount T'ien-t'ung and is said to have attained enlightenment. In 1227 he returned to Japan and stayed at Kennin-ji.

Dōgen strongly asserted that the Zen teaching of sole reliance on seated meditation *(zazen)* was absolute and constituted the essence of the Buddha's teachings. This incurred the hostility of the Tendai priests on Mount Hiei and at Kennin-ji, and around 1230 he was banished from Kennin-ji. He moved to Fukakusa in Kyoto and there around 1233 built Kōshō-ji temple, where he lived for more than ten years, devoting himself to teaching and writing. As his disciples increased in number, oppression by the Tendai priests arose again, and in 1243 he went to Echizen Province to the fief of Hatano Yoshishige, a shogunate official, at Yoshishige's invitation and at the urging of followers there. In Hatano's domain, he founded Daibutsu-ji temple, which was renamed Eihei-ji in 1246 and became a major center of Sōtō Zen. There he devoted himself to training disciples and completing his chief work *The Treasury of Knowledge of the True Law.*

In 1247 Dōgen went to Kamakura at the request of Hōjō Tokiyori, the regent of the Kamakura shogunate, and instructed him in the Zen teachings. In 1250 the Retired Emperor Gosaga sent a messenger to Dōgen at Eihei-ji to bestow on him a purple robe. In 1253 Dōgen returned to Kyoto, where he died of illness. He wrote *The General Teaching for the Promotion of Seated Meditation* and other works.

Dōji [道慈] (d. 744): A priest of the Three Treatises (Sanron) school in Japan. He learned the Three Treatises doctrine from Chizō of Hōryū-ji temple and the Dharma Characteristics (Hossō) doctrine from Gien of Ryūmon-ji temple. In 702 he went to China and studied the Three Treatises teaching under Yüan-k'ang, and Esoteric Buddhism under Shan-wu-wei (Skt Shubhakarasimha). After returning to Japan in 718, Dōji lived at Daian-ji temple and taught the Three Treatises teaching. This is known as the third transmission of the Three Treatises doctrine to Japan. *See also* Three Treatises school.

Dōkyō [道鏡] (d. 772): A priest of the Dharma Characteristics (Hossō) school who lived at Tōdai-ji temple in Nara, Japan. In 761 the Retired Empress Kōken fell ill, and Dōkyō was summoned to court to pray for her recovery. His prayers were regarded as effective, and he won her trust and esteem. When she reassumed the throne as Empress Shōtoku in 764, Dōkyō became her advisor and in time acquired considerable power. It is said that he was planning to usurp the throne, but courtiers such as Wake no Kiyomaro prevented him from doing so. After the death of the empress in 770, he was banished to Yakushi-ji temple in Shimotsuke Province, where he died.

Dōryū [道隆] (1213–1278) (Jpn; Chin Tao-lung): Also known as Rankei (Lan-ch'i) or Rankei Dōryū (Lan-ch'i Tao-lung). A priest of the Lin-chi (Jpn Rinzai) school of Zen in China who became a prominent teacher of that school in Japan. Dōryū is the Japanese reading of his Chinese name. Born in Lan-ch'i, China, he entered the priesthood in 1225 and studied the Zen (Ch'an) teachings. In 1246 he went to Japan, accompanied by several of his disciples. The next year, he arrived in Kyoto and lived there at Sennyū-ji temple. He later went to Kamakura and lived at the temples Jufuku-ji and Jōraku-ji. When Hōjō Tokiyori, the regent of the Kamakura shogunate, built Kenchō-ji temple in Kamakura in 1253, Dōryū was invited to become its first chief priest. There he propagated the Zen teachings for thirteen years. Later he moved to Kennin-ji temple in Kyoto, but returned to Kamakura and lived at Kenchō-ji. Because of a disciple's calumny, he was twice exiled to Kai Province, but was pardoned and returned to Kenchō-ji, where he died of illness. The Japanese imperial court gave him the posthumous title the Meditation Master Daigaku (Great Awakening).

Dōsen [道璿] (702–760) (Jpn; Chin Tao-hsüan): A priest of the Flower Garland (Chin Hua-yen; Jpn Kegon) school in China who introduced the teachings of that school to Japan. Dōsen is the Japanese reading of his Chinese name. In China, he studied the teachings of the Precepts (Lü; Ritsu), Zen (Chin Ch'an), and Flower Garland schools. In 736 he went to Japan, where he introduced the Flower Garland teachings. At that time he also brought with him the teachings of the Precepts and Zen schools and lectured on them as well. He was one of the eminent priests who conducted a grand ceremony to consecrate a new great image of Vairochana Buddha at Tōdai-ji temple in Nara in 752.

Dōshō [道昭] (629–700): A priest of Japan who first introduced the Dharma Characteristics (Hossō) school to his country. A native of Kawachi Province, he entered the priesthood at Gangō-ji temple in Nara. In 653 he went to China, where he studied the Dharma Characteristics doctrine under Hsüan-tsang and the Zen teachings under Hui-man. After an eight-year period of study in China, he returned to Japan and introduced the Dharma Characteristics doctrine. This is regarded as the first transmission of the Dharma Characteristics doctrine to Japan. He also traveled to many provinces to propagate the Dharma Characteristics teaching. He built a meditation hall at Gangō-ji, where he preserved the Buddhist scriptures he had brought from China. In 698 he was appointed general supervisor of priests. After his death, his body was cremated according to his instructions; this is considered the first case of cremation in Japan.

Dōzen-bō [道善房] (d. 1276): A priest of Seichō-ji temple in Tōjō Village of Awa Province, Japan, where Nichiren entered the priesthood. Nichiren studied under Dōzen-bō from age twelve. When Nichiren first declared his teaching at Seichō-ji on the twenty-eighth day of the fourth month, 1253, his refutation of the Nembutsu enraged Tōjō Kagenobu, the steward of the village and an ardent believer in the Pure Land teachings, who ordered his arrest. At that time, Dōzen-bō quietly helped Nichiren escape. Nevertheless, Dōzen-bō was afraid to oppose Kagenobu and for this reason could never bring himself to convert to Nichiren's teachings. Nichiren, however, never forgot his teacher. In the seventh month of 1276, learning of his death, he wrote *On Repaying Debts of Gratitude* as an expression of his gratitude to Dōzen-bō, and sent it to Gijō-bō and Jōken-bō who had been his seniors when they were disciples together at Seichō-ji.

dragon deity [竜神] (Skt, Pali *nāga;* Jpn *ryūjin*): Also, dragon god. A deification of the dragon, one of the eight kinds of nonhuman beings held to be guardians of Buddhism. Dragon deities are said to have various powers, such as the ability to cause rain. The Sanskrit *nāga* means snake or serpent. According to Indian mythology, *nāga*-demons with human faces and serpent-like lower extremities inhabited the waters or lived under the earth. Their ruler, *nāga-rāja* (serpent-king), was feared as a huge poisonous being on the one hand and worshiped as the god who caused rain to fall on the other. When Buddhist scriptures were translated into Chinese, *nāga* was rendered in Chinese as *lung,* or dragon. Hence the terms dragon gods, dragon kings, and the *nāga* girl, or dragon girl.

dragon girl [竜女] (Jpn *ryūnyo*): *See* dragon king's daughter.

Dragon King of the Sea Sutra [海竜王経] (Chin *Hai-lung-wang-ching;* Jpn *Kairyūō-kyō*): A sutra translated into Chinese by Dharmaraksha, a monk from Tun-huang who went to China during the Western Chin dynasty (265–316). In this scripture, Shakyamuni Buddha expounds for the dragon king the teachings of the six *pāramitās* and the non-substantiality of all phenomena and bestows the prophecy of attaining Buddhahood on the dragon king, his daughter, the *asuras,* and others.

dragon kings [竜王] (Skt *nāga-rāja;* Jpn *ryūō*): Kings of the dragons said to live at the bottom of the sea. Eight dragon kings, each with many followers, are depicted in the Lotus Sutra assembling at the ceremony on Eagle Peak to hear the sutra taught. According to the Dragon King of the Sea Sutra, dragons are often eaten by giant birds called *garudas,* which are their natural enemies. *See also* dragon deity; eight great dragon kings.

dragon king's daughter [竜女] (Jpn *ryūnyo*): Also, dragon girl or *nāga* girl. The eight-year-old daughter of Sāgara, one of the eight great dragon kings said to dwell in a palace at the bottom of the sea. According to the "Devadatta" (twelfth) chapter of the Lotus Sutra, the dragon girl conceived the desire for enlightenment when she heard Bodhisattva Manjushrī preach the Lotus Sutra in the dragon king's palace. When Manjushrī asserts that she is capable of quickly attaining the Buddha wisdom, Bodhisattva Wisdom Accumulated challenges him, saying that even Shakyamuni attained enlightenment only after fulfilling the bodhisattva practice for many *kalpas,* and that she cannot become a Buddha so easily. Just then the dragon girl appears in front of the assembly and praises Shakyamuni Buddha. Shāriputra then speaks to her, saying that women are subject to the five obstacles and are incapable of attaining Buddhahood. At that moment, she offers a jewel to the Buddha, transforms herself into a male, and instantaneously perfects the bodhisattva practice.

She then appears in a land to the south called Spotless World and manifests the state of Buddhahood without changing her dragon form. With the thirty-two features and eighty characteristics of a Buddha, she preaches the Lotus Sutra to all living beings there.

The dragon girl's enlightenment has important implications. First, it refutes the idea of the time that women could never attain enlightenment. Second, it reveals that the power of the Lotus Sutra enables all people equally to attain Buddhahood in their present form, without undergoing *kalpas* of austere practices. Perhaps the social circumstances in which the Lotus Sutra was compiled did not allow the dragon girl to be depicted as attaining Buddhahood without first becoming a male. But the transformation occurred instantaneously, not in the next life, and in this respect differs significantly from that of other, provisional teachings, which hold that a woman must be reborn as a man and then practice bodhisattva austerities for innumerable *kalpas* in order to become a Buddha. *See also* dragon deity.

Drona [香姓婆羅門] (Skt; Pali Dona; Jpn Kōshō-baramon): A Brahman who became a follower of Shakyamuni Buddha. According to the Long Āgama Sutra, when the Buddha died, the rulers of several states vied for possession of the Buddha's ashes, wishing to enshrine them in their own states. This would have developed into a conflict had it not been for Drona, who maintained that battling and killing one another over the possession of the Buddha's ashes runs counter to the Buddha's teaching. He was singled out as a mediator in the strife over the Buddha's ashes and was asked to divide them into eight parts. Consequently, the Buddha's ashes were distributed equally among the rulers, who each erected a stupa in his respective domain to enshrine a portion of the ashes. Drona himself obtained the vessel used in the cremation and erected a stupa to house it.

Dronodana [斛飯王] (Skt; Pali Dhotodana; Jpn Kokubonnō): A younger brother of King Shuddhodana, Shakyamuni's father. Dronodana was the father of Devadatta and Ānanda. According to another account, he was the father of Mahānāma and Aniruddha.

duhukha [苦] (Skt; Jpn *ku*): *See* suffering.

dukkha [苦] (Pali; Jpn *ku*): *See* suffering.

Dunhuang [敦煌] (PY; WG Tun-huang; Jpn Tonkō): An oasis town located in the western end of the so-called Kansu Corridor, in the present northwestern Kansu Province of China. *See* Tun-huang.

dust particles of the land [大地微塵] (Jpn *daichi-mijin*): An expression indicating an incalculable number. In Buddhist scriptures, phrases like "as numerous as the dust particles of the land" are often employed to express the incalculable worlds or *kalpas,* the countless number of bodhisattvas at a particular preaching assembly, or the great number of slanderers of the correct teaching. Similar expressions include "the dust particles of a world," "the dust particles of a major world system," and "the dust particles of all the worlds in the ten directions." The phrase "the sands of the Ganges River" is also used to indicate an inconceivable number.

dvesha [瞋恚・瞋] (Skt; Pali *dosa;* Jpn *shinni* or *shin*): Also, *pratigha* or *krodha.* Hatred, dislike, anger, repugnance, aversion, or enmity. *Dvesha,* or anger, is one of the three poisons, or the three sources of vice and suffering, the other two being *rāga* (greed) and *moha* (foolishness). *See also* anger; three poisons.

dvīpa [洲] (Skt; Pali *dīpa;* Jpn *shū*): Island or continent. According to the ancient Indian worldview, four *dvīpas,* or continents, surround Mount Sumeru, which is the center of the world. One continent, Jambudvīpa, situated south of Mount Sumeru, is the continent or island of the *jambu* trees and refers to the world where we live.

E

Eagle Peak [霊鷲山・耆闍崛山・霊山] (Skt Gridhrakūta; Pali Gijjhakūta; Jpn Ryōju-sen, Gishakussen, or Ryō-zen): Also known as Vulture Peak, Holy Eagle Peak, or Sacred Eagle Peak, and simply Holy Mountain, Sacred Mountain, or Holy Peak. A small mountain located northeast of Rājagriha, the capital of Magadha in ancient India. Eagle Peak is known as a place frequented by Shakyamuni, where he is said to have expounded the Lotus Sutra and other teachings. According to *The Treatise on the Great Perfection of Wisdom* by Nāgārjuna, Eagle Peak derived its name from its eagle-shaped summit and the many eagles or vultures inhabiting it. "Eagle Peak" also symbolizes the Buddha land or the state of Buddhahood, as in the expression "the pure land of Eagle Peak." *See also* Gridhrakūta.

Earnest Donor [能施太子] (Skt Mahādāna; Jpn Nōse-taishi): Also known as Great Donor. A prince described as Shakyamuni Buddha in a previous existence, whose story appears in the Sutra on the Wise and the Foolish, *The Treatise on the Great Perfection of Wisdom* by Nāgārjuna, and elsewhere. Prince Earnest Donor felt pity for the poor and suffering people of his country and entreated his father, the king, to give all his treasures to them. When his father had exhausted his treasures, Prince

Earnest Donor went into the sea to look for a fabulous wish-granting jewel belonging to the dragon king. Overcoming many obstacles, he finally obtained the jewel and brought it back with him, causing treasures to rain down upon his people.

earthly desires [煩悩] (Skt *klesha;* Pali *kilesa;* Jpn *bonnō*): Also, illusions, defilements, impurities, earthly passions, or simply desires. A generic term for all the workings of life that cause one psychological and physical suffering and impede the quest for enlightenment, including desires and illusions in the general sense. Earthly desires are also referred to as fetters or bonds (Skt *samyojana* or *bandhana*), because they bind people to the realm of delusion and suffering. Buddhism regards them as the fundamental cause for affliction and suffering, and presents various analyses and perspectives on them. *The Treatise on the Great Perfection of Wisdom* by Nāgārjuna says that the three poisons of greed, anger, and foolishness are the most fundamental earthly desires and give rise to all others. *The Treatise on the Establishment of the Consciousness-Only Doctrine* compiled by Dharmapāla (530–561) divides earthly desires into two types, fundamental and derivative.

The ten fundamental earthly desires consist of the five delusive inclinations of greed, anger, foolishness, arrogance, and doubt, and the five false views. Moreover, there are twenty derivative earthly desires that arise from and accompany these fundamental ones. For example, irritability, the tendency to bear grudges, and the desire to inflict harm derive from anger. T'ien-t'ai (538–597) classified earthly desires and set forth the three categories of illusion: (1) illusions of thought and desire, (2) illusions innumerable as particles of dust and sand, and (3) illusions about the true nature of existence. *See also* five delusive inclinations; five false views; three categories of illusion.

earthly desires are enlightenment [煩悩即菩提] (Jpn *bonnō-soku-bodai*): A Mahayana principle based on the view that earthly desires cannot exist independently on their own; therefore one can attain enlightenment without eliminating earthly desires. This contrasts with the Hinayana view that extinguishing earthly desires is a prerequisite for enlightenment. According to the Hinayana teachings, earthly desires and enlightenment are two independent and opposing factors, and the two cannot coexist; while the Mahayana teachings reveal that earthly desires are one with and inseparable from enlightenment. This is because all things, even earthly desires and enlightenment, are manifestations of the unchanging reality or truth—and thus are non-dual at their source.

The Universal Worthy Sutra, an epilogue to the Lotus Sutra, states, "Without either cutting off earthly desires or separating themselves from the five desires, they can purify all their senses and wipe away all their offenses." T'ien-t'ai (538–597) says in *Great Concentration and Insight,* "The ignorance and dust of desires are enlightenment, and the sufferings of birth and death are nirvana." In *The Record of the Orally Transmitted Teachings,* Nichiren (1222–1282) states: "The idea of gradually overcoming delusions is not the ultimate meaning of the 'Life Span' chapter [of the Lotus Sutra]. You should understand that the ultimate meaning of this chapter is that ordinary mortals, just as they are in their original state of being, are Buddhas," and, "Today, when Nichiren and his followers recite the words Nam-myoho-renge-kyo, they are burning the firewood of earthly desires, summoning up the wisdom-fire of enlightenment."

Earth Repository [地蔵菩薩] (Skt Kshitigarbha; Chin Ti-tsang; Jpn Jizō-bosatsu): A bodhisattva said to have been entrusted by Shakyamuni with the task of saving people during the period from Shakyamuni's death until the enlightenment of Bodhisattva Maitreya. According to the Advent of Maitreya Sutra, Maitreya will make his advent as the next Buddha 5,670 million years after Shakyamuni's death. Bodhisattva Earth Repository was originally an earth god in Indian mythology, and in China he came to be revered as a bodhisattva. The Sanskrit name Kshitigarbha represents the power and function of the earth. *Kshiti* means earth, soil, or abode. *Garbha* means the womb, which symbolizes fertility, protection, and nourishment. Belief in Bodhisattva Earth Repository prevailed in China during the T'ang dynasty (618–907) and was introduced to Japan in the Nara period (710–794), where it won acceptance among the nobility in the Heian period (794–1185). In the Kamakura period (1185–1333) and after, it spread gradually, and Earth Repository became an object of traditional folk belief. He is said to have the power of granting long life and easy childbirth. Because of the many forms he assumes in order to save people, he is sometimes called "Earth Repository of a Thousand Forms." He is usually depicted as a monk with a staff in his right hand and a jewel in his left.

"Easy Practice" chapter [易行品] (Jpn *Igyō-hon*): The ninth chapter of Nāgārjuna's *Commentary on the Ten Stages Sutra,* later treated as an independent text. "Easy practice" means to meditate on Buddhas, and to call upon their names. With this practice, the chapter says, one can reach the stage of non-regression and finally attain enlightenment. The chapter emphasizes salvation through the power of Amida Buddha, saying that one can be saved by meditating on the Buddha and calling his name. Nāgārjuna presented this as an easy form of practice. Thus the "Easy Practice" chapter came to be revered by the patriarchs of the Pure Land school as one of their most important texts. They classified the

Buddhist teachings into two categories, the Sacred Way teachings and the Pure Land teachings. Then, based on the ideas contained in this chapter of Nāgārjuna's commentary, they defined the Sacred Way teachings as the difficult-to-practice way and the Pure Land teachings as the easy-to-practice way, advocating the latter as the only effective means of attaining salvation.

easy-to-practice way [易行道] (Jpn *igyō-dō*): One of the two ways of Buddhist practice mentioned by Nāgārjuna (c. 150–250) in the "Easy Practice" chapter of *The Commentary on the Ten Stages Sutra.* The easy-to-practice way, established for those of inferior capacity, means to call upon the names of Buddhas, relying upon their power of salvation, while the difficult-to-practice way means to engage in strenuous austere practices for many *kalpas* in order to attain enlightenment. On the basis of Nāgārjuna's categorization of the easy-to-practice way and the difficult-to-practice way, the founders of the Pure Land school equated the easy-to-practice way with the Pure Land teachings (the Amida, Buddha Infinite Life, and Meditation on the Buddha Infinite Life sutras) and the practice of calling upon the name of Amida Buddha. They equated the difficult-to-practice way with all the other teachings and practices, maintaining that the former is superior to the latter.

Eben [恵便] (n.d.) (Jpn; Kor Hyepyŏn): A priest of Koguryŏ, a state on the Korean Peninsula, who lived during the sixth century. Eben is his Japanese name. He went to Japan as a priest, but because Buddhism had not spread there yet, he lived there as a layman. In 584 two statues, one of Bodhisattva Maitreya and the other of Shakyamuni Buddha, were brought from another Korean state, Paekche, to Japan. The court official Soga no Umako enshrined the images and ordered Shiba Tatsuto, a naturalized Japanese subject originally from China, to look for a Buddhist priest. He found Eben, who then resumed priestly life under Soga's patronage.

Echi [依智]: A fief held by Homma Rokurō Saemon, the deputy constable of Sado Island in Japan. It was located in what is now Atsugi City in Kanagawa Prefecture. After the Tatsunokuchi Persecution, which occurred on the twelfth day of the ninth month, 1271, Nichiren was held in custody at Homma's residence at Echi before being taken to exile on Sado on the tenth day of the tenth month.

eight arrogances [八慢] (Jpn *hachi-man*): *See* eight types of arrogance.

eight cold hells [八寒地獄] (Jpn *hakkan-jigoku*): Eight hells said to lie under the continent of Jambudvīpa next to the eight hot hells. Residents of these hells are tormented by unbearable cold. According to the Nirvana Sutra, they are (1) the Hahava hell, (2) the Atata hell, (3) the Alalā hell, (4) the Ababa hell, (5) the Utpala hell (the hell of the blue lotus), (6) the Padma hell (the hell of the crimson lotus), (7) the Kumuda hell (the hell of the scarlet lotus), and (8) the Pundarīka hell (the hell of the white lotus). The first four names reflect the cries uttered by sufferers in these hells because of the intolerable cold. The latter four hells are named for the changes one's flesh is said to undergo when exposed to the intense cold there. For instance, in the hell of the crimson lotus the cold is said to be so severe that one's back breaks open and bloody flesh emerges, resembling a crimson lotus flower.

According to *The Dharma Analysis Treasury*, the eight cold hells are (1) the Arbuda hell (the hell of chilblains), (2) the Nirarbuda hell (the hell of enlarged chilblains), (3) the Atata hell, (4) the Hahava hell, (5) the Huhuva hell, (6) the Utpala hell (the hell of the blue lotus), (7) the Padma hell (the hell of the crimson lotus), and (8) the Mahāpadma hell (the hell of the great crimson lotus). In the first hell, the intense cold produces chilblains all over one's body. In the second hell, one's chilblains worsen and finally burst. The following three hells are named for the shrieks of sufferers who inhabit them. In the sixth hell, one's flesh turns blue from the intense cold. In the last two hells, the cold makes one's flesh crack open, resembling a crimson lotus.

eight consciousnesses [八識] (Jpn *hasshiki*): Eight kinds of discernment: (1) sight-consciousness, (2) hearing-consciousness, (3) smell-consciousness, (4) taste-consciousness, (5) touch-consciousness, (6) mind-consciousness, (7) *mano*-consciousness, and (8) *ālaya*-consciousness. The concept of eight consciousnesses was set forth by the Consciousness-Only school. The first six consciousnesses—sight, hearing, smell, taste, touch, and thought—were originally expounded by the Hinayana schools. The Consciousness-Only school of Mahayana tradition delved into the subconscious and postulated the seventh and eighth consciousnesses. The school named them, respectively, the *mano*-consciousness and the *ālaya*-consciousness, and formulated the doctrine of eight consciousnesses. The *mano*-consciousness is the realm of the ego, or where the sense of self resides. The Sanskrit word *manas,* from which *mano* of *mano*-consciousness derives, means to ponder. This consciousness performs the function of abstract thought and discerns the inner world. The *ālaya*-consciousness is regarded as the source of one's body and mind as well as the natural world. *Ālaya* means abode, dwelling, or receptacle. It is also called the storehouse consciousness because all karma created in the present and previous lifetimes is stored there. See also *ālaya*-consciousness; *mano*-consciousness.

eight difficulties [八難・八難処] (Jpn *hachi-nan* or *hachi-nansho*):

Eight places, states, or circumstances wherein one is unable to see a Buddha or to listen to his teaching. They are (1) hell; (2) the realm of hungry spirits; (3) the realm of animals; (4) the heaven of long life (any of the eighteen heavens in the world of form or the four heavens in the world of formlessness where beings live long; or, by another account, the Heaven of No Thought in the fourth meditation heaven in the world of form); (5) Uttarakuru, the continent north of Mount Sumeru where pleasures dominate; (6) obstructions of the sense organs, such as blindness; (7) attachment to and satisfaction with secular knowledge; and (8) the period before a Buddha's birth or after his death.

eight dragon kings [八竜王] (Jpn *hachi-ryūō*): *See* eight great dragon kings.

eighteen elements [十八界] (Jpn *jūhachi-kai*): Also, eighteen realms, eighteen sense-elements, eighteen sense-realms, eighteen sensory elements, or eighteen *dhātus*. The comprehensive concept of three interrelated categories: the six sense organs (eyes, ears, nose, tongue, body, and mind), the six objects they perceive (colors and forms, sounds, odors, tastes, textures, and phenomena), and the six consciousnesses (sight, hearing, smell, taste, touch, and thought) arising through contact between the six sense organs and their respective objects.

eighteen heavens [十八天] (Jpn *jūhachi-ten*): Eighteen heavens in the world of form. The world of form consists of the four meditation heavens, which are further subdivided into eighteen heavens (sixteen or seventeen according to some sources). The eighteen heavens are (1) three heavens in the first meditation heaven—the Heaven of Brahmā's Retinue, the Heaven of Brahmā's Aide, and the Heaven of Great Brahmā, also known as the Heaven of Mahābrahman; (2) three heavens in the second meditation heaven—the Minor Light Heaven, the Infinite Light Heaven, and the Utmost Light and Purity Heaven, also known as the Light Sound Heaven; (3) three heavens in the third meditation heaven—the Minor Purity Heaven, the Boundless Purity Heaven, and the All Pure Heaven; and (4) nine heavens in the fourth meditation heaven—the Cloudless Heaven, the Merit Increasing Heaven, the Large Fruitage Heaven, the Heaven of No Thought, the Heaven of No Vexations, the Heaven of No Heat, the Reward Appearing Heaven, the Heaven of Clear Perception, and the Akanishtha Heaven, also known as the Summit of Being Heaven, or the highest heaven of the world of form.

eighteen Hinayana schools [十八部・小乗十八部] (Jpn *jūhachi-bu* or *shōjō-jūhachi-bu*): Also, eighteen schools. Hinayana schools formed by schisms in the Buddhist Order after Shakyamuni's death. According to *The Doctrines of the Different Schools,* a text of the Sarvāstivāda school, one hundred years after Shakyamuni's death, the first schism occurred in the Buddhist Order and gave rise to the Sthaviravāda (Pali Theravāda) and Mahāsamghika schools. During the following hundred years, eight schools derived from the Mahāsamghika school. They were the Ekavyāvahārika, Lokottaravāda, Kaukkutika, Bahushrutīya, Prajnāptivādin (also, Prajnaptivādin), Chaityavādin, Aparashaila, and Uttarashaila schools.

The Sarvāstivāda school broke away from the Sthaviravāda school about two hundred years after Shakyamuni's death and later gave rise to nine offshoots, totaling ten schools. The nine offshoots were the Vātsīputrīya, Mahīshāsaka, Kāshyapīya, Sautrāntika, Dharmottara, Bhadrayānīya, Sammatīya, Shannāgarika, and Dharmagupta schools. The eight schools that derived from the Mahāsamghika school, plus the ten schools that derived from the Sthaviravāda, or the Sarvāstivāda and its nine offshoots, together constitute the eighteen schools. If the original two schools, Sthaviravāda and Mahāsamghika, are added to the eighteen schools, then they form twenty Hinayana schools. The successive schisms that gave rise to these schools are said to have ceased by the beginning of the first century B.C.E.

eighteen miraculous powers [十八変] (Jpn *jūhachi-hen*): Eighteen kinds of actions and appearances that Buddhas and bodhisattvas are said to manifest. They are: (1) making water come out of the right side of their bodies, (2) making fire come out of the left side of their bodies, (3) making fire come out of the right side of their bodies, (4) making water come out of the left side of their bodies, (5) making water come out of the upper part of their bodies, (6) making fire come out of the lower part of their bodies, (7) making fire come out of the upper part of their bodies, (8) making water come out of the lower part of their bodies, (9) walking on water as though it were land, (10) moving on the ground as though it were water, (11) disappearing into the sky and then suddenly appearing on the ground, (12) disappearing on the ground and then suddenly appearing in the sky, (13) walking in midair, (14) standing in midair, (15) sitting in midair, (16) lying down in midair, (17) manifesting a huge body that fills the sky, and (18) making one's huge body small again. It is said that Buddhas and bodhisattvas manifest these supernatural powers in order to instruct people and lead them to enlightenment. Explanations vary among sources.

eighteen schools [十八部] (Jpn *jūhachi-bu*): *See* eighteen Hinayana schools.

eighteen sense-elements [十八界] (Jpn *jūhachi-kai*): *See* eighteen elements.

eighteenth vow [第十八願] (Jpn *dai-jūhachi-gan*): The eighteenth of forty-eight vows made by Bodhisattva Dharma Treasury (Skt Dharmākara) before he attained enlightenment as Amida Buddha. The forty-eight vows are set forth in the Buddha Infinite Life Sutra. In the eighteenth vow, Bodhisattva Dharma Treasury pledged that, if he attained Buddhahood, all people who placed their trust in him would attain rebirth in his pure land, except those who had committed the five cardinal sins or who had slandered the correct teaching. (Shan-tao [613–681], the third patriarch of the Chinese Pure Land school, interpreted this placing of trust as calling upon the name of Amida Buddha.) Among the forty-eight vows, the Pure Land school regards the eighteenth vow as the most important and calls it the original vow.

eighteen unshared properties [十八不共法 · 十八不共仏法] (Jpn *jūhachi-fugūhō* or *jūhachi-fugūbuppō*): Also, eighteen distinctive characteristics. Eighteen properties that only Buddhas and bodhisattvas possess, and that voice-hearers and cause-awakened ones do not share. Another view holds that Buddhas alone possess these properties. Though they differ among Buddhist scriptures, the eighteen properties commonly consist of the ten powers, the four fearlessnesses, the three kinds of tranquillity, and great pity. Another definition describes them as: (1) no faults in the action of the body, (2) no faults in the action of the mouth, (3) no faults in the action of the mind, (4) impartiality, (5) constant concentration of the mind, (6) insight into all things and absence of attachment to them, (7) untiring intention to lead people to salvation, (8) incessant endeavor, (9) consistency of teachings with those of other Buddhas, (10) perfect wisdom, (11) perfect emancipation, (12) perfect insight, (13) consistency of deeds with wisdom, (14) consistency of words with wisdom, (15) consistency of mind with wisdom, (16) knowledge of the past, (17) knowledge of the future, and (18) knowledge of the present. *See also* four fearlessnesses; ten powers; three kinds of tranquillity.

eight emancipations [八解脱 · 八背捨] (Jpn *hachi-gedatsu* or *hachi-haisha*): Also, eight kinds of liberation. Eight forms of emancipation obtained through the eight kinds of meditation. The ultimate aim is freedom from the earthly desires of the threefold world. They are (1) emancipation from thoughts of external things by meditating on their impurity, (2) further advancement of the first emancipation by continuing meditation on impurity, (3) emancipation obtained by meditating on the pure aspect of things in the outside world, (4) emancipation from thoughts and bonds of material objects and entering meditation on the Realm of Boundless Empty Space, (5) emancipation from thoughts of boundless empty space and entering meditation on the Realm of Boundless Consciousness, (6) emancipation from thoughts of boundless consciousness and entering meditation on the Realm of Nothingness, (7) emancipation from thoughts of nothingness and entering meditation on the Realm of Neither Thought Nor No Thought, and (8) emancipation from, or extinction of, all workings of the mind, which is the source of earthly desires.

eight errors [八邪] (Jpn *hachi-ja*): Eight wrong actions or states, the exact opposite of those defined as the eightfold path. They are wrong views, wrong thinking, wrong speech, wrong action, wrong way of life, wrong endeavor, wrong mindfulness, and wrong meditation.

eightfold path [八正道・八聖道] (Skt *ārya-ashtānga-mārga, ashtānga-mārga,* or *ashtāngika-mārga;* Pali *ariya-atthangika-magga* or *atthangika-magga;* Jpn *hasshō-dō*): Also, noble eightfold path or eightfold holy path. An early teaching of Buddhism setting forth the principles for attaining emancipation. They are (1) right views, or correct views of the Buddha's teaching; (2) right thinking, which includes right thought, right intent, and right aspiration; (3) right speech, or avoidance of falsehood, slander, abuse, and idle talk; (4) right action, or abstaining from all wrong deeds such as taking life and stealing; (5) right way of life, or living while purifying one's thoughts, words, and deeds; (6) right endeavor, to overcome evil in one's own life and make an uninterrupted progress in pursuing the way of truth; (7) right mindfulness, which means always aspiring for the truth and keeping its pursuit in mind; and (8) right meditation. In the doctrine of the four noble truths, the truth of the path to the cessation of suffering is regarded as the discipline of the eightfold path.

eight grave offenses [八重] (Jpn *hachijū*): *See* eight major offenses.

eight great dragon kings [八大竜王] (Jpn *hachidai-ryūō*): Also, eight dragon kings. Eight dragon kings who assembled at the gathering where Shakyamuni preached the Lotus Sutra, as described in the sutra. Kumārajīva's translation of the Lotus Sutra refers to them by their Sanskrit names: Nanda, Upananda, Sāgara, Vāsuki, Takshaka, Anavatapta, Manasvin, and Utpalaka. According to the "Introduction" (first) chapter of the Lotus Sutra, each attends the gathering accompanied by several hundreds of thousands of followers.

eight great hells [八大地獄] (Jpn *hachidai-jigoku*): *See* eight hot hells.

eight hot hells [八熱地獄] (Jpn *hachinetsu-jigoku*): Also, eight great hells or eight major hells. The realms of suffering said to lie beneath the ground of Jambudvīpa. According to *The Dharma Analysis Treasury,* the eighth and lowest hell, the Avīchi hell, or the hell of incessant suffering, is located twenty thousand *yojanas* beneath the ground, and above it are the seven other hot hells. *The Great Commentary on the Abhidharma* presents several differing views on the subject, one of which describes the hell of incessant suffering as being forty thousand *yojanas* beneath the ground. Descriptions of the size of the eight hot hells also differ. One says that the length and breadth of each hell measure ten thousand *yojanas*, except for the lowest, the hell of incessant suffering, which is twenty thousand *yojanas* both in length and breadth. Another view holds that each of the seven hells above the Avīchi hell is only five thousand *yojanas* in length and breadth.

In general, each of these eight major hells is said to have sixteen subsidiary hells. These 128 subsidiary hells plus the eight major hells are called the 136 hells. In order of increasing depth or increasing suffering, the major hells are (1) the hell of repeated rebirth for torture, where inhabitants injure and kill one another, but are brought back to life again and again only to undergo the same torment; (2) the hell of black cords, where offenders are cut and sawed apart according to markings made by heated black iron cords; (3) the hell of crushing, where large numbers of evildoers are crushed between two moving mountain ranges; (4) the hell of wailing, whose inhabitants are thrown into boiling water and continuously utter anguished cries from the pain; (5) the hell of great wailing, whose inhabitants utter cries of greater anguish from greater pain; (6) the hell of burning heat, where evildoers are burned in flames; (7) the hell of great burning heat, where evildoers are burned in hotter, more raging flames; and (8) the hell of incessant suffering, also known as the Avīchi hell, whose inhabitants constantly suffer without respite. It is said that those who commit any of the five cardinal sins or slander the correct teaching undergo torment in this hell.

eight kinds of nonhuman beings [八部衆] (Jpn *hachibu-shu*): Also, eight kinds of beings or eight kinds of guardians. Beings referred to in Buddhist scriptures as protectors of Buddhism. They are *deva*, or heavenly beings; *nāga*, or dragons; a kind of demon called *yaksha;* gods of music called *gandharva;* belligerent demons called *asura; garuda*, birds that prey on dragons; *kimnara*, gods with beautiful voices; and *mahoraga*, gods in snake forms. Buddhist scriptures refer to the eight kinds of nonhuman beings either individually or with expressions such as "heavenly beings (or gods), dragons, and others of the eight kinds of nonhuman beings." The eight kinds of nonhuman beings are often described as attendants at the assembly of the Buddha's preaching.

eight kinds of sufferings [八種の大難] (Jpn *hasshu-no-dainan*): The sufferings that one must undergo as retribution for countless past offenses. They are described in the Mahāparinirvāna Sutra, Fa-hsien's Chinese version of the Nirvana Sutra. They are (1) to be despised, (2) to be cursed with an ugly appearance, (3) to be poorly clad, (4) to be poorly fed, (5) to seek wealth in vain, (6) to be born to an impoverished and lowly family, (7) to be born to a family with erroneous views, and (8) to be persecuted by one's sovereign.

eight major hells [八大地獄] (Jpn *hachidai-jigoku*): *See* eight hot hells.

eight major offenses (1) [八重・八波羅夷] (Jpn *hachijū* or *hachi-harai*): Also, eight grave offenses, eight unpardonable offenses, eight *pārājikas*, or eight *pārājika* offenses. The gravest offenses defined for nuns, punishable by expulsion from the Buddhist Order. They are killing, stealing, sexual relations, lying, touching a male, improper association with a male, concealing the misbehavior of another, and following a monk whose behavior goes against monastic rules.

(2) [八重] (Jpn *hachijū*): Violations of the eight prohibitions for bodhisattvas. They consist of the four offenses of killing, stealing, sexual relations, and lying, plus those of praising oneself and disparaging others, begrudging offerings or withholding one's efforts to expound the teachings, giving way to anger and not accepting apology, and slandering the correct teaching.

eight negations [八不] (Jpn *happu*): Also, middle path of the eight negations. Eight expressions of negation that appear in the opening of Nāgārjuna's *Treatise on the Middle Way:* "Neither birth nor extinction, neither cessation nor permanence, neither uniformity nor diversity, neither coming nor going." The teaching of the eight negations is intended to demonstrate that the true nature of phenomena can be defined neither as existence nor nonexistence, nor, for that matter, as any other fixed concept that one might choose to impose upon it. Rather, the nature of phenomena is non-substantiality, the Middle Way that transcends all dualities.

eight pārājika offenses [八重・八波羅夷] (Jpn *hachijū* or *hachi-harai*): *See* eight major offenses.

eight phases of a Buddha's existence [八相・八相成道・八相作仏] (Jpn *hassō, hassō-jōdō,* or *hassō-sabutsu*): Eight successive phases that a Buddha is said to manifest when appearing in the world in order to save people. They are (1) descending from heaven, (2) entering the mother's womb, (3) emerging from the mother's womb, (4) renouncing the secular world, (5) conquering devils, (6) attaining enlightenment, (7) turning the wheel of the Law, and (8) entering nirvana.

eight precepts [八斎戒] (Jpn *hassaikai*): Precepts that Buddhist lay believers observe for twenty-four hours on specific days of the month. Although they vary somewhat among sources, the eight precepts can be summarized as follows: (1) not to take life, (2) not to steal, (3) to refrain from all sexual relations, (4) not to lie, (5) not to drink intoxicants, (6) not to wear ornaments or perfume, or to listen to singing or watch dancing, (7) not to sleep on a wide or elevated bed, and (8) not to eat after the noon hour. Because these eight precepts are included among the ten precepts for male and female novices of the Buddhist Order, on specific days of the month lay believers effectively live a monastic life in form and spirit by observing the eight precepts.

eight precepts of reverence [八敬戒] (Jpn *hachikyōkai*): Eight monastic regulations for nuns. In essence, they require that nuns revere monks and demonstrate proper attitudes toward them. According to tradition, Shakyamuni set forth these eight precepts when he permitted the formation of a Buddhist community of nuns. They are: (1) even though the time since her ordination may be as long as one hundred years, a nun must pay respect even to a monk who has just been ordained into the Buddhist Order; (2) she must not slander a monk; (3) she must not accuse a monk of any misdeed; (4) she must receive from a monk the entire commandments for nuns; (5) she must confess her offenses before the assembly of monks and accordingly make amends; (6) she must ask for instruction from a monk every half month; (7) she must not spend the summer retreat at a place where there are no monks; and (8) after the summer retreat she must confess her offenses to a monk and make amends.

eight schools [八宗] (Jpn *hasshū*): The eight major schools of Buddhism in Japan before the Kamakura period (1185–1333). They are the Dharma Analysis Treasury (Kusha), Establishment of Truth (Jōjitsu), Precepts (Ritsu), Dharma Characteristics (Hossō), Three Treatises (Sanron), Flower Garland (Kegon), Tendai, and True Word (Shingon) schools. The first six schools flourished in the Nara period (710–794), and the Tendai and True Word schools appeared and rose to prominence during the Heian period (794–1185).

eight sufferings [八苦] (Jpn *hakku*): Eight kinds of universal suffering. They are the four sufferings of birth, aging, sickness, and death, plus the suffering of having to part from those whom one loves, the suffering of having to meet with those whom one hates, the suffering of being unable to obtain what one desires, and the suffering arising from the five components that constitute one's body and mind.

eight teachings [八教] (Jpn *hakkyō*): A system by which T'ien-t'ai (538–597) classified Shakyamuni's teachings. The eight teachings are divided into two groups: the four teachings of doctrine and the four teachings of method. The first is a division by content, and the second, by method of teaching. The four teachings of doctrine are: (1) The Tripitaka teaching, which corresponds to Hinayana, is so called because it consists of the three divisions of the canon (Skt *tripitaka*)—sutras (the Buddha's teachings), *vinaya* (the rules of monastic discipline), and *abhidharma* (commentaries and treatises). The teachings of this category reveal the cause of transmigration in the threefold world and urge one to free oneself from this continual rebirth and enter the state of nirvana in which all desires are extinguished. To help one cast off attachment to the threefold world, they teach the analytical view of non-substantiality, or the perception that all things, when analyzed into their constituent elements (dharmas), prove to be without substance. These teachings were expounded primarily for persons of the two vehicles and secondarily for bodhisattvas. (2) The connecting teaching, or introductory Mahayana, which is so called because it forms a link between the Tripitaka teaching and the specific teaching. Like the Tripitaka teaching, the connecting teaching is concerned with casting off attachment to the threefold world. The teachings of this category deny the view of the Tripitaka teaching that all things, when analyzed, prove to be without substance; instead they teach the view that all things, just as they are, are without substance, because they arise and disappear only by virtue of dependent origination. These teachings are directed primarily to bodhisattvas and secondarily to persons of the two vehicles. (3) The specific teaching, or a higher level of provisional Mahayana, which is so called because it was expounded specifically for bodhisattvas. The teachings of this category set forth a long series of austere practices spanning many *kalpas,* which bodhisattvas must carry out to attain Buddhahood. They address the three truths of non-substantiality, temporary existence, and the Middle Way, but indicate them as separate from and independent of one another. (4) The perfect teaching, which expounds the mutually inclusive relationship of the ultimate reality and all phenomena, and the unification of the three truths. The perfect teaching is directed to people of all capacities and holds that all can attain Buddhahood. According to T'ien-t'ai's system, the Tripitaka, connecting, and specific teachings are all means leading to the perfect teaching, which encompasses and unifies them.

The four teachings of method is a classification of the teachings in terms of the way the Buddha taught them. They are (1) The sudden teaching, or those teachings that Shakyamuni expounded directly from his own enlightenment without giving his disciples preparatory knowledge. This category corresponds to the Flower Garland Sutra, traditionally regarded as the first teaching he expounded after his enlightenment at Buddhagayā. (2) The gradual teaching, or those teachings expounded to gradually elevate people's capacities to an understanding of higher doctrines. The gradual teaching corresponds to the sutras of the Āgama, Correct and Equal, and Wisdom periods. (3) The secret teaching, or those teachings that the listeners understand differently according to their respective capacities and from which they each receive a different benefit without being aware of the difference. (4) The indeterminate teaching, or those teachings that the listeners understand and benefit from differently as above but are aware of the difference. *See also* five periods.

eight types of arrogance [八慢] (Jpn *hachi-man*): Also, eight arrogances. They are (1) thinking that one is superior to others, though one is really inferior; (2) thinking that one is superior to others, when actually one is equal to them; (3) boasting of one's superiority over others and belittling them; (4) thinking that one's life, a temporary union of the five components, is permanent; (5) thinking that one has attained enlightenment when in fact one has not; (6) thinking that one is only slightly inferior to those who far surpass one; (7) thinking that one possesses virtue though one lacks virtue, and (8) thinking little of others or paying no respect to people of virtue or who are superior to oneself.

eight unpardonable offenses [八重・八波羅夷] (Jpn *hachijū* or *hachiharai*): *See* eight major offenses.

eight winds [八風] (Jpn *happū*): Eight conditions that prevent people from advancing along the right path to enlightenment. According to *The Treatise on the Stage of Buddhahood Sutra*—Bandhuprabha's work that was translated into Chinese by Hsüan-tsang—the eight winds are prosperity, decline, disgrace, honor, praise, censure, suffering, and pleasure. People are often swayed either by their attachment to prosperity, honor, praise, and pleasure (collectively known as "four favorites" or "four favorable winds"), or by their aversion to decline, disgrace, censure, and suffering ("four dislikes" or "four adverse winds").

eighty characteristics [八十種好] (Jpn *hachijisshugō*): Extraordinary features that Buddhas and bodhisattvas are said to have. While the thirty-two features are possessed not only by Buddhas and bodhisattvas but also by the gods Shakra and Brahmā and by the wheel-turning kings, the eighty characteristics are found only in Buddhas and bodhisattvas. Descriptions of the eighty characteristics vary. These and the thirty-two features partly overlap.

eighty-four thousand [八万四千] (Jpn *hachiman-shisen*): A figure used in Buddhist texts to represent a large number, or a quantity that is immeasurable or all-inclusive. It is often abbreviated as eighty thousand. Some examples of terms containing this expression are eighty-four thousand earthly desires, eighty-four thousand diseases, eighty-four thousand stupas built by King Ashoka, and the Buddha's eighty-four thousand teachings.

eighty-four thousand teachings [八万四千法門・八万四千法蔵] (Jpn *hachiman-shisen-hōmon* or *hachiman-shisen-hōzō*): Also, eighty thousand teachings. The entire body of teachings that Shakyamuni Buddha expounded during his lifetime. These figures are not to be taken literally, but simply indicate a large number, innumerable, countless, or all.

eighty thousand teachings [八万法門・八万法蔵] (Jpn *hachiman-hōmon* or *hachiman-hōzō*): *See* eighty-four thousand teachings.

Eikan [永観]: Also known as Yōkan. A priest of the Three Treatises (Sanron) school in Japan. *See* Yōkan.

Eisai [栄西] (1141–1215): Also known as Yōsai. The founder of the Rinzai school of Zen in Japan. As a youth he received the precepts and was ordained at Enryaku-ji, the head temple of the Tendai school on Mount Hiei. He traveled to China twice, in 1168 and in 1187, and brought back the Zen teaching of the Lin-chi (Jpn Rinzai) school. He founded a number of Zen temples, including Shōfuku-ji in Hakata, Kennin-ji in Kyoto, and Jufuku-ji in Kamakura. The opposition of the Tendai priests on Mount Hiei made it difficult for him to propagate his teachings in Kyoto, so he went to Kamakura. There he founded Jufuku-ji temple with the support of Hōjō Masako, widow of Minamoto no Yoritomo, the founder of the Kamakura shogunate, and devoted himself to propagation. He also won the patronage of the second shogun, Minamoto no Yoriie, and with his support founded Kennin-ji in Kyoto.

In Kyoto he found it necessary to compromise with the older schools; Kennin-ji, for example, was not a purely Zen institution but included places for Tendai and True Word (Shingon) worship. Though not technically the first to introduce Zen ideas to Japan, Eisai is credited with establishing Zen as an independent school. His works include *The Propagation of Zen for the Protection of the Country.* He also wrote *Drinking Tea to Improve Health and Prolong Life,* the first work on tea in Japan. When the third shogun, Minamoto no Sanetomo, was ill, Eisai offered him a regimen that involved drinking tea.

Eizon [叡尊] (1201–1290): Also known as Eison and Shien. A restorer of the Precepts (Ritsu) school in Japan. Born in Yamato Province, he first studied the teachings of the True Word (Shingon) school at Daigo-ji temple in Kyoto. In 1224 he went to Mount Kōya, the center of the esoteric teachings, to further his study. Awakened to the importance of the Buddhist precepts and grieved at the decline of those precepts, in 1235 he went to Saidai-ji temple of the Precepts school at Nara to restore it to prominence. The following year he accepted the precepts in a self-administered ceremony at Tōdai-ji temple. He also visited various temples in the surrounding areas where he lectured on the teaching of the precepts and administered the precepts to clerics and lay believers.

In 1262, at the request of the former regent Hōjō Tokiyori and other government authorities, Eizon went east to Kamakura, the seat of the shogunate, where he and his disciple Ryōkan disseminated the teaching of the precepts. After half a year, he returned to Saidai-ji temple. Eizon won many followers among the imperial court and shogunate officials. He also undertook a number of social works. On the occasion of the Mongol invasion of Japan in 1274 and 1281, he repeatedly conducted an esoteric prayer ritual to ward off the invasion. Eizon engaged in the practice of both the precepts and the True Word teachings. He is regarded as the founder of the True Word Precepts (Shingon–Ritsu) school based at Saidai-ji temple. He was posthumously given the title Bodhisattva Kōshō (Promoter of the Correct).

Ekan [慧灌] (n.d.) (Jpn; Kor Hyekwan): The founder of the Three Treatises (Sanron) school in Japan. He was a native of Koguryŏ, a kingdom on the Korean Peninsula, in the seventh century. He went to China during the Sui dynasty (581–618) and studied the doctrines of the Three Treatises (Chin San-lun) school under Chi-tsang. In 625 he went to Japan and lived at Gangō-ji temple in Nara, where he lectured on *The Treatise on the Middle Way, The Treatise on the Twelve Gates,* and *The One-Hundred-Verse Treatise,* the three works that form the basis for the Three Treatises school. Although the Korean priests Eji (Hyecha) and Kanroku (Kwallŭk) had introduced the Three Treatises teachings to Japan before Ekan, it was Ekan who gave systematic explanations of the doctrine and laid the foundation of the Three Treatises school in Japan. Ekan on one occasion conducted prayers for rain that were apparently successful and was appointed administrator of priests.

Elephant-Head Mountain [象頭山] (Jpn Zōzu-sen): A hill in India on which Shakyamuni is believed to have preached. *See* Gayāshīrsha, Mount.

Eleven-faced Perceiver of the World's Sounds [十一面観音] (Skt Ekādasha-mukha; Jpn Jūichimen-kannon): One of the various forms in which Bodhisattva Perceiver of the World's Sounds is depicted. Several esoteric sutras refer to different forms of this bodhisattva, including one with eleven faces and another with a thousand arms. Images depicting those various forms were produced to express and to venerate the bodhisattva's great compassion. According to the Mysterious Spells of the Eleven-faced Perceiver of the World's Sounds Sutra, the three faces in the front of the head of this figure are those of bodhisattvas; the three on the left are those of anger; the three on the right are fanged bodhisattvas; the one in the back is an atrocious but laughing face; and the one on top is a Buddha's face. With all these faces, Bodhisattva Perceiver of the World's Sounds keeps watch over the ten directions so that he can rescue all who are suffering. The "Perceiver of the World's Sounds" (twenty-fifth) chapter of the Lotus Sutra depicts his compassion and ability to assume thirty-three forms, from that of a Buddha to a *vajra*-bearing god, with which to save living beings. The bodhisattva's eleven-faced form, however, is not one of those depicted in the sutra.

Eloquence [弁才天・弁天] (Skt Sarasvatī; Jpn Benzai-ten or Benten): A goddess said to possess the virtues of music, wealth, wisdom, and eloquence in preaching. Originally a river goddess in ancient India, she was later incorporated into Buddhism. Some of her images and statues depict her with eight arms and carrying a bow and arrow, sword, ax, and other weapons, while others have only two arms and hold the *biwa,* a Japanese lute. She is regarded as one of the seven beneficent deities.

Ema Mitsutoki [江間光時] (n.d.): Also known as Hōjō Mitsutoki. A Japanese samurai and a grandson of Hōjō Yoshitoki (1163–1224), the second regent of the Kamakura shogunate, and a son of Yoshitoki's son, Hōjō Tomotoki. He was called Ema Mitsutoki because his main fief was located in Ema in Izu Province. He was the feudal lord of Shijō Kingo, a follower of Nichiren. In 1246 Mitsutoki was suspected of plotting treason against the regent Hōjō Tokiyori and was sentenced to confinement at Ema in Izu. At that time, his retainer Nakatsukasa Yorikazu, Shijō Kingo's father, accompanied him as an attendant until his lord returned to Kamakura after being pardoned. Hōjō Chikatoki, who was also known as Ema Chikatoki or Ema no Shirō, was Mitsutoki's son and successor. Shijō Kingo also served this new lord.

emanation Buddhas [分身] (Jpn *funjin*): *See* emanations of the Buddha.

emanations of the Buddha [分身] (Jpn *funjin*): Also, emanation Buddhas or emanations. Buddhas who are separate manifestations of a true Buddha. According to Mahayana belief, a true Buddha can produce infinite emanations who can simultaneously appear in innumerable worlds in order to save the people there. Hence the phrase "the emanation Buddhas of the ten directions" and other similar expressions that appear in the Lotus Sutra and other sutras. In the "Treasure Tower" (eleventh) chapter of the Lotus Sutra, Shakyamuni summons to the assembly the Buddhas who are his emanations in the ten directions in order to commence the Ceremony in the Air.

emancipation [解脱] (Skt *moksha, mukti, vimoksha,* or *vimukti;* Jpn *gedatsu*): Also, liberation or release. Release from delusions and earthly desires that leads to the attainment of freedom. It also means release from transmigration in the world of suffering. There are various stages of emancipation, but emancipation at its ultimate stage is the same as nirvana.

"Emergence of the Treasure Tower" chapter [見宝塔品] (Jpn *Kenhōtō-hon*): Abbreviated as the "Treasure Tower" chapter. The eleventh chapter of the Lotus Sutra. This chapter describes the emergence of the treasure tower of the Buddha Many Treasures, who bears witness to the truth of the Lotus Sutra, and the beginning of the Ceremony in the Air. After the proclamations in the preceding chapters of the sutra that voice-hearers and cause-awakened ones will attain Buddhahood in the future, a magnificent tower adorned with the seven kinds of treasures, 500 *yojanas* in height and 250 *yojanas* each in width and depth, emerges from beneath the earth and hangs suspended in midair. A voice issues from within, praising Shakyamuni Buddha and declaring that all he has taught thus far in the Lotus Sutra is true. Through the person of Bodhisattva Great Joy of Preaching, the assembly asks to know the meaning of this event. Shakyamuni explains that within the tower is the body of a Buddha called Many Treasures who once lived in the land of Treasure Purity, an incalculable number of worlds to the east. Though he has long since entered nirvana, he has made a vow that he will appear in the treasure tower wherever anyone might preach the Lotus Sutra and testify to the truth of that sutra.

Bodhisattva Great Joy of Preaching then requests to see the figure of Many Treasures Buddha. Shakyamuni replies that, in order to open the door to the treasure tower, he must first assemble from throughout the ten directions those Buddhas who are preaching the Law as emanations of himself, and he proceeds to purify the lands three times to make room for the emanations. First he purifies the *sahā* world by removing all the human and heavenly beings other than the members of the assembly to other lands, leaving no one but the assembled multitude. Then he uses his transcendental powers to purify "two hundred ten thousand million *nayutas* of lands in each of the eight directions." In these lands, there are no longer any beings of hell and of the realms of hungry spirits, animals, and *asuras*—that is, no beings of the four evil paths. In addition, Shakyamuni moves the human beings and heavenly beings to other lands so that these purified lands are not inhabited by any beings in the six paths. He then purifies yet "another two hundred ten thousand million *nayutas* of lands in each of the eight directions" in the same manner.

Now that the *sahā* world and two other groups of lands have been transformed into Buddha lands in this way, all the Buddhas assemble from throughout the ten directions, seating themselves on lion seats under jeweled trees. When they all have gathered, Shakyamuni opens the treasure tower, and Many Treasures Buddha invites him to share his seat. Shakyamuni then uses his transcendental powers to raise the entire assembly into open space so that they can see Many Treasures Buddha more clearly, and the Ceremony in the Air begins. Seated beside Many Treasures in the treasure tower, Shakyamuni then makes three pronouncements, calling upon the multitude to propagate the Lotus Sutra after his death. In the course of the third pronouncement, he sets forth "the six difficult and nine easy acts" to emphasize the great difficulty of embracing and propagating the Lotus Sutra after his death.

"Emerging from the Earth" chapter [従地涌出品] (Jpn *Jūji-yujuppon*): The fifteenth chapter of the Lotus Sutra and the beginning of the essential teaching, or the latter fourteen chapters of the sutra. This chapter opens with innumerable great bodhisattvas who have assembled from other worlds vowing to propagate the Lotus Sutra in the *sahā* world after Shakyamuni's death. Shakyamuni stops them, however, saying that there is no need; the *sahā* world already has great bodhisattvas who will carry out this task. With this, the earth trembles and splits open, and a host of bodhisattvas emerge, equal in number to the sands of sixty thousand Ganges Rivers, each with his own retinue. Four bodhisattvas lead this multitude: Superior Practices, Boundless Practices, Pure Practices, and Firmly Established Practices. Bodhisattva Maitreya, astounded at this sight, asks Shakyamuni Buddha on behalf of the assembly who these bodhisattvas are, where they come from and for what purpose, what Buddha they follow and what teaching they practice. Shakyamuni replies that they are his original disciples whom he has been teaching since long ago. Maitreya again asks how, in the mere forty-odd years since his awakening, Shakyamuni has managed to teach so many countless bodhisattvas. He beseeches Shakyamuni to explain further, especially for the sake of people in the future who may have doubts about this point. The "Emerging from the Earth" chapter ends here. To answer Maitreya's question, Shakyamuni reveals in the next chapter, "Life Span," that in reality countless *kalpas* have passed since he first attained enlightenment.

Emma [閻魔] (Jpn): Also known as King Yama. The king of hell who is said to judge the dead on the basis of their deeds while alive. *See* Yama.

Enchin [円珍]: Also known as Chishō. The fifth chief priest of Enryaku-ji, the head temple of the Tendai school in Japan. *See* Chishō.

Enchō [円澄] (772–837): The second chief priest of Enryaku-ji, the head temple of the Tendai school on Mount Hiei in Japan. Born in Musashi Province, he entered the priesthood under the guidance of

Dōchū, a disciple of Ganjin. In 798 he went to Mount Hiei and became a disciple of Dengyō. In 806 he received from Dengyō the precepts of perfect and immediate enlightenment and in 808 became a lecturer on the Golden Light Sutra. In 833 he expounded the Tendai teachings at the imperial court and in the same year was appointed chief priest of Enryaku-ji temple, succeeding Gishin, the first chief priest. His posthumous name and title are the Great Teacher Jakkō (Tranquil Light).

"Encouragements" chapter [勧発品] (Jpn *Kambotsu-hon*): The twenty-eighth and last chapter of the Lotus Sutra. *See* "Encouragements of the Bodhisattva Universal Worthy" chapter.

"Encouragements of the Bodhisattva Universal Worthy" chapter [普賢菩薩勧発品] (Jpn *Fugen-bosatsu-kambotsu-hon*): Abbreviated as the "Universal Worthy" chapter or the "Encouragements" chapter. The twenty-eighth and last chapter of the Lotus Sutra. In the first part of the chapter, Bodhisattva Universal Worthy arrives from the land of the Buddha King Above Jeweled Dignity and Virtue in the east to pay homage to Shakyamuni Buddha and to hear him preach. He says to Shakyamuni, "World-Honored One, when I was in the land of the Buddha King Above Jeweled Dignity and Virtue, from far away I heard the Lotus Sutra being preached in this *sahā* world. In company with this multitude of immeasurable, boundless hundreds, thousands, ten thousands, millions of bodhisattvas I have come to listen to and accept the sutra. I beg that the World-Honored One will preach it for us." He asks how one can acquire the Lotus Sutra after the Buddha's death, and in answer to this Shakyamuni explains four conditions for doing so: to be protected and kept in mind by the Buddhas, to plant the roots of virtue, to enter the stage where one is sure of reaching enlightenment, and to arouse the determination to save all living beings. Bodhisattva Universal Worthy then vows to protect the Lotus Sutra and all those who embrace it in the evil-ridden Latter Day of the Law. Shakyamuni briefly explains the blessings obtained through the practice of the sutra and through the act of offering alms to and praising its practitioners. He says, "Therefore, Universal Worthy, if you see a person who accepts and upholds this sutra, you should rise and greet him from afar, showing him the same respect you would a Buddha." Overjoyed to have heard the Lotus Sutra, all the assembly bow in obeisance to him and depart. In the Lotus Sutra of the Wonderful Law, Kumārajīva's translation of the sutra, this is the final chapter, but in the other versions—the Lotus Sutra of the Correct Law translated by Dharmaraksha and the Supplemented Lotus Sutra of the Wonderful Law by Jnānagupta and Dharmagupta—the "Entrustment" chapter appears at the end of the twenty-seven chapter sutra.

"Encouraging Devotion" chapter [勧持品] (Jpn *Kanji-hon*): The thirteenth chapter of the Lotus Sutra. In the beginning of the chapter, Bodhisattva Medicine King and his retinue of twenty thousand bodhisattvas make a vow before Shakyamuni Buddha to propagate the Lotus Sutra in this *sahā* world after his death. Meanwhile, a vow of propagation in other worlds is made by five hundred arhats who have received a prophecy of enlightenment and by eight thousand other voice-hearers, some still learning and others with nothing more to learn. Shakyamuni then bestows a prophecy of enlightenment on Mahāprajāpatī, his maternal aunt, and Yashodharā, who was his wife before he renounced the secular world. These two and their retinue of six thousand nuns also vow to spread the Lotus Sutra after the Buddha's death. Then "eight hundred thousand million *nayutas* of bodhisattvas" make a vow to teach the sutra in the frightful evil age after the Buddha's death. Their vow is stated in verse form and is often referred to as the twenty-line verse of the "Encouraging Devotion" chapter. It enumerates the types of persecutions that will be met in propagating the Lotus Sutra in that latter age. Miao-lo (711–782) of China later summarized these persecutions and their perpetrators as the "three kinds of enemies" or "three kinds of arrogance and presumption." *See also* three powerful enemies; twenty-line verse.

Endō Saemon-no-jō [遠藤左衛門尉] (n.d.): A lay follower of Nichiren. Little is known about him, though he appears to have been a samurai who lived on Sado, an island in the Sea of Japan. There is only one extant letter by Nichiren addressed to him, dated the twelfth day of the third month, 1274. In it, Nichiren conveys his deep gratitude for Endō's assistance during his time of exile on Sado Island. According to one opinion, Endō was a relative of Abutsu-bō, another lay follower and a native of Sado who assisted Nichiren during his exile.

Endowed with a Thousand Ten Thousand Glowing Marks [具足千万光相如来] (Skt Rashmi-shatasahasra-paripūrna-dhvaja; Jpn Gusoku-semmankōsō-nyorai): The Thus Come One Endowed with a Thousand Ten Thousand Glowing Marks. The name that Yashodharā, formerly the wife of Shakyamuni and mother of Rāhula, will assume when she becomes a Buddha, according to the "Encouraging Devotion" (thirteenth) chapter of the Lotus Sutra. The chapter reads: "The Buddha said to Yashodharā, 'In future ages, amid the Law of hundreds, thousands, ten thousands, millions of Buddhas, you will practice the deeds of a bodhisattva, will be a great teacher of the Law, and will gradually fulfill the Buddha way. Then in a good land you will become a Buddha named Endowed with a Thousand Ten Thousand Glowing Marks.'"

Enemy before Birth [未生怨] (Jpn Mishō'on): Also, Unborn Enemy.

A translation of the Sanskrit name Ajātashatru, king of Magadha in ancient India during Shakyamuni's time, that appears in Chinese Buddhist texts. *Ajāta* means unborn, and *shatru* means enemy. According to the Nirvana Sutra, Prince Ajātashatru asks, "Why do the people denounce me as Enemy before Birth? Who gave me the name?" Devadatta replies, "Before you were born, all the diviners said that, when the child is born, he will kill his father. That is why the others call you Enemy before Birth." The following story is well known, though it is a composition based on several texts. Bimbisāra, king of Magadha, was impatient for the birth of an heir. A diviner predicted that a certain hermit, upon dying, would be reborn as the king's son. To hasten the birth, Bimbisāra had the hermit killed. When the king's wife became pregnant, the diviner foretold that the baby would grow up to be the king's enemy. Hence he was called Ajātashatru, or "Enemy before Birth."

Engaku-ji [円覚寺]: The head temple of the Engaku-ji branch of the Rinzai school of Zen in Kamakura, Japan, built in 1282 by Hōjō Tokimune, the eighth regent of the Kamakura shogunate. The first chief priest was Mugaku Sogen (Chin Wu-hsüeh Tsu-yüan, 1226–1286), a priest from China. In 1283 the temple was designated as an official place of prayer by the shogunate. It is counted as one of the Five Temples of Kamakura. *See also* Five Temples.

Enlightened One [覚者] (Jpn *kakusha*): Also, Awakened One. A Buddha. One who is enlightened to the ultimate truth or principle of life and the universe.

enlightenment [悟] (Jpn *satori*): *See* attainment of Buddhahood.

enlightenment of plants [草木成仏] (Jpn *sōmoku-jōbutsu*): Also, enlightenment of insentient beings. The enlightenment of grass, trees, rocks, the land itself, or anything else that has neither emotion nor consciousness. The doctrine that insentient beings can attain Buddhahood derives from T'ien-t'ai's doctrine of three thousand realms in a single moment of life. One of the component principles of this doctrine is the realm of the environment, or the insentient objective world. The doctrine teaches the mutually inclusive relationship of living beings and their environments, or that of sentient and insentient beings, thereby revealing that both manifest the same state of life. Therefore, when living beings manifest the state of Buddhahood, their environment simultaneously manifests the state of Buddhahood as well. In *The Diamond Scalpel,* Miao-lo (711–782) refuted the arguments of Ch'eng-kuan, the fourth patriarch of the Chinese Flower Garland (Hua-yen) school, who asserted that insentient beings do not possess the Buddha nature. Miao-lo wrote, "A plant, a tree, a pebble, a speck of dust—each has the Buddha nature, and each is endowed with cause and effect and with the function to manifest and the wisdom to realize its Buddha nature."

Enni [円爾] (1202–1280): Also known as Bennen. A priest of the Rinzai school of Zen in Japan. In 1235 he journeyed to China where he studied for six years under Wu-chun Shih-fan. After returning to Japan in 1241, he taught Zen at the imperial court and obtained the patronage of the nobility. He became the first chief priest of Tōfuku-ji, a temple built in Kyoto by the chief minister of the imperial court, Kujō Michiie. Enni's lineage is called the Tōfuku-ji branch of the Rinzai school. In 1311 the imperial court gave him the posthumous name and title Teacher of the Nation Shōichi.

Ennin [円仁]: Also known as Jikaku. The third chief priest of Enryaku-ji, the head temple of the Tendai school in Japan. *See* Jikaku.

En no Ozunu [役小角] (b. 634): Also known as En no Ubasoku or En no Gyōja. The semi-legendary founder of Shugen-dō in Japan, a Buddhistic tradition of ascetic practices in the mountains to obtain supernatural powers that was later coupled with the practice of Esoteric Buddhism. A native of Yamato Province, he began practicing austerities as a youth, living in the mountains. At age thirty-two, he went to Mount Katsuragi where he enshrined an image of the god Peacock King in a cave and engaged in the recitation of magic formulas for more than thirty years. In 699 he was exiled to Izu as the result of an accusation against him by a former disciple who was a court noble, but was later pardoned. It is not known when or where he died. He is the reputed founder of a great many temples in the present-day Kinki district, the area surrounding Kyoto. Some schools that follow his practice still exist.

Enryaku-ji [延暦寺]: The head temple of the Tendai school in Ōtsu in Shiga Prefecture, Japan. Located on Mount Hiei, it was founded by Dengyō in 788 and given the name Enryaku-ji by Emperor Saga in 823. In 794 the capital had been moved from Nara to Kyoto. According to Chinese tradition, the northeast was believed to be the "demon gate," or the direction from which evil influences entered the country. Mount Hiei's location, to the northeast of the new capital, made Enryaku-ji ideally suited as an official temple for the protection of the nation, and it was designated as such. In 805 Dengyō returned from his studies in China and in 806 established the Tendai school. In 822, after Dengyō's death, the school was allowed to erect a Mahayana ordination platform on Mount Hiei, the first such platform in the country. Enryaku-ji prospered for centuries as the center of Japanese Buddhism. Several founders of Japanese Buddhist schools, such as Hōnen, Eisai, Dōgen, and Nichiren, studied there.

Ensai [円載] (d. 877): A priest of the Tendai school in Japan. In 839, seventeen years after the death of Dengyō, his teacher and the school's founder, Ensai made a pilgrimage to Mount T'ien-t'ai in China. There he submitted a list of thirty questions (fifty questions by another account) that had been prepared at Enryaku-ji, the head temple of the Japanese Tendai school, to the priest Kuang-hsiu and his disciple Wei-chüan of the T'ien-t'ai school. Upon receiving their answers, he had two of his disciples take them back to Enryaku-ji in Japan. Ensai stayed in China for nearly forty years. He died while on his way back to Japan with many Buddhist and Confucian scriptures when his ship was wrecked in a storm.

"Entrustment" chapter [嘱累品] (Jpn *Zokurui-hon*): The twenty-second chapter of the Lotus Sutra. In the previous (twenty-first) chapter, "Supernatural Powers," Shakyamuni Buddha makes a "specific transfer" of the Law of supreme perfect enlightenment, the essence of the Lotus Sutra, to the Bodhisattvas of the Earth. In this chapter, the Buddha makes a "general transfer" of the Lotus Sutra to all of the bodhisattvas attending the assembly of the Lotus Sutra. Then all the Buddhas who have gathered from throughout the ten directions return to their respective lands, the treasure tower returns to its original place, and the place of the assembly shifts from the air back to Eagle Peak. In the Lotus Sutra of the Wonderful Law, Kumārajīva's translation of the sutra, this is the twenty-second of the twenty-eight chapters; but in the other versions—the Lotus Sutra of the Correct Law translated by Dharmaraksha and the Supplemented Lotus Sutra of the Wonderful Law by Jnānagupta and Dharmagupta, both containing only twenty-seven chapters—the "Entrustment" chapter is the final chapter.

envoy of the Thus Come One [如来の使] (Skt *tathāgata-dūta;* Jpn *nyorai-no-tsukai*): Also, emissary of the Thus Come One or messenger of the Thus Come One. One whom the Thus Come One, or the Buddha, sends to propagate his teachings after his death. *Tathāgata* and *dūta* correspond to the Thus Come One and envoy, respectively. The "envoy of the Thus Come One" is emphasized in the "Teacher of the Law" (tenth) chapter of the Lotus Sutra. The preceding chapters address persons of the two vehicles, or voice-hearers and cause-awakened ones, and contain the Buddha's prophecies of their future enlightenment. In contrast, the "Teacher of the Law" chapter and ensuing chapters address bodhisattvas and describe the practice and propagation of the sutra after the Buddha's death. In the "Teacher of the Law" chapter, Shakyamuni Buddha speaks of the envoy of the Thus Come One as follows: "Medicine King, you should understand that these persons voluntarily relinquish the reward due them for their pure deeds and, in the time after I have passed into extinction, because they pity living beings, they are born in this evil world so they may broadly expound this sutra. If one of these good men or good women in the time after I have passed into extinction is able to secretly expound the Lotus Sutra to one person, even one phrase of it, then you should know that he or she is the envoy of the Thus Come One. He has been dispatched by the Thus Come One and carries out the Thus Come One's work."

The Buddha also says: "If one is capable of embracing the Lotus Sutra of the Wonderful Law, know that such a person is an envoy of the Buddha who thinks with pity of living beings. Those who are capable of embracing the Lotus Sutra of the Wonderful Law relinquish their claim to the pure land and out of pity for living beings are born here. Know that persons such as these freely choose where they will be born, and choose to be born in this evil world so they may broadly expound the unsurpassed Law. . . . If there are those in a later age who can accept and embrace this sutra, they are my envoys sent out among the people to perform the Thus Come One's work."

The envoy of the Thus Come One is therefore one who is capable of embracing and spreading the sutra in the evil world and who has pity and compassion for living beings. Out of pity for living beings the envoy appears in the evil world and strives to bring benefit to them. In his writings, Nichiren (1222–1282) often refers to himself as the "envoy of the Thus Come One" out of his conviction that he was acting as the true practitioner of the Lotus Sutra who "carries out the Thus Come One's work." He also uses the expression "envoy of the Thus Come One" to describe his disciples who spread the Lotus Sutra.

equal in principle but superior in practice [理同事勝] (Jpn *ridō-jishō*): An interpretation applied in Esoteric Buddhism to the Mahāvairochana Sutra, a primary esoteric sutra. It was formulated by Shan-wu-wei (Skt Shubhakarasimha, 637–735) in China and espoused in Japan by Jikaku (794–864), who established the foundation of Tendai Esotericism. This statement is an assertion that the Mahāvairochana Sutra is equal to the Lotus Sutra in terms of principle and is superior to it in terms of practice. According to this interpretation, both the Mahāvairochana Sutra and the Lotus Sutra reveal the doctrine of three thousand realms in a single moment of life, and therefore these two sutras are equal in terms of principle; however, because the Mahāvairochana Sutra contains descriptions of mudras (hand gestures) and mantras (mystic formulas), Tendai Esotericism argued that it is superior to the Lotus Sutra in terms of practice.

eranda [伊蘭] (Skt, Pali; Jpn *iran*): A plant depicted in Buddhist scriptures as emitting a very foul odor, often mentioned in contrast with the fragrant sandalwood tree. The *eranda* is thought to refer to the castor-oil plant or a close relative, though the castor-oil plant does not emit a foul odor. According to the Ocean of Meditation on the Buddha Sutra, the odor of the *eranda* plant is similar to that of a rotting corpse and reaches a distance of forty *yojanas*. The sutra says that the fragrant sandalwood tree dispels the stench of the *eranda*. The *eranda* and its stench are cited as a metaphor for delusion and suffering, and the sandalwood and its wonderful fragrance as a metaphor for enlightenment or the purifying and beneficial power of the Buddhist Law. *See also* sandalwood tree.

Eryō [慧亮] (802–860): A priest of the Tendai school in Japan. As a youth, Eryō studied at Enryaku-ji, the head temple of the Tendai school on Mount Hiei. In 829 he received the Mahayana bodhisattva precepts under Gishin, Dengyō's designated successor and the first chief priest of Enryaku-ji. He also studied under Enchō and Jikaku, the second and third chief priests of Enryaku-ji, and learned both the exoteric and esoteric Tendai doctrines. Eryō was supervisor of a temple on Mount Hiei called Hōdō-in. One account states that he was born in 812.

Eshin [恵心] : Also known as Genshin, a priest of the Tendai school in Japan. *See* Genshin.

Eshin school [恵心流] (Jpn Eshin-ryū): A branch of the Japanese Tendai school that regards Genshin (942–1017) as its founder. A disciple of Ryōgen, the eighteenth chief priest of the Tendai school, Genshin was also called the Supervisor of Priests Eshin because he lived in a hall called Eshin-in at Enryaku-ji temple on Mount Hiei. Kakuun, another disciple of Ryōgen, is regarded as the founder of the Danna school. Genshin valued the practice of meditation that Dengyō, founder of the Japanese Tendai school, had learned from Tao-sui, while Kakuun attached greater importance to the doctrinal studies that Dengyō had learned from Hsing-man. The Eshin school later gave rise to the Sugiu, Gyōsen-bō, Tsuchimikado Monzeki, and Hōji-bō schools.

Esoteric Buddhism [密教] (Jpn *mikkyō*): Also, esoteric teachings. Those Buddhist teachings that are conveyed secretly or implicitly and are held to be beyond the understanding of ordinary persons. They are defined in contrast to the exoteric teachings, or those teachings that are explicitly revealed and accessible to all. According to the True Word (Jpn Shingon) school, the esoteric teachings are those teachings that Mahāvairochana Buddha preached secretly to Vajrasattva, who compiled them and sealed them in an iron tower in southern India. The school holds that they contain the enlightenment of Mahāvairochana Buddha, which is said to be beyond ordinary understanding.

The line of transmission of Esoteric Buddhism is held to be from Vajrasattva to Nāgārjuna, and then down through Nāgabodhi, Chin-kang-chih (Skt Vajrabodhi), Pu-k'ung (Amoghavajra), Hui-kuo, and finally to Kōbō, the founder of the True Word school in Japan. The school also lists eight patriarchs who upheld Esoteric Buddhism: Nāgārjuna and Nāgabodhi who spread it in India; Chin-kang-chih, Pu-k'ung, and Shan-wu-wei (Shubhakarasimha) who introduced and established it in China; I-hsing and Hui-kuo who propagated it in China; and Kōbō who brought it to Japan. Esoteric Buddhism in India was a form of Tantrism that incorporates indigenous magical and ritualistic elements such as symbolic gestures (mudras) and spells (mantras), as well as diagrams (mandalas) and the worship of numerous deities.

Shan-wu-wei, Chin-kang-chih, and Pu-k'ung introduced Esoteric Buddhism to China. Kōbō (774–835), who went to China and studied under Hui-kuo, a disciple of Pu-k'ung, brought these teachings to Japan. He systematized them as the Japanese True Word school. According to this school, the esoteric teachings are the three mysteries—the mind, mouth, and body—of Mahāvairochana Buddha. Mahāvairochana is believed to be omnipresent, constantly expounding the Law for his own enjoyment. Through the fusion of the common mortal's three categories of action—mind, mouth, and body—with Mahāvairochana's three mysteries, people can understand the Buddha's teachings. Kōbō taught that, by forming mudras with one's hands, chanting mantras with one's mouth, and concentrating one's mind on mandalas as objects of devotion, one could become identical with Mahāvairochana Buddha. That is, Kōbō said that the practice of the three mysteries enabled one to attain Buddhahood in one's present form. Thus his teachings are referred to as esoteric.

Shakyamuni Buddha, on the other hand, who appeared in this world as a human being, expounded his teachings in accordance with the people's capacity. The True Word school claims that, because these teachings were expounded explicitly within the reach of the people's understanding, they are to be called exoteric and are inferior to the teachings of the transcendent Mahāvairochana Buddha. Esoteric teachings were also endorsed by the Tendai school. Tendai Esotericism was developed by Jikaku, the third chief priest of the Tendai school, Chishō, the fifth chief priest, and others. Unlike Kōbō's True Word school, Tendai Esotericism holds that Shakyamuni and Mahāvairochana are two aspects of the same

Buddha. Tendai Esotericism views the three vehicles as exoteric teachings, and the one vehicle as the esoteric teaching. It classifies such sutras as the Lotus and the Flower Garland as one vehicle, and therefore esoteric, sutras. Because they do not mention mudras and mantras, which constitute esoteric practice, however, those sutras are called esoteric teachings in theory, while the Mahāvairochana and Diamond Crown sutras are called esoteric teachings in both theory and practice. Tendai Esotericism claims that, while the Lotus and Mahāvairochana sutras are equal in terms of principle, the Mahāvairochana Sutra is superior in terms of practice.

esoteric teachings in both theory and practice [事理俱密] (Jpn *jiri-kumitsu*): *See* Esoteric Buddhism; esoteric teachings in theory.

esoteric teachings in theory [理秘密] (Jpn *ri-himitsu*): Also, esoteric teachings of theory. A concept set forth in Tendai Esotericism indicating those teachings that can be defined as esoteric teachings in terms of theory, but fail to describe mudras (hand gestures) and mantras (mystic formulas), which constitute esoteric practice. Tendai Esotericism divides the Buddhist teachings into exoteric teachings and esoteric teachings, viewing the three vehicle teaching as exoteric and the one vehicle teaching as esoteric. It goes on to classify esoteric teachings into esoteric teachings in theory and esoteric teachings in both theory and practice (or esoteric teachings of both theory and practice). Tendai Esotericism maintains that esoteric teachings in both theory and practice are superior to esoteric teachings in theory. It defines the Lotus, Flower Garland, and other sutras as esoteric teachings in theory, and the Mahāvairochana, Diamond Crown, and other sutras as esoteric teachings in both theory and practice because the former do not mention mudras and mantras, while the latter describe them. *See also* Tendai Esotericism.

Essay on the Protection of the Nation, An [守護国界章] (Jpn *Shugo-kokkai-shō*): A work written in 818 by Dengyō, the founder of the Japanese Tendai school. It refutes the arguments of Tokuitsu, a priest of the Japanese Dharma Characteristics (Hossō) school. Tokuitsu criticized Dengyō and the Tendai teachings from the standpoint of Dharma Characteristics doctrine. Tokuitsu asserted that the one vehicle teaching of the Lotus Sutra is a provisional teaching, while the three vehicle teachings are true teachings, and that some people are without the potential to attain Buddhahood. Countering this assertion, Dengyō maintained in this work that all people have the Buddha nature, and that the supreme vehicle of Buddhahood, or the one vehicle teaching, of the Lotus Sutra is the true teaching that leads all people to Buddhahood. *An Essay on the Protection of the Nation* is regarded as one of Dengyō's major writings.

essence of the Lotus Sutra in four phrases [四句の要法] (Jpn *shiku-no-yōbō*): The teaching transferred by Shakyamuni Buddha to Bodhisattva Superior Practices and the other Bodhisattvas of the Earth in the "Supernatural Powers" (twenty-first) chapter of the Lotus Sutra. *See* four-phrase essence of the Lotus Sutra.

essential nature of phenomena [法性] (Skt *dharmatā;* Jpn *hosshō*): Also, Dharma nature. The unchanging nature inherent in all things and phenomena. It is a concept equal to the "true aspect" (Jpn *jissō*) of all phenomena, or "the true aspect of reality" *(shinnyo)*. In Buddhism, the term *dharma* means both phenomena and the truth underlying them. A Buddha is defined as one who is enlightened to the essential nature of phenomena, and an ordinary person as one who is ignorant of this nature. Hence both enlightenment and ignorance, or darkness, originate from one source, the essential nature of phenomena.

Essentials of Rebirth in the Pure Land, The [往生要集] (Jpn *Ōjō-yōshū*): A work completed in 985 by Genshin, a priest of the Japanese Tendai school. It is a compilation of passages from more than 160 sutras and treatises regarding the subject of rebirth in the land of Amida Buddha. In this work, Genshin inspires fear of the sufferings of transmigration through the six paths and encourages people to arouse a longing for the Pure Land of Perfect Bliss, stressing meditation on Amida Buddha as the practice for attaining rebirth there. *The Essentials of Rebirth in the Pure Land* became extremely popular and lent tremendous impetus to the rise of Pure Land practices in Japan.

Essentials of the Eight Schools, The [八宗綱要] (Jpn *Hasshū-kōyō*): An outline of the eight schools of Buddhism prominent in Japan before the Kamakura period (1185–1333), written in 1268 by Gyōnen, a priest of the Japanese Flower Garland (Kegon) school. The work begins with an explanation of the fundamentals of Buddhism and the history of the spread of Buddhism from India to China and later to Japan. Then it refers to each of the eight schools: the Dharma Analysis Treasury (Kusha), Establishment of Truth (Jōjitsu), Precepts (Ritsu), Dharma Characteristics (Hossō), Three Treatises (Sanron), Tendai, Flower Garland, and True Word (Shingon) schools that flourished in Japan's Nara period (710–794) and Heian period (794–1185). Each school is described with regard to the meaning and origin of its name, the history of its formation and spread, and its basic scriptures and doctrines in India, China, and Japan. The work concludes with a brief explanation of the Zen and Pure Land schools, which were newer additions to Japanese Buddhism.

Essentials of "The Fourfold Rules of Discipline," The [四分律行事鈔] (Chin *Ssu-fen-lü-hsing-shih-ch'ao;* Jpn *Shibun-ritsu-gyōji-shō*): A commentary on *The Fourfold Rules of Discipline* written in 630 by Tao-hsüan, the founder of the Nan-shan branch of the Precepts (Lü) school in China. This work is regarded as one of the fundamental scriptures of the Nan-shan branch. It exerted a great influence on the establishment of the code of conduct for priests, and many subcommentaries on it were produced.

Essentials of the One Vehicle Teaching, The [一乗要決] (Jpn *Ichijō-yōketsu*): A treatise written around 1006 by Genshin, a priest of the Japanese Tendai school. Based on the Tendai doctrine, it stresses the one vehicle teaching of the Lotus Sutra and asserts that all people possess the Buddha nature. It attacks the "five natures" doctrine of the Dharma Characteristics (Hossō) school, which classifies sentient beings into five groups according to their inborn capacity, three of which it holds can never attain Buddhahood.

essential teaching [本門] (Jpn *hommon*): Also, original teaching. (1) The teaching expounded by Shakyamuni from the perspective of his true identity as the Buddha who attained enlightenment countless *kalpas* ago. It consists of the latter fourteen chapters of the Lotus Sutra, from the "Emerging from the Earth" (fifteenth) through the "Universal Worthy" (twenty-eighth) chapter. In *The Words and Phrases of the Lotus Sutra,* T'ien-t'ai (538–597) classifies the content of the sutra into two parts—the first fourteen chapters, or theoretical teaching (also known as trace teaching), and the latter fourteen chapters, or essential teaching (original teaching). He further explains that Shakyamuni expounded these two teachings from two respectively different identities: The Shakyamuni Buddha who attained enlightenment in India expounded the theoretical teaching, while the Shakyamuni who cast off his transient identity as the Buddha enlightened in that lifetime in India and revealed his true identity as the Buddha who attained enlightenment in the remote past expounded the essential teaching. T'ien-t'ai identified the Buddha of the essential teaching as the true Buddha, and the Buddha of the theoretical teaching as the true Buddha's provisional manifestation, or a provisional Buddha. He respectively compared the relationship between them and between their teachings to that of the moon in the sky and its reflection on the surface of a pond. In contrast with the theoretical teaching, which presents Buddhahood as a potential in the lives of all people, the essential teaching describes it as a reality manifest in the eternal life of the true Buddha. The core of the essential teaching is the "Life Span" (sixteenth) chapter, which reveals Shakyamuni's enlightenment in the distant past. Moreover, it reveals the three mystic principles: the true effect (the original enlightenment that Shakyamuni Buddha attained in the remote past), the true cause (the practice he carried out to attain that enlightenment), and the true land (where the Buddha lives and teaches); together they clarify the reality of the Buddha's enlightenment.

(2) In his writings, Nichiren (1222–1282) sometimes uses the term *essential teaching* to indicate the essential teaching of the Latter Day of the Law; that is, the teaching of Nam-myoho-renge-kyo. *The Object of Devotion for Observing the Mind* reads: "The essential teaching of Shakyamuni's lifetime and that revealed [by Nichiren] at the beginning of the Latter Day are both pure and perfect [in that both lead directly to Buddhahood]. Shakyamuni's, however, is the Buddhism of the harvest, and this is the Buddhism of sowing. The core of his teaching is one chapter and two halves, and the core of mine is the five characters of the daimoku alone" (370). Nichiren thus identified Nam-myoho-renge-kyo, the teaching he revealed at the "beginning of the Latter Day," as the essential teaching for that age. From this viewpoint, in the same treatise, Nichiren states: "The difference between the theoretical and the essential teachings is as great as that between heaven and earth. . . . Nevertheless, even the difference between the doctrine of three thousand realms in a single moment of life of the theoretical teaching and that of the essential teaching pales into insignificance" (368). That "difference . . . pales into insignificance" when it is compared with the difference between the essential teaching that is the latter half of the Lotus Sutra, and the essential teaching revealed by Nichiren at the beginning of the Latter Day of the Law, or Nam-myoho-renge-kyo. Hence he termed his essential teaching "the unique essential teaching" (Jpn *dokuichi-hommon*) in *On the Mystic Principle of the True Cause,* a writing he gave his immediate successor, Nikkō. *See also* fivefold view of revelation.

Essential Works of the Fuji School, The [富士宗学要集] (Jpn *Fuji-shūgaku-yōshū*): A work compiled by Nichikō (1867–1957), the fifty-ninth chief priest of Taiseki-ji, the head temple of Nichiren Shōshū (formerly known as the Fuji school) in Japan. Published in ten volumes in 1939, the work consists of major documents that he selected from his own compilation *The Complete Works of the Fuji School.* It includes the recorded oral teachings of Nichiren, records of debates, writings relating to doctrine, the history of the school, and other related matters.

Establishment of Truth school [成実宗] (Chin Ch'eng-shih-tsung; Jpn Jōjitsu-shū): Also known as the Satyasiddhi school. A school based on *The Treatise on the Establishment of Truth* (Skt *Satyasiddhi-shāstra*) authored by Harivarman (third or fourth century) of India and translated into Chinese in the early fifth century by Kumārajīva. This treatise expounds two levels of truth: the worldly truth, which recognizes the transitory nature of things and analyzes and divides them into eighty-four dharmas, or elements of existence, in five categories; and the supreme truth, which indicates that both the self and the dharmas are empty and without substance. On the basis of this doctrine of non-substantiality, it outlines twenty-seven stages of practice to free oneself from desires and illusions. *The Treatise on the Establishment of Truth* is generally regarded as the pinnacle of Hinayana philosophy and in some respects resembles Mahayana. In China, Kumārajīva's disciples Seng-tao and Seng-sung made an intense study of it, laying the foundation for the Establishment of Truth school. Study of *The Treatise on the Establishment of Truth* flourished during the Ch'i (479–502) and Liang (502–557) dynasties, and twenty-eight commentaries on it were produced during this period. In the Sui dynasty (581–618), however, after the rise of the Three Treatises (Chin San-lun; Jpn Sanron) school, which criticized the school's view of non-substantiality as Hinayanistic, the Establishment of Truth school declined. The doctrines of the school were introduced to Japan together with those of the Three Treatises school. The Establishment of Truth school is known as one of the thirteen schools of Chinese Buddhism, and in Japan it was one of the so-called six schools of Nara. In actuality, however, it never became an independent school in Japan and was always studied in conjunction with the Three Treatises system. A government proclamation of 806 lists the Establishment of Truth school as a branch of the Three Treatises school.

Ever Wailing [常啼菩薩] (Skt Sadāprarudita; Jpn Jōtai-bosatsu): A bodhisattva who appears in the Larger Wisdom Sutra and other Wisdom sutras, as well as the Sutra of Collected Birth Stories concerning the Practice of the Six Pāramitās. He is described as devoted to the pursuit of the perfection of wisdom, unconcerned with worldly fame or fortune. He was called Ever Wailing because he wept when, despite his efforts, he could not find a teacher from whom to seek the teaching of the perfection of wisdom. According to the Larger Wisdom Sutra, Ever Wailing sought the teaching from Bodhisattva Dharmodgata who lived in the City of Fragrances. Having nothing to offer him because of his poverty, Ever Wailing attempted to sell his body in the marketplace to obtain money for alms. The god Shakra decided to test his resolve. Assuming the form of a Brahman, he appeared to Ever Wailing and said that he needed a human heart, blood, and marrow to perform a ritual dedicated to heaven. Ever Wailing agreed to provide them, and voluntarily stabbed his arm with a knife to draw blood. Then, as he cut his thigh, broke open his bones, and was about to obtain the marrow, the daughter of a wealthy householder interrupted him and volunteered to provide whatever offerings Ever Wailing might require. Upon seeing this, Shakra revealed his true form and praised Ever Wailing for his devotion.

evil friend [悪知識] (Jpn *aku-chishiki*): Also, evil companion or evil teacher. One who causes others to fall into the evil paths by misleading them in connection with Buddhism. An evil friend deludes others with false teachings in order to obstruct their correct Buddhist practice. The Nirvana Sutra states: "Bodhisattvas and mahāsattvas, have no fear of mad elephants. What you should fear are evil friends! Why? Because a mad elephant can only destroy your body; it cannot destroy your mind. But an evil friend can destroy both body and mind. A mad elephant can destroy only a single body, but an evil friend can destroy countless bodies and countless minds. A mad elephant merely destroys an impure, stinking body, but an evil friend can destroy both a pure body and a pure mind. A mad elephant can destroy the physical body, but an evil friend destroys the Dharma body. Even if you are killed by a mad elephant, you will not fall into the three evil paths. But if you are killed by an evil friend, you are certain to fall into them. A mad elephant is merely an enemy of your body, but an evil friend is an enemy of the good Law. Therefore, bodhisattvas, you should at all times keep away from evil friends." The term *evil friend* is contrasted with *good friend* who helps lead people to the correct teaching. Evil friends refer to those who influence or approach other people with the intention of leading them away from correct Buddhist practice and to an erroneous teaching. Nichiren (1222–1282) suggests, however, that even the most evil of individuals—those who persecute or harass practitioners of the correct teaching—can function as good friends if one is determined to use their presence as a stimulus to deepen one's faith and practice and attain enlightenment. In *The Actions of the Votary of the Lotus Sutra,* he states, "Devadatta was the foremost good friend to the Thus Come One Shakyamuni. In this age as well, it is not one's allies but one's powerful enemies who assist one's progress" (770). See also *mitra.*

evil path [悪道・悪趣] (Skt *durgati;* Jpn *akudō* or *akushu*): Also, evil path(s) of existence. The realms of suffering into which fall those who have committed evil acts; also the suffering that such people undergo. "Path" here means a state of life or realm of existence. The worlds of hell, hungry spirits, and animals are called the three evil paths, and with the realm of *asuras* they are called the four evil paths.

exclusive practice of the Nembutsu [専修念仏] (Jpn *senju-nembutsu*): Also, single practice of the Nembutsu, exclusive reliance on the Nembutsu, or exclusive devotion to Nembutsu practice. To devote oneself solely to the practice of calling on the name of Amida Buddha in order to attain rebirth in the Pure Land, discarding all other practices. The

Nembutsu here indicates the practice of calling on the name of Amida Buddha. Hōnen (1133–1212), the founder of the Japanese Pure Land (Jōdo) school, defined the exclusive practice of the Nembutsu to be the essence of his teaching and encouraged all people to concentrate on this single practice. In *The Nembutsu Chosen above All,* he maintains that, if people wish to be reborn in the Pure Land of Amida Buddha, they should practice the Nembutsu exclusively.

exoteric teachings [顕教] (Jpn *kenkyō*): Those teachings that were revealed openly or explicitly for all listeners, in contrast with the esoteric teachings, which were taught secretly, implicitly, or exclusively to certain individuals. The True Word (Jpn Shingon) school divides Buddhism into exoteric and esoteric teachings. It defines all the teachings of Shakyamuni Buddha as exoteric teachings expounded in accord with the people's capacity, and the teachings of Mahāvairochana Buddha as esoteric teachings. *See also* Esoteric Buddhism.

expanded replacement of the three vehicles with the one vehicle [広開三顕一] (Jpn *kōkaisan-ken'ichi*): *See* replacement of the three vehicles with the one vehicle.

expedient means [方便] (Skt, Pali *upāya;* Jpn *hōben*): The methods adopted to instruct people and lead them to enlightenment. The concept of expedient means is highly regarded in Mahayana Buddhism, especially in the Lotus Sutra, as represented by its second chapter titled "Expedient Means." This is because expedient means are skillfully devised and employed by Buddhas and bodhisattvas to lead the people to salvation. According to the Lotus Sutra, the three vehicles of the voice-hearer, cause-awakened one, and bodhisattva are provisional teachings and expedient means designed to lead people to the one Buddha vehicle, or the teaching that leads all people to Buddhahood. The teaching that directly reveals the truth of enlightenment is called the true teaching, while the teachings that are expounded in accordance with the people's capacity and as a temporary means of leading people to the truth are called expedient teachings or provisional teachings. *See also* three expedient means.

"Expedient Means" chapter [方便品] (Jpn *Hōben-bon*): The second chapter of the Lotus Sutra, in which Shakyamuni Buddha reveals that the purpose of a Buddha's advent in the world is to lead all people to enlightenment. Shakyamuni shows that all people have the potential for Buddhahood, namely, that Buddhahood is not separate from ordinary people but is inherent in their lives. It is the principal chapter of the theoretical teaching (first half) of the Lotus Sutra and one of the two pivotal chapters of the entire sutra, the other being the "Life Span" (sixteenth) chapter, the core of the essential teaching (latter half). At the beginning of the second chapter, Shakyamuni arises from the deep meditation called the *samādhi* of the origin of immeasurable meanings, and addresses Shāriputra, declaring that the wisdom of the Buddhas is infinitely profound and immeasurable, far beyond the comprehension of voice-hearers and cause-awakened ones. Only Buddhas, he says, can realize the true aspect of all phenomena, which consists of appearance, nature, entity, power, influence, internal cause, relation, latent effect, manifest effect, and consistency from beginning to end. This revelation that all living beings of the Ten Worlds are innately endowed with and can manifest the true aspect identified as "the ten factors of life" establishes a theoretical basis for the subsequent assertion that all people have the potential to attain Buddhahood. Based on this passage, T'ien-t'ai (538–597) established the principle of three thousand realms in a single moment of life.

Shakyamuni then reveals that the Buddhas make their advent for "one great reason": to enable all people to attain the same enlightenment as themselves. According to the chapter, their purpose is "to open the door of Buddha wisdom to all living beings, to show the Buddha wisdom to living beings, to cause living beings to awaken to the Buddha wisdom, and induce living beings to enter the path of Buddha wisdom." Shakyamuni goes on to state that the three vehicles, or the teachings for voice-hearers, cause-awakened ones, and bodhisattvas, are not ends in themselves, but are expedient means by which he leads people to the one Buddha vehicle. This concept is referred to as "the replacement of the three vehicles with the one vehicle."

eye-begging Brahman [乞眼の婆羅門] (Jpn *kotsugen-no-baramon*): (1) A Brahman who begged for Shāriputra's eye when the latter was practicing austerities in a previous existence. The story is found in *The Treatise on the Great Perfection of Wisdom.* In the distant past, Shāriputra, practicing the bodhisattva way, engaged in the offering of alms. When he had practiced almsgiving for sixty *kalpas,* a Brahman came to him and begged for his eye. (*Great Perfection of Wisdom* itself does not depict this beggar as a Brahman, but in later references he is often described as such.) Shāriputra gouged out one of his own eyes and gave it to him. But the Brahman was so revolted by the smell of the eye that he spat on it, dropped it on the ground, and trampled it. Seeing this, Shāriputra thought it too difficult to lead such persons to salvation and decided to seek only his own liberation from the sufferings of birth and death; he withdrew from bodhisattva practice, backsliding into the Hinayana teachings, or the way of voice-hearers.

(2) A Brahman who begged for the eye of Shakyamuni in a previous

existence. This tale of Shakyamuni offering his eye to the Brahman appears in the *Jātaka,* or stories of the previous lives of Shakyamuni Buddha. In one lifetime, Shakyamuni was a king named Shibi who endeavored to donate gold and various other goods to the people. The king, thinking that the true offering was to selflessly donate his body, declared he would give his body to anyone who wanted it. To test his resolve, the god Shakra assumed the form of a blind Brahman and appeared before the king. The Brahman requested one of the king's eyes. The king willingly gave his eye to the Brahman and went on to give the other eye even without being asked. Thereupon Shakra revealed his true form and with his powers restored to the king his eyes and vision.

eye-opening ceremony [開眼供養] (Jpn *kaigen-kuyō*): Also, "opening of the eyes" ceremony. A ceremony to "open the eyes" of, or consecrate, newly created statues or painted images of a Buddha. It is performed in the belief that the image can thereby be endowed with spiritual properties. Through this ceremony, in which a Buddhist teaching is invoked, the image is believed to become equal to the living Buddha. This idea accords with the principle of the attainment of Buddhahood by insentient beings or the enlightenment of plants. "Plants" here refers to all insentient things. Nichiren (1222–1282) attributes the concept of the enlightenment of plants to T'ien-t'ai's doctrine of three thousand realms in a single moment of life derived from the Lotus Sutra, and states that the eye-opening ceremony of a Buddhist statue or image is effective only when conducted on the basis of the Lotus Sutra.

F

face-covering tongue [覆面舌] (Jpn *fumen-zetsu*): One of a Buddha's thirty-two features. *See* long broad tongue.

Fa-chao [法照] (n.d.) (PY Fazhao; Jpn Hōshō or Hosshō): A priest of the Pure Land teaching in China in the eighth century. He initiated a new form of reciting the name of Amida Buddha, the basic practice of that school, in which Amida's name is chanted in five distinct tones. This, he claimed, Amida himself had taught him. He successfully propagated the Pure Land teachings and was honored with the title Teacher of the Nation by the emperor.

Fa-ch'üan [法全] (n.d.) (PY Faquan; Jpn Hassen): A priest of Esoteric Buddhism of the late T'ang dynasty (618–907) in China. He transmitted the esoteric doctrines to Jikaku and Chishō, later respectively the third and the fifth chief priest of Enryaku-ji, the head temple of the Japanese Tendai school, when they journeyed to China (Jikaku in 838 and Chishō in 853). He wrote many treatises on Esoteric Buddhism.

Fa-hsiang school [法相宗] (PY Faxiangzong; Jpn Hossō-shū): *See* Dharma Characteristics school.

Fa-hsien (PY Faxian) (1) [法顯] (c. 340–420) (Jpn Hokken): A Chinese Buddhist pilgrim who traveled to India to seek Buddhist scriptures. Deploring the lack of Buddhist scriptures in China, around age sixty he left Ch'ang-an in 399 and journeyed overland to India, where he studied Sanskrit and the three divisions of the Buddhist canon. In 414 he returned to China by sea, bringing many Buddhist texts and images. With Buddhabhadra, he translated six works in sixty-three volumes including the Mahāparinirvāna Sutra and *The Great Canon of Monastic Rules*. Fa-hsien's *Record of the Buddhistic Kingdoms*, a record of his travels, includes valuable historical material concerning India and Central Asian countries in his time.

(2) [法賢] (d. 1001) (Jpn Hōken): A translator of Buddhist scriptures into Chinese. A native of India, he traveled to China, where he translated seventy-six scriptures into Chinese during the period from 989 through 999. His Sanskrit name is unknown.

faith [信] (Skt *shraddhā;* Pali *saddhā;* Jpn *shin*): A basic attitude emphasized in both early Buddhism and Mahayana Buddhism. Faith constitutes the first of the five roots, or the five elements of practice conducive to enlightenment, expounded in early Buddhism. The five roots are faith, exertion, memory, meditation, and wisdom. Mahayana Buddhism likewise emphasizes the importance of faith. The Flower Garland Sutra says, "Faith is the basis of the way and the mother of blessings." The Mahāparinirvāna Sutra says, "Although there are innumerable practices that lead to enlightenment, if one teaches faith, then that includes all those practices." In the Lotus Sutra, Shakyamuni addresses Shāriputra, who was known as foremost in wisdom, as follows: "Even you, Shāriputra, in the case of this sutra were able to gain entrance through faith alone. How much more so, then, the other voice-hearers." *The Treatise on the Great Perfection of Wisdom* attributed to Nāgārjuna (c. 150–250) reads, "The great ocean of Buddhism can be entered through faith." In *Great Concentration and Insight,* T'ien-t'ai (538–597) states, "Buddhism is like an ocean that one can only enter with faith."

Another Sanskrit word for faith is *adhimukti,* which means confidence and is rendered in Chinese Buddhism as "belief and understanding." It means faith based on understanding; it also means to first take faith in the Buddha's teaching and then to understand it. *Adhimukti* is the Sanskrit title of the "Belief and Understanding" (fourth) chapter of the Lotus Sutra translated by Kumārajīva. The "Distinctions in Benefits" (seventeenth) chapter of the Lotus Sutra says, "Ajita, if there are living beings who, on hearing that the life span of the Buddha is of such long duration, are able to believe and understand it even for a moment, the benefits they gain thereby will be without limit or measure." In *The Record of the Orally Transmitted Teachings,* Nichiren (1222–1282) states: "Belief represents the value or price we attach to a jewel or treasure, and understanding represents the jewel itself. It is through the one word *belief* that we are able to purchase the wisdom of the Buddhas of the three existences. That wisdom is Nam-myoho-renge-kyo." *See also* faith, practice, and study.

faith, practice, and study [信行学] (Jpn *shin-gyō-gaku*): The three fundamentals in the practice of Nichiren's teachings. Faith means to believe in the Gohonzon, or the object of devotion. Practice means to chant the daimoku of Nam-myoho-renge-kyo, as well as to explain Nichiren's teachings to others. Study means to study and understand the Buddhist teachings. Among these three, faith is the most fundamental for the attainment of Buddhahood. Faith gives rise to practice and study, and practice and study serve to deepen faith. In *The True Aspect of All Phenomena,* written in 1273, Nichiren states: "Believe in the Gohonzon, the supreme object of devotion in all of Jambudvīpa. Be sure to strengthen your faith, and receive the protection of Shakyamuni, Many Treasures, and the Buddhas of the ten directions. Exert yourself in the two ways of practice and study. Without practice and study, there can be no Buddhism. You must not only persevere yourself; you must also teach others. Both practice and study arise from faith. Teach others to the best of your ability, even if it is only a single sentence or phrase" (386).

Fa-lang [法朗] (507–581) (PY Falang; Jpn Hōrō): A priest of the Three Treatises (San-lun) school in China. Since he lived at Hsing-huang-ssu temple, he is also known as Hsing-huang. In 527 he renounced secular life and studied meditation under Pao-chih at Ta-ming-ssu temple. After that, he traveled and studied the *vinaya,* or rules of monastic discipline, and the teachings of the Abhidharma (P'i-t'an) and the Establishment of Truth (Ch'eng-shih) schools. At Chih-kuan-ssu temple, he studied *The Treatise on the Great Perfection of Wisdom, The Treatise on the Middle Way, The One-Hundred-Verse Treatise,* and *The Treatise on the Twelve Gates* under Seng-ch'üan. He also studied the Flower Garland and Wisdom sutras. He was revered as one of Seng-ch'üan's four main disciples. In

558, in compliance with imperial decree, he settled at Hsing-huang-ssu temple in the capital and lectured on the above four treatises. Chi-tsang was his successor.

Fa-pao [法宝] (n.d.) (PY Fabao; Jpn Hōbō): A priest of the early T'ang dynasty (618–907) in China. He contributed to the translation of Buddhist scriptures as one of Hsüan-tsang's major disciples. He also wrote *The Annotations on "The Dharma Analysis Treasury."* This work is considered one of the three major annotations on *The Dharma Analysis Treasury,* along with two others written by P'u-kuang and Shen-t'ai.

farther shore [彼岸] (Jpn *higan*): The shore of enlightenment; i.e., nirvana, or the state of enlightenment. *See* other shore.

Fa-shun [法順] (PY Fashun; Jpn Hōjun): Also known as Tu-shun, the founder of the Flower Garland (Hua-yen) school in China. *See* Tu-shun.

Fa-tao [法道] (1086–1147) (PY Fadao; Jpn Hōdō): Also known as Yung-tao or the Tripitaka Master Fa-tao. A Buddhist priest of China who remonstrated with Hui-tsung, the eighth emperor of the Northern Sung dynasty. Emperor Hui-tsung, a confirmed Taoist, revered the philosophy of Lao Tzu and Chuang Tzu and in 1119 decided to replace some terms and titles used in Buddhism with those of Taoism. Fa-tao opposed this move, incurring the emperor's wrath. He was branded on the face and exiled to Tao-chou, south of the Yangtze River.

Fa-tsang [法蔵] (643–712) (PY Fazang; Jpn Hōzō): Also known as Hsien-shou or the Great Teacher Hsien-shou. The third patriarch of the Flower Garland (Hua-yen) school in China. His family was originally from Central Asia. In 659 he entered the Buddhist learning center at Mount T'ai-po as a layman and began to study the Buddhist scriptures. Later he learned the Flower Garland doctrines from Chih-yen at the capital, Lo-yang. In 670 he became a priest in compliance with an imperial directive. In 695 he assisted Shikshānanda with his eighty-volume translation of the Flower Garland Sutra. He contributed greatly to the systematization of the Flower Garland doctrine, wrote many commentaries, and formulated a classification system called the "five teachings and ten doctrines" to demonstrate the superiority of the Flower Garland Sutra. Hence the Hua-yen school is also called the Hsien-shou (Jpn Genju) school. He lectured widely on the Flower Garland Sutra and built Flower Garland temples in Lo-yang, Ch'ang-an, and elsewhere.

Fa-tsu [法祖] (n.d.) (PY Fazu; Jpn Hōso): Also known as Po-yüan or Po Fa-tsu. A priest and a translator of Buddhist texts during the late Western Chin dynasty (265–316) in China. He built a Buddhist monastery at Ch'ang-an, where he translated and lectured on Buddhist scriptures. In 305 he set out for Lung-yu, where he intended to live in retirement. He was killed along the way, however, because of his refusal to work for Chang Fu, the local governor of Ch'in-chou, and also because of accusations lodged by someone he had defeated in debate. The Buddha's Parinirvāna Sutra, one of the Hinayana versions of the Nirvana Sutra, was translated by Fa-tsu.

Fa-yün [法雲] (PY Fayun; Jpn Hōun): (1) (467–529) A priest revered as one of the three great Dharma teachers of China's Liang dynasty, the others being Chih-tsang and Seng-min. He joined the priesthood in 473 and studied under Seng-yin. He gained renown with his lectures on the Lotus Sutra and the Vimalakīrti Sutra in 496, and in 508 Emperor Wu appointed him chief priest of Kuang-che-ssu temple. The emperor often invited him to lecture at court. Emperor Wu built Fa-yün-ssu temple for him in 519, and in 525 Fa-yün was appointed general administrator of priests, the highest rank in the priesthood. He also wrote a commentary on the Lotus Sutra titled *The Meaning of the Lotus Sutra.*

(2) (1087–1158) A priest of China who compiled *A Dictionary of the Pronunciation and Meaning of Buddhist Terms,* a Sanskrit–Chinese Buddhist dictionary, in 1143. He is said to have spent some twenty years compiling the text. He also lectured on the Lotus, Golden Light, Nirvana, and Vimalakīrti sutras.

fearlessness [無畏] (Skt *vaishāradya;* Jpn *mui*): A quality of Buddhas and bodhisattvas. Buddhist scriptures often refer to the virtue of fearlessness, characterizing the Buddha as undaunted by any hardship, obstacle, or suffering, and as fearless in preaching. Buddhist scriptures set forth four kinds of fearlessness, or four fearlessnesses, that come into play while preaching the Law. Buddhist practitioners are required not only to be dauntless in their practice but also to give fearlessness, or security, to those who are in difficult conditions; in other words, to release them from affliction. Bodhisattva Perceiver of the World's Sounds, for example, is called Bestower of Fearlessness. *See also* four fearlessnesses.

field of good fortune [福田] (Skt *punya-kshetra;* Jpn *fukuden*): A field that produces good fortune. It is used as a simile for that which enables people to gain good fortune. A Buddha is often referred to as a great field of good fortune. "Field of good fortune" is also applied to Buddhist practice that gives rise to good fortune, and to one who carries out the Buddhist practice and thereby cultivates good fortune within oneself. The Sanskrit word *punya* means good fortune, blessing, or meritorious act, and *kshetra* means field, land, region, country, sphere of action, or sacred place.

fiery pit [火坑] (Jpn *kakyō* or *kakō*): Also, pit of fire or fire pit. A metaphor for hell, which Buddhist scriptures say burns those who dwell there in its flames. Fiery pit is also a metaphor for earthly desires, which torment and consume people.

fifth five-hundred-year period [後五百歳] (Jpn *go-gohyakusai*): Also, last five-hundred-year period or fifth half-millennium. The last of the five five-hundred-year periods described as following Shakyamuni's death. It corresponds to the beginning of the Latter Day of the Law. The Great Collection Sutra predicts in some detail the course that the development of Buddhism will take in the twenty-five hundred years, or five half-millennia, following the Buddha's death. The fifth five-hundred-year period indicates the first five hundred years of the Latter Day of the Law and is called "the age of quarrels and disputes" or "the age of conflict." The sutra predicts that during this period, various rival Buddhist schools will quarrel incessantly among themselves, and Shakyamuni's correct teachings will be obscured and lost. T'ien-t'ai of China and Dengyō and Nichiren of Japan, however, viewed the fifth five-hundred-year period as the time when the supreme teaching would spread. In the "Medicine King" (twenty-third) chapter of the Lotus Sutra, Shakyamuni states, "After I have passed into extinction, in the last five-hundred-year period you must spread it abroad widely throughout Jambudvīpa and never allow it to be cut off." *See also* three periods.

fifth scroll of the Lotus Sutra [法華経第五の巻] (Jpn *Hokekyō-daigo-no-maki*): Also, scroll of the fifth volume of the Lotus Sutra. The fifth of the eight scrolls, or volumes, of the Lotus Sutra. The fifth scroll contains four chapters—the "Devadatta" (twelfth) chapter through the "Emerging from the Earth" (fifteenth) chapter. Among them, the "Encouraging Devotion" (thirteenth) chapter predicts that those who propagate the sutra after Shakyamuni Buddha's death will be persecuted by the three powerful enemies and attacked with swords and staves. Nichiren mentions in his writings that he was beaten with the fifth scroll of the Lotus Sutra. That incident occurred just before the attempt to execute Nichiren known as the Tatsunokuchi Persecution. When Hei no Saemon, a leading official of the shogunate, came with a group of soldiers to arrest Nichiren at Matsubagayatsu in Kamakura on the twelfth day of the ninth month in 1271, one of his men, Shō-bō, snatched a scroll of the fifth volume of the Lotus Sutra from Nichiren and struck him in the face with it. That scroll was wound around a wooden roller, and Nichiren accordingly interpreted this assault as his being "attacked with staves," one of the hardships predicted in the "Encouraging Devotion" chapter to befall the sutra's votary. Nichiren saw special significance in the fact that the "Encouraging Devotion" chapter is contained in the fifth scroll of the Lotus Sutra.

fifty-two stages of bodhisattva practice [五十二位] (Jpn *gojūni-i*): Also, fifty-two stages of practice. The stages through which bodhisattvas advance from the time of their initial resolve until they finally attain Buddhahood. The fifty-two stages are enumerated in the Jeweled Necklace Sutra and consist of ten stages of faith, ten stages of security, ten stages of practice, ten stages of devotion, ten stages of development, the stage of near-perfect enlightenment, and the stage of perfect enlightenment. The Brahmā Net Sutra divides bodhisattva practice into forty stages. The Benevolent Kings Sutra divides it into fifty-one stages, and there is an explanation elsewhere that sets forth forty-one stages.

figurative lotus [譬喩蓮華] (Jpn *hiyu-renge*): Also, figurative *renge* or lotus as a metaphor. According to T'ien-t'ai's *Profound Meaning of the Lotus Sutra,* the lotus used as a metaphor to explain the essence of the Lotus Sutra. Since the principle expounded in the sutra simultaneously possesses both cause and effect, it is difficult to explain. Therefore the lotus plant, which blooms (cause) and produces fruit (effect) at the same time, is employed as a metaphor to describe this principle of simultaneous causality. The term *figurative lotus* stands in contrast with the *lotus as the entity of the Law,* the latter meaning the lotus that is not a metaphor, but an expression of the Law itself. See also *renge.*

figurative renge [譬喩蓮華] (Jpn *hiyu-renge*): *See* figurative lotus.

fire pit [火坑] (Jpn *kakyō* or *kakō*): *See* fiery pit.

fire-pit meditation [火坑三昧] (Jpn *kakyō-zammai* or *kakō-sammai*): Also, fire pit of meditation. A meditation undisturbed by flames and heat. It is said that even the flames and heat of hell do not affect one who has obtained the fire-pit meditation.

Firmly Established Practices [安立行菩薩] (Skt Supratishthitachāritra; Jpn Anryūgyō-bosatsu): One of the four bodhisattvas who are the leaders of the Bodhisattvas of the Earth. He appears in the "Emerging from the Earth" (fifteenth) chapter of the Lotus Sutra. The chapter says: "Among these bodhisattvas were four leaders. The first was called Superior Practices, the second was called Boundless Practices, the third was called Pure Practices, and the fourth was called Firmly Established Practices. These four bodhisattvas were the foremost leaders and guiding teachers among all the group."

According to Tao-hsien's *Supplement to "The Words and Phrases of the Lotus Sutra,"* the four bodhisattvas represent the four virtues of a Buddha: true self, eternity, purity, and happiness. Bodhisattva Firmly Established Practices represents happiness.

first four flavors [前四味・四味] (Jpn *zen-shimi* or *shimi*): Also, four flavors, four tastes, four inferior flavors, or four preceding flavors. The first four of the five flavors—those of fresh milk, cream, curdled milk, butter, and ghee (the finest clarified butter). T'ien-t'ai (538–597) used the five flavors as a metaphor for the Buddhist teachings of the five periods—the Flower Garland, Āgama, Correct and Equal, Wisdom, and Lotus and Nirvana periods. He compared the process by which Shakyamuni Buddha instructed his disciples and gradually developed their capacity for enlightenment to the process whereby milk is converted into ghee. The four flavors indicate all the sutras expounded before the Lotus and Nirvana period, in other words, the pre-Lotus Sutra teachings. The ghee represents the teachings of the Lotus and the Nirvana sutras. The expression "the four flavors and three teachings" can also indicate the entire body of teachings preached before the Lotus Sutra. The three teachings are the first three of the four teachings of doctrine—the Tripitaka teaching, the connecting teaching, the specific teaching, and the perfect teaching.

first stage of development [初地] (Jpn *shoji*): The first of the ten stages of development, which corresponds to the forty-first of the fifty-two stages of bodhisattva practice. This stage is also called the stage of joy; those at this stage rejoice in realizing a partial aspect of the truth. *See also* ten stages of development.

first stage of security [初住] (Jpn *shojū*): The first of the ten stages of security, which corresponds to the eleventh of the fifty-two stages of bodhisattva practice. At this stage, one arouses the aspiration for Buddhahood. It is regarded as the point at which bodhisattvas no longer regress in practice. The "Life Span" (sixteenth) chapter of the Lotus Sutra reads, "Originally I [Shakyamuni Buddha] practiced the bodhisattva way." In *The Words and Phrases of the Lotus Sutra,* T'ien-t'ai (538–597) interprets the above passage, saying, "When the Buddha carried out the perfect cause (i.e., the cause for attaining the perfect effect—the bodhisattva practice for attaining Buddhahood) and reached the first stage of security, he acquired eternal life." Nichiren (1222–1282) defined the teaching that Shakyamuni practiced to attain the first stage of security as Nam-myoho-renge-kyo. *See also* true cause.

five Āgamas [五部] (Jpn *go-bu*): The five divisions of the Pali Āgama, the sutra section of the canon of Theravāda Buddhism. They are thought to have been set down in writing around the first century B.C.E., having been passed down by way of oral tradition until then. The five Āgamas are *Dīgha-nikāya* (long sutras), *Majjhima-nikāya* (medium-length sutras), *Samyutta-nikāya* (sutras on related topics), *Anguttara-nikāya* (sutras of numerical doctrines), and *Khuddaka-nikāya* (minor sutras). The first four correspond respectively to the four Chinese Āgama sutras: the Long Āgama Sutra, the Medium-Length Āgama Sutra, the Miscellaneous

Āgama Sutra, and the Increasing by One Āgama Sutra. *See also* four Āgama sutras.

five aggregates [五陰] (Jpn *go-on*): *See* five components.

five ascetic practices [五法] (Jpn *go-hō*): Five rules of conduct for monks referred to in *The Fourfold Rules of Discipline* and *The Great Commentary on the Abhidharma.* They are (1) to wear clothing of patched rags, (2) to subsist only on alms, (3) to eat only one meal a day, (4) to remain always outdoors, and (5) to refrain from eating sweet, sour, bitter, spicy, or salty food.

five ascetics [五比丘] (Jpn *go-biku*): The first converts of Shakyamuni Buddha. Their names are Ājnāta Kaundinya, Ashvajit, Mahānāma, Bhadrika, and Vāshpa, though these differ somewhat according to the source. The Buddha's Preaching Life Sutra lists Dashabala Kāshyapa as one of the five ascetics instead of Vāshpa. When Shakyamuni renounced secular life, his father, Shuddhodana, anxious about his son's safety, dispatched these five men to accompany him. Together with Shakyamuni they engaged in ascetic practice. When Shakyamuni rejected asceticism, they thought that he had abandoned the search for truth altogether and left him, going to Deer Park in Vārānasī to continue their austere practice. After he attained enlightenment, Shakyamuni sought them out as the first people to whom he would preach. According to scriptural accounts, the five at first resolved to greet him with coolness, regarding him as a backslider. But when Shakyamuni approached them, they were struck by his dignified bearing and welcomed him in spite of themselves. They listened to his teachings and became his first disciples.

five Buddhas [五仏] (Jpn *go-butsu*): Buddhas depicted on the Diamond Realm and Womb Realm mandalas, the two objects of devotion in the True Word (Jpn Shingon) school. The five Buddhas on the Diamond Realm mandala are Mahāvairochana in the center, Akshobhya in the east, Jewel Born in the south, Amida (also known as Infinite Life) in the west, and Infallible Realization in the north. The five Buddhas on the Womb Realm mandala are Mahāvairochana in the center, Jeweled Banner in the east, Florescence King in the south, Infinite Life (Amida) in the west, and Heavenly Drum Thunder in the north. In either case, the four Buddhas of the four directions represent the attributes of Mahāvairochana, whom the True Word school holds to be all-encompassing. *See also* five wisdom Buddhas.

five cardinal sins [五逆・五逆罪] (Jpn *go-gyaku* or *go-gyakuzai*): The five most serious offenses in Buddhism. Explanations vary according to the sutras and treatises. The most common is (1) killing one's father, (2) killing one's mother, (3) killing an arhat, (4) injuring a Buddha, and

(5) causing disunity in the Buddhist Order. It is said that those who commit any of the five cardinal sins invariably fall into the hell of incessant suffering. The last three offenses are collectively referred to as the three cardinal sins. Devadatta is well known for committing these three.

five categories of Buddhas [五仏] (Jpn *go-butsu*): The five kinds of Buddhas indicated in the "Expedient Means" (second) chapter of the Lotus Sutra. They are all Buddhas, past Buddhas, present Buddhas, future Buddhas, and Shakyamuni Buddha. According to this chapter, all these Buddhas preach in a uniform manner. That is, the Buddhas all employ a similar process by which to lead people to the one Buddha vehicle. With the purpose of enabling people to attain Buddhahood, they first expound various vehicles or teachings as expedient means to develop people's capacity, after which they reveal the one Buddha vehicle, the direct path to Buddhahood.

five components [五陰・五蘊] (Skt *pancha-skandha;* Jpn *go-on* or *go-un*): Also, five components of life, five aggregates, or five *skandhas.* The five components are form, perception, conception, volition, and consciousness. Buddhism holds that these constituent elements unite temporarily to form an individual living being. Together they also constitute one of the three realms of existence, the other two being the realm of living beings and the realm of the environment. (1) Form means the physical aspect of life and includes the five sense organs—eyes, ears, nose, tongue, and body—with which one perceives the external world. (2) Perception is the function of receiving external information through the six sense organs (the five sense organs plus the "mind," which integrates the impressions of the five senses). (3) Conception is the function of creating mental images and concepts out of what has been perceived. (4) Volition is the will that acts on the conception and motivates action. (5) Consciousness is the cognitive function of discernment that integrates the components of perception, conception, and volition. Form represents the physical aspect of life, while perception, conception, volition, and consciousness represent the spiritual aspect. Because the physical and spiritual aspects of life are inseparable, there can be no form without consciousness, and no consciousness without form. All life carries on its activities through the interaction of these five components. Their workings are colored by the karma one formed in previous lifetimes and at the same time create new karma.

five correct practices [五正行・五種の正行] (Jpn *go-shōgyō* or *goshu-no-shōgyō*): Also, five kinds of correct practices. Practices for attaining rebirth in the Pure Land, expounded by Shan-tao (613–681) in his *Commentary on the Meditation on the Buddha Infinite Life Sutra.* According to that work, correct practices are those related to Amida Buddha. They are (1) to read and recite the three basic scriptures of the Pure Land school—the Buddha Infinite Life Sutra, the Meditation on the Buddha Infinite Life Sutra, and the Amida Sutra; (2) to meditate on Amida Buddha and his Pure Land; (3) to worship Amida Buddha; (4) to call on Amida Buddha's name; and (5) to praise and give offerings to Amida Buddha. Among these, Shan-tao designated the practice of calling on Amida Buddha's name as the primary practice, and the other four as auxiliary practices. Shan-tao used the term "correct practices" in contrast with "sundry practices," the latter signifying all Buddhist practices not related to Amida Buddha. *See also* five sundry practices.

five defilements [五濁] (Jpn *go-joku*): *See* five impurities.

five delusive inclinations [五鈍使] (Jpn *go-donshi*): Greed, anger, foolishness, arrogance, and doubt. According to *The Dharma Analysis Treasury*, the five delusive inclinations constitute the most fundamental of illusions or earthly desires. Dharmapāla (530–561), an Indian scholar of the Consciousness-Only doctrine, defined the five delusive inclinations and the five false views together as the ten fundamental earthly desires, and T'ien-t'ai (538–597) included them among the illusions of thought and desire, which constitute the first of the three categories of illusion. *See also* earthly desires.

five desires [五欲] (Jpn *go-yoku*): (1) The desires that arise from the contact of the five sense organs (eyes, ears, nose, tongue, and body) with their respective objects (color and form, sound, smell, taste, and texture). (2) The desires for wealth, sexual love, food and drink, fame, and sleep.

five elements [五大] (Jpn *go-dai*): According to ancient Indian belief, the five constituents of all things in the universe. They are earth, water, fire, wind, and space. The first four correspond respectively to the physical states of solid, liquid, heat, and gas. Space is interpreted as integrating and harmonizing the other four elements.

five false views [五利使] (Jpn *go-rishi*): According to *The Treatise on the Establishment of the Consciousness-Only Doctrine*, the five views that, along with the five delusive inclinations, constitute the ten fundamental earthly desires. T'ien-t'ai (538–597) included these ten in the illusions of thought and desire, the first of the three categories of illusion. The five false views are: (1) Though the mind and body are no more than a temporary union of the five components, one regards them as possessing a self that is absolute; and though nothing in the universe can belong to an individual, one views one's mind and body as one's own possession; (2) the belief in one of two extremes concerning existence: that life ends with death, or that life persists after death in some eternal and unchanging form; (3) denial of the law of cause and effect; (4) adhering to misconceptions and viewing them as truth, while regarding inferior views as superior; and (5) viewing erroneous practices or precepts as the correct way to enlightenment. *See also* earthly desires.

five five-hundred-year periods [五箇の五百歳] (Jpn *goka-no-gohyaku-sai*): Five consecutive periods following Shakyamuni's death, during which Buddhism is said to spread, prosper, and eventually decline. These five periods are described in the Great Collection Sutra and predict the course of Buddhism in the first twenty-five hundred years following Shakyamuni's death. In chronological sequence, the five five-hundred-year periods are (1) the "age of attaining liberation," in which many people attain emancipation through practicing the Buddha's teachings; (2) the "age of meditation," when meditation is widely practiced; (3) the "age of reading, reciting, and listening," in which the people study and recite the sutras and hear lectures on them as their central practice; (4) the "age of building temples and stupas," when many temples and stupas are built, but the spirit of seeking the Buddhist teachings declines; and (5) the "age of quarrels and disputes," also known as the age of conflict, when strife occurs among the various rival schools and Shakyamuni Buddha's teachings become obscured and lost. In terms of the three periods, the age of attaining liberation and the age of meditation correspond to the Former Day of the Law; the age of reading, reciting, and listening and the age of building temples and stupas correspond to the Middle Day of the Law; and the age of quarrels and disputes corresponds to the beginning of the Latter Day of the Law. Regarding this fifth period, Shakyamuni says in the Great Collection Sutra, "Quarrels and disputes will arise among the adherents to my teachings, and the pure Law will become obscured and lost."

five flavors [五味] (Jpn *go-mi*): Also, five tastes. The flavors of fresh milk, cream, curdled milk, butter, and ghee—the five stages in the process by which milk is made into ghee, or the finest clarified butter. In the Mahāparinirvāna Sutra, Shakyamuni says, "Good man, milk comes from the cow, cream is made from milk, curdled milk is made from cream, butter is made from curdled milk, and ghee is made from butter. Ghee is the finest of all. One who eats it will be cured of all illnesses, just as if all kinds of medicinal properties were contained in it." T'ien-t'ai (538–597) used these five flavors as a metaphor for his doctrine of the five periods. The "five periods" is a classification of Shakyamuni's entire body of teachings according to the order in which T'ien-t'ai believed they were expounded. They are the Flower Garland period, the Āgama period, the Correct and Equal period, the Wisdom period, and the Lotus and Nirvana period. T'ien-t'ai compared this process by which Shakyamuni instructed his disciples and elevated their understanding to the process of converting milk into ghee.

fivefold bodies of the Law [五分法身] (Jpn *gobun-hosshin*): Five meritorious attributes or aspects of arhats and Buddhas. They are precept body, meditation body, wisdom body, emancipation body, and knowledge-of-emancipation body. This term is interpreted to mean that the bodies and lives of persons in the stages of arhat and Buddhahood naturally possess moral discipline, concentration, wisdom, emancipation from illusions and suffering, and knowledge of emancipation (the insight to know that one is free from delusion).

fivefold comparison [五重の相対] (Jpn *gojū-no-sōtai*): Five successive levels of comparison set forth by Nichiren (1222–1282) in *The Opening of the Eyes* to demonstrate the superiority of his teaching of Nam-myoho-renge-kyo over all other teachings.

(1) Buddhism is superior to non-Buddhist teachings. Nichiren takes up Confucianism and Brahmanism, and concludes that these non-Buddhist religions are not as profound as Buddhism in that they do not reveal the causal law of life that penetrates the three existences of past, present, and future.

(2) Mahayana Buddhism is superior to Hinayana Buddhism. Hinayana Buddhism is the teaching for persons of the two vehicles, or voice-hearers (Skt *shrāvaka*) and cause-awakened ones *(pratyekabuddha)*, who aim at personal emancipation; its ultimate goal is to put an end to the cycle of rebirth in the threefold world by eliminating all earthly desires. It is called Hinayana (Lesser Vehicle) because it saves only a limited number of people. In contrast, Mahayana Buddhism is the teaching for bodhisattvas who aim at both personal enlightenment and the enlightenment of others; it is called Mahayana (Great Vehicle) because it can lead many people to enlightenment. In this sense, the Mahayana teachings are superior to the Hinayana teachings.

(3) True Mahayana is superior to provisional Mahayana. Here *true Mahayana* means the Lotus Sutra, while *provisional Mahayana* indicates the Mahayana teachings that, according to T'ien-t'ai's system of classification, were expounded before the Lotus Sutra. In the provisional Mahayana teachings, the people of the two vehicles, women, and evil persons are excluded from the possibility of attaining enlightenment; in addition, Buddhahood is attained only by advancing through progressive stages of bodhisattva practice over incalculable *kalpas*. In contrast, the Lotus Sutra reveals that all people have the Buddha nature inherently, and that they can attain Buddhahood immediately by realizing that

nature. Furthermore, the provisional Mahayana teachings assert that Shakyamuni attained enlightenment for the first time in India and do not reveal his original attainment of Buddhahood in the remote past, nor do they reveal the principle of the mutual possession of the Ten Worlds, as does the Lotus Sutra. For these reasons, the true Mahayana teachings are superior to the provisional Mahayana teachings.

(4) The essential teaching of the Lotus Sutra is superior to the theoretical teaching of the Lotus Sutra. The theoretical teaching consists of the first fourteen chapters of the Lotus Sutra, and the essential teaching, the latter fourteen chapters. The theoretical teaching takes the form of preaching by Shakyamuni who is still viewed as having attained enlightenment during his lifetime in India. In contrast, the essential teaching takes the form of preaching by Shakyamuni who has discarded this transient status and revealed his true identity as the Buddha who attained Buddhahood in the remote past. This revelation implies that all the Ten Worlds of ordinary people are eternal just as the Buddha's are, and confirms that Buddhahood is an ever-present potential of human life. For these reasons, the essential teaching is superior to the theoretical teaching.

(5) The Buddhism of sowing is superior to the Buddhism of the harvest. Nichiren established this comparison based on the concept of sowing, maturing, and harvesting that T'ien-t'ai (538–597) set forth in *The Words and Phrases of the Lotus Sutra.* In *The Profound Meaning of the Lotus Sutra,* T'ien-t'ai cites the process by which the Buddha teaches, described in the "Parable of the Phantom City" (seventh) chapter of the Lotus Sutra, as well as the relationship of the Buddha and his disciples from the remote past explained in the "Life Span" (sixteenth) chapter of the sutra. All these ideas illustrate how the Buddha begins teaching his disciples by sowing the seeds of Buddhahood in their lives, helps those seeds mature, and finally harvests their fruit by leading them to the final stage of enlightenment or Buddhahood.

The Lotus Sutra describes this process as ranging over countless *kalpas.* The sutra does not, however, explain the nature of these original seeds, though it is clear that the seed of Buddhahood is essential for attaining Buddhahood. Nichiren identifies the seed as Nam-myoho-renge-kyo and states that it can be found only in the depths of the "Life Span" chapter. By implanting this seed in one's life, one can attain Buddhahood. From this viewpoint, Nichiren identifies his teaching as the Buddhism of sowing (the teaching aimed at implanting the seed of Buddhahood) and Shakyamuni's as the Buddhism of the harvest (the teaching aimed at harvesting the fruit of enlightenment borne from the seed planted in the remote past). He explains that Shakyamuni appeared in India in order to harvest the fruit of Buddhahood borne from the seed he had sown and caused to mature in the lives of his disciples until that time. The people of the Latter Day of the Law who have no such seed implanted in their lives cannot harvest its fruit. Nichiren states, "Now, in the Latter Day of the Law, neither the Lotus Sutra nor the other sutras lead to enlightenment. Only Nam-myoho-renge-kyo can do so" (903).

fivefold meditation [五相成身観] (Jpn *gosō-jōshin-kan*): Also, fivefold meditation for attaining Buddhahood. The practices of meditation set forth in Esoteric Buddhism. The fivefold meditation consists of (1) perceiving the mind of enlightenment, (2) arousing the mind of enlightenment, (3) achieving the adamantine mind, (4) obtaining the adamantine body, and (5) obtaining the body of the Buddha.

Fivefold Rules of Discipline, The [五分律] (Chin *Wu-fen-lü;* Jpn *Gobun-ritsu*): Also known as *The Mahīshāsaka Vinaya* or *The Mahīshāsaka Fivefold Vinaya.* A work of the *vinaya* (rules of monastic discipline) of the Mahīshāsaka school, one of the eighteen Hinayana schools and one of the divisions of the Sarvāstivāda school. It was translated by Buddhajīva, an Indian monk of the Mahīshāsaka school who came to China in 423, together with Tao-sheng and Hui-yen, disciples of Kumārajīva, at Lung-kuang-ssu temple in Chien-k'ang. "Fivefold" in the title refers to the fact that the work consists of five sections. According to tradition, it is a translation of the Sanskrit text that Fa-hsien, a Chinese Buddhist pilgrim, brought from Sri Lanka in the early fifth century.

fivefold view of revelation [五重三段] (Jpn *gojū-sandan*): An analysis of the Buddhist teachings that appears in *The Object of Devotion for Observing the Mind,* a treatise completed in 1273 by Nichiren. *Revelation* means the truth that Buddhas impart. A teaching of revelation is preceded by a teaching of preparation, which readies people to receive the truth; and is followed by a teaching of transmission, which urges that the truth revealed be transmitted to posterity. Chinese Buddhist scholars classified the sutras according to these three divisions: preparation, revelation, and transmission. In the above treatise, Nichiren applies the three divisions to (1) all of Shakyamuni's teachings, (2) the threefold Lotus Sutra (the Immeasurable Meanings Sutra, the eight-volume Lotus Sutra, and the Universal Worthy Sutra), (3) the theoretical teaching (first half) of the Lotus Sutra, (4) the essential teaching (latter half) of the sutra, and (5) the teaching implicit in the "Life Span" (sixteenth) chapter of the sutra. His purpose in so doing is to show that Nam-myoho-renge-kyo is the very teaching to be practiced and propagated in the Latter Day of the Law.

A summary of the fivefold view of revelation is as follows: (1) From the standpoint of all of Shakyamuni's teachings, preparation is represented by the sutras of the Flower Garland, Āgama, Correct and Equal, and Wisdom periods, that is, the pre-Lotus Sutra teachings; revelation is represented by the threefold Lotus Sutra, and transmission by the Nirvana Sutra. (2) From the standpoint of the threefold Lotus Sutra, preparation consists of the Immeasurable Meanings Sutra and the "Introduction" (first) chapter of the Lotus Sutra, revelation extends from the "Expedient Means" (second) chapter through the first half of the "Distinctions in Benefits" (seventeenth) chapter, and transmission includes the second half of the "Distinctions in Benefits" chapter through the "Universal Worthy" (twenty-eighth) chapter and includes the Universal Worthy Sutra. (3) In terms of the theoretical teaching, preparation comprises the Immeasurable Meanings Sutra and the "Introduction" chapter of the Lotus Sutra, revelation extends from the "Expedient Means" chapter through the "Prophecies" (ninth) chapter, and transmission, from the "Teacher of the Law" (tenth) chapter through the "Peaceful Practices" (fourteenth) chapter. (4) From the viewpoint of the essential teaching, preparation comprises the first half of the "Emerging from the Earth" (fifteenth) chapter, revelation includes the second half of the "Emerging from the Earth" chapter, the "Life Span" chapter, and the first half of the "Distinctions in Benefits" chapter (collectively known as "one chapter and two halves"), and transmission extends from the second half of the "Distinctions in Benefits" chapter through the "Universal Worthy" chapter and includes the Universal Worthy Sutra. (5) In terms of the teaching implicit in the "Life Span" chapter, that is, Nam-myoho-renge-kyo, preparation is represented by the teachings of all the Buddhas of the ten directions throughout the three existences; revelation by Nam-myoho-renge-kyo, the Law implicit in the "Life Span" chapter; and transmission by the teachings of all the Buddhas read in the light of Nam-myoho-renge-kyo.

five great wisdom kings [五大明王] (Jpn *godai-myō'ō*): Also, five great honored ones or five honored ones. Immovable, Conqueror of the Threefold World, Kundalī, Great Awesome Virtue, and Diamond Yaksha. Wisdom kings (Skt *vidyā-rāja*) are a group of deities who are said to remove all obstacles. Depicted as angry figures, the five great wisdom kings are especially revered in Esoteric Buddhism. In Japan, an esoteric prayer ritual known as the "ceremony of the five altars" was performed in order to defeat enemies during the Heian (794–1185) and the Kamakura (1185–1333) periods. In this ceremony, images of the five great wisdom kings were enshrined in five altars and were worshiped.

five guides for propagation [五綱] (Jpn *go-kō*): Five criteria for propagating Buddhism: (1) the teaching, (2) the people's capacity, (3) the time, (4) the country, and (5) the sequence of propagation. Nichiren (1222–1282) established these five guides as a standard to demonstrate the correct way to propagate his teaching of Nam-myoho-renge-kyo in his time and in the future. They are set forth in his writings *The Teaching, Capacity, Time, and Country* and *What It Means to Slander the Law*. While Nichiren discusses the five guides in reference to what teaching one should propagate in Japan in his day, they are universally applicable. The five may be briefly explained as follows:

(1) A correct understanding of the teaching. This means to recognize the differences among the many Buddhist teachings and discern which are profound and which are superficial. Nichiren established the fivefold comparison for this purpose. Ultimately, to recognize that the Lotus Sutra stands supreme among all the sutras, and that Nam-myoho-renge-kyo of the Three Great Secret Laws implicit in the "Life Span" (sixteenth) chapter of the Lotus Sutra is the teaching that enables all people in the Latter Day of the Law to attain Buddhahood, is to have a correct understanding of the teaching.

(2) A correct understanding of the people's capacity. Capacity means the life-tendency of the people, the nature of their connection to Buddhism (or lack thereof), and their ability to understand and believe in the Buddhist teachings. In short, to understand the people's capacity means to know by what teaching they can attain Buddhahood. According to Nichiren, the people of Shakyamuni's time and of the Former Day and the Middle Day of the Law had already received the seed of Buddhahood from him in the remote past and nurtured it through Buddhist practice in previous existences. Therefore Shakyamuni's Lotus Sutra was the teaching most appropriate to benefit them by enabling them to reap the "harvest" of Buddhahood. In contrast, the people of the Latter Day have not yet received the seed of Buddhahood, and must therefore receive the seed of enlightenment by practicing the Buddhism of sowing. To recognize this is to have a correct understanding of the people's capacity.

(3) A correct understanding of the time. The development of Buddhism following Shakyamuni's death is divided into three periods, known as the Former Day, Middle Day, and Latter Day of the Law. The Former Day is the time in which Shakyamuni's teaching is transmitted correctly and leads many people to enlightenment. The Middle Day is the period in which, though Shakyamuni's teaching is practiced, the practice gradually becomes a formality and benefits fewer and fewer people. In

the Latter Day, the teaching is obscured and lost, no longer leading people to enlightenment. Shakyamuni offered enlightenment for the people of the Latter Day, however. In the Lotus Sutra, he implied the teaching to be propagated in that age and the person who would propagate it. The Law that is to spread in this time period is Nam-myoho-renge-kyo, the essence of the Lotus Sutra, and the person who will spread it is Bodhisattva Superior Practices, the leader of the Bodhisattvas of the Earth, to whom Shakyamuni has entrusted the task. To know this is to correctly understand the time. Nichiren regards himself as fulfilling the mission of Bodhisattva Superior Practices.

(4) A correct understanding of the country. This means to discern the nature of a particular nation's or society's connection to Buddhism. Nichiren states that some countries actively slander the correct teaching, some are completely ignorant of it, some are exclusively Hinayana, some exclusively Mahayana, and others both Hinayana and Mahayana. Japan is an exclusively Mahayana country, he says, that is filled with people who slander the correct teaching. He concludes, therefore, that the Mystic Law of Nam-myoho-renge-kyo, which can save all people including even those who oppose it, should be spread in Japan.

(5) A correct understanding of the sequence of propagation. The point of this criterion is that one should not propagate a teaching inferior to those that have already spread. Nichiren points out that in a country such as Japan, where the theoretical teaching (first half) of the Lotus Sutra has already been spread (by Dengyō, the founder of the Tendai school, during the Middle Day of the Law), the essential teaching (latter half) of the sutra—specifically, the teaching implicit in the "Life Span" chapter—should be propagated. To recognize this is to have a correct understanding of the sequence of propagation.

five heavens of purity [五浄居天] (Skt *shuddhāvāsa;* Jpn *go-jōgo-ten*): Also, five pure-dwelling heavens or heavens of purity. The five highest heavens among the eighteen heavens in the world of form. They are (1) the Heaven of No Vexations (Skt Avriha); (2) the Heaven of No Heat (Atapa), a realm that is free of distress; (3) the Reward Appearing Heaven (Sudrisha), where one is able to receive the reward of one's good deeds; (4) the Heaven of Clear Perception (Sudarshana); and (5) the Akanishtha Heaven, the highest heaven of the world of form. Those reaching the stage of the non-returner, or the second highest of the four stages of enlightenment taught in early Buddhism, are said to be reborn among these heavens.

five honored ones [五大尊] (Jpn *godaison*): *See* five great wisdom kings.

"Five Hundred Disciples" chapter [五百弟子品] (Jpn *Gohyaku-deshi-hon*): The eighth chapter of the Lotus Sutra. *See* "Prophecy of Enlightenment for Five Hundred Disciples" chapter.

five hundred precepts [五百戒] (Jpn *gohyaku-kai*): The rules of monastic discipline to be observed by fully ordained nuns of Hinayana Buddhism. "Five hundred" is not a literal figure; the actual number differs from one source to another. *The Fourfold Rules of Discipline* lists 348 precepts that fall into seven categories: (1) Eight prohibitions. The prohibition of the eight major, or unpardonable, offenses (Skt *pārājika*), punishment for which is expulsion from the Buddhist Order. These offenses are killing, stealing, having sexual relations, lying (particularly, claiming to have attained insight that one does not in fact possess), touching a male, improper association with a male, hiding another nun's *pārājika* offenses, and following a monk whose behavior goes against monastic rules. These eight unpardonable offenses are also called the eight major offenses, the eight grave offenses, the eight *pārājikas*, or the eight *pārājika* offenses. (2) Seventeen major prohibitions, violation of which results in suspension from the Buddhist Order for a specified period. This second category forbids such acts as matchmaking and initiating lawsuits. (3) Thirty standards that, if broken, cause one's property to be forfeited to the Buddhist Order. (4) One hundred seventy-eight lesser standards, such as telling simple lies. (5) Eight minor regulations (concerned with meals). (6) One hundred disciplines pertaining to meals, clothing, preaching, etc. (7) Seven rules for the settling of disputes within the Buddhist Order.

five improper ways of livelihood [五邪・五種邪命] (Jpn *go-ja* or *goshu-jamyō*): Five ways of gaining a livelihood deemed improper for monks: (1) assuming an air of superiority, (2) advertising one's powers and virtue, (3) fortune telling, (4) hectoring and bullying, and (5) praising an almsgiver in order to obtain alms. In any event, preaching for the purpose of gaining wealth was forbidden to monks.

five impurities [五濁] (Jpn *go-joku*): Also, five defilements. Impurity of the age, of desire, of living beings, of thought (or view), and of life span. The "Expedient Means" (second) chapter of the Lotus Sutra says, "The Buddhas appear in evil worlds of five impurities. . . . In this evil world of the five impurities those who merely delight in and are attached to the desires, living beings such as this in the end will never seek the Buddha way." (1) Impurity of the age includes repeated disruptions of the social or natural environment. (2) Impurity of desire is the tendency to be ruled by the five delusive inclinations, i.e., greed, anger, foolishness, arrogance, and doubt. (3) Impurity of living beings is the physical and spiritual decline of human beings. (4) Impurity of thought, or impurity of view, is the prevalence of wrong views such as the five false views. (5) Impurity of life span is the shortening of the life spans of living beings. According to *The Words and Phrases of the Lotus Sutra,* the most fundamental of these five are the impurities of thought and desire, which result in the impurity of living beings and the impurity of life span. These in turn give rise to the impurity of the age.

five kinds of correct practices [五正行・五種の正行] (Jpn *go-shōgyō* or *goshu-no-shōgyō*): *See* five correct practices.

five kinds of sundry practices [五種の雑行] (Jpn *goshu-no-zōgyō*): *See* five sundry practices.

five kinds of wisdom [五智] (Jpn *go-chi*): Also, five types of wisdom. The five aspects of Mahāvairochana Buddha's wisdom in Esoteric Buddhism. They are (1) "the wisdom of the essence of the phenomenal world," which perceives the phenomenal world as composed of the six elements of earth, water, fire, wind, space, and consciousness; (2) "the great round mirror wisdom," which perceives the world without distortion, just as a clear mirror accurately reflects all images; (3) "the non-discriminating wisdom," which observes the essential equality of all things without discrimination; (4) "the wisdom of insight into the particulars," which distinguishes the particulars of all phenomena and observes the capacities of living beings so that one may preach to them and resolve the various doubts they have; and (5) "the wisdom of perfect practice," which enables one to develop the power of benefiting others as well as oneself. The last four are considered aspects of the first. Esoteric Buddhism asserts that the wisdom of the Thus Come One Mahāvairochana is perfect and encompasses all five aspects. The five kinds of wisdom are represented by the five wisdom Buddhas of the Diamond Realm mandala.

five major principles [五重玄] (Jpn *gojū-gen*): The five viewpoints from which T'ien-t'ai (538–597) interpreted the Lotus Sutra: name, essence, quality, function, and teaching. In *The Profound Meaning of the Lotus Sutra,* T'ien-t'ai explains that *Myoho-renge-kyo,* the title of the Lotus Sutra, is not only the name, but also the essence of the sutra, and is endowed with a unique quality, function, and position among all teachings. "Name" signifies the meaning of the title of a sutra. The "Interpretation of the Name" section of *Profound Meaning* gives a detailed explanation of the title *Myoho-renge-kyo* and explains why it represents the essence of the Lotus Sutra. "Essence" signifies the ultimate principle of a sutra. The "Clarification of the Essence" section defines the substance of *Myoho-renge-kyo* to be the true aspect of all phenomena. "Quality" indicates the principal doctrines of a sutra. The section "Elucidation of Quality" defines the principal doctrine of the theoretical teaching (first half) of the Lotus Sutra to be the replacement of the provisional teachings with the true teaching, and the principal doctrine of the essential teaching (latter half) to be the revelation of the Buddha's true identity, i.e., his original attainment of enlightenment, as well as the revelation of the true cause and true effect of his enlightenment. This section of *Profound Meaning* also states that the quality, or main point, of the sutra as a whole is the causality of the supreme vehicle of Buddhahood. "Function" indicates the benefit and power of a sutra. The "Discussion of Function" section says that the theoretical teaching dispels belief in the three vehicles (teachings for voice-hearers, cause-awakened ones, and bodhisattvas) and arouses faith in the one vehicle of Buddhahood, and that the essential teaching denies the Buddha's attainment of enlightenment in this life and arouses faith in his original attainment of enlightenment in the remote past. Moreover, the function of the Lotus Sutra as a whole is to lead all people to Buddhahood. "Teaching" refers to the position and influence of a sutra with respect to other sutras. The section "Evaluation of the Teaching" asserts that the Lotus Sutra encompasses all other teachings, and that its influence permeates all phenomena. This section introduces the systems of classifying the sutras advocated by the three schools of southern China and the seven schools of northern China, and refutes them with T'ien-t'ai's own classification of "five periods and eight teachings," a system that defines *Myoho-renge-kyo* as the supreme sutra. T'ien-t'ai's five major principles are based on the passage of the "Supernatural Powers" (twenty-first) chapter of the Lotus Sutra that begins the transfer of the essence of the sutra to the Bodhisattvas of the Earth. It reads: "To put it briefly, all the doctrines possessed by the Thus Come One [name], all the freely exercised supernatural powers of the Thus Come One [function], the storehouse of all the secret essentials of the Thus Come One [essence], all the most profound matters of the Thus Come One [quality]—all these are proclaimed, revealed, and clearly expounded in this sutra [teaching]."

five major writings [五大部] (Jpn *godai-bu*): The five most important writings of Nichiren (1222–1282), as identified by Nichiren's successor, Nikkō. They are (1) *On Establishing the Correct Teaching for the Peace of the Land,* (2) *The Opening of the Eyes,* (3) *The Object of Devotion for Observing the Mind,* (4) *The Selection of the Time,* and (5) *On Repaying Debts of Gratitude. See also* ten major writings.

five meditations [五停心観] (Jpn *gojōshin-kan*): Also, five meditations for stopping the mind. Five meditative practices for quieting the mind and eliminating delusion. They are (1) meditation on the vileness of the body, (2) meditation on compassion, (3) meditation on dependent origination, (4) meditation on the correct discernment of the phenomenal world, and (5) breath-counting meditation. Meditation on the vileness of the body serves to eliminate greed by contemplating the impurity of the body and severing one's attachment to it. Meditation on compassion serves to eliminate anger and hatred by contemplating compassion. Meditation on dependent origination serves to eliminate foolishness or ignorance by contemplating the twelve-linked chain of causation. Meditation on the correct discernment of the phenomenal world enables one to gain an understanding that no phenomena or existences have any permanent intrinsic substance, by contemplating the five components and the eighteen elements. Breath-counting meditation serves to calm the mind by counting one's breaths.

five meditations for stopping the mind [五停心観] (Jpn *gojōshin-kan*): *See* five meditations.

five mighty bodhisattvas [五大力菩薩] (Jpn *godairiki-bosatsu*): Five bodhisattvas enumerated in the Benevolent Kings Sutra. According to Kumārajīva's Chinese translation, they are Diamond Roar, Dragon King's Roar, Roar of Fearlessness and Ten Powers, Thunderbolt Roar, and Infinitely Powerful Roar. Pu-k'ung's Chinese translation lists them as Diamond Hand, Diamond Treasure, Diamond Benefit, Diamond Yaksha, and Diamond Pāramitā. According to the sutra, if a ruler embraces the three treasures of Buddhism, namely, the Buddha, his teachings, and the Order—the community of believers who protect and transmit the Buddha's teachings—these five powerful bodhisattvas will protect him and the people of his country.

five natures [五性] (Jpn *go-shō*): (1) Also, five distinct natures. A doctrine set forth by the Dharma Characteristics (Chin Fa-hsiang; Jpn Hossō) school, dividing human beings into five groups according to their inborn capacity for enlightenment. The five groups are (a) those predestined to be voice-hearers, (b) those predestined to be cause-awakened ones, (c) those predestined to be bodhisattvas, (d) an indeterminate group, and (e) those without the nature of enlightenment. The first group can eventually attain the state of arhat, and the second group, that of cause-awakened ones, or *pratyekabuddha*. Neither of these first two groups can attain Buddhahood, however. The third group, those predestined for the realm of bodhisattvas, seeks Buddhahood and will eventually attain it. These three are called the determinate groups because the kind of enlightenment they will achieve is predetermined. People in the fourth group possess two or all of the three natures of voice-hearers, cause-awakened ones, and bodhisattvas, but which of these natures will develop is not predetermined; therefore they are called the indeterminate group. Among them, only those who develop the nature of the bodhisattva can eventually attain Buddhahood. Those in the fifth group cannot attain Buddhahood, nor can they attain the enlightenment of voice-hearers or cause-awakened ones; instead they can only transmigrate through the six paths for eternity. Thus only those predestined as bodhisattvas and those among the indeterminate group who develop the bodhisattva nature can attain Buddhahood. This doctrine is based on the Lankāvatāra Sutra and the Revelation of the Profound Secrets Sutra. It led to an intense dispute with the Tendai school, which asserted that all living beings possess the Buddha nature and therefore can attain Buddhahood.

(2) Another similar classification of people's inborn capacities set forth in the Perfect Enlightenment Sutra: (a) the nature of common mortals, (b) the nature of those of the two vehicles (voice-hearers and cause-awakened ones), (c) the nature of bodhisattvas, (d) the indeterminate nature, and (e) the nature of non-Buddhists.

five obscurations [五蓋] (Jpn *go-gai*): Also, five covers. Five mental impediments that cloud people's minds and prevent good from arising within them. They are greed, anger, drowsiness and languor, excitement and depression (emotional instability), and doubt.

five obstacles [五障] (Jpn *go-shō*): Also, five hindrances. Five obstructions to women's attainment. The view that a woman cannot become a Brahmā, a Shakra, a devil king, a wheel-turning king, or a Buddha. This concept is referred to in a number of Buddhist writings, and is mentioned and then refuted in the "Devadatta" (twelfth) chapter of the Lotus Sutra. This refutation takes place through the example of the dragon king's daughter who instantaneously attains Buddhahood, the most difficult of all five, when challenged by Shāriputra on the grounds that women are subject to these five obstacles. The expression "five obstacles and three obediences" is often used in reference to the hindrances that prevent women from attaining Buddhahood. The "three obediences," also known as the "three submissions," was a code of conduct derived from Brahmanism and Confucianism that required women to obey their parents in childhood, their husbands after marriage, and their sons in old age.

five obstacles and three obediences [五障三従] (Jpn *goshō-sanjū* or *goshō-sanshō*): *See* five obstacles.

five or seven characters [五字七字] (Jpn *goji-shichiji*): The "five characters" indicating Myoho-renge-kyo, which consists of five Chinese characters (pronounced in Japanese)—*myō, hō, ren, ge,* and *kyō,* and the "seven characters," Nam-myoho-renge-kyo, which comprises two additional

Chinese characters, *nan* or *na*, and *mu*. Nichiren (1222–1282) often uses Myoho-renge-kyo synonymously with Nam-myoho-renge-kyo in his writings. *Nam* or *namu* is a compound of the two Chinese characters of *nan* and *mu*. In his work *On Offering Prayers to the Mandala of the Mystic Law*, Nichiren states: "I have offered prayers to the Gohonzon of Myoho-renge-kyo. Though this mandala has but five or seven characters, it is the teacher of all Buddhas throughout the three existences and the seal that guarantees the enlightenment of all women. It will be a lamp in the darkness of the road to the next world and a fine horse to carry you over the mountains of death. . . . It is the teacher who leads all people to Buddhahood and enlightenment" (414).

five pāramitās [五波羅蜜] (Jpn *go-haramitsu*): Almsgiving, keeping the precepts, forbearance, assiduousness, and meditation. Five of the six *pāramitās*, or six practices required of Mahayana bodhisattvas in order to attain Buddhahood, omitting the *pāramitā* of obtaining wisdom.

five paths [五道・五趣] (Jpn *go-dō* or *go-shu*): The five realms or worlds into which living beings are born in accord with the law of causality. Their good or bad deeds in this life determine the realm of their rebirth. The five realms correspond to five of the Ten Worlds: the realms of hell, hungry spirits, animals, human beings, and heavenly beings. As such, they can also be interpreted as states or conditions of life. With the realm of *asuras* they constitute the six paths.

five patriarchs of the Chinese Pure Land school [浄土五祖] (Jpn *Jōdo-goso*): T'an-luan (476–542), Tao-ch'o (562–645), Shan-tao (613–681), Huai-kan (n.d.), and Shao-k'ang (d. 805). Hōnen (1133–1212), the founder of the Pure Land (Jōdo) school in Japan, designated these individuals as the five patriarchs of the Chinese Pure Land school, according to Shinran's record of Hōnen's remarks. This must have been Hōnen's own assessment, since no such list is known to have existed in China.

five periods [五時] (Jpn *go-ji*): Also, five periods of preaching or five periods of teachings. A classification by T'ien-t'ai (538–597) of Shakyamuni Buddha's teachings according to the order in which he believed they had been expounded. They are as follows: (1) The Flower Garland period, or the period of the Flower Garland Sutra, which according to T'ien-t'ai was the first teaching Shakyamuni expounded after his enlightenment. The Flower Garland teaching represents a very high level of teaching, second only to the teachings of the Lotus and Nirvana period. With this teaching, the Buddha awakens his listeners to the greatness of Buddhism, though it was too profound for them to grasp. The Flower Garland period is also referred to as the Flower Ornament period or the Avatamsaka period. The Avatamsaka Sutra is the Sanskrit title of the

Flower Garland Sutra. (2) The Āgama period, or the period of the Āgama sutras. Perceiving that his disciples' capacity was not yet ready for the Flower Garland teaching, Shakyamuni next expounded the Āgama teachings as a means to develop their capacity. These teachings reveal the four noble truths—the truth of suffering, the truth of the origin of suffering, the truth of the cessation of suffering, and the truth of the path to the cessation of suffering—that free people from the six paths and correspond to the Hinayana teachings. The Āgama period is also called the Deer Park period, or the period of the sermon in Deer Park, because the Buddha preached the Āgama teachings at Deer Park. (3) The Correct and Equal period, or the period of the introductory Mahayana sutras. In this period, Shakyamuni refuted his disciples' attachment to Hinayana doctrines and directed them toward provisional Mahayana with such teachings as the Amida, Mahāvairochana, and Vimalakīrti sutras. The Correct and Equal period is also referred to as the Vaipulya period or the Extended period. The Sanskrit word *vaipulya* means largeness or spaciousness. (4) The Wisdom period, or the period of the Wisdom sutras. In this period, Shakyamuni expounded a higher level of provisional Mahayana and refuted his disciples' attachment to the distinction between Hinayana and Mahayana by teaching the doctrine of non-substantiality. The Wisdom period is also referred to as the Prajnā period because in this period the *Prajnā-pāramitā,* or Perfection of Wisdom, sutras were preached. (5) The Lotus and Nirvana period, or period of the Lotus and Nirvana sutras, in which Shakyamuni taught directly from the standpoint of his enlightenment, fully revealing the truth. In this eight-year interval, he expounded the Lotus Sutra and the Nirvana Sutra, the latter a restatement of the teachings in the Lotus Sutra.

According to T'ien-t'ai, the Flower Garland period lasted for twenty-one days, the Āgama period for twelve years, the Correct and Equal period for eight or sixteen years, the Wisdom period for twenty-two or fourteen years, and the Lotus and Nirvana period for eight years. In fact there is no way to verify the historical accuracy of these figures or, for that matter, of the order of the five periods. The five periods could perhaps best be described as T'ien-t'ai's account of the process by which Shakyamuni led his disciples to an understanding of his ultimate teaching.

five periods and eight teachings [五時八教] (Jpn *goji-hakkyō*): A system of classification of the Buddhist teachings set forth by T'ien-t'ai (538–597) in *The Profound Meaning of the Lotus Sutra* to demonstrate the superiority of the Lotus Sutra over all the other sutras. The *five periods* is a classification of Shakyamuni Buddha's sutras according to the order in which they were expounded and consists of the Flower Garland,

Āgama, Correct and Equal, Wisdom, and Lotus and Nirvana periods. The *eight teachings* is an organization of the Buddha's teachings by content and method of presentation. It consists of two sub-classifications—the four teachings of doctrine and the four teachings of method. The four teachings of doctrine, a classification by content, are the Tripitaka teaching, the connecting teaching, the specific teaching, and the perfect teaching. The four teachings of method, a classification by method of teaching, are the sudden teaching, the gradual teaching, the secret teaching, and the indeterminate teaching. *See also* eight teachings; five periods.

five powers [五力] (Jpn *go-riki*): Five attributes obtained by the practice of the five roots—faith, exertion, memory, meditation, and wisdom. The five powers are the power of faith, the power of exertion, the power of memory, the power of meditation, and the power of wisdom. Along with the five roots, which are similarly named, they constitute ten of the thirty-seven aids to the way, or the thirty-seven practices leading to enlightenment. *See also* five roots; thirty-seven aids to the way.

five practices [五種の修行] (Jpn *goshu-no-shugyō*): Five kinds of practice described in the "Teacher of the Law" (tenth) chapter of the Lotus Sutra. They are to embrace, read, recite, expound, and transcribe the Lotus Sutra. The "Teacher of the Law" chapter says that one who embraces, reads, recites, expounds, and transcribes even a single verse of the sutra will attain Buddhahood without fail. In this chapter, Shakyamuni says to the bodhisattva Medicine King: "You should understand that such persons [who carry out the five practices] have already offered alms to a hundred thousand million Buddhas and in the place of the Buddhas have fulfilled their great vow, and because they take pity on living beings they have been born in this human world. Medicine King, if someone should ask what living beings will be able to attain Buddhahood in a latter-day existence, then you should show him that all these people in a latter-day existence are certain to attain Buddhahood." Various categories of five practices are set forth in Buddhism.

five precepts [五戒] (Jpn *go-kai*): The basic precepts to be observed by laypersons. They are (1) not to kill, (2) not to steal, (3) not to engage in sexual misconduct (such as adultery), (4) not to lie, and (5) not to consume intoxicants. The five precepts are regarded as the most fundamental of Buddhist precepts; in addition, Buddhism views them as basic moral guidelines for humanity. The word *precept* is interpreted as "preventing error and putting an end to evil." A layperson was required to vow to observe the five precepts upon becoming a Buddhist. The Sanskrit word *shīla* for precept also means custom, disposition, integrity, morality, piety, virtue, or rules of moral conduct.

five proclamations of the Buddha [五箇の鳳詔] (Jpn *goka-no-hōshō*): The three pronouncements in the "Treasure Tower" (eleventh) chapter of the Lotus Sutra and the two admonitions in the "Devadatta" (twelfth) chapter, in which Shakyamuni exhorts the assembly to propagate the Lotus Sutra after his death. *See also* three pronouncements; two admonitions.

five pure-dwelling heavens [五浄居天] (Jpn *go-jōgo-ten*): *See* five heavens of purity.

five regions of India [五天竺・五天] (Jpn *go-tenjiku* or *go-ten*): A term used in China and Japan to mean all of ancient India. The eastern, western, southern, northern, and central regions of India.

five roots [五根] (Jpn *go-kon*): Five kinds of action or cause that are conducive to enlightenment. The root of faith, the root of exertion, the root of memory, the root of meditation, and the root of wisdom. The five roots are often listed simply as faith, exertion, memory, meditation, and wisdom. Practice of the five roots gives rise to the five powers, which are similarly named. The five roots and the five powers together constitute ten of the thirty-seven aids to the way, or the thirty-seven practices leading to enlightenment. *See also* five powers; thirty-seven aids to the way.

five schools of Zen [五家] (Jpn *go-ke*): A generic term for the branches of the Southern school of Zen (Ch'an) Buddhism in China. The five are the Lin-chi (Jpn Rinzai), Kuei-yang (Igyō), Ts'ao-tung (Sōtō), Yün-men (Ummon), and Fa-yen (Hōgen) schools. The five plus the Huang-lung (Ōryū) and Yang-ch'i (Yōgi) schools, both of which broke away from the Lin-chi school, are together called the seven schools. All of the Southern Zen schools trace their lineage to Hui-neng (638–713), the sixth of the Chinese Zen patriarchs, who received the transmission from Hung-jen. Hui-neng propagated Zen in the southern part of China; therefore his lineage is called the Southern school of Zen. Another of Hung-jen's disciples, Shen-hsiu (606–706), spread Zen Buddhism in northern China. His lineage came to be called the Northern school. *See also* Zen school.

five senior priests [五老僧] (Jpn *go-rōsō*): Five of the six senior priests, excluding Nikkō (1246–1333), designated by Nichiren shortly before his death as his principal disciples. They are Nisshō (1221–1323), Nichirō (1245–1320), Nikō (1253–1314), Nitchō (1252–1317), and Nichiji (b. 1250). On the eighth day of the tenth month, 1282, at the residence of his lay follower and supporter Ikegami Munenaka in Musashi Province, Nichiren named six senior priests whom he entrusted with the responsibility of propagation in their respective areas after his death. He selected them because of the outstanding efforts and contributions they had made to the dissemination of his teachings. Among them, he formally designated Nikkō as his successor. After Nichiren's death, however, the other five refused to follow Nikkō. They gradually departed from Nichiren's teachings, compromising with schools their teacher had refuted as erroneous and misleading. *On Refuting the Five Priests,* completed in 1328 by Nichijun, the second chief instructor of Omosu Seminary, describes the differences between Nikkō and the five senior priests from six viewpoints: (1) While the five officially declared themselves to be priests of the Tendai school, Nikkō identified himself as a disciple of Nichiren, whom he regarded as the reincarnation of the bodhisattva Superior Practices. (2) While the five belittled those letters of Nichiren that were written in a mixture of Chinese characters and Japanese *kana* syllabary, Nikkō treasured them, calling them *Gosho,* honorable writings. In those days formal documents were written in classical Chinese. (3) While the five regarded the theoretical teaching (first half) and the essential teaching (latter half) of the Lotus Sutra as equal in merit, Nikkō held that the former is inferior to the latter. (4) While the five revered images of Shakyamuni Buddha as the object of devotion, Nikkō revered Nichiren's mandala (i.e., Gohonzon). (5) While the five read the entire Lotus Sutra in their practice, Nikkō recited only the key chapters (i.e., the "Expedient Means" and the "Life Span" chapters). (6) While the five worshiped at Shinto shrines, Nikkō prohibited such worship. See also *Guidelines for Believers of the Fuji School, The; On Refuting the Five Priests.*

five sense organs [五根] (Skt, Pali *pancha-indriya;* Jpn *go-kon*): Also, five sensory organs or five faculties. The eyes, ears, nose, tongue, and body, which perform the corresponding five sensory functions of sight, hearing, smell, taste, and touch. The Sanskrit word *indriya* means faculty, organ, or power.

five signs of decay [五衰] (Jpn *go-sui*): Also, five types of decay. Five signs of decline displayed by heavenly beings when their lives are about to end. These signs differ according to the sutras. The Nirvana Sutra describes these five: (1) their clothes become soiled, (2) the flowers on their heads wither, (3) their bodies become dirty and smell bad, (4) they sweat under the armpits, and (5) they do not feel happy, wherever they may be.

five skandhas [五陰] (Jpn *go-on*): Form, perception, conception, volition, and consciousness. *See* five components.

five spicy foods [五辛] (Jpn *go-shin*): *See* five strong-flavored foods.

five stages of practice [五品] (Jpn *go-hon*): Five progressive stages of practice to be followed after Shakyamuni's death described by T'ien-t'ai (538–597) in *The Words and Phrases of the Lotus Sutra.* T'ien-t'ai formulated them based on the content of the "Distinctions in Benefits" (seventeenth) chapter of the Lotus Sutra. They are (1) to rejoice on hearing the Lotus Sutra, (2) to read and recite the sutra, (3) to expound the sutra to others, (4) to embrace the sutra and practice the six *pāramitās,* and (5) to perfect one's practice of the six *pāramitās.* For example, the first stage derives from the passage in the "Distinctions in Benefits" chapter that reads, "If after the Thus Come One has entered extinction there are those who hear this sutra and do not slander or speak ill of it but feel joy in their hearts, they should know that this is a sign that they have already shown deep faith and understanding."

five strong-flavored foods [五辛] (Jpn *go-shin*): Also, five spicy foods. Five kinds of pungent vegetables: garlic, scallions, leeks, rocamboles, and a plant of the dropwort family. The list of the five strong-flavored foods differs among sources. According to another account, they are garlic, scallions, leeks, onions, and ginger. In the Buddhist Order, they were forbidden because of their strong odor and their stimulating effect when eaten. The five strong-flavored foods were said to produce irritability and sexual desire.

five sundry practices [五種の雑行] (Jpn *goshu-no-zōgyō*): Also, five kinds of sundry practices. The Pure Land school regards these practices as preventing rebirth in Amida's Pure Land. Based on Shan-tao's *Commentary on the Meditation on the Buddha Infinite Life Sutra,* Hōnen (1133–1212), the founder of the Japanese Pure Land (Jōdo) school, explained them in his work *The Nembutsu Chosen above All.* They are (1) to read and recite any sutra other than the three Pure Land sutras (the Buddha Infinite Life, Meditation on the Buddha Infinite Life, and Amida sutras), (2) to meditate on any Buddha other than Amida, (3) to worship any Buddha other than Amida, (4) to call on the name of any Buddha other than Amida, and (5) to praise and give offerings to any Buddha other than Amida. The five sundry practices are contrasted with the five correct practices, which are directed toward Amida Buddha. *See also* five correct practices.

five supernatural powers [五神通 · 五通] (Jpn *go-jinzū* or *go-tsū*): *See* five transcendental powers.

five tastes [五味] (Jpn *go-mi*): *See* five flavors.

five teachings and ten doctrines [五教十宗] (Jpn *gokyo-jisshu*): A classification of Buddhist sutras set forth by the Chinese Flower Garland (Hua-yen) school. Fa-tsang (643–712), the third patriarch of the school, established this classification. He classified the sutras into five groups according to the level of their teaching, and the Buddhist schools into ten groups according to their doctrines. The five teachings are (1) the Hinayana teaching, (2) the elementary Mahayana teaching, (3) the final Mahayana teaching, (4) the sudden teaching, and (5) the perfect teaching. "The Hinayana teaching" corresponds to the Āgama sutras. These teachings set forth the four noble truths and the twelve-linked chain of causation. They also hold that, while the self has no independent existence of its own, the dharmas (elements of existence) are real. "The elementary Mahayana teaching" is divided into two: the teaching that analyzes the specific and distinct characters of the dharmas, and the teaching that regards all dharmas as non-substantial. The former is found in the Revelation of the Profound Secrets Sutra, and the latter in the Wisdom sutras. "The final Mahayana teaching" maintains the essentially unchanging nature of all things and the ability of all beings to attain Buddhahood. This teaching is found in the Lankāvatāra Sutra and *The Awakening of Faith in the Mahayana.* "The sudden teaching" expounds the abrupt realization of the ultimate truth without relying upon verbal explanations or progression through various stages of practice. This teaching is found in the Vimalakīrti Sutra. "The perfect teaching" indicates the Flower Garland and Lotus sutras, which expound the one vehicle. "The perfect teaching" is further divided into two: the one vehicle of the identical doctrine and the one vehicle of the distinct doctrine. The former is the one vehicle that is identical in part to the other teachings, the final Mahayana and the sudden in particular, and corresponds to the Lotus Sutra. The latter is the one vehicle that is entirely distinct or separate from the other teachings, and corresponds to the Flower Garland Sutra. The one vehicle of the distinct doctrine is held to be superior to that of the identical doctrine. Hence the Flower Garland school asserts that the Flower Garland Sutra is superior to all the other sutras.

The ten doctrines are: (1) The doctrine of the reality of both the self and the dharmas. This is espoused by the rather unorthodox Vātsīputrīya school. (2) The doctrine that the self is non-substantial but the dharmas are real, and that the past, present, and future exist independently. This is the position of the Sarvāstivāda school. (3) The doctrine that the reality of the dharmas exists only in the present and not in the past or the future, which is upheld by the Mahāsamghika school. (4) The doctrine that the present contains both reality and unreality. That is, the five components of life are real, but the six sense organs, six sense objects, and six senses are temporary, or unreal. The Prajnāptivādin school holds this position. (5) The doctrine that worldly truth is unreal, but that Buddhist truth is real, taught by the Lokottaravāda school. (6) The doctrine that all things and phenomena are mere names without self-nature, taught by the Ekavyāvahārika school. The first six of the ten doctrines correspond to the first of the five teachings, that is, the Hinayana teaching. The remaining four doctrines belong to Mahayana: (7) The doctrine that maintains the non-substantiality of all things. This doctrine corresponds to the elementary Mahayana teaching and is found in the Wisdom sutras. It is also the view of the Three Treatises (Chin San-lun) school. (8) The doctrine that recognizes an unchanging truth that is the essence of all things. This doctrine corresponds to the final Mahayana teaching and is espoused by the T'ien-t'ai school. (9) The doctrine that the truth lies in the mystic realm beyond the polarity of subject and object. This doctrine corresponds to the sudden teaching and is found in the Zen, or Ch'an, school. (10) The doctrine that all things exist in perfect harmony and interrelation. This doctrine corresponds to the perfect teaching and is found in the Lotus and Flower Garland sutras. In particular, it indicates the doctrine of the Flower Garland school.

With this system of classification, Fa-tsang asserted the superiority of the Flower Garland Sutra over all the other sutras, and the doctrine of the Flower Garland school over those of all other schools.

five teachings of Mahādeva [大天の五事] (Jpn *Daiten-no-goji*): Five modifications of the Buddhist teachings advanced by Mahādeva about one hundred years after Shakyamuni's death concerning the concept of the arhat; in essence, that even arhats retain certain human weaknesses. On the basis of these, he and his supporters called for a more flexible interpretation of the monastic rules. The five teachings are as follows: (1) An arhat may experience sexual orgasm while sleeping, when tempted by a devil in a dream. (2) An arhat may lack certain knowledge. (3) An arhat may have doubts. (4) An arhat may lack a penetrating eye of wisdom and become aware of his level of enlightenment only when it is pointed out by another. (5) An arhat may cry out under the strain of unbearable trials. According to *The Great Commentary on the Abhidharma*, controversy over Mahādeva's interpretations contributed to the first schism in the Buddhist Order, the Sthaviravāda (Pali Theravāda) school condemning them as false views and the Mahāsamghika school hailing them as a new perspective.

Five Temples [五山] (Jpn Gozan or Gosan): Either of two groups, one in Kamakura and the other in Kyoto, of five principal temples of the Rinzai school of Zen in Japan. They are respectively called the Five Temples of Kamakura and the Five Temples of Kyoto. In the fourteenth century, the shogunate designated these ten temples the highest-ranking Zen temples in Japan. This ranking system was modeled after the one applied to official Zen (Ch'an) temples in China. The Japanese term *gozan* literally means "five mountains," mountain in this context being synonymous with a temple or monastery. Though the five temples and their order of ranking in each of the two cities changed, in 1341 the Five Temples of Kamakura were Kenchō-ji, Engaku-ji, Jufuku-ji, Jōchi-ji, and Jōmyō-ji; the Five Temples of Kyoto were Nanzen-ji, Tenryū-ji, Kennin-ji, Tōfuku-ji, and Manju-ji. In 1386 Nanzen-ji was raised to a special position, and the newly built Shōkoku-ji was included to form the five temples in Kyoto. The order of ranking was, from highest to lowest: Tenryū-ji, Shōkoku-ji, Kennin-ji, Tōfuku-ji, and Manju-ji. Nanzen-ji occupied a rank above both the Five Temples of Kamakura and those of Kyoto.

five thousand and forty-eight volumes [五千四十八巻] (Jpn *gosen-shi-jūhachi-kan*): The number of volumes of the Chinese versions of Buddhist scriptures, known to have existed in the eighth century. *The K'ai-yüan Era Catalog of the Buddhist Canon,* compiled by Chih-sheng in 730, the eighteenth year of the K'ai-yüan era (713–741) of the T'ang dynasty, lists this number of extant works. Thereafter "five thousand and forty-eight volumes," "five thousand volumes," or "more than five thousand volumes" came to refer to the entire body of Buddhist scriptures. A later catalog, *The Chen-yüan Era Catalog of the Buddhist Canon,* compiled by Yüan-chao in 800, the sixteenth year of the Chen-yüan era (785–804) of the T'ang dynasty, lists 7,388 volumes of Buddhist scriptures. This number was also employed in referring to the entire body of Buddhist texts as the "five thousand or seven thousand volumes of Buddhist scriptures."

five thousand arrogant persons [五千の上慢] (Jpn *gosen-no-jōman*): Also, five thousand persons of overweening pride, five thousand persons of overbearing arrogance, or five thousand arrogant members of the assembly. Five thousand arrogant monks, nuns, laymen, and laywomen described in the "Expedient Means" (second) chapter of the Lotus Sutra as refusing to listen any longer to Shakyamuni Buddha preach the teaching of the sutra and leaving the assembly. The chapter states: "When the Buddha had spoken these words, there were some five thousand monks, nuns, laymen, and laywomen in the assembly who immediately rose from their seats, bowed to the Buddha, and withdrew. What was the reason for this? These persons had roots of guilt that were deep and manifold, and in addition they were overbearingly arrogant. What they had not attained they supposed they had attained, what they had not understood they supposed they had understood." In the sutra, the Buddha goes on to describe them as "monks and nuns who behave with overbearing arrogance, laymen full of self-esteem, laywomen who are lacking in faith" and all those who "fail to see their own errors, are heedless and remiss with regard to the precepts, clinging to their shortcomings, unwilling to change." Referring to them as chaff, leaves, and branches, the Buddha states that the assembly is now "made up only of those steadfast and truthful." This event is termed "the rising from the seats and withdrawal of the five thousand persons."

five transcendental powers [五神通 · 五通] (Jpn *go-jinzū* or *go-tsū*): Also, five supernatural powers. They are (1) the power to be anywhere at will, (2) the power to see anything anywhere, (3) the power to hear any sound anywhere, (4) the power to know the thoughts of all other minds, and (5) the power to know past lives. These constitute five of the six transcendental powers, the sixth being the power to eradicate illusions and earthly desires.

five types of decay [五衰] (Jpn *go-sui*): *See* five signs of decay.

five types of vision [五眼] (Jpn *go-gen*): Also, five types of eyes. Five kinds of perceptive faculty. They are (1) the eye of ordinary people, also called the physical eye, which distinguishes color and form; (2) the heavenly eye, also called the divine eye, which perceives things in the darkness, at a distance, or beyond the physical limits of obstruction; (3) the wisdom eye, or the ability of those in the two vehicles to perceive that nothing has independent existence of its own and all phenomena are non-substantial; (4) the Dharma eye, with which bodhisattvas perceive the nature of all teachings in order to save the people; and (5) the Buddha eye, which perceives the true nature of life spanning past, present, and future. The Buddha eye includes all the other four eyes, or perceptive faculties. In other words, Buddhas possess all five types of vision.

five types of wisdom [五智] (Jpn *go-chi*): *See* five kinds of wisdom.

five vehicles [五乗] (Jpn *go-jō*): Five kinds of teaching expounded in accordance with the people's capacity. *Vehicle* means a teaching that brings people to a particular stage of attainment. The five vehicles are the vehicles of ordinary people, heavenly beings, voice-hearers, cause-awakened ones, and bodhisattvas. (1) The vehicle of ordinary people enables one to be reborn a human being through honoring the three treasures of Buddhism and upholding the five precepts. (2) The vehicle of heavenly beings enables one to reach the heavenly realms through the observance of the ten good precepts and the practice of the four stages of meditation. (3) The vehicle of voice-hearers enables one to attain the state of arhat through awakening to the four noble truths. (4) The vehicle of cause-awakened ones leads one to the state of *pratyekabuddha,* or the insight of the cause-awakened one, through awakening to the doctrine of the twelve-linked chain of causation. (5) The vehicle of bodhisattvas brings one to Buddhahood through the practice of the six *pāramitās*. There are several differing explanations of the five vehicles.

five wisdom Buddhas [五智如来] (Jpn *gochi-nyorai*): Also, five wisdom Thus Come Ones. In Esoteric Buddhism, the five Buddhas of the Diamond Realm mandala, who represent the five aspects of Mahāvairochana Buddha's wisdom. They are (1) Mahāvairochana Buddha, who represents "the wisdom of the essence of the phenomenal world" that penetrates the nature of the phenomenal world; (2) Akshobhya Buddha, who symbolizes "the great round mirror wisdom" that accurately perceives the world; (3) Jewel Born Buddha, who stands for "the non-discriminating wisdom" that recognizes the fundamental equality of all things; (4) Amida Buddha, who represents "the wisdom of insight into the particulars" that discerns the capacities of all beings; and (5) Infallible Realization Buddha, who symbolizes "the wisdom of perfect practice" that benefits both oneself and others. *See also* five kinds of wisdom.

fixed karma [定業] (Jpn *jōgō*): Also, immutable karma. The opposite of unfixed karma. Karma that inevitably produces a fixed or set result, whether negative or positive. *The Dharma Analysis Treasury* lists the four causes of fixed karma. They are (1) actions motivated by exceptionally strong earthly desires or by a profoundly pure mind; (2) actions, whether good or evil, done habitually; (3) actions, whether good or evil, performed in relation to such sources of benefit as the three treasures of Buddhism; and (4) actions causing harm to one's parents. Fixed karma may also be interpreted as karma whose effects are destined to appear at a fixed time. In this case, fixed karma may be of three types depending on when its effects will appear: (1) karma whose effects are destined to appear in the same lifetime; (2) karma whose effects are destined to appear in the next lifetime; and (3) karma whose effects are destined to appear in a third or even later lifetime. As a general rule, lighter karma is said to manifest itself in the same lifetime that it was created, while exceptionally good or bad karma will be carried over into subsequent lifetimes. Fixed karma was traditionally considered unchangeable, but Nichiren states in his writing *On Prolonging One's Life Span*, "Karma also may be divided into two categories: fixed and unfixed. Sincere repentance will eradicate even fixed karma, to say nothing of karma that is unfixed" (954).

Fixed Light [錠光仏] (Jpn Jōkō-butsu): Another name for the Buddha Burning Torch. *See* Burning Torch.

flame-emitting meditation [火生三昧] (Jpn *kashō-zammai*): A meditation in which flames are said to emerge from the body. It is known specifically as the kind of meditation entered into by the wisdom king

Immovable, a main deity among a group of deities called wisdom kings who are said to be capable of destroying all obstacles. In this meditation, the wisdom king Immovable emits flames from his body that destroy all devils, obstacles, and earthly desires.

Flower Garland period [華厳時] (Jpn Kegon-ji): The period of the Flower Garland Sutra. The first of the five periods, a classification of Shakyamuni's teachings by T'ien-t'ai. *See* five periods.

Flower Garland school [華厳宗] (Chin Hua-yen-tsung; Jpn Kegon-shū): A school based on the Flower Garland Sutra. Tu-shun (557–640) is usually regarded as the founder of the Flower Garland school in China. His successor was Chih-yen. Chih-yen's disciple Fa-tsang (also known as the Great Teacher Hsien-shou) systematized the doctrines of the school. Hence the Flower Garland school is also called the Hsien-shou (Jpn Genju) school. Fa-tsang was followed by Ch'eng-kuan, who was in turn succeeded by his disciple Tsung-mi. These five persons are regarded as the first five patriarchs of the Chinese Flower Garland school. Fa-tsang, the third patriarch, formulated a classification of the Buddhist teachings called the "five teachings and ten doctrines" to show the superiority of the Flower Garland Sutra over all the other sutras. His system arranged the Buddhist sutras into five categories according to their degree of profundity, and the Buddhist schools into ten categories according to their doctrines. The Flower Garland school was introduced to Japan by Tao-hsüan (702–760), a priest from China, in 736. In 740 Shinjō (Kor Simsang), a priest from Silla on the Korean Peninsula, who had studied under Fa-tsang, lectured on the Flower Garland Sutra in Japan. He is regarded as the founder of the Japanese Flower Garland school. Tōdai-ji in Nara is the head temple of the school. The Flower Garland school teaches that all phenomena interpenetrate without obstruction; one permeates all and all are contained in one. Unlike the Tendai school, which elucidates the relationship between phenomena and the ultimate reality, the Flower Garland school is primarily concerned with the relationships among phenomena. *See also* six forms; ten mysteries.

Flower Garland Sutra [華厳経] (Skt *Buddha-avatamsaka-nāma-mahā-vaipulya-sūtra;* Chin *Hua-yen-ching;* Jpn *Kegon-gyō*): Also known as the Avatamsaka Sutra. The basic text of the Flower Garland (Chin Hua-yen; Jpn Kegon) school. According to this sutra, Shakyamuni expounded the teaching it contains immediately after he attained enlightenment under the *bodhi* tree in the kingdom of Magadha, India. Its full title is the Great and Vast Buddha Flower Garland Sutra. There are three Chinese translations: the sixty-volume sutra translated by Buddhabhadra (359–429), the eighty-volume sutra by Shikshānanda (652–710), and the forty-volume sutra by Prajnā (b. 734). Prajnā's translation consists only of the "Entering the Dharma Realm" chapter of the sutra. In the Flower Garland Sutra, Bodhisattva Dharma Wisdom and others teach other bodhisattvas of superior capacity that all things constantly interrelate and give rise to one another, that one permeates all and all are contained in one, and so on. The sutra also sets forth many stages of bodhisattva practice.

Flower Glow [華光如来] (1) (Skt Padmaprabha; Jpn Kekō-nyorai): Flower Glow Thus Come One or Flower Glow Buddha. The name that Shāriputra will bear when he attains enlightenment, according to Shakyamuni's prediction in the "Simile and Parable" (third) chapter of the Lotus Sutra. The chapter reads: "Shāriputra, in ages to come, after a countless, boundless, inconceivable number of *kalpas* have passed, you will make offerings to some thousands, ten thousands, millions of Buddhas, and will honor and uphold the correct Law. You will fulfill every aspect of the way of the bodhisattva and will be able to become a Buddha with the name Flower Glow Thus Come One . . . Your realm will be called Free from Stain, the land will be level and smooth, pure and beautifully adorned, peaceful, bountiful, and happy. . . . And this Flower Glow Thus Come One will employ the three vehicles to teach and convert living beings. Shāriputra, when this Buddha appears, although it will not be an evil age, because of his original vow he will preach the Law through the three vehicles. His *kalpa* will be called Great Treasure Adornment."

(2) (Skt unknown; Jpn Kekō-nyorai): The name of a Buddha who appeared in the Glorious Kalpa, which immediately preceded the present Wise Kalpa. A thousand Buddhas are said to have appeared in succession during the Glorious Kalpa; Flower Glow Buddha is known as the first in that succession. *See also* Glorious Kalpa.

Fo-lung-ssu [仏隴寺] (PY Folongsi; Jpn Butsurō-ji): Also known as Fo-lung Monastery. A temple of the T'ien-t'ai school located on the southwest peak of Mount T'ien-t'ai in China, founded by T'ien-t'ai in 575. It was later renamed Hsiu-ch'an-ssu. Dengyō, who later became the founder of the Japanese Tendai school, traveled to China at the beginning of the ninth century and received the transmission of the T'ien-t'ai teachings from Hsing-man, the chief priest of this temple.

foolishness [愚癡・癡・無明] (Skt, Pali *moha;* Jpn *guchi, chi,* or *mumyō*): One of the three poisons, or the three sources of vice and suffering, the other two being greed and anger. It is also interpreted as delusion, illusion, ignorance, or error, and indicates the unenlightened state that causes one to take the false for the true and the seeming for the real, and thus prevents one from perceiving the true nature of things or from discerning the truth. *See also* three poisons.

forbearance [忍・忍辱] (Skt *kshānti;* Jpn *nin* or *ninniku*): Also, patience or endurance. One of the six *pāramitās,* or six practices required of bodhisattvas. In practicing the *pāramitā,* or perfection, of forbearance, bodhisattvas are required to bear persecutions and difficulties and remain unperturbed. The Sutra on the Wise and the Foolish tells the story of an ascetic named Forbearance (Skt Kshāntivādin), who was Shakyamuni Buddha in a previous incarnation. This ascetic, when engaged in the practice of forbearance, suffered mutilation at the hands of the ruler and yet remained unperturbed. A forbearing mind is compared to a robe or armor; hence expressions such as "the robe of forbearance" and "the armor of perseverance." They enable one to bear insult and all persecutions and to protect oneself against evils and obstructions. *See also* Forbearance.

Forbearance [忍辱仙人] (Skt Kshāntivādin; Jpn Ninniku-sennin): The ascetic Forbearance. The name of Shakyamuni in a past existence when he carried out the *pāramitā* of forbearance. This story appears in the Sutra on the Wise and the Foolish. Once King Kāli of Vārānasī, accompanied by his wife, ministers, and maids in waiting, went on a pleasure excursion to a mountain and grew so tired that he fell asleep. While the king was sleeping, the maids happened to meet an ascetic and listened reverently to his preaching. King Kāli awoke and found the ascetic preaching, and asked him what benefits he could bestow. The ascetic humbly replied that he could bestow no benefit. The king therefore wrongly assumed that the ascetic had been trying to seduce the maids and flew into a rage. When the king was informed that the ascetic was engaged in the practice of forbearance, he cut off the ascetic's hands, legs, ears, and nose. But the ascetic did not flinch, maintaining a look of composure. His blood turned into milk, and his body restored itself. Seeing this, the king repented his conduct and thereafter protected the ascetic wholeheartedly. *See also* Kāli.

foreign invasion [他国侵逼難] (Jpn *takoku-shimpitsu-nan*): One of the seven disasters described in the Medicine Master Sutra. *See* calamity of invasion from foreign lands; seven disasters.

foremost worldly stage [世第一法・世第一法位] (Jpn *sedaiippō* or *sedaiippō-i*): Also, stage of the foremost worldly good root. The fourth of the four good roots, which are stages of Hinayana practice. In this stage, one obtains the highest of the four good roots, though these are still tainted by outflows, or earthly desires; hence the name "foremost worldly stage." One who has reached this stage will in time enter the way of insight, or the first of the three ways, and become a sage. The third and last of the three ways is the way of the arhat. *See also* four good roots; three stages of worthiness.

Forest of Gems in the Garden of the Law, The [法苑珠林] (Chin *Fa-yüan-chu-lin;* Jpn *Hō'on-jurin*): A one-hundred-volume Buddhist encyclopedia compiled in 668 by the Chinese priest Tao-shih. This work organizes terms and concepts appearing in various Buddhist texts into one hundred general categories, each with more detailed subheadings, and explains them. This work contains passages from the Buddhist scriptures that have been lost, as well as passages from non-Buddhist writings. It is regarded as a valuable reference for the study not only of Buddhism but of Chinese history and literature as well.

Forest of Meanings in the Mahayana Garden of the Law, The [大乘法苑義林章] (Chin *Ta-ch'eng-fa-yüan-i-lin-chang;* Jpn *Daijō-hō'on-girin-jō*): Abbreviated as *The Forest of Meanings in the Garden of the Law.* A seven-volume work by Tz'u-en (632–682), the founder of the Dharma Characteristics (Fa-hsiang) school in China, explaining the major doctrines of the school. It compares non-Buddhist, Hinayana, and Mahayana teachings, and asserts the supremacy of the Mahayana Consciousness-Only doctrine.

Forest of Merits [功徳林菩薩] (Jpn Kudokurin-bosatsu): One of the four great bodhisattvas depicted in the Flower Garland Sutra, the other three being Dharma Wisdom, Diamond Banner, and Diamond Storehouse. The preaching of the Flower Garland Sutra is described as occurring in eight successive assemblies in seven different locations, beginning at the place of Shakyamuni Buddha's enlightenment and then shifting to various heavens. At the fourth assembly, held in the Yāma Heaven, the bodhisattva Forest of Merits expounds the doctrine of the ten stages of practice, or the twenty-first through the thirtieth of the fifty-two stages of bodhisattva practice.

"Former Affairs of King Wonderful Adornment" chapter [妙荘厳王本事品] (Jpn *Myōshōgonnō-honji-hon*): Abbreviated as the "King Wonderful Adornment" chapter. The twenty-seventh chapter of the Lotus Sutra, in which Shakyamuni relates the story of King Wonderful Adornment. In the remote past, Shakyamuni says, there was a Buddha named Cloud Thunder Sound Constellation King Flower Wisdom who expounded the Lotus Sutra. The king's two sons, Pure Storehouse and Pure Eye, begged their mother Pure Virtue to come with them to listen to the Buddha. She replied that they must first persuade their father, a devout believer in Brahmanism, and suggested that they perform magical feats to demonstrate to him the power of Buddhism. They then displayed transcendental powers before the king, awakening in him a desire to hear the Buddha's teaching. Together with his wife, two sons, ministers, and attendants, King Wonderful Adornment went to make offerings to the Buddha Cloud Thunder Sound Constellation King Flower Wisdom and received from him a prophecy of Buddhahood. The king proclaimed that his sons were what Buddhism calls his good friends because they had led him to Buddhism. Then he, his wife and sons, and his entire retinue renounced the secular world and became the Buddha's disciples.

In the concluding part of this chapter, King Wonderful Adornment is identified as the present Bodhisattva Flower Virtue, who is among the assembly at Eagle Peak; Queen Pure Virtue as the bodhisattva Light Shining Adornment Marks; and Pure Storehouse and Pure Eye as the bodhisattvas Medicine King and Medicine Superior. In *The Words and Phrases of the Lotus Sutra,* T'ien-t'ai (538–597) tells the following story about the past relationship between Wonderful Adornment and his wife and sons. In the remote past, there were four religious practitioners carrying out austerities in search of the way. They found themselves hindered, however, by the daily routines of cooking and cleaning. To assist the practice of the other three, one of them abandoned his austerities and took all these chores upon himself. The other three continued their practice and obtained the way to Buddhahood, but he did not. As his karmic reward for having supported the others' practice, however, he was reborn as King Wonderful Adornment, and the other three were reborn as his wife and sons to lead him to the Buddha way and thus repay their debt to him.

"Former Affairs of the Bodhisattva Medicine King" chapter [薬王菩薩本事品] (Jpn *Yakuō-bosatsu-honji-hon*): Abbreviated as the "Medicine King" chapter. The twenty-third chapter of the Lotus Sutra. Following the Ceremony in the Air, the assembly returns to Eagle Peak and this chapter begins. It opens with Bodhisattva Constellation King Flower imploring Shakyamuni Buddha to talk about the past practices of Bodhisattva Medicine King. In reply, the Buddha explains that there was once a bodhisattva named Gladly Seen by All Living Beings who heard the Lotus Sutra from the Buddha Sun Moon Pure Bright Virtue. In gratitude, he burned his body as an offering to the Buddha and the Lotus Sutra for twelve hundred years. Born again in the land of the Buddha Sun Moon Pure Bright Virtue, he burned his arms as a further offering for seventy-two thousand years. After relating this story, Shakyamuni Buddha sets forth ten similes and twelve analogies illustrating the supremacy of the Lotus Sutra and the benefit of faith in the sutra. Toward the end of the chapter, he urges propagation of the sutra in the future.

This section includes the passage: "After I have passed into extinction, in the last five-hundred-year period you must spread it abroad widely throughout Jambudvīpa and never allow it to be cut off." According to Chang-an's *Biography of the Great Teacher T'ien-t'ai Chih-che of the Sui Dynasty,* T'ien-t'ai (538–597) obtained a great awakening through the "Medicine King" chapter after practicing for fourteen days the recitation of and meditation on the Lotus Sutra he had learned from his teacher, Nan-yüeh.

Former Day of the Law [正法] (Jpn *shōbō*): Also, age of the Correct Law or age of the True Dharma. The first of three periods following Shakyamuni's death. In this age, the teaching, practice, and proof of Shakyamuni's teachings are all present, and those who practice Buddhism and attain enlightenment are more numerous than in the ages that follow. According to *The Annotations on "The Treatise on the Middle Way"* and other works, the Former Day of the Law of Shakyamuni Buddha lasts for one thousand years, though other sources state its length as five hundred. The Great Collection Sutra defines the first five hundred years of the Former Day of the Law as the "age of attaining liberation," in which many people are sure to attain emancipation through practicing the Buddha's teachings. It defines the second five hundred years as the "age of meditation," in which meditation will be widely practiced. *See also* three periods.

forty-eight minor precepts [四十八軽戒] (Jpn *shijūhachi-kyōkai*): Precepts for Mahayana bodhisattvas enumerated in the Brahmā Net Sutra. The forty-eight minor precepts are so called because they concern relatively minor evils, in contrast with the ten major precepts expounded in the same sutra. For example, they prohibit drinking intoxicants and eating meat or pungent vegetables, such as leeks and onions, avoiding nursing the sick, keeping implements for killing living creatures, etc.

forty-eight vows [四十八願] (Jpn *shijūhachi-gan*): The vows that Amida Buddha is said to have made while still engaged in bodhisattva practice as Bodhisattva Dharma Treasury. They are listed in the Buddha Infinite Life Sutra. According to the sutra, Bodhisattva Dharma Treasury wished to create a splendid Buddha land in which he would live after attaining Buddhahood. Under the guidance of the Buddha World Freedom King, he studied the characteristics of "the lands of two hundred ten million Buddhas" and then meditated for five *kalpas,* pondering the features that should dignify his own Buddha land. After completing this meditation, Bodhisattva Dharma Treasury made forty-eight vows concerning the characteristics of his Buddha land, thus ensuring its sublimity. For example, the first vow states, "If, after I attain Buddhahood, there are any beings of hell, the realm of hungry spirits, or the realm of animals to be found in my land, then let me not attain supreme enlightenment." Among these vows, the eighteenth vow—that all who place their trust in Amida Buddha will obtain rebirth in the Pure Land, excepting only those who commit the five cardinal sins and those who slander the correct teaching—is the one most emphasized by the Pure Land school.

forty-two levels of ignorance [四十二品の無明] (Jpn *shijūnihon-no-mumyō*): Also, forty-two levels of illusion. There are two versions of this concept. (1) The specific illusions associated with each of the final forty-two stages of bodhisattva practice, from the ten stages of security through the highest stage of perfect enlightenment. After eliminating all those illusions, one attains perfect enlightenment as a Buddha. (2) The forty-two levels of illusion into which T'ien-t'ai (538–597) divided the third of the three categories of illusion, "illusions about the true nature of existence." They are kinds of ignorance concerning the true nature of life—illusions that prevent bodhisattvas from attaining enlightenment. The last and most deeply rooted of the forty-two is called fundamental darkness or fundamental ignorance. According to T'ien-t'ai, one attains enlightenment by eradicating these successive levels of ignorance or illusions and finally freeing oneself from fundamental darkness.

Fo-t'u-teng [仏図澄] (232–348) (PY Fotudeng; Jpn Buttochō): A monk of Central Asia who went to Lo-yang in China in 310, where he propagated Buddhism. He was highly esteemed by the ruler of the Later Chao dynasty, whom he advised on such matters as military administration, culture, and politics. He is said to have built about nine hundred temples and helped lay the foundation for the spread of Buddhism in China.

four activities of daily life [四威儀] (Jpn *shi-igi*): Also, four daily activities or four modes of conduct. Walking, standing, sitting, and lying down. The activity of standing means the state of standing still and also the motion of standing up. The same applies to the other three. The term "four activities of daily life" is often used to refer to all modes of human behavior. In Buddhism, the various rules of conduct were prescribed with regard to the four activities of daily life, and it was required that monks and nuns be correct in all their modes of behavior, and that their four daily activities accord with the rules of conduct.

four Āgama sutras [四阿含経] (Jpn *shi-agon-gyō*): The extant Chinese versions of the Āgama sutras. The Long Āgama Sutra, the Medium-Length Āgama Sutra, the Miscellaneous Āgama Sutra, and the Increasing by One Āgama Sutra. Each of these four Āgama sutras is not a single sutra but a collection of individual sutras. The Long Āgama Sutra is a collection of comparatively long sutras. The Medium-Length Āgama

Sutra is a collection of medium-length sutras. The Miscellaneous Āgama Sutra is a collection of short sutras; these sutras are grouped by doctrines or themes. The Increasing by One Āgama Sutra is also a collection of short sutras; these sutras are categorized in eleven groups, each group comprising doctrines with numerical themes such as the four noble truths. For instance, the first group contains sutras on themes related to the word *single,* such as the [single] practice of meditating on the Buddha or the elimination of greed; the second group contains sutras concerning pairs, such as the two kinds of almsgiving; the third group contains sutras dealing with triplets, such as the three treasures; and the fourth group contains sutras concerning principles in groups of four, such as the four noble truths and the four forms of birth; and so on. These four Chinese Āgama sutras correspond respectively to the first four of the five Āgamas of the Pali canon: *Dīgha-nikāya* (long sutras), *Majjhima-nikāya* (medium-length sutras), *Samyutta-nikāya* (sutras on related topics), *Anguttara-nikāya* (sutras of numerical doctrines), and *Khuddaka-nikāya* (minor sutras). *See also* Āgama sutras.

four bases of transcendental powers [四如意足・四神足] (Jpn *shi-nyoisoku* or *shi-jinsoku*): *See* four steps to transcendental powers.

four bodhisattvas [四菩薩] (Jpn *shi-bosatsu*): Different groups of four bodhisattvas who are referred to in various Buddhist scriptures. In the Lotus Sutra, they are the four leaders of the Bodhisattvas of the Earth described in the "Emerging from the Earth" (fifteenth) chapter: Superior Practices, Boundless Practices, Pure Practices, and Firmly Established Practices. According to Tao-hsien's *Supplement to "The Words and Phrases of the Lotus Sutra,"* they signify respectively the four virtues of the Buddha's life: true self, eternity, purity, and happiness. The four bodhisattvas described in the Flower Garland Sutra are Dharma Wisdom, Forest of Merits, Diamond Banner, and Diamond Storehouse. Other sets of four bodhisattvas to which this term applies are Manjushrī, Universal Worthy, Perceiver of the World's Sounds, and Maitreya; and Manjushrī, Universal Worthy, Medicine King, and Perceiver of the World's Sounds.

four categories of Buddhists [四衆] (Jpn *shi-shu*): Monks, nuns, laymen, and laywomen. *See also* four kinds of believers.

four continents [四洲] (Jpn *shi-shū*): Also, four great continents. The continents located in the outermost circular sea surrounding Mount Sumeru, according to the ancient Indian worldview. They are Pūrvavideha in the east, Aparagodānīya in the west, Uttarakuru in the north, and Jambudvīpa in the south. According to *The Dharma Analysis Treasury,* the shapes of these continents are, respectively, semicircular, circular, square, and roughly triangular with the base in the north and the apex in the south. Human beings inhabit them all, the shape of their faces resembling that of the continent in which they live. Among the four continents, Jambudvīpa is said to be the only continent where Buddhas appear.

four-continent world [四天下] (Jpn *shi-tenge*): Also, four-continent realm, or simply four continents. A world of four continents surrounding a Mount Sumeru. According to Buddhist cosmology, there exist countless four-continent worlds in the universe. *See also* four continents.

four daily activities [四威儀] (Jpn *shi-igi*): Walking, standing, sitting, and lying down. *See* four activities of daily life.

four debts of gratitude [四恩] (Jpn *shi-on*): The debts owed to one's parents, to all living beings, to one's sovereign, and to the three treasures of Buddhism. These four are set forth in the Contemplation on the Mind-Ground Sutra. The definition of the four debts of gratitude varies somewhat according to the source. The Meditation on the Correct Teaching Sutra defines them as the debts owed to one's father, to one's mother, to the Thus Come One or Buddha, and to the teacher of the Law. In his work *The Four Debts of Gratitude,* Nichiren (1222–1282) refers to the four debts of gratitude described in the Contemplation on the Mind-Ground Sutra. In *On Repaying Debts of Gratitude,* he lists the four debts of gratitude as the debts owed to one's father and mother, to one's teacher, to the three treasures, and to one's sovereign.

four devils [四魔] (Jpn *shi-ma*): Four evil or debilitating functions described in Buddhist scriptures as afflicting practitioners and obstructing their practice. They are (1) the devil of the five components (Skt *skandha-māra*), or hindrances arising from the five components of life; (2) the devil of earthly desires *(klesha-māra),* hindrances arising from earthly desires; (3) the devil of death (also called the devil death, *mrityu-māra*), the hindrance arising from the death of oneself or another practitioner; and (4) the heavenly devil *(devaputra-māra),* hindrances attributed to the workings of the devil king of the sixth heaven. The Sanskrit word *māra* means devil, obstacle, killing, death, or pestilence. Together with the three obstacles of earthly desires, karma, and retribution, the four devils are referred to as the "three obstacles and four devils." *See also* three obstacles and four devils.

four Dharma seals [四法印] (Jpn *shi-hōin*): Four identifying principles of Buddhism: impermanence, non-self, nirvana, and suffering. *See* three Dharma seals.

four dhyāna heavens [四禅天] (Jpn *shizenten*): The four heavens that constitute the world of form. *See* four meditation heavens.

four dictums [四箇の格言] (Jpn *shika-no-kakugen*): Also, four maxims. Four statements with which Nichiren (1222–1282) denounced the four most influential Buddhist schools of his time in Japan—the Pure Land (Jōdo) school (also, the Nembutsu school), the Zen school, the True Word (Shingon) school, and the Precepts (Ritsu) school. Based on his understanding of the supremacy of the Lotus Sutra and his perception of the slander of these schools against the sutra, he repudiated their doctrines and declared as follows: (1) "Nembutsu leads to the hell of incessant suffering," (2) "Zen is the invention of the heavenly devil," (3) "True Word will ruin the nation," and (4) "Precepts is a traitor to the nation."

four different views of the grove of sal trees [沙羅の四見] (Jpn *shara-no-shiken*): *See* four views of the sal grove.

four easy practices [四安楽行] (Jpn *shi-anraku-gyō*): *See* four peaceful practices.

four elements [四大] (Jpn *shi-dai*): Also, four basic elements. The four constituent elements of all things, according to ancient Indian belief. They are earth, water, fire, and wind. These are also understood in terms of their natures or functions. Each corresponds to a quality of matter: earth to solidity, water to moisture, fire to heat, and wind to motion. Their respective functions correspond to four intrinsic functions of the universe itself: to sustain and preserve, to gather and contain, to mature, and to cause growth. Disharmony among the four elements in the human body was said to cause illness. Space, which functions to integrate and harmonize the four elements, is added to these four to make the five elements.

four encounters [四門遊観・四門出遊] (Jpn *shimon-yūkan* or *shimon-shutsuyū*): *See* four meetings.

four evil paths [四悪趣・四悪道] (Jpn *shi-akushu* or *shi-akudō*): The four realms of hell, hungry spirits, animals, and *asuras*. Considered the lowest four of the Ten Worlds, they are called evil because they are characterized by suffering. Nevertheless, the world of *asuras* is counted as one of the three good paths, because those in it possess a will that is not entirely controlled by the environment. Yet those who remain in this state ultimately do harm to themselves through their own arrogance. Traditionally, the four evil paths were considered the physical realms into which people fall because of the evil karma they had created by the commission of evil acts.

four fearlessnesses [四無所畏・四無畏] (Jpn *shi-mushoi* or *shi-mui*): Four types of confidence possessed by Buddhas and bodhisattvas. The four fearlessnesses of a Buddha are distinct from those of bodhisattvas. The four fearlessnesses of a Buddha are (1) fearlessness in declaring oneself to be enlightened to the truth of all phenomena, (2) fearlessness in proclaiming oneself to have extinguished all desires and illusions, (3) fearlessness in proclaiming oneself to have elucidated the obstacles to Buddhist practice and enlightenment, and (4) fearlessness in declaring oneself to have clarified the way of liberation from the world of suffering, and thus the way of attaining emancipation.

The four fearlessnesses of the bodhisattva are (1) fearlessness in continually memorizing the Buddhist teachings, and in expounding the meaning of these teachings, (2) fearlessness in perceiving the people's inherent capacities, and in expounding the teachings according to those capacities, (3) fearlessness in resolving the people's doubts, and (4) fearlessness in answering any question. The term *fearlessness* derives from the Sanskrit word *vaishāradya,* and here implies dauntless courage and unwavering confidence; it is regarded as one of the virtues of Buddhas and bodhisattvas.

four flavors [前四味・四味] (Jpn *zen-shimi* or *shimi*): *See* first four flavors; four flavors and three teachings.

four flavors and three teachings [四味三教] (Jpn *shimi-sankyō*): According to T'ien-t'ai's doctrine, the entire body of Shakyamuni Buddha's teachings preached prior to the Lotus Sutra, or the Buddha's provisional teachings. The "four flavors" refers to the first four of the five flavors—fresh milk, cream, curdled milk, butter, and ghee (the finest clarified butter). T'ien-t'ai (538–597) used the five flavors as a metaphor for the teachings of the five periods—the Flower Garland, Āgama, Correct and Equal, Wisdom, and Lotus and Nirvana periods. Thus he compared the process by which Shakyamuni instructed his disciples and gradually developed their capacity to that of converting milk into ghee. The three teachings are the first three of the four teachings of doctrine, a classification by T'ien-t'ai of Shakyamuni's teachings according to their content, which are the Tripitaka, connecting, specific, and perfect teachings. The perfect teaching, which is not included in the three teachings, refers to that revealed in the Lotus Sutra. *See also* five periods; four teachings of doctrine.

fourfold rise and fall [四重の興廃] (Jpn *shijū-no-kōhai*): Four levels of comparison that clarify the principle that, when a superior teaching rises, inferior teachings decline. They are as follows: (1) When the great doctrine of the pre-Lotus Sutra teachings rises, non-Buddhist teachings fall. (2) When the great teaching of the Lotus Sutra rises, the pre-Lotus Sutra teachings fall. (3) When the great doctrine of the essential teaching (latter half) of the Lotus Sutra rises, the theoretical teaching (first half) of the sutra falls. (4) When the great teaching of the observation of the mind rises, the essential teaching falls. This fourfold comparison is expounded in T'ien-t'ai's *Profound Meaning of the Lotus Sutra.* Nichiren (1222–1282) accepted this standard of comparison and defined the teaching of the observation of the mind as the teaching of Nam-myoho-renge-kyo, the practice of which he said enables all people in the Latter Day of the Law to manifest the Buddhahood inherent in their lives. The fourfold rise and fall is equivalent to the fivefold comparison that Nichiren set forth, except that it lacks the comparison of the Mahayana teachings with the Hinayana teachings.

Fourfold Rules of Discipline, The [四分律] (Chin *Ssu-fen-lü;* Jpn *Shibun-ritsu*): A text of the Indian Dharmagupta school on the *vinaya,* or rules of monastic discipline, translated into Chinese in the early fifth century by Buddhayashas and Chu Fo-nien. The Dharmagupta school was one of the twenty Hinayana schools of ancient India. *The Fourfold Rules of Discipline* is so called because it divides the monastic rules into four sections; it sets forth 250 precepts for monks and 348 for nuns. This work is the *vinaya* text of the Precepts (Lü; Ritsu) school in China and Japan.

four forms of birth [四生] (Jpn *shi-shō*): A classification of the ways of coming into existence. They are (1) birth from the womb, as in the case of mammals; (2) birth from eggs, as in the case of birds; (3) birth from dampness (or moisture)—the way worms were thought to be generated; and (4) birth by transformation, that is, spontaneous birth without the womb, eggs, or dampness, as in the cases of deities and beings in the hells. It is said that, after their previous lives end, such beings suddenly appear in this fashion due to their karma, without the help of parents or any other agency. The term "four forms of birth" often appears in conjunction with the six paths, such as in "transmigrating through the six paths and the four forms of birth" and "the living beings of the six paths and the four forms of birth."

four forms of meditation [四種三昧] (Jpn *shishu-sammai* or *shishu-zammai*): Also, four kinds of meditation or four kinds of *samādhi.* Four methods of meditation described in T'ien-t'ai's *Great Concentration and Insight.* T'ien-t'ai (538–597) classified the various types of meditation referred to in the Buddhist sutras into four comprehensive categories: (1) constant sitting meditation, in which one engages in seated meditation for ninety days; (2) constant active meditation, in which one meditates while walking around a statue of the Buddha in a monastery for ninety days; (3) half-active and half-sitting meditation, in which one engages in the two practices of seated meditation and of walking around a meditation platform. (This third practice is further divided into that based upon the Great Correct and Equal Dhāranī Sutra and that based on the Lotus Sutra. The former practice is carried out for seven days, and the latter, for twenty-one days); and (4) meditation in an unspecified posture for an unspecified period, in which one practices meditation of an unspecified length of time or form. All meditations not covered in the first three categories are included in the last.

four good roots [四善根・四善根位] (Jpn *shi-zengon* or *shi-zengon-i*): Also, four roots of goodness, four roots of good, or the stages of the four good roots. Stages of practice taught in Hinayana Buddhism. The preparatory practices leading to the way of insight, the first of the three ways. The way of insight is the stage at which one gains insight into the four noble truths. It is followed by the way of practice and the way of the arhat, or having no more to learn. One who has attained the four good roots enters the way of insight. *Root* here means the source of an attribute or virtue. Because these four form the foundation or source of the capacity to enter the way of insight, they are called roots. The four good roots, along with the three stages of worthiness, constitute the seven expedient means. Both the four good roots and the three stages of worthiness refer to the stage of ordinary people, and the way of insight and the subsequent stages, to the stage of sages. The stage of ordinary people is divided into two: the inner rank and the outer rank. The former, or the higher rank of ordinary practitioners, corresponds to the four good roots, and the latter, or the lower rank of ordinary practitioners, corresponds to the three stages of worthiness.

The four good roots are (1) the heat stage, or the stage in which one approaches wisdom without outflows, or earthly desires, and obtains the type of good roots still tainted by outflows, just as one approaches a fire and obtains heat from it; (2) the peak stage, or the stage in which one's good roots are still unsettled but one obtains the highest of the unsettled good roots; though the peak stage is the stage of possible regression, even if persons in this stage recede from it and fall into hell, the good roots represented by the peak stage cannot be wiped out; (3) the perception stage, or the stage in which one understands the doctrine of the four noble truths, and one's good roots are settled; one who has entered this stage will never fall into the evil paths of existence; and (4) the foremost worldly stage, or the stage in which one obtains the highest of the four good roots, though these good roots are still tainted by outflows. One who has reached this stage in time will enter the way of insight and become a sage. The concept of the four good roots was later applied to the stages of Mahayana practice with some modification.

four grave offenses [四重罪・四波羅夷罪] (Jpn *shi-jūzai* or *shi-harai-zai*): *See* four major offenses.

four grave prohibitions [四重禁・四重] (Jpn *shijūkin* or *shijū*): Prohibitions against the four major offenses, i.e., the offenses of (1) killing a human being, (2) stealing, (3) having sexual relations, and (4) lying (particularly, lying about one's level of insight or spiritual attainment). *See also* four major offenses.

four great continents [四大洲] (Jpn *shidai-shū*): *See* four continents.

four great heavenly kings [四大天王] (Jpn *shidai-tennō*): *See* four heavenly kings.

four great rivers [四大河] (Jpn *shidai-ga*): *See* four rivers.

four great seas [四大海] (Jpn *shidai-kai*): *See* four seas.

four great voice-hearers [四大声聞] (Jpn *shidai-shōmon*): Mahākāshyapa, Subhūti, Maudgalyāyana, and Kātyāyana, whose attainment of Buddhahood is predicted in the "Bestowal of Prophecy" (sixth) chapter of the Lotus Sutra. These four belong to the group of intermediate capacity among Shakyamuni's voice-hearer disciples. They constitute the second of the three groups of voice-hearer disciples who understood the teaching of "replacement of the three vehicles with the one vehicle" through the parable of the three carts and the burning house related in the "Simile and Parable" (third) chapter of the Lotus Sutra. They express their understanding of this teaching in the "Belief and Understanding" (fourth) chapter of the sutra by relating the parable of the wealthy man and his poor son. In that chapter, after having related this parable, Mahākāshyapa says: "We today have heard the Buddha's voice teaching and we dance for joy, having gained what we never had before. The Buddha declares that the voice-hearers will be able to attain Buddhahood. This cluster of unsurpassed jewels has come to us unsought. . . . Now we have become voice-hearers in truth, for we will take the voice of the Buddha way and cause it to be heard by all."

four guidelines [四釈・四種釈] (Jpn *shi-shaku* or *shishu-shaku*): Four guidelines or standpoints for interpreting the words and phrases of the Lotus Sutra. They are causes and conditions, correlated teachings, the theoretical and essential teachings, and the observation of the mind. T'ien-t'ai (538–597) employed these four guidelines in *The Words and Phrases of the Lotus Sutra. Causes and conditions* means to interpret the words and phrases of the sutra in terms of the causes and conditions that prompted the Buddha to expound them, and to grasp them in terms of the four ways of preaching. *Correlated teachings* means to interpret the sutra's words and phrases from the standpoint of the four teachings of doctrine and the five periods. *The theoretical and essential teachings* means to interpret them in light of the theoretical teaching (first half) and the essential teaching (latter half) of the sutra. *The observation of the mind* means to perceive the truth within one's own mind through the practice of meditation and also to interpret the words and phrases of the sutra from the standpoint of this perception of the truth.

four heavenly kings [四天王] (Jpn *shi-tennō*): Also, four great heavenly kings. The lords of the four quarters who are said to serve the god Shakra as his generals and protect the four quarters of the world. They are Upholder of the Nation (Skt Dhritarāshtra), who protects the east; Wide-Eyed (Virūpāksha), who guards the west; Hearer of Many Teachings (Vaishravana), who watches over the north; and Increase and Growth (Virūdhaka), who defends the south. They are called the guardians of the world and are said to live halfway up the four sides of Mount Sumeru, on whose summit Shakra dwells. Their respective functions are to protect the world; to discern and punish evil and encourage the aspiration for enlightenment; to listen to the Buddhist teachings and protect the place where the Buddha expounds them; and to relieve people of their sufferings. Various sutras, such as the Golden Light Sutra, refer to them as guardians of Buddhism. In the ceremony of the Lotus Sutra, these four heavenly gods appear with their ten thousand retainer gods, and in the "Dhāranī" (twenty-sixth) chapter of the sutra, Hearer of Many Teachings and Upholder of the Nation pledge to protect those who embrace the sutra.

four heavens of the world of formlessness [四無色天] (Jpn *shi-mushiki-ten*): *See* four realms of the world of formlessness.

four imperial persecutions of Buddhism in China [三武一宗の法難] (Jpn Sambu-issō-no-hōnan): The wholesale suppression of Buddhism carried out on four occasions from the fifth through the tenth century by four Chinese emperors. They are (1) the persecution by Emperor T'ai-wu (r. 423–452) of the Northern Wei dynasty, a believer in Taoism; it lasted for seven years, beginning in 446; (2) the persecution by Emperor Wu (r. 560–578) of the Northern Chou dynasty, enacted twice, in 574 and 577; Wu also abolished Taoism, and this event prompted Buddhists to define this time as marking the beginning of the Latter Day of the Law in China; (3) the persecution in 845 by Emperor Wu-tsung (r. 840–846) of the T'ang dynasty, which was instigated by Taoists; and (4) the persecution in 955 by Emperor Shih-tsung (r. 954–959) of the Later Chou dynasty, in which a total of 3,336 temples were destroyed (with 2,694 temples surviving). In these persecutions, priests and nuns were killed or made to return to secular life, and Buddhist temples, statues, and sutras destroyed. In addition to the conflict between Taoists and Buddhists, moral decline in the clergy also contributed to the persecutions. Moreover, from around the time of Emperor Wu-tsung of the T'ang dynasty, the increase in the number of temples and priests and nuns put financial pressure on the state, which prompted the successive dynasties to regulate Buddhism. Finally Emperor Shih-tsung of the Later Chou dynasty carried out one of the greatest destructions.

four improper ways of livelihood [四邪命食・四不浄食・四食] (Jpn *shi-jamyōjiki, shi-fujōjiki,* or *shi-jiki*): Four illicit ways for a monk to obtain a living. They are to earn his livelihood (1) by cultivating the land or selling herbs, (2) by making astrological predictions, (3) by fawning on persons of authority or persons of wealth, and (4) by fortune-telling.

four inferior flavors [前四味・四味] (Jpn *zen-shimi* or *shimi*): *See* first four flavors.

four infinite virtues [四無量心] (Jpn *shi-muryōshin*): Boundless pity, boundless compassion, boundless joy, and boundless impartiality (or indifference). Pity, or *maitrī* in Sanskrit, here is interpreted as giving living beings delight or happiness; compassion, or *karunā,* as removing their suffering; and joy, or *muditā,* as rejoicing at seeing beings become free from suffering and gain happiness. Impartiality, or *upekshā,* is interpreted as abandoning attachments to love and hatred and being impartial toward everyone. By the practice of these four virtues, one is said to be able to attain rebirth in the Brahma Heaven.

four inverted views [四顛倒] (Jpn *shi-tendō*): Also, four wrong-headed views or four topsy-turvy views. They are called "inverted" because one takes an opposite view of the truth. Mistaking impermanence for permanence, suffering for happiness, non-self for self, and impurity for purity. This indicates the inverted views of ordinary people who do not recognize the world of delusion for what it is. The term *inverted views* also means to mistake permanence for impermanence, happiness for suffering, self for non-self, and purity for impurity. This indicates the inverted views of voice-hearers and cause-awakened ones, who recognize the world of delusion for what it is but do not recognize the world of enlightenment for what it is. Taken together, the above are referred to as the eight inverted views.

four kalpas [四劫] (Jpn *shi-kō*): In Buddhist cosmology, the four periods of time corresponding to the four stages in the cycle of formation, continuance, decline, and disintegration that a world is said to undergo. The four *kalpas* are explained in the Long Āgama Sutra and *The Dharma Analysis Treasury*. In the *kalpa* of formation, a world takes shape in space, and a variety of sentient beings appear on it. In the *kalpa* of continuance, living beings conduct their life-activities. In the *kalpa* of decline, the land is destroyed by natural disasters, and living beings gradually diminish and then disappear completely. In the *kalpa* of disintegration, complete destruction has taken place, and nothing exists. One complete cycle of the four *kalpas* is called a major *kalpa*. See also *kalpa* of continuance; *kalpa* of decline; *kalpa* of disintegration; *kalpa* of formation.

four kinds of believers [四衆] (Jpn *shi-shu*): Also, four kinds of Buddhists, four categories of Buddhists, four categories of believers, four types of Buddhist believers, or four kinds of people. (1) Four categories of people who believe in Buddhism—monks (Skt *bhikshu*), nuns *(bhikshunī)*, laymen *(upāsaka)*, and laywomen *(upāsikā)*. (2) Four kinds of people in the assembly where Shakyamuni Buddha preaches: those who ask the Buddha to expound the teaching; those who praise it; those who, having attained sufficient maturity, listen to the Buddha's teaching and immediately benefit from it; and those who attain no immediate benefit, but nevertheless form a bond with the Buddha's teaching and benefit from it at a later time.

four kinds of Buddhists [四衆] (Jpn *shi-shu*): Monks, nuns, laymen, and laywomen. *See also* four kinds of believers.

four kinds of flowers [四華] (Jpn *shi-ke*): *Māndārava* (also, *māndāra*), great *māndārava*, *manjūshaka*, and great *manjūshaka* flowers. Fragrant red and white flowers that, according to Indian tradition, bloom in heaven. The Lotus Sutra says that when the sutra was about to be preached these four kinds of flowers rained down from the heavens.

four kinds of lands [四土] (Jpn *shi-do*): A classification established by the T'ien-t'ai school of the various types of lands mentioned in the sutras. They are: (1) The Land of Sages and Common Mortals, also referred to as the Land of Enlightened and Unenlightened Beings. Here ordinary people of the six paths, or the six lower of the Ten Worlds, live together with the sages of the four noble worlds, or the four higher of the Ten Worlds. (2) The Land of Transition, which is inhabited by voice-hearers, cause-awakened ones, and bodhisattvas in the lower stages of practice. (3) The Land of Actual Reward, a realm inhabited by bodhisattvas in the higher stages of practice. (4) The Land of Eternally Tranquil Light, or simply the Land of Tranquil Light, where a Buddha lives. This Buddha land is free from impermanence and impurity.

four kinds of meditation [四種三昧] (Jpn *shishu-sammai* or *shishu-zammai*): *See* four forms of meditation.

four kinds of offerings [四事・四事供養] (Jpn *shiji* or *shiji-kuyō*): Offerings of food and drink, clothing, bedding, and medicine made in support of the Buddha and the Buddhist Order. Another definition replaces "bedding" with "monks' quarters."

four-line verse [四句偈] (Jpn *shiku-ge*): Also, four-phrase verse. A grouping of four phrases comprising a verse in Chinese translations of Buddhist sutras and treatises. A number of such four-line or four-phrase verses constitute a complete verse section. The Lotus Sutra mentions the great benefits to be gained by accepting and upholding a single four-line verse of the sutra. For example, the sutra's "Medicine King" (twenty-third) chapter reads, "Even if a person were to fill the entire major world system with the seven kinds of treasures as an offering to the Buddha and the great bodhisattvas, *pratyekabuddhas* and arhats, the benefits gained by such a person cannot match those gained by accepting and upholding this Lotus Sutra, even just one four-line verse of it! The latter brings the most numerous blessings of all." The "Dhāranī" (twenty-sixth) chapter reads, "If there are good men or good women who, with regard to this sutra, can accept and uphold even one four-line verse, if they read and recite it, understand the principle, and practice it as the sutra directs, the benefits will be very many."

four major disciples [四大弟子] (Jpn *shidai-deshi*): Shakyamuni's four leading disciples; the list differs among Buddhist scriptures. They are variously identified as Mahākāshyapa, Shāriputra, Maudgalyāyana, and Subhūti; Mahākāshyapa, Kātyāyana, Maudgalyāyana, and Subhūti; Shāriputra, Maudgalyāyana, Subhūti, and Pūrna; and Mahākāshyapa, Maudgalyāyana, Aniruddha, and Pindolabhāradvāja.

four major offenses [四重罪・四波羅夷罪] (Jpn *shi-jūzai* or *shi-harai-zai*): Also, four grave offenses, four unpardonable offenses, or four *pārājika* offenses. The offenses of (1) killing a human being, (2) stealing, (3) having sexual relations, and (4) lying (particularly, lying about one's level of insight or spiritual attainment). These four acts are the gravest of all the offenses proscribed by monastic discipline, warranting automatic expulsion from the Buddhist Order. The Sanskrit word *pārājika* means "deserving of expulsion."

four meditation heavens [四禅天] (Jpn *shizenten*): Also, four *dhyāna* heavens. The four heavens that constitute the world of form. They are named ordinally—the first meditation heaven, the second meditation heaven, and so on—in ascending order of altitude and quality. They are further subdivided into eighteen heavens. When, by practicing the four stages of meditation, one frees oneself of the illusions of the world of desire, one can be reborn among these four meditation heavens. The four meditation heavens are also regarded as four levels of consciousness that one can attain by practicing the corresponding meditation. *See also* four stages of meditation.

four meditations [四念処・四念住] (Jpn *shi-nenjo* or *shi-nenjū*): Also, four states of mindfulness. Four types of meditation on the body, sensation, mind, and phenomena. (1) Meditation on the body means to perceive the body as impure, (2) meditation on sensation is to perceive all sensation as suffering, (3) meditation on the mind is to perceive the mind as impermanent, and (4) meditation on phenomena is to perceive that they are without a self, that is, without any intrinsic nature of their own. The concept of the four meditations negates the ideas of purity (seeing the body as pure), pleasure (seeing all sensation as pleasure), permanence (seeing the mind as permanent), and ego (seeing phenomena as possessing a self) that were prevalent in India before the appearance of Buddhism. The four meditations are divided into specific meditation and general meditation. Specific meditation means to meditate on each of the four objects of meditation individually. General meditation means to meditate on them as a whole. The four meditations refer to the first of the seven constituent categories of the thirty-seven aids to the way, or the thirty-seven practices leading to enlightenment.

four meditations on formlessness [四無色定・四空定・四空処定] (Jpn *shi-mushiki-jō, shi-kū-jō,* or *shi-kūsho-jō*): Four levels of meditation leading to the four realms of the world of formlessness. They are intended to enable one to gain release from the bonds and limitations of matter and deliverance from all thought of matter. The four realms of the world of formlessness are, in ascending order of quality, the Realm of Boundless Empty Space, the Realm of Boundless Consciousness, the Realm of Nothingness, and the Realm of Neither Thought Nor No Thought. By practicing the four meditations on formlessness, one can be reborn among these four realms. The deeper the meditation, the higher the realm one attains upon rebirth. The four levels of meditation are named for their four corresponding realms. The first meditation, which leads to rebirth in the Realm of Boundless Empty Space, is called meditation on the Realm of Boundless Empty Space, the second meditation is called meditation on the Realm of Boundless Consciousness, and so on. The four realms of the world of formlessness are often interpreted as the levels of awareness that these four meditations enable their practitioners to attain.

four meetings [四門遊観・四門出遊] (Jpn *shimon-yūkan* or *shimon-shutsuyū*): Also, four encounters. A story that appears in various sutras concerning Shakyamuni's motivation for renouncing the secular world and pursuing a religious life. According to tradition, Prince Siddhārtha, the young Shakyamuni, was mostly confined to the palace of his father, who shielded him from the sight of any worldly suffering that might arouse in him a desire for a religious life. One day, however, emerging from the eastern gate of the palace on what was intended to be a pleasure outing, the prince encountered a man withered with age. Exiting from the southern gate on another occasion, he saw a sick person. A third time, going out from the western gate, he saw a corpse. Through these encounters, the prince awakened to the four sufferings of birth, aging, sickness, and death. Finally, going out through the northern gate, he encountered a religious ascetic whose air of serene dignity awoke in him the resolve to embark on a religious life and attain enlightenment.

four methods of winning people [四摂法・四摂事] (Jpn *shi-shōbō* or *shi-shōji*): Four methods employed by bodhisattvas to attract others to Buddhism. They are (1) expounding the Buddha's teachings and/or giving material things; (2) speaking in a kindly manner; (3) acting to benefit others; and (4) sharing others' hardships and cooperating with them. Bodhisattvas carry out these four kinds of conduct to win people's friendship and trust and finally to lead them to the way of the Buddha.

four modes of conduct [四威儀] (Jpn *shi-igi*): Walking, standing, sitting, and lying down. *See* four activities of daily life.

four noble truths [四諦・四聖諦] (Skt *chatur-ārya-satya;* Jpn *shi-tai* or *shi-shōtai*): A fundamental doctrine of Buddhism clarifying the cause of suffering and the way of emancipation. The four noble truths are the truth of suffering, the truth of the origin of suffering, the truth of the cessation of suffering, and the truth of the path to the cessation of suffering. Shakyamuni is said to have expounded the four noble truths at Deer Park in Vārānasī, India, during his first sermon after attaining enlightenment. They are: (1) all existence is suffering; (2) suffering is caused by selfish craving; (3) the eradication of selfish craving brings about the cessation of suffering and enables one to attain nirvana; and (4) there is a path by which this eradication can be achieved, namely, the discipline of the eightfold path. The eightfold path consists of right views, right thinking, right speech, right action, right way of life, right endeavor, right mindfulness, and right meditation.

four noble worlds [四聖] (Jpn *shi-shō* or *shi-sei*): The highest four of the Ten Worlds—the realms of voice-hearers, cause-awakened ones, bodhisattvas, and Buddhas. The term is contrasted with the six paths, or six lowest of the Ten Worlds. These four noble worlds are also regarded as the states in which one makes efforts to transcend the uncertainty of the six paths, where one is controlled by earthly desires and governed by an ever-changing environment, and to establish independence or release from the control of earthly desires and external changes.

four objects of faith [四信] (Jpn *shi-shin*): The objects of faith set forth in *The Awakening of Faith in the Mahayana.* They are the essential truth of things, and the three treasures, namely, the Buddha, the Law (his teachings), and the Order, or community of believers who protect and transmit his teachings.

four pārājika offenses [四重罪・四波羅夷罪] (Jpn *shi-jūzai* or *shi-haraizai*): *See* four major offenses.

four peaceful practices [四安楽行] (Jpn *shi-anraku-gyō*): Also, four easy practices, four comfortable practices, or four peaceful ways of practice. The practices for bodhisattvas in the evil age after Shakyamuni Buddha's death, set forth in the "Peaceful Practices" (fourteenth) chapter of the Lotus Sutra. While the descriptions of these practices in the sutra text are lengthy, T'ien-t'ai (538–597) categorized these as the four peaceful practices. They are (1) the peaceful practice of the body, which means to avoid temptations and meditate in a quiet and secluded place; (2) the peaceful practice of the mouth, or to teach the Lotus Sutra without despising or speaking of the faults of other people or scriptures; (3) the peaceful practice of the mind, or to discard a mind of jealousy or contention toward other sutras or those who embrace them; and (4) the peaceful practice of vows, which means to vow to save all people through great compassion. The "Encouraging Devotion" (thirteenth) chapter, which precedes "Peaceful Practices," sets forth a more difficult bodhisattva practice in which bodhisattvas are required to endure all hardships and persecutions, propagating the sutra without begrudging their bodies and lives. When contrasted with this kind of practice, T'ien-t'ai viewed the four peaceful practices set forth in the "Peaceful Practices" chapter as passive and less difficult, and therefore as disciplines for bodhisattvas still in the early stages of practice.

Four Peaceful Practices, The [四安楽行] (Jpn *Shi-anraku-gyō*): See *On the Peaceful Practices of the Lotus Sutra.*

four peaceful ways of practice [四安楽行] (Jpn *shi-anraku-gyō*): *See* four peaceful practices.

four-phrase essence of the Lotus Sutra [四句の要法] (Jpn *shiku-no-yōbō*): Also, essence of the Lotus Sutra in four phrases. The teaching transferred by Shakyamuni Buddha to Bodhisattva Superior Practices and the other Bodhisattvas of the Earth in the "Supernatural Powers" (twenty-first) chapter of the Lotus Sutra. The chapter conveys these words of the Buddha: "The supernatural powers of the Buddhas, as you have seen, are immeasurable, boundless, inconceivable. If in the process of entrusting this sutra to others I were to employ these supernatural powers for immeasurable, boundless hundreds, thousands, ten thousands, millions of *asamkhya kalpas* to describe the benefits of the sutra, I could never finish doing so. To put it briefly, [1] all the doctrines possessed by the Thus Come One, [2] all the freely exercised supernatural powers of the Thus Come One, [3] the storehouse of all the secret essentials of the Thus

Come One, [4] all the most profound matters of the Thus Come One—all these are proclaimed, revealed, and clearly expounded in this sutra." Concerning the last sentence, T'ien-t'ai (538–597), in *The Words and Phrases of the Lotus Sutra,* defined the four-phrase description it contains as an essential summary of the Lotus Sutra, and Nichiren (1222–1282) interpreted the same passage as indicating Nam-myoho-renge-kyo of the Three Great Secret Laws. In *The Record of the Orally Transmitted Teachings,* Nichiren identified the teaching, or the "four-phrase essence of the Lotus Sutra" entrusted to Bodhisattva Superior Practices for its propagation in the Latter Day of the Law, as "the five characters of Myoho-renge-kyo."

four-phrase verse [四句偈] (Jpn *shiku-ge*): *See* four-line verse.

four powers [四力] (Jpn *shi-riki*): (1) The power of the Buddha, the power of the Law, the power of faith, and the power of practice. In Nichiren's teachings, the four powers are known as the four powers of the Mystic Law, whose interaction enables one to have one's prayers answered and attain Buddhahood. The power of the Buddha is the Buddha's compassion in saving all people. The power of the Law indicates the boundless capacity of the Mystic Law to lead all people to enlightenment. The power of faith is to believe in the Gohonzon, the object of devotion that embodies the power of the Buddha and the power of the Law, and the power of practice is to chant Nam-myoho-renge-kyo oneself and teach others to do the same. To the extent that one brings forth one's powers of faith and practice, one can manifest the powers of the Buddha and the Law within one's own life.

(2) The power of self, the power of another, the power of good karma, and the power of expedient means. The four powers expounded in the Upholding the Bodhisattva Stage Sutra that enable one to arouse the aspiration for enlightenment. The power of self means arousing the aspiration for enlightenment through one's own devoted effort in practice. The power of another means arousing the aspiration for enlightenment through being taught and inspired by another. The power of good karma means that, because of one's practice of the great vehicle teaching in past existences and because of good causes accumulated thereby, one encounters a Buddha or bodhisattva in this lifetime and so conceives the aspiration for enlightenment. The power of expedient means indicates that one seeks a good friend or teacher who skillfully expounds the Buddha's teaching in the way best suited to one's capacity, thus awakening in one the desire for enlightenment.

four preceding flavors [前四味・四味] (Jpn *zen-shimi* or *shimi*): *See* first four flavors.

four ranks of bodhisattvas [四依の菩薩] (Jpn *shie-no-bosatsu*): Bodhisattvas who embrace and propagate the correct teaching after Shakyamuni Buddha's death. *See also* four ranks of sages.

four ranks of sages [四依] (Jpn *shie*): Buddhist teachers to be relied upon after Shakyamuni Buddha's death. They are explained in the Nirvana and other sutras, which classify them into four ranks according to their level of understanding. The first rank refers to the voice-hearers who have yet to attain any of the four stages of Hinayana enlightenment. The second rank refers to those who have attained the first stage, that of the stream-winner (Skt *srota-āpanna*), or one who has entered the metaphorical river leading to nirvana; and to those of the second stage, that of the once-returner *(sakridāgāmin),* or one who must undergo only one more rebirth in the human world before entering nirvana. The third rank refers to those who have attained the third stage, that of the non-returner *(anāgāmin),* or one who will never be reborn in this world. The fourth rank refers to those who have eliminated the illusions of thought and desire and attained the fourth and highest stage, that of arhat. T'ien-t'ai (538–597) and Chang-an (561–632) correlated the four ranks to the fifty-two stages of bodhisattva practice in *The Profound Meaning of the Lotus Sutra* and *The Annotations on the Nirvana Sutra,* respectively. From this viewpoint, persons of the first rank correspond to those who have not yet attained the first stage of security. Persons of the second rank correspond to those in the ten stages of security. Persons of the third rank correspond to those in the ten stages of practice and the ten stages of devotion. Persons of the fourth rank correspond to those in the ten stages of development and the stage of near-perfect enlightenment, in which one has almost reached the enlightenment of the Buddha. Though the four ranks represent the four levels of understanding, "the four ranks of sages" is also a general term for reliable Buddhist teachers, irrespective of how they fit into the above classification. If they are bodhisattvas, they are also referred to as the four ranks of bodhisattvas.

four realms of the world of formlessness [四無色界・四無色天・四無色処・四空処] (Jpn *shi-mushiki-kai, shi-mushiki-ten, shi-mushiki-sho,* or *shi-kū-sho*): Also, four heavens of the world of formlessness. The four heavens composing the world of formlessness, the highest division of the threefold world. They are said to be realms free from the bonds and limitations of matter and from all thought of matter. The four heavens or realms are, in ascending order of quality, the Realm of Boundless Empty Space, the Realm of Boundless Consciousness, the Realm of Nothingness, and the Realm of Neither Thought Nor No Thought. The practice of meditation leads to rebirth among these four realms; the deeper the meditation, the more superior the realm one attains. The four levels of meditation leading to their respective realms are termed the four meditations on formlessness. Each meditation is named for the realm it leads to, with the first being meditation on the Realm of Boundless Empty Space, the second, meditation on the Realm of Boundless Consciousness, and so on. The Realm of Neither Thought Nor No Thought is also called the Summit of Being Heaven because it is the highest heaven in the threefold world, that is, the highest heaven in the entire realm of being or existence.

four reliances [四依] (Jpn *shie*): *See* four standards.

four right efforts [四正勤・四正断] (Jpn *shi-shōgon* or *shi-shōdan*): Also, four correct exertions or four types of correct effort. The four right efforts are (1) to put an end to existing evil, (2) to prevent evil from arising, (3) to bring good into existence, and (4) to encourage existing good. In short, they indicate efforts to put an end to evil acts that block the way to enlightenment and to perform good acts that lead to enlightenment. The four right efforts are the second of the seven constituent groups of the thirty-seven aids to the way, or the thirty-seven practices leading to enlightenment. *See also* thirty-seven aids to the way.

four rivers [四河] (Jpn *shi-ga*): Also, four great rivers. In the ancient Indian worldview, the four rivers in Jambudvīpa that originate from Anavatapta (Heat-Free) Lake: the Gangā River, the Sindhu River, the Vakshu River, and the Shītā River. The Gangā River and the Sindhu River are identified respectively as the Ganges River and the Indus River. As for the identity of the other two rivers, opinions differ, but generally the Vakshu River is presumed to be the Amu Darya River flowing into the Aral Sea, and the Shītā River, the Syr Darya River, also flowing into the Aral Sea. According to Buddhist texts, the Gangā, Sindhu, Vakshu, and Shītā rivers flow respectively from a silver ox's mouth on the eastern side of Anavatapta Lake, a gold elephant's mouth on the southern side, an emerald horse's mouth on the western side, and a crystal lion's mouth on the northern side. These four rivers flow respectively eastward, southward, westward, and northward into the ocean.

four roots of goodness [四善根・四善根位] (Jpn *shi-zengon* or *shi-zengon-i*): *See* four good roots.

four seas [四海] (Jpn *shi-kai*): Also, four great seas or four great oceans. Seas that surround Mount Sumeru to the north, south, east, and west. Actually, the four seas are said to compose one of eight large seas said to encircle Mount Sumeru concentrically. According to the ancient Indian worldview, Mount Sumeru stands at the center of the world and is surrounded by eight concentric mountain ranges. Eight concentric seas separate these eight mountain ranges. The "four seas" refers to four regions of one of these eight seas—the sea that lies between the seventh mountain range and the eighth, or outermost, mountain range. The seventh mountain range is called Nimimdhara, and the outermost range, Chakravāda-parvata, or the Iron Encircling Mountains. This outermost sea, which lies between these two mountain ranges, is a salt-water sea, while the innermost seven seas are fresh water. Moreover, the distance between the Nimimdhara range and the Iron Encircling Mountains is 322,000 *yojanas*. In this salt-water sea, there are the four continents of Pūrvavideha, Aparagodānīya, Uttarakuru, and Jambudvīpa, located to the east, west, north, and south of Mount Sumeru, respectively. The expression *four seas* refers to the waters surrounding each of these continents. It also refers to an entire land, region, country, or the entire world.

four stages of enlightenment [四果] (Jpn *shi-ka*): *See* four stages of Hinayana enlightenment.

four stages of faith [四信] (Jpn *shi-shin*): Stages of faith of those who embrace the Lotus Sutra during Shakyamuni's lifetime. T'ien-t'ai (538–597) formulated these four stages in *The Words and Phrases of the Lotus Sutra* on the basis of the "Distinctions in Benefits" (seventeenth) chapter of the Lotus Sutra. They are (1) to believe in and understand the sutra even for a moment, (2) to generally understand the import of the words of the sutra, (3) to expound the teaching of the sutra widely for others, and (4) to realize with deep faith the truth expounded by the Buddha. The first stage, for example, derives from the passage of the "Distinctions in Benefits" chapter that reads, "If there are living beings who, on hearing that the life span of the Buddha is of such long duration, are able to believe and understand it even for a moment, the benefits they gain thereby will be without limit or measure." The remaining stages similarly derive from passages in the "Distinctions in Benefits" chapter.

four stages of faith and the five stages of practice [四信五品] (Jpn *shishin-gohon*): Stages of faith in and practice of the Lotus Sutra formulated by T'ien-t'ai (538–597) in *The Words and Phrases of the Lotus Sutra* on the basis of the "Distinctions in Benefits" (seventeenth) chapter of the Lotus Sutra. The four stages of faith are for those who embrace the Lotus Sutra during Shakyamuni's lifetime, and the five stages of practice are for believers in the sutra after Shakyamuni's death. The four stages of faith are (1) to believe in and understand the sutra even for a moment, (2) to generally understand the import of the words of the sutra, (3) to expound the teaching of the sutra widely for others, and (4) to realize with deep faith the truth expounded by the Buddha.

The five stages of practice are (1) to rejoice on hearing the Lotus Sutra, (2) to read and recite the sutra, (3) to expound the sutra to others, (4) to embrace the sutra and practice the six *pāramitās,* and (5) to perfect one's practice of the six *pāramitās.* In *On the Four Stages of Faith and the Five Stages of Practice,* Nichiren (1222–1282) defines the correct stage for practitioners in the Latter Day of the Law to be the first of the four stages of faith and the first of the five stages of practice, that is, to believe in and understand the Lotus Sutra even for a moment and to rejoice on hearing the sutra. *See also* four stages of faith.

four stages of Hinayana enlightenment [四果] (Jpn *shi-ka*): Also, four stages of enlightenment or four fruits. Four levels of enlightenment that voice-hearers aim to attain, according to the Hinayana teachings. In ascending order, they are the stage of the stream-winner (Skt *srota-āpanna*), the stage of the once-returner *(sakridāgāmin),* the stage of the non-returner *(anāgāmin),* and the stage of arhat. The stage of the stream-winner indicates one who has entered the stream of the sages, in other words, the river leading to nirvana. At this stage, one has eradicated the illusions of thought in the threefold world. At the stage of the once-returner, one has eradicated six of the nine illusions of desire in the world of desire. Due to the remaining illusions, one will be born next in the realm of heavenly beings and then once again in the human world before entering nirvana; hence the name *once-returner.* Someone at the stage of the non-returner has eliminated the other three illusions of desire and will not be reborn in the world of desire. At the stage of arhat, one has eliminated all the illusions of thought and desire in the threefold world and has freed oneself from transmigration in the threefold world or the six paths. *See also* four ranks of sages.

four stages of meditation [四禅定] (Skt *chatur-dhyāna;* Jpn *shi-zenjō*): Also, four stages of *dhyāna* or four *dhyānas.* Four levels of meditation that enable those in the world of desire to throw off illusions and be reborn among the four meditation heavens in the world of form. The first meditation leads one to the first heaven, and so on. In the first meditation, one is freed from the desires of the senses and the commitment of evil deeds and thus experiences pleasure. In the second meditation, one experiences concentration of mind and inner serenity, which also produces pleasure. In the third meditation, one feels true joy and equanimity. In the fourth meditation, one gains the state that transcends both suffering and joy. The meditation heavens are also interpreted as the states of consciousness attained by practitioners of the corresponding meditations.

four standards [四依] (Jpn *shie*): Also, four reliances. Four standards that Buddhists must follow. According to the Nirvana Sutra and the Vimalakīrti Sutra, the four standards are (1) to rely on the Law and not upon persons; (2) to rely on the meaning of the teaching and not upon the words; (3) to rely on wisdom and not upon discriminative thinking; and (4) to rely on sutras that are complete and final and not upon those that are not complete and final.

four steps to transcendental powers [四如意足 · 四神足] (Jpn *shi-nyoi-soku* or *shi-jinsoku*): Also, four bases of transcendental powers. Four elements or attributes conducive to obtaining transcendental powers. They are zeal, exertion, memory, and meditative insight. The Sanskrit *riddhi-pāda* indicates a step toward attaining transcendental powers; *riddhi* means wealth, prosperity, or transcendental or supernatural power; *pāda* means foot, root, or base. The four steps to transcendental powers are the third of the seven constituent groups of the thirty-seven aids to the way, or the thirty-seven practices leading to enlightenment. *See also* thirty-seven aids to the way.

four sufferings [四苦] (Jpn *shi-ku*): The four universal sufferings: birth, aging, sickness, and death. Various sutras describe Shakyamuni's quest for enlightenment as motivated by a desire to find a solution to these four sufferings. Shakyamuni awakened to these sufferings through four encounters known as the "four meetings" that took place around the grounds of his father's palace when he was a young prince. This awakening is what motivated him to renounce secular life and pursue the religious path in order to attain enlightenment. Later four more sufferings came to be added to these four sufferings, yielding the concept of "eight sufferings." The four additions are the sufferings of having to part with loved ones, of having to meet those one hates, of being unable to obtain one's desires, and suffering arising from the five components of life. The "four sufferings" and the "eight sufferings" often indicate all human suffering. *See also* eight sufferings; four meetings.

four tastes [前四味 · 四味] (Jpn *zen-shimi* or *shimi*): *See* first four flavors.

four teachers of the three countries [三国四師] (Jpn *sangoku-shishi*): The four teachers Nichiren (1222–1282) listed as having revealed and transmitted the Lotus Sutra correctly. They are Shakyamuni of India, T'ien-t'ai (538–597) of China, and Dengyō (767–822) and Nichiren of Japan. Buddhism originated in India, was brought to China, and made its way to Japan. Thus, these three countries were regarded as the lands of the transmission and spread of Buddhism. In *On the Buddha's Prophecy,* Nichiren writes: "The Great Teacher Dengyō says: 'Shakyamuni taught that the shallow is easy to embrace, but the profound is difficult. To discard the shallow and seek the profound is the way of a person of courage. The Great Teacher T'ien-t'ai trusted and obeyed Shakyamuni and worked to uphold the Lotus school, spreading its teachings throughout China. We of Mount Hiei inherited the doctrine from T'ien-t'ai and work to uphold the Lotus school and to disseminate its teachings throughout Japan.' I, Nichiren of Awa Province, have doubtless inherited the teachings of the Law from these three teachers, and in this era of the Latter Day I work to uphold the Lotus school and disseminate the Law. Together we should be called the four teachers of the three countries" (402).

four teachings of doctrine [化法の四教] (Jpn *kehō-no-shikyō*): Also, four teachings. A classification by T'ien-t'ai (538–597) of Shakyamuni Buddha's teachings according to their content. Together with the four teachings of method, a classification by method of preaching, it constitutes the system of classification called the eight teachings. The four teachings of doctrine are: (1) The Tripitaka teaching, which consists of the three divisions of the Buddhist canon—sutras, *vinaya,* or rules of monastic discipline, and *abhidharma,* or doctrinal treatises and commentaries—and corresponds to the Hinayana, or pre-Mahayana, teachings. Teachings of this category aim to awaken people to the sufferings of birth and death in the threefold world and urge practitioners to rid themselves of earthly desires in order to escape the cycle of rebirth. (2) The connecting teaching, or introductory Mahayana, which forms a link between the Tripitaka teachings and the later, more sophisticated, Mahayana teachings. Teachings of this category stress the perception of the non-substantiality of all things, or that nothing has an independent existence of its own, in order to eliminate illusions. While the Tripitaka teaching is addressed to voice-hearers and cause-awakened ones and the specific teaching to bodhisattvas, the connecting teaching is addressed to all of them. (3) The specific teaching, a higher level of Mahayana addressed specifically to bodhisattvas, which enumerates the fifty-two stages of bodhisattva practice spanning innumerable *kalpas.* The teachings of this category reveal the three truths of non-substantiality, temporary existence, and the Middle Way, but show them as separate from and independent of one another. (4) The perfect teaching, which expounds the mutually inclusive relationship of the ultimate truth and all phenomena, as well as the unification of the three truths. It reveals that all people have the potential for

Buddhahood, and that they can attain enlightenment through the perception of the unification of the three truths. The perfect teaching is further subdivided into two: the perfect teaching of the sutras expounded before the Lotus Sutra, and the perfect teaching of the Lotus Sutra, or the sutra itself. Both teach that one can attain Buddhahood as an ordinary person, but the former, unlike the Lotus Sutra, does not show the way to achieve it. The full expression of the perfect teaching is found only in the Lotus Sutra.

In *The Profound Meaning of the Lotus Sutra,* T'ien-t'ai defined the relationship between the four teachings of doctrine and the first four of the five periods with the terms "combining, excluding, corresponding, and including." These terms also describe the characteristics of the various sutras that came before the Lotus Sutra, and differentiate between them and the Lotus Sutra. The Flower Garland period combines the specific teaching with the perfect teaching ("combining"). The Āgama period consists of the Tripitaka teaching only and excludes the connecting, specific, and perfect teachings ("excluding"). In the Correct and Equal period, all four teachings were taught in a manner corresponding to the people's capacity ("corresponding"). The Wisdom period consists of the perfect teaching, but includes the connecting and specific teachings ("including"). The purpose of clarifying these relationships is to show that the Lotus Sutra alone is the pure and perfect teaching, or the perfect teaching in the true sense of the term.

four teachings of method [化儀の四教] (Jpn *kegi-no-shikyō*): A classification by T'ien-t'ai (538–597) of Shakyamuni Buddha's teachings according to how they were expounded. Together with the four teachings of doctrine, it forms the system of classification known as the eight teachings. The four teachings of method are: (1) The sudden teaching, in which the Buddha preached directly from the standpoint of his own enlightenment, independently of his listeners' capacity, and without giving them preparatory knowledge. This category corresponds to the Flower Garland Sutra. (2) The gradual teaching, which the Buddha expounded progressively to gradually elevate his disciples' capacity to understand higher teachings. This category includes the teachings of the Āgama, Correct and Equal, and Wisdom periods. (3) The secret teaching (more precisely, the secret indeterminate teaching), in which the Buddha preaches in such a way that his listeners understand according to their individual capacities and thereby each receive different benefits without being aware of the differences. (4) The indeterminate (or non-fixed) teaching (more precisely, the explicit indeterminate teaching), in which the Buddha's listeners understand his teaching differently and thereby receive different benefits in the same way as above, but are aware of the differences. This teaching is called indeterminate because the benefits that the listeners receive are not fixed but vary with their respective capacities.

fourteen slanders [十四誹謗・十四謗法] (Jpn *jūshi-hibō* or *jūshi-hōbō*): Fourteen types of slander enumerated in *The Annotations on "The Words and Phrases of the Lotus Sutra"* by Miao-lo (711–782) based on the contents of the "Simile and Parable" (third) chapter of the Lotus Sutra. They consist of fourteen offenses against the Law, or the Buddha's teachings, and against the people who believe in and practice it. They are (1) arrogance, (2) negligence, (3) wrong views of the self, (4) shallow understanding, (5) attachment to earthly desires, (6) not understanding, (7) not believing, (8) scowling with knitted brows, (9) harboring doubts, (10) slandering, (11) despising, (12) hating, (13) envying, and (14) bearing grudges. According to the "Simile and Parable" chapter, the last four offenses are leveled at the practitioners of the Lotus Sutra. The chapter reads, "If this person should slander a sutra such as this, or on seeing those who read, recite, copy, and uphold this sutra, should despise, hate, envy, or bear grudges against them, the penalty this person must pay—listen, I will tell you now: When his life comes to an end he will enter the Avīchi hell."

four topsy-turvy views [四顛倒] (Jpn *shi-tendō*): *See* four inverted views.

four treatises [四論] (Jpn *shi-ron*): Four Buddhist treatises; usually a reference to Nāgārjuna's three treatises, *The Treatise on the Middle Way, The Treatise on the Twelve Gates,* and *The Treatise on the Great Perfection of Wisdom,* plus *The One-Hundred-Verse Treatise* by Āryadeva, Nāgārjuna's disciple and successor. *The Profound Meaning of the Four Mahayana Treatises* by Hui-chün of the early T'ang dynasty (618–907) in China is an exposition of the essential meanings of these four treatises.

four types of Buddhist believers [四衆] (Jpn *shi-shu*): Monks, nuns, laymen, and laywomen. *See also* four kinds of believers.

four types of correct effort [四正勤・四正断] (Jpn *shi-shōgon* or *shi-shōdan*): *See* four right efforts.

four types of mandalas [四種曼荼羅] (Jpn *shishu-mandara*): Four kinds of mandalas of the Japanese True Word (Shingon) school described by its founder Kōbō (774–835) in his *Doctrine of Attaining Buddhahood in One's Present Form.* They are the great mandala, the *samaya* mandala, the Dharma mandala, and the karma mandala. (1) The great mandala is one on which the figures of Buddhas and bodhisattvas are painted. (2) The *samaya* mandala depicts *samayas,* objects held by Buddhas and bodhisattvas that represent their vows to lead all people to enlightenment, or their mudras (gestures by hands). *Samayas* include a sword, a lotus, and a diamond-pounder. (3) The Dharma mandala depicts those Sanskrit letters that represent Buddhas and bodhisattvas and that are believed to possess supernatural powers. (4) The karma mandala depicts the actions of Buddhas and bodhisattvas who lead living beings to enlightenment. *Karma* means action.

four types of wheel-turning kings [四輪王] (Jpn *shi-rinnō*): *See* wheel-turning king.

four universal vows [四弘誓願] (Jpn *shigu-seigan*): Also, four great vows, or simply four vows. Vows that every bodhisattva makes when he or she first resolves to embark upon the Buddhist practice. They are (1) to save innumerable living beings, (2) to eradicate countless earthly desires, (3) to master immeasurable Buddhist teachings, and (4) to attain supreme enlightenment.

four unlimited kinds of knowledge [四無礙智・四無礙] (Jpn *shi-muge-chi* or *shi-muge*): Also, four unlimited (or unhindered) powers of knowledge, four unlimited kinds of understanding, or four unlimited kinds of eloquence. Powers of understanding and teaching that Buddhas and bodhisattvas are said to possess. They are (1) complete understanding of the Law, or teachings; (2) complete mastery of the meanings deriving from the Law; (3) complete freedom in expressing the teachings in various languages and dialects; and (4) the ability to preach to all people at will by employing the first three powers. The four unlimited kinds of knowledge represent being unhindered in understanding and teaching.

four unpardonable offenses [四重罪・四波羅夷罪] (Jpn *shi-jūzai* or *shi-haraizai*): *See* four major offenses.

four views of the sal grove [沙羅の四見] (Jpn *shara-no-shiken*): Also, four views or four perspectives. The sal grove refers to that located in the northern part of Kushinagara, India, where Shakyamuni Buddha died. Because of differences in people's capacities and their states of life, they are said to perceive the same sal grove in four different ways: as the Land of Sages and Common Mortals, as the Land of Transition, as the Land of Actual Reward, and as the Land of Eternally Tranquil Light. This expression appears often in Buddhist texts and indicates that people view a particular thing or phenomenon in different ways according to their individual capacity and state of life. *See also* four kinds of lands.

four virtues [四徳] (Jpn *shi-toku*): (1) Four noble qualities of a Buddha's life—eternity, happiness, true self, and purity. These describe the true nature of a Buddha's life, which is pure and eternal, and which manifests the true self and enjoys absolute happiness. Because ordinary people possess the Buddha nature, they too can develop the four virtues when they attain Buddhahood by fulfilling the Buddha's teachings. (2) Four virtues of a wheel-turning king: great wealth, admirable features and form, freedom from worries, and long life.

four ways of preaching [四悉檀] (Jpn *shi-shitsudan*): Also, four ways of teaching. Four ways in which Buddhas expound their teachings, explained in *The Treatise on the Great Perfection of Wisdom* by Nāgārjuna (c. 150–250). They are (1) to teach Buddhism in secular terms, explaining to people that it will fulfill their desires, thus arousing their willingness to take faith; (2) to teach according to people's respective capacities, thus enabling them to increase their store of good karma; (3) to help people abandon their illusions and free themselves from the three poisons of greed, anger, and foolishness. This is done by teaching those caught up in greed to recognize the impurity of their attachments, those dominated by anger to practice compassionate acts, and those blinded by the poison of foolishness to perceive the causal law; and (4) to reveal the ultimate truth directly, causing people to realize it. Compared to this way of teaching, the first three are regarded as temporary means.

four wheel-turning kings [四輪王] (Jpn *shi-rinnō*): Also, four wheel-turning sage kings. A gold-wheel-turning king, a silver-wheel-turning king, a copper-wheel-turning king, and an iron-wheel-turning king. *See* wheel-turning king.

four wrong-headed views [四顚倒] (Jpn *shi-tendō*): *See* four inverted views.

Fragrant, Mount [香酔山・香山] (Skt, Pali Gandhamādana; Jpn Kōsui-sen or Kō-sen): Also known as the Fragrant Mountain. A mountain in Jambudvīpa, said to lie to the north of the Snow Mountains, according to the ancient Indian worldview. Mount Fragrant is also said to be the abode of *gandharvas*, gods of music, and the trees in this mountain are said to issue fragrance. Between the Fragrant Mountain and the Snow Mountains is Anavatapta (Heat-Free) Lake from which four great rivers flow.

Fragrant Mountain [香酔山・香山] (Jpn Kōsui-sen or Kō-sen): *See* Fragrant, Mount.

Freely Enjoying Things Conjured by Others [他化自在天] (Jpn Take-jizai-ten): Also known as the devil king of the sixth heaven. *See* devil king of the sixth heaven.

Freely Perceiving [観自在菩薩] (Skt Avalokiteshvara; Jpn Kanjizai-bosatsu): Another name for the bodhisattva Perceiver of the World's Sounds. *See* Perceiver of the World's Sounds.

Fudō [不動] (Jpn): The wisdom king Immovable (Fudō-myō'ō). *See* Immovable (1).

Fuji school [富士門流] (Jpn Fuji-monryū): A Buddhist school in Japan derived from Nikkō (1246–1333), one of the six senior priests appointed by Nichiren and his designated successor. In 1289 Nikkō left Kuon-ji temple, which Nichiren had founded at Minobu, and moved to a place at the foot of Mount Fuji. He did this because Nikō, another of the six senior priests, had influenced Hakiri Sanenaga, the steward of the Minobu area and a follower of Nichiren, to engage in actions and practices that deviated substantially from Nichiren's teachings. Though Nikkō warned them repeatedly on this account, they disregarded him. After leaving Minobu, Nikkō settled in the Fuji district on the southwestern flank of Mount Fuji, where Nanjō Tokimitsu, one of Nichiren's lay followers and a strong supporter of Nikkō, ruled as steward. Nikkō established a temple there named Taiseki-ji; this became the head temple of the Fuji school, which revered Nichiren and Nikkō as its founders. This school was the origin of what is today Nichiren Shōshū.

Fuju Fuse Kōmon school [不受不施講門派] (Jpn Fuju Fuse Kōmon-ha): The No Alms Accepting or Giving Nichikō school, an offshoot of the Nichiren school founded by Nichikō. *See* Nichikō.

Fuju Fuse school [不受不施派] (Jpn Fuju Fuse-ha): The No Alms Accepting or Giving school, a branch of the Nichiren school founded by Nichiō. *See* Nichiō.

full commandments [具足戒] (Jpn *gusoku-kai*): The complete set of rules of monastic discipline for monks and for nuns. *See* complete precepts.

Funamori Yasaburō [船守弥三郎] (n.d.): A lay follower of Nichiren and a fisherman at Kawana on the Izu Peninsula in Japan. On the twelfth day of the fifth month, 1261, the Kamakura shogunate exiled Nichiren to the Izu Peninsula. He was taken to Kawana, a small fishing village on the northeastern coast of Izu, where Funamori Yasaburō and his wife became steadfast believers in his teachings. The couple gave him shelter and food for more than thirty days until he was summoned to the residence of the steward of Itō District in Izu, Itō Sukemitsu, who was suffering from a serious illness. There he offered prayers at the steward's request for his recovery. Yasaburō sent a messenger to Nichiren at Itō with various offerings. In reply, Nichiren wrote him a letter known as *The Izu Exile*. *See also* Izu Exile.

fundamental darkness [元品の無明] (Jpn *gampon-no-mumyō*): Also, fundamental ignorance or primal ignorance. The most deeply rooted illusion inherent in life, said to give rise to all other illusions. *Darkness* in this sense means inability to see or recognize the truth, particularly, the true nature of one's life. The term *fundamental darkness* is contrasted with the fundamental nature of enlightenment, which is the Buddha nature inherent in life. According to the Shrīmālā Sutra, fundamental darkness is the most difficult illusion to surmount and can be eradicated only by the wisdom of the Buddha. T'ien-t'ai (538–597) interprets darkness as illusion that prevents one from realizing the truth of the Middle Way, and divides such illusion into forty-two types, the last of which is fundamental darkness. This illusion is only extirpated when one attains the stage of perfect enlightenment, the last of the fifty-two stages of bodhisattva practice. Nichiren (1222–1282) interprets fundamental darkness as ignorance of the ultimate Law, or ignorance of the fact that one's life is essentially a manifestation of that Law, which he identifies as Nam-myoho-renge-kyo. In *The Treatment of Illness,* Nichiren states: "The heart of the Lotus school is the doctrine of three thousand realms in a single moment of life, which reveals that both good and evil are inherent even in those at the highest stage of perfect enlightenment. The fundamental nature of enlightenment manifests itself as Brahmā and Shakra, whereas the fundamental darkness manifests itself as the devil king of the sixth heaven" (1113). Nichiren thus regards fundamental darkness as latent even in the enlightened life of the Buddha, and the devil king of the sixth heaven as a manifestation or personification of life's fundamental darkness. *The Record of the Orally Transmitted Teachings* reads, "Belief is a sharp sword that cuts off fundamental darkness or ignorance."

fundamental nature of enlightenment [元品の法性] (Jpn *gampon-no-hosshō*): Enlightenment to the fundamental nature of all things and phenomena. It is contrasted with fundamental darkness. Also, the Buddha nature that is inherent in life. *See also* fundamental darkness.

Further Anthology of the Propagation of Light, The [広弘明集] (Chin *Kuang-hung-ming-chi;* Jpn *Kō-gumyō-shū*): A collection of essays on Buddhism and other documents compiled in 664 by Tao-hsüan, a priest of the Precepts (Lü) school in China, some of which are found only in this work. This thirty-volume work contains essays, biographies, letters, epitaphs, or literary writings that were written from the third through the seventh century and were considered useful in protecting Buddhism against attacks from Taoists and Confucianists. Along with *The Anthology of the Propagation of Light,* a collection of essays on Buddhism compiled by Seng-yu (445–518), this work is considered invaluable in the study of Chinese Buddhism and the contact between Buddhism and the teachings of Taoism and Confucianism.

fusion of reality and wisdom [境智冥合] (Jpn *kyōchi-myōgō*): The fusion of the objective reality or truth and the subjective wisdom to realize that truth, which is the Buddha nature inherent within one's life. Since enlightenment, or Buddhahood, is defined as the state in which one fully realizes the ultimate reality, the fusion of reality and wisdom means enlightenment. T'ien-t'ai (538–597) discusses this principle in *The Words and Phrases of the Lotus Sutra.* In *The Annotations on "The Words and Phrases of the Lotus Sutra,"* Miao-lo (711–782) associates Shakyamuni Buddha and Many Treasures Buddha as they are portrayed in the "Treasure Tower" (eleventh) chapter of the Lotus Sutra with the fusion of reality and wisdom. This chapter describes Shakyamuni Buddha seated side by side with Many Treasures Buddha in the treasure tower. Miao-lo writes that these two Buddhas seated in this manner signify the fusion of reality and wisdom. Nichiren (1222–1282) identifies the Law that underlies the fusion of reality and wisdom as Nam-myoho-renge-kyo, and asserts that he embodied his enlightenment to that Law—the fusion of reality and wisdom—in the form of the Gohonzon, the object of devotion he established. In terms of Buddhist practice for people in the Latter Day of the Law, Nichiren maintained that, when they chant Nam-myoho-renge-kyo with deep faith in the Gohonzon, they achieve the fusion of reality and wisdom within their own lives and are thus able to manifest the Buddha nature and attain Buddhahood. According to Nichiren, the Buddha nature constitutes reality, and faith in the Gohonzon, the embodiment of that nature, corresponds to wisdom. Nichiren states: "Reality means the true nature of all phenomena, and wisdom means the illuminating and manifesting of this true nature. Thus when the riverbed of reality is infinitely broad and deep, the water of wisdom will flow ceaselessly. When this reality and wisdom are fused, one attains Buddhahood in one's present form. . . . What then are these two elements of reality and wisdom? They are simply the five characters of Nam-myoho-renge-kyo" (746).

Fu Ta-shih [傅大士] (497–569) (PY Fu Dashi; Jpn Fu-daishi): A lay Buddhist in China who was revered as a reincarnation of Bodhisattva Maitreya. He won the respect of Emperor Wu of the Liang dynasty, who was a devout Buddhist. His real name was Fu Hsi, and he was commonly known as Fu Ta-shih (*ta-shih* means great man). A layperson with a wife and children, he was not only an earnest practitioner of Buddhism but also a philanthropist, generously bestowing his own wealth upon the people. When he erected Shuang-lin-ssu temple, he built a sutra repository on the premises to house the entire collection of Buddhist scriptures. The repository was unique in that it had a revolving stand with eight faces for storing the scriptures. Later many temples adopted this type of sutra repository.

G

Gadgadasvara [妙音菩薩] (Skt; Jpn Myō'on-bosatsu): The bodhisattva Wonderful Sound. A bodhisattva described in the "Wonderful Sound" (twenty-fourth) chapter of the Lotus Sutra. *See* Wonderful Sound.

Gainer of Great Authority [得大勢菩薩] (Skt Mahāsthāmaprāpta; Jpn Tokudaisei-bosatsu): Another name for the bodhisattva Great Power. In the "Introduction" (first) chapter of the Lotus Sutra, Bodhisattva Gainer of Great Authority appears as one of those who assembled on Eagle Peak to listen to Shakyamuni Buddha preach. *See also* Great Power.

Gakkō [月光] (Jpn): The bodhisattva Moonlight (Gakkō-bosatsu). One of the two bodhisattvas who attend Medicine Master Buddha, the other being Nikkō (Sunlight). *See* Moonlight.

gandha [香・乾陀] (Skt, Pali; Jpn *kō* or *kenda*): Incense, fragrance, smell, scent, odor, or perfume. *Gandha* constituted important offerings to the Buddha and the Buddhist Order along with such offerings as *pushpa* (flowers) and *dīpa* (lamps). In ancient India, incense had a variety of customary uses: as a deodorant that was rubbed on the body, as a room freshener, and used to scent clothing, etc. Incense was produced from sandalwood, aloes wood, wood from other aromatic trees, and from flowers such as *kunkuma* (saffron). The "Teacher of the Law" (tenth) chapter of the Lotus Sutra reads: "If there are persons who embrace, read, recite, expound, and copy the Lotus Sutra of the Wonderful Law, even only one verse, and look upon this sutra with the same reverence as they would the Buddha, presenting various offerings of flowers, incense, necklaces, powdered incense, paste incense, incense for burning, silken canopies, streamers and banners, clothing and music, and pressing their palms together in reverence, then, Medicine King, you should understand that such persons have already offered alms to a hundred thousand million Buddhas and in the place of the Buddhas have fulfilled their great vow, and because they take pity on living beings they have been born in this human world." The word *gandha* is an element of a number of Sanskrit Buddhist terms and proper names. For example, the Wisdom sutras describe Gandhavatī, City of Fragrances, as the place where Bodhisattva Dharmodgata preached on the perfection of wisdom. Gandhamādana, Mount Fragrant, is said to lie to the north of the Snow Mountains in Jambudvīpa. The trees on this mountain are said to give off a beautiful fragrance. *Gandhakutī*, hall of fragrance, means a room where the Buddha dwells. Tamālapattra-chandana-gandha, or Tamālapattra Sandalwood Fragrance, is the name Maudgalyāyana will have as a Buddha in a future life according to a prediction in the Lotus Sutra. Gods of music called *gandharva,* one of the eight kinds of nonhuman beings who protect Buddhism, are said to subsist on *gandha,* or fragrance.

Gandhara [ガンダーラ・健駄羅国] (Skt, Pali Gandhāra; Jpn Gandāra or Kendara-koku): A historic region that includes the present Peshawar Division in the North-West Frontier Province of Pakistan. Gandhara had long been a crossroads of Indian, Iranian, Greek, and Roman cultural influences and also a center of Buddhist culture. Around the sixth century B.C.E., it was one of the sixteen great states of the Indian subcontinent. In the late sixth century B.C.E., it was annexed by the Persian Achaemenian Empire and remained under its rule for about two centuries. Gandhara fell under Greek rule after being conquered by Alexander the Great in the late fourth century B.C.E., and then was ruled by the Maurya dynasty of India. During the reign of King Ashoka of the Maurya dynasty in the third century B.C.E., Madhyāntika, a Buddhist monk, was sent by the king to Gandhara to disseminate the teachings of Buddhism. Later Gandhara was ruled by Indo-Greek kings, then by the Shakas, Parthians, and the Kushans. Kushan rule began in the first century; King Kanishka of that dynasty, who is generally believed to have reigned in the second century, made Purushapura, the present-day Peshawar, the capital of his empire. With his support Buddhism flourished in the new capital and reached its height during his reign. Both Hinayana and Mahayana Buddhism were studied and practiced. Among the various schools, the Sarvāstivāda school of Hinayana particularly prospered. In the fourth century (the fifth century according to another account), Asanga and Vasubandhu lived in Gandhara where they contributed greatly to the propagation of Mahayana Buddhism. During the period of Kushan rule, many monasteries and stupas were built, but were destroyed by the Hephthalites, also known as the White Huns, who invaded the area in the fifth century. Hsüan-tsang, a Chinese priest who visited Gandhara in the seventh century, wrote in *The Record of the Western Regions* that it was a dependency of the Kapisha kingdom, and that more than one thousand monasteries had been devastated and a number of stupas reduced to ruins. In the twentieth century, archaeological expeditions into the Gandhara region were undertaken by John Marshall (1876–1958) and Alfred Foucher (1865–1952).

Gandhara is also known as the birthplace of Gandhara art, a predominantly Buddhist style of art that flourished from the first through the fifth century. Artworks of this style have been found in what was ancient Gandhara and its surrounding regions extending to Taxila and Swat to the east and north, respectively, and to eastern Afghanistan to the west. Gandhara art, influenced by Greek and Roman artistic style, produced the earliest images of Shakyamuni Buddha. Before the rise of Gandhara art in the first century, relief sculptures depicting the events of the Buddha's life existed but did not portray the Buddha himself. A wheel, an empty throne, a *bodhi* tree, an umbrella, or a pair of footprints were used as symbols to represent the Buddha. Gandhara art, however, depicted the Buddha for the first time in human form. Gandhara art had an important effect on Buddhist art as a whole in India, Central Asia, and China.

gandharva [乾闥婆] (Skt; Jpn *kendatsuba*): A heavenly musician or a god of music. In Buddhism, *gandharvas* constitute one of the eight kinds of nonhuman beings who protect Buddhism. They are said to serve the god Indra, known also as Shakra, as heavenly musicians and live on *gandha,* which means fragrance, scent, or perfume. *Gandharva* was rendered in Chinese as "god of fragrance."

Gangā [恒河・ガンジス河] (Skt, Pali; Jpn Gōga or Ganjisu-gawa): *See* Ganges River.

Ganges River [恒河・ガンジス河] (Jpn Gōga or Ganjisu-gawa): The great river of the northern and northeastern Indian subcontinent, which originates in the Himalayas and flows southeast across the vast Ganges Valley, emptying into the Bay of Bengal through the Ganges Delta. Its length is about 2,500 kilometers. In Sanskrit the river is called Gangā. Depicted as a beautiful river goddess in Indian mythology, Gangā originally flowed only through heaven, but was brought to earth by the gods Brahmā and Shiva. In Buddhist scriptures, the Ganges is counted as one of the four great rivers in Jambudvīpa. The Rigveda, the earliest Vedic scripture, took root here and gave rise to India's Vedic religion and culture. The fertile Ganges Valley also supported a flourishing agriculture and commerce. Many cities were built and prospered in the Ganges Valley, which constituted the cradle and the center of successive Indian civilizations. Around the time of Shakyamuni, a number of new kingdoms emerged, the most powerful of which were Kosala in the middle Ganges Valley and Magadha in the lower Ganges Valley. Shakyamuni spread his teachings widely in the region, and his followers increased rapidly in number. As a result, monasteries were built in many cities in the valley. The Mauryan dynasty, renowned for its ruler Ashoka of the third century B.C.E., established the city of Pātaliputra (present-day Patna) as the center of its empire on the banks of the Ganges. The Gupta dynasty, which began in the fourth century C.E., also made Pātaliputra its capital.

The Ganges has long been held sacred, and today is still revered as a holy river by Hindus who believe that they can eradicate their sins by immersing themselves in its waters. Crematoriums have been built along the banks of the Ganges, and the Hindus cast the ashes of the dead into the river, believing this will deliver the deceased straight to heaven. Along the basin of the Ganges are some of the most prominent Indian cities, such as Varanasi (the holy city of the Hindus), Patna, and Calcutta on the bank of an arm of the Ganges River called the Hooghly.

Ganges sands [恒河沙] (Jpn *gōga-sha*): An expression used to indicate an incalculably large number. *See* sands of the Ganges.

Gangō-ji [元興寺] : A temple of the Flower Garland (Kegon) school in Nara, Japan. Originally located in Asuka, then the seat of the imperial court, its construction was commissioned by the court official Soga no Umako and was completed in 596. It was called Asuka-dera temple and also Hōkō-ji. After the imperial court moved to Nara, the temple was moved there in 718 and renamed Gangō-ji. Gangō-ji prospered as a center of Buddhist learning and came to be counted among the so-called seven major temples of Nara. In the Nara period (710–794), earnest study of the doctrines of the Three Treatises (Sanron) and Dharma Characteristics (Hossō) schools was carried out at the temple. Its prosperity began to wane, however, in the middle of the Heian period (794–1185). It declined further after being damaged by fire in 1451 and was finally destroyed by fire in 1859.

Ganjin [鑑真] (688–763) (Jpn; Chin Chien-chen): The founder of the Precepts (Chin Lü; Jpn Ritsu) school in Japan. Originally from China, Ganjin is the name by which he became known in Japan and is the Japanese reading of his Chinese name, Chien-chen. At age fourteen, he entered the priesthood at Ta-yün-ssu temple in Yang-chou and studied the T'ien-t'ai and Precepts teachings in Lo-yang and Ch'ang-an. After returning to Yang-chou, he lived at Ta-ming-ssu temple. While lecturing there in 742, two Japanese priests, Yōei and Fushō, implored him to come to Japan and instruct priests and nuns there in the precepts. Yōei and Fushō had been dispatched to China by the Japanese emperor Shōmu to invite Chinese priests well versed in Buddhist teachings and precepts to teach in Japan and to establish there an authentic Buddhist ordination platform, which Japan lacked. In defiance of a Chinese imperial prohibition, Ganjin attempted to leave the country, but was unsuccessful in five separate attempts due to storms, pirates, and other obstacles. After eleven years of hardship, however, he finally arrived in Japan in 753, though he had lost his eyesight. In addition to the scriptures of the Precepts school, he brought with him those of the T'ien-t'ai school, which Dengyō (767–822), the founder of the Japanese Tendai school, later studied. The following year Ganjin had an ordination platform erected at Tōdai-ji temple and conducted ceremonies conferring the precepts on the Retired Emperor Shōmu and some four hundred others. In the fifth month of the same year, he established the Precepts school. In the fifth month of 756, he was appointed general supervisor of priests, and in the eighth month, general administrator of priests. In 759 he founded Tōshōdai-ji temple under the patronage of Empress Kōken. He died in 763 and was posthumously called the Great Teacher Kakai, or the Great Teacher Who Crossed the Sea. His biography, *The Life of the Great Priest of T'ang China Who Journeyed to the East,* was written in 779 by Ōmi no Mifune, a scholar and court official.

garbhadhātu [胎蔵界] (Skt; Jpn *taizō-kai*): The Womb Realm, a realm that represents the Dharma body of Mahāvairochana Buddha. *See* Womb Realm.

garment-snatching demoness [奪衣婆] (Jpn *datsueba*): A female demon said to dwell on the bank of the river of three crossings who strips off the clothes of the dead as they proceed from this world to the next. She hands the clothes of the dead to a male partner, called the garment-suspending demon. The garment-suspending demon then hangs the clothes on a branch of a tree and determines the weight of the offenses that the dead committed while alive by the droop of the branch. The dead are said to encounter these demons on the bank of the river of three crossings on the seventh day after their death. The garment-snatching demoness, the garment-suspending demon, and the river of three crossings do not appear in the scriptures of Indian Buddhism but are first mentioned in Chinese Buddhist texts. In Japan, belief in them became popular from the middle of the Heian period (794–1185) through the Kamakura period (1185–1333).

garment-suspending demon [懸衣翁] (Jpn *kenneō*): A male demon said to dwell on the bank of the river of three crossings. *See* garment-snatching demoness.

garuda [迦楼羅] (Skt; Jpn *karura*): In Indian mythology, a giant bird that feeds on dragons and is regarded as the king of birds. It is depicted in Buddhist artworks as having the head and wings of an eagle and the body of a man. The god Vishnu was believed to ride a *garuda,* which was revered as a deification of the sun's fire. The *garuda* was incorporated into Buddhism and came to be counted as one of the eight kinds of nonhuman beings, along with dragons and *asuras.* In Chinese translations of Buddhist scriptures, *garuda* is often rendered as "golden-winged bird."

gātha [偈・伽陀] (Skt, Pali; Jpn *ge* or *kada*): *See* verse.

gati [趣・道] (Skt, Pali; Jpn *shu* or *dō*): *See* path.

Gautama [瞿曇] (Skt; Pali Gotama; Jpn Kudon): The family name of the historical Buddha, Shakyamuni. In Buddhist scriptures, Shakyamuni is often referred to as Gautama. Shakyamuni is an honorific name meaning "sage of the Shākyas." The Shākyas were the clan to which the Gautamas belonged.

Gautamī [憍曇弥] (Skt; Jpn Kyōdommi): Also known as Mahāprajāpatī. The aunt and foster mother of Shakyamuni. *See* Mahāprajāpatī.

Gayā [伽耶城] (Skt, Pali; Jpn Gaya-jō): A city of the Magadha kingdom in ancient India, south of Pātaliputra (present-day Patna) on the Ganges River. Present-day Gaya is located in central Bihar, a state in northeastern India. Today it is a center of Hindu belief that attracts many pilgrims. There are numerous Hindu temples in the city, and the principal shrine is the Vishnu temple. Gayā was formerly a center of Buddhism, but from the second through the fourth century, Hinduism gradually displaced Buddhism. Near the city, however, are a number of sites associated with Shakyamuni Buddha, such as Buddhagayā (now Bodh Gaya, also called Buddh Gaya), where Shakyamuni attained enlightenment, and Mount Gayāshīrsha (the hill now called Brahmayoni or Brahmajini), where the Buddha is believed to have preached.

Gayā Kāshyapa [伽耶迦葉] (Skt; Pali Gayā Kassapa; Jpn Gaya-kashō): One of three brothers of Uruvilvā in India who converted to Shakyamuni's teachings in his early days of preaching. The two others were Uruvilvā Kāshyapa and Nadī Kāshyapa. All three were leaders among Brahman ascetics, and Gayā Kāshyapa's two hundred disciples are said to have converted to Buddhism with him.

Gayāshīrsha, Mount [伽耶山・象頭山] (Skt; Pali Gayāsīsa; Jpn Gaya-sen or Zōzu-sen): A hill in India on which Shakyamuni is believed to have preached. It has been identified as the hill known today as Brahmayoni, located 1.5 kilometers southwest of Gaya city in northeastern India. In Chinese Buddhist scriptures, Mount Gayāshīrsha is rendered as the Elephant-Head Mountain. According to Chinese scriptures, it was on Elephant-Head Mountain that Devadatta plotted to create a schism within the Buddhist Order and to form his own Buddhist community.

Gembō [玄昉] (d. 746): A priest of the Dharma Characteristics (Hossō) school in Japan. He is numbered among the seven superior disciples of Gien, a Dharma Characteristics scholar, the other six being Gyōki, Senkyō, Ryōbin, Gyōtatsu, Ryūson, and Rōben. After entering the priesthood, he studied the Consciousness-Only doctrine and then went to China in 716 or 717 where he studied the Dharma Characteristics teachings. He returned to Japan in 735, bringing with him images of the Buddha as well as sutras, treatises, and commentaries totaling more than five thousand volumes. In 737 he was appointed administrator of priests by the imperial court. He won the favor of the imperial court and served as court priest to Emperor Shōmu. Because of political intrigue, however, he was banished to Kanzeon-ji temple in Chikuzen Province in 745, and died there the following year.

general and specific viewpoints [総別の二義] (Jpn *sōbetsu-no-nigi*): Also, two categories of general and specific. A set of criteria for interpreting Buddhist teachings. "General" refers to an overall or surface view of a particular teaching or doctrine, and "specific," to a more sharply delineated and profound view. In Nichiren's doctrine, from the general viewpoint, the five periods and eight teachings, or Shakyamuni's lifetime teachings, all reveal the truth, but from a specific viewpoint, only the Lotus Sutra represents the truth. Again, generally speaking, the entire Lotus Sutra is the Buddha's true teaching, but more specifically, it is the essential teaching (latter fourteen chapters) of the sutra that contains the truth. Yet again, from the general viewpoint, the essential teaching represents the truth, but specifically, the Law implied in the "Life Span" (sixteenth) chapter of the essential teaching is the ultimate truth.

The terms *general* and *specific* also apply to the transfer or entrustment of the teachings of the Lotus Sutra as described in the sutra. In the "Entrustment" (twenty-second) chapter, Shakyamuni makes a general transfer of the sutra to all the bodhisattvas present, but in the "Supernatural Powers" (twenty-first) chapter, he entrusts it specifically to the Bodhisattvas of the Earth. Again, while he transfers the sutra to the Bodhisattvas of the Earth in general, he specifically entrusts it to Bodhisattva Superior Practices alone.

general transfer [総付嘱] (Jpn *sō-fuzoku*): Also, general transfer of the Lotus Sutra or general transmission. The transfer of the Lotus Sutra by Shakyamuni Buddha to all the assembled bodhisattvas as described in the "Entrustment" (twenty-second) chapter of the sutra. This is used in contrast to the specific transfer described in the preceding chapter, "Supernatural Powers," in which the sutra is entrusted specifically to Bodhisattva Superior Practices and the other Bodhisattvas of the Earth. *See also* general and specific viewpoints.

Genkō Era Biographies of Eminent Priests, The [元亨釈書] (Jpn *Genkō-shakusho*): A work compiled by Kokan Shiren, a priest of the Rinzai Zen school of Japan, in the second year of the Genkō era (1321–1324) in the late Kamakura period. It contains the biographies of some four hundred eminent priests who lived during the seven hundred years or so following the introduction of Buddhism to Japan. It also contains chronological tables of Japanese Buddhist history from 540 to 1221.

Genkū [源空] : Another name for Hōnen, the founder of the Pure Land (Jōdo) school in Japan. *See* Hōnen.

Gennin [源仁] (818–887): A priest of the True Word (Shingon) school in Japan. At first he studied the doctrine of the Dharma Characteristics (Hossō) school, but later studied True Word Esotericism under Shinga and Shūei. In 885 he became the chief priest of Tō-ji temple. He built Nanchi-in temple in the Tō-ji temple complex and was revered as a great scholar of the esoteric teachings. He is also known as the Supervisor of Priests Nanchi-in and the Supervisor of Priests Ikegami.

Genshin [源信] (942–1017): Also known as Eshin. A priest of the Tendai school in Japan. A native of Yamato Province, he entered Enryaku-ji, the head temple of the Tendai school on Mount Hiei, in 950 and was ordained in 954. There he studied under Ryōgen who later became the eighteenth chief priest of the temple. He was also called Eshin because he practiced at a temple called Eshin-in on Mount Hiei. Valuing the practice of meditation, Genshin founded the Eshin branch of the Tendai school. He also practiced Nembutsu, meditating on Amida Buddha and chanting his name, while he read and recited such sutras as the Lotus, Amida, and Wisdom sutras. In 985 he completed *The Essentials of Rebirth in the Pure Land*, a work that had contributed considerably to the establishment and development of the Pure Land school in Japan. Later he wrote *The Essentials of the One Vehicle Teaching*, in which he clarified the one vehicle teaching of the Lotus Sutra and the universal possession of the Buddha nature by all people, thereby refuting the three vehicle teachings.

geya [祇夜・重頌] (Skt; Jpn *giya* or *jūju*): *See* verse.

ghee [醍醐味] (Jpn *daigo-mi*): The finest clarified butter, or the last of the five flavors (milk, cream, curdled milk, butter, and ghee), the stages in the process by which milk is made into ghee. The five flavors are compared to the five levels of Buddhist teachings, and the word *ghee* is used to indicate the fifth and highest level of teaching, or the supreme teaching. In his doctrine of the five periods, T'ien-t'ai (538–597) used ghee as a metaphor for the period of the Lotus and Nirvana sutras, defining the Lotus Sutra as the highest of all the sutras.

Ghoshila [瞿師羅] (Skt; Pali Ghosita; Jpn Kushira): A wealthy man in Kaushāmbī, India, who became a follower of Shakyamuni Buddha. He built a monastery in a grove that he owned, and offered both the monastery and grove to the Buddha. They were named Ghoshila Grove and Ghoshila Monastery. According to the Buddha's Preaching Life Sutra, five hundred Brahmans met Ghoshila on their way to Shrāvastī to see Sudatta, a wealthy merchant and the Buddha's patron, and Ghoshila, who also wanted to see Sudatta, traveled with them. When they arrived in Shrāvastī and met Sudatta, he was on his way to see Shakyamuni Buddha at Jetavana Monastery. They accompanied Sudatta to the monastery, where they saw the Buddha. Hearing the Buddha preach, the five hundred Brahmans attained the stage of non-returner, the level directly below the stage of arhat, while Ghoshila obtained the Dharma eye.

Ghoshila wanted to invite Shakyamuni to Kaushāmbī, so he converted one of his residences into a monastery so that the Buddha could stay there and preach. The story of the five hundred Brahmans and Ghoshila, who attained insight after hearing Shakyamuni preach, is found also in the Stories of the Words of Truth Sutra. This sutra, however, does not mention Ghoshila's desire to invite Shakyamuni to Kaushāmbī or his grove and monastery. In Chinese Buddhist scriptures, including the Chinese translation of the Stories of the Words of Truth Sutra, Ghoshila's name is rendered as "Beautiful Sound." According to *The Record of the Western Regions,* when its author, Hsüan-tsang, visited Kaushāmbī in the first half of the seventh century, the monastery built by Ghoshila and a stupa erected by King Ashoka on its compound were still standing. Hsüan-tsang says that Shakyamuni preached there for several years.

Gien [義淵] (d. 728): Also known as Giin. A priest of the Dharma Characteristics (Hossō) school in Japan. A native of Yamato Province, he studied the Consciousness-Only doctrine under Chihō at Gangō-ji temple. He devoted himself to propagating the Dharma Characteristics teachings. He founded temples in his native province including Ryūmon-ji at Yoshino and Ryūgai-ji (also known as Oka-dera) at Asuka. In 703 he was appointed administrator of priests by the imperial court. He had many disciples, among whom Gembō, Gyōki, Senkyō, Ryōbin, Gyōtatsu, Ryūson, and Rōben were called the "seven superior disciples of Gien."

Gijō-bō [義浄房] (n.d.): A disciple of Dōzen-bō at Seichō-ji temple in Awa Province, Japan, where Nichiren entered the priesthood. In *On Repaying Debts of Gratitude,* Nichiren wrote, "Now you two, Jōken-bō and Gijō-bō, were my teachers in my youth" (729). When Nichiren refuted the errors of the dominant schools and revealed his teaching at Seichō-ji temple on the twenty-eighth day of the fourth month, 1253, Tōjō Kagenobu, the steward of the village and a passionate believer in the Pure Land teachings, ordered his arrest. At that time, Gijō-bō and another priest named Jōken-bō helped Nichiren escape. They continued to correspond with Nichiren and sought his teachings. Nichiren sent them several letters and treatises, including *On Repaying Debts of Gratitude, The Tripitaka Master Shan-wu-wei,* and *Flowering and Bearing Grain.* A letter Nichiren sent him is known as *Letter to Gijō-bō.*

Girika [耆利柯・耆利] (n.d.) (Skt; Jpn Girika or Giri): A notorious man in the state of Magadha, India, who killed his own parents and many others. He became a retainer to King Ashoka before the king converted to Buddhism and later became a chief jailor. He attempted to kill King Ashoka, but was killed by the king. He is mentioned in *The Story of King Ashoka,* translated into Chinese by An Fa-ch'in in 306.

Gishin [義真] (781–833): The first chief priest of Enryaku-ji, the head temple of the Tendai school on Mount Hiei, in Japan. Born in Sagami Province, he went to Mount Hiei as a child and studied there under Dengyō. When Dengyō traveled to China in 804, Gishin, who was versed in Chinese, accompanied him as his interpreter. In 806, the year after they returned to Japan, Dengyō established the Tendai school and in 822, prior to his death, designated Gishin as his successor. Dengyō had tried to obtain imperial permission for the building of a Mahayana ordination center on Mount Hiei in the face of determined opposition from the older schools of Nara. Permission was granted a week after his death. In 823 Gishin began performing ordination ceremonies. In 824, by imperial decree, he became the first chief priest of Enryaku-ji and in 827 established a Mahayana ordination center on Mount Hiei, thereby fulfilling Dengyō's wishes.

Gladly Seen [喜見菩薩] (Jpn Kiken-bosatsu): The bodhisattva Gladly Seen by All Living Beings. *See* Gladly Seen by All Living Beings (2).

Gladly Seen by All Living Beings (Skt Sarva-sattva-priyadarshana) (1) [一切衆生喜見如来] (Jpn Issai-shujō-kiken-nyorai): The Thus Come One Gladly Seen by All Living Beings. The name that Mahāprajāpatī (also known as Gautamī or Gotamī), foster mother of Shakyamuni, will bear when she becomes a Buddha, according to the "Encouraging Devotion" (thirteenth) chapter of the Lotus Sutra. In this chapter, Shakyamuni tells Mahāprajāpatī: "Now if you would like to know the prophecy [of the attainment of enlightenment] for you, I will say that in ages to come, amid the Law of sixty-eight thousands of millions of Buddhas, you will be a great teacher of the Law, and the six thousand nuns, some still learning, some already sufficiently learned, will accompany you as teachers of the Law. In this manner you will bit by bit fulfill the way of the bodhisattva until you are able to become a Buddha with the name Gladly Seen by All Living Beings Thus Come One . . . Gautamī, this Gladly Seen by All Living Beings Buddha will confer a prophecy upon the six thousand bodhisattvas, to be passed from one to another, that they will attain supreme perfect enlightenment."

(2) [一切衆生喜見菩薩] (Jpn Issai-shujō-kiken-bosatsu): The bodhisattva Gladly Seen by All Living Beings, also known simply as Gladly

Seen. A bodhisattva described as a previous incarnation of Bodhisattva Medicine King in the "Medicine King" (twenty-third) chapter of the Lotus Sutra. According to this chapter, he learned the Lotus Sutra from a Buddha named Sun Moon Pure Bright Virtue and thereby gained supernatural powers. In gratitude Gladly Seen used his powers to make offerings of heavenly flowers and precious scents to this Buddha and to the sutra. He decided, however, that such offerings were less worthy than the offering of his own body. Anointing himself with oil and once again employing his transcendental powers, he burned his body as an offering of light for twelve hundred years, illuminating the entire universe. When his body was consumed, he was reborn in the land of the Buddha Sun Moon Pure Bright Virtue and again served this Buddha. After this Buddha's death, he burned his arms for seventy-two thousand years as a further offering.

Glorious Kalpa [荘厳劫] (Jpn Shōgon-kō): One of the three *kalpas,* the other two being the present Wise Kalpa and the future Constellation Kalpa. The major *kalpa* immediately preceding the present one. Each major *kalpa* consists of four medium *kalpas*—a *kalpa* of formation, a *kalpa* of continuance, a *kalpa* of decline, and a *kalpa* of disintegration. According to *The Record of the Three Thousand Buddhas of the Three Kalpas,* the *kalpa* of continuance of the Glorious Kalpa was graced by the advent of a thousand Buddhas in succession, the first named Flower Glow Buddha, and the last, Vishvabhū Buddha.

Godānīya [瞿耶尼 · 牛貨洲] (Skt; Jpn Kuyani or Goke-shū): One of the four continents said to surround Mount Sumeru. It is located to the west of the mountain. *See* Aparagodānīya.

god of fragrance [香神] (Jpn *kōjin*): One of the eight kinds of nonhuman beings, whose original Sanskrit name is *gandharva.* See *gandharva.*

god of the moon [月天] (Jpn Gatten): *See* moon, god of the.

god of the sun [日天] (Jpn Nitten): *See* sun, god of the.

Gohonzon [御本尊] (Jpn): The object of devotion. The word *go* is an honorific prefix, and *honzon* means object of fundamental respect or devotion. In Nichiren's (1222–1282) teaching, the object of devotion has two aspects: the object of devotion in terms of the Law and the object of devotion in terms of the Person. These may be described as follows: (1) The object of devotion in terms of the Law: Nichiren's mandala that embodies the eternal and intrinsic Law of Nam-myoho-renge-kyo. That Law is the source of all Buddhas and the seed of Buddhahood for all people. In other words, Nichiren identified Nam-myoho-renge-kyo as the ultimate Law permeating life and the universe, and embodied it in the form of a mandala. In his *Questions and Answers on the Object of Devo-*

tion, Nichiren refers to the object of devotion for people in the Latter Day of the Law as "the title (daimoku) of the Lotus Sutra." He further describes the title as the essence of the Lotus Sutra, or Nam-myoho-renge-kyo to be found only in the depths of the "Life Span" (sixteenth) chapter of the sutra. *The Object of Devotion for Observing the Mind* reads, "Myoho-renge-kyo appears in the center of the [treasure] tower with the Buddhas Shakyamuni and Many Treasures seated to the right and left, and, flanking them, the four bodhisattvas, followers of Shakyamuni, led by Superior Practices. Manjushrī, Maitreya, and the other bodhisattvas, who are followers of the four bodhisattvas, are seated below" (366). In this passage, Nichiren clarifies the relationship between the Law of Nam-myoho-renge-kyo, the Buddhas Shakyamuni and Many Treasures, and the various bodhisattvas depicted on the Gohonzon. In this way he emphasizes Nam-myoho-renge-kyo as the fundamental object of devotion. *The Real Aspect of the Gohonzon* explains that all living beings of the Ten Worlds "display the dignified attributes that they inherently possess" (832) through the benefit of Nam-myoho-renge-kyo. Nichiren viewed the Dai-Gohonzon, the object of devotion he inscribed for all humanity on the twelfth day of the tenth month in 1279, as the purpose of his life. This can be gleaned from his statement in *On Persecutions Befalling the Sage,* written in the tenth month of 1279: "The Buddha fulfilled the purpose of his advent in a little over forty years, the Great Teacher T'ien-t'ai took about thirty years, and the Great Teacher Dengyō, some twenty years. I have spoken repeatedly of the indescribable persecutions they suffered during those years. For me it took twenty-seven years, and the great persecutions I faced are well known to you all" (996). The object of devotion in terms of the Law is explained in greater detail in Nichiren's writings such as *The Object of Devotion for Observing the Mind* and *The Real Aspect of the Gohonzon.*

(2) The object of devotion in terms of the Person: In his *Reply to Kyō'ō,* Nichiren writes, "I, Nichiren, have inscribed my life in *sumi* ink, so believe in the Gohonzon with your whole heart. The Buddha's will is the Lotus Sutra, but the soul of Nichiren is nothing other than Nam-myoho-renge-kyo" (412). Nichiren here expresses his realization that Nam-myoho-renge-kyo is the origin and basis of his life, which he embodied in *sumi* ink in the form of the mandala he calls the Gohonzon. In *The Record of the Orally Transmitted Teachings,* he says, "The object of devotion is thus the entity of the entire body of the votary of the Lotus Sutra." "The votary" here refers to Nichiren himself. He also says, "The Buddha of the Latter Day of the Law is an ordinary person and an ordinary priest." "An ordinary priest" here refers to Nichiren. Because Nichiren revealed and spread

Nam-myoho-renge-kyo, which is manifest as the Person and the Law, he is regarded by his disciple and designated successor Nikkō and his followers as the Buddha of the Latter Day of the Law. Nichiren himself writes in *The Opening of the Eyes:* "On the twelfth day of the ninth month of last year [1271], between the hours of the rat and the ox [11:00 P.M. to 3:00 A.M.], this person named Nichiren was beheaded. It is his soul that has come to this island of Sado and, in the second month of the following year, snowbound, is writing this to send to his close disciples" (269). He states that he "was beheaded," though actually he survived the execution at Tatsunokuchi, implying that the ordinary person Nichiren ceased to exist. In this context, the passage "It is his soul that has come to this island of Sado [his place of exile]" means that Nichiren described himself as having revealed a deeper, true identity in the course of his attempted execution. Again Nikkō and his followers equate that identity with the Buddha of the Latter Day of the Law.

(3) The oneness of the Person and the Law: This means that the object of devotion in terms of the Person and the object of devotion in terms of the Law are one in their essence. The Law is inseparable from the Person, and vice versa. The object of devotion in terms of the Law is the physical embodiment, as a mandala (the Gohonzon), of the eternal and intrinsic Law of Nam-myoho-renge-kyo. Nichiren writes in his *Reply to Kyō'ō,* "I, Nichiren, have inscribed my life in *sumi* ink, so believe in the Gohonzon with your whole heart" (412). This passage indicates that Nichiren embodied in the Gohonzon the state of life he enjoyed as the eternal Buddha who personified the Law, so that people could attain the same state of enlightenment. *The Record of the Orally Transmitted Teachings* reads: "The 'body that is freely received and used [also, the Buddha of limitless joy]' is none other than the principle of three thousand realms in a single moment of life: The Great Teacher Dengyō says: 'A single moment of life comprising the three thousand realms is itself the "body that is freely received and used"; this Buddha has forsaken august appearances. The Buddha who has forsaken august appearances is the Buddha eternally endowed with the three bodies.' Now Nichiren and his followers who chant Nam-myoho-renge-kyo are just this." "The Buddha who has forsaken august appearances" means a Buddha who is no different from an ordinary person in form and appearance.

(4) The core of the Three Great Secret Laws: The Gohonzon, or the object of devotion of the essential teaching, is the core of the Three Great Secret Laws in Nichiren's doctrine and represents the purpose of his life. The Three Great Secret Laws are the object of devotion of the essential teaching, the invocation, or daimoku, of the essential teaching, and the

sanctuary of the essential teaching. Here, "essential teaching" refers to the teaching of Nam-myoho-renge-kyo, not to the essential teaching (latter half) of the Lotus Sutra. Nichiren expressed the Law of Nam-myoho-renge-kyo he realized within his own life in these three forms, which correspond to the three types of learning in Buddhism—precepts, meditation, and wisdom. The object of devotion corresponds to meditation, the invocation to wisdom, and the sanctuary to precepts. Sanctuary is a translation of the Japanese word *kaidan*, which is also translated as "ordination platform." This is a platform where practitioners vow to uphold the Buddhist precepts. In Nichiren's teaching, to embrace the object of devotion is the only precept, and the place where one enshrines the object of devotion and chants the daimoku is called the sanctuary. Again to keep faith in the object of devotion and chant the daimoku while teaching others to chant it is called the invocation. Both the sanctuary and the invocation derive from the object of devotion. Hence the object of devotion is the core of all three. For this reason the Gohonzon, or object of devotion, is also referred to as the One Great Secret Law.

(5) The inscriptions on the Gohonzon: In the center of the Gohonzon are written the Chinese characters "Nam-myoho-renge-kyo Nichiren." This indicates the oneness of the Person and the Law. On either side there are characters for the names of beings representing each of the Ten Worlds. At the top of the Gohonzon, the names of Shakyamuni Buddha and Many Treasures Buddha appear respectively to the immediate left and right (when facing the Gohonzon) of these central characters. They represent the realm or world of Buddhahood. The four bodhisattvas—Superior Practices, Boundless Practices, Pure Practices, and Firmly Established Practices—who lead the other Bodhisattvas of the Earth are positioned to the left and right of the two Buddhas. They, along with other bodhisattvas in the second row from the top such as Universal Worthy and Manjushrī, represent the realm of bodhisattvas. Also in the second row are persons of the two vehicles—voice-hearers and cause-awakened ones, such as Shāriputra and Mahākāshyapa—and flanking them are representatives of the realm of heavenly beings, such as Brahmā, Shakra, the devil king of the sixth heaven, and the gods of the sun and moon. In the third row appear a wheel-turning king, representing the realm of human beings; an *asura* king, representing the realm of *asuras;* a dragon king, representing the realm of animals; the Mother of Demon Children and the ten demon daughters, representing the realm of hungry spirits; and Devadatta, representing the realm of hell. Moreover, the four heavenly kings are positioned in the four corners of the Gohonzon: (again, when facing the Gohonzon) Vaishravana in the upper

left, Upholder of the Nation in the upper right, Wide-Eyed in the lower right, and Increase and Growth in the lower left. While all other figures on the Gohonzon are represented in Chinese characters, the names of the wisdom king Craving-Filled and the wisdom king Immovable are written below Vaishravana and Upholder of the Nation respectively in Siddham, a medieval Sanskrit script. Here the wisdom king Craving-Filled represents the principle that earthly desires are enlightenment, and the wisdom king Immovable, the principle that the sufferings of birth and death are nirvana. Other characters on the Gohonzon include the names of Great Bodhisattva Hachiman and the Sun Goddess. All these names express the principles that the Ten Worlds exist within the eternal Buddha's life, and that living beings of the Ten Worlds can attain Buddhahood. Not all of the above names appear on every Gohonzon that is transcribed from the Dai-Gohonzon, but whichever ones do appear represent all of the Ten Worlds.

The names of the Great Teacher T'ien-t'ai and the Great Teacher Dengyō are inscribed in the lower part of the Gohonzon representing those who transmitted the true lineage of Buddhism. There are two inscriptions gleaned from Miao-lo's *Annotations on "The Words and Phrases of the Lotus Sutra,"* which Nichiren used to describe the power of the Gohonzon and the Law it embodies. One, placed in the upper right (facing the Gohonzon), reads, "Those who vex or trouble [the practitioners of the Law] will have their heads split into seven pieces." The other, in the upper left, reads, "Those who give alms [to them] will enjoy good fortune surpassing the ten honorable titles." The ten honorable titles are epithets applied to the Buddha expressing his virtue, wisdom, and compassion. In the lower right is Nichiren's declaration that "This is the great mandala never before known in the entire land of Jambudvīpa in the more than 2,230 years since the Buddha's passing."

Gokuraku-ji [極楽寺]: Literally, "Temple of Perfect Bliss." A temple of the True Word Precepts (Shingon–Ritsu) school in Kamakura, Japan, built in 1259 by Hōjō Shigetoki, the third son of Hōjō Yoshitoki, the second regent of the Kamakura government. Later Hōjō Nagatoki, a son of Hōjō Shigetoki and the sixth regent of the Kamakura shogunate, invited Ryōkan to act as chief priest. Ryōkan, while widely respected, had great animosity for Nichiren, who sought to engage him in a public religious debate. He conspired with authorities to have Nichiren and his followers persecuted. The temple was destroyed by fire in 1275, and was rebuilt in 1281 by the eighth regent Hōjō Tokimune as the shogunate's official place of prayer. In 1332 it became affiliated with the imperial court, and its priests were charged with the responsibility of praying for the peace of the country and the good health of the emperor. It was destroyed by an earthquake in 1433 but later restored. *See also* Ryōkan.

gold circle [金輪] (Skt *kānchana-mandala;* Jpn *konrin*): Also, gold wheel. In ancient Indian cosmology, a circle of gold that supports the world. According to *The Dharma Analysis Treasury*, the gold circle is 320,000 *yojanas* thick and 1,203,450 *yojanas* across. This gold circle is the uppermost of three circles said to be located beneath the earth's surface that rest upon the cosmic void and support the world. The three circles are the windy circle, the watery circle, and the gold circle. The windy circle, which floats in space, supports the watery circle just above it. Upon this sits the gold circle, which directly supports the land with its Mount Sumeru, seas, and mountains. The Sanskrit word *kānchana* means gold, and *mandala* means disk or circle.

Golden Color [金色王] (Jpn Konjiki-ō): The name of Shakyamuni as a king in a previous existence. According to the King Golden Color Sutra, Shakyamuni was once a king who ruled over his people with wisdom and benevolence. When the nation suffered twelve years of drought and many of his subjects were dying of starvation, the king gathered all the grain to be found in the country and distributed it equally among the people. At that time, a *pratyekabuddha,* or a cause-awakened one, who had dedicated himself to Buddhist practice for forty *kalpas* appeared and begged for something to eat. The king gave him his last bit of food as an offering. This good deed caused various kinds of grain to fall like rain from the skies for seven days. Thereafter seven kinds of treasures as well as clothing, food, and other necessities rained down every seven days, putting an end to the people's destitution.

Golden Light Sutra [金光明経] (Skt *Suvarnaprabhāsa-sūtra* or *Suvarnaprabhāsottama-sūtra;* Chin *Chin-kuang-ming-ching;* Jpn *Konkōmyō-kyō*): A sutra that takes the form of a discourse by Shakyamuni on Eagle Peak in Rājagriha, India. There were five Chinese translations, of which three are extant. One is the four-volume Golden Light Sutra translated in the early fifth century by Dharmaraksha. Another is the ten-volume Sovereign Kings of the Golden Light Sutra (also called the Sovereign Kings Sutra) translated in the early eighth century by I-ching. A third is an eight-volume text translated in the late sixth century by Pao-kuei. The Golden Light Sutra teaches that those who embrace this sutra will obtain the protection of the four heavenly kings and other benevolent deities, and that, if a ruler takes faith in the correct teaching, these deities will protect his country. On the other hand, if he fails to protect the correct teaching, the benevolent deities will abandon the nation, and calamities and disasters will occur. In Japan, this sutra was revered as one of the three sutras for the protection of the nation, the other two being the Lotus Sutra and the Benevolent Kings Sutra. Nichiren (1222–1282) quoted from this sutra to support his contention, found in his work *On Establishing the Correct Teaching for the Peace of the Land*, that Japan in his time was suffering and would continue to suffer calamities and disasters because the benevolent deities had abandoned the nation due to the ruler's slander of the correct teaching. The Sanskrit text and a Tibetan translation also exist.

golden-winged bird [金翅鳥] (Jpn *konji-chō*): One of the eight kinds of nonhuman beings, whose original Sanskrit name is *garuda*. *See* eight kinds of nonhuman beings; *garuda*.

gold-wheel treasure [金輪宝] (Jpn *konrin-hō*): One of the seven treasures that a gold-wheel-turning king, or an ideal ruler in ancient India, was said to possess. The seven treasures are a gold wheel, elephants, horses, jewels, jewel-like women, excellent ministers of financial affairs, and generals. A wheel-turning king possesses one of the four kinds of wheels—gold, silver, copper, and iron. A gold wheel is the most superior of the four kinds of wheels, and a gold-wheel-turning king who possesses a gold-wheel treasure rules all the four continents surrounding Mount Sumeru.

gold-wheel-turning king [金輪王・金輪聖王] (Jpn *konrin-ō* or *konrin-jō'ō*): Also, gold-wheel-turning sage king. The foremost ruler among the four types of wheel-turning kings, the other three being silver-wheel-turning kings, copper-wheel-turning kings, and iron-wheel-turning kings. The number of continents each king rules differs according to his rank. A gold-wheel-turning king rules over the four continents surrounding Mount Sumeru. A silver-wheel-turning king rules three of the four continents, a copper-wheel-turning king rules two, and an iron-wheel-turning king rules one continent. While turning his gold wheel, a gold-wheel-turning king advances at will and establishes peace. The term *wheel-turning king* often indicates a gold-wheel-turning king. *See also* wheel-turning king.

Gomyō [護命] (750–834): A priest of the Dharma Characteristics (Hossō) school in Japan. In 759 he became a disciple of Dōkō, a priest of the official temple of that school in Mino Province. Thereafter he learned the Consciousness-Only doctrine from Man'yō and Shōgu, priests of Gangō-ji temple in Nara. He received the precepts from Fa-chin (Jpn Hasshin) of Tōshōdai-ji temple, who had come to Japan from China with his teacher Chien-chen (Ganjin). In 818 Dengyō, the founder of the Japanese Tendai school, sought permission from the emperor to construct a Mahayana ordination center on Mount Hiei. The next year Gomyō condemned the project as contrary to the Buddhist teachings in a petition to the throne. He also competed with Dengyō in praying for rain, but lost. In 827 Gomyō was designated administrator of priests by the imperial court.

gongyō [勤行] (Jpn): Literally, to "exert [oneself in] practice." Generally speaking, *gongyō* refers to the practice of reciting Buddhist sutras in front of an object of devotion. The content and method of *gongyō* differ according to the school of Buddhism. In Nichiren's (1222–1282) teaching, *gongyō* means to chant the daimoku of Nam-myoho-renge-kyo and recite portions of the "Expedient Means" (second) chapter and the "Life Span" (sixteenth) chapter of the Lotus Sutra with faith in the object of devotion called the Gohonzon. In *The Recitation of the "Expedient Means" and "Life Span" Chapters,* Nichiren states: "Though no chapter of the Lotus Sutra is negligible, among the entire twenty-eight chapters, the 'Expedient Means' chapter and the 'Life Span' chapter are particularly outstanding. The remaining chapters are all in a sense the branches and leaves of these two chapters. . . . If you recite the 'Life Span' and 'Expedient Means' chapters, then the remaining chapters will naturally be included even though you do not recite them" (71). In the *gongyō* of Nichiren's practice, chanting the daimoku constitutes the fundamental practice, and therefore it is called the primary practice. Recitation of the "Expedient Means" and "Life Span" chapters helps bring forth the benefits of the primary practice and is hence called the supporting practice.

Gonsō [勤操] (758–827): Also known as Gonzō. A priest of the Three Treatises (Sanron) school in Japan. In 769 he began to study under Shinrei, a priest of Daian-ji temple, and at sixteen he went to Mount Kōya. After that, he studied the three treatises—*The Treatise on the Middle Way, The Treatise on the Twelve Gates,* and *The One-Hundred-Verse Treatise*—under Zengi, a priest of Tōdai-ji temple. In 802 he and other learned priests of the seven major temples of Nara engaged Dengyō, the founder of the Japanese Tendai school, in religious debate at Takao-dera temple. Dengyō won the debate. Gonsō was later appointed supervisor of priests by the imperial court, in which capacity he administrated Tōdai-ji and Saidai-ji temples and founded a temple named Iwabuchi-dera. In 826 he was appointed general supervisor of priests, and after his death he was named the Administrator of Priests Iwabuchi. Gonsō is also known as a teacher of Kōbō, the founder of the True Word (Shingon) school.

Gon'yo [厳誉] (n.d.): The administrator of Shijūku-in, a temple of the Tendai school, in Kambara in Suruga Province, Japan, during the Kamakura period (1185–1333). Nikkō, who was later to become Nichiren's successor, had originally entered the priesthood at Shijūku-in and studied there. In the course of his propagation efforts in the Fuji area in the

1270s, Nikkō often visited the temple, and he converted several of its young priests including Nichiji, Kenshū, and Shōken. Shortly before the Atsuhara Persecution, Gon'yo expelled Nikkō, Kenshū, Shōken, and Nichiji from the temple, asserting that they were preaching erroneous teachings.

good friend [善知識] (Skt *kalyāna-mitra;* Jpn *zen-chishiki*): Also, good companion. One who leads others to the correct teaching, or helps them in their practice of the correct teaching. In this sense, *good friend* may also be called good teacher. A good friend is contrasted with an evil friend, who leads people away from the way of Buddhist practice and into the evil paths, that is, into suffering. Buddhism teaches that, in pursuing the way to enlightenment, one should associate with a good friend to strengthen one's faith and practice. In the "Devadatta" (twelfth) chapter of the Lotus Sutra, Shakyamuni Buddha describes Devadatta, who tried to kill him, as a good friend who in a past life instructed him in the Lotus Sutra. Shakyamuni states that it is therefore because of Devadatta that he was able to attain enlightenment and save living beings. The "King Wonderful Adornment" (twenty-seventh) chapter of the sutra describes the two brothers Pure Storehouse and Pure Eye as good friends to their father, King Wonderful Adornment, because they converted their father to the correct teaching. This chapter defines a good friend as "the great cause and condition by which one is guided and led, and which enables one to see the Buddha and to conceive the desire for supreme perfect enlightenment." *See also* evil friend.

Good Kalpa [善劫] (Jpn Zen-kō): *See* Wise Kalpa.

Good Law Hall [善法堂] (Jpn Zembō-dō): A structure said to be located to the southwest of the god Shakra's palace on the peak of Mount Sumeru. *See* Hall of the Good Law.

good man [善男子] (Skt *kula-putra;* Jpn *zen-nanshi*): In the Buddhist scriptures, a man of correct faith. The Sanskrit *kula-putra* means son of a noble family, young man of a good family, or virtuous and noble man. The phrase "good man and good woman (Skt *kula-duhitri*)" also appears. "Good man" generally refers to a male lay believer, and also a bodhisattva. Buddhist scriptures record Shakyamuni as addressing bodhisattvas with the phrase "good men."

good root [善根] (Skt *kushala-mūla;* Jpn *zengon* or *zenkon*): Also, root of goodness, root of merit, good act, good cause, or act of merit. A cause, or action, that produces a good effect or reward. Good acts are compared to the roots that nourish the plants and trees so that they bear flowers and fruit. In Buddhism, "good roots" are necessary for the attainment of Buddhahood. Greed, anger, and foolishness are called the three bad roots or the three poisons. In contrast, "no greed, no anger, and no foolishness" are called the three good roots.

Good to See [善見城] (Jpn Zenken-jō): The god Shakra's palace located on the peak of Mount Sumeru, also known as Correct Views or Joyful to See. *See* Correct Views.

Good Treasures [善財童子] (Skt Sudhana-shreshthi-dāraka or Sudhana; Jpn Zenzai-dōji): A bodhisattva described in the Flower Garland Sutra. According to the sutra, when he was born, gold, silver, emeralds, and other treasures suddenly appeared in his father's house; therefore he was called Good Treasures. On meeting Bodhisattva Manjushrī, he conceived the desire for enlightenment and then sought out one teacher after another to receive their instruction. Finally he met the fifty-third teacher, Bodhisattva Universal Worthy, and on hearing his ten great vows, attained enlightenment. Good Treasures' pilgrimage was popularized in both art and literature, and in Japan it is thought to have inspired the building of the fifty-three post stations along the Tōkaidō Road, the highway linking Edo (now Tokyo) and Kyoto, during the Edo period (1600–1867).

good woman [善女人] (Skt *kula-duhitri;* Jpn *zen-nyonin*): In the Buddhist scriptures, a woman of correct faith. *See* good man.

Gopikā [瞿夷] (Skt; Jpn Kui): Also known as Gopī or Gopā. Shakyamuni's wife while he was a prince, before he renounced secular life to seek enlightenment. The Twelve-year Journey Sutra describes Gopikā as Shakyamuni's principal wife, and Yashodharā, the mother of his son and disciple Rāhula, as his second wife. In the Sutra of Collected Birth Stories concerning the Practice of the Six Pāramitās, however, Gopikā is the mother of Rāhula and is identified with Yashodharā.

Gōsanze [降三世] (Jpn): The wisdom king Conqueror of the Threefold World (Gōsanze-myō'ō), one of the five great wisdom kings. *See* Conqueror of the Threefold World.

Gosho [御書] (Jpn): The individual and collected writings of Nichiren (1222–1282). *Gosho* literally means honorable writings; *go* is an honorific prefix, and *sho* means writings. In general the word is used in Japanese as an honorific for certain books and writings, particularly for those of the founders and patriarchs of some Buddhist schools. Nikkō, Nichiren's successor, used the word *gosho* to refer to Nichiren's works and made efforts to collect, copy, and preserve them as sacred texts. As a result, a remarkable number of Nichiren's works have been passed down to the present, and many are extant in his own hand. In terms of content, the Gosho may be divided into four groups: (1) treatises setting forth doctrine, (2) writings remonstrating with government authorities, (3) letters offering advice, encouragement, or consolation to believers, or written in answer to questions (many in this category also include expressions of gratitude for offerings and support received), and (4) written records of Nichiren's oral teachings, including his lectures on the Lotus Sutra.

Gotama [瞿曇] (Pali; Jpn Kudon): The family name of the historical Buddha, Shakyamuni. *See* Gautama.

Gotamī [憍曇弥] (Pali; Jpn Kyōdommi): Also known as Mahāprajāpatī. The aunt and foster mother of Shakyamuni. *See* Mahāprajāpatī.

gradual teaching [漸教] (Jpn *zen-kyō*): Teachings expounded progressively to gradually develop people's capacities to understand higher doctrines. The concept of gradual teaching was adopted by scholars of various schools in China in their classification of Shakyamuni Buddha's teachings. In T'ien-t'ai's doctrine, "gradual teaching" constitutes one of the four teachings of method. *See also* four teachings of method.

Great Adornment (1) [大荘厳仏] (Jpn Daishōgon-butsu): A Buddha mentioned in the Buddha Treasury Sutra. According to the sutra, the Buddha Great Adornment lived in the remote past. His life lasted for "sixty-eight hundred ten thousand million years," and he amassed a following of "sixty-eight hundred ten thousand million disciples." One hundred years after this Buddha's death, his followers split into five schools. Only the monk Universal Practice, the leader of one of the five schools, correctly upheld what Great Adornment had taught. The leaders of the four other schools, such as the monk Shore of Suffering, held erroneous views and, along with their followers, hated and reviled Universal Practice. For this reason, the sutra says, these four monks and their followers fell into hell.

(2) [大荘厳菩薩] (Jpn Daishōgon-bosatsu): A bodhisattva appearing in the Immeasurable Meanings Sutra. He represents the assembly on Eagle Peak and addresses Shakyamuni Buddha. Their ensuing dialogue constitutes the content of that sutra, which is considered an introductory teaching to the Lotus Sutra. In the Immeasurable Meanings Sutra, the Buddha entrusts the sutra to Great Adornment and the other eighty thousand bodhisattvas present, who then vow to propagate it.

Great Arrogant Brahman [大慢婆羅門] (n.d.) (Jpn Daiman-baramon): A Brahman in the kingdom of Mālava in India, described in *The Record of the Western Regions,* Hsüan-tsang's record of his travels through Central Asia and India in the seventh century. Having mastered a great many Buddhist and non-Buddhist scriptures, he was overly proud of his erudition and boasted that he surpassed all scholars of the past, present, and future. He made four statues—one each of the Hindu gods Maheshvara, Vishnu, and Nārāyana, and one of the Buddha—and used them as the pillars of his preaching platform, asserting that his wisdom far surpassed that of these four. He was defeated in debate, however, by Bhadraruchi, a Mahayana Buddhist monk of western India. The king of Mālava realized that he had been completely deceived by the Brahman and sentenced him to death. The Brahman was spared his life at Bhadraruchi's request to the king. Consumed by rancor against Bhadraruchi, however, the Great Arrogant Brahman slandered him and the Mahayana teachings when Bhadraruchi came to visit. According to *The Record of the Western Regions,* while he was still spewing abuse, the earth split open and he fell into hell alive.

Great Awesome Virtue [大威徳明王] (Skt Yamāntaka; Jpn Daiitoku-myō'ō): The wisdom king Great Awesome Virtue. One of the five great wisdom kings. The wisdom kings are a group of deities revered in Esoteric Buddhism as the removers of all obstacles. The other four of the five great wisdom kings are Immovable, Conqueror of the Threefold World, Kundalī, and Diamond Yaksha. The wisdom king Great Awesome Virtue is said to defeat all poisonous snakes and evil dragons. He is depicted as an angry figure, holding weapons such as a sword, a lance, and a bow and arrow. In Japan, an esoteric rite called the Great Awesome Virtue ceremony was conducted for the purpose of subduing enemies.

Great Canon of Monastic Rules, The [摩訶僧祇律] (Chin *Mo-ho-seng-chih-lü;* Jpn *Maka-sōgi-ritsu*): A work of the *vinaya,* or rules of monastic discipline, of the Mahāsamghika school, translated into Chinese in 416 by Buddhabhadra, a monk from northern India, and Fa-hsien, a Chinese Buddhist pilgrim. Fa-hsien left Ch'ang-an in 399 and journeyed to India to seek Buddhist texts. He obtained the Sanskrit text of *The Great Canon of Monastic Rules* and brought it back to China. This work divides the Buddhist precepts into two large categories—those for monks and those for nuns.

great citadel of the Avīchi hell [阿鼻大城] (Jpn Abi-daijō): *See* Avīchi hell.

great citadel of the hell of incessant suffering [無間大城] (Jpn Muken-daijō): *See* hell of incessant suffering.

Great Collection Sutra [大集経] (Chin *Ta-chi-ching;* Jpn *Daijikkyō*): A collection of sutras translated into Chinese by Dharmaraksha (385–433) and others. These sutras were compiled into a single sutra, or the sixty-volume Great Collection Sutra, by a Chinese priest named Seng-chiu in 586. Among the better-known sections are the twenty-fourth volume, which refers to the three calamities, and the fifty-fifth volume, which predicts in some detail how the spread of Buddhism will unfold, describing its rise, prosperity, and decline over the five five-hundred-year periods following Shakyamuni's death. It also discusses the significance of the

Latter Day of the Law, when Shakyamuni's teachings become obscured and lost. Its contents take the form of Shakyamuni Buddha preaching to a great assembly of Buddhas and bodhisattvas who have gathered from the worlds in the ten directions. *See also* five five-hundred-year periods.

Great Commander [太元帥明王] (Skt Āṭavaka; Jpn Taigensui-myō'ō, better known as Taigen-myō'ō): The wisdom king Great Commander. Great Commander is one of the deities collectively called the wisdom kings who are said to remove all obstacles. In Esoteric Buddhism, Great Commander is revered as a deity who protects the nation by dispelling disasters and troubles. He is depicted as an angry figure surrounded by flames and bearing weapons such as a sword. In Japan, a ceremony of Esoteric Buddhism called the ceremony of Great Commander was performed to protect the nation.

Great Commentary on the Abhidharma, The [阿毘達磨大毘婆沙論] (Skt *Abhidharma-mahāvibhāshā-shāstra;* Chin *A-p'i-ta-mo-ta-p'i-p'o-sha-lun;* Jpn *Abidatsuma-daibibasha-ron*): An exhaustive commentary on the Hinayana doctrines. This work was compiled in Kashmir in the former half of the second century. According to tradition, the compilation was carried out by five hundred arhats under the guidance of Pārshva and the support of King Kanishka at the time of the Fourth Buddhist Council; the compilation took twelve years. This two-hundred-volume work is a commentary on Kātyāyanīputra's *Treatise on the Source of Wisdom,* the basic doctrinal text of the Sarvāstivāda school, and was translated into Chinese by Hsüan-tsang in the mid-seventh century. There is another Chinese translation, which is the sixty-volume *Commentary on the Abhidharma,* made by Buddhavarman and Tao-t'ai of the Northern Liang dynasty (397–439). This work corresponds to the first half of *The Great Commentary on the Abhidharma. The Great Commentary on the Abhidharma* sets forth the doctrine of the conservative Sarvāstivāda school of Kashmir and refutes the positions of the more progressive Gandhara Sarvāstivāda school, the Mahāsamghika school, the non-Buddhist Sāmkhya school, and other non-Buddhist schools. It serves as a record of the doctrinal development of the Sarvāstivāda school from the time of the writing of *The Treatise on the Source of Wisdom.* This work systematized the Sarvāstivāda doctrine; however, because it was so voluminous, it later prompted the compilation of a condensed version, *The Heart of the Abhidharma.*

Great Compassion Sutra [大悲経] (Chin *Ta-pei-ching;* Jpn *Daihi-kyō*): A sutra translated into Chinese in 558 by Narendrayashas. This sutra describes how Shakyamuni Buddha, about to enter nirvana, transfers the Law to the gods Brahmā and Shakra and to his disciples Mahākāshyapa and Ānanda. It extols the blessings of chanting the Buddha's name and making offerings to his relics. In this sutra, Shakyamuni instructs Ānanda to work with Mahākāshyapa to compile his teachings after his death, so that they will be transmitted to posterity. A Tibetan translation is also extant.

Great Concentration and Insight [摩訶止観] (Chin *Mo-ho-chih-kuan;* Jpn *Maka-shikan*): Also known as *Great Calming and Contemplation.* One of T'ien-t'ai's three major works, the others being *The Profound Meaning of the Lotus Sutra* and *The Words and Phrases of the Lotus Sutra.* "Concentration" means focusing one's mind on one point without any distractions, and "insight" means seeing all things as they are—having perception that penetrates the ultimate reality, or true aspect, of all phenomena. This work is a compilation of lectures delivered by T'ien-t'ai at Yü-ch'üan-ssu temple in Ching-chou of China in 594. Chang-an, T'ien-t'ai's disciple who compiled this work, wrote in his introduction to it, "*Great Concentration and Insight* reveals the teaching that T'ien-t'ai Chih-che himself practiced in the depths of his being." This work clarifies the principle of three thousand realms in a single moment of life based on the Lotus Sutra and elucidates the method of practice for observing one's mind in order to realize this principle within oneself.

In contrast with *Profound Meaning* and *Words and Phrases,* Chang-an's compilations of T'ien-t'ai's theoretical explanation of the Lotus Sutra, *Great Concentration and Insight* reveals T'ien-t'ai's enlightenment to the essence of the sutra and the practice by which this enlightenment can be obtained. *Great Concentration and Insight* consists of ten chapters in ten volumes; among these Miao-lo, the sixth patriarch of the T'ien-t'ai school, as well as Chang-an and other scholars regard the seventh chapter, titled "Correct Practice," as the core of the work that clarifies the practice of concentration and insight. It describes ten objects of meditation and ten corresponding meditations as the ultimate way to realize "the region of the unfathomable," or the principle of three thousand realms in a single moment of life. The relationship between the mind or life and all phenomena is explained through the "threefold contemplation in a single mind." The sixth chapter, titled "Preparatory Practices," prepares one for the practice of the ten meditations on the ten objects by describing twenty-five preparatory exercises. These aim to enable one to regulate one's daily life through the observance of precepts, appropriate food and clothing, and controlling of the body and mind. *See also* ten meditations; ten objects.

Great Forest Monastery [大林精舎] (Skt Mahāvana-vihāra; Jpn Dairin-shōja): Also known as Mahāvana Monastery. A monastery located in a forest called Mahāvana, or Great Forest, near Vaishālī, India, during the time of Shakyamuni Buddha. In the monastery stood a two-story hall. Shakyamuni Buddha frequented Great Forest Monastery and preached there.

great impartial wisdom [平等大慧] (Jpn *byōdō-daie*): The wisdom of the Buddhas that perceives the truth that all beings and phenomena are essentially equal and without distinction. Also the Buddhas' teachings based on that wisdom. *See* great wisdom of equality.

Greatly Enlightened World-Honored One [大覚世尊] (Jpn Daikaku-seson): *See* World-Honored One of Great Enlightenment.

Great Ornament of Tales, The [大荘厳論経] (Skt *Kalpanā-manditikā;* Chin *Ta-chuang-yen-lun-ching;* Jpn *Daishōgon-rongyō*): A work generally attributed to Ashvaghosha and translated into Chinese by Kumārajīva in the early fifth century. A collection of ninety Buddhist tales, it contains stories about the deeds of Buddhist kings such as Ashoka and Kanishka, anecdotes about Buddhist monks and lay believers, and stories about Shakyamuni Buddha in previous incarnations and of his compassionate deeds in his historic life. The stories deal with a variety of subjects, such as the virtues of almsgiving and the spirit to seek Buddhism. A number of them derive from the Āgama sutras. The Sanskrit text is extant.

Great Perfection of Wisdom Sutra (1) [摩訶般若波羅蜜経] (Skt *Panchavimshatisāhasrikā-prajnāpāramitā;* Chin *Mo-ho-pan-jo-po-lo-mi-ching;* Jpn *Makahannya-haramitsu-kyō*): One of the major Wisdom sutras, translated into Chinese by Kumārajīva in 404. Also known as the Larger Wisdom Sutra, in contrast with the Smaller Wisdom Sutra (also translated by Kumārajīva). The formal Chinese titles of these two sutras are the same; hence they are commonly distinguished by the shortened titles above. The Larger Wisdom Sutra expounds the doctrine of supreme wisdom (Skt *prajnā*) and the non-substantiality of all phenomena. The text consists of ninety chapters. In the first six chapters, Shakyamuni Buddha expounds the doctrine of supreme wisdom to his disciples of superior capacity, including Shāriputra. In the subsequent chapters, Subhūti preaches to bodhisattvas and others on behalf of the Buddha. *The Treatise on the Great Perfection of Wisdom* is Nāgārjuna's commentary on the Sanskrit text of this sutra.

(2) [摩訶般若波羅蜜経] (Skt *Ashtasāhasrikā-prajnāpāramitā;* Chin *Mo-ho-pan-jo-po-lo-mi-ching;* Jpn *Makahannya-haramitsu-kyō*): Also known as the Smaller Wisdom Sutra. A sutra translated by Kumārajīva in 408, the Chinese title of which is also rendered as the Great Perfection of Wisdom Sutra. It consists of twenty-nine chapters. Though con-

siderably different in length, the Larger and Smaller Wisdom sutras basically set forth the same doctrines.

(3) [大般若波羅蜜多経・大般若経] (Skt *Mahāprajnāpāramitā-sūtra;* Chin *Ta-pan-jo-po-lo-mi-to-ching;* Jpn *Daihannya-haramitta-kyō* or *Daihannya-kyō*): Also known as the Great Wisdom Sutra. *See* Great Wisdom Sutra.

Great Power [勢至菩薩] (Skt Mahāsthāmaprāpta; Jpn Seishi-bosatsu): The bodhisattva Great Power, also known as Gainer of Great Authority. According to the Meditation on the Buddha Infinite Life Sutra and the Buddha Infinite Life Sutra, a bodhisattva who attends Amida Buddha together with Bodhisattva Perceiver of the World's Sounds. The former sutra describes him as illuminating all with the light of his wisdom, saving people from the sufferings of the three evil paths and endowing them with unmatched power. In the "Introduction" (first) chapter of the Lotus Sutra, Bodhisattva Great Power appears under the name of Bodhisattva Gainer of Great Authority as one of those assembled on Eagle Peak to listen to Shakyamuni Buddha preach. In the "Never Disparaging" (twentieth) chapter of the sutra, Shakyamuni addresses him as the representative of the whole assembly.

great pure Law [大白法] (Jpn *daibyakuhō*): In Nichiren's (1222–1282) teaching, the Law of Nam-myoho-renge-kyo. Nichiren uses this term in his writings to indicate the ultimate Law implied in the "Life Span" (sixteenth) chapter of the Lotus Sutra, in contrast with the pure Law, or Shakyamuni's teachings. To illustrate, Nichiren writes in *The Selection of the Time:* "There is no doubt that our present age corresponds to the fifth five-hundred-year period described in the Great Collection Sutra, when 'the pure Law will become obscured and lost.' But after the pure Law is obscured and lost, the great pure Law of Nam-myoho-renge-kyo, the heart and core of the Lotus Sutra, will surely spread and be widely declared throughout the land of Jambudvīpa" (541).

great south gate [南大門] (Jpn *nandaimon*): A term for the front or main gate of a temple in Japan. Temples usually face south, so the great south gate stands in the middle front of the temple grounds facing south and is regarded as the most important of the outer gates of the grounds. The inner gate stands directly to its north and forms the entrance to the inner and main precinct where the main hall and the pagoda stand. In some of the earlier temples, the great south gate was smaller than the inner gate, but later it was made proportionately larger than the inner gate.

Great T'ang Dynasty Catalog of Buddhist Scriptures, The [大唐内典録] (Chin *Ta-t'ang-nei-tien-lu;* Jpn *Daitō-naiten-roku*): Also known as

The Catalog of Buddhist Scriptures. A catalog of the Buddhist canon compiled in 664 by Tao-hsüan, the founder of the Nan-shan branch of the Precepts (Lü) school in China. It is composed of ten volumes.

great teacher [大師] (Chin *ta-shih;* Jpn *daishi*): An honorific title awarded to priests of virtue in China and Japan by the imperial court, usually after their death. In Japan, Saichō, the founder of the Tendai school, was given the name and title the Great Teacher Dengyō (Jpn Dengyō Daishi) in 866, and Ennin, the third chief priest of Enryaku-ji, the head temple of the Tendai school, the Great Teacher Jikaku (Jikaku Daishi) in the same year. Kūkai, the founder of the True Word (Shingon) school, was given the name and title the Great Teacher Kōbō (Kōbō Daishi) in 921. These were the first instances of the bestowal of the honorific title "great teacher" in Japan.

Great Treasure Chamber [大宝坊] (Jpn Daihō-bō): The vast court where the Great Collection Sutra was preached. According to this sutra, when Shakyamuni was on Eagle Peak in Magadha, India, using his powers of meditation, he made a great court adorned with precious treasures appear between the world of desire and the world of form. He ascended to that court, the Great Treasure Chamber, and expounded his teachings there.

Great Universal Wisdom Excellence [大通智勝仏] (Skt Mahābhijnājnānābhibhū; Jpn Daitsūchishō-butsu): A Buddha described in the "Parable of the Phantom City" (seventh) chapter of the Lotus Sutra as having taught the Lotus Sutra in the inconceivably distant past. According to this chapter, after seating himself in the place of practice and defeating the armies of the devil, he continued to meditate for ten small *kalpas* and at last attained perfect enlightenment. At the request of his sixteen sons and the Brahmā kings, Great Universal Wisdom Excellence Buddha expounded the four noble truths and the twelve-linked chain of causation. His sixteen sons renounced secular life to follow him and begged him to reveal the teaching of perfect enlightenment. After twenty thousand *kalpas,* he acceded to their request and finally preached the Lotus Sutra for a period of eight thousand *kalpas.* Apart from his sixteen sons and a number of voice-hearers, however, many others gave way to doubt and confusion. At that time, Great Universal Wisdom Excellence Buddha entered into meditation and dwelt in meditation for eighty-four thousand *kalpas.* During this period, each of his sixteen sons preached the Lotus Sutra in his stead, enabling innumerable people to set their minds upon enlightenment. Their preaching is called the restatement of Great Universal Wisdom Excellence Buddha's teaching (Jpn *Daitsū-fukkō*). After eighty-four thousand *kalpas,* Great Universal Wisdom

Excellence Buddha emerged from meditation and declared that whoever had taken faith in the teaching related by his sixteen sons would surely attain enlightenment. From then on, the people who had heard the Law from one or another of these sixteen bodhisattvas were always reborn together with their respective teachers. All sixteen sons later became Buddhas and, according to this chapter, taught the Law in various lands in the ten directions of the universe. The youngest was reborn in this *sahā* world as Shakyamuni.

great vehicle [大乘] (Jpn *daijō*): Also, Great Vehicle. The Mahayana teachings. The Sanskrit word Mahayana means great vehicle. Great vehicle indicates a teaching capable of carrying many people to enlightenment. The term is used in contrast with the lesser vehicle, Hinayana, a name given by Mahayanists to the more conservative monastic forms of Buddhism of their time and indicating a teaching that can carry only a limited number of people to enlightenment.

great white ox cart [大白牛車] (Jpn *daibyaku-gosha*): A carriage adorned with jewels and drawn by a great white ox. It appears in the parable of the three carts and the burning house in the "Simile and Parable" (third) chapter of the Lotus Sutra, where it represents the one Buddha vehicle, or the supreme vehicle of Buddhahood. *See also* parable of the three carts and the burning house.

great wisdom of equality [平等大慧] (Jpn *byōdō-daie*): Also, great impartial wisdom or great impartially perceiving wisdom. A Buddha's wisdom, which perceives the truth that all beings and phenomena are essentially equal and without distinction. Also, the teaching or Law expounded by a Buddha based on that wisdom, which is capable of saving and benefiting all beings impartially. This phrase appears in the "Treasure Tower" (eleventh) chapter of the Lotus Sutra, where it is spoken by the Buddha Many Treasures from his seat in the treasure tower in praise of Shakyamuni Buddha's preaching of the Lotus Sutra, which he calls the great wisdom of equality.

Great Wisdom Sutra [大般若経] (Skt *Mahāprajnāpāramitā-sūtra;* Chin *Ta-pan-jo-ching;* Jpn *Daihannya-kyō*): A Chinese translation by Hsüan-tsang (602–664) of the compilation of the various Wisdom (Skt *prajnā*) sutras into one sutra. Its full title is the Great Perfection of Wisdom Sutra. The six-hundred-volume text addresses the perfection of wisdom and the non-substantiality of all phenomena; it takes the form of Shakyamuni Buddha's preaching in sixteen assemblies at four locations.

Great Yüeh-chih [大月氏] (Jpn Dai-gesshi): *See* Yüeh-chih.

greed [貪・貪欲・愛] (Skt, Pali *rāga;* Jpn *ton, ton'yoku,* or *ai*): One of the three poisons, the three sources of vice and suffering, the other two being anger and foolishness. T'ien-t'ai (538–597) says in *The Words and Phrases of the Lotus Sutra,* "Because greed increases in intensity, famine arises." *See also* three poisons.

greed and stinginess [慳貪] (Jpn *kendon*): An offense mentioned in Chinese translations of Buddhist scriptures. *Greed and stinginess* is described as the cause of falling into the realm of hungry spirits. The term is also applied to the fault of unwillingness to share one's knowledge of Buddhist truth. In the "Expedient Means" (second) chapter of the Lotus Sutra, Shakyamuni Buddha says: "The Buddha himself dwells in this great vehicle, and adorned with the power of meditation and wisdom that go with the Law he has attained, he uses it to save living beings. He himself testifies to the unsurpassed way, the great vehicle, the Law in which all things are equal. If I used a lesser vehicle to convert even one person, I would be guilty of stinginess and greed."

Gridhrakūta [耆闍崛山・霊鷲山] (Skt; Pali Gijjhakūta; Jpn Gishakussen or Ryōju-sen): The Sanskrit name for Eagle Peak near Rājagriha, the capital of Magadha in ancient India. *Gridhra* means vulture, and *kūta* means summit or peak. Accordingly, *Gridhrakūta* means Vulture Peak. In the Chinese translations of Buddhist scriptures, Gridhrakūta is rendered as Ling-chiu-shan, Sacred Eagle Peak, or Holy Eagle Peak. *See also* Eagle Peak.

griha-pati [居士] (Skt; Jpn *koji*): In Buddhist scriptures, a male lay practitioner of Buddhism. *Griha-pati,* meaning the master of a house, referred in particular to wealthy householders of the Vaishya class. *See* householder.

Guidelines for Believers of the Fuji School, The [富士一跡門徒存知の事] (Jpn *Fuji-isseki-monto-zonchi-no-koto*): A record of the differences between Nikkō's teachings and those of the other five of the six senior priests named by Nichiren. This record was set down by Nitchō (1262–1310), the first chief instructor of Omosu Seminary in the Fuji District of Suruga Province, Japan, under the direction of Nikkō, Nichiren's designated successor. In it, Nikkō refutes the teachings and actions of the five senior priests by clarifying the true meaning of Nichiren's teachings. *See also* five senior priests.

Gunabhadra [求那跋陀羅] (394–468) (Skt; Jpn Gunabaddara): A monk of central India and a translator of Buddhist scriptures into Chinese. He was born to a Brahman family, but converted to Buddhism. He first studied the Hinayana teachings and later studied the Mahayana. In 435 he went to China by sea, where he devoted himself to teaching and translating Buddhist scriptures. He translated a total of 52 scriptures in

134 volumes, including the Miscellaneous Āgama Sutra, the Shrīmālā Sutra, and the Buddha Infinite Life Sutra.

Gunamati [徳慧] (n.d.) (Skt; Jpn Tokue): A monk of the Consciousness-Only school who lived in southern India around the sixth century, revered as one of the ten great scholars of the school. According to *The Record of the Western Regions,* Hsüan-tsang's account of his travels in Central Asia and India in the seventh century, Gunamati refuted the non-Buddhist scholar Mādhava who enjoyed the respect and patronage of the king of Magadha, and converted the king to Buddhism. Later he lived at Nālandā Monastery. He is the author of *The Commentary on "The Thirty-Stanza Treatise on the Consciousness-Only Doctrine."*

Gunaprabha [徳光] (n.d.) (Skt; Jpn Tokukō): A monk and scholar of India. His story appears in *The Record of the Western Regions*—Hsüan-tsang's account of his travels through Central Asia and India in the seventh century in which he wrote about the religion, customs, folklore, etc., of the areas he visited. Gunaprabha was said to have first studied the Mahayana teachings but converted to the Hinayana after reading a Hinayana treatise, and wrote scores of treatises in which he criticized the Mahayana teachings. He was believed to have ascended to the Tushita Heaven to resolve his remaining doubts concerning the differences between the Hinayana and the Mahayana; there he met Bodhisattva Maitreya, but did not respect or learn from him because Maitreya was not an ordained monk.

Gunavarman [求那跋摩] (367–431) (Skt; Jpn Gunabatsuma): A monk of Kashmir and a translator of Buddhist scriptures into Chinese. He was a member of a royal family, but entered the Buddhist Order at age twenty and mastered the three divisions of the Buddhist canon. At age thirty, upon the king's death he was offered the throne but refused it. He traveled to various places to preach, including Java, where he played an important role in establishing Buddhism. He went to China in 424. Emperor Wen of the Liu Sung dynasty heard of Gunavarman's fame and invited him to his capital, Chien-k'ang, in 431. There Gunavarman lectured on the Lotus Sutra, the Ten Stages Sutra, and other sutras. He translated altogether ten works in eighteen volumes.

Gurupādaka, Mount [尊足山] (Skt; Jpn Sonsoku-sen): A mountain in the state of Magadha in ancient India. Also known as Mount Kukkutapāda. *See* Kukkutapāda, Mount.

Gyōchi [行智] (n.d.): A lay priest and a member of the ruling Hōjō clan in Japan during the time of Nichiren (1222–1282). Though not ordained, he acted as the deputy chief priest of Ryūsen-ji, a temple of the Tendai school in Atsuhara Village of Suruga Province. His full name and title were Hei no Sakon Nyūdō Gyōchi. He privatized some of the temple's property, extracted bribes from a thief he made a priest and allowed him to reside at the temple, and had farmers of his parish hunt and cook quails, raccoon dogs, and deer, and serve the meat to him at the chief priest's quarters. Nikkō, later Nichiren's successor, converted several priests of the temple, including Nisshū, Nichiben, and Nichizen, to Nichiren's teaching. This angered Gyōchi, who unlawfully instigated official harassment of Nichiren's followers that led to the imprisonment of twenty of them, all farmers. They were sent to Kamakura, where three of them were beheaded and the others banished from Atsuhara in 1279. These acts of oppression became known collectively as the Atsuhara Persecution. *See also* Atsuhara Persecution.

Gyōhyō [行表] (724–797): A priest of Yamato Province in Japan. He entered the priesthood in 741 and studied the teachings of the Precepts (Ritsu), Zen, Dharma Characteristics (Hossō), and Flower Garland (Kegon) schools. Later he moved to Sūfuku-ji temple in Ōmi Province and became its chief priest. Esteemed for his learning, Gyōhyō was appointed provincial teacher by the imperial court. In 778 he performed the ceremony in which Dengyō, who later founded the Tendai school, was ordained a priest. Gyōhyō later went to Daian-ji temple in Nara, where he spent the remainder of his life.

Gyōki [行基] (668–749): A priest of Yakushi-ji temple in Nara, Japan. He entered the priesthood in 682 and studied the doctrines of the Dharma Characteristics (Hossō) school. He traveled throughout the provinces to teach these doctrines and is said to have gained some one thousand converts. The imperial court became uneasy about his propagation activities and persecuted him as an agitator. Later, however, after a change in imperial policy, such religious activities were permitted. When Emperor Shōmu proclaimed his vow to build a great image of Vairochana Buddha in 743, Gyōki traveled widely with his disciples, soliciting contributions for its construction. In 745 he was appointed general administrator of priests. In his travels, he also built bridges and embankments, repaired roads, and carried out reclamation and irrigation work. Because of his contributions to public welfare, people highly revered and respected him, calling him Bodhisattva Gyōki.

Gyōnen [凝然] (1240–1321): A priest of the Flower Garland (Kegon) school in Japan. In 1257 he became a disciple of Enshō, a priest of the Kaidan-in hall of Tōdai-ji temple in Nara. Under Enshō and others, he studied the doctrines of the Precepts (Ritsu), Tendai, True Word (Shingon), Flower Garland, Dharma Characteristics (Hossō), Three Treatises

(Sanron), Pure Land (Jōdo), Zen, and other schools, becoming well versed in a wide range of Buddhist doctrines. He lectured on the Flower Garland and Precepts teachings. He wrote *The Essentials of the Eight Schools* and *A History of the Transmission and Propagation of Buddhism in Three Countries*, a work on the history of Buddhism in India, China, and Japan. His works amount to more than 160 in more than 1,000 volumes.

H

Hachiman [八幡]: Also known as Great Bodhisattva Hachiman. One of Japan's main deities. The first known shrine to Hachiman was built in Usa, Buzen Province, on Japan's southernmost main island, Kyushu, sometime between the sixth and the eighth century. Later this god became famous for his oracles, one of which declared that Hachiman would protect the construction of the great image of Vairochana Buddha at Tōdai-ji temple in Nara in the mid-eighth century. For this the god was given the Buddhist title Great Bodhisattva in 781, making him the first Japanese deity to receive this title. This event is seen as symbolic of the emerging syncretism of Buddhism and Japan's indigenous religion, Shinto, at the time. In the Heian period (794–1185), Hachiman was widely revered as the deified spirit of Emperor Ōjin, and a derivative shrine called Iwashimizu Hachiman Shrine was built in 860 in the suburbs of Kyoto, the capital. This shrine, along with Ise Shrine, came to be devoted to the imperial ancestors. Later the Minamoto clan adopted Hachiman as its patron deity, and Minamoto no Yoritomo, the founder of the Kamakura shogunate, established a shrine to Hachiman at Tsurugaoka in Kamakura in the late twelfth century. With this, Hachiman came to be known as the deity of warriors or the god of war. As worship of Hachiman spread, he also came to be regarded as the guardian deity of many respective communities. Hachiman's incorporation as a protective deity of Buddhism signifies the transition of Buddhism from its early status in Japan as a foreign religion to a mainstay of Japan's spiritual culture.

Hakiri Sanenaga [波木井実長] (1222–1297): Also known as Hakii Sanenaga, Hakiri Rokurō Sanenaga, or Nambu Rokurō Sanenaga. The steward of the southern part of Kai Province that included the Minobu area and its three villages, Hakiri, Mimaki, and Iino. He was converted by Nikkō to Nichiren's teachings around 1269. When Nichiren resolved to leave Kamakura, Hakiri eagerly welcomed him to Minobu and constructed a small dwelling for him. In 1281 he built a temple and donated it to Nichiren, who named it Kuon-ji. After Nichiren's death, he served Nichiren's successor, Nikkō. Influenced by Nikō, then the chief instructor of priests, however, he later strayed from Nikkō's instruction. Nikō seems to have lost Nichiren's spirit to strictly distinguish between the true and provisional teachings and later disassociated himself from Nichiren's teachings and Nikkō by, among other things, identifying himself as a priest of the Tendai school. As a result of his relationship with Nikō, Hakiri deviated from Nichiren's teachings by committing four acts Nichiren had forbidden as inappropriate for practitioners of the correct teaching: He commissioned a statue of Shakyamuni Buddha, made pilgrimages to Shinto shrines, made donations for the construction of a stone tower of the Pure Land teaching in Fukushi Village, and had a Pure Land seminary built. These actions prompted Nikkō, who felt responsible for protecting the purity of Nichiren's teachings, to leave Minobu in 1289.

Haklenayashas [鶴勒夜那・鶴勒夜奢] (n.d.) (Skt; Jpn Kakurokuyana or Kakurokuyasha): Also known as Haklena or Haklenayasha. The twenty-second of Shakyamuni's twenty-three, or the twenty-third of his twenty-four, successors. Born to a Brahman family in India during the sixth century, he entered the Buddhist Order at age twenty-two. He received the Buddha's teachings from Manorhita. He propagated Buddhism in central India and transferred the teachings to Āryasimha.

Hall of the Good Law [善法堂] (Skt Sudharman; Jpn Zembō-dō): According to *The Dharma Analysis Treasury*, a structure said to be located to the southwest of a palace called Correct Views, the dwelling of the god Shakra in the center of the Heaven of the Thirty-three Gods on the peak of Mount Sumeru. It is said that Shakra and the other gods of this heaven gather in the Hall of the Good Law to judge the good and evil actions of humans and gods.

Han-kuang [含光] (n.d.) (PY Hanguang; Jpn Gankō): A priest of Esoteric Buddhism who lived in China in the eighth century. According to one account, Han-kuang was a native of India. A senior disciple of Pu-k'ung (Skt Amoghavajra), a patriarch of Esoteric Buddhism, he traveled to India and Sri Lanka with his teacher. After returning to China, he lived at Pao-shou-ssu temple in Ch'ang-an, the capital, and assisted Pu-k'ung in various activities including the translation of Sanskrit Buddhist scriptures into Chinese. He was regarded as foremost among the forty-nine most virtuous priests of Ta-hsing-shan-ssu temple, the largest of the temples in Ch'ang-an. With Pu-k'ung, he built Chin-ko-ssu, or Gold Pavilion Temple, on Mount Wu-t'ai and made it a center of Esoteric Buddhism.

Harivarman [訶梨跋摩] (n.d.) (Skt; Jpn Karibatsuma): An Indian monk in the third or fourth century, regarded as the founder of the Establishment of Truth (Ch'eng-shih) school in China. He was born to a Brahman family and originally studied the doctrines of the Sāmkhya school, one of the six main schools of Brahmanism. Later he studied under Kumāralāta, the founder of the Sautrāntika school, one of the eighteen schools of Hinayana Buddhism. He also studied the Mahayana teachings and wrote *The Treatise on the Establishment of Truth,* which was later translated into Chinese by Kumārajīva in the early fifth century and became the basis of the Establishment of Truth school in China.

Harsha [戒日王] (Skt; Jpn Kainichi-ō): Also known as Shīlāditya. An Indian king who established an empire that included most of northern India in the seventh century. At first an adherent of Hinduism, he later converted to Buddhism, and built many temples and stupas, and is said to have governed compassionately based on Buddhist principles. *See* Shīlāditya.

Healing Buddha [薬師仏] (Jpn Yakushi-butsu): Also known as the Thus Come One Medicine Master. *See* Medicine Master.

Hearer of Many Teachings [多聞天] (Jpn Tamon-ten): Also known as Vaishravana, one of the four heavenly kings. *See* Vaishravana.

Heart of the Abhidharma, The [阿毘曇心論] (Skt *Abhidharma-hridaya-shāstra;* Chin *A-p'i-t'an-hsin-lun;* Jpn *Abidon-shin-ron*): A 250-verse compendium of the *abhidharma* doctrine of the Sarvāstivāda school, written in the third century by Dharmashrī (also known as Dharmashreshthin) and translated into Chinese in 384 by Samghadeva. Dharmashrī, a scholar of the Sarvāstivāda school, was from the Tukhāra kingdom. *The Heart of the Abhidharma* is an abridgment of the doctrinal teachings contained in the massive *Great Commentary on the Abhidharma,* one of the basic texts of the Sarvāstivādins. The Sarvāstivāda school first compiled *The Treatise on the Source of Wisdom* and six other doctrinal texts to clarify its fundamental tenets, and later produced *The Great Commentary on the Abhidharma* as a comprehensive survey and compilation of studies concerning its doctrine. The production of *The Heart of the Abhidharma* followed.

Heart of Wisdom Sutra [般若心経] (Jpn *Hannya-shingyō*): *See* Heart Sutra.

Heart Sutra [般若心経] (Skt *Prajnāpāramitā-hridaya-sūtra;* Chin *Pan-jo-hsin-ching;* Jpn *Hannya-shingyō*): Also known as the Heart of Wisdom Sutra. A short sutra containing the essence of the Wisdom sutras and briefly describing the non-substantiality or emptiness of all phenomena. Translated into Chinese by Hsüan-tsang in 649, its full title is the Heart of the Perfection of Wisdom Sutra. The original Sanskrit text and its Tibetan translation are extant, and there are several other Chinese translations, including that of Kumārajīva. Many commentaries on the Heart Sutra were produced in China and Japan, and in Japan it is one of the most popular sutras, revered particularly by the Zen and True Word (Shingon) schools.

Heat-Free Lake [無熱池] (Jpn Munetchi): A lake said to give rise to the four rivers that nurture the soil in the four quarters of Jambudvīpa. *See* Anavatapta Lake.

heat stage [煖位・煖法] (Jpn *nan-i* or *nampō*): Also, heat root, heat method, warmth stage, etc. The first of the four good roots, or preparatory practices leading to the way of insight. In the heat stage, one approaches wisdom that is free from outflows, or earthly desires, and obtains good roots that are still tainted by outflows. This process is compared to approaching a fire and being warmed by it. The fire itself is compared to pure wisdom (wisdom without outflows), and the warmth one feels from it is compared to good roots that still retain outflows. After having accomplished the stage of the four good roots, one proceeds to the way of insight, or the first of the "three ways"—the three stages of Hinayana practice. *See also* four good roots.

heaven [天] (Skt, Pali *deva-loka;* Jpn *ten*): In Buddhism, a realm of heavenly beings. Buddhism describes twenty-eight heavens or heavenly realms (twenty-six or twenty-seven according to different sources) in the threefold world. In ascending order, there are the six heavens in the world of desire, the eighteen heavens in the world of form, and the four heavens in the world of formlessness. These heavens are ranked in quality according to their elevation. The first and lowest heaven is the Heaven of the Four Heavenly Kings, located halfway up Mount Sumeru. The highest heaven is the Heaven of Neither Thought Nor No Thought. This heaven is regarded as the realm where those who have accumulated good fortune will be reborn, though it still belongs to the six paths of existence, a realm still encumbered by transmigration and delusion. Heaven, or the world of heavenly beings, is also the sixth of the Ten Worlds. Based on the philosophy of the Lotus Sutra, this can be viewed as a potential state or condition of human life. In *The Object of Devotion for Observing the Mind,* Nichiren (1222–1282) writes, "Joy is [the world] of heaven" (358). This describes the condition of contentment and joy one feels when released from suffering or upon satisfaction of some desire. Such joy disappears with the passage of time or with even a slight change in the circumstances. "Heaven" is therefore included within the six paths—states of life that are relatively passive and subject to changes in one's surroundings.

heavenly being among heavenly beings [天中天] (Skt, Pali *devātideva;* Jpn *tenchū-ten*): An honorific title for a Buddha, who is held to be peerless among heavenly beings. Similar titles are applied to Buddhas to express their superior nobility and wisdom in comparison to all other beings. "The most honored of heavenly and human beings" is another such title.

heavenly devil [天魔] (Jpn *temma*): *See* devil king of the sixth heaven.

heavenly gods and benevolent deities [諸天善神] (Jpn *shoten-zenjin*): Also, Buddhist gods, protective gods, tutelary gods, guardian deities, etc. The gods that protect the correct Buddhist teaching and its practitioners. Gods who function to protect the people and their land and bring good fortune to both. *Heavenly gods and benevolent deities* is a generic term for the Buddhist pantheon that includes Brahmā, Shakra, the four heavenly kings, the Sun Goddess, the gods of the sun and moon, and other deities. Many of these gods and deities were traditionally revered in India, China, and Japan. They became part of Buddhist thought as Buddhism flourished in those areas. Rather than primary objects of belief or devotion, Buddhism tends to view them as functioning to support and protect the Buddha, the Law, or Buddhist teachings, and practitioners.

The "Introduction" (first) chapter of the Lotus Sutra describes a scene in which the heavenly beings or gods gather to hear the preaching of the sutra. The "Peaceful Practices" (fourteenth) chapter of the sutra says, "The heavenly beings day and night will for the sake of the Law constantly guard and protect [those who practice as the sutra teaches]." In the Lotus Sutra, the gods are regarded as the guardians of those who embrace the sutra. In *The Treatment of Illness,* Nichiren (1222–1282) writes, "The fundamental nature of enlightenment manifests itself as Brahmā and Shakra, whereas the fundamental darkness manifests itself as the devil king of the sixth heaven" (1113). Here the gods are viewed as manifestations of the Buddha nature in one's life. The Golden Light Sutra reads: "Though this sutra exists in the nation, its ruler has never allowed it to be propagated. In his heart he turns away from it, and he takes no pleasure in hearing its teachings. . . . In the end, he makes it impossible for us [the four heavenly kings] and the other countless heavenly beings who are our followers to hear this profound and wonderful teaching. He deprives us of the sweet dew of its words and cuts us off from the flow of the correct teaching, so that our majesty and strength are drained away. . . . And once we and the others abandon and desert this nation, then many different types of disasters will occur in the country, and the ruler will fall from power." This passage may be interpreted as indicating that the gods gain their strength from the Buddhist Law, and that they are the inherent functions of nature and society that protect those who uphold that Law.

Heavenly King [天王如来] (Skt Devarāja; Jpn Tennō-nyorai): The Thus Come One Heavenly King. The name that Devadatta will bear when he attains Buddhahood in a future existence, according to Shakyamuni's prediction in the "Devadatta" (twelfth) chapter of the Lotus Sutra. The chapter reads: "Devadatta, after immeasurable *kalpas* have passed, will attain Buddhahood. He will be called Heavenly King Thus Come One. . . . His world will be called Heavenly Way, and at that time Heavenly King Buddha will abide in the world for twenty medium *kalpas*, broadly preaching the wonderful Law for the sake of living beings." Devadatta came to personify evil in the Buddhist teachings because of his opposition to the Buddha, which included attempts on the Buddha's life. The attainment of Buddhahood by Devadatta expresses the power of the Lotus Sutra to enable all people, even the most evil, to attain enlightenment eventually. It is a declaration of the universality of the potential for Buddhahood. The Sanskrit title *Devarāja* means king of the gods. *Deva* means deity, god, heavenly, or divine, and *rāja* means king.

Heaven of Boundless Consciousness [識無辺処天] (Jpn Shikimuhenjo-ten): The second lowest of the four realms of the world of formlessness. *See* Realm of Boundless Consciousness.

Heaven of Boundless Empty Space [空無辺処天] (Jpn Kūmuhenjo-ten): The first and the lowest of the four realms of the world of formlessness. *See* Realm of Boundless Empty Space.

Heaven of Enjoying the Conjured [化楽天・楽変化天] (Skt Nirmānarati; Jpn Keraku-ten or Rakuhenge-ten): Also, Nirmānarati Heaven. The fifth of the six heavens in the world of desire. It is located above the Tushita Heaven and below the Heaven of Freely Enjoying Things Conjured by Others, the highest heaven of the world of desire. In this heaven, the occupants conjure objects of pleasure and enjoy various delights. Inhabitants of the Heaven of Enjoying the Conjured are said to live for eight thousand years, one day of which is equal to eight hundred human years. The life span of beings in this heaven, then, is equal to about 2.3 billion human years.

Heaven of Freely Enjoying Things Conjured by Others [他化自在天] (Skt Paranirmita-vasha-vartin; Jpn Takejizai-ten): Also, sixth heaven. In ancient Indian cosmology, the sixth and highest of the six heavens in the world of desire. Its dwellers make free use of things conjured by others for their own pleasure, hence the name of this heaven. Their life span is sixteen thousand years, one day of which is equal to sixteen hundred human years. Their life span is therefore equal to about 9.3 billion human years. The Heaven of Freely Enjoying Things Conjured by Others is the abode of the devil king, called Māra in Sanskrit, and therefore it is known as the Heaven of Māra or the Heaven of the Devil. The devil king abiding in this sixth heaven at the top of the world of desire is often referred to as the devil king of the sixth heaven. He is said to harass practitioners of Buddhism himself or through his subordinates to dissuade them from practice and prevent their attaining Buddhahood. *See also* devil king of the sixth heaven.

Heaven of Great Brahmā [大梵天] (Jpn Daibon-ten): Also, Great Brahmā Heaven or Mahābrahman Heaven. In ancient Indian cosmology, the uppermost of the three realms of the first meditation heaven in the world of form. This heaven is the abode of the god Brahmā and is located 10,160,000 *yojanas* above the summit of Mount Sumeru, or 10,240,000 *yojanas* above the surface of the sea. The three realms are all under the reign of the god Brahmā, and therefore all generally called the Brahma Heaven. They are specifically called the Heaven of Brahmā's Retinue, or the realm where the followers of Brahmā dwell; the Heaven of Brahmā's Aide, or the realm where Brahmā's assistants such as ministers and high officials dwell; and the Heaven of Great Brahmā, or the realm where the god Brahmā himself lives. The Heaven of Brahmā's Retinue is located 1,280,000 *yojanas* above the sixth or highest heaven of the world of desire. The sixth heaven is called the Heaven of Freely Enjoying Things Conjured by Others, and is where the devil king dwells. The Heaven of Brahmā's Aide is 2,560,000 *yojanas* above the Heaven of Brahmā's Retinue, and the Heaven of Great Brahmā is 5,120,000 *yojanas* above the Heaven of Brahmā's Aide.

Heaven of Māra [魔天] (Jpn Ma-ten): *See* Heaven of Freely Enjoying Things Conjured by Others.

Heaven of Neither Thought Nor No Thought [非想非非想天] (Jpn Hisō-hihisō-ten): The highest heaven in the world of formlessness. *See* Realm of Neither Thought Nor No Thought.

Heaven of Nothingness [無所有処天] (Jpn Mushousho-ten): The second highest of the four realms of the world of formlessness. *See* Realm of Nothingness.

Heaven of the Four Heavenly Kings [四王天] (Skt Chātur-mahārāja-kayika; Jpn Shio-ten): The abode of the four heavenly kings—Upholder of the Nation, Wide-Eyed, Hearer of Many Teachings (Skt Vaishravana), and Increase and Growth—and their followers. This heaven is the lowest of the six heavens of the world of desire, located halfway up Mount Sumeru. Upholder of the Nation, Wide-Eyed, Hearer of Many Teachings, and Increase and Growth abide halfway up the eastern, western, northern, and southern slopes of Mount Sumeru, respectively. It is said that the life span of beings in this heaven is five hundred years, and that one day in the life of beings in this heaven is equal to fifty years in the life of a human being. This means that their life span is equal to about nine million human years. *See also* four heavenly kings.

Heaven of the Thirty-three Gods [三十三天] (Jpn Sanjūsan-ten): Also, Trāyastrimsha Heaven. According to ancient Indian cosmology, the second lowest of the six heavens in the world of desire. The Sanskrit word *trāyastrimsha* means thirty-three. This heaven is located on a plateau at the top of Mount Sumeru, where thirty-three gods, including the lord Shakra, live. Shakra rules from his palace in the center, and the other thirty-two gods live on four peaks, eight gods to a peak, in each of the plateau's four corners. The beings in this heaven have a life span of one thousand years, each day of which is equal to a hundred years in the human, or *sahā,* world. This means that their life span is equal to about 36.5 million human years.

heavens of purity [浄居天] (Jpn *jōgo-ten*): The five highest heavens among the eighteen heavens in the world of form. *See* five heavens of purity.

Hei no Saemon [平左衛門] (d. 1293): Also known as Taira no Yoritsuna or by his full name and title, Hei no Saemon-no-jō Yoritsuna. (*Hei* is another pronunciation of the character for Taira.) A leading official of the Hōjō regency, the de facto ruling body of Japan during the Kamakura period. He served two successive regents, Hōjō Tokimune and Hōjō Sadatoki, and wielded tremendous influence as deputy chief of the Office of Military and Police Affairs (the chief being the regent himself). He collaborated with Ryōkan and other leading priests to persecute Nichiren and his followers. In 1268, when the first envoy from the Mongol empire arrived to demand that Japan pay tribute or face invasion, Nichiren sent letters to Hei no Saemon and ten other leading political and religious figures. In these letters he reminded them that his prediction of foreign invasion made eight years earlier in his work *On Establishing the Correct Teaching for the Peace of the Land* was about to be fulfilled, and requested a public religious debate. All ignored his request.

On the tenth day of the ninth month in 1271, Hei no Saemon summoned Nichiren to court to answer accusations against him. Nichiren refuted these charges and again requested a public debate, asserting that ruin would overtake the country if the government punished him unreasonably. His words enraged the official. On the twelfth day of the same month, leading a company of armed men, Hei no Saemon rode to Matsubagayatsu in Kamakura and arrested Nichiren. Maneuvering to do away with him, Hei no Saemon had his men take Nichiren that night to the execution ground in Tatsunokuchi. Their attempt to behead him failed, however, and Nichiren was exiled to the island of Sado. Nichiren stayed there for nearly two and a half years until he was pardoned and left for Kamakura in the third month of 1274. On the eighth day of the next month, Hei no Saemon again summoned him to ask on behalf of the regent about the impending Mongol invasion. Nichiren replied that it would take place within the year and repeated his warnings, which again went unheeded; thereafter Nichiren left Kamakura. In 1279 Gyōchi, the deputy chief priest of Ryūsen-ji temple, plotted to have twenty peasant-believers in Nichiren's teachings arrested at Atsuhara in Suruga Province. Gyōchi made false accusations against them, and they were brought to Hei no Saemon's residence in Kamakura. There without investigating the charges, Hei no Saemon tried to force them to recant, eventually beheading three of them as a warning to the others.

In 1284, two years after Nichiren died, Hōjō Sadatoki became regent and Hei no Saemon became steward to the main family of the Hōjō clan. He arranged the death of Adachi Yasumori, who sat on the regent's council, and seized the reins of power for himself. His influence at one point surpassed even that of the regent. In 1293, however, Hei no Saemon was attacked by the forces of Hōjō Sadatoki on the charge of attempted revolt, and Hei no Saemon and his second son Sukemune killed themselves. The eldest son Munetsuna was exiled to Sado Island.

hell [地獄] (Skt, Pali *naraka* or *niraya;* Jpn *jigoku*): The first and lowest of the three evil paths, the six paths, and the Ten Worlds. Buddhist scriptures describe various kinds of hells, such as the eight hot hells and the eight cold hells. They depict hell as a realm beneath the earth where those who have committed evil are reborn and undergo different degrees of suffering for varying periods of time according to the nature and weight of their offenses. The expression "136 hells" is used to describe the array of hells, this number representing the eight hot hells, each with its sixteen subsidiary hells. T'ien-t'ai (538–597) and Nichiren (1222–1282) interpreted hell, or any other of the Ten Worlds, as a condition inherent within life and manifest at any moment. Viewed in this manner, hell describes a condition of utmost suffering and despair. *See also* eight cold hells; eight hot hells.

hell of black cords [黒縄地獄] (Skt Kālasūtra; Jpn Kokujō-jigoku): The second of the eight hot hells. It is said that in this hell the bodies of offenders are wrapped with heated black iron cords, and with these cords as guides are sawed or slashed to pieces. The Sanskrit word *kāla-sūtra* means the thread of death. *Kāla* means death and fate, and *sūtra* means thread, cord, wire, or measuring line. Explanations of the hell of black cords differ slightly according to the source. *See also* eight hot hells; hell.

hell of burning heat [焦熱地獄] (Skt Tapana; Jpn Shōnetsu-jigoku): Also, hell of searing heat. The sixth of the eight hot hells. It is said that in this hell offenders are surrounded by iron walls and consumed by flames. In Buddhist works, the fierce flames of this hell and of the hell of great burning heat often symbolize the suffering of hell in general. The Sanskrit word *tapana* means heat or burning. *See also* eight hot hells; hell.

hell of incessant suffering [無間地獄] (Skt, Pali Avīchi; Jpn Muken-jigoku): Also, Avīchi hell. The eighth and most horrible of the eight hot hells. It is so called because its inhabitants are said to suffer without a moment's respite. This hell is often referred to as the great citadel of the hell of incessant suffering because seven iron walls surround it so that no one can escape. The hell of incessant suffering is situated at the lowest level of the world of desire. It measures eighty thousand *yojanas* (twenty thousand *yojanas* according to another source) on each side. Those who commit even one of the five cardinal sins or slander the correct teaching are said to fall into this hell. *See also* eight hot hells; hell.

hell of repeated rebirth for torture [等活地獄] (Skt Samjīva; Jpn Tōkatsu-jigoku): Also, hell of repeated rebirth, hell of regeneration, or hell of repeated misery. The first of the eight hot hells. It is said that dwellers in this hell are constantly injuring and killing one another. When a cold wind blows over the bodies of those killed, however, they immediately regenerate and begin to fight again, in this way repeatedly undergoing the same torment. The Sanskrit word *samjīva* means reviving or reanimating. Explanations of the hell of repeated rebirth for torture differ slightly according to the source. *See also* eight hot hells; hell.

hell of the crimson lotus [紅蓮地獄] (Skt Padma; Jpn Guren-jigoku): One of the eight cold hells. It is said that the intense cold of this hell makes one's flesh crack open so that it has the appearance of crimson lotus flowers. According to *The Great Commentary on the Abhidharma* and *The Dharma Analysis Treasury*, this hell and the hell of the great crimson lotus constitute the seventh and the eighth of the eight cold hells. The Sanskrit word *padma* means lotus flower or red lotus flower. *See also* eight hot hells; hell.

heritage of the Law [血脈] (Jpn *kechimyaku* or *ketsumyaku*): Originally blood vessel, lifeblood, or lineage. In Buddhism, (1) the lineage of a teaching passed on from teacher to disciple. It is transmitted either in written form, orally, or from mind to mind. This tradition was valued in various Buddhist schools such as Zen, Pure Land, and Nichiren. (2) The transmission or transfer of the Law from teacher to disciple. In addition, the heritage of the Law refers to the Law or teaching that is transmitted. *The Minobu Transfer Document,* which Nichiren wrote at Minobu in 1282, reads in part, "Order of the heritage: from Nichiren to Nikkō." This is the transmission of the heritage of the Law from Nichiren to Nikkō, his disciple and designated successor. (3) In Nichiren's teachings, the heritage of the Law is Nam-myoho-renge-kyo. In *The Heritage of the Ultimate Law of Life,* Nichiren describes three conditions that enable one to receive the heritage of the Law as follows: (a) "Shakyamuni Buddha who attained enlightenment countless *kalpas* ago, the Lotus Sutra that leads all people to Buddhahood, and we ordinary human beings are in no way different or separate from one another. To chant Myoho-renge-kyo with this realization is to inherit the ultimate Law of life and death" (216). (b) "The heritage of the Lotus Sutra flows within the lives of those who never forsake it in any lifetime whatsoever" (217). (c) That practitioners should "chant Nam-myoho-renge-kyo with the spirit of many in body but one in mind, transcending all differences among themselves to become as inseparable as fish and the water in which they swim. This spiritual bond is the basis for the universal transmission of the ultimate Law of life and death" (217).

hero of the world [世雄] (Jpn *seō*): An honorific title for a Buddha. *See* world hero.

Hiei, Mount [比叡山] (Jpn Hiei-zan): A mountain located to the northeast of Kyoto, Japan, on which Enryaku-ji, the head temple of the Tendai school, is situated. Dengyō, the founder of the Tendai school, went to live on Mount Hiei in 785, and in 788 he built a small temple there called Hieisan-ji. Hieisan-ji was renamed Enryaku-ji by Emperor Saga in 823, the year after Dengyō's death. Its first chief priest was Gishin, Dengyō's successor. A number of important figures in Japanese Buddhism, including Hōnen, Eisai, Dōgen, and Nichiren, the founders of newer Japanese Buddhist schools, studied at this temple.

high grain prices [穀貴] (Jpn *kokki*): Also, calamity of high grain prices. One of the three calamities described in the Great Collection Sutra. The sutra says: "Though for countless existences in the past the ruler of a state may have practiced the giving of alms, observed the precepts, and cultivated wisdom, if he sees that my teaching is in danger of perishing and stands idly by without doing anything to protect it, then all the inestimable roots of goodness that he has planted through the practices just mentioned will be entirely wiped out, and his country will become the scene of three inauspicious occurrences. The first is high grain prices, the second is warfare, and the third is epidemics." The calamity of high grain prices is identified with the calamity of famine.

Hiki Yoshimoto [比企能本] (1202–1286): Also known as Daigaku Saburō. An official teacher of Confucianism to the Kamakura shogunate in Japan. His full name was Hiki Daigaku Saburō Yoshimoto. He studied Confucianism in Kyoto and is said to have been the son of Hiki Yoshikazu, an important figure in the establishment of the Kamakura shogunate. It is said that Yoshimoto converted to Nichiren's teachings upon reading a draft of Nichiren's treatise *On Establishing the Correct Teaching for the Peace of the Land.* He and his wife both became strong believers. Yoshimoto built Myōhon-ji temple at Hikigayatsu in Kamakura and entered the priesthood, taking the name Nichigaku.

Himatala [雪山下王] (Skt; Jpn Sessenge-ō): A ruler of the ancient kingdom of Tukhāra in northern India about six hundred years after Shakyamuni Buddha's death. According to *The Record of the Western Regions,* Hsüan-tsang's record of his travels through Central Asia and India in the seventh century, King Krita of Kashmir persecuted Buddhist monks and suppressed Buddhism. Hearing this, Himatala, a devout patron of Buddhism, marched on Kashmir at the head of three thousand warriors. He selected five hundred to accompany him to the palace. There, on the pretense of offering gifts, they approached the king and killed him with swords they had hidden in their robes. While Himatala banished Krita's high-ranking officials for their offense, he secured peace for the people, made offerings to the monks, and built temples for their sake. After that, Buddhism prospered again in Kashmir.

Hinayana Buddhism [小乘仏教] (Jpn Shōjō-bukkyō): One of the two major streams of Buddhism, the other being Mahayana. Teachings that aim at attaining the state of arhat. After Shakyamuni Buddha's death, the Buddhist Order experienced several schisms and eventually split into eighteen or twenty schools. The monks of these schools were concerned with preserving the Buddha's teachings as they understood them, and devoted themselves to doctrinal studies. As a result, they produced *abhidharma* works, or doctrinal treatises and commentaries on the Buddha's teachings. Over time, however, they tended toward reclusiveness, while placing greater emphasis on asceticism and doctrinal analysis. Around the end of the first century B.C.E. or the beginning of the first century C.E., a new Buddhist movement began to emerge among those who were dissatisfied with what they perceived as the sterile academicism and rigidity of the existing schools. Feeling it was important to model their behavior after that of the Buddha himself, they advocated bodhisattva practice, or practice to benefit others, and engaged themselves in instructing laypersons while practicing among them. These practitioners called themselves bodhisattvas and their teachings Mahayana (Great Vehicle), indicating that their teaching was the vehicle to transport a great many people to enlightenment. In contrast, they referred to the earlier schools as Hinayana (Lesser Vehicle), implying that these teachings could only address a selected few and could not lead to the ultimate goal of enlightenment. The designation *Hinayana* was derogatory, and these schools naturally did not apply the name to themselves. The Sanskrit *hīna* means lesser, and *yāna*, vehicle or teaching. Mahayana Buddhists regarded Hinayana teachings as the way of voice-hearers and cause-awakened ones who seek their own emancipation from delusion and suffering yet lack practice to benefit others. They held that Hinayana teachings were inferior to Mahayana teachings, which set forth the way of bodhisattvas who strive to attain enlightenment for themselves and help others achieve it as well.

Hiranyavatī [熈連河] (Skt, Pali; Jpn Kiren-ga): A river flowing through Kushinagara in India. *See* Ajitavatī.

History of the Buddha's Successors, A [付法蔵因縁伝] (Chin *Fu-fa-tsang-yin-yüan-chuan;* Jpn *Fuhōzō-innen-den*): Also known as the Buddha's Successors Sutra. A record of the twenty-three monks in India said to have successively inherited Shakyamuni Buddha's teachings and propagated them. Kinkara (Chin Chi-ch'ieh-yeh) and T'an-yao produced the Chinese translation of this work in 472. The Sanskrit text is not extant. According to this account, the Buddha first transferred his teachings to Mahākāshyapa, who in turn entrusted them to Ānanda. Ānanda transferred the Buddha's teachings to Shānavāsa, who in turn transferred them to Upagupta. In this way, the teachings were passed down to Āryasimha, the twenty-third and last successor. Āryasimha was beheaded by King Mirakutsu (Jpn; Sanskrit unknown) and the line of succession ceased. According to *A History of the Buddha's Successors,* Ānanda transferred the Buddha's teachings to not only Shānavāsa but Madhyāntika as well, who propagated them in Kashmir and Gandhara. Because Shānavāsa transmitted the Buddha's teachings inherited from Ānanda to the fourth successor, Upagupta, he is regarded as the third successor. Based on this explanation, Chang-an (561–632), T'ien-t'ai's disciple and successor, listed the twenty-three successors (not including Madhyāntika) in his preface to T'ien-t'ai's *Great Concentration and Insight.* He added that because Madhyāntika and Shānavāsa had both inherited the Buddha's teachings from Ānanda, if Madhyāntika is included among the Buddha's successors, they number twenty-four. Thereafter the T'ien-t'ai school (and its Japanese counterpart, the Tendai school) came to refer both to the twenty-three and the twenty-four successors.

Hōjō Yagenta [北条弥源太] (n.d.): A lay follower of Nichiren who lived in Kamakura, Japan. He was a samurai who belonged to the ruling Hōjō clan. Yagenta was a recipient of one of eleven letters Nichiren wrote in 1268 remonstrating with top government officials and religious leaders after a delegate from the Mongol Empire arrived demanding tribute from Japan. The letters briefly restated the declaration Nichiren made eight years previously in his treatise *On Establishing the Correct Teaching for the Peace of the Land*—that the country would suffer foreign invasion and internal strife if the government continued to give its support to erroneous teachings. Nichiren urged Yagenta to help realize the holding of an open religious debate and thus contribute to ending the disasters. Yagenta received another letter from Nichiren called *The Swords of Good and Evil* when he offered two fine swords to Nichiren.

Hōki-bō [伯耆房]: Also known as Hōki-bō Nikkō. The Buddhist name that Nikkō, Nichiren's designated successor, received in 1258 on becoming Nichiren's disciple. *See* Nikkō.

Hokke school [法華宗] (Jpn Hokke-shū): *See* Lotus school.

Holy Eagle Peak [霊鷲山] (Jpn Ryōju-sen): *See* Eagle Peak; Gridhrakūta.

Homma Rokurō Saemon [本間六郎左衛門] (n.d.): A retainer of Hōjō Nobutoki, the constable of the island province of Sado, Japan. His full name and title were Homma Rokurō Saemon-no-jō Shigetsura. His fief was at Echi in Sagami Province, but he was also steward of Niiho on Sado Island and deputy constable of the entire island. Nichiren was detained at Homma's residence in Echi for nearly a month after the abortive attempt to execute him at Tatsunokuchi in 1271. He was then exiled to Sado in Homma's custody. On the occasion of the Tsukahara Debate on Sado early in 1272, Nichiren urged Homma to hurry with his men to Kamakura, as a battle would soon break out there. Homma doubted this prediction, but when a messenger came with a report of a rebellion the following month, he abandoned his belief in the Pure Land teaching, as Nichiren describes in his work *The Actions of the Votary of the Lotus Sutra*.

Hōnen [法然] (1133–1212): Also known as Genkū. The founder of the Pure Land (Jōdo) school in Japan. Born in Mimasaka Province, in 1141 Hōnen became a disciple of his uncle, Kankaku, a priest of the Tendai school in the province, in accord with the wishes of his assassinated father. In 1145 (1147 according to another account) he entered Enryaku-ji temple on Mount Hiei, where he studied the teachings of the Tendai school under Genkō and Kōen. In 1150 he began to study the Pure Land teachings under Eikū. He left Kurodani on Mount Hiei, where Eikū lived, and went to study the doctrines of other schools. On his return he read through the Buddhist canon. He is said to have reached an awakening in 1175 upon reading *The Commentary on the Meditation on the Buddha Infinite Life Sutra* by Shan-tao, a patriarch of the Chinese Pure Land school. Thereafter he dedicated himself solely to the Pure Land practice of Nembutsu, or the chanting of Amida Buddha's name. The Pure Land school in Japan considers this awakening by Hōnen as the date of its founding. Hōnen then moved to Yoshimizu in Kyoto where he devoted himself to the exclusive practice of Nembutsu and attracted a great number of followers. In 1186, at the request of Kenshin, later the chief priest of Enryaku-ji on Mount Hiei, Hōnen preached the Pure Land teachings at Shōrin-in temple in Ōhara, Kyoto, where he is said to have refuted priests of the Dharma Characteristics (Hossō), Three Treatises (Sanron), Flower Garland (Kegon), and other schools. This event is known as the Ōhara Discourse. Alarmed at the spread of his teachings, the priests of Mount Hiei and Kōfuku-ji temple, a major temple in Nara, petitioned the throne against Hōnen. Matters came to a head in 1206, when two court ladies were persuaded to become nuns of the Pure Land school at a prayer service conducted by Hōnen's disciples Junsai and Jūren. This incident aroused the anger of the Retired Emperor Gotoba, who banned the Pure Land teaching and exiled Hōnen to Tosa in 1207. In 1211 he was permitted to return to the capital, where he died the following year. Hōnen's best-known work is *The Nembutsu Chosen above All,* written in 1198. In it, he defines the cause for attaining rebirth in the Pure Land to be the exclusive practice of Nembutsu, and urges that people discard all sutras other than the three basic sutras of the Pure Land teaching (the Buddha Infinite Life Sutra, the Meditation on the Buddha Infinite Life Sutra, and the Amida Sutra). He also wrote commentaries on the three Pure Land sutras and on *The Essentials of Rebirth in the Pure Land* by Genshin.

Hongan-ji [本願寺]: The head temple of the True Pure Land (Jōdo Shin) school in Japan. After the school's founder, Shinran, died, the nun Kakushin, his youngest daughter, and his disciples built a memorial hall in 1272 and there enshrined an image of Shinran. Shinran's great-grandson, Kakunyo, had it officially recognized as a temple and named it Hongan-ji (Original Vow Temple). He regarded Shinran as the temple's founding patriarch and first chief priest, Shinran's grandson, Nyoshin, as the second chief priest, and himself as the third chief priest.

The temple's prosperity declined for a time, but was restored by the eighth chief priest, Rennyo (1415–1499). It came to wield considerable secular, military, and religious power, until in the sixteenth century its eleventh chief priest, Kennyo, waged a military struggle against the warrior chieftain Oda Nobunaga. After years of conflict, the imperial court commanded Kennyo, who, in addition to being a priest was also a functionary of the court, to make peace with Nobunaga to whom he surrendered the massive temple, which had served as a fortress. In 1602 Kyōnyo, the elder brother of the twelfth chief priest, Junnyo, founded a temple of the same name under the patronage of Tokugawa Ieyasu, the first in the line of Tokugawa shoguns. From then on, the original temple was called Nishi (West) Hongan-ji, and the new one, Higashi (East) Hongan-ji. Higashi Hongan-ji is the head temple of the Ōtani branch of the True Pure Land school, and Nishi Hongan-ji, that of the Hongan-ji branch. Both are located in Kyoto.

Hōren [法蓮]: The Buddhist name for Soya Kyōshin, a follower of Nichiren. *See* Soya Kyōshin.

horse-headed demons [馬頭] (Skt *ashvashīrsha;* Jpn *mezu*): Also, horse-headed beings. Jailors of hell who have the body of a human and the head of a horse, they stand guard with similar ox-headed demons. The Sanskrit word *ashva* means horse, and *shīrsha* means head.

Hōryū-ji [法隆寺]: Also known as Ikaruga-dera. A temple located at Ikaruga in Nara, Japan. According to an inscription on the back of the halo on the statue of Medicine Master Buddha in the main hall, the temple was founded in 607 by Prince Shōtoku and Empress Suiko. They built it and enshrined the statue there in accord with the wishes of the late Emperor Yōmei. Though the year of its founding is disputable, it is certain that the temple was built by Shōtoku during the reign of Empress Suiko (592–628). *The Chronicles of Japan* records the donation of rice fields to Ikaruga-dera in 606. It is thought that the temple was probably built at the beginning of the seventh century. In 622 Prince Shōtoku died at the palace of Ikaruga, and in his memory statues of Shakyamuni and Shakyamuni's two attendants were enshrined at Hōryū-ji. The statues were made in 623 by the sculptor Tori at the request of the prince's family. According to *The Chronicles of Japan,* Hōryū-ji was destroyed by fire in 670, but it is generally agreed that the temple was rebuilt around the beginning of the eighth century. It was at first the headquarters for the study of the Three Treatises (Sanron) teachings, and later the Dharma Characteristics (Hossō) school's doctrine was also studied there. It became one of the seven major temples of Nara. The temple has many historical buildings and treasures of art as well as precious documents.

Hoshina Gorō Tarō [星名五郎太郎] (n.d.): A lay follower of Nichiren (1222–1282), who lived in Kazusa Province, Japan, which bordered Awa Province, Nichiren's birthplace. Hoshina is said to have been a retainer of Sakuma Hyōgo, the lord of Okitsu in Kazusa, and converted to Nichiren's teaching when Nichiren returned to his native province in the autumn of 1264 and propagated his teachings in the vicinity. From the single extant letter called *Reply to Hoshina Gorō Tarō* sent to him by Nichiren in 1267, Hoshina seems to have previously been a follower of the True Word (Shingon) school before converting to Nichiren's teachings.

Hossō school [法相宗] (Jpn Hossō-shū): *See* Dharma Characteristics school.

householder [居士] (Skt *griha-pati;* Pali *gaha-pati;* Jpn *koji*): In Buddhist scriptures, a male lay practitioner of Buddhism. *Griha-pati,* which means the master of a house, referred especially to wealthy householders of the Vaishya class, one of the four castes in ancient India and the class of merchants and artisans. *Griha* means house, and *pati* means master, owner, or ruler. The term *householder* also refers in general to a layman well versed in Buddhism, or simply a layman.

Hsien-shou [賢首] (PY Xianshou; Jpn Genju): Also known as Fa-tsang, the third patriarch of the Flower Garland (Hua-yen) school in China. *See* Fa-tsang.

Hsi-ming-ssu [西明寺] (PY Ximingsi; Jpn Saimyō-ji): A temple built in Ch'ang-an, China, in 658 at the command of Emperor Kao-tsung of the T'ang dynasty. It was founded by Hsüan-tsang and modeled, according to tradition, after Jetavana Monastery in India. The temple produced many eminent priests, including Tao-sui, who studied there.

Hsing-huang [興皇] (PY Xinghuang; Jpn Kōkō): Another name of Fa-lang, a priest of the Three Treatises (San-lun) school in China. *See* Fa-lang.

Hsing-man [行滿] (n.d.) (PY Xingman; Jpn Gyōman): A priest of the T'ien-t'ai school in China during the eighth and ninth centuries. He studied T'ien-t'ai's three major works under Miao-lo. After Miao-lo's death in 782, he lived at Fo-lung Monastery on Mount T'ien-t'ai. When Dengyō arrived at Mount T'ien-t'ai from Japan in the ninth month of 804 to further his studies, Hsing-man taught him the T'ien-t'ai doctrine and entrusted him with the major works of the school, including *The Annotations on "The Profound Meaning of the Lotus Sutra," Great Concentration and Insight, The Annotations on "The Words and Phrases of the Lotus Sutra,"* and commentaries on the Lotus and Nirvana sutras. Hsing-man wrote *A Personal Commentary on "The Annotations on the Nirvana*

Sutra" and *The Meaning of the Six Stages of Practice.* According to *The Biography of the Great Teacher of Mount Hiei,* Hsing-man said to Dengyō: "The sacred words will not become extinct. Now I have encountered this man! All the doctrines that I have learned I will transfer to this *āchārya* from the country of Japan." After his return from China, Dengyō founded the Tendai (Chin T'ien-t'ai) school based at Mount Hiei.

Hsin-hsing [信行] (540–594) (PY Xinxing; Jpn Shingyō): Also known as the Meditation Master San-chieh, or simply San-chieh. A priest who founded the Three Stages (San-chieh-chiao) school in China. His concept of the three stages was closely related to the three periods following Shakyamuni Buddha's death, i.e., the Former Day, the Middle Day, and the Latter Day of the Law. In China, from the end of the Northern and Southern Dynasties period (439–589) through the period of the Sui dynasty (581–618), discussions of the three periods prevailed with emphasis on the Latter Day of the Law. The Former Day was believed to last five hundred years, the Middle Day, a thousand years, and the Latter Day, ten thousand years. Moreover, it was widely believed that the Latter Day had begun in the mid-sixth century.

Hsin-hsing taught in a time that was considered the very beginning of the Latter Day. He maintained that his teaching was the teaching appropriate to the third stage, or the Latter Day of the Law, when the people's capacity was most limited, and that only his teaching, being the most universal, could save the people in that age. According to Hsin-hsing, during the first stage, or the Former Day of the Law, the one vehicle teaching was practiced; during the second stage, or the Middle Day of the Law, the three vehicle teaching was practiced; and during the third stage, or the Latter Day of the Law, his teaching would spread. Hsin-hsing taught that the people should direct their faith and allegiance to all Buddhas and all teachings and also held that the Buddha nature was inherent in all living beings. Thus he and his followers looked upon the people as potential or future Buddhas, and as a practice prostrated themselves in veneration before those they met. His teaching spread widely, but after his death the school was often persecuted because its doctrine and activities contradicted those of the earlier schools as well as government policy. It died out during the Sung dynasty (960–1279). *See also* Three Stages school.

Hsiu-ch'an-ssu [修禅寺] (PY Xiuchansi; Jpn Shuzen-ji): Also known as Fo-lung-ssu. A temple of the T'ien-t'ai school on Mount T'ien-t'ai in China. It was originally Fo-lung Monastery, founded by T'ien-t'ai in 575. Emperor Hsüan of the Ch'en dynasty supported the monastery and named it Hsiu-ch'an-ssu in 578. A part of this temple was destroyed in

845 during the nationwide suppression of Buddhism initiated by Emperor Wu-tsung of the T'ang dynasty, but was rebuilt in 867. The temple is no longer in existence.

Hsüan-lang [玄朗] (673–754) (PY Xuanlang; Jpn Genrō): The fifth patriarch of the T'ien-t'ai school in China. He engaged in the T'ien-t'ai practice of concentration and insight under Hui-wei at T'ien-kung-ssu temple in Tung-yang. Thereafter he continued this practice on Mount Tso-hsi for more than thirty years. In his later years, he lectured on the T'ien-t'ai doctrines and devoted himself to training his disciples. Hsüan-lang transmitted the teaching to his disciple, Miao-lo, who, as the sixth patriarch, clarified and further developed T'ien-t'ai's teaching and contributed to the restoration of the school.

Hsüan-tsang [玄奘] (602–664) (PY Xuanzang; Jpn Genjō): A Chinese priest and a translator of Buddhist scriptures known for his travels through Central Asia and India. In 614 he entered the priesthood and studied Buddhism at Ching-t'u-ssu temple in Lo-yang. In 622 he was formally ordained and studied the *vinaya,* or the rules of monastic discipline, as well as Buddhist scriptures including the Nirvana Sutra and *The Summary of the Mahayana* under various teachers. Perplexed by the differences in their views, however, he left for India in 629 (627 according to another account) to study Buddhism in Sanskrit. He traveled throughout India visiting many teachers in search of greater understanding. At Nālandā Monastery, the greatest Buddhist monastery in India, he studied the Consciousness-Only doctrine under Shīlabhadra. Hsüan-tsang himself is said to have lectured on the Consciousness-Only doctrine before four thousand monks of the Mahayana and Hinayana traditions, and his fame spread throughout India.

In 645 Hsüan-tsang returned to China with Buddhist images and more than 650 Sanskrit Buddhist scriptures. He translated 75 Buddhist scriptures in 1,335 volumes into Chinese, including the 600-volume Great Wisdom Sutra. His work marked a new epoch in the history of the translation of sutras; and his translations and those produced thereafter are called the "new translations," in contrast with the "old translations" done before him. He also recorded his seventeen-year journey through India and Central Asia in *The Record of the Western Regions,* the most comprehensive account of its kind ever written in the Orient. Hsüan-tsang, himself a follower of the Consciousness-Only school, is often regarded as the founder of the Dharma Characteristics (Fa-hsiang) and Dharma Analysis Treasury (Chü-she) schools in China. He had brought from India and translated principal texts of these two schools, including the Profound Secrets Sutra of the former and *The Dharma Analysis Treasury* of the latter. Among his three thousand disciples, Tz'u-en, who formally established the Dharma Characteristics school, was the most prominent and is regarded as his successor.

Huai-kan [懐感] (n.d.) (PY Huaigan; Jpn Ekan): A priest of the Pure Land school in China during the seventh century who lived at Ch'ien-fu-ssu temple in Ch'ang-an. He first studied the Dharma Characteristics (Fa-hsiang) doctrines and the Buddhist precepts, but, dissatisfied with these, he turned to the Pure Land teaching. Unable to believe that one could directly be reborn in the Pure Land by meditating on Amida Buddha, however, he sought out Shan-tao, the third patriarch of the Pure Land school, and confessed his doubts. Following Shan-tao's guidance, he meditated upon Amida Buddha for three years and is said to have realized the essence of the Pure Land teaching. He began writing *The Treatise Resolving Numerous Doubts about the Pure Land Teachings,* but died before he could finish it. Huai-yün, another disciple of Shan-tao, completed it.

Hua-yen school [華厳宗] (PY Huayanzong; Jpn Kegon-shū): *See* Flower Garland school.

Hui-ch'ang Persecution [会昌の廃仏] (Jpn Kaishō-no-haibutsu): Also, Hui-ch'ang Era Persecution. In general, the wholesale suppression of Buddhism carried out by Wu-tsung (r. 840–846), the fifteenth emperor of the T'ang dynasty, that took place from 842 through 845 during the Hui-ch'ang era (841–846). In particular, the Hui-ch'ang Persecution refers to the persecution of 845 that involved the destruction of Buddhist temples. A Taoist named Chao Kuei-chen won special favor from the emperor and incited the emperor to abolish Buddhism. The emperor complied because he regarded the increase of nonproductive Buddhist priests and nuns and their temples and lands, which were exempt from taxation, as economic problems. He also recognized corruption among Buddhist priests and nuns.

In 845 he issued a decree calling for the destruction of all Buddhist temples except four temples each in Ch'ang-an and Lo-yang and one temple in each province. Priests and nuns were ordered to return to the laity except for a small number of priests who were permitted to serve the remaining temples. Jikaku, later the third chief priest of Enryaku-ji, the head temple of the Japanese Tendai school, happened to be in China during the Hui-ch'ang Persecution and recorded these events in his work *The Record of a Pilgrimage to China in Search of the Law.* The Hui-ch'ang Persecution of Buddhism is counted as one of the four imperial persecutions of Buddhism in China. The other three were carried out by Emperor T'ai-wu (r. 423–452) of the Northern Wei dynasty, Emperor

Wu (r. 560–578) of the Northern Chou dynasty, and Emperor Shih-tsung (r. 954–959) of the Later Chou dynasty. Among these four persecutions, the Hui-ch'ang Persecution included all of T'ang-dynasty China. The other three persecutions were limited to northern China. *See also* four imperial persecutions of Buddhism in China.

Hui-k'o [慧可] (487–593) (PY Huike; Jpn Eka): The second patriarch of the Zen (Ch'an) school in China. As a young man, he studied Confucianism, Taoist philosophy, and the Buddhist scriptures. He entered the Buddhist Order under the guidance of Pao-ching at Mount Hsiang. He then practiced Buddhism in a number of places before returning to Mount Hsiang in 518. At age forty, he went to Shao-lin-ssu temple on Mount Sung to seek the guidance of Bodhidharma, the putative founder of Zen in China. Tradition has it that, when refused admittance to Bodhidharma's dwelling even after waiting outside all night in the snow, Hui-k'o demonstrated his seriousness by cutting off his own left arm. Hui-k'o practiced at Shao-lin-ssu for six years and was eventually entrusted by Bodhidharma with the teachings of Zen. After Bodhidharma's death, Hui-k'o went to Yeh, capital of the Eastern Wei dynasty, and there spread the Zen teachings. Opposition from other Buddhist schools and later the wholesale persecution of Buddhists by Emperor Wu (r. 560–578) of the Northern Chou dynasty forced him to retire to Mount Wan-kung, where he transferred the Zen teachings to Seng-ts'an.

Hui-kuan [慧観] (n.d.) (PY Huiguan; Jpn Ekan): A Chinese priest who lived during the fourth and fifth centuries. He studied under Hui-yüan at Mount Lu. Hearing of the master translator Kumārajīva, who had come to Ch'ang-an in 401, Hui-kuan became his disciple and joined in his translation work. He wrote *An Introduction to the Essentials of the Lotus Sutra,* which won Kumārajīva's high praise. Kumārajīva exhorted him to propagate Buddhism in the south, and after Kumārajīva's death he went to Ching-chou and later to Chien-k'ang, where he lived at Tao-ch'ang-ssu temple. Hence he was known as Hui-kuan of Tao-ch'ang-ssu temple. It is said that in Chien-k'ang he assisted Buddhabhadra with his translation of the Flower Garland Sutra. Together with Hsieh Ling-yün and Hui-yen, he revised the two existing Chinese translations of the Nirvana Sutra and produced what is called the southern version of the sutra. He also devised a classification of Shakyamuni Buddha's lifetime teachings into five periods according to the order in which he believed they had been expounded. He defined the Nirvana Sutra in this system as the teaching of the eternity of the Buddha nature, regarding it as the teaching of the fifth and last period, and the Lotus Sutra as the teaching of the fourth period. His concept of the five periods was widely known in

China and was incorporated into other scholars' systems of classification. Hui-kuan held that enlightenment is achieved gradually in the course of practice. He thus opposed Tao-sheng, another disciple of Kumārajīva who held that enlightenment is attained suddenly and completely. He wrote *The Discrimination of Teachings* and *The Treatise on the Doctrines of Immediate Attainment of Enlightenment and Gradual Attainment of Enlightenment.*

Hui-kuang [慧光] (468–537) (PY Huiguang; Jpn Ekō): The founder of the Fourfold Rules of Discipline (Ssu-fen-lü) school in China. In 480 he became a priest and studied chiefly the Buddhist *vinaya,* or rules of monastic discipline, propagating the precepts set forth in *The Fourfold Rules of Discipline,* the *vinaya* of the Dharmagupta school. When Bodhiruchi and Ratnamati translated *The Treatise on the Ten Stages Sutra* into Chinese, Hui-kuang assisted in its translation and wrote a commentary on this treatise. He is therefore also regarded as the founder of the Treatise on the Ten Stages Sutra (Ti-lun) school, which took that treatise as its foundational text. Later he was appointed national superintendent of priests and called discipline master of the nation. Among the teachers of the three schools of the south and seven schools of the north, he was one of the seven teachers of the north and lived just prior to T'ien-t'ai's birth in 538. His works include *The Annotations on the Benevolent Kings Sutra* and *The Annotations on "The Fourfold Rules of Discipline."*

Hui-kuo [恵果] (746–805) (PY Huiguo; Jpn Keika): A priest of Esoteric Buddhism in China. As a boy, he became a disciple of Pu-k'ung (Skt Amoghavajra), and in 765 received from him the esoteric doctrines of the Womb Realm and the Diamond Realm. Later he was appointed to serve at the altar of the imperial palace and lived at Ch'ing-lung-ssu temple in Ch'ang-an. He had many disciples. In 805 he transmitted the teachings of Esoteric Buddhism to Kōbō, who had come to China and would later found the True Word (Shingon) school in Japan.

Hui-neng [慧能] (638–713) (PY Huineng; Jpn Enō): The sixth patriarch of the Zen (Ch'an) school in China. He was also known as the Great Teacher Ts'ao-ch'i because he lived at Pao-lin-ssu temple in Ts'ao-ch'i. According to Zen tradition, he became a disciple of Hung-jen, the fifth patriarch of Chinese Zen. Hung-jen eventually chose Hui-neng as his successor over his most senior disciple, Shen-hsiu. Hui-neng then moved south to Pao-lin-ssu where he devoted himself to training disciples. After Hung-jen's death in 674, the Zen school split into two—the Northern school, headed by Shen-hsiu, and the Southern school, headed by Hui-neng. The Southern school quickly became the predominant school of

Zen. Hui-neng's words are preserved in a work called *The Platform Sutra of the Sixth Patriarch.*

Hui-ssu [慧思] (PY Huisi; Jpn Eshi): Also known as Nan-yüeh. The teacher of T'ien-t'ai. *See* Nan-yüeh.

Hui-tz'u [慧次] (434–490) (PY Huici; Jpn Eji): A priest famed for his mastery of the doctrines of the Establishment of Truth (Ch'eng-shih) and Three Treatises (San-lun) schools in China. Among the teachers of the three schools of the south and seven schools of the north, he was known as one of the three teachers of the south. He lived at Hsieh-ssu temple in Chien-k'ang, the capital of the Liu Sung dynasty (420–479), and won respect from the imperial court. Chih-tsang, Seng-min, and Fa-yün, who were revered as the three great Dharma teachers of the Liang dynasty (502–557), studied under Hui-tz'u.

Hui-wen [慧文] (n.d.) (PY Huiwen; Jpn Emon): A priest of China who lived in the sixth century. Hui-wen studied Nāgārjuna's *Treatise on the Middle Way* and *Treatise on the Great Perfection of Wisdom* and devoted himself to the practice of meditation. He is said to have awakened to the three kinds of wisdom in a single mind and the three truths of non-substantiality, temporary existence, and the Middle Way. Hui-wen transferred his teachings to Nan-yüeh. One view regards him as the founder of the T'ien-t'ai school, Nan-yüeh as its second patriarch, and T'ien-t'ai, its third patriarch. Another view regards Hui-wen as its second patriarch, in which case Nāgārjuna is considered the founder. *See also* three kinds of wisdom; three truths.

Hui-yen [慧厳] (363–443) (PY Huiyan; Jpn Egon): A disciple of Kumārajīva and a translator of Buddhist scriptures in China. Together with Hui-kuan and Hsieh Ling-yün, he revised the forty-volume Mahāparinirvāna Sutra, the Chinese translation by Dharmaraksha, in light of the Mahāparinirvāna Sutra translated by Fa-hsien and Buddhabhadra. He produced this revision as thirty-six volume Mahāparinirvāna Sutra in 436.

Hui-yüan (1) [慧遠] (334–416) (PY Huiyuan; Jpn Eon): The founder of the Pai-lien-she, or White Lotus Society, a group that practiced meditation on the Buddha Amida to attain rebirth in Amida's Pure Land. Born in northern China in what is today Shansi Province, Hui-yüan became a priest and went to see Tao-an in 354, learning the teachings of the Wisdom sutras under his tutelage. Later he went to Mount Lu (in present-day Kiangsi Province), where he founded Tung-lin-ssu temple. Admiring his virtues, many people followed him to Mount Lu. In 402 he founded the Pai-lien-she together with 123 priests and laypersons who engaged in the Pure Land practices. This is the origin of the Pure Land school in

China. As the Buddhist community came to the fore, Huan Hsüan, who had usurped the throne of the Chin dynasty, showed intentions of placing Buddhism under his authority. Opposing this, Hui-yüan wrote a treatise titled *A Priest Does Not Bow before a King,* asserting that Buddhist priests, who had renounced the secular world, did not have to pay customary homage to the sovereign or subordinate themselves to secular authority. Hui-yüan also corresponded with Kumārajīva, who was in Ch'ang-an, asking about various Buddhist concepts such as the Dharma body and non-substantiality; these letters were compiled as *The Essay on the Grand Meaning of the Mahayana.* He lived on Mount Lu for about thirty years until his death.

(2) [慧遠] (523–592) (PY Huiyuan; Jpn Eon): A priest of the Treatise on the Ten Stages Sutra (Ti-lun) school in China. Born in Tun-huang in northwestern China, he is noted for having remonstrated with Emperor Wu of the Northern Chou dynasty (557–581) when the emperor threatened to abolish Buddhism. Emperor Wu eventually outlawed both Buddhism and Taoism. This persecution is known as one of the four imperial persecutions in the history of Chinese Buddhism. The other three took place under Emperor T'ai-wu of the Northern Wei dynasty in the fifth century, Emperor Wu-tsung of the T'ang dynasty in the ninth century, and Emperor Shih-tsung of the Later Chou dynasty in the tenth century. After the suppression of Buddhism ended, Hui-yüan preached Buddhism in various locations. During the Sui dynasty (581–618), he enjoyed the favor of Emperor Wen who sought to restore Buddhism. He wrote commentaries on *The Treatise on the Ten Stages Sutra,* the Nirvana Sutra, the Vimalakīrti Sutra, the Shrīmālā Sutra, and other sutras. His *Treatise on the Meaning of the Mahayana* is highly valued as an example of contemporary Buddhist study. In his later years, he lived in Ching-ying-ssu temple and devoted himself to expounding the Buddhist doctrines.

(3) [慧苑] (n.d.) (PY Huiyuan; Jpn Eon): A priest of the Flower Garland (Hua-yen) school in China during the late-seventh and mid-eighth centuries. He became a disciple of Fa-tsang, the third patriarch of the Flower Garland school, who systematized the school's doctrine. Fa-tsang established a system of classification that asserted the supremacy of the Flower Garland Sutra. In it, he divided all the Buddhist sutras into the following five categories of teachings: the Hinayana teaching, the elementary Mahayana teaching, the final Mahayana teaching, the sudden teaching, and the perfect teaching. Hui-yüan criticized this system as too heavily influenced by the T'ien-t'ai school and formulated a new classi-

fication of four teachings based on *The Treatise on the Treasure Vehicle of Buddhahood,* a work by Sāramati. The four teachings of Hui-yüan's classification are the non-Buddhist teaching, the Hinayana teaching, the partially true and complete teaching (lower Mahayana), and the fully true and complete teaching (higher Mahayana).

hundred blessings [百福] (Jpn *hyaku-fuku*): Also, hundredfold merit, hundred meritorious acts, or hundred kinds of good fortune. The blessings needed to obtain any one of a Buddha's thirty-two features, which can be acquired by accumulating a hundred blessings, i.e., performing a hundred meritorious acts. According to *The Great Commentary on the Abhidharma,* to obtain all thirty-two features and become a Buddha requires continuous practice for a hundred major *kalpas.* The "Parable of the Phantom City" (seventh) chapter of the Lotus Sutra reads, "World hero without peer, you who adorn yourself with a hundred blessings, you have attained unsurpassed wisdom—we beg you to preach for the sake of the world."

hundred worlds and thousand factors [百界千如] (Jpn *hyakkai-sennyo*): Component principles of "three thousand realms in a single moment of life," a philosophical system established by T'ien-t'ai (538–597) on the basis of the Lotus Sutra. "Hundred worlds" means the mutual possession of the Ten Worlds—the principle that each of the Ten Worlds from the world of hell through that of Buddhahood possesses the potential for all ten within itself, thus making one hundred possible worlds. Each of the hundred worlds in turn encompasses the ten factors of appearance, nature, entity, power, influence, internal cause, relation, latent effect, manifest effect, and their consistency from beginning to end, thus constituting a "thousand factors." In contrast with "three thousand realms in a single moment of life," which includes all things in the universe, both sentient and insentient, the "hundred worlds and thousand factors" refers to sentient beings alone because it does not include the realm of the environment, or that of insentient beings.

Hung-jen [弘忍] (601–674) (PY Hongren; Jpn Kōnin): The fifth patriarch of the Zen (Ch'an) school in China. In 607, as a young child, he became a disciple of the fourth patriarch, Tao-hsin, and inherited his teachings after practicing under him for thirty years. Hung-jen had many disciples, and Zen Buddhism prospered in his time. Among his most outstanding disciples was Hui-neng, who became the sixth patriarch. Shen-hsiu, another major disciple, founded the Northern school of Zen, while Hui-neng's teaching came to be called the Southern school.

hungry spirits [餓鬼] (Skt *preta;* Jpn *gaki*): Also, hungry ghosts. Spirits who suffer from hunger and thirst as karmic retribution for their greed, selfishness, and jealousy while they were alive. Buddhist scriptures describe hungry spirits as beings with throats as small as needles and distended bellies. The realm of hungry spirits is said to be located five hundred *yojanas* beneath the earth, above the realm of hell. In that realm, food and drink turn into flames and torment the inhabitants. The realm of hungry spirits is one of the three or the four evil paths. From the standpoint of the doctrine of the Ten Worlds and their mutual possession, it represents a potential state or condition of life in which one is tormented by relentless craving. Hungry spirits are called *preta* in Sanskrit, which in ancient India meant the spirits of the dead. In China and Japan, the story of Maudgalyāyana's saving his mother from the realm of hungry spirits is well known. *See also* service for deceased ancestors.

I

icchantika [一闡提] (Skt; Jpn *issendai*): A person of incorrigible disbelief. *Icchantika* means one who is filled with desires or cravings. Originally *icchantika* meant a hedonist or one who cherishes only secular values. In Buddhism, the term came to mean those who neither believe in Buddhism nor aspire for enlightenment and therefore have no prospect of attaining Buddhahood. Many sutras say that *icchantikas* are inherently and forever incapable of reaching enlightenment, but some sutras hold that even *icchantikas* can become Buddhas. This discrepancy concerning the potential of such people to attain enlightenment became a source of considerable debate among Buddhist schools over the centuries.

The term *icchantika* also refers to one who slanders the correct teaching of the Buddha and does not repent and rectify the error. The Nirvana Sutra translated by Dharmaraksha says: "Chunda spoke once more, asking, 'What is the meaning of the term *icchantika*?' The Buddha said: 'Chunda, suppose there should be monks or nuns, laymen or laywomen who speak careless and evil words and slander the correct teaching, and that they should go on committing these grave acts without ever showing any inclination to reform or any sign of repentance in their hearts. Persons of this kind I would say are following the path of the *icchantika*. Again there may be those who commit the four grave offenses or are guilty of the five cardinal sins, and who, though aware that they are guilty of serious faults, from the beginning have no trace of fear or contrition in their hearts or, if they do, give no outward sign of it. When it comes to the correct teaching, they show no inclination to protect, treasure, and establish it over the ages, but rather speak of it with malice and contempt, their words replete with error. Persons of this kind too I would say are following the path of the *icchantika*.'" It also says, "Good man, there are *icchantikas*, or persons of incorrigible disbelief. They pretend to be arhats, living in deserted places and speaking slanderously of the correct and equal sutras of the great vehicle. When ordinary people see them, they all suppose that they are true arhats and speak of them as great bodhisattvas."

In this sense, *icchantika* refers not simply to those who have no exposure to or interest in Buddhism, but to those who feign Buddhist faith and understanding for self-serving ends. The Nirvana Sutra, however, says, "All living beings alike possess the Buddha nature," thus revealing that *icchantikas* can also attain Buddhahood. The Lotus Sutra says, "At the start I [the Buddha] took a vow, hoping to make all persons equal to me, without any distinction between us, and what I long ago hoped for has now been fulfilled." In this sutra, Devadatta, who symbolizes the *icchantika*, is assured of becoming a Buddha in the future.

ichinen [一念] (Jpn; Chin *i-nien*): A single moment of life, one instant of thought, or the mind or life at a single moment. Also, life-moment, thought-moment, or simply a single moment or instant. *Ichinen* has various meanings in Buddhism: (1) A moment, or an extremely short period comparable to the Sanskrit term *kshana*. *The Treatise on the Great Perfection of Wisdom* defines one *kshana* or moment as a sixtieth of the time it takes to snap one's fingers. (2) The functioning of the mind for one moment. The "Distinctions in Benefits" (seventeenth) chapter of the Lotus Sutra speaks of a single moment of belief and understanding. (3) To focus one's mind on meditating on a Buddha; Shan-tao (613–681), a patriarch of the Chinese Pure Land school, defined *ichinen* (one instant of thought) as chanting Amida Buddha's name once. (4) T'ien-t'ai (538–597) philosophically interprets *ichinen* in his doctrine of three thousand realms in a single moment of life (Jpn *ichinen-sanzen;* Chin *i-nien san-ch'ien*). In this doctrine, *ichinen* indicates the mind of an ordinary person, which at each moment is endowed with the potential of three thousand realms; its characteristics are: (a) it pervades the entire universe; (b) it includes both body and mind; (c) it includes both self and environment; (d) it gives rise to good and evil; and (e) it encompasses cause and effect simultaneously. Nichiren (1222–1282) embodied this philosophical framework in the form of a mandala known as the

Gohonzon. By this he aimed to establish a practical way for ordinary people to manifest Buddhahood from among the Ten Worlds of their own lives.

ichinen-sanzen [一念三千] (Jpn): *See* three thousand realms in a single moment of life.

I-ching [義浄] (635–713) (PY Yijing; Jpn Gijō): A Chinese priest who traveled to India in 671 to study Buddhism and returned to China to translate Buddhist scriptures. He studied both Hinayana and Mahayana teachings at Nālandā Monastery and visited many Buddhist sites. He recorded his travels in *The Record of Southern Countries*. In 695 he returned to Lo-yang with some four hundred Sanskrit scriptures and devoted himself to translating them. He translated fifty-six Buddhist texts in 230 volumes in all, including the Sovereign Kings of the Golden Light Sutra.

Ichinosawa, the lay priest [一谷入道] (d. 1278) (Jpn Ichinosawa-nyūdō): A resident of Ichinosawa on Sado, an island province in the Sea of Japan, who supported Nichiren during his exile to that province. In the fourth month of 1272, Nichiren, who was in exile on Sado, was moved from his dismal accommodations at Tsukahara to the home of the lay priest Ichinosawa, where he lived for nearly two years until he was pardoned and left Sado in the third month of 1274. The lay priest Ichinosawa, though himself a believer of the Pure Land school, apparently was impressed by Nichiren and protected him.

In 1275 Nichiren wrote from Minobu to the wife of Ichinosawa: "The lay priest felt deeply concerned about the life to come and had for a long time devoted himself to chanting the Nembutsu. Moreover, he had constructed an Amida hall and dedicated his lands in offering to Amida Buddha. He was also afraid of how the steward of the area might react, and so he did not come forward and take faith in the Lotus Sutra. From his point of view, this was probably the most reasonable course to take. But at the same time, he will without doubt fall into the great citadel of the hell of incessant suffering. I had thought, for example, that, even if I were to send him a copy of the Lotus Sutra, he would not be willing to abandon the practice of the Nembutsu out of his fear of worldly opinion, and so it would be like combining water with fire. There was no doubt that the flood of his slander of the Law would extinguish the small flame of his faith in the Lotus Sutra. And if he were to fall into hell, I, Nichiren, would in turn be to blame. Thus, while asking myself anxiously again and again what ought to be done, I have so far not sent him a copy of the Lotus Sutra. . . . and yet I am afraid that people may think I am given to irresponsible and deceitful behavior. Therefore, I feel I have no choice but to send a copy of the entire Lotus Sutra in ten volumes. Since the lay priest's grandmother seems at heart to be more deeply drawn to the sutra than does the lay priest himself, I entrust it to you for her sake" (529–30).

ignorance [無明] (Skt *avidyā;* Pali *avijjā;* Jpn *mumyō*): Also, illusion or darkness. In Buddhism, ignorance about the true nature of existence. Ignorance is the first of the twelve-linked chain of causation, the sequence of causal relationships connecting ignorance with suffering. In the concept of the twelve-linked chain of causation, ignorance is the fundamental cause of delusion, suffering, and transmigration in the realm of delusion and suffering. In the T'ien-t'ai school, ignorance is regarded as that which prevents one from perceiving the Middle Way. Buddhist schools defined various levels of ignorance, teaching that, by cutting off increasingly deeper levels of ignorance, one can gradually gain understanding of the true aspect of existence and finally attain enlightenment. *See also* forty-two levels of ignorance; fundamental darkness; twelve-linked chain of causation.

I-hsing [一行] (683–727) (PY Yixing; Jpn Ichigyō): A Chinese priest of Esoteric Buddhism and a disciple of Shan-wu-wei (Skt Shubhakarasimha). He assisted Shan-wu-wei in translating the Sanskrit version of the Mahāvairochana Sutra into Chinese and compiled his teacher's oral teachings as *The Annotations on the Mahāvairochana Sutra.* This commentary is highly esteemed by the True Word (Shingon) school, a school of Esoteric Buddhism in Japan. I-hsing wrote some twenty works on Esoteric Buddhism and was also well versed in the Zen (Chin Ch'an) teaching, the T'ien-t'ai teaching, and the *vinaya* (rules of monastic discipline), as well as Taoism, mathematics, astronomy, and calendrical studies. Dengyō (767–822), the founder of the Japanese Tendai school, in defense of the T'ien-t'ai school's doctrines, later criticized elements of I-hsing's translations and writings as containing important errors. He argued that I-hsing had incorporated key elements of the T'ien-t'ai school's teachings into his Chinese descriptions of the True Word doctrine and on this basis asserted the supremacy of True Word (in Japan, Chinese Esoteric Buddhism was equated with the True Word school, though the school itself originated in Japan).

Ikegami Munenaga [池上宗長] (d. 1283): A follower of Nichiren. His full name and title were Ikegami Hyōe no Sakan Munenaga. He was the younger son of Ikegami Saemon no Tayū Yasumitsu (also, Ikegami Saemon no Taifu Yasumitsu), who held an important post in the Office of Construction and Repairs of the Kamakura shogunate. He is thought to have embraced Nichiren's teachings around 1256, shortly after the conversion of his elder brother, Munenaka. Their father was an ardent supporter of Ryōkan, chief priest of Gokuraku-ji temple of the True Word Precepts (Shingon–Ritsu) school, and violently objected to their practice. Twice he disowned Munenaka when the latter refused to give up his faith in Nichiren's teachings, each time tempting Munenaga to abandon his faith and take his brother's place as the next head of the family. Though Munenaga may have wavered temporarily on this account, ultimately he persisted in his beliefs and, together with his brother, finally converted their father to Nichiren's teachings in 1278.

Ikegami Munenaka [池上宗仲] (d. 1293): A follower of Nichiren. His full name and title were Ikegami Uemon no Tayū Munenaka. He was the elder son of Ikegami Saemon no Tayū Yasumitsu (also, Ikegami Saemon no Taifu Yasumitsu), who held an important post in the Office of Construction and Repairs of the Kamakura shogunate. Munenaka is thought to have become Nichiren's follower around 1256, and his younger brother, Munenaga, shortly thereafter. Their father, Yasumitsu, was an earnest supporter of Ryōkan, chief priest of Gokuraku-ji temple of the True Word Precepts (Shingon–Ritsu) school, and vehemently opposed their beliefs for more than twenty years. When Munenaka refused to renounce his faith in Nichiren's teachings in 1275, Yasumitsu disowned him. Nichiren sent a letter to Munenaka and Munenaga, titled *Letter to the Brothers,* encouraging them to unite their efforts and persist in faith. Around 1276 Munenaka was forgiven, but the next year, he was disowned again. Although Munenaka faced this hardship courageously, his younger brother, Munenaga, seems to have wavered in his faith for a while. During this trying period, Nichiren sent the brothers and their wives letters of guidance and encouragement. In 1278 the brothers finally succeeded in converting their father to Nichiren's teachings. Nichiren died in Munenaka's residence in Ikegami in present-day Tokyo in 1282.

Ikegami Transfer Document, The [池上相承書] (Jpn *Ikegami-sōjō-sho*): Also known as *The Document for Entrusting Minobu-san.* A document that Nichiren wrote at the residence of Ikegami Munenaka at Ikegami in Musashi Province (present-day Tokyo) on the thirteenth day of the tenth month, 1282, the day of his death. In it, he names Nikkō as his successor and chief priest of Minobu-san Kuon-ji temple. It also declares that those priests and lay believers who disregard its contents are acting in defiance of Nichiren's teachings. It is one of the two transfer documents defining the transmission of Nichiren's teachings, the other being *The Minobu Transfer Document,* written in the ninth month of 1282. See also *Minobu Transfer Document, The.*

Ikkō school [一向宗] (Jpn Ikkō-shū): The Single-minded Practice school. Another name for the True Pure Land (Jōdo Shin) school in Japan. *See* Single-minded Practice school.

illusions of thought and desire [見思惑] (Jpn *kenji-waku*): Also, delusions of thought and desire. Errors or afflictions of perception and emotion that cause people to suffer in the lower realms or states of existence described as the six paths and the threefold world. People of the two vehicles are said to rid themselves of these illusions and gain freedom from rebirth in the threefold world. In general, the illusions of thought are regarded as distorted perceptions of reality, and the illusions of desire as base inborn inclinations such as greed, anger, and arrogance: (1) In the Dharma Analysis Treasury (Chin Chü-she; Jpn Kusha) school, the illusions of thought are described as those arising from ignorance of the four noble truths, and the illusions of desire as those arising from attachment. (2) In the Consciousness-Only school, the illusions of thought are regarded as those caused by erroneous teachers and misleading doctrines, and the illusions of desire as those inherent in life. (3) In the T'ien-t'ai school, illusions of thought and desire are one of three categories of illusion, the other two being illusions innumerable as particles of dust and sand and illusions about the true nature of existence.

I-lung [遺竜] (n.d.) (PY Yilong; Jpn Iryō): A master calligrapher in China, a story about whom appears in *The Lotus Sutra and Its Traditions* written in the eighth century by Seng-hsiang. Wu-lung, I-lung's father, was also an outstanding calligrapher. The father was a firm believer in Taoism and detested Buddhism. On his deathbed he forbade his son ever to transcribe any Buddhist scriptures, especially the Lotus Sutra. At the command of Ssu-ma, the lord of Ping-chou, however, I-lung was forced to write the sixty-four Chinese characters that comprise the titles of the eight volumes of the Lotus Sutra. That night he dreamed that the sixty-four characters he had written all turned into Buddhas and saved his father, Wu-lung, who had been suffering in hell for his slander of Buddhism.

Immeasurable Meanings Sutra [無量義経] (Chin *Wu-liang-i-ching;* Jpn *Muryōgi-kyō*): Also known as the Sutra of Immeasurable Meanings. A sutra regarded as the introductory teaching, or prologue, to the Lotus Sutra. It was translated into Chinese in 481 by Dharmagathayashas, a monk from central India. The sutra describes the Buddha's preaching on Eagle Peak and consists of three chapters. In the first, or "Virtuous Practices," chapter, Bodhisattva Great Adornment praises Shakyamuni Buddha in verse on behalf of the assembly. This verse section contains the passage known as the thirty-four negations, referring to the substance or essence of the Buddha. In the second chapter, "Preaching the Law," Shakyamuni explains that all principles and meanings derive from a single Law. He then declares: "Because their [people's] natures and desires are not alike, I preached the Law in various different ways. Preaching the Law in various different ways, I made use of the power of expedient means. But in these more than forty years, I have not yet revealed the truth," indicating that all the prior teachings were provisional and expedient. The final, "Ten Benefits," chapter explains that by practicing this sutra one can obtain ten kinds of blessings. The Buddha encourages Bodhisattva Great Adornment and the other eighty thousand bodhisattvas present to propagate the sutra, and they vow to do so.

Immovable (1) [不動明王] (Skt Achala or Achalanātha; Jpn Fudō-myō'ō): The wisdom king Immovable. Immovable is a main deity among the wisdom kings, a group of deities who are said to remove all obstacles and defeat all devils that hinder Buddhist practice. He is regarded as the leader of the five great wisdom kings, the other four being Conqueror of the Threefold World, Kundalī, Great Awesome Virtue, and Diamond Yaksha, as well as of the eight great wisdom kings (the above five deities plus Ucchushma, Unconquerable, and Horse-Headed). It is said that he enters the flame-emitting meditation in which he emits flames that destroy all karmic hindrances. Because he remains unperturbed by obstacles, he is called Immovable. He is popularly depicted as an angry figure surrounded by flames, holding a rope and a sword. The Sanskrit name *achala* means immovable, and *nātha* means a lord or a protector. *See also* flame-emitting meditation.

(2) [不動仏] (Jpn Fudō-butsu): The Buddha Immovable, also known as Akshobhya Buddha. *See* Akshobhya.

(3) [不動智仏] (Jpn Fudōchi-butsu): The Buddha Immovable. A shortened name for the Buddha Immovable Wisdom. *See* Immovable Wisdom.

Immovable Wisdom [不動智仏] (Jpn Fudōchi-butsu): Also known as the Buddha Immovable. A Buddha said to live in the Golden-colored World in the east. According to the Flower Garland Sutra, Bodhisattva Manjushrī is carrying out the practice there under Immovable Wisdom Buddha.

immutable karma [定業] (Jpn *jōgō*): *See* fixed karma.

impure land [穢土] (Jpn *edo*): Any land inhabited by those who are afflicted with earthly desires. The term is contrasted with "pure land," meaning a tranquil and blissful realm where a Buddha lives. Many Buddhist scriptures describe the present world as an impure land and speak of distant pure lands inhabited by Buddhas and bodhisattvas. From this developed the idea that the present world, an impure realm of suffering and desire, is a place to be abhorred, and that one should seek rebirth in a pure land. Among others, the three sutras that form the doctrinal basis of the Pure Land school—the Buddha Infinite Life, Meditation on the Buddha Infinite Life, and Amida sutras—encourage people to aspire for rebirth in Amida Buddha's Pure Land, the Western Paradise. In contrast, such scriptures as the Vimalakīrti Sutra teach that the purity or impurity of a land depends on the enlightenment or delusion of those who inhabit it. The "Life Span" (sixteenth) chapter of the Lotus Sutra says that the Buddha has always dwelt in the *sahā* world (this world, where one must endure suffering), which is, from the Buddha's perspective, a pure land. *See also* pure land.

Inaba-bō [因幡房] (n.d.): Also known as Nichiei or Inaba-bō Nichiei. A follower of Nichiren who lived in Shimoyama Village of Kai Province in Japan. Originally a Pure Land believer, he was converted by Nikkō, Nichiren's successor, and became Nichiren's disciple. He attempted to convert Shimoyama Hyōgo Gorō Mitsumoto, his father (his lord according to one account), who was the steward of Shimoyama, and met with intense opposition. In 1277 Nichiren wrote a letter to the steward on Inaba-bō's behalf, under the latter's name. Titled *Letter to Shimoyama,* it was later classified by Nikkō as one of Nichiren's ten major writings. Later Shimoyama Mitsumoto converted to Nichiren's teachings.

inclusion of Buddhahood in the nine worlds [九界即仏界・九界所具の仏界] (Jpn *kukai-soku-bukkai* or *kukai-shogu-no-bukkai*): The principle that the world of Buddhahood is inherent in the nine worlds. That is, all beings of the nine worlds possess the potential for Buddhahood (i.e., the Buddha nature). The nine worlds refer to the realms of hell, hungry spirits, animals, *asuras,* human beings, heavenly beings, voice-hearers, cause-awakened ones, and bodhisattvas. These realms also signify inherent conditions or states of life that beings manifest at any given moment. The nine worlds are contrasted with the world of Buddhahood in that they are realms or states of illusion and suffering, while Buddhahood is a state of enlightenment free from illusion and suffering. The principle of Buddhahood as a potential within the nine worlds means that the beings of the nine worlds, i.e., those who are deluded, inherently possess the state of Buddhahood and can manifest Buddhahood from within their lives. This concept is derived from the Lotus Sutra, particularly the "Expedient Means" (second) chapter. Together with the inclusion of the nine worlds within Buddhahood, it explains T'ien-t'ai's concept of the mutual possession of the Ten Worlds. The chapter reads, "The Buddhas, the World-Honored Ones, wish to open the door of Buddha wisdom to all living beings." Nichiren says, "This refers to the world of Buddhahood inherent in the nine worlds" (356). That is, Buddhahood is inherent in all living beings. *See also* "Expedient Means" chapter.

inclusion of the nine worlds in Buddhahood [仏界即九界・仏界所具の九界] (Jpn *bukkai-soku-kukai* or *bukkai-shogu-no-kukai*): The principle that the nine worlds are inherent in Buddhahood. That is, the world of Buddhahood possesses the nine worlds, i.e., the world of hell, the world of hungry spirits, the world of animals, the world of *asuras*, the world of human beings, the world of heavenly beings, the world of voice-hearers, the world of cause-awakened ones, and the world of bodhisattvas. The nine worlds indicate realms or states of life that are tainted by illusions and suffering. According to this principle, a Buddha does not eradicate the nine worlds even after attaining enlightenment, but retains and uses them to save the people. In other words, even when one has attained Buddhahood, the nine worlds continue to exist in one's life, as does the potential for suffering and illusions. This principle is derived from the Lotus Sutra, particularly the "Life Span" (sixteenth) chapter, and with the inclusion of Buddhahood in the nine worlds, it explains T'ien-t'ai's concept of the mutual possession of the Ten Worlds. The "Life Span" chapter reads: "The scriptures expounded by the Thus Come One are all for the purpose of saving and emancipating living beings. Sometimes I speak of myself, sometimes of others; sometimes I present myself, sometimes others; sometimes I show my own actions, sometimes those of others. All that I preach is true and not false." T'ien-t'ai (538–597) interprets "myself" in the quotation as the Buddha's Dharma body and "others" as his manifested body. He says that, when the Buddha teaches directly from the standpoint of his enlightenment, he speaks of "myself" (Buddhahood), and when he teaches in accord with the people's capacity, he speaks of "others" (the nine worlds).

inconspicuous benefit [冥益] (Jpn *myōyaku*): Benefit deriving from Buddhist practice that accumulates over a period of time and is not immediately recognizable. The term is contrasted with conspicuous benefit, or benefit that appears in clearly recognizable form. In *The Teaching, Practice, and Proof,* Nichiren (1222–1282) explains conspicuous and inconspicuous benefit, respectively, as the benefit of the Buddhism of the harvest and that of the Buddhism of sowing. Those who attained Buddhahood during Shakyamuni's lifetime and in the subsequent two thousand years of the Former Day and Middle Day of the Law had already received the seed of Buddhahood from Shakyamuni in the remote past and nurtured it over many *kalpas* until their capacity for enlightenment had all but matured. Therefore, they were able to reap the fruit of enlightenment when they practiced Shakyamuni Buddha's teachings during his lifetime or in the Former Day and Middle Day of the Law. The fruit or benefit of their enlightenment was conspicuous and ready for harvest.

In the Latter Day of the Law, however, people receive the seed of Buddhahood in their lives for the first time. The growth of this seed is not immediately recognizable. Therefore, the benefit of the Buddhism of sowing is called inconspicuous benefit. Practically speaking, conspicuous and inconspicuous benefits are not two different types of benefit but two different ways in which benefit appears. Inconspicuous benefit is likened to the gradual growth of a tree—the growth is real, but difficult to recognize in the short run. In the long run, however, the shade or fruit the tree provides can be conspicuously appreciated. In a similar manner, the inconspicuous benefit that derives from the practice of the correct teaching in the Latter Day eventually finds conspicuous expression in the present life of the practitioner.

incorrigible disbelief, persons of [一闡提] (Jpn *issendai*): See *icchantika.*

Increase and Growth [増長天] (Skt Virūdhaka; Jpn Zōjō-ten or Zōchō-ten): One of the four heavenly kings of Buddhist mythology. This god is said to live halfway up the southern side of Mount Sumeru, on whose summit Shakra dwells, and guard the south. He reigns over two kinds of spirits, called *kumbhānda* and *preta.* In Buddhist scriptures, he often appears as a guardian of the Buddha's teachings and protector of the world along with the other three heavenly kings, Upholder of the Nation, Wide-Eyed, and Hearer of Many Teachings (also known as Vaishravana). *See also* four heavenly kings.

Increasing by One Āgama Sutra [増一阿含経] (Chin *Tseng-i-a-han-ching;* Jpn *Zōichi-agon-gyō*): One of the four Chinese Āgama sutras. The Increasing by One Āgama Sutra consists of 471 smaller sutras in 52 sections. It was translated and compiled in 51 volumes by Samghadeva, a monk from Kashmir, in 397. This Chinese text corresponds to the Pali text *Anguttara-nikāya,* and categorizes various doctrines into eleven groups, numbered one through eleven, each of which contains doctrines whose name or description contains that number. For example, the third group includes doctrines such as the three treasures and the three categories of action; the fourth group includes the four noble truths, the four forms of birth, etc. This incremental organization of its contents is the source of the sutra's title, "Increasing by One."

independent of words or writing [不立文字] (Jpn *furyū-monji*): Also, no dependence on words or writing, not expressed in words or writing.

It often accompanies the phrase "a separate transmission outside the sutras." Both are attributed to Bodhidharma, the founder of the Chinese Zen (Ch'an) school. They express the school's teaching that the Buddha's enlightenment has been transmitted from mind to mind, independent of words or writing, and that enlightenment is attained not through the study of Buddhist scriptures but through meditation alone.

Indra [因陀羅] (Skt; Jpn Indara): Also known as Shakra Devānām Indra or Shakra. The most prominent god in the Rigveda, the oldest Indian scripture. In Vedic mythology, Indra was the god of thunder and rain and the powerful god of war. Buddhism later adopted this god as its defender, and Buddhist scriptures refer to him as either Shakra or Indra. The Rigveda characterizes the god Indra as a great hero, and many of its hymns are addressed to him. He wields a weapon called a *vajra* fashioned by the artisan god Tvashtri. He fights a heroic battle against and slays a dragon demon named Vritra, or "The Enveloper," because the demon envelops and withholds all the waters of the land, causing a severe drought.

In later Indian mythology, Indra's status declined; a later version of the above story has him being initially defeated by Vritra and requiring the help of the gods Vishnu and Shiva to slay him. Other stories portray him as inferior to the gods Brahmā, Vishnu, and Shiva. Indra was also believed to be the guardian of the eastern quarter and to ride a white elephant named Airāvata. *See also* Shakra.

Indra's net [因陀羅網・帝網] (Skt *Indra-jāla;* Jpn *Indara-mō* or *Tai-mō*): Also, Shakra's net. A net that adorns the palace of the god Indra, or Shakra. Each intersection of the net has a reflecting jewel that mirrors all the other countless jewels in the net. Indra's net is frequently employed as a metaphor for the interrelation or mutual inclusiveness of all phenomena.

indriya [根] (Skt, Pali; Jpn *kon*): Faculty, faculty of sense, organ of sense, or power. *See* six sense organs.

inferior manifested body [劣応身] (Jpn *retsu-ōjin*): Also, Buddha of the inferior manifested body. One of the two types of manifested body, the other being the superior manifested body. *See* superior manifested body.

Infinite Life [無量寿仏] (Jpn Muryōju-butsu): The Buddha Infinite Life, another name for Amida Buddha. *See* Amida.

Infinite Light [無量光仏] (Jpn Muryōkō-butsu): The Buddha Infinite Light, another name for Amida Buddha. *See* Amida.

Ingen [隠元] (1592–1673) (Jpn; Chin Yin-yüan): Also known as Ryūki or Ingen Ryūki. The founder of the Ōbaku school of Zen in Japan. Ingen is the Japanese reading of his Chinese name. Born in China, he entered the Zen (Ch'an) center at Mount Huang-po (Jpn Ōbaku) in 1620 and studied there under Zen Master Chien-yüan. In 1654 he went to Japan at the request of Itsunen (Chin I-jan), another Chinese priest who had gone to Japan in 1644. Ingen preached at Kōfuku-ji and other temples, and won the respect of both the Tokugawa shogunate and the imperial court. The shogunate gave him a manor at Uji, Kyoto, where he founded Mampuku-ji temple in 1661. He established the Ōbaku school by incorporating the practice of Nembutsu into the teachings of the Rinzai school of Zen.

inherent enlightenment [本覚] (Jpn *hongaku*): Also, original enlightenment; or, depending on context, originally enlightened or eternally enlightened. Enlightenment, or Buddhahood, that is originally inherent in human life. Often used as an equivalent of the Buddha nature. The concept of inherent or original enlightenment is contrasted with acquired enlightenment *(shikaku),* the view that enlightenment occurs as a result of carrying out Buddhist practice, dispelling illusions, and developing wisdom. In the Tendai school of Japan, the doctrine of inherent or original enlightenment was taken to the extreme with the argument that ordinary people are already Buddhas even before engaging in Buddhist practice, and that the world as it is equals the world of enlightenment. Critics assert that this view led to complacency in Buddhist practice.

initial stage of rejoicing [初随喜品・初随喜] (Jpn *shozuiki-hon* or *shozuiki*): Also, stage of rejoicing. The initial stage of practice of the Lotus Sutra, in which one rejoices on hearing the sutra. It is the first of five stages of practice for believers of the Lotus Sutra after Shakyamuni Buddha's death, a concept set forth by T'ien-t'ai (538–597) based on the sutra's "Distinctions in Benefits" (seventeenth) chapter. The chapter reads, "If after the Thus Come One has entered extinction there are those who hear this sutra and do not slander or speak ill of it but feel joy in their hearts, they should know that this is a sign that they have already shown deep faith and understanding." *See also* five stages of practice.

insentient beings [非情] (Jpn *hijō*): Those beings or objects that have no emotions or consciousness, such as trees and stones. The term is contrasted with sentient beings, those forms of life that possess senses, emotions, or consciousness. Buddhism classifies all existences into two categories: sentient and insentient. A dispute arose in Chinese Buddhism with regard to whether insentient beings possess a Buddha nature, but the view that Buddhahood exists as a potential in all things and phenomena prevailed in China. This idea also became widespread in Japan. *See also* enlightenment of plants.

integration of the three mystic principles [三妙合論] (Jpn *sammyō-gōron*): *See* three mystic principles.

Interfusing Nembutsu school [融通念仏宗] (Jpn Yūzū Nembutsu-shū): A branch of the Nembutsu school in Japan, founded on the teachings of Ryōnin (1073–1132). "Interfusing" here means the union of self and others, a reference to the doctrine of the school that one's own recitation of the Nembutsu (the invocation of Amida Buddha's name) influences all others, and that other people's recitation of the Nembutsu influences oneself, interacting to help bring about the rebirth of all in the Pure Land. This doctrine is based on the idea that all people and phenomena are mutually related and interdependent. The Interfusing Nembutsu movement spread throughout the country with Shūraku-ji temple (later renamed Dainembutsu-ji) in Settsu Province as its center. Dainembutsu-ji is now its head temple.

internal strife [自界叛逆難] (Jpn *jikai-hongyaku-nan*): One of the seven disasters described in the Medicine Master Sutra. *See* calamity of revolt within one's own domain; seven disasters.

"Introduction" chapter [序品] (Jpn *Jo-hon*): The first chapter of the Lotus Sutra. Like a great many Buddhist sutras, it begins with the sentence "This is what I heard." It then goes on to identify the setting as Eagle Peak in Rājagriha and names representatives of the countless arhats, bodhisattvas, heavenly gods, *asuras, garudas,* and other beings, human and nonhuman, who have gathered there to hear Shakyamuni Buddha preach. According to this chapter, the Buddha has finished preaching the Immeasurable Meanings Sutra and enters into profound meditation. At that time, four kinds of exquisite flowers rain down from the heavens, and the earth trembles in six different ways. The members of the whole assembly gain what they never had before, are filled with joy, and, pressing their palms together, gaze at the Buddha with a single mind. Then the Buddha emits a beam of light from the tuft of white hair between his eyebrows, illuminating eighteen thousand worlds to the east. All the living beings in the six paths of existence as well as the Buddhas and their disciples in all these worlds are clearly visible, and the entire assembly is astonished at these fabulous portents. Bodhisattva Maitreya then speaks on behalf of them all, asking Bodhisattva Manjushrī, who has already practiced under an incalculable number of Buddhas, to explain their meaning. Manjushrī replies that he has seen other Buddhas emit a beam of light in this way in the past, after which they have always expounded a great teaching.

Countless *kalpas* ago, he says, there once appeared twenty thousand Buddhas in succession, each with the same name, Sun Moon Bright. The last and twenty-thousandth Sun Moon Bright Buddha had once preached a scripture known as the Immeasurable Meanings Sutra, after which he entered into deep meditation and the very same portents appeared. Then this Buddha immediately expounded a sutra called the Lotus Sutra of the Wonderful Law. At that time, Manjushrī says, there was a bodhisattva in the assembly named Wonderfully Bright, accompanied by his eight hundred disciples, among whom was one named Seeker of Fame. Bodhisattva Wonderfully Bright, says Manjushrī, is now himself, and Bodhisattva Seeker of Fame is the present Bodhisattva Maitreya. The portents they are now witnessing are identical with those they saw in the past. Bodhisattva Manjushrī concludes that Shakyamuni Buddha is about to expound the Lotus Sutra of the Wonderful Law.

"Introduction" is also the title of the first chapter of the Chinese versions of many other sutras. In general, the "Introduction" chapter contains descriptions of the circumstances under which the Buddha is about to preach a sutra and of the causes and conditions that prompt him to preach it. *See also* six auspicious happenings.

Invincible [無勝童子] (Jpn Mushō-dōji): The boy Invincible. A child who, together with the boy Virtue Victorious, offered a mud pie to Shakyamuni Buddha as a gesture of sincerity when the Buddha was begging in Rājagriha. It is said that by virtue of this offering, one hundred years after the Buddha's death, the boy Virtue Victorious was reborn as King Ashoka and the boy Invincible as his consort. This story appears in *The Story of King Ashoka,* translated into Chinese by An Fa-ch'in in 306.

Ippen [一遍] (1239–1289): Also known as Chishin. The founder of the Time (Ji) school, a school of the Pure Land teachings in Japan. He studied under Shōtatsu, a priest of the Seizan branch of the Pure Land (Jōdo) school, which Hōnen established. He returned to secular life in 1263 when his father died, but later resumed the role of priest. In 1275 he went to Kumano Shrine. There, it is said, he received a divine oracle, changed his name from Chishin to Ippen, and began to travel throughout many provinces, distributing talismans with an inscription indicating that the invocation of Namu Amida Butsu ("Homage to Amida Buddha") will ensure rebirth in the Pure Land. The Time school considers Ippen's receipt of this oracle as its founding. He also propagated the Pure Land teachings with the practice of "dancing Nembutsu" *(odori-nembutsu),* an invocation of Amida's name performed while dancing to music in the streets. He was also known as Yugyō Shōnin, or the Wandering Sage.

Iron Encircling Mountains [鉄囲山・鉄輪囲山] (Skt Chakravāda-parvata or Chakravāda; Jpn Tetchi-sen or Tetsurin'i-sen): The mountain range that forms the circular periphery of the world, according to the ancient Indian worldview. It is 312.5 *yojanas* in height and 3,610,350 *yojanas* in circumference. Located at the center of the world, Mount Sumeru is surrounded by eight concentric mountain ranges, which are separated by eight concentric seas. The Iron Encircling Mountains are the eighth and outermost of these mountain ranges and are made of iron, while the other seven are made of gold. The sea that lies between this eighth mountain range and the seventh mountain range is salty, while the other seven seas are of fresh water. The distance between the seventh range and the Iron Encircling Mountains, and hence the width of this sea, is 322,000 *yojanas*. In this outermost sea are four continents: Pūrvavideha, Aparagodānīya, Uttarakuru, and Jambudvīpa, located respectively to the east, west, north, and south of Mount Sumeru.

Īshāna [伊舎那天] (Skt; Jpn Ishana-ten): One of the twelve gods in Buddhism said to protect the world and the universe in all directions. Īshāna protects the northeastern quarter. The Sanskrit word *īshāna* means ruler or master. Īshāna is considered another name for or an avatar of the god Maheshvara.

Ishikawa Monastery [石川精舎] (Jpn Ishikawa-shōja): The first Buddhist temple in Japan, built in what is presently Takaichi in Nara Prefecture. According to *The Chronicles of Japan,* the court official Soga no Umako built this temple near his residence in Ishikawa in 584 to enshrine a stone image of Bodhisattva Maitreya brought from the Korean state of Paekche.

Ishikawa no Hyōe, the lay priest [石河の兵衛入道] (n.d.) (Jpn Ishikawa no Hyōe-nyūdō): A follower of Nichiren and the steward of Omosu in Fuji District in Suruga Province, Japan. His full name was Ishikawa Shinbei Yoshisuke. His wife was an elder sister of Nanjō Tokimitsu (1259–1332), the steward of Ueno in the same province and Nichiren's loyal follower, and it is thought that he converted to Nichiren's teachings through this relationship.

Izu Exile [伊豆流罪] (Jpn Izu-ruzai): Banishment of Nichiren by the Kamakura shogunate to Itō in Izu Province, Japan, from the twelfth day of the fifth month, 1261, to the twenty-second day of the second month, 1263. In the eighth month of 1260, a group of Nembutsu believers, infuriated at Nichiren's criticism of the Pure Land school in *On Establishing the Correct Teaching for the Peace of the Land,* attacked his dwelling at Matsubagayatsu in Kamakura in an attempt to assassinate him. Nichiren narrowly escaped and fled to Toki Jōnin's house in Shimōsa Province. When he reappeared in Kamakura in the spring of 1261 and resumed his propagation activities, the shogunate arrested him and, without due investigation, ordered him exiled to Itō on the Izu Peninsula. Later Nichiren wrote, "[The regent Hōjō] Nagatoki, the lord of Musashi, who was a son of the lay priest of Gokuraku-ji [Hōjō Shigetoki] and aware of his father's feelings in the matter, quite unreasonably had me exiled to the province of Izu" *(Reply to the Nun Myōhō).*

The boatmen charged with his transport apparently did not take him to Itō, but abandoned him at a beach called Kawana, where a fisherman named Funamori Yasaburō found him. Yasaburō and his wife secretly fed and sheltered Nichiren for about thirty days, and in the process became his steadfast followers. At that time the steward of the Itō area, Itō Sukemitsu, was seriously ill. Hearing that Nichiren had been exiled to Itō, Sukemitsu summoned him and requested that he pray for his recovery. Nichiren agreed and prayed for him. Itō recovered, and by way of appreciation offered Nichiren the statue of Shakyamuni Buddha he had treasured. About two years after arriving in Izu, Nichiren was pardoned and returned to Kamakura. His writings during this exile include *The Four Debts of Gratitude; The Teaching, Capacity, Time, and Country;* and *What It Means to Slander the Law.*

J

Jakunichi-bō [寂日房]: *See* Jakunichi-bō Nikke (1).

Jakunichi-bō Nikke (1) [寂日房日家] (n.d.): A disciple of Nichiren, also known as Jakunichi-bō. He was a younger brother of Sakuma Hyōgo-no-suke Shigesada, a follower of Nichiren who lived in Okitsu in Isumi District in Kazusa Province, Japan. In 1265 he became a follower of Nichiren. Nichiren addressed his *Letter to Jakunichi-bō* to him in 1279.

(2) [寂日房日華] (1252–1334): A disciple of Nichiren, also known as Nikke. According to one account, he was the son of Akiyama Nobutsuna, the lord of Kajikazawa in Kai Province, Japan. He entered the priesthood under Nikkō, and in 1276 went to Mount Minobu to serve Nichiren. After Nichiren's death, he was assigned to the twelfth-month shift in the rotation system for attending to Nichiren's tomb. In 1289, when Nikkō left Minobu to establish what later became Taiseki-ji temple at the foot of Mount Fuji, Nikke accompanied him. He was one of Nikkō's six elder disciples.

Jakushō [寂照] (d. 1034): A priest of the Tendai school in Japan. His wife's death awoke him to the impermanence of life, motivating him to leave secular life and become a priest. He studied the Tendai doctrine under Genshin and Esoteric Buddhism under Ningai. In 1003 he journeyed to China, and the following year he met Emperor Chen-tsung, who gave him the title Great Teacher Yüan-t'ung (Jpn Entsū). He brought with him a list of twenty-seven questions from Genshin concerning the T'ien-t'ai doctrine, which he submitted to the T'ien-t'ai master Chih-li. After having studied under Chih-li, Jakushō intended to return to Japan, but at the urging of the provincial official Ting Wei, he remained at Wu-men-ssu temple. Ting Wei honored him and gave him alms and support. He died in Hang-chou in 1034.

In addition to Genshin's questions, Jakushō brought with him a copy of Nan-yüeh's work *The Mahayana Method of Concentration and Insight,* a text that had been lost for centuries in China. In that country, the work was known only as an entry in a catalog of Buddhist scriptures. Tsun-shih, a priest of the T'ien-t'ai school, was so delighted to read it that he wrote an introduction to this work in which he stated: "It [Buddhism] came first from the west [India], like the moon appearing. Now it is returning from the east [Japan], like the sun rising."

Jambudvīpa [閻浮提・贍部洲] (Skt; Pali Jambudīpa; Jpn Embudai or Sembu-shū): One of four continents situated in the four directions around Mount Sumeru, according to the ancient Indian worldview. Jambudvīpa is the southern continent. *Jambu* (or *jambū*) is the name of a tree said to abound in Jambudvīpa; *dvīpa* means continent. The shape of Jambudvīpa is that of an almost equilateral triangle (precisely, a trapezoid whose southern end is far narrower than its northern end). That is, the northern part of the continent is broad, tapering to a very narrow breadth in the south, a shape that suggests the Indian subcontinent. In the northern part of Jambudvīpa are the Snow Mountains, and to the north of the Snow Mountains lies Heat-Free Lake (also known as Anavatapta Lake). The four great rivers of the Gangā, Sindhu, Vakshu, and Shītā originate from Heat-Free Lake and nurture the soil on Jambudvīpa. Mount Fragrant stands to the north of Heat-Free Lake. Within Jambudvīpa, there are sixteen great states, five hundred middle-sized states, and a hundred thousand small states (ten thousand small states according to another source). The joys of Jambudvīpa are fewer than those of the other three continents, for this continent is populated with people of bad karma. It is said, therefore, that the Buddhas appear only in Jambudvīpa in order to save the people.

Jambūnada gold [閻浮檀金] (Skt; Jpn *embudan-gon*): Also, Jāmbūnada gold. Gold produced from the gold dust found in rivers running through the forest of *jambu* trees in Jambudvīpa. The Sanskrit name *Jambūnada* indicates a river flowing through *jambu* trees. This gold is said to be found also under the *jambu* trees in Jambudvīpa. Buddhist scriptures regard it as the finest among all kinds of gold.

Jāmbūnada Gold Light [閻浮那提金光如来] (Skt Jāmbūnadaprabhāsa; Jpn Embunadai-konkō-nyorai): The Thus Come One Jāmbūnada Gold Light. The name that Kātyāyana, one of Shakyamuni's ten major disciples, will bear when he becomes a Buddha, according to Shakyamuni's prediction in the "Bestowal of Prophecy" (sixth) chapter of the Lotus Sutra. The chapter reads: "Great Kātyāyana here in future existences will present various articles as offerings and will serve eight thousand million Buddhas, paying honor and reverence to them. . . . When he has finished offering alms to all the Buddhas, he will fulfill the way of the bodhisattva and will become a Buddha with the title Jāmbūnada Gold Light Thus Come One." The Sanskrit name *Jāmbūnadaprabhāsa* means the brilliance of the Jāmbūnada gold. Jāmbūnada gold, found in a river running through the forest of *jambu* trees in Jambudvīpa, was believed to be the finest of all gold. *Prabhāsa* means light, glow, brightness, or splendor.

jambu tree [閻浮樹] (Skt, Pali; Jpn *embu-ju*): A tree described in Buddhist scriptures as a lofty and enormous tree that abounds in Jambudvīpa. Jambudvīpa literally means "continent of *jambu* trees." The *jambu* tree is also said to produce sweet purple-colored fruit. This tree is identified with a tree called *jambu* or *jambo,* which is found widely in India today. The Sanskrit and Pali word *jambu* is also written *jambū.*

Jātaka [本生話] (Skt, Pali; Jpn *Honjō-wa*): Also, *Jātaka Tales* or "Birth Stories." The stories of the previous lives of Shakyamuni Buddha. One of the traditional twelve divisions of the Buddhist canon. The Pali canon contains a collection of 547 such stories, which are generally referred to as the *Jātaka.* These stories depict the good acts carried out by Shakyamuni in previous lifetimes that enabled him to be reborn as the Buddha in India. The *Jātaka* story is traditionally divided into three parts. The first part introduces an incident or anecdote from the life of Shakyamuni Buddha in India. The second, or main, part relates an act that he performed in one of his past existences. The third part describes the causal relationship between the past act and the present (Shakyamuni's historic life in India) and identifies the persons involved in the past incident with his contemporaries.

Jayata [闍夜多・闍夜那] (n.d.) (Skt; Jpn Jayata or Jayana): The nineteenth of Shakyamuni's twenty-three, or the twentieth of his twenty-four, successors. *The Record of the Lineage of the Buddha and the Patriarchs* describes him as a native of northern India. According to *A History of the Buddha's Successors,* he was widely revered for his meticulous observance of the precepts. Both documents state that he received the Buddha's teachings from Kumārata (also known as Kumāralāta) and transferred them to Vasubandhu.

Jeta [祇陀太子] (Pali; Jpn Gida-taishi): Jetri in Sanskrit. A prince who offered Shakyamuni a grove and land he owned as a site for the monastery, which came to be called Jetavana Monastery. *Vana* of Jetavana means a grove. *See* Jetri.

Jetavana Monastery [祇園精舎] (Skt Jetavana-vihāra; Jpn Gion-shōja): A monastery in Shrāvastī, India, where Shakyamuni Buddha is said to have lived and taught during the rainy season for the last twenty-five years of his life. Sudatta, a wealthy lay patron of the Buddha and his Order, built it as an offering on land provided by Prince Jetri. Jetavana Monastery was one of the two major centers of the Buddha's propagation activities, the other being Bamboo Grove Monastery in Rājagriha. The story of Jetavana Monastery is related in the Miscellaneous Āgama Sutra, the Sutra on the Wise and the Foolish, and other sutras. The wealthy merchant Sudatta, seeking the most suitable land on which to build a monastery for the Buddha and his disciples, sought to purchase a piece of land called Jetavana (Jetri's Grove). Prince Jetri was unwilling to part with the land and told Sudatta in jest that he would sell it if the merchant could cover the area in question with gold. When he saw Sudatta actually begin to do so, he was astonished, and on learning his purpose for wanting it, the prince gave him both the land and the grove and helped him build the monastery.

Jetri [祇陀太子] (Skt; Pali Jeta; Jpn Gida-taishi): A son of Prasenajit, ruler of the Kosala kingdom in ancient India. When Sudatta, a wealthy Buddhist lay practitioner, sought to build a monastery as an offering to Shakyamuni Buddha, Prince Jetri offered a grove and land he owned as a site for the monastery and helped Sudatta build it. It came to be called Jetavana Monastery, Jetavana meaning "Jetri's Grove." Jetri was later killed by his younger brother, Virūdhaka, because Jetri disapproved of Virūdhaka's massacre of the Shākyas, the tribe to which Shakyamuni belonged. *See also* Jetavana Monastery.

Jeweled Dignity [宝威仏] (Jpn Hōi-butsu): Also known as King Above Jeweled Dignity and Virtue. A Buddha who, according to the "Universal Worthy" (twenty-eighth) chapter of the Lotus Sutra, lives in a land in the east and is the teacher of Bodhisattva Universal Worthy. *See also* "Encouragements of the Bodhisattva Universal Worthy" chapter.

Jeweled Necklace Sutra [瓔珞経] (Jpn *Yōraku-kyō*): *See* Bodhisattva Practice Jeweled Necklace Sutra.

Jewel Sign [宝相如来] (Skt Ratnaketu; Jpn Hōsō-nyorai): The Thus

Come One Jewel Sign. The name that two thousand voice-hearers will bear when they become Buddhas, according to Shakyamuni's prediction in the "Prophecies" (ninth) chapter of the Lotus Sutra. The chapter reads: "These persons [the two thousand learners and adepts] will offer alms to Buddhas and Thus Come Ones equal in number to the dust particles of fifty worlds, paying honor and reverence to them, guarding and upholding their Dharma storehouses. In their final existence they will all at the same time succeed in becoming Buddhas in lands in the ten directions. All will have the identical designation, being called Jewel Sign Thus Come One." *Ratna* in the Sanskrit name means jewel or treasure, and *ketu* means a sign.

Jibu-bō [治部房] (1257–1318): A disciple of Nichiren who was originally a priest at Shijūku-in, a temple of the Tendai school, in Suruga Province, Japan. He took faith in Nichiren's teachings and studied under Nichiji, later one of the six senior priests designated by Nichiren. He was one of the eighteen priests charged with the responsibility of attending to Nichiren's tomb. According to a record dated 1298 by Nikkō listing the disciples on whom he bestowed the Gohonzon (object of devotion), Jibu-bō was among the recipients but turned against Nikkō.

Jie [慈慧]: Also known as Ryōgen. The eighteenth chief priest of Enryaku-ji, the head temple of the Tendai school in Japan. He is regarded as a restorer of the Tendai school. *See* Ryōgen.

Jien [慈円] (1155–1225): A priest of the Tendai school in Japan. He was a son of the imperial regent Fujiwara Tadamichi. In 1167 he received the precepts from Myōun, the chief priest of the Tendai school, and in 1203 he was appointed general administrator of priests. He held the position of chief priest of Enryaku-ji, the head temple of the Tendai school, on four occasions. After his death the imperial court gave him the name Jichin. A noted poet, Jien left a collection of poems titled *The Gathering of Jewels*. Ninety of his poems appear in *A New Collection of Ancient and Modern Poetry* compiled in 1205 at the order of the imperial court. He also wrote a historical work titled *A Personal View*.

Jiga-ge [自我偈] (Jpn): The verse section that concludes the "Life Span" (sixteenth) chapter of the Lotus Sutra. *See* verse section of the "Life Span" chapter.

Jih-chao [日照] (PY Rizhao; Jpn Nisshō): The Chinese name of Divākara, a monk of central India who went to China around 676. *See* Divākara.

Jikaku [慈覚] (794–864): Also known as Ennin or the Great Teacher Jikaku. The third chief priest of Enryaku-ji, the head temple of the Tendai school on Mount Hiei in Japan. Born in Shimotsuke Province, in 802 he began to study under Kōchi at Daiji-ji temple. In 808 he entered Mount Hiei and became a disciple of Dengyō, the founder of the Japanese Tendai school. In 838 he journeyed to China, where he studied Sanskrit and Esoteric Buddhism. He was anointed in an Esoteric Buddhist ritual by Ch'üan-ya. He also studied the T'ien-t'ai doctrine and received a copy of T'ien-t'ai's *Great Concentration and Insight* from Chih-yüan at Mount Wu-t'ai. He proceeded to Ch'ang-an, where he was instructed in the esoteric doctrines of the Diamond Realm and the Womb Realm by Yüan-cheng, I-chen, and Fa-ch'üan. Jikaku also studied the doctrines of the T'ien-t'ai school under Tsung-ying. In 847 he returned to Japan and in 854 became third chief priest of the Tendai school.

He had great esteem for the teachings of Esoteric Buddhism and asserted that they were equal to the perfect teaching of the Lotus Sutra. During his time the Tendai school incorporated Esoteric Buddhism into its original doctrines. This was called Tendai Esotericism, as distinguished from Kōbō's True Word Esotericism. Jikaku developed the idea that the Lotus Sutra and the Mahāvairochana Sutra are equal in terms of doctrine because they share the principle of three thousand realms in a single moment of life, but that the latter is superior in practice because it expounds mantras and mudras, which are lacking in the Lotus Sutra. Jikaku recorded his decade of travels in China under the title *The Record of a Pilgrimage to China in Search of the Law.*

Jikoku-ten [持国天] (Jpn): The heavenly king Upholder of the Nation. One of the four heavenly kings. *See* Upholder of the Nation.

Jimon school [寺門派] (Jpn Jimon-ha): *See* Temple school.

Ji school [時宗] (Jpn Ji-shū): *See* Time school.

Jissō-ji [実相寺]: A temple at Iwamoto in Fuji City, Shizuoka Prefecture, Japan. Founded by Chiin in the mid-twelfth century, it belonged to the Tendai school. In 1258 Nichiren visited this temple to do research in its sutra library in preparation for writing his treatise *On Establishing the Correct Teaching for the Peace of the Land.* At that time Nikkō, who studied at nearby Shijūku-in, another Tendai temple across the Fuji River, had an opportunity to serve Nichiren at Jissō-ji and decided to become his disciple. Jissō-ji later converted to the Nichiren school.

Jitsue [実慧] (786–847): A priest of the True Word (Shingon) school in Japan, also known as the Supervisor of Priests Hino'o or the Great Teacher Dōkō. He first studied the doctrine of the Dharma Characteristics (Hossō) school under Taiki of Daian-ji temple. When Kōbō, who was later to found the True Word school in Japan, returned from China to Japan, Jitsue became his disciple. He helped establish Kongōbu-ji temple on Mount Kōya and, in 823, moved to Tō-ji temple in Kyoto. Thereafter he founded Kanshin-ji temple at Hino'o in Kawachi Province. He was regarded highly by the imperial court and revered as foremost among Kōbō's ten major disciples. His works are *The Orally Transmitted Teachings on Meditation on the Character* अ (अ represents the vowel sound "ă"), *The Teachings Orally Transmitted to Hino'o,* and *The Treatise on the Diamond Realm.*

Jīvaka [耆婆] (Skt, Pali; Jpn Giba): A skilled physician of the state of Magadha in India in Shakyamuni's time. As a court physician, Jīvaka served Bimbisāra, the king of Magadha, and his son, Ajātashatru. He was also a devout Buddhist and patron of the Buddhist Order. As a physician he treated Shakyamuni Buddha and his disciples, in addition to ordinary patients. According to one account, his father was Bimbisāra, and his mother, Ambapālī, who lived in Vaishālī. According to *The Fourfold Rules of Discipline,* his father was Prince Abhaya, who was a son of Bimbisāra, and his mother was a courtesan in Rājagriha, the capital of Magadha. The courtesan gave birth to the son of Prince Abhaya and, wishing for someone to adopt him, left him on the roadside. Abhaya happened to find the baby and took him into his palace to raise him. Abhaya named him Jīvaka and cherished him dearly. When Jīvaka grew up, he decided to study the medical arts. Knowing that a skilled physician named Pingala lived in Takshashilā (present-day Taxila in Pakistan), Jīvaka went there to receive instruction from him. After several years of study, having mastered the practice of medicine, he returned to Rājagriha.

It is said that Jīvaka cured various kinds of illnesses, some serious and chronic, thus earning renown, and that he performed a number of different surgical treatments. Ajātashatru, whom Jīvaka served as minister, then killed his father, King Bimbisāra. When Ajātashatru was about to kill his mother, Vaidehī, Jīvaka dissuaded him. Later, when King Ajātashatru broke out in malignant sores that covered his body, Jīvaka persuaded him to repent his evil conduct and seek out the Buddha's teaching. Ajātashatru did so, overcame his illness, and became a devout follower of the Buddha.

jīvamjīvaka [命命鳥・共命鳥] (Skt, Pali; Jpn *myōmyō-chō* or *gumyō-chō*): Also, *jīvajīvaka, jīvamjīva, jīvajīva,* or *jīvakajīvaka.* A two-headed bird said to live in the Snow Mountains. It is mentioned in various sutras for its melodious song and depicted in Buddhist art as resembling a pheasant.

Jizō [地蔵] (Jpn): The bodhisattva Earth Repository (Jizō-bosatsu) said to have been entrusted by Shakyamuni with the task of saving people during the period from Shakyamuni's death until the enlightenment of Bodhisattva Maitreya. *See* Earth Repository.

Jnānagupta [闍那崛多] (523–c. 600) (Skt; Jpn Janakutta): A monk of Gandhara in northwestern India who went to Ch'ang-an in China around the mid-sixth century and engaged in the translation of Buddhist scriptures under the patronage of the emperor. In 575 he went to Central Asia in search of Buddhist scriptures and returned to Ch'ang-an with 260 Sanskrit texts. In the period of the Sui dynasty (581–618), he lived at Ta-hsing-shan-ssu temple at Ch'ang-an where he continued his translation efforts. He collaborated with Dharmagupta on a Chinese translation of the Lotus Sutra titled the Supplemented Lotus Sutra of the Wonderful Law. Altogether, Jnānagupta is credited with the translation of 37 works in 176 volumes that include the above-mentioned Chinese version of the Lotus Sutra, the Sutra of the Collected Stories of the Buddha's Deeds in Past Lives, and the Origin of the World Sutra.

Jnānaprabha [智光] (n.d.) (Skt; Jpn Chikō): A leading disciple of Shīlabhadra who lived in the state of Magadha in central India around the seventh century. Jnānaprabha studied Buddhism at Nālandā Monastery. Well versed in both Hinayana and Mahayana teachings and non-Buddhist literature, he was famous throughout India. He is said to have later followed Nāgārjuna's doctrine of the Middle Way and debated with his former teacher, Shīlabhadra, who belonged to the Consciousness-Only school.

Jōdo school [浄土宗] (Jpn Jōdo-shū): *See* Pure Land school.

Jōdo Shin school [浄土真宗] (Jpn Jōdo Shin-shū): *See* True Pure Land school.

Jōjin [成尋] (1011–1081): A priest of the Tendai school in Japan. He wrote commentaries on the Lotus Sutra and *The Treatise on the Observation of the Mind.* In 1072 he journeyed to China of the Northern Sung dynasty and made a pilgrimage to Mount T'ien-t'ai and Mount Wu-t'ai. Emperor Shen-tsung regarded him highly. He had sutras, texts of the rules of monastic discipline, and doctrinal treatises brought from China to Japan in 527 volumes. He died in 1081 at K'ai-pao-ssu temple in Pien-ching, the capital of the Northern Sung dynasty. His work *The Record of the Pilgrimage to Mount T'ien-t'ai and Mount Wu-t'ai* is a description of his journey to China and his stay, and is valued highly in Japan as a record of that period in China.

Jōjitsu school [成実宗] (Jpn Jōjitsu-shū): *See* Establishment of Truth school.

Jōkaku-bō [成覚房]: Another name for Kōsai, a priest of the Pure Land (Jōdo) school in Japan. *See* Kōsai.

Jōkan [静観]: Also known as Zōmyō, the tenth chief priest of Enryaku-ji, the head temple of the Tendai school in Japan. *See* Zōmyō.

Jōken-bō [浄顕房] (n.d.): A disciple of Dōzen-bō at Seichō-ji temple in Awa Province, Japan, where Nichiren entered the priesthood in his childhood. When Nichiren declared his teaching at that temple on the twenty-eighth day of the fourth month, 1253, Tōjō Kagenobu, the steward of the area and an ardent Pure Land believer, attempted to harm him. Jōken-bō and another priest, Gijō-bō, helped Nichiren escape from Seichō-ji. In 1264 Tōjō Kagenobu again tried to kill Nichiren in an ambush that became known as the Komatsubara Persecution, which Nichiren survived. On the fourteenth day of the eleventh month, 1264, three days after that attack, Jōken-bō, accompanying his teacher Dōzen-bō, again met Nichiren at Renge-ji temple in Hanabusa. Though he remained at Seichō-ji, he seemed to believe in Nichiren's teachings, for in the cover letter to *On Repaying Debts of Gratitude,* Nichiren wrote, "I have inscribed the Gohonzon for you" (737). He and Gijō-bō received several of Nichiren's writings, including *On Repaying Debts of Gratitude, The Tripitaka Master Shan-wu-wei,* and *Flowering and Bearing Grain.*

Jōkōmyō-ji [浄光明寺]: A temple in Kamakura, Japan, built in 1251 by Hōjō Nagatoki, later the sixth regent of the Kamakura shogunate. The first chief priest was Shin'a, and the doctrines of the True Word (Shingon), Tendai, Zen, and Precepts (Ritsu) schools were studied there. Later it became a temple of the True Word school.

Joyful to See [喜見城] (Jpn Kiken-jō): The palace Joyful to See, also known as Correct Views or Good to See. The abode of the god Shakra located on the peak of Mount Sumeru. *See* Correct Views.

Jufuku-ji [寿福寺]: A Zen temple of the Rinzai school located in Kamakura in Japan. It was built in 1200 by Hōjō Masako, the widow of Minamoto no Yoritomo, the founder of the Kamakura shogunate, and opened by the priest Eisai. It is counted as one of the Five Temples of Kamakura and played a remarkable role in the early development of Zen in Japan. *See also* Five Temples.

Junsai [遵西] (d. 1207): Also known as Anraku or Anraku-bō. A disciple of Hōnen, the founder of the Pure Land (Jōdo) school in Japan. Born in Kyoto, Junsai actively propagated the Pure Land, or Nembutsu, teachings (centering on the Nembutsu, or the invocation of Amida Buddha's name), journeying to Kamakura to disseminate them. Hōnen wrote *The Nembutsu Chosen above All* in 1198, and as his followers gradually increased in number, criticism from older Buddhist schools intensified. The priests at Kōfuku-ji in Nara, Enryaku-ji on Mount Hiei, and other temples repeatedly petitioned the imperial court to outlaw the Pure Land school. In 1206, when the Retired Emperor Gotoba was away from Kyoto on a pilgrimage to Kumano Shrine, disciples of Hōnen including Junsai and Jūren held a Nembutsu ceremony at Shishigatani in Kyoto. A number of court ladies in the service of Gotoba attended this ceremony and without court consent renounced secular life to become nuns. This incident incurred the anger of the retired emperor, and in the second month of the following year, Hōnen was sent into exile, while Junsai and Jūren were executed along with two other disciples of Hōnen.

Jūren [住蓮] (d. 1207): A disciple of Hōnen, the founder of the Japanese Pure Land (Jōdo) school. *See* Junsai.

K

Kacchāyana [迦旃延] (Pali; Jpn Kasennen): Also known as Kātyāyana. One of Shakyamuni's ten major disciples, respected as foremost in debate. *See* Kātyāyana.

K'ai-yüan Era Catalog of the Buddhist Canon, The [開元釈教録] (Chin *K'ai-yüan-shih-chiao-lu;* Jpn *Kaigen-shakkyō-roku*): Also known as *The K'ai-yüan Era Catalog.* A twenty-volume index of Chinese Buddhist scriptures compiled by Chih-sheng. It was completed in 730, the eighteenth year of the K'ai-yüan era (713–741), during the reign of the emperor Hsüan-tsung of the T'ang dynasty. This catalog consists of two sections. The first includes all the recorded scriptures, even those not extant at the time of this compilation, and lists 2,275 works in 7,046 volumes translated into Chinese by 176 individuals between 67 and 730. Chih-sheng divided this period into nineteen eras. The section for each era contains a brief description of that age followed by a chronological list of the translators of that era with a brief biography of each and the titles of their translations. Multiple translations of the same text are noted, as are the titles of translations that had been lost, with no copies extant in Chih-sheng's time. The second section lists 1,076 works in 5,048 volumes, only those that were extant at the time of this compilation. Based on this number, the entire body of Buddhist scriptures was customarily said to consist of "5,048 volumes," "5,000 volumes," or "more than 5,000 volumes." *The K'ai-yüan Era Catalog of the Buddhist Canon* served as a basis for subsequent catalogs. See also *Chen-yüan Era Catalog of the Buddhist Canon, The.*

K'ai-yüan-ssu [開元寺] (PY Kaiyuansi; Jpn Kaigen-ji): The name given to a number of Buddhist temples, one in each prefecture of China by order of the emperor Hsüan-tsung of the T'ang dynasty. The name K'ai-yüan derives from the date of this imperial edict, which was issued in the twenty-sixth year of the K'ai-yüan era (738). Some of these temples were newly built, and others were existing temples that were renamed K'ai-yüan-ssu. These official temples, along with Buddhism in general, were placed under state control, and they were used also for imperial birthday ceremonies and other national rites and celebrations.

Kakuban [覚鑁] (1095–1143): Also known as Shōkaku-bō. The precursor of the New Doctrine (Shingi) school in Japan, a branch of the True Word (Shingon) school. Born in Hizen Province, he entered Ninna-ji temple in Kyoto in 1107 and studied under Kanjo. He also studied at Nara and received instruction in the True Word teachings at Kongōbu-ji, Mii-dera, and Daigo-ji temples. He entered Kongōbu-ji on Mount Kōya in 1114. In 1132 he founded and presided over two new temples there, known as Daidembō-in and Mitsugon-in. In 1134 he concurrently became the chief priest of Kongōbu-ji. This incurred the enmity of the other priests of Mount Kōya, however, and he and his followers were forced to flee. They went to Mount Negoro, where he founded Emmyō-ji temple. Because of differences in doctrinal interpretation, his followers founded the New Doctrine branch of the True Word school in the late thirteenth century, in opposition to the traditional teachings of Mount Kōya and Tō-ji temple in Kyoto. Those traditional temples and their teachings came to be known as the Old Doctrine (Kogi) school.

Kakumyō [覚明]: Another name for Chōsai, a priest of the Japanese Pure Land (Jōdo) school. *See* Chōsai.

Kakuun [覚運] (953–1007): The founder of the Danna school, a branch of the Tendai school in Japan. He was popularly called the Supervisor of Priests Danna and the Administrator of Priests Danna, because he lived in Danna-in temple on Mount Hiei. After renouncing secular life, he studied under Ryōgen, the eighteenth chief priest of Enryaku-ji, the head temple of the Tendai school. Later he studied Tendai Esotericism under Jōshin and Kōkei. In 1004 he was appointed the supervisor of priests by the emperor Ichijō. He and Genshin (also known as Eshin, later the founder of the Eshin school, another branch of the Tendai school) were regarded as the two leading Tendai scholars of the day. After his death, the imperial court gave Kakuun the title administrator of priests. His lineage, which later became known as the Danna school, was regarded as one of the two major branches of the Tendai school, the other being the Eshin school. His works include *The Treatise on the Enlightenment of Plants.*

kālakula [迦羅求羅] (Skt; Jpn *karakura* or *karagura*): According to *The Treatise on the Great Perfection of Wisdom,* mythical insects whose small bodies swell rapidly in a strong wind until they are large enough to swallow any living being. The *kālakula* is also described as a kind of lizard.

Kalandaka [迦蘭陀] (Skt; Jpn Karanda): A wealthy man of the state of Magadha in India who is said to have donated a bamboo grove in the suburbs of Rājagriha to Shakyamuni Buddha. On the land donated by Kalandaka, Bimbisāra, king of Magadha, built a Buddhist monastery and donated it to Shakyamuni and his Order. This monastery was known as Bamboo Grove Monastery. There are several conflicting accounts of this story, including one that has Bimbisāra donating both the site and the monastery. Still another account has it that both the land and the monastery were offered by Kalandaka.

kalavinka [迦陵頻伽] (Skt; Jpn *karyōbinga*): A bird said to possess a voice more beautiful and melodious than any other bird. The *kalavinka* is cited in Buddhist sutras and other works for its beautiful voice, which is often used as a metaphor for the Buddha's voice. The "Parable of the Phantom City" (seventh) chapter of the Lotus Sutra reads, "Sage lord, heavenly being among heavenly beings, voiced like the *kalavinka* bird, you who pity and comfort living beings, we now pay you honor and reverence." The *kalavinka* is said to start singing even before leaving its shell and to live in the valleys of the Himalayas as well as in Amida's Pure Land of Perfect Bliss. Some have equated it with real birds of India, though its origin is not clear, and some Buddhist art depicts it as having the body of a bird and a human head.

Kālayashas [畺良耶舎] (383–442) (Skt; Jpn Kyōryōyasha): A monk of Central Asia, renowned for excelling in meditation and mastery of the three divisions of the Buddhist canon. In 424 he went to Chien-k'ang, the capital of the Liu Sung dynasty in China, where Emperor Wen welcomed him. He translated into Chinese the Meditation on the Buddha Infinite Life Sutra and the Meditation on the Two Bodhisattvas Medicine King and Medicine Superior Sutra.

Kāli [迦利王] (Skt; Jpn Kari-ō): A violent king who appears in a story about one of Shakyamuni Buddha's previous lives. According to the Sutra on the Wise and the Foolish, in the remote past there lived an ascetic named Forbearance, who was engaged in the practice of forbearance, one of the six *pāramitās*. One day, Kāli, king of Vārānasī in Jambudvīpa, went into the mountains to pass the time with his wife, ministers, and maids-in-waiting. Feeling tired at one point, he lay down and fell asleep. The maids wandered about freely looking at flowers and happened upon the ascetic Forbearance, who was absorbed in meditation. They paid him their respects and listened to the ascetic preach. Awakening from his sleep, King Kāli and his ministers searched for the maids and found them sitting before the ascetic. He asked the ascetic about the types of meditation he had attained, but the ascetic said that he had attained none.

Angered, Kāli said to the ascetic that he was nothing but an ordinary mortal, and that he had suspicions about the ascetic's intentions with the maids. Asked what kind of practice he was engaged in, the ascetic said that he was carrying out the practice of forbearance. The suspicious king then decided to test his forbearance by cutting off his hands, feet, ears, and nose, but the ascetic remained unperturbed. The blood that poured from his wounds changed into milk and his body was restored. Kāli deeply repented his actions and to make amends he frequently invited the ascetic to his palace and gave him offerings. According to the sutra, having related this story, Shakyamuni reveals that the ascetic was himself in a past existence, and the king was Ājnāta Kaundinya, one of Shakyamuni's first converts.

Kalmāshapāda [斑足王・鹿足王] (Skt; Jpn Hansoku-ō or Rokusoku-ō): The king Spotted Feet, also known as Deer Feet. *See* Spotted Feet.

Kālodāyin [迦留陀夷] (Skt; Jpn Karudai): A disciple of Shakyamuni Buddha. When Shakyamuni was a prince, Kālodāyin was his subject. Later Kālodāyin renounced secular life and became a disciple of the Buddha. He is said to have failed to observe the precepts, but later attained the state of arhat and converted 999 families in Shrāvastī. According to *The Ten Divisions of Monastic Rules,* Kālodāyin was killed and his head buried in horse dung by the jealous husband of a woman who gave him offerings when he was begging for alms in Shrāvastī. According to another account, Kālodāyin happened to discover a young Brahman woman's love affair. Fearing he would tell her husband, she feigned sickness and asked him, as a Buddhist monk, to come to care for her. When he arrived, she had her servant behead him.

kalpa [劫] (Skt; Jpn *kō*): In ancient Indian cosmology, an extremely long period of time. There are various views on the length of a *kalpa.* According to *The Treatise on the Great Perfection of Wisdom,* a *kalpa* is longer than the time required to wear away a cube of rock forty *ri* (one *ri* being about 450 meters) on each side, by brushing it with a piece of cloth once every hundred years. *Great Perfection of Wisdom* also defines a *kalpa* as being longer than the time needed to remove all the mustard seeds filling a city forty *ri* square, if one takes away one seed every hundred years. Nearly identical explanations appear in the Miscellaneous Āgama Sutra, where the length of each side of the rock is given as one *yojana* (about 7 kilometers), and the size of the city as one *yojana* square.

The word *kalpa* is also used in describing the formation and disintegration of the world. According to Buddhist cosmology, a world perpetually repeats a four-stage cycle of formation, continuance, decline, and disintegration. The periods corresponding to these four stages are called the four *kalpas.* Each of these four *kalpas*—the *kalpa* of formation, the *kalpa* of continuance, the *kalpa* of decline, and the *kalpa* of disintegration—lasts for twenty small *kalpas.* A small *kalpa* is defined in terms of cyclical changes said to occur repeatedly in the human life span during the *kalpa* of continuance. Over the course of a small *kalpa,* the human life span increases from 10 to 80,000 years and then decreases from 80,000 to 10 years. The increase of life span occurs at the rate of one year every hundred years, and the decrease of life span also occurs in the same way. During the *kalpa* of continuance, a world and its inhabitants continue to exist for twenty small *kalpas,* that is, while the human life span repeats its increase and decrease in this way. The time required for the life span to increase from 10 to 80,000 years is 79,990 years multiplied by 100, which equals 7,999,000 years. Exactly the same number of years is necessary for the decrease in life span from 80,000 to 10 years; that is, 7,999,000 is multiplied by two, equaling 15,998,000 years. Thus, this number represents the length of a small *kalpa.* Because a small *kalpa* is often described simply as a *kalpa,* 15,998,000 years, or about 16,000,000 years, is often given as the definition of the length of a *kalpa.*

kalpa of continuance [住劫] (Jpn *jū-kō*): One of the four *kalpas.* The second period of the four-stage cycle of formation, continuance, decline, and disintegration, which a world is said to undergo repeatedly. In the *kalpa* of continuance, a world continues to exist in a relatively stable state along with its inhabitants. The *kalpa* of continuance consists of twenty small *kalpas,* measured in terms of cyclical changes said to occur in human longevity. According to *The Dharma Analysis Treasury,* in the first small *kalpa,* the human life span is immeasurably long and steadily decreases to 10 years. In the second small *kalpa,* it increases from 10 to 80,000 years and then again diminishes to 10. From the third through the nineteenth small *kalpas,* the increase and decrease of life span repeats itself in the same way as in the second small *kalpa.* In the twentieth small *kalpa,* the life span increases from 10 to 80,000 years. Though the above descriptions of one small *kalpa* differ, *The Dharma Analysis Treasury* determines that the first and the last of these twenty small *kalpas* are of the same duration and both equal to each of the other eighteen intervening small *kalpas* in duration. Later a new explanation was devised to the effect that the rate of increase and decrease in the second through the nineteenth small *kalpas* was one year every hundred years, which would make each of these small *kalpas* equal to 15,998,000 years. Whenever the human life span diminishes to 10 years—which happens 19 times in the *kalpa* of continuance—the three lesser calamities (war, pestilence, and famine) are said to occur. According to another explanation, these three occur alternately, that is, pestilence in one small *kalpa*, war in the next, and famine in the next. See also *kalpa*.

kalpa of decline [壊劫] (Jpn *e-kō*): One of the four *kalpas*. The period in which a world collapses. The third period of the four-stage cycle of formation, continuance, decline, and disintegration, which a world is said to undergo repeatedly. The time it takes to complete this four-*kalpa* cycle is called a major *kalpa*. The *kalpa* of decline, like the other three *kalpas* of the cycle, lasts for twenty small *kalpas*. Each small *kalpa* is said to last nearly sixteen million years. In the first nineteen small *kalpas* of the *kalpa* of decline, sentient beings in the six lower worlds from hell through the world of heavenly beings gradually disappear. In the last small *kalpa*, the world is destroyed by the three greater calamities caused by water, fire, and wind. See also *kalpa*.

kalpa of decrease [減劫] (Jpn *gen-kō*): A period in which the human life span is said to diminish. In the *kalpa* of continuance—the second of the four *kalpas* of formation, continuance, decline, and disintegration that a world undergoes—the human life span repeats a cycle of change, decreasing by a factor of one year every 100 years until it reaches 10 years, and then increasing at the same rate until it reaches 80,000 years. Then it begins to decrease again until it reaches 10 years, and so on. This pattern of decrease and increase is said to occur repeatedly in the *kalpa* of continuance. Any period of diminution is called a *kalpa* of decrease. Any of the periods in which the human life span is increasing is called a *kalpa* of increase. It is said that Shakyamuni appeared in the present *kalpa* of continuance, in the ninth *kalpa* of decrease, when the life span of human beings was a hundred years long. See also *kalpa*.

kalpa of disintegration [空劫] (Jpn *kū-kō*): One of the four *kalpas*. The fourth and last period of the four-stage cycle of formation, continuance, decline, and disintegration, which a world is said to undergo repeatedly. The time it takes to complete this four-*kalpa* cycle is called a major *kalpa*. The *kalpa* of disintegration is the period lasting from the annihilation of a world at the end of the *kalpa* of decline until the formation of a new world. This *kalpa*, like the other three *kalpas* of the cycle, lasts for twenty small *kalpas*. Each small *kalpa* is said to last nearly sixteen million years. See also *kalpa*.

kalpa of formation [成劫] (Jpn *jō-kō*): One of the four *kalpas*. The period of the first stage in the cycle of formation, continuance, decline, and disintegration that a world is said to undergo repeatedly. In this *kalpa*, a world takes shape and living beings appear in it. According to *The Dharma Analysis Treasury*, the power of the karma of living beings first causes a small wind to arise in space. This wind grows and forms the windy circle thought to lie at the base of a world. Upon this windy circle, a watery circle and then a gold circle take shape, and upon them forms the land, with a Mount Sumeru, seas, and mountains. Then living beings begin to appear, first in the heavens, then in the human world, and successively in the lower of the six worlds, until finally beings appear in the hell of incessant suffering. This *kalpa,* like the other three *kalpas* of the cycle, lasts for twenty small *kalpas.* Each small *kalpa* is said to last nearly sixteen million years. See also *kalpa.*

kalpa of increase [増劫] (Jpn *zō-kō*): A period in which the human life span is said to increase. See *kalpa* of decrease.

kāma-dhātu [欲界] (Skt, Pali; Jpn *yokkai* or *yoku-kai*): The world of desire, the lowest level of the threefold world. *See* world of desire.

Kanāda [カナーダ] (Skt; Jpn Kanāda): Another name for Ulūka, the founder of the Vaisheshika school of Brahmanism. *See* Ulūka.

Kānadeva [迦那提婆] (Skt; Jpn Kanadaiba): Another name for Āryadeva, a scholar of the Mādhyamika school in India. *See* Āryadeva.

Kanakamuni [倶那含仏] (Skt; Jpn Kunagon-butsu): According to the Long Āgama Sutra and other Buddhist texts, the fifth of the seven Buddhas of the past, the seventh and last of whom was Shakyamuni. The Wise Kalpa Sutra describes Kanakamuni as the second of the thousand Buddhas who appear in the world in the present Wise Kalpa.

K'ang-seng-hui [康僧会] (d. 280) (PY Kangsenghui; Jpn Kōsōe): A monk originally of Sogdiana in Central Asia. His family had moved to Indochina because of his father's business. There he lost both parents and decided to become a monk. In 247 he went to Chien-yeh, the capital of Wu, one of the Three Kingdoms of China at the time, and there propagated Buddhism. He was revered by Sun Ch'üan, the ruler of Wu, who built a temple called Chien-ch'u-ssu for him. There he taught Buddhism and translated Buddhist sutras. He is known for a Chinese translation of the Sutra of Collected Birth Stories concerning the Practice of the Six Pāramitās.

Kanishka [迦弐色迦王] (n.d.) (Skt; Jpn Kanishika-ō): The third and most influential king of the Kushan or Kushāna dynasty, which ruled over the northern part of the Indian subcontinent, Afghanistan, and regions north of Kashmir in Central Asia. It is generally thought that Kanishka reigned during the second century, though differing accounts place his ascension between 78 and 144. His reign is believed to have lasted for about twenty-five years. According to one influential account, he was born in Khotan and came from a family line different from that of Kushan dynasty founder Kujūla Kadphises and his successor, Vīma

Kadphises. He made Purushapura (present-day Peshawar in Pakistan) the capital of his Kushan kingdom, which prospered as a transit-caravan center and a crossroad for Eastern and Western civilizations to meet. As the most powerful monarch of the Kushan kingdom, he expanded his territory, bringing the influence of the Kushan kingdom to its height.

Most of the information concerning him has been gleaned from Buddhist literature, and he is best remembered as a great patron of Buddhism, together with King Ashoka who lived four hundred years earlier. He studied Buddhism under the Buddhist poet Ashvaghosha and convened the Fourth Buddhist Council in Kashmir with five hundred monks, including Pārshva, Vasumitra, and Dharmatrāta. That council compiled *The Great Commentary on the Abhidharma.* He also built a great stupa in the suburbs of his capital at Purushapura. Kanishka maintained contacts with Rome, and during his reign, Gandhara Buddhist art, influenced by Greco-Roman style, prospered. The neighboring Gandhara region became the center of Buddhism, and the doctrinal study of the Sarvāstivāda school flourished there. Charaka, to whom the medical treatise *Charaka-samhitā* is attributed, is said to have been King Kanishka's physician. Though Kanishka greatly honored Buddhism, he is said to have protected the teachings of Zoroastrianism and Hinduism as well. The coins used during Kanishka's reign are engraved with images of Iranian, Greek, and Brahmanic deities. His kingdom was so affluent that large numbers of gold coins were issued during his reign.

Kannon [観音] (Jpn): The bodhisattva Perceiver of Sounds (Kannon-bosatsu), an abbreviation of Perceiver of the World's Sounds (Kanzeon-bosatsu). *See* Perceiver of the World's Sounds.

Kanroku [観勒] (n.d.) (Jpn; Kor Kwallŭk): A priest of Paekche, an ancient state on the Korean Peninsula, who went to Japan in 602. He lived at Hōkō-ji temple in Asuka. He introduced the teachings of the Three Treatises (Jpn Sanron) and the Establishment of Truth (Jōjitsu) schools, as well as works relating to the calendar, astronomy, and geography. In 624 the imperial court gave him the title administrator of priests. It was the first time this title was bestowed in Japan. *See also* administrator of priests.

Kanzeon [観世音] (Jpn): The bodhisattva Perceiver of the World's Sounds (Kanzeon-bosatsu). *See* Perceiver of the World's Sounds.

Kanzeon-ji [観世音寺]: A temple of the Tendai school located in Chikuzen Province in Japan. Though Emperor Tenchi (626–671) ordered its construction, it was not completed until 746, well after his death. In 761 an ordination hall was added, making it one of the three ordination centers in Japan, the other two being at Tōdai-ji in Nara and Yakushi-ji in Shimotsuke Province. In 1064 the temple was destroyed by fire but was later rebuilt. Today, however, only the main hall and the Amida hall remain.

Kao-ch'ang [高昌国] (PY Gaochang; Jpn Kōshō-koku): An ancient kingdom of the Turfan region of what is now the eastern part of the Sinkiang Uighur Autonomous Region in northwestern China. The Kao-ch'ang kingdom, which lasted from the fifth through the seventh century, was situated on the northern side of the Turfan Depression at the foot of the southern slope of the Tien Shan range. Buddhism prospered there from early on under the reign of the Ch'ü clan. In the early seventh century, on the way to India, the Chinese priest Hsüan-tsang was invited to visit Kao-ch'ang by the king and ruler of the Ch'ü clan, and he was accorded a hospitable welcome. Control by the Ch'ü clan lasted from 498 until 640, when T'ang-dynasty China conquered the Kao-ch'ang kingdom. Today a number of Buddhist temple ruins can be found in Karakhoja (also spelled Karakhojo) near the present-day city of Turfan. Buddhist texts written in the Uighur script and Manichaean wall paintings have been excavated there. Many caves once used as Buddhist temples also exist near Karakhoja.

Kapila [迦毘羅] (Skt; Jpn Kabira): A Vedic sage and the founder of the Sāmkhya school, one of the six major schools of Brahmanism in ancient India, held to be a legendary figure.

Kapilavastu [迦毘羅衛国] (Skt; Pali Kapilavatthu; Jpn Kabirae-koku): The ancient kingdom of the Shākya tribe; a small state on the Indian–Nepalese border. The capital was also called Kapilavastu. Based on archaeological findings, it was believed that the capital was located at Tilaurakot in southern Nepal. More recent excavations, however, indicate that it was more likely located at the site of present-day Piprahwa (also spelled Piprava) just south (on the Indian side) of the India–Nepal border. Lumbinī, Shakyamuni's birthplace, is the present-day Rummindei, located east of Piprahwa just inside Nepal's southern border. A stone pillar erected by King Ashoka on his visit to this spot still remains. In Shakyamuni's later years, Virūdhaka, the king of Kosala, destroyed the Shākya kingdom. Early in the fifth century, Fa-hsien, a Chinese Buddhist priest, visited the former capital at Kapilavastu and noted in his travel record that the capital was devastated and only a few dozen houses remained.

Kapimala [迦毘摩羅・毘羅尊者] (n.d.) (Skt; Jpn Kabimara or Bira-sonja): A native of Pātaliputra in the Indian state of Magadha in the second century. The twelfth of Shakyamuni's twenty-three, or the thirteenth of his twenty-four, successors. Kapimala was originally a teacher of Brahmanism and tried to harass Ashvaghosha with his supernatural powers. Ashvaghosha refuted his tenets, however, and he converted to Buddhism along with his three thousand disciples. Later Kapimala propagated Buddhism in southern and western India and refuted many non-Buddhist teachers in debate.

karma [業] (Skt; Pali *kamma;* Jpn *gō*): Potentials in the inner, unconscious realm of life created through one's actions in the past or present that manifest themselves as various results in the present or future. Karma is a variation of the Sanskrit *karman,* which means act, action, a former act leading to a future result, or result. Buddhism interprets karma in two ways: as indicating three categories of action, i.e., mental, verbal, and physical, and as indicating a dormant force thereby produced. That is, one's thought, speech, and behavior, both good and bad, imprint themselves as a latent force or potential in one's life.

This latent force, or karma, when activated by an external stimulus, produces a corresponding good or bad effect, i.e., happiness or suffering. There are also neutral acts that produce neither good nor bad results. According to this concept of karma, one's actions in the past have shaped one's present reality, and one's actions in the present will in turn influence one's future. This law of karmic causality operates in perpetuity, carrying over from one lifetime to the next and remaining with one in the latent state between death and rebirth.

It is karma, therefore, that accounts for the circumstances of one's birth, one's individual nature, and in general the differences among all living beings and their environments. It was traditionally viewed as a natural process in which no god or deity could intervene. The Hindu gods, in fact, were subject to the same law of karma as people, having become gods supposedly through the creation of good karma. The idea of karma predates Buddhism and was already prevalent in Indian society well before the time of Shakyamuni. This pre-Buddhist view of karma, however, had an element of determinism, serving more to explain one's lot in life and compel one to accept it than inspiring hope for change or transformation. The Brahmans, who were at the top of the Indian class structure by birth, may well have emphasized this view to secure their own role. The idea of karma was further developed, however, in the Buddhist teachings.

Shakyamuni maintained that what makes a person noble or humble is not birth but one's actions. Therefore the Buddhist doctrine of karma is not fatalistic. Rather, karma is viewed not only as a means to explain the present, but also as the potential force through which to influence one's future. Mahayana Buddhism holds that the sum of actions and experiences of the present and previous lifetimes are accumulated and stored as karma in the depths of life and will form the framework of individual existence in the next lifetime. Buddhism therefore encourages people to create the best possible karma in the present in order to ensure the best possible outcome in the future. In terms of time, some types of karma produce effects in the present lifetime, others in the next lifetime, and still others in subsequent lifetimes. This depends on the nature, intensity, and repetitiveness of the acts that caused them. Only those types of karma that are extremely good or bad will last into future existences. The other, more minor, types will produce results in this lifetime. Those that are neither good nor bad will bring about no results.

Karma is broadly divided into two types: fixed and unfixed. Fixed karma is said to produce a fixed result—that is, for any given fixed karma there is a specific effect that will become manifest at a specific time. In the case of unfixed karma, any of various results or general outcomes might arise at an indeterminate time. Irrespective of these differences, the Buddhist philosophy of karma, particularly that of Mahayana Buddhism, is not fatalistic. No ill effect is so fixed or predetermined that good karma from Buddhist practice in the present cannot transform it for the better. Moreover, any type of karma needs interaction with the corresponding conditions to become manifest. *See also* fixed karma; unfixed karma.

karma mandala [羯磨曼荼羅] (Jpn *katsuma-mandara*): (1) One of the four types of mandala. The karma mandala depicts the actions of Buddhas and bodhisattvas who lead living beings to enlightenment.

(2) The various arrangements of statues of Buddhas and bodhisattvas enshrined on altars.

karunā [悲・慈悲] (Skt, Pali; Jpn *hi* or *jihi*): *See* compassion.

Kashgar [疏勒国] (Jpn Soroku-koku): An oasis city in Central Asia on the western end of the Tarim Basin, in what is now the Sinkiang Uighur Autonomous Region of northwestern China. Most of the inhabitants are Uighurs, people of Turkic origin. Kashgar was an important location along the Silk Road as a center of trade and traffic between the East and the West. Over the last two millennia, it has been the subject of frequent conquests by different peoples. China occupied it, lost control, and regained control several times. According to *The Record of the Western Regions* by Hsüan-tsang, who visited Kashgar in the seventh century, agriculture and textile manufacturing prospered there. There were hundreds of Buddhist monasteries and more than ten thousand monks studying the doctrines of the Sarvāstivāda school. Though Hinayana Buddhism flourished there, it is noteworthy that fragments of the Sanskrit text of the Lotus Sutra, a Mahayana sutra, were recently uncovered in Kashgar.

In the tenth century, Kashgar fell under the domination of the Turkish-Islamic Qarakhanid dynasty and became one of its two capitals. As a result, Turkish and Islamic culture and religion took root there. Kashgar fell under the rule of the Karakitai dynasty in the twelfth century and of the Mongols in the thirteenth and later centuries. In the mid-eighteenth century, Kashgar was occupied by the Chinese Ch'ing dynasty.

Kāshī [迦尸国] (Skt; Pali Kāsī; Jpn Kashi-koku): Also known as the Vārānasī kingdom. One of the sixteen great states of India in the sixth century B.C.E. Its capital was Vārānasī (present-day Varanasi, also known as Benares), a flourishing center of commerce in northern India. Deer Park, now Sarnath, where Shakyamuni gave his first sermon, was located a few miles north of Varanasi. Kāshī was situated in the middle Ganges Valley on the fertile Indo-Gangetic Plain, where water transportation was conducive to trade and agriculture thrived. During the time of Shakyamuni, Kāshī fell under the rule of Kosala, another kingdom in the middle Ganges Valley. Later, as the Magadha kingdom in the lower Ganges Valley expanded its political power, its king, Ajātashatru annexed Kāshī.

Kashmir [迦湿弥羅国・罽賓国] (Skt Kashmīra or Kāshmīra; Jpn Kashumira-koku or Keihin-koku): An ancient country in the northwestern part of the Indian subcontinent. According to tradition, King Ashoka sent the Buddhist monk Madhyāntika to this region to introduce Buddhism in the third century B.C.E. Later King Kanishka built monasteries there and sponsored the Fourth Buddhist Council at which the Buddhist scriptures were compiled. Kashmir also produced a number of noteworthy Buddhist monks who traveled to China, where they engaged in the translation of the Buddhist scriptures.

Kāshyapa (Skt) (1) [迦葉菩薩] (Jpn Kashō-bosatsu): A bodhisattva who appears in the Mahāparinirvāna Sutra to whom Shakyamuni Buddha addresses the "Bodhisattva Kāshyapa" chapter of that sutra and who, in the sutra, asks Shakyamuni thirty-six questions.

(2) [迦葉仏] (Jpn Kashō-butsu): According to the Long Āgama Sutra and others, the sixth of the seven Buddhas of the past, the seventh and last of whom is Shakyamuni. The Wise Kalpa Sutra lists the names of a thousand Buddhas appearing in the present Wise Kalpa and describes Kāshyapa Buddha as the third of them. According to the Mahāparinirvāna Sutra, the monk Realization of Virtue, who upheld the correct teaching, was reborn as Kāshyapa Buddha, and the king Possessor of Virtue, who was killed defending him, was reborn as Shakyamuni.

Kāshyapa Mātanga [迦葉摩騰] (n.d.) (Skt; Jpn Kashō-matō): Also known as Mātanga. The Indian monk believed to have been the first to introduce Buddhism to China. According to Chinese tradition, he traveled from India to Lo-yang in China with another Indian monk, known by his Chinese name Chu Fa-lan. They came in C.E. 67 at the invitation of Emperor Ming of the Later Han dynasty. Born to a Brahman family in central India, Mātanga was well versed in the Hinayana and Mahayana sutras. It is said that Emperor Ming had dreamed about the Buddha and dispatched emissaries to bring his teachings to China. These emissaries invited Mātanga and Chu Fa-lan to China, and the two arrived in that country with white horses carrying Buddhist scriptures. Because of this, Buddhism was referred to as the "teaching brought by white horses." The first Buddhist temple in China was built for these two monks in the suburbs of Lo-yang in 67, and was given the name of Pai-ma-ssu (White Horse Temple). At this temple, Mātanga and Chu Fa-lan are said to have translated five sutras including the Sutra of Forty-two Sections.

Kāshyapīya school [飲光部・迦葉遺部] (Skt; Jpn Onkō-bu or Kashōi-bu): An offshoot of the Sarvāstivāda school, and one of the so-called twenty Hinayana schools. According to *The Doctrines of the Different Schools,* the Kāshyapīya school branched out from the Sarvāstivāda school in the third one-hundred-year period after Shakyamuni Buddha's death. *See* twenty Hinayana schools.

Kataumi [片海]: The birthplace of Nichiren (1222–1282). A place on the Pacific coast of thirteenth-century Japan in Tōjō Village of Awa Province (the southern part of present-day Chiba Prefecture). In his writing *The Tripitaka Master Shan-wu-wei,* Nichiren states, "I, Nichiren, am the son of a humble family, born along the shore in Kataumi of Tōjō in the province of Awa, a person who has neither authority nor virtue" (169).

Kātyāyana [迦旃延] (Skt; Pali Kacchāyana or Kacchāna; Jpn Kasennen): Also known as Mahākātyāyana (Pali Mahākacchāyana or Mahākacchāna). One of Shakyamuni Buddha's ten major disciples, respected as foremost in debate. He was a native of Ujjayinī, the capital of Avanti in west-central India. A Brahman by birth, he held the position of religious advisor to the ruler of state. The first native of Avanti to become a disciple of the Buddha, he converted at Shrāvastī, where the Buddha was preaching. The ruler of Avanti had heard reports of Shakyamuni's teachings and sent Kātyāyana there to investigate. After becoming Shakyamuni's disciple, he returned to Avanti, where he converted the king and many others. In the Lotus Sutra, Kātyāyana is one of the four great voice-hearers who understood the Buddha's true intention through the parable of the three carts and the burning house in the sutra's "Simile and Parable" (third) chapter. The "Bestowal of Prophecy" (sixth) chapter predicts that in the future he will become a Buddha named Jāmbūnada Gold Light.

Kātyāyanīputra [迦多衍尼子] (n.d.) (Skt; Jpn Kataennishi): A monk of the Sarvāstivāda school in India around the second century B.C.E. Born to a Brahman family, he later converted to Buddhism. A great scholar, he wrote *The Treatise on the Source of Wisdom,* a principal doctrinal text of the school, and contributed greatly to the systematization of the school's doctrine. He is often regarded as the founder of the Sarvāstivāda school.

Kaundinya [憍陳如] (Skt; Jpn Kyōjinnyo): One of the five ascetics who heard Shakyamuni Buddha's first sermon and became his disciples. *See* Ājnāta Kaundinya.

Kaushāmbī [憍賞弥国] (Skt; Pali Kosambī; Jpn Kyōshōmi-koku): The capital of Vatsa, one of the sixteen great states in India in Shakyamuni's time. Kaushāmbī was one of the major cities in India, and one of the places where Shakyamuni Buddha concentrated his teaching efforts. Buddhist scriptures identify the king of Kaushāmbī in Shakyamuni's time as Udayana, who converted to Buddhism and became a patron of Shakyamuni. King Udayana is celebrated in Buddhist scriptures for having fashioned an image of the Buddha, which is described as the first such image ever made. Another resident of Kaushāmbī described in Buddhist texts is a wealthy man named Ghoshila, also the Buddha's follower. He built a monastery in a grove that he owned and offered the monastery and grove to the Buddha. They are named after him, respectively Ghoshila Grove and Ghoshila Monastery.

Kaushika [憍尸迦] (Skt; Jpn Kyōshika): The name of the god Shakra, or Indra, when he was once a Brahman, according to *The Treatise on the Great Perfection of Wisdom.* Buddhist scriptures often refer to Shakra as Kaushika. *See* Shakra.

Kawanobe, the lay priest of [河野辺の入道] (n.d.) (Jpn Kawanobe-no-nyūdō): A follower of Nichiren. He is thought to have been arrested and imprisoned because of his association with Nichiren at the time of the Tatsunokuchi Persecution in 1271.

Kegon school [華厳宗] (Jpn Kegon-shū): *See* Flower Garland school.

Kenchō-ji [建長寺]: The head temple of the Kenchō-ji branch of the Rinzai school of Zen, located in Kamakura in Japan, regarded as the first in rank among the Five Temples of Kamakura. In 1249 Hōjō Tokiyori, the fifth regent of the Kamakura shogunate, sponsored its construction. Upon its completion in 1253, Tokiyori invited Dōryū (Chin Tao-lung), a priest from China, to be its first chief priest. Mugaku Sogen (Wu-hsüeh Tsu-yüan), another priest from China, also resided there. *See also* Five Temples.

Kennin-ji [建仁寺]: The head temple of the Kennin-ji branch of the Rinzai school of Zen, located in Kyoto, Japan. This temple is regarded as one of the Five Temples of Kyoto. Eisai founded it in 1202 after being commissioned to do so by the shogun Minamoto no Yoriie. Although Kennin-ji was the first Zen temple in Kyoto, the doctrines of the Tendai and True Word (Shingon) schools were also taught there because of pressure from these older schools. After staying thirteen years at Kenchō-ji temple in Kamakura, in 1265 Dōryū (Chin Tao-lung), a priest originally from China, took up residence at Kennin-ji as its eleventh chief priest. From that time on it was used exclusively for Zen practice. *See also* Five Temples.

Kenshin [顕真] (1130–1192): The sixty-first chief priest of Enryaku-ji, the head temple of the Tendai school on Mount Hiei in Japan. He studied the exoteric teachings under Myōun and the esoteric teachings under Sōjitsu. In 1173 he retired to a temple at Ōhara, and in 1186 he invited Hōnen there to answer questions about the Pure Land teachings from himself and other priests (an event known as the Ōhara Discourse) and devoted himself to the exclusive practice of Nembutsu, or the chanting of Amida Buddha's name. In 1190, against his wishes, he was appointed chief priest of Enryaku-ji and then under-administrator of priests.

Kharadīya, Mount [伽羅陀山] (Skt; Jpn Karada-sen): Also, Kharādīya. The abode of Bodhisattva Earth Repository. *Pronunciation and Meaning in the Buddhist Scriptures* by Hui-lin (737–820) describes Mount Kharadīya as one of seven concentric gold mountain ranges that, according to ancient Indian and Buddhist cosmology, surround Mount Sumeru.

Khotan [于闐・和田] (Jpn Uten or Hōtan): An oasis city in Central Asia, located in the present Sinkiang Uighur Autonomous Region of China. The oasis of Khotan lies on the southern edge of the Takla Makan Desert, which forms the greater part of the Tarim Basin at the foot of the northern slope of the Kunlun Mountains. The Chinese knew Khotan in the time of the Former Han dynasty (202 B.C.E.–C.E. 8) as Yü-t'ien, and China occupied it for a time around C.E. 70. Khotan flourished as a trading center on routes connecting China and India, and China and regions to the west.

Along with Kucha, which was on the road along the northern edge of the Takla Makan Desert, Khotan played a major role in the transmission of Buddhism from India to China and prospered as a center of Buddhism from the fifth to the eighth century. When Fa-hsien and Hsüan-tsang went to Khotan in the early fifth and mid-seventh centuries, respectively, Khotan was a center of Mahayana Buddhism and home to a number of great monasteries where tens of thousands of monks resided. It is known from Buddhist and other texts discovered in Khotan that, from the sixth through the tenth century, the people of Khotan spoke Khotanese, a Middle Iranian language of the Indo–European language family.

The Chinese occupied Khotan again in the seventh century under the T'ang dynasty, but left when they were defeated by the Arabs and driven out of Central Asia in the eighth century. In the tenth century the Qarakhanids, a Turkish dynasty, occupied the neighboring state of Kashgar to the west; as a result, Khotan came under the influence of the Qarakhanids, and people began to convert to Islam, bringing about the decline of Buddhism. Finally, the Qarakhanids conquered Khotan during the late tenth and early eleventh centuries. It was occupied by the Karakitai dynasty, rivals of the Qarakhanids, in the twelfth century, and then by the Mongols in the thirteenth century.

In the following centuries, Khotan fell under the domination of different kingdoms, and in the mid-eighteenth century, it came under the control of China again under the Ch'ing dynasty (1644–1912). Archaeologist Aurel Stein (1862–1943) carried out excavations in Khotan and discovered valuable Buddhist and other artifacts there. Khotan has long been famous as a source of jade, and is well known for its silks and rugs.

Khuddaka-nikāya [小部] (Pali; Jpn Shō-bu): A collection of minor sutras. One of the five Āgamas. *See* five Āgamas.

Kichijō-ten [吉祥天] (Jpn): Auspicious, the goddess of fortune and beauty, who is said to bestow fortune and benefit on living beings. In Japan, prayers for peace and agricultural fertility were offered to the goddess. *See* Auspicious.

Kimbara [金原] (n.d.): The Dharma Bridge Kimbara (Kimbara-hokkyō). Also known as the Dharma Bridge Kanahara. A follower of Nichiren who lived in Shimōsa Province, Japan. He actively spread Nichiren's teaching there together with Ōta Saemon and Soya Kyōshin. "Dharma Bridge" was a title established in the mid-ninth century as an official rank for priests, but later became simply a title of honor. In 1271 Nichiren addressed a letter, known as *Lessening One's Karmic Retribution,* to Kimbara, Ōta, and Soya, which he wrote while being held in detention at Echi in Sagami Province prior to his exile on Sado Island.

kimnara [緊那羅] (Skt; Jpn *kinnara*): Also, *kinnara.* According to Indian mythology, musicians of the deity Kuvera who excel in singing and dancing and have a human body and the head of a horse. They were regarded as the gods of music. In Buddhism, they are one of the eight kinds of nonhuman beings who protect the Buddha's teachings, as are the heavenly musicians called *gandharvas.*

King Above Jeweled Dignity and Virtue [宝威徳上王仏] (Skt Ratnatejobhyudgatarāja; Jpn Hōitokujō'ō-butsu): Also known as Jeweled Dignity. A Buddha who, according to the "Universal Worthy" (twenty-eighth) chapter of the Lotus Sutra, lives in a land in the east and is the teacher of Bodhisattva Universal Worthy. *See also* "Encouragements of the Bodhisattva Universal Worthy" chapter.

"King Wonderful Adornment" chapter [妙荘厳王品] (Jpn *Myōshōgon-nō-hon*): The twenty-seventh chapter of the Lotus Sutra. *See* "Former Affairs of King Wonderful Adornment" chapter.

Kinkara [吉迦夜] (n.d.) (Skt; Jpn Kikkaya): A monk from Central Asia who translated Buddhist texts in China. In 472, together with T'an-yao, who held the position of national director of the clergy, Kinkara translated the Storehouse of Various Treasures Sutra and *A History of the Buddha's Successors.*

Kishimojin [鬼子母神] (Jpn): Mother of Demon Children. Originally regarded as a demonness, she was later revered as a god of procreation and easy delivery. In the "Dhāranī" (twenty-sixth) chapter of the Lotus Sutra, she pledges before Shakyamuni Buddha to safeguard the votaries of the sutra. *See* Mother of Demon Children.

Kiyomizu-dera [清水寺]: A temple of the Dharma Characteristics (Hossō) school located in Higashiyama Ward in Kyoto, Japan. According to that temple's tradition, a priest named Enchin (different from the Enchin who was the fifth chief priest of Enryaku-ji) came to the Higashiyama section of Kyoto to practice Buddhism in 778. Sakanoue no Tamuramaro (who later was commissioned to pacify the northeast of Japan's mainland and given the imperial title *Seii-taishōgun* or "great general who subdues the barbarians" for doing so, which became the origin of the title *shōgun*) happened to pass by while seeking water on a hunting trip, met Enchin, and became his follower. They worked together to arrange the making of a golden image of the eleven-faced, forty-armed Bodhisattva Perceiver of the World's Sounds. When it was completed in 798, a temporary hall was built to enshrine it. This structure was called Kiyomizu-dera. In 810 it was made into a national temple and designated by the imperial court as an official place of prayer for the protection of the nation. It became affiliated with Kōfuku-ji temple of the Dharma Characteristics school and was consequently burned on several occasions by the priests of Enryaku-ji on Mount Hiei, who were hostile toward Kōfuku-ji. The present main hall of Kiyomizu-dera was rebuilt in 1633.

Kizil caves [キジル石窟] (Jpn Kijiru-sekkutsu): The Buddhist cave-temples located about seventy kilometers west of Kucha, a city in the Sinkiang Uighur Autonomous Region of China. The Kizil Buddhist caves, more than 230 of them, are the largest such cluster of caves in the Tarim Basin. The wall paintings preserved in these caves are second in number only to the Mo-kao Caves at Tun-huang. These paintings depict legends of Shakyamuni's previous births and events of his life, including his entrance into nirvana. Research conducted there in the early twentieth century made the Kizil caves a focus of attention. Although opinions differ as to the dates of their creation, it is generally thought that these caves were built over a period beginning in the fourth century and ending in the eighth century.

klesha [煩悩] (Skt; Jpn *bonnō*): *See* earthly desires.

knot of flesh on the head [肉髻相] (Skt *ushnīsha-shiraskatā;* Jpn *nikkei-sō*): Also, protuberant knot of flesh or fleshy protuberance. A knot of flesh resembling a topknot said to exist on the crown of a Buddha's head; one of a Buddha's thirty-two features. This feature is identified with "the unseen crown of the head," one of a Buddha's eighty characteristics, indicating that the crown of a Buddha's head cannot be seen by ordinary people. This knot of flesh is often depicted in Buddhist images and sculptures. *See also* eighty characteristics; thirty-two features.

Kō, the lay nun of [国府尼] (n.d.) (Jpn Kō-ama or Kō-no-ama): A follower of Nichiren who lived in the capital of the island province of Sado in the Sea of Japan. *Kō* means provincial office or seat of government; hence she and her husband were commonly known, respectively, as the lay nun of Kō and the lay priest of Kō. The government seat of Sado Province is thought to have been at the site of the present-day town of Mano. While Nichiren was in exile on Sado from 1271 through 1274, she converted to his teachings together with her husband. They gave Nichiren offerings and helped protect him. After Nichiren was pardoned and left Sado, she sent her husband to Minobu to visit him and continued to send him offerings.

Kō, the lay priest of [国府入道] (Jpn Kō-nyūdō): A follower of Nichiren, who lived in Sado Island, Japan. *See* Kō, the lay nun of.

kōan [公案] (Jpn; Chin *kung-an*): Originally, in China, a government decree or public notice. In the Zen (Chin Ch'an) school, it refers to a master's statements, including questions and answers directed at his disciples. A famous example of *kōan* is the statement "Listen to the sound of one hand clapping." The purpose of *kōan* is to help Zen practitioners transcend the rational intellect and develop intuition. They are used as objects of meditation for developing insight and also as tests of whether a student has obtained a certain level of insight. In China, the use of *kōan* began in the T'ang dynasty (618–907).

Kōben [高弁]: Also known as Myōe, a priest of the Flower Garland (Kegon) school in Japan. *See* Myōe.

Kōbō [弘法] (774–835): Also known as Kūkai. The founder of the True Word (Shingon) school in Japan. His posthumous honorific name and title are the Great Teacher Kōbō. A native of Sanuki Province in Shikoku in southern Japan, he went to Nara in 788 and studied the Chinese classics, including *Analects* by Confucius, under the Confucian scholar Ato no Ōtari, his maternal uncle. In 791 he entered the Confucian college at Nara and continued his study of the Chinese classics. Around that time, a priest (Gonsō according to one view) taught him the Esoteric Buddhist practice of chanting a certain mantra one million times with belief in Bodhisattva Space Treasury. This practice, it was said, would enable one to understand all the Buddhist teachings and memorize all the sutras. Kōbō devoted himself to this practice. After this, he was ordained a Buddhist priest by Gonsō in 793. In 797 he wrote *The Essentials of the Three Teachings,* proclaiming the superiority of Buddhism over Taoism and Confucianism.

In 804 Kōbō traveled to China and studied Esoteric Buddhism at Ch'ang-an under Hui-kuo. Hui-kuo schooled him in the esoteric doctrines of the Womb Realm and the Diamond Realm, gave him the name Universal Illumination and Diamond, and qualified him to transmit the secret doctrines. In 806, the year after Hui-kuo's death, Kōbō returned to Japan, bringing with him copies of the two mandalas of Esoteric Buddhism, esoteric scriptures, and ritual prayer implements. After his arrival, he stayed at Kanzeon-ji temple in Chikuzen Province and elsewhere, and then went to the capital, Kyoto. In 810 he was appointed the chief priest of Tōdai-ji temple in Nara, and in 816 the imperial court granted him Mount Kōya in Kii Province. There he built Kongōbu-ji temple and devoted himself to the dissemination of Esoteric Buddhism. In 823 the imperial court presented him with Tō-ji temple in Kyoto, which he made into a center for the study and practice of Esoteric Buddhism. His works include *A Comparison of Exoteric and Esoteric Buddhism, The Doctrine of Attaining Buddhahood in One's Present Form,* and *The Treatise on the Ten Stages of the Mind.* Kōbō was also an accomplished calligrapher.

Kōchi [広智] (n.d.): A priest of the Tendai school in Japan during the late eighth and early ninth centuries. He began his studies under Dōchū, who was a disciple of Ganjin (688–763; Chin Chien-chen), founder of the Japanese Precepts (Ritsu) school. Kōchi lived at Daiji-ji temple in Shimotsuke Province. After Dōchū's death, he became a central figure in the Precepts school in the Kanto area. He was widely revered for his outstanding virtue and was called Bodhisattva Kōchi. When Dengyō traveled to Kanto, Kōchi learned the Tendai meditation and the doctrines of the Lotus Sutra from him. Following Dengyō's instruction, he devoted himself to propagating the Tendai doctrines in Kanto. Kōchi is said to have assisted Dengyō in copying sutras. He conducted the tonsure ceremony for Jikaku, a native of Shimotsuke Province, and introduced him to Dengyō. Jikaku later became the third chief priest of Enryaku-ji, the head temple of the Tendai school.

Kōfuku-ji [興福寺]: One of the two head temples of the Dharma Characteristics (Hossō) school in Nara, Japan, the other being Yakushi-ji temple. Both were counted among the so-called seven major temples of Nara. The Fujiwara clan, which would come to dominate Japan's imperial government from the ninth to the twelfth century, built the temple in 669. At that time it was known as Yamashina-dera. In 672 it was moved to Umayasaka and renamed Umayasaka-dera. In 710, when the capital moved to Nara, Umayasaka-dera temple was also moved to Nara and renamed Kōfuku-ji. There it prospered as the family temple of the Fujiwara clan. It also became an important center for the study of the doctrines of the Dharma Characteristics and Dharma Analysis Treasury (Kusha) schools, and produced many learned scholars. With the decline of the Fujiwara clan, Kōfuku-ji declined, and after the Meiji Restoration (1868), it was briefly linked with the True Word (Shingon) school. In 1882, however, Kōfuku-ji became independent as a head temple of the Dharma Characteristics school. It is known for its large collection of national art treasures.

Kōjō [光定] (779–858): A priest of the Tendai school and a native of Iyo Province in Japan. In 808 he went to Enryaku-ji, the head temple of the Tendai school on Mount Hiei, and became Dengyō's disciple. In 812 he received the precepts at Tōdai-ji temple and learned the teachings of the Womb Realm and the Diamond Realm from Kōbō, founder of the Japanese True Word (Shingon) school, in a ceremony performed at Takaosan-ji temple. He exerted himself to help realize his teacher's desire to establish a Mahayana ordination center on Mount Hiei. Imperial permission for construction was finally granted seven days after Dengyō's death in 822. In 854 Kōjō became the superintendent of Enryaku-ji temple. He wrote *The Record of the Precepts of the One Mind*, an account of the efforts that led to the establishment of a Mahayana ordination center that is regarded as the primary history of those events.

Kokālika [瞿伽利] (Skt, Pali; Jpn Kugyari or Kukari): A member of the Shākya tribe of ancient India and an enemy of Shakyamuni Buddha. He became a disciple of Shakyamuni but, falling under Devadatta's influence, slandered the Buddha's disciples Shāriputra and Maudgalyāyana. According to *The Treatise on the Great Perfection of Wisdom*, Kokālika was always looking for fault or error on the part of Shāriputra and Maudgalyāyana. One day, caught in a heavy rain, Shāriputra and Maudgalyāyana stayed overnight at a potter's house. Kokālika, who happened to pass by this house the next morning and to know that a woman also lived there, spread false rumors to the effect that Shāriputra and Maudgalyāyana had had relations with a woman, which was forbidden them as monks. Shakyamuni admonished Kokālika against spreading false rumors, but Kokālika refused to heed his admonition. It is said that on that day boils broke out all over his body and that he died that night in a fit of agony, falling into the hell of the great crimson lotus, the most terrible of the eight cold hells.

Kokan Shiren [虎関師錬] (1278–1346): Also known as Shiren. A priest of the Rinzai school of Zen in Japan. He received the precepts at Enryaku-ji, the head temple of the Tendai school, and later went to Kamakura where he studied under I-shan I-ning, a priest of the Lin-chi (Jpn Rinzai) school who had come from China to Japan in 1299. In 1313 he returned to his birthplace, Kyoto, and lived at Tōfuku-ji, Nanzen-ji, and other temples. He enjoyed the confidence of the Retired Emperor Gofushimi and often preached the Zen teachings at the imperial court. He was also a distinguished poet and scholar of so-called Gozan literature (Chinese learning that developed in medieval Japan at key Zen temples in Kyoto and Kamakura). He was posthumously granted the title Teacher of the Nation Hongaku by the imperial court. His works include *The Genkō Era Biographies of Eminent Priests,* a biographical history of Buddhism in Japan.

Kokūzō [虚空蔵] (Jpn): The bodhisattva Space Treasury (Kokūzō-bosatsu), whose wisdom and good fortune are said to be as vast and boundless as the universe. *See* Space Treasury.

Komatsubara Persecution [小松原の法難] (Jpn Komatsubara-no-hōnan): An attempt by Tōjō Kagenobu and his men to kill Nichiren at Komatsubara in Awa Province, Japan, on the eleventh day of the eleventh month, 1264. Kagenobu, the steward of Tōjō Village and a believer of the Pure Land teachings, had tried but failed to harm Nichiren earlier when the latter publicly proclaimed his teaching and denounced the Pure Land teachings in 1253. Nichiren was helped to escape at that time. After being pardoned from his exile in Izu (1261–1263), Nichiren returned to Kamakura. In 1264 he visited his native village in Awa. His father had already died in 1258, and his mother was now seriously ill. Nichiren prayed for her, and she recovered from her illness, living four more years. Nichiren stayed in Awa for a while, taking lodging at a temple called Renge-ji. At that time, a believer named Kudō Yoshitaka invited Nichiren to stay at his home. At dusk, en route to Yoshitaka's residence, Nichiren and his party of about ten people were ambushed by Kagenobu and his men at a place known as Komatsubara. In the ensuing fight,

Nichiren suffered a sword cut to his forehead, and his left hand was broken; among his followers, Kyōnin-bō was killed, and Kudō Yoshitaka died of the wounds he suffered.

Kōmoku-ten [広目天] (Jpn): The heavenly king Wide-Eyed. One of the four heavenly kings. *See* Wide-Eyed.

Kongōbu-ji [金剛峯寺]: The head temple of the True Word (Shingon) school, located on Mount Kōya in Wakayama Prefecture, Japan. Its full name is Kōya-san Kongōbu-ji. In 816 Kōbō, the school's founder, requested and was granted Mount Kōya by the imperial court. Thereafter he set about building the temple structures, which were completed after his death, late in the ninth century.

Kōnichi, the lay nun [光日尼] (Jpn Kōnichi-ama): A follower of Nichiren. *See* Kōnichi-bō.

Kōnichi-bō [光日房] (n.d.): Also known as the lay nun Kōnichi or the Honorable Kōnichi. A follower of Nichiren who lived in Amatsu of Awa Province, Japan. Several letters to her from Nichiren are extant. Her son Yashirō converted her to Nichiren's teachings. While Nichiren was in exile on Sado Island between 1271 and 1274, she sent him robes and other articles, and continued to send him offerings after he took up residence at Mount Minobu in the fifth month of 1274. Her son Yashirō died that year. From Mount Minobu, Nichiren sent her a letter known as *Letter to Kōnichi-bō*. In it, he wrote that, though her son was a warrior, he would be saved from the evil paths of existence because of her prayers, and that "because he [himself] believed in the Lotus Sutra, he may have become the one who will lead his parents to Buddhahood" (664). She apparently maintained strong faith in Nichiren's teachings and enjoyed his trust. Nichiren sent her *The Actions of the Votary of the Lotus Sutra,* an autobiographical account covering the nine years of his life from 1268 to 1277.

Kōsai [幸西] (1163–1247): Also known as Jōkaku-bō. A priest of the Pure Land (Jōdo) school in Japan and a disciple of the school's founder Hōnen. He first studied the Tendai doctrine on Mount Hiei, but converted to the Pure Land teachings in 1198. He advocated the doctrine of one-time recitation of the Nembutsu. This doctrine states that rebirth in the Pure Land is assured with a single recitation of the Nembutsu—the invocation of Amida Buddha's name with the phrase Namu Amida Butsu ("Homage to Amida Buddha"); therefore, there is no need for repeated recitation or chanting of this phrase. Kōsai is regarded as the originator of the doctrine of one-time recitation. In contrast, Ryūkan, another disciple of Hōnen, taught the many-time recitation of the Nembutsu. In 1206, when disciples of Hōnen held a prayer gathering at Shishigatani in

Kyoto, two court ladies who served the Retired Emperor Gotoba attended the ceremony and decided to become nuns of the Pure Land school. This angered the retired emperor, who punished Hōnen and his main disciples. Four disciples were executed, and Hōnen was exiled. In the second month of the next year, Kōsai was exiled to the island of Shikoku, but later pardoned. In 1227, when the Pure Land school was again persecuted, Kōsai was exiled to the island of Iki. Later he was pardoned and propagated the Pure Land teachings in Shimōsa Province.

Kosala [憍薩羅国] (Skt, Pali; Jpn Kyōsara-koku): Also known as Koshala. A kingdom of ancient India, in the eastern part of what is now Uttar Pradesh, India's northern state. Around the sixth century B.C.E., i.e., during Shakyamuni's lifetime, Kosala was one of the sixteen great states in India and, along with Magadha, one of the two greatest powers in the subcontinent. The capital was Shrāvastī. Kosala was a center for Shakyamuni's activities; after his enlightenment, he frequently visited and preached in Shrāvastī, and often spent the rainy season there. In Shakyamuni's time, the king of Kosala was Prasenajit, a follower of the Buddha who aided the spread of Buddhism. Kapilavastu, the small kingdom of the Shākyas from which Shakyamuni came, was a subject state of Kosala. Jetavana Monastery, donated by Sudatta to the Buddhist Order, was on the outskirts of Shrāvastī. Kosala expanded its frontiers, placing its southern neighbor, the kingdom of Kāshī, under its rule and vying with Magadha for control of the Ganges Valley. When Ajātashatru, the son of the Magadhan king Bimbisāra, ascended the throne, he waged war on Kosala. Though they had competed for territory until that time, these two kingdoms had been on generally good terms because the wife of Bimbisāra was the sister of Prasenajit. The war turned out to be a long one, and Ajātashatru defeated Kosala during the reign of Prasenajit's son, Virūdhaka.

Kosambī [憍賞弥国] (Pali; Jpn Kyōshōmi-koku): The capital of Vatsa, one of the sixteen great states in India in Shakyamuni's time. *See* Kaushāmbī.

kōsen-rufu [広宣流布] (Jpn): Wide propagation, or wide proclamation and propagation. A term from the Lotus Sutra that literally means to declare and spread widely. The "Medicine King" (twenty-third) chapter of the Lotus Sutra reads, "After I [Shakyamuni Buddha] have passed into extinction, in the last five-hundred-year period you must spread it abroad widely *(kōsen-rufu)* throughout Jambudvīpa and never allow it to be cut off." Nichiren (1222–1282), identifying himself as the votary of the Lotus Sutra, made it his lifelong mission to fulfill the above injunction of the Buddha, that is, *kōsen-rufu*. He saw widely propagating his teaching of

Nam-myoho-renge-kyo, which he identified as the essence of the sutra, as the fulfillment of that mission.

Nichiren writes in his *Selection of the Time,* "Can there be any doubt that, after this period described in the Great Collection Sutra when 'the pure Law will become obscured and lost,' the great pure Law of the Lotus Sutra will be spread far and wide *(kōsen-rufu)* throughout Japan and all the other countries of Jambudvīpa?" (550). In *The True Aspect of All Phenomena,* he also writes, "At the time when the Law has spread far and wide *(kōsen-rufu),* the entire Japanese nation will chant Nam-myoho-renge-kyo, as surely as an arrow aimed at the earth cannot miss the target" (385).

In *On Practicing the Buddha's Teachings,* he writes: "The time will come when all people will abandon the various kinds of vehicles and take up the single vehicle of Buddhahood, and the Mystic Law alone will flourish throughout the land. When the people all chant Nam-myoho-renge-kyo, the wind will no longer buffet the branches, and the rain will no longer break the clods of soil. The world will become as it was in the ages of Fu Hsi and Shen Nung" (392). He meant that the spread of the Mystic Law would bring about peace in society and nature.

koti [倶胝] (Skt, Pali; Jpn *kutei*): An ancient Indian numerical unit. There are various interpretations of the value of a *koti,* which is defined as ten million, one hundred million, etc. The term appears in Buddhist sutras often as a factor of an astronomically large number describing an incomprehensible expanse of time or space.

Kōya, Mount [高野山] (Jpn Kōya-san): The location of Kongōbu-ji, the head temple of the True Word (Shingon) school, in Japan. *See* Kongōbu-ji.

Krakucchanda [拘留孫仏] (Skt; Jpn Kuruson-butsu): The fourth of the seven Buddhas of the past described in the Long Āgama Sutra, the Seven Buddhas Sutra, and other Buddhist texts. The first three are said to have appeared in the past Glorious Kalpa, and the other four, the last being Shakyamuni, in the present Wise Kalpa. Krakucchanda is the first of the four Buddhas in the present Wise Kalpa. The Wise Kalpa Sutra describes Krakucchanda as the first of the thousand Buddhas in the present Wise Kalpa.

Kriki [訖哩枳王] (Skt; Jpn Kiriki-ō): A king who was a devout follower of Kāshyapa Buddha. Kāshyapa Buddha is the sixth of the seven Buddhas of the past, the last being Shakyamuni, according to the Long Āgama Sutra and other texts. The Protection of the Sovereign of the Nation Sutra describes King Kriki's dreams and their interpretation by Kāshyapa Buddha. According to the sutra, on one night the king had two dreams, one about ten monkeys and the other about a white elephant. The ten monkeys lived as a group. Nine of them harassed people in the city by stealing their food and drink. The tenth refused to join them and contented himself with what little he had. For this, the other nine monkeys ostracized him. In the other dream, there was a white elephant with an extra mouth at his tail that continuously devoured food yet the elephant always remained thin. King Kriki asks Kāshyapa Buddha about the meaning of the two dreams.

The Buddha explains that the dreams represent the conditions of the Buddhist world following the death of Shakyamuni Buddha, who will appear in an age defiled by the five impurities. The ten monkeys represent ten kinds of monk-followers of Shakyamuni; the ostracized one who has little desire and knows satisfaction represents the true *shramana,* or seeker of the way. The other nine kinds of monks, represented by the nine greedy monkeys, will slander the true monk to the ruler and ministers, accusing him of performing evil acts and violating the precepts. As a result, the ruler will banish that monk, and Shakyamuni's teaching will be lost. These monks have nine different ulterior motives, such as the desire for fame and profit. The white elephant with two mouths represents those government officials in an age after Shakyamuni Buddha's death who always seek recognition and material reward from their ruler while harassing the common people. Ultimately, when they bring ruin upon themselves and their homes, they will renounce secular life and become evil monks, embrace erroneous ideas, and fall into hell. In this sutra, Shakyamuni Buddha relates the story of King Kriki's dreams to King Ajātashatru.

Krita [訖利多王] (n.d.) (Skt; Jpn Kirita-ō): A king of Kashmir in ancient India who suppressed Buddhism. He banished Buddhist monks and destroyed their temples, annihilating Buddhism in that area. For this, Himatala, king of Tukhāra and a patron of Buddhism, killed him. This story appears in *The Record of the Western Regions,* Hsüan-tsang's account of his travels through Central Asia and India in the seventh century. This work describes Krita as a person who appeared six hundred years after Shakyamuni's death.

krosha [倶盧舎] (Skt; Jpn *kurosha*): A unit of measurement in ancient India. The distance from which the lowing of a great ox or the sound of a drum can be heard. It is said to be one-fourth or one-eighth of a *yojana,* or around one or two kilometers. The word *krosha* means a cry or yell. *Krosha* is also described as the length of five hundred archery bows arranged end to end.

kshānti [忍・忍辱] (Skt; Jpn *nin* or *ninniku*): Forbearance, one of the six *pāramitās,* or six practices required of bodhisattvas. *See* forbearance.

Kshatriya [刹帝利] (Skt; Jpn *setsuteiri*): The second highest of the four castes in ancient Indian Brahmanic society, just below the Brahmans, or priestly caste. Also, a member of this caste. The Kshatriyas consisted of nobles and warriors and were the ruling class in secular affairs.

kshetra [国土・刹土] (Skt; Jpn *kokudo* or *setsudo*): Land, field, region, country, sphere of action, or sacred place. *Kshetra* is a component of a number of Buddhist terms, e.g., *punya-kshetra* (field of blessing or field of good fortune) and *buddha-kshetra* (the Buddha land).

Kshitigarbha [地蔵菩薩] (Skt; Jpn Jizō-bosatsu): The bodhisattva Earth Repository. *See* Earth Repository.

kū [空] (Jpn): *See* non-substantiality.

Kuang-che-ssu [光宅寺] (PY Guangzhesi; Jpn Kōtaku-ji): A temple built in 502 (504 according to another account) for the priest Fa-yün by Emperor Wu of the Liang dynasty in China at the capital Chien-k'ang. Kuang-che means "abode of light." Fa-yün lectured there on the Lotus Sutra, and for this Kuang-che-ssu gained wide renown. His lectures on the Lotus Sutra were recorded and compiled by his disciples as *The Meaning of the Lotus Sutra.* Fa-yün was also known as Kuang-che. In 587 T'ien-t'ai stayed at Kuang-che-ssu, where he lectured on the Lotus Sutra and the Benevolent Kings Sutra. His disciple Chang-an later compiled his lectures on the Lotus Sutra at the temple in a work called *The Words and Phrases of the Lotus Sutra.*

Kuang-hsiu [広脩・広修] (771–843) (PY Guangxiu; Jpn Kōshū or Kōshu): A priest of the T'ien-t'ai school in China. He became a disciple of Tao-sui, under whom he studied the T'ien-t'ai teachings. He lectured on *Great Concentration and Insight* by T'ien-t'ai. When Ensai, a priest of the Tendai school in Japan, brought with him to China a list of thirty questions (fifty questions according to another account) about the T'ien-t'ai teachings in 839, Kuang-hsiu provided the answers. Among his disciples were Wu-wai, Wei-chüan, and Liang-hsü.

Kuan-ting [灌頂] (PY Guanding; Jpn Kanjō): Also known as Chang-an, successor of T'ien-t'ai. *See* Chang-an.

Kuan-yin [観音菩薩] (PY Guanyin; Jpn Kannon-bosatsu): The popular Chinese name of the bodhisattva Perceiver of the World's Sounds. *See* Perceiver of the World's Sounds.

Kubo, the lay nun of [窪尼] (n.d.) (Jpn Kubo-no-ama): A follower of Nichiren who lived in Suruga Province, Japan, during the thirteenth century. From the contents of the several letters Nichiren addressed to her, she appears to have been a sincere believer who frequently sent offerings to him. One explanation identifies the lay nun of Kubo with the wife of the lay priest Takahashi Rokurō Hyōe, and another with the lay nun Myōshin. The contents of the twelve letters Nichiren addressed to these three women, however, suggest that they were all the same woman. These letters suggest that the lay nun Myōshin was a member of the Yui family and the wife of the lay priest Takahashi. The same person was also an aunt of Nikkō, Nichiren's successor. She became a lay nun and assumed the name Myōshin when her husband, the lay priest, was ill. In 1277, after his death, she went with her young daughter to live with the Yui family in a place called Kubo, from which the designation "the lay nun of Kubo" probably derives.

Kucha [亀茲・庫車] (Jpn Kiji or Kosha): An oasis city in the Sinkiang Uighur Autonomous Region of China. In ancient times, it was inhabited by a people who spoke Kuchean, or Tocharian B, one of two forms of Tocharian, an Indo-European language. Kucha was an important center on the road that ran along the southern foot of the Tien Shan range on the northern rim of the Tarim Basin. This road is now known as the northern route of the Silk Road. Kucha accommodated the eastward spread of Buddhism, which originated in India and was introduced to Kucha around the beginning of the first century.

From around the fourth century, the exchange between Kucha and the Buddhist community in the northwestern regions of India increased; Kucha became a major Buddhist center in Central Asia, along with Khotan on the southern route of the Silk Road along the southern rim of the Tarim Basin. In the fourth and fifth centuries, many Buddhists emerged from Kucha, including Kumārajīva, one of the most important translators of Buddhist scriptures into Chinese. Kumārajīva's mother was a younger sister of the king of Kucha. In Kucha, the Hinayana and Mahayana traditions existed side by side, but Hinayana was predominant when the Chinese priest Hsüan-tsang visited there around 630 on his way to India. He noted in his *Record of the Western Regions* that more than one hundred monasteries existed there, where more than five thousand monks lived and studied the doctrines of the Sarvāstivāda school, a major Hinayana school. He also noted that Kucha grew various grains, grapes, peaches, pomegranates, and other fruits; that it produced gold, copper, iron, and other minerals; and that the performance of orchestral music was a specialty there. In 658 China's T'ang dynasty made Kucha a Chinese protectorate. In the ninth century Kucha came under Uighur control, and eventually Islam superseded Buddhism. The Kizil caves, about seventy kilometers west of Kucha, still remain, preserving artifacts from the age when Buddhism flourished there. These Buddhist cave-temples were made in the period from the fourth to the eighth century, and they contain many murals depicting the events of Shakyamuni Buddha's life and the legends of his previous births. About thirty kilometers southwest of Kucha are the Kumtura caves, dating from the eighth or ninth century. The murals in these Buddhist caves depict Amida Buddha's Pure Land and Medicine Master Buddha, among other themes.

Kudō Yoshitaka [工藤吉隆] (d. 1264): A follower of Nichiren and the lord of Amatsu in Awa Province, Japan. His name and title were Kudō Sakon-no-jō Yoshitaka. Nichiren sent him a letter, known as *The Four Debts of Gratitude,* which he wrote while in exile in Izu. On the eleventh day of the eleventh month, 1264, Nichiren was en route with some of his followers to Kudō Yoshitaka's residence at Yoshitaka's invitation. When the party reached a place called Komatsubara in Tōjō Village, Tōjō Kagenobu, the steward of the village and a believer of the Pure Land teachings, attacked them with a band of his men. Intent on protecting Nichiren, Kudō Yoshitaka hastened to the scene and fought the attackers, but was seriously wounded and died. *See also* Komatsubara Persecution.

K'uei-chi [窺基] (PY Kuiji; Jpn Kiki): Also known as Tz'u-en. The founder of the Dharma Characteristics (Fa-hsiang) school in China. *See* Tz'u-en.

Kūkai [空海]: Also known as Kōbō. The founder of the True Word (Shingon) school in Japan. *See* Kōbō.

Kukkutapāda, Mount [鶏足山] (Skt; Jpn Keisoku-sen): Also known as Mount Kukkutapada or Mount Gurupādaka. A mountain in the state of Magadha in ancient India, where Mahākāshyapa, one of Shakyamuni's ten major disciples, died. The name of Mount Kukkutapāda was rendered into Chinese as Chicken Leg Mountain, and Mount Gurupādaka as Honored Foot Mountain. The Chinese priest Fa-hsien, who traveled to India to study the Buddhist scriptures in the beginning of the fifth century, described the mountain as a dangerous place inhabited by tigers, wolves, and other savage animals. Tradition has it that Mahākāshyapa is still living on Mount Kukkutapāda and waiting for the appearance of the future Buddha, Maitreya; when Maitreya appears, Mahākāshyapa will present him with Shakyamuni Buddha's robe.

Kukkutārāma Monastery [鶏頭摩寺] (Skt, Pali; Jpn Keizuma-ji): Also known as Kurkutārāma Monastery. A monastery built by King Ashoka in the third century B.C.E. and located southeast of Pātaliputra, the capital of the Maurya dynasty, in India. According to *The Record of the Western Regions,* Hsüan-tsang's record of his travels through Central Asia and India in the seventh century, King Ashoka often visited the monastery with his retainers and made various offerings such as robes, food, and drink to the monks. Later King Pushyamitra, the founder of the Shunga dynasty, destroyed Kukkutārāma Monastery and killed many monks. *See also* Pushyamitra.

Kumārajīva [鳩摩羅什] (344–413) (Skt; Jpn Kumarajū): A Buddhist scholar and a translator of Buddhist scriptures into Chinese. Another account has him living from 350 through 409. His father was Kumārayāna, the son of a former minister of an Indian kingdom, who had renounced his right to his father's position in order to become a monk. His mother was Jīvakā, a younger sister of the king of Kucha in Central Asia. When Kumārajīva was seven years old, his mother renounced secular life and traveled with him to India and several other countries to study Buddhism. As a result, Kumārajīva mastered several languages. He first studied Hinayana Buddhism and later received instruction in the Mahayana teachings from Shūryasoma. When he returned home, he spread Mahayana Buddhism, and his reputation became known as far away as China.

In 382 Fu Chien, ruler of the Former Ch'in dynasty, ordered General Lü Kuang and his army to invade Kucha and other countries, and to bring Kumārajīva back to Ch'ang-an, the dynastic capital. Lü Kuang took Kumārajīva prisoner but on the way back learned of the fall of the Former Ch'in dynasty. He decided to remain in Liang-chou, where he held Kumārajīva for some sixteen years. Finally, however, Kumārajīva made his way to Ch'ang-an in 401 at the invitation of Yao Hsing, ruler of the Later Ch'in dynasty. There he was given the position of teacher of the nation and immersed himself in the translation of Buddhist scriptures. According to *A Collection of Records concerning the Tripitaka,* he translated 35 works in 294 volumes, accomplishing this in a mere ten years. Prominent among his translations were those of the Lotus Sutra, the Larger Wisdom Sutra, the Smaller Wisdom Sutra, the Vimalakīrti Sutra, the Benevolent Kings Sutra, the Amida Sutra, *The Ten Divisions of Monastic Rules, The Treatise on the Great Perfection of Wisdom, The Treatise on the Middle Way, The One-Hundred-Verse Treatise, The Treatise on the Twelve Gates,* and *The Treatise on the Establishment of Truth.* Prized by later generations for their excellence and clarity, Kumārajīva's translations profoundly influenced the subsequent development of Buddhism in China and Japan. Kumārajīva also fostered many disciples, more than three thousand by some accounts.

Kumāralāta [鳩摩羅駄] (Skt; Jpn Kumarada): Also known as Kumārata. *See* Kumārata.

Kumārata [鳩摩羅駄] (n.d.) (Skt; Jpn Kumarada): Also known as Kumāralāta or Kumāralabdha. The eighteenth of Shakyamuni's twenty-three, or the nineteenth of his twenty-four, successors. According to *A History of the Buddha's Successors,* he was born in Takshashilā in the northwestern part of ancient India and was very wise even as a child. He became a monk and is said to have later inherited Shakyamuni Buddha's teachings from Samghayashas. His wisdom and scholarship were famed throughout India and attracted numerous people to Buddhism. Hsüan-tsang's *Record of the Western Regions* lists Kumārata as one of the "four suns," the others being Ashvaghosha, Nāgārjuna, and Āryadeva. They were called "suns" because they were considered to illuminate the world with the light of wisdom. Kumārata is regarded as the founder of the Sautrāntika school. He transferred the Buddha's teachings to Jayata. It is said that he lived near the late third century, but there is no clear evidence confirming that date.

Kumārayāna [鳩摩羅炎] (n.d.) (Skt; Jpn Kumaraen): The father of Kumārajīva. He lived in the fourth century and was the son of a minister of an Indian kingdom, but forsook his position to enter the Buddhist Order. He left India and crossed the Pamir range to the north, traveling toward China. In the Central Asian kingdom of Kucha, he was officially welcomed by the king and was designated as teacher of the nation. In compliance with royal decree, he married Jīvakā, the king's younger sister, and called their son Kumārajīva, combining their names. According to legend, when Kumārayāna left India, he brought with him a statue of Shakyamuni Buddha. It is said that he carried the statue during the day, and at night the statue carried him.

kumbhānda [鳩槃荼] (Skt; Jpn *kuhanda*): A class of demons. *Kumbhāndas* are regarded as evil spirits who devour human vitality. They are also said to attend the heavenly king Increase and Growth, one of the four heavenly kings.

Kundalī [軍荼利明王] (Skt; Jpn Gundari-myō'ō): The wisdom king Kundalī. One of the five great wisdom kings revered in Esoteric Buddhism. The other four are the wisdom kings Immovable, Conqueror of the Threefold World, Great Awesome Virtue, and Diamond Yaksha. The wisdom kings are a group of deities said to destroy all obstacles. Kundalī is depicted as an angry figure and is believed to subdue all demons including *asuras.*

Kuntī [皐諦・皐諦女] (Skt; Jpn Kōdai or Kōdai-nyo): One of the ten demon daughters who appear in the "Dhāranī" (twenty-sixth) chapter of the Lotus Sutra. After the ten demon daughters pledge in the presence of Shakyamuni Buddha to guard the practitioners of the sutra, the Buddha tells them: "If you can shield and guard those who accept and uphold the mere name of the Lotus Sutra, your merit will be immeasurable.

How much more so if you shield and guard those who accept and uphold it in its entirety . . . Kuntī, you and your attendants should shield and guard the teachers of the Law such as these!" *See also* ten demon daughters.

Kuo-ch'ing-ssu [国清寺] (PY Guoqingsi; Jpn Kokusei-ji): A temple of the T'ien-t'ai school on Mount T'ien-t'ai in China. It was built in 598, the year after T'ien-t'ai's death (601 according to another account), by Prince Kuang of the Sui dynasty (later known as Emperor Yang of that dynasty) in compliance with T'ien-t'ai's will. Chang-an, T'ien-t'ai's successor, lived at Kuo-ch'ing-ssu, which prospered as the school's main center of practice. When Dengyō, who later founded the Japanese Tendai school, and his disciple Gishin went to China in 804, they studied at this temple. Many other Japanese priests studied there as well, among them Enchin (the fifth chief priest of the Tendai school head temple Enryaku-ji) and Eisai (the founder of the Rinzai school of Zen in Japan).

kuon-ganjo [久遠元初] (Jpn): Literally *kuon* means the remote past, and *ganjo,* beginning or foundation. This term appears in *On the Mystic Principle of the True Cause,* a work written by Nichiren in 1282. This work refers to "the Mystic Law, uncreated and eternal, of the Buddha of beginningless time *(kuon-ganjo),*" and states that the Mystic Law lies in the depths of the "Life Span" (sixteenth) chapter of the Lotus Sutra. Nichiren interprets *kuon-ganjo* on two different levels: (1) In the context of the "Life Span" chapter, *kuon* refers to the remote past when Shakyamuni originally attained enlightenment, and *ganjo,* to the foundation of his original enlightenment. (2) In *The Record of the Orally Transmitted Teachings,* Nichiren's oral teachings on the Lotus Sutra compiled by Nikkō in 1278, it is stated: "*Kuon* means something that was not worked for, that was not improved upon, but that exists just as it always has." *Orally Transmitted Teachings* continues: "Because we are speaking here of the Buddha eternally endowed with the three bodies, it is not a question of something attained for the first time at a certain time, or of something that was worked for. This is not the kind of Buddhahood that is adorned with the thirty-two features and eighty characteristics or that needs to be improved on in any way. Because this is the eternal and immutable Buddha in his original state, he exists just as he always has. This is what is meant by *kuon.*" The same section of *Orally Transmitted Teachings* concludes, "*Kuon* is Nam-myoho-renge-kyo, and 'true attainment' means awakening to the fact that one is eternally endowed with the three bodies." In essence, for Nichiren, *kuon,* or *kuon-ganjo,* means the eternal Law of Nam-myoho-renge-kyo and the original state of life that embodies Buddhahood.

Kuon-ji [久遠寺]: The head temple of the Nichiren school. Originally the Nichiren school was the generic term for all the schools derived from Nichiren's teachings, but today it is also the name of the school based at Kuon-ji on Mount Minobu in Yamanashi Prefecture, Japan. The temple's full name is Minobu-san Kuon-ji. It was founded by Nichiren on a site slightly removed from its present location in 1281, the year before his death. Hakiri Sanenaga, who was the steward of the area and one of Nichiren's followers, built the temple and donated it to Nichiren, who named it Minobu-san Kuon-ji. After Nichiren's death, however, Hakiri Sanenaga violated Nichiren's teachings, and in 1289 Nichiren's successor, Nikkō, left Minobu for the Ueno area. After that, Kuon-ji belonged to the lineage of Nikō, one of the six senior priests designated by Nichiren. In 1474, during the time of the eleventh chief priest, Nitchō, it was moved to its present location. *See also* five senior priests; Nikō.

Kurkutārāma Monastery [鶏頭摩寺] (Skt; Jpn Keizuma-ji): Also known as Kukkutārāma Monastery. *See* Kukkutārāma Monastery.

Kuru [倶盧洲] (Skt, Pali; Jpn Kuru-shū): Commonly known as Uttarakuru. One of the four continents surrounding Mount Sumeru in the ancient Indian worldview. It is located to the north of the mountain. *See* Uttarakuru.

kusha grass [吉祥草] (Skt; Jpn *kichijō-sō*): A grass regarded as sacred in ancient India and believed to possess powers of purification. *Kusha* grass, reaching up to sixty centimeters in height, was made into brooms used to sweep and purify ritual sites. Performers of rituals would often seat themselves or place offerings upon a mat made of *kusha* grass. It is said that Shakyamuni sat on a mat of *kusha* grass when he meditated and attained enlightenment under the *bodhi* tree.

Kushan [クシャーナ朝・貴霜朝] (Jpn Kushāna-chō or Kisō-chō): Also known as Kushāna. A dynasty that existed from the mid-first through the mid-third century in the area that included Afghanistan, the northwestern part of the Indian subcontinent, and parts of Central Asia. The territory of the Kushan kingdom contained an important section of the great trade route leading from China to India and westward to Parthia and Rome. Generally, the people of Kushan are regarded as having been of Iranian stock. In the second century B.C.E., the Yüeh-chih people, driven out of their territory by the Hsiung-nu (known to Europeans as the Huns), moved westward and established their kingdom in the region around the northern part of present-day Afghanistan. The Chinese knew it as the Great Yüeh-chih kingdom. The kingdom was then divided into five domains under five chieftains. One of the five chiefdoms was that of the Kushans. In the latter half of the first century C.E., the Kushans increased their power under the reign of Kujūla Kadphises, who conquered the other four chieftains and established his own dynasty. He extended his territory southward into Gandhara and the surrounding area, and the successive Kushan rulers expanded their dynastic territory still farther. During the reign of King Kanishka around the second century, the Kushan kingdom reached its height.

From the third century onward, Kushan power was limited by the rise of the Sasanids in Iran and local powers in northern India. Eventually the Kushan kingdom was attacked by the Sasanids, leading to its rapid decline and collapse in the mid-third century. Under Kushan rule, the northwestern region of the Indian subcontinent witnessed a prospering of the Hinayana Buddhist schools, especially the Sarvāstivāda, and the flourishing of Mahayana Buddhism as well. Images of the Buddha were created for the first time, and Gandhara Buddhist art developed. King Kanishka is known as a great patron of Buddhism, along with King Ashoka. Ashvaghosha, the renowned Buddhist scholar and poet from Kushan, actively spread Mahayana Buddhism.

Kusha school [俱舍宗] (Jpn Kusha-shū): *See* Dharma Analysis Treasury school.

Kushinagara [拘尸那揭羅・俱尸那城] (Skt; Pali Kusinārā; Jpn Kushinagara or Kushina-jō): The capital city of Malla in northern India, one of the sixteen great states of India during Shakyamuni's lifetime. Kushinagara is equated with the present-day city of Kasia in the northeastern part of Uttar Pradesh state. Shakyamuni died in a grove of sal trees in the northern part of Kushinagara. For this reason, Kushinagara is considered one of the four most sacred places associated with Shakyamuni, the others being the place of his birth, of his attainment of enlightenment, and of his first sermon. Shakyamuni's remains were cremated at Kushinagara, and his ashes were divided into eight parts, one of which was kept with the Mallas. It is said that the Mallas erected a stupa at Kushinagara to enshrine these ashes.

Kusinārā [拘尸那揭羅・俱尸那城] (Pali; Jpn Kushinagara or Kushina-jō): *See* Kushinagara.

Kūya [空也] (903–972): An early exponent of the Pure Land teachings in Japan who disseminated the worship of Amida Buddha. He was tonsured as a novice priest around age twenty at the provincial temple in Owari Province and assumed the name Kūya. He traveled the provinces chanting the name of Amida Buddha while dancing in the streets. He was therefore called the "Sage of the Streets." He also involved himself in such forms of social work as repairing roads and building bridges. In

948 he went to Mount Hiei, where he was ordained as a priest and given the name Kōshō. After that he began to receive support from members of the imperial court. In 963 he founded Saikō-ji temple, later known as Rokuharamitsu-ji, or the Six Pāramitās Temple, in Higashiyama in Kyoto, where he is said to have resided until he died.

Kyōnin-bō [鏡忍房] (d. 1264): A priest and a disciple of Nichiren in Japan. He was killed defending Nichiren when Tōjō Kagenobu, the steward of Tōjō Village and a believer of the Pure Land teachings, and his men attacked their party at Komatsubara on the eleventh day of the eleventh month, 1264. *See also* Komatsubara Persecution.

Kyō'ō [経王] (b. 1272): A daughter of Shijō Kingo and his wife Nichigen-nyo, both of whom were Nichiren's followers. They had two children, an older daughter named Tsukimaro (literally, Full Moon) born in the fifth month of 1271, and Kyō'ō (Sutra King), who was born in 1272. *Reply to Kyō'ō,* a letter from Nichiren, was written in the eighth month of 1273 in response to news that Kyō'ō had become seriously ill. Nichiren, who was living in exile on Sado Island, encouraged the couple with this letter to firmly believe in the Gohonzon, the object of devotion he inscribed, writing: "Nam-myoho-renge-kyo is like the roar of a lion. What sickness can therefore be an obstacle?" (412).

Kyō'ō Gokoku-ji [教王護国寺]: Also known as Tō-ji, the head temple of the Tō-ji branch of the True Word (Shingon) school, located in Kyoto, Japan. *See* Tō-ji.

L

Lalitavistara [普曜経] (Skt; Jpn *Fuyō-kyō*): *See* Multitudinous Graceful Actions Sutra.

Lamenting Heresy [歎異抄] (Jpn *Tan'ni-shō*): A work thought to have been written in the thirteenth century by Yuien, a disciple of Shinran, the founder of the True Pure Land (Jōdo Shin) school in Japan. Some have also attributed it to either Nyoshin or Kakunyo, respectively, the second and third chief priests of Hongan-ji temple, but Yuien's authorship is now generally accepted. Deploring the erroneous and divergent views proliferating among Shinran's followers after his death, Yuien compiled the teachings he had heard from Shinran in person. The work consists of eighteen chapters. The first nine chapters cite the late teacher's words, which came to constitute the core doctrines of the True Pure Land school. The latter nine refute what Yuien saw as the mistaken views of contemporary believers. This work is regarded as a concise statement of the school's belief in the all-importance of faith in "the power of another," or Amida's grace.

Lan-ch'i Tao-lung [蘭渓道隆] (PY Lanqi Daolong; Jpn Rankei Dōryū): A priest of the Rinzai (Lin-chi) school of Zen (Ch'an) in China who went to live in Japan. *See* Dōryū.

Land of Actual Reward [実報土] (Jpn *jippō-do*): One of the four kinds of lands. A realm inhabited by bodhisattvas in the higher stages of practice. *See also* four kinds of lands.

Land of Enlightened and Unenlightened Beings [凡聖同居土] (Jpn *bonshō-dōgo-do*): Also, Land of Sages and Common Mortals. Here ordinary people of the six paths live together with the sages of the four noble worlds. *See* Land of Sages and Common Mortals.

Land of Eternally Tranquil Light [常寂光土] (Jpn *jōjakkō-do*): Also, Land of Tranquil Light or Land of Eternal Light. The Buddha land, which is free from impermanence and impurity. The Land of Eternally Tranquil Light is one of the four kinds of lands described in the doctrine of the T'ien-t'ai school, the other three being the Land of Sages and Common Mortals, the Land of Transition, and the Land of Actual Reward. In many sutras, this *sahā* world is described as an impure land filled with delusions and sufferings, and the Buddha land as a pure land free from these and far removed from this *sahā* world. In contrast, the Lotus Sutra reveals the *sahā* world to be the Buddha land, or the Land of Eternally Tranquil Light, and explains that the nature of a land is determined by the minds of its inhabitants.

Land of Joy [歓喜国] (Skt Abhirati; Jpn Kangi-koku): Also, Land of Wonderful Joy. The land of the Buddha Akshobhya in the east. *See also* Akshobhya.

Land of Sages and Common Mortals [凡聖同居土] (Jpn *bonshō-dōgo-do*): Also, Land of Enlightened and Unenlightened Beings. Literally, "the land where common mortals and sages dwell together" and thus called "land of co-dwelling" for short. One of the four kinds of lands described in the doctrine of the T'ien-t'ai school. This is divided into two categories: impure lands of co-dwelling and pure lands of co-dwelling. The impure lands include this *sahā* world, where common mortals of the six paths (the realms of hell, hungry spirits, animals, *asuras,* human beings, and heavenly beings) and sages of the four noble worlds (the realms of voice-hearers, cause-awakened ones, bodhisattvas, and Buddhas) dwell together. The pure lands include Amida Buddha's Pure Land of Perfect Bliss, where human beings and heavenly beings are said to live together with the people of the three vehicles (voice-hearers, cause-awakened ones, and bodhisattvas) and the Buddha.

Land of Tranquil Light [寂光土] (Jpn *jakkō-do*): Also, Land of Eternally Tranquil Light. The land where a Buddha lives. One of the four kinds of lands. *See* Land of Eternally Tranquil Light.

Land of Transition [方便土] (Jpn *hōben-do*): One of the four kinds of lands. A realm inhabited by voice-hearers, cause-awakened ones, and bodhisattvas in the lower stages of practice. *See also* four kinds of lands.

Land of Wonderful Joy [妙喜国] (Jpn Myōki-koku): The land of the Buddha Akshobhya in the east. *See also* Akshobhya.

Lankāvatāra Sutra [楞伽経] (Skt; Chin *Leng-ch'ieh-ching;* Jpn *Ryōga-kyō*): A Mahayana sutra that discusses the Consciousness-Only doctrine, especially the *ālaya*-consciousness, and the inherent potential for Buddhahood. The Sanskrit text of the Lankāvatāra Sutra is thought to have been composed around C.E. 400. It represents the integration of two doctrines—that of the matrix of the Thus Come One and the Consciousness-Only doctrine—and asserts that all people possess the matrix of the Thus Come One, or the potential for Buddhahood. It equates the matrix of the Thus Come One with the *ālaya*-consciousness. The sutra takes the form of a discourse by Shakyamuni Buddha on Mount Lankā, the actual location of which is unknown. Some scholars identify Lankā with Sri Lanka, while others place it in southern or central India. In addition to the Sanskrit manuscript and two Tibetan translations, there are three extant Chinese versions: (1) one translated in 443 by Gunabhadra, a monk from central India; (2) another, in 513 by Bodhiruchi, a monk from northern India; and (3) a third produced between 700 and 704 by Shikshānanda, a monk of Khotan in Central Asia. A fourth, actually the earliest version, translated in the early fifth century by Dharmaraksha, a monk from central India, is lost. An important text for the early Zen (Ch'an) school in China, the Lankāvatāra Sutra was related to the development of the Zen school during the T'ang dynasty (618–907). Many commentaries on the sutra were produced during the T'ang, Sung (960–1279), and Ming (1368–1644) dynasties.

Larger Wisdom Sutra [大品般若経] (Skt *Panchavimshatisāhasrikā-prajnāpāramitā;* Chin *Ta-p'in-pan-jo-ching;* Jpn *Daibon-hannya-kyō*): Another name for the Great Perfection of Wisdom Sutra, translated into Chinese in 404 by Kumārajīva. The title "Larger Wisdom Sutra" is used to distinguish it from a much shorter text also called the Great Perfection of Wisdom Sutra. This shorter scripture, also translated in 408 by Kumārajīva, is known as the Smaller Wisdom Sutra. *See also* Great Perfection of Wisdom Sutra.

last five-hundred-year period [後五百歳] (Jpn *go-gohyakusai*): The fifth five-hundred-year period, or the first five hundred years of the Latter Day of the Law. *See* fifth five-hundred-year period.

Latter Day of the Law [末法] (Jpn *mappō*): Also, age of the Decadent Law, age of the Final Law, or latter age. The last of the three periods—the Former Day of the Law, the Middle Day of the Law, and the Latter Day of the Law—following Shakyamuni Buddha's death, when his teachings are said to fall into confusion and lose the power to lead people to enlightenment. The Latter Day of the Law is said to last for ten thousand years. The fifth of five five-hundred-year periods following Shakyamuni's death described in the Great Collection Sutra corresponds to the beginning of the Latter Day of the Law. The sutra predicts that it will be an "age of quarrels and disputes," when monks will disregard the precepts and feud constantly among themselves, when erroneous views will prevail, and when Shakyamuni's teachings will "be obscured and lost."

In contrast, the Lotus Sutra views the Latter Day of the Law as the time when the teaching it contains will be propagated. The "Medicine King" (twenty-third) chapter of the Lotus Sutra says, "After I have passed into extinction, in the last five-hundred-year period you must spread it abroad widely throughout Jambudvīpa and never allow it to be cut off." T'ien-t'ai (538–597) states in *The Words and Phrases of the Lotus Sutra,* "In the last five-hundred-year period, the mystic way will spread and benefit humankind far into the future," and Dengyō (767–822) says in *An Essay on the Protection of the Nation,* "The Former and Middle Days are almost over, and the Latter Day is near at hand." It was believed in Japan that the Latter Day would begin in 1052; this was based on an account in *The Record of Wonders in the Book of Chou* that places Shakyamuni's death in 949 B.C.E. Modern research suggests, however, that he died in the early fifth century B.C.E.

The concept of the Latter Day of the Law is also applied to Buddhas other than Shakyamuni, and Buddhist scriptures often refer to the "Latter Day of the Law" of a particular Buddha as the age in which that Buddha's teachings are lost. *See also* fifth five-hundred-year period.

Law [法] (Skt *dharma;* Jpn *hō*): The Law or truth of life and the universe, and a Buddha's teachings on it. *See* dharma.

Law Bright [法明如来] (Skt Dharmaprabhāsa; Jpn Hōmyō-nyorai): The Thus Come One Law Bright. The name under which Pūrna, one of Shakyamuni Buddha's ten major disciples, will attain Buddhahood in the future, according to Shakyamuni's prophecy in the "Five Hundred Disciples" (eighth) chapter of the Lotus Sutra. In this chapter, concerning Pūrna's future enlightenment, Shakyamuni says: "In the future too he will protect, uphold, aid, and proclaim the Law of immeasurable, boundless Buddhas, teaching, converting, and enriching immeasurable living beings, and causing them to turn toward supreme perfect enlightenment. To purify the Buddha lands he will constantly apply himself with diligence, teaching and converting living beings. Little by little, he will become fully endowed with the way of the bodhisattva, and when immeasurable *asamkhya kalpas* have passed, here in the land where he is dwelling he will attain supreme perfect enlightenment. He will be called Law Bright Thus Come One." *Prabhāsa* in the Sanskrit name Dharmaprabhāsa means light, brightness, or splendor; *dharma* means the Law.

Law-devouring hungry spirit [食法餓鬼] (Jpn *jikihō-gaki*): One of the thirty-six types of hungry spirits listed in the Meditation on the Correct Teaching Sutra. According to this sutra, one who preaches the Buddhist Law, or teachings, out of the desire to gain fame or profit is reborn as a Law-devouring hungry spirit. The sutra details the karmic causes of Law-devouring hungry spirits. During their lives as human beings, they are so greedy that they expound teachings to the people for the purpose of earning a livelihood and accumulating riches. They violate the precepts and have no respect for the Buddhist Law. They expound impure and erroneous teachings and propagate false views; for instance, the view that, though one may rob others of their possessions, one will not be subject to retribution. While disseminating false views, they accumulate riches that they use only for their own benefit. As a result, in the next life they are reborn as Law-devouring hungry spirits.

In *The Origin of the Service for Deceased Ancestors,* a letter written in 1271, Nichiren applies this term to certain priests, saying: "Law-devouring hungry spirits are people who renounce the world and spread Buddhism. They think that if they preach the Law people will respect them, and because of their ambition for fame and profit, they spend their entire present lifetime striving to be thought of as better than others. They neither help other human beings nor have a mind to save their parents. Such people are called Law-devouring hungry spirits, or hungry spirits who use the Buddhist teachings to satisfy their own desires" (191).

Law-wheel [法輪] (Jpn *hōrin*): *See* wheel of the Law.

lay nun [尼] (Jpn *ama*): A female believer of Buddhism who has shaven her head in the manner of a Buddhist nun, but continues to live in society as a layperson. Lay nun is the female equivalent of lay priest *(nyūdō)*. "Lay nun" was often affixed to the names of women who had been tonsured yet retained their lay status.

lay priest [入道] (Jpn *nyūdō*): One whose head is shaven in the manner of a Buddhist priest, but continues to live in society as a layperson.

Lay priest is a translation of the Japanese term *nyūdō,* which literally means to "enter the way," i.e., to "enter the way of the Buddha." In Japan, from the Heian period (794–1185) on, a distinction was made between lay priests and those who formally renounced the secular world and lived in temples. Later an increasing number of samurai took the tonsure as priests did, but continued to live as laypersons.

Learned Youth [儒童] (Skt Mānava or Mānavaka; Jpn Judō): The name of Shakyamuni Buddha in a previous life when he is said to have practiced as a bodhisattva. The Sanskrit word *mānava* or *mānavaka* means a youth, lad, Brahman youth, pupil, or scholar. The story of Bodhisattva Learned Youth appears in the Sutra of the Buddha's Marvelous Deeds in Previous Lifetimes, the Sutra of Collected Birth Stories concerning the Practice of the Six Pāramitās, and other works. Details differ slightly from one source to another.

According to the Sutra of the Buddha's Marvelous Deeds in Previous Lifetimes, Learned Youth happened to hear that a Buddha named Fixed Light (Skt Dīpamkara, also known as Burning Torch) was in the world. Rejoicing, he set out for the country where the Buddha lived. At length he reached a village where he met five hundred religious practitioners and he expounded a teaching to them. They were delighted to receive this teaching, and each gave him one silver coin when he left the village. Then he went to a city that was decorated as though for a festival, and was told that the Buddha would soon arrive there. In the street, he passed a woman named Gopī who was carrying seven lotus blossoms. So eager was Learned Youth to make an offering to the Buddha that he offered her his five hundred silver coins in exchange for just five blossoms. On learning that he wanted them as an offering to the Buddha, she was deeply moved and asked him to make her his wife in their next existence. She also gave him her remaining two lotus blossoms. When Fixed Light Buddha reached the city, the king and his ministers all bowed and reverently threw flowers before him as an offering. The flowers fell down to the ground. The five lotus blossoms offered by Learned Youth remained floating in the air, however, and the other two lotus flowers given to Learned Youth by Gopī came to rest on the Buddha's shoulders. Fixed Light Buddha then perceived the sincere faith of Learned Youth and Gopī, and predicted that Learned Youth would in the distant future attain enlightenment as Shakyamuni Buddha.

lecture hall [講堂] (Jpn *kōdō*): One of the main structures on the compound of a Buddhist temple, in which sutras are read, Buddhist doctrines taught, and rituals performed. The lecture hall has traditionally been one of the seven structures on the grounds of Buddhist temples in Japan. Located behind the main hall on the temple compound, it is generally more spacious than the other buildings, including the main hall. It is the building where priests assemble to listen to sermons and attend rituals. Some of the oldest surviving lecture halls in Japan are the hall called Dempō-dō in the eastern precinct of Hōryū-ji temple in Nara, built in 739; the hall at Tōshōdai-ji temple in Nara, built around 760; and the hall in the western precinct of Hōryū-ji temple, built in 990.

Legacy Teachings Sutra [遺教経] (Chin *I-chiao-ching;* Jpn *Yuikyō-gyō*): Also known as the Buddha's Legacy Teachings Sutra. A sutra translated into Chinese by Kumārajīva in the early fifth century. It purports to have been preached by Shakyamuni Buddha as his final instruction to his disciples under the sal trees just before his death. This sutra says that, after the Buddha's death, one should observe the precepts in order to control the five sense organs and regulate the mind, and devote oneself to Buddhist practice without succumbing to laziness and sloth. Though an extremely short sutra, Kumārajīva's translation of it is regarded as one of the best among Chinese sutra translations because of its polished style and excellent wording. The Legacy Teachings Sutra was widely favored and read by many people, and a number of commentaries on it were produced. The Zen school, in particular, values this sutra.

lessening one's karmic retribution [転重軽受] (Jpn *tenjū-kyōju*): The principle that one can experience the effects of bad karma from the past to a lesser degree because of Buddhist faith and practice. In general, Buddhism attributes one's present sufferings to one's past actions or causes that remain in one's life as karma, asserting that one must suffer the effect of every negative cause made in the past. The Mahāparinirvāna Sutra, Fa-hsien's Chinese translation of the Nirvana Sutra, states, however, "It is due to the blessings obtained by protecting the Law that they can diminish in this lifetime their suffering and retribution." This passage suggests that, due to the benefits accumulated through faith and practice, one can diminish in terms of both time and intensity negative karmic retribution that would otherwise torment one harshly over a longer period, even several lifetimes. Nichiren (1222–1282) states in his writing *Lessening One's Karmic Retribution:* "If one's heavy karma from the past is not expiated within this lifetime, one must undergo the sufferings of hell in the future, but if one experiences extreme hardship in this life [because of the Lotus Sutra], the sufferings of hell will vanish instantly. And when one dies, one will obtain the blessings of the human and heavenly worlds, as well as those of the three vehicles and the one vehicle"

(199). According to this principle, Buddhist faith and practice may cause one suffering and hardship, but will relieve one of the hellish suffering that is one's due.

lesser vehicle [小乗] (Jpn *shōjō*): Also, Lesser Vehicle. The Hinayana teachings. *See* Hinayana Buddhism.

Letter to Shimoyama [下山御消息] (Jpn *Shimoyama-goshōsoku*): One of the ten major writings of Nichiren. *See* ten major writings.

Liang Dynasty Biographies of Eminent Priests, The [梁高僧伝] (Chin *Liang-kao-seng-chuan;* Jpn *Ryō-kōsō-den*): Abbreviated as *The Biographies of Eminent Priests.* A biographical compilation written in 519 by Hui-chiao in China. It recounts the biographies of noteworthy priests who lived during the period of about 450 years from C.E. 67 when Buddhism was introduced to China to the year of the work's compilation. It includes the biographies of five hundred individuals. Several similar biographies were produced in China prior to *The Liang Dynasty Biographies of Eminent Priests,* but this was the most comprehensive and formed the basis of subsequent collections of biographies produced during the T'ang, Sung, and Ming dynasties. The title *The Biographies of Eminent Priests* sometimes refers to other such collections.

Liang-hsü [良諝] (n.d.) (PY Liangxu; Jpn Ryōjo): A priest of the T'ien-t'ai school in China during the ninth century. He taught the doctrines of his school to Chishō, who was later to become the fifth chief priest of Enryaku-ji, the head temple of the Japanese Tendai school, when Chishō came to China in 853.

Liang-pi [良賁] (717–777) (PY Liangbi; Jpn Ryōhi): A priest of Ch'ing-lung-ssu temple in Ch'ang-an, China. He assisted Pu-k'ung, also known by the Indian name Amoghavajra, in his translation of the Benevolent Kings Sutra into Chinese in 765, and wrote a commentary on that sutra.

Licchavi [離車] (Skt, Pali; Jpn Risha): A tribe that dwelt in an area north of the Ganges River in northeastern India. The Licchavis, with their capital at Vaishālī, maintained a republican form of government and had a general assembly consisting of heads of the leading families. They were rivals of the Magadha kingdom to the south. The Licchavis, along with the Videhas and other tribes, constituted the Vriji confederacy, known as one of the sixteen great states in ancient India. After Shakyamuni's death, the Licchavis received a share of his relics, which had been divided into eight portions. Ajātashatru, king of Magadha, later conquered the Licchavis.

life-liberating practice [放生会] (Jpn *hōjō-e*): Also, life-releasing ceremony. A Buddhist ceremony of releasing living things, such as fish and birds, from captivity. This practice was conducted in China and Japan as a work of merit and as an expression of pity for living beings. Performers of this ceremony would release captured birds and fish in mountains, forests, rivers, lakes, and ponds. In China, this ceremony began to prevail in the Northern and Southern Dynasties period (439–589), and an imperial command was issued to build ponds where purchased fish were set free. In Japan, the life-liberating ceremony was carried out during the time of Emperor Bidatsu (r. 572–585). The life-liberating practice is closely related to the Buddhist idea of not taking life. The Brahmā Net Sutra says that, because all living beings were people's fathers and mothers in past lives, captured beings should be set free rather than killed or eaten. The Golden Light Sutra speaks of Water Carrier, a skilled physician who lived countless *kalpas* ago. According to the sutra, he encountered a dried-up pond and saw many fish dying there. Feeling pity for the fish, he had elephants carry water to the pond and fill it with water, saving them.

"Life Span" chapter [寿量品] (Jpn *Juryō-hon*): The sixteenth chapter of the Lotus Sutra. *See* "Life Span of the Thus Come One" chapter.

"Life Span of the Thus Come One" chapter [如来寿量品] (Jpn *Nyorai-juryō-hon*): Abbreviated as the "Life Span" chapter. The sixteenth chapter of the Lotus Sutra, in which Shakyamuni Buddha reveals that he originally attained enlightenment in the far distant past rather than in his present life in India as his listeners generally thought. The chapter title "The Life Span of the Thus Come One" means the duration of Shakyamuni's life as a Buddha, that is, how much time has passed since he originally attained Buddhahood. T'ien-t'ai (538–597) of China ranks it as the key chapter of the essential teaching, or the latter fourteen chapters of the sutra. The chapter opens with three exhortations and four entreaties, in which the Buddha three times admonishes the multitude to believe and understand his truthful words, and the assembly four times begs him to preach. Shakyamuni then says, "You must listen carefully and hear of the Thus Come One's secret and his transcendental powers." He proceeds to explain that, while all heavenly and human beings and *asuras* believe that he first attained enlightenment in his present lifetime under the *bodhi* tree, it has actually been an incalculable length of time since he attained enlightenment. He then offers a dramatic description of the magnitude of this immeasurably long period. He describes taking a vast number of worlds, grinding them to dust, and then traversing the universe, dropping a particle each time one passes an equally vast number of worlds. Having exhausted all the dust particles, one takes all the worlds traversed, whether they have received a dust particle or not, and grinds them to dust. Then Shakyamuni says: "Let one particle represent one *kalpa.* The time that has passed since I attained Buddhahood surpasses this by a hundred, a thousand, ten thousand, a million *nayuta asamkhya kalpas.*" Commentaries on this chapter refer to this cosmically immense period as "numberless major world system dust particle *kalpas.*" In the essential teaching of the Lotus Sutra, Shakyamuni thus refutes the view that he attained enlightenment for the first time in this life in India and reveals his original attainment of enlightenment in the remote past. T'ien-t'ai refers to this in *The Words and Phrases of the Lotus Sutra* and *The Profound Meaning of the Lotus Sutra* as "opening the near and revealing the distant," "casting off the transient and revealing the true," and "opening the transient and revealing the true." Here, "the transient" means Shakyamuni's transient status, and "the true" means his true identity. From his original attainment of Buddhahood, Shakyamuni declares, he has constantly been here in this *sahā* world preaching the Law, appearing as many different Buddhas and using various means to save living beings. Though he says that he enters nirvana, he merely uses his death as a means to arouse in people the desire to seek a Buddha. He then illustrates this idea with the parable of the skilled physician and his sick children. In the parable, the children of a skilled physician have accidentally swallowed poison. Having lost their senses, they refuse the medicine their father offers them as an antidote. The father then goes off to a remote place and sends a message informing his children he has died. Shocked to their senses, the children take the medicine their father has left for them and are cured. The Buddha is compared to the father in this parable, living beings to the children who have drunk poison, and the Buddha's entry into nirvana to the father's report of his own death—an expedient means to arouse in people the aspiration for enlightenment. The chapter concludes with a verse section, which restates the important teachings of the preceding prose section.

In *Profound Meaning,* T'ien-t'ai interprets the "Life Span" chapter as revealing the three mystic principles of the true cause (the cause for Shakyamuni's original attainment of enlightenment), the true effect (his original enlightenment), and the true land (the place where the Buddha lives and teaches). He interprets the passage "Originally I practiced the bodhisattva way . . . " as indicating the stage of non-regression, or the eleventh of the fifty-two stages of bodhisattva practice, which he explained as the true cause that enabled Shakyamuni to attain Buddhahood. In answer to the question of what Shakyamuni practiced in order to reach the stage of non-regression, Nichiren (1222–1282) identified it as the Law of Nam-myoho-renge-kyo.

Light Bright [光明如来] (Skt Rashmiprabhāsa; Jpn Kōmyō-nyorai): The Thus Come One Light Bright. The name that Mahākāshyapa, one of Shakyamuni's ten major disciples, will bear when he attains enlightenment, according to Shakyamuni's prediction in the "Bestowal of Prophecy" (sixth) chapter of the Lotus Sutra. The chapter reads: "This disciple of mine Mahākāshyapa in future existences will be able to enter the presence of three thousand billion Buddhas, World-Honored Ones, to offer alms, pay reverence, honor and praise them, widely proclaiming the innumerable great doctrines of the Buddhas. And in his final incarnation he will be able to become a Buddha named Light Bright Thus Come One . . . His land will be called Light Virtue and his *kalpa* will be called Great Adornment." *Rashmi* of the Sanskrit name Rashmiprabhāsa means light and beam; *prabhāsa* means brightness, splendor, or light.

Light Sound Heaven [光音天] (Skt Ābhāsvara; Jpn Kō'on-ten): Also known as Ābhāsvara Heaven, or Utmost Light and Purity Heaven. One of the eighteen heavens in the world of form, specifically the highest of the three heavens in the second meditation heaven of the world of form. The world of form comprises the four meditation heavens and is further subdivided into eighteen heavens. The three heavens of the second meditation heaven are, in ascending order, the Minor Light Heaven (Skt Parīttābha), the Infinite Light Heaven (Apramānābha), and the Light Sound Heaven. The inhabitants in this last heaven, or the heavenly beings in this realm, converse by means of light. When they speak, they emit rays of pure light, rather than sound, which function as words. *Ābhā* of the Sanskrit name Ābhāsvara means light, and *svara* means voice or sound.

Lin-chi school [臨済宗] (PY Linjizong; Jpn Rinzai-shū): A branch of the Zen (Ch'an) school in China. It is counted as one of the five branches of the Southern school of Zen. The Lin-chi school was founded by I-hsüan (d. 867; 866 by another account) of Lin-chi-yüan temple. Though Chinese Zen is said to have begun with Bodhidharma, who lived in the fifth and sixth centuries, it did not become firmly established until the days of its sixth patriarch, Hui-neng (638–713). The Lin-chi school is in the lineage of Huai-jang, a disciple of Hui-neng. During the Northern Sung dynasty (960–1127), two more schools, the Huang-lung and the Yang-ch'i, broke away from the Lin-chi school. Hui-nan founded the former, and Fang-hui, the latter. These two founders were disciples of Ch'u-yüan, the seventh in the lineage of the Lin-chi school. *See also* Rinzai school.

lion seat [師子座・獅子座] (Skt *simhāsana;* Jpn *shishi-za*): Also, lion throne. The place where a Buddha is seated. A Buddha's preaching is likened to a lion's roar and the Buddha to a lion because he preaches the Law without fear. The Sanskrit term *simhāsana* is a compound of *simha* (lion) and *āsana* (seat).

Lion Sound King [師子音王仏] (Skt Simhanādarāja; Jpn Shishionnō-butsu): A Buddha who is said to have appeared immeasurable *kalpas* ago. He is mentioned in the Non-Substantiality of All Phenomena Sutra and *The Treatise on the Great Perfection of Wisdom*. These works describe his land, in which all trees issue the Dharma sound that leads people to attain the way. After the death of Lion Sound King, however, the sound stops. In the latter age of this Buddha's teaching, the monk Root of Joy carries out only the practice of expounding the doctrine of the true aspect of all phenomena. In spite of being slandered by the monk Superior Intent for that, Root of Joy persists in his beliefs and attains Buddhahood.

lion's roar [師子吼・獅子吼] (Skt *simhanāda;* Jpn *shishi-ku*): Also, roar of a lion. The voice or preaching of a Buddha. A Buddha's preaching is likened to the roar of a lion, because a Buddha preaches the Law without fear, refutes erroneous doctrines, and fills persons who uphold erroneous doctrines with awe. The Sanskrit term *simhanāda* is a compound of *simha* (lion) and *nāda* (roar).

Lion's Roar of Queen Shrīmālā Sutra [勝鬘師子吼経] (Jpn *Shōman-shishiku-kyō*): *See* Shrīmālā Sutra.

lion throne [師子座・獅子座] (Jpn *shishi-za*): *See* lion seat.

little desire and contentment with a little gain [少欲知足] (Jpn *shō-yoku-chisoku*): A virtue that monks should possess. This concept is expressed variously in English as "contentment while desiring little," "wanting little and being content," "desiring little and knowing satisfaction," etc. It means to have few personal desires and to be satisfied or content with what one has. Buddhist scriptures condemn monks who are desirous of worldly fame and profit and attached to worldly pleasures. The Mahāparinirvāna Sutra reads: "After I [Shakyamuni Buddha] have passed away . . . there will be monks who will give the appearance of abiding by the rules of monastic discipline. But they will scarcely ever read or recite the sutras, and instead will crave all kinds of food and drink to nourish their bodies. . . . Though they wear the clothes of a monk, they will go about searching for alms like so many huntsmen who, narrowing their eyes, stalk softly. They will be like a cat on the prowl for mice. And they will constantly reiterate these words, 'I have attained arhatship!' . . . Outwardly they will seem to be wise and good, but within they will harbor greed and jealousy. . . . They are not true monks—they merely have the appearance of monks. Consumed by their erroneous views, they slander the correct teaching." The "Encouraging Devotion" (thirteenth) chapter of the Lotus Sutra describes monks who pretend to be sages but are greedy. It says, "Greedy for profit and support, they will preach the Law to white-robed laymen and will be respected and revered by the world as though they were arhats who possess the six transcendental powers. These men with evil in their hearts, constantly thinking of worldly affairs, . . ." Nichiren (1222–1282) wrote: "A good teacher is a priest who is free from any fault in secular affairs, who never fawns upon others even in the slightest, who desires and is satisfied with little, and who is compassionate; a priest who reads and upholds the Lotus Sutra precisely as it teaches and also encourages and leads others to embrace it. Such a priest the Buddha has praised among all priests as the finest teacher of the Law" (880).

lobha [貪・貪欲] (Skt, Pali; Jpn *ton* or *ton'yoku*): Greed, covetousness, or avarice. *Lobha,* greed, is one of the three poisons, the three sources of vice and suffering; the other two being *dvesha* (anger) and *moha* (foolishness). *See also* three poisons.

Lokakshema [支婁迦讖] (n.d.) (Skt; Jpn Shirukasen): A monk of Yüeh-chih, a kingdom in Central Asia, who is regarded as the earliest of the translator-monks from that country to journey to China. Lokakshema went to Lo-yang in China around C.E. 150 and translated many Mahayana sutras into Chinese. He was famed for his strict observance of precepts and diligent practice. His translations include the Shūramgama Sutra, the Sutra of the Meditation to Behold the Buddhas, and the Practice of Wisdom Sutra, the earliest of the Chinese translations of the Wisdom sutras.

Lokāyata [順世外道] (Skt, Pali; Jpn Junse-gedō or Junsei-gedō): One of the non-Buddhist schools in ancient India, also known as the Chārvāka school. It held that human existence is no more than a temporary combination of the four elements of earth, water, fire, and wind. The Lokāyata followers denied the existence of both past and future lives, and advocated the pursuit of pleasure in this life as the highest goal. Ajita Kesakambala, one of the so-called six non-Buddhist teachers in Shakyamuni's time, is regarded as a forerunner of this school.

Lokeshvararāja [世自在王仏] (Skt; Jpn Sejizaiō-butsu): The Buddha Lokeshvararāja (World Freedom King), under whom Amida Buddha, in a previous existence, carried out Buddhist practice. *See* World Freedom King.

Long Āgama Sutra [長阿含経] (Chin *Ch'ang-a-han-ching;* Jpn *Jō-agon-gyō*): One of the four Chinese Āgama sutras. The other three are the Medium-Length Āgama Sutra, the Miscellaneous Āgama Sutra, and the

Increasing by One Āgama Sutra. Translated into Chinese by Buddhayashas and Chu Fo-nien of the Later Ch'in dynasty (384–417) of China, the Long Āgama Sutra consists of thirty sutras, each of which is relatively lengthy. The Long Āgama Sutra in its entirety corresponds to the Pali text *Dīgha-nikāya,* one of the five Āgamas of the Pali canon, which contains thirty-four long sutras. The Sutra of Preaching Travels, one of the thirty sutras in the Long Āgama Sutra, describes Shakyamuni Buddha's travels during the year preceding his death. This sutra corresponds to the Pali text *Mahāparinibbāna-suttanta,* or the Pali Nirvana Sutra. The Description of the World Sutra, the last of the thirty sutras, explains Buddhist cosmology.

long broad tongue [広長舌] (Jpn *kōchō-zetsu*): One of a Buddha's thirty-two features. It symbolizes the truth of a Buddha's words, or his attitude never to tell falsehoods. The "Supernatural Powers" (twenty-first) chapter of the Lotus Sutra states that Shakyamuni Buddha extended his tongue up to the Brahma Heaven along with the other Buddhas from the ten directions, who were his emanations. It is also referred to as a face-covering tongue or a face-veiling tongue because a Buddha's tongue is said to be large enough to cover his face.

lord of teachings [教主] (Jpn *kyōshu*): A Buddha. Lord of teachings often refers to Shakyamuni Buddha, the founder of Buddhism and expounder of its teachings. In Mahayana Buddhism, however, it refers also to numerous Buddhas who dwell in their own lands throughout the universe and preach doctrines to instruct and convert beings. For example, Medicine Master Buddha teaches in the Pure Emerald World in the east, and Amida Buddha in the land of Perfect Bliss in the west. The Buddha who is revered in a particular Buddhist school is usually considered the lord of teachings for that school.

Lotus and Nirvana period [法華涅槃時] (Jpn Hokke-nehan-ji): The period of the Lotus and Nirvana sutras. The fifth of the five periods, a classification of Shakyamuni's teachings by T'ien-t'ai. *See* five periods.

lotus as a metaphor [譬喩蓮華] (Jpn *hiyu-renge*): The lotus used as a metaphor to explain the essence of the Lotus Sutra. *See* figurative lotus.

Lotus meditation [法華三昧] (Jpn *hokke-sammai* or *hokke-zammai*): A form of meditation based on the Lotus Sutra. In the T'ien-t'ai school of China and the Tendai school of Japan, the Lotus meditation refers particularly to meditation practiced to perceive the true aspect of the Middle Way based on the Lotus Sutra. The Lotus meditation is categorized as "half-active and half-sitting" meditation, one of the four forms of meditation set forth by T'ien-t'ai (538–597). It is carried out over a twenty-one-day period, and combines both walking and seated meditation. Specifically, the Lotus meditation involves walking around the place of meditation while reciting the Lotus Sutra, as well as seated meditation. *See also* four forms of meditation.

lotus of the entity [当体蓮華] (Jpn *tōtai-renge*): A reference in the T'ien-t'ai doctrine to the lotus that is the essence of the Lotus Sutra and also the people who are entities of, or who embody, this essence. Nichiren (1222–1282) described this essence as Myoho-renge-kyo, or Nam-myoho-renge-kyo. He states in *The Entity of the Mystic Law:* "The supreme principle [that is the Mystic Law] was originally without a name. When the sage was observing the principle and assigning names to all things, he perceived that there is this wonderful single Law *[myōhō]* that simultaneously possesses both cause and effect *[renge],* and he named it Myoho-renge" (421). The term *lotus of the entity* is contrasted with the *figurative lotus,* or the lotus as a metaphor for the Law. Since the lotus of the entity, or lotus of the Law that simultaneously possesses both cause and effect, is difficult to understand, the lotus plant, which blooms and produces fruit at the same time, is employed as a metaphor. See also *renge.*

Lotus school [法華宗] (Chin Fa-hua-tsung; Jpn Hokke-shū): (1) Another name for the Chinese T'ien-t'ai school and for its Japanese counterpart, the Tendai school. The name Lotus school derives from the fact that these schools made the Lotus Sutra central to their doctrine. Dengyō (767–822), the founder of the Japanese Tendai school, stated in his work *The Outstanding Principles of the Lotus Sutra:* "The Great Teacher T'ien-t'ai trusted and obeyed Shakyamuni and worked to uphold the Lotus school, spreading its teachings throughout China. We of Mount Hiei inherited the doctrine from T'ien-t'ai and work to uphold the Lotus school and to disseminate its teachings throughout Japan."

(2) Nichiren (1222–1282), who asserted the supremacy of the Lotus Sutra among all the teachings of Shakyamuni, also referred to himself and the followers of his teachings as the Lotus school.

Lotus Sutra [法華経] (Skt *Saddharma-pundarīka-sūtra;* Chin *Fa-hua-ching;* Jpn *Hoke-kyō*): One of the Mahayana sutras. Several Sanskrit manuscripts are extant, and Sanskrit fragments have been discovered in Nepal, Kashmir, and Central Asia. There is also a Tibetan version. Six Chinese translations of the sutra were made, of which three are extant. They are (1) the Lotus Sutra of the Correct Law, in ten volumes and twenty-seven chapters, translated by Dharmaraksha in 286; (2) the Lotus Sutra of the Wonderful Law, in eight volumes and twenty-eight chapters, translated by Kumārajīva in 406; and (3) the Supplemented Lotus Sutra of the Wonderful Law, in seven volumes and twenty-seven chapters, translated by Jnānagupta and Dharmagupta in 601. Among these,

Kumārajīva's Lotus Sutra of the Wonderful Law has known the greatest popularity. Therefore, in China and Japan, the name Lotus Sutra usually indicates the Lotus Sutra of the Wonderful Law (Chin *Miao-fa-lien-hua-ching;* Jpn *Myoho-renge-kyo*).

In India, Nāgārjuna (c. 150–250) often cited the Lotus Sutra in his *Treatise on the Great Perfection of Wisdom,* and Vasubandhu wrote a commentary on the Lotus Sutra known as *The Treatise on the Lotus Sutra of the Wonderful Law.* In China, Kumārajīva's Lotus Sutra of the Wonderful Law exerted a great influence and was widely read. Many scholars, including Fa-yün (467–529), wrote commentaries on it. T'ien-t'ai (538–597), in *The Profound Meaning of the Lotus Sutra,* formulated a system of classification of the entire body of Buddhist sutras called the "five periods and eight teachings," which ranks the Lotus Sutra above all the other sutras. His lectures on the sutra's text are compiled as *The Words and Phrases of the Lotus Sutra,* and on his method of practice as *Great Concentration and Insight.* These two works and *Profound Meaning* are the records of T'ien-t'ai's lectures compiled by his disciple Chang-an and are together known as T'ien-t'ai's three major works.

In Japan, Prince Shōtoku (574–622) designated the Lotus, Shrīmālā, and Vimalakīrti sutras as the three sutras that could protect the country, and he wrote commentaries on each of them. After that, the Lotus Sutra gained wide acceptance in Japan. Emperor Shōmu (701–756) built provincial temples for priests and nuns throughout the country. In the temples for nuns, the Lotus Sutra was honored above all other sutras for its teaching that women can attain Buddhahood. Dengyō (767–822) established the Tendai (Chin T'ien-t'ai) school, which was based on the Lotus Sutra and became one of the major Buddhist schools in Japan. Nichiren (1222–1282) also upheld the Lotus Sutra, which describes all living beings as potential Buddhas, and identified its essence as Nam-myoho-renge-kyo, spreading this teaching. In his later years he lectured on the Lotus Sutra, and his lectures were compiled by his disciples, by Nikkō as *The Record of the Orally Transmitted Teachings* and by Nikō as *The Recorded Lectures. See also* Lotus Sutra of the Wonderful Law.

Lotus Sutra and Its Traditions, The [法華伝記] (Chin *Fa-hua-chuan-chi;* Jpn *Hokke-denki*): A work written by Seng-hsiang, a priest of China, in the eighth century. This work maintains the superiority of Kumārajīva's Chinese translation of the Lotus Sutra over all the other Chinese translations of the sutra. Moreover, it contains various stories concerning benefits and salvation to be gained by performing such deeds as expounding, reading and reciting, transcribing, listening to, and making offerings to the Lotus Sutra.

Lotus Sutra of the Correct Law [正法華経] (Chin *Cheng-fa-hua-ching;* Jpn *Shō-hoke-kyō*): A Chinese translation of the Lotus Sutra by Dharmaraksha, a priest from Tun-huang. Translated in 286, it is the oldest of the three extant Chinese versions of the Lotus Sutra and consists of twenty-seven chapters. In this translation, the content of what appears as the "Devadatta" (twelfth) chapter in Kumārajīva's version, the Lotus Sutra of the Wonderful Law, is not treated as an independent chapter but is included in the "Seven-Treasure Tower" (eleventh) chapter, which corresponds to the "Emergence of the Treasure Tower" (eleventh) chapter in Kumārajīva's version.

Lotus Sutra of the Wonderful Law [妙法蓮華経] (Skt *Saddharma-pundarīka-sūtra;* Chin *Miao-fa-lien-hua-ching;* Jpn *Myoho-renge-kyo*): Also known as the Sutra of the Lotus of the Wonderful Law or the Sutra of the Lotus Blossom of the Fine Dharma. A Chinese translation of the Sanskrit scripture *Saddharma-pundarīka-sūtra,* known in English as the Lotus Sutra, produced by Kumārajīva in 406. It consists of eight volumes and twenty-eight chapters. Six Chinese translations are recorded as having been made of the *Saddharma-pundarīka-sūtra,* three of which survive today. Among these, Kumārajīva's Lotus Sutra of the Wonderful Law is by far the most popular and is the basis of the T'ien-t'ai teachings that spread in China and Japan. Nichiren (1222–1282) also regarded the Lotus Sutra of the Wonderful Law as the best of the Chinese translations.

The titles of the twenty-eight chapters are (1) Introduction, (2) Expedient Means, (3) Simile and Parable, (4) Belief and Understanding, (5) The Parable of the Medicinal Herbs, (6) Bestowal of Prophecy, (7) The Parable of the Phantom City, (8) Prophecy of Enlightenment for Five Hundred Disciples, (9) Prophecies Conferred on Learners and Adepts, (10) The Teacher of the Law, (11) The Emergence of the Treasure Tower, (12) Devadatta, (13) Encouraging Devotion, (14) Peaceful Practices, (15) Emerging from the Earth, (16) The Life Span of the Thus Come One, (17) Distinctions in Benefits, (18) The Benefits of Responding with Joy, (19) Benefits of the Teacher of the Law, (20) The Bodhisattva Never Disparaging, (21) Supernatural Powers of the Thus Come One, (22) Entrustment, (23) Former Affairs of the Bodhisattva Medicine King, (24) The Bodhisattva Wonderful Sound, (25) The Universal Gateway of the Bodhisattva Perceiver of the World's Sounds, (26) Dhāranī, (27) Former Affairs of King Wonderful Adornment, and (28) Encouragements of the Bodhisattva Universal Worthy.

The sutra opens with Shakyamuni Buddha and an assembly of his countless listeners gathered on Eagle Peak. The "Introduction" (first) chapter through the first half of the "Treasure Tower" (eleventh) chapter is set on Eagle Peak. The latter half of the "Treasure Tower" chapter through the "Entrustment" (twenty-second) chapter describes the so-called Ceremony in the Air in which the entire gathering is suspended in space. Finally, the "Medicine King" (twenty-third) chapter through the "Encouragements" (twenty-eighth) chapter is set again on Eagle Peak. These divisions are referred to as the "two places and three assemblies."

In *The Words and Phrases of the Lotus Sutra,* T'ien-t'ai (538–597) divided the Lotus Sutra of the Wonderful Law into two parts: the first fourteen chapters, which he called the theoretical teaching, and the latter fourteen chapters, which he called the essential teaching. The theoretical teaching takes the form of preaching by the historical Shakyamuni who is depicted as having first attained enlightenment during this lifetime in India. The essential teaching takes the form of preaching by the Buddha who discards his transient role as the historical Shakyamuni and reveals his true identity as the Buddha who actually attained enlightenment in the unimaginably remote past.

In the theoretical teaching, the Buddha declares that the three vehicles—the teachings for voice-hearers, cause-awakened ones, and bodhisattvas stressed in the pre-Lotus Sutra teachings—are not ends in themselves but only means to lead people to the one supreme vehicle of Buddhahood. T'ien-t'ai defines this revelation, known as the "replacement of the three vehicles with the one vehicle," to be the principal doctrine of the theoretical teaching. This doctrine is first revealed in the "Expedient Means" (second) chapter, which T'ien-t'ai regards as the principal chapter of the theoretical teaching. This chapter reveals "the true aspect of all phenomena," indicating theoretically that there is no essential difference between an ordinary person of the nine worlds and a Buddha, and that the potential for enlightenment exists in everyone. The chapter further clarifies this by declaring that all Buddhas appear in the world for one reason alone: to expound the one Buddha vehicle, that is, to enable all people to attain the Buddha wisdom. In the ensuing chapters up until the "Prophecies" (ninth) chapter, Shakyamuni explains the same idea through the parable of the three carts and the burning house and by revealing the connections he formed with his disciples in the distant past. Thus three times he explains the teachings—elucidating the principle, parable, and connections, respectively—and each time one of the three groups of his voice-hearer disciples, groups of progressively lesser capacity, understands, and he in turn pronounces prophecies of their enlightenment.

The remaining five chapters of the theoretical teaching refer to the time after Shakyamuni Buddha's death and the propagation of the Lotus

Sutra in that period. The "Teacher of the Law" (tenth) chapter explains both the difficulty and the great benefit of propagating the sutra, and the "Treasure Tower" (eleventh) chapter describes the Buddha urging the bodhisattvas present to spread the sutra after his death. The "Devadatta" (twelfth) chapter illustrates dramatically the principle that all people can equally attain Buddhahood. It does this with the examples of the enlightenment of Devadatta, an evil man, and the dragon king's daughter, a woman in reptile form. In the "Encouraging Devotion" (thirteenth) chapter, the assembled bodhisattvas respond to the Buddha's earlier call and vow to propagate the sutra in the face of any obstacles that will occur after his death. The "Peaceful Practices" (fourteenth) chapter sets forth the four peaceful practices to be employed in propagating the sutra. This concludes the theoretical teaching.

The essential teaching begins with the "Emerging from the Earth" (fifteenth) chapter. The most important doctrine in the essential teaching, T'ien-t'ai says, is the revelation of Shakyamuni Buddha's original enlightenment in the remote past. Though explicitly stated in the "Life Span" (sixteenth) chapter, the whole process of this revelation begins with the latter half of the "Emerging from the Earth" chapter, continues through the entire "Life Span" chapter, and ends in the first half of the "Distinctions in Benefits" (seventeenth) chapter. T'ien-t'ai terms this part of the sutra the "one chapter and two halves" and regards it as the core of the Lotus Sutra. At the beginning of the "Emerging from the Earth" chapter, countless Bodhisattvas of the Earth appear, and Bodhisattva Maitreya addresses the Buddha, asking by whom these bodhisattvas were taught. Shakyamuni replies that they are his original disciples whom he has been teaching since long ago. This revelation T'ien-t'ai terms "opening the near and revealing the distant in concise form." The latter half of the chapter begins with Maitreya's second question: How could Shakyamuni possibly have trained all these bodhisattvas in the mere forty-odd years since his enlightenment? This opens the way for the Buddha's revelation in the "Life Span" chapter in which he discloses that he actually attained enlightenment in the inconceivably distant past. This revelation T'ien-t'ai terms "opening the near and revealing the distant in expanded form." The Buddha then describes in some detail the magnitude of the time that has elapsed since his enlightenment, a period known as numberless major world system dust particle *kalpas.* Ever since this original enlightenment, Shakyamuni says, he has been always in this *sahā* world, appearing as Buddhas of different names and using various expedient means to teach and convert the people. The first half of the "Distinctions in Benefits" chapter describes the distinct benefits obtained by those who listened to the Buddha's description of his immeasurable life span.

The latter half of the "Distinctions in Benefits" chapter and the final eleven chapters are concerned with the propagation of the sutra after Shakyamuni's death. The portion of the sutra from the latter half of the "Distinctions in Benefits" chapter through the "Never Disparaging" (twentieth) chapter urges that the sutra be propagated and declares the benefits of doing so. The "Supernatural Powers" (twenty-first) and "Entrustment" (twenty-second) chapters describe Shakyamuni Buddha's transfer of the sutra respectively to the Bodhisattvas of the Earth in particular and to all the bodhisattvas in general. The remaining six chapters further stress the necessity and benefits of propagation.

Lotus Treasury World [蓮華藏世界・華藏世界] (Skt Kusuma-tala-garbha-vyūhālamkāra-loka-dhātu-samudra or Padma-garbha-loka-dhātu; Jpn Rengezō-sekai or Kezō-sekai): (1) The pure land described in the Flower Garland Sutra where Vairochana Buddha is said to live after fulfilling his bodhisattva vows and practices. According to the sutra, the Lotus Treasury World exists in a huge lotus flower growing in a sea of perfume that is supported by many layers of windy circles. This Lotus Treasury World consists of twenty layers of worlds in the center, the thirteenth (counting from below) of which is called the *sahā* world where Vairochana Buddha dwells. These are surrounded by 111 peripheral worlds each of which also has twenty layers of worlds. Each of these many worlds is ornamented with treasures and inhabited by a Buddha and a great many living beings.

(2) A similar world described in the Brahmā Net Sutra. The world in the Brahmā Net Sutra is a thousand-petaled lotus. Each of the thousand petals is itself a world consisting of a billion smaller worlds, each with a sun, a moon, a Mount Sumeru, and four continents. Vairochana Buddha sits in the center of the lotus. In each of the thousand petals dwells a Shakyamuni Buddha who is regarded as a transformation body of Vairochana Buddha. In each of the numerous smaller worlds in each petal dwells a bodhisattva who is a transformation body of Shakyamuni. Each bodhisattva preaches the teaching under a *bodhi* tree.

Lou-lan [樓蘭] (PY Loulan; Jpn Rōran): An oasis city-state in Central Asia during the Han dynasty (202 B.C.E.–C.E. 220) of China. The remains of Lou-lan are in the present-day Sinkiang Uighur Autonomous Region of China. Lou-lan lay by the northwestern shore of the lake Lop Nor (Lop Lake) on the eastern rim of the Tarim Basin and prospered as a center of East–West trade along the Silk Road. Because Lou-lan occupied an important position, the Hsiung-nu (known in Europe as the Huns) and the Han Chinese often warred with each other over its possession;

consequently, it fell at different times under the rule of the Hsiung-nu or the Han. In 77 B.C.E. the Han killed the ruler of the Lou-lan kingdom and renamed it Shan-shan. From the first century onward, Shan-shan gradually annexed the oasis city-states lying to its south and southwest and along the foot of the northern slope of the Kunlun Mountains. From the fifth century onward, however, the Shan-shan kingdom was invaded by various tribes and gradually declined, until ultimately it was buried under the desert sands. Through excavation and research conducted early in the twentieth century, it became clear that Lou-lan had at one time been a great center of Buddhism in Central Asia.

Lumbinī [藍毘尼] (Skt, Pali; Jpn Rambini): The birthplace of Shakyamuni. Buddhist scriptures often refer to it as Lumbinī Gardens. It was a grove in what is today the village of Rummindei just inside the southern border of Nepal. Lumbinī is one of the four sacred sites connected with Shakyamuni, the other three being Buddhagayā (the place of his enlightenment), Deer Park (the place of his first sermon), and Kushinagara (the site of his death, or entry into nirvana). The remains of Lumbinī were discovered at Rummindei in 1896, and inscriptions on the stone pillar found there show that King Ashoka made a pilgrimage to Lumbinī and erected the pillar to commemorate Shakyamuni Buddha's birthplace. Hsüan-tsang, a Chinese priest who visited the site of Lumbinī in the seventh century, said in his travel records that lightning had broken the pillar, and only the lower half remained. According to Buddhist legend, Māyā gave birth to Shakyamuni here when she reached for a branch of an *ashoka* tree to obtain its blossoms.

Lung-men caves [竜門石窟] (PY Longmen; Jpn Ryūmon-sekkutsu): A large-scale grouping of Buddhist cave-temples located south of the city of Lo-yang in China. The Lung-men caves extend one kilometer from north to south. The construction of the caves began after Emperor Hsiao-wen of the Northern Wei dynasty had transferred the capital from P'ing-ch'eng to Lo-yang in 494. The Lung-men caves were carved into rocky cliff faces on both banks of the Yi River. Within the cave-temples, statues of the Buddha, bodhisattvas, and other figures were carved out of the rock walls. Among them, a statue of Vairochana Buddha is the tallest, standing more than seventeen meters. The construction continued over a four-hundred-year period into the late T'ang dynasty (618–907). In the thirty years before the transfer of the capital in 494, a number of cave-temples were also built at a site west of P'ing-ch'eng with the support of the same dynasty. These are known as the Yün-kang caves. *See also* Yün-kang caves.

Lü school [律宗] (PY Lüzong; Jpn Risshū): *See* Precepts school.

M

Madhura [摩奴羅] (Skt; Jpn Manura): Also known as Manorhita. The twenty-first of Shakyamuni Buddha's twenty-three successors. *See* Manorhita.

madhya (Skt) (1) [末陀] (Jpn *mada*): An ancient Indian numerical unit meaning one hundred million.

(2) [中] (Jpn *chū*): Middle, central, neutral, intermediate, impartial, or standing between. In Buddhist philosophy, the concept of *madhya,* also known as the Middle Way, denies extremes, indicating a state that transcends polar categories such as existence and nonexistence, cessation and permanence. The concept of *madhya* encourages practice aimed at transcending attachments to extreme or one-sided views. *Mādhya, madhyama,* and *mādhyama* are equivalent Sanskrit terms. *See also* Middle Way.

Madhyamaka-kārikā [中頌・中論頌・中論] (Skt; Jpn *Chūju, Chūron-ju,* or *Chū-ron*): Also known as *Mādhyamika-kārikā* or *Mūla-madhyamaka-kārikā.* A work by Nāgārjuna that became the principal text of the Mādhyamika (Middle Way) school in India. See *Verses on the Middle Way.*

Mādhyamika school [中観派] (Skt; Jpn Chūgan-ha): Also known as the Madhyamaka school. A Mahayana school based on Nāgārjuna's *Madhyamaka-kārikā,* or *Verses on the Middle Way.* The Mādhyamika school was one of the two major Mahayana schools in India, the other being the Vijnānavāda, or Consciousness-Only, school, also known as the Yogāchāra school. It upholds the doctrines of non-substantiality and dependent origination, which maintain that all phenomena arise interdependently and are without distinctive natures of their own, i.e., that they are non-substantial. In addition, it teaches that, by recognizing the interdependence of all phenomena, one can rid oneself of illusions and perceive the ultimate truth of the Buddha—the Middle Way that is beyond the two extremes of existence and nonexistence. Nāgārjuna (c. 150–250) is regarded as the founder of the school, from which emerged later important figures such as Āryadeva, Rāhulabhadra, and Pingala.

In the sixth century, two scholars, Buddhapālita and Bhāvaviveka, wrote conflicting commentaries on the *Madhyamaka-kārikā.* Their opinions differed on the method of approaching and demonstrating the truth of non-substantiality. As a result, the Mādhyamika school divided into two—the Prāsangika school, led by Buddhapālita, and the Svātantrika school, led by Bhāvaviveka. From the Prāsangika school emerged the scholar Chandrakīrti; and from the Svātantrika school, Avalokitavrata, Shāntarakshita, and his disciple Kamalashīla. Later Shāntarakshita and Kamalashīla established close doctrinal ties with the Vijnānavāda, or Yogāchāra, school, which gave rise to the Yogāchāra-Mādhyamika school. In China and Japan, the Three Treatises (Chin San-lun; Jpn Sanron) school inherited the philosophy of the Mādhyamika school. Mādhyamika philosophy spread also to Tibet, and its concept of non-substantiality formed a basis for Tibetan Buddhism.

Madhyāntika [末田提 · 末田地] (Skt; Jpn Madendai or Madenji): Also known as Madhyantika. A monk in India who received the Buddha's teachings from Ānanda and propagated them in Kashmir. *A History of the Buddha's Successors* lists the twenty-three successors of the Buddha from the first, Mahākāshyapa, through the last, Āryasimha. The text describes Ānanda as the second successor and Shānavāsa as the third. It also refers to Madhyāntika as a successor of Ānanda, though not as the formal one. Chang-an, T'ien-t'ai's successor, writes in his preface to *Great Concentration and Insight* that Madhyāntika and Shānavāsa are contemporaries who inherited the Buddha's teachings from Ānanda, and that, if both are included among the Buddha's successors, they number twenty-four. Among these twenty-four successors, Madhyāntika is regarded as the third and Shānavāsa as the fourth.

Magadha [摩揭陀国] (Skt, Pali; Jpn Makada-koku): The most powerful of the sixteen great states in India in the time of Shakyamuni Buddha. Magadha, with Rājagriha as its capital, covered an area south of the Ganges River in what is now the state of Bihar in northeastern India. Eagle Peak, Buddhagayā (the place of Shakyamuni's enlightenment), and Bamboo Grove Monastery were located in this kingdom. Magadha was ruled in the Buddha's lifetime by Bimbisāra and then by his son Ajātashatru. Shakyamuni taught widely in the kingdom, which became the center of Buddhism and Buddhist culture. Bimbisāra and later Ajātashatru became followers of Shakyamuni Buddha. It is said that Shakyamuni preached in the Magadhi dialect of that region. The capital, Rājagriha, was the base of his religious activities. King Ajātashatru succeeded in annexing the neighboring kingdom of Kosala, Magadha's only rival. According to one view, when Udāyibhadra, a son of Ajātashatru (a grandson according to another view), was king of Magadha, he moved the capital to Pātaliputra. Another account holds that Ajātashatru himself moved the capital from Rājagriha to Pātaliputra. In the third century B.C.E., King Ashoka of the Maurya dynasty ruled the area of Magadha. Ashoka, who was a Buddhist, is famous for basing his government on humane Buddhist principles while maintaining an atmosphere of religious freedom. Magadha is also known as the birthplace of Jainism.

mahā [摩訶] (Skt, Pali; Jpn *maka*): Great, superior, large, numerous, or major. It is often a component of Sanskrit Buddhist terms and proper nouns, such as *mahāyāna* (great vehicle, or great teaching), *mahāsattva* (great being, an honorific title for a bodhisattva), *mahāprajnā* (great wisdom), *mahāparinirvāna* (great complete nirvana), and Mahākāshyapa (Great Kāshyapa).

Mahābrahmā [大梵天] (Skt, Pali; Jpn Daibon-ten): The great heavenly king Brahmā, a god said to live in the first and lowest of the four meditation heavens in the world of form above Mount Sumeru and who rules over the *sahā* world. *See also* Brahmā.

Mahābrahman Heaven [大梵天] (Skt; Jpn Daibon-ten): In ancient Indian cosmology, the uppermost of the three realms of the first meditation heaven in the world of form. The abode of the god Mahābrahmā (also known as Brahmā). *See* Heaven of Great Brahmā.

Mahādeva [摩訶提婆・大天] (Skt; Jpn Makadaiba or Daiten): A monk of Mathurā in India who lived about one hundred years after Shakyamuni. He instigated the first division within the Buddhist Order. According to *The Great Commentary on the Abhidharma,* before becoming a Buddhist, Mahādeva committed incest with his mother and killed his father. He also killed an arhat. Later, discovering that his mother was having relations with another man, he killed her as well. He deeply regretted his evil deeds, however, and entered the Buddhist Order. He mastered the three divisions of the Buddhist canon and, an eloquent speaker, converted many people in Pātaliputra to Buddhism. He later advanced the so-called five new opinions, involving the view that those who have attained the stage of arhat retain certain human weaknesses. Controversy over whether or not to accept Mahādeva's interpretations helped precipitate the first schism in the Order that resulted in the formation of two separate schools: the conservative Sthaviravāda (Pali Theravāda) school, and the more liberal Mahāsamghika school, which supported Mahādeva. Another account, however, traces this split to contention over ten modifications of the monastic rules proposed by monks in Vaishālī. *See also* five teachings of Mahādeva.

Mahākacchāyana [摩訶迦旃延] (Pali; Jpn Makakasennen): One of Shakyamuni's ten major disciples, known as foremost in debate. *See* Kātyāyana.

Mahākāla [摩訶迦羅天] (Skt; Jpn Makakara-ten): The original Sanskrit name for Daikoku or Daikoku-ten, one of the seven beneficent deities. *See* Daikoku.

Mahākāshyapa [摩訶迦葉] (Skt; Pali Mahākassapa; Jpn Makakashō): Also known as Kāshyapa. One of Shakyamuni's ten major disciples, known as foremost in the ascetic practices called *dhūta*. He was born to a Brahman family in a village near Rājagriha, the capital of the Indian kingdom of Magadha. He married Bhaddā Kapilānī and with her later renounced secular life and became Shakyamuni Buddha's disciple. Only eight days later, Mahākāshyapa is said to have attained the state of arhat. He persisted in Buddhist practice and won Shakyamuni's deep trust to the extent that the Buddha sometimes asked him to preach in his stead. He is said to have been almost the same age as Shakyamuni. Shortly after Shakyamuni's death, Mahākāshyapa, as the head of the Buddhist Order, presided over the First Buddhist Council, at which the Buddha's teachings were compiled. He died at Mount Kukkutapāda in Magadha after transferring leadership of the Order to Ānanda, another of Shakyamuni's ten major disciples. In the Lotus Sutra, Mahākāshyapa belongs to the second of the three groups of voice-hearers, having understood the Buddha's true intention through the parable of the three carts and the burning house related in the sutra's "Simile and Parable" (third) chapter. The "Bestowal of Prophecy" (sixth) chapter states that he will become a Buddha named Light Bright Thus Come One. He is regarded as the first of the Buddha's twenty-three or twenty-four successors.

Mahākātyāyana [摩訶迦旃延] (Skt; Jpn Makakasennen): Also known as Kātyāyana. One of Shakyamuni's ten major disciples, known as foremost in debate. *See* Kātyāyana.

Mahāmaudgalyāyana [摩訶目犍連・大目犍連] (Skt; Jpn Makamokkenren or Daimokkenren): Also known as Maudgalyāyana. One of Shakyamuni's ten major disciples, known as foremost in transcendental powers. *See* Maudgalyāyana.

Mahāmāyā [摩訶摩耶] (Skt, Pali; Jpn Makamaya): Also known as Māyā. The wife of King Shuddhodana of the Shākya tribe in India, and the mother of Shakyamuni. *See* Māyā.

Mahānāma [摩訶男] (Skt, Pali; Jpn Makanan): (1) One of the five ascetics who heard Shakyamuni Buddha's first sermon and became his first converts. The Increasing by One Āgama Sutra describes him as excelling in supernatural powers. The Medium-Length Āgama Sutra describes him as one of the virtuous and venerable senior monks of the Buddhist Order. While Shakyamuni was still a prince, Mahānāma served him and his father, King Shuddhodana. When Shakyamuni renounced the secular world and embarked on his religious quest for truth, King Shuddhodana ordered Mahānāma and four others to accompany him. All five engaged in ascetic practice together with Shakyamuni. When Shakyamuni realized that such austere practices would not lead to enlightenment and gave them up, the five continued without him. Later, after attaining enlightenment, Shakyamuni delivered his first sermon to Mahānāma and the other four ascetics at Deer Park, and all five became the Buddha's disciples.

(2) A member of the Shākya tribe in Kapilavastu, India. He gave his maidservant's daughter away in marriage to Prasenajit, the king of Kosala, claiming her to be his own daughter. Virūdhaka, the son of Prasenajit and this woman, motivated by a grudge he bore against the Shākyas because of this deception, later killed the majority of the Shākyas. According to the Increasing by One Āgama Sutra, when King Virūdhaka attacked the Shākyas, Mahānāma asked the king to grant him one wish. That was that the king allow the Shākyas to escape for as long as he, Mahānāma, could remain under water. Virūdhaka granted his wish, and Mahānāma remained under water for so long the king wondered what had happened. The king sent some attendants into the water to find him, and they discovered Mahānāma tied his hair to the root of a tree and drowned. Mahānāma had sacrificed his life to save the Shākyas. It is also said that Mahānāma frequently offered medicine to the Buddhist monks. According to *The Fivefold Rules of Discipline,* Mahānāma was Shakyamuni's cousin and Aniruddha's brother.

Mahāpanthaka [摩訶槃特] (Skt, Pali; Jpn Makahandoku): The elder of two brothers who were disciples of Shakyamuni Buddha. He was bright, but his brother Chūdapanthaka was so dull-witted he was unable to memorize even a single verse of the Buddhist teachings. According to one account, they were sons of a Brahman living in Shrāvastī. Mahāpanthaka attained the state of arhat and led his slow-witted brother to become a follower of the Buddha. Because his brother could not commit to memory even a single verse, Mahāpanthaka thought him unable to follow the Buddha's teachings or adapt to monastic life and was going to expel him from the monastery. At that time, Shakyamuni gave instruction to Chūdapanthaka, who then reached the state of arhat. According to *The Monastic Rules of the Sarvāstivāda School,* when Mahāpanthaka was born, his father prayed for him to lead a long and healthy life, and had a maidservant place the infant by the side of a main road so that a passing religious practitioner could bless him. When Chūdapanthaka was born, the father gave the same instructions to the maidservant, but she put the baby by the side of an alley. According to another account, the daughter of a wealthy man had relations with a servant and ran away with him. Later she became pregnant and wanted to return home. On her way home, she bore a son, Mahāpanthaka, on the roadside. Later she gave birth to a second son, Chūdapanthaka, also on the roadside. *See also* Chūdapanthaka.

Mahāparinirvāna Sutra: A reference to several Chinese translations of different texts, both Mahayana and Hinayana. The Sanskrit title Mahāparinirvāna Sutra literally means the Great Complete Nirvana Sutra and has two kinds of Chinese and Japanese transliteration: that accompanying (1) and (3) below, and that accompanying (2).

(1) [大般涅槃経] (Chin *Ta-pan-nieh-p'an-ching;* Jpn *Daihatsu-nehan-gyō*): Also known as the Great Complete Nirvana Sutra, the Great Nirvana Sutra, or simply the Nirvana Sutra. Either of the two Chinese versions of the Mahayana Nirvana Sutra: the northern version, translated by Dharmaraksha in 421; and the southern version, translated by Hui-kuan, Hui-yen, and Hsieh Ling-yün in 436. The latter is a revision of the former. The northern version consists of forty volumes and the southern version of thirty-six volumes. Both concern teachings Shakyamuni expounded immediately before his death. The Mahāparinirvāna Sutra teaches that the Dharma body of the Buddha is eternal, that all people possess the Buddha nature, and that even *icchantikas,* persons of incorrigible disbelief, can attain Buddhahood. It also contains the stories of the boy Snow Mountains, who offered his body to a demon in exchange for a Buddhist teaching, and of Ajātashatru, who put his father to death but later repented and became Shakyamuni's disciple. Fragments of the Sanskrit text are extant.

(2) [大般泥洹経] (Chin *Ta-pan-ni-yüan-ching;* Jpn *Daihatsu-naion-gyō*): Also known as the Parinirvāna Sutra, the six-volume Parinirvāna Sutra, or the six-volume Nirvana Sutra. A Chinese version of the Mahayana Nirvana Sutra, translated by Fa-hsien and Buddhabhadra around 417. This sutra consists of six volumes and corresponds in content to the first ten volumes of the forty-volume (northern version) Mahāparinirvāna Sutra translated by Dharmaraksha in 421. Comparing these two versions, Hui-kuan, Hui-yen, and Hsieh Ling-yün produced the thirty-six volume (southern version) Mahāparinirvāna Sutra as a revised version in 436.

(3) [大般涅槃経] (Chin *Ta-pan-nieh-p'an-ching;* Jpn *Daihatsu-nehan-gyō*): A Chinese version of the Hinayana Nirvana Sutra, translated by Fa-hsien around 417. This sutra consists of three volumes and records the final events of Shakyamuni Buddha's life and what took place after his death such as the cremation of his body and the erection of stupas

to enshrine his ashes. There is an extant Pali text called the *Mahāparinibbāna-suttanta,* but this is not thought to be the text from which Fa-hsien translated his version. *See also* Nirvana Sutra.

Mahāprajāpatī [摩訶波闍波提] (Skt; Pali Mahāpajāpatī; Jpn Makahajahadai): The aunt and foster mother of Shakyamuni, the younger sister of Māyā, Shakyamuni's birth mother. She is also known as Gautamī or Gotamī. Gautamī is the feminine form of Gautama, the surname of Shakyamuni's family. Mahāprajāpatī was a daughter of Suprabuddha, a wealthy man of the Shākya tribe who lived in Devadaha near Kapilavastu. Suprabuddha is also said to have been the ruler of Devadaha. When Māyā, the consort of King Shuddhodana of Kapilavastu, died seven days after giving birth to Shakyamuni, Mahāprajāpatī became Shuddhodana's wife and raised Shakyamuni. She bore Shuddhodana a son, Nanda. After the death of Shuddhodana, Mahāprajāpatī wished to renounce secular life, imploring the Buddhist Order to receive her. Initially, however, Shakyamuni Buddha would not allow women to join the Buddhist Order. Mahāprajāpatī begged the Buddha earnestly and persistently to grant her request. Ānanda also asked the Buddha to comply. Finally, Shakyamuni admitted Mahāprajāpatī to the Order as the first Buddhist nun. She gave instruction to a number of nuns and was respected as their elder. The "Encouraging Devotion" (thirteenth) chapter of the Lotus Sutra predicts that she will become a Buddha named Gladly Seen by All Living Beings. She is said to have died three months before Shakyamuni.

Mahāsamghika school [大衆部] (Skt; Jpn Daishu-bu): Also known as Mahāsāmghika, Mahāsanghika, or Mahāsānghika. One of the two schools formed by the first split in the Buddhist Order about a century after Shakyamuni's death. The other was the Sthaviravāda (Pali Theravāda) school. *The Great Commentary on the Abhidharma* attributes the cause of the schism to controversy over five new opinions set forth by a monk named Mahādeva concerning the modification of doctrine. One opinion held that those who have attained the stage of arhat retain certain human weaknesses. Another account of the split regards it as arising from a controversy over a new interpretation of the monastic rules known as the ten unlawful revisions, set forth by the monks of the Vriji tribe in Vaishālī. In either case, the Mahāsamghika school accepted the new opinions or interpretations, while the more conservative Sthaviravāda school opposed them. The Mahāsamghika school was the more liberal of the two in its interpretation of monastic rules and doctrine. According to one view, it was the forerunner of the Mahayana movement. The Mahāsamghika school divided repeatedly, and eventually gave rise to eight additional schools. *See also* five teachings of Mahādeva; ten unlawful revisions.

mahāsattva [摩訶薩・大士] (Skt; Jpn *makasatsu* or *daishi*): A great being. An honorific title for bodhisattvas. The "Simile and Parable" (third) chapter of the Lotus Sutra reads: "If there are living beings who attend the Buddha, the World-Honored One, hear the Law, believe and accept it, and put forth diligent effort, seeking comprehensive wisdom, Buddha wisdom, wisdom that comes of itself, teacherless wisdom, the insight of the Thus Come One, powers and freedom from fear, who pity and comfort countless living beings, bring benefit to heavenly and human beings, and save them all, they shall be called [those who ride] the great vehicle. Because the bodhisattvas seek this vehicle, they are called mahāsattvas." The term *mahāsattva* often accompanies bodhisattva in Buddhist scriptures, in such expressions as "the bodhisattva and mahāsattva Manjushrī" and "the bodhisattvas and mahāsattvas who gathered from the lands of the other directions."

Mahāsattva [摩訶薩埵・薩埵王子] (Skt; Jpn Makasatta or Satta-ōji): Also known as Sattva. A prince who sacrificed himself to save a starving tigress, according to the Golden Light Sutra. Mahāsattva is identified as a previous incarnation of Shakyamuni Buddha. This story is cited in several Buddhist scriptures as an illustration of compassion, and it is depicted in a number of ancient Buddhist artworks. According to the Golden Light Sutra, Mahāsattva was the third son of King Mahāratha. One day when Prince Mahāsattva was walking in a bamboo grove with his two elder brothers, Mahāpranāda and Mahādeva, he found a dying tigress that had given birth to seven cubs seven days earlier and was too weak with hunger to feed them. After his elder brothers hastily returned to the palace in fear, Prince Mahāsattva presented his flesh and blood as an offering to the starving tigress and thus saved her and her cubs.

Mahāsthāmaprāpta [勢至菩薩] (Skt; Jpn Seishi-bosatsu): The bodhisattva Great Power. According to the Meditation on the Buddha Infinite Life Sutra and the Buddha Infinite Life Sutra, a bodhisattva who attends Amida Buddha, together with Bodhisattva Perceiver of the World's Sounds. *See* Great Power.

Mahāvairochana [大日如来] (Skt; Jpn Dainichi-nyorai): The Thus Come One Mahāvairochana. A Buddha worshiped in Esoteric Buddhism. The Sanskrit name Mahāvairochana is a compound of *mahā*, meaning great, and *vairochana*, meaning that which is of, related to, or luminous like the sun. It is translated in Chinese Buddhist scriptures as "Great Sun." This Buddha appears in the Mahāvairochana Sutra and the Diamond Crown Sutra. He is regarded as the Buddha of the Dharma body who personifies the unchanging truth of all phenomena and is the source from which all Buddhas and bodhisattvas spring. Esoteric Buddhism holds that Mahāvairochana is always expounding the teaching, and that common mortals can become one with this Buddha through the practice of the three mysteries—the forming of mudras with the hands, the recitation of mantras (magical formulas), and meditation on an esoteric mandala or one of the figures appearing in it. Mahāvairochana has two aspects, the Mahāvairochana of the Womb Realm, who represents the fundamental truth of the universe, and the Mahāvairochana of the Diamond Realm, who represents wisdom. These two are fundamentally one. In Japan, Tendai Esotericism and True Word (Shingon) Esotericism differ in their interpretations of Mahāvairochana. The former holds that Mahāvairochana is the Buddha of the Dharma body, and that Shakyamuni is the Buddha of the manifested body, or a temporary manifestation of the Buddha of the Dharma body. The latter maintains that they are two entirely distinct and separate Buddhas.

Mahāvairochana Sutra [大日経] (Skt; Chin *Ta-jih-ching;* Jpn *Dainichi-kyō*): A Chinese translation of a Sanskrit text made in 725 by Shan-wu-wei (Skt Shubhakarasimha) with his disciple I-hsing's assistance. The Sanskrit text is unknown. It is generally supposed that the Sanskrit text dates from the seventh century. A Tibetan translation also exists. This sutra and the Diamond Crown Sutra formed the two fundamental scriptures of the True Word (Jpn Shingon) school. Tendai Esotericism added the Susiddhikara Sutra to these, forming its three principal scriptures. These became known as the three True Word sutras, following the model of the Pure Land (Jōdo) school, which had designated three Pure Land sutras.

The Mahāvairochana Sutra and the Diamond Crown Sutra respectively describe the Womb Realm and the Diamond Realm of Esoteric Buddhism. In the Mahāvairochana Sutra, Mahāvairochana Buddha explains, in a dialogue with Vajrasattva, the way of obtaining the Buddha wisdom. He defines the aspiration for enlightenment as the cause, great compassion as the foundation, and skillful means as the way to realize that wisdom. The sutra teaches that to observe the true nature of one's mind is to obtain the Buddha wisdom. It also describes rituals and various aspects of practice, such as mudra (hand gesture), mantra (magical formula), and mandala. There are several commentaries on the text, including *The Annotations on the Mahāvairochana Sutra,* which is I-hsing's record of Shan-wu-wei's lectures on the sutra, and *The Commentary on the Meaning of the Mahāvairochana Sutra,* a revision by Chih-yen and

Wen-ku of *The Annotations on the Mahāvairochana Sutra*. In Japan, True Word Esotericism adopts the former text, and Tendai Esotericism, the latter.

Mahāvamsa [大史・大王統史] (Pali; Jpn *Daishi* or *Dai-ōtōshi*): "The Great Chronicle." A historical chronicle of Sri Lanka compiled by Mahānāma in the fifth century. Written in Pali verse style, the *Mahāvamsa* is at once a chronological record of dynastic succession in Sri Lanka and a Buddhist history. This work was based on the *Dīpavamsa* ("The History of the Island"), an older chronicle of Sri Lanka and Buddhism. It ends with the time of the king Mahāsena, who reigned from the late third through the early fourth century. *The Chūlavamsa* ("The Little Chronicle") is a sequel to the *Mahāvamsa,* continuing the history of Sri Lanka to the nineteenth century. The name *Mahāvamsa* is often applied to the original *Mahāvamsa* together with its sequel, *Chūlavamsa.*

Mahāvana Monastery [大林精舎] (Skt, Pali; Jpn Dairin-shōja): Also known as Great Forest Monastery. *See* Great Forest Monastery.

Mahāvastu [大事] (Skt; Jpn *Daiji*): "The Great Event." A Sanskrit writing depicting the life of Shakyamuni Buddha. A work of the Lokottaravāda school, an offshoot of the Mahāsamghika school. The title *Great Event* refers specifically to the birth of Shakyamuni Buddha. This work consists of three sections. The first describes the Buddha's previous life as a bodhisattva in the age of the Buddha Burning Torch. The second relates the Buddha's life from his birth through his enlightenment. It tells of how he entered his mother's womb, emerged from her body, renounced secular life, conquered devils, and attained enlightenment, or Buddhahood. The third section describes how he taught, or "turned the wheel of the Law," and established the Buddhist Order.

Mahayana Buddhism [大乗仏教] (Jpn Daijō-bukkyō): Buddhism of the Great Vehicle. The Sanskrit *mahā* means great, and *yāna,* vehicle. One of the two major divisions of the Buddhist teachings, Mahayana and Hinayana. Mahayana emphasizes altruistic practice—called the bodhisattva practice—as a means to attain enlightenment for oneself and help others attain it as well. In contrast, Hinayana Buddhism (Buddhism of the Lesser Vehicle, *hīna* meaning lower or lesser), as viewed by Mahayanists, aims primarily at personal awakening, or attaining the state of arhat through personal discipline and practice. After Shakyamuni's death, the Buddhist Order experienced several schisms, and eventually eighteen or twenty schools formed, each of which developed its own doctrinal interpretation of the sutras.

As time passed, the monks of these schools tended toward monastic lifestyles that were increasingly reclusive, devoting themselves to the practice of precepts and the writing of doctrinal exegeses. This tendency was criticized by those who felt the monks were too conservative, rigid, and elitist, believing they had lost the Buddha's original spirit of working among the people for their salvation. Around the end of the first century B.C.E. and the beginning of the first century C.E., a new Buddhist movement arose. Its adherents called it *Mahayana*, indicating a teaching that can serve as a vehicle to carry a great number of people to a level of enlightenment equal to that of the Buddha. They criticized the older conservative schools for seeking only personal enlightenment, derisively calling them *Hinayana* (Lesser Vehicle) indicating a teaching capable of carrying only a select few to the lesser objective of arhat. According to one opinion, the Mahayana movement may have originated with the popular practice of stupa worship—revering the relics of the Buddha—that spread throughout India during the reign of King Ashoka. In any event, it seems to have arisen at least in part as a popular reform movement involving laypersons as well as clergy. *See also* Hinayana Buddhism.

Mahayana Method of Concentration and Insight, The [大乗止観法門] (Chin *Ta-ch'eng-chih-kuan-fa-men;* Jpn *Daijō-shikan-hōmon*): A work attributed to Nan-yüeh (515–577) of China. It deals with the theory and method of meditation in Mahayana Buddhism. Some scholars question Nan-yüeh's authorship. *See also* Nan-yüeh.

Mahayana ordination platform [大乗戒壇] (Jpn *daijō-kaidan*): Also, Mahayana ordination hall or Mahayana ordination center. A place for conducting the ceremony conferring the Mahayana precepts. The first Mahayana ordination platform built in Japan was the one at Enryaku-ji temple on Mount Hiei. Before that, priests had been ordained exclusively in the Hinayana precepts. Dengyō, the founder of the Japanese Tendai school, repeatedly sought imperial permission to establish a Mahayana ordination center at Mount Hiei over the objections of the Buddhist schools based at Nara. Permission was finally granted in 822 seven days after Dengyō's death, and a building housing the Mahayana ordination platform was erected there in 827.

Mahendra [摩哂陀] (n.d.) (Skt; Pali Mahinda; Jpn Mahinda): A son of the Indian king Ashoka, he brought Buddhism to Sri Lanka in the third century B.C.E. He became a monk at age twenty under the guidance of Moggaliputta Tissa. Obeying Ashoka's wishes, Mahendra went to Sri Lanka to propagate Buddhism. Under the patronage of the king of Sri Lanka, a convert to Buddhism, he built Mahāvihāra (Great Monastery), the first Buddhist monastery in Sri Lanka, in the capital of Anurādhapura. He spent the remainder of his life in Sri Lanka and is attributed with establishing Buddhism there with the aid of his sister Samghamitrā.

Maheshvara [摩醯首羅天] (Skt; Jpn Makeishura-ten): A god said to reign over the major world system. An incorporation of the major Hindu god Shiva into Buddhism. Shiva (Auspicious One) is one of the main deities of Hinduism, embodying seemingly contradictory qualities. He is both the destroyer and the restorer of the world. The Sanskrit name Maheshvara was rendered in China as "God of Great Freedom." He is usually depicted as having three eyes and eight arms and riding a white ox.

Mahinda [摩哂陀] (Pali; Jpn Mahinda): Mahendra in Sanskrit. A son of the Indian king Ashoka, he brought Buddhism to Sri Lanka in the third century B.C.E. *See* Mahendra.

Mahīshāsaka school [化地部・弥沙塞部] (Skt; Jpn Keji-bu or Misha-soku-bu): An offshoot of the Sarvāstivāda school and one of the so-called twenty Hinayana schools. According to *The Doctrines of the Different Schools,* the Mahīshāsaka school was formed out of the Sarvāstivāda school in the third one-hundred-year period after Shakyamuni Buddha's death. Other offshoots of the Sarvāstivāda school were the Vātsīputrīya, Kāshyapīya, and Sautrāntika schools. The Mahīshāsaka school acknowledged the reality of the present, but denied the reality of past and future, though its parent, the Sarvāstivāda school, recognized the reality of past, present, and future. *The Fivefold Rules of Discipline* is the *vinaya* text, or the text of monastic rules, of the Mahīshāsaka school. The Dharmagupta school eventually branched off from the Mahīshāsaka school.

mahoraga [摩睺羅伽] (Skt, Pali; Jpn *magoraga*): One of the eight kinds of nonhuman beings who protect Buddhism. *Mahoraga* means a great serpent. *See also* eight kinds of nonhuman beings.

maintaining-consciousness [執持識] (Jpn *shūji-shiki*): The eighth and deepest of the eight consciousnesses according to the Consciousness-Only school. The maintaining-consciousness is so named because it maintains the life and body of a sentient being beyond physical death. Also known as *ālaya*-consciousness. See *ālaya*-consciousness.

Maitreya (Skt) (1) [弥勒菩薩] (Jpn Miroku-bosatsu): A bodhisattva predicted to succeed Shakyamuni as a future Buddha. Also known as Ajita, meaning invincible. In China, Maitreya was rendered as Compassionate One or Compassionate Honored One. The Sanskrit word *maitreya* means friendly, benevolent, affectionate, or amicable. He is said to have been reborn in the Tushita Heaven and to reside in the inner court of this heaven, where he now teaches the heavenly beings. According to the Advent of Maitreya Sutra, he is to reappear in the world 5,670 million years after Shakyamuni's death, attain Buddhahood, and save the people in Shakyamuni's stead. For this reason, he is also sometimes called Maitreya Buddha. Belief in Maitreya prevailed in India around the beginning of the first century and spread to China and Japan.

(2) [弥勒] (Jpn Miroku): The founder of the Consciousness-Only school, thought to have been the teacher of Asanga and to have lived around 270–350 (350–430 according to another account). Various ancient works of India, China, and Tibet mention that Asanga ascended to the Tushita Heaven where he learned the Mahayana doctrines from Bodhisattva Maitreya and thereby attained enlightenment. Nevertheless, scholars have come to identify Asanga's teacher with a historical personage named Maitreya. Asanga is thought to have inherited Maitreya's teachings and advanced the systematization of the Consciousness-Only doctrine. Maitreya's works include *The Treatise on the Stages of Yoga Practice, The Treatise on the Discrimination of the Middle and the Extreme,* and *The Ornament of Mahayana Sutras.*

maitrī [慈] (Skt; Pali *mettā;* Jpn *ji*): Kindness, friendship, love, benevolence, or pity. *Maitrī* is one of the four infinite virtues, or the four aspects of a compassionate and altruistic mind, the other three being *karunā* (compassion), *muditā* (joy), and *upekshā* (impartiality). It is construed as giving others delight or happiness. Maitreya, the name of the bodhisattva, derives from the word *maitrī.* A benevolent and compassionate mind is a quality that Buddhism has always encouraged its practitioners to cultivate and nurture. *See also* four infinite virtues.

Majjhima-nikāya [中部] (Pali; Jpn Chū-bu): A collection of medium-length sutras, one of the five Āgamas. *See* five Āgamas.

major kalpa [大劫] (Jpn *dai-kō*): The period required for a world to undergo the entire four-stage cycle of formation, continuance, decline, and disintegration. These four stages themselves constitute periods called the *kalpa* of formation, the *kalpa* of continuance, the *kalpa* of decline, and the *kalpa* of disintegration. According to ancient Indian cosmology, a world perpetually repeats this four-stage cycle, and the four *kalpas* from formation through disintegration together constitute a major *kalpa.* Each of these four *kalpas* lasts for twenty small *kalpas,* and so a major *kalpa* consists of eighty small *kalpas.* One small *kalpa* equals 15,998,000 years, which makes a major *kalpa* approximately 1,280 million years. *See also* four *kalpas; kalpa.*

major world system [三千大千世界] (Skt *trisāhasra-mahāsāhasraloka-dhātu;* Jpn *sanzen-daisen-sekai*): Also, thousand-millionfold world. One of the world systems described in ancient Indian cosmology. A world consists of a Mount Sumeru, its surrounding seas and mountain ranges, a sun, a moon, and other heavenly bodies, extending upward to the first meditation heaven in the world of form and downward to the windy circle that is its foundation. This concept might be compared in modern terms to the concept of a solar system from the standpoint of the planet one lives on. One thousand worlds make a minor world system; one thousand minor world systems compose an intermediate world system; and one thousand intermediate world systems form a major world system. Therefore, one major world system comprises one billion worlds, and hence it is referred to as the thousand-millionfold world. The universe was conceived of as containing countless major world systems.

major world system dust particle kalpas [三千塵点劫] (Jpn *sanzen-jintengō* or *sanzen-jindengō*): An immensely long period of time described in the "Parable of the Phantom City" (seventh) chapter of the Lotus Sutra to indicate how much time has passed since Shakyamuni preached the sutra to his voice-hearer disciples as the sixteenth son of the Buddha Great Universal Wisdom Excellence. A "major world system" is that of ancient Indian cosmology (*see* previous entry). The "Parable of the Phantom City" chapter explains the duration called major world system dust particle *kalpas* as follows: If a person should use his strength to smash a major world system, should completely crush its earth particles and reduce them all to powdered ink, and if when he passed through a thousand lands he should drop one speck of ink, and if he continued in this manner until he had exhausted all the specks of ink, and if one then took all the lands he had passed through, both those he dropped a speck in and those he did not, and once more ground their earth into dust, and then took one grain of dust to represent one *kalpa* (approximately sixteen million years)—the number of tiny grains of dust would be less than the number of *kalpas* in the past when that Buddha lived.

In this explanation, "that Buddha" refers to Great Universal Wisdom Excellence Buddha, and an immeasurable number of *kalpas* that elapsed since his extinction is commonly described by the term *major world system dust particle kalpas*. In the "Parable of the Phantom City" chapter, Shakyamuni declares that, major world system dust particle *kalpas* in the past, he was born as the last of the sixteen sons of Great Universal Wisdom Excellence Buddha, who was formerly a king. This Buddha expounded the Lotus Sutra, and his sons, blessed by the chance to hear their father's teaching, transmitted it to a great number of people. Those who were taught by the Buddha's sixteenth son were later reborn in India together with Shakyamuni, the son's reincarnation, to complete their Buddhist practice for attaining enlightenment.

makara [摩竭] (Skt, Pali; Jpn *makatsu*): A huge fish often mentioned in Buddhist scriptures. The Great Compassion Sutra relates the story of a merchant seaman whose ship is about to be swallowed by a *makara*. Though his shipmates are in despair, he fixes his mind on the Buddhas and calls upon their mercy. Seeing him, the others join him in prayer, and the *makara* ceases its attack.

Makkhali Gosāla [末伽梨拘舍梨] (Pali; Jpn Makkari-kushari): An influential non-Buddhist thinker during Shakyamuni's time. *See* six non-Buddhist teachers.

Malaya, Mount [摩黎山・摩羅耶山] (Skt; Jpn Mari-sen, Marei-sen, or Maraya-sen): A mountain in southern India. It was noted for its sandalwood trees.

Malla [末羅] (Skt, Pali; Jpn Matsura): One of the sixteen great states in ancient India in Shakyamuni's time. Malla is also the name of the tribe that occupied that state, in what is the present-day state of Uttar Pradesh in northern India. Kushinagara was the capital of the Mallas, and Pāvā was another great Malla city. Unlike the monarchies that surrounded it, Malla is said to have employed a republican form of government, where assemblies were held to decide important matters. When Shakyamuni died in a grove of sal trees in the northern part of Kushinagara, his body was received and cremated by the Mallas who were overcome with grief. Shakyamuni's ashes were then divided into eight parts, one of which was distributed to the Mallas, who built a stupa to house them.

Mallikā [末利] (Skt, Pali; Jpn Mari): The wife of Prasenajit, a king of Kosala in ancient India. According to *The Fourfold Rules of Discipline*, she was a maidservant of a Brahman at Shrāvastī, the capital of Kosala. One day, Prasenajit encountered Mallikā who made a deep impression on him. He took her as one of his consorts, among whom she came to hold the foremost place. Later she visited Shakyamuni Buddha at Jetavana Monastery in Shrāvastī in the Kosala kingdom to receive his instruction and converted to his teachings. She led Prasenajit to the Buddha's teachings. In the Increasing by One Āgama Sutra, Mallikā is described as foremost among laywomen who made offerings to the Buddha. Mallikā appears with Prasenajit in many Buddhist works. According to one account, she was the mother of Virūdhaka, who later seized the throne from his father Prasenajit and killed the great majority of the Shākyas. Shrīmālā, the protagonist of the Shrīmālā Sutra, is known as a daughter of Mallikā and King Prasenajit. *See also* Virūdhaka.

māna [慢] (Skt, Pali; Jpn *man*): *See* arrogance.

mandala [曼荼羅] (Skt; Jpn *mandara*): An object of devotion on which Buddhas and bodhisattvas are depicted or on which a doctrine is expressed. Many Buddhist schools regard a mandala specific to their respective schools as the embodiment of enlightenment or truth. It was rendered in Chinese as "perfectly endowed" or "cluster of blessings."

māndāra flower [曼陀羅華] (Skt; Jpn *mandara-ke*): Also, *māndārava* flower. A flower said to bloom in heaven. It is fragrant, and its beauty delights those who see it. The Sanskrit term *mahāmāndāra* (also *mahāmāndārava*) indicates great or large *māndāra* flowers, a distinct kind of flower in Buddhist scriptures. In Buddhist sutras, *māndāras* and other heavenly flowers rain down from the heavens when a Buddha preaches or when other wonderful events occur. The *māndāra* flower is one of the four kinds of flowers said to bloom in heaven, the other three being the great *māndāra* flower, the *manjūshaka* flower, and the great *manjūshaka* flower. See also *manjūshaka* flower.

Māndhātri [頂生王・曼陀多王] (Skt; Jpn Chōshō-ō or Mandata-ō): A king who ruled all four continents surrounding Mount Sumeru, but, failing in an attempt to conquer the heaven of the god Shakra, is said to have fallen to the ground. *See* Born from the Crown of the Head.

mani [摩尼] (Skt, Pali; Jpn *mani*): A jewel. Also, a particular kind of jewel said to have the power to remove misfortune, clarify muddy water, and cure illness. It is often identified with the wish-granting jewel, which is said to possess the power to produce whatever one desires.

manifested body [応身] (Skt *nirmāna-kāya;* Jpn *ōjin*): One of the three bodies of a Buddha, the others being the Dharma body and the reward body. The Sanskrit term *nirmāna-kāya* literally means body of transformation. The manifested body is the physical form that a Buddha assumes in this world in order to save people. In other words, it is the body with which a Buddha carries out compassionate actions to lead people to enlightenment. A Buddha of this kind is called a Buddha of the manifested body. The T'ien-t'ai school distinguishes two types of manifested body: the inferior manifested body, or the Buddha who appears for the sake of ordinary people, persons of the two vehicles, and bodhisattvas who have not yet reached the first stage of development (the forty-first stage of bodhisattva practice); and the superior manifested body, or the Buddha who appears for the sake of bodhisattvas at the first stage of development and beyond. *See also* three bodies.

manjūshaka flower [曼殊沙華] (Skt; Jpn *manjusha-ge*): A soft white flower said to bloom in heaven and to have the power to remove the evil karma of those who see it. *Manjūshaka* flowers are said to rain down from the heavens when a Buddha preaches or when other wonderful events occur. In the "Introduction" (first) chapter of the Lotus Sutra, an event that heralds the preaching of the sutra is depicted as follows: "At that time heaven rained down *māndārava* flowers, great *māndārava* flowers, *manjūshaka* flowers, and great *manjūshaka* flowers, scattering them over the Buddha and over the great assembly." These flowers are collectively known as the four kinds of flowers. See also *māndāra* flower.

Manjushrī [文殊師利菩薩・文殊菩薩] (Skt; Jpn Monjushiri-bosatsu or Monju-bosatsu): A bodhisattva who appears in the sutras as the leader of the bodhisattvas and is regarded as symbolic of the perfection of wisdom. Sutras depict him as one of the two bodhisattvas who attend Shakyamuni Buddha, the other being Samantabhadra, or Universal Worthy. Manjushrī is generally shown in Buddhist art riding a lion at the Buddha's left, and represents the virtues of wisdom and enlightenment. Shakyamuni's right-hand attendant, Bodhisattva Universal Worthy, shown riding a white elephant, represents the virtues of truth and practice. According to the Flower Garland Sutra, Manjushrī lives on Mount Clear and Cool in the east, which came to be identified with Mount Wu-t'ai in China. Belief in Manjushrī flourished in China from the Eastern Chin dynasty (317–420) and in Japan from the Heian period (794–1185).

mano-consciousness [末那識] (Skt *mano-vijnāna;* Jpn *mana-shiki*): The seventh of the eight consciousnesses. The Sanskrit word *mano,* a variation of *manas,* means the mind, thought, perception, cognition, and pondering. This consciousness performs the function of abstract thought and discerns the inner world. Awareness of self is said to originate at this level. The passionate attachment to the ego that helps create evil karma is also viewed as the working of the *mano*-consciousness.

man of pure faith [清信士] (Skt, Pali *upāsaka;* Jpn *shōshin-ji*): A Buddhist layman who has faith in the three treasures of the Buddha, the Law (his teachings), and the Buddhist Order, and has received the five precepts. "Man of pure faith" is the Chinese translation of the Sanskrit word *upāsaka,* a Buddhist layman. "Woman of pure faith" *(upāsikā)* is the female counterpart. See also *upāsaka.*

Manoratha [摩奴羅他・如意] (n.d.) (Skt; Jpn Manurata or Nyoi): A monk of Gandhara in northern India thought to have lived around the fourth or fifth century; the teacher of Vasubandhu. He was well versed in the three divisions of the Buddhist canon and was widely respected for his learning and eloquence in preaching. According to Hsüan-tsang's *Record of the Western Regions,* King Vikramāditya of Shrāvastī, famed for his generosity, gave a hundred thousand coins to a person who looked for and captured the wild boar the king had missed while hunting. On the other hand, Manoratha gave the same amount of money to a person who simply shaved his head. This incurred the king's abiding displeasure.

One day the king conceived the idea of humiliating the monk in the presence of a great audience. He recruited a hundred non-Buddhist scholars to debate with Manoratha. Prior to the debate, the king said, "If the Buddhist monk wins, I will convert to the Buddha's teaching, but if he is defeated, he will be put to death." The monk defeated ninety-nine of the scholars. The last scholar looked down upon the monk and argued with him violently. When they took up the topic of "fire and smoke," the king joined the scholar and together they insisted that the monk was wrong. When Manoratha began to explain, he was shouted down. Humiliated, he bit off his tongue, admonished his disciple Vasubandhu not to debate with persons who rely on their number or discuss the truth among the ignorant, and then died. Shortly thereafter King Vikramāditya lost his throne and kingdom. When the new king restored the country, Vasubandhu asked him for the chance to vindicate his teacher. The king praised his resolution and sponsored a debate between Vasubandhu and the hundred non-Buddhist scholars who had argued with Manoratha. Vasubandhu won, and the scholars admitted their defeat.

Manorhita [摩奴羅] (n.d.) (Skt; Jpn Manura): Also known as Madhura. A monk of the Nadī kingdom in India around the fourth and fifth centuries. The twenty-first of Shakyamuni Buddha's twenty-three, or the twenty-second of his twenty-four, successors. According to *A History of the Buddha's Successors,* though he was born as a crown prince of the kingdom, he renounced secular life and studied Buddhism under Vasubandhu, his teacher and predecessor. Well versed in the three divisions of the Buddhist canon, he practiced Buddhism chiefly in southern India, refuting the doctrines of Hinayana schools and spreading Mahayana Buddhism. He transferred the Buddha's teachings to Haklenayashas.

mantra [真言] (Skt; Jpn *shingon*): A formula consisting of secret words or syllables said to embody mysterious powers. Mantra was rendered into Chinese as "true word." True Word (Jpn Shingon) later became the name of an influential school of Esoteric Buddhism in Japan. Mantras are employed in the practice and ritual of Esoteric Buddhism, where they are believed to help achieve union with Mahāvairochana Buddha. Esoteric Buddhism views them as the distillation of Buddhist truth.

many in body, one in mind [異体同心] (Jpn *itai-dōshin*): A concept used to describe ideal unity. Nichiren (1222–1282) used the phrase to encourage unity among his followers. In his writing known as *Many in Body, One in Mind,* Nichiren states, "If the spirit of many in body but one in mind prevails among the people, they will achieve all their goals, whereas if one in body but different in mind, they can achieve nothing remarkable" (618). Another writing of Nichiren, *The Heritage of the Ultimate Law of Life*, says: "All disciples and lay supporters of Nichiren should chant Nam-myoho-renge-kyo with the spirit of many in body but one in mind, transcending all differences among themselves to become as inseparable as fish and the water in which they swim. This spiritual bond is the basis for the universal transmission of the ultimate Law of life and death. Herein lies the true goal of Nichiren's propagation" (217). This expression can also be translated as "different in body, same in spirit." "Different in body" can be interpreted as suggesting the uniqueness of individuals, and "same in spirit," a goal or commitment shared among individuals.

Many Treasures [多宝如来] (Skt Prabhūtaratna; Jpn Tahō-nyorai): A Buddha depicted in the Lotus Sutra. Many Treasures appears, seated within his treasure tower, in order to lend credence to Shakyamuni's teachings in the sutra. According to the "Treasure Tower" (eleventh) chapter of the Lotus Sutra, Many Treasures Buddha lives in the World of Treasure Purity in the east. While still engaged in bodhisattva practice, he pledges that, even after entering nirvana, he will appear with his treasure tower in order to attest to the validity of the Lotus Sutra, wherever it might be taught. In the "Treasure Tower" chapter, Shakyamuni assembles all the Buddhas from the ten directions. He then opens the treasure tower and, at the invitation of the Buddha Many Treasures, seats himself beside this Buddha. Shakyamuni then employs his supernatural powers to lift the assembly into the air, and the sequence of events known as the Ceremony in the Air begins. *See also* Ceremony in the Air.

māra [魔] (Skt, Pali; Jpn *ma*): *See* devil.

Marīchi [摩利支天] (Skt; Jpn Marishi-ten): A god originally thought of as a personification of the sun's rays. He also appears as a god of wind in Indian mythology. Regarded as a child of Brahmā, he was widely venerated in India. The Marīchi Sutra of Esoteric Buddhism depicts this god as female, and thus Marīchi sometimes appears as a woman in sculpture, painting, and various writings. Buddhism generally represents Marīchi as the male vassal of the sun god who precedes him in his advance across the sky. Marīchi was said to possess the power to become invisible and defeat an enemy without being captured. For this reason, he was revered by warriors in Japan. Marīchi is also depicted as riding a wild boar and having three faces and six or eight arms.

markings of the thousand-spoked wheel [千輻輪相] (Jpn *sempukurin-sō*): One of the thirty-two features that a Buddha is said to possess, appearing on the sole of each foot. *See* thousand-spoked wheel.

Mātanga [摩騰迦・摩騰] (Skt; Jpn Matōga or Matō): Also known as

Kāshyapa Mātanga. The Indian monk believed to have been the first to introduce Buddhism to China. *See* Kāshyapa Mātanga.

Mathura [摩突羅国] (Skt Mathurā; Jpn Matora-koku): A city in northern India on the bank of the Yamuna River, located about 140 kilometers south-southeast of New Delhi. It was the capital of Shūrasena, one of the sixteen great states of India in the sixth century B.C.E., around the time of Shakyamuni. It prospered as a trading center and became an important center for Buddhism and Jainism. Mathura, long regarded as sacred by Hindus, is also the birthplace of Krishna, venerated as an avatar of the god Vishnu. Shakyamuni himself went to Mathura several times to preach. Later, according to *A History of the Buddha's Successors,* Upagupta, the fourth of Shakyamuni's twenty-three successors and a native of Mathura, contributed greatly to the rise of Buddhism in this area. The Sarvāstivāda school also flourished there. Mathura prospered as a center of the Kushan dynasty especially during the reign of King Kanishka in the second century.

Mathura was also one of the two birthplaces of unique Buddhist artistic styles that flourished during the Kushan dynasty, the other being Gandhara. Mathuran Buddhist art reached its height after Kanishka's accession, which presumably was around C.E. 130, though another view places it in 144. Buddhist art in Mathura maintained its prominence for about one hundred years after this. The earliest production of Buddha images is thought to have occurred in Gandhara near the end of the first century, and in Mathura such art began to appear in the early second century. By another account, the Mathuran and Gandharan images of the Buddha were contemporaneous, distinctively different in style. The Mathuran style is predominantly Indian, while the Gandharan style reveals a considerable Western, or Greco-Roman, influence. According to *The Record of the Western Regions,* Hsüan-tsang's account of his travels through Central Asia and India in the seventh century, there were monasteries at that time in more than twenty locations in Mathura. More than two thousand monks lived in them and studied both Hinayana and Mahayana teachings.

matrix of the Tathāgata [如来蔵] (Jpn *nyorai-zō*): *See* matrix of the Thus Come One.

matrix of the Thus Come One [如来蔵] (Skt *tathāgata-garbha;* Jpn *nyorai-zō*): Also, matrix of the Tathāgata, womb of the Thus Come One, womb of the Tathāgata, or Tathāgata-store. An expression that refers to all people or living beings as potential Buddhas. *Tathāgata-garbha* means that all living beings have the pure mind of the Thus Come One, or Buddha, hidden within the "matrix" or "womb" of their earthly desires.

That all living beings are "the womb of the Thus Come One" means that all have the potential for attaining Buddhahood. This concept is found in various sutras and treatises, such as the Matrix of the Thus Come One Sutra, Shrīmālā Sutra, Secret Solemnity Sutra, *The Treatise on the Treasure Vehicle of Buddhahood,* and *The Treatise on the Buddha Nature.* For example, the Matrix of the Thus Come One Sutra states that all living beings are "the matrix of the Thus Come One," the womb in which the Thus Come One is formed. The Sanskrit *garbha* means womb or embryo. According to the Shrīmālā Sutra, translated into Chinese by Gunabhadra, the Dharma body is buried or stored amid one's earthly desires. When this store is opened, the Dharma body appears.

Matrix of the Thus Come One Sutra [如来蔵経] (Skt *Tathāgatagarbha-sūtra;* Chin *Ju-lai-tsang-ching;* Jpn *Nyoraizō-kyō*): A sutra that sets forth the concept of the matrix of the Thus Come One, i.e., that each person is the matrix, womb, or embryo of a Thus Come One, or Buddha. This means that all persons possess the Buddha nature, that all people are potential Buddhas.

The Sanskrit text is generally thought to have been produced in the early third century, but is not extant. A Tibetan translation and two Chinese translations exist. Of the Chinese translations, Buddhabhadra (359–429) produced one, and Pu-k'ung (Skt Amoghavajra, 705–774), the other. The "matrix of the Thus Come One" became a core concept of Mahayana Buddhism, and this sutra is regarded as one of the earliest to address it. Around the fourth or fifth century, Vasubandhu and Sāramati delved into the concept in their respective treatises *The Treatise on the Buddha Nature* and *The Treatise on the Treasure Vehicle of Buddhahood.* The principle that "all living beings alike possess the Buddha nature," which appears repeatedly in the Nirvana Sutra, and the Lotus Sutra's teaching of the one Buddha vehicle are related to the concept of the matrix of the Thus Come One.

Matsubagayatsu [松葉ケ谷]: The place of Nichiren's residence in Kamakura, Japan. Nichiren had a dwelling there that served as the center of his religious activities in Kamakura. He is thought to have lived there for most of the period from 1253, shortly after he publicly declared his teaching, until 1271, the year of the Tatsunokuchi Persecution and his subsequent exile to Sado Island. This period was punctuated by his nearly two-year exile to the province of Izu, and his time spent in what is now Chiba Prefecture spreading his teachings.

Matsubagayatsu Persecution [松葉ケ谷の法難] (Jpn Matsubagayatsu-no-hōnan): An attempt on Nichiren's life by believers of the Pure Land (Jōdo) school at his dwelling at Matsubagayatsu in Kamakura, Japan, on the twenty-seventh day of the eighth month, 1260. The attack was motivated by anger at Nichiren's criticism of Hōnen, the founder of the Pure Land school, and his teachings. Nichiren had publicly expressed these criticisms in *On Establishing the Correct Teaching for the Peace of the Land,* which he submitted to Hōjō Tokiyori, the retired regent but de facto leader of the shogunate, on the sixteenth day of the seventh month in 1260. In this treatise, he called upon the rulers to stop patronizing Buddhist schools whose teachings he described as provisional, especially the Pure Land school, which encouraged people to abandon the Lotus Sutra. Turning against the correct teaching, he said, was the basic cause for the disasters facing Japan in his time, and upholding it would stem these disasters. This apparently incensed Hōjō Shigetoki, father of the regent Nagatoki, and other members of the ruling Hōjō clan who were ardent followers of the Pure Land teaching and its priests. These shogunate officials apparently played a role in inciting Pure Land followers to attack and attempt to kill Nichiren. On the night of the attack, a group of several hundred people besieged Nichiren's dwelling at Matsubagayatsu, though he had already managed to escape. He then went to the home of his follower Toki Jōnin in Shimōsa Province, where he spread his teachings for nearly half a year until he returned to Kamakura the following spring.

Matsuno Rokurō Saemon [松野六郎左衛門] (d. 1278): Also known as the lay priest Matsuno Rokurō Saemon. A follower of Nichiren who lived in the village of Matsuno in Ihara District of Suruga Province, Japan. His daughter married Nanjō Hyōe Shichirō, the father of Nanjō Tokimitsu. Nanjō Hyōe Shichirō and his family were strong followers and supporters of Nichiren. Matsuno converted to Nichiren's teachings through his relationship with the Nanjō family. Though Matsuno had many children, the known members of his family are Matsuno Rokurō Saemon himself; his wife; his eldest son Rokurō Saemon-no-jō and his wife; Nichiji, another of Rokurō Saemon's sons, who became one of the six senior priests named by Nichiren; and the daughter who married Nanjō. More than ten letters from Nichiren to the Matsuno family are extant.

Maudgalyāyana [目連・目犍連] (Skt; Pali Moggallāna; Jpn Mokuren or Mokkenren): Also known as Mahāmaudgalyāyana or Kolita. One of Shakyamuni Buddha's ten major disciples, known as foremost in transcendental powers. Born to a Brahman family in the suburbs of Rājagriha in the kingdom of Magadha, India, he was a close friend of Shāriputra from childhood. Maudgalyāyana and Shāriputra were previously disciples of Sanjaya Belatthiputta, a skeptic and one of the so-called six non-Buddhist teachers. Later they became followers of Shakyamuni and entered the Buddhist Order, bringing all of Sanjaya's 250 disciples with them. Maudgalyāyana and Shāriputra came to be revered as the Buddha's two leading disciples.

When Devadatta fomented a schism in the Buddhist Order and lured away five hundred monks, these two persuaded the monks to leave Devadatta and return to Shakyamuni Buddha. Maudgalyāyana and Shāriputra died before Shakyamuni, the former killed by a hostile Brahman while begging for alms in Rājagriha and the latter dying of an illness. In the Lotus Sutra, Maudgalyāyana belongs to the second of the three groups of voice-hearers to understand the Buddha's true intention as related in the parable in the "Simile and Parable" (third) chapter of the sutra. The "Bestowal of Prophecy" (sixth) chapter predicts that he will attain enlightenment in the future as a Buddha named Tamālapattra Sandalwood Fragrance. The Service for the Deceased Sutra details the story of how Maudgalyāyana saved his deceased mother from the world of hungry spirits. This story spread widely in China, where the service for deceased ancestors (Chin *yü-lan-p'en;* Jpn *urabon*) became a Buddhist observance based upon it. This tradition was adopted in Japan and Korea as well.

Māyā [摩耶] (Skt, Pali; Jpn Maya): Also known as Mahāmāyā. The wife of King Shuddhodana of the Shākya tribe in India, and the mother of Shakyamuni. She died seven days after giving birth to Shakyamuni at the Lumbinī grove, and her younger sister Mahāprajāpatī raised the young prince. According to the Sutra of the Collected Stories of the Buddha's Deeds in Past Lives, Māyā was the eldest of the eight daughters of a man named Suprabuddha who lived in Devadaha near Kapilavastu. She married into the royal family of the Shākya tribe at Kapilavastu along with her seven younger sisters. Māyā and her youngest sister Mahāprajāpatī were married to Shuddhodana and the other six sisters to Shuddhodana's three brothers. A differing account appears in the Mahāsammata Sutra, which states that Suprabuddha had two daughters, Māyā and Mahāmāyā, and that it was Mahāmāyā who married Shuddhodana and gave birth to Shakyamuni. According to the Miscellaneous Āgama Sutra, Shakyamuni, having attained enlightenment, ascended to the Heaven of the Thirty-three Gods to preach his teaching to his mother, Māyā, who had been reborn in this heaven. The Causality of Past and Present Sutra states that, when the pregnant Māyā reached out with her right arm for a branch of an *ashoka* tree at the Lumbinī grove to pick some blossoms, Shakyamuni was born out of her right side.

Māyā Sutra [摩耶経] (Skt; Chin *Mo-ya-ching;* Jpn *Maya-kyō*): Also known as the Mahāmāyā Sutra. A sutra about Māyā, the mother of

Shakyamuni, translated into Chinese by T'an-ching during the Ch'i dynasty (479–502). The text from which this translation was made is not extant. The first half of the sutra relates how Shakyamuni used his supernatural powers to ascend to the Heaven of the Thirty-three Gods. There he expounded his teachings for three months to his mother Māyā, who had died seven days after giving him birth and was reborn in that heaven. The latter half describes Shakyamuni's entry into nirvana after his travels for preaching through many kingdoms, and how, knowing of her son's death, Māyā descended from the Heaven of the Thirty-three Gods. Wishing to view the body for the last time, she approached the coffin. At that moment it opened, a thousand luminous Buddhas, emanations of Shakyamuni, appeared, and mother and son were reunited. The sutra subsequently tells of those who will propagate Buddhism during the fifteen hundred years following Shakyamuni Buddha's death and predicts the time of their advent and their deeds. Among those predictions are the advent of Ashvaghosha and his propagation of Buddhism six hundred years after the Buddha's death, and of Nāgārjuna and his teaching activities seven hundred years after the Buddha's death.

Meaning of the Four Teachings, The [四教義] (Chin *Ssu-chiao-i;* Jpn *Shikyō-gi*): A work by T'ien-t'ai (538–597) that interprets the names of the four teachings of doctrine (the Tripitaka teaching, the connecting teaching, the specific teaching, and the perfect teaching), a classification of Shakyamuni's teachings that he established, and clarifies the doctrines contained in each. Miao-lo's *Annotations on "The Words and Phrases of the Lotus Sutra"* identifies this work with six volumes of T'ien-t'ai's ten-volume *Profound Meaning of the Vimalakīrti Sutra,* a lost work that T'ien-t'ai later shortened and revised into the still-extant *Annotations on the Profound Meaning of the Vimalakīrti Sutra* in six volumes.

Meaning of the Lotus Sutra, The [法華経義記・法華義記] (Chin *Fa-hua-ching-i-chi* or *Fa-hua-i-chi;* Jpn *Hokekyō-giki* or *Hokke-giki*): A commentary by Fa-yün (467–529) on Kumārajīva's Chinese translation of the Lotus Sutra. It is the second among extant commentaries on the Lotus Sutra produced in China; the first is by Tao-sheng (d. 434), a disciple of Kumārajīva. *The Meaning of the Lotus Sutra* is said to have been expounded orally by Fa-yün and recorded by a disciple. Because this work contains no commentary on the "Devadatta" chapter of the Lotus Sutra, it is thought to be based on a version of Kumārajīva's translation in which the content of the "Devadatta" chapter did not appear as a separate, distinct chapter. *The Meaning of the Lotus Sutra* greatly influenced Prince Shōtoku (574–622) in Japan, who wrote a commentary on the sutra based upon it.

Medicine King [薬王菩薩] (Skt Bhaishajyarāja; Jpn Yakuō-bosatsu): A bodhisattva said to possess the power to cure physical and mental diseases. The Sanskrit *bhaishajya* means curativeness, medicine, or remedy; *rāja* means king. According to the Meditation on the Two Bodhisattvas Medicine King and Medicine Superior Sutra, in the remote past, in the Middle Day of the Law of a Buddha named Lapis Lazuli Brightness, Bodhisattva Medicine King was a rich man named Constellation Light. He heard the teaching of the Buddha wisdom from the monk Sun Repository. Rejoicing, he presented beneficial medicines as an offering to Sun Repository and his fellow monks, and vowed that when he attained Buddhahood all those who heard his name would be cured of illness. Constellation Light had a younger brother Lightning Glow, who also offered beneficial medicines to Sun Repository and others, vowing to attain Buddhahood. The people praised the two brothers, calling the elder brother Medicine King and the younger brother Medicine Superior. Constellation Light and Lightning Glow, the sutra says, were reborn respectively as Bodhisattva Medicine King and Bodhisattva Medicine Superior and will in the future attain enlightenment as the Buddhas Pure Eye and Pure Storehouse.

Bodhisattva Medicine King also figures prominently in the Lotus Sutra. The "Teacher of the Law" (tenth) chapter is addressed to Bodhisattva Medicine King. In the "Encouraging Devotion" (thirteenth) chapter, he and Bodhisattva Great Joy of Preaching lead the host of bodhisattvas in vowing to propagate the sutra in the evil age after Shakyamuni's death. The "Medicine King" (twenty-third) chapter describes the austerities he performed in a previous lifetime as a bodhisattva named Gladly Seen by All Living Beings, or simply Gladly Seen. In the remote past, Bodhisattva Gladly Seen heard the Lotus Sutra from the Buddha Sun Moon Pure Bright Virtue. As a result, he mastered a form of meditation that enabled him to manifest any physical form. In gratitude, Gladly Seen entered this meditation and caused flowers and incense to rain down from the heavens as an offering to the Buddha Sun Moon Pure Bright Virtue and the Lotus Sutra, but he felt dissatisfied with this offering and decided that it would be more meaningful to offer his own body. After steeping himself in scents and fragrances for twelve hundred years, he anointed his body with fragrant oil and set himself ablaze in the presence of the Buddha.

The blaze illuminated worlds equal in number to the sands of eighty million Ganges Rivers, and the Buddhas within them praised his act as the supreme offering. His body burned for twelve hundred years, and after it was consumed, he was reborn in the land of Sun Moon Pure

Bright Virtue Buddha, whom he found at the point of entering nirvana. The Buddha transferred his teachings to Bodhisattva Gladly Seen and then died. Gladly Seen cremated the Buddha's body and built eighty-four thousand stupas to enshrine his ashes, to which he then made offerings. Not satisfied, he proceeded to burn his arms as a further offering for seventy-two thousand years. All the bodhisattvas, gods, people, and other beings he had converted grieved to see him without arms, but he declared to them that having offered his own flesh, he would surely attain Buddhahood, whereupon his arms were restored. Later he was reborn as Bodhisattva Medicine King. The "King Wonderful Adornment" (twenty-seventh) chapter says that the bodhisattvas Medicine King and Medicine Superior are reincarnations of Pure Storehouse and Pure Eye who converted their father, King Wonderful Adornment, to the correct teaching.

The Biography of the Great Teacher T'ien-t'ai Chih-che of the Sui Dynasty by Chang-an states that T'ien-t'ai (538–597) was a reincarnation of Bodhisattva Medicine King because he had attained a great awakening through the "Medicine King" chapter of the Lotus Sutra.

"Medicine King" chapter [薬王品] (Jpn *Yakuō-hon*): The twenty-third chapter of the Lotus Sutra. *See* "Former Affairs of the Bodhisattva Medicine King" chapter.

Medicine Master [薬師如来] (Skt Bhaishajyaguru; Jpn Yakushi-nyorai): Also known as the Buddha of Medicine, the Buddha of Healing, or the Healing Buddha. The Thus Come One Medicine Master, the Buddha of the Pure Emerald World in the east. The Sanskrit *bhaishajya* means curativeness, medicine, or remedy; *guru* means teacher, master, or venerable person. Before he attained enlightenment, Medicine Master made twelve vows to cure all illnesses and lead all people to enlightenment. Belief in this Buddha was popular in both China and Japan, and many statues were made of him. He is often depicted as being flanked by the bodhisattvas Sunlight and Moonlight.

Medicine Master Sutra [薬師経] (Skt *Bhaishajyaguru-vaidūryaprabharāja-sūtra;* Chin *Yao-shih-ching;* Jpn *Yakushi-kyō*): A sutra that explains the blessings of the Buddha Medicine Master. The Medicine Master Sutra refers to any of four extant Chinese translations, though usually to the translation produced in 650 by Hsüan-tsang. In this work, Shakyamuni Buddha explains to Bodhisattva Manjushrī the virtues of the Buddha Medicine Master. First, the sutra recounts a previous life of the Buddha Medicine Master in which, as a bodhisattva, he made twelve vows to benefit the people. The great benefit of invoking his name is then described. The sutra also describes seven disasters that making offerings to the Buddha Medicine Master can avert, and how by doing so one can restore peace to the land. The Sanskrit text and a Tibetan translation are extant.

Medicine Superior [薬上菩薩] (Skt Bhaishajyarājasamudgata or Bhaishajyasamudgata; Jpn Yakujō-bosatsu): One of the two bodhisattvas said to heal physical and spiritual illnesses, the other being Medicine King. According to the "King Wonderful Adornment" (twenty-seventh) chapter of the Lotus Sutra, in a previous life these two bodhisattvas were the princes Pure Storehouse and Pure Eye who converted their father, King Wonderful Adornment, to the correct teaching. The Sanskrit name Bhaishajyarājasamudgata means one who "has come forth from the king of medicine," and Bhaishajyasamudgata, one who "has come forth from medicine." *Bhaishajya* means medicine, *rāja,* king, and *samudgata,* appeared, risen up, or come forth. *See also* Medicine King.

meditation [禅・禅定] (Skt *dhyāna;* Pali *jhāna;* Jpn *zen* or *zenjō*): The practice of focusing the mind on one point in order to purify the spirit, eradicate illusions, and perceive the truth. Meditation was practiced widely in India before Shakyamuni, and was later incorporated into Buddhism, which developed its own forms and approaches. In Mahayana Buddhism, *dhyāna,* meaning meditation, is the fifth of the six *pāramitās,* six practices required of Mahayana bodhisattvas. In China, T'ien-t'ai (538–597) established a system of meditative practice he named "concentration and insight." China also saw the appearance of the Ch'an, or Zen, school, which places primary emphasis on meditation as the practice for attaining enlightenment. *See also* seated meditation; Zen school.

meditation master [禅師] (Jpn *zenji*): A priest who has attained the level of meditation that enables one to focus the mind on one point, remaining in that state of concentration in order to eradicate illusions and contemplate the truth. "Meditation Master" was often applied as an honorific title, as were the titles "Dharma Teacher" and "Discipline Master." The imperial courts of China and Japan awarded the title "Meditation Master" to priests they considered to be of outstanding virtue. This title in Chinese and Japanese is also used to refer to eminent priests of the Ch'an, or Zen, school, to whom the term "Zen Master" is often applied in English.

Meditation on the Buddha Infinite Life Sutra [観無量寿経] (Chin *Kuan-wu-liang-shou-ching;* Jpn *Kammuryōju-kyō*): Abbreviated as the Meditation Sutra. A sutra said to have been translated into Chinese by Kālayashas between 424 and 442. The Buddha Infinite Life is also known as the Buddha Amida. This sutra is one of the three basic scriptures of the Pure Land school, which reveres that Buddha. According to the Chinese text, Shakyamuni Buddha expounded it in the royal palace at Rājagriha in Magadha, India, at the request of Vaidehī, who was grieving in prison over the evil acts of her son Ajātashatru, who had also imprisoned his father, King Bimbisāra, in order to become the new king. Shakyamuni employed supernatural powers to show her various pure lands, including Amida's Pure Land of Perfect Bliss. Since Vaidehī preferred Amida's Pure Land to all the others, Shakyamuni expounded sixteen types of meditation to attain rebirth there. This sutra inspired Shan-tao (613–681), a patriarch of the Pure Land school in China, when he was young, and he later wrote *The Commentary on the Meditation on the Buddha Infinite Life Sutra.* This commentary moved Hōnen to establish the Pure Land (Jōdo) school in Japan based on the sole practice of reciting the name of Amida Buddha. Only one Chinese translation of the sutra exists, and neither a Sanskrit text nor a Tibetan version is extant. Hence contemporary scholars view this sutra as having originated in either Central Asia or China.

Meditation on the Buddha Sutra [観仏三昧経] (Jpn *Kambutsu-sammai-kyō*): *See* Ocean of Meditation on the Buddha Sutra.

Meditation on the Correct Teaching Sutra [正法念処経] (Chin *Cheng-fa-nien-ch'u-ching;* Jpn *Shōbōnenjo-kyō*): A sutra that details the karmic cause of transmigration within the six paths, or six lower worlds (from hell through the world of heavenly beings), and exhorts people to liberate themselves from the suffering of this transmigration. Translated into Chinese by Prajnāruchi in the sixth century, it is noted particularly for a detailed description of the worlds of hell, hungry spirits, and animals.

meditation on the five elements [五輪観] (Jpn *gorin-kan*): A form of meditation in Esoteric Buddhism aimed at realizing that self and environment are composed of the five elements—earth, water, fire, wind, and space; that the five parts of the body, namely, the crown of the head, face, chest, abdomen, and knees, are none other than the five syllables of the esoteric mantra *avarahakha (a-va-ra-ha-kha),* which represent the five elements of Mahāvairochana Buddha; and that one's body ultimately is one with the five Buddhas who embody the five aspects of Mahāvairochana Buddha's wisdom.

meditation on the vileness of the body [不浄観] (Jpn *fujō-kan*): Also, meditation on the impurity of the body, or simply meditation on impurity. The practice of meditating on the inherent impurity of the human body in order to overcome craving and greed. One of the five meditations, which are aimed at stemming desire and quieting the mind. Regarding meditation on the vileness of the body, a man, for example, may aim to sever his attachment to the physical beauty of a woman and stifle his desire for her by meditating on the image of her as a corpse undergoing the process of decay until finally only bones remain.

Meditation Sutra [観経] (Jpn *Kan-gyō*): An abbreviation of the Meditation on the Buddha Infinite Life Sutra. *See* Meditation on the Buddha Infinite Life Sutra.

meditation to behold the Buddhas [般舟三昧] (Skt *pratyutpanna-samādhi;* Jpn *hanju-zammai*): Also, Buddha-beholding meditation. A form of meditation in which one clearly perceives the Buddhas of the ten directions, as if standing face to face with them.

medium kalpa [中劫] (Jpn *chū-kō*): A unit of time in ancient Indian cosmology. Medium *kalpa* can refer to either of two different periods of time. One is any of the twenty *kalpas* that constitute each of the four *kalpas* of formation, continuance, decline, and disintegration. (According to one account, a medium *kalpa* is 15,998,000 years.) The other is a total of those twenty *kalpas* or the period of any of the four *kalpas* mentioned above.

Medium-Length Āgama Sutra [中阿含経] (Chin *Chung-a-han-ching;* Jpn *Chū-agon-gyō*): One of the four Chinese Āgama sutras. Samghadeva, a monk from Kashmir, translated and compiled it between 397 and 398. A compilation of 222 sutras of medium length, it explains such basic doctrines as the four noble truths and the twelve-linked chain of causation. The Medium-Length Āgama Sutra corresponds to the Pali text *Majjhima-nikāya,* which contains 152 sutras of medium length. *See also* four Āgama sutras.

Miao-lo [妙楽] (711–782) (PY Miaole; Jpn Myōraku): Also known as Chan-jan. The sixth patriarch of the T'ien-t'ai school in China, in the tradition that counts T'ien-t'ai as the first patriarch. Another tradition, which regards Nāgārjuna as the founder, counts Miao-lo as the ninth patriarch. He is revered as the restorer of the T'ien-t'ai school. He was called the Great Teacher Miao-lo because he lived at Miao-lo-ssu temple, or the Venerable Ching-hsi (also the Great Teacher Ching-hsi) after his birthplace. Born to a Confucian family, at age twenty Miao-lo studied the doctrine of the T'ien-t'ai school under its fifth patriarch, Hsüan-lang. In 748 he entered the priesthood. At that time, the Zen (Ch'an), Flower Garland (Hua-yen), Dharma Characteristics (Fa-hsiang), and other schools were flourishing, and the T'ien-t'ai school was in a slight decline. Miao-lo reasserted the supremacy of the Lotus Sutra and wrote commentaries on T'ien-t'ai's major works, helping clarify and bring about a revival of interest in the school's teachings. He maintained the superiority of the T'ien-t'ai teachings over the doctrines of other schools. In his later years, he lived at Kuo-ch'ing-ssu temple and died at Fo-lung

Monastery, both on Mount T'ien-t'ai. His commentaries on T'ien-t'ai's three major works are titled *The Annotations on "The Profound Meaning of the Lotus Sutra," The Annotations on "The Words and Phrases of the Lotus Sutra,"* and *The Annotations on "Great Concentration and Insight."*

Middle Day of the Law [像法] (Jpn *zōbō*): Also, age of the Counterfeit Law, age of the Simulated Law, or age of the Semblance of the Law. The second of the three consecutive periods following Shakyamuni Buddha's death. During this time, the Buddha's teaching gradually becomes formalized, the people's connection to it weakens, and progressively fewer people are able to gain enlightenment through its practice. According to *The Forest of Meanings in the Mahayana Garden of the Law,* in the Former Day of the Law, the Buddha's teaching, its practice, and proof of its efficacy (people's attainment of enlightenment through its practice) all exist; in the Middle Day of the Law, only the teaching and practice exist, but no longer any proof. That is, the Buddhist teaching and its practitioners exist, but among those practitioners few if any achieved enlightenment. Sources differ as to the length of the Middle Day of the Law. The Great Collection Sutra defines it as lasting a thousand years and the Compassionate White Lotus Flower Sutra as five hundred years. The Middle Day of the Law corresponds to two of the five five-hundred-year periods defined in the Great Collection Sutra: the age of reading, reciting, and listening and the age of building temples and stupas. In these ages, the spirit of seeking the Buddhist teachings declines.

The three stages following Shakyamuni Buddha's death, that is, the three successive periods of the Former Day, the Middle Day, and the Latter Day of the Law were applied to the other Buddhas appearing in Buddhist scriptures. Accordingly, the teaching of each Buddha has its own Middle Day of the Law.

middle path of the eight negations [八不中道] (Jpn *happu-chūdō*): *See* eight negations.

Middle Way [中道] (Skt *madhyamā-pratipad;* Jpn *chūdō*): The way or path that transcends polar extremes. The Middle Way also indicates the true nature of all things, which cannot be defined by the absolutes of existence or nonexistence. It transcends the extremes of polar and opposing views, in other words, all duality. However, interpretations of this concept vary considerably from one text or school to another. The three major interpretations of the Middle Way follow:

(1) In the Hinayana teachings, it is the rejection of the two extremes of self-indulgence and self-mortification. While still a prince, Shakyamuni lived in luxury in his father's palace, but after renouncing the secular world, he abandoned worldly diversions and for years practiced as

an ascetic, leading a life of deprivation and austerity. Eventually he rejected asceticism as well, and after attaining enlightenment he preached a way of life that avoids the extremes of indulgence and denial. The Medium-Length Āgama Sutra, one of the four Chinese Āgama sutras, terms this path the Middle Way. It is exemplified by the doctrine of the eightfold path.

(2) According to Nāgārjuna's *Treatise on the Middle Way*, the true nature of all things is that they are neither born nor die, and cannot be defined by either of the two extremes of existence or nonexistence. This true nature of things is non-substantiality, also referred to as the Middle Way. *The Treatise on the Middle Way* begins: "Neither birth nor extinction, neither cessation nor permanence, neither uniformity nor diversity, neither coming nor going. . . ." This passage is termed the eight negations, or the middle path of the eight negations, and is intended to clarify the concept of the Middle Way.

(3) In terms of T'ien-t'ai's doctrine of the three truths, the truth of the Middle Way means that the true nature of all things is neither non-substantiality nor temporary existence, but exhibits the characteristics of both.

Mihirakula [大族王] (n.d.) (Skt; Jpn Daizoku-ō): A king of ancient Cheka, also known as Takka, in India. According to *The Record of the Western Regions*, Hsüan-tsang's record of his travels through Central Asia and India in the seventh century, he was a brave and intelligent ruler who extended his domain to include the neighboring kingdoms. He originall desired to study Buddhism and commanded that a learned and virtuous monk be recommended to him. The monks of those days were humble and did not aspire to high honors, so none came forward in response to the king's request. Eventually his ministers found a man of outstanding virtue who had served as a menial in the king's household before becoming a monk.

On learning that the monk sent to instruct him had formerly been his servant, the king lost his reverence for Buddhism and instead turned against it, banishing the Buddhist monks from the kingdom. He later attempted to conquer Magadha, but was instead captured by its king, Bālāditya, who was a Buddhist. Bālāditya was about to have him killed, but Bālāditya's mother interceded, entreating her son to be merciful, and saved him. Mihirakula then fled to Kashmir where he was warmly received, but later he fomented a rebellion and killed the king, assuming power himself. He went on to attack Gandhara where he had the royal family and ministers put to death. He destroyed Buddhist temples and stupas and killed more than half of the people on account of their Buddhist faith. Mihirakula died that same year, however, and he was said to have fallen into the hell of incessant suffering.

Mii-dera [三井寺]: Another name for Onjō-ji, the head temple of the Temple (Jimon) branch of the Tendai school in Japan. *See* Onjō-ji.

Mikkaka [弥遮迦] (Skt; Jpn Mishaka): Also known as Micchaka. The sixth of Shakyamuni Buddha's twenty-three, or the seventh of his twenty-four, successors. Born in central India, he was originally a teacher of Brahmanism with a following of eight thousand disciples. When he heard the preaching of Dhritaka, his predecessor among the Buddha's successors, he converted to Buddhism with his followers. Known for his scholarship and eloquence, Mikkaka spread the Buddha's teachings in northern India and transmitted them to his successor, Buddhananda.

Mikuni no Taifu [三国太夫] (d. 1258): Also known as Mikuni no Tayū. The father of Nichiren, according to *The Transmission on the First Cleaning Bath* written by Nikkō, Nichiren's immediate disciple and successor. A fisherman at Kominato in Awa Province, Japan. Nichiren publicly declared his teaching in the fourth month of 1253 at Seichō-ji temple in Awa. He left the temple immediately afterward, escaping an attack by Tōjō Kagenobu, the steward of the area and a believer of the Pure Land teachings. Before making his way to Kamakura, he first went to visit his parents and converted them to his teaching. At that time, it is said, he gave his father the Buddhist name Myōnichi (Wonderful Sun) and his mother the name Myōren (Wonderful Lotus), both of which derive from his own name, Nichiren, or Sun Lotus.

Milinda [弥蘭陀] (n.d.) (Pali; Jpn Miranda-ō): The Indian name of the Greco-Bactrian king Menander, or Menandros, who ruled the region that is the present-day Afghanistan and northern India in the latter half of the second century B.C.E. Milinda had a series of discussions with the Buddhist monk Nāgasena concerning Buddhist doctrines, and these were compiled into a Pali work titled *Milindapanha*, or *The Questions of King Milinda.* Their dialogue is famous as both a text of Buddhist philosophy and an example of an early encounter between Buddhism and Hellenistic thought and culture. According to the *Milindapanha,* Milinda eventually became a Buddhist. See also *Milindapanha.*

Milindapanha [ミリンダ王問経] (Pali; Jpn *Mirindaō-monkyō*): *The Questions of King Milinda.* A record of the dialogues of the Buddhist monk Nāgasena and the learned Greco-Bactrian king Menander or Menandros (Pali Milinda), who ruled the region that is the present-day Afghanistan and northern India in the latter half of the second century B.C.E. The questions put by King Menander to the monk Nāgasena cover a wide range of subjects, such as the nature of self, wisdom and desire, transmigration, karma, the Buddha as a historical figure, the Buddhist Order, the qualifications of monks, the respective roles of monks and lay people, and nirvana. This work is valued as one of the first recorded encounters between Hellenistic and Buddhist thought and culture. It states that Menander dedicated a monastery to Nāgasena and abdicated the throne in favor of his son, entering the Buddhist Order and eventually attaining the state of arhat. Menander's renunciation of the secular world is questionable in light of historical evidence, but it appears that he gained a great understanding of Buddhism and his influence helped it to prosper. The Chinese text titled the Monk Nāgasena Sutra corresponds to the first three chapters of the *Milindapanha*. It was translated sometime during the Eastern Chin dynasty (317–420). The translator is unknown.

Ming-sheng [明勝] (n.d.) (PY Mingsheng; Jpn Myōshō): A priest of the Three Treatises (San-lun) school in China from the sixth through the seventh century. Along with Chi-tsang, he was a disciple of Fa-lang (507–581). According to one account, Shan-tao, the third patriarch of the Chinese Pure Land school, first entered the priesthood as Ming-sheng's disciple and studied the Lotus and Vimalakīrti sutras under him.

Minobu, Mount [身延山] (Jpn Minobu-san): A mountain in what is today Yamanashi Prefecture, Japan. Nichiren lived there during the later years of his life, from the fifth month of 1274 through the ninth month of 1282, just prior to his death. After his return from exile to Sado, Nichiren remonstrated for a third time with the rulers, represented by Hei no Saemon, deputy chief of the Office of Military and Police Affairs (the chief being the regent himself). When his advice was rejected once again, Nichiren went to live at Minobu. According to his work *On Repaying Debts of Gratitude,* he based this choice on an ancient custom, which he described as follows: "If a worthy man makes three attempts to warn the rulers of the nation and they still refuse to heed his advice, then he should retire to a mountain forest" (728).

Minobu at the time was under the jurisdiction of Hakiri Sanenaga, Nichiren's follower and the steward of the area. Nichiren remained in Minobu and devoted himself to educating his disciples, directing propagation efforts, and writing doctrinal treatises. It was also there that he inscribed the Dai-Gohonzon, the object of devotion he established for all humankind, and which he referred to as the purpose of his advent. During Nichiren's later years, Mount Minobu was the center of his teaching, but after his death, Nichiren's successor, Nikkō, moved the center to the foot of Mount Fuji. Nikkō did this out of his concern that offenses committed by Hakiri had violated Nichiren's teachings and made the location inappropriate as an enduring base for those teachings. Though Hakiri was converted by Nikkō, he had begun to follow Nikō, chief instructor of the priests, who had been lax in upholding Nichiren's instructions and had permitted Hakiri to actively support other teachings and schools that Nichiren had deemed erroneous. *See also* Kuon-ji.

Minobu Transfer Document, The [身延相承書] (Jpn *Minobu-sōjō-sho*): Also known as *The Document for Entrusting the Law that Nichiren Propagated throughout His Life.* A document written by Nichiren at Minobu in the ninth month of 1282, about a month before his death, transferring the entirety of his teachings to Nikkō. Together with *The Ikegami Transfer Document,* also known as *The Document for Entrusting Minobu-san,* written on the thirteenth day of the tenth month, 1282, it is one of the two transfer documents by Nichiren specifying the transmission of his teachings to Nikkō and designating him as his successor.

The originals of these documents in Nichiren's own hand are not extant. Criticisms arose, therefore, as to the legitimacy of Nikkō being viewed as Nichiren's designated successor. Records support the authenticity of the content of these documents, however, and the circumstances under which they were lost in the midst of a military conflict in 1581 are clearly noted. A copy each of the transfer documents made by Nisshin (1508–1576) of Yōbō-ji temple, Kyoto, is extant. There are also records in which other priests read the original two transfer documents.

Mirakutsu [弥羅掘]: Also known as Dammira. A king of Kashmir in ancient India. He destroyed Buddhist temples and stupas in his kingdom, killing many monks including Āryasimha, the last of Shakyamuni's twenty-three successors. *See* Dammira.

Miran [ミーラーン] (Jpn Mīrān): The capital of the ancient kingdom of Shan-shan in eastern Turkestan in Central Asia. Miran, now a historic site famous for its ruins of Buddhist monasteries, is southwest of Lop Nor (Lop Lake) in the Sinkiang Uighur Autonomous Region in northwestern China. In 77 B.C.E., the Han dynasty killed the ruler of a kingdom called Lou-lan. The Han renamed the kingdom Shan-shan and made Miran its capital. Miran was on the easternmost part of the trade route running along the southern rim of the Tarim Basin. This route linked China, the lands to the west, and India. It later became known as the southern route of the Silk Road. Miran is said to have fallen into ruin around the fourth century. Murals depicting legends of Shakyamuni Buddha's previous births and the events of the Buddha's life remain in the Buddhist monasteries. Ancient documents have also been discovered there, including those written in the ancient Indian Kharoshthī and Brāhmī scripts and in the Old Tibetan and Old Turkish languages.

Miroku [弥勒] (Jpn): The bodhisattva Maitreya (Miroku-bosatsu). *See* Maitreya (1).

Misawa Kojirō [三沢小次郎] (n.d.): A lay follower of Nichiren. He was the lord of Misawa in Fuji District of Suruga Province, Japan. Two letters to him from Nichiren are extant. One was written in 1278 and suggests that he kept his distance from Nichiren for fear of antagonizing and arousing the suspicions of the Kamakura shogunate. Nichiren understood his position, however, and encouraged him to continue to exercise discretion, promising never to abandon him.

Miscellaneous Āgama Sutra [雑阿含経] (Chin *Tsa-a-han-ching;* Jpn *Zō-agon-gyō*): One of the four Chinese Āgama sutras. It is a Chinese translation in fifty volumes by Gunabhadra (394–468), a monk from central India. It is actually a collection of about thirteen hundred short sutras of succinct content that address doctrines on suffering, emptiness, impermanence, and non-self, as well as the eightfold path. The Miscellaneous Āgama Sutra is thought to correspond to the Pali text *Samyutta-nikāya,* a collection of about twenty-nine hundred short sutras.

mitra [知識] (Skt; Jpn *chishiki*): Friend, companion, or ally. *Mitra* was translated into Chinese as *chih-shih* (Jpn *chishiki*), meaning acquaintance or friend. *Kalyāna-mitra* means a good friend, friend of virtue, or good counselor; *pāpa-mitra* means a bad friend. In Buddhism, *good friend* indicates one who leads others to the correct teaching or helps them in its practice, i.e., in the attainment of enlightenment. *Bad friend* refers to one who instructs others in an incorrect teaching, leading them away from enlightenment and toward the evil paths or suffering. *See also* evil friend; good friend.

Mogao Caves [莫高窟] (PY; WG Mo-kao; Jpn Bakkō-kutsu): *See* Mo-kao Caves.

Moggallāna [目連・目犍連] (Pali; Jpn Mokuren or Mokkenren): Maudgalyāyana in Sanskrit. One of Shakyamuni Buddha's ten major disciples. *See* Maudgalyāyana.

moha [愚癡・癡・無明] (Skt, Pali; Jpn *guchi, chi,* or *mumyō*): Foolishness, delusion, illusion, ignorance, or error. *Moha* indicates the unenlightened state that causes one to take the false for the true and the seeming for the real, thus preventing one from perceiving the real nature of things and from discerning the truth. *Moha,* or foolishness, is also one of the three poisons, or the three sources of vice and suffering, the other two being *rāga* (greed) and *dvesha* (anger). *See also* three poisons.

Mo-kao Caves [莫高窟] (PY Mogao; Jpn Bakkō-kutsu): Also known as the Cave of the Thousand Buddhas. The Buddhist caves at Tun-huang in northwestern Kansu Province, China. They are located at the base of a cliff on the eastern side of a hill called Ming-sha-shan southeast of the town of Tun-huang. Tun-huang was a principal station for entry into China from Central Asia. In 366 a monk named Le-tsun dug into the hillside and established the first cave; subsequently a monk named Fa-liang built a second cave. This began a period of cave construction that spanned one thousand years through the fourteenth century. The oldest existing caves date to the early fifth century. Today about five hundred caves remain, spanning an area that measures about 1.6 kilometers from north to south. Many Buddhist images are preserved within them.

Wall paintings inside the caves depict events of Shakyamuni Buddha's life, legends of his previous lives, and other themes. These wall paintings are valued in the study of Buddhism and the Buddhist arts. In 1900, in a cave now known as Cave No. 16, an enclosed area was accidentally uncovered, revealing tens of thousands of ancient documents and manuscripts. This new space is now known as Cave No. 17. The uncovered materials, dating from the fifth century, are largely Buddhist scriptures, though Confucian, Taoist, Manichaean, and Nestorian scriptures were found as well. This collection also includes secular documents on administration, economics, and literature. The majority of these religious and secular texts are Chinese, while some are written in Brāhmī script, Tibetan, Khotanese, Kuchean, Sogdian, Turkish, Uighur, and the writing system of the Hsi-hsia kingdom. Together they constitute an important historical resource.

moksha [解脱] (Skt; Jpn *gedatsu*): *See* emancipation; *vimoksha.*

Mongaku [文覚] (n.d.): A priest of the True Word (Shingon) school in Japan who lived from the twelfth through the thirteenth century. He is known as a restorer of Jingo-ji temple in Kyoto. Once a warrior and a guard of the imperial court in Kyoto, he renounced the secular world at age eighteen and devoted himself to austere Buddhist practice. In 1168 he began rebuilding the dilapidated Jingo-ji temple. In 1173, in an attempt to raise funds for this project, he persistently demanded that the Retired Emperor Goshirakawa provide financial assistance. This angered Goshirakawa, and Mongaku was exiled to Izu, where he met and won the patronage of Minamoto no Yoritomo, the eventual founder of the Kamakura shogunate. Mongaku urged Yoritomo to raise an army against the ruling Taira family. After Yoritomo defeated the Tairas and founded the Kamakura shogunate, Mongaku restored Jingo-ji, Tō-ji, and other temples with the support of Yoritomo. In 1199, however, upon Yoritomo's death, he was implicated in a plot against the shogunate. He was exiled to the island of Sado and then to the island of Tsushima, but is said to have died in Chinzei (present-day Kyushu) en route to Tsushima at age eighty.

Monju [文殊] (Jpn): The bodhisattva Manjushrī (Monju-bosatsu). The abbreviated name of Monjushiri, the name by which Manjushrī became known in Japan. *See* Manjushrī.

Monjushiri [文殊師利] (Jpn): The bodhisattva Manjushrī (Monju-shiri-bosatsu) who appears as the chief of the bodhisattvas in the sutras and is regarded as symbolic of the perfection of wisdom. *See* Manjushrī.

moon, god of the [月天] (Skt Chandra; Jpn Gatten): A deification of the moon in Indian mythology, incorporated into Buddhism as a tutelary god. The moon played an important role in Indian civilization, which employed a lunar calendar. Hindu and later Buddhist rites were observed in accord with this calendar, which was based on a year defined by complete cycles of the moon's phases. These rites were held regularly, for instance, on the day of a full moon or a new moon. Buddhist scriptures often mention the god of the moon in conjunction with the god of the sun.

Moonlight [月光菩薩] (Skt Chandraprabha; Jpn Gakkō-bosatsu): One of the two bodhisattvas who attend Medicine Master Buddha, the other being Sunlight. Moonlight is depicted on Medicine Master's right, and Sunlight on his left, both as the leaders of the bodhisattvas who appear in the Medicine Master Sutra. *Chandra* of the Sanskrit name Chandraprabha means the moon, and *prabha,* light, glow, brightness, or radiance.

moon-loving meditation [月愛三昧] (Jpn *gatsuai-zammai*): The type of meditation Shakyamuni entered to save Ajātashatru, the king of Magadha, from his suffering. Ajātashatru was ill with virulent boils that broke out over his entire body. These were the effect of his various evil deeds, which included killing his father, Bimbisāra, and attempting to kill Shakyamuni Buddha and his disciples. This story is related in the Nirvana Sutra, which reads: "Then the World-Honored One, the compassionate and merciful teacher, entered into the moon-loving meditation for the king's sake. Upon entering meditation, he emitted a brilliant ray of light. This ray of clear coolness fell upon the body of the king, and instantly the boils were healed." The boundless compassion of the Buddha is compared to moonlight, which illuminates the night, relieving anxiety and bringing peace of mind.

Moon of Deliverance [解脱月菩薩] (Skt Vimuktichandra; Jpn Gedatsu-gatsu-bosatsu): A bodhisattva who appears in the Flower Garland Sutra. The preaching of the Flower Garland Sutra is described as occurring in eight successive assemblies in seven different locations, beginning at the place of Shakyamuni Buddha's enlightenment and then shifting to various heavens. At the sixth assembly, held in the Heaven of Freely Enjoying Things Conjured by Others, the bodhisattva Diamond Storehouse mentions only the names of the ten stages of development, or the forty-first through the fiftieth of the fifty-two stages of bodhisattva practice, and then remains silent. The other bodhisattvas present wish to hear the meaning of the ten stages of development. Knowing their wish, Bodhisattva Moon of Deliverance earnestly and repeatedly begs Diamond Storehouse to preach on the ten stages of development, and the latter responds by elucidating them.

most honored of two-legged beings [両足尊・二足尊] (Jpn *ryōsoku-son, ryōzoku-son,* or *nisoku-son*): Also, supremely honored among two-legged beings. An honorific title of a Buddha. It expresses the idea that a Buddha is the most worthy of respect among human (two-legged) beings. The two legs mentioned in this title have been interpreted as indicating such pairs of qualities as wisdom and compassion, knowledge and conduct, vows and practice, and merit and wisdom. A Buddha was regarded as having these kinds of two legs, that is, as fully possessed of both qualities in the pairs mentioned above.

Mother of Demon Children [鬼子母神] (Skt Hārītī; Jpn Kishimojin): A demoness said to be a daughter of a *yaksha* demon in Rājagriha. She had five hundred children (one thousand or ten thousand by other accounts). According to the Mother of Demon Children Sutra and *The Monastic Rules on Various Matters,* she killed other people's babies to feed her own children. Terrified and grieving, the people begged Shakyamuni Buddha for help. The Buddha then hid Priyankara (also known as Piyankara or Pingala), the youngest son of the Mother of Demon Children. She sought him desperately for seven days, but to no avail. In despair, she finally asked the Buddha where he was. Shakyamuni rebuked her for her cruel and evil conduct and made her vow never to kill another child. Then he returned her son to her. According to *The Record of Southern Countries,* I-ching's record of his travels to India and Southeast Asia in the late seventh century, the Mother of Demon Children was revered in India as a goddess who could bestow the blessings of childbirth and easy delivery. Worship of her became popular in Japan in the Kamakura period (1185–1333). In the "Dhāranī" (twenty-sixth) chapter of the Lotus Sutra, she pledges before the Buddha to safeguard the votaries of the sutra.

Mountain King [山王] (Jpn Sannō): The guardian deity of Enryaku-ji temple on Mount Hiei in Japan, the head temple of the Tendai school.

Hie Shrine at the foot of Mount Hiei has been dedicated to the god Mountain King since the time of Dengyō (767–822), the founder of Enryaku-ji.

Mountain Order school [山門派] (Jpn Sammon-ha): *See* Mountain school (1).

Mountain school (1) [山門派] (Jpn Sammon-ha): Also known as the Mountain Order school. A division of the Tendai school based at Enryaku-ji temple on Mount Hiei in Japan. A rival branch centered at Onjō-ji temple (also known as Mii-dera) is called the Temple (Jimon) school. After the death in 985 of Ryōgen, the eighteenth chief priest of Enryaku-ji who is known as a restorer of the Tendai school, serious discord arose between those in the line of Jikaku (the third chief priest) and those in the line of Chishō (the fifth chief priest), as both sides claimed the vacant position of chief priest. In 993 those in Chishō's line finally left Mount Hiei and established themselves at Onjō-ji temple. Thereafter Enryaku-ji temple called itself the Mountain school, and Onjō-ji temple, the Temple school.

(2) [山家派] (Chin Shan-chia-p'ai; Jpn Sange-ha): A branch of the T'ien-t'ai school in China. Ch'ing-sung, the eleventh patriarch of the school, had two major disciples, I-chi and Chih-yin, whose views diverged. I-chi's teachings were transmitted to I-t'ung and then to Chih-li (960–1028), who called his group the Mountain (Shan-chia) school, asserting its orthodoxy as the school of Mount T'ien-t'ai where the founder T'ien-t'ai had lived. The other branch was pejoratively called the Outside-the-Mountain (Shan-wai) school by adherents of the Mountain school. The name was a double entendre referring to the school's physical location in Ch'ien-t'ang, outside of Mount T'ien-t'ai, and to its presumed divergence from T'ien-t'ai orthodoxy. Though their points of controversy were rather complex, in essence the Mountain school asserted that practitioners should first master various preparatory meditations prior to perceiving the mystic truth of life, while the Outside-the-Mountain school asserted that one should aim to observe the mystic truth directly. The Mountain school criticized its opponents' position as leaning too heavily toward the Flower Garland (Hua-yen) school's position and deviating from the original T'ien-t'ai doctrine. The dispute between these two schools continued for decades. While the Mountain school prospered, the Outside-the-Mountain school gradually declined.

Mountain Sea Wisdom Unrestricted Power King [山海慧自在通王如来] (Skt Sāgara-vara-dhara-buddhi-vikrīditābhijna; Jpn Sengaie-jizaitsūō-nyorai): The name that Ānanda, one of Shakyamuni Buddha's ten major disciples, will bear when he attains enlightenment, according to

Shakyamuni's prediction in the "Prophecies" (ninth) chapter of the Lotus Sutra. The chapter reads: "In a future existence you will become a Buddha with the name Mountain Sea Wisdom Unrestricted Power King Thus Come One . . . You will offer alms to sixty-two million Buddhas and will guard and uphold their Dharma storehouses, and after that you will attain supreme perfect enlightenment. You will teach and convert bodhisattvas as numerous as twenty thousand ten thousand million Ganges sands and will cause them to attain supreme perfect enlightenment. Your land will be named Ever Standing Victory Banner, its soil will be clean and pure and made of lapis lazuli. The *kalpa* will be named Wonderful Sound Filling Everywhere. The life span of that Buddha will be immeasurable thousands, ten thousands, millions of *asamkhyas* of *kalpas*."

Mrigadāva [鹿野苑] (Skt; Jpn Rokuya-on): Also known as Deer Park. A park in Vārānasī in India, where Shakyamuni delivered his first sermon. *See* Deer Park.

mudra [印契] (Skt *mudrā;* Jpn *ingei*): Signs and gestures made with hands and fingers that symbolize the enlightenment and vows of Buddhas and bodhisattvas. Mudras are commonly employed in Esoteric Buddhism, which regards them as a way of achieving union with Mahāvairochana Buddha.

Mugaku Sogen [無学祖元] (1226–1286) (Jpn; Chin Wu-hsüeh Tsu-yüan): A priest of the Rinzai (Chin Lin-chi) school of Zen from China, who went to live in Japan. At age thirteen, he entered the priesthood at Ching-tz'u-ssu temple. Soon afterward, in 1239, he visited Wu-chun Shih-fan, under whom he studied the Zen teachings. Thereafter he visited other Zen teachers to further his studies. In 1279 he went to Japan to propagate Zen at the invitation of Hōjō Tokimune, the eighth regent of the Kamakura shogunate. There he lived at Kenchō-ji temple in Kamakura with Tokimune's support. In 1282, when Hōjō Tokimune built Engaku-ji temple in Kamakura, he invited Sogen to be the founding priest. Two years later, Sogen returned to Kenchō-ji temple where he died. He exerted great spiritual influence on the leaders and warriors of Kamakura.

mukti [解脱] (Skt; Jpn *gedatsu*): *See* emancipation; *vimoksha.*

Multitudinous Graceful Actions Sutra [普曜経] (Skt *Lalitavistara;* Chin *P'u-yao-ching;* Jpn *Fuyō-kyō*): A biography of Shakyamuni Buddha written from the standpoint of the Mahayana tradition. In this work, the Buddha is pictured as a sublime being who performs supernatural marvels. "Graceful actions" indicates those miraculous deeds of the Buddha. The work describes the Buddha's birth, renunciation of secular life, awakening, preaching of the Law, and so on, up to the time of his return to his home country, Kapilavastu. The Multitudinous Graceful Actions Sutra was translated into Chinese in 308 by Dharmaraksha, a monk from Tun-huang. Another Chinese version of the *Lalitavistara,* known as the Correct and Vast Great Adornment Sutra, was translated in 683 by Divākara, a monk from central India. The Sanskrit text *Lalitavistara* and a Tibetan translation are also extant.

muni [聖者・聖人・牟尼] (Skt, Pali; Jpn *seija, shōnin,* or *muni*): Sage, saint, holy person, seer, ascetic, monk, hermit, or recluse. The name Shakyamuni means the sage of the Shākya tribe. The word *muni* was widely used in the religious world in India. The Sanskrit words *sādhu* and *ārya* are synonymous with *muni; sādhu* means holy person or sage, and *ārya,* noble person, wise person, loyal person, or sage.

Mūrdhagata [頂生王・曼陀多王] (Skt; Jpn Chōshō-ō or Mandata-ō): The king Born from the Crown of the Head. A king who ruled all four continents surrounding Mount Sumeru, but, failing in an attempt to conquer the heaven of the god Shakra, fell to the ground. *See* Born from the Crown of the Head.

mustard-seed kalpa [芥子劫] (Jpn *keshi-kō*): A designation for the time period known as a *kalpa,* named for a way of illustrating its duration. According to the Miscellaneous Āgama Sutra, a *kalpa* is longer than the time needed to remove all the mustard seeds filling a city one *yojana* (about 7 kilometers) square, if one takes away one seed every hundred years. A mustard-seed *kalpa* is also illustrated in *The Treatise on the Great Perfection of Wisdom,* in which the size of the city is described as forty *ri* square (one *ri* being about 450 meters). In Buddhist scriptures, the mustard seed is often used as a symbol for minuteness. For example, the "Devadatta" (twelfth) chapter of the Lotus Sutra says: "I [Bodhisattva Wisdom Accumulated] observe that, throughout the major world system, there is not a single spot tiny as a mustard seed where this bodhisattva [a previous incarnation of Shakyamuni Buddha] failed to sacrifice body and life for the sake of living beings. Only after he had done that was he able to complete the way to enlightenment."

mutable karma [不定業] (Jpn *fujō-gō*): *See* unfixed karma.

mutual possession of the Ten Worlds [十界互具] (Jpn *jikkai-gogu*): A principle formulated by T'ien-t'ai (538–597) on the basis of the Lotus Sutra stating that each of the Ten Worlds possesses the potential for all ten within itself. One of the component principles of T'ien-t'ai's doctrine of three thousand realms in a single moment of life. "Mutual possession" means that life is not fixed in one or another of the Ten Worlds, but can manifest any of the ten, from hell to the state of Buddhahood, at any given moment. While one of the ten is manifest, the other nine remain latent, in the state of non-substantiality. The important point of this principle is that all beings in any of the nine worlds possess the Buddha nature. This means that every person has the potential to manifest Buddhahood, while a Buddha also possesses the nine worlds and in this sense is not separate or different from ordinary people.

From another viewpoint, the mutual possession of the Ten Worlds can be seen as indicating "the world of Buddhahood inherent in the nine worlds," or "inclusion of Buddhahood in the nine worlds," and "the nine worlds inherent in Buddhahood," or "inclusion of the nine worlds in Buddhahood." In his treatise *The Object of Devotion for Observing the Mind,* Nichiren (1222–1282) writes: "The 'Expedient Means' chapter in volume one of the Lotus Sutra states, 'The Buddhas wish to open the door of Buddha wisdom to all living beings.' This refers to the world of Buddhahood inherent in the nine worlds. The 'Life Span' chapter states: 'Thus, since I attained Buddhahood, an extremely long period of time has passed. My life span is an immeasurable number of *asamkhya kalpas,* and during that time I have constantly abided here without entering extinction. Good men, originally I practiced the bodhisattva way, and the life span that I acquired then has yet to come to an end but will last twice the number of years that have already passed.' Here the sutra refers to the nine worlds inherent in Buddhahood" (356–57).

myō [妙] (Jpn): Wonderful, mystic, without peer, or beyond conception. This term is used to describe the Buddhist Law, which is wonderful and beyond ordinary understanding. In *The Profound Meaning of the Lotus Sutra,* T'ien-t'ai (538–597) interprets the word *myō* (wonderful) of the title *Myoho-renge-kyo,* or the Lotus Sutra of the Wonderful Law, from two perspectives to show the profundity of the sutra. The first is the relative *myō,* also referred to as the comparative *myō.* The relative *myō* means that the Lotus Sutra is wonderful or mystic because, when compared with all other teachings, it is superior. *Myō* does not merely mean that the Lotus Sutra is superior to all other teachings, however. Hence the second interpretation, the absolute *myō.* This means that the Lotus Sutra cannot be compared with any other teaching because it encompasses and integrates all other teachings; no teaching exists outside it, and thus none can be called superior or inferior to it. From this viewpoint, all teachings when based on the Lotus Sutra express various aspects of the ultimate truth. Nichiren (1222–1282) interpreted *myō* as referring to Nam-myoho-renge-kyo, which he deemed the essence of the Lotus Sutra. In *The Daimoku of the Lotus Sutra,* he explains three meanings of the character *myō:* to open, to be fully endowed, and to revive. "To open" means to open up the darkness of illusion and reveal the Buddha nature. "To be fully endowed" means to possess all Ten Worlds and three thousand realms, while permeating and integrating the whole of the phenomenal world. It can also mean possessing the practices and resulting virtues of all Buddhas. "To revive" means enabling one to attain Buddhahood. For example, women, evil men, and those of the two vehicles (voice-hearers and cause-awakened ones), who were denied the possibility of enlightenment in the provisional teachings, can all attain Buddhahood through the daimoku of the Lotus Sutra. "To revive" also means that all teachings and doctrines, when based upon the Mystic Law, assume their correct perspective and fulfill their intrinsic purpose. *See also* Nam-myoho-renge-kyo.

Myōe [明恵] (1173–1232): Also known as Kōben. A priest of the Flower Garland (Kegon) school in Japan. He is the founder of Kōzan-ji temple in Kyoto and is viewed as a restorer of the Flower Garland school. Having lost both parents in 1180, he went to Mount Takao where he studied under Mongaku and Jōkaku, one of Mongaku's major disciples and Myōe's uncle. Myōe also received instruction in the Flower Garland doctrines and Esoteric Buddhism from Keiga and Sonjitsu, respectively. In 1188 he was ordained at Tōdai-ji temple and there studied the Flower Garland teachings. In 1195 he went to Mount Shirakami in Kii Province for further training. In 1206 he was granted an estate in Togano'o, Kyoto, by the Retired Emperor Gotoba. He renewed the old temple there and named it Kōzan-ji, establishing it as a temple of the Flower Garland school. Myōe was venerated by the imperial court and by Hōjō Yasutoki, the third regent of the Kamakura shogunate. He wrote more than seventy treatises, among them *A Refutation of Erroneous Doctrines,* a criticism of the Pure Land doctrines of Hōnen, the founder of the Pure Land (Jōdo) school in Japan.

Myōhō, the lay nun [妙法尼] (Jpn Myōhō-ama): Several of Nichiren's (1222–1282) followers were called by this name. Myōhō means the Wonderful Law, or Mystic Law. Among the various individuals known as the lay nun Myōhō are: (1) A woman who lived in Okamiya in Suruga Province, who had lost her husband and elder brother. She had strong faith and received several letters from Nichiren, who apparently placed great trust in her. (2) The mother of Shijō Kingo, a samurai and a loyal follower of Nichiren. (3) The mother of the lay priest of Nakaoki who lived at Nakaoki on Sado Island. She converted to Nichiren's teaching while he was in exile on Sado. (4) The paternal grandmother of Nichimoku; as the successor of Nikkō, Nichimoku inherited the lineage of Nichiren's teaching.

Myoho-renge-kyo [妙法蓮華経] (Jpn): (1) The Japanese reading of the

Chinese title of the Lotus Sutra of the Wonderful Law *(Miao-fa-lien-hua-ching)*, which is the translation of the Sanskrit Lotus Sutra, the *Saddharma-pundarīka-sūtra*, produced by Kumārajīva in 406; it consists of eight volumes and twenty-eight chapters. *See also* Lotus Sutra of the Wonderful Law.

(2) The Mystic Law, or Nam-myoho-renge-kyo. It is the essence of Nichiren's teaching, which comprises the Three Great Secret Laws, and which, he assures, enables all people to attain Buddhahood. *On the Four Stages of Faith and the Five Stages of Practice,* written in 1277 by Nichiren, reads, "The five characters of Myoho-renge-kyo do not represent the sutra text, nor are they its meaning. They are nothing other than the intent of the entire sutra" (788). In *Earthly Desires Are Enlightenment,* Nichiren writes, "Practicing only the seven characters of Nam-myoho-renge-kyo seems limited, but since they are the master of all the Buddhas of the three existences, the teacher of all bodhisattvas in the ten directions, and the guide that enables all living beings to attain the Buddha way, it is profound" (317). *See also* five or seven characters; Nam-myoho-renge-kyo.

Myōichi, the lay nun [妙一尼] (Jpn Myōichi-ama): Either of two followeres of Nichiren (1222–1282) known by this name. Both lived in Kamakura, Japan, in the thirteenth century. (1) A relative of Nisshō, one of the six senior priests named by Nichiren. A few extant letters to her from Nichiren indicate that she was an earnest believer and fairly well educated, though in poor health. While Nichiren was in exile on Sado Island during the years between 1271 and 1274, she sent her servant to attend him.

(2) A believer in Kamakura whose husband was also a believer but died while Nichiren was in exile on Sado Island. In a letter Nichiren addressed to her in 1275, he writes: "Your husband gave his life for the Lotus Sutra. His entire livelihood depended on a small fief, and that was confiscated because of his faith in the Lotus Sutra. Surely that equals giving his life for the Lotus Sutra" (536). Though she had to raise their two children alone, she sent her servant to Nichiren with offerings while he was in Sado and at Minobu. Nichiren's letter known as *Winter Always Turns to Spring* was addressed to her. One account identifies these two women as the same person. *See also* Myōichi-nyo.

Myōichi-nyo [妙一女] (n.d.): A follower of Nichiren. Very little is known about her. Two of Nichiren's letters to her are extant, dated respectively the fourteenth day of the seventh month, 1280, and the fifth day of the tenth month of the same year. The former is known as *The Doctrine of Attaining Buddhahood in One's Present Form,* and the latter is a reply to her questions about the same subject. One account identifies her with the lay nun Myōichi, who received a letter from Nichiren titled *Winter Always Turns to Spring. See also* Myōichi, the lay nun.

Myōjō Pond [明星が池] (Jpn Myōjō-ga-ike): A pond said to have been located at Seichō-ji temple in Awa Province, Japan, where Nichiren (1222–1282) entered the priesthood. *The Transmission of Seven Teachings on the Gohonzon,* a document attributed to Nichiren and Nikkō, says that, when Nichiren was praying to Bodhisattva Space Treasury to understand what form the object of devotion in the Latter Day of the Law should take, a venerable priest appeared and told him to look into Myōjō Pond. When he did so, he saw his image reflected on the water as the mandala he later inscribed called the Gohonzon.

Myōmitsu [妙密] (n.d.): A follower of Nichiren (1222–1282) who lived in Kuwagayatsu in Kamakura, Japan. While little information on Myōmitsu is available, it appears that he and his wife were sincere believers in Nichiren's teachings. The contents of *The Blessings of the Lotus Sutra,* a letter Nichiren addressed to Myōmitsu in 1276, indicate that the couple frequently made offerings to Nichiren at his small dwelling in the wilderness of Mount Minobu.

Myōren [妙蓮]: (1) (d. 1267) The Buddhist name of Nichiren's mother, Umegiku-nyo. Myōren means Wonderful Lotus. His father Mikuni no Taifu's Buddhist name was Myōnichi, or Wonderful Sun. *See also* Umegiku-nyo.

(2) (d. 1323) A follower of Nichiren and the wife of Nanjō Tokimitsu, the steward of Ueno Village in Fuji District of Suruga Province, Japan. Myōren (Wonderful Lotus) is the Buddhist name given her by Nichiren; her real name was Otozuru. During the Atsuhara Persecution, she helped her husband protect and support Nichiren's followers despite government pressures imposed on them, such as unreasonably heavy taxes. They had nine sons and four daughters. The couple consistently made offerings to Nichiren. After Nichiren's death, they remained loyal to his designated successor, Nikkō, offering a part of their fief, an area called Ōishigahara, for the building of a temple that was the origin of Taiseki-ji. Myōren spent her later years in comfort and died peacefully on the thirteenth day of the eighth month, 1323. In the third month of the following year, Tokimitsu built Myōren-ji temple in Myōren's honor. Their children persisted in faith as they carried on their parents' efforts to spread Nichiren's teachings. *See also* Nanjō Tokimitsu.

Myōshin, the lay nun [妙心尼] (n.d.) (Jpn Myōshin-ama): A follower of Nichiren (1222–1282) who lived in Fuji District of Suruga Province, Japan. From the four extant letters sent to her by Nichiren, it appears that she maintained very pure faith in his teachings. Her husband, who is referred to as "the lay priest" in the letters, was troubled for a long time by some illness, which prompted him to practice sincerely. Regarding this, Nichiren states in one of those letters, titled *The Good Medicine for All Ills:* "Illness gives rise to the resolve to attain the way" (937). After her husband's death, the lay nun Myōshin continued to send offerings frequently to Nichiren at Mount Minobu. One account identifies her as the wife of the lay priest Takahashi Rokurō Hyōe, and another as the wife of the lay priest of Nishiyama, both followers of Nichiren.

Myōun [明雲] (1115–1183): The fifty-fifth and fifty-seventh chief priest of Enryaku-ji, the head temple of the Tendai school on Mount Hiei in Japan. He studied both the exoteric and esoteric teachings under Benkaku and in 1167 became the fifty-fifth chief priest of Enryaku-ji. In 1176 the so-called warrior-monks of Enryaku-ji made a direct appeal to the imperial court protesting the destruction of a branch temple of the school by a provincial lord. The Retired Emperor Goshirakawa, angered by the illegal appeal, had Myōun exiled to Izu. En route, however, he was rescued by his armed disciples. Thereafter Goshirakawa pardoned him, and Myōun became the fifty-seventh chief priest in 1179. When Myōun visited the retired emperor at his palace, it was attacked by forces led by Minamoto no Yoshinaka, a general of the Minamoto clan, and Myōun was struck and killed by a stray arrow.

Mystic Law [妙法] (Chin *miao-fa;* Jpn *myōhō*): The ultimate law, principle, or truth of life and the universe in Nichiren's teachings; the Law of Nam-myoho-renge-kyo. This term derives from Kumārajīva's Chinese translation of the Sanskrit word *saddharma,* from the title of the *Saddharma-pundarīka-sūtra,* or the Lotus Sutra. It has been translated into English also as Wonderful Law, Wonderful Dharma, Fine Dharma, etc. (In this dictionary, in accord with published translations, it is rendered as Wonderful Law when referring to the title of the Lotus Sutra, and as Mystic Law when referring to the underlying principle it represents in Nichiren's teaching.) *See also* Nam-myoho-renge-kyo.

N

Nadī Kāshyapa [那提迦葉] (Skt; Pali Nadī Kassapa; Jpn Nadai-kashō): An ascetic who practiced fire worship and lived in the village of Uruvilvā near Gayā, a city in Magadha, India, during the time of Shakyamuni Buddha. He converted to Shakyamuni's teaching along with his two brothers, Uruvilvā Kāshyapa and Gayā Kāshyapa, when Shakyamuni went to their village to preach soon after attaining enlightenment. Nadī Kāshyapa had three hundred disciples of his own who all converted to Buddhism at the same time as their teacher.

Nāgabodhi [竜智] (n.d.) (Skt; Jpn Ryūchi): A native of southern India regarded as the fourth in the lineage of the transfer of Esoteric Buddhism. According to the True Word (Jpn Shingon) school, he inherited Esoteric Buddhism from Nāgārjuna and transferred it to Chin-kang-chih (Skt Vajrabodhi), although it is difficult to distinguish fact from legend concerning this and other details about his life. Nāgārjuna is said to have transferred the esoteric teachings to Nāgabodhi and the exoteric teachings to Āryadeva. Nāgabodhi is said to have lived for hundreds of years.

Nāgārjuna [竜樹] (n.d.) (Skt; Jpn Ryūju): A Mahayana scholar of southern India, thought to have lived between the years 150 and 250. Born to a Brahman family, he first studied Hinayana Buddhism but later converted to Mahayana. According to *The Biography of Bodhisattva Nāgārjuna,* he converted to Mahayana while studying the Mahayana teachings under an elderly monk in the Himalayas. Thereafter Nāgārjuna traveled throughout India to master all the Mahayana sutras. *The Biography of Bodhisattva Nāgārjuna* states that he obtained a most profound and secret scripture in the palace of the dragon king, and realized the Law by studying this scripture and engaging in meditation. Nāgārjuna wrote many important treatises on a great number of Mahayana sutras and organized the theoretical foundation of Mahayana thought, thus making an inestimable contribution to its development. He is especially known for his systematization of the doctrine of non-substantiality. His treatises include *The Treatise on the Middle Way, The Treatise on the Great Perfection of Wisdom, The Commentary on the Ten Stages Sutra,* and *The Treatise on the Twelve Gates.* His philosophy was called the Mādhyamika (Middle Way) doctrine. Since his doctrine is integral to Mahayana Buddhism, Nāgārjuna is revered in Japan as the "founder of the eight schools"—the Dharma Analysis Treasury (Kusha), Establishment of Truth (Jōjitsu), Precepts (Ritsu), Dharma Characteristics (Hossō), Three Treatises (Sanron), Flower Garland (Kegon), Tendai, and True Word (Shingon). In his later years, he lived in Bhramaragiri on the upper reaches of the Kistna River and trained disciples, transferring the teachings to Āryadeva. Nāgārjuna is counted as the thirteenth of Shakyamuni's twenty-three, or the fourteenth of his twenty-four, successors.

Nāgasena [那先比丘] (n.d.) (Skt, Pali; Jpn Nasen-biku): An Indian monk of the second century B.C.E. According to the *Milindapanha,* or *The Questions of King Milinda,* he was born to a Brahman family but entered the Buddhist Order and studied under Rohana. He debated on various subjects with the Greek king Menander (known as Milinda in Pali), who ruled northern India, and is said to have converted the king to Buddhism. This debate, depicted in the *Milindapanha,* is famous as one of the earliest recorded encounters between Hellenistic and Buddhist thought. It also is viewed as an authoritative text on Buddhist philosophy of the time. A Chinese text exists as the Monk Nāgasena Sutra, translated during the Eastern Chin dynasty (317–420). See also *Milindapanha.*

Nagoe, the lay nun of [名越の尼] (n.d.) (Jpn Nagoe-no-ama): A follower of Nichiren (1222–1282) who lived in Nagoe in Kamakura, Japan. Her name appears in Nichiren's letter known as *The Workings of Brahmā and Shakra,* which reads: "Shō-bō, Noto-bō, and the lay nun of Nagoe were once Nichiren's disciples. Greedy, cowardly, and foolish, they nonetheless pass themselves off as wise persons. When persecutions befell me, they took advantage of these to convince many of my followers to drop out" (800). Nothing else is known about her. She was once considered the same person as Ōama (elder nun), but further research has shown there is no certain evidence to support this. *See also* Ōama.

Nairanjanā River [尼連禅河] (Skt; Pali Neranjarā; Jpn Nirenzen-ga): The present-day Lilaja River in the state of Bihar, India. This body of water proceeds northward and flows finally into the Ganges River. After leaving the royal palace, Shakyamuni practiced austerities for six years (ten or twelve according to some accounts) on the shore of this river in a forest that was part of the village Uruvilvā. Eventually he became aware that practicing austerities would never lead to enlightenment. He bathed in the Nairanjanā River, and then, accepting milk curds offered by a girl named Sujātā, recovered his strength. He proceeded to the nearby *pippala* tree and sat beneath it. There he entered meditation and attained enlightenment. Hence the tree was later called the *bodhi* (enlightenment) tree, and this site, Buddhagayā, or Bodh Gaya.

Naivasamjnānāsamjnā Realm [非想非非想処] (Skt; Jpn Hisō-hihisō-sho): The highest heaven in the world of formlessness. *See* Realm of Neither Thought Nor No Thought.

Nakaoki, the lay priest of [中興入道] (n.d.) (Jpn Nakaoki-nyūdō): A follower of Nichiren who lived at Nakaoki on Sado Island in Japan. His father, the lay priest Nakaoki no Jirō, who had status in the community and the confidence of the people in that area and who was a believer in the Pure Land (Jōdo) school, apparently embraced Nichiren's teachings when they met during the latter's exile on Sado. The young Nakaoki and his wife became Nichiren's followers shortly afterward, in 1272. Even after

Nichiren was pardoned and went to live at Minobu in 1274, Nakaoki continued to send him letters and sought his guidance.

Nālandā Monastery [那爛陀寺] (Skt; Jpn Naranda-ji): Also, Nālanda Monastery. A Buddhist monastery that was located at the site of present-day Bargaon in Bihar, northeastern India. It prospered as a center of Buddhist learning from the fifth through the twelfth century. Founded in the fifth century by Kumāragupta (also known as Shakrāditya), king of the Gupta dynasty; the monastery was enlarged by the kings of the late Gupta period. Nālandā Monastery was in reality a Buddhist university, where many learned monks came to further their study of Buddhism. Hsüan-tsang and I-ching, Chinese priests who traveled to India in the seventh century, wrote in their records of the imposing structure and prosperity of this monastery. Many outstanding Mahayana Buddhist scholars, such as Dharmapāla and Shīlabhadra, studied there.

Nambu Rokurō Sanenaga [南部六郎実長]: Also known as Hakiri Sanenaga. The steward of the southern part of Kai Province, Japan, including the Minobu area, where Nichiren lived for the last nine years of his life. *See* Hakiri Sanenaga.

Nam-myoho-renge-kyo [南無妙法蓮華経]: The ultimate Law or truth of the universe, according to Nichiren's teaching. Nichiren first taught the invocation of Nam-myoho-renge-kyo to a small group of people at Seichō-ji temple in his native province of Awa, Japan, on the twenty-eighth day of the fourth month in 1253. It literally means devotion to Myoho-renge-kyo. Myoho-renge-kyo is the Japanese reading of the Chinese title of the Lotus Sutra, which Nichiren regards as the sutra's essence, and appending *nam* (a phonetic change of *namu*) to that phrase indicates devotion to the title and essence of the Lotus Sutra. Nichiren identifies it with the universal Law or principle implicit in the meaning of the sutra's text.

The meaning of Nam-myoho-renge-kyo is explained in the opening section of *The Record of the Orally Transmitted Teachings,* the record of Nichiren's lectures on the Lotus Sutra compiled by his disciple and successor, Nikkō. It states that *namu* derives from the Sanskrit word *namas* and is translated as devotion, or as "dedicating one's life." What one should dedicate one's life to, he says, are the Person and the Law. The Person signifies "Shakyamuni," which means the eternal Buddha, and the Law is "the Lotus Sutra," which means the ultimate truth, or Myoho-renge-kyo. According to *Orally Transmitted Teachings,* the act of devotion *(namu)* has two aspects: One is to devote oneself to, or fuse one's life with, the eternal and unchanging truth; the other is that, through this fusion of one's life with the ultimate truth, one simultaneously draws forth inexhaustible wisdom that functions in accordance with changing circumstances.

Orally Transmitted Teachings further states: "We may also note that the *nam* of Nam-myoho-renge-kyo is a Sanskrit word, while Myoho-renge-kyo are Chinese words. Sanskrit and Chinese join in a single moment to form Nam-myoho-renge-kyo. If we express the title [of the Lotus Sutra] in Sanskrit, it will be *Saddharma-pundarīka-sūtra.* This is Myoho-renge-kyo. *Sad* (a phonetic change of *sat*) means *myō,* or wonderful. *Dharma* means *hō,* Law or phenomena. *Pundarīka* means *renge,* or lotus blossom. *Sūtra* means *kyō,* or sutra. The nine Chinese characters [that represent the Sanskrit title] are the Buddha bodies of the nine honored ones. This expresses the idea that the nine worlds are none other than the Buddha world.

"*Myō* stands for the Dharma nature, or enlightenment, while *hō* represents darkness, or ignorance. Together as *myōhō,* they express the idea that ignorance and the Dharma nature are a single entity, or one in essence. *Renge* stands for the two elements of cause and effect. Cause and effect are also a single entity.

"*Kyō* represents the words and voices of all living beings. A commentary says, 'The voice carries out the work of the Buddha, and it is called *kyō.*' *Kyō* may also be defined as that which is constant and unchanging in the three existences of past, present, and future. The Dharma realm is *myōhō,* the wonderful Law; the Dharma realm is *renge,* the lotus blossom; the Dharma realm is *kyō,* the sutra."

As Nichiren states, *namu* derives from Sanskrit, and Myoho-renge-kyo comes from Chinese. Nam-myoho-renge-kyo is, therefore, not simply a Japanese phrase, but a Japanese reading of a Sanskrit and Chinese phrase. In this sense, it contains aspects of the languages of three countries in which Mahayana Buddhism spread. According to Nichiren's treatise *The Entity of the Mystic Law,* Nan-yüeh and T'ien-t'ai of China and Dengyō of Japan recited the invocation meaning devotion to the Lotus Sutra of the Wonderful Law, or Nam-myoho-renge-kyo, as their private practice, but they did not spread this practice to others.

In *On the Three Great Secret Laws,* Nichiren states that the daimoku Nichiren chants today in the Latter Day of the Law is different from that of the previous ages—the daimoku T'ien-t'ai and others chanted in the Former Day and Middle Day of the Law—because the practice of daimoku in the Latter Day of the Law involves chanting it oneself and teaching others to do so as well. Nichiren not only established the invocation (daimoku) of Nam-myoho-renge-kyo but embodied it as a mandala, making it the object of devotion called Gohonzon. In *Reply to Kyō'ō,* he states, "I, Nichiren, have inscribed my life in *sumi* ink, so believe in the Gohonzon with your whole heart. The Buddha's will is the Lotus Sutra, but the soul of Nichiren is nothing other than Nam-myoho-renge-kyo" (412).

namu [南無] (Jpn; Skt *namas*): Also pronounced *nam*. A transliteration of the Sanskrit word *namas*, meaning devotion. The word *namu* expresses a feeling of reverence and devotion and is placed before the names of objects of veneration such as Buddhas, bodhisattvas, deities, sutras, the truth, and the three treasures of Buddhism (the Buddha, his teachings, and the Buddhist Order). "Namu Amida Butsu," the phrase invoked in the Pure Land school in general, means "Homage to Amida Buddha" or "I take refuge in Amida Buddha." "Nam-myoho-renge-kyo" is the invocation in Nichiren's teachings, meaning devotion to Myoho-renge-kyo, or the title and essence of the Lotus Sutra.

Namu Amida Butsu [南無阿弥陀仏]: "Homage to Amida Buddha" or "I take refuge in Amida Buddha." Also known as the Nembutsu. The phrase invoked by followers of the Pure Land school in Japan. The Pure Land school asserts that one can attain rebirth in the Pure Land of Amida Buddha by simply chanting this phrase. This practice was firmly established by Shan-tao (613–681), a Chinese patriarch of the school, who equated contemplation on Amida Buddha with the chanting of that Buddha's name. In Japan, Hōnen (1133–1212), who was revered by his followers as Shan-tao reborn, wrote *The Nembutsu Chosen above All*, thereby refuting all practices other than the Nembutsu, and spread the single practice of chanting the name of Amida Buddha. *See also* Nembutsu.

Nanda [難陀] (Skt; Jpn Nanda): (1) Shakyamuni's disciple and younger half brother, the son of Shuddhodaṇa and Shakyamuni's maternal aunt Mahāprajāpatī. He is said to have been particularly handsome and was known as Sundarananda (Beautiful Nanda). After Shakyamuni renounced the secular world, Nanda took his place as heir to King Shuddhodana. When Shakyamuni returned to Kapilavastu for the first time following his awakening, Nanda was persuaded to join the Buddhist Order. He was for some time tormented because he loved his wife Sundarī wholeheartedly. Under Shakyamuni's guidance, however, he renounced secular life and dedicated himself to Buddhist practice, attaining the state of arhat.

(2) A disciple of Shakyamuni, known also as the cowherd Nanda because that was his vocation before entering the Buddhist Order. It is said that King Bimbisāra, while playing host to Shakyamuni Buddha and his disciples for three months, called upon Nanda the cowherd to furnish them daily with milk and other dairy products. Nanda complied,

and to reward his industry Bimbisāra introduced him to Shakyamuni. When Nanda heard Shakyamuni, a former prince, speak knowledgeably about cowherding, he was convinced of the Buddha's all-encompassing wisdom and became his disciple.

(3) A poor woman in Shrāvastī who was a follower of Shakyamuni Buddha. According to the Sutra on the Wise and the Foolish, she wished to make an offering to the Buddha. Only able to afford to buy oil for a single lamp, she offered this with the vow to eliminate the darkness of the sufferings of all people. Other lamps offered to the Buddha eventually went out, but hers continued to burn throughout the night. Maudgalyāyana, known as foremost in transcendental powers, attempted to blow it out but could not. Shakyamuni Buddha then prophesied that the poor woman would attain enlightenment, and thereafter she was revered by the people of the country.

(4) One of the ten great scholars of the Consciousness-Only school in India who wrote commentaries on Vasubandhu's *Thirty-Stanza Treatise on the Consciousness-Only Doctrine*. He is thought to have lived in the sixth century.

Nanjō Hyōe Shichirō [南条兵衛七郎] (d. 1265): A lay follower of Nichiren and the father of Nanjō Tokimitsu. A retainer of the Kamakura shogunate, he governed Nanjō Village in Izu Province, Japan. Later he moved to Ueno Village in Fuji District of Suruga Province. As steward of the village, he was also called Ueno. He married a daughter of Matsuno Rokurō Saemon, and they had five sons and four daughters. Sometime between 1260 and 1264, while on an official tour of duty in Kamakura, Nanjō met Nichiren and converted to his teachings. Later, when he became a lay priest, he took the Buddhist name Gyōzō (Practice Increasing). In 1264 he became ill and was confined to bed. Concurrently, in the eleventh month of that year, at Komatsubara in Awa Province, Nichiren was assaulted and wounded by a party of men led by Tōjō Kagenobu, the steward of Tōjō Village and a staunch believer in the Pure Land teachings. On the thirteenth day of the twelfth month, one month after the Komatsubara Persecution, learning about Nanjō's illness, Nichiren wrote him a letter of encouragement in which he urged Nanjō to strengthen his faith in the Lotus Sutra without being disturbed by his relatives who still upheld the Pure Land teachings. It is said that he died on the eighth day of the third month, 1265, and maintained strong faith in Nichiren's teaching until the end. At that time, his second son, Tokimitsu, was seven years old, and his youngest son, Shichirō Gorō, was not yet born. Grieved at his death, Nichiren traveled from Kamakura to Ueno Village to offer prayers for his repose. His wife and family carried on the practice of Nichiren's teachings, and Tokimitsu in particular contributed greatly to their perpetuation.

Nanjō Shichirō Gorō [南条七郎五郎] (1265–1280): The fifth son of Nanjō Hyōe Shichirō, the steward of Ueno Village in Fuji District of Suruga Province, Japan, and a younger brother of Nanjō Tokimitsu. His mother was a daughter of Matsuno Rokurō Saemon. He was the youngest of Nanjō Hyōe Shichirō's five sons and four daughters. His father, Hyōe Shichirō, died before he was born, in the third month of 1265. On the fifteenth day of the sixth month, 1280, he and his elder brother Tokimitsu visited Nichiren at Minobu. Because of Shichirō Gorō's pure faith and fine character, Nichiren was optimistic about his future. Shichirō Gorō died suddenly, however, on the fifth day of the ninth month, 1280, at age sixteen. From letters sent by Nichiren to Tokimitsu and his mother, it is clear that Nichiren was greatly disappointed and grieved by his death.

Nanjō Tokimitsu [南条時光] (1259–1332): Also known as Ueno, because he lived in Ueno Village in Fuji District of Suruga Province, Japan, and became the steward of that village. A lay follower of Nichiren and the second son of Nanjō Hyōe Shichirō. His full name was Nanjō Shichirō Jirō Taira no Tokimitsu. He began practicing Nichiren's teachings quite early in life. In 1265 his father, an official of the Kamakura shogunate, died, and he lost his eldest brother, Shichirō Tarō, in 1274. This forced Tokimitsu to assume the duties of the steward of Ueno while still in his teens. Tokimitsu was an infant when his father met Nichiren and became a follower of his teaching. Upon the elder Nanjō's death, Nichiren traveled from Kamakura to Ueno Village to offer prayers for his repose. It was then, at age seven, that Tokimitsu is said to have first met Nichiren. In 1274, immediately after Nichiren took up residence at Minobu, Tokimitsu went to see him again. This encounter seems to have deepened his faith in Nichiren's teachings. In 1275 Nikkō, later Nichiren's designated successor, visited the grave of the late Nanjō Hyōe Shichirō on Nichiren's behalf; from that time on, Tokimitsu looked up to Nikkō as his teacher in the practice of Nichiren's teachings and aided him in propagating them. Propagation proceeded energetically, especially in the Ueno and Atsuhara areas, and many people converted. Tokimitsu offered his residence for use as a center of propagation activities. As the number of converts, which included local priests and farmers, increased under Nikkō's leadership, official and private opposition increased. During what came to be known as the Atsuhara Persecution, Tokimitsu used his influence to protect other believers, sheltering some in his home. Nichiren honored him for his courage and tireless efforts by calling him "Ueno the Worthy," though he was only about twenty at the time. In retaliation for Tokimitsu's support of Nichiren and his followers, the shogunate levied exorbitant taxes upon him. Official pressure continued for several years, and the Nanjō family was forced to live in extreme poverty. Even under these circumstances, and while struggling to raise their nine sons and four daughters, Tokimitsu and his wife, Otozuru (also known as Myōren), consistently made offerings to Nichiren.

When Nichiren died on the thirteenth day of the tenth month, 1282, Tokimitsu attended the funeral ceremony along with such long-time followers as Shijō Kingo, Toki Jōnin, the Ikegami brothers, and Ōta Jōmyō. In 1289 Nikkō left Minobu and went to live at Tokimitsu's residence in Ueno Village at the latter's invitation. Tokimitsu donated to him the tract of land called Ōishigahara, on which a temple called Dai-bō was completed on the twelfth day of the tenth month, 1290. This was the origin of Taiseki-ji temple. In his later years, Tokimitsu became a lay priest and assumed the name Daigyō (Great Practice). On the thirteenth day of the eighth month, 1323, his wife died. In the third month of the following year, Tokimitsu built Myōren-ji temple in her honor, naming it after her Buddhist name Myōren (Wonderful Lotus); it is thought that this temple had formerly been Tokimitsu's residence. Tokimitsu died on the first day of the fifth month, 1332. Nichiren's extant letters to Tokimitsu number more than thirty, the largest number among those addressed to any of his followers.

Nan-yüeh [南岳] (515–577) (PY Nanyue; Jpn Nangaku): Also known as Hui-ssu. T'ien-t'ai's teacher and the third patriarch of the T'ien-t'ai school in China, in the tradition that counts Nāgārjuna as the school's founder. A native of Nan-yü-chou in north China, he entered the priesthood in 529 and concentrated on the study of the Lotus Sutra. Later he learned from Hui-wen the meditation for observing the mind and mastered the Lotus meditation, a meditation based on the Lotus Sutra. In 548 a malicious priest who had opposed Nan-yüeh in debate poisoned him, and he nearly died. In 553 another rival priest poisoned him. He survived this attempt, too, and in the next year moved to K'ai-yüeh-ssu temple in Kuang-chou where he lectured on the Great Perfection of Wisdom Sutra. In 555 he moved to Mount Ta-su in Kuang-chou. There he devoted himself to lecturing on the Wisdom and the Lotus sutras and engaged in the practice of the Lotus Sutra and the training of his disciples; one of those disciples was T'ien-t'ai. In 568 he moved to Nan-yüeh, the mountain after which he gained the name the Great Teacher Nan-yüeh, and received the title great meditation master from the emperor. His works include *The Mahayana Method of Concentration and Insight* and *On the Peaceful Practices of the Lotus Sutra.*

naraka [地獄・奈落] (Skt, Pali; Jpn *jigoku* or *naraku*): *See* hell.

Nārāyana [那羅延] (Skt; Jpn Naraen): Originally the god Vishnu in Hindu mythology. He was incorporated into Buddhism as a protective deity said to possess great physical strength, and thus he appears as a symbol of strength in Buddhist scriptures.

Narendrayashas [那連提耶舎] (490–589) (Skt; Jpn Narendaiyasha): Also, Narendrayasha. A monk of northern India who went to China in 556 and engaged in the translation of Buddhist scriptures. With the support of the emperor of the Northern Ch'i dynasty, he carried out his translation work at T'ien-p'ing-ssu temple in Yeh, the capital of the dynasty. Thereafter he moved to Ch'ang-an where he continued his translation while living at Ta-hsing-shan-ssu temple. His translations include the Great Compassion Sutra, the Lotus-like Face Sutra, and the Prayer for Rain Sutra. Narendrayashas is also known for his translation of twenty-five volumes of the sixty-volume Great Collection Sutra.

nayuta [那由多] (Skt; Jpn *nayuta*): An Indian numerical unit. Explanations of its magnitude differ. *The Dharma Analysis Treasury* defines it as one hundred billion. Other sources define it as ten million.

near-perfect enlightenment [等覚] (Jpn *tōgaku*): The fifty-first of the fifty-two stages of bodhisattva practice. The stage nearly equal to the Buddha's perfect enlightenment, the last stage before a bodhisattva attains Buddhahood. *See also* fifty-two stages of bodhisattva practice.

Nembutsu [念仏] (Jpn): (1) To meditate on a Buddha. Later interpreted as invoking or reciting a Buddha's name, especially that of the Buddha Amida. Contemplation on Shakyamuni Buddha was an important practice in early Buddhism. Later Mahayana sutras came to describe various Buddhas, and people's desire to see them led to the development of meditation aimed at envisioning these Buddhas. The idea also developed that meditation on a specific Buddha would enable one to be reborn in that Buddha's land. Eventually the Buddha Amida came to be the most popular object of such meditation. The Meditation on the Buddha Infinite Life Sutra states that even an evil person can attain rebirth in Amida Buddha's Pure Land by reciting the Buddha's name on his or her deathbed. Thus, Nembutsu primarily concerns Amida Buddha. The practice of the Nembutsu is believed by its practitioners to lead to rebirth in Amida Buddha's land, or the Pure Land of Perfect Bliss. While it initially meant meditation on Amida, it later came to mean the recitation of Amida's name. In China, from the time of Shan-tao in the seventh century, the latter usage became more prevalent, for he equated meditation on Amida with the recitation of his name. In Japan, Hōnen (1133–1212) followed the example of Shan-tao and went further to establish the practice of reciting the name of Amida Buddha as the only means for attaining rebirth in the Pure Land of Perfect Bliss.

(2) The Nembutsu school, another name of the Pure Land school in general. A Pure Land believer is also called a Nembutsu believer. *See also* Nembutsu school; Pure Land school.

Nembutsu Chosen above All, The [選択集] (Jpn *Senchaku-shū* or *Senjaku-shū*): A work written in 1198 by Hōnen, the founder of the Pure Land (Jōdo) school in Japan. Its full title is *The Nembutsu of the Original Vow Chosen above All.* This work advocates the practice called Nembutsu above all other ways of achieving rebirth in the Pure Land. Nembutsu, literally, "meditation on a Buddha," is interpreted to mean invoking the name of a Buddha, especially that of Amida Buddha, i.e., reciting the invocation Namu Amida Butsu ("Homage to Amida Buddha"). In *The Nembutsu Chosen above All,* Hōnen explains the doctrine behind this practice, citing passages chiefly from the three Pure Land sutras and Shan-tao's *Commentary on the Meditation on the Buddha Infinite Life Sutra.* Following Shan-tao, a patriarch of the Chinese Pure Land school, he divides Buddhist teachings into the Sacred Way teachings and the Pure Land teachings, the difficult-to-practice way and the easy-to-practice way, and correct practices and sundry practices. He identifies the Nembutsu doctrine alone as the Pure Land teaching, the easy-to-practice way, and the correct practice. He enjoins people to "discard, close, ignore, and abandon" (as Nichiren later summarized Hōnen's terminology) all Buddhist teachings other than the three Pure Land sutras and all Buddhist practices other than that of calling upon the name of Amida Buddha in order to be reborn in Amida's Pure Land. Nichiren strongly criticized the content of *The Nembutsu Chosen above All* in his work of 1259, *On the Protection of the Nation,* and other writings as being destructive to Buddhism and thus to the people's welfare.

Nembutsu school [念仏宗] (Jpn Nembutsu-shū): A generic term for those Buddhist schools in Japan that teach that one should seek to attain rebirth in the Pure Land by practicing Nembutsu, or invoking the name of Amida Buddha, i.e., chanting the phrase Namu Amida Butsu ("Homage to Amida Buddha" or "I take refuge in Amida Buddha"). Here the Pure Land refers to Amida's Pure Land of Perfect Bliss. The major branches in Japan are the Pure Land (Jōdo) school, True Pure Land (Jōdo Shin) school, Time (Ji) school, and Interfusing Nembutsu (Yūzū Nembutsu) school. The term "Nembutsu school" often refers particularly to the Pure Land school founded in the twelfth century by Hōnen.

Nen'a [然阿]: Another name for Ryōchū, the third patriarch of the Japanese Pure Land (Jōdo) school. *See* Ryōchū.

Neranjarā River [尼連禅河] (Pali; Jpn Nirenzen-ga): The present-day Lilaja River in the state of Bihar, India. Also known as Nairanjanā River. *See* Nairanjanā River.

Never Disparaging [常不軽菩薩・不軽菩薩] (Skt Sadāparibhūta; Jpn Jōfukyō-bosatsu or Fukyō-bosatsu): A bodhisattva described in the "Never Disparaging" (twentieth) chapter of the Lotus Sutra. According to the sutra, he lived after the death of a Buddha named Awesome Sound King, in the Middle Day of that Buddha's teachings. Buddhism was then in decline, and arrogant monks held great authority. This bodhisattva deeply respected everyone, and his practice consisted of addressing all he met in the following manner: "I have profound reverence for you, I would never dare treat you with disparagement or arrogance. Why? Because you are all practicing the bodhisattva way and are certain to attain Buddhahood." This statement is known as the twenty-four-character Lotus Sutra, because in Kumārajīva's Chinese translation it consists of twenty-four characters.

The sutra describes his practice as follows: "This monk did not devote his time to reading or reciting the scriptures, but simply went about bowing to people." Although people ridiculed him and attacked him with staves and stones, he regarded all people with utmost respect because of their innate potential to become Buddhas. Therefore he was dubbed Never Disparaging. Toward the end of his life he heard the Lotus Sutra that had been preached by the Buddha Awesome Sound King, and embraced it fully. As a result, he purified his six sense organs and extended his life span by "two hundred ten thousand million *nayutas* of years," preaching the Lotus Sutra to countless millions of people. Those people who had slandered Bodhisattva Never Disparaging now followed him and took faith in the sutra, but due to their past offenses of harboring anger and grudges against him, for two hundred million *kalpas* they never encountered a Buddha, heard of the Law, or saw the community of monks. They languished in the hell of incessant suffering for one thousand *kalpas*. Eventually, however, after they had finished expiating their offenses, they once more encountered Never Disparaging who instructed them in supreme enlightenment. In the "Never Disparaging" chapter, Shakyamuni identifies Bodhisattva Never Disparaging as himself in a previous lifetime.

Nichiren (1222–1282) often cites the story of Bodhisattva Never Disparaging to illustrate the principle of attaining enlightenment through reverse relationship, or the connection that one forms with the correct teaching by opposing or slandering it. Nichiren often refers to Bodhisattva Never Disparaging as an example of the true spirit of bodhisattva practice. In his writing *The Three Kinds of Treasure,* he states: "The heart of the Buddha's lifetime of teachings is the Lotus Sutra, and the heart of the practice of the Lotus Sutra is found in the 'Never Disparaging' chapter. What does Bodhisattva Never Disparaging's profound respect for people signify? The purpose of the appearance in this world of Shakyamuni Buddha, the lord of teachings, lies in his behavior as a human being" (851–52).

"Never Disparaging" chapter [不軽品] (Jpn *Fukyō-bon*): The twentieth chapter of the Lotus Sutra. *See* "Bodhisattva Never Disparaging" chapter.

new translations [新訳] (Jpn *shin'yaku*): Also, newer translations. Buddhist sutras and treatises translated into Chinese by Hsüan-tsang (602–664) and those after him. Translations that were completed before Hsüan-tsang by contrast are referred to as "old translations." Generally speaking, the new translations tend to be more literal, while the old translations are more interpretive and attempt to translate the Buddhist texts in a style that is easier to understand.

nibbāna [涅槃] (Pali; Jpn *nehan*): *See* nirvana.

Nichiben [日弁] (1239–1311): A disciple of Nichiren. Born in Kai Province, Japan, he became a priest at Ryūsen-ji, a temple of the Tendai school in Atsuhara Village of Fuji District in Suruga Province. There Nikkō converted him and another priest, Nisshū, to Nichiren's teachings. Though threatened by the deputy chief priest, Gyōchi, they remained at Ryūsen-ji, preaching Nichiren's teachings to the people in that area. When the Atsuhara Persecution took place, Nichiren sent Nichiben and Nisshū to Guhō-ji temple in Shimōsa Province for their safety. The chief priest of the temple was Nitchō, who would later be designated by Nichiren as one of the six senior priests. Nichiben is said to have spread Nichiren's teachings in the neighboring province of Kazusa and in Mutsu Province to the north. Nikkō's record shows that he eventually turned against Nikkō after Nichiren's death.

Nichidai [日代] (1297–1394): One of the six new disciples of Nikkō. Nichidai was a member of the Yui family from Kawai of Fuji District in Japan. He became Nikkō's disciple at a young age. He studied under Nikkō at Omosu Seminary and devoted himself to propagation in Kawai and Ueno. In 1334, one year after Nikkō's death, he had an impromptu debate with Nissen, another of Nikkō's disciples, about whether or not the "Expedient Means" (second) chapter of the Lotus Sutra should be recited as a daily practice. Nichidai maintained that it should; however, in attempting to support his argument he took the untenable position that the theoretical teaching (first fourteen chapters) of the Lotus Sutra is not inferior but equal to the essential teaching (latter fourteen chapters). He later left Omosu and went to Nishiyama, where he built Nishiyama Hommon-ji temple.

Nichigen-nyo [日眼女] (1242–1303): A lay follower of Nichiren and the wife of Shijō Kingo, a samurai who lived in Kamakura in Japan and served the Ema family of the ruling Hōjō clan. Nichigen-nyo (literally, Lady Sun Eye) is most likely the name Nichiren gave her. Their first daughter Tsukimaro (Full Moon) and the second, Kyō'ō (Sutra King), were named by Nichiren. Nichigen-nyo received several letters from Nichiren. When Shijō Kingo visited Nichiren, who was then in exile on Sado Island, Nichiren praised Nichigen-nyo for her faith and her willingness to send her husband to Sado, even though, in such perilous times, she had no one else on whom to rely.

Nichigō [日郷・日毫] (1293–1353): One of the six new disciples of Nikkō. A native of Echigo in Japan, when young he was led by a follower of Nichiren in the neighboring village to Taiseki-ji temple at the foot of Mount Fuji and entered the priesthood under Nisse of the Kujō-bō lodging temple at Taiseki-ji. He later served Nichimoku, the chief priest of Taiseki-ji, and at the same time frequented Omosu Seminary where he met Nikkō, Nichiren's immediate successor, and studied under him. In 1333 he and Nichizon accompanied Nichimoku to remonstrate with the imperial court in Kyoto. Nichimoku died on the way and the two disciples went on to Kyoto in his stead. Nichizon remained there, and Nichigō returned to Taiseki-ji with their teacher's ashes. Before his departure for Kyoto, Nichimoku had named Nichidō to succeed him as the chief priest of Taiseki-ji. Nichigō then claimed the Renzō-bō lodging temple and its vicinity in Taiseki-ji, stating that Nichimoku had willed it to him on his deathbed. Nichigō eventually left Taiseki-ji and moved to Yoshihama in Awa Province, where he built a temple named Myōhon-ji. He continued pressing his claim on the Renzō-bō, and this conflict between Nichigō and Nichidō and their respective successors lasted for some seventy years.

Nichiji [日持] (b. 1250): Also known as Kai-kō. One of the six senior priests designated by Nichiren. Born in Matsuno Village of Ihara District in Suruga Province, Japan, he was the second son of Matsuno Rokurō Saemon. In his boyhood, he entered Shijūku-in temple and studied under Hōki-bō (later called Nikkō), taking the name Kai-kō. In 1270 he entered the priesthood and, on the advice of Hōki-bō, became Nichiren's follower. He was later given the name of Nichiji, and was especially active in Matsuno Village, where he built a temple called Ren'ei-ji. In 1295 he set out on a journey to propagate Nichiren's teachings and is said to have gone to Hokkaido, northern China, and even to Mongolia. What happened to him is not known.

Nichijū [日什] (1314–1392): The founder of the Nichijū branch of the Nichiren school in Japan. At age nineteen, he entered Enryaku-ji, the head temple of the Tendai school on Mount Hiei, where he studied under Jihen. Later he was inspired by reading Nichiren's works *The Opening of the Eyes* and *On Practicing the Buddha's Teachings,* and took faith in Nichiren's teachings. Nichijū eventually claimed to have received the direct transmission of Nichiren's teachings by reading Nichiren's works, and founded Myōman-ji temple in Kyoto. His school was known as the Nichijū branch or the Myōman-ji branch. It is the origin of the present-day Truth-Revealed Lotus (Kempon Hokke) school.

Nichijun [日順] (1294–1356): A disciple of Nikkō, Nichiren's successor. Born in Kai Province, Japan, he became a disciple of Nitchō (1262–1310) in his boyhood. Nitchō was originally a disciple of Nikō, one of the six senior priests designated by Nichiren. After Nikō violated a number of Nichiren's teachings and refused to support Nikkō, whom Nichiren had designated as his successor, Nitchō left Nikō to become Nikkō's disciple, and Nichijun followed suit. Around 1317 he was appointed the chief instructor of Omosu Seminary, a position formerly held by Nitchō. In 1327, representing Nikkō, he went to Kyoto and submitted a letter of remonstration to the imperial court urging the court to accept Nichiren's teachings. In 1328, under Nikkō's direction, he wrote *On Refuting the Five Priests,* pointing out the errors made by five of the six senior priests. In 1329 he was afflicted with an eye disease. He eventually lost sight in one eye and went to live in retirement in Ōsawa in Kai Province. In obedience to Nikkō's last wishes, however, he again began to lecture on Nichiren's writings at Omosu Seminary after Nikkō's death. He left a number of works, including commentaries on *The Selection of the Time* and *The Opening of the Eyes.*

Nichikan [日寛] (1665–1726): The twenty-sixth chief priest of Taiseki-ji, the head temple of the Nikkō school (also known as the Fuji school), or what today is called Nichiren Shōshū, in Japan. He is revered as a restorer of Nichiren's teachings because he worked to clarify their true meaning. His father was a retainer of the lord of Maebashi in Kōzuke Province, and his childhood name was Itō Ichinoshin. Around age fifteen, he moved to Edo (now Tokyo) and served at the residence of a direct retainer of the Tokugawa shogunate. In 1683, however, he entered the priesthood and studied under Nichiei, the twenty-fourth chief priest of Taiseki-ji. Thereafter he devoted himself to the practice and study of

Nichiren's teachings, and in 1689 entered Hosokusa Seminary in Kazusa Province, where priests were instructed in Nichiren's teachings. In 1708 he became head of the seminary and took the name Nichikan. In 1711 he was appointed the chief instructor of Taiseki-ji by Nichiei.

During the four centuries after Nichiren's death, a number of errors and misconceptions had arisen as his followers split into many schools, beginning with the dissension of the five senior priests, whom Nichiren had designated as his senior disciples along with Nikkō, his successor. Nichikan worked tirelessly to clarify the true meaning of Nichiren's teachings. He completed exegeses on Nichiren's five major writings and other works, and authored *The Six-Volume Writings*, which distinguishes the correct interpretations of Nichiren's teachings from misleading ones. He thus contributed greatly to the doctrinal clarification and study of Nichiren's teachings. In 1718 Nichikan became the twenty-sixth chief priest of Taiseki-ji, and in 1720 he retired from that post and devoted himself solely to lecturing on Nichiren's works and instructing priests. Three years later, however, the chief priest who had succeeded him died, and Nichikan again assumed that responsibility. He also collected funds and promoted the repair and construction of buildings at Taiseki-ji.

Nichikō [日講] (1626–1698): The founder of the No Alms Accepting or Giving Nichikō (Fuju Fuse Kōmon) school, a branch of the No Alms Accepting or Giving (Fuju Fuse) school, in Japan. Both schools derive from the Nichiren school. A native of Kyoto, Nichikō entered Myōkaku-ji temple in 1635 and studied there under Ankoku Nisshū, a disciple of Nichiō of the No Alms Accepting or Giving school. In 1661 he lectured on T'ien-t'ai's *Profound Meaning of the Lotus Sutra* at Noro Seminary in Shimōsa Province. In 1665 the Tokugawa shogunate ordered that all temples submit a document stating that temple estates authorized by the shogunate for temple possession would be acknowledged as offerings from the shogunate. Nichikō embraced the doctrine of non-acceptance of alms and non-giving of alms promulgated by Nichiō, which held that priests and laypersons who are followers of Nichiren should neither give alms to, nor receive them from, those who do not accept Nichiren's teachings. Nichikō therefore objected to the shogunate decree and consequently, in 1666, was exiled to Hyūga in the southern part of Japan for the remainder of his life. There he obtained the patronage of a local lord and engaged in writing commentaries on Nichiren's works. In 1695 he completed a thirty-six-volume commentary on Nichiren's writings, the fruit of five years of study. In it, he took the position that the theoretical teaching (first fourteen chapters) of the Lotus Sutra is not inferior but equal to the essential teaching (latter fourteen chapters), a position that contradicted Nichiren's own statements such as that in *The Treatment of Illness,* where he writes: "Further, the Lotus Sutra itself is divided into two distinct categories, the theoretical teaching and the essential teaching. One is as different from the other as fire is from water or heaven from earth" (1112).

Nichimoku [日目] (1260–1333): The chief priest of Taiseki-ji temple in Japan who inherited Nichiren's teachings from Nikkō, Nichiren's immediate successor. He was born in Hatake Village in Nitta District of Izu Province. His father was Niida Gorō Shigetsuna, and his mother, Ren'a-ni, was an elder sister of Nichiren's follower Nanjō Tokimitsu. His childhood name was Toraō-maru. In 1272 he went to study at a temple called Izu-san, and in 1274 witnessed a religious debate between the Supervisor of Priests Shikibu, the most learned priest of that temple, and Nichiren's disciple Nikkō. On the spot he resolved to become Nikkō's disciple. In 1276 he went to Minobu where Nichiren was living.

For the next six years until Nichiren's death, Nichimoku served him. Whenever Nichiren preached, he was invariably there. He spared no effort in supporting Nichiren, and it is said that he was so diligent in making his several daily trips to fetch water from the mountain stream that his head developed a slight depression from supporting the weight of the water bucket. He also excelled in doctrinal debate. In 1282, when Nichiren went to the residence of Ikegami Munenaka shortly before his death, a learned priest of the Tendai school called the Dharma Seal Ise challenged him to debate. Nichiren appointed Nichimoku to represent him, and the young priest defeated the Tendai scholar. After Nichiren died, Nichimoku supported Nikkō and took part in the rotation system for attending to Nichiren's tomb. He also devoted himself to propagation in Izu Province and in the Ōshū area in the north, converting many people and building a number of temples. In 1289, when Nikkō left Minobu, Nichimoku worked with Nanjō Tokimitsu and others to help construct their temple. This was the origin of Taiseki-ji. When the Dai-bō (Grand Lodging) was completed in 1290, he privately received the transfer of Nichiren's teachings from Nikkō and in turn built a lodging temple called Renzō-bō. In 1298 Nikkō, having entrusted Nichimoku with all responsibility for Taiseki-ji, went to live at Omosu and dedicated himself to training disciples. In 1332, one year before his death, Nikkō gave Nichimoku a transfer document titled *Matters to Be Observed after Nikkō's Death,* officially appointing him chief priest and transferring to him the object of devotion (referred to as the Dai-Gohonzon in his transfer document) that

Nichiren had inscribed in 1279 for the attainment of Buddhahood of all humankind. In the document, Nikkō charged his successor with the observance of daily prayer for widespread propagation.

On behalf of Nichiren and Nikkō, Nichimoku remonstrated with the Kamakura shogunate and leading warriors, urging them to heed Nichiren's teachings. In the fifth month of 1333, the shogunate fell and power reverted to the imperial court in Kyoto. Nichimoku resolved to remonstrate with the new authorities and urge them to accept Nichiren's teachings. In the eleventh month of that year, having transferred the office of chief priest of Taiseki-ji to Nichidō, he set out for Kyoto, accompanied by his disciples Nichizon and Nichigō. It was a cold, grueling journey, and Nichimoku died en route at Tarui in Mino Province. His two disciples went on to Kyoto to submit a letter of remonstration in his stead; Nichizon remained there, and Nichigō returned to Taiseki-ji with Nichimoku's ashes.

Nichimyō [日妙] (n.d.): A lay follower of Nichiren who lived in Kamakura, Japan. Widowed, she traveled alone with her infant daughter, Oto, all the way from Kamakura to visit Nichiren while he was living in exile on Sado Island. In recognition of her pure faith, Nichiren sent a letter to her in Kamakura in the fifth month of 1272, in which he wrote: "You are the foremost votary of the Lotus Sutra among the women of Japan. Therefore, following the example of Bodhisattva Never Disparaging, I bestow on you the Buddhist name Sage Nichimyō [Sun Wonderful]" (325).

Nichinyo [日女] (n.d.): A lay follower of Nichiren in Japan. She is thought to have been either the wife of Ikegami Munenaka, the elder of the two Ikegami brothers, or a daughter of the lay priest Matsuno Rokurō Saemon, a believer in Suruga Province. Little information about her exists outside of two extant letters to her from Nichiren in 1277 and 1278, respectively. One of these explains the object of devotion he inscribed, and the other gives an overview of the principal teachings of the Lotus Sutra. From the content of these letters, it appears that she had firm faith, was well educated, and enjoyed some measure of wealth.

Nichiō [日奥] (1565–1630): The founder of the No Alms Accepting or Giving (Fuju Fuse) school, a branch of the Nichiren school in Japan. A native of Kyoto, he became the head of Myōkaku-ji, a local temple of the Nichiren school in 1592. When Toyotomi Hideyoshi, the ruler of the country, held a Buddhist ceremony in 1595, priests of the Nichiren school attended along with priests of other schools. Nichiō refused to attend the ceremony, however, asserting that a follower of Nichiren should neither accept alms from nonbelievers, even the ruler, nor give alms to them. His doctrinal stand having been rejected by other priests of the Nichiren school, he left the temple and secluded himself in the countryside. In 1599 Tokugawa Ieyasu, who later founded the shogunate in Edo (now Tokyo), summoned him to debate with priests of the Nichiren school, whose views were opposed to his. Because Nichiō persisted in his assertion, challenging the idea of the ultimate supremacy of secular power, in 1600 he was exiled to the island of Tsushima. In 1612, however, he was pardoned and returned to Myōkaku-ji in Kyoto. His position instigated a schism in the Nichiren school with regard to the precedence of religious tenets over secular authority.

Nichiren [日蓮] (1222–1282): The founder of the Buddhist tradition that is based on the Lotus Sutra and urges chanting the phrase Nam-myoho-renge-kyo as a daily practice. Nichiren revealed that Nam-myoho-renge-kyo (Myoho-renge-kyo being the title of the Lotus Sutra) represents the essence of the Lotus's teaching. He embodied it in a mandala called the Gohonzon and taught that chanting that phrase with faith in the Gohonzon is the practice that enables people in the present age, the Latter Day of the Law, to attain Buddhahood.

Nichiren was born on the sixteenth day of the second month, 1222, in Tōjō Village of Awa Province, Japan. His father was Mikuni no Taifu, and his mother, Umegiku-nyo. His childhood name was Zennichi-maro (also called Zennichi-maru). In 1233 he entered a nearby temple of the Tendai school called Seichō-ji, where he studied both Buddhist and secular teachings under the senior priest Dōzen-bō. According to Nichiren's *Letter to the Priests of Seichō-ji,* written in 1276, Zennichi-maro prayed before a statue of Bodhisattva Space Treasury at Seichō-ji to become the wisest person in Japan. As a result, the letter says, he obtained "a great jewel," or a jewel of wisdom that later enabled him to grasp the essence of all the sutras.

In 1237 he was formally ordained and took the name Zeshō-bō Renchō. Soon after, he left for Kamakura, the seat of the shogunate, to further his studies. Thereafter he returned briefly to Seichō-ji and then set out again for such major centers of Buddhist learning as Mount Hiei, Mount Kōya, Onjō-ji temple, and other temples in the Kyoto and Nara areas. During these years he studied all of the available sutras and commentaries, as well as the teachings of the different Buddhist schools. He became firmly convinced that the highest of Shakyamuni's teachings is the Lotus Sutra, and that the great pure Law that leads directly to enlightenment in the Latter Day of the Law is implicit in that sutra. He was also convinced that his was the mission of Bodhisattva Superior Practices, who, according to the Lotus Sutra, was entrusted with the task of propagating that Law in the Latter Day. He resolved to declare the sutra's supremacy and point out the misconceptions of the prevailing Buddhist schools, though he knew that the Lotus Sutra predicts its votary will experience severe persecutions.

In 1253 he returned to Seichō-ji. There at noon on the twenty-eighth day of the fourth month, he preached to an assembly of priests and villagers who had gathered to hear the results of his studies. In that first sermon, he declared that the Lotus Sutra is the true teaching of Shakyamuni Buddha, and that its essence, Nam-myoho-renge-kyo, is the very teaching in the Latter Day of the Law that enables all people to attain Buddhahood in this lifetime. On this occasion he renamed himself Nichiren (Sun Lotus). He also severely criticized the widespread Nembutsu (or Pure Land) doctrine as one that drives people into the hell of incessant suffering. Tōjō Kagenobu, the steward of the area and an ardent Nembutsu believer, became furious on hearing this. He ordered his warriors to seize Nichiren, who narrowly managed to escape with the help of the priests, Jōken-bō and Gijō-bō, who were his seniors when they were disciples together at Seichō-ji. After converting his parents and giving the Buddhist name Myōnichi (Wonderful Sun) to his father and Myōren (Wonderful Lotus) to his mother, he headed for Kamakura to launch his efforts to spread his teaching. In Kamakura he lived in a dwelling at a place called Matsubagayatsu in Nagoe. He devoted the next several years primarily to converting individuals, eventually gaining a number of followers. Among the first priests to become his disciples were Nisshō and Nichirō. Laypersons who converted were mostly samurai, including Toki Jōnin, Shijō Kingo, Kudō Yoshitaka, and the Ikegami brothers.

Japan at that time was experiencing a succession of unusually severe storms, earthquakes, drought, famine, epidemics, and other disasters. Corpses littered the streets. Government relief measures and the prayers offered by shrines and temples were no help. An earthquake that struck Kamakura in the eighth month of 1257 destroyed the greater part of the city. Nichiren, determined to clarify a solution to these calamities based on Buddhist principles, went to Jissō-ji temple in Suruga Province to do research in its sutra library. During his stay there, Nikkō, then a boy of thirteen studying at the nearby Shijūku-in temple, became Nichiren's disciple. He would later become his successor. On the sixteenth day of the seventh month, 1260, Nichiren submitted a treatise titled *On Establishing the Correct Teaching for the Peace of the Land* to Hōjō Tokiyori, the retired regent who was nevertheless the most influential man in the

Kamakura shogunate. In that work, he attributed the disasters ravaging the country to slander of the correct teaching and belief in false teachings. In particular, he criticized the dominant Nembutsu school. Of the three calamities and seven disasters described in the sutras, he predicted that the two disasters that had yet to occur—internal strife and foreign invasion—would befall the nation without fail if it persisted in supporting misleading schools. He urged that the one vehicle teaching of the Lotus Sutra be embraced immediately. The submission of *On Establishing the Correct Teaching* is regarded as the first of his several remonstrations with Japan's rulers.

There was no official response to this document, but a crowd of Nembutsu believers, incited by priests and high government officials, attacked Nichiren's dwelling on the night of the twenty-seventh day of the eighth month. He narrowly escaped with a few disciples and went to stay at the residence of Toki Jōnin in Shimōsa Province. His sense of mission, however, would not allow him to remain there long. The next spring Nichiren returned to Kamakura. This time leaders of the Nembutsu priests accused him of defamation, and the shogunate, without trial or further investigation, sentenced him to exile in Itō on the Izu Peninsula.

The boatmen charged with his transport did not take him to Itō, but abandoned him on a beach called Kawana to the mercy of the local inhabitants, many of whom were Nembutsu believers and were in any case hostile to exiles. Nichiren was sheltered for a time by a fisherman named Funamori Yasaburō and his wife. Later Nichiren won the favor of the steward of Itō, when he successfully prayed for the steward's recovery from a serious illness. Nichiren was pardoned and returned to Kamakura in the second month of 1263. Concerned about his aged mother (his father had died in 1258), Nichiren returned to his native Awa in the autumn of 1264. He found his mother critically ill. He prayed for her, and she recovered and lived four more years. He stayed in Awa for awhile to conduct propagation activities.

On the eleventh day of the eleventh month, while still in Awa, he set out with a group of followers to visit Kudō Yoshitaka, one of his samurai believers, at Yoshitaka's invitation. En route, Nichiren and his party were ambushed by Tōjō Kagenobu and his men at a place called Komatsubara. Nichiren's disciple Kyōnin-bō was killed, and Kudō Yoshitaka, who came rushing to the scene, died of wounds he suffered in the fight. Nichiren sustained a sword cut on his forehead and a broken hand. This incident is called the Komatsubara Persecution.

During the next three years or so, Nichiren devoted himself to propagation in Awa, Kazusa, Shimōsa, and Hitachi provinces, and then returned to Kamakura. Early in 1268, an official letter from the Mongol Empire arrived in Japan with a demand that Japan acknowledge fealty to it or prepare to be invaded. The arrival of the letter from the Mongols substantiated Nichiren's earlier prophecy of foreign invasion.

In the fourth month Nichiren sent his newly written rationale for having completed the treatise *On Establishing the Correct Teaching* to a government official named Hōgan, pointing out that the prediction made in the treatise was beginning to come true and urging the shogunate to heed his admonitions. On the eleventh day of the tenth month, he sent eleven letters to influential political and religious leaders, including the regent Hōjō Tokimune, urging them to abandon their faith in erroneous teachings and demanding the opportunity for a public religious debate. There was no response.

In 1271 the country was troubled by persistent drought, and the shogunate ordered Ryōkan of Gokuraku-ji temple to pray for rain. Hearing of this, Nichiren sent Ryōkan a written challenge, offering to become his disciple if Ryōkan succeeded; on the other hand, if Ryōkan failed, he should become Nichiren's disciple. Ryōkan readily agreed, but despite his prayers and those of hundreds of attendant priests, no rain fell. Far from keeping his promise, he vindictively began to spread false rumors about Nichiren, using his influence among the wives and widows of shogunate officials. On the tenth day of the ninth month, Nichiren was summoned to court and interrogated by Hei no Saemon, the deputy chief of the Office of Military and Police Affairs (the chief being the regent himself). He reemphasized the errors of the True Word (Shingon), Zen, and Nembutsu schools and repeated his prediction that the country would face ruin if it continued to reject the correct teaching.

On the evening of the twelfth day of the ninth month, Hei no Saemon, with a large group of his soldiers, attacked and arrested Nichiren. As he later wrote, Nichiren said to Hei no Saemon at the time: "Nichiren is the pillar and beam of Japan. Doing away with me is toppling the pillar of Japan!" (579). Hei no Saemon then maneuvered to have Nichiren beheaded and had him taken late that night to the execution grounds at Tatsunokuchi. Just as the executioner had raised his sword to strike, a brilliant object shot across the sky, illuminating everyone like bright moonlight. Nichiren wrote later: "The executioner fell on his face, his eyes blinded. The soldiers were filled with panic" (767). In the end, they abandoned the execution. Nichiren wrote about this incident, called the Tatsunokuchi Persecution, in *The Opening of the Eyes:* "On the twelfth day of the ninth month of last year [1271], between the hours of the rat and the ox [11:00 P.M. to 3:00 A.M.], this person named Nichiren was beheaded. It is his soul that has come to this island of Sado and, in the second month of the following year, snowbound, is writing this to send to his close disciples" (269). Nichikan (1665–1726), the twenty-sixth chief priest of Taiseki-ji temple, interpreted this passage to mean that the ordinary person Nichiren died at Tatsunokuchi, but the Buddha of the Latter Day of the Law Nichiren survived. This is called "casting off the transient [status] and revealing the true [identity]" (Jpn *hosshaku-kempon*). After this, Nichiren began to inscribe the object of devotion known as the Gohonzon.

On the tenth day of the tenth month, after an almost one-month stay in Echi in Sagami Province, Nichiren left under escort for Sado Island, his designated place of exile, and arrived at Tsukahara on Sado on the first day of the eleventh month. There he was assigned as his dwelling a dilapidated hut in a graveyard, exposed to the wind and snow. On the sixteenth day of the first month in the following year, several hundred priests from Sado and the mainland came to confront him in religious debate. In what is known as the Tsukahara Debate, Nichiren refuted those priests and won converts. In the second month of that year, Nichiren's prediction of internal strife came true when Hōjō Tokisuke, an elder half brother of Regent Hōjō Tokimune, made an abortive attempt to seize power. In the fourth month Nichiren was transferred from Tsukahara to the more comfortable residence of the lay priest Ichinosawa. While on Sado he wrote many of his most important works, including *The Opening of the Eyes, The Object of Devotion for Observing the Mind, The Heritage of the Ultimate Law of Life, The True Aspect of All Phenomena, The Entity of the Mystic Law, On the Buddha's Prophecy,* and *On Practicing the Buddha's Teachings.*

In the second month of 1274, the shogunate issued a pardon for Nichiren, and he returned to Kamakura the next month. On the eighth day of the fourth month, Hei no Saemon summoned Nichiren and, in a deferential manner, asked his opinion regarding the impending Mongol invasion. Nichiren said that it would occur within the year and reiterated that this calamity was the result of slandering the correct teaching. On this occasion the shogunate offered to build him a large temple and establish him on an equal footing with all the other Buddhist schools, but Nichiren refused. He instead again refuted the errors of the shogunate.

The shogunate continued its support of the True Word and other schools. Convinced that he had done all he could to warn the nation's leaders of their religious errors and of what would ensue as a result,

Nichiren now turned his efforts to ensuring the correct transmission of his teachings to posterity. In keeping with an old maxim that a worthy man who warns his sovereign three times and still is not heeded should withdraw to a mountain forest, he left Kamakura on the twelfth day of the fifth month, and went to take up residence at the foot of Mount Minobu in Kai Province. There he gave lectures on the Lotus Sutra and devoted himself to training his disciples. He also continued to write, producing such important documents as *On Taking the Essence of the Lotus Sutra, The Selection of the Time,* and *On Repaying Debts of Gratitude.*

In the tenth month of 1274, the Mongols launched a massive attack against the southern Japanese islands of Iki and Tsushima and advanced to Kyushu. Japanese losses were staggering, but one night when the Mongol forces returned to their battleships, an unexpected storm arose and heavily damaged the Mongol fleet, which then withdrew. In the fourth month of the next year, however, the Mongols sent an envoy relaying a threat of another invasion if the Japanese government did not acknowledge fealty to their empire. During this period, Nichiren was busy at Minobu writing letters, training his disciples, and lecturing on the Lotus Sutra. Nikkō assumed active leadership in disseminating Nichiren's teachings, concentrating his efforts in Kai, Izu, and Suruga provinces. These activities led to an increase in converts among both the priesthood and laity, and eventually to more oppression. In Atsuhara Village of the Fuji area, in particular, believers were repeatedly threatened and harassed, and some were finally executed. In what later became known as the Atsuhara Persecution, twenty believers, all farmers, were arrested on false charges on the twenty-first day of the ninth month, 1279. Though tortured to force them to recant their beliefs, not one of the twenty farmers yielded. Three of them were beheaded on the fifteenth day of the tenth month (by another account, the eighth day of the fourth month, 1280). Nichiren, seeing that his followers now had the strength to uphold their faith even at the cost of their lives, determined that the time had come to fulfill the ultimate purpose of his life. On the twelfth day of the tenth month, 1279, he inscribed the object of devotion (known as the Dai-Gohonzon) and dedicated it for the attainment of Buddhahood by all humanity.

Subsequently, his health began to fail. Sensing that death was near, Nichiren designated Nikkō as his successor in a transfer document dated the ninth month of 1282. On the eighth day of the ninth month, he left Minobu at the urging of his followers to visit a hot spring in Hitachi. When he reached the residence of Ikegami Munenaka at Ikegami in Musashi Province, he realized that his death was imminent. There he lectured for his followers on *On Establishing the Correct Teaching.* On the eighth day of the tenth month, he named six senior priests and entrusted them with the responsibility for propagation after his death. Early on the morning of the thirteenth day of the tenth month, he appointed Nikkō as the chief priest of Kuon-ji temple in Minobu, directing all believers to follow him. He died that morning, in the company of his disciples, both priests and laity.

Nichiren school [日蓮宗] (Jpn Nichiren-shū): In general, any Buddhist school that regards Nichiren as its founder, or all such schools taken together. Specifically, the school whose head temple is Kuon-ji in Minobu of Yamanashi Prefecture, Japan. Nichiren nominated six senior priests among his disciples to lead the propagation of his teachings after his death. They were Nisshō (1221–1323), Nichirō (1245–1320), Nikkō (1246–1333), Nikō (1253–1314), Nitchō (1252–1317), and Nichiji (b. 1250). Among them, he specifically appointed Nikkō as his successor and chief priest of Kuon-ji temple, which he had founded at Minobu. After Nichiren died, however, divergent opinions developed among the six. Most of the Nichiren schools that exist today can trace their roots to this initial division. The major Nichiren schools can be classified as follows:

(1) The Nikkō school. Nikkō left Kuon-ji temple on Mount Minobu and with his disciples established a temple called Taiseki-ji at the foot of Mount Fuji. Though founded by Nichiren, Kuon-ji had fallen under the influence of Nikō, whom Nikkō had concluded misunderstood and misrepresented Nichiren's teachings, and who had succeeded in making the steward of the Minobu area his patron. Nikkō enshrined the object of devotion Nichiren inscribed in 1279 (commonly known as the Dai-Gohonzon) at the new location. Later Nikkō founded a seminary at nearby Omosu and educated his disciples there. Nikkō's disciples and followers spread out, while those of the other five senior priests tended to remain localized. Among the temples derived from Nikkō and his disciples, seven major temples including Kitayama Hommon-ji, originally Omosu Seminary, in 1941 became affiliated with Kuon-ji temple on Mount Minobu by the order of the militarist government.

(2) The Nikō school, deriving from Nikō and his disciples. Also called the Minobu school. After Nikkō left Mount Minobu in 1289, Nikō became the chief priest of Kuon-ji temple with the support of Hakiri Sanenaga, the steward of the area. The eleventh chief priest Nitchō (1422–1500) rebuilt Kuon-ji at its present location, on the flank of Mount Minobu. During the Edo period (1600–1867) Minobu enjoyed the support of the Tokugawa shogunate and thereby extended its influence. Prior

to the Second World War, many smaller Nichiren schools merged with this school as part of the government effort to consolidate and control religious groups.

(3) The Nichirō school begun by Nichirō and his disciples, which was originally based at Hommon-ji temple in Ikegami and Myōhon-ji temple in Hikigayatsu in Kamakura. In the late Kamakura period (1185–1333), Nichirō's disciple Nichizō went to Kyoto for propagation. Although repeatedly expelled from that city due to the political influence of other Buddhist schools, he eventually won recognition in Kyoto and in 1321 built Myōken-ji temple there. In 1326 the emperor gave him a tract of land in Shijō in Kyoto; hence his school came to be called the Shijō school. The offshoots of the Nichirō school include the Eight Chapters (Happon) school, which is also known as the Essential Teaching Lotus (Hommon Hokke) school, the Buddha-Founded (Butsuryū) school, and the Nisshin branch of the Lotus (Hokke-shū Shimmon) school.

(4) The Nakayama school, which originally centered around three temples in Shimōsa: Mama Guhō-ji, Nakayama Hommyō-ji, and Wakamiya Hokke-ji. Nakayama Hommyō-ji had been Ōta Jōmyō's residence, and Wakamiya Hokke-ji had been Toki Jōnin's family temple. Ōta's son Nikkō (different from Nichiren's successor) served as chief priest of both temples. Mama Guhō-ji was at first a temple of the Tendai school; when Toki Jōnin converted it, his adopted son Nitchō, who was one of the six senior priests designated by Nichiren, became its chief priest. Much later, a priest named Nitchū and his disciple Nichigen propagated the Nakayama school in Kyoto.

(5) The Nisshō school, also known as the Hama school, deriving from Nisshō and his disciples. Originally it was centered at Hokke-ji temple at Hamado, Kamakura, and Myōhō-ji temple at Nase, both in Sagami Province. Later it became affiliated with the Minobu school.

(6) In addition, there is the No Alms Accepting or Giving (Fuju Fuse) school, founded by Nichiō (1565–1630), a native of Kyoto, and the No Alms Accepting or Giving Nichikō (Fuju Fuse Kōmon) school founded by Nichikō (1626–1698). (*See* Nichikō; Nichiō.)

Nichiren Shōshū [日蓮正宗]: Literally, "Nichiren Correct school." One of the Nichiren schools, whose head temple is Taiseki-ji in Shizuoka Prefecture, Japan. This school regards Nichiren as the Buddha of the Latter Day of the Law and recognizes his teaching of "sowing" implicit in the "Life Span" (sixteenth) chapter of the Lotus Sutra. Along with the body of his teachings, Nichiren transferred to Nikkō the Dai-Gohonzon, literally the great object of devotion, which he inscribed on the twelfth day of the tenth month, 1279. Nikkō then established a center for

Nichiren's teachings at the foot of Mount Fuji. Hence, the group of Nikkō's followers came to be called the Nikkō school or the Fuji school.

In 1876 eight major temples in the line of Nikkō and his disciples, including Taiseki-ji, united as one group and called themselves the Nikkō branch of the Nichiren school. In 1899 this group was renamed the Essential Teaching (Hommon) school. The next year, however, Taiseki-ji became independent of the Essential Teaching school, taking the name Fuji branch of the Nichiren school. In 1912 they changed their name to Nichiren Shōshū.

Nichiren Shōshū regards Nichiren as its founder and Nikkō as his rightful successor. Nikkō lived up to the mission Nichiren entrusted to him of widely propagating his teachings. He established Taiseki-ji when he found it no longer possible to preserve Nichiren's teachings purely at Kuon-ji temple, Minobu. Minobu had fallen under the influence of another of Nichiren's senior disciples, Nikō, and the steward of the area, Hakiri Sanenaga, who together had rejected and subverted certain essential elements of Nichiren's doctrine. Nikkō tried to preserve Nichiren's original writings, making copies by hand, and designated among them the ten major writings he deemed most important. At the same time, he devoted himself to propagating Nichiren's teachings.

In 1333 Nichimoku, who succeeded Nikkō as the chief priest of Taiseki-ji, died on his way to Kyoto to submit a letter of remonstration to the emperor. Nichigō, who had accompanied him, claimed a portion of the land of Taiseki-ji. This resulted in a conflict that lasted some seventy years and led to Taiseki-ji's decline. Later Nichiu (1402–1482), the ninth chief priest, contributed to the restoration of the temple, repairing its buildings and educating the priests. Nichikan (1665–1726), the twenty-sixth chief priest, worked to restore rigorous observance of Nichiren's teachings at Taiseki-ji. He is noted for his clear analysis of and commentaries on Nichiren's works and teachings.

In 1930 the Soka Kyōiku Gakkai (Value-Creating Education Society) was inaugurated by Tsunesaburō Makiguchi (1871–1944) and Jōsei Toda (1900–1958), who had converted to Nichiren Shōshū. From the early 1930s through the Second World War, imperial Japan tried to unify the people with State Shinto as the spiritual backbone of wars it fought and the Peace Preservation Law of 1925 as the means for thought control. Under this system, the Nichiren Shōshū priesthood complied with the militarist government's command of Shinto worship, which Makiguchi refused despite the urging of the priesthood. As a result, charged with violation of the Peace Preservation Law and with lese majesty against the emperor and his ancestral god, twenty-one top leaders of the society were arrested and imprisoned. Most of them abandoned their faith and renounced their association with Makiguchi and Toda. Makiguchi upheld his faith and died in prison in 1944. His disciple, Toda, was finally released on parole just before the end of the war and then embarked on the reconstruction of their lay movement, which he renamed Soka Gakkai (Value-Creating Society), and of Nichiren Shōshū, which had been left destitute.

In the ensuing years, the Soka Gakkai grew into a substantial worldwide movement with a membership of several million. The priesthood of Nichiren Shōshū, however, found itself ill-prepared to deal with an active and socially engaged membership body of this scale. Its 67th chief priest, Nikken, sought to disband the organization and bring its membership directly under his control. The Soka Gakkai resisted this plan and was excommunicated in 1991 by Nikken. Contrary to Nikken's plans, however, the Soka Gakkai continued to grow and flourish after the excommunication. Nichiren Shōshū maintained a posture of appealing to Soka Gakkai members to leave the organization and directly believe in and support the Nichiren Shōshū priesthood. To do so, they promulgated a doctrine ascribing to their chief priest certain unique and special powers and implied that he alone was the living equivalent of Nichiren. The Soka Gakkai held that this doctrine had nothing to do with the teachings of Nichiren, the spiritual founder of both groups, and thus constituted a misrepresentation of his teachings. *See also* Soka Gakkai; Taiseki-ji.

Nichirō [日朗] (1245–1320): Also known as Chikugo-bō. One of the six senior priests nominated by Nichiren to be responsible for disseminating his teachings. He was born in Shimōsa Province, Japan. In 1254 he converted to Nichiren's teachings along with his father and became a priest under his uncle Nisshō, another of the six senior priests. On the occasion of the Tatsunokuchi Persecution in the ninth month of 1271, the Kamakura shogunate imprisoned him and four other disciples. At this time he received what is known as *Letter to Priest Nichirō in Prison* from Nichiren. After Nichiren's death, however, he did not observe his turn in the rotation system for attending to Nichiren's tomb, and he turned against Nikkō, Nichiren's designated successor. In a letter he submitted to the shogunate in 1285, in which he pledged to pray for the protection of the nation with the Lotus Sutra, Nichirō proclaimed himself to be a priest of the Tendai school rather than of Nichiren's teaching. He built Hommon-ji temple at Ikegami, the place where Nichiren had died. He apparently longed for Nichiren to such an extent that in 1310 and 1317 he went to visit Nikkō to see the main statue of Nichiren. He did not change his mind, however, about doctrinal matters or with regard to supporting Nikkō.

Nichiu [日有] (1402–1482): The ninth chief priest of Taiseki-ji, the head temple of the Nikkō school (also known as the Fuji school), or what today is called Nichiren Shōshū, in Japan. A land dispute between two factions of priests had lasted for seventy years at the temple after the death of Nichimoku, the third chief priest. Nichiu contributed to the restoration of Taiseki-ji, repairing its buildings and educating the priests. He went to Echigo, on the Sea of Japan, and to Kyoto to propagate the teachings. In 1432 he submitted a letter of remonstration to the emperor. He instructed the priests from various areas on the formalities of the school, and his disciple Nanjō Nichijū compiled those instructions as *Reverend Nichiu's Teachings on the Formalities.*

Nichizen [日禅] (d. 1331): Also known as Shō-bō or Shō-bō Nichizen. A disciple of Nichiren. He was a member of the Yui family of Kawai in the Fuji area, Japan. Originally a priest at Ryūsen-ji temple of the Tendai school in Atsuhara Village of Suruga Province, Nichizen took faith in Nichiren's teachings in 1275 with his fellow priests Nisshū and Nichiben through Nikkō's persuasion. He personally converted a number of laypersons in Atsuhara and remonstrated with Gyōchi, the deputy chief priest of Ryūsen-ji, during the Atsuhara Persecution. Nichizen served Nichiren at Minobu and later became one of Nikkō's six elder disciples.

Nichizon [日尊] (1265–1345): A disciple of Nikkō. A native of Tamano in Mutsu Province, Japan, he studied Buddhism at a nearby temple of the Tendai school. In 1283 Nichimoku, who was visiting Mutsu Province, converted him to Nichiren's teaching. The next year, Nichizon accompanied Nichimoku to Minobu, where he served Nikkō, Nichiren's successor. In 1289, when Nikkō decided to leave Minobu, Nichizon accompanied him. In the autumn of 1299, he was expelled from among Nikkō's disciples for letting his attention wander to the falling leaves of a pear tree while Nikkō was lecturing on Nichiren's teachings. In Nichizon's inattention, Nikkō sensed a lack of earnestness. As an act of penance, Nichizon journeyed to various districts throughout Japan to spread Nichiren's teaching, and in the next twelve years converted or built many temples (a total of thirty-six according to one source). As a result, Nikkō finally forgave him. In 1333, after Nikkō's death, he accompanied Nichimoku together with Nichigō to remonstrate with the imperial court in Kyoto. Nichimoku died en route, but Nichizon and Nichigō went on to Kyoto in his stead. Nichizon remained in Kyoto and in 1336 built Jōgyō-in temple (a foundation for present-day Yōbō-ji temple) there. In 1341 he enshrined statues of Shakyamuni Buddha and his ten major disciples, an act that ran counter to the teachings of Nichiren and Nikkō.

Nigantha Nātaputta [尼乾陀若提子] (Pali; Jpn Nikenda-nyakudaishi):

An influential non-Buddhist thinker during Shakyamuni's time. *See* six non-Buddhist teachers.

Niiama [新尼] (n.d.): A follower of Nichiren who practiced his teachings along with her mother-in-law, Ōama (whose name means elder nun). Her name, Niiama, means younger nun. Ōama is regarded as the wife of the proprietary lord of Tōjō Village of Nagasa District in Awa Province. Although Ōama renounced her faith in Nichiren's teachings around the time of the Tatsunokuchi Persecution of 1271, Niiama remained steadfast and was granted a Gohonzon by Nichiren in 1275. She also received a letter from Nichiren, known as *Reply to Niiama,* in which he explained the significance of the Gohonzon, or object of devotion in his teachings, and why he did not give one to Ōama.

Niida Shirō Nobutsuna [新田四郎信綱] (n.d.): A follower of Nichiren who lived in Hatake Village of Nitta District of Izu Province, Japan. He was an elder brother of Nichimoku (1260–1333), who succeeded Nikkō, Nichiren's designated successor. Niida's mother was an elder sister of Nanjō Tokimitsu, the steward of Ueno and one of the leading followers of Nichiren. He converted to Nichiren's teachings through this relationship with the Nanjō family and, with Nanjō Tokimitsu and others, endeavored to propagate Nichiren's teachings.

Niike Saemon-no-jō [新池左衛門尉] (n.d.): A follower of Nichiren who lived at Niike in Iwata District of Tōtōmi Province, Japan, and an official of the Kamakura shogunate. Nikkō converted him and his wife, known as the lay nun Niike, to Nichiren's teachings, and the two appear to have persisted in their faith and practice. In 1280 he received from Nichiren a letter known as *Letter to Niike,* which stresses the potential of Buddhahood within each human life, the importance of faith in realizing this potential, and the pitfalls of negligence in Buddhist practice.

Nikke [日華] : A disciple of Nichiren. *See* Jakunichi-bō Nikke (2).

Nikkō (1) [日興] (1246–1333): Nichiren's designated successor, also known as Hōki-kō or Hōki-bō. The founder of Taiseki-ji temple at the foot of Mount Fuji in Japan. He was born at Kajikazawa in Koma District of Kai Province. His father's name was Ōi no Kitsuroku, and his mother belonged to the Yui family in Fuji. His father died while he was a child, and his mother married into another family, so his maternal grandfather raised him. In his boyhood, he entered Shijūku-in, a temple of the Tendai school, in Suruga Province. There, in addition to the Tendai doctrine, he studied Chinese classics, Japanese literature, poetry, calligraphy, and other subjects. Shijūku-in was closely affiliated with Jissō-ji, another Tendai temple in nearby Iwamoto. In 1258 Nichiren visited Jissō-ji to do research in its sutra library in preparation for writing *On Establishing the Correct Teaching for the Peace of the Land.* Nikkō had an opportunity to serve Nichiren there, and decided to become his disciple.

Though still quite young, from that time on, he devotedly served Nichiren. He joined Nichiren in his place of exile, Izu, in 1261, and while there converted a priest of the True Word (Shingon) school named Kongō-in Gyōman to Nichiren's teachings. Gyōman renamed his temple Daijō-ji and made Nikkō its founder. In 1271 Nikkō accompanied Nichiren in his exile to Sado Island. In 1274 Nichiren was released from the exile and in Kamakura remonstrated with Hei no Saemon, the deputy chief of the Office of Military and Police Affairs (the chief being the regent himself).

Because all of his remonstrations with the rulers went unheeded, Nichiren decided to leave Kamakura. At that time Nikkō arranged with one of his converts, Hakiri Sanenaga, for Nichiren to live in the Minobu area where Sanenaga was steward. Nikkō recorded the lectures Nichiren gave on the Lotus Sutra to his disciples at Minobu and compiled them as *The Record of the Orally Transmitted Teachings* in the first month of 1278. He also led a great propagation effort in Kai, Suruga, and Izu, which spread to other provinces. Because of his propagation activities in the Suruga area, priests at Shijūku-in and Ryūsen-ji, a Tendai temple in Atsuhara, converted to Nichiren's teachings. As the number of converts increased, so did the pressure on Nichiren's followers. First, in 1278 Nikkō and other priests such as Nichiji and Shōken were expelled from Shijūku-in. Nikkō submitted a joint petition to the shogunate, asking for an open debate with Gon'yo, the temple's secretary. At Ryūsen-ji temple, the deputy chief priest Gyōchi expelled the priests Nikkō had converted, including Nisshū, Nichiben, and Nichizen, and harassed their lay converts, most of them farmers. Eventually, on the twenty-first day of the ninth month, 1279, twenty of these farmers were arrested on false charges and sent to Kamakura. Nikkō immediately drafted a petition with Nichiren, who wrote the first part of it, and had Nisshū and Nichiben copy and submit it jointly to the shogunate. Three of the arrested believers were beheaded, and the others were banished from Atsuhara. This incident is known as the Atsuhara Persecution. Their courageous faith is said to have motivated Nichiren to inscribe the object of devotion for all humanity (commonly known as the Dai-Gohonzon), which he alluded to in his writing as the purpose of his life.

In 1282 Nichiren, sensing that his death was near, designated Nikkō as his successor with two transfer documents, one written in the ninth month at Minobu and the other on the day of his death, the thirteenth day of the tenth month at Ikegami. The latter document also stated that Nikkō should be chief priest of Kuon-ji temple at Minobu. After Nichiren's funeral, Nikkō brought his ashes to Minobu and placed them in a tomb. On the hundredth day after Nichiren's death, he held a memorial service. At that time eighteen priests—the six senior priests and twelve of their disciples—assumed the responsibility of attending to the tomb in rotation, one of the six senior priests or two of his disciples watching over it each month.

The five senior priests other than Nikkō then left for their respective areas. None of them, however, returned to fulfill their commitment to attend to Nichiren's tomb. Under pressure from the authorities, they gradually began to disassociate themselves from Nichiren's teachings and worshiped images of Shakyamuni Buddha, declaring themselves to be priests of the Tendai school. Nikō, one of the six senior priests, returned to Minobu around 1285, and Nikkō appointed him the chief instructor of priests. Under Nikō's influence, however, Hakiri Sanenaga, the steward of the area and one of Nichiren's followers, commissioned a statue of Shakyamuni Buddha, made pilgrimages to Shinto shrines, contributed to the erecting of a tower of the Pure Land (Jōdo) school, and even had a Pure Land temple built. Nikkō repeatedly warned them that such acts flagrantly contradicted Nichiren's teachings, but to no avail. Convinced that Minobu would not be the place to preserve Nichiren's teachings, Nikkō left in the spring of 1289, taking the Dai-Gohonzon, Nichiren's ashes, and other treasures with him. He stayed for awhile at the home of his maternal grandfather in Kawai of Fuji District, but soon moved to Nanjō Tokimitsu's estate at the latter's invitation. In 1290 Nikkō built a temple called Dai-bō (Grand Lodging) on a tract of land donated by Tokimitsu. His disciples also established their lodging temples surrounding Dai-bō. This was the origin of Taiseki-ji. Nikkō concentrated all his efforts on promoting Nichiren's teachings, educating disciples, and collecting and transcribing Nichiren's writings, which he called the *Gosho,* or honorable writings.

In 1298 Nikkō established a seminary at nearby Omosu, moved there, and devoted himself to training his disciples. Nichimoku, Nikke, Nisshū, Nichizen, Nissen, and Nichijō are known as his six elder disciples, whom he assigned to protect the Dai-Gohonzon. At this point, Nichimoku functionally became the chief priest of Taiseki-ji. Nikkō also designated six new disciples (Nichidai, Nitchō, Nichidō, Nichimyō, Nichigō, and Nichijo), whom he charged with the task of propagation after his death. In the eleventh month of 1332, Nikkō officially appointed

Nichimoku as his successor and wrote *Matters to Be Observed after Nikkō's Death.* Shortly before his death, he left *The Twenty-six Admonitions of Nikkō* as a warning to believers in general and priests in particular to preserve and uphold Nichiren's teachings correctly.

(2) [日光] (Jpn): The bodhisattva Sunlight (Nikkō-bosatsu). One of the two bodhisattvas who attend Medicine Master Buddha, the other being Gakkō (Moonlight). *See* Sunlight.

Nikō [日向] (1253–1314): One of the six senior priests designated by Nichiren; he was also known as Sado-kō or Sado-bō. Born in Nagasa District of Awa Province (Mobara Village in Kazusa Province, according to another account) in Japan, he became Nichiren's disciple in 1265. In 1276, when Nichiren learned of the death of Dōzen-bō, his former teacher at Seichō-ji temple, he wrote *On Repaying Debts of Gratitude* in Dōzen-bō's honor and dispatched Nikō to read it in front of his grave. Between 1278 and 1280, when Nichiren delivered a series of lectures on the Lotus Sutra, Nikō wrote those down and compiled them in a work called *The Recorded Lectures.* After Nichiren's death, he propagated Nichiren's teachings in Kazusa Province, using Myōkō-ji temple in Mobara as his base, but neglected to come to Minobu to take his turn in the rotation system for attending to Nichiren's tomb. Around 1285, however, he changed his mind and returned to Minobu, and Nikkō appointed him the chief instructor of priests.

Nikō did not exercise diligence in refuting or refusing to support teachings that Nichiren had taught were erroneous. He permitted Hakiri Sanenaga, a believer and the steward of the area, to worship at Shinto shrines, donate to the Pure Land school, and engage in other acts Nichiren would never have sanctioned. Nikkō cautioned the two repeatedly, but Hakiri preferred Nikō's compliant attitude to Nikkō's strictness and refused to heed Nikkō's warnings. In 1289 Nikkō left Minobu to maintain the purity of Nichiren's teachings. After that, Nikō became the chief priest of Kuon-ji temple at Minobu. In 1313 he transferred his position to his disciple Nisshin and retired to Mobara, where he died.

Nikō's Records [日向記] (Jpn *Nikō-ki*): Another title for *The Recorded Lectures* compiled by Nikō. A compilation of Nichiren's lectures on the Lotus Sutra. See *Recorded Lectures, The.*

nine arrogances [九慢] (Jpn *ku-man*): *See* nine types of arrogance.

nine consciousnesses [九識] (Jpn *ku-shiki*): Nine kinds of discernment. "Consciousness" is the translation of the Sanskrit *vijnāna,* which means discernment. The nine consciousnesses are (1) sight-consciousness (Skt *chakshur-vijnāna*), (2) hearing-consciousness *(shrota-vijnāna),* (3) smell-consciousness *(ghrāna-vijnāna),* (4) taste-consciousness *(jihvā-*

vijnāna), (5) touch-consciousness *(kāya-vijnāna),* (6) mind-consciousness *(mano-vijnāna),* (7) *mano*-consciousness *(mano-vijnāna),* (8) *ālaya*-consciousness *(ālaya-vijnāna),* and (9) *amala*-consciousness *(amala-vijnāna).* (The Sanskrit is the same for both the sixth and seventh consciousnesses.)

The first five consciousnesses correspond to the five senses of sight, hearing, smell, taste, and touch. The sixth consciousness integrates the perceptions of the five senses into coherent images and makes judgments about the external world. In contrast with the first six consciousnesses, which deal with the external world, the seventh, or *mano*-consciousness, corresponds to the inner spiritual world. Awareness of and attachment to the self are said to originate from the *mano*-consciousness, as does the ability to distinguish between good and evil. The eighth, or *ālaya*-consciousness, exists in what modern psychology calls the unconscious; all experiences of present and previous lifetimes—collectively called karma—are stored there. The *ālaya*-consciousness receives the results of one's good and evil deeds and stores them as karmic potentials or "seeds," which then produce the rewards of either happiness or suffering accordingly. Hence it was rendered as "storehouse consciousness" in Chinese. The *ālaya*-consciousness thus forms the framework of individual existence. The Dharma Characteristics (Chin Fa-hsiang; Jpn Hossō) school regards the eighth consciousness as the source of all spiritual and physical phenomena. The Summary of the Mahayana (She-lun; Shōron) school, the T'ien-t'ai school, and the Flower Garland (Hua-yen; Kegon) school postulate a ninth consciousness, called *amala*-consciousness, which lies below the *ālaya*-consciousness and remains free from all karmic impurity. This ninth consciousness is defined as the basis of all life's functions. Hence it was rendered as "fundamental pure consciousness" in Chinese.

nine divisions of the scriptures [九分経]. (Jpn *kubun-kyō*): Also, nine divisions of the sutras or nine divisions of the teachings. A classification of Shakyamuni Buddha's teachings according to style and content, of which there are four different traditions. According to one tradition, the nine divisions of the teachings are (1) *sūtra,* or teachings in prose style; (2) *geya,* restatements of *sūtra* in verse; (3) *vyākarana,* the Buddha's predictions of the future enlightenment of his disciples; (4) *gāthā,* teachings set forth by the Buddha in verse; (5) *udāna,* teachings that the Buddha preaches spontaneously without request or query from his disciples; (6) *itivrittaka,* discourses beginning with the words "This is what the World-Honored One said"; (7) *jātaka,* stories of the Buddha's previous lives; (8) *vaipulya,* expansion of doctrine; and (9) *adbhutadharma,* descriptions of marvelous events that concern the Buddha or his disciples. According to another tradition, *nidāna* replaces *jātaka;* in a third tradition, *nidāna* replaces *udāna;* and in a fourth tradition, *nidāna, avadāna,* and *upadesha* replace *vyākarana, udāna,* and *vaipulya. Nidāna* means descriptions of the purpose, cause, and occasion on which teachings and rules of monastic discipline are propounded. *Avadāna* refers to tales of the previous lives of persons other than the Buddha, and *upadesha* to discourses on the Buddha's teachings. It is generally believed that the nine divisions of the teachings developed into the concept of twelve divisions of the teachings. *See also* twelve divisions of the scriptures.

nine divisions of the teachings [九分教] (Jpn *kubun-kyō*): *See* nine divisions of the scriptures.

nine great ordeals [九横の大難] (Jpn *kuō-no-dainan*): Also, nine great persecutions. The major hardships that Shakyamuni Buddha underwent. They are listed in *The Treatise on the Great Perfection of Wisdom* and other Buddhist works, but differ slightly according to the source. A well-known account of the nine ordeals follows:

(1) At the instigation of a group of Brahmans, a beautiful woman named Sundarī spread rumors to the effect that she was having an affair with Shakyamuni.

(2) Brahmans mocked Shakyamuni when a maidservant gave him an offering of stinking rice gruel in a Brahman city.

(3) Agnidatta, a Brahman in Vairanjā, invited Shakyamuni and five hundred disciples to his mansion, but was so completely absorbed in the pursuit of pleasure that he neglected to make them any offerings. For a period of ninety days, they had nothing to eat but oats used as horse fodder.

(4) King Virūdhaka of Kosala killed a great many members of the Shākya clan, to which Shakyamuni belonged.

(5) When Shakyamuni entered a Brahman city, the king forbade the people to make offerings or listen to him.

(6) A Brahman woman named Chinchā tied a tub to her belly under her robe and claimed that she was pregnant by Shakyamuni.

(7) Devadatta pushed a boulder from atop a cliff on Shakyamuni in an attempt to crush him. It missed its mark, however, injuring only his toe.

(8) Once, around the time of the winter solstice, an icy wind rose and continued to blow for eight days. Shakyamuni and his disciples were particularly vulnerable since they were away from the monastery and had no permanent shelter. Shakyamuni protected himself from the cold wind

by wearing three robes made of discarded rags, the only garments permitted a monk.

(9) King Ajātashatru loosed a drunken elephant and set it upon Shakyamuni and his disciples in an attempt to have them trampled to death.

nine great persecutions [九横の大難] (Jpn *kuō-no-dainan*): The major persecutions Shakyamuni is said to have undergone. *See* nine great ordeals.

nine honored ones on the eight-petaled lotus [八葉九尊] (Jpn *hachiyō-kuson*): Buddhas and bodhisattvas in the court of the eight-petaled lotus in the center of the Womb Realm mandala, one of the objects of devotion in Esoteric Buddhism. The Womb Realm mandala comprises twelve sections called great courts or halls. The central court is the court of the eight-petaled lotus. Mahāvairochana Buddha sits in the center of the lotus, with four Buddhas and four bodhisattvas on the eight petals. Jeweled Banner Buddha is in the east, Florescence King Buddha in the south, Infinite Life Buddha in the west, and Heavenly Drum Thunder Buddha in the north. Bodhisattva Universal Worthy is in the southeast, Bodhisattva Manjushrī in the southwest, Bodhisattva Perceiver of the World's Sounds in the northwest, and Bodhisattva Maitreya in the northeast. The four Buddhas and four bodhisattvas represent the virtues of Mahāvairochana Buddha.

nine mountains and eight seas [九山八海] (Jpn *kusen-hakkai*): The mountains and seas that constitute the world, according to ancient Indian cosmology. The nine mountains are Mount Sumeru at the center of the world and eight concentric mountain ranges that surround it. Eight concentric seas separate these mountain ranges. According to *The Dharma Analysis Treasury*, the eight circular mountain ranges are, from the innermost out, Yugamdhara, Īshādhāra, Khadiraka, Sudarshana, Ashvakarna, Vinataka, Nimimdhara, and Chakravāda-parvata. All these mountain ranges are made of gold except the outermost, Chakravāda-parvata, also known as the Iron Encircling Mountains, which is made of iron. Mount Sumeru and the eight mountain ranges are each separated from one another by a sea. The distance between Mount Sumeru and Mount Yugamdhara is eighty thousand *yojanas*. The inner seven seas are of fresh water, while the outermost sea, just inside the iron mountain range, is salty. In this sea are four continents—Pūrvavideha in the east, Jambudvīpa in the south, Aparagodānīya in the west, and Uttarakuru in the north. *See also* four continents.

nine schools [九宗] (Jpn *ku-shū*): Nine major Buddhist schools often referred to in Japanese Buddhist works. The Dharma Analysis Treasury (Kusha), Establishment of Truth (Jōjitsu), Precepts (Ritsu), Dharma

Characteristics (Hossō), Three Treatises (Sanron), Flower Garland (Kegon), Tendai, True Word (Shingon), plus either the Zen or the Pure Land (Jōdo) school. The first eight schools and the Pure Land school appeared in Japan before the Kamakura period (1185–1333), while the Zen school emerged in the early Kamakura period.

ninety-five non-Buddhist schools [九十五種の外道] (Jpn *kujūgoshu-no-gedō*): Non-Buddhist schools that, according to some Buddhist scriptures, existed in India during Shakyamuni's time. Their names and particular doctrines are unknown. Moreover, it is unclear whether the number ninety-five indicates an exact number. The figure ninety-six appears in some texts. The "ninety-five non-Buddhist schools" is also referred to as "the ninety-five schools of Brahmanists."

nine types of arrogance [九慢] (Jpn *ku-man*): Also, nine arrogances. Nine kinds of arrogance explained in *The Treatise on the Source of Wisdom* and *The Dharma Analysis Treasury*. They are (1) thinking that one surpasses one's equals; (2) thinking that one is equal to those who are superior; (3) thinking that one is only slightly inferior to those who are far superior; (4) assuming false humility in affirming the superiority of those in fact superior to oneself; (5) asserting equality with one's equals; (6) asserting the inferiority of one's equals; (7) thinking that one is not surpassed by one's equals; (8) thinking that one's equals are not equal to oneself, i.e., that they are inferior; and (9) humbly acknowledging the superiority of superiors and vaunting one's inferiority (a form of false humility).

nine worlds [九界] (Jpn *ku-kai* or *kyū-kai*): Nine of the Ten Worlds; those other than the world of Buddhas, or Buddhahood. The nine worlds are contrasted with the world of Buddhas to indicate the realm of delusion and impermanence. They are the worlds or realms of hell, hungry spirits, animals, *asuras*, human beings, heavenly beings, voice-hearers, cause-awakened ones, and bodhisattvas. In the Lotus Sutra, both the nine worlds and the world of Buddhas are viewed as different states or potential states of life rather than physical realms or locations. The nine worlds and the world of Buddhahood are mutually inclusive: the world of Buddhas, or the state of Buddhahood, is inherent within the nine worlds, and the nine worlds all exist within the state of Buddhahood. Thus, the sutra holds that all beings of the nine worlds possess the potential for Buddhahood, and that Buddhas are not without the nine worlds. *See also* mutual possession of the Ten Worlds.

Ninshō [忍性]: Also known as Ryōkan, a priest of the True Word Precepts (Shingon-Ritsu) school in Japan. *See* Ryōkan.

ninth period of decrease in the kalpa of continuance [住劫第九の減]

(Jpn *jūkō-daiku-no-gen*): The period in Buddhist cosmology during which Shakyamuni Buddha is said to have been born. It is the ninth period of decrease in the human life span in the *kalpa* of continuance. The *kalpa* of continuance, one of the four *kalpas,* is the period in which living beings exist and conduct their life-activities. The *kalpa* of continuance consists of twenty small *kalpas.* In the beginning of the first small *kalpa,* the human life span is immeasurable and gradually decreases to 10 years. This first small *kalpa* is the first *kalpa* of decrease. In the second small *kalpa,* the human life span increases from 10 to 80,000 years, and then decreases from 80,000 to 10 years. The first half of the second small *kalpa* is the first *kalpa* of increase, and the latter half is the second *kalpa* of decrease. Each of the following seventeen small *kalpas* follows the same pattern as the second. The last, or twentieth, small *kalpa* is the *kalpa* of increase; in it the human life span increases from 10 years to 80,000 years. It is said that Shakyamuni appeared in the *kalpa* of continuance, in the ninth *kalpa,* or period, of decrease, when the life span of human beings was 100 years long. See also *kalpa.*

nirmāna-kāya [応身] (Skt; Jpn *ōjin*): The manifested body, one of the three bodies of a Buddha. *See* manifested body.

nirvana [涅槃] (Skt; Pali *nibbāna;* Jpn *nehan*): Enlightenment, the ultimate goal of Buddhist practice. The Sanskrit word *nirvāna* means "blown out" and is variously translated as extinction, emancipation, cessation, quiescence, or non-rebirth. Nirvana was originally regarded as the state in which all illusions and desires as well as the cycle of birth and death are extinguished. Hinayanists distinguish two types of nirvana. The first is that of the arhat who has eliminated all illusions and will no longer be reborn in the six paths, but who is still bound to the world of suffering in that he possesses a body. This is called the nirvana of remainder or incomplete nirvana. The second is that which the arhat achieves at death, when both body and mind—the sources of suffering—are extinguished. This is called the nirvana of no remainder or complete nirvana. Because Hinayana Buddhism teaches that the ultimate goal of practice can only be achieved at death, it was called the teaching of "reducing the body to ashes and annihilating consciousness." Mahayanists criticized the practice directed toward this goal as escapist and indifferent to the salvation of others, and probably derogatively coined the above phrase. In Mahayana Buddhism, nirvana came to mean not so much an exit from the phenomenal world as an awakening to the true nature of phenomena, or the attainment of Buddha wisdom. Even in Mahayana sutras, however, this attainment is regarded as requiring the elimination of earthly desires in the same manner as expounded in the Hinayana teachings. Therefore, it is taught that nirvana requires an immeasurably long period to achieve.

In contrast, the Lotus Sutra teaches that, by awakening to one's innate Buddha nature, one can reach the state of nirvana in his or her present form as an ordinary person who possesses earthly desires and undergoes the sufferings of birth and death. It reveals the principle that the sufferings of birth and death are none other than nirvana. From the standpoint of the Lotus Sutra, birth and death are two integral phases of eternal life. Nirvana, therefore, is not the cessation of birth and death, but a state of enlightenment experienced as one repeats the cycle of birth and death. The sufferings of birth and death and nirvana, or enlightenment, are inseparable: it is not necessary to extinguish one in order to attain the other. These sufferings belong to the nine worlds, and nirvana, to the world of Buddhahood. The nine worlds and the world of Buddhahood are mutually inclusive. By manifesting the state of Buddhahood, one enjoys nirvana while repeating the cycle of birth and death.

nirvana of no remainder [無余涅槃] (Jpn *muyo-nehan*): *See* nirvana.

nirvana of remainder [有余涅槃] (Jpn *uyo-nehan*): *See* nirvana.

Nirvana school [涅槃宗] (Chin Nieh-p'an-tsung; Jpn Nehan-shū): A school based on the Nirvana Sutra that flourished primarily in southern China. One of the thirteen major schools of Chinese Buddhism. In the fourth and fifth centuries, Tao-sheng, Hui-kuan, and other disciples of Kumārajīva defined the Nirvana Sutra as Shakyamuni Buddha's ultimate teaching and maintained, based on that sutra, that the Dharma body is eternal and the Buddha nature is inherent in all beings. T'ien-t'ai (538–597) later established the system of classifying the sutras into five periods and eight teachings and defined the Nirvana Sutra as subordinate to the Lotus Sutra. T'ien-t'ai, for instance, cited the passage from the Nirvana Sutra that reads: "When this [Nirvana] sutra was preached . . . the prediction had already been made in the Lotus Sutra that the eight thousand voice-hearers would attain Buddhahood, a prediction that was like a great harvest. Thus, the autumn harvest was over and the crop had been stored away for winter [when the Nirvana Sutra was expounded], and there was nothing left of it [but a few gleanings]." Thus, with the rise of the T'ien-t'ai school in the Sui dynasty (581–618), the Nirvana school began to decline and was eventually absorbed by the T'ien-t'ai school. The teachings of the Nirvana school were transmitted to Japan, but it did not become an independent school there.

Nirvana Sutra [涅槃経] (Chin *Nieh-p'an-ching;* Jpn *Nehan-gyō*): Any of the sutras either recording the teachings that Shakyamuni Buddha expounded immediately before his death or describing the events surrounding his death, or entry into nirvana. There are both Mahayana and Hinayana Nirvana sutras in Chinese translation. (Note: Where the titles of Chinese Nirvana sutras are phonetic transliterations from Sanskrit, the Sanskrit names are given for convenience's sake. Those titles that were translated into Chinese are given in English.) Chinese Mahayana versions include: (1) The Mahāparinirvāna Sutra, a translation by Dharmaraksha of the Northern Liang dynasty (397–439). This is the so-called northern version, consisting of forty volumes and thirteen chapters. It teaches that the Dharma body of the Buddha is indestructible and eternal; that the state of nirvana is endowed with the four virtues of eternity, happiness, true self, and purity; that all living beings possess the Buddha nature; and that even *icchantikas,* or persons of incorrigible disbelief, can attain Buddhahood. (2) The Mahāparinirvāna Sutra (southern version), a translation by Hui-kuan, Hui-yen, and Hsieh Ling-yün of the Liu Sung dynasty (420–479). This is a revision of the northern version in light of the Mahāparinirvāna Sutra translated by Fa-hsien and Buddhabhadra, and consists of thirty-six volumes and twenty-five chapters. (3) The Mahāparinirvāna Sutra, a translation by Fa-hsien and Buddhabhadra in the Eastern Chin dynasty (317–420). This work consists of six volumes and corresponds to the first ten volumes of Dharmaraksha's version. It is also called the Parinirvāna Sutra or the six-volume Parinirvāna Sutra. (4) The Epilogue to the Mahāparinirvāna Sutra, a two-volume translation by Jnānabhadra and Hui-ning of the T'ang dynasty (618–907), in which Shakyamuni Buddha describes the practice his disciples should carry out after his death. This sutra also describes the cremation of the Buddha's body, the distribution of his ashes, etc. Fragments of the Sanskrit texts from which these translations were made are extant.

The Hinayana Nirvana sutras are not so much expositions of Shakyamuni Buddha's teachings as descriptions of the final events of his life, his entry into nirvana, and the distribution of his remains. There are five Chinese versions: (1) the two-volume Buddha's Parinirvāna Sutra, a translation by Po Fa-tsu of the Western Chin dynasty (265–316); (2) the two-volume Parinirvāna Sutra, translator unknown; (3) the three-volume Mahāparinirvāna Sutra, a translation by Fa-hsien of the Eastern Chin dynasty; (4) the one-volume Legacy Teachings Sutra, a translation by Kumārajīva in the Later Ch'in dynasty (384–417); and (5) the Sutra of Preaching Travels contained in the Long Āgama Sutra, one of the four Chinese Āgama sutras, which was translated by Buddhayashas and Chu Fo-nien in the Later Ch'in dynasty. Among these five Chinese translations, only the Legacy Teachings Sutra is devoted to the expounding of doctrine rather than descriptions of the Buddha's final travels. Therefore, some scholars do not regard it as one of the Hinayana Nirvana sutras. The thirty-fifth through fortieth volumes of *The Monastic Rules of the Sarvāstivāda School on Various Matters,* a translation by I-ching, is similar in content to the four Hinayana versions other than the Legacy Teachings Sutra. In addition to these Chinese versions, there is also a Pali text called the *Mahāparinibbāna-suttanta,* whose content resembles that of the Chinese Hinayana versions. *See also* Mahāparinirvāna Sutra.

Nishiyama, the lay priest of [西山入道] (n.d.) (Jpn Nishiyama-nyūdō): A follower of Nichiren (1222–1282) who lived in Nishiyama Village in Fuji District of Suruga Province, Japan. Nichiren addressed six extant letters to him, including *Three Tripitaka Masters Pray for Rain.* According to one account, Nishiyama was a relative of Ōuchi Tasaburō Yasukiyo, the steward of Nishiyama Village, but another view identifies him as the lay priest Yui, Nikkō's maternal grandfather, who lived in Kawai, Fuji District.

Nissen [日仙] (1262–1357): A disciple of Nichiren; after Nichiren's death one of Nikkō's six elder disciples. A native of Kai Province in Japan, he studied under Jakunichi-bō Nikke, also later one of the six elder disciples. In 1334, the year after Nikkō's death, Nissen had a debate with Nichidai, another disciple of Nikkō, on the topic of whether or not it is necessary to recite the "Expedient Means" (second) chapter of the Lotus Sutra as a daily practice. Nissen insisted that it is not, basing his argument on the position that one cannot attain Buddhahood through the theoretical teaching, or the first half of the sutra, which includes the "Expedient Means" chapter. They did not reach a definite conclusion. Nissen later went to Sanuki Province, where he devoted himself to propagation. *See also* Nichidai.

Nisshō [日昭] (1221–1323): One of the six senior priests designated by Nichiren. He was Nichiren's first convert among the priesthood. A native of Shimōsa Province in Japan, he began his study of Buddhism at a temple of the Tendai school around 1235. Later he continued his study of the Tendai doctrine at Mount Hiei. Hearing that Nichiren had proclaimed a new teaching, Nisshō went to visit him at Matsubagayatsu in Kamakura and became his disciple in the eleventh month of 1253. He devoted himself to propagation mainly in Kamakura. After the memorial service at Minobu on the hundredth day following Nichiren's death, Nisshō returned to Kamakura where he built Hokke-ji temple at a place called Hamado. Because of governmental pressures on Nichiren's followers, however, he eventually pronounced himself to be a priest of the Tendai school and turned against Nikkō, Nichiren's designated successor.

Nisshū [日秀] (d. 1329): A disciple of Nichiren. Before his conversion to Nichiren's teachings, he was called Shimotsuke-bō. He was a priest at Ryūsen-ji, a temple of the Tendai school in Atsuhara of Suruga Province, Japan. Nikkō, later to become Nichiren's designated successor, converted him and his fellow priests Nichiben and Nichizen to Nichiren's teachings. Though the deputy chief priest Gyōchi ordered them to leave the temple, Nisshū and Nichiben secretly remained at Ryūsen-ji and converted many people in neighboring villages, an effort that eventually led to the Atsuhara Persecution. Nichiren and Nikkō drafted a petition on behalf of the two priests, who copied and signed it and submitted it to the shogunate. To protect them from governmental pressures following the Atsuhara Persecution, Nichiren sent Nisshū and Nichiben to Shimōsa Province. There they stayed at Guhō-ji temple, where the chief priest was Nitchō, Toki Jōnin's adopted son. After Nichiren's death, when Nikkō left Minobu in 1289, Nisshū accompanied him and engaged in propagation. He was named one of Nikkō's six elder disciples. *See also* Atsuhara Persecution.

Nitchō (1) [日頂] (1252–1317): Also known as Iyo-bō. One of the six senior priests designated by Nichiren. He was born in Omosu Village of Fuji District of Suruga Province, Japan. After his father's death, he and his mother went to live in Kamakura. She later married Toki Jōnin, who adopted Nitchō as his own son. In 1267 Nitchō became a disciple of Nichiren. When Toki Jōnin converted Guhō-ji, a temple of the Tendai school, to Nichiren's teaching in 1277, Nitchō became its first chief priest. During the Atsuhara Persecution, at the request of Nichiren, he temporarily sheltered Nisshū and Nichiben, the priests who had been expelled from Ryūsen-ji temple. After Nichiren's death, Nitchō failed to appear for his turn in the rotation system for attending to Nichiren's tomb, and for this Toki Jōnin disowned him. In 1291 he declared himself a priest of the Tendai school and disassociated himself from Nichiren's teaching. In 1302, however, he returned to serve Nikkō at Omosu.

(2) [日澄] (1262–1310): A disciple of Nikkō, Nichiren's designated successor. He was a son of Toki Jōnin, one of the leading followers of Nichiren who lived in Shimōsa Province in Japan. Though originally a disciple of Nikō, Nitchō found that Nikō had gone against Nichiren's teachings and in 1300 gave his allegiance to Nikkō. He was very learned and well versed in both Buddhist and non-Buddhist literature, and became the first chief instructor of Omosu Seminary. Nikkō had him write the draft of *The Guidelines for Believers of the Fuji School.*

noble eightfold path [八正道] (Jpn *hasshō-dō*): *See* eightfold path.

non-duality of body and mind [色心不二] (Jpn *shikishin-funi*): *See* oneness of body and mind.

non-duality of delusion and enlightenment [迷悟不二・迷悟一体] (Jpn *meigo-funi* or *meigo-ittai*): *See* oneness of delusion and enlightenment.

non-duality of good and evil [善悪不二] (Jpn *zen'aku-funi*): *See* oneness of good and evil.

non-duality of life and its environment [依正不二] (Jpn *eshō-funi*): *See* oneness of life and its environment.

non-duality of living beings and Buddhas [生仏不二・生仏一如] (Jpn *shōbutsu-funi* or *shōbutsu-ichinyo*): *See* oneness of living beings and Buddhas.

Nōnin [能忍] (n.d.): Also known as Dainichi or Dainichi Nōnin. A Japanese priest who was among the first to spread the Zen teachings in Japan during the twelfth century. Although the Rinzai school established by Eisai (1141–1215) was the first official Japanese Zen school, Nōnin preceded him in introducing the Zen teachings. He founded Sambō-ji temple in Settsu Province. Criticized for not having received his teachings from any authorized master, he dispatched two disciples to China in 1189 and obtained authorization of his views from the Zen master Cho-an Te-kuang. Nōnin called his following the Japanese Bodhidharma (Nihon Daruma) school, though it did not in fact become an independent school.

non-returner [阿那含・不還] (Skt, Pali *anāgāmin;* Jpn *anagon* or *fugen*): The third of the four stages of Hinayana enlightenment. The fourth and highest stage is the stage of arhat. The stage of the non-returner is the stage in which one has eliminated the desires and delusions of the world of desire. At this stage, one will not be reborn in the world of desire; hence the term "non-returner." Instead one will be reborn in the world of form or the world of formlessness. The Sanskrit word *anāgāmin* means not coming, not arriving, or not subject to returning.

non-substantiality [空] (Skt *shūnya* or *shūnyatā;* Jpn *kū*): A fundamental Buddhist concept, also translated as emptiness, void, latency, or relativity. The Sanskrit *shūnya* or *shūnyatā* means emptiness. *Shūnya* also means "empty" and "empty of." It is the concept that things and phenomena have no fixed or independent nature or existence of their own. Non-substantiality is neither negative nor world-negating but teaches the importance of perceiving the true nature of phenomena, which are on the surface transient. The Wisdom sutras developed the Mahayana concept of non-substantiality and Nāgārjuna (c. 150–250) systematized it based on them. This concept originated in connection to those of dependent origination and of the nonexistence of self-nature. Dependent origination means that, because phenomena arise only by virtue of their relationship with other phenomena, they have no distinct nature or existence of their own. Nonexistence of self-nature means that there is no independent entity that exists alone, apart from other phenomena. The common message is that the true nature of all phenomena is non-substantiality, and that it cannot be defined in terms of the concepts of existence and nonexistence. Nāgārjuna explained it as the Middle Way, a perspective that regards the categories of existence and nonexistence as extremes, and aims to transcend them. The practical purpose behind the teaching of non-substantiality lies in eliminating attachments to transient phenomena and to the ego, or the perception of self as an independent and fixed identity.

Northern Buddhism [北方仏教・北伝仏教] (Jpn Hoppō-bukkyō or Hokuden-bukkyō): The teachings of Buddhism that spread north from India to Central Asia, Tibet, China, and Korea, and then to Japan. The term *Northern Buddhism* is contrasted with *Southern Buddhism,* the Buddhism that spread south to Sri Lanka and Southeast Asian countries, such as Myanmar, Thailand, Laos, and Cambodia. This distinction was applied originally in the nineteenth century by European scholars of Buddhism; the division of Buddhism based on the Pali scriptures preserved in Sri Lanka was called Southern Buddhism, and the division of Buddhism mainly based on the Sanskrit scriptures transmitted from India to Central Asia and China was referred to as Northern Buddhism. Southern Buddhism is also called Theravāda Buddhism. In the areas where Northern Buddhism spread, Mahayana Buddhism is predominant. Tibetan Buddhism, also known as Lamaism, is classified as Northern Buddhism. It is a mixture of the teachings on monastic discipline of early Buddhism, Mahayana, and Tantric Buddhism, and is practiced mostly in Tibet and Mongolia. From early on, Northern Buddhism was transmitted from India to Central Asia, but it was not until around the first century that Buddhism spread eastward to China. Thereafter the translation of the Buddhist scriptures into Chinese proceeded in earnest, giving rise to numerous Chinese versions of the scriptures. In the later fourth century, Buddhism made its way eastward to Korea, which was then divided into three kingdoms—Koguryŏ, Paekche, and Silla. From Korea it was introduced to Japan in the sixth century. Northern and Southern Buddhism are designations related to the development of Buddhism from a geographical viewpoint and not a classification based on teaching.

Though this classification remains somewhat ambiguous, it is indisputable that, in the countries where Northern Buddhism spread, Mahayana has been prevalent, and in the countries where Southern Buddhism spread, Theravāda has prevailed.

Northern school of Zen [北宗禅] (Jpn Hokushū Zen): One of the two schools formed by the first schism in the Zen (Ch'an) school in China. The other school is called the Southern school of Zen. The fifth Chinese Zen patriarch Hung-jen had two capable disciples. One was Shen-hsiu (606–706), who propagated Zen in northern China and upheld the traditional doctrine of gradual enlightenment. His school became the Northern school of Zen. The other disciple was Hui-neng (638–713), who became the sixth patriarch and spread Zen in southern China. He formulated and taught the doctrine of sudden enlightenment (also known as abrupt, or immediate, enlightenment), and his school came to be called the Southern school of Zen. The Northern school rapidly declined, while Hui-neng produced many able disciples and his Southern school became the mainstream of Chinese Zen. The Japanese Zen schools derive from the Southern school.

numberless major world system dust particle kalpas [五百塵点劫] (Jpn *gohyaku-jintengō* or *gohyaku-jindengō*): An incredibly long period of time described in the "Life Span" (sixteenth) chapter of the Lotus Sutra to indicate how long ago Shakyamuni Buddha originally attained enlightenment. In the "Life Span" chapter, Shakyamuni reveals that he attained enlightenment not for the first time in this life under the *bodhi* tree in Gayā, India, but in the inconceivably remote past. He then explains the duration since his original attainment of Buddhahood as follows: "Suppose a person were to take five hundred, a thousand, ten thousand, a million *nayuta asamkhya* major world systems and grind them to dust. Then, moving eastward, each time he passes five hundred, a thousand, ten thousand, a million *nayuta asamkhya* worlds he drops a particle of dust. He continues eastward in this way until he has finished dropping all the particles. . . . Suppose all these worlds, whether they received a particle of dust or not, are once more reduced to dust. Let one particle represent one *kalpa*. The time that has passed since I attained Buddhahood surpasses this by a hundred, a thousand, ten thousand, a million *nayuta asamkhya kalpas*." *Numberless major world system dust particle kalpas* is the term applied to the length of time described in the above passage. The Japanese term for this concept, *gohyaku-jintengō*, literally means "five hundred dust particle *kalpas*." "Five hundred" here is an abbreviation for "five hundred, a thousand, ten thousand, a million *nayuta asamkhya* major world systems," which is described as "numberless major world systems." *See also* major world system; major world system dust particle *kalpas*.

Nyagrodha [尼俱律陀] (Skt; Jpn Nikurida): A Brahman of the state of Magadha in ancient India. A legend concerning him is recorded in *A History of the Buddha's Successors*. According to that work, his virtuous deeds in past lifetimes resulted in his being endowed with matchless intelligence and a thousand times the wealth of the king. He had no children, however, and though he prayed repeatedly to a tree god for a child, he was not blessed with one. Finally he grew angry and threatened to chop down the tree the god inhabited if his prayer was not answered. In fear, the god of the tree reported to the four heavenly kings, who in turn sought the help of the god Shakra. Shakra searched the world, but could find no one worthy enough to become the child of someone of such great fortune, so he went to the great heavenly king Brahmā for advice. Brahmā then discovered a heavenly being in his domain who was on the point of death and asked him to be reborn as Nyagrodha's child. The heavenly being at first objected that he did not want to be born among Brahmans as their teachings were erroneous, but after being assured of Nyagrodha's virtue and Shakra's protection, he finally agreed. Nyagrodha's wife gave birth to a son. The son was Mahākāshyapa, who became one of Shakyamuni Buddha's leading disciples and the Buddha's successor as head of the Buddhist Order after his death.

nyagrodha tree [尼拘律樹・尼俱類樹] (Skt; Jpn *nikuritsu-ju* or *nikurui-ju*): A tree cited in Buddhist works, often as a symbol for great size. *The Treatise on the Great Perfection of Wisdom* by Nāgārjuna (c. 150–250) states that the *nyagrodha* tree is large enough to provide shade for more than five hundred carts. *The Fourfold Rules of Discipline* describes a scene in which the people take rest under a *nyagrodha* tree located near Kaushāmbī in India, under which they also fit their elephants and horses and the carts they are drawing. The *nyagrodha* tree also symbolizes the principle that a seemingly insignificant cause can produce a great effect, just as the tiny seed of the *nyagrodha* develops into an expansive tree. The *nyagrodha* tree is identified with the banyan tree found in tropical and subtropical Asiatic regions, which is around thirty meters tall. Its abundant foliage offers cool shade from the tropical sun, and its branches send shoots down to the earth that take root and form new trunks, enabling one tree to expand outward.

Nyohō [如宝] (d. 814 or 815) (Jpn; Chin Ju-pao): A priest who brought the scriptures of the Precepts (Chin Lü; Jpn Ritsu) school from China to Japan. He arrived at Japan's capital, Nara, in 754, accompanying his teacher, Chien-chen, who became known as Ganjin in Japan. Nyohō lived at Yakushi-ji temple in Shimotsuke Province and also at Tōshōdai-ji temple in Nara. Renowned as a lecturer and practitioner of the precepts, he won respect from Emperor Kammu and conferred the precepts upon him, his consort, and his crown prince.

nyūdō [入道] (Jpn): *See* lay priest.

O

Ōama [大尼] (n.d.): A follower of Nichiren (1222–1282). The wife of the lord of Tōjō Village of Nagasa District in Awa Province, Japan. In his writings, Nichiren also refers to her simply as "the wife of the lord of the manor" and as the lay nun of Ryōke, *ryōke* meaning the family of the local proprietary lord who owned and managed the estate. She had known Nichiren and his parents and is said to have helped him enter Seichō-ji temple. Later Ōama became a believer in Nichiren's teaching but abandoned her faith around the time of the Tatsunokuchi Persecution in 1271. After Nichiren returned from his exile on Sado Island and situated himself at Minobu in 1274, she again changed her mind and asked Nichiren to inscribe the object of devotion called Gohonzon for her. He refused, however, knowing her faith to be unstable. He did nevertheless present a Gohonzon to her daughter-in-law, Niiama (Younger Nun). She was called Ōama (Elder Nun) in relation to Niiama. Though Ōama and the lay nun of Nagoe were previously regarded as the same person, further research has shown there is no certain evidence to support this.

Ōbaku school [黄檗宗] (Jpn Ōbaku-shū): One of the three principal schools of Zen in Japan, the other two being the Rinzai and Sōtō schools. Its head temple is Mampuku-ji at Uji in Kyoto. In 1654 the Chinese priest Yin-yüan came to Japan, where he became known as Ingen. In 1661 Ingen built Mampuku-ji and established what was later called the Ōbaku school. The name of this school derives from Mount Huang-po (Ōbaku), where Ingen had studied in China. Since Ingen was trained in the Lin-chi (Rinzai) school, the teachings of the Ōbaku school are identical with those of the Rinzai school except that they incorporate the Nembutsu, i.e., the invoking of the name of Amida Buddha, and other elements of the Pure Land teachings concerning rebirth in the Pure Land.

Object of Devotion for Observing the Mind, The [観心本尊抄] (Jpn *Kanjin-no-honzon-shō*): The abbreviated title of one of Nichiren's five or ten major writings, *The Object of Devotion for Observing the Mind Established in the Fifth Five-Hundred-Year Period after the Thus Come One's*

Passing. It explains the object of devotion in Nichiren's teaching, or the Gohonzon. It was written at Ichinosawa on Sado Island, Japan, dated the twenty-fifth day of the fourth month, 1273, and addressed to Toki Jōnin, one of Nichiren's influential followers who lived in Shimōsa Province. In the previous year, Nichiren wrote *The Opening of the Eyes,* which identifies the object of devotion in his teaching in terms of the "Person," describing himself as being endowed with the Buddha's three virtues of sovereign, teacher, and parent, or as the person to lead people in the Latter Day of the Law to Buddhahood with wisdom and compassion. In contrast, *The Object of Devotion for Observing the Mind* reveals the object of devotion in terms of the "Law"—as the embodiment of the Law of Nam-myoho-renge-kyo—and describes the practice for attaining Buddhahood. This writing can be divided into four parts. The first establishes that the doctrine of three thousand realms in a single moment of life is revealed only in the fifth volume of T'ien-t'ai's work *Great Concentration and Insight.* The second discusses the Ten Worlds, especially Buddhahood, inherent in the lives of all people and the meaning of observation of the mind, defining it as "to observe one's own mind and find the Ten Worlds within it." Nichiren describes the way to achieve this as follows: "Shakyamuni's practices and the virtues he consequently attained are all contained within the five characters of Myoho-renge-kyo. If we believe in these five characters, we will naturally be granted the same benefits as he was" (365). In this passage, "believe in these five characters" means to chant Nam-myoho-renge-kyo with faith in the Gohonzon. This is known as the principle that embracing the Gohonzon is in itself observing one's own mind, i.e., attaining enlightenment.

The third section explains the Gohonzon from the standpoint of the "fivefold view of revelation," an analysis of the Buddhist teachings. The final revelation in the above view is described as follows: "The essential teaching of Shakyamuni's lifetime and that revealed at the beginning of the Latter Day are both pure and perfect [in that both lead directly to Buddhahood]. Shakyamuni's, however, is the Buddhism of the harvest, and this is the Buddhism of sowing. The core of his teaching is one chapter and two halves, and the core of mine is the five characters of the daimoku alone" (370). In this passage, "the five characters of the daimoku" means the essence of the Lotus Sutra, or the Gohonzon of Nam-myoho-renge-kyo. This section identifies who will spread the teaching and concludes, "At this time the countless Bodhisattvas of the Earth will appear and establish in this country [Japan] the object of devotion, foremost in Jambudvīpa, that depicts Shakyamuni Buddha of the essential teaching attending [the eternal Buddha]" (376). The fourth section concludes the treatise by stating, "Showing profound compassion for those unable to comprehend the gem of the doctrine of three thousand realms in a single moment of life, the Buddha [who made his advent in the Latter Day of the Law] wrapped it within the five characters [of Myoho-renge-kyo], with which he then adorned the necks of the ignorant people of the latter age" (376). *See also* Gohonzon; oneness of the Person and the Law.

object of devotion of the essential teaching [本門の本尊] (Jpn *hommon-no-honzon*): One of the Three Great Secret Laws. *See* Gohonzon.

observation of the mind [観心] (Jpn *kanjin*): To perceive or awaken to the ultimate reality inherent in one's life. Also, the method of practice that makes this possible. In contrast with doctrinal study of the Buddhist sutras, observation of the mind means to perceive in the depths of one's being the truth that is beyond verbal explanation. Observing the mind is particularly stressed in T'ien-t'ai's practice, in which meditation is focused on the true nature of the mind rather than upon some exterior object. In *Great Concentration and Insight,* T'ien-t'ai (538–597) taught meditation to perceive "the region of the unfathomable," which is interpreted as either the unification of the three truths in a single mind or three thousand realms in a single moment of life. This means, in essence, to perceive one's inherent Buddhahood, which is the goal of the T'ien-t'ai system of meditation.

Nichiren (1222–1282) defined T'ien-t'ai's observation of the mind as follows: "The observation of the mind means to observe one's own mind and to find the Ten Worlds within it" (356). Nichikan, the twenty-sixth chief priest of Taiseki-ji temple, interpreted the above statement in his *Exegesis on "The Object of Devotion for Observing the Mind"* as follows: "'To observe one's own mind' means to believe in the Gohonzon [the object of devotion in Nichiren's teaching]. 'To find the Ten Worlds within it' means to chant [the daimoku of] the Mystic Law. If only you believe in the Gohonzon and chant the Mystic Law, then the Ten Worlds of the Gohonzon will become the Ten Worlds of your own life." This interpretation is based on the passage from Nichiren's *Object of Devotion for Observing the Mind* that reads: "Shakyamuni's practices and the virtues he consequently attained are all contained within the five characters of Myoho-renge-kyo. If we believe in these five characters, we will naturally be granted the same benefits as he was" (365). In Nichiren's teaching, the observation of the mind means to believe in the Gohonzon, the embodiment of three thousand realms in a single moment of life, and chant the daimoku. This is the teaching that embracing the Gohonzon is in itself observing one's own mind, i.e., attaining enlightenment.

Observation of the mind also means to interpret the sutras from the viewpoint of the truth one realizes in one's life. In Nichiren's teaching, it means to read the sutras from the viewpoint of the principle of Nam-myoho-renge-kyo.

ocean-imprint meditation [海印三昧] (Jpn *kaiin-zammai*): A kind of meditation expounded in the Flower Garland Sutra, the Great Collection Sutra, and other sutras. In this meditation, all phenomena of the three existences of past, present, and future are clearly observed in the mind, just as all things are reflected on the calm surface of the ocean.

Ocean of Meditation on the Buddha Sutra [観仏三昧海経] (Chin *Kuan-fo-san-mei-hai-ching;* Jpn *Kambutsu-sammai-kai-kyō*): Abbreviated as the Meditation on the Buddha Sutra. A Chinese translation made in the early fifth century by Buddhabhadra, a monk from northern India. The Sanskrit original is not extant. According to the text of this sutra, Shakyamuni preached the Ocean of Meditation on the Buddha Sutra at Nyagrodha Monastery in Kapilavastu to his father, King Shuddhodana, his aunt and foster mother, Mahāprajāpatī, and others. The sutra teaches that, by settling into meditation on a Buddha, one can attain emancipation, and describes how to meditate on a Buddha, explaining the benefit of such meditation. It also describes a Buddha's thirty-two features and eighty characteristics, as well as the way to meditate on these qualities.

offering [供養] (Jpn *kuyō*): To donate, with a sense of veneration, various things to the Buddha and the Buddhist Order; also, that which is donated. Offerings included food, drink, clothing, bedding, medicine, flowers, incense, lamps, and necessary utensils. Among these, clothing, food and drink, bedding, and medicine were called the four kinds of offerings. Buddhist sutras and their commentaries list various sets of offerings. For example, the two kinds of offerings indicate the offering of goods and the offering of the Law, i.e., the preaching of the Buddha's teachings. The three kinds of offerings are the offering of goods, the offering of the Law, and the offering of fearlessness. The offering of fearlessness means to relieve others' fears and give them courage. Another set of the three kinds of offerings is the offering of goods, the offering of praise and reverence, and the offering of the Law. A third set of the three kinds of offerings is the offering of food and drink, the offering of rare treasures, and the offering of body and life. The offerings described in the "Teacher of the Law" (tenth) chapter of the Lotus Sutra are generally called the ten kinds of offerings, that is, the offering of flowers, incense, necklaces, powdered incense, paste incense, incense for burning, silken canopies, streamers and banners, clothing, and music. In this chapter, these offerings are described as being made to the Lotus Sutra. Another view of the ten kinds of offerings regards "silken canopies" and "streamers and banners" as one offering, and adds an act of "pressing one's palms together."

Ōhara Discourse [大原問答・大原談義] (Jpn Ōhara-mondō or Ōhara-dangi): Also known as the Ōhara Debate. A discourse on the Pure Land teachings between Hōnen, who later founded the Japanese Pure Land (Jōdo) school, and the priests of other Buddhist schools. It was held at Shōrin-in temple in Ōhara, Kyoto, in 1186, at the request of Kenshin, later the chief priest of Enryaku-ji, the head temple of the Tendai school. There Hōnen expounded on the exclusive practice of the Pure Land teachings and won many converts.

old translations [旧訳] (Jpn *kuyaku*): Also, older translations. Chinese translations of the Buddhist sutras and treatises produced before those of Hsüan-tsang (602–664). "Old translations" is contrasted with "new translations," those translations produced by Hsüan-tsang and persons after him. The works of Kumārajīva and Paramārtha belong to the group of old translations. It is generally held that the old translations tend to be more interpretative, yet readily comprehensible, while the new translations tend to be more literal yet less accessible. In actuality, however, the quality of any given translation depends mostly on the understanding and capability of its translators, rather than to which of these two categories it belongs.

om [唵] (Skt; Jpn *on*): A mystic syllable expressing affirmation, uttered at the beginning of a Vedic prayer, recitation, or chanting. *Om* is regarded as a combination of the three sounds of *a, u,* and *m,* representing respectively beginning, continuation, and end. These three component sounds were identified respectively with the Brahman trinity, the three deities of Brahmā the Creator, Vishnu the Sustainer, and Shiva the Destroyer. *Om* was later incorporated into Esoteric Buddhism as a mystic formula. The Protection of the Sovereign of the Nation Sutra, an esoteric sutra, identifies the sounds *a, u,* and *m* respectively with the Dharma body, the reward body, and the manifested body, which together constitute the Buddha's three bodies.

Omosu Seminary [重須談所] (Jpn Omosu-dansho): A seminary that Nikkō, Nichiren's successor, established in Omosu Village of Fuji District, Suruga Province, Japan, 1298. He lived and lectured there to his disciples and supervised their training. Nikkō appointed his disciple Nitchō as the first chief instructor of Omosu Seminary. After Nitchō's death, Nikkō appointed Nichijun, a disciple of Nitchō, as the second chief instructor of the seminary.

The training at Omosu emphasized an intensive study of Nichiren's teachings, distinguishing between the correct interpretation of Nichiren's teachings and the incorrect interpretations set forth by five of the six senior priests designated by Nichiren other than Nikkō. There the disciples trained for public debate aimed at the propagation of Nichiren's teachings. Many new disciples were attracted to the seminary, which they called "the temple at Omosu," and the priests of nearby Taiseki-ji also attended in order to learn from Nikkō.

In 1483 the seminary severed its ties with Taiseki-ji and became affiliated with Koizumi Kuon-ji temple, the origin of which was the dwelling inhabited by Nichigō during his dispute over the possession of part of Taiseki-ji with its fourth chief priest, Nichidō. In 1515 it was renamed Hommon-ji and returned to the Nikkō school (based at Taiseki-ji). In 1899 it was renamed Kitayama Hommon-ji and the school connected with it became the Hommon (Essential Teaching) school. In 1941 it merged into the Minobu school in response to a government order.

once-returner [斯陀含・一来] (Skt *sakridāgāmin;* Pali *sakadāgāmin;* Jpn *shidagon* or *ichirai*): The second of the four stages of Hinayana enlightenment. The fourth and highest stage is that of arhat. In the stage of the once-returner, one has eradicated six of the nine illusions of desire in the world of desire. Due to the remaining illusions, one will be born next in the realm of heavenly beings and then once again in the human world before entering nirvana; hence the name once-returner.

On Chanting the Daimoku of the Lotus Sutra [唱法華題目抄] (Jpn *Shōhokke-daimoku-shō*): One of the ten major writings of Nichiren. *See* ten major writings.

one Buddha vehicle [一仏乗] (Jpn *ichi-butsujō*): The teaching that leads all people to Buddhahood. *See* one vehicle.

one chapter and two halves [一品二半] (Jpn *ippon-nihan*): The core of the Lotus Sutra, comprising the latter half of the "Emerging from the Earth" (fifteenth) chapter, the entire "Life Span" (sixteenth) chapter, and the first half of the "Distinctions in Benefits" (seventeenth) chapter. This section reveals Shakyamuni Buddha's original attainment of enlightenment. At the beginning of the "Emerging from the Earth" chapter, the Bodhisattvas of the Earth make their appearance, and Bodhisattva Maitreya, on behalf of the assembly, asks Shakyamuni who they are. The Buddha replies that they are his disciples whom he has been teaching since the time of his enlightenment in this *sahā* world, though he alludes to having taught them since the "long distant past." Unsatisfied, Bodhisattva Maitreya persists: How could Shakyamuni have possibly trained so many countless bodhisattvas in the mere forty-odd years since his awakening under the *bodhi* tree? He implores Shakyamuni to explain further for the sake of future generations who may harbor doubts. To comply, the Buddha explains in the next chapter, "Life Span," that he actually attained enlightenment in the unimaginably distant past—what is known as numberless major world system dust particle *kalpas* in the past—and that since then he has always been in this world teaching the people. The first part of the "Distinctions in Benefits" chapter explains that the bodhisattvas and others who heard this revelation have all thereby received great benefits that will ensure their enlightenment.

T'ien-t'ai (538–597) and Nichiren (1222–1282) interpreted the concept of "one chapter and two halves" differently. According to T'ien-t'ai's interpretation, the latter half of the "Emerging from the Earth" chapter begins with Shakyamuni's statement that the Bodhisattvas of the Earth are his disciples whom he has been teaching since the long distant past. Hearing this brief statement, T'ien-t'ai says, Shakyamuni's disciples have understood that his enlightenment occurred in the remote past. In the Lotus Sutra, however, this implication is followed by Bodhisattva Maitreya's second question: How could the Buddha have taught so many bodhisattvas in the short space of a few decades? Based on the sutra's text, Nichiren interprets this question as being asked for the sake of those who will come after Shakyamuni's death. Thus Nichiren does not include Shakyamuni's initial brief allusion in his answer to this question—his statement that he has been teaching the Bodhisattvas of the Earth since the "long distant past"—in the latter half of the "Emerging from the Earth" chapter, or in the one chapter and two halves. In other words, Nichiren defines the one chapter and two halves as beginning with Bodhisattva Maitreya's second question.

This difference in the interpretations of T'ien-t'ai and Nichiren relates to the distinction Nichiren made between the Buddhism of the harvest and the Buddhism of sowing. Shakyamuni's reference to the remote past in this chapter is intended to resolve the doubts of the assembly. That is, it is a teaching directed toward Shakyamuni's contemporary disciples and therefore falls into the category of the Buddhism of the harvest (the teaching meant to enable Shakyamuni's contemporaries to "harvest" the seeds of Buddhahood planted in their previous lives). In contrast, Bodhisattva Maitreya's second question is asked on behalf of those who will appear after Shakyamuni's death. In reply, Shakyamuni reveals his enlightenment in the remote past in the next chapter, "Life Span." According to Nichiren's interpretation, this revelation implies the seed of Buddhahood or the cause that enabled Shakyamuni to attain enlightenment; that is, the ultimate truth or Law of life and the universe. Nichiren identified this Law as Nam-myoho-renge-kyo, which enables all people to attain Buddhahood. Nichiren's "one chapter and two halves" refers to the essence of the "Life Span" chapter, or Nam-myoho-renge-kyo, the Buddhism of sowing meant for people in the Latter Day of the Law. In *The Object of Devotion for Observing the Mind,* Nichiren writes: "The essential teaching of Shakyamuni's lifetime and that revealed at the beginning of the Latter Day are both pure and perfect [in that both lead directly to Buddhahood]. Shakyamuni's, however, is the Buddhism of the harvest, and this is the Buddhism of sowing. The core of his teaching is one chapter and two halves, and the core of mine is the five characters of the daimoku alone" (370).

one-eyed turtle [一眼の亀] (Jpn *ichigen-no-kame*): A reference in the "King Wonderful Adornment" (twenty-seventh) chapter of the Lotus Sutra, which says that encountering a Buddha's teaching is as rare as a one-eyed turtle finding a floating sandalwood log with a hollow in it to hold him. The Nirvana Sutra uses the same image to express the rarity of being born human and encountering a Buddha's teaching. The story behind this reference is found in the parable of the blind turtle in the Miscellaneous Āgama Sutra. A blind turtle, whose life span is immeasurable *kalpas,* lives at the bottom of the sea. Once every one hundred years he rises to the surface. There is only one log floating in the sea with a suitable hollow in it. Since the turtle is blind and the log is tossed about by the wind and waves, the likelihood of the turtle reaching the log is extremely remote. It is even rarer, says Shakyamuni, to be born a human being; having been born human, one should use the opportunity to master the four noble truths and attain emancipation.

A much more elaborate version of this story appears in Nichiren's letter *The One-eyed Turtle and the Floating Log,* where he uses it to describe the difficulty of encountering the Lotus Sutra and of encountering the daimoku, or essence, of the Lotus Sutra. The turtle in this case is described as one-eyed and limbless. His belly is as hot as heated iron, and his back as cold as the Snow Mountains. There is a sacred red sandalwood tree that can cool his belly. Day and night the turtle yearns to find a hollowed-out sandalwood log so that he can cool his belly in its hollow while warming his back in the sun. However, he can rise to the surface only once in a thousand years, and even if he should happen to find a floating log at that time, it may not necessarily be red sandalwood. Even if he finds a red sandalwood log, it rarely has a hollow in it, and even if it does, the hollow is rarely of the right size to accommodate him. And even if he should be fortunate enough to find the perfect log, because he is lacking one eye, he has trouble moving in the proper direction. Here

Nichiren interprets the sea as the sufferings of birth and death, and the turtle as humankind. His lack of limbs indicates lack of good fortune from previous lifetimes, the heat of his belly signifies the eight hot hells, and the cold of his back, the eight cold hells. Having one eye indicates the distorted perception that sees inferior teachings as superior, and vice versa. The ability to surface only once every thousand years indicates how difficult it is to emerge from the lower worlds of existence and be born human, especially to be born in an age when a Buddha has been present. The floating logs other than red sandalwood are the provisional teachings that are comparatively easy to encounter, and the red sandalwood is the Lotus Sutra. The proper-sized hollow in the log is the daimoku of that sutra, Nam-myoho-renge-kyo.

one great reason [一大事] (Jpn *ichidaiji*): Also, one great matter. The ultimate reason for a Buddha's appearance in the world, as expounded in the "Expedient Means" (second) chapter of the Lotus Sutra. In this chapter, Shakyamuni reveals that Buddhas make their advent for "one great reason," namely, to enable all people to attain the same enlightenment they have. Concerning this "one great reason," he goes on to say that Buddhas appear in the world in order to open the door of Buddha wisdom to all living beings, to show it to them, to cause them to awaken to it, and induce them to enter into it.

One Great Secret Law [一大秘法] (Jpn *ichidai-hihō*): The object of devotion of the essential teaching, one of the Three Great Secret Laws in Nichiren's teaching. The other two of the Three Great Secret Laws are the daimoku of the essential teaching and the sanctuary of the essential teaching. Here, the essential teaching refers to the teaching of Nam-myoho-renge-kyo implicit in the "Life Span" (sixteenth) chapter of the Lotus Sutra. The object of devotion of the essential teaching is the basis of the Three Great Secret Laws. Chanting Nam-myoho-renge-kyo with faith in the object of devotion is the daimoku of the essential teaching, and the place where one enshrines the object of devotion and chants the daimoku is the sanctuary of the essential teaching. Thus the object of devotion encompasses all Three Great Secret Laws within itself and is called the One Great Secret Law.

One Hundred Records of the Great Teacher T'ien-t'ai, The [国清百録] (Chin *Kuo-ch'ing-pai-lu;* Jpn *Kokusei-hyakuroku*): A collection of 104 historical records and documents that includes the monastic rules of discipline in the T'ien-t'ai school, imperial edicts, and correspondence between T'ien-t'ai and Emperor Hsüan of the Ch'en dynasty (557–589), Emperor Yang of the Sui dynasty (581–618), and eminent priests such as Chi-tsang. Its compilation was planned and initiated by Chih-chi, a disciple of T'ien-t'ai, but because Chih-chi died while the work was in progress, it was continued by Chang-an, T'ien-t'ai's successor, and completed around 605. Together with *The Biography of the Great Teacher T'ien-t'ai Chih-che of the Sui Dynasty,* which was also compiled by Chang-an, it is regarded as an essential source for the study of T'ien-t'ai and his school in its early phase.

One-Hundred-Verse Treatise, The [百論] (Chin *Pai-lun;* Jpn *Hyaku-ron*): A treatise consisting of one hundred verses attributed to Āryadeva and translated into Chinese in 404 by Kumārajīva. It is one of the three treatises of the Three Treatises (Chin San-lun; Jpn Sanron) school, the other two being Nāgārjuna's *Treatise on the Middle Way* and his *Treatise on the Twelve Gates. The One-Hundred-Verse Treatise* reaffirms the doctrine of non-substantiality expounded in *The Treatise on the Middle Way,* refuting the Sāmkhya, Vaisheshika, Nyāya, and other schools of Hindu philosophy in light of the teachings of Buddhism.

oneness of body and mind [色心不二] (Jpn *shikishin-funi*): Also, non-duality of body and mind. The principle that the two seemingly distinct phenomena of body, or the physical aspect of life, and mind, or its spiritual aspect, are essentially non-dual, being two integral phases of a single reality. One of the ten onenesses formulated by Miao-lo (711–782) in his *Annotations on "The Profound Meaning of the Lotus Sutra."* In the Japanese term *shikishin-funi, shiki* means that which has form and color, or physical existence, while *shin* means that which has neither form nor color, or spiritual existence, such as the mind, heart, and soul. *Funi* is an abbreviation of *nini-funi,* which indicates "two (in phenomena) but not two (in essence)." This means that the material and the spiritual are two separate classes of phenomena, but non-dual and indivisible in essence, because they are both aspects of the same reality. In the above annotations, Miao-lo states that, from the viewpoints of the whole and its components, life at a single moment is the whole, while body and mind are its components. Neither body nor mind is a separate entity; there is not one without the other. They are inseparable components of life.

In the Lotus Sutra, the principle of the ten factors of life represents the oneness of body and mind. The ten factors are listed in the "Expedient Means" (second) chapter of the sutra, where it states that the true aspect of all phenomena consists of "appearance, nature, entity, power, influence, internal cause, relation, latent effect, manifest effect, and their consistency from beginning to end." *On "The Profound Meaning"* states: "Appearance exists only in what is material; nature exists only in what is spiritual. Entity, power, influence, and relation in principle combine both the material and the spiritual. Internal cause and latent effect are purely spiritual; manifest effect exists only in what is material." *The Record of the Orally Transmitted Teachings* reads, "[Concerning the term *dedication of one's life*] 'dedication' refers to the element of physical form as it pertains to us, while 'life' refers to the element of mind as it pertains to us. But the ultimate teaching tells us that form and mind are not two." *See also* ten onenesses.

oneness of delusion and enlightenment [迷悟不二・迷悟一体] (Jpn *meigo-funi* or *meigo-ittai*): Also, non-duality of delusion and enlightenment. The principle that delusion and enlightenment are, though different in aspect, one and the same in their essential nature. A bad cause or influence gives rise to delusion, and a good cause or influence, to enlightenment. Delusion and enlightenment are two different workings, but both arise from the essential nature of life. This Mahayana concept contrasts with the Hinayana view that enlightenment and delusion, or enlightenment and earthly desires, are mutually exclusive and incompatible.

oneness of good and evil [善悪不二] (Jpn *zen'aku-funi*): Also, non-duality of good and evil. The principle that good and evil are not separate and distinct, but are inherent in all phenomena. "Good" in Buddhism means that which benefits oneself and others, while "evil" means that which harms oneself and others. Good and evil are not two mutually exclusive entities but are two different functions of life. The principle of three thousand realms in a single moment of life elucidates that all possible conditions or states of existence reside within life at each moment. Life therefore simultaneously possesses the potential for both good and evil, and even when manifesting one, it is never devoid of the potential for the other.

oneness of life and its environment [依正不二] (Jpn *eshō-funi*): Also, non-duality of life and its environment. The principle that life and its environment, though two seemingly distinct phenomena, are essentially non-dual; they are two integral phases of a single reality. In the Japanese term *eshō-funi*, *eshō* is a compound of *shōhō*, meaning life or a living being, and *ehō*, its environment. *Funi*, meaning "not two," indicates oneness or non-duality. It is short for *nini-funi*, which means "two (in phenomena) but not two (in essence)." *Hō* of *shōhō* and *ehō* means reward or effect. It indicates that "life" constitutes a subjective self that experiences the effects of its past actions, and "its environment" is an objective realm in which individuals' karmic rewards find expression. Each living being has its own unique environment. The effects of karma appear in oneself and in one's objective environment, because self and environment are two integral aspects of an individual. *The Treatise on the Great Perfection of Wisdom* by Nāgārjuna (c. 150–250) introduces the concept of the three realms of existence, which views life from three different standpoints and explains the manifestation of individual lives in the real world. These three are the realm of the five components of life, the realm of living beings, each as a temporary combination of these components, and the realm of the environment. T'ien-t'ai (538–597) included this concept in his doctrine of three thousand realms in a single moment of life. According to Miao-lo's *Annotations on "The Profound Meaning of the Lotus Sutra,"* two of these three realms—the realm of the five components and the realm of living beings—represent "life," and, naturally, the realm of the environment represents "environment" in terms of the principle of oneness of life and its environment. These three realms exist in a single moment of life and are inseparable from one another. Therefore, a living being and its environment are non-dual in their ultimate reality. Nichiren (1222–1282) writes in his letter *On Omens:* "The ten directions are the 'environment,' and living beings are 'life.' To illustrate, environment is like the shadow, and life, the body. Without the body, no shadow can exist, and without life, no environment. In the same way, life is shaped by its environment" (644). He also writes in *On Attaining Buddhahood in This Lifetime:* "If the minds of living beings are impure, their land is also impure, but if their minds are pure, so is their land. There are not two lands, pure or impure in themselves. The difference lies solely in the good or evil of our minds" (4).

oneness of living beings and Buddhas [生仏不二・生仏一如] (Jpn *shōbutsu-funi* or *shōbutsu-ichinyo*): Also, oneness of ordinary people and Buddhas, or non-duality of living beings and Buddhas. The principle that living beings and Buddhas are not two different things but are essentially one. "Living beings" here indicates life in its unenlightened form, or beings who are afflicted with delusion. This principle is set forth in several Mahayana Buddhist scriptures. The Flower Garland Sutra states, "The mind, the Buddha, and all living beings—these three things are without distinction." The Nirvana Sutra states, "All living beings alike possess the Buddha nature." The Lotus Sutra reveals the true aspect of all phenomena, indicating that, though different, all living beings, the Buddha included, are manifestations of the ultimate reality. The sutra also reads, "The Buddhas . . . wish to open the door of Buddha wisdom to all living beings . . . to induce living beings to enter the path of Buddha wisdom," because Buddha wisdom is inherent in all living beings, i.e., all living beings are potential Buddhas. In China, based on the Lotus Sutra, T'ien-t'ai (538–597) set forth the principle of the mutual possession of the Ten Worlds, from Buddhahood through hell, and the doctrine of three thousand realms in a single moment of life.

oneness of the Person and the Law [人法一箇] (Jpn *nimpō-ikka*): A principle established by Nichikan (1665–1726), the twenty-sixth chief priest of Taiseki-ji temple in Japan, with regard to Nichiren's (1222–1282) teaching, indicating that the object of devotion in terms of the Person and the object of devotion in terms of the Law are one in their essence. The Law is inseparable from the Person and vice versa. The "Treasure Tower" (eleventh) chapter of the Lotus Sutra states, "If one upholds this [sutra], one will be upholding the Buddha's body." This means that the Lotus Sutra is the Buddha's body; that is, the Buddha (Person) and the teaching (Law) he expounded are one and inseparable. Nichiren revealed and spread the Law of Nam-myoho-renge-kyo and inscribed it in the form of a mandala, known as the Gohonzon, to enable all people in the Latter Day of the Law to attain Buddhahood; for this reason he is regarded as the Buddha of the Latter Day of the Law. This is the object of devotion in terms of the Law, or the physical embodiment of the eternal and intrinsic Law of Nam-myoho-renge-kyo that Nichiren realized and manifested within his own life. Hence Nichiren is the object of devotion in terms of the Person. In his *Reply to Kyō'ō,* Nichiren writes, "The soul of Nichiren is nothing other than Nam-myoho-renge-kyo" (412). This means that Nichiren realized Nam-myoho-renge-kyo as the origin and basis of his life and embodied it as a mandala. Nichiren also writes in the same reply, "I, Nichiren, have inscribed my life in *sumi* ink, so believe in the Gohonzon with your whole heart" (412). Ultimately, Nichiren's life embodied the principle of the oneness of the Person and the Law, as does the Gohonzon, the object of devotion he established.

On Establishing the Correct Teaching for the Peace of the Land [立正安国論] (Jpn *Risshō-ankoku-ron*): Abbreviated as *On Establishing the Correct Teaching.* One of Nichiren's five or ten major writings. Nichiren submitted this treatise to Hōjō Tokiyori, the retired regent but still the most powerful figure in Japan's ruling clan, through the offices of shogunate official Yadoya Mitsunori on the sixteenth day of the seventh month, 1260. Around the 1250s, Kamakura and Japan as a whole experienced a series of floods and landslides, epidemics and famine, and an earthquake of unprecedented scale in 1257. In an effort to clarify the fundamental cause of these disasters, Nichiren visited Jissō-ji temple at Iwamoto in Suruga Province in 1258 to do research in its sutra library in preparation for writing this treatise. As a result, he found ample documentary support for his arguments in such sutras as the Benevolent Kings, Medicine Master, Great Collection, and Golden Light.

The treatise begins by depicting the misery caused by the frequent disasters ravaging Japan, and regards the fact that the whole nation is turning against the correct teaching as a major factor responsible for the unprecedented disasters. Nichiren explains that the people should abandon their faith in erroneous teachings and embrace the correct teaching, asserting that this is the basis for establishing a peaceful land. *On Establishing the Correct Teaching* was written in classical Chinese and consists of a dialogue between a host and a visitor. It is generally considered that the host represents Nichiren, and the visitor, Hōjō Tokiyori. In this treatise, Nichiren presents numerous scriptural references to the disasters that will befall a nation that follows incorrect teachings. He makes an unsparing criticism of the Pure Land teachings of Hōnen. The Medicine Master Sutra lists the seven disasters, of which Nichiren points out that five have already occurred. The remaining two—internal strife and foreign invasion—will happen without fail, he says, if the rulers continue to support erroneous doctrines. Later these prophecies were fulfilled when Hōjō Tokisuke revolted against his younger half brother, Regent Hōjō Tokimune, in the second month of 1272, and when the Mongol forces attacked Japan twice, in 1274 and 1281. During the years he resided at Minobu, Nichiren created an expanded version of this treatise by adding scriptural passages, but the keynote remained the same as in the 1260 version. In the ninth month of 1282, shortly before his death, Nichiren lectured on this treatise to his followers. The attention he continued to give it long after it was submitted, including making several copies and having his disciple Nikkō copy it also, demonstrates the importance he attached to this work, and that he intended it for future generations as well as his contemporaries.

one vehicle [一乗] (Skt *ekayāna;* Jpn *ichijō*): Also, single vehicle, Buddha vehicle, one Buddha vehicle, one vehicle of Buddhahood, or supreme vehicle. The teaching that leads all people to Buddhahood. It is taught in the Flower Garland Sutra and other Mahayana sutras, but the Lotus Sutra places the greatest emphasis on it. The Buddha's teaching is compared to a vehicle (Skt *yāna*) that carries one to a particular state of enlightenment. In accordance with people's capacities, the pre-Lotus Sutra teachings expound and emphasize the voice-hearer vehicle *(shrāvaka-yāna),* which leads one to the state of arhat; the cause-awakened one vehicle *(pratyekabuddha-yāna),* which leads one to the state of *pratyekabuddha;* and the bodhisattva vehicle *(bodhisattva-yāna),* which after many *kalpas* of practice leads one to Buddhahood. The voice-hearer vehicle and the cause-awakened one vehicle are together termed the two vehicles, and with the addition of the bodhisattva vehicle, the three vehicles.

The Lotus Sutra teaches that these three vehicles are not ends in themselves but means to lead people to the one vehicle, which unifies and refines the three vehicle teachings. The "Expedient Means" (second) chapter of the sutra says that the Buddhas employ only a single vehicle to preach the Law to living beings. It also says that the Buddhas, utilizing the power of expedient means, divide the one vehicle and preach as though it were three. The chapter again says that there is only one vehicle in all the Buddha lands throughout the universe, and the Buddha's sole purpose is to lead all beings to Buddhahood. The T'ien-t'ai school called this the "replacement of the three vehicles with the one vehicle." In the Lotus Sutra, the term *one vehicle* is synonymous with the Buddha's true teaching.

one vehicle teaching [一乗法] (Jpn *ichijō-hō*): The teaching that leads all people to Buddhahood. *See also* one vehicle.

One Who Can Endure [能忍] (Jpn *nōnin*): An honorific title for Shakyamuni Buddha. Shakyamuni Buddha is so called because he appears in the *sahā* world, or the world of endurance, in order to lead the people to Buddhahood and, in so doing, endures all the hardships he encounters there.

Ōnichi-nyo [王日女] (n.d.): A lay follower of Nichiren. Little information about her exists, at least under this name. From the content of a letter sent to her by Nichiren in 1280, it appears that she had some connection with Nisshō, Nichiren's first convert among the priesthood and later one of his designated six senior priests. Another view identifies her with the lay nun Myōichi, the mother of Nisshō.

Onjō-ji [園城寺]: Also known as Mii-dera. The head temple of the Temple (Jimon) branch of the Tendai school, located in Ōtsu in Shiga Prefecture, Japan. According to the temple's tradition, it was built in 686 by Ōtomo no Yotamaro, a son of Prince Ōtomo, but it is widely thought that a local lord called Ōtomo built it as a family temple in the late Nara period (710–794). Chishō, later the fifth chief priest of Enryaku-ji, the head temple of the Tendai school on Mount Hiei, restored Onjō-ji in 859, and it became affiliated with Enryaku-ji temple. Later friction arose between priests in the lineage of Jikaku, the third chief priest of Enryaku-ji, and those in Chishō's lineage. In 993, one hundred years after Chishō's death, his followers left Mount Hiei and moved to Onjō-ji temple, where they declared their independence from Enryaku-ji and established the Temple school.

On Refuting the Five Priests [五人所破抄] (Jpn *Gonin-shoha-shō*): A work written in 1328 by Nichijun, chief instructor of Omosu Seminary in Suruga Province, Japan, and approved by Nikkō, Nichiren's successor. It refutes as incorrect the views that the five senior priests, or five of the six senior priests designated by Nichiren other than Nikkō, developed after Nichiren's death, and explains as correct the views of Nikkō. Originally Nikkō entrusted this task to Nitchō (1262–1310), Nichijun's predecessor, but he died after he had finished the draft. Based on the draft, Nichijun completed the work. Nitchō's draft remains as *The Guidelines for Believers of the Fuji School. See also* five senior priests.

On Repaying Debts of Gratitude [報恩抄] (Jap *Hō'on-shō*): One of Nichiren's five or ten major writings, dated the twenty-first day of the seventh month of 1276, a little more than two years after he had moved to Minobu in Kai Province, Japan. It was prompted by the news of the death of Dōzen-bō who had been Nichiren's teacher at Seichō-ji temple in Awa Province. Nichiren wrote this treatise in memory of the deceased Dōzen-bō and sent it to Jōken-bō and Gijō-bō, his former seniors at Seichō-ji who now regarded Nichiren as their teacher. He entrusted this writing to Nikō, later one of the six senior priests he designated, and requested that it be read aloud at Kasagamori on the summit of Mount Kiyosumi where he is said to have first chanted Nam-myoho-renge-kyo, and again before the tomb of his late teacher.

Nichiren begins this treatise by emphasizing the need to repay one's obligations to one's parents, teacher, the three treasures of Buddhism, and one's sovereign. Of these four debts of gratitude, this work stresses specifically repaying that owed to one's teacher. Nichiren states that to repay such debts one must dedicate oneself single-mindedly to Buddhist practice and attain enlightenment. To this end, Nichiren traces the development of the various schools of Buddhism in India, China, and Japan, focusing on the sutras upon which these schools base their doctrines. He next identifies the Lotus Sutra as the highest of all the teachings of Shakyamuni Buddha. He then refutes the doctrines of the various schools, especially of the True Word (Shingon) school, a Japanese form of Esoteric Buddhism. In this work, Nichiren also criticizes Jikaku and Chishō, patriarchs of the Tendai school who incorporated the doctrines and rituals of Esoteric Buddhism into the school's teachings, which were based originally on the Lotus Sutra. Nichiren determines that the essence of the Lotus Sutra is its title, or daimoku, Nam-myoho-renge-kyo, and reveals the Three Great Secret Laws or teachings to be propagated in the Latter Day of the Law. They are the invocation, or daimoku, the object of devotion, and the sanctuary, of the essential teaching. Then he states, "If Nichiren's compassion is truly great and encompassing, Nam-myoho-renge-kyo will spread for ten thousand years and more, for all eternity" (736).

On Taking the Essence of the Lotus Sutra [法華取要抄] (Jpn *Hokke-shuyō-shō*): One of the ten major writings of Nichiren. *See* ten major writings.

On the Formalities [化儀抄] (Jpn *Kegi-shō*): See *Reverend Nichiu's Teachings on the Formalities.*

On the Four Stages of Faith and the Five Stages of Practice [四信五品抄] (Jpn *Shishin-gohon-shō*): One of the ten major writings of Nichiren. *See* ten major writings.

On the Peaceful Practices of the Lotus Sutra [法華経安楽行義] (Chin *Fa-hua-ching-an-lo-hsing-i;* Jpn *Hokekyō-anrakugyō-gi*): Also known as *The Four Peaceful Practices.* A work authored by Nan-yüeh of China during the sixth century. It explains practices set forth in the Lotus Sutra such as meditation on the true aspect of all phenomena, the reading and reciting of the sutra, and the four peaceful practices. The four peaceful practices are those of deeds, words, thoughts, and vows set forth in the "Peaceful Practices" (fourteenth) chapter of the sutra. Nan-yüeh identifies the four peaceful practices as the basis for bodhisattva practice. *See also* four peaceful practices.

Opening of the Eyes, The [開目抄] (Jpn *Kaimokū-sho*): One of Nichiren's five or ten major writings. It consists of two volumes and was completed at Tsukahara on Sado, an island in the Sea of Japan, in the second month of 1272. According to Nichikan (1665–1726), the twenty-sixth chief priest of Taiseki-ji temple, in this work Nichiren reveals his identity as the Buddha of the Latter Day of the Law who possesses the three virtues of sovereign, teacher, and parent. Thus he says it reveals the object of devotion in terms of the Person, while *The Object of Devotion for Observing the Mind,* written in 1273, reveals the object of devotion in terms of the Law. *The Opening of the Eyes* begins with the words: "There are three categories of people that all human beings should respect. They are the sovereign, the teacher, and the parent" (220). In the concluding part, Nichiren says, "I, Nichiren, am sovereign, teacher, and father and mother to all the people of Japan" (287). Because in this statement Nichiren identifies himself with the three virtues the Buddhas possess, it is viewed as his declaration that he is the Buddha of the Latter Day of the Law. He also states: "On the twelfth day of the ninth month of last year [1271], between the hours of the rat and the ox [11:00 P.M. to 3:00 A.M.], this person named Nichiren was beheaded. It is his soul that has come to this island of Sado and, in the second month of the following year, snowbound, is writing this to send to his close disciples" (269). "This person named Nichiren" means the ordinary person Nichiren. "It is his soul that has come to this island of Sado" is taken to mean that the individual who arrived alive at Sado was Nichiren in his true identity—the Buddha Nichiren.

The title *The Opening of the Eyes* means to open the eyes of the people and awaken them to the three virtues of the Buddhism of the harvest and finally to those of the Buddhism of sowing, severing their blind attachment to the provisional teachings. In doing so, Nichiren discusses the relative superiority of the lifetime teachings of Shakyamuni (with the doctrine known as the fivefold comparison), determines the superiority of the Lotus Sutra over all other sutras, and reveals the Mystic Law, the teaching for attaining Buddhahood in the Latter Day of the Law. He says: "The doctrine of three thousand realms in a single moment of life [i.e., the Mystic Law] is found in only one place, hidden in the depths of the 'Life Span' chapter of the essential teaching of the Lotus Sutra. Nāgārjuna and Vasubandhu were aware of it but did not bring it forth into the light. T'ien-t'ai Chih-che alone embraced it and kept it ever in mind" (224). Based on this passage, Nichikan later established the doctrine of the threefold secret teaching. In his work known as *The Actions of the Votary of the Lotus Sutra,* Nichiren writes: "I began to put into shape a work in two volumes called *The Opening of the Eyes,* which I had been working on since the eleventh month of the previous year. I wanted to record the wonder of Nichiren, in case I should be beheaded" (772). *The Opening of the Eyes,* which was intended for posterity, was given to Shijō Kingo, a lay disciple who had accompanied Nichiren to the execution site at Tatsunokuchi and resolved to die there by his side. *See also* fivefold comparison; threefold secret teaching.

opening the near and revealing the distant [開近顕遠] (Jpn *kaigon-kennon*): Discarding the assumption that Shakyamuni attained enlightenment for the first time in India and revealing that he originally gained enlightenment in the immensely distant past. In *The Profound Meaning of the Lotus Sutra,* T'ien-t'ai (538–597) of China defines the principal doctrine of the theoretical teaching (first half) of the Lotus Sutra to be the "replacement of the three vehicles with the one vehicle," and that of the essential teaching (latter half) of the sutra to be "opening the near and revealing the distant." This term describes a revelation made in the essential teaching of the Lotus Sutra. At the beginning of the "Emerging from the Earth" (fifteenth) chapter, countless bodhisattvas rise up from beneath the earth. The bodhisattvas already present in the assembly are surprised by the sudden appearance of this great multitude. On behalf of the others, Bodhisattva Maitreya asks Shakyamuni Buddha to explain the identity of these newly arrived bodhisattvas. In reply, Shakyamuni announces, "Ever since the long distant past I have been teaching and converting this multitude." This revelation is called "opening the near and revealing the distant in concise form."

Hearing this statement, however, the assembled bodhisattvas are dubious and perplexed, and Maitreya again asks Shakyamuni Buddha how he could have taught and trained so many bodhisattvas in the scant forty-odd years since his awakening under the *bodhi* tree. This opens the way for the Buddha's explicit revelation in the following (sixteenth) chapter, "Life Span," in which he says: "In all the worlds the heavenly and human beings and *asuras* all believe that the present Shakyamuni Buddha, after leaving the palace of the Shākyas, seated himself in the place of meditation not far from the city of Gayā and there attained supreme perfect enlightenment. But good men, it has been immeasurable, boundless hundreds, thousands, ten thousands, millions of *nayutas* of *kalpas* since I in fact attained Buddhahood." Shakyamuni then describes in some detail the immensity of the span of time since he actually attained enlightenment. The name given to that time span—numberless major world system dust particle *kalpas*—is an abbreviation of that description. This revelation in the "Life Span" chapter of the Buddha's original attainment of enlightenment in the remote past is called "opening the near and revealing the distant in expanded form." *See also* numberless major world system dust particle *kalpas.*

opening the provisional and revealing the true [開権顕実] (Jpn *kaigon-kenjitsu*): Also, "opening the provisional teachings and revealing the true teaching," "discarding the provisional and revealing the true," or the "replacement of the provisional teachings with the true teaching." A reference to the doctrine of opening expedient or provisional teachings and revealing the true teaching of the Lotus Sutra, which is set forth in the theoretical teaching (first half) of the sutra. The "Teacher of the Law" (tenth) chapter says, "This sutra opens the gate of expedient means and shows the form of true reality." Depending on what is indicated by "expedient means" or provisional teaching, this principle can mean that persons of the two vehicles who were denied attainment of Buddhahood in the provisional teachings can attain Buddhahood in the Lotus Sutra; that the sutra opens the three vehicles and reveals the one Buddha vehicle; and that, while the provisional teachings state that the Ten Worlds are distinct and separate, the Lotus Sutra reveals the mutual possession of the Ten Worlds. These principles are expounded in the theoretical teaching.

opening the three vehicles and revealing the one vehicle [開三顕一] (Jpn *kaisan-ken'ichi*): *See* replacement of the three vehicles with the one vehicle.

opposite shore [彼岸] (Jpn *higan*): The shore of enlightenment; nirvana, or the state of enlightenment. *See* other shore.

ordinary person [凡夫] (Skt *prithag-jana* or *bāla;* Jpn *bompu* or *bombu*): Also, common mortal, ordinary mortal, ordinary (human) being, or worldling. In Buddhism, an unenlightened person who is bound by earthly desires and karma and therefore repeats the cycle of birth and death in the realm of delusion, or the six paths. Also, one who is ignorant of the Buddhist teachings and concerned only with secular matters, whose life is ruled by earthly desires and illusions. The exact meaning varies among the Buddhist teachings. One view defines an ordinary person as someone who is ignorant of the four noble truths and thus deluded. In the Sarvāstivāda school, an ordinary person is one who has yet to attain any of the stages of sagehood—the stage of the stream-winner, the stage of the once-returner, the stage of the non-returner, and the stage of arhat. The Sanskrit *prithag-jana* means a commoner or a fool; in contrast, *ārya* means a person of respect, wisdom, or noble birth. *Bāla* means an ignorant or foolish person.

ordination platform [戒壇] (Jpn *kaidan*): Also, sanctuary. A place where the ceremony for conferring Buddhist precepts is conducted. Originally the ceremony for conferring precepts was held at a particular site or location designated as sacred. Later platforms were erected for this purpose. Tradition has it that the ordination platforms in China emulated those at Jetavana Monastery and Nālandā Monastery in India. According to one account, the first ordination platform in China was erected in 434 at Nan-lin-ssu temple in Chien-k'ang. In 667 Tao-hsüan, the founder of the Nan-shan branch of the Precepts (Lü) school, erected an ordination platform at Ching-yeh-ssu temple on the outskirts of Ch'ang-an. He also wrote a work in which he expanded upon the origin and forms of the ordination platform. Ordination platforms were also built in Lo-yang and other areas of China.

In Japan, the first ordination platform was built in 754 at the command of the Retired Emperor Shōmu at Tōdai-ji temple in Nara under the supervision of Ganjin (Chien-chen), a naturalized priest from China. There Ganjin conferred precepts upon about four hundred persons including the Retired Emperor Shōmu and his consort. This ordination platform was a temporary structure, and a permanent ordination hall was thereafter established within the precincts of Tōdai-ji temple. In 761 two more ordination platforms were built at Yakushi-ji temple in Shimotsuke Province and at Kanzeon-ji temple in Chikuzen Province. These were known as "the three ordination platforms" or "the three ordination platforms of the nation." The whole country was divided into three ordination districts for the ordination of priests. At all three centers, priests were customarily ordained in the Hinayana precepts. Dengyō, the founder of the Tendai school, exerted himself to secure imperial approval for the erection of a Mahayana ordination platform at Enryaku-ji, the head temple of the Tendai school on Mount Hiei, but was opposed by the eminent priests of Nara. Permission was finally granted in 822, seven days after Dengyō's death, and a Mahayana ordination platform was erected there in 827. This was the first Mahayana ordination platform in the history of Buddhism. In the period of the Northern and Southern Courts (1336–1392), ordination platforms were established at four temples of the Tendai school in the provinces of Sagami, Higo, Kaga, and Iyo, as branches of the ordination hall at Enryaku-ji. These four platforms were all later destroyed by fire and were never rebuilt.

original Buddha [本仏] (Jpn *hombutsu*): *See* Buddha of beginningless time; true Buddha.

original enlightenment [本覚] (Jpn *hongaku*): (1) A reference to the enlightenment Shakyamuni attained countless *kalpas* ago, as described in the "Life Span" (sixteenth) chapter of the Lotus Sutra. (2) Enlightenment or Buddhahood originally inherent in human life. *See also* "Life Span of the Thus Come One" chapter for (1); inherent enlightenment for (2).

original vows [本願] (Skt *pūrvapranidhāna;* Jpn *hongan*): The vows made by a Buddha in the past while still engaged in bodhisattva practice. Of these, the forty-eight vows of Amida Buddha and the twelve vows of Medicine Master Buddha are especially well known. In the Pure Land school, "original vow" in the singular indicates the eighteenth vow of Amida Buddha—his promise to enable all people who invoke his name to be reborn in the Pure Land of Perfect Bliss in the west, excepting those who have committed the five cardinal sins and those who have slandered the correct teaching. The Sanskrit word *pūrva* of *pūrvapranidhāna* means former or prior, and *pranidhāna* means vow or prayer.

Ornament of Mahayana Sutras, The [大乗荘厳経論] (Skt *Mahāyāna-sūtrālamkāra;* Chin *Ta-ch'eng-chuang-yen-ching-lun;* Jpn *Daijō-shōgon-kyō-ron*): A commentary on the Consciousness-Only doctrine translated into Chinese by the Indian monk Prabhākaramitra, who went to China in 626. This work consists of verse and a prose commentary on it. The verse is attributed to Maitreya (c. 270–350 or 350–430), the founder of the Consciousness-Only school, and the prose commentary to Vasubandhu who lived around the fourth or fifth century. One account attributes *The Ornament of Mahayana Sutras* to Asanga, a disciple of Maitreya. The Sanskrit text and a Tibetan translation are also extant.

Ōta Jōmyō [大田乗明] (1222–1283): Also known as Ōta Kingo, the lay priest Ōta, or Ōta Saemon-no-jō. A follower of Nichiren who lived in Nakayama of Shimōsa Province, Japan. His full name and title were Ōta Gorō Saemon-no-jō Jōmyō. From the content of a letter sent to him by Nichiren, it appears that he and Nichiren were the same age. He was an official employed in the Office of Legal Affairs of the Kamakura shogunate and converted to Nichiren's teachings by Toki Jōnin. With Toki Jōnin and Soya Kyōshin, he was a pillar among the believers of Shimōsa Province. In 1275 he arranged for his second son to enter the priesthood as a disciple of Nichiren. This son took the Buddhist name Nikkō (written differently from that of Nichiren's designated successor). Around 1278 Jōmyō himself became a lay priest and was given the name Myōnichi (Wonderful Sun) by Nichiren. He called the place where he lived Hommyō-ji temple. Nichiren gave him several important writings including *On the Three Great Secret Laws* and *Lessening One's Karmic Retribution*.

other shore [彼岸] (Jpn *higan*): Also, farther shore or opposite shore. The shore of enlightenment; nirvana, or the state of enlightenment. The other shore contrasts with "this shore," which means the realm of the sufferings of birth and death, or the state of delusion. The Sanskrit term *pāramitā*, a practice required of bodhisattvas, was rendered in Chinese as "to reach the other shore," i.e., "to cross over from this shore of delusion to the other shore of enlightenment." *Pāramitā* is usually translated into English as perfection.

Oto [乙] (n.d.): A daughter of Nichimyō, a follower of Nichiren who lived in Kamakura, Japan. When she was a child, her mother took her on the long journey to visit Nichiren, who was in exile on Sado Island. Nichiren addressed a letter known as *The Supremacy of the Law*, dated the fourth day of the eighth month of 1275, to her, though its content was intended for her mother. *See also* Nichimyō.

outflows [漏] (Skt *āsrava;* Jpn *ro*): An equivalent term for earthly desires. "Outflows" refers to that which flows out from the six sense organs; i.e., earthly desires, illusions, or defilements. To become free of outflows means liberation from earthly desires, illusions, or defilements. In Buddhist scriptures, the presence of or freedom from outflows describes various related yet contrasting qualities or states. For example, there are wisdom that retains outflows and wisdom that is free of outflows, meditation accompanied by outflows and meditation without outflows, and a body with outflows and a body without outflows.

Outside-the-Mountain school [山外派] (Chin Shan-wai-p'ai; Jpn Sangai-ha): A reference to the Shan-wai school, a branch of the T'ien-t'ai school in China. In the tenth century, the T'ien-t'ai school divided into two branches. One, headed by Chih-yüan and Ch'ing-chao, was called the Outside-the-Mountain school. This was a pejorative epithet applied by the other school, which called itself the Mountain (Chin Shan-chia; Jpn Sange) school. The implication was that they, the Mountain school, were within the legitimate stream of Mount T'ien-t'ai. The name "outside-the-mountain" suggested departure from the orthodox T'ien-t'ai doctrine, though it is also thought to have indicated geographical location, since that school's center was in Ch'ien-t'ang outside Mount T'ien-t'ai. Each of the two schools produced a number of treatises and commentaries criticizing the position of the other. The dispute between them continued for decades, but the Outside-the-Mountain school gradually declined.

Outstanding Principles of the Lotus Sutra, The [法華秀句] (Jpn *Hokke-shūku*): A work written in 821 by Dengyō, the founder of the Japanese Tendai school. It explains why the Tendai school, which is based on the Lotus Sutra, is superior to the Dharma Characteristics (Hossō), Three Treatises (Sanron), Flower Garland (Kegon), True Word (Shingon), and other schools. It was written to refute the arguments of Tokuitsu, a priest of the Dharma Characteristics school, who asserted that some people are by nature eternally incapable of attaining Buddhahood, and that the three vehicle teachings are true while the one vehicle teaching is provisional. In this work, Dengyō lists ten superior characteristics of the Lotus Sutra, in light of which he argues its supremacy over all other teachings.

The ten superior characteristics of the Lotus Sutra are as follows: (1) Shakyamuni Buddha reveals the truth only in this sutra. (2) The title of the sutra as well as various names later given to the sutra has profound meaning. (3) In this sutra, the Buddha spontaneously expounds the teaching of his enlightenment without being asked to do so. (4) The sutra reveals that the five categories of Buddhas (all Buddhas, past Buddhas, present Buddhas, future Buddhas, and Shakyamuni Buddha) employ a similar device to lead people to the one Buddha vehicle; that is, they first expound the teachings that serve as expedient means to develop the people's capacity, and then reveal the one Buddha vehicle, the direct path to Buddhahood. (5) Shakyamuni declares the Lotus Sutra to be foremost among all the sutras. (6) He expounds ten similes to illustrate the superiority of the Lotus Sutra over all other sutras. (7) The sutra can purify the workings of the six sense organs. (8) The sutra enables people to attain Buddhahood in their present form. (9) In the assembly of the Buddha Many Treasures and the Buddhas of the ten directions who are Shakyamuni's emanations, Shakyamuni declares that he will entrust the sutra to someone to ensure that it will be perpetuated. (10) The sutra expounds the encouragements of Bodhisattva Universal Worthy who said to Shakyamuni Buddha that he will guard and protect those who accept and uphold the sutra after the Buddha's death.

Ōwa Debate [応和の宗論] (Jpn Ōwa-no-shūron): A debate on Buddhist doctrine held between priests of the Tendai school and the Dharma Characteristics (Hossō) school at the imperial court in Japan in 963 (the third year of the Ōwa era). A central issue of the doctrinal arguments presented was whether all people possess the Buddha nature, i.e., whether all people have the capacity to attain Buddhahood. The Dharma Characteristics priests, including Anshū, Hōzō, and Chūzan, asserted that persons of the two vehicles (voice-hearers and cause-awakened ones) cannot attain Buddhahood; the Tendai priests, who included Yokei, Kakukei, and Ryōgen, insisted that all people, including persons of the two vehicles, possess the Buddha nature and can become Buddhas.

ox-headed demons [牛頭] (Skt *goshīrsha;* Jpn *gozu*): Also, ox-headed beings. With horse-headed demons, beings said to act as jailors in hell. These two kinds of jailors are depicted as having the bodies of human beings and the heads of oxen and horses. The Sanskrit word *go* means ox, and *shīrsha* means head.

ox-head sandalwood [牛頭栴檀] (Skt *goshīrsha-chandana;* Jpn *gozu-sendan*): A particular kind of sandalwood that grows in southern India. It is reddish in color and has medicinal properties. Ox-head sandalwood is said to have the finest fragrance of all sandalwood. The Sanskrit word *go* means ox, and *shīrsha* means head; *chandana* means sandalwood. The name of this sandalwood is said to derive from either the shape or the name of a mountain upon which it grew.

P

pagoda [塔] (Jpn *tō*): A tower-like structure usually associated with temples or monasteries in East and Southeast Asia. The English word pagoda derives from the Portuguese *pagode,* the origin of which is unclear, but which also indicates this kind of structure. The pagoda developed from the ancient Indian stupa, which was dome- or mound-shaped and housed the remains or relics of kings, sages, or holy persons. After the death of Shakyamuni Buddha, stupas were built to house the Buddha's ashes, which were divided among the various Indian states. As Buddhism spread through India and made its way into other countries, new forms of stupa, or pagoda, architecture developed. Initially, the pagoda was the focal point of a temple compound, housing sacred relics believed to be those of the Buddha. In China, the pagoda came to house the Buddha's teachings, rather than his relics, in the form of sutras. The pagoda dates back to the fourth or fifth century in China, where they were built of brick, wood, or stone with multiple stories. A great wooden pagoda was built at Yung-ning-ssu temple in Lo-yang in 519. The oldest surviving wooden pagoda in China is the five-storied pagoda of Fo-kung-ssu temple in Shansi Province, built in 1056. The oldest standing brick pagoda was built in 520 at Sung-yüeh-ssu temple in Honan Province, and the oldest remaining stone pagoda is that built in 544 at Shen-t'ung-ssu temple in Shantung Province.

Pagoda architecture and construction techniques came to Japan through the Korean Peninsula with the transmission of Buddhism. There, as in China, wooden pagodas of three, five, seven, and nine stories were built, though the majority were either three or five stories. Seven-storied pagodas were erected at Tōdai-ji temple and provincial temples, but in Japan today none above five stories remains. The oldest among the remaining pagodas is the five-storied pagoda at Hōryū-ji temple, built in the late seventh century. The oldest standing three-storied pagoda in Japan is the one built in 706 at Hokki-ji temple. The three-storied pagoda at Yakushi-ji temple was built in 730. These oldest structures are located in Nara, the ancient capital of Japan. Pagodas of various designs can be found throughout East and Southeast Asia. One example is the ancient Shwe Dagon pagoda in Yangon, Myanmar, which was rebuilt in the eighteenth century and towers approximately a hundred meters.

Pai-lien-she [白蓮社] (PY Bailianshe; Jpn Byakuren-sha): "White Lotus Society." A Chinese religious group that practiced meditation on the Buddha Amida, established in 402 by Hui-yüan at Tung-lin-ssu temple on Mount Lu. Hui-yüan, a leading disciple of Tao-an, went to Mount Lu in 384 with a group of his disciples. In 402 he along with 123 priests and lay practitioners made a vow before an image of Amida, and tradition identifies this with the founding of Pai-lien-she, or White Lotus Society. The group was so named after the white lotus flowers that grew in the ponds of the temple. The Pai-lien-she is regarded as a precursor of the Pure Land school of Buddhism.

Pai-ma-ssu [白馬寺] (PY Baimasi; Jpn Hakuba-ji): "White Horse Temple," said to have been the first Buddhist temple built in China. According to tradition, Emperor Ming of the Later Han dynasty built this temple in C.E. 67 at Lo-yang for Kāshyapa Mātanga and Chu Fa-lan, Buddhist monks who had come from India at his invitation to teach Buddhism. In this temple, it is said, they accomplished the first Chinese translation of a Buddhist scripture—the Sutra of Forty-two Sections. The temple was named Pai-ma-ssu, or White Horse Temple, because the two Indian monks were said to have brought Buddhist scriptures from India on the backs of white horses. Later in China, in accordance with this tradition, temples with the name Pai-ma-ssu were built at Ch'ang-an, Chien-k'ang, and elsewhere.

Painfully Acquired [苦得] (Jpn Kutoku): A follower of Jainism mentioned in the Chinese version of the Mahāparinirvāna Sutra. The sutra describes Painfully Acquired as having lived at Rājagriha, the capital of the kingdom of Magadha, India, in the time of Shakyamuni Buddha and having misled the monk Sunakshatra, Shakyamuni's disciple and son. Sunakshatra revered him as being supreme among arhats. His Sanskrit name is unknown. In Chinese Buddhist texts, Painfully Acquired is also the name of a non-Buddhist school that emphasized rigorous asceticism as the cause of emancipation; this school is identified with Jainism.

Pakudha Kacchāyana [迦羅鳩駄迦旃延] (Pali; Jpn Karakuda-kasen-nen): An influential non-Buddhist thinker during Shakyamuni's time. *See* six non-Buddhist teachers.

pāpīyas [波旬] (Skt; Jpn *hajun*): A devil, especially a devil king. *Pāpīyas* is often synonymous with the Sanskrit word *māra,* and is identified with the devil king of the sixth heaven in the world of desire. In Buddhist scriptures, Pāpīyas often appears as the proper name of this devil king, who is said to constantly harass Shakyamuni Buddha and his disciples. He attempts to obstruct people's Buddhist practice and prevent them from attaining enlightenment. He is also said to lure people toward evil and on to destruction. The Sanskrit *pāpīyas* also means villain, or evil spirit.

parable of the blind men and the elephant [群盲評象の譬] (Jpn *gummō-hyōzō-no-tatoe*): A parable that appears in the Mahāparinirvāna Sutra, in which it is related by Shakyamuni Buddha, and in other Buddhist texts. A king instructed his high minister to assemble a group of blind men, bring an elephant before them, and have each of them touch it. The king then asked each of them to describe the elephant to him. One blind man, stroking the elephant's trunk, insisted that the animal resembled a pestle; another, pressing his hands against the elephant's stomach, said that it was like a pot; a third, who touched the elephant's tail, reported that the elephant resembled a rope; and so on. In the sutra, Shakyamuni likens the king, who knows the true form of the elephant, to the Buddha's wisdom, the high minister to the Mahāparinirvāna Sutra, the elephant to the Buddha nature inherent in all living beings, and the blind men to ordinary people who are ignorant of the reality of their own Buddha nature.

parable of the bright jewel in the topknot [髻中明珠の譬] (Jpn *keichū-myōju-no-tatoe*): Also, parable of the priceless gem in the topknot. One of the seven parables in the Lotus Sutra. It appears in the "Peaceful Practices" (fourteenth) chapter. After a battle, a wheel-turning king rewards those who have fought successfully with fields, houses, robes, gold, silver, and other treasures. There is one object he does not give away easily, a bright jewel he wears hidden in his topknot. Finally he takes the jewel from his hair and gives it to the soldier who has gained truly great distinction. Shakyamuni compares the jewel in the topknot to the Lotus Sutra, which the Buddha conceals while expounding preparatory teachings, and the treasures previously bestowed to the provisional teachings.

parable of the burning house [火宅の譬] (Jpn *kataku-no-tatoe*): *See* parable of the three carts and the burning house.

parable of the jewel in the robe [衣裏珠の譬] (Jpn *eriju-no-tatoe*): Also, parable of the gem in the robe or parable of the jewel sewn in the poor man's robe. One of the seven parables in the Lotus Sutra. It is related in the "Five Hundred Disciples" (eighth) chapter by five hundred arhats to demonstrate their understanding of the one vehicle teaching. It tells of an impoverished man who goes to visit a close wealthy friend. Being treated to wine, he becomes drunk and falls asleep. The wealthy friend must go out on business, but before leaving, he sews a priceless jewel into the lining of his sleeping friend's robe. When the poor man awakens, he has no idea that he has been given the jewel. He then sets out on a journey. To provide himself with food and clothing, he searches with all his energy, encountering great hardship. Being always in want, he is content with whatever little he can obtain. Later he happens to meet his old friend, who is shocked at his poverty and shows him the jewel in the robe. The man realizes for the first time that he possesses a priceless jewel and is overjoyed. The five hundred arhats explain that, just as this man was ignorant of the treasure he possessed, so the Buddha's disciples were unaware that the Buddha had caused them to plant the seeds of an unsurpassed aspiration and were instead satisfied with provisional teachings and a small portion of nirvana.

parable of the medicinal herbs [薬草喩] (Jpn *yakusō-yu*): *See* parable of the three kinds of medicinal herbs and two kinds of trees.

"Parable of the Medicinal Herbs" chapter [薬草喩品] (Jpn *Yakusōyu-hon*): The fifth chapter of the Lotus Sutra. In this chapter, Shakyamuni Buddha relates the parable of the three kinds of medicinal herbs and two kinds of trees to illustrate that, although the Buddha's teaching is the same, people who encounter it understand it differently and develop in different ways. According to the parable, rain falls equally upon all kinds of plants and trees, but they absorb the moisture differently and grow to varying heights according to their individual natures. In the same way, the Buddha impartially expounds only the one Buddha vehicle for all people, but their understanding and benefits differ according to their respective capacities.

parable of the phantom city [化城喩] (Jpn *kejō-yu*): *See* parable of the phantom city and the treasure land.

parable of the phantom city and the treasure land [化城宝処の譬] (Jpn *kejō-hōsho-no-tatoe*): Also, parable of the phantom city. One of the seven parables in the Lotus Sutra, related in the "Parable of the Phantom City" (seventh) chapter to illustrate the principle of replacing the three vehicles with the one vehicle. It tells of a group of people who want to travel five hundred *yojanas* to reach a remote place where there are rare treasures. Their leader is wise, experienced, and very familiar with the route, but the road they must take is steep and treacherous; midway they lose heart and want to turn back. Seeing this, their leader uses his powers of expedient means and, when they have gone three hundred *yojanas* along the steep road, he conjures up a city. There they go to rest and regain their spirits, convinced they can escape the dreadful road. Knowing they have recovered from their exhaustion, the leader wipes out the phantom city and tells them that the treasure land, their true destination, is close by. In the "Parable of the Phantom City" chapter, the phantom city is compared to the three vehicles, or expedient means by which the Buddha leads people to Buddhahood, and the treasure land, the group's destination, is compared to the one vehicle of Buddhahood. The meaning of the parable is that, just as the guide conjures a city to lead his party of travelers to the treasure land, the Buddha employs the expedient means of the three vehicles to lead the people to the one vehicle of Buddhahood.

"Parable of the Phantom City" chapter [化城喩品] (Jpn *Kejōyu-hon*): The seventh chapter of the Lotus Sutra, in which Shakyamuni reveals the relationship he formed with his disciples in the remote past when he was the sixteenth and youngest son of a Buddha named Great Universal Wisdom Excellence. In the chapter, Shakyamuni describes the magnitude of time that has passed since then, a period referred to as major world system dust particle *kalpas*. That long ago, he explains, he and his fifteen brothers each expounded the Lotus Sutra, which their father had taught them. His present disciples to whom he now preaches, he explains, were among those to whom he taught the Lotus Sutra and converted at that time. In explaining this past relationship, Shakyamuni points out that the ultimate purpose of his advent is to expound the one vehicle of Buddhahood (the Lotus Sutra), and that it is only faith in the one vehicle that enables all his voice-hearer disciples to attain nirvana, or enlightenment. In this way, the "Parable of the Phantom City" chapter further validates the doctrine of the "replacement of the three vehicles with the one vehicle" set forth in the preceding chapters.

Those who heard the Lotus Sutra from Shakyamuni in the distant past when he was the sixteenth son of Great Universal Wisdom Excellence Buddha fall into three categories or groups: The first consists of those who took faith, embraced the sutra without faltering, and attained Buddhahood. The second includes those who at first took faith in the sutra, but later abandoned it and accepted lower Buddhist teachings. The third group includes those who heard the sutra, but did not take faith in it. Those of the second group were later reborn as voice-hearers in India with Shakyamuni, who again instructed them and finally led them to the one Buddha vehicle of the Lotus Sutra.

The same chapter illustrates the doctrine of the "replacement of the three vehicles with the one vehicle" with a parable. A leader is guiding a multitude of people traveling over a difficult road to a treasure land. Seeing that they are too exhausted and discouraged to continue, he employs the power of expedient means to conjure up a phantom city where they can rest. When they have recovered their strength and courage, he dissolves the city and leads them the rest of the way to their destination. In this parable, the guiding leader represents the Buddha, the phantom city indicates the three vehicles of voice-hearers, cause-awakened ones, and bodhisattvas, and the treasure land is the one vehicle of Buddhahood. *See also* major world system dust particle *kalpas;* parable of the phantom city and the treasure land.

parable of the skilled physician and his sick children [良医病子の譬] (Jpn *rōi-byōshi-no-tatoe*): Also, parable of the skilled physician. One of the seven parables in the Lotus Sutra. Shakyamuni relates it in the "Life Span" (sixteenth) chapter to explain that the Buddha uses his own death as a means to awaken in people a desire to seek his teaching. The parable describes a skilled physician who has a great many children. One day while he is away from home, the children mistakenly drink poison.

Returning to find them writhing on the ground in agony, he quickly prepares for them a medicine that possesses excellent color, fragrance, and flavor. Some of the children take the medicine and are cured instantly, but others, their reasoning distorted by the working of the poison, refuse it despite their great agony. The father therefore devises an expedient to induce them to take the medicine. Telling them, "I will leave this good medicine here," he sets off for another land. From there he dispatches a messenger, who informs the children that their father has died. Grief-stricken, they finally come to their senses, take the medicine their father has left them, and are immediately cured. Thereupon their father returns. Shakyamuni explains that the Buddha is like this physician: If he were always present in the world, people would begin to take him for granted and would no longer seek his teaching. Therefore, although the Buddha's life is eternal, he uses his death as a means to arouse in people an aspiration for enlightenment.

parable of the three carts and the burning house [三車火宅の譬] (Jpn *sansha-kataku-no-tatoe*): Also, parable of the burning house. One of the seven parables in the Lotus Sutra. It appears in the "Simile and Parable" (third) chapter. Shakyamuni relates this parable to illustrate his statement in the "Expedient Means" (second) chapter that the sole purpose of the Buddhas' advent is to enable all people to attain Buddhahood, and that the three vehicles of voice-hearers, cause-awakened ones, and bodhisattvas are simply means to lead people to the one Buddha vehicle.

Suppose, he says, there is a very rich man who has many children. One day a fire suddenly breaks out in his spacious but decaying house, and his children, totally absorbed in playing games, do not know that the house is in flames and ignore his cries of warning. He therefore resorts to an expedient means to induce them to come out of the burning house. He shouts to them that outside he has three kinds of carts they have long wanted: a cart pulled by a goat, another by a deer, and a third by an ox. Immediately they race outside. Having coaxed them to safety in this way, the rich man gives each of his children a cart—not one of the three kinds he had promised, but a much finer carriage, adorned with numerous jewels and drawn by a white ox. Shakyamuni compares the burning house in the parable to the threefold world, and the flames to the sufferings of birth and death. The rich man is the Buddha, who appears in this troubled world to save the people, the children are all living beings, and the games in which they are so absorbed are worldly pleasures. The three kinds of carts originally promised represent the three vehicles, or the provisional teachings, and the great white ox carriage symbolizes the supreme vehicle of Buddhahood, that is, the Lotus Sutra.

parable of the three kinds of medicinal herbs and two kinds of trees [三草二木の譬] (Jpn *sansō-nimoku-no-tatoe*): Also, parable of the medicinal herbs. One of the seven parables in the Lotus Sutra. Shakyamuni relates this parable to Mahākāshyapa and others in the "Parable of the Medicinal Herbs" (fifth) chapter to reiterate his teaching in the previous three chapters ("Expedient Means," "Simile and Parable," and "Belief and Understanding") that the Buddha's true purpose is the revelation of the one vehicle of Buddhahood, but that, because of the differences in people's capacity, he first expounds the three vehicles and the five vehicles as provisional teachings. In the parable, a great cloud envelops the world and sends down life-giving rain equally upon all the grasses, flowers, trees, and medicinal herbs. Though the rain is the same, the plants, trees, and medicinal herbs absorb the moisture differently and grow to varying heights according to their individual natures. Similarly, the Buddha impartially expounds only the one vehicle of Buddhahood for all people, but they understand and benefit from it differently according to their respective capacities.

The three kinds of medicinal herbs appearing in the parable are inferior medicinal herbs, intermediate medicinal herbs, and superior medicinal herbs; the two kinds of trees are small trees and big trees. Based on the description in the text, T'ien-t'ai (538–597), in *The Words and Phrases of the Lotus Sutra,* interprets the inferior medicinal herbs as ordinary people and heavenly beings, the intermediate medicinal herbs as persons of the two vehicles (voice-hearers and cause-awakened ones), and the superior medicinal herbs, small trees, and big trees as bodhisattvas. Among these, T'ien-t'ai says, the superior medicinal herbs represent bodhisattvas of the Tripitaka teaching, the small trees indicate bodhisattvas of the connecting teaching, and the big trees, bodhisattvas of the specific teaching.

parable of the wealthy man and his poor son [長者窮子の譬] (Jpn *chōja-gūji-no-tatoe*): One of the seven parables in the Lotus Sutra. It appears in the "Belief and Understanding" (fourth) chapter. The four great voice-hearers—Subhūti, Kātyāyana, Maudgalyāyana, and Mahākāshyapa—relate this parable to show that they have understood the teaching of replacing the three vehicles with the one vehicle that Shakyamuni recounted in the "Simile and Parable" (third) chapter using the parable of the three carts and the burning house. Briefly, it tells of a wealthy man's son who runs away from his father in childhood. For some fifty years he wanders from one place to another in abject poverty, hiring himself out as a menial laborer. One day in his wanderings he chances upon his father's mansion. The rich old man is overjoyed to see his son again, as he wants to bequeath to him all his wealth and possessions. The son, however, does not recognize his father and runs away, overwhelmed by the splendor of the rich man's estate. The rich man sends a messenger to bring him back, but the son thinks the messenger has come to arrest him and faints in terror. Hearing this, the father tells the messenger to release him and instead sends two of his servants dressed in dirty clothes to offer the son the work of clearing away excrement. The impoverished son happily accepts this employment on his father's estate. After a while, his father disguises himself in dirty clothes so he can approach his son. He tells him that he can always work there, and that he will treat him like his own son. For twenty years the son works at clearing away excrement and gradually gains self-confidence. The rich man then promotes him, charging him with the administration of his property, and gradually he comes to understand all the rich man's affairs. Eventually the rich man senses death approaching. He invites his relatives, the king of the country, the high ministers, and others, and declares to them that his servant is actually his true son. He then transfers to his son the whole of his estate. The rich man in this parable represents the Buddha, whose sole desire is to let all people enjoy the same sublime state as his own, just as the rich man wishes to bequeath all his wealth to his son. The poor son represents ordinary people, who "wander about" transmigrating in the threefold world without encountering the one Buddha vehicle. To lead them to enlightenment, the Buddha first employs expedient means and preaches what is appropriate to their capacities, just as the rich man trains his son gradually. Thus the Buddha leads them gradually to higher teachings and ultimately reveals the one Buddha vehicle of the Lotus Sutra.

pārājika [波羅夷] (Skt, Pali; Jpn *harai*): The gravest offenses proscribed by monastic rules of discipline, the commission of which may result in expulsion from the Buddhist Order. *Pārājika* is the first section of the *vinaya,* or monastic rules. There are four *pārājikas* for monks, and eight *pārājikas* for nuns. The four *pārājikas,* also known as the four major offenses or the four grave prohibitions, are killing, stealing, having sexual relations, and lying (in particular, lying about one's level of insight or spiritual attainment). The eight *pārājikas,* also known as the eight major offenses, consist of the four grave offenses plus those of touching a male, improper association with a male, concealing the misbehavior of another, and following a monk who goes against monastic rules.

Paramārtha [真諦] (499–569) (Skt; Jpn Shindai): Also known as Kulanātha. A translator of Buddhist scriptures and the founder of the Summary of the Mahayana (She-lun) school in China. Originally from western India, he was welcomed by Emperor Wu of the Liang dynasty and traveled to various parts of China to teach Buddhism. His Chinese translations of Buddhist scriptures are said to have amounted to either 64 texts in 278 volumes or 49 texts in 142 volumes, which include *The Summary of the Mahayana, The Treatise on the Buddha Nature,* and *The Awakening of Faith in the Mahayana.* Paramārtha is counted as one of the four great translators of Buddhist scriptures into Chinese, the other three being Kumārajīva, Hsüan-tsang, and Pu-k'ung.

pāramitā [波羅蜜] (Skt, Pali; Jpn *haramitsu*): Practices that Mahayana bodhisattvas must undertake to attain enlightenment. Generally, *pāramitā* is interpreted as "perfection" or "having reached the opposite shore." These practices were so called because by perfecting them one was said to cross from the shore of delusion and suffering to the shore of enlightenment. They are usually divided into six or ten. *See also* six *pāramitās;* ten *pāramitās.*

parinirvāna [般涅槃 · 涅槃] (Skt; Pali *parinibbāna;* Jpn *hatsu-nehan* or *nehan*): Complete nirvana. Also called *mahāparinirvāna* (great complete nirvana). *Mahā* means great, and *pari* means round, complete, or final. *Nirvana* refers to the death, or "passing into extinction," of a Buddha. *Parinirvāna* in this sense is the same as "nirvana of no remainder," in which both body and mind, the sources of desire and suffering, are extinguished. *Nirvana* also means emancipation from delusion and suffering, or enlightenment. Accordingly, *parinirvāna* can also indicate complete emancipation, perfect tranquillity, or perfect enlightenment. *See also* nirvana.

Parinirvāna Sutra [般泥洹経] (Jpn *Hatsu-naion-gyō*): *See* Mahāparinirvāna Sutra (2).

Pārshva [脇比丘 · 脇尊者] (n.d.) (Skt; Jpn Kyō-biku or Kyō-sonja): A monk of the Sarvāstivāda school in India during the second century who is considered the ninth of Shakyamuni Buddha's twenty-three, or the tenth of his twenty-four, successors. *The Record of the Lineage of the Buddha and the Patriarchs* gives his birthplace as central India. According to this work, he renounced secular life and received the precepts under the guidance of Buddhamitra, his predecessor among the Buddha's successors, and later transferred the Buddha's teachings to Punyayashas, who in turn transferred them to Ashvaghosha. Tradition has it that, under the patronage of King Kanishka, Pārshva and Vasumitra summoned some five hundred monks and convened the Fourth Buddhist Council in Kashmir, at which Buddhist scriptures were compiled and *The Great Commentary on the Abhidharma* produced.

Parthia [安息国] (Jpn Ansoku-koku): An ancient empire of Asia. It was known in China as An-hsi. Established in the mid-third century B.C.E., the Parthian Empire lasted for about four and a half centuries. At its greatest extent it spread from northwestern India or Bactria in the east, encompassing the entire region between the Caspian Sea in the north and the Persian Gulf in the south, and extending to the Euphrates River and Armenia in the west. An Shih-kao and An Hsüan, who engaged in translating Buddhist scriptures into Chinese in second-century China, are known to have been natives of Parthia; the "An" in their names is an abbreviation of An-hsi, the Chinese name for Parthia.

Pasenadi [波斯匿王] (Pali; Jpn Hashinoku-ō): Also known as Prasenajit. The king of Kosala of ancient India in Shakyamuni's time. *See* Prasenajit.

Pātaliputra [華氏城] (Skt; Pali Pātaliputta; Jpn Keshi-jō): The capital of Magadha in ancient India. It is today the city of Patna. During the reign of King Bimbisāra in the time of Shakyamuni Buddha, the capital of Magadha was Rājagriha. Bimbisāra's son, Ajātashatru, moved it, however, to Pātaliputra near the Ganges after assuming the throne. According to another account, it was Udāyibhadra, the son or grandson of Ajātashatru, who moved the capital from Rājagriha to Pātaliputra. Pātaliputra later flourished as the capital of the Maurya dynasty (c. 317 B.C.E.–C.E. 180) and the Gupta dynasty (c. 320–570), during which periods lived the kings Ashoka and Chandragupta II, respectively. The Third Buddhist Council was held at Pātaliputra about two hundred years after Shakyamuni's death. The Chinese priests Fa-hsien and Hsüan-tsang, who chronicled their journeys to India, visited Pātaliputra in the fifth and seventh centuries, respectively. Fa-hsien wrote that the city was prosperous and Buddhism flourished there, but Hsüan-tsang noted that Pātaliputra was in ruins by the time he visited it.

path [趣・道] (Skt, Pali *gati;* Jpn *shu* or *dō*): In Buddhism, the state of existence into which one is reborn as a result of karma or causes formed through one's actions in the previous existence. The Sanskrit *gati* derives from the root *gam,* which means "to go." Buddhism set forth the concept of the six paths *(gatis),* or six paths of existence: the realms or states of hell, hungry spirits, animals, *asuras,* human beings, and heavenly beings. Originally these were thought of as physical locations; later they came to represent the states or conditions of life that living beings experience. These correspond to the lowest six of the Ten Worlds. The first three or four are called evil paths, *durgati* in Sanskrit, because one is reborn into them as a consequence of one's past evil actions or bad karma. There is also a concept of five paths, which excludes the realm of *asuras.* *See also* Ten Worlds.

path of insight [見道] (Jpn *ken-dō*): *See* way of insight.

pātra [鉢] (Skt; Jpn *hachi* or *hatsu*): A begging bowl used by monks. *See* alms bowl.

patriarchal Zen [祖師禅] (Jpn *soshi-zen*): Also, patriarchal meditation. A reference to the seated meditation of Bodhidharma, the founder and first patriarch of the Zen (Ch'an) school in China. This form of meditation aims to perceive the Buddha-mind intuitively and directly. Originally the Zen meditation that Bodhidharma introduced to China in the early sixth century was called Thus Come One Zen and was regarded in the Zen school as the highest form of meditation. Eventually, however, an opinion became predominant in the Zen school that the Buddha's enlightenment had been transmitted wordlessly, outside the sutras, from Shakyamuni Buddha to Mahākāshyapa and finally to Bodhidharma in the lineage of Zen masters in India. With this, the expression Thus Come One Zen was criticized as based on the sutras and therefore limited. The seated meditation of Bodhidharma, the patriarch of Chinese Zen, came to be called patriarchal Zen. Patriarchal Zen is considered supreme and held to constitute the correct transmission of the Zen teachings.

pattra [貝多羅] (Skt; Jpn *baitara*): A leaf; specifically a tree leaf used for writing upon. In ancient India, the leaves of the *tāla* tree were usually used for this purpose. The tree called *tāla* in Sanskrit is now known as the palmyra palm. It grows to more than twenty meters tall, and its leaves are large and leathery. They were dried and cut into rectangles of uniform size, about thirty to sixty centimeters long and six centimeters wide. Text was inscribed on both sides with a bamboo or iron stylus. The leaves were then pierced with holes, bound with string, and secured between wooden boards. In Buddhist countries where this tree grew, such as India, Myanmar, and Sri Lanka, Buddhist scriptures were preserved and transmitted this way. Today they are referred to as palm-leaf scriptures. See also *tāla* tree.

Peace and Delight [安楽世界] (Skt Sukhāvatī; Jpn Anraku-sekai): Another name for Perfect Bliss, the land of Amida Buddha, said to be located "a hundred thousand million Buddha lands away in the west." "Peace and Delight" is one of the Chinese translations of the Sanskrit name Sukhāvatī, which was also rendered as Perfect Bliss and as Peace and Sustenance. Sukhāvatī means land of happiness or pleasure. *See also* Peace and Sustenance; Perfect Bliss.

Peace and Sustenance [安養国] (Skt Sukhāvatī; Jpn An'yō-koku or Annyō-koku): Another name for Perfect Bliss, the land where Amida Buddha is said to dwell. The Sanskrit name Sukhāvatī, which means land of happiness or pleasure, was rendered in Chinese as Peace and Sustenance, Perfect Bliss, or Peace and Delight. The Buddha Infinite Life Sutra, a Chinese translation done by the Indian monk Samghavarman in 252, contains both the names Peace and Sustenance and Peace and Delight, but does not refer to Perfect Bliss. In the Amida Sutra, translated by Kumārajīva in 402, only the name Perfect Bliss appears. The Lotus Sutra also refers to the land of Amida Buddha: The Lotus Sutra of the Correct Law, Dharmaraksha's Chinese translation produced in 286, the oldest of the three extant Chinese versions, employs the name Peace and Sustenance. The Lotus Sutra of the Wonderful Law, translated into Chinese by Kumārajīva in 406, uses Peace and Delight. Eventually, the name Perfect Bliss became the most common rendering. *See also* Peace and Delight; Perfect Bliss.

"Peaceful Practices" chapter [安楽行品] (Jpn *Anraku-gyō-hon*): The fourteenth chapter of the Lotus Sutra and the last chapter of the theoretical teaching (first half) of the sutra. In response to a question from Bodhisattva Manjushrī about how bodhisattvas should practice Buddhism in the evil age after Shakyamuni Buddha's death, the Buddha expounds four rules or peaceful practices to be observed. While the sutra's descriptions of these four practices are rather lengthy, T'ien-t'ai (538–597) summarized them as the peaceful practice of the body, the peaceful practice of the mouth, the peaceful practice of the mind, and the peaceful practice of vows. T'ien-t'ai regarded these four peaceful practices as a development of the three rules of preaching described in the "Teacher of the Law" (tenth) chapter. The "Peaceful Practices" chapter also contains the parable of the bright jewel in the topknot. In the parable, a great wheel-turning king rewards his soldiers who have shown merit in battle with a variety of treasures, but withholds a bright jewel that he keeps in his topknot. Only when he sees someone who has achieved particularly great distinction does he remove the jewel and give it to that person. The Buddha is likened to the king, the soldiers of merit are his disciples, and the ordinary treasures he gives away are the provisional, or pre-Lotus Sutra, teachings. Those of great distinction represent his disciples who have developed their capacity through the provisional teachings and are now ready to receive the supreme teaching. The bright jewel in the topknot is the Buddha's highest teaching, the Lotus Sutra, which the Buddha has withheld until last. The Sanskrit title of this chapter is "Sukhavihāra," which means an easy, comfortable, or peaceful life. *See also* four peaceful practices; three rules of preaching.

peak stage [頂位・頂法] (Jpn *chō-i* or *chō-hō*): Also, peak method. The second of the four good roots, or the four stages of Hinayana practice that immediately precede the higher stage called the way of insight. In the peak stage, one obtains the highest of the "unsettled good roots." Though one may possibly regress from the peak stage, even if one should do so and fall into hell, the good roots developed in that stage cannot be erased. After having reached the stages of the four good roots, one proceeds to the way of insight, or the first of the three ways, in which one beholds the four noble truths. The second of the three ways is the way of practice, and the third and last is the way of the arhat. *See also* four good roots.

Perceiver of Sounds [観音菩薩] (Jpn Kannon-bosatsu): *See* Perceiver of the World's Sounds.

Perceiver of the World's Sounds [観世音菩薩] (Skt Avalokitasvara or Avalokiteshvara; Jpn Kanzeon-bosatsu): Also known as Perceiver of Sounds. Widely known by his Chinese name Kuan-yin (Perceiver of Sounds), he is one of the most popular bodhisattvas in the Buddhist world and revered as the bodhisattva of infinite compassion. The bodhisattva is the protagonist of the "Perceiver of the World's Sounds" (twenty-fifth) chapter of the Lotus Sutra, which is also known as an independent sutra. According to that chapter, this bodhisattva is called Perceiver of the World's Sounds because he perceives the sounds and voices of those who are suffering and compassionately releases them from that suffering. He assumes various forms and appears wherever is necessary to save people from danger or fear. In the chapter, Shakyamuni Buddha says: "Suppose there are immeasurable hundreds, thousands, ten thousands, millions of living beings who are undergoing various trials and suffering. If they hear of this bodhisattva Perceiver of the World's Sounds and single-mindedly call his name, then at once he will perceive the sound of their voices and they will all gain deliverance from their trials." The chapter lists specifically thirty-three among the variety of different forms Bodhisattva Perceiver of the World's Sounds assumes in accordance with people's needs to relieve their suffering; it also states that he is called Bestower of Fearlessness because he liberates people from fear and gives them security. The chapter states, "This bodhisattva and mahāsattva Perceiver of the World's Sounds can bestow fearlessness on those who are in fearful, pressing, or difficult circumstances. That is why in this *sahā* world everyone calls him Bestower of Fearlessness."

In the Buddha Infinite Life Sutra and the Meditation on the Buddha Infinite Life Sutra, Perceiver of the World's Sounds appears with Bodhisattva Great Power as an attendant of Amida Buddha. In Esoteric Buddhism, he is one of the nine honored ones in the central court of the Womb Realm mandala. Because he was said to assume various forms, he is depicted in a number of ways. Several esoteric sutras refer to different forms of this bodhisattva, such as an eleven-faced Perceiver of the World's Sounds and a thousand-armed Perceiver of the World's Sounds. The bodhisattva was generally regarded as male, but in China, apparently as early as the seventh century, Perceiver of the World's Sounds came to be thought of as female. Among other powers, the bodhisattva was said to protect women during childbirth. Popular worship of this bodhisattva began in India and became widespread in China, Japan, and other countries.

Perceiver of the World's Sounds is also known by the name Freely Perceiving (Jpn Kanjizai), which is a rendering of Hsüan-tsang's (602–664) Chinese translation of the Sanskrit name Avalokiteshvara. The name of Perceiver of the World's Sounds derives from Kumārajīva's Chinese translation of Avalokitasvara. Avalokiteshvara is a compound of *avalokita,* meaning the act of looking or "having been seen," and *īshvara,* meaning "able to do," "master," or "lord." Avalokitasvara is a compound of *avalokita* and *svara; svara* means sound and voice. It is generally believed that Avalokitasvara came into use before Avalokiteshvara, and in the history of Chinese translations of Buddhist scriptures, "Perceiver of the World's Sounds" preceded "Freely Perceiving." Kumārajīva used the former in his translation of the Lotus Sutra. In China and Japan, this chapter of Kumārajīva's translation circulated as an independent sutra titled Perceiver of the World's Sounds Sutra. It is perhaps for these reasons that the name Perceiver of the World's Sounds is so popular today. Many Chinese refer to this bodhisattva as Kuan-yin (Jpn Kannon), an abbreviation of Kuan-shih-yin (Kanzeon).

"Perceiver of the World's Sounds" chapter [観音品] (Jpn *Kannon-bon*): The twenty-fifth chapter of the Lotus Sutra. *See* "Universal Gateway of the Bodhisattva Perceiver of the World's Sounds" chapter.

Perceiver of the World's Sounds Sutra [観音経] (Chin *Kuan-yin-ching;* Jpn *Kannon-gyō*): Another name for the "Perceiver of the World's Sounds" (twenty-fifth) chapter of the Lotus Sutra, translated into Chinese by Kumārajīva in 406. In China and Japan, this chapter circulated as an independent sutra. It praises Bodhisattva Perceiver of the World's Sounds, who benefits and saves people out of profound compassion. *See also* Perceiver of the World's Sounds; "Universal Gateway of the Bodhisattva Perceiver of the World's Sounds" chapter.

perception of the truth of the birthlessness of all phenomena [無生法忍] (Jpn *mushō-bōnin*): *See* realization of the non-birth and non-extinction of all phenomena.

perception stage [忍位 · 忍法] (Jpn *nin-i* or *nin-pō*): Also, stage of perception. The third of the four good roots that are stages of Hinayana practice. In this stage, one understands the doctrine of the four noble truths, and one's good roots become settled. One who has entered this stage will never fall into the evil paths of existence. After having reached the stages of the four good roots, one proceeds to the way of insight, the first of the three ways, which is followed by the way of practice and the way of the arhat. *See also* four good roots.

Perfect Bliss [極楽] (Skt Sukhāvatī; Jpn Gokuraku): The name of the land of Amida Buddha, said to be located "a hundred thousand million Buddha lands away in the west." According to the Buddha Infinite Life Sutra, when the Buddha Infinite Life (another name for Amida) was engaged in Buddhist practice as a bodhisattva, he vowed to create his own Buddha land that would combine the most outstanding features of various pure lands, where he would live when he attained Buddhahood. The Sanskrit name Sukhāvatī means land of happiness or pleasure. In Chinese, it was rendered as Perfect Bliss, Peace and Delight, or Peace and Sustenance. It is also called the Western Pure Land, the Western Paradise, or simply the Pure Land. The splendor of this land is described in detail in the Amida Sutra and the Buddha Infinite Life Sutra. In this land, there is no suffering; there is only comfort and delight, or "perfect bliss." Belief in Amida Buddha and his Pure Land prevailed widely in China and Japan, and the Pure Land of Perfect Bliss became a more popular focus of aspiration than the pure lands of other Buddhas. Thus the term Pure Land came to mean Amida's Pure Land of Perfect Bliss.

perfect enlightenment [妙覚 · 円覚] (Jpn *myōgaku* or *engaku*): Also, supreme perfect enlightenment. The enlightenment of a Buddha. "Perfect enlightenment" also refers to the last and highest of the fifty-two stages of bodhisattva practice, or Buddhahood. *See also* fifty-two stages of bodhisattva practice.

Perfect Enlightenment Sutra [円覚経] (Chin *Yüan-chüeh-ching;* Jpn *Engaku-kyō*): An abbreviation of the Complete and Final Teaching on Perfect Enlightenment Sutra. A sutra translated into Chinese in 693 by Buddhatāra who had gone to China from Kashmir. In this sutra, Shakyamuni explains the mystic principle of perfect enlightenment and the practice for its attainment to an audience of twelve bodhisattvas including Manjushrī, Universal Worthy, and Maitreya. Contemporary scholars view this sutra as a work produced in China, where this sutra was widely read and a number of commentaries written on it. It had considerable influence on the Flower Garland (Hua-yen) and Zen (Ch'an) schools, and was regarded highly by the Zen school in particular.

Perfection of Wisdom sutras [般若波羅蜜経] (Jpn *Hannya-haramitsu-kyō*): *See* Wisdom sutras.

perfect precepts [円戒] (Jpn *en-kai*): *See* precepts of perfect and immediate enlightenment.

perfect teaching [円教] (Jpn *en-gyō*): Also, round teaching. A teaching lacking in nothing, one that is full and complete. The supreme teaching of Buddhism. Buddhist sutras were introduced from India to China virtually at random over the centuries, and many attempts were made to organize and classify this vast array of teachings into coherent systems. In such systems of classification, the sutra that was ranked highest was called the perfect teaching. For example, Hui-kuang (468–537) divided the Buddhist teachings into three categories—gradual, sudden, and perfect—and designated the Flower Garland Sutra as the perfect teaching. T'ien-t'ai (538–597) also classified Shakyamuni's teachings according to content and established the four teachings of doctrine. In this system of classification, he termed the last of the four teachings of doctrine the perfect teaching, the other three being the Tripitaka teaching, connecting teaching, and specific teaching. In addition, he defined two categories of perfect teaching: that expounded in the pre-Lotus Sutra teachings and that taught in the Lotus Sutra. Though both teach the concept of the attainment of Buddhahood by ordinary persons, T'ien-t'ai points out that the former teaches it in name only, that is, with no example of it ever having occurred, and draws various distinctions and exceptions; the latter teaches that all people can without exception attain enlightenment, illustrating it with examples. The term *perfect teaching* is synonymous with the Lotus Sutra in traditions stemming from T'ien-t'ai's, including Nichiren's. *See also* four teachings of doctrine.

persons of incorrigible disbelief [一闡提] (Jpn *issendai*): See *icchantika.*

phantom city [化城] (Jpn *kejō*): A magically conjured city described in the "Parable of the Phantom City" (seventh) chapter of the Lotus Sutra. In the parable presented in that chapter, a guide with supernatural powers conjures up the city to allow his party of weary travelers to rest en route to the treasure land, which is their true destination. The phantom city represents the three vehicles, or expedient means; the guide represents the Buddha; and the treasure land, the one vehicle of Buddhahood. The *phantom city* also represents the Hinayana concept of nirvana. Nichiren's *Conversation between a Sage and an Unenlightened Man,* reads in part, "Long ago, when the Buddha taught the Hinayana doctrines in

Deer Park, he was opening the gate to a phantom city" (102). *See also* parable of the phantom city and the treasure land.

Pilindavatsa [畢陵伽婆蹉] (Skt; Jpn Hitsuryōgabasha): One of Shakyamuni's disciples, born to a Brahman family in Shrāvastī, India. It is said that prior to joining the Buddhist Order he had been overbearingly arrogant and contemptuous of others. He had had transcendental powers and been renowned for his practice of magic, but he lost these powers when he met Shakyamuni Buddha and converted to the Buddha's teachings. The "Introduction" (first) chapter of the Lotus Sutra includes him among those who attended the assembly of the sutra.

Pindolabhāradvāja [賓頭盧] (Skt, Pali; Jpn Binzuru): Also known as Pindola. A follower of Shakyamuni Buddha. Although he was the son of a minister to Udayana, the king of Kaushāmbī in India, he renounced the secular world to enter the Buddhist Order and attained the state of arhat. It is said that he excelled in supernatural powers, but that Shakyamuni Buddha rebuked him for using them when he should not and for terrifying others, though not intentionally, with those powers. Pindolabhāradvāja is counted among the sixteen arhats entrusted by Shakyamuni Buddha with his teaching and who vowed to protect it after his death. Pindolabhāradvāja is also written Pindola Bhāradvāja. *See also* sixteen arhats.

Pingala [青目・賓伽羅] (n.d.) (Skt; Jpn Shōmoku or Bingara): An Indian scholar of the Mādhyamika school who lived from the late third through the early fourth century and a commentator on Nāgārjuna's *Madhyamaka-kārikā*, or *Verses on the Middle Way*. The *Madhyamaka-kārikā* was regarded as the principal work of the Mādhyamika (Middle Way) school, and Pingala's commentary on it was one of a number written by Mādhyamika scholars. Though the Sanskrit original is not extant, a Chinese translation titled *The Treatise on the Middle Way* exists. *The Treatise on the Middle Way*, translated by Kumārajīva in 409, consists of Nāgārjuna's *Verses on the Middle Way* and Pingala's prose commentary on these verses. The study of *Verses on the Middle Way* in China and Japan developed on the basis of Pingala's commentary.

pipal tree [インドボダイジュ] (Skt *pippala;* Jpn *Indo-bodaiju*): A *bodhi* tree. See *pippala* tree.

pippala tree [畢鉢羅樹] (Skt; Jpn *hippara-ju*): A *bodhi* tree. The *pippala* tree came to be called the *bodhi* tree because it was under one such tree that Shakyamuni attained enlightenment (*bodhi* in Sanskrit). It is said that *pippala* was originally the name of the fruit of the *ashvattha* tree, but that later came to refer to the tree itself. In India, even before the rise of Buddhism, both the *ashvattha* tree and its close relative, the banyan, had been considered sacred. Today the *bodhi* tree is also known as the pipal tree or the peepul tree, names that derive from *pippala*. See also *bodhi* tree.

Pippalī Cave [畢鉢羅窟] (Skt; Jpn Hippara-kutsu): A cave located near Rājagriha in Magadha, India. According to one Buddhist tradition, Pippalī Cave was the site of the First Buddhist Council, held to compile Shakyamuni Buddha's teachings immediately after his death. A different tradition has it that the site of the First Buddhist Council was Saptaparna Cave, or Cave of the Seven Leaves, also located near Rājagriha. Some suppose that Pippalī Cave is another name for the Cave of the Seven Leaves. It is said that Mahākāshyapa, one of Shakyamuni's ten major disciples, who led the compilation of the sutras and the *vinaya* (rules of monastic discipline) at the First Buddhist Council, used this cave as his dwelling and place of practice.

pishācha [毘舎闍] (Skt; Jpn *bishaja*): A demon that eats human flesh. In some Buddhist scriptures, *pishācha* appear as retainers of Upholder of the Nation, one of the four heavenly kings, and as protectors of Buddhism.

P'i-t'an school [毘曇宗] (PY Pitanzong; Jpn Bidon-shū): *See* Abhidharma school.

pit of fire [火坑] (Jpn *kakyō* or *kakō*): A metaphor for hell. *See* fiery pit.

place of practice [道場] (Jpn *dōjō*): A place where one carries out Buddhist practice to gain enlightenment. This term, which appears often in Chinese translations of Buddhist scriptures, may also be translated as "place of the way." Initially, this referred to the place where one gains "the way" or enlightenment, and specifically the place under the *pippala*, or *bodhi*, tree where Shakyamuni entered into meditation and gained enlightenment. This is referred to in Sanskrit as *bodhimanda*, literally, the seat of enlightenment. Hence it is also called the place of meditation, or the place of enlightenment.

planting the seeds of Buddhahood [下種] (Jpn *geshu*): Also, sowing the seeds of Buddhahood. One of the three benefits described in T'ien-t'ai's teachings based on the Lotus Sutra: the benefits of sowing, maturing, and reaping. The process of attaining Buddhahood is compared to that of cultivating plants. In this regard, Nichiren (1222–1282) states, "The Lotus Sutra is like the seed, the Buddha like the sower, and the people like the field" (748). In teaching people, the Buddha begins by sowing the seeds of Buddhahood in their lives. The phase of sowing is divided into two stages: First, the Buddha causes the people to hear his teaching, and second, he leads them to take faith in it. These are termed respectively "sowing the seeds by letting one hear the teaching" (Jpn *mompō-geshu*) and "sowing the seeds by leading one to arouse faith in the teaching" *(hosshin-geshu)*.

There are cases in which a person takes faith immediately upon hearing the teaching. There are also cases in which someone hears the teaching and later takes faith. In either case, the Buddha's teaching has the power to influence one's life, whether or not one takes faith in it immediately. In *The Annotations on "The Words and Phrases of the Lotus Sutra,"* Miao-lo (711–782) states: "Whether one accepts or rejects the teaching, it enters one's ears and one thus establishes a bond with it. And then, though one may comply with or go against it, in the end one will be able to achieve liberation because of this bond." "Sowing the seeds by letting one hear the teaching" in this sense means that simply by hearing the Law one forms the cause, or seed, for attaining Buddhahood eventually, even if one should reject it initially. *See also* sowing, maturing, and harvesting.

Platform Sutra, The [壇経] (Jpn *Dan-kyō*): See *Platform Sutra of the Sixth Patriarch, The.*

Platform Sutra of the Sixth Patriarch, The [六祖壇経] (Chin *Liu-tsu-t'an-ching;* Jpn *Rokuso-dan-kyō*): Also known as *The Platform Sutra.* A collection of the sermons of Hui-neng (638–713), the sixth patriarch of the Chinese Zen (Ch'an) school. It was called a "sutra" by Hui-neng's disciples who recorded and compiled his sermons. In this work, Hui-neng expounds the Zen doctrine of the immediate attainment of enlightenment and the doctrine of perceiving one's true nature and attaining Buddhahood.

Po Fa-tsu [帛法祖] (PY Bo Fazu; Jpn Haku-hōso): Also known as Fa-tsu. A priest and a translator of Buddhist scriptures in ancient China. *See* Fa-tsu.

poison-drum relationship [毒鼓の縁] (Jpn *dokku-no-en*): A reverse relationship, or relationship formed through rejection. A bond formed with the Lotus Sutra by opposing or slandering it. One who opposes the Lotus Sutra when it is preached will still form a relationship with the sutra by virtue of opposition, and will thereby attain Buddhahood eventually. A "poison drum" is a mythical drum daubed with poison; this is a reference to a statement in the Nirvana Sutra that once the poison drum is beaten, all those who hear it will die, even if they are not of the mind to listen to it. Similarly, when the correct teaching is preached, both those who embrace it and those who oppose it will equally receive the seeds of Buddhahood, and even those who oppose it will attain Buddhahood eventually. *See also* reverse relationship.

poshadha [布薩] (Skt; Jpn *fusatsu*): Also, *uposhadha*. A gathering for self-reflection and repentance, held regularly within the Buddhist Order. See *uposhadha*.

Possessor of Virtue [有徳王] (Jpn Utoku-ō): The name of Shakyamuni in a previous lifetime when he was a king in Kushinagara, according to a story related in the "Diamond-like Body" chapter of the forty-volume Chinese version of the Mahāparinirvāna Sutra translated by Dharmaraksha in 421. His Sanskrit name is unknown, since only fragments of the Sanskrit text are extant. According to this sutra, Possessor of Virtue lived a great many years after the death of a Buddha named Joy Increasing. When the teaching of the Buddha Joy Increasing was destined to perish in forty years, many evil monks who violated the Buddhist precepts armed themselves and attacked a monk called Realization of Virtue while he was preaching that teaching. King Possessor of Virtue rushed to his protection, enabling Realization of Virtue to escape unharmed, but the king received wounds all over his body and died. As a result, the king was reborn in the land of Akshobhya Buddha and became that Buddha's chief disciple, while Realization of Virtue became Akshobhya's second disciple. Later King Possessor of Virtue was reborn as Shakyamuni Buddha, and Realization of Virtue, as Kāshyapa Buddha.

Potalaka, Mount [補陀落山] (Skt; Jpn Fudaraku-sen): A mountain said to be located on the southern coast of India, regarded as the home of Bodhisattva Perceiver of the World's Sounds. According to the Flower Garland Sutra, the boy Good Treasures, who was traveling in search of the Law, encountered Bodhisattva Perceiver of the World's Sounds on this mountain.

power of another [他力] (Jpn *tariki*): The power of a Buddha or a bodhisattva one relies upon for salvation. Also, the protection afforded by a Buddha or bodhisattva. In the Pure Land (Jōdo) school, the power of another specifically means the power of the Buddha Amida to bring his believers to rebirth in his pure land. The Pure Land school encourages its followers to place all their trust solely in the power of another, or the power of salvation of the Buddha Amida. Shinran (1173–1262), founder of the True Pure Land (Jōdo Shin) school in Japan, asserted that one's power of faith is also provided by the absolute power of Amida Buddha. Power of another is contrasted with the power of self, which means to seek to achieve enlightenment through one's own efforts in Buddhist practice. *See also* power of self.

power of self [自力] (Jpn *jiriki*): One's own power or effort to seek enlightenment. Power of self is contrasted with power of another, or the absolute power of a Buddha or a bodhisattva to save people. The power of self refers to the power of one's own virtuous acts and efforts in Buddhist practice to produce benefit and enable one to attain enlightenment. *See also* power of another.

Po-yüan [帛遠] (PY Boyuan; Jpn Hakuon): Another name for Fa-tsu. A priest and a translator of Buddhist scriptures in ancient China. *See* Fa-tsu.

practice for oneself and others [自行化他] (Jpn *jigyō-keta*): Also, practice for oneself and practice for others, benefiting oneself and benefiting others, or practicing for oneself and converting others. The two kinds or aspects of Buddhist practice. Practice for oneself means to engage in Buddhist practice in order to personally enjoy the benefits of the Law and attain enlightenment. Practice for others means to teach and convert other people so that they too can enjoy the benefits of the Law and attain enlightenment. The Mahayana Buddhist tradition sets forth these two kinds of practice as an ideal for bodhisattvas, who endeavor to practice the correct teaching themselves and to lead others to the correct teaching. This concept contrasts with what Mahayanists considered the inclination of Hinayana practitioners to seek only personal emancipation.

Praising Rebirth in the Pure Land [往生礼讃] (Chin *Wang-sheng-li-tsan;* Jpn *Ōjō-raisan*): Also known as *The Verses Praising Rebirth in the Pure Land.* A work by Shan-tao (613–681), the third patriarch of the Chinese Pure Land school, which describes the way of practice for attaining rebirth in the Pure Land of Amida Buddha. In it, Shan-tao formulates a method of reciting verses of praise, including those by Nāgārjuna and Vasubandhu, six times a day in worship of Amida Buddha.

Praising the Buddha's Deeds [仏所行讃] (Skt *Buddhacharita;* Chin *Fo-so-hsing-tsan;* Jpn *Busshogyō-san*): An epic written by Ashvaghosha who lived in India from the first through the second century. It was translated into Chinese by Dharmaraksha in the early fifth century. It recounts the life of Shakyamuni Buddha from his birth to the distribution of his ashes after his death. The Sanskrit original, *Buddhacharita* (literally, the Buddha's deeds), is written in the style known as *kāvya* employed in the epic poetry associated with the court in India and is regarded as a masterpiece of Sanskrit poetry. Only the first thirteen chapters and a portion of the fourteenth chapter of the Sanskrit original are extant, ending with a description of Shakyamuni's awakening. These correspond to the same chapters of the twenty-eight-chapter Chinese text.

Praising the Profundity of the Lotus Sutra [法華玄賛] (Chin *Fa-hua-hsüan-tsan;* Jpn *Hokke-genzan*): A commentary on the Lotus Sutra by Tz'u-en (632–682), the founder of the Chinese Dharma Characteristics (Fa-hsiang) school, written from the viewpoint of the Consciousness-Only doctrine. It criticizes T'ien-t'ai's interpretation of the Lotus Sutra, asserting that the one vehicle teaching set forth in the sutra is a mere expedient, and that the three vehicle teaching represents the truth.

prajnā [般若] (Skt; Jpn *hannya*): The wisdom that perceives the true nature of all things. Because *prajnā* leads to enlightenment, it is regarded as the mother or source of all Buddhas, and obtaining *prajnā* as the goal of Buddhist practice. Buddhism sets forth three types of learning that practitioners should aim to master: the observance of *shīla* (precepts), the practice of *dhyāna* (meditation), and the cultivation of *prajnā.* The Wisdom, or *Prajnā,* sutras, in particular, emphasize the cultivation of *prajnā,* or the perfection of wisdom. *See also* three types of learning.

Prajnā [般若] (b. 734) (Skt; Jpn Hannya): A monk from the state of Kapisha in northern India and a translator of Buddhist scriptures into Chinese. He traveled in India and studied both Hinayana and Mahayana teachings in a number of places, including Nālandā Monastery. In 781 he went to Kuang-chou in China and the next year proceeded to Ch'ang-an. There, at Hsi-ming-ssu and other temples, he translated many Buddhist scriptures. His translations include the Six Pāramitās Sutra, the Contemplation on the Mind-Ground Sutra, the Heart Sutra, and the forty-volume Flower Garland Sutra.

prajnā-pāramitā [般若波羅蜜] (Skt; Jpn *hannya-haramitsu*): The perfection of wisdom. One of the six *pāramitās. Prajnā* means wisdom that penetrates the essential nature of all things. *Pāramitā* means perfection. Thus *prajnā-pāramitā* is rendered as perfection of wisdom. *Pāramitā* also means having reached the opposite shore, i.e., having arrived at the shore of enlightenment, the opposite of the shore of delusion. Among the six *pāramitās,* or six practices for Mahayana bodhisattvas, *prajnā-pāramitā* is defined as the mother and father of all Buddhas. This *pāramitā* is therefore regarded as the most important of the six, the other five serving as means to achieve it.

Prajnāpāramitā sutras [般若経] (Skt; Jpn *Hannya-kyō*): Also known as the Perfection of Wisdom sutras or the Wisdom sutras. *See* Wisdom sutras.

Prajnāruchi [般若流支] (n.d.) (Skt; Jpn Hannyarushi): A monk from southern India who was active in China as a translator in the sixth century. Born to a Brahman family, in 516 he went to Lo-yang in China. From 538 through 543 he translated Buddhist scriptures into Chinese at

Chin-hua-ssu and Ch'ang-ting-ssu temples in Yeh, the capital of the Eastern Wei dynasty. His translations include the Meditation on the Correct Teaching Sutra, *The Accordance with "The Treatise on the Middle Way,"* and *The Refutation of Objections.*

pranidhāna [誓願] (Skt; Jpn *seigan*): Vows that bodhisattvas take upon commencing their practice. *See* vow.

Prāsangika school [帰謬論証派] (Skt; Jpn Kibyūronshō-ha): One of the two schools of Mādhyamika (Middle Way) philosophy in India. The Prāsangika school was founded by Buddhapālita (c. 470–540). Buddhapālita and his contemporary Bhāvaviveka wrote separate commentaries on Nāgārjuna's *Madhyamaka-kārikā,* or *Verses on the Middle Way,* taking different approaches to explaining the truth of non-substantiality. As a result, the Mādhyamika school divided into two schools—the Prāsangika school, led by Buddhapālita, and the Svātantrika school, headed by Bhāvaviveka. The Prāsangika school employed what might be described as a dialectic approach, pointing out contradictions in the arguments of an opponent school to demonstrate the truth of non-substantiality. Chandrakīrti (c. 600–650), whose works defined the school's position, continued its tradition. *See also* Svātantrika school.

Prasenajit [波斯匿王] (Skt; Pali Pasenadi; Jpn Hashinoku-ō): The king of Kosala of ancient India in Shakyamuni's time. He is also known as the father of Shrīmālā, the Indian queen noted for her devotion to Buddhism. According to the Medium-Length Āgama Sutra, King Prasenajit was the same age as Shakyamuni. He ruled the middle Ganges Valley from Shrāvastī, the capital of Kosala. Under his reign, Kosala rose to prominence as one of the two most powerful kingdoms in India, the other being Magadha. Prasenajit had a sister named Vaidehī whom he gave in marriage to Bimbisāra, king of Magadha. Because of this relationship, Kosala and Magadha were on friendly terms. According to one account, however, after Bimbisāra's death, Prasenajit battled with Bimbisāra's son Ajātashatru over possession of a tract of land in Kāshī that Prasenajit had given to Bimbisāra as his sister's dowry. This turned into a protracted conflict.

At the urging of his wife, Mallikā, Prasenajit became a follower of Shakyamuni Buddha and endeavored to protect and support the Buddhist Order. He often visited the Buddha while the latter was staying at the capital of Shrāvastī. According to the Increasing by One Āgama Sutra, shortly after Shakyamuni attained enlightenment, Prasenajit ascended the throne and wished to take a wife from the Shākyas, the tribe from which Shakyamuni had come and whose people were believed to be of noble birth. A man named Mahānāma, a member of the Shākyas, gave the king his maidservant's beautiful daughter in marriage, falsely claiming that she was his own daughter. She bore him a prince, who was named Virūdhaka. When Virūdhaka was eight years old, he went to Kapilavastu, the domain of the Shākyas, where he was informed of the truth behind his birth and thereby put to shame. Later, when he ascended the throne, this led him to destroy the great majority of the Shākyas.

There are different accounts from Buddhist sources concerning Prasenajit's later years. According to one, his throne was usurped by Virūdhaka and he fled from his own country to Rājagriha, the capital of Magadha, but died on the outskirts of that city. Another account says that Virūdhaka succeeded him in due course upon his death.

pratigha [瞋恚・瞋] (Skt; Jpn *shinni* or *shin*): Anger, wrath, enmity, or repugnance. *Pratigha* is one of the three poisons, the other two being *rāga* (greed) and *moha* (foolishness). *Pratigha,* or anger, has been considered a great obstacle to Buddhist practice and therefore regarded as a poison. *See also* three poisons.

pratītya-samutpāda [縁起・因縁] (Skt; Jpn *engi* or *innen*): A Buddhist doctrine expressing the interdependence of all things. *See* dependent origination.

pratyekabuddha [縁覚・独覚・辟支仏] (Skt; Jpn *engaku, dokkaku,* or *byakushibutsu*): *See* cause-awakened one.

pravārana [自恣] (Skt; Pali *pavāranā;* Jpn *jishi*): Also, *pravāranā.* A ceremony performed by monks in India on the last day of the rainy-season retreat, in which they publicly confessed their offenses and repented their errors. *Pravārana* in Sanskrit means fulfillment of a wish. During the three months of the Indian rainy season in summer, monks ceased to move about the countryside and stayed in one location, where they devoted themselves to study and practices such as meditation. This is what Buddhist texts refer to as the rainy-season retreat, the summer retreat, or the three-month retreat. On the last day of this retreat, all the monks at that location assembled to engage in voluntary mutual confession and repentance of their monastic errors and improper acts. Today, the custom of the annual retreat and the *pravārana* ceremony is still practiced in Theravāda Buddhist countries.

prayer beads [数珠] (Jpn *juzu*): A circular string of beads held in the hands during Buddhist prayer or worship or when counting the number of recitations of a Buddha's name or Buddhist incantations such as *dhāranī* (mystic formulas). The basic number of beads is 108, which is said to represent the number of earthly desires humans possess. The origin of prayer beads in Buddhism is uncertain. In Southern Buddhism, there is no tradition of using prayer beads, but in countries such as Tibet, Mongolia, China, Korea, and Japan, they have long been used as an implement essential to Buddhist practice.

Prayer for Rain Sutra [請雨経] (Chin *Ch'ing-yü-ching;* Jpn *Shōu-kyō*): A sutra that details the ritual of prayer for rain and how to perform it properly. Translated into Chinese in the eighth century by Pu-k'ung (Skt Amoghavajra), a patriarch of Chinese Esoteric Buddhism from India, it was used in China and Japan in prayer rituals to bring rain, typically conducted at the request of the sovereign to alleviate drought or ensure a rich harvest. There are two additional Chinese versions, one translated by Narendrayashas in 585 and the other by Jnānayasha in 550. There is also a Tibetan translation.

preaching in accordance with one's own mind [随自意] (Jpn *zuijii*): The Buddha's direct preaching of his enlightenment, irrespective of the capacity of his listeners. It contrasts with "preaching in accordance with the minds of others," or preaching that accords with the capacities of the listeners. These two concepts come from the Mahāparinirvāna Sutra. In *Great Concentration and Insight* and *The Profound Meaning of the Lotus Sutra,* T'ien-t'ai (538–597) categorizes the Lotus Sutra as a teaching that accords with the Buddha's own mind and the other sutras as teachings that accord with the minds of others. He defines the Lotus Sutra as a teaching that directly reveals the Buddha's enlightenment regardless of the people's varying capacities to understand it, and the other sutras as expedient means, taught in accordance with the capacity of the people.

In *The Outstanding Principles of the Lotus Sutra,* Dengyō (767–822), the founder of the Japanese Tendai school, adheres to T'ien-t'ai's interpretation of the Lotus Sutra as a teaching in which the Buddha directly revealed what he had attained. In *A Comparison of the Lotus and Other Sutras,* Nichiren says: "The teachings expounded in accordance with the people's capacity are the sutras that the Buddha preached in response to the wishes of the people of the nine worlds, just as a wise father instructs an ignorant son in a way suited to the child's understanding. On the other hand, the teaching expounded in accordance with the Buddha's enlightenment is the sutra that the Buddha preached directly from the world of Buddhahood, just as a sage father guides his ignorant son to his own understanding" (1038).

preaching in accordance with the minds of others [随他意] (Jpn *zuitai*): *See* preaching in accordance with one's own mind.

precept for benefiting sentient beings [饒益有情戒・摂衆生戒] (Jpn *nyōyaku-ujō-kai* or *shō-shujō-kai*): Also, precept that encompasses all living beings. One of the three comprehensive precepts for Mahayana bodhisattvas. The other two are the precept that encompasses all the rules and standards of behavior set forth by the Buddha, i.e., to observe all those precepts and prevent evil; and the precept that encompasses all good deeds, i.e., to strive to perform good deeds. The precept for benefiting sentient beings is an exhortation to instruct and benefit all people.

precept of adapting to local customs [随方毘尼] (Jpn *zuihō-bini*): A Buddhist precept indicating that, in matters the Buddha did not expressly either permit or forbid, one may act in accordance with local custom so long as the fundamental principles of Buddhism are not violated. The precept of adapting to local customs was employed when Buddhism made its way to various regions that differed in culture, tradition, manners and customs, climate, and other natural and human aspects. While this guidance does not prohibit or prescribe any specific behavior, it is described as a precept.

precept of the diamond chalice [金剛宝器戒] (Jpn *kongō-hōki-kai*): Also, diamond precept or diamond-treasure precept. The precept that, like a diamond chalice, is impossible to break. The term appears in the Brahmā Net Sutra, which states, "This precept of the diamond chalice is the source of all Buddhas, the source of all bodhisattvas, and the seed of the Buddha nature." In *The Secret Commentary on the Aspect of the Diamond Precept,* Dengyō (767–822) interpreted the Buddha nature, or the true aspect of all phenomena mentioned in the Lotus Sutra, as the diamond chalice. The precept of the diamond chalice thus means to embrace the Lotus Sutra. Nichiren (1222–1282) interpreted the embracing of the Law of Myoho-renge-kyo, the essence of the Lotus Sutra, as the precept of the diamond chalice and taught that, by observing this single precept, one can manifest the three bodies of a Buddha—the Dharma body, the reward body, and the manifested body—and receive benefit equal to that of observing all other good precepts. In *The Teaching, Practice, and Proof,* Nichiren writes: "The five characters of Myoho-renge-kyo, the heart of the essential teaching of the Lotus Sutra, contain the benefit amassed through the countless practices and meritorious deeds of all Buddhas throughout the three existences. Then, how can these five characters not include the benefits obtained by observing all of the Buddhas' precepts? Once the practitioner embraces this perfectly endowed wonderful precept, he cannot break it, even if he should try. It is therefore called the precept of the diamond chalice" (481).

precepts [戒] (Skt *shīla;* Pali *sīla;* Jpn *kai*): Rules of discipline. One of the three types of learning that Buddhists should master. The word *precept* in Buddhism has the connotation of preventing error and putting an end to evil. Broadly speaking, Buddhist precepts can be divided into those of Hinayana and those of Mahayana. The Hinayana precepts consist of several categories or groupings, such as the five precepts, eight precepts, ten precepts, two hundred and fifty precepts, and five hundred precepts. The most fundamental of these are the five precepts: (1) not to kill, (2) not to steal, (3) not to engage in sexual misconduct, (4) not to lie, and (5) not to drink intoxicants. One who observes these precepts is said to be reborn as a human being. The eight precepts comprise these five precepts (the third of which is replaced by "not to engage in any sexual relations") plus three others: (6) not to wear ornaments or perfume, nor to listen to singing or watch dancing, (7) not to sleep on an elevated or broad bed, and (8) not to eat at an improper hour, i.e., after noon. The eight precepts are for lay believers and are observed only on specified days. The ten precepts are for both male and female novices of the Buddhist Order. They consist of the eight precepts described above, plus two others: (9) not to listen to singing or watch dancing (which is part of [6] above, but is here made an independent precept), and (10) not to own valuables such as gold and silver. The two hundred and fifty precepts and the five hundred precepts are the complete rules of discipline for fully ordained monks and nuns, respectively.

Mahayana precepts include the three comprehensive precepts, the ten major precepts, and the forty-eight minor precepts. The three comprehensive precepts are for Mahayana bodhisattvas, whether laity or clergy. They are (1) the precept that encompasses all the rules and standards of behavior set forth by the Buddha for Mahayana bodhisattvas, i.e., to observe all those precepts and prevent evil; (2) the precept that encompasses all good deeds, i.e., to strive to perform good deeds; and (3) the precept that encompasses all living beings, i.e., to instruct and benefit all living beings. The third is also called the precept for benefiting sentient beings. The ten major precepts are for clergy. They are (1) not to kill, (2) not to steal, (3) not to engage in any sexual relations, (4) not to lie, (5) not to sell liquor, (6) not to speak of the past misdeeds of other Buddhists, (7) not to praise oneself or disparage others, (8) not to begrudge offerings or spare one's efforts for the sake of Buddhism, (9) not to give way to anger, and (10) not to speak ill of the three treasures of Buddhism. The forty-eight minor precepts are set forth in the Brahmā Net Sutra and deal with matters of less importance than those covered by the ten major precepts.

In China, priests of the T'ien-t'ai and other Mahayana schools received the Hinayana precepts at their ordination, though they interpreted these in light of Mahayana doctrine. In Japan, however, Dengyō (767–822), the founder of the Tendai school, pointed out the contradiction of Mahayana priests having to receive the Hinayana ordination ceremony and, based on the Lotus Sutra, adopted the three comprehensive precepts, the ten major precepts, and the forty-eight minor precepts as the specific rules of Mahayana discipline that priests were to uphold. Because these precepts were based on the Lotus Sutra, which is known in T'ien-t'ai's doctrine as the perfect teaching, they were called the perfect precepts.

precepts, meditation, and wisdom [戒定慧] (Jpn *kai-jō-e*): *See* three types of learning.

precepts of perfect and immediate enlightenment [円頓戒] (Jpn *endon-kai*): Also, perfect precepts. One of the three types of learning based on the teaching for perfect and immediate enlightenment, or the Lotus Sutra. The other two are perfect meditation and perfect wisdom. Dengyō (767–822), the founder of the Japanese Tendai school, adopted the Mahayana precepts, specifically the ten major precepts and forty-eight minor precepts set forth in the Brahmā Net Sutra, and interpreted them based on the Lotus Sutra, known in the T'ien-t'ai or Tendai doctrine as the teaching for perfect and immediate enlightenment, or perfect teaching. He thus laid the foundation for the establishment of an ordination platform for administering the precepts of perfect and immediate enlightenment.

Precepts school [律宗] (Chin Lü-tsung; Jpn Risshū): Also known as the Vinaya school. A school based on the *vinaya,* the Buddhist rules of monastic discipline, or precepts. *Vinaya* was translated in Chinese scriptures as *lü,* pronounced *ritsu* in Japanese, meaning rule, statute, or principle. The Precepts school emphasizes strict adherence to the rules of monastic discipline. In Japan, the Precepts school was one of the six schools of Nara. In China, the most prosperous branch of the Precepts school was the Nan-shan school founded by Tao-hsüan in the seventh century and based on the work *The Fourfold Rules of Discipline,* the *vinaya* text of the Indian Dharmagupta school. The Chinese priest Chien-chen (known as Ganjin in Japan), who had studied the teaching of the Nan-shan school, went to Japan in 753, entered the capital, Nara, in 754, and founded the Precepts school there. He built an ordination platform at Tōdai-ji temple and founded Tōshōdai-ji temple as a center for the study of the monastic rules of discipline. Thereafter ordination platforms were built at Yakushi-ji temple in Shimotsuke Province and at Kanzeon-ji temple in Chikuzen Province as branches of the ordination center at Tōdai-ji. Priests and nuns in Japan were ordained at one of these three platforms, and the Precepts school flourished as a major school of Japanese Buddhism. During the Heian period (794–1185) the school gradually declined, but it reemerged during the Kamakura period (1185–1333), when the priest Shunjō in Kyoto strove to revive the practice of the precepts. He founded the Precepts school of the Northern Capital (Kyoto). Kakujō and Eizon also worked to revive precepts practice, and their lineage was known as the Precepts school of the Southern Capital (Nara). Eizon advocated the practice of both the precepts and the esoteric teachings, a conviction that later led to the founding of the True Word Precepts (Shingon–Ritsu) school based at Saidai-ji temple in Nara. There are two major precepts-based schools in Japan today: the Precepts school, whose head temple is Tōshōdai-ji, and the True Word Precepts school, whose head temple is Saidai-ji.

precept that encompasses all good deeds [摂善法戒] (Jpn *shō-zembō-kai*): One of the three comprehensive precepts. The precept that enjoins one to strive to perform good deeds. *See* three comprehensive precepts.

precept that encompasses all living beings [摂衆生戒] (Jpn *shō-shujō-kai*): One of the three comprehensive precepts. The precept for instructing and benefiting all living beings. *See* precept for benefiting sentient beings; three comprehensive precepts.

Precious Key to the Secret Treasury, The [秘蔵宝鑰] (Jpn *Hizō-hōyaku*): A three-volume work by Kōbō (774–835), the founder of the Japanese True Word (Shingon) school. In the Tenchō era (824–834), when Emperor Junna ordered the Flower Garland (Kegon), Dharma Characteristics (Hossō), Three Treatises (Sanron), Precepts (Ritsu), Tendai, and True Word schools to submit a written statement of their fundamental teachings, Kōbō presented *The Treatise on the Ten Stages of the Mind* in ten volumes, setting forth the essential doctrines of the school. Because *The Treatise on the Ten Stages of the Mind* was so comprehensive, the emperor ordered Kōbō to make a summary of this work. The condensed version he produced in response is *The Precious Key to the Secret Treasury.* In it, Kōbō recapitulates the ten stages of the mind and asserts the superiority of the esoteric over the exoteric teachings. *See also* ten stages of the mind.

pre-Lotus Sutra teachings [爾前教] (Jpn *nizen-kyō*): The teachings that Shakyamuni Buddha expounded during the first forty-two years of his preaching life, from the time following his enlightenment up until he began to expound the Lotus Sutra. According to T'ien-t'ai's classification of the Buddha's teachings into five periods, the teachings of the first four periods—the Flower Garland, Āgama, Correct and Equal, and Wisdom periods—constitute the pre-Lotus Sutra teachings, all of which he identified as provisional teachings, or expedient means to lead people to the Lotus Sutra. *See also* five periods.

preparation section [序分] (Jpn *jo-bun*): Also, preparation. One of the three sections or divisions of a sutra, the other two being revelation and transmission, into which the text of a sutra is divided for the purpose of interpreting its teachings. The preparation section consists of introductory remarks clarifying the reasons for expounding the sutra, preparing the way for the revelation of the core teaching of the sutra, and readying people to accept that teaching. *See also* three divisions of a sutra.

preta [餓鬼・薜茘・薜茘多] (Skt; Jpn *gaki, heirei,* or *heireita*): Originally, in ancient India, spirits of the deceased. Incorporated into Buddhism, *preta* came to mean hungry spirits. In Buddhist scriptures, they are depicted as having human form with swollen bellies and throats as small as needles. Persons who lead lives of unrestrained desire or selfishness were said to be reborn as *preta.* The realm of *preta* is the second of the Ten Worlds, in which dwellers are tormented physically or spiritually by relentless craving, particularly hunger and thirst. This realm is also interpreted as representing the state of life of someone consumed with insatiable desire. *See also* hungry spirits.

preventing error and putting an end to evil [防非止悪] (Jpn *bōhi-shiaku*): One aspect of precepts that prevents the evils of the three categories of action—deed, speech, and thought. In Buddhism, an important purpose of the precepts is to conquer earthly desires and cease committing any evil act.

Principle of Wisdom Sutra [理趣経] (Skt *Ārya-prajnāpāramitā-nayashatapanchashatikā;* Chin *Li-ch'ü-ching;* Jpn *Rishu-kyō*): A sutra that depicts Mahāvairochana Buddha preaching to Vajrasattva, who is regarded as one of the eight original patriarchs of Esoteric Buddhism by the True Word (Jpn Shingon) school. The sutra teaches that the true nature of all desires, including sexual desires, is purity, and that this purity of all things and phenomena is realized through the wisdom, or *prajnā,* that penetrates the truth. It also praises the compassionate actions of bodhisattvas. There exists a Sanskrit text, as well as six Chinese and three Tibetan versions. The translators of the Chinese versions are Hsüan-tsang, Bodhiruchi, Chin-kang-chih (Skt Vajrabodhi), Pu-k'ung (Amoghavajra), Dānapāla, and Fa-hsien, all of whom, with the exception of Hsüan-tsang, were of Indian origin. Fa-hsien's Sanskrit name is unknown. Of these six versions, Pu-k'ung's translation is the most popular and is recited in the True Word school. Hsüan-tsang's version is included in the six-hundred-volume Great Wisdom Sutra.

Profound Meaning of the Four Mahayana Treatises, The [大乗四論玄義] (Chin *Ta-ch'eng-ssu-lun-hsüan-i;* Jpn *Daijō-shiron-gengi*): A work by Hui-chün, also known as Chün-cheng, of the early T'ang dynasty (618–907) in China. The four Mahayana treatises are *The Treatise on the*

Middle Way, The One-Hundred-Verse Treatise, The Treatise on the Twelve Gates, and *The Treatise on the Great Perfection of Wisdom.* This text explains the doctrine of the Three Treatises (Chin San-lun; Jpn Sanron) school and attempts to refute that of the Establishment of Truth (Ch'eng-shih; Jōjitsu) school and the Summary of the Mahayana (She-lun; Shōron) school.

Profound Meaning of the Lotus Sutra, The [法華玄義] (Chin *Fa-hua-hsüan-i;* Jpn *Hokke-gengi*): One of T'ien-t'ai's three major works, the others being *The Words and Phrases of the Lotus Sutra* and *Great Concentration and Insight.* This work was originally a lecture series given in 593 by T'ien-t'ai at Yü-ch'üan-ssu temple in Ching-chou, China, and was compiled into ten volumes by his disciple Chang-an. On the premise that the sutra's title expresses the essence of the entire sutra, T'ien-t'ai discusses the title of the Lotus Sutra, *Myoho-renge-kyo,* in light of the five major principles of name, entity or essence, quality, function, and teaching. From the viewpoint of name, for example, he gives an exhaustive interpretation of each of the five characters *myō, hō, ren, ge,* and *kyō.* This explanation of the name composes a great part of *The Profound Meaning of the Lotus Sutra.*

Profound Meaning of the "Perceiver of the World's Sounds" Chapter, The [観音玄義] (Chin *Kuan-yin-hsüan-i;* Jpn *Kannon-gengi*): A work compiled from lectures T'ien-t'ai gave on the "Perceiver of the World's Sounds" (twenty-fifth) chapter of the Lotus Sutra by his disciple Chang-an. T'ien-t'ai comments on this chapter in light of the five major principles of name, entity or essence, quality, function, and teaching, and explains the three realms of existence, the Ten Worlds, the one hundred worlds, and the one thousand factors. Since this work does not refer to the principle of three thousand realms in a single moment of life, it is thought to have been compiled prior to *Great Concentration and Insight,* a compilation of lectures T'ien-t'ai delivered in 594.

Profound Meaning of the Three Treatises, The [三論玄義] (Chin *San-lun-hsüan-i;* Jpn *Sanron-gengi*): A work written around 597 by Chi-tsang, a systematizer of the doctrines of the Three Treatises (San-lun) school in China. This work explains the teachings of the three basic treatises of the school—*The Treatise on the Middle Way, The Treatise on the Twelve Gates,* and *The One-Hundred-Verse Treatise.* The first two treatises are works by Nāgārjuna (c. 150–250), and the third is the work of his disciple Āryadeva. Kumārajīva translated all three of these texts into Chinese in the beginning of the fifth century. *The Profound Meaning of the Three Treatises,* which discusses the principles of non-substantiality and the Middle Way, is known for its clear and concise explanation of the doctrinal system of the Three Treatises school. In Japan, this work was highly regarded, and many commentaries on it were produced.

Profound Secrets Sutra [深密経] (Jpn *Jimmitsu-kyō*): *See* Revelation of the Profound Secrets Sutra.

Pronunciation and Meaning in the Buddhist Scriptures [一切経音義] (Chin *I-ch'ieh-ching-yin-i;* Jpn *Issaikyō-ongi*): (1) A Buddhist dictionary compiled by Hsüan-ying in China around the middle of the seventh century. It gave Chinese readers transliterations and definitions of Sanskrit Buddhist terms appearing in some 450 Buddhist texts. It is the oldest extant Buddhist dictionary.

(2) A Buddhist dictionary compiled by Hui-lin (737–820), based on Hsüan-ying's dictionary of the same title. It defines and gives transliterations for Buddhist terms appearing in some 1,220 texts.

Propagation of Zen for the Protection of the Country, The [興禅護国論] (Jpn *Kōzen-gokoku-ron*): A work written in 1198 by Eisai, the founder of the Rinzai school of Zen in Japan. When Eisai attempted to spread the Zen teachings, the priests of the established schools in Nara and of Mount Hiei opposed him. In response, he produced this work in which he asserts the legitimacy of Zen and outlines its basic teaching, arguing also that Zen is conducive to the general welfare and security of the nation. It is regarded as a declaration of the founding of Zen as a Buddhist school in Japan, though it apparently was not written with that specific purpose in mind.

"Prophecies" chapter [人記品] (Jpn *Ninki-hon*): The ninth chapter of the Lotus Sutra. *See* "Prophecies Conferred on Learners and Adepts" chapter.

"Prophecies Conferred on Learners and Adepts" chapter [授学無学人記品] (Jpn *Jugaku-mugaku-ninki-hon*): Abbreviated as the "Prophecies" chapter. The ninth chapter of the Lotus Sutra, in which Shakyamuni Buddha prophesies the enlightenment of Ānanda, Rāhula, and two thousand other voice-hearer disciples in the far distant future. The chapter begins with Ānanda and Rāhula, inspired by Shakyamuni's prediction of enlightenment for the five hundred arhats in the previous (eighth) chapter, requesting that Shakyamuni bestow on them a prophecy of enlightenment. Shakyamuni complies and predicts that Ānanda will become a Buddha named Mountain Sea Wisdom Unrestricted Power King, and Rāhula, a Buddha named Stepping on Seven Treasure Flowers. He then bestows a prophecy of enlightenment on the two thousand voice-hearer disciples, who include both learners and adepts. Adepts are those who, having mastered the enlightenment of the voice-hearer and become arhats, have nothing more to learn. All of these two thousand disciples, he declares, will become Buddhas with the name Jewel Sign. This chapter concludes Shakyamuni's teaching of the replacement of the three vehicles with the one vehicle. The subsequent chapters deal with the practice and propagation of the sutra after the Buddha's death and its transmission to future ages.

"Prophecy of Enlightenment for Five Hundred Disciples" chapter [五百弟子受記品] (Jpn *Gohyaku-deshi-juki-hon*): Abbreviated as the "Five Hundred Disciples" chapter. The eighth chapter of the Lotus Sutra. At the beginning of the chapter, Pūrna rejoices at having understood the teaching of the one vehicle by hearing Shakyamuni tell, in the "Parable of the Phantom City" (seventh) chapter, of their relationship in the remote past when Shakyamuni was the sixteenth son of the Buddha Great Universal Wisdom Excellence. In this (eighth) chapter, Shakyamuni predicts that Pūrna will attain enlightenment in a future existence as a Buddha named Law Bright. Subsequently he prophesies that the twelve hundred arhat disciples in the assembly, including Kaundinya, will also attain Buddhahood. He first bestows this prophecy on five hundred arhats, and then on the remaining seven hundred. All twelve hundred, he says, will become Buddhas with the name Universal Brightness. To show their understanding of the one vehicle teaching, these five hundred arhats then relate the parable of the jewel in the robe.

prophecy of future enlightenment [授記・記別・和伽羅那] (Skt *vyākarana;* Pali *veyyākarana;* Jpn *juki, kibetsu,* or *wagarana*): A Buddha's prediction that a disciple (or disciples) will attain enlightenment in the future. One of the twelve divisions of the teachings, *vyākarana* is rendered as the prophecy of future enlightenment and indicates the part of a sutra in which Shakyamuni Buddha pronounces that a practitioner will attain Buddhahood in a future existence. Such prophecies are common in Mahayana sutras. The Lotus Sutra contains a number of passages in which the Buddha predicts enlightenment for his disciples and foretells what their titles as future Buddhas will be as well as the names of their respective *kalpas* (eras) and Buddha lands. In the "Simile and Parable" (third) chapter of the Lotus Sutra, Shakyamuni Buddha predicts the enlightenment of Shāriputra, and in the "Bestowal of Prophecy" (sixth) chapter, Shakyamuni predicts enlightenment for the four great voice-hearers, Mahākāshyapa, Subhūti, Kātyāyana, and Maudgalyāyana. In the "Five Hundred Disciples" (eighth) and the "Prophecies" (ninth) chapters, Shakyamuni predicts enlightenment for other individual disciples as well as for groups of disciples, thousands in all. According to the *Jātaka,* stories of the Buddha's previous lives, in a past existence Shakyamuni himself received a prophecy of enlightenment from the Buddha Burning Torch (Skt Dīpamkara).

Protection of the Sovereign of the Nation Sutra [守護国界経] (Chin *Shou-hu-kuo-chieh-ching;* Jpn *Shugo-kokkai-kyō*): Also known as the Protection Sutra. A sutra that expounds a *dhāranī,* or a spell or mystic formula, for protecting the sovereign, and describes the benefit this *dhāranī* confers. The full title is the Dhāranī for the Protection of the Sovereign of the Nation Sutra. It was translated into Chinese by Prajnā and Munishrī in the eighth century, and introduced to Japan in the early ninth century by Kōbō, the founder of the Japanese True Word (Shingon) school, which treasured this sutra.

Protection Sutra [守護経] (Jpn *Shugo-kyō*): *See* Protection of the Sovereign of the Nation Sutra.

protuberant knot of flesh [肉髻相] (Jpn *nikkei-sō*): One of a Buddha's thirty-two features. *See* knot of flesh on the head.

provincial temples [国分寺] (Jpn *kokubun-ji*): Temples established in the provinces of Japan by an edict Emperor Shōmu issued in 741. These temples were for offering prayers for the peace and prosperity of the nation. They consisted of temples for priests and temples for nuns, with one of each located in each province. Formally, those for priests were called "temples for the protection of the nation by the power of the Golden Light Sutra and the four heavenly kings," and those for nuns, "temples for the eradication of past offenses by the power of the Lotus Sutra." The temples for priests were headed by Tōdai-ji temple and those for nuns, by Hokke-ji, both in Nara. As their names suggest, the Sovereign Kings of the Golden Light Sutra and the Lotus Sutra were recited at these temples.

provincial temples for nuns [国分尼寺] (Jpn *kokubun-niji*): Temples for nuns established in the provinces of Japan by an edict of Emperor Shōmu in 741. Nuns at these temples were expected to seek, through the power of the Lotus Sutra, to remove the sufferings and obstacles of the women of Japan. The temples for nuns were formally called "temples for the eradication of past offenses by the power of the Lotus Sutra." *See also* provincial temples.

provisional Buddha [迹仏] (Jpn *shakubutsu*): Also, transient Buddha. A Buddha who does not reveal his true identity, but assumes a transient status or role in order to save the people. The term is used in contrast with "true Buddha," a Buddha who has revealed his true identity. A true Buddha can be compared to the moon in the sky, and a provisional Buddha to its reflection on the surface of water. A provisional Buddha does not expound the truth in its entirety, but only partial aspects of the truth. From the standpoint of the essential teaching (latter half) of the Lotus Sutra, the Shakyamuni Buddha depicted in the pre-Lotus Sutra teachings and in the theoretical teaching (first half) of the sutra is a provisional Buddha because he has yet to reveal his true identity. In these teachings, Shakyamuni is presented as having attained Buddhahood for the first time under the *bodhi* tree during his lifetime in India. In the essential teaching, however, Shakyamuni declares that he actually attained Buddhahood in the inconceivably remote past. The Shakyamuni who has revealed this truth is called the true Buddha. *See also* true Buddha.

provisional Mahayana teachings [権大乗教] (Jpn *gon-daijō-kyō*): The Mahayana teachings expounded as a means to lead people to the true Mahayana teaching, or the Lotus Sutra, which fully reveals Shakyamuni Buddha's enlightenment. Provisional Mahayana teachings reveal only partial aspects of the truth to which the Buddha was awakened. In his classification of Shakyamuni's teachings into five periods, T'ien-t'ai (538–597) termed the teachings of the Flower Garland, Correct and Equal, and Wisdom periods provisional Mahayana, and the teachings of the Lotus and Nirvana period true Mahayana.

provisional manifestation [権化] (Jpn *gonge*): Also, temporary manifestation, manifestation in temporal form. The provisional transformation of a Buddha or a bodhisattva into various forms in order to benefit living beings and lead them from suffering to enlightenment. The "Perceiver of the World's Sounds" (twenty-fifth) chapter of the Lotus Sutra describes the bodhisattva Perceiver of the World's Sounds as appearing in thirty-three different forms in order to save the people. The concept of a deity incarnating into various forms is found in Hindu or Vedic belief well before Buddhism; this kind of incarnation is called *avatāra* in Sanskrit, from which derives the English word avatar. The ten avatars of the god Vishnu, which include a fish, a tortoise, Rāma (a hero of Hinduism), Krishna, and even the Buddha, are well known. In Japan, belief that deities of Japan were provisional manifestations of Buddhas or bodhisattvas began to spread in the late Heian period (794–1185).

provisional sutras [権経] (Jpn *gon-kyō*): The sutras of the provisional teachings that Shakyamuni Buddha expounded as expedient means to prepare people for the true teaching. This contrasts with the true sutra, or the sutra of the true teaching. According to T'ien-t'ai's doctrine, all sutras expounded prior to the Lotus Sutra are provisional sutras. *See also* pre-Lotus Sutra teachings; provisional teachings.

provisional teachings [権教] (Jpn *gon-kyō*): The teachings that Shakyamuni Buddha expounded as expedient means to lead people to the true teaching. According to T'ien-t'ai's doctrine, all the teachings expounded before the Lotus Sutra. The provisional teachings reveal only partial aspects of the truth that the Buddha attained, while the true teaching expounds the truth in its entirety. T'ien-t'ai (538–597) states in *Great Concentration and Insight,* "'Provisional' means a temporary expedient, which is to be employed temporarily and then discarded. 'True' means a true teaching; it is the ultimate goal to be reached." From the viewpoint of T'ien-t'ai's classification of the Buddha's teachings into five periods, the provisional teachings correspond to the teachings of the first four periods—the Flower Garland, Āgama, Correct and Equal, and Wisdom periods—and the true teaching, to the Lotus Sutra. Provisional teachings, which include Hinayana and provisional Mahayana, were set forth in accord with the people's capacity as a means to lead them to the true teaching of the Lotus Sutra, in which the Buddha directly reveals his enlightenment. Although various Buddhist schools in China divided Shakyamuni's teachings into two categories—provisional and true—what constituted each of these differed according to that school's system of classification. The Dharma Characteristics (Chin Fa-hsiang; Jpn Hossō) school regarded the one vehicle teaching of the Lotus Sutra as a provisional teaching and the three vehicle teaching as the true teaching, while the T'ien-t'ai school regarded the three vehicle teaching as provisional and the one vehicle teaching as true.

P'u-kuang [普光] (n.d.) (PY Puguang; Jpn Fukō): A Chinese priest and a translator of Buddhist scriptures. One of Hsüan-tsang's major disciples. During the period from 645 through 664, he assisted Hsüan-tsang in his translation of Buddhist scriptures into Chinese. When Hsüan-tsang translated *The Dharma Analysis Treasury,* P'u-kuang wrote the thirty-volume *Commentary on "The Dharma Analysis Treasury,"* considered one of the three major commentaries on this treatise. Fa-pao and Shen-t'ai, also Hsüan-tsang's major disciples, produced the other two. With Fa-pao and others, P'u-kuang promoted the study of the Sarvāstivāda doctrine and helped establish the Dharma Analysis Treasury (Chü-she) school in China.

Pu-k'ung [不空] (705–774) (PY Bukong; Skt Amoghavajra; Jpn Fukū): An Indian monk who went to China to disseminate Esoteric Buddhism. Pu-k'ung is his Chinese name. Born in northern India (Central Asia or Sri Lanka according to some accounts), in 720 he journeyed to Lo-yang in China and became a disciple of Chin-kang-chih (Skt Vajrabodhi). In 741, after Chin-kang-chih's death, he went to India and Sri Lanka in search of esoteric scriptures. In 746 he returned to China, where he won the patronage of Emperor Hsüan-tsung and his successors, and conducted esoteric rituals for the protection of the nation. Pu-k'ung propagated Esoteric Buddhism and also translated many esoteric scriptures, including the Diamond Crown Sutra, into Chinese. He is regarded as the sixth patriarch in the lineage of Esoteric Buddhism by the True Word (Jpn Shingon) school. Among his six major disciples was Hui-kuo, who transferred Esoteric Buddhism to Kōbō, the founder of the True Word school.

punya [功徳・福徳] (Skt; Jpn *kudoku* or *fukutoku*): Virtue, benefit, good fortune, blessing, meritorious act, good, or right. *Punya* is a component of a number of Buddhist terms. For example, the Sanskrit word *punya-kshetra* was rendered in China as "field of good fortune" or "field of blessing." The seventeenth chapter of Kumārajīva's translation of the Lotus Sutra is titled "Distinctions in Benefits," and its Sanskrit title is *Punya-paryāya. Paryāya* means arrangement, disposition, or distinction. The Sanskrit title of the "Benefits of Responding with Joy" (eighteenth) chapter of the same work is *Anumodanā-punya-nirdesha. Anumodanā* means joyful acceptance, and *nirdesha,* description or explanation. Thus *Anumodanā-punya-nirdesha* indicates a description of benefits accruing from joyful acceptance. One of the eighteen heavens in the world of form is called Punya-prasava, which means increase of merit. *See also* benefit.

Punyatāra [弗若多羅] (n.d.) (Skt; Jpn Futsunyatara): A monk from Kashmir famed for his observance of, and his learning regarding, the precepts. During the period from 399 until 416, he went to China and participated with Kumārajīva in the translation of *The Ten Divisions of Monastic Rules.* He died before its completion.

Punyayashas [富那奢] (n.d.) (Skt; Jpn Funasha): A native of Pātaliputra in Magadha, India. The tenth of Shakyamuni Buddha's twenty-three, or the eleventh of his twenty-four, successors. He became a disciple of Pārshva, his predecessor among the Buddha's successors, and received the teachings from him. Later he instructed and passed the teachings on to Ashvaghosha. Punyayashas is noted for having made skillful use of expedient means to lead many people to the Buddhist way.

Pūrana Kassapa [富蘭那迦葉] (Pali; Jpn Furanna-kashō): An influential non-Buddhist thinker during Shakyamuni's time. *See* six non-Buddhist teachers.

pure and far-reaching voice [梵音声] (Skt *brahma-svara;* Jpn *bonnonjō*): Also, *brahma* sound. The voice of a Buddha. One of a Buddha's thirty-two features. The voice of the Buddha is said to be pure and to reach all the worlds in the ten directions. This is symbolic of the power of a Buddha's voice to delight those who hear it, deeply touch people's hearts, and inspire a sense of reverence.

Pure Emerald World [浄瑠璃世界] (Jpn Jōruri-sekai): Also known as the Pure Emerald Land. The pure land of Medicine Master Buddha, who is said to dwell as many Buddha lands away in the east as the grains of sand of ten Ganges Rivers. According to the Medicine Master Sutra, its ground is made of emerald, ropes of gold mark the boundaries of roads, and the seven kinds of gems adorn its buildings. Two bodhisattvas, Sunlight and Moonlight, are described as the leaders of the countless bodhisattvas in this land and also as upholders and guardians of the teachings of Medicine Master Buddha.

Pure Eye [浄眼] (Skt Vimalanetra; Jpn Jōgen): One of the two sons of King Wonderful Adornment who appear in the "King Wonderful Adornment" (twenty-seventh) chapter of the Lotus Sutra. *See* Pure Storehouse.

pure land [浄土] (Jpn *jōdo*): A Buddha's land. The term is contrasted with *impure land,* meaning the *sahā* world, this world that is tainted with suffering and desire. A Buddha's land is said to be blissful and free from impurity and is therefore called a pure land. Buddhism sets forth two views concerning the relationship of the *sahā* world and the pure land. The first is that the pure land is another realm entirely, physically removed from the *sahā* world. Examples of this view are belief in the Pure Emerald World of Medicine Master Buddha in the east, and in Amida Buddha's Pure Land of Perfect Bliss in the west. (The term *Pure Land* in capitals generally indicates Amida's land.) The second view, represented in the Lotus Sutra and the Vimalakīrti Sutra, is that no pure land exists apart from the *sahā* world: the *sahā* world reveals either its pure aspect or impure aspect in response to the purity or impurity of the hearts and minds of those inhabiting it. One with a pure heart thus dwells in a pure land here and now. Collectively, when people purify their hearts and minds, the society or world where they live becomes a pure land.

Pure Land of Perfect Bliss [極楽浄土] (Jpn Gokuraku-jōdo): The land of Amida Buddha. *See* Perfect Bliss.

Pure Land of Secret Solemnity [密厳浄土] (Jpn Mitsugon-jōdo): The pure land described in the Secret Solemnity Sutra. It symbolizes awakening to the *ālaya*-consciousness, which is equated in this sutra with the Buddha nature. The Pure Land of Secret Solemnity is also identified with the land of Mahāvairochana Buddha.

Pure Land school (1) [浄土門・浄土教・浄土宗] (Jpn Jōdo-mon, Jōdo-kyō, or Jōdo-shū): Also, Pure Land (Chin Ching-t'u; Jpn Jōdo) teachings. A general term for the Buddhist denominations of the Pure Land teachings in China and Japan. The Pure Land school teaches the attainment of rebirth in the Pure Land of Amida Buddha by means of devotion to Amida Buddha, especially, the recitation of Amida's name. The

Buddha Infinite Life Sutra, the Meditation on the Buddha Infinite Life Sutra, and the Amida Sutra are known as the three Pure Land sutras.

(a) China: The Pai-lien-she (White Lotus Society), a religious group dedicated to Amida worship, was founded in 402 by Hui-yüan. This is said to have been the origin of Pure Land practices in China. In the early sixth century, T'an-luan received the Meditation on the Buddha Infinite Life Sutra from Bodhiruchi and thereafter propagated faith in Amida Buddha, asserting that one could be reborn in the Pure Land through Amida's grace. During the seventh century, T'an-luan's teaching was systematized by Tao-ch'o and his disciple Shan-tao.

(b) Japan: The Pure Land teachings including the Nembutsu, or meditation on Amida Buddha, were first adopted by the Tendai school when in 848 Jikaku, who was later the third chief priest of Enryaku-ji, the school's head temple, established a hall for constant active meditation (a form of walking meditation) on Mount Hiei and there practiced meditation on Amida Buddha. Ryōgen (912–985), the eighteenth chief priest of Enryaku-ji, was probably the first to try systematizing the Pure Land doctrines. His disciple Genshin wrote *The Essentials of Rebirth in the Pure Land,* in which he systematized the teachings of meditation on Amida Buddha within the framework of Tendai doctrines. Later Yōkan (1033–1111) of the Three Treatises (Sanron) school practiced the recitation of Amida's name. Hōnen (1133–1212), who was inspired by the works of Shan-tao of China and the Tendai priest Genshin of Japan, established the Pure Land school. He wrote *The Nembutsu Chosen above All,* in which he defined the sole cause of rebirth in the Pure Land to be the practice of calling upon the name of Amida Buddha. After his death, the school split into five schools: Chinzei, Seizan, Chōraku-ji, Kuhon-ji, and a group centering around Hōnen's disciple Kōsai. In addition to these schools, Shinran (1173–1262), who was a disciple of Hōnen, founded the True Pure Land (Jōdo Shin) school. Ippen (1239–1289), who studied under Shōtatsu, Hōnen's second-generation disciple, founded a school of the Pure Land teachings known as the Time (Ji) school. Besides these schools, there exists the Interfusing Nembutsu (Yūzū Nembutsu) school founded on the teachings of Ryōnin (1073–1132), which saw a revival during the Edo period (1600–1867). In Japan, the Pure Land school is also known as the Nembutsu school. "Nembutsu" refers to the invocation of Amida's name—the words *Namu Amida Butsu* ("Homage to Amida Buddha")—chanted by the school's adherents.

(2) [浄土宗] (Jpn Jōdo-shū): The Japanese Buddhist school established by Hōnen (1133–1212). Its head temple is Chion-in in Kyoto. The school's principal doctrine is that its followers revere Amida Buddha,

believe in his original vow, and invoke Amida Buddha's name in order to be reborn in his Pure Land. In 1198 Hōnen wrote *The Nembutsu Chosen above All*, in which he defined the sole cause for attaining rebirth in Amida Buddha's Pure Land to be the practice of invoking that Buddha's name. Hōnen revered the patriarchs of the Chinese Pure Land school—T'an-luan, Tao-ch'o, and Shan-tao—and followed their example in dividing Shakyamuni Buddha's teachings into two categories, the Pure Land teachings (the three Pure Land sutras—the Buddha Infinite Life, Meditation on the Buddha Infinite Life, and Amida sutras) and the Sacred Way teachings (all other sutras). The Pure Land teachings are defined as the easy-to-practice way, or salvation through Amida's power, and the Sacred Way teachings as the difficult-to-practice way, or attaining enlightenment through personal power. The Pure Land school holds that the easy-to-practice way is the one way appropriate for the people of the Latter Day of the Law who are inferior in their capacity to understand Buddhism. Again, the practice of the Pure Land teachings is regarded as the correct practice, and that of the other teachings as sundry practices. Hōnen identified as the principal texts of his school the above three sutras and *The Treatise on the Pure Land* (also known as *The Treatise on Rebirth in the Pure Land*) by Vasubandhu. Hōnen's teaching quickly spread throughout Japan, but was banned in 1207 when the influential Enryaku-ji temple on Mount Hiei and Kōfuku-ji temple in Nara protested strongly, and Hōnen was exiled to Tosa. His disciple, Shinran, later established the True Pure Land (Jōdo Shin) school.

Pure Land teachings [浄土門・浄土教] (Jpn Jōdo-mon or Jōdo-kyō): *See* Pure Land school (1).

pure Law [白法] (Jpn *byakuhō*): The teachings of Shakyamuni Buddha. The Great Collection Sutra states that in the fifth and last half-millennium after Shakyamuni Buddha's death (the beginning of the Latter Day of the Law) "quarrels and disputes will arise among the adherents to my teachings, and the pure Law will become obscured and lost." *See also* great pure Law.

Pure Practices [浄行菩薩] (Skt Vishuddhachāritra; Jpn Jōgyō-bosatsu): One of the four leaders of the Bodhisattvas of the Earth, who appear in the "Emerging from the Earth" (fifteenth) chapter of the Lotus Sutra. *The Supplement to "The Words and Phrases of the Lotus Sutra"* by Tao-hsien, an eighth-century priest of the T'ien-t'ai school in China, says that the four bodhisattvas represent the four virtues of the Buddha's life—true self, eternity, purity, and happiness. Of these virtues, Bodhisattva Pure Practices represents purity.

Pure Storehouse [浄蔵] (Skt Vimalagarbha; Jpn Jōzō): One of the two sons of King Wonderful Adornment who appear in the "King Wonderful Adornment" (twenty-seventh) chapter of the Lotus Sutra. According to this chapter, Pure Storehouse and his brother, Pure Eye, heard the Lotus Sutra from a Buddha named Cloud Thunder Sound Constellation King Flower Wisdom. They begged their mother, Pure Virtue, to go with them to hear him preach the sutra. She agreed, but urged them first to convince their father, King Wonderful Adornment, to go with them. The king was a devout believer in Brahmanism, so their mother suggested that they display supernatural powers to awaken him to the greatness of Buddhism. They followed her advice and demonstrated a number of feats before the king, such as walking in space and walking on water. Delighted, he asked to meet their teacher and went with his sons, his wife, his ministers and retinue, and many others to see the Buddha. Thereafter the king abdicated the throne in favor of his younger brother and renounced the secular world along with his wife, his sons, and subjects to practice the Buddha way. The "King Wonderful Adornment" chapter says that he is present at the ceremony of the Lotus Sutra on Eagle Peak as Bodhisattva Flower Virtue, and his queen Pure Virtue, as Bodhisattva Light Shining Adornment Marks, and his sons Pure Storehouse and Pure Eye, as Bodhisattva Medicine King and Bodhisattva Medicine Superior, respectively.

Pure Virtue [浄德] (Skt Vimaladattā; Jpn Jōtoku): Also known as Lady Pure Virtue or Queen Pure Virtue. The wife of King Wonderful Adornment, who appears in the "King Wonderful Adornment" (twenty-seventh) chapter of the Lotus Sutra. *See* Pure Storehouse.

purification of the six sense organs [六根清浄] (Jpn *rokkon-shōjō*): Also, purification of the six senses. Eradication of earthly desires caused by the workings of the six sense organs—eyes, ears, nose, tongue, body, and mind. The "Benefits of the Teacher of the Law" (nineteenth) chapter of the Lotus Sutra says that one can purify the functions of the six sense organs by carrying out the five practices of embracing, reading, reciting, teaching, and transcribing the Lotus Sutra.

Pūrna [富楼那] (Skt; Pali Punna; Jpn Furuna): One of Shakyamuni Buddha's ten major disciples. Noted as foremost in preaching the Law, he is said to have converted five hundred people of his tribe. His full name is Pūrna Maitrāyanīputra, but he is commonly referred to simply as Pūrna. According to the Sutra of the Collected Stories of the Buddha's Deeds in Past Lives and other sutras, he was born to a rich Brahman family near Kapilavastu, the kingdom of the Shakyas, but renounced secular life to seek enlightenment and entered the Snow Mountains where he practiced austerities. As a result, he achieved a degree of awakening. When he heard that Shakyamuni had attained Buddhahood, he became the Buddha's disciple and attained the state of arhat. According to another explanation, Pūrna was originally a merchant in the seaport town of Sunāparanta in western India and first heard of Shakyamuni's teachings when he joined a commercial voyage with some Shrāvastī merchants who were lay Buddhists. The divergence between these two accounts has led some scholars to conclude that there were actually two individuals named Pūrna. It has been established that there was a monk in Sunāparanta named Pūrna, but whether he was the Pūrna who was one of Shakyamuni's major disciples is unclear. In the Lotus Sutra, Pūrna belongs to the last of the three groups of voice-hearers who, in the "Parable of the Phantom City" (seventh) chapter of the sutra, understand the Buddha's teaching by hearing about their relationship with Shakyamuni countless *kalpas* in the past. The "Five Hundred Disciples" (eighth) chapter predicts that Pūrna will attain enlightenment as the Buddha Law Bright.

Pūrvavideha [弗婆提・勝身洲] (Skt; Jpn Hotsubadai or Shōshin-shū): One of the four continents of the world, according to the ancient Indian worldview. Pūrvavideha is located to the east of Mount Sumeru in the outermost of the eight concentric seas surrounding the mountain, which is at the center of the world. Within Pūrvavideha, there are two large states, Deha and Videha, and five hundred smaller states. Pūrvavideha is said to be in the shape of a semicircle. *See also* four continents.

Pushyamitra [弗沙弥多羅王] (n.d.) (Skt; Jpn Hosshamittara-ō): A king in India around the second century B.C.E. who became an enemy of Buddhism. A descendant of King Ashoka, he originally served as commander in chief of the armies of Brihadratha, the last king of the Maurya dynasty. He murdered Brihadratha in 183 B.C.E. and assumed the throne, founding the Shunga dynasty and ruling northern India from his capital at Pātaliputra. He disparaged Buddhism, killed many monks, and destroyed Kukkutārāma Monastery, a major center of Buddhism built by Ashoka.

pūtana [富単那] (Skt; Jpn *futanna*): A class of spirits described in Buddhist scriptures. *Pūtanas* can be either evil or good spirits. As evil spirits, they are said to inflict harm upon humans and animals. Depicted as ugly and foul-smelling, in China they are known as "stinking spirits," or as "stinking demons." In the "Universal Worthy" (twenty-eighth) chapter of the Lotus Sutra, Bodhisattva Universal Worthy addresses Shakyamuni Buddha: "World-Honored One, in the evil and corrupt age of the last five-hundred-year period, if there is someone who accepts and upholds this sutra, I will guard and protect him, free him from decline and harm, see that he attains peace and tranquillity, and make certain that no one can spy out and take advantage of his shortcomings. No devil, devil's son, devil's daughter, devil's minion, or one possessed by the devil, no *yaksha, rākshasa, kumbhānda, pishācha, kritya, pūtana, vetāda,* or other being that torments humans will be able to take advantage of him." A *pūtanā* (pronounced with a prolonged final "a"), the female form, is said to inflict a particular illness upon children. As good, or benevolent, spirits, however, *pūtanas* are said to work to protect Buddhism. They are regarded as retainers of Wide-Eyed, one of the four heavenly kings said to protect the Buddha's teachings.

Q

Questions and Answers on the Object of Devotion [本尊問答抄] (Jpn *Honzon-mondō-shō*): One of the ten major writings of Nichiren. *See* ten major writings.

Questions of Brahmā Excellent Thought Sutra [思益梵天所問経] (Chin *Ssu-i-fan-t'ien-so-wen-ching;* Jpn *Shiyaku-bonten-shomon-gyō*): Abbreviated as the Brahmā Excellent Thought Sutra. The Chinese version of the non-extant Sanskrit sutra translated by Kumārajīva in 402. This sutra is cited in many Mahayana treatises, including *The Treatise on the Great Perfection of Wisdom* attributed to Nāgārjuna (c. 150–250). There are two other Chinese translations, one by Dharmaraksha in 286 and the other by Bodhiruchi in the early sixth century, as well as a Tibetan translation. It tells of a Brahmā king named Excellent Thought who comes to the *sahā* world from an eastern realm of the universe and listens to Shakyamuni Buddha's preaching of the bodhisattva way. The sutra explains the doctrines of non-substantiality and non-duality.

Questions of King Milinda, The [ミリンダ王問経] (Jpn *Mirindaō-monkyō*): A record of the dialogues of the Buddhist monk Nāgasena and the Greco-Bactrian king Menander (Pali Milinda). See *Milinda-panha.*

R

rāga [貪・貪欲・愛] (Skt, Pali; Jpn *ton, ton'yoku,* or *ai*): Greed, desire, emotion, feeling, love, or passion. *Rāga,* indicating greed or avarice, is a component of the three poisons, the three sources of vice and suffering;

the other two are *dvesha* (anger) and *moha* (foolishness). *See also* three poisons.

Rāhula [羅睺羅] (Skt, Pali; Jpn Ragora): The son of Shakyamuni and Yashodharā. One of Shakyamuni's ten major disciples, respected as foremost in inconspicuous practice. He entered the Buddhist Order in his youth upon seeing Shakyamuni Buddha when the latter returned home to Kapilavastu for the first time after attaining enlightenment. Thereafter Rāhula devoted himself to the inconspicuous practice of observing the precepts and reciting and preaching the Buddha's teachings under the guidance of Shāriputra and Maudgalyāyana. He did not pride himself on being the Buddha's son, and the other monks revered him for his earnestness in Buddhist practice. In the Lotus Sutra, Rāhula belongs to the third of the three groups of voice-hearers who understand the Buddha's teaching when they hear him reveal, in the "Parable of the Phantom City" (seventh) chapter, their relationship with him in a remote time described as major world system dust particle *kalpas* in the past. The "Prophecies" (ninth) chapter states that he will in the future become a Buddha named Stepping on Seven Treasure Flowers.

Rāhulabhadra [羅睺羅跋陀羅・羅睺羅] (n.d.) (Skt; Jpn Ragorabaddara or Ragora): Also known as Rāhulatā. A scholar of the Mādhyamika school in India during the third century. A native of Kapilavastu, he studied under Āryadeva and awakened to the truth of non-substantiality. He is said to have converted many monks and laypersons to Mahayana Buddhism. He also wrote a commentary on Nāgārjuna's *Madhyamaka-kārikā,* or *Verses on the Middle Way.* He is regarded as the fifteenth of Shakyamuni Buddha's twenty-three, or the sixteenth of his twenty-four, successors and is said to have transferred the Buddha's teachings to Samghanandi.

Rāhulatā [羅睺羅跋陀羅・羅睺羅] (Skt; Jpn Ragorabaddara or Ragora): Also known as Rāhulabhadra. *See* Rāhulabhadra.

rainy-season retreat [安居] (Jpn *ango*): *See* three-month retreat.

Raiyu [頼瑜] (1226–1304): A priest who developed the doctrinal basis of the New Doctrine (Shingi) branch of the True Word (Shingon) school in Japan, and the restorer of Daidembō-in temple, also known as Negoro-ji temple. After becoming a priest of Daidembō-in at Mount Kōya, Raiyu engaged in the doctrinal study of Esoteric Buddhism. Beginning around 1249, he visited Tōdai-ji, Kōfuku-ji, Ninna-ji, and other temples to further his studies not only in Esoteric Buddhism but also in other doctrines. In 1266 he became chief instructor of Daidembō-in and later founded a school of esoteric practice named the Chūshō-in school after his lodging temple. In 1288 Raiyu moved Daidembō-in from Mount Kōya to Mount Negoro. Kakuban (1095–1143), the founder of Daidembō-in at Mount Kōya, had once resided at Mount Negoro in his later years. The moving of Daidembō-in to Mount Negoro effectively put an end to a 150-year dispute between that temple and Kongōbu-ji on Mount Kōya.

Rājagriha [王舍城] (Skt; Pali Rājagaha; Jpn Ōsha-jō): The capital of the kingdom of Magadha in ancient India. One of the largest cities in India in Shakyamuni's time, it was a center of culture and philosophical studies. King Bimbisāra and his son Ajātashatru lived in this capital, and Shakyamuni often preached there. Rājagriha and its environs were also the location of many important Buddhist sites such as Eagle Peak, Bamboo Grove Monastery, and the Cave of the Seven Leaves, where the First Buddhist Council was held. Rājagriha was located at the site of present-day Rajgir in the Indian state of Bihar. Rājagriha means "royal palace" (*rāja* meaning king, and *griha,* house).

rākshasa [羅刹] (Skt; Jpn *rasetsu*): A type of demon. In Vedic literature, *rākshasas* are demons that attempt to kill unborn children and infants. Later incorporated into Buddhism, some sutras describe them as guardian deities of Buddhism, and others, as demons. A female *rākshasa* is a *rākshasī.* In the "Dhāranī" (twenty-sixth) chapter of the Lotus Sutra, the ten *rākshasīs* known as the ten demon daughters are depicted as deities who, together with the Mother of Demon Children, protect those who uphold the sutra. Later Buddhist commentaries depict *rākshasas* as beings that eat human flesh; male demons are described as ugly and terrifying, and female demons, as beautiful. *See also* demon.

Rankei Dōryū [蘭渓道隆] (Jpn; Chin Lan-ch'i Tao-lung): A Chinese priest of the Rinzai school of Zen Buddhism who went to Japan in 1246 and was naturalized. *See* Dōryū.

Rare Form [名相如来] (Skt Shashiketu; Jpn Myōsō-nyorai): The name that Subhūti will bear when he attains Buddhahood, according to Shakyamuni's prediction in the "Bestowal of Prophecy" (sixth) chapter of the Lotus Sutra. Subhūti is one of Shakyamuni's ten major disciples. The chapter states that in future existences Subhūti will constantly carry out Buddhist practice and fulfill the bodhisattva way, and in his final incarnation he will become a Buddha named Rare Form. Shashiketu, the Sanskrit name of this Buddha, has various meanings, such as moonlight, marks of the moon, and moon-decorated banner. One of the Sanskrit manuscripts of the Lotus Sutra refers to him as Yashasketu, which means beautiful light or excellent form.

ratna [宝] (Skt; Jpn *hō* or *takara*): Jewel, gem, treasure, or anything precious. *Ratna* is a component of a number of Sanskrit Buddhist terms and names. For example, Ratnaketu, or Jewel Sign, is the name that two thousand voice-hearers will bear when they become Buddhas, according to the "Prophecies" (ninth) chapter of the Lotus Sutra. Prabhūtaratna is the name of the Buddha Many Treasures, who appears in the "Treasure Tower" (eleventh) chapter of the Lotus Sutra to lend credence to the sutra, which Shakyamuni Buddha is preaching. The word *prabhūta* means abundant, numerous, etc. *Sapta-ratna* is the term for the seven kinds of treasures or gems often mentioned in the Buddhist scriptures. *Tri-ratna* is the three treasures—the Buddha, the Law (his teachings), and the Buddhist Order (community of believers).

Ratnamati [勒那摩提] (n.d.) (Skt; Jpn Rokunamadai): A monk of central India and a translator of Buddhist scriptures. He is said to have memorized a great many verses of the sutras. In 508 he went to Lo-yang in China and, with Bodhiruchi, translated *The Treatise on the Ten Stages Sutra* into Chinese. The Chinese translations of *The Treatise on the Lotus Sutra* and *The Treatise on the Treasure Vehicle of Buddhahood* are also accredited to him.

realization of the non-birth and non-extinction of all phenomena [無生法忍] (Jpn *mushō-bōnin*): Also, perception of the truth of the birthlessness of all phenomena. The stage at which one realizes the truth that nothing is born and nothing dies. At this stage, one attains peace and contentment by perceiving the non-birth and non-extinction of the phenomenal world.

Realization of Virtue [覚徳比丘] (Jpn Kakutoku-biku): A monk described in the "Diamond-like Body" (second) chapter of the Mahāparinirvāna Sutra, the forty-volume Chinese version of the Nirvana Sutra translated by Dharmaraksha in 421. His Sanskrit name is unknown, for only fragments of the Sanskrit text are extant. According to the sutra, a considerable time after the death of the Buddha Joy Increasing, the correct teaching of Buddhism was about to perish. Realization of Virtue strove to protect the teaching and was attacked by many evil monks and their followers. The king Possessor of Virtue defended him, enabling Realization of Virtue to escape, but the king died of the wounds he sustained. According to the sutra, because of their devotion to Buddhism, the king Possessor of Virtue was reborn as Shakyamuni Buddha and the monk Realization of Virtue as Kāshyapa Buddha. *See also* Possessor of Virtue.

Realm of Boundless Consciousness [識無辺処] (Skt Vijnānānantyāyatana; Jpn Shikimuhen-jo): Also, Vijnānānantya Realm, or Heaven of Boundless Consciousness. The second lowest of the four realms of the world of formlessness. Meditation that leads to rebirth in this heaven is called meditation on the Realm of Boundless Consciousness. The life span of beings in this realm is said to be forty thousand *kalpas*. *See also* world of formlessness.

Realm of Boundless Empty Space [空無辺処] (Skt Ākāshānantyāyatana; Jpn Kūmuhen-jo): Also, Ākāshānantya Realm, or Heaven of Boundless Empty Space. The first and the lowest of the four realms of the world of formlessness. Meditation leading to rebirth in this heaven is termed meditation on the Realm of Boundless Empty Space. In this meditation, one becomes free from all thought of matter, meditating on the limitless space where no matter exists. The life span of beings in the Realm of Boundless Empty Space is said to be twenty thousand *kalpas*. *See also* world of formlessness.

Realm of Neither Thought Nor No Thought [非想非非想処] (Skt Naivasamjnānāsamjnāyatana; Jpn Hisō-hihisō-sho): Also, Naivasamjnānāsamjnā Realm, Heaven of Neither Thought Nor No Thought, or Heaven Where There Is Neither Thought Nor No Thought. This realm, known as the Summit of Being Heaven, is the highest heaven in the world of formlessness. Meditation leading to rebirth in this realm is called meditation on the Realm of Neither Thought Nor No Thought. The life span of beings in the Realm of Neither Thought Nor No Thought is said to be eighty thousand *kalpas*. *See also* world of formlessness.

Realm of Nothingness [無所有処] (Skt Ākimchanyāyatana; Jpn Mushou-sho): Also, Ākimchanya Realm, Heaven of Nothingness, or the realm where nothing exists. The second highest of the four realms of the world of formlessness. Meditation that leads to rebirth in this realm is called meditation on the Realm of Nothingness. The life span of beings in the Realm of Nothingness is sixty thousand *kalpas*. *See also* world of formlessness.

Recorded Lectures, The [御講聞書] (Jpn *Okō-kikigaki*): Also known as *Nikō's Records*. A compilation of lectures on the Lotus Sutra that Nichiren gave for his disciples at Minobu in Kai Province, Japan, between 1278 and 1280. Nikō, one of the six senior priests designated by Nichiren, recorded these lectures and compiled them as *The Recorded Lectures*.

Record of a Pilgrimage to China in Search of the Law, The [入唐求法巡礼行記] (Jpn *Nittō-guhō-junrei-kō-ki*): An account by Jikaku, the third patriarch of the Japanese Tendai school, of the nine years he spent in China from 838 to 847. It is considered an especially valuable reference on Buddhism and on China during the T'ang dynasty. It describes the state of Buddhism at that time, as well as the history, geography, social conditions, and customs of China. It also records Jikaku's encounter at the capital, Ch'ang-an, with a nationwide drive to destroy Buddhism led by Emperor Wu-tsung of the T'ang dynasty in 845. This is known as the third of the four imperial persecutions of Buddhism in China.

Record of Southern Countries, The [南海寄帰内法伝] (Chin *Nan-hai-chi-kuei-nei-fa-chuan;* Jpn *Nankai-kiki-naihō-den*): A work by the Chinese priest I-ching recording his travels to India and Southeast Asia from 671 to 695. I-ching traveled by sea to India, where he studied Hinayana and Mahayana teachings at Nālandā Monastery and other Buddhist centers. En route back to China, he stayed in Shrīvijaya, a country on the island that is now Sumatra, Indonesia. There, in 691, he set down this record and had Ta-chin, a Chinese priest he met in Shrīvijaya, take it to Ch'ang-an in China. The work describes the daily lives of monks and nuns, their observance of the precepts and rules of monastic discipline, and is considered a valuable reference for the study of India and Southeast Asia of that period. An English translation of this work by the Japanese scholar Junjirō Takakusu was published in 1896 under the title *A Record of the Buddhist Religion as Practiced in India and [the] Malay Archipelago (A.D. 671–695) by Itsing.*

Record of the Buddhistic Kingdoms, The [仏国記] (Jpn *Bukkoku-ki*): A record of Fa-hsien's travels in India and other countries in the early fifth century. See *Travels of Fa-hsien, The.*

Record of the Lineage of the Buddha and the Patriarchs, The [仏祖統紀] (Chin *Fo-tsu-t'ung-chi;* Jpn *Busso-tōki*): A work compiled in 1269 by the Chinese priest Chih-p'an, tracing the history of Buddhism from the viewpoint of the T'ien-t'ai school. It includes biographies of the eminent priests of India and China and a history of the transmission of the T'ien-t'ai doctrine. The first part concerns the life of Shakyamuni Buddha and the compilation of his teachings. The next part contains the biographies of the Buddha's twenty-four successors in India, beginning with Mahākāshyapa and ending with Āryasimha. Chih-p'an then traces the lineage of the T'ien-t'ai school beginning with its first nine patriarchs: Nāgārjuna, Hui-wen, Nan-yüeh, T'ien-t'ai, Chang-an, Chih-wei, Hui-wei, Hsüan-lang, and Miao-lo. Priests of the Pure Land, Zen (Chin Ch'an), Flower Garland (Hua-yen), Dharma Characteristics (Fa-hsiang), and other schools are represented as well.

Record of the Orally Transmitted Teachings, The [御義口伝] (Jpn *Ongi-kuden*): Nichiren's oral teachings on the Lotus Sutra, recorded and compiled by his disciple and successor Nikkō. At Minobu in Kai Province, Japan, Nichiren gave a series of lectures for his disciples on important sentences and phrases from the Lotus Sutra. This work, dated the first month of 1278, consists of two parts and reveals the essential principles of Nichiren's teachings. When explaining the meaning of a passage of the sutra, he cited as references the major works of T'ien-t'ai and

Miao-lo; he then interpreted the passage to clarify essential tenets of his teaching. *The Record of the Orally Transmitted Teachings* begins with a lecture on the meaning of Nam-myoho-renge-kyo and then proceeds through each of the twenty-eight chapters of the Lotus Sutra as well as the Immeasurable Meanings Sutra and the Universal Worthy Sutra. It concludes with two separate lectures: "The Essential Passage in Each of the Twenty-eight Chapters of the Lotus Sutra" and "All the Twenty-eight Chapters of the Lotus Sutra Are Nam-myoho-renge-kyo."

Record of the Western Regions, The [西域記] (Jpn *Saiiki-ki*): See *Record of the Western Regions of the Great T'ang Dynasty, The.*

Record of the Western Regions of the Great T'ang Dynasty, The [大唐西域記] (Chin *Ta-t'ang-hsi-yü-chi;* Jpn *Daitō-saiiki-ki*): Abbreviated as *The Record of the Western Regions.* A twelve-volume account by the Chinese priest Hsüan-tsang, recording his travels through Central Asia and India between 629 and 645 in search of Buddhist scriptures. Based on firsthand observation of the places he visited and reports he collected about those he did not, Hsüan-tsang's work describes in detail the topography, culture, language, folklore, history, situation of Buddhism, and politics of 138 states. The first volume includes his preface and covers thirty-four countries in Central Asia. The first half of the second volume describes the geography, language, manners, and customs of India; the latter half of the second volume through the first half of the fourth volume deal with northern India; and the latter half of the fourth volume through the first half of the tenth volume cover central India. Since Hsüan-tsang's primary interest was Buddhism, volumes eight and nine are devoted to Magadha, where Buddhism was first established. The latter half of the tenth volume gives an account of the eastern part of India, and the eleventh volume, of the western part. The twelfth volume describes the Central Asian countries through which Hsüan-tsang passed on his return journey. *The Record of the Western Regions* is one of the most comprehensive records of travel to India ever written in the Orient, and it is still valued as a major reference for Central Asian and Indian studies.

Record of Wonders in the Book of Chou, The [周書異記] (Chin *Chou-shu-i-chi;* Jpn *Shūsho-iki*): A Chinese work often cited for the information it contains pertaining to Buddhist events, such as the dates of Shakyamuni's birth and death. The entire work is no longer extant, but quotations from it are found in a number of Buddhist writings. These place Shakyamuni Buddha's birth in 1029 B.C.E., the twenty-fourth year of the reign of King Chao of China's Chou dynasty, and his death in 949 B.C.E., the fifty-second year of the reign of King Mu of the same dynasty.

This account was traditionally adopted in China and Japan. It is generally agreed that this work was written before the early sixth century C.E.

reducing the body to ashes and annihilating consciousness [灰身滅智] (Jpn *keshin-metchi*): Also, "annihilating consciousness and reducing the body to ashes." A reference to the Hinayana doctrine asserting that one can attain nirvana only upon extinguishing one's body and mind. Hinayanists defined the eradication of all earthly desires, which requires the extinction of both the mind and the body, as "nirvana of no remainder" (complete nirvana). This contrasts with "nirvana of remainder" (incomplete nirvana), in which the body still exists. Body and mind were regarded as the sources of earthly desires, illusions, and sufferings, and the extinction of body and mind as release from the sufferings of the endless cycle of birth and death. Mahayanists derided this Hinayana teaching as "reducing the body to ashes and annihilating consciousness." They asserted that, in pursuit of this concept of nirvana, Hinayana practitioners became occupied with eradicating their body and mind and abandoned the salvation of others.

Refutation of Erroneous Doctrines, A [摧邪輪] (Jpn *Sai-jarin*): A work written in 1212 by Myōe, a priest of the Flower Garland (Kegon) school in Japan, in response to Hōnen's work *The Nembutsu Chosen above All,* which sets forth the doctrine that the Nembutsu, or the invoking of the name of Amida Buddha, alone should be practiced. Myōe attacked Hōnen's treatise mainly for denying the necessity of arousing the aspiration for enlightenment and for comparing adherents of all teachings other than the Pure Land teachings to a band of robbers who prevent travelers from completing their journey, that is, who prevent practitioners of the Pure Land teachings from reaching the Pure Land.

Refutation of "The Nembutsu Chosen above All," A [弾選択] (Jpn *Dan-senchaku*): A work written in 1225 by Jōshō, a priest of the Japanese Tendai school. It attacks Hōnen's *Nembutsu Chosen above All,* which sets forth the doctrine of the exclusive practice of Nembutsu, or calling on the name of Amida Buddha. At Enryaku-ji temple, Jōshō was appointed an interpreter of the doctrines, whose function it was to elucidate and expand on subjects of discussion and answer questions from the other priests. One view assigns credit for *A Refutation of "The Nembutsu Chosen above All"* to Ryūshin, also a Tendai priest, though others hold this to be a misunderstanding arising from the fact that Ryūshin wrote a postscript to the work. Still another view holds that there were two works titled *A Refutation of "The Nembutsu Chosen above All,"* one by Jōshō and one by Ryūshin. In any event, Ryūkan, a disciple of Hōnen, challenged the content of this work in his *Clarification of "The Nembutsu Chosen above All."*

Regulations for Students of the Mountain School, The [山家学生式] (Jpn *Sange-gakushō-shiki*): Abbreviated as *The Regulations for Students.* A three-part work by Dengyō (767–822), the founder of the Japanese Tendai school, specifying regulations for students appointed by the imperial court (two each year) to study the Tendai teachings at the temple on Mount Hiei, and setting forth the Mahayana precepts into which the students were to be initiated upon their ordination as priests. The first part contains six articles and was presented independently to Emperor Saga on the thirteenth day of the fifth month of 818. It stipulates that all annually appointed students will be initiated into the ten good precepts before becoming novices; that after their ordination they shall remain on Mount Hiei for twelve years and study both the type of meditation called concentration and insight and the Vairochana disciplines, based chiefly on the Mahāvairochana Sutra; and that after completing their twelve-year practice they shall be appointed to responsible positions according to their ability. The second part contains eight articles and was presented to Emperor Saga on the twenty-seventh day of the eighth month of the same year. It gives a more concrete and detailed explanation of the regulations. The third part comprises four articles and was presented to Emperor Saga on the fifteenth day of the third month of 819. It classifies the precepts into those of Hinayana and those of Mahayana, and the methods of ordination into the Hinayana way and the Mahayana way. It moreover asserts that the annually appointed students of the Tendai school are required to receive the precepts of Mahayana bodhisattvas, and that the ceremony of receiving the precepts should be performed under Mahayana regulations. In *The Regulations for Students,* Dengyō expressed his wish that the ordination ceremony for conferring the Mahayana precepts be performed at the temple on Mount Hiei independently of the six schools of Nara. At that time the six Nara schools alone were privileged to perform Buddhist ordination ceremonies, which they conducted according to the Hinayana regulations. Dengyō's request provoked intense opposition from the Nara priests. He rebutted their arguments in *A Clarification of the Precepts,* which he wrote in 820. *See also* Mahayana ordination platform.

Reiyūkai [霊友会]: Literally, "Society of Friends of the Spirits." A Buddhist lay organization in Japan founded in 1925 by Kakutarō Kubo (1892–1944), an employee of the Imperial Household Ministry, his elder brother Yasukichi Kotani (1885–1929), and Kotani's wife, Kimi

(1901–1971). The Reiyūkai stresses ancestor veneration and Buddhist tradition centering on the Lotus Sutra. The group has no clergy and no formal affiliation with any Buddhist school but relies on lay teachers who lead small group meetings. Kubo devised an ancestral ritual to be performed twice daily by reciting a selection of the Lotus Sutra and the repeated chanting of its name. During the years before and after the Second World War, several groups split off from the Reiyūkai, of which the Risshō Kōseikai, founded in 1938, became the most prominent.

relative myō [相待妙] (Jpn *sōdai-myō*): One of the two perspectives to show the profundity of the Lotus Sutra. See *myō*.

removing suffering and giving joy [抜苦与楽] (Jpn *bakku-yoraku*): The practice of compassion in Buddhism. Compassion is interpreted as encompassing the two merciful deeds: saving other people from their sufferings and giving them peace and delight. From its inception Buddhism encourages its followers to rescue people from suffering and give them peace and joy.

renge [蓮華] (Jpn; Chin *lien-hua*): Lotus or lotus flower. Also called the Oriental lotus, Indian lotus, East Indian lotus or sacred lotus. An aquatic plant with flowers of white, pink, and other colors, often mentioned in Indian Buddhist scriptures and their Chinese translations. For example, in the Compassionate White Lotus Flower Sutra (Skt *Karunā-pundarīka-sūtra;* Jpn *Hike-kyō*), Shakyamuni Buddha is compared to the white lotus flower *(pundarīka),* described in the sutra as a symbol of great compassion. The white lotus flower, traditionally the most highly regarded variety, also appears in the Sanskrit title of the Lotus Sutra, *Saddharma-pundarīka-sūtra.* In his Chinese translation of that sutra, Kumārajīva rendered the Sanskrit title as the Lotus Sutra of the Wonderful Law, or *Myoho-renge-kyo* in Japanese. Here *pundarīka* is translated as lotus, or *renge. Renge* simply means lotus flower, without reference to the color or variety. The meaning of *renge* is of particular importance in Buddhist traditions deriving from the Lotus Sutra, such as those of T'ien-t'ai in China and Nichiren in Japan. Both interpret *renge* in various ways, examples of which follow:

(1) In *The Profound Meaning of the Lotus Sutra,* T'ien-t'ai (538–597) interprets the meaning of *renge* of *Myoho-renge-kyo* in two ways: as the figurative lotus and as the lotus that is the entity of the Law. He states, "Now the name *renge* is not intended as a symbol for anything. It is the teaching expounded in the Lotus Sutra. The teaching expounded in the Lotus Sutra is pure and undefiled and explains the subtleties of cause and effect. Therefore, it is called *renge,* or lotus. This name designates the true entity that the meditation based on the Lotus Sutra reveals and is

not a metaphor or figurative term." He then explains, "Because [the lotus that is] the essence of the Lotus Sutra is difficult to understand, the metaphor of the lotus plant is introduced." Here T'ien-t'ai refers to the three groups of voice-hearers portrayed in the Lotus Sutra and designated by their respective capacities: those of superior capacity understand the principle of the lotus directly, while those of intermediate and inferior capacities understand it only through its metaphor, the figurative lotus. T'ien-t'ai regards the parables of the Lotus Sutra as metaphors for the lotus that is the entity of the Law.

(2) In the same work, T'ien-t'ai refers to the two meanings of the lotus. The first regards the fact that the lotus grows and blossoms from muddy water. This, he says, symbolizes voice-hearers emerging from the muddy water of the lesser teachings and realizing, through the Lotus Sutra, that they are entities of the wonderful Law. Second, the lotus blooming symbolizes the Buddha revealing his pure and wonderful Dharma body in order to cause people to arouse faith. Thus, he is showing them the lotus that opens through a mystic cause.

(3) In *The Profound Meaning of the Lotus Sutra,* the figurative lotus is explained with three metaphors: the lotus blossom enfolding the fruit, the lotus blossom opening to reveal the fruit inside, and the lotus blossom falling and the fruit ripening. Each can be interpreted in two ways: First, from the perspective of the theoretical teaching (first half) of the Lotus Sutra, the three metaphors respectively mean that one cannot see the fruit of the true teaching because it is covered by the blossom of the provisional teachings; that the blossom opens to reveal the fruit of the true teaching; and that the blossom of the three vehicles is replaced by the fruit of the one Buddha vehicle. Second, from the perspective of the essential teaching (latter half) of the sutra, the three metaphors mean that the blossom of the theoretical teaching contains the fruit of the essential teaching; that the blossom of the theoretical teaching opens to reveal the fruit of the essential teaching; and that the blossom of the theoretical teaching is replaced by the fruit of the essential teaching.

(4) Nichiren (1222–1282) refers to the lotus plant as symbolizing the simultaneous nature of cause and effect. In a letter to the lay nun Ueno, he states: "Thus there are all manner of plants, but the lotus is the only one that bears flowers and fruit simultaneously. The benefit of all the other sutras is uncertain, because they teach that one must first make good causes and only then can one become a Buddha at some later time. With regard to the Lotus Sutra, when one's hand takes it up, that hand immediately attains Buddhahood, and when one's mouth chants it, that mouth is itself a Buddha, as, for example, the moon is reflected in the

water the moment it appears from behind the eastern mountains, or as a sound and its echo arise simultaneously" (1099).

(5) In *The Entity of the Mystic Law,* Nichiren states: "The Buddha who is the entity of Myoho-renge-kyo, of the 'Life Span' chapter of the essential teaching, who is both inhabiting subject and inhabited realm, life and environment, body and mind, entity and function, the Buddha eternally endowed with the three bodies—he is to be found in the disciples and lay believers of Nichiren. Such persons embody the true entity of Myoho-renge-kyo" (420).

Repaying Debts of Gratitude Sutra [報恩経] (Chin *Pao-en-ching;* Jpn *Hō'on-kyō*): A sutra that defines the repaying of moral obligations from the standpoint of Mahayana Buddhism. Brahmans criticized Shakyamuni Buddha as unfilial for leaving his parents and entering a religious life. The Repaying Debts of Gratitude Sutra refutes this criticism with the argument that by renouncing the secular world and awakening to the truth that leads all people to Buddhahood one can truly repay all one's obligations to others. The Chinese translation is said to date from the Later Han dynasty (25–220). The translator of this sutra is unknown, however, and the Sanskrit manuscript is not extant.

repentance [懺悔] (Skt *kshama* or *deshanā;* Jpn *sange*): Also, apology. An act of acknowledging one's faults, shortcomings, or past misdeeds, and seeking to correct or make amends for them. In Indian monasteries, a gathering called *uposhadha* was held every half month, at which members of the Buddhist Order who had violated the precepts apologized before the Buddha or before the other monks with the aim of purifying their minds. In addition, an annual ceremony called *pravārana* was performed at the end of the rainy-season retreat (three-month retreat). At the ceremony held on the last day of the retreat, monks publicly repented the errors they had committed during that three-month period. In the Buddhist community, various rules concerning the practice and ceremony of repentance were set forth as the *vinaya,* or rules of monastic discipline. With the rise of Mahayana, however, less emphasis was placed on monastic rules, and the meaning of repentance changed accordingly. The Universal Worthy Sutra, regarded as the epilogue to the Lotus Sutra, states, "If one wishes to carry out repentance, sit upright and ponder the true aspect. Then the host of sins, like frost or dew, can be wiped out by the sun of wisdom." In short, since one's wrong acts ultimately stem from ignorance of the true nature of life, to awaken to that nature, or the true aspect of all phenomena, and bring forth one's inherent Buddha wisdom, thereby purifying one's life, is the ultimate act of repentance.

replacement of the three vehicles with the one vehicle [開三顕一] (Jpn *kaisan-ken'ichi*): Also, "opening the three vehicles and revealing the one vehicle." A reference to Shakyamuni's statement in the Lotus Sutra that the three vehicles are not ends in themselves—though other, provisional, sutras teach that they are—but expedient means by which he leads people to the one vehicle of Buddhahood. The three vehicles are the teachings expounded for voice-hearers, cause-awakened ones, and bodhisattvas, respectively. The one vehicle of Buddhahood means the teaching that enables all people to attain Buddhahood and corresponds to the Lotus Sutra. Shakyamuni Buddha first preached the various provisional teachings, or the three vehicle teachings, as an expedient means to help people develop the capacity to understand and receive the one vehicle teaching. In the Lotus Sutra, he declares that the earlier teachings have been set forth as expedient means to prepare people for the teaching of the sutra, which is the supreme vehicle of Buddhahood, the goal of the Buddhist practice. This concept is expressed as the replacement of the three vehicles with the one vehicle. T'ien-t'ai (538–597) explains the meaning of replacing the three vehicles with the one vehicle in *The Profound Meaning of the Lotus Sutra,* where he defines it as the principal doctrine of the theoretical teaching (first half) of the Lotus Sutra. T'ien-t'ai further divided the principle into two—the concise replacement of the three vehicles with the one vehicle and the expanded replacement of the three vehicles with the one vehicle. The concise replacement refers to the first part of the "Expedient Means" (second) chapter (through the end of the fifth verse section of that chapter, which concludes with Shāriputra's words, "When we hear this Law / we will be filled with great joy"). This part centers on "the true aspect of all phenomena," that is, the ten factors of life. The expanded replacement refers to Shakyamuni's further elaboration on his meaning from a variety of angles, using parables and other means of explanation. This elaboration lasts from the latter half of the "Expedient Means" chapter, which begins with Shakyamuni's words to Shāriputra, "Three times you have stated your earnest request," through the end of the "Prophecies" (ninth) chapter.

"Responding with Joy" chapter [随喜品] (Jpn *Zuiki-hon*): The eighteenth chapter of the Lotus Sutra. *See* "Benefits of Responding with Joy" chapter.

restatement of Great Universal Wisdom Excellence Buddha's teaching [大通覆講] (Jpn *Daitsū-fukkō*): *See* Great Universal Wisdom Excellence.

Revata [離婆多] (Skt, Pali; Jpn Ribata): (1) A monk in India who lived about one hundred years after Shakyamuni's death. At that time, the monks of the Vriji tribe in Vaishālī were advocating a freer interpretation of the precepts, a move that disturbed more conservative monks. The council headed by Yasa, in which Revata was a leading figure, rejected the Vriji monks' proposal as ten unlawful revisions, and controversy over this issue eventually led to the first schism in the Buddhist Order. The monks who were dissatisfied with this decision formed the Mahāsāmghika school. *See also* five teachings of Mahādeva; ten unlawful revisions.

(2) Also known as Revata-khadiravaniya. Shāriputra's younger brother and a disciple of Shakyamuni Buddha. He was known as having few desires and being diligent in the practice of meditation.

Revelation of the Profound Secrets Sutra [解深密経] (Skt *Samdhinirmochana-sūtra;* Chin *Chieh-shen-mi-ching;* Jpn *Gejimmitsu-kyō*): Abbreviated as the Profound Secrets Sutra. A five-volume sutra translated into Chinese by Hsüan-tsang in 647. This sutra is the principal text of the Dharma Characteristics (Chin Fa-hsiang; Jpn Hossō) school. It is written in question-and-answer format and deals with such topics as the nature of the dharmas (phenomena), Consciousness-Only doctrine, and the *ālaya*-consciousness. There are three Chinese translations in addition to the one by Hsüan-tsang: the five-volume version translated by Bodhiruchi in the early sixth century, and two abridged versions, the two-volume translation by Gunabhadra in the mid-fifth century and the one-volume translation by Paramārtha in the latter part of the sixth century.

revelation section [正宗分] (Jpn *shōshū-bun*): Also, revelation. One of the three sections or divisions of a sutra, the other two being preparation and transmission, into which the text of the sutra is divided for the purpose of interpreting its teachings. The revelation section is the main part of a sutra in which the core subject matter is discussed. *See also* three divisions of a sutra.

reverse relationship [逆縁] (Jpn *gyaku-en*): Another term for poison-drum relationship. Also translated as reverse relation, relationship of rejection, or connection through rejection. A bond formed with the correct teaching by opposing or slandering it. When the correct teaching is preached to the people, some may reject and slander it and fall into hell as a consequence. Because of the relationship formed with the correct teaching in the process, however, they will eventually attain Buddhahood. That is, the act of rejecting and slandering the correct teaching is a cause to establish a connection with it and receive the seeds of Buddhahood. Miao-lo's (711–782) work *The Annotations on "The Words and Phrases of the Lotus Sutra"* says: "Even if one reviles the correct teaching and falls into the evil paths, one can create causes for the eventual attainment of benefit. It is like the case of a person who falls to the ground, but who then pushes himself up from the ground and rises to his feet again. Thus, even though one may slander the correct teaching, one will eventually be saved from the evil paths." The reverse relationship contrasts with a relationship of acceptance (Jpn *jun-en*), which is formed by those who put their faith in the correct teaching on hearing about it, without slandering or opposing it. *See also* poison-drum relationship.

Reverend Nichiu's Teachings on the Formalities [有師化儀抄] (Jpn *Ushi-kegi-shō*): Also known as *On the Formalities*. A Japanese work setting forth the observances and rituals to be performed by priests of the Fuji school of Nichiren's teachings as systematized by Nichiu (1409–1482), the ninth chief priest of Taiseki-ji, the head temple of the school. Nichiu gave detailed guidance and instruction on this subject to priests of the school who had come to Taiseki-ji from throughout Japan to further their studies. His words were recorded by his disciple Nanjō Nichijū and compiled after his death as *Reverend Nichiu's Teachings on the Formalities*. This work consists of 121 articles concerning the daily life of priests, rituals, way of preaching, how to observe *gongyō* (the practice of reciting part of the Lotus Sutra and chanting of the daimoku, or Nam-myoho-renge-kyo), treatment of the Gohonzon (the object of devotion in Nichiren's teaching), etc. It also clarifies the differences between Shakyamuni's and Nichiren's Buddhism, Nichiren's identity as the eternal Buddha, and other doctrinal points.

reward body [報身] (Skt *sambhoga-kāya;* Jpn *hōshin* or *hōjin*): One of the three Buddha bodies, the other two being the Dharma body and the manifested body. The reward body means a body obtained as a reward of completing bodhisattva practices. As the concept of three bodies developed, questions arose as to which Buddha possessed which body. Amida Buddha and Medicine Master Buddha were categorized as Buddhas of the reward body. Amida, for example, was believed to have been the bodhisattva Dharma Treasury in a past existence, but was reborn as a Buddha in reward for his Buddhist practice. In contrast with this early stage of the doctrine of the three bodies, it was later held that a single Buddha possesses all three bodies; in this sense, the three bodies can be regarded as three properties inherent in a Buddha, the reward body representing the property of wisdom. The Sanskrit word *sambhoga-kāya* literally means body of enjoyment or bliss body. When *sambhoga-kāya* was translated into Chinese, it was rendered as "reward body." *See also* three bodies.

Rida [利吒]: Also known as Rita. In an account of a previous lifetime of Aniruddha, one of Shakyamuni's ten major disciples, Aniruddha's elder brother. In that story, which appears in the Storehouse of Various Treasures Sutra and elsewhere, Aniruddha is called Arida, and his elder brother, Rida. Rida and Arida are Japanese renderings of their names; their Sanskrit names are unknown. *See* Arida.

Rinda [輪陀] (Jpn): A king who appears in a story of a previous lifetime of Ashvaghosha, related in Nāgārjuna's *Commentary on the Mahayana Treatise.* In ancient times, there lived a king named Rinda (Sanskrit unknown) who ruled a kingdom where there were a thousand white swans, each with a beautiful voice. When he heard the swans sing, he acquired dignity and strength. These swans, however, sang only when they saw white horses. One day, the white horses disappeared. The king searched for them, but to no avail. He declared that, if non-Buddhists could make the swans sing, he would revere their teachings only and destroy Buddhism; if, however, a Buddhist could make the swans sing, he would revere Buddhism only and destroy the non-Buddhist teachings. At that time, a bodhisattva named Ashvaghosha (meaning "horse neigh") employed supernatural powers to induce the appearance of a thousand white horses, and the thousand swans sang. As a result, this bodhisattva enabled the correct teaching to prosper, securing its ceaseless flow.

Nichiren (1222–1282) mentions the story of King Rinda in writings such as *King Rinda* and *White Horses and White Swans.* According to his account, the roles of the white horses and white swans are reversed. Rinda is described as having acquired and maintained his dignity and strength by listening to the neighing of white horses. These white horses neighed only when they saw white swans. One day, all the swans suddenly disappeared from the kingdom; consequently, the white horses stopped neighing. Feeling his powers begin to wane, King Rinda issued a mandate, and in response, all the non-Buddhist teachers gathered and offered prayers but to no effect. Then Bodhisattva Ashvaghosha prayed to all the Buddhas in the ten directions. The swans immediately reappeared, the white horses began to neigh again, and the king regained his powers.

Rinzai school [臨済宗] (Jpn Rinzai-shū): One of the major Zen schools in Japan. It was founded by Eisai, who introduced the Huang-lung (Jpn Ōryū) branch of the Lin-chi (Rinzai) school to Japan from China. In China, the Lin-chi school was founded by I-hsüan (d. 867) who lived at Lin-chi-yüan temple. Eisai brought the teachings of the Lin-chi school to Japan in 1191, and in 1202 founded Kennin-ji temple, the first Zen temple in Kyoto. Other branches of Rinzai were established by Enni who went to China in 1235 and studied Lin-chi, and by the naturalized Japanese priests Rankei Dōryū (Chin Lan-ch'i Tao-lung), Mugaku Sogen (Wu-hsüeh Tsu-yüan), and others who came from China in the thirteenth century to propagate the Zen teachings. The Rinzai school became popular among the samurai and nobility and prospered through the support of the Kamakura shogunate. At present, the Rinzai school has fourteen branches. In addition to the seated meditation (Jpn *zazen*) emphasized by the Sōtō school, Rinzai employs a form of training called *kōan* in Japanese (Chin *kung-an*), problems comprising sutra passages, presentations from Zen teachers, questions and answers, short exchanges, etc., that are beyond logical solution. *Kōan* employs paradox as a means of transcending rational reasoning and stimulating intuitive insight. The famous question "What is the sound of one hand clapping?" which in the West has come to characterize Zen thinking, is an example of a *kōan*. *See also* Lin-chi school.

Rishipatana [仙人堕処] (Skt; Jpn Sennin-dasho): Sage Ascetics-Gathering. Another name for Deer Park, where Shakyamuni delivered his first sermon. *See* Deer Park.

Risshō Kōseikai [立正佼成会]: Literally, "Society for Establishing Righteousness and Friendly Relations." A Japanese Buddhist lay organization. Headquartered in Tokyo, it was founded in 1938 by Nikkyō Niwano (1906–1999), a son of a farming family in Niigata Prefecture, and Myōkō Naganuma (1889–1957), a housewife from Saitama Prefecture. Based on the Lotus Sutra and inspired by the Nichiren Buddhist tradition, Risshō Kōseikai has no clergy and no formal affiliation with any other Nichiren school. It is an offshoot of the Reiyūkai, from which it separated in 1938, and emphasizes devotion to the Lotus Sutra and the efficacy of chanting its title, as well as veneration of one's ancestors. Members believe in Shakyamuni Buddha and recite selections from the Lotus Sutra morning and evening. In terms of activities, they gather in small groups for counseling and the study of Buddhist doctrine.

Ritsu school [律宗] (Jpn Risshū): *See* Precepts school.

river of three crossings [三途の河] (Jpn *sanzu-no-kawa*): A river that people are said to cross on the seventh day after their death. It has three crossing points—a bridge, a ford, and a spot where there is only deep serpent-infested water. Where one crosses depends on the weight of one's offenses while alive. Those who performed acts of good while alive cross over a bridge adorned with seven precious substances. Those whose karmic balance of good and evil is relatively even cross at a ford. Those who committed great evil must wade through deep water infested with hideous serpents. On the bank, a male demon and a female demon dwell under a large tree. The female, called the garment-snatching demoness, strips the dead of their clothes, and the male, called the garment-suspending demon, hangs the clothes on a branch of the tree to determine the weight of their offenses. The concept of the river of three crossings is not found in Indian Buddhism, and therefore it is thought to have originated in China. In Japan, it became popular from the middle of the Heian period (794–1185) through the Kamakura period (1185–1333). Accounts of the river of three crossings differ slightly according to the source.

roar of a lion [師子吼・獅子吼] (Jpn *shishi-ku*): The voice or preaching of a Buddha. *See* lion's roar.

Rōben [良弁] (689–773): The second patriarch of the Japanese Flower Garland (Kegon) school and the first chief priest of Tōdai-ji temple in Nara. He originally studied the teachings of the Dharma Characteristics (Hossō) school under Gien and lived at Konshō-ji temple. In 740 he invited Shinjō, who was living at Daian-ji temple in Nara, to come to Konshō-ji and lecture on the Flower Garland Sutra. Since this was the first lecture on the Flower Garland Sutra ever given in Japan, Shinjō is regarded as the founder of the Flower Garland school in that country. Rōben became his successor. Under the patronage of Emperor Shōmu, he devoted himself to the building of Tōdai-ji temple. In 752 he was appointed the temple's first chief priest and later was given the title administrator of priests.

robe of forbearance [忍辱の衣] (Jpn *ninniku-no-koromo*): Also, robe of patience or robe of endurance. A simile for the spirit of forbearance required to teach the Lotus Sutra, and with which one bears abuse, insult, and any other persecution, remaining unperturbed and composed. The robe is one of the three essentials, or rules, for preaching the Lotus Sutra—the robe, seat, and room of the Thus Come One—mentioned in the "Teacher of the Law" (tenth) chapter of the sutra. A forbearing mind is compared to a robe because it protects against external hindrances. The "Teacher of the Law" chapter speaks of "the robe of gentleness and patience," saying that one who desires to expound the Lotus Sutra after Shakyamuni Buddha's death should put on "the Thus Come One's robe," and that "the Thus Come One's robe is the mind that is gentle and forbearing." *See also* robe, seat, and room; three rules of preaching.

robe of rags [糞掃衣・納衣] (Jpn *funzōe* or *nōe*): A monk's garment. *See* clothes of patched rags.

robe, seat, and room [衣座室] (Jpn *e-za-shitsu*): Also referred to as the three rules of preaching. The robe, the seat, and the room of the Thus Come One—the three essentials for propagating the Lotus Sutra after Shakyamuni Buddha's death that are mentioned in the "Teacher of the Law" (tenth) chapter of the Lotus Sutra. The chapter states: "These good men and good women should enter the Thus Come One's room, put on the Thus Come One's robe, sit in the Thus Come One's seat, and then for the sake of the four kinds of believers [i.e., monks, nuns, laymen, and laywomen] broadly expound this sutra. The 'Thus Come One's room' is the state of mind that shows great pity and compassion toward all living beings. The 'Thus Come One's robe' is the mind that is gentle and forbearing. The 'Thus Come One's seat' is the emptiness of all phenomena." In effect, this passage means that one who wishes to expound the Lotus Sutra after the Buddha's death should abide in gentleness and forbearance, possess insight into the emptiness or non-substantiality of all phenomena, and dwell in pity and compassion. *See also* three rules of preaching.

rock kalpa [磐石劫] (Jpn *banjaku-gō*): Also, rock-rubbing *kalpa*. One of several definitions of a *kalpa* used to illustrate its measureless length. According to *The Treatise on the Great Perfection of Wisdom*, a *kalpa* is longer than the time required to wear away an immense cube of rock forty *ri* (one *ri* is about 450 meters) on each side if one were to brush it with a piece of cloth once every hundred years. In the Miscellaneous Āgama Sutra, the length of each side of the rock is given as one *yojana* (about 7 kilometers).

root of goodness [善根] (Jpn *zengon* or *zenkon*): *See* good root.

Root of Joy [喜根比丘] (Skt Prasannendriya; Jpn Kikon-biku): A monk said to have lived in the latter age after the death of a Buddha named Lion Sound King. He is referred to in the Non-Substantiality of All Phenomena Sutra and *The Treatise on the Great Perfection of Wisdom*. He did not value ascetic practices, but taught only the doctrine of the true aspect of all phenomena. Because of this, the monk Superior Intent insulted him in front of many other monks. Root of Joy upheld his beliefs and attained Buddhahood, while Superior Intent is said to have fallen into hell.

root teaching [根本法輪] (Jpn *kompon-hōrin*): (1) One component of the "thrice turned wheel of the Law," a division of Shakyamuni Buddha's teachings into three categories set forth by Chi-tsang (549–623), a systematizer of the doctrines of the Three Treatises (San-lun) school in China. *See* thrice turned wheel of the Law.

(2) A term that Fa-tsang (643–712), the third patriarch of the Flower Garland (Hua-yen) school in China, applied to the Flower Garland Sutra. In contrast to the root teaching, he called the Lotus and other sutras branch teachings to express his conviction that the Flower Garland Sutra was superior to the other sutras.

rotten seeds [敗種] (Jpn *haishu*): Also, decayed seeds or spoiled seeds. In Mahayana scriptures, persons of the two vehicles—voice-hearers and cause-awakened ones—are often compared to rotten seeds that will never sprout, implying that they are incapable of attaining Buddhahood. Similarly, they are likened to scorched seeds that can never sprout and to rotten roots that can never put forth shoots. Persons of the two vehicles are described as those who, content with the rewards accruing from their practice, claim that their enlightenment as arhats is true and supreme and do not seek the true enlightenment of Buddhahood. The Lotus Sutra overturns the idea that persons of the two vehicles cannot attain enlightenment when Shakyamuni prophesies that such individuals will become Buddhas in the future.

rūpa-dhātu [色界] (Skt, Pali; Jpn *shiki-kai*): The world of form, the middle division of the threefold world. *See* world of form.

Ryōchū [良忠] (1199–1287): Also known as Nen'amidabutsu or Nen'a. The third patriarch of the Japanese Pure Land (Jōdo) school, after Hōnen and Benchō. A native of Iwami Province, he entered Gakuen-ji temple to study in 1211 and received the precepts at Enryaku-ji, the head temple of the Tendai school on Mount Hiei in 1214. He studied the doctrines of the Dharma Analysis Treasury (Kusha), Tendai, True Word (Shingon), Dharma Characteristics (Hossō), Zen, and Precepts (Ritsu) schools until 1232 when he went to his native place and began to practice the Pure Land teaching. In 1236 he traveled west to Chikugo to learn the Pure Land doctrine from Benchō and then went east to the Kanto region to propagate that teaching. He won the support of Hōjō Tsunetoki, the fourth regent of the Kamakura shogunate, and other members of the Hōjō clan and founded Goshin-ji temple (later renamed Renge-ji and then Kōmyō-ji) in Kamakura in 1243. He made this temple the center of propagation of the Pure Land teaching and went on to win support from other shogunate authorities.

Ryōgen [良源] (912–985): Also known as the Great Teacher Jie. The eighteenth chief priest of Enryaku-ji, the head temple of the Tendai school on Mount Hiei in Japan. He is regarded as a restorer of the Tendai school. A native of Ōmi Province, he began his Buddhist practice at Mount Hiei in 923. In 937 he defeated the priest Gishō of the Dharma Characteristics (Hossō) school in debate, and in 963 he prevailed over the priest Hōzō of the same school in what became known as the Ōwa Debate, held at the imperial court. (It is called the Ōwa Debate because it took place in the third year of the Ōwa era, 963). Thus he won nationwide fame. In 966 he became chief priest of Enryaku-ji temple, and in 981 was appointed general administrator of priests, the highest rank in the priesthood. He was often ordered by the imperial court to conduct a prayer ritual for the security of the imperial family. He also rebuilt dilapidated temples on Mount Hiei and helped restore the Tendai school. His major disciples Genshin and Kakuun founded the Eshin branch and the Danna branch, respectively, of the Tendai school.

Ryōkan [良観] (1217–1303): Also known as Ninshō. A priest of the True Word Precepts (Shingon-Ritsu) school in Japan. Born in Yamato Province, he began to study at Gakuan-ji temple in 1232 and in the following year received the precepts to become a priest at Tōdai-ji temple in Nara. In 1240 he became a disciple of Eizon, who was revered as a restorer of the Precepts (Ritsu) school. Eizon advocated the practice of both the precepts and the True Word (Shingon) esoteric teaching. This later led to the establishment of the True Word Precepts school, which regards Eizon as its founder. In 1252 Ryōkan traveled east to the Kanto region, which included the city of Kamakura, where the shogunate was headquartered, and propagated the Precepts teaching there. In 1261 he settled in Kamakura, and his activities in the Kanto region fostered a connection with the ruling Hōjō clan. Hōjō Tokiyori, the former regent who still held the reins of government, built Kōsen-ji temple and named Ryōkan its first chief priest. In 1262, at the request of Hōjō Tokiyori and other government officials, Ryōkan's teacher, Eizon, came from Saidai-ji temple in Nara to Kamakura, where he stayed for half a year. Eizon and Ryōkan together promoted the teaching of the precepts and administered the precepts to priests and lay believers. In 1267 Ryōkan became chief priest of Gokuraku-ji temple, which had been established by Hōjō Shigetoki, a high official of the Kamakura shogunate. Gokuraku-ji thus became Ryōkan's permanent abode. He undertook a number of social welfare projects, building hospitals, roads, etc. The people of Kamakura revered him, and he enjoyed great influence. The ruling Hōjō family recommended him for a post as superintendent of great temples; it also bestowed manors on him and invested him with the authority to collect tolls on ports and barrier stations. At the command of the shogunate, Ryōkan often conducted esoteric prayer rituals to bring about rain and to ward off invasion by the Mongols. During the great drought of 1271, Ryōkan vied with Nichiren in praying for rain and failed. After that he contrived to have accusations brought against Nichiren, which eventually led to the Tatsunokuchi Persecution, in which Nichiren came near to being executed, and Nichiren's subsequent exile to the island of Sado. For many years Ryōkan harassed Nichiren and his disciples, both openly and covertly.

Ryōnin [良忍] (1073–1132): A priest who spread the Pure Land teachings before Hōnen founded the Pure Land (Jodo) school in Japan. He is regarded as the founder of the Interfusing Nembutsu (Yūzū Nembutsu) school. A native of Owari Province, in his childhood he went to Enryaku-ji, the head temple of the Tendai school on Mount Hiei, to become a priest and study the Tendai doctrine. Later he moved to Ōhara in Kyoto and there built two temples, Raigō-in and Jōrenge-in. He devoted himself to the practice of the Nembutsu, or recitation of Amida Buddha's name, to attain rebirth in Amida's Pure Land. In 1117 he asserted that he had received instruction directly from Amida Buddha, the gist of which was that one's personal practice of the Nembutsu influences all people, and that others' practice of the Nembutsu influences oneself; this mutual interaction works to bring about the rebirth of all people in the Pure Land. The Interfusing Nembutsu school regards this event as the origin of the school. Thereafter Ryōnin propagated this teaching and encouraged the people to recite the name of Amida Buddha, thus winning numerous converts. Ryōnin is also known for reviving and systematizing the Tendai school's tradition of musical recitation of sutras, called *shōmyō* in Japanese.

Ryūkan [隆寛] (1148–1227): Also known as Kaikū or Muga. A priest of the Pure Land (Jōdo) school in Japan; a disciple of Hōnen, the school's founder. Because he lived at Chōraku-ji temple in Kyoto, the doctrinal lineage he is regarded as having founded is known as the Chōraku-ji branch of the Pure Land school. Ryūkan first studied the Tendai doctrine at Enryaku-ji temple on Mount Hiei. Later he was attracted by the Pure Land teachings and became a disciple of Hōnen. After Hōnen's death, he wrote *A Clarification of "The Nembutsu Chosen above All"* in rebuttal to *A Refutation of "The Nembutsu Chosen above All"* by Jōshō, a Tendai priest of Enryaku-ji. This incurred the wrath of Enryaku-ji priests and persecution by the shogunate. He was exiled to Ōshū in northern Japan in 1227, but died en route at Iiyama in Sagami Province. His teaching advocates the doctrine of many-time recitation, the belief that one should recite the Nembutsu, or the name of the Buddha Amida, as many times as possible to ensure rebirth in the Pure Land. This teaching stands in opposition to the doctrine of one-time recitation advocated by Kōsai, another disciple of Hōnen, which holds that a single recitation is sufficient. Ryūkan wrote *A Comparison of One-time Recitation and Many-time Recitation.*

Ryūsen-ji [滝泉寺]: A temple of the Tendai school located in Atsuhara Village in Fuji District of Suruga Province during the Kamakura period (1185–1333) in Japan. The temple's deputy chief priest, Gyōchi, displayed great hostility toward Nichiren's followers, who had won many converts in the area, including the temple's young priests. That hostility eventually led to a three-year-long series of threats and violent acts that began in earnest in 1278 and was later known as the Atsuhara Persecution.

Ryūshin [隆真] (n.d.): Also known as Butchō-bō. A priest of the Tendai school in the early Kamakura period (1185–1333) who lived at Enryaku-ji temple on Mount Hiei in Japan. At Enryaku-ji he was appointed discussion supervisor, whose function it was to select topics for and oversee Buddhist discussions among the priests. He criticized as evil the exclusive practice of the Nembutsu, or calling on the name of Amida Buddha, set forth by Hōnen, the founder of the Japanese Pure Land (Jōdo) school. Some credit *A Refutation of "The Nembutsu Chosen above All,"* a work critical of the doctrine of the exclusive practice of the Nembutsu, to Ryūshin. See also *Refutation of "The Nembutsu Chosen above All," A.*

Ryūzō-bō [竜象房] (n.d.): Also known as Ryūzō. A priest of the Tendai school during the Kamakura period (1185–1333) in Japan. He lived at Enryaku-ji, the head temple of the Tendai school on Mount Hiei, but was expelled from Mount Hiei when it was disclosed that he had eaten human flesh, the flesh of those who had died of hunger. This is recounted in the records of the chief priests of the Tendai school, in an entry dated the twenty-seventh day of the fourth month in the first year of Kenji (1275). Later he appeared in Kamakura and won the patronage of Ryōkan, the chief priest of Gokuraku-ji temple. Ryūzō-bō was defeated in debate by Sammi-bō, a disciple of Nichiren, at Kuwagayatsu in Kamakura in 1277, before a great number of his followers. This incident is known as the Kuwagayatsu Debate. Shijō Kingo, a lay follower of Nichiren and a samurai, happened to be an observer at the debate, and jealous colleagues reported falsely to Kingo's lord, Ema Chikatoki (or his father Mitsutoki according to another account), that he had forcibly disrupted Ryūzō-bō's preaching. This led Ema to threaten to confiscate Kingo's fief unless he abandoned faith in the Lotus Sutra.

S

Sacred Way teachings [聖道門] (Jpn Shōdō-mon): The teachings that hold that attaining enlightenment depends upon one's own power. The term *Sacred Way teachings* is used in contrast with *Pure Land teachings,* which assert that enlightenment depends upon the power of another, specifically, Amida Buddha. Tao-ch'o (562–645), a patriarch of the Chinese Pure Land school, formulated the classification of the Buddhist teachings into these two categories in his *Collected Essays on the World of Peace and Delight.* He asserted that the Sacred Way teachings were too difficult and profound for ordinary people to practice, and that only through the recitation of Amida Buddha's name as expounded in the Pure Land teachings could they attain salvation.

Sadāprarudita [常啼菩薩] (Skt; Jpn Jōtai-bosatsu): The bodhisattva known by the name of Ever Wailing in Chinese Buddhist scriptures. *See* Ever Wailing.

Saddharma-pundarīka-sūtra [法華経] (Skt; Jpn *Hoke-kyō*): *See* Lotus Sutra.

sādhu [善哉] (Skt, Pali; Jpn *zenzai* or *yokikana*): "Excellent," "Very good," or "Well done." An expression of praise and approval. A Buddha or a Buddhist teacher might use this word when praising or expressing approval, usually toward a disciple. In Buddhist scriptures, this word is often repeated for emphasis, appearing in English translations as "Excellent, excellent!" or "Well done, well done!" In the "Treasure Tower" (eleventh) chapter of the Lotus Sutra, the Buddha Many Treasures speaks from within the jeweled tower, saying: "Excellent *(sādhu)*, excellent *(sādhu)!* Shakyamuni, World-Honored One, that you can take the great wisdom of equality, a Law to instruct the bodhisattvas, guarded and kept in mind by the Buddhas, the Lotus Sutra of the Wonderful Law, and preach it for the sake of the great assembly! It is as you say, as you say. Shakyamuni, World-Honored One, all that you have expounded is the truth!" *Sādhu* also means upright, good, honorable, righteous, or correct, and also indicates a holy man or a sage.

Sado-bō [佐渡房]: Another name for Nikō, one of the six senior priests designated by Nichiren. *See* Nikō.

Sado Exile [佐渡流罪] (Jpn Sado-ruzai): The exile of Nichiren to Sado Island in the Sea of Japan from 1271 through 1274. The priest Ryōkan of Gokuraku-ji temple in Kamakura was challenged by Nichiren to a contest praying for rain. But when Ryōkan's prayers failed to have an effect, he spread false rumors about Nichiren, using his influence with the wives and widows of high government officials. This led to Nichiren's confrontation with Hei no Saemon, deputy chief of the Office of Military and Police Affairs of the Kamakura shogunate, who arrested him and maneuvered to have him executed at Tatsunokuchi. The execution attempt failed, however, and Nichiren was then confined for nearly a month at the residence in Echi, on the mainland, of Homma Rokurō Saemon, the deputy constable of the island province of Sado. Finally the shogunate ordered Nichiren exiled to the island.

On the tenth day of the tenth month, 1271, Nichiren was taken by Homma's warriors from Echi to Sado. They reached Sado on the twenty-eighth day of the tenth month in winter, and, on the first day of the eleventh month, arrived at Tsukahara. Nichiren's quarters were a dilapidated shrine called Sammai-dō in the middle of a graveyard. Exposed to the wind, snow fell in through gaping holes in the roof. Nichiren stayed there for nearly half a year. On the sixteenth day of the first month, 1272, Nichiren debated with several hundred priests of other Buddhist schools who had assembled in the field before Sammai-dō. His impressive victory in what became known as the Tsukahara Debate won a number of converts to his teachings. The next day, Benjō of the Pure Land (Jōdo) school returned to debate further, only to be refuted. A record of their debate exists, signed by both Nichiren and Benjō. In the second month, Nichiren's prediction of internal strife came true when Hōjō Tokisuke, an elder half brother of the regent, attempted to seize power. Battles broke out in Kyoto and Kamakura between factions of the ruling Hōjō family. In the fourth month, Nichiren was transferred to the residence of the lay priest Ichinosawa at Ichinosawa on Sado.

While on Sado, Nichiren won many converts, inscribed the object of devotion of his teaching (the Gohonzon) for individual believers, maintained frequent correspondence with his followers on the mainland, and wrote a number of treatises. The most important of these are *The Opening of the Eyes,* completed in the second month of 1272, and *The Object of Devotion for Observing the Mind,* written in the fourth month of 1273. The former reveals the concept traditionally called "casting off the transient [status] and revealing the true [identity]" (Jpn *hosshaku-kempon*), meaning that he disclosed his true identity as the Buddha of the Latter Day of the Law. In *Letter to Misawa,* he wrote, "As for my teachings, regard those before my exile to the province of Sado as equivalent to the Buddha's pre-Lotus Sutra teachings" (896).

On the eighth day of the third month in 1274, a government official arrived at Sado Island with a pardon. Nichiren left Ichinosawa on the thirteenth day of the third month and returned to Kamakura on the twenty-sixth day of the third month.

Sāgara [沙竭羅竜王] (Skt; Jpn Shakara-ryūō, Shakatsura-ryūō, or Shagara-ryūō): One of the eight great dragon kings assembled at the ceremony of the Lotus Sutra. In the "Devadatta" (twelfth) chapter of the Lotus Sutra, the dragon king Sāgara is described as the father of a dragon girl who attained enlightenment at age eight. The Sanskrit word *sāgara* means the ocean. According to the Long Āgama Sutra, he lives in the dragon palace on the bed of the ocean, which, adorned with seven kinds of gems, measures eighty thousand *yojanas* in length and width. The Flower Garland Sutra describes Sāgara as the dragon who causes rain to fall throughout the world.

Sage Ascetics-Gathering [仙人堕処] (Jpn Sennin-dasho): Another name for Deer Park, where Shakyamuni delivered his first sermon. *See* Deer Park.

sahā world [娑婆世界] (Skt; Jpn *shaba-sekai*): This world, which is full of suffering. Often translated as the world of endurance. *Sahā* means the earth; it derives from a root meaning "to bear" or "to endure." For this reason, in the Chinese versions of Buddhist scriptures, *sahā* is rendered as endurance. In this context, the *sahā* world indicates a world in which people must endure suffering. It is also defined as an impure land, a land defiled by earthly desires and illusions, in contrast with a pure land. The *sahā* world describes the land where Shakyamuni Buddha makes his appearance and instructs living beings. In Buddhist scriptures, the *sahā* world indicates either Jambudvīpa, which is one of the four continents of ancient Indian cosmology, or the entire world containing all four continents. It also indicates the major world system, considered to be the realm of Shakyamuni's instruction. In some Buddhist scriptures, including the Lotus and Vimalakīrti sutras, it is held that the *sahā* world, this world full of distress and suffering, is in itself a pure land, the Land of Eternally Tranquil Light. In the "Life Span" (sixteenth) chapter of the Lotus Sutra, Shakyamuni states, "Ever since then I have been constantly in this *sahā* world, preaching the Law, teaching and converting," indicating that the place where the Buddha dwells, the Buddha land, is in fact the *sahā* world.

Saichō [最澄]: Also known as Dengyō. The founder of the Tendai school in Japan. *See* Dengyō.

Saidai-ji [西大寺]: The head temple of the True Word Precepts (Shingon-Ritsu) school in Japan. It was one of the seven major temples of Nara, the capital of Japan from 710 to 784. Built in 765 in response to a decree issued the previous year by Empress Shōtoku, it was named Saidai-ji (West Great Temple), because it was located in the western part of the capital. It had two main halls, one enshrining an image of Medicine Master Buddha and the other, an image of Bodhisattva Maitreya. Though it enjoyed prosperity along with Tōdai-ji (East Great Temple) in the eastern part of the capital, Saidai-ji was damaged by a fire in 846 and 860, and declined late in the Heian period (794–1185). The priest Eizon took up residence at Saidai-ji in 1235, and restored the temple as a center for the teachings on the precepts. In 1502 the main buildings in the temple precinct burned down, and the temple again declined, but was revitalized by Tokugawa Ieyasu (1542–1616), the founder of the Tokugawa shogunate, who gave it financial support. Saidai-ji preserves bronze images of the four heavenly kings produced late in the Nara period (710–794), and other Buddhist art works.

Saimyō-ji [最明寺]: A temple of the Rinzai school of Zen, located within the precincts of Kenchō-ji temple in Kamakura, Japan. It was built by Hōjō Tokiyori (1227–1263), the fifth regent of the Kamakura shogunate, in 1256. Hōjō Tokiyori invited Dōryū to become the chief priest. That year, he retired from office and took up residence at Saimyō-ji temple. Tokiyori was thus known as the lay priest of Saimyō-ji. From there, though officially retired, he continued to exercise political authority. He invited Zen priests to the temple to listen to them preach, and remained at Saimyō-ji until his death. The temple declined for a time, but was restored by Hōjō Tokimune (1251–1284), Tokiyori's son and the eighth regent of the Kamakura shogunate, and was renamed Zenkō-ji temple. The temple no longer exists.

Sairen-bō [最蓮房] (n.d.): Also known as Sairen-bō Nichijō. A disciple of Nichiren (1222–1282). Born in Kyoto, Japan, he was a priest of the Tendai school who, for an unknown reason, had been exiled to Sado Island. There he met Nichiren and converted to his teachings in the second month of 1272, shortly after the Tsukahara Debate. From the letters Nichiren sent to him, it appears that he had a profound knowledge of Buddhism but was in poor health. After Nichiren left Sado and went to live at Mount Minobu in 1274, Sairen-bō was also pardoned and returned to Kyoto. Thereafter he is said to have gone to Shimoyama in Kai Province and founded Honkoku-ji temple. He received from Nichiren a number of important writings including *The Heritage of the Ultimate Law of Life, The Enlightenment of Plants, On Prayer, The True Aspect of All Phenomena, The Entity of the Mystic Law,* and *On the Eighteen Perfections.*

Sajiki, the lady of [桟敷女房] (n.d.) (Jpn Sajiki-nyōbō): Also known as the lay nun of Sajiki. A follower of Nichiren who lived at Sajiki in Kamakura, Japan. In a letter written by Nichiren to her in 1275, her husband is called Hyōe no Saemon (probably Indō Saburō Saemon Sukenobu), and he was also a follower of Nichiren. According to one account, she was related to Nisshō, one of the six senior priests designated by Nichiren. From the two extant letters Nichiren wrote to her, it appears that she made him an offering of robes on two occasions.

sakridāgāmin [斯陀含・一来] (Skt; Jpn *shidagon* or *ichirai*): The second of the four stages of Hinayana enlightenment. *See* once-returner.

sal tree [沙羅樹] (Skt *shāla;* Pali *sāla;* Jpn *shara-ju*): A tree native to India and Nepal that grows to more than thirty meters in height and produces pale yellow blossoms. The sal is a deciduous tree belonging to the dipterocarp family. In India, it is a valuable source of timber, and its aromatic resin is used in religious rituals and also as a surface coating. Shakyamuni Buddha died in a sal grove in Kushinagara. According to one tradition, Shakyamuni laid himself down on a couch between twin sal trees and entered nirvana. Another account has it that there were twin sal trees on each of the four sides of the area where Shakyamuni entered nirvana. When he entered nirvana, one of each pair of trees withered. Yet another tradition says that, upon Shakyamuni's entrance into nirvana, four twin sal trees, or eight sal trees, turned as white as cranes. For this reason, the place where Shakyamuni died is also called the crane grove.

samādhi [三昧] (Skt, Pali; Jpn *sammai*): A state of intense concentration of mind, or meditation, said to produce inner serenity. The term *samādhi* is translated as meditation, contemplation, or concentration. Numerous types of meditation are described in the Buddhist sutras, such as moon-loving meditation, ocean-imprint meditation, and Buddha-beholding meditation.

samādhi of the origin of immeasurable meanings [無量義処三昧] (Skt *ananta-nirdesha-pratishthāna-samādhi;* Jpn *muryōgisho-sammai*): Also, *samādhi* of the place of immeasurable meanings. The *samādhi,* or meditation, into which the Lotus Sutra describes Shakyamuni Buddha as entering before preaching the sutra. The "Introduction" (first) chapter of the Lotus Sutra says: "At that time the World-Honored One, surrounded by the four kinds of believers, received offerings and tokens of respect and was honored and praised. And for the sake of the bodhisattvas he preached the great vehicle sutra titled Immeasurable Meanings, a Law to instruct the bodhisattvas, one that is guarded and kept in mind by the Buddhas. When the Buddha had finished preaching this sutra, he sat with his legs crossed in lotus position and entered into the *samādhi* of the origin of immeasurable meanings, his body and mind never moving." The Immeasurable Meanings Sutra, which is regarded as a prologue to the Lotus Sutra, says, "These immeasurable meanings are born from a single Law." *Ananta* of the Sanskrit for this term, *ananta-nirdesha-pratishthāna,* means immeasurable, *nirdesha* means description, elucidation, or explanation, and *pratishthāna* means basis, foundation, dwelling, or support.

sāmanera [沙弥] (Pali; Jpn *shami*): A male novice in the Buddhist Order who has renounced secular life and vowed to uphold the ten precepts. See *shrāmanera.*

sāmanerī [沙弥尼] (Pali; Jpn *shamini*): A female novice in the Buddhist

Order who has renounced secular life and vowed to uphold the ten precepts. See *shrāmanerī*.

Samantabhadra [普賢菩薩] (Skt; Jpn Fugen-bosatsu): The bodhisattva Universal Worthy, depicted in various sutras and thought to symbolize the virtues of truth and practice. *See* Universal Worthy.

samaya [三昧耶形・三摩耶形] (Skt; Jpn *sammaya-gyō* or *samaya-gyō*): Objects and mudras (hand gestures) displayed by Buddhas and bodhisattvas that represent their vows to lead all people to enlightenment. Buddhas and bodhisattvas are sometimes depicted as holding various objects such as a bow, an arrow, a pagoda, a jewel, or a sword. Particularly well known are the sword of Bodhisattva Manjushrī and the lotus of Bodhisattva Perceiver of the World's Sounds. The Sanskrit *samaya* means time, assembly, doctrine, agreement, rule, covenant, etc. Esoteric Buddhism interprets *samaya* as the vows made by Buddhas and bodhisattvas and as symbols of their vows. The esoteric True Word (Jpn Shingon) school goes further to interpret *samaya* as indicating four things—equality between a Buddha and the people, a Buddha's vow to lead all people to supreme enlightenment, his ridding the people of earthly desires and hindrances, and his awakening them from delusion.

sambhoga-kāya [報身] (Skt; Jpn *hōshin* or *hōjin*): The reward body, one of the three Buddha bodies. *See* reward body.

Same Birth and Same Name [同生同名] (Jpn Dōshō Dōmyō): Two gods said to dwell on one's shoulders from the time of birth, recording all of one's acts, good and evil, and reporting them to King Yama, who judges the dead. Described in the Flower Garland Sutra, Same Birth and Same Name symbolize the workings of the law of cause and effect within one's life. In *Great Concentration and Insight,* T'ien-t'ai (538–597) says: "The deities Same Name and Same Birth protect people. If one's faith is strong, then their protection is great." According to Miao-lo's *Annotations on "Great Concentration and Insight,"* Same Birth means "born at the same time [as the person he protects]," and Same Name, "bearing the same name [as the person he (or she) protects]." One view regards Same Birth as a male god and Same Name as a female god. Concerning these gods' power of protection, Miao-lo also says, "The stronger one's faith, the greater the protection of the gods."

samgha [僧伽] (Skt; Jpn *sōgya*): Also, *sangha*. The Buddhist Order, or the community of Buddhist believers. One of the three treasures of Buddhism, the other two being the Buddha and his teachings. *Samgha* refers specifically to the group of monks and nuns who renounced secular life and dedicated themselves to Buddhist practice night and day, but in a broad sense includes all Buddhist practitioners: monks, nuns, laymen, and laywomen. The Sanskrit term originally meant a collective body or assembly and later came to refer to the body of Buddhist practitioners. In the early stage of Buddhism, a body of at least four monks or nuns living in a communal arrangement was called a *samgha,* designation of a community for practicing the Buddha's teaching, preserving it, and transmitting it to the future. Because this role was considered so important, the *samgha* was regarded together with the Buddha and his teachings as deserving of devotion and protection. With the rise of Mahayana Buddhism, the *samgha* came to refer to the body of Mahayana practitioners, or bodhisattvas, including monks, nuns, or laypersons. *See also* three treasures.

Samghabhadra [僧伽跋陀羅・衆賢] (n.d.) (Skt; Jpn Sōgyabaddara or Shugen): A monk and scholar of the Sarvāstivāda school thought to have lived in India around the fourth or fifth century. Born in Kashmir, he is known as the author of *The Treatise on Accordance with the Correct Doctrine* and *A Clarification of Doctrine.* To rebut Vasubandhu's *Dharma Analysis Treasury,* which was at once a systematic exposition on and a criticism of Sarvāstivāda doctrine, Samghabhadra wrote *The Treatise on Accordance with the Correct Doctrine.* This was itself a detailed exposition of Sarvāstivāda doctrine as well as a defense and exaltation of its orthodoxy. Samghabhadra wanted to confront Vasubandhu in debate, but died before realizing that wish.

Samghadeva [僧伽提婆] (n.d.) (Skt; Jpn Sōgyadaiba): A monk of Kashmir and a translator of Buddhist scriptures into Chinese. Samghadeva went to Ch'ang-an in China between the years 365 and 384, and translated Buddhist scriptures there. From Ch'ang-an he moved to Lo-yang and then went to Mount Lu at the invitation of Hui-yüan who had heard of his reputation. Samghadeva's translations include the Medium-Length Āgama Sutra, the Increasing by One Āgama Sutra, *The Eight-part Treatise,* and *The Heart of the Abhidharma.*

Samghanandi [僧伽難提] (n.d.) (Skt; Jpn Sōgyanandai): A monk of Shrāvastī in India around the third century. He is regarded as the sixteenth of Shakyamuni Buddha's twenty-three, or the seventeenth of his twenty-four, successors. Born a prince, he renounced the royal life at age seven and entered the Buddhist Order. He received the transmission of the Buddha's teachings from Rāhulabhadra and later transmitted them to Samghayashas.

Samghavarman (Skt) (1) [康僧鎧] (n.d.) (Jpn Kōsōgai): A monk and a translator of Buddhist scriptures active in China during the third century. Described by some accounts as a native of India, another view holds that he was a native of a kingdom known by the Chinese as K'ang-chü that included the city of Samarkand and its neighboring areas in Central Asia. The Chinese name for Samghavarman is K'ang-seng-k'ai; K'ang is a name generally thought to have been given to those from the K'ang-chü kingdom. In 252 he went to Lo-yang in the Wei kingdom, one of the three kingdoms in China at the time, and settled at Pai-ma-ssu temple. According to a Buddhist source, he translated the Buddha Infinite Life Sutra and other sutras into Chinese. Some believe, however, that the Buddha Infinite Life Sutra was translated in a later period.

(2) [僧伽跋摩] (n.d.) (Jpn Sōgyabatsuma): A monk from India who traveled to Chien-k'ang in China in 433 where he conferred the Buddhist precepts upon hundreds of priests and nuns. He also translated five Buddhist works, including *The Supplement to "The Heart of the Abhidharma."* In 442 he left China and returned to India by sea.

Samghayashas [僧伽耶舍] (n.d.) (Skt; Jpn Sōgyayasha): A monk of Magadha in India regarded as the seventeenth of Shakyamuni Buddha's twenty-three, or the eighteenth of his twenty-four, successors. Described as wise and eloquent, Samghayashas was entrusted with the Buddha's teachings by Samghanandi and later transmitted them to Kumārata.

Sammi-bō [三位房] (n.d.): Also known as Sammi-bō Nichigyō. One of Nichiren's earliest disciples. A native of Shimōsa Province in Japan, he received a Buddhist education at Mount Hiei and was highly esteemed among Nichiren's followers for his learning and debating skill. These were evident in his victory over Ryūzō-bō, a priest of the Tendai school, in the Kuwagayatsu Debate of 1277. He tended to be arrogant about his knowledge and desirous of social recognition and status, however. Nichiren found it necessary to admonish him about this on several occasions, such as when he appeared excessively proud of having preached before the court aristocracy in Kyoto. During the Atsuhara Persecution, he renounced his belief in Nichiren's teachings and turned against Nichiren and his supporters. In several letters, Nichiren refers to Sammi-bō's untimely and tragic death, though details of this are unknown.

Sammon school [山門派] (Jpn Sammon-ha): Mountain school. A division of the Tendai school based at Enryaku-ji temple on Mount Hiei in Japan. *See* Mountain school (1).

samsāra [輪廻] (Skt, Pali; Jpn *rinne*): Transmigration. The cycle of birth and death that ordinary people undergo in the world of illusion and suffering. In India, the theory of transmigration first appeared in Upanishad philosophy, before the rise of Buddhism, in the eighth or seventh century B.C.E. Buddhism holds that ordinary people undergo an endless cycle of birth and death within the threefold world (the worlds of desire, form, and formlessness) and among the six paths (the realms of hell, hungry spirits, animals, *asuras,* human beings, and heavenly beings). This repeated cycle of birth and death in the realms of illusion and suffering is referred to as "transmigration in the six paths." Unenlightened beings are born into one of the six paths in accordance with their actions in their previous existence; when the present life is over, they are reborn in the same or another of the six paths, repeating this process so long as they fail to free themselves from it.

The Buddhist concept of emancipation (Skt *vimoksha*) means liberation from this repeated cycle of birth and death in the realms of illusion and suffering. Freeing oneself from transmigration in the six paths was considered the goal of Buddhist practice. The causes for such transmigration were regarded as ignorance of the true nature of life and selfish craving. Liberation from them required awakening to the truth and eliminating selfish craving, and was considered to lead to the attainment of nirvana, or emancipation.

Samyutta-nikāya [相応部] (Pali; Jpn Sō'ō-bu): One of the five Āgamas. A collection of sutras on related topics. *See* five Āgamas.

San-chieh, the Meditation Master [三階禅師] (PY Sanjie; Jpn Sangai-zenji): Another name for Hsin-hsing, the Chinese priest who founded the Three Stages (San-chieh-chiao) school. *See* Hsin-hsing.

San-chieh-chiao [三階教] (PY Sanjiejiao; Jpn Sangai-kyō): A school founded in China by Hsin-hsing. *See* Three Stages school.

sanctuary of the essential teaching [本門の戒壇] (Jpn *hommon-no-kaidan*): In Nichiren's teachings, the place for enshrining the object of devotion of the essential teaching, i.e., the Gohonzon that Nichiren inscribed, and chanting the daimoku of Nam-myoho-renge-kyo. One of the Three Great Secret Laws, the other two being the object of devotion of the essential teaching and the daimoku or invocation of the essential teaching. Nichiren associated these three with the three types of learning in Buddhism—precepts, meditation, and wisdom—among which the sanctuary corresponds to precepts. The purpose of keeping Buddhist precepts is to prevent error and put an end to evil within oneself. Sanctuary, in this context, originally meant an ordination platform where one vowed to observe the monastic precepts. In Nichiren's teachings, however, there are no precepts other than to believe in the object of devotion and chant the daimoku, Nam-myoho-renge-kyo; therefore, the place where one enshrines the object of devotion and chants Nam-myoho-renge-kyo is the sanctuary.

The sanctuary of the essential teaching is called the "spacelike immovable precept," indicating the certainty and expansiveness of the benefit derived from embracing the object of devotion and chanting Nam-myoho-renge-kyo. *See also* Three Great Secret Laws.

sandalwood tree [栴檀] (Skt, Pali *chandana;* Jpn *sendan*): An aromatic tree found in India. The sandalwood tree grows to be ten meters in height, and its fragrant heartwood is used for making incense. It is often mentioned in Buddhist scriptures, which refer to its superior fragrance.

sands of the Ganges [恒河沙] (Skt *Gangā-nadī-vāluka* or *Gangā-nadī-vālikā;* Jpn *gōga-sha*): Also, Ganges sands. An expression indicating an incalculable number. In Buddhist scriptures, "the sands of the Ganges" often appears as an analogy for an uncountable number. This expression is used to represent, for example, the incalculable number of worlds in the universe or the countless bodhisattvas at a particular preaching assembly. "The sands of sixty thousand Ganges" and similar expressions are also common.

sangha [僧伽] (Skt, Pali; Jpn *sōgya*): The Buddhist Order. See *samgha.*

Sanjaya Belatthiputta [刪闍耶毘羅胝子] (Pali; Jpn Sanjaya-birateishi): An influential non-Buddhist thinker during Shakyamuni's time. *See* six non-Buddhist teachers.

San-lun school [三論宗] (PY Sanlunzong; Jpn Sanron-shū): *See* Three Treatises school.

Sannō [山王] (Jpn): The god Mountain King, the guardian deity of Enryaku-ji, the head temple of the Tendai school in Japan. *See* Mountain King.

Sanron school [三論宗] (Jpn Sanron-shū): *See* Three Treatises school.

Sāramati [堅慧] (n.d.) (Skt; Jpn Kenne or Ken'e): A Mahayana scholar in central India, thought to have lived during the fourth and fifth centuries. He is generally considered the author of *The Treatise on the Treasure Vehicle of Buddhahood.* See also *Treatise on the Treasure Vehicle of Buddhahood, The.*

Sāriputta [舎利弗] (Pali; Jpn Sharihotsu): Shāriputra in Sanskrit. One of the ten major disciples of Shakyamuni. *See* Shāriputra.

Sarvāstivāda school [説一切有部] (Skt; Jpn Setsu-issaiu-bu): Also known as Sarvāstivādin school. A major early Buddhist school that broke away from the Sthaviravāda (Pali Theravāda) school. One of the twenty Hinayana schools. Its followers are called Sarvāstivādins. According to *The Doctrines of the Different Schools,* the schism that formed this school occurred about two hundred years after Shakyamuni's death. Kātyāyanīputra is often regarded as the founder. The Sarvāstivāda school sets forth the view that everything has an existence of its own. It holds that since living beings are formed by a temporary union of the five components there is no real or permanent self, but that the dharmas, or elements of existence that compose the living being, are real and have their own existence throughout the past, present, and future.

The Sarvāstivādins developed the *abhidharma,* the section of the canon composed of doctrinal commentaries, to an extent surpassing that of any other Hinayana school. They produced a total of seven *abhidharmas,* including *The Treatise on the Source of Wisdom.* Further commentaries were later written on these seven, the most famous of which is *The Great Commentary on the Abhidharma,* an exhaustive statement of Sarvāstivāda thought. Vasubandhu included the essentials of this work in his *Dharma Analysis Treasury. The Dharma Analysis Treasury,* however, departs from the traditional Sarvāstivāda position and interprets the school's doctrine more broadly, drawing on the views of other schools, particularly the Sautrāntika. The Sarvāstivāda school gave rise to a total of nine other schools. It was the most influential school of Hinayana in India, and had an important influence on Mayahana thought as well. Its doctrines were widely studied in China and Japan.

Sasshō [薩生] (n.d.): A priest of the Pure Land (Jōdo) school who lived in Kamakura in Japan during the thirteenth century. Originally a Tendai priest, he later practiced the Pure Land teachings under Hōnen's disciple Jōkaku and studied the doctrine of one-time recitation. Later he followed Shōkū of the Seizan branch of the Pure Land school. In 1227, when the imperial court prohibited the practice of the Nembutsu (the recitation of Amida Buddha's name), Sasshō was banished from Kyoto. He moved to Kamakura and eventually founded his own school, which upheld the doctrine of meditation on Amida Buddha. The details of his teachings are unknown.

sattva [薩埵] (Skt; Pali *satta;* Jpn *satta*): Being, existence, a living being, consciousness, spirit, or character. In Chinese translations of Buddhist sutras, the term *sattva* is rendered as living being or sentient being. "Sentient beings" refers to those living beings endowed with emotion and consciousness. *Sattva* is a component of such Buddhist terms as *bodhisattva* (a being who aspires to *bodhi* or enlightenment) and *mahāsattva* (a great being, an honorific title for a bodhisattva).

Sattva [薩埵王子] (Skt; Jpn Satta-ōji): A prince who sacrificed himself to save a starving tigress, according to the Golden Light Sutra. *See* Mahāsattva.

Satyasiddhi school [成実宗] (Skt; Jpn Jōjitsu-shū): *See* Establishment of Truth school.

Satyasiddhi-shāstra [成実論] (Skt; Jpn *Jōjitsu-ron*): See *Treatise on the Establishment of Truth, The.*

Sautrāntika school [経量部] (Skt; Jpn Kyōryō-bu): One of the twenty

Hinayana schools. The Sautrāntika school broke away from the Sarvāstivāda school. Unlike the Sarvāstivādins, who valued *abhidharma* works, or Buddhist treatises, the Sautrāntikas relied only on the sutras. Whereas the Sarvāstivāda school held that the dharmas, or elements of existence, are real and have an abiding existence of their own, the Sautrāntika school taught that the dharmas have actual existence only in the present and that only the present exists. The Sautrāntika doctrine is similar in several aspects to Mahayana thought and is regarded by some scholars as the origin of the Consciousness-Only, or Yogāchāra, teaching because the two share in common the concept of "karmic seeds," the causes or sources of all phenomena, which are inherent in life.

Sāvatthī [舍衛城] (Pali; Jpn Shae-jō): Shrāvastī in Sanskrit. The capital of the Kosala kingdom of ancient India in Shakyamuni's time. *See* Shrāvastī.

scorched seeds [焦種] (Jpn *shōshu*): A reference to persons of the two vehicles. Mahayana sutras often describe persons of the two vehicles—voice-hearers and cause-awakened ones—as being incapable of attaining Buddhahood, likening them to scorched or rotten seeds that will never sprout. *See also* rotten seeds.

scroll of the fifth volume of the Lotus Sutra [法華経第五の巻] (Jpn *Hoke-kyō daigo-no-maki*): *See* fifth scroll of the Lotus Sutra.

seal of the Dharma [法印] (Jpn *hōin*): A standard for judging whether a certain doctrine is Buddhist; also, basic principles applied to this standard. *See* Dharma seal.

sea of the sufferings of birth and death [生死の苦海] (Jpn *shōji-no-kukai*): Also, sea of suffering. The sufferings of transmigration in the six paths, which are endless and difficult to overcome. They are compared to the ocean, which is vast and difficult to cross. In this context, the term *other shore* or *reaching the other shore* is used as an analogy for enlightenment, or emancipation from transmigration in the six paths.

seated meditation [坐禅] (Jpn *zazen*): The practice of meditation in a sitting posture to perceive the truth by keeping the mind concentrated and unperturbed. This type of concentration exercise was carried out widely in ancient India and was incorporated into Buddhism by Shakyamuni, who sat in meditation when he attained enlightenment under the *bodhi* tree. This practice was introduced to China, and T'ien-t'ai (538–597) taught it as part of an integrated system of disciplines aimed at perceiving the true nature of one's mind. The Zen, or Ch'an, school attaches primary importance to the practice of seated meditation.

Secret Solemnity [密厳] (Jpn Mitsugon): The name of the pure land described in the Secret Solemnity Sutra. It symbolizes awakening to the *ālaya*-consciousness, which is equated in this sutra with the Buddha nature. The Pure Land of Secret Solemnity is also identified with the land of Mahāvairochana Buddha. *See also* Secret Solemnity Sutra.

Secret Solemnity Sutra [密厳経] (Chin *Mi-yen-ching;* Jpn *Mitsugon-gyō*): A Mahayana sutra that depicts the Pure Land of Secret Solemnity, a world of bodhisattvas who have overcome the illusions of the threefold world. Its full title is the Mahayana Secret Solemnity Sutra. The sutra teaches that all phenomena originate from the *ālaya*-consciousness, which it equates with the matrix of the Thus Come One (Skt *tathāgata-garbha*), or potential for Buddhahood. It also asserts that one must awaken to the *ālaya*-consciousness in order to be reborn in the Pure Land of Secret Solemnity. Two Chinese versions exist, one translated by Divākara in the late seventh century and the other by Pu-k'ung (Amoghavajra) in 765. A Tibetan translation also exists.

seed of Buddhahood [仏種] (Jpn *busshu*): The cause for attaining Buddhahood. The Buddha nature inherent in ordinary people, or the innate potential to become a Buddha; also the Buddha's teaching, which clarifies and enables people to realize their Buddha nature. Bodhisattva practice, the practice required of a bodhisattva, is also regarded as the seed of Buddhahood. One ensures the cause for realizing enlightenment by receiving the Buddha's teaching, the seed of Buddhahood. Based on the Lotus Sutra, T'ien-t'ai (538–597) interpreted the seed of Buddhahood as the doctrine of three thousand realms in a single moment of life, and Nichiren (1222–1282) defined it as the Law of Nam-myoho-renge-kyo. *See also* sowing, maturing, and harvesting.

Seichō-ji [清澄寺]: Also known as Kiyosumi-dera, an alternative pronunciation of the Chinese characters that form the name. A head temple of the Nichiren school based at Minobu since 1949. Located on Mount Kiyosumi in Kominato of Awa Province, in what is today Chiba Prefecture, Japan, the temple was founded in 771 by a priest named Fushigi who enshrined there an image of Bodhisattva Space Treasury he carved from an oak tree. In the next century, Jikaku, the third chief priest of the Tendai school's Enryaku-ji temple, paid a visit there, after which it gained prestige in the area. In 1233 Nichiren entered Seichō-ji and studied Buddhism there under Dōzen-bō, a senior priest at the temple. There he chanted Nam-myoho-renge-kyo for the first time and proclaimed his teaching on the twenty-eighth day of the fourth month, 1253.

Seiryō-ji [清凉寺]: A temple of the Pure Land (Jōdo) school in Kyoto, Japan. Originally a villa belonging to Minamoto no Tōru, a son of Emperor Saga, it was converted into a temple and founded in 896 with the name Seika-ji. In 983 Chōnen, a priest of Tōdai-ji temple, traveled to China. There he had an image of Shakyamuni Buddha made, a copy of the Buddha image enshrined at K'ai-yüan-ssu temple in that country. In China, it was believed that the K'ai-yüan-ssu image had been sculpted in Shakyamuni's time by order of King Udayana of Kaushāmbī in India. In 987 Chōnen brought his copy of the image back with him to Japan, and after his death his disciple Jōsan enshrined it in the Shakyamuni Buddha Hall in the Seika-ji compound. This hall was named Seiryō-ji. As worship of the image became popular, Seiryō-ji became the main hall on the grounds of the original Seika-ji, and later the entire temple was renamed Seiryō-ji.

Seishi [勢至] (Jpn): The bodhisattva Great Power (Seishi-bosatsu), who attends Amida Buddha. *See* Great Power.

Selection of the Time, The [撰時抄] (Jpn *Senji-shō*): One of Nichiren's five or ten major writings. Nichiren composed this treatise at Minobu in Kai Province, Japan, in 1275 and sent it to a believer named Yui who lived in Nishiyama of Suruga Province. As with a number of his other important works, it takes the form of a dialogue between the author and a hypothetical questioner. "Time" in the title refers to the Latter Day of the Law, when the "pure Law" of Shakyamuni's teaching is destined to become obscured and lost, and the "great pure Law" of Nam-myoho-renge-kyo is to be spread.

In the treatise, Nichiren discusses the five five-hundred-year periods following the death of Shakyamuni, which are described in the Great Collection Sutra. He outlines the events pertaining to Buddhism during each period, as Buddhism spread from India to China and then to Japan, and the age shifted from the Former Day to the Middle Day and finally to the Latter Day of the Law. Nichiren then proclaims that during the last of the five five-hundred-year periods, or the first five hundred years of the Latter Day, the great pure Law will spread far and wide throughout the world. He describes the great pure Law as "a correct Law that is supremely profound and secret, one that, though expounded in full by the Buddha, in the time since his passing has never yet been propagated by Mahākāshyapa, Ānanda, Ashvaghosha, Nāgārjuna, Asanga, or Vasubandhu, nor even by T'ien-t'ai or Dengyō" (560). Nichiren sees himself in this context as the votary of the Lotus Sutra destined to propagate this Law. In this regard, he writes: "A person who spreads the Lotus Sutra is father and mother to all the living beings in Japan. For, as the Great Teacher Chang-an says, 'One who rids the offender of evil is acting as his parent.' If so, then I, Nichiren, am the father and mother of the present emperor of Japan, and the teacher and lord of the Nembutsu believers, the Zen followers, and the True Word priests" (551).

The latter half of the treatise exposes what Nichiren sees as the errors of the Pure Land (Jpn Jōdo), Zen, and True Word (Shingon) schools, referring to them as the root causes of the calamities besetting Japan at that time. Nichiren holds the leading priests of the True Word school particularly responsible for all of this. Not only does he take them to task for incorporating T'ien-t'ai's doctrine of three thousand realms in a single moment of life into their own teaching, but also for asserting the superiority of their Mahāvairochana Sutra over the Lotus Sutra. Making the point that Buddhist and non-Buddhist texts define a sage as one who knows the future, Nichiren declares that he is a great sage, because the predictions he made on the three occasions he remonstrated with the authorities all came true. These are his predictions of internal strife and foreign invasion. He declares that he has lived the passage in the "Encouraging Devotion" (thirteenth) chapter of the Lotus Sutra, which foretells the appearance of the three powerful enemies, and without begrudging his life he has struggled continually to spread the great pure Law of Nam-myoho-renge-kyo.

self-awakened one [独覚] (Jpn *dokkaku*): *See* cause-awakened one.

self-nature [自性] (Skt *svabhāva;* Jpn *jishō*): The individual nature that all things maintain; their unchanging identities. Also, the notion that things or beings exist independently, separate from all others.

Seng-chao [僧肇] (384–414) (PY Sengzhao; Jpn Sōjō): A priest of Ch'ang-an in China and a disciple of Kumārajīva. He first studied the Taoist philosophy of Lao Tzu and Chuang Tzu. On reading the Vimalakīrti Sutra, however, he took a deep interest in Buddhism and resolved to become a Buddhist priest. Later he heard of Kumārajīva and became one of his most outstanding disciples, assisting Kumārajīva in the translation of Buddhist scriptures. He wrote *The Treatises of Seng-chao,* which elucidates the concepts of non-substantiality, wisdom, and nirvana, and *The Afterword to the Lotus Sutra Translation,* which describes Kumārajīva translating the Lotus Sutra.

Seng-ch'üan [僧詮] (n.d.) (PY Sengquan; Jpn Sōsen): A priest of the Three Treatises (San-lun) school in China in the sixth century. He studied its doctrine under Seng-lang, the master of the Three Treatises teachings. He had four main disciples: Fa-lang, Hui-pu, Chih-pien, and Hui-yung. He transmitted the Three Treatises teaching to Fa-lang, who in turn transmitted it to Chi-tsang.

Seng-jou [僧柔] (431–494) (PY Sengrou; Jpn Sōnyū): A priest of Ting-lin-ssu temple at Chien-k'ang, the capital of the Southern Ch'i dynasty in China. Under Hung-ch'eng, who was famed for his knowledge of Buddhist sutras and treatises, Seng-jou studied sutras, practiced meditation, and observed the precepts. Later he lectured on Buddhist sutras and treatises and at the request of Wen Hsüan, a son of Emperor Wu of the Southern Ch'i dynasty, resided at Ting-lin-ssu temple in the capital.

Seng-jui [僧叡] (n.d.) (PY Sengrui; Jpn Sōei): One of Kumārajīva's major disciples. He became a priest and first studied Buddhism under Seng-hsien. When Kumārajīva went to Ch'ang-an in China in 401, Seng-jui became his disciple. He assisted Kumārajīva in translating the Lotus Sutra into Chinese. He had a deep understanding of Buddhist scriptures and wrote prefaces to many Chinese translations of Buddhist texts, such as the Lotus Sutra and *The Treatise on the Great Perfection of Wisdom.*

Seng-lang [僧朗] (n.d.) (PY Senglang; Jpn Sōrō): A priest of the Three Treatises (San-lun) school in China who lived from the fifth through the sixth century. A native of Koguryŏ, a kingdom that ruled the northern Korean Peninsula and a part of northeastern China, Seng-lang propagated the Three Treatises doctrine in southern China. His teachings were successively transmitted by Seng-ch'üan, Fa-lang, and Chi-tsang.

Seng-min [僧旻] (467–527) (PY Sengmin; Jpn Sōbin or Sōmin): A priest who was revered as one of the three great Dharma teachers of the Liang dynasty (502–557) in China, the other two being Fa-yün and Chih-tsang. In 482 Seng-min went to the capital, Chien-k'ang, where he studied under T'an-ching at Chuang-yen-ssu temple. He also received instruction from Seng-jou, Hui-tz'u, and other eminent priests. He later became renowned for his lectures on *The Treatise on the Establishment of Truth,* the Wisdom sutras, and the Shrīmālā Sutra.

Seng-ts'an [僧璨] (d. 606) (PY Sengcan; Jpn Sōsan): Also known as the Meditation Master Chien-chih. The third patriarch in the lineage of Zen (Ch'an) Buddhism in China. He studied the Zen teachings under the second patriarch, Hui-k'o. When Buddhism was suppressed by Emperor Wu (r. 560–578) of the Northern Chou dynasty, he hid himself on a mountain where he continued his practice. Seng-ts'an transferred the Zen teachings to Tao-hsin. He authored the work *On Trust in the Heart.*

Seng-yu [僧祐] (445–518) (PY Sengyou; Jpn Sōyū): The priest who compiled the Chinese work *A Collection of Records concerning the Tripitaka,* which he did on the basis of Tao-an's *Comprehensive Catalog of Sutras,* the first index of Chinese translations of the Buddhist scriptures. Because *The Comprehensive Catalog of Sutras* was lost, his *Collection of Records concerning the Tripitaka* is the oldest extant Chinese catalog of the Buddhist canon. This work is a valuable reference not only for the study of Buddhist literature but also for historical studies, as it includes prefaces to the various translations and biographies of the early translators.

Senkan [千観] (918–983): A priest of the Tendai school in Japan. He first entered the priesthood at Onjō-ji temple and studied the exoteric and esoteric teachings of the Tendai school. Later he came to practice the Pure Land teachings and taught them to many. In 962 (963 according to another account) Senkan offered prayers for rain at the request of the imperial court to save the country from a drought, and it is said that rain fell immediately. Thereafter he founded Konryū-ji temple in Settsu Province and lived there.

Sennichi, the lay nun [千日尼] (n.d.) (Jpn Sennichi-ama): The wife of Abutsu-bō (d. 1279) and a follower of Nichiren. She and her husband lived in Sado, an island in the Sea of Japan. Her origins are unclear. According to one account, the lay nun Sennichi served as an attendant to a court lady who had accompanied the Retired Emperor Juntoku, when he was banished to Sado after the Jōkyū Disturbance of 1221. Another, more likely, account says that she was a native of the island. While Nichiren was in exile on Sado Island in late 1271, Sennichi and her husband Abutsu-bō converted to his teaching. The couple frequently visited Nichiren in his forlorn dwelling at Tsukahara on the island and supplied him with food, writing materials, and other necessities. Their support continued for more than two years until his pardon in 1274. After Nichiren moved to Mount Minobu, the lay nun Sennichi sent her husband to visit him there with offerings on three or more occasions.

sentient beings [有情] (Skt *sattva;* Jpn *ujō*): Those living things endowed with feelings, emotion, and consciousness; that is, most of the animal kingdom including human beings. Buddhism broadly classifies all existence into sentient and insentient beings. "Insentient beings," while including plants, also includes non-living things such as stones and water.

Sen'yo [仙予] (Jpn): The name of Shakyamuni Buddha when he was a king in a previous existence, according to the "Noble Practice" chapter of the Nirvana Sutra. The chapter describes King Sen'yo (Sanskrit unknown; Chin Hsien-yü) as the ruler of a great kingdom who had deep reverence for the great vehicle, or Mahayana, sutras. In his heart, he was pure and good, free from evil thoughts, jealousy, or stinginess. He continued to make offerings to Brahmans for twelve years. One day, when he heard Brahmans slander the great vehicle teachings, he put them to death to protect the teachings. Because of this act, the sutra says, he was never thereafter in danger of falling into hell. In his 1260 work *On Establishing the Correct Teaching for the Peace of the Land,* Nichiren says that this story should not be taken as condoning the killing of slanderers, but rather as demonstrating the gravity of slandering the correct teaching and the importance of protecting it. He says, "According to the Buddhist teachings, prior to Shakyamuni slanderous monks would have incurred the death penalty. But since the time of Shakyamuni, the One Who Can Endure, the giving of alms to slanderous monks is forbidden in the sutra teachings" (23).

separate transmission outside the sutras [教外別伝] (Jpn *kyōge-betsu-den*): A doctrine of the Zen school stating that the Buddha's enlightenment and his true teaching have been transmitted apart from the sutras. This phrase is often accompanied by the phrase "independent of words or writing." "Transmission from mind to mind" is a similar oft-quoted phrase. The Zen school asserts that the Buddha's enlightenment has been wordlessly transmitted from mind to mind and in this way handed down from one Zen patriarch to the next. In referring to this tenet, sometimes the word "special" replaces "separate," or "scriptures" replaces "sutras" in the above.

separation of the three truths [隔歴の三諦] (Jpn *kyakuryaku-no-santai*): A view of the three truths found in the specific teaching, one of the four teachings of doctrine as classified by T'ien-t'ai (538–597). It holds the three truths of non-substantiality, temporary existence, and the Middle Way to be separate from and independent of one another. This doctrine is contrasted with the unification of the three truths, another view formulated by T'ien-t'ai, which perceives the three truths as three perspectives of an integrated whole. The unification of the three truths is a view revealed in the perfect teaching, the highest of the four teachings of doctrine. *See also* three truths.

service for deceased ancestors [盂蘭盆] (Skt *ullambana;* Jpn *urabon*): A Buddhist service in which offerings are made to the three treasures of Buddhism for the benefit of the deceased. Such ceremonies were conducted annually, usually on the fifteenth day of the seventh month. In Japan today, it is a Buddhist observance honoring the spirits of deceased ancestors, which is held July 13–15 (August in some areas). According to the Service for the Deceased Sutra, this tradition began with Shakyamuni's disciple Maudgalyāyana, known as foremost in transcendental powers. That sutra states that Maudgalyāyana perceived with his divine eyesight that his deceased mother was suffering in the world of hungry spirits. He tried to send her food to ease her hunger by means of his transcendental abilities, but it turned into flames and instead burned her. Accordingly, he sought the advice of Shakyamuni Buddha, who urged him to make offerings to the monks on her behalf on the fifteenth day of the seventh month (the last day of the three-month rainy-season retreat, on which monks met and publicly acknowledged and repented of any violation of the precepts). Maudgalyāyana made offerings of food to the

Buddhist Order as instructed, and his mother was relieved of her agony.

It is said that the first service for deceased ancestors was held in China in 538, and in Japan in 606. Some interpret the Sanskrit *ullambana,* which means "hanging upside down," as a metaphor for the suffering that a deceased person is said to undergo in the world of hungry spirits. Hence the Buddhist observance was conducted to save the dead from that suffering. The Service for the Deceased Sutra is now regarded as having originated in China, as is the tradition of *urabon,* or the *bon* festival.

Service for the Deceased Sutra [盂蘭盆経] (Chin *Yü-lan-p'en-ching;* Jpn *Urabon-kyō*): A sutra that explains the origin of the service for deceased ancestors. When Maudgalyāyana asked Shakyamuni Buddha how to save his mother who had died and fallen into the world of hungry spirits, he was exhorted to offer various foods of a hundred flavors to the monks of the Order on the fifteenth day of the seventh month (the last day of the three-month rainy-season retreat, when monks would come together and publicly repent any violation of the precepts). Maudgalyāyana did as the Buddha had instructed, and his mother was relieved of her suffering. In China and Japan, this story gave rise to the service for deceased ancestors, an annual Buddhist ceremony held on the fifteenth day of the seventh month. Today this sutra is generally regarded as having originated in China, though its translation into Chinese was traditionally attributed to Dharmaraksha sometime in the third or fourth century.

seven aids to enlightenment [七覚支・七菩提分] (Jpn *shichi-kakushi* or *shichi-bodaibun*): Seven practices conducive to enlightenment. They are memory, discrimination, exertion, joy, lightness and ease, meditation, and impartiality (also referred to as indifference). *Memory* here means to recollect one's own past deeds and states, and keep them in mind. *Discrimination* means to discern the true from the false. *Exertion* means to be ever diligent in the practice of true teachings, and *joy* to delight in the practice of true teachings. *Lightness and ease* means that one's body and mind are at peace and free from burden. *Meditation* means to keep the mind concentrated and unperturbed, and *impartiality* to abandon feelings of attachment and keep the mind detached and calm. The "seven aids to enlightenment" constitutes the sixth of the seven categories within the thirty-seven aids to the way, or the thirty-seven practices leading to enlightenment. The Sanskrit for "aid to enlightenment" is *bodhyanga.*

seven arrogances [七慢] (Jpn *shichi-man*): *See* seven types of arrogance.

seven beneficent deities [七福神] (Jpn *shichi-fukujin*): Also, seven deities of good fortune or seven gods of luck. Seven gods of good fortune and long life. They include deities of Indian, Chinese, and Japanese origin. Belief in the seven beneficent deities prevailed in Japan in the early eighteenth century as a popular cult. They are called, in Japanese, Ebisu, Daikoku-ten (Skt Mahākāla), Bishamon-ten (Vaishravana), Benzai-ten (Sarasvatī), Hotei (Chin Pu-tai), Fukurokuju, and Jurōjin. Ebisu, Daikoku-ten, and Bishamon-ten are considered gods of fortune; Ebisu is also venerated as the deity of fishing. Benzai-ten is the deity of water and music, and Fukurokuju and Jurōjin are deities of long life.

seven Buddhas of the past [過去七仏] (Jpn *kako-shichi-butsu*): Also, seven Buddhas. Shakyamuni and six Buddhas said to have preceded him. The six Buddhas are Vipashyin, Shikhin, Vishvabhū, Krakucchanda, Kanakamuni, and Kāshyapa. The first three Buddhas appeared in the past Glorious Kalpa, while the other four Buddhas including Shakyamuni appeared in the present Wise Kalpa. The seven Buddhas are mentioned in the Long Āgama Sutra, the Seven Buddhas Sutra, and other sutras.

seven cardinal sins [七逆] (Jpn *shichi-gyaku*): The seven gravest offenses in Buddhism. According to the Brahmā Net Sutra, they are (1) injuring a Buddha, (2) killing one's father, (3) killing one's mother, (4) killing a monk of high virtue, (5) killing an *āchārya* (a Buddhist teacher), (6) causing disunity in the Buddhist Order, and (7) killing a sage. Lists of the seven cardinal sins differ slightly among the Buddhist sutras and commentaries. Miao-lo's work *The Annotations on "Great Concentration and Insight"* lists the five cardinal sins as killing one's father, killing one's mother, killing an arhat, injuring a Buddha, and causing disunity in the Buddhist Order, and adds to those killing a monk of high virtue and killing an *āchārya* to make the seven cardinal sins.

seven deities of good fortune [七福神] (Jpn *shichi-fukujin*): *See* seven beneficent deities.

seven disasters [七難] (Jpn *shichi-nan*): Disasters said to be caused by slander of the correct Buddhist teaching. In the Benevolent Kings Sutra, they are (1) extraordinary changes of the sun and moon, (2) extraordinary changes of the stars and planets, (3) fires, (4) unseasonable floods, (5) storms, (6) drought, and (7) war, including enemy attacks from without and rebellion from within. The Medicine Master Sutra defines the seven disasters as (1) pestilence, (2) foreign invasion, (3) internal strife, (4) extraordinary changes in the heavens, (5) solar and lunar eclipses, (6) unseasonable storms, and (7) drought. The seven disasters are often cited together with the three calamities in Nichiren's works as "the three calamities and seven disasters." The "Perceiver of the World's Sounds" (twenty-fifth) chapter of the Lotus Sutra also lists seven disasters from which people can be saved by the power of Bodhisattva Perceiver of the

World's Sounds: (1) fire, (2) flood, (3) *rākshasa* demons, (4) attack by swords and staves, (5) attack by *yaksha* and other demons, (6) imprisonment, and (7) attack by bandits. *See also* three calamities.

seven expedient means [七方便・七方便位] (Jpn *shichi-hōben* or *shichi-hōben-i*): (1) Seven stages of Hinayana practice, also referred to as seven expedients, seven stages of worthiness, seven worthies, or seven categories of worthy persons. The seven expedient means belong to the level of ordinary practitioners. They lead to the way of insight, the first of the three ways leading to nirvana, and are divided into two groups: the three stages of worthiness and the four good roots. They constitute practice preparatory to entering the way of insight. *See also* four good roots; three stages of worthiness.

(2) Seven expedients or expedient means, a concept set forth by the T'ien-t'ai school. T'ien-t'ai (538–597) defined two different sets of seven expedient means. One is that of the seven vehicles, or teachings, preached prior to the perfect teaching of the Lotus Sutra. These are teachings for (a) human beings, (b) heavenly beings, (c) voice-hearers, (d) cause-awakened ones, (e) bodhisattvas of the Tripitaka teaching, (f) bodhisattvas of the connecting teaching, and (g) bodhisattvas of the specific teaching. The other refers to practitioners: (a) voice-hearers and (b) cause-awakened ones of the Tripitaka teaching; (c) voice-hearers, (d) cause-awakened ones, and (e) bodhisattvas of the connecting teaching; (f) bodhisattvas of the specific teaching; and (g) bodhisattvas of the perfect teaching. In this context, the seven expedient means also refer to the seven stages or levels attained by these practitioners.

seven gods of luck [七福神] (Jpn *shichi-fukujin*): *See* seven beneficent deities.

seven guardian spirits [七鬼神] (Jpn *shichi-kijin*): Spirits said to end epidemics. According to the Mysterious Spells for Eliminating the Illnesses of the Five Components Sutra, calling upon the names of the seven guardian spirits puts an end to epidemics and releases people from suffering and affliction. In Japanese transliteration, they are called Mudanan, Akani, Nikashi, Akana, Harani, Abira, and Hadairi. In his work of 1260 titled *On Establishing the Correct Teaching for the Peace of the Land,* Nichiren portrays the misery accruing from the epidemics that afflicted Japan in his time. In listing the various ways people turned to religion and ritual in a desperate but futile attempt to abate them, he says: "Some write out the names of the seven guardian spirits and paste them on a thousand gates" (6).

seven-halled temple [七堂伽藍] (Jpn *shichidō-garan*): A type of Buddhist temple with seven basic structures. Though these seven structures and their designations differ according to the Buddhist school and historical period, the oldest arrangement consisted of the pagoda (main tower), the main hall (called golden hall), the lecture hall, the bell tower, the sutra repository, the dormitory for priests, and the dining hall. The pagoda originally housed the relics believed to be those of the Buddha. Later pagodas were used to house Buddhist scriptures instead. The main hall contained the temple's principal object of devotion.

In Zen temples, the main hall was called the Buddha hall. The pagoda and the main hall were the most important buildings in the early temple complex, though gradually the main hall became the central component. In the lecture hall, lectures on the Buddhist scriptures and discourse on the Buddhist doctrines were conducted, and the priests of the temple assembled to listen to sermons and perform rituals. The bell tower held the temple bell, which was traditionally sounded to assemble priests and to mark their daily routine. The sutra repository housed a collection of Buddhist texts. The dormitory was usually a long and narrow building where priests lived, some temples having more than one. The priests took their meals in the dining hall. Besides those buildings, temple compounds had an inner gate and an outer gate. The outer gate was the front entrance of the temple grounds and was called the "great south gate" because it faced south. The seven-halled temple style originated in China and was prevalent in Japan.

Asuka-dera temple, built by Soga no Umako (d. 626), a leading imperial court official, was the earliest among the full-fledged temple complexes in Japan. Early types of the seven structures, though with somewhat different layout, exist at Shitennō-ji and Hōryū-ji temples, built about the same time as Asuka-dera; at Yakushi-ji temple built in the late seventh century; and at Tōdai-ji in the mid-eighth century.

seven kinds of believers [七衆] (Jpn *shichi-shu*): Seven categories of members of the Buddhist Order. The seven kinds of believers are (1) monks, age twenty and older (Skt *bhikshu*), (2) nuns, age twenty and older *(bhikshunī)*, (3) male novices under twenty years of age *(shrāmanera)*, (4) female novices under twenty *(shrāmanerī)*, (5) female novices from eighteen to nineteen preparing for the nunhood *(shikshamānā)*, (6) male lay believers *(upāsaka)*, and (7) female lay believers *(upāsikā)*. The first five categories correspond to those who have left home, i.e., renounced secular life to live with the Buddhist Order. The remaining two—laymen and laywomen—remain at home, practicing Buddhism while maintaining their family and community responsibilities. In terms of precepts to observe, both laymen and laywomen observe the five precepts, and *shrāmaneras* and *shrāmanerīs* observe the ten precepts. *Shi-*

kshamānās observe the six precepts. Monks and nuns are those who have pledged to observe the entire set of monastic precepts, i.e., 250 for monks and 348 (commonly referred to as 500) for nuns.

seven kinds of treasures (1) [七宝] (Jpn *shichi-hō* or *shippō*): Also, seven treasures or seven kinds of gems. Precious substances mentioned in the sutras. The list differs among the Buddhist scriptures. According to the Lotus Sutra, the seven are gold, silver, lapis lazuli, seashell, agate, pearl, and carnelian. In the "Treasure Tower" (eleventh) chapter of the sutra, the treasure tower adorned with these seven kinds of treasures appears from beneath the earth. In a letter known as *On the Treasure Tower,* Nichiren associates the seven kinds of treasures that adorn the treasure tower with the seven elements of practice, writing: "It is the treasure tower adorned with the seven kinds of treasures—hearing the correct teaching, believing it, keeping the precepts, engaging in meditation, practicing assiduously, renouncing one's attachments, and reflecting on oneself" (299).

(2) [七財・七聖財] (Jpn *shichi-zai* or *shichi-shōzai*): Seven indispensable elements of Buddhist practice, which are compared to treasures. They are hearing the correct teaching, believing it, keeping the precepts, engaging in meditation, practicing assiduously, renouncing one's attachments, and reflecting on oneself.

seven major temples of Nara [南都七大寺] (Jpn *nanto-shichidai-ji*): Also, seven great temples of Nara. The main temples of Buddhism in Nara, the capital of Japan during the Nara period (710–794). They are Tōdai-ji, Kōfuku-ji, Gangō-ji, Daian-ji, Yakushi-ji, Saidai-ji, and Hōryū-ji.

seven parables [七譬] (Jpn *shichi-hi*): The seven parables that appear in the Lotus Sutra. They are (1) the parable of the three carts and the burning house, related in the "Simile and Parable" (third) chapter; (2) the parable of the wealthy man and his poor son, in the "Belief and Understanding" (fourth) chapter; (3) the parable of the three kinds of medicinal herbs and two kinds of trees, in the "Parable of the Medicinal Herbs" (fifth) chapter; (4) the parable of the phantom city and the treasure land, in the "Parable of the Phantom City" (seventh) chapter; (5) the parable of the jewel in the robe, in the "Five Hundred Disciples" (eighth) chapter; (6) the parable of the bright jewel in the topknot, in the "Peaceful Practices" (fourteenth) chapter; and (7) the parable of the skilled physician and his sick children, in the "Life Span" (sixteenth) chapter. The first, third, fourth, sixth, and seventh parables are related by Shakyamuni Buddha, and the second and fifth parables, by his disciples. The second parable is told by the four great voice-hearers (Maudgalyāyana, Mahākāshyapa, Kātyāyana, and Subhūti), while the fifth parable is shared by five hundred arhats. *See* the entry for each of the seven parables for a description of that parable.

seven schools [七宗] (Jpn *shichi-shū*): Seven prominent schools of Buddhism in Japan. Lists of the seven schools differed: One includes the Dharma Analysis Treasury (Kusha), Establishment of Truth (Jōjitsu), Precepts (Ritsu), Dharma Characteristics (Hossō), Three Treatises (Sanron), Flower Garland (Kegon), and True Word (Shingon) schools. The first six schools in the above list are known as the six schools of Nara, which flourished during the Nara period (710–794); the seventh, the True Word school, rose to prominence during the early Heian period (794–1185). A second list consists of the six schools of Nara plus the Tendai school (instead of the True Word school). The Tendai and True Word schools became popular during the same period. A third list names the Precepts, Dharma Characteristics, Three Treatises, Flower Garland, Tendai, True Word, and Zen schools; it excludes the Dharma Analysis Treasury school and the Establishment of Truth school because they were not regarded as fully independent.

seven stages of worthiness [七賢] (Jpn *shichi-ken*): *See* seven expedient means (1).

seven treasures [七宝] (Jpn *shichi-hō* or *shippō*): (1) Seven precious possessions of a wheel-turning king, an ideal ruler in ancient Indian mythology. They are a wheel (Skt *chakra*), elephants, horses, jewels, jewel-like women, excellent ministers of financial affairs, and generals. (2) *See* seven kinds of treasures (1).

seven types of arrogance [七慢] (Jpn *shichi-man*): Also, seven arrogances. Enumerated in *A Basic Treatise for the Explanation of Buddhist Concepts* and in *The Dharma Analysis Treasury*, they are (1) to think that one is superior to those inferior to oneself and that one is equal to one's equals; (2) to think that one is superior to one's equals and equal to those who are superior to oneself; (3) to think that one is superior to those superior to oneself; (4) to be attached to the self based on the delusion that one's life, which is a temporary combination of the five components, is a permanent entity; (5) to think that one has gained a truth that one has not yet perceived; (6) to think that one is not much inferior to those who far surpass oneself; and (7) to pretend to possess virtue when one lacks virtue. *See also* nine types of arrogance.

seven worthies [七賢] (Jpn *shichi-ken*): Seven stages of Hinayana practice, also referred to as seven expedient means. *See* seven expedient means (1).

Shāketa [娑祇多] (Skt; Jpn Shagita): A city in Kosala, one of the sixteen great states of ancient India around the sixth century B.C.E., which Shakyamuni Buddha often visited to preach. Scholars generally maintain that Shāketa is another name for Ayodhyā, the capital of Kosala before Shrāvastī. The Mahāparinirvāna Sutra lists the six great cities in the sixteen great states of India as Shāketa, Shrāvastī, Champā, Vaishālī, Vārānasī, and Rājagriha. Shrāvastī was another flourishing city in the kingdom of Kosala. Shāketa is commonly regarded as having been at the site of modern Oudh in northeastern Uttar Pradesh, a northern state of India.

Shakra [帝釈] (Skt; Jpn Taishaku): Also known as Shakra Devānām Indra, or simply Indra. The lord or king of gods in early Vedic and Hindu belief, and one of the two principal protective gods of Buddhism, the other being Brahmā. The Sanskrit word *shakra* means powerful. Indra was originally the god of thunder in Vedic mythology, and Shakra was one of his many titles. Buddhist texts adopted Shakra as his primary name, though the name Indra also appears. He is also one of the twelve gods of Esoteric Buddhism said to protect the world. Residing in a palace called Joyful to See in the Heaven of the Thirty-three Gods on the summit of Mount Sumeru and served by the four heavenly kings, he is said to govern the other thirty-two gods of that heaven. Shakra is depicted in many sutras as testing Buddhist practitioners' resolve. This he often does by assuming various forms, such as that of a Brahman or a demon. The *Jātaka* and other scriptures depict him as testing Shakyamuni when the latter was engaged in bodhisattva practices in previous lifetimes. According to the "Introduction" (first) chapter of the Lotus Sutra, he took part in the assembly on Eagle Peak at which the sutra was preached, with twenty thousand retainers accompanying him. Shakra Devānām Indra means "Shakra, the Indra of the Gods," i.e., "Shakra, the Lord of the Gods." Buddhist scriptures also refer to him as Kaushika.

Shakra Devānām Indra [釈提桓因・帝釈] (Skt; Jpn Shakudai-kan'in or Taishaku): *See* Shakra.

shakubuku [折伏] (Jpn): A method of expounding Buddhism, the aim of which is to suppress others' illusions and to subdue their attachment to error or evil. This refers to the Buddhist method of leading people, particularly its opponents, to the correct Buddhist teaching by refuting their erroneous views and eliminating their attachment to opinions they have formed. The practice of *shakubuku* thus means to correct another's false views and awaken that person to the truth of Buddhism.

The term *shakubuku* is used in contrast with *shōju,* which means to lead others to the correct teaching gradually, according to their capacity and without directly refuting their religious misconceptions. These two methods of propagation are described in the Shrīmālā Sutra, *Great Concentration and Insight* by T'ien-t'ai (538-597), and other works. Nichiren, who employed *shakubuku* in his propagation, writes in his 1272 treatise *The Opening of the Eyes:* "When the country is full of evil people without wisdom, then *shōju* is the primary method to be applied, as described in the 'Peaceful Practices' chapter [of the Lotus Sutra]. But at a time when there are many people of perverse views who slander the Law, then *shakubuku* should come first, as described in the 'Never Disparaging' chapter [of the sutra]" (285). Here "evil people without wisdom" means those who are ignorant of the Buddhist teachings. "Evil" means the unhappiness of acquiring no roots of goodness. It is contrasted with "people of perverse views who slander the Law," i.e., those who have a biased view of Buddhism and slander its correct teaching.

Nichiren describes Bodhisattva Never Disparaging, who bowed in respect to everyone he met and praised them as potential Buddhas, as a practitioner of *shakubuku*. In citing Never Disparaging as an example, Nichiren made clear that *shakubuku* is not a form of verbal or rhetorical aggression, but an expression of reverence for the truth that everyone possesses a Buddha nature, and of compassion for people. At the same time, in bowing and praising people as potential Buddhas, Never Disparaging was in effect challenging and refuting their misconceptions about Buddhahood, and was for this reason attacked.

Shākya [釈迦族] (Skt; Jpn Shaka-zoku): A tribe that lived in the area along the modern Indian-Nepalese border in the southern foothills of the Himalayas. Shakyamuni Buddha came from this tribe; his name, Shakyamuni, means "sage of the Shākyas." According to tradition, the Shākyas were descended from a royal family that belonged to the Kshatriyas, the warrior or ruling class, the second highest of the four castes in ancient Indian society. They had their capital at Kapilavastu. In Shakyamuni's time, the Shākyas were subjects of their adjacent kingdom, Kosala. During Shakyamuni's later years, the majority of the Shākya tribe was destroyed by Kosala's king Virūdhaka.

Shakyamuni [釈尊・釈迦牟尼] (Skt; Jpn Shakuson or Shakamuni): Also known as Gautama Buddha. The founder of Buddhism. "Shakyamuni" means "sage of the Shākyas," Shākya being the name of the tribe or clan to which his family belonged. Opinions differ concerning the dates of his birth and death. According to Buddhist tradition in China and Japan, he was born on the eighth day of the fourth month of 1029 B.C.E. and died on the fifteenth day of the second month of 949 B.C.E., but recent studies have him living nearly five hundred years later. The view prevalent among scholars is that Shakyamuni lived from about 560 to about 480 B.C.E., though some scholars hold that he lived from about 460 to about 380 B.C.E. He was the son of Shuddhodana, the king of the Shākyas, a small tribe whose kingdom was located in the foothills of the Himalayas south of what is now central Nepal. Shakyamuni's family name was Gautama (Best Cow), and his childhood or given name was Siddhārtha (Goal Achieved), though some scholars say the latter is a title bestowed on him by later Buddhists in honor of the enlightenment he attained.

According to the Buddhist scriptures, Shakyamuni was born in Lumbinī Gardens, in what is now Rummindei in southern Nepal. His mother, Māyā, died on the seventh day after his birth, and he was raised thereafter by her younger sister Mahāprajāpatī. In his boyhood and adolescence, he is said to have excelled in both learning and the martial arts. Though raised amid the luxuries of the royal palace, he seems to have very soon become aware of and been profoundly troubled by the problem of human suffering. As a young man, he married the beautiful Yashodharā, who bore him a son, Rāhula. He became increasingly possessed, however, by a longing to abandon the secular world and go out in search of a solution to the inherent sufferings of life. Buddhist scriptures describe four encounters, which served to awaken in him an awareness of these four sufferings common to all people—birth, aging, sickness, and death—and a desire to seek their solution. Eventually he renounced his princely status and embarked on the life of a religious mendicant.

Having left the palace of the Shākyas at Kapilavastu, Shakyamuni traveled south to Rājagriha, the capital of the kingdom of Magadha, where he studied first with Ālāra Kālāma and then with Uddaka Rāmaputta, both teachers of yogic meditation. Though he quickly mastered their respective forms of meditation, he did not find the answers to his questions in these disciplines. Leaving Rājagriha, he proceeded to the bank of the Nairanjanā River near the village of Uruvilvā, where he began to engage in ascetic practices in the company of other ascetics. For six years, he subjected himself to disciplines of appalling severity, far surpassing those of his companions, but he found it entirely impossible to reach emancipation through such self-mortification and eventually rejected these practices as well. To restore his body, which had been weakened by long fasting, he accepted milk curds offered him by a girl named Sujātā. Then, near the city of Gayā, he seated himself under a pipal tree and entered meditation. There he attained an awakening, or enlightenment, to the true nature of life and all things. It was because of this enlightenment that he came to be called Buddha, or "Awakened One." According to Buddhist tradition in China and Japan, Siddhārtha renounced secular life at age nineteen and attained enlightenment at thirty. (Modern scholars generally place these ages at twenty-nine and thirty-five, respectively.) The pipal tree was later called the *bodhi* tree, *bodhi* meaning enlightenment, and the site itself came to be called Buddhagayā.

After his awakening, Shakyamuni is said to have remained for a while beneath the tree, rejoicing in his emancipation yet troubled by the knowledge of how difficult it would be to communicate what he had realized to others. For a while, he vacillated as to whether he should attempt to teach others what he had achieved. At length, however, he resolved that he would strive to do so, so that the way to liberation from the sufferings of birth and death would be open to all people. First he made his way to Deer Park in Vārānasī, where he preached and converted five ascetics who had formerly been his companions.

After that, Shakyamuni's efforts to propagate his teaching advanced rapidly. In Vārānasī he converted Yashas, the son of a rich man, and about sixty others. Then he headed back toward the site of his enlightenment, the village of Uruvilvā near Gayā. There he converted three brothers—Uruvilvā Kāshyapa, Nadī Kāshyapa, and Gayā Kāshyapa—who were leaders among Brahman ascetics, along with their one thousand followers. The Buddha then set out for Rājagriha in Magadha, where he converted its king, Bimbisāra, as well as Shāriputra and Maudgalyāyana, who would become two of the Buddha's leading disciples. The latter two were at that time followers of Sanjaya, one of the six non-Buddhist teachers. Together with Shāriputra and Maudgalyāyana, all of Sanjaya's followers—said to number 250—forsook him and entered the Buddhist Order. Mahākāshyapa also became another of the Buddha's disciples in Rājagriha shortly thereafter.

The Buddha made several trips to his childhood home, Kapilavastu, resulting in the conversion of many people, including his younger half brother Nanda, his son Rāhula, his cousins Ānanda, Aniruddha, and Devadatta, and a barber named Upāli. Shakyamuni's father, Shuddhodana, and his former wife, Yashodharā, are also said to have embraced the Buddhist teachings. The Buddha permitted his foster mother, Mahāprajāpatī, to enter the Buddhist Order, and thus the order of Buddhist nuns was established. At that time there was a powerful kingdom called Kosala that rivaled Magadha. In Shrāvastī, the capital of Kosala, a wealthy and influential merchant named Sudatta became the Buddha's lay follower and patron. He had met Shakyamuni while on business in Rājagriha and converted. Sudatta built Jetavana Monastery in Shrāvastī as an offering to the Buddha, and Shakyamuni is said to have spent twenty-five rainy seasons at this monastery with his disciples. Prasenajit, the king of Kosala, also became a Buddhist.

In the fifty years (forty-five according to modern scholars) from the time of his awakening until he died, Shakyamuni continued to travel through much of India to disseminate his teachings. Among the places where he concentrated his efforts were the cities of Rājagriha in Magadha; Shrāvastī in Kosala; Vaishālī, capital of the Vriji confederacy; and Kaushāmbī, the capital of Vatsa. The Buddha's disciples in the monastic order were also active in spreading his teachings. Mahākātyāyana was a native of the kingdom of Avanti in the western part of central India and made several converts there, including the king. Pūrna propagated Shakyamuni's teachings in Sunāparanta in western India north of present-day Bombay.

Thus even during Shakyamuni's lifetime, his teachings spread not only in central India but also to more remote areas, and people of all classes converted to Buddhism. The new religious movement, however, was perceived by many as a threat to the old Brahmanic order, and in the course of his efforts Shakyamuni personally underwent numerous hardships, representative of which are the so-called nine great ordeals. Persevering in the face of adversity, he continued to preach his message of emancipation, expounding the teachings in various ways according to the circumstances and capacity of his listeners. The teachings he left are so numerous that they later came to be called the eighty thousand teachings.

Shakyamuni died at age eighty. The year before his death, he stayed at Gridhrakūta (Eagle Peak) near Rājagriha. Then he set out on his last journey, proceeding northward across the Ganges River to Vaishālī. He spent the rainy season in Beluva, a village near Vaishālī. During this retreat he became seriously ill, but recovered and continued to preach in many villages. Eventually he came to a place called Pāvā in Malla. There he again became ill after eating a meal prepared as an offering by the village blacksmith, Chunda. Despite his pain, he continued his journey until he reached Kushinagara, where in a grove of sal trees he calmly lay down and spoke his last words. He admonished his disciples, saying: "You must not think that your teacher's words are no more, or that you are left without a teacher. The teachings and precepts I have expounded to you shall be your teacher." His final words are said to have been, "Decay is inherent in all composite things. Work out your salvation with diligence." His body was received by the Mallas of Kushinagara and cremated seven days later. The ashes were divided into eight parts, and eight stupas were erected to enshrine them. Two more stupas were built to house the vessel used in the cremation and the ashes of the fire. In the same year, the First Buddhist Council was held in the Cave of the Seven Leaves near Rājagriha to compile Shakyamuni's teachings.

shāla tree [沙羅樹] (Skt; Jpn *shara-ju*): A sal tree native to India and Nepal. *See* sal tree.

Shānavāsa [商那和修] (Skt; Jpn Shōnawashu): Also known as Shānavāsin, Shānakavāsa, or Shānakavāsin. He is regarded as the third of Shakyamuni Buddha's twenty-three, or the fourth of his twenty-four, successors. According to *A History of the Buddha's Successors,* he was a wealthy man of Rājagriha, the capital of Magadha in India. Extremely wise and valiant, as a lay practitioner of Buddhism, he made offerings of buildings and other things to the Buddhist Order. Finally he renounced the secular world to devote himself as a monk to practicing the Buddha's teachings. Shānavāsa inherited Shakyamuni's teachings from Ānanda, the second of the Buddha's twenty-three successors, and devoted himself to spreading the teachings, traveling to Mathurā and Kashmir to do so. He transferred the teachings to Upagupta. *A History of the Buddha's Successors* also describes Madhyāntika as a successor of Ānanda together with Shānavāsa. Although Madhyāntika propagated Buddhism in Kashmir, no distinct lineage or successorship emerged from his efforts and the recorded transmission of the teachings he had received from Ānanda ended. Madhyāntika, however, is sometimes included among the Buddha's successors, bringing the total number of successors to twenty-four; among these twenty-four successors, Shānavāsa is traditionally regarded as the fourth, and Madhyāntika, as the third.

Shan-chia school [山家派] (PY Shanjiapai; Jpn Sange-ha): A branch of the T'ien-t'ai school in China. *See* Mountain school (2).

Shan-tao [善導] (613–681) (PY Shandao; Jpn Zendō): The third patriarch of the Pure Land school in China. Shan-tao entered the priesthood at age ten and studied the Lotus, Vimalakīrti, and other sutras. Later he studied the Meditation on the Buddha Infinite Life Sutra and embraced the Pure Land teachings. In 641 he visited Tao-ch'o at Hsüan-chung-ssu temple, and was influenced deeply by Tao-ch'o's lecture on the Meditation on the Buddha Infinite Life Sutra. Thereafter he went to the capital Ch'ang-an, where he disseminated the practice of chanting the name of Amida Buddha. In his work *The Commentary on the Meditation on the Buddha Infinite Life Sutra,* Shan-tao classified Buddhist practices into the categories of correct and sundry. He defined the correct practices to be those directed toward Amida Buddha and regarded all other practices as sundry. In Japan, Hōnen (1133–1212) studied Shan-tao's *Commentary* *on the Meditation on the Buddha Infinite Life Sutra* and founded the Pure Land (Jōdo) school. Shan-tao also wrote *Praising Rebirth in the Pure Land* and other works.

Shan-wai school [山外派] (PY Shanwaipai; Jpn Sangai-ha): A branch of the T'ien-t'ai school in China. *See* Outside-the-Mountain school.

Shan-wu-wei [善無畏] (637–735) (PY Shanwuwei; Skt Shubhakarasimha; Jpn Zemmui): The Indian monk who first introduced Esoteric Buddhism to China. Shan-wu-wei is his Chinese name. Born a prince in Udyāna (Udra according to another account) in India, he became king at age thirteen. He abdicated the throne, however, in favor of a jealous elder brother and entered the Buddhist Order. He studied Esoteric Buddhism under Dharmagupta at Nālandā Monastery. In 716 he went to China and was welcomed by Emperor Hsüan-tsung of the T'ang dynasty, who named him teacher of the nation. There Shan-wu-wei translated a number of esoteric scriptures, including the Mahāvairochana and Susiddhikara sutras.

Shāriputra [舍利弗] (Skt; Pali Sāriputta; Jpn Sharihotsu): One of Shakyamuni Buddha's ten major disciples, known as foremost in wisdom. Shāriputra means "son of Shārī" (Shārī was his mother). Shāriputra is also known as Upatishya (Pali Upatissa). Born to a Brahman family in Nālaka in the suburbs of Rājagriha, the capital of Magadha, he was a close friend of Maudgalyāyana from childhood. Together they had both become followers of Sanjaya Belatthiputta, a skeptic and one of the six non-Buddhist teachers. Not long after Shakyamuni attained enlightenment, Shāriputra happened to meet Ashvajit, a disciple of Shakyamuni, at Rājagriha. Ashvajit taught him about the law of causation, and Shāriputra was so impressed by the implication of this doctrine and by Ashvajit's noble bearing that he became Shakyamuni's disciple. Maudgalyāyana followed his friend into the Buddhist Order, and the two brought all of Sanjaya's 250 disciples with them. From early on in Shakyamuni's preaching life, both were reckoned by the Buddha as his foremost disciples. Shāriputra in particular was esteemed by the Buddha so highly as to be regarded by him as his successor. He fell ill, however, and died several months before Shakyamuni in his native village, Nālaka. In the Lotus Sutra, Shāriputra alone constitutes the first of the three groups of voice-hearers to have grasped the Buddha's teaching, for he understood the Buddha's intention on hearing him preach the true aspect of all phenomena in the "Expedient Means" (second) chapter of the sutra. The "Simile and Parable" (third) chapter predicts that he will in a future existence become a Buddha named Flower Glow.

shāsana [教] (Skt; Pali *sāsana;* Jpn *kyō*): Teaching or doctrine. *Buddha-shāsana* means the Buddha's teaching or Buddhism.

She-lun school [摂論宗] (PY Shelunzong; Jpn Shōron-shū): *See* Summary of the Mahayana school.

Shen-hsiu [神秀] (d. 706) (PY Shenxiu; Jpn Jinshū): The founder of the Northern school of Zen (Ch'an) in China. As a young man, he studied Buddhism and the Taoist philosophy of Lao Tzu and Chuang Tzu. In 625 he entered the priesthood at Lo-yang. In 655 he met Hung-jen, the fifth patriarch of Chinese Zen, and practiced seated meditation under his guidance. Thereafter he left his teacher and continued his practice alone for fifteen years. In 700, at the invitation of Empress Wu, he propagated Zen in Ch'ang-an and Lo-yang in the north, teaching the traditional Zen doctrine of the gradual attainment of enlightenment. The lineage of his teaching therefore came to be called the Northern school of Zen. The Northern school rapidly declined after his death, however. The Southern school of Zen, carried on by Hui-neng, who formulated the doctrine of sudden enlightenment, came to predominate in China.

Shen-t'ai [神泰] (n.d.) (PY Shentai; Jpn Jintai): A priest and translator of the early T'ang dynasty (618–907) in China. As a disciple of Hsüan-tsang, he engaged in the translation of Buddhist scriptures and in 657 became the chief priest of Hsi-ming-ssu temple. He wrote *The Annotations on "The Summary of the Mahayana"* and *The Annotations on "The Dharma Analysis Treasury."* The latter is regarded as one of the three major annotations on *The Dharma Analysis Treasury,* the other two of which were written by P'u-kuang and Fa-pao.

Shiba Tatsuto [司馬達等] (n.d.) (Jpn; Chin Ssu-ma Ta-teng): Also known as Shiba Tatto. A native of China (a native of the Korean Peninsula according to another account) who in 522 brought to Japan an image of Shakyamuni Buddha and enshrined it in a grass hut in Takaichi District of Yamato Province. Shiba Tatsuto remained in Japan and worked with the courtier Soga no Umako, who supported Buddhism, to foster the new religion. He also contributed to introducing the culture of China to Japan. His daughter Shima became a Buddhist nun, and his son Tasuna became a priest. The daughter assumed the Buddhist name Zenshin and is said to have been the first nun in Japan. Tasuna's son, Kuratsukuri no Tori, was a famous sculptor of Buddhist images.

Shibi [尸毘王] (Skt; Jpn Shibi-ō): The name of Shakyamuni in a past existence when he was the ruler of a great kingdom, according to *The Garland of Birth Stories.* That work compares King Shibi's love for the people to a mother's love for her children. He was seeking the teachings of a Buddha, and one day the god Vishvakarman and the god Shakra decided to test him. They disguised themselves respectively as a dove and a hawk, the hawk relentlessly pursuing the dove, which flew into King Shibi's robes for protection. The hungry hawk demanded the dove as food, and Shibi decided that to save the dove he would offer the hawk an amount of his own flesh equal to the weight of the dove. He sliced off a piece of his flesh, placed it on one side of a balance, and placed the dove on the other. Strangely enough, although he continued slicing off his flesh and placing it on the scale, he could not equal the weight of the dove. Finally he placed himself on the scale, demonstrating his willingness to offer his entire body, and felt such delight and satisfaction as he had never experienced. At that time, Vishvakarman and Shakra reverted to their original forms as Buddhist gods and praised his practice of almsgiving. After Shakyamuni relates this story to his disciples, he reveals that King Shibi was himself in a past existence.

Shien [思円]: Another name for Eizon. A restorer of the Precepts (Ritsu) school in Japan. *See* Eizon.

Shiiji Shirō [椎地四郎] (n.d.): A follower of Nichiren who lived in the province of Suruga, Japan. Letters written by Nichiren in the twelfth month of 1280 and in the tenth month of 1281 indicate that he was acquainted with two of Nichiren's leading disciples, Shijō Kingo and Toki Jōnin. Shiiji Shirō received a letter, titled *A Ship to Cross the Sea of Suffering,* from Nichiren in the fourth month of 1261.

Shijō Kingo [四条金吾] (c. 1230–1300): A follower of Nichiren who lived in Kamakura, Japan. His full name and title were Shijō Nakatsukasa Saburō Saemon-no-jō Yorimoto. Kingo is an equivalent of the title Saemon-no-jō. His wife was Nichigen-nyo and they had two daughters, Tsukimaro and Kyō'ō. As a samurai retainer, he served the Ema family, a branch of the ruling Hōjō clan. Kingo was well versed in both medicine and the martial arts, and in temperament was straightforward, loyal, and passionate. He is said to have converted to Nichiren's teachings around 1256, at about the same time as Kudō Yoshitaka and the brothers Ikegami Munenaka and Ikegami Munenaga. When Nichiren was taken to Tatsunokuchi to be beheaded in 1271, Shijō Kingo accompanied him, resolved to die by his side. After Nichiren was exiled to Sado Island, Shijō Kingo sent a messenger to him with various offerings. Through this messenger Nichiren entrusted Shijō Kingo with his treatise *The Opening of the Eyes,* which he had completed in the second month of 1272. A few months later, Kingo himself made the journey to Sado to visit Nichiren.

Sometime after Nichiren returned from Sado and moved to Minobu in 1274, Shijō Kingo tried to convert his lord, Ema, who was a believer of the Pure Land (Jōdo) school and a follower of the priest Ryōkan of Gokuraku-ji temple. Lord Ema did not take kindly to his retainer's belief in the Lotus Sutra or support of Nichiren, whom Ryōkan hated, and harassed him on that account. At one point, he ordered Kingo to abandon his faith in Nichiren's teaching, threatening to transfer him to the remote province of Echigo if he did not obey. In 1277 Shijō Kingo happened to observe a debate at Kuwagayatsu in Kamakura in which Sammi-bō, a disciple of Nichiren, defeated Ryūzō-bō, a Tendai priest and a protégé of Ryōkan. Fellow samurai jealous of Kingo saw a chance to disgrace him in the eyes of his lord and reported falsely to Lord Ema that Kingo had forcibly disrupted the debate. This led Lord Ema to threaten to confiscate Kingo's fief.

Nichiren drafted a petition to Lord Ema on behalf of Shijō Kingo, which he sent to his loyal disciple. Before long, Lord Ema fell ill, and eventually had to ask Shijō Kingo for treatment. He recovered under Kingo's care and thereafter placed renewed trust in him. In 1278 Kingo received from Ema another estate three times larger than his original one. When Nichiren became ill in his later years, Shijō Kingo attended to him at Minobu. Kingo also attended Nichiren on his deathbed and participated in his funeral. After Nichiren's death, he lived in retirement at Utsubuna in Kai Province.

Shijūku-in [四十九院]: A temple of the Tendai school in Kambara of Suruga Province, Japan, where Nikkō, Nichiren's eventual successor, entered the priesthood and spent his childhood. After Nichiren went to live at Mount Minobu in 1274, Nikkō used the temple as a center for his propagation activities in the Fuji area. Gon'yo, the temple's administrator, became antagonistic toward Nikkō and other followers of Nichiren including Nichiji, Shōken, and Kenshū, and expelled them from the temple, claiming that their teachings were false. Nikkō sent a joint petition to the Kamakura shogunate condemning the expulsion as unreasonable and requesting an official religious debate with Gon'yo.

shikshamānā [式叉摩那・正学女・学法女] (Skt; Jpn *shikishamana, shōgakunyo,* or *gakuhōnyo*): A female novice in the Buddhist Order from eighteen to nineteen years of age who is preparing to take a vow to obey the entire set of monastic precepts for women and thereby become a fully ordained nun (Skt *bhikshunī*). A *shikshamānā* observes the six precepts against killing, stealing, having sexual relations, lying, drinking intoxicants, and eating after noon. A female novice under twenty years of age is called *shrāmanerī;* among *shrāmanerī,* those ages eighteen and nineteen are called *shikshamānā.* During these two years, the *shikshamānās* receive rigorous instruction to determine whether they can live as nuns.

Shikshānanda [実叉難陀] (652–710) (Skt; Jpn Jisshananda): A monk from Khotan in Central Asia. He was versed in Hinayana and Mahayana Buddhism as well as non-Buddhist learning. At the request of Empress Wu of T'ang-dynasty China, he brought the Sanskrit text of the Flower Garland Sutra to Lo-yang and began translating the sutra there. Bodhiruchi, I-ching, and others also joined the project, and in 699 the eighty-volume Chinese translation was completed. Thereafter Shikshānanda translated some twenty scriptures, including the Lankāvatāra Sutra. He also produced a second Chinese translation of *The Awakening of Faith in the Mahayana,* the first having been done by Paramārtha. In 704 he returned to Khotan to look after his elderly mother. He later returned to China and resumed his translation efforts in Ch'ang-an, but died a short time later.

shīla [戒] (Skt; Jpn *kai*): *See* precepts.

Shīlabhadra [戒賢] (529–645) (Skt; Jpn Kaigen): An Indian scholar of the Consciousness-Only (Skt Vijnānavāda) school. Born to the royal family of the kingdom of Samatata in eastern India, he studied the Consciousness-Only doctrine under Dharmapāla at Nālandā Monastery and was widely known as an outstanding scholar. According to *The Biography of the Tripitaka Master of Ta-tz'u-en-ssu Temple,* when the Chinese priest Hsüan-tsang visited the monastery to study in the early seventh century, Shīlabhadra taught him the doctrines of the Consciousness-Only school. Hsüan-tsang then brought them back to China, thereby establishing the basis of the Dharma Characteristics (Chin Fa-hsiang; Jpn Hossō) school.

Shīlāditya [戒日王] (r. 606–647) (Skt; Jpn Kainichi-ō): Also known as Harsha or Harshavardhana. An Indian king who, through inheritance and conquest, formed an empire that included most of northern India in the seventh century. Kanyākubja was its capital. At first an adherent of Hinduism, Shīlāditya later converted to Buddhism. He built many temples and stupas, supported Nālandā Monastery, and is said to have governed compassionately based on Buddhist principles. He is known through the biographical work *Harsha-charita* ("The Deeds of Harsha") written by the poet Bāna, and by Hsüan-tsang's detailed accounts of him and his kingdom in *The Record of the Western Regions.* Hsüan-tsang, the Chinese Buddhist priest who traveled extensively in India and Central Asia during the seventh century, became a friend and confidant of King Shīlāditya, who is also known for establishing the first diplomatic ties between India and China. Shīlāditya was also a poet and playwright and composed several dramas including *Nāgānanda* ("The Joy of the Dragon King").

Shinga [真雅] (801–879): Also known as the Administrator of Priests Jōgan-ji. A priest of the True Word (Shingon) school in Japan and the founder of Jōgan-ji temple in Kyoto. In 809 he renounced secular life and studied Esoteric Buddhism under his elder brother, Kōbō, the founder of the True Word school. In 825 he was invested with the rank of *ajari* (Skt *āchārya*), or teacher, in Esoteric Buddhism. In 847 he was appointed superintendent of Tōdai-ji temple, and in 860 became the chief priest of Tō-ji temple. In 862 he founded Jōgan-ji temple in the capital, Kyoto, and in 864 he was appointed administrator of priests. After Kōbō's death, he became an influential leader in the True Word school and headed Shingon-in temple at Tōdai-ji. He was often called on by the rulers to perform esoteric rituals for the protection of the country. He wrote *The Treatise on the Womb Realm*.

Shingon-Ritsu school [真言律宗] (Jpn Shingon Risshū): *See* True Word Precepts school.

Shingon school [真言宗] (Jpn Shingon-shū): *See* True Word school.

Shinjō [審祥] (n.d.) (Jpn; Kor Simsang): The founder of the Japanese Flower Garland (Kegon) school in the eighth century. He was believed to be a native of Silla, a kingdom on the Korean Peninsula, but recent research suggests he was a Japanese priest who had traveled to Silla to study Buddhism. From Japan he went to China, where he studied the Flower Garland doctrine under Fa-tsang, the third patriarch of the Chinese Flower Garland (Hua-yen) school. After returning to Japan, he lived at Daian-ji temple in Nara. In 740 he lectured on the Flower Garland Sutra at Konshō-ji temple, later known as Tōdai-ji temple, at the request of that temple's founder, Rōben. This was the first lecture on the Flower Garland Sutra to be given in Japan. Shinjō propagated the Flower Garland teaching with the support of Emperor Shōmu and fostered many disciples. Rōben was his successor.

Shinran [親鸞] (1173–1262): The founder of the True Pure Land (Jōdo Shin) school in Japan. His father was Hino Arinori, a court noble in Kyoto. Orphaned, he entered the priesthood in 1181 and as a youth studied the teachings of the Tendai school at Mount Hiei and the teachings of other schools in Nara. Dissatisfied, however, he went to Kyoto in 1201 and confined himself to a temple called the Rokkaku-dō (hexagonal hall) for one hundred days of prayer. It is said that, on the morning of the ninety-fifth day, Prince Shōtoku appeared before him in a dream and advised him to go to see Hōnen, the founder of the Japanese Pure Land (Jōdo) school. He visited Honen at Yoshimizu in Kyoto and became his disciple. Shinran was ardent in the Pure Land practice of Nembutsu—recitation of Amida Buddha's name—and soon became one of Hōnen's favorite disciples. Hōnen entrusted him with transcribing his major work *The Nembutsu Chosen above All.* When the Pure Land teachings were banned in 1207, Hōnen and Shinran were both divested of their priestly status; Hōnen was exiled to Tosa, and Shinran, to Echigo. There Shinran married the daughter of the Miyoshi family, a powerful clan in Echigo Province. His wife was called the nun Eshin. Shinran was pardoned in 1211 and went to Hitachi Province to propagate the Pure Land teaching. Around 1234 he returned to Kyoto, where he concentrated on writing. His main work was *The Teaching, Practice, Faith, and Proof.*

Shinsen-en garden [神泉苑] (Jpn Shinsen-en): A garden established on the grounds of the imperial palace in Kyoto, Japan. When the capital was moved to Kyoto by Emperor Kammu (r. 781–806), Shinsen-en garden was established for the banquets and other amusements of the emperor and court nobles. Kōbō, the founder of the Japanese True Word (Shingon) school, conducted a ritual of prayer for rain in this garden during the disastrous drought of 824, and thereafter it became a place of religious observance, particularly, ritual prayer for rain. Whenever a drought occurred, True Word priests were summoned to the garden to pray for rain. In 1607 a temple of the True Word school was built there.

Shinzei [真済] (800–860): A priest of the True Word (Shingon) school in Japan. He renounced secular life in childhood and became a disciple of Kōbō (also known as Kūkai), the founder of the True Word school. In 824 he was granted the position of *ajari* (Skt *āchārya*), which qualifies one to transmit the secret doctrines of True Word. After Kōbō's death, he took full responsibility for Jingo-ji temple on Mount Takao. Shinzei set out for China to further his studies, but his ship was wrecked by a storm and he returned to Jingo-ji. In 856 he was appointed administrator of priests, the first True Word priest to receive that title. He wrote *The Life of the Supervisor of Priests Kūkai.* He also collected Kōbō's writings, including prose and poetry, and compiled *The Collected Works of the Universally Illuminating Soul-Inspiring One.*

Shiren [師錬]: Also known as Kokan Shiren. A priest of the Rinzai school of Zen in Japan. *See* Kokan Shiren.

Shītavana [尸陀林・寒林] (Skt; Jpn Shidarin or Kanrin): A forest near Rājagriha, the capital of Magadha in ancient India. Shītavana is known as a place where the dead were abandoned.

Shitennō-ji [四天王寺]: The head temple of the Harmony (Wa) school, an offshoot of the Tendai school, in Osaka, Japan. It is the oldest extant Buddhist temple in Japan, founded by Prince Shōtoku in 587. Prince Shōtoku is said to have built it in gratitude for his victory in alliance with Soga no Umako over Mononobe no Moriya, the leader of the anti-Buddhist faction at court. According to tradition, Prince Shōtoku enshrined statues of the four heavenly kings (Jpn *shi-tennō*) there because he had won the victory as a result of his prayer to those gods; hence the name Shitennō-ji, or "Temple of the Four Heavenly Kings." Later Shitennō-ji became a branch temple of Enryaku-ji, the head temple of the Tendai school. It broke away from the Tendai school in 1949.

shloka [首盧迦] (Skt; Jpn *shuroka*): A kind of meter employed in Sanskrit literature, including Buddhist scriptures. In the *shloka* style, a verse consists of two lines, each with sixteen syllables. Each line is further divided into two eight-syllable parts, so that each verse contains four eight-syllable parts. *Shloka* style conforms to the following rule: In each line, the sixth, seventh, and fourteenth syllables must contain long vowels, and the fifth, thirteenth, and fifteenth syllables must contain short vowels. The other syllables can contain either long or short vowels. There are also irregular forms of *shloka* that depart to some degree from this standard form.

Shōbō [聖宝] (832–909): The priest who is recognized as the precursor of the Ono branch of the True Word (Shingon) school in Japan. In 847 he entered the priesthood under Kōbō's disciple Shinga, and later he studied the Three Treatises (Sanron), Flower Garland (Kegon), and Consciousness-Only doctrines. Thereafter he engaged in the practice of the esoteric teachings and in 876 founded Daigo-ji temple. After Shinga's death, he practiced the esoteric teachings under Shinnen and Gennin and thus distinguished himself among the community of the True Word school. In the lineage of Shōbō, Ningai (951–1046) later established the Ono school, so called because Ningai founded Mandara-ji temple in Ono of Kyoto and based his activities there.

Shō-bō [少輔房]: The name of individuals mentioned in the writings of Nichiren. The Japanese component *shō* is a title indicating the deputy or vice chief of a government ministry, and there were likely many persons called Shō-bō. *Bō* means a priest, lay priest, or a samurai who became a lay priest.

(1) Though originally Nichiren's disciple, he abandoned his belief in Nichiren's teachings around the time of the Izu Exile in 1261 and eventually turned against Nichiren. According to one account, he died around 1269.

(2) On the twelfth day of the ninth month, 1271, when Hei no Saemon, the deputy chief of the Office of Military and Police Affairs of the shogunate, went to arrest Nichiren at Matsubagayatsu in Kamakura, a person named Shō-bō accompanied him with other retainers and struck Nichiren in the face with a scroll, wrapped around a heavy wooden roller,

of the fifth volume of the Lotus Sutra. Nichiren saw special significance in this act of violence against him, because the fifth volume of the Lotus Sutra includes the "Encouraging Devotion" (thirteenth) chapter, which predicts that the votaries of the Lotus Sutra will be attacked with swords and staves.

(3) Shō-bō Nichizen, one of the six elder disciples of Nikkō. A priest of Ryūsen-ji, a temple of the Tendai school in Atsuhara, who was converted by Nikkō in 1275. *See* Nichizen.

Shōichi [聖一]: Also known as Enni. A priest of the Rinzai school of Zen in Japan. *See* Enni.

Shōjari [尚闍梨] (Jpn): The ascetic Shōjari (Shōjari-sennin). The name of Shakyamuni in a past existence, when he was an ascetic practicing the *pāramitā* of meditation. Nāgārjuna's *Treatise on the Great Perfection of Wisdom* describes Shōjari as an ascetic engaged in meditation and in whose hair a bird happened to build a nest and lay several eggs. One day he gained a great insight, but, aware of the eggs on his head, he did not move until they had hatched and the baby birds flew away. Some scholars regard his Sanskrit name as Shankhāchārya, but this is uncertain.

shōju [摂受] (Jpn): A method of expounding Buddhism in which one gradually leads another to the correct teaching according to that person's capacity and without refuting his or her attachment to mistaken views. The term is used in contrast with *shakubuku,* or directly awakening another to the correct teaching by refuting that person's mistaken views. These two methods are explained in the Shrīmālā Sutra, *Great Concentration and Insight,* and elsewhere. The *shōju* method was generally employed in the Former Day and Middle Day of the Law, but is also used in the Latter Day among those who have little or no knowledge of, or no prejudices against, Buddhism. In his 1272 treatise *The Opening of the Eyes,* Nichiren states: "When the country is full of evil people without wisdom, then *shōju* is the primary method to be applied, as described in the 'Peaceful Practices' chapter [of the Lotus Sutra]. But at a time when there are many people of perverse views who slander the Law, then *shakubuku* should come first, as described in the 'Never Disparaging' chapter [of the sutra]" (285). Here "evil people without wisdom" means people who are ignorant of the Buddhist teachings. "Evil" implies the unhappiness of not acquiring roots of goodness.

Shōkaku-bō [正覚房]: Another name for Kakuban. The precursor of the New Doctrine (Shingi) school in Japan, a branch of the True Word (Shingon) school. *See* Kakuban.

Shōkō [聖光]: Another name for Benchō. The second patriarch of the

Japanese Pure Land (Jōdo) school and founder of the Chinzei branch of that school. *See* Benchō.

Shōkū [証空] (1177–1247): Also known as Zenne-bō. The founder of the Seizan branch of the Pure Land (Jōdo) school in Japan. He became a disciple of Hōnen, the founder of the Japanese Pure Land school, in 1190. He made a profound study of the Pure Land teachings and assisted his teacher in composing *The Nembutsu Chosen above All.* After Hōnen's death, he devoted himself to spreading faith in Amida Buddha among the nobility. Unlike Hōnen, however, Shōkū did not deny practices other than the Nembutsu (the invocation of Amida Buddha's name), believing that observance of the precepts and other good acts also assisted rebirth in the Pure Land.

Shōmu, Emperor [聖武天皇] (701–756) (Jpn Shōmu-tennō): The forty-fifth emperor (r. 724–749) of Japan, who contributed greatly to the prosperity of Buddhism in the country. He was the first son of Emperor Mommu, the forty-second emperor. He had deep faith in the power of Buddhism to safeguard the nation and established a temple and a nunnery in each province of the country. Moreover, he built Tōdai-ji temple in Nara as the center of these provincial temples and nunneries and erected a great image of Vairochana Buddha there.

Shore of Suffering [苦岸比丘] (Jpn Kugan-biku): A monk said to have lived one hundred years after the death of the Buddha Great Adornment in the remote past, according to the Buddha Treasury Sutra. In those days, the followers of Great Adornment had split into five schools, but only one, led by the monk Universal Practice, maintained the Buddha's teachings correctly and enabled its followers to attain Buddhahood. The leaders of the other four schools, including the monk Shore of Suffering, departed from the Buddha's teachings and denounced Universal Practice, thereby falling into hell.

Shōron school [摂論宗] (Jpn Shōron-shū): *See* Summary of the Mahayana school.

Shōtoku, Prince [聖徳太子] (574–622) (Jpn Shōtoku-taishi): Also known as Prince Jōgū. The second son of Japan's thirty-first emperor, Yōmei, and the regent under the reign of Empress Suiko. He carried out numerous reforms and governed wisely in both domestic and international affairs. In 604 he promulgated the Seventeen-Article Constitution, whose second article stresses reverence for the three treasures of Buddhism. In order to enter into diplomatic relations with Sui-dynasty China, the prince appointed Ono no Imoko to head an embassy there, opening the way for the widespread introduction of Buddhism and other elements of Chinese culture to Japan. Shōtoku had devout faith in Buddhism and contributed greatly to its establishment in Japan. He revered the Lotus, Shrīmālā, and Vimalakīrti sutras, and is credited with having written commentaries on them. He founded Hōryū-ji and Shitennō-ji temples.

shramana [沙門] (Skt; Pali *samana;* Jpn *shamon*): A seeker of the way. In India, the word originally referred to any ascetic, recluse, mendicant, or other religious practitioner who renounced secular life and left home to seek the truth. Later it came to mean chiefly one who renounces the world to practice Buddhism.

shrāmanera [沙弥] (Skt; Pali *sāmanera;* Jpn *shami*): A male novice in the Buddhist Order who has renounced secular life and vowed to uphold the ten precepts. *Shrāmanera* refers to a novice from age seven to nineteen, before he has received all the precepts and become a full-fledged monk (Skt *bhikshu*). The female equivalent is *shrāmanerī* or *shrāmanerikā.* According to *The Great Canon of Monastic Rules,* a *shrāmanera* belongs to one of three categories, depending on his age. The first category covers those from seven to thirteen years of age, when one is old enough to drive away crows from the dining area, and the second, from fourteen to nineteen, when one is old enough to pursue monastic life. The third category covers those twenty and older, when they have not yet taken vows to observe the complete commandments of full-fledged monks and still remain novices. In Japan, the title *shami,* the Japanese transliteration of *shrāmanera,* came to mean a lay priest. Though they shaved their heads and possessed religious names, priests with the title *shami* had wives and children and lived as laypersons.

shrāmanerī [沙弥尼] (Skt; Pali *sāmanerī;* Jpn *shami-ni*): A female novice in the Buddhist Order who has left home, shaved her head, and taken a vow to observe the ten precepts. The male equivalent is *shrāmanera. Shrāmanerī* refers to a novice from age seven to nineteen before she becomes a full-fledged nun (Skt *bhikshunī*), i.e., an observer of all the precepts specified for nuns. Among *shrāmanerī,* those of ages eighteen and nineteen are called *shikshamānā;* they engage in the rigorous final preparation for nunhood during those two years.

shrāvaka [声聞] (Skt; Jpn *shōmon*): *See* voice-hearer.

Shrāvastī [舎衛城] (Skt; Pali Sāvatthī; Jpn Shae-jō): The capital of the Kosala kingdom of ancient India. In Shakyamuni's time, Kosala was under the rule of King Prasenajit; along with Magadha, it was one of the greatest political powers in India. Shrāvastī was among India's most prosperous cities, along with Rājagriha in Magadha. Shakyamuni is said to have made Shrāvastī the center of his activities, and there he converted King Prasenajit and many others. The wealthy Sudatta, a resident of Shrāvastī, built Jetavana Monastery on the outskirts of Shrāvastī as an offering to Shakyamuni Buddha.

The city later declined; according to an account by Fa-hsien, a Chinese priest who visited Shrāvastī in the early fifth century, it was by that time in ruins and only about two hundred families lived there. Excavations carried out in the nineteenth century in the twin villages of Sahet and Mahet near Balrampur in Uttar Pradesh state uncovered the remains of Shrāvastī. *The Treatise on the Great Perfection of Wisdom* attributed to Nāgārjuna refers to the three hundred thousand families of Shrāvastī who met Shakyamuni Buddha. At that time, the treatise says, nine hundred thousand families lived in the city: one third had actually seen the Buddha, another third had only heard of him, and the remaining third had neither heard of nor seen the Buddha. Nāgārjuna indicates that, such being the case in the city where the Buddha was physically present for twenty-five years, it would have been all the more difficult for those living far away from Shrāvastī to encounter the Buddha.

Shrīmālā [勝鬘夫人] (Skt; Jpn Shōman-bunin): Also known as Lady Shrīmālā or Queen Shrīmālā. A daughter of King Prasenajit of Kosala in India and his consort Mallikā, in the time of Shakyamuni. Shrīmālā married Mitrayashas (also known as Yashomitra), the king of Ayodhyā. She is the protagonist of the Shrīmālā Sutra, which depicts her conversion to Buddhism by her parents, her encounter with Shakyamuni Buddha, and her vows to the Buddha to propagate the one vehicle teaching. *See also* Shrīmālā Sutra.

Shrīmālā Sutra [勝鬘経] (Skt *Shrīmālādevī-simhanāda-sūtra;* Chin *Sheng-man-ching;* Jpn *Shōman-gyō*): Also known as the Lion's Roar of Queen Shrīmālā Sutra. A sutra translated into Chinese in 436 by Gunabhadra. Fragments of the Sanskrit text and a Tibetan translation exist. This sutra takes the form of preaching, with the aid of Shakyamuni Buddha's power, by Lady Shrīmālā, the daughter of King Prasenajit of Kosala who became the consort of King Mitrayashas (also known as Yashomitra) of Ayodhyā in India. She expounds the one vehicle teaching and makes clear that the matrix of the Thus Come One (Skt *tathāgata-garbha*), or the Buddha nature, is inherent in all living beings. Along with the Vimalakīrti Sutra, it is valued as a scripture for lay Buddhists. Another Chinese translation, by Bodhiruchi (d. 727), is contained in the Accumulated Treasures Sutra, a compilation of a number of smaller sutras. According to this sutra, Prasenajit and Mallikā, both followers of Shakyamuni, wished to lead their daughter Shrīmālā to the Buddha way. They sent a messenger to Shrīmālā in Ayodhyā with a letter from them praising the Buddha and his virtues. Reading her parents' letter, Shrīmālā was overjoyed and desired to listen to the Buddha preach. Shakyamuni, who was staying at Jetavana Monastery in Shrāvastī of Kosala, perceived Shrīmālā's wish and suddenly appeared before her. She respectfully and reverently praised the Buddha and his virtues, and Shakyamuni prophesied that in a future existence she would become a Buddha named Universal Light. At that time, she vowed to protect the correct teaching with her life and work to save the people from suffering.

Shrutasoma [須陀須摩王・普明王] (Skt; Jpn Shudasuma-ō or Fumyō-ō): The king Universal Brightness. The name of Shakyamuni in a past existence, when he was a king engaged in the *pāramitā,* or practice, of observing precepts. *See* Universal Brightness (1).

Shubhakarasimha [善無畏] (Skt; Jpn Zemmui): An Indian monk who first introduced Esoteric Buddhism to China and became known in China as Shan-wu-wei. *See* Shan-wu-wei.

Shubin [守敏] (n.d.): A priest of the True Word (Shingon) school in Japan during the ninth century. He studied the teachings of the Three Treatises (Sanron) and Dharma Characteristics (Hossō) schools under Gonsō and other priests and also pursued Esoteric Buddhism. In 823 he was given Sai-ji temple in the capital, Kyoto, by Emperor Saga, while Kōbō, the founder of the True Word school, was given Tō-ji temple, also in Kyoto. In 824, during a drought, Shubin competed with Kōbō in praying for rain. It is said that Shubin succeeded in making some rain fall, but that Kōbō failed. The two are said to have been on bad terms thereafter, with Kōbō claiming that whatever rain eventually fell resulted from his prayers.

Shuddhodana [浄飯王] (Skt; Pali Suddhodana; Jpn Jōbonnō): A king of Kapilavastu in northern India and the father of Shakyamuni. According to the Sutra of the Collected Stories of the Buddha's Deeds in Past Lives, Shuddhodana was the eldest son of King Simhahanu. Shuddhodana's wife, Māyā, died seven days after giving birth to Shakyamuni, after which he married Māyā's younger sister, Mahāprajāpatī. With Mahāprajāpatī, he had another son, Nanda. Shuddhodana originally opposed his son Shakyamuni's desire to renounce the secular world and lead a religious life, but when Shakyamuni returned to his home Kapilavastu as the Buddha after his awakening, Shuddhodana converted to the Buddha's teachings. Five years after Shakyamuni's enlightenment, Shuddhodana is said to have died of illness at age seventy-nine (ninety-seven according to another account). The name Shuddhodana is rendered in Chinese translations of sutras as "Pure Rice."

Shūei [宗叡] (809–884): Also known as Shuei. A priest of the True Word (Shingon) school in Japan. Born in Kyoto, he entered the priesthood under Saichin on Mount Hiei in 822 and studied the Tendai doctrine under Gishin, the Dharma Characteristics (Hossō) doctrine under Gien, and Esoteric Buddhism under Chishō. He furthered his study of Esoteric Buddhism under Jitsue and received the status of *ajari* (Skt *āchārya*), or Buddhist teacher, from Shinshō. In 862 he went to China where he studied Esoteric Buddhism, and in 865 he returned to Japan. In 879 the imperial court appointed him the superintendent of Tō-ji temple and then administrator of priests.

Shūen [修円] (771–835): A priest of the Dharma Characteristics (Hossō) school in Japan. In 812 he became the superintendent of Kōfuku-ji temple in Nara. In 819, with Gomyō and others, he submitted a petition to the emperor opposing Dengyō's proposal for the construction of a Mahayana ordination center on Mount Hiei. Among his disciples was Tokuitsu, who is well known for his dispute with Dengyō regarding the supremacy of the one vehicle doctrine versus the three vehicle doctrine.

Shugendō school [修験道] (Jpn Shugen-dō): Also, Shugen school. A Buddhist school in Japan that teaches ascetic practices in the mountains aimed at obtaining supernatural powers. The founding of this school is attributed to En no Ozunu, a semi-legendary ascetic of the seventh century. The Shugendō school developed in the middle or late Heian period (794–1185) as a combination of indigenous beliefs such as mountain worship, and elements of Esoteric Buddhism, Taoism, and other religious influences. Adherents engage in the recitation of magic spells and the practice of ascetic disciplines on mountains they deem to be sacred.

Shuklodana [白飯王] (Skt; Pali Sukkodana; Jpn Byakubonnō): A younger brother of Shuddhodana, father of Shakyamuni. Shuklodana was a son of Simhahanu, king of Kapilavastu in northern India. According to *The Treatise on the Great Perfection of Wisdom,* he was the second son of Simhahanu and had two sons, Bhadrika and Tirnabhasya. According to *The Fivefold Rules of Discipline,* his two sons were Ānanda and Devadatta, who became Shakyamuni's closest assistant and greatest enemy, respectively. The name Shuklodana was rendered as "White Rice" in Chinese versions of the sutras.

Shun-hsiao [順暁] (n.d.) (PY Shunxiao; Jpn Jungyō): A priest of Esoteric Buddhism in China who lived from the eighth through the ninth century. After renouncing secular life, he became a student of I-lin, who was a disciple of Shan-wu-wei (Skt Shubhakarasimha), and lived at Ling-yen-ssu temple. Later he moved to Lung-hsing-ssu temple. It is said that Shun-hsiao imparted the doctrines of Esoteric Buddhism to Dengyō, who later founded the Japanese Tendai school, when Dengyō visited China in 804.

Shunjō [俊芿] (1166–1227): The founder of Sennyū-ji temple in Kyoto, Japan. Born in Higo Province, in 1184 he received the precepts to become a priest at Kanzeon-ji temple in Chikuzen Province. Thereafter he studied the teachings on the Buddhist precepts in Nara and Kyoto and returned to Higo where he founded Shōbō-ji temple and spread the teachings on the precepts. In 1199, deploring the decline of the practice of the precepts, he went to China where for twelve years he studied not only teachings on the precepts but also those of the T'ien-t'ai, Zen (Ch'an), and Pure Land schools. In 1211 he returned to Japan with more than two thousand volumes of Buddhist and non-Buddhist works. At the invitation of Eisai, the founder of the Japanese Rinzai school of Zen, Shunjō stayed at Kennin-ji temple in Kyoto for a time. In 1218 one of his followers donated to him a temple named Sen'yū-ji in Kyoto. At the time, Sen'yū-ji was in a state of disrepair, but Shunjō moved in, worked to repair it, and later renamed it Sennyū-ji temple. He made it into a center for the practice of the Precepts (Ritsu), Tendai, Zen, and Pure Land (Jōdo) teachings. He enjoyed respect and support from the Retired Emperor Gotoba, the court aristocracy, and the third regent of the Kamakura shogunate, Hōjō Yasutoki. He strove to revive the practice of precepts, and his doctrinal lineage was later called the Precepts school of the Northern Capital (Kyoto).

shūnya [空] (Skt; Jpn *kū*): *See* non-substantiality.

shūnyatā [空] (Skt; Jpn *kū*): *See* non-substantiality.

shūramgama meditation [首楞厳三昧] (Skt; Jpn *shuryōgon-zammai*): *Shūramgama-samādhi,* or resolute meditation, described in the Shūramgama Sutra. *See* Shūramgama Sutra.

Shūramgama Sutra [首楞厳経] (Chin *Shou-leng-yen-ching;* Jpn *Shuryōgon-kyō*): Also, Shūrangama Sutra. (1) A sutra translated into Chinese by Kumārajīva in the early fifth century. Its full title is the Shūramgama Meditation Sutra. According to this sutra, Bodhisattva Firm Will asked Shakyamuni Buddha what meditation would enable him to dispel earthly desires, illusions, and all other obstacles, and to attain enlightenment. In reply the Buddha taught him the *shūramgama-samādhi,* or resolute meditation, and explained its power. The Shūramgama Sutra describes this as the source of all types of meditation. One who masters the *shūramgama* meditation is said to be able to master all other kinds of meditation and overcome any obstacle such as desire, illusion, or diabolical influence.

(2) A sutra traditionally thought to have been translated into Chinese by Pan-la-mi-ti in the early eighth century. Also known as the Great Crown of the Buddha's Head Sutra or the Great Crown of the Buddha's Head Shūramgama Meditation Sutra, the sutra explains the power accru-

ing from meditation and *dhāranī* (mystic formulas). Many commentaries were written on it, though today it is regarded as a scripture produced originally in China during the T'ang dynasty (618–907) and not a translation of an Indian sutra.

Shūryasoma [須利耶蘇摩] (n.d.) (Skt; Jpn Suriyasoma or Shuriyasoma): A prince of Yarkand who lived in Central Asia in the fourth century and a teacher of Kumārajīva. He instructed Kumārajīva in the Mahayana teachings. According to *The Afterword to the Lotus Sutra Translation* by Seng-chao, one of Kumārajīva's major disciples, Shūryasoma was well versed in the Mahayana sutras and bequeathed the Lotus Sutra to Kumārajīva, saying: "The sun of the Buddha has set in the west, but its lingering rays shine over the northeast. This text is destined for the northeast. You must make certain that it is transmitted there."

Shuzen-ji [修禅寺]: A temple of the Sōtō school of Zen in Izu in Shizuoka Prefecture, Japan. It was founded by Gōrin (b. 767), a disciple of Kōbō, the founder of the Japanese True Word (Shingon) school. Another account identifies the founder as Kōbō himself. Thus it originally belonged to the True Word school. In the Kenchō era (1249–1256), Dōryū (Chin Tao-lung), a Zen priest from China, lived at this temple and converted it to the Rinzai school of Zen. At the end of the fifteenth century, Shuzen-ji was converted to the Sōtō school.

Siddhārtha [悉達多] (Skt; Pali Siddhattha; Jpn Shiddatta): "Goal Achieved." Another name for Shakyamuni, possibly his childhood or given name. According to tradition, Shakyamuni was so called because upon his birth the kingdom of the Shākyas became prosperous and all the wishes of his father Shuddhodana were fulfilled. Some scholars believe that it was not his actual name, but a title bestowed by later Buddhists in recognition of his having achieved the goal of enlightenment and become a Buddha. Shakyamuni is often referred to as Siddhārtha Gautama, the latter being his family name. Shakyamuni, meaning "sage of the Shākyas," was an honorific name applied to him.

sīla [戒] (Pali; Jpn *kai*): *See* precepts.

Silk Road [シルクロード] (Jpn Shiruku-rōdo): Also known as the Silk Route. The ancient travel route through Central Asia, linking Lo-yang and Ch'ang-an in China with the regions of ancient Syria and the Roman territory in the west. The Silk Road was a caravan route along which silk and other goods from China were carried to the West for trading, and gold, silver, glass vessels, and other goods from the West to China. In addition to goods, the route also facilitated an exchange of culture and religion, and was a principal route along which Buddhism reached China from India and Central Asia. In China, the route began in Lo-yang and

Ch'ang-an, and passed through the Kansu Corridor to Tun-huang. The road then passed through the Tarim Basin, a broad valley lying between the lofty mountain range Tien Shan in the north and the Kunlun Mountains in the south.

The oases around the Tarim Basin were watered by the rivers flowing from these two mountain ranges, and became the centers of a number of oasis city-states throughout history. The Silk Road divided into northern and southern routes along the perimeter of the Tarim Basin. The northern route linked the oasis cities or states that lay on the northern rim of the basin along the foot of the southern slope of the Tien Shan range. The southern route passed through the oasis cities on the southern rim of the basin along the foot of the northern slope of the Kunlun Mountains. The northern route extended to Kashgar on the western end of the Tarim Basin, and then crossed the Pamirs and continued through the Fergana Valley. It then passed through the western regions of Asia, by the Black Sea, and finally to the east coast of the Mediterranean Sea, where silk and other trade items were shipped to and from ports on the Mediterranean. The southern route extended to Yarkand at the western end of the Tarim Basin, passed through the southern Pamirs to Bactria, and continued on to northern Iran. This road also had a branch extending southward into northwestern India.

The northern and southern routes through the Tarim Basin flourished in the latter part of the second century B.C.E., during which time the Chinese official Chang Ch'ien was sent westward by Emperor Wu, the ruler of the Former Han dynasty, to form an alliance with a people who lived to the west of the Pamirs and were known to the Chinese as the Yüeh-chih. Buddhism entered China from India and Central Asia along both the northern and southern routes of the Silk Road. Other religions also made their way to China along the same routes, including Nestorian Christianity, Manichaeism, and Islam.

In recent times, several archaeological expeditions into Central Asia have shed light on the importance of these trade routes in fostering contact between Eastern and Western civilizations. Beside the route through the Tarim Basin, two other routes connecting East and West are now known. One ran through the vast steppes or grasslands of central Eurasia, westward through Mongolia, and then through the regions lying north of the Tien Shan range, the Aral Sea, and the Caspian Sea, and toward the Black Sea in southeastern Europe. This route dates to the last centuries B.C.E. The other route was a seaborne route across the South China Sea, the Indian Ocean, the Arabian Sea, and on to the Persian Gulf or the Red Sea. This route can be traced back to the third century

B.C.E. Thus, the passage between East and West known generally as the Silk Road consisted of several main routes and numerous branches.

Silver-Colored Woman Sutra [銀色女経] (Chin *Yin-se-nü-ching;* Jpn *Gonjikinyo-kyō*): A short sutra translated into Chinese in 539 by Buddhashānta, a monk from India. It teaches the benefits of the practice of almsgiving. According to this sutra, Shakyamuni Buddha in a past existence was a woman known as Silver-Colored or Silver-Colored Woman. One day she encountered another woman who had just given birth but who was about to devour the child because of her extreme hunger. Silver-Colored begged the woman to wait until she could fetch something for her to eat, but realized that, if she took the baby with her, the mother would die of starvation before they could return with food. If she left the baby with the mother, however, the mother would surely eat it. She then asked for a knife, and with it cut off her breasts and offered them to the mother to eat, saving both mother and child. When Silver-Colored returned home, she was asked if she had any regrets at what she had done, for if she had regrets, her act of almsgiving would not be valid. She replied that she had no regrets, whereupon her breasts were immediately restored. The god Shakra, hearing of this, appeared before her in the guise of a Brahman and questioned her. She replied again that she had no regrets and said she was determined to devote herself to the salvation of all living beings. Thereupon she changed into a man. The king of the country then died, leaving no heir. Silver-Colored, now a man, was chosen to succeed him as king. In the next life, he was born the son of a wealthy man and offered his flesh to feed starving birds and beasts. He was then reborn to a Brahman family and this time offered his body to a starving mother tiger. The sutra says that he never once regretted his acts of almsgiving, and that because of such practice, he was reborn as Shakyamuni Buddha.

Simhahanu [師子頰王] (Skt; Pali Sīhahanu; Jpn Shishikyō-ō): A king of Kapilavastu and the Shākya tribe in ancient India, the father of Shuddhodana and grandfather of Shakyamuni. The Sutra of the Collected Stories of the Buddha's Deeds in Past Lives and *The Treatise on the Great Perfection of Wisdom* say that Simhahanu had four sons and one daughter. The first son was Shuddhodana, the second Shuklodana, the third Dronodana, and the fourth Amritodana; the daughter was Amrita. Simhahanu was also the grandfather of Ānanda, Aniruddha, and Devadatta.

"Simile and Parable" chapter [譬喩品] (Jpn *Hiyu-hon*): The third chapter of the Lotus Sutra. It begins with Shāriputra expressing his joy at having understood Shakyamuni's teaching of "the true aspect of all phenomena" in the previous chapter, "Expedient Means," and stating the following realization: "Today at last I understand that truly I am the Buddha's son, born from the Buddha's mouth, born through conversion to the Law, gaining my share of the Buddha's Law!" Shakyamuni then prophesies that, in the far distant future, Shāriputra will become a Buddha named Flower Glow.

This prophecy is significant because Shāriputra represents the people of the two vehicles (voice-hearers and cause-awakened ones), who in the provisional Mahayana teachings are barred from ever attaining Buddhahood. In predicting that Shāriputra will attain Buddhahood, Shakyamuni substantiates the message in the "Expedient Means" chapter that all people can become Buddhas.

Up until this point in the sutra, only Shāriputra has grasped what Shakyamuni Buddha is expounding. So that others might understand, the Buddha relates the following parable of the three carts and the burning house: There is a very rich man who has many children. One day a fire suddenly breaks out in his spacious but decaying house, and his children, totally absorbed in playing games, do not know that the house is in flames and ignore his cries of warning. He therefore resorts to an expedient means to induce them to come out of the burning house. He shouts to them that outside he has three kinds of carts they have long wanted, pulled respectively by a goat, a deer, and an ox. Immediately the children race one another out of the door. Having coaxed them to safety in this way, the rich man gives each of his children a cart, not of the three kinds he had promised, but a much finer carriage adorned with numerous jewels and drawn by a white ox.

In this parable, the father represents the Buddha, his children represent the people, and the burning house represents this world, which is filled with suffering; the three kinds of carts originally promised represent the three vehicles, or the provisional teachings, and the great white ox carriage symbolizes the supreme vehicle of Buddhahood, i.e., the Lotus Sutra. The parable is employed to illustrate that the three vehicles of voice-hearers, cause-awakened ones, and bodhisattvas are simply means to lead people to the one Buddha vehicle. The latter part of this chapter emphasizes the importance of faith, pointing out that even Shāriputra, known as foremost in wisdom, could "gain entrance through faith alone" and not through his own wisdom or understanding. The "Simile and Parable" chapter also describes the terrible consequences of slandering the Lotus Sutra and its practitioners.

simultaneity of cause and effect [因果俱時] (Jpn *inga-guji*): (1) The principle that both cause and effect exist together simultaneously in a single moment of life. It contrasts with the concept of non-simultaneity of cause and effect, or cause and effect as they appear in the phenomenal world, where there inevitably seems to be a time gap between an action and its result. From the viewpoint that all phenomena exist in a single moment of life, there is no time gap between cause and effect; in other words, cause and effect are simultaneous.

(2) Cause (the nine worlds) and effect (Buddhahood) simultaneously exist in one's life. In this sense, the simultaneity of cause and effect is revealed in the mutual possession of the Ten Worlds and the three thousand realms in a single moment of life. Nichiren's work *The Entity of the Mystic Law* discusses the simultaneity of cause and effect as an attribute of the Mystic Law. It states: "He [the Buddha] perceived that there is this wonderful single Law *[myōhō]* that simultaneously possesses both cause and effect *[renge]*, and he named it Myoho-renge. This single Law that is Myoho-renge encompasses within it all the phenomena comprising the Ten Worlds and the three thousand realms, and is lacking in none of them. Anyone who practices this Law will obtain both the cause and the effect of Buddhahood simultaneously" (421). Because the Law of Myoho-renge encompasses all phenomena comprising the Ten Worlds, it simultaneously possesses both the cause, or the nine worlds characterized by delusion, and the effect, the world of Buddhahood. To "obtain both the cause and the effect of Buddhahood simultaneously" means that by practicing this Law one will obtain both the cause (or practice) for attaining Buddhahood and the effect of actualizing Buddhahood simultaneously within oneself. Specifically, Nichiren is referring here to the practice of chanting Nam-myoho-renge-kyo and its function to instantaneously tap and bring forth one's innate Buddhahood.

Single-minded Practice school [一向宗] (Jpn Ikkō-shū): Another name for the True Pure Land (Jōdo Shin) school founded by Shinran (1173–1262) in Japan. "Single-minded" reflects the school's belief that the single-minded invocation of Amida's name and devotion to Amida Buddha lead to rebirth in that Buddha's Pure Land. Because of pressure from the Pure Land school and other related schools, however, the school refrained from publicly naming itself the True Pure Land school. Instead it used the name Single-minded Practice school until 1872, when the name True Pure Land school was officially adopted. *See also* True Pure Land school.

single vehicle [一乗] (Jpn *ichijō*): The teaching that leads all people to Buddhahood. *See* one vehicle.

six auspicious happenings [六瑞] (Jpn *roku-zui*): Also, six portents or six omens. Occurrences that herald the preaching of the Lotus Sutra, depicted in the "Introduction" (first) chapter of the sutra. There are two categories of six auspicious happenings: the six auspicious happenings occurring in this world and those occurring in other worlds. The six auspicious happenings in this world are as follows: (1) the Buddha preaches the Immeasurable Meanings Sutra, an introductory teaching to the Lotus Sutra; (2) he enters a profound meditation called the *samādhi* of the origin of immeasurable meanings; (3) four kinds of exquisite flowers rain down from the heavens; (4) the earth trembles in six different ways; (5) seeing these portents, the whole assembly rejoice and, placing their palms together, single-mindedly behold the Buddha; and (6) the Buddha emits a beam of light from the tuft of white hair between his eyebrows, illuminating eighteen thousand worlds to the east.

The "Introduction" chapter goes on to describe the six auspicious happenings occurring in the worlds the Buddha has just illuminated, which differ from the six events listed above. They are: (1) the light emitted by the Buddha reaches as high as the Akanishtha Heaven and as deep as the Avīchi hell, so that the living beings of the six paths in all the illuminated worlds are clearly visible to those at the assembly of the sutra; (2) the Buddhas present in the other worlds can be seen; (3) the preaching of these Buddhas can be heard; (4) the four kinds of believers—monks, nuns, laymen, and laywomen—who have carried out Buddhist practices and attained the way can be seen; (5) bodhisattvas practicing the bodhisattva way can be seen; and (6) it can be seen that, after the Buddhas have entered nirvana, towers adorned with the seven kinds of treasures are built to house the Buddhas' relics.

six consciousnesses [六識] (Jpn *roku-shiki*): Sight, hearing, smell, taste, touch, and thought. Six kinds of perception that occur when the six sense organs make contact with their respective objects. The Hinayana teachings explain only those six consciousnesses and regard the sixth consciousness as the basis of all mental functions. The Consciousness-Only school of Mahayana postulated a seventh and eighth consciousness, and the Summary of the Mahayana (Chin She-lun; Jpn Shōron) school, the Flower Garland (Hua-yen; Kegon) school, and the T'ien-t'ai school added a ninth consciousness. The seventh, eighth, and ninth consciousnesses are called *mano*-consciousness, *ālaya*-consciousness, and *amala*-consciousness, respectively. *See also* nine consciousnesses.

six days of purification [六斎日] (Jpn *roku-sainichi*): Six days designated monthly on which lay followers purify their bodies and minds by observing eight precepts. They are the 8th, 14th, 15th, 23rd, 29th, and 30th days of the month. The eight precepts to be observed are (1) not to take life, (2) not to steal, (3) to refrain from all sexual relations, (4) not to lie, (5) not to drink intoxicants, (6) not to wear ornaments or perfume, or to listen to singing or watch dancing, (7) not to sleep on a wide or elevated bed, and (8) not to eat after noon. According to the Four Heavenly Kings Sutra, on these days the four heavenly kings and other gods take note of human conduct. On other days, laypersons observe the five precepts, which accord with the first five of the eight precepts listed above, except that the precept concerning sexual activity prohibits only improper (such as adultery), not all, sexual relations. *See also* five precepts.

six desires [六欲] (Jpn *roku-yoku*): (1) The desires associated with the six sense organs (eyes, ears, nose, tongue, body, and mind). (2) The desires induced by colors, shapes, carriage, voices, smooth skin, and attractive features. These are the desires caused by the opposite sex.

six difficult and nine easy acts [六難九易] (Jpn *rokunan-kui*): A series of comparisons set forth by Shakyamuni in the "Treasure Tower" (eleventh) chapter of the Lotus Sutra to show how difficult it will be to embrace and propagate the sutra in the evil age after his death. The six difficult acts are (1) to propagate the Lotus Sutra widely, (2) to copy it or cause someone else to copy it, (3) to recite it even for a short while, (4) to teach it even to one person, (5) to hear of and accept it and inquire about its meaning, and (6) to maintain faith in it.

The nine easy acts are (1) to teach innumerable sutras other than the Lotus Sutra; (2) to take up Mount Sumeru and hurl it across countless Buddha lands; (3) to kick a major world system into a different quarter with one's toe; (4) to stand in the Summit of Being Heaven and preach innumerable sutras other than the Lotus Sutra; (5) to grasp the sky with one's hand and travel around with it; (6) to place the earth on one's toenail and ascend to the Brahma Heaven; (7) to carry dry grass on one's back into the great fires occurring at the end of the *kalpa* without being burned; (8) to preach eighty-four thousand teachings and enable one's listeners to obtain the six transcendental powers; and (9) to enable innumerable people to reach the stage of arhat and acquire the six transcendental powers. By citing these impossible feats as "easy," Shakyamuni emphasizes the extreme difficulty of embracing the sutra and teaching it to others in the evil age that he predicts will come after his death.

six elder disciples of Nikkō [本六] (Jpn *hon-roku*): Six priests selected by Nikkō, Nichiren's immediate disciple and successor, to attend to and protect the object of devotion Nichiren inscribed for the sake of all humankind on the twelfth day of the tenth month, 1279. They were Nichimoku, Nikke, Nisshū, Nichizen, Nissen, and Nichijō. They all had met Nichiren in person. According to one account, Nikkō designated the six around 1298. *See also* six new disciples of Nikkō.

six elements [六大] (Jpn *roku-dai*): Also, six great elements. Six constituent elements of all things in the universe, both material and spiritual. They are the five elements of earth, water, fire, wind, and space, plus consciousness. The concept of the six elements is used notably by Esoteric Buddhism. Esoteric Buddhism maintains that the six elements of Mahāvairochana Buddha and those of ordinary people mutually interfuse and that the six elements themselves interpenetrate without obstruction and are always united. *See also* five elements.

six forms [六相] (Jpn *roku-sō*): Also, sixfold nature. A doctrine of the Flower Garland (Chin Hua-yen; Jpn Kegon) school that analyzes the phenomenal world from the standpoints of both difference and identity. The six forms are six inseparable aspects inherent in all things: (1) universality—the whole that is composed of parts; (2) particularity—each part that composes the whole; (3) similarity—the parts are all related to the whole; (4) diversity—though similar in that they are all related to the whole, each part's relation to the whole is unique; (5) formation—the harmonization of unique parts forms the whole; and (6) differentiation—while harmonizing to form the whole, each part still retains its particular characteristics. The term *six forms* is often used in conjunction with the *ten mysteries.* The two explain the phenomenal world from different perspectives. *See also* ten mysteries.

six heavens of the world of desire [六欲天] (Jpn *rokuyoku-ten*): Also, six desire heavens or six heavens of desire. In ancient Indian cosmology as adopted by Buddhism, the six heavens located in the world of desire and situated between the earth and the Brahma Heaven. Beings in the six heavens are dominated by desire. The six heavens are, in ascending order, the Heaven of the Four Heavenly Kings, the Heaven of the Thirty-three Gods, the Yāma Heaven, the Tushita Heaven, the Heaven of Enjoying the Conjured, and the Heaven of Freely Enjoying Things Conjured by Others. The Heaven of the Four Heavenly Kings is located halfway up Mount Sumeru, and the Heaven of the Thirty-three Gods, at its summit. The other four heavens are in the air, that is, between the summit of Mount Sumeru and the Brahma Heaven. Among them, the Heaven of Freely Enjoying Things Conjured by Others, often called the sixth heaven, is known as the abode of the devil king. *See also* threefold world.

six kinds of contemplation [六念] (Jpn *roku-nen*): Six meditative practices referred to in the Universal Worthy Sutra and in the Nirvana Sutra. They are contemplations on the Buddha, the Law, the Buddhist Order, the observance of the precepts, the benefit of almsgiving, and rebirth in heaven.

six major offenses [六重罪] (Jpn *roku-jūzai*): Violations of the six precepts. The offenses of killing, stealing, lying, sexual misconduct, talking about the misdeeds of other Buddhists, and selling intoxicants. The six precepts are prohibitions of these acts.

six metaphors of the theoretical and essential teachings [本迹の六譬] (Jpn *honjaku-no-roppi*): Metaphors T'ien-t'ai (538–597) used in interpreting the word *renge* (lotus plant) of *Myoho-renge-kyo*, or the Lotus Sutra of the Wonderful Law (the title of Kumārajīva's Chinese version of the Lotus Sutra), in *The Profound Meaning of the Lotus Sutra*. In this work, T'ien-t'ai explains the figurative lotus with three metaphors: the lotus blossom enfolding the fruit, the lotus blossom opening to reveal the fruit inside, and the lotus blossom falling and the fruit ripening. Each of these can be interpreted in two ways: as the three metaphors of the theoretical teaching (first half) of the Lotus Sutra, which illustrate the relationship between the Lotus Sutra (true teaching) and the provisional teachings, and as the three metaphors of the essential teaching (latter half) of the sutra, which show the relationship between the essential teaching and the theoretical teaching.

In the three metaphors of the theoretical teaching, *ren* (the fruit of the lotus) corresponds to the true teaching, and *ge* (the lotus blossom) to the provisional teachings. The three metaphors respectively mean (1) that one cannot see the fruit of the true teaching because it is covered by the blossom of the provisional teachings, (2) that the blossom opens to reveal the fruit of the true teaching, and (3) that the blossom of the three vehicles is replaced by the fruit of the one Buddha vehicle.

In the three metaphors of the essential teaching, *ren* (the lotus fruit) corresponds to the essential teaching, and *ge* (the lotus blossom) to the theoretical teaching. The three metaphors mean (1) that the blossom of the theoretical teaching contains the fruit of the essential teaching, (2) that the blossom of the theoretical teaching opens to reveal the fruit of the essential teaching, and (3) that the blossom of the theoretical teaching is replaced by the fruit of the essential teaching.

six ministers [六大臣・六臣] (Jpn *roku-daijin* or *roku-shin*): Also, six royal ministers. The ministers of Ajātashatru, a king of Magadha in India during Shakyamuni's time. In Chinese scriptures, their names are rendered as Famed for the Moon, Virtue Contained, Truly Attaining, Complete Understanding of Meanings, Auspicious Virtue, and Fearlessness. The original Sanskrit names are unknown, although Famed for the Moon is thought to be Chandrakīrti or Chandrayashas. According to the Mahāparinirvāna Sutra, Ajātashatru was suffering from virulent sores all over his body because of his offense of killing his father, King Bimbisāra, a patron of Shakyamuni Buddha. Ajātashatru's six ministers each recommended to him that he consult a different one of the six non-Buddhist teachers. The minister Famed for the Moon exhorted the king to see the teacher Pūrana Kassapa; Virtue Contained advised him to consult Makkhali Gosāla; Truly Attaining, to see Sanjaya Belatthiputta; Complete Understanding of Meanings, Ajita Kesakambala; Auspicious Virtue, Pakudha Kacchāyana; and Fearlessness urged him to see Nigantha Nātaputta. The great physician Jīvaka, however, exhorted the king to see Shakyamuni Buddha and receive his instruction. According to the sutra, when the king decided to seek out Shakyamuni Buddha, the Buddha was far off in a grove of sal trees. Nevertheless, he perceived the king's desire and entered the so-called moon-loving meditation in order to relieve his suffering. A brilliant ray of light then shone forth from the Buddha's body and reached the palace, falling on the king's body. As a result, Ajātashatru was completely cured of his sores.

six monks, group of [六群比丘] (Jpn *rokugun-biku*): Six monks of Shakyamuni Buddha's Order in India. Buddhist texts on the rules of monastic discipline cite the improper conduct of this group of six monks as the reason for the Buddha's establishment of many of the monastic precepts or prohibitions. Though their names differ among Buddhist scriptures, they are most often listed as Nanda, Upananda, Kālodāyin, Chanda, Ashvaka, and Punarvasu.

six new disciples of Nikkō [新六] (Jpn *shin-roku*): Six priests to whom Nikkō, Nichiren's immediate disciple and successor, entrusted the task of propagation after his death. Nikkō selected them in 1332, one year before his death, when he was residing at Omosu Seminary in Fuji District of Suruga Province. They were Nichidai, Nitchō, Nichidō, Nichimyō, Nichigō, and Nichijo. *See also* six elder disciples of Nikkō.

six non-Buddhist teachers [六師外道] (Jpn *rokushi-gedō*): Also, six teachers of the non-Buddhist doctrines. Influential thinkers in India during Shakyamuni's time who openly broke with old Vedic tradition and challenged Brahman authority in the Indian social order. Their names are usually listed in Pali, rather than Sanskrit. They are as follows: (1) Pūrana Kassapa (Skt Pūrana Kāshyapa), who denied the existence of causality, rejecting the idea that one's good or bad deeds yield corresponding gain or loss. Therefore he rejected all concepts of morality. (2) Makkhali Gosāla (Maskarin Goshālin or Maskarin Goshālīputra), who asserted that all events are predetermined by fate, and that no amount of devotional effort or religious practice can alter them. He therefore advised people to resign themselves to the process of *samsāra,* or transmigration. (3) Sanjaya Belatthiputta (Samjayin Vairatīputra), a skeptic who gave no definite answers to metaphysical questions. For example, when asked whether life continues after death, he is said to have replied that it might and yet again it might not, denying the possibility of certain knowledge in such areas. (4) Ajita Kesakambala (Ajita Keshakambala or Ajita Keshakambalin), who maintained a simple materialism according to which all things in the universe are formed of earth, water, fire, and wind. Since the world is composed of these elements alone, he said, life ends when the body dies, and it is therefore of no consequence whether one does evil or good in this life. For this reason, Ajita encouraged hedonism. He is regarded as the forerunner of the Lokāyata school. (5) Pakudha Kacchāyana (Kakuda Kātyāyana), who asserted that human beings are composed of seven unchangeable elements: earth, water, fire, wind, suffering, pleasure, and soul. He argued that one could not really kill another with a sword, since it would simply cut through the space between those elements composing the person. (6) Nigantha Nātaputta (Nirgrantha Jnātiputra), founder of Jainism, who sought liberation through rigorous asceticism and absolutely forbade the killing of any living being.

six objects [六境] (Jpn *rokkyō*): Also, six sense objects. Color and form, sound, odor, taste, texture, and phenomena. The six objects are those perceived by the six sense organs—eyes, ears, nose, tongue, body, and mind. *Phenomena* is a translation of dharmas, which means all things, physical and spiritual, of the past, present, and future. It is used here to indicate any thing or occurrence that can be perceived or conceived of by the mind. This also includes purely mental or spiritual elements, such as feelings, ideas, and thoughts. Contact between the six sense organs and their respective objects gives rise to the six consciousnesses.

six omens [六瑞] (Jpn *roku-zui*): Occurrences that herald the preaching of the Lotus Sutra. *See* six auspicious happenings.

six pāramitās [六波羅蜜] (Jpn *roku-haramitsu* or *ropparamitsu*): Six practices required of Mahayana bodhisattvas in order to attain Buddhahood. The Sanskrit word *pāramitā* is interpreted as "perfection" or "having reached the opposite shore," i.e., to cross from the shore of delusion to the shore of enlightenment. The six *pāramitās* are (1) almsgiving (Skt *dāna*), which includes material almsgiving, almsgiving of the Law, and almsgiving of fearlessness (meaning to remove fear and give relief); (2) keeping the precepts *(shīla);* (3) forbearance *(kshānti),* or to bear up patiently and continue one's Buddhist practice under all opposition and hardships; (4) assiduousness *(vīrya),* to practice the other five *pāramitās* ceaselessly, with utmost physical and spiritual effort; (5) meditation *(dhyāna),* to focus the mind and contemplate the truth with a tranquil mind; and (6) the obtaining of wisdom *(prajnā),* which enables one to perceive the true nature of all things.

Six Pāramitās Sutra [六波羅蜜経] (Chin *Liu-po-lo-mi-ching;* Jpn *Roku-haramitsu-kyō* or *Ropparamitsu-kyō*): A sutra translated into Chinese in 788 by Prajnā, a monk from northern India. It explains in detail the six *pāramitās,* or six kinds of practice, that bodhisattvas must carry out to attain enlightenment. *See also* six *pāramitās.*

six paths [六道] (Skt *shad-gati;* Jpn *roku-dō*): The realms of hell, hungry spirits, animals, *asuras,* human beings, and heavenly beings. "Path" here means the path a life follows in the process of transmigration; it also indicates a realm or state of existence. The six paths were viewed traditionally as realms within which unenlightened beings repeatedly transmigrate. When regarded as conditions of life, they indicate states of delusion or suffering. The term *six paths* is used in contrast with the *four noble worlds*—the worlds of voice-hearers, cause-awakened ones *(pratyekabuddhas),* bodhisattvas, and Buddhahood—in which one makes efforts to transcend the delusions of the six paths.

Beings in the six paths are governed mostly by their responses to external stimuli and are therefore never really independent or free but constantly at the mercy of changing circumstances. Among the six paths, the three paths—the realms of hell, hungry spirits, and animals—are collectively termed the three evil paths. Beings are reborn into these states of suffering due to their evil actions in a previous lifetime. The three paths of *asuras,* human beings, and heavenly beings are termed the three good paths because beings are reborn into these states due to their good and virtuous actions in a previous lifetime. The concept of the six paths is universally accepted in Mahayana Buddhism. The Sarvāstivāda school, a major Hinayana school, teaches the five paths—the realms of hell, hungry spirits, animals, human beings, and heavenly beings, arguing that the realm of *asuras* was included within the realms of hungry spirits and heavenly beings.

six portents [六瑞] (Jpn *roku-zui*): Occurrences that herald the preaching of the Lotus Sutra. *See* six auspicious happenings.

six precepts (1) [六法戒・六法] (Jpn *roppō-kai* or *roppō*): Also, six prohibitions or six commandments. The precepts for *shikshamānā,* female novices of eighteen and nineteen years of age preparing to become fully ordained nuns. The six precepts are prohibitions against killing, stealing, having sexual relations, lying, drinking intoxicants, and eating after noon. Descriptions of the six precepts vary slightly among Buddhist texts. *See also* precepts; *shikshamānā.*

(2) [六重戒・六重の法] (Jpn *rokujū-kai* or *rokujū-no-hō*): Prohibitions against killing, stealing, lying, sexual misconduct, talking about the misdeeds of other Buddhists, and selling intoxicants, which are set forth in the Precepts for Laymen Sutra.

six royal ministers [六大臣・六臣] (Jpn *roku-daijin* or *roku-shin*): *See* six ministers.

six schools of Nara [南都六宗] (Jpn *nanto-rokushū*): Also, six schools. Six schools of Buddhism that flourished in Nara, the capital of Japan, during the Nara period (710–794). They are the Dharma Analysis Treasury (Kusha), Establishment of Truth (Jōjitsu), Three Treatises (Sanron), Precepts (Ritsu), Dharma Characteristics (Hossō), and Flower Garland (Kegon) schools. These were not so much independent religious schools as philosophical or doctrinal systems, and more than one of these traditions were usually studied at each of the seven major temples of Nara. At Tōdai-ji temple, for example, all six were studied. Later, however, when the great statue of Vairochana Buddha, the principal Buddha of the Flower Garland teachings, was completed and enshrined there, the Flower Garland school became preeminent at Tōdai-ji. The Three Treatises school was based primarily at Daian-ji and Gangō-ji temples, and the Dharma Characteristics school at Gangō-ji and Kōfuku-ji. Though Establishment of Truth and Dharma Analysis Treasury are called schools also, their doctrines were studied in conjunction with the doctrines of the Three Treatises and Dharma Characteristics schools, respectively, and they did not become independent schools. The Precepts school was established in Japan by the Chinese priest Chien-chen (Jpn Ganjin) who arrived there in 753.

six senior priests [六老僧] (Jpn *roku-rōsō*): Six priests whom Nichiren designated as his major disciples on the eighth day of the tenth month, 1282, shortly before his death. In order of conversion, they were Nisshō (1221–1323), Nichirō (1245–1320), Nikkō (1246–1333), Nikō (1253–1314), Nitchō (1252–1317), and Nichiji (b. 1250). Of these six, Nikkō was appointed as Nichiren's successor. After Nichiren's death, the other five gradually departed from his teachings and, under pressure from the government, declared themselves to be priests of the Tendai school, an established school of the day. Hence, in contrast with Nikkō, they are referred to as the five senior priests. The fundamental differences between Nikkō and the other five lay in their understanding of Nichiren's teachings. Nikkō regarded Nichiren's writings as foundational scriptures, calling them *Gosho* (literally, honorable writings; *go* is an honorific prefix, and *sho* means writing), while the five based themselves primarily on T'ien-t'ai's works. Nikkō revered Nichiren's mandala called the Gohonzon as the object of devotion, while the five worshiped images of Shakyamuni Buddha. *See also* five senior priests.

six sense objects [六境] (Jpn *rokkyō*): Color and form, sound, odor, taste, texture, and phenomena. *See* six objects.

six sense organs [六根] (Skt *shad-indriya;* Jpn *rokkon*): Also, six sensory organs. The eyes, ears, nose, tongue, body, and mind. The contact of the six sense organs with their corresponding six objects gives rise to the six consciousnesses—sight, hearing, smell, taste, touch, and thought. In Hinayana Buddhism, the six sense organs are regarded as the source of earthly desires. The Lotus Sutra says that one can purify the workings of the six sense organs by embracing and reciting the sutra. With the six sense organs purified, one is free of attachment to and delusion about their corresponding objects—color and form, sound, odor, taste, texture, and phenomena. The Sanskrit word *indriya* means faculty, faculty of sense, sense organ, or power.

six stages of practice [六即] (Jpn *roku-soku*): Also, six identities. Six stages in the practice of the Lotus Sutra formulated by T'ien-t'ai (538–597) in *Great Concentration and Insight.* They are as follows: (1) The stage of being a Buddha in theory. At this stage one has not yet heard the correct teaching and is ignorant of Buddhism. Nevertheless, a single moment of life is in itself identical to the truth of the matrix of the Thus Come One; in other words, one is a potential Buddha. (2) The stage of hearing the name and words of the truth. At this stage through the spoken or written word one comes to an intellectual understanding that one has the Buddha nature and that all phenomena are manifestations of the Buddhist Law. This may take place through reading or hearing the words of the sutras. (3) The stage of perception and action. Here one perceives the truth [of the Buddha nature] within oneself through practice, the truth and the wisdom to perceive it are in accord with each other, and one's words match one's actions. (4) The stage of resemblance to enlightenment. At this stage, one eliminates the first two of the three categories of illusion and attains purification of the six sense organs. Having advanced this far, one's wisdom resembles that of a Buddha. In terms of the fifty-two stages of practice, this stage corresponds to the first ten stages, the ten stages of faith. (5) The stage of progressive awakening. This is the stage at which one eradicates all illusions except fundamental darkness and awakens progressively to the truth of one's Buddha nature. In terms of the fifty-two stages, it corresponds to the eleventh (the first stage of security) through the fifty-first (the stage of near-perfect enlightenment). (6) The stage of ultimate enlightenment, or the highest stage of practice. At this stage, one finally eliminates fundamental darkness and fully manifests the Buddha nature. This corresponds to the stage of perfect enlightenment, the last of the fifty-two stages.

T'ien-t'ai taught that all people at whatever stage of practice are equally endowed with the potential for Buddhahood. In this way he prevented his disciples from falling into the error of self-deprecation or becoming discouraged. On the other hand, possessing the Buddha nature is not the same as attaining Buddhahood. T'ien-t'ai therefore divided practice into six progressive stages to prevent his disciples from falling into the error of arrogance and relaxing their efforts. In *Great Concentration and Insight,* he states: "If one lacks faith, one will object that it pertains to the lofty realm of the sages, something far beyond the capacity of one's own wisdom to understand. If one lacks wisdom, one will become puffed up with arrogance and will claim to be the equal of the Buddha."

The Record of the Orally Transmitted Teachings gives Nichiren's (1222–1282) interpretation of the six stages of practice: "Speaking in terms of the six stages of practice, the Thus Come One in this ['Life Span'] chapter is an ordinary mortal who is in the first stage, that of being a Buddha in theory. When one reverently accepts Nam-myoho-renge-kyo, one is in the next stage, that of hearing the name and words of the truth. That is, one has for the first time heard the daimoku. When, having heard the daimoku, one proceeds to put it into practice, this is the third stage, that of perception and action. In this stage, one perceives the object of devotion that embodies the three thousand realms in a single moment of life. When one succeeds in overcoming various illusions and obstacles, this is the fourth stage, that of resemblance to enlightenment. When one sets out to convert others, this is the fifth stage, that of progressive awakening. And when one comes at last to the realization that one is a Buddha eternally endowed with the three bodies, then one is a Buddha of the sixth and highest stage, that of ultimate enlightenment.

"Speaking of the chapter as a whole, the idea of gradually overcoming delusions is not the ultimate meaning of the 'Life Span' chapter. You should understand that the ultimate meaning of this chapter is that ordinary mortals, just as they are in their original state of being, are Buddhas.

"And if you ask what is the action or practice carried out by the Buddha eternally endowed with the three bodies, it is Nam-myoho-renge-kyo."

six supernatural powers [六神通・六通] (Jpn *roku-jinzū* or *roku-tsū*): *See* six transcendental powers.

six teachers of the non-Buddhist doctrines [六師外道] (Jpn *rokushi-gedō*): Influential thinkers in India during Shakyamuni's time. *See* six non-Buddhist teachers.

sixteen arhats [十六羅漢] (Jpn *jūroku-rakan*): Arhats designated by Shakyamuni Buddha to protect his teachings for the benefit of the people after his death. According to Hsüan-tsang's Chinese translation of *The Record of Ensuring the Abiding of the Law*, they continued to live after Shakyamuni's entry into nirvana in order to fulfill this mission. They are Pindolabhāradvāja, Kanakavatsa, Kanakabhāradvāja, Subinda, Nakula, Bhadra, Kālika, Vajraputra, Jīvaka, Panthaka, Rāhula, Nāgasena, Angaja, Vanavāsin, Ajita, and Chūdapanthaka. In China and Japan, the sixteen arhats were often depicted artistically and these images enshrined in temples, in particular of the Zen school.

sixteen great states [十六大国] (Jpn *jūroku-daikoku*): Also, sixteen major states, sixteen great kingdoms, or sixteen great countries. Sixteen countries that existed in India during the time of Shakyamuni. Most were located in the northern part of the Indian subcontinent, particularly the Ganges Valley. The names of the sixteen countries differ among Buddhist sutras. The Long Āgama Sutra lists them as Anga, Magadha, Kāshī, Kosala, Vriji, Malla, Chedi, Vatsa, Kuru, Panchāla, Ashvaka, Avanti, Matsya, Shūrasena, Gandhara, and Kamboja. In Shakyamuni's time, the two greatest powers were Magadha, in the lower Ganges Valley, and Kosala, in the middle Ganges Valley. Control of the Kāshī kingdom, which was situated between Magadha and Kosala, became a point of conflict between those two countries. The Magadha kingdom conquered many other countries in Shakyamuni's time and thereafter established its supremacy as an empire.

sixteen princes [十六王子] (Jpn *jūroku-ōji*): The sixteen sons of the Buddha Great Universal Wisdom Excellence, who appeared in the remote past as described in the "Parable of the Phantom City" (seventh) chapter of the Lotus Sutra. According to the chapter, Great Universal Wisdom Excellence was a king with sixteen sons. When he renounced secular life and attained enlightenment, his sons also renounced secular life to follow their father and heard the Lotus Sutra from him. They embraced faith in the sutra and preached it for the people. Their preaching is sometimes referred to as the restatement of Great Universal Wisdom Excellence Buddha's teaching. The above chapter states that these sixteen sons presently live in their respective lands in the ten directions and preach the Law as Buddhas, and lists the names of these Buddhas. They are Akshobhya Buddha and Sumeru Peak Buddha in the east, Lion Voice Buddha and Lion Appearance Buddha in the southeast, Void-Dwelling

Buddha and Ever Extinguished Buddha in the south, Emperor Appearance Buddha and Brahmā Appearance Buddha in the southwest, Amitāyus Buddha (Amida Buddha) and Saving All from Worldly Suffering Buddha in the west, Tamālapattra Sandalwood Fragrance Transcendental Power Buddha and Sumeru Appearance Buddha in the northwest, Cloud Freedom Buddha and Cloud Freedom King Buddha in the north, Destroying All Worldly Fears Buddha in the northeast, and Shakyamuni Buddha in this *sahā* world.

sixteen types of meditation [十六観] (Jpn *jūroku-kan*): According to the Meditation on the Buddha Infinite Life Sutra, the sixteen practices of meditation leading to rebirth in the Land of Perfect Bliss, or the land of Amida Buddha. The first thirteen types of meditation involve concentrating one's mind on the splendor of the Land of Perfect Bliss, the features of Amida Buddha, and the bodhisattvas in this pure land. The other three types of meditation are directed at the image of Amida Buddha. In the Pure Land school, the first thirteen types of meditation are regarded as "concentrated meditation." In contrast, the remaining three can be practiced even with an unfocused mind and are therefore called "unconcentrated meditation."

sixth heaven [第六天] (Jpn *dairoku-ten*): The sixth and highest of the six heavens in the world of desire. *See* Heaven of Freely Enjoying Things Conjured by Others.

six transcendental powers [六神通・六通] (Jpn *roku-jinzū* or *roku-tsū*): Also, six supernatural powers. Powers that Buddhas, bodhisattvas, and arhats are said to possess. They are (1) the power to be anywhere at will, (2) the power to see anything anywhere, (3) the power to hear any sound anywhere, (4) the power to know the thoughts of all other minds, (5) the power to know past lives, and (6) the power to eradicate illusions and earthly desires.

six types of harmony and reverence [六和敬] (Jpn *roku-wakyō* or *roku-wagyō*): Also, six types of harmonious respect. Six ways or areas in which Buddhist practitioners should work in harmony and be respectful of one another. They are in (1) action, (2) word, (3) mind, (4) observance of the precepts, (5) doctrinal views, and (6) practice (or the possession and use of goods, according to another account). The list of these six varies among Buddhist texts.

Six-Volume Writings, The [六巻抄] (Jpn *Rokkan-shō*): A work by Nichikan, the twenty-sixth chief priest of Taiseki-ji temple and scholar of Nichiren's teachings, completed in 1725. During the four hundred years after Nichiren's death, various interpretations of his teachings were adopted by different Nichiren schools, and Nichikan held that the true meaning of Nichiren's teachings had become obscured. He wrote this work to refute what he felt were serious misconceptions and to clarify the true meaning of Nichiren's teachings. As the title indicates, it is a collection of six treatises:

(1) "The Threefold Secret Teaching," which explains the teaching for the Latter Day of the Law by interpreting the meaning of the passage from *The Opening of the Eyes,* one of Nichiren's major works, that reads, "The doctrine of three thousand realms in a single moment of life is found in only one place, hidden in the depths of the 'Life Span' chapter of the essential teaching of the Lotus Sutra" (224). Nichikan thus established the concept of the threefold secret teaching, or threefold comparison: first, the "doctrine of three thousand realms in a single moment of life," which Nichiren himself identified as Nam-myoho-renge-kyo, is found in the Lotus Sutra and not in any of the other sutras; second, it is found in the "Life Span" (sixteenth) chapter of the essential teaching (latter half) of the Lotus Sutra and not in its theoretical teaching (first half); and third, it is found in the depths of the "Life Span" chapter. "Secret" in this context indicates that the Law of Nam-myoho-renge-kyo hidden in the depths of the "Life Span" chapter had been kept secret, or remained hidden, until it was revealed by Nichiren.

(2) "The Meanings Hidden in the Depths," which clarifies that the teaching hidden in the depths of the "Life Span" chapter is Nam-myoho-renge-kyo of the Three Great Secret Laws. It discusses the Three Great Secret Laws in detail.

(3) "Interpreting the Text Based upon Its Essential Meaning," which interprets important passages of the Lotus Sutra from the standpoint of the teaching of Nam-myoho-renge-kyo of the Three Great Secret Laws.

(4) "The Teaching for the Latter Day," which sets forth the correct object of devotion to be established in the Latter Day of the Law. This treatise explains why the object of devotion inscribed by Nichiren, rather than an image of Shakyamuni Buddha, is the correct object of faith in the Latter Day of the Law. This treatise also indicates that the correct practice of reading and reciting the Lotus Sutra in the Latter Day of the Law is to read and recite its two key chapters, "Expedient Means" (second) and "Life Span," and not the entire sutra.

(5) "The Practices of This School," which explains that correct practice in the Latter Day of the Law consists of two kinds: primary and supporting. The primary practice is the chanting of the daimoku, or the invocation of Nam-myoho-renge-kyo, and the supporting practice is the reading and recitation of the "Expedient Means" and "Life Span" chapters. This work explains why these two chapters are recited as a daily prac-

tice. It also defines the three treasures in the Latter Day of the Law and describes the great benefits of chanting the daimoku.

(6) "The Three Robes of This School," which defines the "three robes" as the traditional gray robe, the white surplice, and the prayer beads of the priests of the Fuji school, and explains their significance.

slander [謗法] (Jpn *hōbō*): More specifically, slander of the Law. To deny, oppose, disparage, or vilify the correct Buddhist teaching. The "Simile and Parable" (third) chapter of the Lotus Sutra reads: "If a person fails to have faith but instead slanders this sutra, immediately he will destroy all the seeds for becoming a Buddha in this world. . . . When his life comes to an end he will enter the Avīchi hell." Miao-lo (711–782) says in his *Annotations on "The Words and Phrases of the Lotus Sutra"*: "This [Lotus] sutra opens the seeds of Buddhahood inherent in the beings of each of the six paths. But if one slanders the sutra, then the seeds will be destroyed." According to the Nirvana Sutra, not to reproach those who slander the Law amounts to committing slander oneself. The sutra reads: "If even a good monk sees someone destroying the teaching and disregards him, failing to reproach him, to oust him, or to punish him for his offense, then you should realize that that monk is betraying the Buddha's teaching. But if he ousts the destroyer of the Law, reproaches him, or punishes him, then he is my disciple and a true voice-hearer." Nichiren (1222–1282) states, "Those who put their faith in it [the Lotus Sutra] will surely attain Buddhahood, while those who slander it will establish a 'poison-drum relationship' with it and will likewise attain Buddhahood" (882). *See also* fourteen slanders.

Smaller Wisdom Sutra [小品般若経] (Skt *Ashtasāhasrikā-prajnā-pāramitā;* Chin *Hsiao-p'in-pan-jo-ching;* Jpn *Shōbon-hannya-kyō*): Another name for the Great Perfection of Wisdom Sutra, translated into Chinese by Kumārajīva in the early fifth century. It is called the Smaller Wisdom Sutra in contrast with the Larger Wisdom Sutra, a longer text that Kumārajīva also translated under the same title, the Great Perfection of Wisdom Sutra. The setting of the Smaller Wisdom Sutra is Eagle Peak. In the first section, Subhūti preaches on behalf of Shakyamuni Buddha the teaching of the perfection of wisdom (Skt *prajnā-pāramitā*) and describes how Shakyamuni's practice of this teaching in past existences enabled him to attain Buddhahood. He asserts the superiority of the *prajnā-pāramitā,* (the *pāramitā,* or perfection, of *prajnā,* or wisdom) over the other five of the six *pāramitās.* Shakyamuni then says that the *prajnā-pāramitā* is equal to the supreme wisdom and is the mother of all bodhisattvas; if a bodhisattva takes faith in the teaching of the perfection of wisdom, he will never fail to attain Buddhahood. After emphasizing the supremacy of *prajnā-pāramitā,* the sutra ends with the story of Bodhisattva Ever Wailing, who travels about seeking this teaching.

small kalpa [小劫] (Jpn *shō-kō*): According to *The Treatise on the Rise of the World,* each of the twenty *kalpas* that constitute each of the four *kalpas* of formation, continuance, decline, and disintegration. During a small *kalpa,* the life span of human beings is said to gradually increase from 10 years to 80,000 and then diminish at the same rate again to 10. Both increase and decrease occur at the rate of one year every 100 years. Calculating from this, a small *kalpa* would be 15,998,000 years. According to *The Dharma Analysis Treasury,* however, this small *kalpa* is called a medium *kalpa.* See also *kalpa* of continuance.

Snow Mountains [雪山] (Skt Himālaya or Himavat; Jpn Sessen): In Buddhist scriptures, a reference to the Himalayas. Himālaya is a compound of two Sanskrit words, *hima* (snow) and *ālaya* (repository or abode). In Buddhist texts, the Snow Mountains are often described as being in the northern part of the continent of Jambudvīpa; to the north of the Snow Mountains is Heat-Free Lake, from which flow the rivers that nurture the soil of the four quarters of Jambudvīpa.

Snow Mountains, the boy [雪山童子] (Jpn Sessen-dōji): The name of Shakyamuni Buddha in a previous lifetime when he was practicing austerities in the Snow Mountains in pursuit of enlightenment. His story appears in the "Noble Practice" chapter of the Chinese version of the Mahāparinirvāna Sutra translated by Dharmaraksha, a monk from central India, in the early fifth century. The boy Snow Mountains had mastered all the non-Buddhist teachings, but had yet to hear of Buddhism. The god Shakra decided to test his resolve. He appeared before the boy Snow Mountains in the form of a hungry demon and recited half a verse from a Buddhist teaching: "All is changeable, nothing is constant. This is the law of birth and death." Inspired by this, the boy begged the demon to tell him the second half of the verse. The demon agreed, but demanded flesh and blood in payment. The boy Snow Mountains gladly promised to offer his own body to the demon, who in turn gave him the latter half of the teaching: "Extinguishing the cycle of birth and death, one enters the joy of nirvana." The boy Snow Mountains scrawled this teaching on rocks and trees for the sake of those who might pass by and then, to fulfill his promise, jumped from a tall tree to give his body to the demon. Just at that moment the demon changed back into Shakra and caught him. He praised the boy Snow Mountains' willingness to give his life for the Law and predicted that he would certainly attain Buddhahood.

Soka Gakkai [創価学会]: "Value-Creating Society." A Buddhist lay organization founded in Japan on November 18, 1930, by Tsunesaburō

Makiguchi (1871–1944), who became its first president, and his disciple, Jōsei Toda (1900–1958), later its second president. Makiguchi was an educator and scholar who had been developing an original pedagogical philosophy gleaned from his long experience as a teacher and elementary school principal. He regarded the creation of values that are conducive to a happy life as the purpose of education. In 1928 he encountered the teachings of Nichiren (1222–1282) and the Lotus Sutra and found in them resonance with his philosophy of value. In June of that year he converted to Nichiren Shōshū, one of the Nichiren schools.

Toda, also an educator, quickly followed his mentor in conversion. Makiguchi made the Lotus Sutra the foundation of his philosophy of education and wrote *The System of Value-Creating Pedagogy*, which Toda published. The publisher of the work was listed as the Soka Kyōiku Gakkai (Value-Creating Education Society) by the two educators, and its publication date, November 18, 1930, is regarded as the founding date of the Soka Gakkai. At that time, the group consisted principally of teachers and educators interested in Makiguchi's educational theories and practice.

Although the society met informally, it was not until 1937 that its inaugural ceremony was held in Tokyo with more than sixty attending. At its first general meeting, in December 1939, Makiguchi was named president of the society and Toda general director. Three hundred to four hundred members gathered at the second general meeting in 1940. By this time, Makiguchi was focusing his attention on Buddhism, specifically the teachings and practice of Nichiren, as a means for leading a life of the highest values and greatest good. He conducted discussion meetings at which members talked about the results of their Buddhist faith and practice, which he referred to as experimental evidence of its efficacy. The membership of the Soka Kyōiku Gakkai increased to some three thousand by the early 1940s.

By the 1930s, Japan was following the path of militarism, pursuing a war with China, and finally, in 1941, sparking the Pacific War with its attack on Pearl Harbor. To unite and rally the people for the war effort, the militarist government had adopted Shinto as the state religion as well as various measures to restrict freedom of thought, expression, and religion. In line with this, the government ordered all religious denominations to enshrine Shinto talismans in their places of worship, and private citizens to do so in their homes. People were required to worship the Sun Goddess, the legendary progenitor of the imperial line. Makiguchi refused such Shinto worship as contradictory to Nichiren's teachings. This led to his being detained by police in May 1943 for a week.

The following month, Soka Kyōiku Gakkai leaders were summoned to Taiseki-ji, the head temple of Nichiren Shōshū. Not only did the Nichiren Shōshū priesthood submit to the government demand but its administrators also suggested in the presence of its chief priest that Soka Kyōiku Gakkai members also accept the Shinto talisman. President Makiguchi refused to comply on the grounds that this would violate the teachings of Nichiren and his successor, Nikkō. The priesthood's response to this was virtually to expel them from Nichiren Shōshū by barring them from visiting Taiseki-ji on pilgrimage.

In July 1943, charged with violation of the Peace Preservation Law of 1925, and with lese majesty against the emperor, Makiguchi and Toda were arrested and imprisoned; subsequently, nineteen other leaders of the organization were rounded up and imprisoned. Makiguchi died in prison at age seventy-three on November 18, 1944, having continued to challenge the religious and political views of his captors until the end.

While in prison, Toda immersed himself in the study of the Lotus Sutra, prayer, and contemplation, and experienced two kinds of realization. First, he came to realize that the Buddha described in the sutra is life itself. Second, he awakened to his identity as a Bodhisattva of the Earth as described in the Lotus Sutra. Consequently, he resolved to propagate the sutra's teachings as widely as possible and to reconstruct the organization he and Makiguchi had founded.

Toda was released on parole on July 3, 1945. Amid a war-ravaged Japan, he set out to reconstruct the organization, renaming it the Soka Gakkai in 1946. His dropping of "Kyōiku," or "Education," from the name reflected the objective he envisioned for the organization to include people from and contribute to all fields and strata of society, transcending its role as a society of educators. Toda became the second president on May 3, 1951, pledging on that occasion to achieve a membership of 750,000 households. At that time, the membership was only around 3,000. In August 1952, the Soka Gakkai was legally incorporated as an independent religious organization. By 1957, the membership had reached the goal of 750,000 set by Toda.

In September 1957, Toda issued a declaration calling for the abolition of atomic and hydrogen bombs, urging young people to work toward that end. In addition, Toda had a Grand Lecture Hall built and donated to Taiseki-ji, and events to celebrate the opening of this structure lasted throughout March 1958. On March 16, Toda attended a gathering of six thousand young people at Taiseki-ji, where he entrusted them with the future of the Soka Gakkai and propagation of Nichiren's teachings. He died on April 2, 1958.

On May 3, 1960, Daisaku Ikeda (1928–) became the third president at age thirty-two. Ikeda had worked and studied under Toda for more than ten years, helping him rebuild his businesses after the war and playing a key role in achieving the membership target Toda had set for the Soka Gakkai. Under Ikeda's leadership, the organization grew rapidly during the 1960s and 1970s and expanded abroad. It broadened its focus to include activities in support of peace, culture, and education. In January 1975, in response to the needs of an increasing international membership, the Soka Gakkai International (SGI) was established, and Ikeda became its first president. As of 2002, it became a worldwide network of more than twelve million members in 183 countries and territories. Ikeda resigned as the third president of the Soka Gakkai in 1979 and became its honorary president, while retaining his position as president of the SGI. He was succeeded as Soka Gakkai president by Hiroshi Hōjō (1923–1981), who was followed by Einosuke Akiya (1930–) in 1981.

In pursuit of a lasting peace, Ikeda has tirelessly conducted dialogues and exchanges with scholars and cultural as well as political leaders from around the world. He has made various proposals concerning global issues such as disarmament, the abolition of nuclear weapons, and environmental protection. In 1968 Ikeda proposed the normalization of China–Japan relations and the conclusion of a bilateral peace and friendship treaty. He also acted to realize his proposals and build lasting friendship with China at the grassroots level. During his second visit to China in 1974, he met with Premier Zhou Enlai.

Ikeda has also established several institutions to promote peace, culture, and education, including Soka University and other Soka schools, the Min-On Concert Association, the Tokyo Fuji Art Museum, and the Institute of Oriental Philosophy. In the 1990s he founded the Boston Research Center for the 21st Century and the Toda Institute for Global Peace and Policy Research, both dedicated to peace studies. In addition, as nongovernmental organizations (NGOs) of the United Nations dedicated to peace, the Soka Gakkai and the SGI actively encourage support for the United Nations and sponsor peace and anti-nuclear weapons exhibits and fund-raising campaigns for refugees. The Soka Gakkai publishes numerous books and periodicals; its daily newspaper, *Seikyo Shimbun,* had a circulation of about 5.5 million as of 2002.

In the 1950s, the Soka Gakkai sponsored candidates for political office, and in 1962 a political group supported by the Soka Gakkai was formed. In 1964 the political party Komeitō (Clean Government Party) was founded. In 1970 Kōmeitō became completely separate and independent from the Soka Gakkai. While Soka Gakkai members continued to form its prime constituency, it was stipulated that no members of Kōmeitō could hold positions in the religious organization.

In 1964 the Soka Gakkai built and donated a Grand Reception Hall to Taiseki-ji, and in 1972 the Grand Main Temple, or Shō-Hondō. Around 1977 a group of Nichiren Shōshū priests began to attack the Soka Gakkai, in a failed effort to establish direct control over the membership. Again, at the end of 1990, the priesthood, headed by Nikken Abe, launched a series of measures against the Soka Gakkai aimed at its dissolution, culminating in excommunication of the Soka Gakkai without prior notice in November 1991. In the process, the priesthood refused all requests for dialogue with the lay organization. Nikken Abe then began a program of destroying key temples and structures at Taiseki-ji that had been donated by the Soka Gakkai, including the celebrated Grand Main Temple. The Soka Gakkai outspokenly condemned these acts, pointing out the doctrinal and moral errors of the priesthood. Ultimately, however, these events marked a new era of self-determination and freedom for the Soka Gakkai, which was no longer bound by the priests' conservative ritualism or their authoritarian and dogmatic interpretations of doctrine.

Based on the practice and philosophy of Nichiren's teachings, the Soka Gakkai advocates an individual inner reformation it calls "human revolution," the ultimate goal of which is a peaceful world and the happiness of humanity. It upholds the Lotus Sutra philosophy that all people inherently possess within them the Buddha nature, the potential for attaining Buddhahood, and can bring it forth through Buddhist practice. Based on this teaching, the Soka Gakkai has been endeavoring to establish the sanctity of life and the dignity of humanity as fundamental universal ideals. The Soka Gakkai does not view Buddhism as an exclusively spiritual or metaphysical pursuit, but as an applied philosophy of life. It encourages Buddhist practice as a means for people to develop the character, wisdom, and strength to improve themselves and their circumstances, to contribute to society, and to help bring about happiness and peace in the world.

soma [蘇摩] (Skt, Pali; Jpn *soma*): A drink with a stimulating effect used as an offering to the gods at Brahmanic rituals in ancient India. Also the name of the plant from which this drink is made. *Soma* was highly praised in Vedic scriptures. Later the moon came to be regarded as a heavenly vessel for *soma,* and was itself called Soma. In Buddhism as well, the god of the moon was called Soma or Soma-deva, *deva* meaning god.

sons of the Buddha [仏子] (Jpn *busshi*): *See* children of the Buddha.

Sō'ō [相応] (831–918): A priest of the Tendai school in Japan. He studied under Jikaku, the third chief priest of Enryaku-ji, the head temple of the Tendai school on Mount Hiei. He is said to have excelled in the performance of the esoteric prayer rituals. In 865 he founded Mudō-ji temple on Mount Hiei, in which a statue of the wisdom king Immovable was enshrined. In 866 he petitioned Emperor Seiwa to grant the title "great teacher" to Dengyō and Jikaku. This was the first instance of the title "great teacher" being bestowed in Japan. Sō'ō is also regarded as the founder of the Tendai practice of visiting the assigned shrines and halls on Mount Hiei every day for one thousand days (known as *kaihō-gyō*, "making a round on the mountain").

sorrowless tree [無憂樹] (Jpn *muu-ju*): A tall leguminous tree that produces beautiful orange- or scarlet-colored blossoms. The name of the *ashoka* tree was rendered in Chinese as "the sorrowless tree." See *ashoka* tree.

sotoba [卒塔婆] (Jpn): The Japanese transliteration of stupa, a kind of shrine in India. See *tōba*.

Sōtō school [曹洞宗] (Jpn Sōtō-shū): One of the major schools of Zen in Japan. The founder was Dōgen, who went to China in 1223 and introduced the Ts'ao-tung (Jpn Sōtō) school, one of the five schools of Chinese Zen, to Japan. After returning from China in 1227, he lived at Kennin-ji temple in Kyoto. Thereafter he moved to Fukakusa, where he founded Kōshō-ji temple and taught Zen, stressing the continued practice of seated meditation *(zazen)*. Later he established Eihei-ji temple in Echizen Province as the principal monastery of Sōtō Zen practice. Tettsū Gikai, the third patriarch of Sōtō Zen, left Eihei-ji and lived at Daijō-ji in Kaga Province. His disciple Keizan Jōkin is revered as the founder of Sōji-ji temple in Noto Province. Sōji-ji was relocated and now stands in Kanagawa Prefecture as one of the two head temples of the school, the other being Eihei-ji. Sōtō emphasizes the continued practice of seated meditation, as opposed to meditation on *kōan* (Chin *kung-an*), questions for meditation inaccessible to logical solution taught in the Rinzai school of Zen.

Southern Buddhism [南方仏教・南伝仏教] (Jpn Nampō-bukkyō or Nanden-bukkyō): Buddhism that spread from India to Sri Lanka and Southeast Asian countries such as Myanmar, Thailand, Laos, and Cambodia. The term *Southern Buddhism* contrasts with *Northern Buddhism*, which spread to Central Asia, Tibet, China, Korea, and Japan. Southern Buddhism is also called Theravāda Buddhism or Southern Theravāda Buddhism. Southern Buddhism is placed in the category of Hinayana. Hinayana, or Lesser Vehicle, was originally a pejorative term employed by Mahayana Buddhists. In the areas where Theravāda Buddhism was disseminated, Mahayana Buddhism also spread, but it was ultimately superseded by Theravāda.

Theravāda Buddhism is based upon the Pali canon called *Tipitaka* (Skt *Tripitaka*), which consists of sutras, texts on rules of monastic discipline, and doctrinal commentaries. Theravāda Buddhists revere Shakyamuni Buddha, the founder of Buddhism, as the sole perfect master and teacher. Based on the Pali canon, monks strive to adhere to the doctrines and practices taught by Shakyamuni Buddha, endeavor to observe the precepts, and involve themselves in charitable activities. Laypersons accumulate benefits through offerings to monasteries and monks. Many people hold faith in Theravāda Buddhism while retaining indigenous beliefs that are regarded as compatible with Buddhism. The introduction of Buddhism into Sri Lanka dates back to the third century B.C.E. During the reign of the Indian king Ashoka, the king's son Mahendra brought Theravāda Buddhism to Sri Lanka. The Sri Lankan king, Devānampiya Tissa, built for Mahendra the Mahāvihāra monastery in the capital of Anurādhapura. That monastery is the center of Theravāda Buddhism among Southeast Asian countries, and Theravāda Buddhists in these countries maintain close contact with fellow Buddhists in Sri Lanka.

In the first century B.C.E., another monastery called Abhayagiri was built, which eventually led to the split of the Buddhist Order in Sri Lanka into the Mahāvihāra school and the Abhayagiri school. In the Abhayagiri monastery, Mahayana Buddhism was also studied. In the fifth century, Buddhaghosa went from India to Sri Lanka and systematized the Theravāda doctrines in accordance with the Mahāvihāra lineage. The first people in Myanmar to receive Theravāda Buddhism were the Mons in the cities of Thaton and Pegu. Theravāda Buddhism took firm root within that Burmese tribe in the eleventh century during the reign of Anawrahta of the Pagan kingdom. Anawrahta declared himself the champion of Theravāda Buddhism. He unified the area that is today Myanmar and founded the first Burmese Empire.

In Thailand, Theravāda Buddhism had been introduced by the thirteenth century, when Sukhothai, the first kingdom of the Thai, emerged. It took root within the Sukhothai kingdom and continued to prosper in the Ayutthaya kingdom, which emerged in the mid-fourteenth century. To date, Theravāda Buddhism has continued to be a major pillar of Thai society. For a short period sometime during their lifetime, Buddhist laymen join a monastery to receive instruction. Currently, in Sri Lanka, Myanmar, and Thailand, the greater part of the population are Theravāda Buddhists. It is a predominant religion in Cambodia and Laos, and there are followers of Theravāda in Bangladesh, Indonesia, Malaysia, and Singapore.

Southern school of Zen [南宗禅] (Jpn Nanshū Zen): The school derived from Hui-neng (638–713), the sixth patriarch of Chinese Zen (Ch'an). His teacher was Hung-jen, the fifth patriarch. Hung-jen had another able disciple named Shen-hsiu, who spread Zen in northern China and started what came to be called the Northern school of Zen. While the Northern school soon declined, the Southern school prospered and became the mainstream of Chinese Zen. It is divided into five branches—Ts'ao-tung (Jpn Sōtō), Yün-men (Ummon), Fa-yen (Hōgen), Kuei-yang (Igyō), and Lin-chi (Rinzai). The Lin-chi school eventually produced two more schools, the Huang-lung (Ōryū) and Yang-ch'i (Yōgi).

Sovereign Kings of the Golden Light Sutra [金光明最勝王経] (Skt *Suvarnaprabhāsa-sūtra* or *Suvarnaprabhāsottama-sūtra;* Chin *Chin-kuang-ming-tsui-sheng-wang-ching;* Jpn *Konkōmyō-saishō'ō-kyō*): Abbreviated as the Sovereign Kings Sutra. A sutra in ten volumes and thirty-one chapters, translated in 703 by the Chinese priest I-ching. According to the sutra, it was preached by Shakyamuni Buddha on Eagle Peak northeast of Rājagriha, the capital of the Magadha kingdom. The sutra dwells on the protection of the four heavenly kings and other benevolent deities. It says that the benevolent deities will protect the country of a ruler who upholds and protects the correct teaching, but will abandon the country of a ruler who does not; as a result, numerous disasters such as pestilence, earthquake, storm, and invasion from other countries will occur. In Japan, this sutra was counted as one of the three scriptures for the protection of the nation, the other two being the Lotus Sutra and the Benevolent Kings Sutra. When separate provincial temples for priests and temples for nuns were established by Emperor Shōmu in the mid-eighth century, the Sovereign Kings of the Golden Light Sutra was recited at the temples for priests to ensure the peace and prosperity of the country. The sutra contains a well-known story of two excellent physicians, Water Holder and his son Water Carrier, and the story of Prince Mahāsattva, who sacrificed himself to save a starving tigress. *See also* Golden Light Sutra.

Sovereign Kings Sutra [最勝王経] (Jpn *Saishō-ō-kyō*): *See* Sovereign Kings of the Golden Light Sutra.

sovereign, teacher, and parent [主師親] (Jpn *shu-shi-shin*): *See* three virtues.

sowing, maturing, and harvesting [種熟脱] (Jpn *shu-juku-datsu*):

The three-phase process by which a Buddha leads people to Buddhahood. In *The Words and Phrases of the Lotus Sutra,* T'ien-t'ai (538–597) set forth this concept based on the Lotus Sutra, comparing the process of people attaining Buddhahood to the growth of a plant. In the first stage, "sowing," the Buddha plants the seeds of Buddhahood in the lives of the people, just as a gardener sows seeds in the soil. Nichiren (1222–1282) states in *The Essentials for Attaining Buddhahood,* "The Buddha [is] like the sower, and the people like the field" (748). In the second stage, the Buddha nurtures the seeds he has planted by helping the people practice the teaching and leading them gradually to Buddhahood. This stage is compared to the gardener's care for the sprouting and growth of a plant and is called "maturing." In the third and final stage, the Buddha leads the people to reap the harvest of enlightenment, enabling them to attain Buddhahood. This is comparable to the gardener reaping the fruit of a plant and is called "harvesting."

The process of sowing, maturing, and harvesting is described as taking place over countless *kalpas.* From the viewpoint of the essential teaching (latter half) of the Lotus Sutra, Shakyamuni first planted the seeds of enlightenment in the lives of his disciples numberless major world system dust particle *kalpas* in the past. He then nurtured them as the sixteenth son of the Buddha Great Universal Wisdom Excellence major world system dust particle *kalpas* in the past and later as the Buddha in India by preaching the pre-Lotus Sutra teachings and the theoretical teaching (first half) of the Lotus Sutra. He finally brought them to fruition, or enlightenment, with the "Life Span" (sixteenth) chapter of the Lotus Sutra. Seen from this perspective, Shakyamuni's essential teaching was expounded for the purpose of reaping the harvest of enlightenment and accordingly is called the teaching of the harvest. The pre-Lotus Sutra teachings and the theoretical teaching, through which Shakyamuni nurtured his disciples' capacity for enlightenment, are regarded as the teaching of maturing. As a whole, Nichiren refers to Shakyamuni's teachings as the Buddhism of the harvest.

In *The Object of Devotion for Observing the Mind,* Nichiren states: "He [Shakyamuni] planted the seeds of Buddhahood in their lives in the remote past [numberless major world system dust particle *kalpas* ago] and nurtured the seeds through his preaching as the sixteenth son of the Buddha Great Universal Wisdom Excellence [major world system dust particle *kalpas* ago] and through the first four flavors of teachings [the pre-Lotus Sutra teachings] and the theoretical teaching in this life. Then with the essential teaching he brought his followers to the stage of near-perfect enlightenment and finally to that of perfect enlightenment" (369–70). In the same work, Nichiren writes: "The essential teaching of Shakyamuni's lifetime and that revealed at the beginning of the Latter Day are both pure and perfect [in that both lead directly to Buddhahood]. Shakyamuni's, however, is the Buddhism of the harvest, and this is the Buddhism of sowing. The core of his teaching is one chapter and two halves, and the core of mine is the five characters of the daimoku alone" (370). Though "one chapter and two halves" indicates that Shakyamuni planted the seeds of Buddhahood in the lives of his followers, the teaching of sowing is "hidden in the depths of the 'Life Span' chapter" of the Lotus Sutra. More specifically, it is hidden in the sentence "Originally I practiced the bodhisattva way."

Nichiren referred to the hidden teaching as "the seed of Buddhahood, that is, the three thousand realms in a single moment of life" in *The Object of Devotion for Observing the Mind* (365). In *The Opening of the Eyes,* he writes: "This is the doctrine of original cause and original effect. It reveals that the nine worlds are all present in beginningless Buddhahood and that Buddhahood is inherent in the beginningless nine worlds. This is the true mutual possession of the Ten Worlds, the true hundred worlds and thousand factors, the true three thousand realms in a single moment of life" (235). This indicates the eternal Mystic Law that enables people to reveal Buddhahood from their beginningless nine worlds. Originally Shakyamuni practiced the bodhisattva way as a common mortal with this Law as his teacher and thus realized and manifested his inherent Buddhahood.

In contrast with Shakyamuni's Buddhism, Nichiren identified his teaching as the Buddhism of sowing and defined the daimoku of Nam-myoho-renge-kyo as the teaching for planting the seeds of enlightenment. Because Nam-myoho-renge-kyo is the law of the simultaneity of cause and effect, it contains within it all three stages of sowing, maturing, and harvesting. *The Words and Phrases of the Lotus Sutra* refers to two types of people: those who [received the seeds of Buddhahood and] have good roots and those who do not. According to Nichiren, people in the Latter Day of the Law never received the seeds of Buddhahood from the Buddha in the past and must therefore first receive the seeds of Buddhahood in their lives. Then they can complete the whole process of maturing and harvesting in this lifetime. Nichiren established the object of devotion called the Gohonzon, embodying in it the Law of Nam-myoho-renge-kyo as a means for people to plant the seeds of Buddhahood in their lives and reap the fruit of Buddhahood. In Nichiren's teaching, the practice for doing so involves chanting Nam-myoho-renge-kyo with faith in the Gohonzon. *See also* teacher of the true cause; teacher of the true effect.

Soya, the lay priest [曾谷入道] (Jpn Soya-nyūdō): A devout follower of Nichiren. *See* Soya Kyōshin.

Soya Dōsō [曾谷道宗] (n.d.): A follower of Nichiren and a son of Soya Kyōshin who lived in Shimōsa Province, Japan. His name and title were Soya Shirō Saemon-no-jō Naohide. He converted to Nichiren's teaching early in life and changed his name to Tensō after becoming a lay priest. Some time later, he changed his name again to Dōsō. In 1276 he founded Myōkō-ji temple at what is now Noro in present-day Chiba Prefecture, the place where he lived.

Soya Kyōshin [曾谷教信] (1224–1291): Also known as the lay priest Soya or Kyōshin-bō. A follower of Nichiren. His full name and title were Soya Jirō Hyōe-no-jō Kyōshin. A samurai who lived in Soya of Katsushika District in Shimōsa Province, Japan. He converted to Nichiren's teaching around 1260 and became a leading believer in the area with Toki Jōnin and Ōta Jōmyō. In 1271 he became a lay priest, and Nichiren gave him the Buddhist name Hōren Nichirai. Soya Kyōshin received eight writings (extant) from Nichiren in which important teachings are outlined; their content would seem to indicate that he was well educated. He built two temples, Ankoku-ji and Hōren-ji.

Space Treasury [虚空蔵菩薩] (Skt Ākāshagarbha; Jpn Kokūzō-bosatsu): A bodhisattva whose wisdom and good fortune are said to be as vast and boundless as the universe. In the True Word (Jpn Shingon) school, he appears as the central deity of the Space Treasury court of the Womb Realm mandala, where he is pictured seated on a lotus blossom wearing a crown adorned with jewels representing five kinds of wisdom; in his right hand he holds a sword of wisdom, while in his left he holds a lotus blossom of fortune and a wish-granting jewel. Space Treasury was also worshiped in Japan independently of the True Word school from early on.

specific teaching [別教] (Jpn *bekkyō*): One of the four teachings of doctrine formulated by T'ien-t'ai (538–597) of China. A higher level of provisional Mahayana taught specifically and exclusively for bodhisattvas, which expounds the fifty-two stages of practice to be carried out over a period of countless *kalpas*. The specific teaching is so called because it is specific and distinct both from the preceding two of the four teachings of doctrine (i.e., the Tripitaka teaching and the connecting teaching) and from the subsequent perfect teaching, or the fourth and last of the four teachings of doctrine. The specific teaching elucidates the three truths of non-substantiality, temporary existence, and the Middle Way. In the specific teaching, however, the above three truths are viewed as separate from one another, and the Middle Way is regarded as transcendent. For this reason, the specific teaching is also called the teaching of the Middle Way that is independent of the other two truths, while the Tripitaka teaching is called the exclusive teaching on non-substantiality, or emptiness. *See also* eight teachings; four teachings of doctrine.

specific transfer [別付嘱] (Jpn *betsu-fuzoku*): Also, specific transmission. A transfer of the essence of the Lotus Sutra by Shakyamuni Buddha to Bodhisattva Superior Practices and the other Bodhisattvas of the Earth that takes place in the "Supernatural Powers" (twenty-first) chapter of the sutra. The specific transfer is so called because the essence of the sutra was transferred specifically to the Bodhisattvas of the Earth. It is contrasted with the general transfer, which takes place in the subsequent (twenty-second) chapter, "Entrustment." In that chapter, the Lotus Sutra is transferred to all the assembled bodhisattvas.

specks of dirt on a fingernail [爪上の土] (Jpn *sōjō-no-do*): The number of particles of dirt that can be placed or balanced on a fingernail, an expression used in Buddhist texts to represent extreme scarcity or rarity. In particular, it symbolizes the rarity of being born a human being, encountering the Buddha's teachings, and attaining Buddhahood. The phrase is often contrasted with expressions such as "the specks of dirt in all the lands of the ten directions." The Nirvana Sutra says that those who do not believe in the correct teaching are as numerous as the specks of dirt in all the lands of the ten directions, while those who believe in the correct teaching are as few as the specks of dirt that can be placed on a fingernail. "Specks of dirt" is also translated as particles of dust, etc.

spirits [鬼神] (Jpn *kijin*): Beings said to possess supernatural powers. Buddhism describes two kinds of spirits—good and evil. Good spirits are those that work to protect the people and the Buddha's teachings, while evil spirits are malevolent and try to harm people and the Buddha's teachings. The latter are often referred to as "demons."

spoiled seeds [敗種] (Jpn *haishu*): In Mahayana scriptures, persons of the two vehicles—voice-hearers and cause-awakened ones—are often compared to seeds that will never sprout, implying that they are incapable of attaining Buddhahood. *See also* rotten seeds.

Spotted Feet [斑足王] (Skt Kalmāshapāda; Pali Kammāsapāda; Jpn Hansoku-ō or Hanzoku-ō): Also known as Deer Feet. A king described in the Benevolent Kings Sutra, the Sutra on the Wise and the Foolish, and *The Treatise on the Great Perfection of Wisdom*. According to the Sutra on the Wise and the Foolish, he was a prince born of the king of a country and a lioness. Though human in form, he had spotted feet. According to the Benevolent Kings Sutra, he was the crown prince of a kingdom called Devala and was about to become the king. One day a non-Buddhist teacher suggested to him that he take the heads of a thousand kings and dedicate them to a certain deity. Prince Spotted Feet responded by capturing and imprisoning 999 kings. He then captured the thousandth and last king, who was named Universal Brightness. King Universal Brightness begged Spotted Feet for a day's grace before being killed so that he could return to his country to offer food to Buddhist monks. This granted, he built a hundred preaching platforms and invited a hundred monks to lecture from them. The monks lectured on the *prajnā-pāramitā,* or the teaching of the perfection of wisdom. Universal Brightness listened as the foremost of the monks preached verses for him, and he thereby gained great insight. The next day he returned as promised to Spotted Feet, who had already ascended the throne. He proceeded to teach the Buddhist verses he had learned to the other imprisoned kings and to Spotted Feet as well. The latter was so delighted that he admitted being led astray by a non-Buddhist teacher and urged all the kings to invite the monks to lecture on the perfection of wisdom. Releasing the kings, Spotted Feet became a monk himself and strove in Buddhist practice until he finally awakened to the non-birth and non-extinction of all phenomena. The details of the story differ according to the text. For example, in *The Treatise on the Great Perfection of Wisdom,* King Spotted Feet appears as King Deer Feet who captured the king Universal Brightness and 99 other kings and granted Universal Brightness seven days' grace to fulfill a promise he had made to give offerings to a Brahman. *See also* Universal Brightness.

srota-āpanna [須陀洹・預流] (Skt; Jpn *shudaon* or *yoru*): The first of the four stages of Hinayana enlightenment. *See* stream-winner.

stage of being a Buddha in theory [理即] (Jpn *ri-soku*): The first of the six stages of practice. *See* six stages of practice.

stage of hearing the name and words of the truth [名字即] (Jpn *myōji-soku*): The second of the six stages of practice, stages in the practice of the Lotus Sutra formulated by T'ien-t'ai (538–597). The stage at which one hears the name of the truth (i.e., one hears a Buddhist term for the ultimate reality such as "the true aspect of all phenomena") and/or reads the words of the sutras and thereby understands intellectually that all beings are potential Buddhas and that all phenomena are manifestations of the universal Law. *See also* six stages of practice.

stage of non-regression [不退位] (Skt *avaivartika, avivartika,* or *avini-*

vartanīya; Jpn *futai-i*): Also, stage of non-retrogression. One of the stages of bodhisattva practice. One who reaches this stage never backslides, always advancing in Buddhist practice toward the goal of Buddhahood. In the stage of non-regression, a bodhisattva neither retreats to a lower stage of bodhisattva practice nor regresses to the stages of voice-hearers and cause-awakened ones or to the four evil paths—the realms of hell, hungry spirits, animals, and *asuras.* T'ien-t'ai (538–597) defined the first stage of security among the fifty-two stages of bodhisattva practice as the stage of non-regression. *See also* three kinds of non-regression.

stage of perception and action [観行即] (Jpn *kangyō-soku*): The third of the six stages of practice. *See* six stages of practice.

stage of progressive awakening [分真即] (Jpn *bunshin-soku*): The fifth of the six stages of practice. *See* six stages of practice.

stage of resemblance to enlightenment [相似即] (Jpn *sōji-soku*): The fourth of the six stages of practice. *See* six stages of practice.

stage of the foremost worldly good root [世第一法・世第一法位] (Jpn *sedaiippō* or *sedaiippō-i*): *See* foremost worldly stage.

stage of the four good roots [四善根・四善根位] (Jpn *shi-zengon* or *shi-zengon-i*): *See* four good roots.

stage of ultimate enlightenment [究竟即] (Jpn *kukyō-soku*): The sixth of the six stages of practice. *See* six stages of practice.

Stepping on Seven Treasure Flowers [蹈七宝華如来] (Skt Saptaratna-padma-vikrāntagāmin; Jpn Tōshippōke-nyorai): The Thus Come One Stepping on Seven Treasure Flowers. The name that Rāhula, Shakyamuni's son, will bear when he becomes a Buddha, according to Shakyamuni's prediction in the "Prophecies" (ninth) chapter of the Lotus Sutra.

Sthaviravāda school [上座部] (Skt; Jpn Jōza-bu): The Theravāda school in Pali. One of two schools formed by the first split in the Buddhist Order about one hundred years after Shakyamuni's death, the other being the Mahāsamghika school. *See* Theravāda school.

Sthiramati [安慧] (n.d.) (Skt; Jpn An'ne): A scholar of the Consciousness-Only school in southern India, who lived sometime during the fifth or sixth century. He is counted among the ten great scholars of the Consciousness-Only (Skt Vijnānavāda) school who wrote commentaries on Vasubandhu's *Thirty-Stanza Treatise on the Consciousness-Only Doctrine.* Among all the commentaries written on the treatise, Sthiramati's is the only one still extant in Sanskrit.

stinginess and greed [慳貪] (Jpn *kendon*): *See* greed and stinginess.

stone footprints of the Buddha [仏足石] (Jpn *bussoku-seki*): Imprints of the soles of the Buddha's feet carved in stone. The Buddha's footprints in stone symbolized the Buddha himself, and worship of such stone footprints was popular in India, China, and Japan. For centuries after Shakyamuni Buddha's death, there was no attempt to create an image of the Buddha, for it was thought improper to graphically depict the Buddha himself. Shakyamuni Buddha was instead depicted in carvings symbolically as a wheel, an empty throne, a *bodhi* tree, an umbrella, or a pair of footprints. The Buddha was represented only in this manner until the first century, when Gandhara carvings began to depict him in human form. This was followed by the sculpting of statues of the Buddha. Nevertheless, stone footprints, an early traditional symbol of the Buddha, remained popular and were transmitted along with the teachings from one country to the next.

storehouse consciousness [蔵識] (Jpn *zō-shiki*): Another name for the *ālaya*-consciousness, the eighth and deepest of the eight consciousnesses. It is so called because the results of one's actions, good or evil, are stored there as a potential force, or karmic "seeds." These seeds are said to sprout in the future; in other words, stored karma eventually manifests as happiness or suffering. See also *ālaya*-consciousness.

stream-winner [須陀洹・預流] (Skt *srota-āpanna;* Pali *sota-āpanna;* Jpn *shudaon* or *yoru*): The first of the four stages of Hinayana enlightenment. The fourth and highest stage is that of arhat. The stream-winner is the stage in which one enters the stream of the sages, i.e., in which one joins the ranks of sages advancing toward nirvana. At this stage, one has eradicated the illusions of thought in the threefold world. *See also* four stages of Hinayana enlightenment; illusions of thought and desire.

stupa [塔] (Skt *stūpa;* Jpn *tō*): A kind of shrine in India where the relics of Shakyamuni Buddha or other sage monks are housed. Stupas are usually dome- or mound-shaped. The first stupas were built after Shakyamuni's death, when his ashes were divided into eight parts and eight stupas were erected in eight districts to hold the Buddha's relics. In the third century B.C.E., King Ashoka of the Maurya dynasty supported and protected Buddhism and erected stupas and stone pillars at sites associated with Shakyamuni Buddha. According to Buddhist legend, Ashoka divided the Buddha's ashes that were housed by seven of the eight stupas among eighty-four thousand stupas that he erected throughout India. Among the oldest surviving stupas is the one at Sanchi in central India called the Great Stupa. Stupas were made of brick or stone, and their construction and maintenance were considered meritorious deeds that produced benefit.

Lay believers held stupas in deep reverence, and contributed to their construction. According to some scholars, the monks were originally indifferent to such stupa veneration and the Mahayana movement began with a group of Buddhist believers who practiced stupa worship. In the third century B.C.E., Buddhism was introduced to Sri Lanka along with the practice and techniques of stupa construction. Southern, or Theravāda, Buddhism was first transmitted to Sri Lanka and from there spread to Southeast Asian countries such as Myanmar and Thailand. The stupas of these countries are known to Westerners as pagodas, and in Myanmar and Thailand they are bell-shaped. Northern Buddhism made its way into Central Asia, China, and Japan, where stupas, or pagodas, and other types of Buddhist architecture were introduced. The pagodas of China are multi-leveled, towerlike structures, the architectural style of which has been traced to stupas of the Gandharan era of Indian Buddhist art and architecture. *Sotoba* or *tōba*, a wooden memorial tablet bearing inscriptions set up at gravesites in Japan to honor the deceased, is the Japanese transliteration of the word *stupa*. *See also* pagoda.

Subhadra [須跋陀羅] (Skt; Pali Subhadda; Jpn Shubaddara): The last convert of Shakyamuni Buddha mentioned in Buddhist scriptures. Shakyamuni continued his preaching until he died at Kushinagara in northern India. According to *Mahāparinibbāna-suttanta*, the Pali version of the Nirvana Sutra, Subhadra heard that the Buddha might die that night in Kushinagara, and he went to see him. Though fatigued and weak, Shakyamuni preached for Subhadra, who was deeply impressed with Shakyamuni's teaching and immediately became his follower. According to *The Treatise on the Great Perfection of Wisdom*, Subhadra had a dream in which all people were deprived of their eyesight and left standing naked in the darkness, the sun fell from the sky, the earth cracked, the seas went dry, and Mount Sumeru was toppled by a great wind. In the morning, hearing that the Buddha would enter nirvana "before the next day," he went to Shakyamuni and joined the Buddhist Order; that night he attained the state of arhat.

Subhūti [須菩提] (Skt, Pali; Jpn Shubodai): One of Shakyamuni's ten major disciples. He is said to have been a nephew of Sudatta, the wealthy patron of Shakyamuni Buddha in Shrāvastī, India, who donated Jetavana Monastery. Another account says that Subhūti was born to a Brahman family in that city. On the day of the donation of the monastery, Subhūti heard Shakyamuni preach there and became his disciple. The Wisdom sutras depict him as foremost in understanding the doctrine of non-substantiality. He also appears in the Lotus Sutra as one of the four great voice-hearers who understood the Buddha's one vehicle teaching through the parable of the three carts and the burning house related in the "Simile and Parable" (third) chapter. The "Bestowal of Prophecy" (sixth) chapter predicts his future enlightenment as a Buddha named Rare Form.

substituting faith for wisdom [以信代慧] (Jpn *ishin-daie*): The principle that faith is the true cause for gaining supreme wisdom, and faith alone leads to enlightenment. In general, Buddhism describes supreme wisdom as the cause of enlightenment. According to the Lotus Sutra, however, even Shāriputra, who was revered as foremost in wisdom, could attain enlightenment only through faith, not through wisdom. The "Simile and Parable" (third) chapter of the sutra states: "Even you, Shāriputra, in the case of this sutra were able to gain entrance through faith alone. How much more so, then, the other voice-hearers. Those other voice-hearers—it is because they have faith in the Buddha's words that they can comply with this sutra, not because of any wisdom of their own." In *Great Concentration and Insight,* T'ien-t'ai (538–597) says, "Buddhism is like an ocean that one can only enter with faith." In his 1277 treatise *On the Four Stages of Faith and the Five Stages of Practice,* Nichiren states, "Because our wisdom is inadequate, he [Shakyamuni Buddha] teaches us to substitute faith for wisdom, making this single word 'faith' the foundation" (785).

Sudāna [須大拏太子] (Skt, Pali; Jpn Shudaina-taishi): The name of Shakyamuni Buddha in a former life as a prince carrying out the practice of almsgiving. The story of Prince Sudāna appears in several Buddhist scriptures, including the Sudāna Sutra, which is part of the Sutra of Collected Birth Stories concerning the Practice of the Six Pāramitās. Prince Sudāna valued almsgiving and unselfishly gave food, clothing, and valuables to those of his kingdom who desired them. He presented the people with anything they wanted—gold, silver, horses, houses, and land. The king, his father, had a white elephant that was powerful enough to defend the kingdom from enemies.

Enemy rulers attempted to exploit Sudāna's generosity and his practice of almsgiving to obtain the white elephant. Eight envoys were sent to his country to carry out this mission. They asked Prince Sudāna to give them the white elephant, which he did. The ministers and other officials of the kingdom were apprehensive because they had lost the powerful elephant, and because the prince would not stop giving alms. Finally the king ordered his son Sudāna to leave the country and live in retreat on Mount Dandaka. Sudāna then left with his wife, son, and daughter. On his way to Mount Dandaka, he had three encounters with Brahmans who begged for various items; he granted the requests of each, giving clothes and ornaments to the first, the horse that drew his carriage to the second, and the carriage to the third. He and his family arrived at Mount Dandaka with nothing left.

One day Sudāna received a visit from a Brahman who wished to have Sudāna's children. Sudāna granted this wish. The god Shakra then tested his resolve by assuming the form of a Brahman and asking Sudāna to give him his wife. Sudāna granted this wish as well. Shakra thereupon revealed his true identity and praised Sudāna for his resolve. The Brahman who earlier had taken Sudāna's two children sold them to the king, their grandfather. Hearing about Sudāna from them, the king wished to see his son and sent for him. Finally the king gave Sudāna all of his wealth to support his practice of almsgiving. Sudāna gave treasures and other possessions to the people to support their well-being, and in this way perfected the practice of almsgiving. *The Treatise on the Great Perfection of Wisdom* also mentions Sudāna's act of offering his two children and then his wife to Brahmans as an example of the practice of almsgiving.

The story of Prince Sudāna is depicted in relief on the south gateway leading to the Great Stupa in Sanchi, central India, built in the third century B.C.E., and in a surviving relief found among the ruins of the large second-century stupa in Amaravati in southeast India. A mural depicting the story of Sudāna is found among the ruins of a Buddhist monastery in Miran in Central Asia.

Sudatta [須達] (Skt, Pali; Jpn Shudatsu): A merchant of Shrāvastī in Kosala, India, and a lay patron of Shakyamuni Buddha. He is said to have been one of the wealthiest men in the kingdom of Kosala. Since he often made donations of food and clothing to the poor and friendless, he was also called Anāthapindada (Pali Anāthapindika), Supplier of the Needy. Hearing Shakyamuni preach at Bamboo Grove Monastery in Rājagriha, he converted to Buddhism. Sudatta decided to invite Shakyamuni to Shrāvastī and, with the assistance of Prince Jetri, built Jetavana Monastery as an offering to the Buddha. Shakyamuni often visited Jetavana Monastery to preach, which contributed greatly to the spread of Buddhism in Kosala.

sudden teaching [頓教] (Jpn *ton-gyō* or *ton-kyō*): The category of teachings that Shakyamuni Buddha expounded directly from the standpoint of his enlightenment, without giving his disciples preparatory knowledge. In T'ien-t'ai's system of classification, the sudden teaching is one of the four teachings of method and applied to the Flower Garland Sutra. Various schools adopted the term *sudden teaching*, and applied it in accord with their own doctrines to different sutras.

Suddhodana [浄飯王] (Pali; Jpn Jōbonnō): Shuddhodana in Sanskrit. The king Suddhodana, father of Shakyamuni. *See* Shuddhodana.

suffering [苦] (Skt *duhukha;* Pali *dukkha;* Jpn *ku*): Buddhism describes various categories of suffering, such as the four sufferings and the eight sufferings. The Sanskrit term *duhukha* (*duḥkha* according to standard alphabetization) is rendered as suffering. It also means uneasiness, pain, sorrow, trouble, or difficulty. Shakyamuni's renunciation of the world and quest for enlightenment was motivated by a desire to find a solution to the four sufferings of birth, aging, sickness, and death. The first of the four noble truths, which Shakyamuni is said to have taught in his first sermon after attaining enlightenment, is the truth of suffering, i.e., the truth that all existence is suffering. Thus, the seeking and attaining of the way of release from suffering became the object of Buddhist practice. The doctrine that all existence is suffering constitutes one of the four Dharma seals, the four basic identifying principles of Buddhism; the other three are that all existence is impermanent, that nothing has an independent existence of its own, and that nirvana, enlightenment, is tranquil and quiet. *See also* four sufferings; eight sufferings.

sufferings of birth and death are nirvana [生死即涅槃] (Jpn *shōji-soku-nehan*): A principle derived from the Lotus Sutra. *See* nirvana.

Sujātā [須闍多] (Skt, Pali; Jpn Shujata): A girl who offered food to Shakyamuni before he entered meditation to attain enlightenment. Shakyamuni had engaged in ascetic practices in Uruvilvā for twelve years (six years according to another view) and, realizing that asceticism fails to lead to the true way, he abandoned it. He then bathed in the Nairanjanā River and, offered milk curds by Sujātā, ate them and recovered his strength. Thereafter he entered meditation under a pipal *(bodhi)* tree and attained enlightenment.

Sukhāvatī [極楽] (Skt; Jpn Gokuraku): Perfect Bliss, the Pure Land of the Buddha Amida. *See* Perfect Bliss.

Sukhāvatīvyūha [スカーヴァティーヴューハ] (Skt; Jpn *Sukābatībyūha*): "Splendor of the Blissful Land." Either of the two Sanskrit sutras that describe Amida Buddha and his Pure Land. Sukhāvatī, the name of Amida Buddha's Pure Land, is rendered in Chinese as Perfect Bliss. The two sutras by this title are generally distinguished as the smaller *Sukhāvatīvyūha* and the larger *Sukhāvatīvyūha.* The Chinese translation of the shorter text is called the Amida Sutra, and that of the longer text is called the Buddha Infinite Life Sutra.

sumanā [須摩那・須曼那・蘇摩那] (Skt, Pali; Jpn *shumana, shumanna,* or *somana*): Also, *sumanas.* A shrub with fragrant light yellow flowers, from which a fragrant oil was extracted. Buddhist scriptures mention *sumanā* oil and *sumanā* fragrance among the offerings made to the Buddha. *Sumanā* is thought to be a variety of jasmine.

Sumeru, Mount [須弥山] (Skt; Jpn Shumi-sen): Also known as Mount Meru. In ancient Indian cosmology, the mountain that stands at the center of the world. The Sanskrit name *Sumeru* was rendered into Chinese as "Wonderful High," "Wonderful Bright," or "Calm and Bright." Explanations of Mount Sumeru differ slightly among the Buddhist scriptures. For example, the Long Āgama Sutra describes its height—from its base at the bottom of the sea to the summit—as 168,000 *yojanas,* rising to 84,000 *yojanas* above the surface of the sea and reaching 84,000 *yojanas* below. *The Dharma Analysis Treasury* describes its height as 160,000 *yojanas,* 80,000 *yojanas* above and 80,000 *yojanas* below the sea. According to *The Dharma Analysis Treasury,* Mount Sumeru is composed of gold, silver, emerald, and crystal, with four sides facing respectively north, south, east, and west. The god Shakra resides on the summit with his thirty-two retainer gods, while the four heavenly kings live halfway up, one to each of its four sides.

Mount Sumeru is surrounded by seven concentric mountain ranges made of gold, alternating with seven concentric seas of fresh water. The seventh gold mountain range is surrounded by a saltwater ocean, in which four continents—Pūrvavideha, Aparagodānīya, Uttarakuru, and Jambudvīpa—are situated respectively to the east, west, north, and south of Mount Sumeru. It is said that Buddhism appears and spreads only in Jambudvīpa. The saltwater ocean is in turn bounded by the Iron Encircling Mountains, an iron range that runs along the circular rim of the world. A sun and a moon move around Mount Sumeru. A world with a Mount Sumeru at its center is called a Sumeru world, and the universe is said to consist of countless such worlds.

Sumeru world [須弥山世界] (Jpn Shumisen-sekai): *See* Sumeru, Mount.

Summary of the Mahayana, The [摂大乗論] (Skt *Mahāyāna-samgraha;* Chin *She-ta-ch'eng-lun;* Jpn *Shō-daijō-ron*): A work by Asanga, an Indian Buddhist teacher of the fourth or fifth century, that constitutes the basic teaching of the Summary of the Mahayana (She-lun) school in China. It expounds the Consciousness-Only doctrine and mentions ten points in which Mahayana teachings are superior to those of Hinayana. There are three Chinese translations, attributed to Buddhashānta (completed in 531), Paramārtha (in 564), and Hsüan-tsang (in the mid-seventh century), respectively.

Summary of the Mahayana school [摂論宗] (Chin She-lun-tsung; Jpn Shōron-shū): One of the thirteen Buddhist schools said to have existed in China. A school based on Asanga's *Summary of the Mahayana* that expounds the Consciousness-Only doctrine. This school upholds the doctrine of the nine consciousnesses; it defines the first eight consciousnesses as the realm of delusion and regards the ninth, the *amala*-consciousness, as the realm of perfect purity. In the sixth century, Paramārtha, a monk from western India, brought the Sanskrit texts of *The Summary of the Mahayana* and Vasubandhu's *Commentary on "The Summary of the Mahayana"* to China and translated them into Chinese. Thereafter Paramārtha's followers propagated the doctrine of *The Summary of the Mahayana*, and as a result, the Summary of the Mahayana (She-lun) school was formed. Paramārtha is regarded as the founder. In the mid-seventh century, Hsüan-tsang made a new translation of *The Summary of the Mahayana*, and his disciple Tz'u-en founded the Dharma Characteristics (Fa-hsiang) school, which also taught the Consciousness-Only doctrine. Thereafter the Summary of the Mahayana school gradually declined. *See also* thirteen schools of China.

summer retreat [安居] (Jpn *ango*): *See* three-month retreat.

Summit of Being Heaven [有頂天] (Jpn Uchō-ten): (1) (Skt Akanishtha) Another name for the Akanishtha Heaven, or the highest heaven in the world of form. The living beings in this heaven are said to possess pure bodies that are free from all suffering and illness.

(2) (Skt Bhava-agra or Bhavāgra) Another name for the Heaven of Neither Thought Nor No Thought, or the highest heaven in the world of formlessness. The Sanskrit word *bhava* means being, existence, or realm of existence, and *agra* means summit or the uppermost. *See also* Realm of Neither Thought Nor No Thought.

sun, god of the [日天] (Skt Sūrya; Jpn Nitten): A deification of the sun in Indian mythology, adopted in Buddhism as a protective god. The Sanskrit word *sūrya* means sun. Buddhist scriptures often mention the god of the sun in conjunction with the god of the moon.

Sunakshatra [善星比丘] (Skt; Jpn Zenshō-biku): One of Shakyamuni's disciples, regarded as one of his sons from before becoming a monk. According to the Mahāparinirvāna Sutra, Sunakshatra joined the Buddhist Order, freed himself from all ties with the world of desire, and mastered the four stages of meditation. Influenced by evil teachers, however, he lost his mastery of the four stages of meditation and became attached to the mistaken view that there is no Buddha, no Law, and no attainment of nirvana. The Parinirvāna Sutra says: "At that time the Thus Come One and [Bodhisattva] Kāshyapa went to where Sunakshatra was. The monk Sunakshatra saw them coming from afar and immediately evil thoughts arose in his mind. And because of this evil in his mind, he fell alive into the Avīchi hell."

Sundarananda [孫陀羅難陀] (Skt; Jpn Sondara-nanda): Shakyamuni's disciple and younger half brother. *See* Nanda (1).

Sundarī [孫陀利] (Skt, Pali; Jpn Sondari): A woman who slandered Shakyamuni Buddha. According to the Commitment of Previous Deeds Sutra, when Shakyamuni was at Jetavana Monastery in Shrāvastī, several Brahmans and their followers plotted to discredit him. They persuaded the courtesan Sundarī to frequent the place where Shakyamuni was staying and then spread rumors that she was having an affair with him. Later these Brahmans killed Sundarī and buried her under a tree in Jetavana Monastery in order to implicate the Buddha's followers. The public at first blamed Shakyamuni, but soon perceived the Brahmans' plot and banished them. This incident is counted as one of the nine great ordeals Shakyamuni underwent.

sundry practices [雑行] (Jpn *zō-gyō*): Also, diverse practices. One of two categories of practices defined by Shan-tao (613–681), a patriarch of the Pure Land school in China, in his *Commentary on the Meditation on the Buddha Infinite Life Sutra.* The other category is correct practices. "Sundry practices" means all Buddhist practices not directed toward Amida Buddha, i.e., the practices of all schools and teachings other than Pure Land. "Correct practices" means those directed toward Amida Buddha, such as reading and reciting the Pure Land sutras centered on Amida Buddha, worshiping Amida Buddha, and invoking Amida Buddha's name. *See also* five sundry practices.

Sung Dynasty Biographies of Eminent Priests, The [宋高僧伝] (Chin *Sung-kao-seng-chuan;* Jpn *Sō-kōsō-den*): A compilation of biographies produced by Tsan-ning, a priest of the Precepts (Lü) school in China. A continuation of *The Liang Dynasty Biographies of Eminent Priests* and *The T'ang Dynasty Biographies of Eminent Priests,* it contains the biographies of eminent priests who lived from the Chen-kuan era (627–649) of the T'ang dynasty to the reign of Emperor T'ai-tsung (r. 976–997) of the Northern Sung dynasty. Having begun the compilation in 982 by imperial order, Tsan-ning presented this thirty-volume collection to Emperor T'ai-tsung in 988. The work contains biographies of 533 priests and mentions 130 other priests. It is one of the four major collections of the biographies of eminent priests that were compiled in the four dynasties, the other three being *The Liang Dynasty Biographies of Eminent Priests, The T'ang Dynasty Biographies of Eminent Priests,* and *The Great Ming Dynasty Biographies of Eminent Priests.*

Sun Goddess [天照大神] (Jpn Tenshō Daijin or Amaterasu Ōmikami): The central deity in Japanese mythology. According to the oldest extant

Japanese histories, *The Records of Ancient Matters* and *The Chronicles of Japan,* she is the progenitor of the imperial line and is said to live in Takamagahara (High Celestial Plain). The Sun Goddess was later adopted as a protective deity in Japanese Buddhism.

Sunlight [日光菩薩] (Skt Sūryaprabha; Jpn Nikkō-bosatsu): One of the two bodhisattvas who attend Medicine Master Buddha, the other being Moonlight. Bodhisattva Sunlight attends on Medicine Master's left, and Bodhisattva Moonlight, on his right. According to the Medicine Master Sutra, these two bodhisattvas are leaders of the innumerable bodhisattvas in the pure land of Medicine Master Buddha and are upholders of all the Buddha's teachings.

Sun Moon Bright [日月燈明仏] (Skt Chandra-sūrya-pradīpa; Jpn Nichigatsu-tōmyō-butsu): A Buddha who, according to the "Introduction" (first) chapter of the Lotus Sutra, appeared in the distant past to preach the correct teaching. That chapter refers to twenty thousand Buddhas who appeared successively, all bearing the same name, Sun Moon Bright. The last Sun Moon Bright Buddha expounded the Lotus Sutra to Bodhisattva Wonderfully Bright, a previous incarnation of Bodhisattva Manjushrī. After this Buddha's death, his eight sons practiced under the guidance of Wonderfully Bright and thus attained enlightenment. In the Sanskrit name, *chandra* means the moon, *sūrya,* the sun, and *pradīpa,* light, lamp, or glow.

Sun Moon Pure Bright Virtue [日月浄明徳仏] (Skt Chandra-sūrya-vimala-prabhāsa-shrī; Jpn Nichigatsu-jōmyōtoku-butsu): A Buddha mentioned in the "Medicine King" (twenty-third) chapter of the Lotus Sutra. That chapter describes him as having expounded the Lotus Sutra to Bodhisattva Medicine King when Medicine King was carrying out ascetic practices in a past existence as a bodhisattva named Gladly Seen by All Living Beings. *See also* Gladly Seen by All Living Beings (2).

sun of wisdom [慧日] (Jpn *enichi*): A metaphor for the Buddha's wisdom. The wisdom of the Buddha is called the sun of wisdom because it brings light to all living beings, dispelling all darkness of delusion and suffering. "Sun of wisdom" is also a metaphor for the Buddha or his teaching. The Universal Worthy Sutra reads, "If one wishes to carry out repentance, sit upright and ponder the true aspect. Then the host of sins, like frost or dew, can be wiped out by the sun of wisdom."

Superior Intent [勝意比丘] (Skt Agramati; Jpn Shōi-biku): A monk said to have lived in the latter age after the death of the Buddha Lion Sound King. According to the Non-substantiality of All Phenomena Sutra and *The Treatise on the Great Perfection of Wisdom,* he slandered the monk Root of Joy, who upheld the correct teaching, in front of many other monks, saying that Root of Joy was instructing the people in false doctrines. As a result, the earth split open and he fell into hell alive.

superior manifested body [勝応身] (Jpn *shō-ōjin*): Also, Buddha of the superior manifested body. One of two types of manifested body, the physical form in which a Buddha appears in order to save the people; the other is the inferior manifested body. The manifested body, the Dharma body, and the reward body constitute the three bodies of a Buddha. The Buddha of the superior manifested body is the Buddha who appears for the sake of bodhisattvas at or above the first stage of development, i.e., the forty-first of the fifty-two stages of bodhisattva practice. The Buddha of the inferior manifested body is the Buddha who appears for the benefit of ordinary people, persons of the two vehicles (voice-hearers and cause-awakened ones), and bodhisattvas below the first stage of development.

Superior Practices [上行菩薩] (Skt Vishishtachāritra; Jpn Jōgyō-bosatsu): The first of the four leaders of the Bodhisattvas of the Earth who appear from beneath the earth in the "Emerging from the Earth" (fifteenth) chapter of the Lotus Sutra. Shakyamuni transfers the essence of the sutra to those bodhisattvas, headed by Superior Practices, in the "Supernatural Powers" (twenty-first) chapter. In *The Supplement to "The Words and Phrases of the Lotus Sutra,"* Tao-hsien, a priest of the T'ien-t'ai school in China in the eighth century, states that the four bodhisattvas represent the four virtues of the Buddha's life: true self, eternity, purity, and happiness. Among these, Superior Practices represents the virtue of true self. In his writings, Nichiren (1222–1282) associates himself with Bodhisattva Superior Practices, saying that he has fulfilled the mission entrusted to the bodhisattva by Shakyamuni, and he refers to his propagation efforts as the work of Bodhisattva Superior Practices. Nichikan (1665–1726), the twenty-sixth chief priest of Taiseki-ji temple, regarded Nichiren as the reincarnation of Bodhisattva Superior Practices in terms of his outward behavior, and as the Buddha of the Latter Day of the Law, in terms of his inner enlightenment.

"Supernatural Powers" chapter [神力品] (Jpn *Jinriki-hon*): The twenty-first chapter of the Lotus Sutra. *See* "Supernatural Powers of the Thus Come One" chapter.

"Supernatural Powers of the Thus Come One" chapter [如来神力品] (Jpn *Nyorai-jinriki-hon*): Abbreviated as the "Supernatural Powers" chapter. The twenty-first chapter of the Lotus Sutra, in which Shakyamuni transfers the essence of the sutra to the Bodhisattvas of the Earth led by Superior Practices. At the beginning of the chapter, the Bodhisattvas of the Earth vow to propagate the sutra widely after Shakyamuni

Buddha's death. Then the Buddha, displaying his supernatural powers, states that, although those supernatural powers are vast and great, they are not enough to describe the benefit of the Lotus Sutra. He then declares to Superior Practices and the other Bodhisattvas of the Earth: "To put it briefly, all the doctrines possessed by the Thus Come One, all the freely exercised supernatural powers of the Thus Come One, the storehouse of all the secret essentials of the Thus Come One, all the most profound matters of the Thus Come One—all these are proclaimed, revealed, and clearly expounded in this sutra." (These lines are often referred to as the "four-phrase essence of the Lotus Sutra.") After this statement, he transfers the sutra to Bodhisattva Superior Practices and the other Bodhisattvas of the Earth.

Based on this passage, T'ien-t'ai (538–597) formulated the five major principles of name, essence, quality, function, and teaching. In T'ien-t'ai's interpretation, "All the doctrines possessed by the Thus Come One" indicates name, "all the freely exercised supernatural powers of the Thus Come One" indicates function, "the storehouse of all the secret essentials of the Thus Come One" indicates essence, "all the most profound matters of the Thus Come One" indicates quality, and "all these are proclaimed, revealed, and clearly expounded in this sutra" indicates the teaching. In his 1273 treatise *The Object of Devotion for Observing the Mind,* Nichiren states that Nam-myoho-renge-kyo, the heart of the "Life Span" (sixteenth) chapter of the Lotus Sutra, is endowed with these five principles. Nichiren thus interprets the five major principles as the attributes of Nam-myoho-renge-kyo.

In *The Words and Phrases of the Lotus Sutra,* T'ien-t'ai refers to the transfer in the "Supernatural Powers" chapter as the transfer of the essence of the Lotus Sutra. It is also referred to as the specific transfer because it was made specifically to Bodhisattva Superior Practices and to the other Bodhisattvas of the Earth. In contrast, the general transfer of the sutra was made to all the assembled bodhisattvas in the subsequent (twenty-second) chapter, "Entrustment." *See also* five major principles; four-phrase essence of the Lotus Sutra.

supervisor of priests [僧都] (Jpn *sōzu*): An official position conferred by the government on distinguished priests, designating them responsible for supervising priests and nuns under the direction of the administrators of priests. The title *supervisor of priests* was first conferred in China. In Japan, the imperial court established three such ranks in 624. In descending order of importance, these were administrator of priests *(sōjō),* supervisor of priests *(sōzu),* and Dharma magistrate *(hōzu).* At that time, Kuratsukuri no Tokusaka, a layman, was appointed supervisor of priests. Later these ranks became honorary and lost their functional significance.

Supplemented Lotus Sutra of the Wonderful Law [添品法華経] (Chin *T'ien-p'in-fa-hua-ching;* Jpn *Tembon-hoke-kyō*): One of the three extant Chinese versions of the Lotus Sutra, translated in 601 by Jnānagupta and Dharmagupta. This version generally accords with Kumārajīva's Chinese translation of the Lotus Sutra, the Lotus Sutra of the Wonderful Law, although there are some differences between the two. For example, the content of the "Devadatta" chapter in Kumārajīva's version is included in the preceding chapter, "Treasure Tower" (eleventh), in Jnānagupta and Dharmagupta's translation; accordingly the Supplemented Lotus Sutra of the Wonderful Law has only twenty-seven chapters while the Lotus Sutra of the Wonderful Law has twenty-eight. In addition, the "Entrustment" chapter, the twenty-second chapter of the Lotus Sutra of the Wonderful Law, is placed as the last chapter in the Supplemented Lotus Sutra of the Wonderful Law, and the "Dhāranī," or twenty-sixth, chapter of the Lotus Sutra of the Wonderful Law, as the twenty-first chapter in the Supplemented Lotus Sutra of the Wonderful Law. Furthermore, the "Parable of the Medicinal Herbs" chapter of the Jnānagupta-Dharmagupta version contains an additional parable not found in Kumārajīva's translation.

Supplement to the Meanings of the Commentaries on the Lotus Sutra, The [法華経疏義纘] (Chin *Fa-hua-ching-shu-i-tsuan;* Jpn *Hokekyō-shogisan*): Also known as *Tung-ch'un,* after the place where the author lived. A commentary on the Lotus Sutra written in the eighth century by Chih-tu, a priest of the Chinese T'ien-t'ai school. In this work, Chih-tu presents a general discussion of the five major principles of name, essence, quality, function, and teaching on the basis of T'ien-t'ai's *Profound Meaning of the Lotus Sutra,* and comments in detail on the Lotus Sutra, T'ien-t'ai's *Words and Phrases of the Lotus Sutra,* and Miao-lo's *Annotations on "The Words and Phrases of the Lotus Sutra."*

Supplement to the Three Major Works on the Lotus Sutra, The [法華三大部補註] (Chin *Fa-hua-san-ta-pu-pu-chu;* Jpn *Hokke-sandaibu-fuchū*): Also known as *The Supplement to T'ien-t'ai's Three Major Works.* A commentary by Ts'ung-i (1042–1091), a priest of the Chinese T'ien-t'ai school, on T'ien-t'ai's three major works (*Great Concentration and Insight, The Profound Meaning of the Lotus Sutra,* and *The Words and Phrases of the Lotus Sutra*), as well as Miao-lo's commentaries on them.

Supplement to "The Words and Phrases of the Lotus Sutra," The [法華文句輔正記] (Chin *Fa-hua-wen-chü-fu-cheng-chi;* Jpn *Hokke-mongu-fushō-ki*): A work written in the eighth century by Tao-hsien, a priest of the Chinese T'ien-t'ai school. In it, based chiefly on Miao-lo's *Anno-*

tations on "The Words and Phrases of the Lotus Sutra," Tao-hsien annotates passages from the Lotus Sutra and T'ien-t'ai's *Words and Phrases of the Lotus Sutra.* This work is regarded as a useful reference for studying *The Words and Phrases of the Lotus Sutra.*

Supplement to T'ien-t'ai's Three Major Works, The [天台三大部補註] (Jpn *Tendai-sandaibu-fuchū*): See *Supplement to the Three Major Works on the Lotus Sutra, The.*

Suprabuddha [善覚] (Skt; Jpn Zenkaku): The father of Māyā, Shakyamuni's mother. According to the Sutra of the Collected Stories of the Buddha's Deeds in Past Lives, Suprabuddha was a member of the Shākya tribe, a wealthy man who lived in Devadaha near Kapilavastu, India. He had eight daughters, the eldest of whom was Māyā, and the youngest, Mahāprajāpatī. Both Māyā and Mahāprajāpatī married Shuddhodana, king of Kapilavastu. The other six married his three brothers, two sisters to each of the three. Among them, Māyā gave birth to Shakyamuni. The Mahāsammata Sutra describes Suprabuddha as the ruler of the affluent city of Devadaha and as having two daughters, the elder named Māyā and the younger, Mahāmāyā. According to this account, Mahāmāyā became Shuddhodana's consort and gave birth to Shakyamuni. In the Pali work *Mahāvamsa* ("The Great Chronicle"), Suprabuddha is referred to as the brother of Māyā, Shakyamuni's mother, and Mahāprajāpatī.

supremely honored among two-legged beings [両足尊・二足尊] (Jpn *ryōsoku-son, ryōzoku-son,* or *nisoku-son*): An honorific title of a Buddha. *See* most honored of two-legged beings.

supreme perfect enlightenment [阿耨多羅三藐三菩提・無上正等正覚] (Jpn *anokutara-sammyaku-sambodai* or *mujō-shōtō-shōgaku*): The enlightenment of a Buddha. See *anuttara-samyak-sambodhi.*

Sūryaprabha [日光菩薩] (Skt; Jpn Nikkō-bosatsu): The bodhisattva Sunlight. One of the two bodhisattvas who attend Medicine Master Buddha. *See* Sunlight.

Susiddhikara Sutra [蘇悉地経] (Skt; Chin *Su-hsi-ti-ching;* Jpn *Soshitsuji-kyō*): "Wonderful Accomplishment Sutra." A sutra of Esoteric Buddhism translated into Chinese by Shan-wu-wei (Skt Shubhakarasimha) in the eighth century. There are two other Chinese translations. The Susiddhikara Sutra is one of the three principal scriptures of Esoteric Buddhism, the other two being the Mahāvairochana and Diamond Crown sutras. In Japan, the tradition of Esoteric Buddhism within the Tendai school affords it particular reverence, while the True Word (Shingon) school ranks it below the other two sutras. The Susiddhikara Sutra gives detailed instructions on the performance of incantations and prayers directed toward the so-called three divisions, or three groups, of honored ones. These are the Buddha division, the Lotus division, and the Diamond division, symbolizing respectively the enlightenment, compassion, and wisdom of Mahāvairochana Buddha. The sutra also divides the purposes of those rituals into three: safety, the increase of benefit, and the subjugation of evil.

sutra library [経蔵] (Jpn *kyōzō*): *See* sutra repository.

Sutra of Forty-two Sections [四十二章経] (Chin *Ssu-shih-erh-chang-ching;* Jpn *Shijūni-shō-kyō*): A sutra translated into Chinese in the Yung-p'ing era (C.E. 58–75) of the Later Han dynasty by Kāshyapa Mātanga and Chu Fa-lan. This sutra is said to have been the first Buddhist scripture brought to China and the first translated into Chinese. Some scholars, however, maintain that it was produced in China. Consisting, as its name indicates, of forty-two sections, it explains the fundamental teachings of Buddhism and gives instructions relating to daily practice.

Sutra of the Buddha Answering the Great Heavenly King Brahmā's Questions [大梵天王問仏決疑経] (Chin *Ta-fan-t'ien-wang-wen-fo-chüeh-i-ching;* Jpn *Daibontennō-mombutsu-ketsugi-kyō*): A sutra esteemed by the Zen (Ch'an) school in China and Japan. It describes how Shakyamuni transmitted his enlightenment without words to Mahākāshyapa. The Zen school regards this transmission as its origin. Because the translator of the sutra is unknown, and because it does not appear in any of the catalogs of Chinese translations of Buddhist scriptures, there is a strong possibility that it originated in China.

Sutra of the Collected Stories of the Buddha's Deeds in Past Lives [仏本行集経] (Chin *Fo-pen-hsing-chi-ching;* Jpn *Butsu-hongyō-jikkyō*): A work in sixty volumes translated into Chinese by Jnānagupta during the period from 587 to 591, containing the biography of Shakyamuni and those of many of his disciples as well as descriptions of Shakyamuni's deeds in his past existences. It is one of the most detailed accounts of Shakyamuni's life in Chinese translation. This sutra is divided into three parts. The first part speaks of Shakyamuni in his past existences, his arousal of the aspiration for enlightenment, his subsequent rebirth in the Tushita Heaven, and his descent from that heaven to enter the body of his mother, Māyā. The second part covers the period from Shakyamuni's birth through his first turning of the wheel of the Law, i.e., his first sermon. The third part concerns his teaching activities and the lives of his disciples.

Sutra of the Lotus of the Wonderful Law [妙法蓮華経] (Jpn *Myoho-renge-kyo*): *See* Lotus Sutra of the Wonderful Law.

Sutra of the Meditation to Behold the Buddhas [般舟三昧経] (Skt *Pratyutpanna-buddha-sammukhāvasthita-samādhi-sūtra;* Chin *Pan-chou-san-mei-ching;* Jpn *Hanju-zammai-kyō*) A sutra translated into Chinese in 179 by Lokakshema, a monk from Central Asia. In it, Shakyamuni explains that by practicing "the meditation to behold the Buddhas" (Skt *pratyutpanna-samādhi*) one can see Amida and all other Buddhas. This sutra belongs to the earliest period of Mahayana and is said to have been produced sometime from the first century B.C.E. through the first century C.E. It is one of the first sutras to mention Amida Buddha. Another translation of the same scripture is also attributed to Lokakshema, and there are two additional translations by other translators.

Sutra of Verses [出曜経] (Skt *Udāna-varga;* Chin *Ch'u-yao-ching;* Jpn *Shutsuyō-kyō*): A work translated into Chinese by Chu Fo-nien in the late fourth century. It consists of instructive verses and accompanying prose-style anecdotes concerning the points made in verse. For example, a verse on falsehood is followed by the anecdote in prose of a woman named Chinchā who tied a tub to her belly under her robe and publicly declared that she was pregnant by Shakyamuni.

Sutra on How to Practice Meditation on the Bodhisattva Universal Worthy [観普賢菩薩行法経] (Jpn *Kan-fugen-bosatsu-gyōhō-kyō*): The full title of the Universal Worthy Sutra. *See* Universal Worthy Sutra.

Sutra on Resolving Doubts about the Middle Day of the Law [像法決疑経] (Chin *Hsiang-fa-chüeh-i-ching;* Jpn *Zōbō-ketsugi-kyō*): A sutra in Chinese that describes the characteristics of the Middle Day of the Law and stresses the practice of almsgiving. The original Sanskrit text and the translator are unknown; the work is thought to have originated in China. In it, Shakyamuni addresses Bodhisattva Constant Donations. He explains that in the Middle Day of the Law the practice of almsgiving should be directed toward the poor and friendless, and that one cannot attain enlightenment without almsgiving. The sutra also adds that in the Middle Day there will be many evil monks who do not understand the Buddha's intention but cling to their own arbitrary views and despise the three treasures of Buddhism. In such an age, it says, both clergy and laity alike should devote themselves with great compassion to the salvation of others.

Sutra on the Conversion of Barbarians by Lao Tzu [老子化胡経] (Chin *Lao-tzu-hua-hu-ching;* Jpn *Rōshi-keko-kyō*): A fictitious sutra written by Wang Fu, a Taoist of the Western Chin dynasty (265–316) of China with the intention of asserting the superiority of Taoism over Buddhism. According to this work, Lao Tzu, regarded as the founder of Taoism, traveled back and forth between China and India by means of his supernatural powers, instructing more than eighty kings in the western regions. It also asserts that Shakyamuni was instructed by Lao Tzu.

Sutra on the Wise and the Foolish [賢愚経] (Chin *Hsien-yü-ching;* Jpn *Kengu-kyō* or *Gengu-kyō*): A sutra translated into Chinese in 445 by Hui-chüeh and others. It contains sixty-two Buddhist tales (sixty-nine tales, in a separate extant edition). *A Collection of Records concerning the Tripitaka,* the catalog of the Buddhist canon compiled by Seng-yu (445–518), ascribes the translation of the Sutra on the Wise and the Foolish to others. According to that work, T'an-hsüeh, Wei-te, and six other priests went westward from northwestern China to Khotan on the southern edge of the Takla Makan Desert to seek Buddhist scriptures. They happened upon a great Buddhist ceremony that was held once every five years at a monastery. There they heard the learned monks expound the Buddhist scriptures and rules of monastic discipline in the language of Khotan. T'an-hsüeh and the others translated and recorded the lectures in Chinese. Later they returned from Khotan and, upon reaching the region of Turfan, compiled the lectures given by the monks in Khotan as a single sutra, which is known as the Sutra on the Wise and the Foolish. The sutra contains stories explaining the causal relationship between incidents in one's past existence and those in one's present existence. In each of these stories, Shakyamuni Buddha makes a connection between someone living in the present and a person involved in a past incident.

sutra repository [経蔵] (Jpn *kyōzō*): Also, sutra library, sutra storehouse, or sutra storage hall. A building in which sutras and other Buddhist scriptures, such as texts of the rules of monastic discipline and commentaries, are stored. In the earlier temple compounds in China and Japan, the sutra repository was one of the most important buildings.

sutra storehouse [経蔵] (Jpn *kyōzō*): *See* sutra repository.

Suttanipāta [経集] (Pali; Jpn *Kyōshū*): One of the earliest scriptures of the Pali canon. It is part of the *Khuddaka-nikāya,* one of the five Āgamas that constitute the sutra section of the Pali canon. *Suttanipāta* means collection of *suttas* or sutras, i.e., collection of discourses. Largely written in verse form, it is divided into five sections and comprises about seventy sutras. *Suttanipāta* is regarded as an invaluable resource for the study of early Buddhist ideas and the early Buddhist Order.

Suzudan [須頭檀] (Jpn): A king who appears in the "Devadatta" (twelfth) chapter of the Lotus Sutra. Although the king's name does not appear in any extant Sanskrit or Chinese texts of the sutra, for unknown reasons he was so named in Japan. According to the sutra, when Shakyamuni was a king in a past life, he renounced the throne to seek the correct teaching and selflessly devoted himself to serving the seer Asita for a thousand years, as a result of which he was able to learn the Lotus Sutra from the seer. This king was later reborn as Shakyamuni, and the seer as Devadatta.

Svātantrika school [自立論証派] (Skt; Jpn Jiritsuronshō-ha): One of the two schools of Mādhyamika (Middle Way) philosophy in India. The Svātantrika school was founded by Bhāvaviveka (c. 490–570), and the other Mādhyamika school, the Prāsangika, was founded by Buddhapālita. Bhāvaviveka wrote *The Treatise on the Lamp of Wisdom* (Skt *Prajnā-pradīpa*), a commentary on Nāgārjuna's *Verses on the Middle Way (Madhyamaka-kārikā)* in which he criticized Buddhapālita's method of demonstrating the truth of non-substantiality. Bhāvaviveka based his reasoning on the system of Buddhist logic developed by Dignāga, which had become very influential in the world of Indian thought. *See also* Prāsangika school.

T

Ta-hsing-shan-ssu [大興善寺] (PY Daxingshansi; Jpn Daikōzen-ji): Also known as Hsing-shan-ssu temple. A temple built in Ch'ang-an in 582 by Emperor Wen, the founder of the Sui dynasty and a restorer of Buddhism, to serve as the center of Buddhism in China. During the reign of Emperor Wen, Indian monks such as Narendrayashas and Jnānagupta engaged in the translation of Buddhist scriptures into Chinese at this temple, and many other eminent priests visited or lived there. It was the largest temple in China during the Sui and T'ang dynasties. During the reign of Hsüan-tsung (r. 712–756), the eighth emperor of the T'ang dynasty, Pu-k'ung (Skt Amoghavajra), who had brought Esoteric Buddhism from India to China, resided at this temple, and thereafter it prospered as a center of Esoteric Buddhism. In the ninth century, Jikaku and Chishō, later respectively the third and fifth chief priests of the Japanese Tendai school, went to China and studied Esoteric Buddhism at Ta-hsing-shan-ssu temple.

Taiseki-ji [大石寺]: The head temple of Nichiren Shōshū, located in Fujinomiya, Shizuoka Prefecture, Japan. It was founded by Nikkō (1246–1333), Nichiren's designated successor. After Nichiren's death in 1282, in accord with his will, Nikkō became the chief priest of Kuon-ji temple, which Nichiren had founded at Minobu. Hakiri Sanenaga, steward of the Minobu area whom Nikkō had converted around 1269, had welcomed Nikkō to the temple. Because Hakiri violated Nichiren's teachings, however, and refused to heed Nikkō's warnings in this regard, Nikkō left Minobu in 1289 with the great mandala Nichiren had inscribed (known as the Dai-Gohonzon), Nichiren's ashes, writings, and other precious items. His intention was to find a place where he could preserve Nichiren's teachings in their correct form.

Nanjō Tokimitsu, the steward of the Fuji area, invited Nikkō to his estate and donated a tract of land at a place called Ōishigahara (Great Stone Field). In 1290 Nikkō, with other believers, built a temple called Dai-bō (Grand Lodging), and this is considered the origin of Taiseki-ji (*taiseki* is another reading of the characters *ōishi,* meaning great stone). Nikkō founded this new temple in accordance with Nichiren's instruction that the sanctuary of Hommon-ji (Temple of the Essential Teaching) be built at the foot of Mount Fuji. Thereafter Nikkō's disciples began to establish lodging temples surrounding Dai-bō.

The Dai-bō had a main hall, a place for the training and education of priests, and priests' living quarters. In 1298, when Nikkō moved to the nearby Omosu Seminary he had established, Nikkō's six elder disciples, including Nichimoku, managed Taiseki-ji. Nichimoku, who privately received the transfer of Nichiren's teachings from Nikkō, stayed at Taiseki-ji. In 1332 Nikkō officially appointed Nichimoku chief priest of Taiseki-ji. In 1333 Nichimoku, having transferred the office of chief priest to Nichidō, set out for Kyoto with the priests Nichigō and Nichizon to remonstrate with the imperial court. Nichimoku died en route, however, at Tarui in Mino Province. The two priests who had accompanied him went on to Kyoto to fulfill the purpose of their journey; Nichizon remained there and Nichigō returned to Taiseki-ji. Nichigō then claimed ownership of the Renzō-bō, previously Nichimoku's lodging temple, and its environs, stating that Nichimoku had willed it to him. This sparked a dispute that lasted for some seventy years, during which time Taiseki-ji declined. Nichiu (1402–1482), the ninth chief priest, restored stability to Taiseki-ji for a time, but in the ensuing centuries it saw further periods of decline and recovery. From the mid-fifteenth through the early sixteenth century, a number of structures were added, including a reception hall, a temple to house an image of Nichiren, and a five-storied pagoda.

In the latter half of the twentieth century, Taiseki-ji was completely remodeled, and modern buildings erected in architectural harmony with the older structures. The Hōan-den, enshrining the Dai-Gohonzon, was built in 1955; the Grand Lecture Hall in 1958; the Grand Transient Castle, a rest house for visitors, in 1960; the Grand Reception Hall in 1964; and in 1972 the Grand Main Temple, or Shō-Hondō, which was intended to serve as the sanctuary referred to in Nichiren's writings. These buildings were all constructed through the financial contributions of Soka Gakkai members.

During the tenure of Nikken, the sixty-seventh chief priest, however, most of these structures—those completed during the tenure of his predecessor, Nittatsu—were demolished: the Grand Transient Castle in 1989, the Grand Reception Hall in 1995, and the Grand Main Temple in 1998. Moreover, in 1991 Nikken excommunicated the Soka Gakkai, which, in the latter half of the twentieth century, had revived the practice of and had been widely propagating Nichiren's teachings, thereby bringing about the prosperity of Taiseki-ji and Nichiren Shōshū.

Contrary to Nikken's plans, which were intended to disband the Soka Gakkai and bring many of its members directly under Nichiren Shōshū, the Soka Gakkai continued to grow and flourish after the excommunication. *See also* Nichiren Shōshū; Soka Gakkai.

Taishaku [帝釈] (Jpn): The heavenly king Shakra. A leading Buddhist god. *See* Shakra.

Takahashi Rokurō Hyōe, the lay priest [高橋六郎兵衛入道] (n.d.) (Jpn Takahashi Rokurō Hyōe-nyūdō): A follower of Nichiren (1222–1282), also known as the lay priest Takahashi. He lived in Kajima in Fuji District of Suruga Province, Japan. His wife was an aunt of Nikkō, Nichiren's disciple and designated successor who converted him to Nichiren's teachings. A letter to Takahashi from Nichiren entrusts him with the responsibility of propagation in the area where he was living, which would indicate that he enjoyed Nichiren's trust and was a leading figure among the lay believers in Fuji District.

Takshashilā [徳叉尸羅] (Skt; Jpn Tokushashira): A city in ancient India. In Greek literature, Takshashilā is rendered as Taxila. It was located about thirty-five kilometers northwest of present-day Rawalpindi in Pakistan. Takshashilā prospered for about ten centuries, beginning in the sixth century B.C.E., largely due to its location at what was then an intersection of important trade routes connecting India to Central and Western Asia. The city was also a center of learning in northern India. In 326 B.C.E. Takshashilā was conquered by Alexander the Great, and in the third century B.C.E. it fell under the rule of the Maurya dynasty. King Ashoka is said to have governed Takshashilā while a prince, during which time Buddhism was introduced to this region. Afterward Takshashilā passed successively from rule by the Indo-Greek kingdom of Bactria to that by the Shakas of Central Asia, and then to the Parthians and later to the Kushan dynasty. Under Kushan rule from the first through the third century, Buddhist culture thrived, and numerous stupas, temples, and monasteries were built. Takshashilā became a great center of Buddhism where Gandhara Buddhist art flourished. In the early fifth century Fa-hsien visited the city and in the record of his travels described its people, including the rulers, as making offerings to Buddhist stupas. Later in the same century, the Hephthalites invaded and destroyed the city. Hsüan-tsang wrote that, when he visited the region in the seventh century, Takshashilā lay in ruins. Archaeological excavations began in the nineteenth century and continued into the twentieth century. They revealed the ruins of the ancient city and the remains of its Buddhist architecture and art, including numerous objects of the Gandhara artistic style. Among the relics uncovered at the site of Takshashilā are dozens of Buddhist temples, the oldest and largest of which is Dharmarājika. The great Dharmarājika stupa is at the center of the temple compound. Although the stupa had been rebuilt at some point, its origin dates back to the Mauryan Empire.

tāla tree [多羅樹] (Skt; Jpn *tara-ju*): Now known as palmyra palm. A tree whose leaves were used as a writing surface in ancient India and surrounding regions. Buddhist scriptures were recorded on these leaves. The *tāla* tree belongs to the palm family and reaches more than twenty meters in height. Its fan-shaped leaves are tough and nearly two meters in length. They were dried and cut into rectangles of the same size, about six centimeters wide and thirty to sixty centimeters long. Text was inscribed on both sides with a bamboo or iron stylus. The leaves were pierced at the end with holes, bound with string, and secured between two wooden covers. *Tāla* leaves were used to record and preserve Buddhist scriptures in countries where the trees were prevalent, such as India, Myanmar, and Sri Lanka. Recently discovered Buddhist texts that were preserved and transmitted in this form are referred to as "palm-leaf scriptures." Sutras and other Buddhist scriptures often mention the *tāla* tree as a measure of height, with phrases like "as high as eight *tāla* trees," etc.

Tamālapattra Sandalwood Fragrance [多摩羅跋栴檀香如来] (Skt Tamālapattra-chandana-gandha or Tamālapatra-chandana-gandha; Jpn Tamarabatsu-sendankō-nyorai or Tamaraba-sendankō-nyorai): The Thus Come One Tamālapattra Sandalwood Fragrance. The name that Maudgalyāyana, one of Shakyamuni's ten major disciples, will bear when he attains enlightenment, according to Shakyamuni's prediction in the "Bestowal of Prophecy" (sixth) chapter of the Lotus Sutra. The chapter states that, after making offerings to eight thousand Buddhas and then to "two hundred ten thousand million Buddhas," Maudgalyāyana will become a Buddha with the name Tamālapattra Sandalwood Fragrance, whose *kalpa* and realm will be named Joy Replete and Mind Delight, respectively. The Sanskrit word *tamālapattra* or *tamālapatra* means the leaf of the *tamāla* tree.

Tamon-ten [多聞天] (Jpn): The heavenly king Hearer of Many Teachings. Also known as Vaishravana, one of the four heavenly kings. *See* Vaishravana.

T'ang Dynasty Biographies of Eminent Priests, The [唐高僧伝] (Jpn Tō-kōsō-den): Another title for *The Continued Biographies of Eminent Priests.* See *Continued Biographies of Eminent Priests, The.*

T'an-luan [曇鸞] (476–542) (PY Tanluan; Jpn Donran): The founder of the Chinese Pure Land school. Initially, he studied four treatises—*The Treatise on the Middle Way, The One-Hundred-Verse Treatise, The Treatise on the Twelve Gates,* and *The Treatise on the Great Perfection of Wisdom.* He further undertook the task of writing a commentary on the Great Collection Sutra, but his health failed and he traveled south to visit a Taoist teacher, T'ao Hung-ching, to master the secrets of immortality. After receiving a Taoist scripture about immortality, he returned north and at Lo-yang met Bodhiruchi, who was versed in the Pure Land teachings. Bodhiruchi taught him that one could attain everlasting life only through the Pure Land teachings, giving him a Pure Land scripture, the Meditation on the Buddha Infinite Life Sutra. T'an-luan was so impressed by it that he discarded the Taoist text and devoted himself to the practice of the Pure Land teachings. He stressed the practice of the Pure Land teachings as the "easy-to-practice way" that enables all people to attain rebirth in Amida Buddha's Pure Land, and rejected all other practices as the "difficult-to-practice way," and wrote *The Commentary on "The Treatise on the Pure Land," The Hymn in Verse to Amida Buddha,* and other works. He is revered as the first of the five patriarchs of the Chinese Pure Land school and also regarded as the founder of the Four Treatises (Ssu-lun) school, which was based upon the above four treatises.

Tantric Buddhism [タントラ仏教] (Jpn Tantora-bukkyō): Also, Vajrayāna, Mantrayāna, or Esoteric Buddhism. A stream of Buddhist thought and practice that became formalized in India and flourished from the seventh to the eleventh century. Tantric Esotericism became a part of the broader Mahayana movement and represents an infusion of popular magic, mysticism, and ritual into the Indian schools of Buddhism. The Sanskrit word *tantra* means loom or warp of cloth, essential part, or doctrine.

Tantra also refers to a class of Hindu or Buddhist scriptures on esoteric practices that developed rather late in the history of the literatures of those religions. They emphasize benefits that accrue from the recitation of mantras (magical formulas), the formation of mudras (hand gestures), the performance of rituals, the use of mandalas (ritual diagrams), and other practices. Tantric thought became a formalized stream within Mahayana Buddhism around the seventh century and spread to Central Asia, China, and Tibet. Tantric tradition is an important element of Tibetan Buddhism.

Bu-ston, a Tibetan scholar of the fourteenth century, classified Indian Buddhist tantras into four general categories: *Kriyā-tantra,* dealing with ritual acts; *Charyā-tantra,* which combines ritual acts with meditation; *Yoga-tantra,* dealing chiefly with meditation; and *Anuttarayoga-tantra,* or supreme yoga tantras. The fourth form, *Anuttarayoga-tantra,* which was not introduced to China and Japan, is the strongest in sexual symbolism, identifying *prajnā,* or wisdom, as a female principle; *upāya,* or expedient means, as a male principle; and enlightenment as a union of these two. Some of its practitioners interpreted this symbolism literally and sought enlightenment in the sexual union of man and woman.

The earliest esoteric Buddhist tantras, such as the Sanskrit texts of the Mahāvairochana Sutra and the Diamond Crown Sutra, were produced in India in the seventh century. In China, Esoteric Buddhism was introduced and established by the Indian monks Shan-wu-wei (Skt Shubhakarasimha, 637–735), Chin-kang-chih (Vajrabodhi, 671–741), Pu-k'ung (Amoghavajra, 705–774), and others. Its teachings were systematized to enable the attainment of Buddhahood in one's present body. The Sanskrit Buddhist tantras were translated into Chinese and spread as esoteric sutras and teachings featuring mudras, mantras, and mandalas. In Japan, Kōbō (774–835; also known as Kūkai) formulated his own systematization of these teachings, founding the True Word (Shingon) school based upon them. Esoteric Buddhism was also accepted and developed by the Tendai school in Japan.

T'an-yao [曇曜] (n.d.) (PY Tanyao; Jpn Don'yō): A priest and a translator of Buddhist scriptures in China noted for his establishment of the Yün-kang cave-temples. When Emperor T'ai-wu (also known as Emperor Wu) of the Northern Wei dynasty abolished Buddhism in 446, T'an-yao secluded himself in a mountain forest. Thereafter Buddhism was restored by Emperor Wen-ch'eng who held T'an-yao in high esteem and in 460 appointed him national director of the clergy. Around the same year, he initiated construction of the earliest among the Yün-kang cave-temples. T'an-yao resided at one of these cave-temples, where he worked with Kinkara, a monk from Central Asia, to translate into Chinese *A History of the Buddha's Successors* and the Storehouse of Various Treasures Sutra.

Tao-an [道安] (PY Daoan; Jpn Dōan): (1) (312–385) A priest and scholar of Buddhism in China. At age twelve, he became a priest and studied

Buddhism under Fo-t'u-teng. He won renown for his lectures on the Wisdom sutras. In 379, when Fu Chien, the ruler of the Former Ch'in dynasty, invaded Hsiang-yang, where Tao-an was living, Tao-an went to Ch'ang-an at Fu Chien's request. He also exhorted Fu Chien to invite Kumārajīva to Ch'ang-an, which he did. In Ch'ang-an, Tao-an lived at Wu-chung-ssu temple and devoted himself to the study and propagation of Buddhism. He compiled *The Comprehensive Catalog of Sutras,* an index of existing Chinese translations of the Buddhist scriptures together with the names of the translators and the dates of the translations. This work, which is no longer extant, was the first catalog of Buddhist scriptures in China and served as the basis for the catalogs of Chinese-language Buddhist scriptures made thereafter. Tao-an also systematized the precepts for priests and nuns, devoted himself to the translation of Buddhist scriptures, and wrote commentaries on various sutras. In addition, he is credited with having established the concept of three divisions of a sutra, or the practice of dividing the content of a Buddhist sutra into three parts: preparation, revelation, and transmission. He had several hundred disciples, among whom Hui-yüan was the most prominent.

(2) (n.d.) A priest of China during the sixth century. He lectured on the Nirvana Sutra and *The Treatise on the Great Perfection of Wisdom* by Nāgārjuna. He submitted to Emperor Wu (r. 560–578) of the Northern Chou dynasty *The Treatise on the Two Teachings* (Buddhism and Taoism), in which he asserted the superiority of Buddhism over Taoism and criticized Confucianism. In 574, however, Emperor Wu issued a decree proscribing Buddhism and Taoism, and called for the destruction of Buddhist temples, images, and scriptures. Tao-an avoided persecution and devoted himself to instructing his disciples.

Tao-ch'o [道綽] (562–645) (PY Daochuo; Jpn Dōshaku): The second of the five patriarchs of the Pure Land school in China. Originally a teacher of the Nirvana Sutra, he was deeply moved by T'an-luan's epitaph on a monument at Hsüan-chung-ssu temple and took faith in the Pure Land teachings. Thereafter he is said to have lectured on the Meditation on the Buddha Infinite Life Sutra two hundred times and taught the practice of calling upon the name of Amida Buddha. He classified the Buddhist teachings into two categories: Pure Land teachings and Sacred Way teachings. He asserted that the Sacred Way teachings, which expound the achievement of enlightenment through one's own power, are too difficult for ordinary people of the latter age, and that only the Pure Land teachings, which expound rebirth in Amida Buddha's Pure Land solely by reliance on Amida's power, can offer salvation. He wrote

The Collected Essays on the World of Peace and Delight. Shan-tao was his disciple.

Tao-hsien [道暹] (n.d.) (PY Daoxian; Jpn Dōsen): A priest of the T'ien-t'ai school in China. He is said to have been a disciple of Miao-lo. Sometime in the Ta-li era (766–779), he went to the capital Ch'ang-an, where he devoted himself to writing *The Supplement to "The Words and Phrases of the Lotus Sutra,"* a commentary on both T'ien-t'ai's *Words and Phrases of the Lotus Sutra* and Miao-lo's *Annotations on "The Words and Phrases of the Lotus Sutra."*

Tao-hsin [道信] (580–651) (PY Daoxin; Jpn Dōshin): The fourth patriarch of the Zen (Ch'an) school in China. After studying under the third patriarch, Seng-ts'an, he trained his successor, Hung-jen, and other disciples. T'ai-tsung, the second emperor of the T'ang dynasty, heard of his virtue and three times summoned him to the capital, but Tao-hsin refused each time. Eventually the emperor threatened to behead him, but Tao-hsin remained adamant; impressed, the emperor forgave him.

Tao-hsüan (PY Daoxuan) (1) [道宣] (596–667) (Jpn Dōsen): The founder of the Nan-shan branch of the Precepts (Lü) school in China. In 611 he entered the priesthood and studied the *vinaya,* or rules of monastic discipline, under Chih-shou. In 624 he went to a mountain called Chung-nan-shan to study and practice and eventually founded a school based on the precepts of *The Fourfold Rules of Discipline,* the *vinaya* text of the Dharmagupta school. The name Nan-shan derives from the name of that mountain. The Nan-shan school was the only branch of the Precepts school to survive, and later it became synonymous with the Precepts school. From 645 Tao-hsüan assisted Hsüan-tsang with his translation work. He also authored several books on precepts, as well as a number of historical works. His works include *The Essentials of "The Fourfold Rules of Discipline,"* which is the principal text of the Nan-shan school, and *The Further Anthology of the Propagation of Light,* a thirty-volume anthology of essays on Buddhism by various Chinese Buddhists. Because some of these essays are found only in this work, it is considered invaluable in the study of Chinese Buddhism. Tao-hsüan's *Continued Biographies of Eminent Priests* carries on from *The Biographies of Eminent Priests* and contains the biographies of five hundred priests active from 502 to 645. Tao-hsüan also compiled *The Great T'ang Dynasty Catalog of Buddhist Scriptures,* a ten-volume catalog of the Buddhist canon.

(2) [道璿] (Jpn Dōsen): A priest of China who introduced the Flower Garland (Chin Hua-yen; Jpn Kegon) school to Japan. *See* Dōsen.

Tao-sheng [道生・竺道生] (d. 434) (PY Daosheng; Jpn Dōshō or Jiku-dōshō): Also known as Chu Tao-sheng. A disciple of Kumārajīva in China. According to one account, Tao-sheng was born in 355. In his youth he became a priest and studied Buddhism under Fa-t'ai, assuming the position of lecturer by age fifteen. He then studied under Hui-yüan on Mount Lu. Eventually he went to Ch'ang-an, where he joined Kumārajīva in his translation work and became one of his major disciples. In 409 he advocated the doctrine of immediate attainment of Buddhahood. Moreover, based on his study of Fa-hsien's Chinese version of the Nirvana Sutra, he argued that all people possess the Buddha nature and that even *icchantikas,* those of incorrigible disbelief, can attain Buddhahood. The elder priests attacked him for these views and expelled him from the community of priests, and he retired to a mountain in Su-chou. Later, when Dharmaraksha translated the Nirvana Sutra into Chinese, Tao-sheng's assertions were proven and widely accepted. In collaboration with Buddhajīva, Tao-sheng translated *The Fivefold Rules of Discipline,* the *vinaya* text of the Mahīshāsaka school, from Sanskrit into Chinese.

Tao-sui [道邃] (n.d.) (PY Daosui; Jpn Dōsui or Dōzui): A priest of the T'ien-t'ai school in China. He became a disciple of Miao-lo, under whom he studied T'ien-t'ai's teachings. In 796 he went to Mount T'ien-t'ai, where he studied for nine years, thereafter taking up residence at Lung-hsing-ssu temple. When Dengyō, who later founded the Japanese counterpart of the T'ien-t'ai school, came to China from Japan in 804, Tao-sui taught him the T'ien-t'ai meditation. His works include *A Personal Commentary on "The Annotations on the Mahāparinirvāna Sutra"* and *A Personal Commentary on "The Annotations on the Vimalakīrti Sutra."*

Tarim Basin [タリム盆地] (Jpn Tarimu-bonchi): A broad geological depression in Eastern Turkestan. Now part of the Sinkiang Uighur Autonomous Region of China, it is surrounded on the north and south by the Tien Shan and Kunlun mountain ranges, respectively. The greater part of the Tarim Basin consists of the Takla Makan Desert. From ancient times, the Chinese referred to the area of the Tarim Basin as the "Western Regions." Buddhism was transmitted eastward to China through the Tarim Basin, while Chinese priests went westward through this vast basin, seeking Buddhist scriptures. At the eastern rim of the Tarim Basin, the road from China divided into two branches and ran westward along the northern and southern edges of the Takla Makan Desert. These constituted the northern and southern branches of the caravan route known as the Silk Road that connected East and West and served as a passageway of commerce and culture. Moving west on the northern road, one encountered such oasis cities as Turfan, Karashar, Kucha, and Kashgar; and going west on the southern road, one passed through the oasis cities of Lou-lan, Miran, and Khotan. These cities fostered unique cultures merging aspects of Eastern and Western civilizations. There are a large number of Buddhist remains along the northern and southern roads. In recent years, numerous manuscripts of Buddhist scriptures and other ancient texts in various languages have been excavated there.

tathāgata [如来] (Skt, Pali; Jpn *nyorai*): The Thus Come One, an honorable title of a Buddha. *See* Thus Come One.

tathatā [真如・如如] (Skt, Pali; Jpn *shinnyo* or *nyonyo*): Thusness, suchness, essential nature, true nature, or truth. *Tathatā* is a fundamental concept in Mahayana philosophy and is interpreted as the true nature of all phenomena or as the original state of things. A Buddha is regarded as one who observes things exactly as they are and who perceives the true nature of all things.

Tatsunokuchi Persecution [竜の口の法難] (Jpn Tatsunokuchi-no-hōnan): An unsuccessful attempt to execute Nichiren at Tatsunokuchi on the western outskirts of Kamakura in Japan in the ninth month of 1271. It is described in Nichiren's works *The Actions of the Votary of the Lotus Sutra* and *The Letter of Petition from Yorimoto*. From early in 1271 Japan had been suffering a drought, and the shogunate ordered the priest Ryōkan of Gokuraku-ji temple to pray for rain. Nichiren sent him a challenge, stating that if Ryōkan's prayers could produce rain in seven days he would become Ryōkan's disciple, but if Ryōkan failed he should become Nichiren's disciple. Ryōkan accepted the challenge, but failed to produce rain even after fourteen days of prayer he offered with several hundreds of priests; instead, fierce gales arose. Humiliated, he ignored his promise and began using his influence among the wives and widows of top shogunate officials to make accusations against Nichiren. As a result, Nichiren was summoned for interrogation by the deputy chief of the Office of Military and Police Affairs, Hei no Saemon, on the tenth day of the ninth month, 1271. Nichiren took the opportunity to remonstrate with Hei no Saemon, predicting the outbreak of internal strife and foreign invasion if the rulers punished him unlawfully.

On the twelfth day of the ninth month, two days later, Hei no Saemon and a group of warriors rushed to Nichiren's dwelling at Matsubagayatsu and arrested him. Around midnight, Nichiren was taken by Hei no Saemon's men to the execution grounds on the beach at Tatsunokuchi.

As the party passed the shrine of the god Hachiman, Nichiren requested that he be given a moment. His request was granted, and he turned to address the deity of the shrine. Nichiren reprimanded Hachiman for failing to protect him, saying that he was the votary of the Lotus Sutra, whom Hachiman had vowed to protect in the presence of Shakyamuni Buddha. He also sent a messenger to Shijō Kingo, a samurai who was a staunch believer and supporter; Kingo hurried to Nichiren's side, determined to die with him. After they reached the execution site, just before dawn on the thirteenth day, at the moment Nichiren was about to be beheaded, a luminous object shot across the sky, brightly illuminating the surroundings. Terrified, the soldiers called off the execution. Nichiren was then placed in custody at the Echi (about twenty kilometers from Tatsunokuchi) residence of Homma Shigetsura, deputy constable of the island province of Sado, for about one month. On the tenth day of the tenth month, 1271, he was sent into exile on Sado. Reflecting on the event, he wrote in *The Opening of the Eyes:* "On the twelfth day of the ninth month of last year . . . this person named Nichiren was beheaded. It is his soul that has come to this island of Sado" (269), and later in *Letter to Misawa,* "As for my teachings, regard those before my exile to the province of Sado as equivalent to the Buddha's pre-Lotus Sutra teachings" (896). This is interpreted by Nichikan, the twenty-sixth chief priest of Taiseki-ji temple, to mean that the ordinary person Nichiren ceased to exist after the Tatsunokuchi Persecution, but the Buddha Nichiren went to Sado alive. Hence Nichiren asserts, the teachings he had expounded before his exile to Sado should be regarded not as true but provisional. This process has been described as Nichiren's "casting off the transient and revealing the true" (Jpn *hosshaku-kempon*), i.e., discarding his transient status and revealing his true identity.

Ta-tz'u-en-ssu [大慈恩寺] (PY Daciensi; Jpn Daijion-ji): Also known as Tz'u-en-ssu. A temple built in Ch'ang-an, China, in 648 by Emperor Kao-tsung of the T'ang dynasty. *See* Tz'u-en-ssu.

Taxila [タクシラ] (Jpn Takushira): A city in ancient India that was a great center of Buddhism where Gandhara Buddhist art flourished. *See* Takshashilā.

teacherless wisdom [無師智] (Jpn *mushi-chi*): Also, self-attained wisdom. Wisdom obtained without a teacher, i.e., the wisdom of the Buddha.

Teacher of Heavenly and Human Beings [天人師] (Skt *shāstā-deva-manushyānām;* Jpn *tennin-shi*): One of the ten honorable titles of a Buddha. The "Parable of the Phantom City" (seventh) chapter of the Lotus Sutra says: "World-Honored One, very rarely met with, one whom it is difficult to encounter, endowed with immeasurable blessings, capable of saving everyone, great teacher of heavenly and human beings, you bestow pity and comfort on the world. Living beings in the ten directions all receive benefit everywhere."

"Teacher of the Law" chapter [法師品] (Jpn *Hosshi-hon*): The tenth chapter of the Lotus Sutra. In it, Shakyamuni Buddha addressed Bodhisattva Medicine King, and through him the eighty thousand bodhisattvas. In contrast to the preceding chapters, which reveal that the voice-hearer disciples will attain Buddhahood in the future, the "Teacher of the Law" and the ensuing four chapters deal with the practice and propagation of the Lotus Sutra after Shakyamuni Buddha's death. Shakyamuni accordingly addresses these chapters not to his voice-hearer disciples but to the great bodhisattvas who work to save the people as the Buddha's emissaries, praising the great benefit of embracing and teaching the sutra. One who hears even a single verse or phrase of it and devotes to it even a single moment of rejoicing, he declares, will without fail attain supreme enlightenment. Moreover, one who secretly teaches to another even a single phrase of the sutra should be regarded as the Buddha's envoy, sent to carry out his work. This chapter sets forth the so-called "three rules of preaching" of the Lotus Sutra. These are to enter the room of the Thus Come One, to put on the robe of the Thus Come One, and to sit in the seat of the Thus Come One. The room of the Thus Come One means profound compassion; his robe, a gentle and forbearing heart; and his seat, the ability to perceive the non-substantiality of all phenomena. This chapter also mentions the five practices of the Lotus Sutra: to embrace, read, recite, expound, and copy it.

teacher of the nation [国師] (Jpn *kokushi*): A title conferred by the ruler of a nation upon distinguished Buddhist monks who were regarded as models of virtue for their country. According to *A Collection of Records concerning the Tripitaka,* Kumārayāna, the father of Kumārajīva, was designated teacher of the nation by the ruler of Kucha. In Japan, the title teacher of the nation was bestowed for the first time in 1311 on the Zen priest Enni (1202–1280) after his death; his posthumous name and title are the Teacher of the Nation Shōichi.

teacher of the true cause [本因妙の教主] (Jpn *honnin-myō-no-kyōshu*): In Nichiren's teachings, the Buddha who expounds the fundamental Law, or the true cause, that enables all people to attain Buddhahood. In the "Life Span" (sixteenth) chapter of the Lotus Sutra, Shakyamuni reveals the true effect, or the Buddhahood that he attained numberless major world system dust particle *kalpas* ago. He does not, however, fully clarify the true cause of, i.e., the practice that led to, his enlightenment. Hence, he is called the teacher of the true effect. In contrast, Nichiren taught that Nam-myoho-renge-kyo is the Law implicit in the "Life Span" chapter and is the cause of enlightenment for all people. Because he clarified the true cause for attaining Buddhahood, he is called the teacher of the true cause, and his Buddhism, the Buddhism of the true cause, or the Buddhism of sowing that implants the seeds of enlightenment in the lives of those who practice it.

teacher of the true effect [本果妙の教主] (Jpn *honga-myō-no-kyōshu*): In Nichiren's teachings, Shakyamuni Buddha. In the "Life Span" (sixteenth) chapter of the Lotus Sutra, Shakyamuni reveals the true effect, the Buddhahood he attained numberless major world system dust particle *kalpas* ago. He alludes to the cause of that enlightenment only with the words "Originally I practiced the bodhisattva way," and does not clarify the teaching or Law that he practiced to attain Buddhahood. Shakyamuni Buddha is called the teacher of the true effect because he revealed his original enlightenment as a result already achieved—as an effect—and did not specify its cause. Nichiren defined the true cause that enabled Shakyamuni and all other Buddhas to attain enlightenment as the Law of Nam-myoho-renge-kyo; he is therefore called the teacher of the true cause.

teaching of gleaning [捃拾教] (Jpn *kunjū-kyō*): A reference to the Nirvana Sutra. According to the doctrine of the five periods and eight teachings set forth by T'ien-t'ai (538–597), the preaching of the Lotus Sutra was followed by that of the Nirvana Sutra. The T'ien-t'ai school compared the Lotus Sutra to the harvest and the Nirvana Sutra to the gleaning that comes after the harvest. That is, the Nirvana Sutra was preached to extend enlightenment to those who had been left out during the exposition of the Lotus Sutra and failed to benefit from it. Hence the Nirvana Sutra is termed the teaching of gleaning.

teaching, practice, and proof [教行証] (Jpn *kyō-gyō-shō*): The Buddha's teaching, the practice of the teaching, and the proof, or merit—strictly speaking, enlightenment—resulting from the practice of the teaching. This concept is addressed in *The Treatise on the Ten Stages Sutra, The Profound Meaning of the Lotus Sutra,* and elsewhere. Tz'u-en (632–682) of the Chinese Dharma Characteristics (Fa-hsiang) school, in his *Forest of Meanings in the Mahayana Garden of the Law,* discusses teaching, practice, and proof in terms of each of the three periods of the Former Day, Middle Day, and Latter Day of the Law. In the Former Day of the Law, he says, there exist the Buddhist teaching, its practice, and proof of its efficacy (attainment of enlightenment); in the Middle Day, teaching and practice remain, but there is no longer proof; and in the Latter Day, only the teaching remains—there is neither practice nor proof. This became a standard way of describing the three periods, but the concept differs depending on the "teaching."

Nichiren (1222–1282) says in *On the Buddha's Prophecy:* "In the Latter Day of the Law, no benefit is derived from either Mahayana or Hinayana.

Hinayana retains nothing but its teaching; it has neither practice nor proof. Mahayana still has its teaching and practice, but no longer provides any proof of benefit, either conspicuous or inconspicuous" (399). Concerning proof in the Latter Day of the Law, he says in *The Teaching, Practice, and Proof*: "Now in the Latter Day of the Law, only the teaching remains; there is neither practice nor proof. There is no longer a single person who has formed a relationship with Shakyamuni Buddha. Those who possessed the capacity to gain enlightenment through either the provisional or true Mahayana sutras have long since disappeared. In this impure and evil age, Nam-myoho-renge-kyo of the 'Life Span' chapter, the heart of the essential teaching, should be planted as the seeds of Buddhahood for the first time in the hearts of all those who commit the five cardinal sins and [those who] slander the correct teaching" (473).

Teaching, Practice, Faith, and Proof, The [教行信証] (Jpn *Kyō-gyō-shin-shō*): A major work by Shinran (1173–1262), the founder of the True Pure Land (Jōdo Shin) school in Japan. In it, Shinran sought to systematize the doctrine of his teacher, Hōnen, in the context of all Buddhist teachings. In contrast to Hōnen, however, Shinran emphasized the element of faith. The True Pure Land school regards this work as its fundamental doctrinal text. It consists of six volumes, the first four of which respectively discuss the teaching, practice, faith, and proof in terms of the Pure Land teachings. (For example, the first volume defines the Buddha Infinite Life Sutra as the sutra of the true teaching and therefore as foremost among all the sutras.) The fifth volume explains the true Buddha and true land from the standpoint of the Pure Land teachings. The sixth volume deals with provisional Buddhas and provisional lands. To support his arguments, Shinran quotes from sutras, treatises, and commentaries. These quotations comprise the greater part of the work.

teachings of the three periods [三時教] (Jpn *sanji-kyō*): *See* three periods, teachings of the.

teaching that unites the branch teaching with the root teaching [摂末帰本法輪] (Jpn *shōmatsu-kihon-hōrin*): One component of the "thrice turned wheel of the Law," a division of Shakyamuni's lifetime teachings into three categories set forth by Chi-tsang (549–623), a systematizer of the doctrines of the Three Treatises (San-lun) school in China. *See* thrice turned wheel of the Law.

Temple school [寺門派] (Jpn Jimon-ha): Also known as the Temple Order school. A branch of the Tendai school based at Onjō-ji temple in Ōtsu, Japan. The Temple (Jimon) school traces its lineage from Chishō (814–891), the fifth chief priest of Enryaku-ji, the head temple of the

Tendai school on Mount Hiei. Friction over doctrinal differences between priests in the line of Chishō and those in the line of the third chief priest Jikaku led to a violent dispute over succession after the death of Ryōgen, the eighteenth chief priest of Enryaku-ji. In 993 the priests in Chi-shō's line left Enryaku-ji and established themselves at Onjō-ji, where Chi-shō had once been chief priest, founding the Temple school there. In contrast, the Tendai school of Mount Hiei was called the Mountain (Sammon) school. *See also* Tendai school.

ten analogies [十喻] (Jpn *jū-yu*): *See* ten similes.

ten comparisons [十喻] (Jpn *jū-yu*): *See* ten similes.

Tendai Esotericism [台密] (Jpn Taimitsu): The esoteric teachings of the Japanese Tendai school. In 804 Dengyō, who would later become the school's founder, went to China, where he received the essentials of T'ien-t'ai's teachings from Miao-lo's disciples Tao-sui and Hsing-man. He also received the Zen teachings from Hsiao-jan and the anointment ceremony of Esoteric Buddhism from Shun-hsiao. In 805 he returned to Japan and the next year established the Tendai school. Dengyō included the study of esoteric teachings in the school's curricula. His disciples, Jikaku and Chishō, who later respectively became the third and fifth chief priests of Enryaku-ji temple, went to China in 838 and 853 respectively and brought various texts of Esoteric Buddhism, notes concerning rituals, and mandalas back to Japan. They incorporated the esoteric teachings into the Tendai doctrines and promoted them. Annen (b. 841), a disciple of Jikaku, is known as the priest who systematized the practices and doctrines of Tendai Esotericism.

Tendai Hokke school [天台法華宗] (Jpn Tendai Hokke-shū): *See* Tendai school.

Tendai Lotus school [天台法華宗] (Jpn Tendai Hokke-shū): Another name for the Tendai school, so called because it ranks the Lotus Sutra above all other sutras and bases itself upon that sutra. *See* Tendai school.

Tendai school [天台宗] (Jpn Tendai-shū): Also known as the Tendai Lotus school or the Tendai Hokke school. The Japanese counterpart of the Chinese T'ien-t'ai (Jpn Tendai) school, founded in the early ninth century by Dengyō, also known as Saichō. Its head temple is Enryaku-ji on Mount Hiei. The basic teaching of the school consists of two aspects, doctrine and meditation. The Tendai school reveres the Lotus Sutra, ranking it above all other sutras based on T'ien-t'ai's system of classification called the five periods and eight teachings. The school also teaches the principle of the unification of the three truths and that of three thousand realms in a single moment of life, which clarify the universality of the Buddha nature. The way to attain Buddhahood, it holds, is the practice of the meditation to observe one's mind and see those principles in it.

The writings of the T'ien-t'ai school were brought to Japan from China in 753 by the priest Chien-chen known in Japan as Ganjin, but not until the time of Dengyō was the school formally established. In 804 Dengyō journeyed to China, where he studied the T'ien-t'ai teachings under Tao-sui and Hsing-man. He returned to Japan in 805 and in the following year obtained imperial permission to admit two government-sponsored priest candidates annually to his school. This is regarded as the founding of the Tendai school. Dengyō also petitioned the emperor for permission to build a Mahayana ordination center on Mount Hiei, but for years his request was not granted because of opposition from the priests of Nara. On the eleventh day of the sixth month, 822, seven days after Dengyō's death, permission was finally given, and the ordination center was completed in the fifth month of 827 by his disciple and successor, Gishin.

Jikaku and Chishō, respectively the third and fifth chief priests of Enryaku-ji, incorporated teachings of Esoteric Buddhism into the doctrines of the Tendai school. Hence the Tendai school in Japan rapidly assumed the character of Esoteric Buddhism, differing in this respect from the Chinese T'ien-t'ai school. The esoteric teachings of the Tendai school are called Tendai Esotericism to distinguish them from those of the True Word (Shingon) school. While Tendai Esotericism divided into what are known as thirteen schools, the orthodox Tendai teaching also split into the Eshin school and the Danna school. The former is in the lineage of Genshin, also called Eshin. The latter is in the lineage of Kakuun. Both were disciples of Ryōgen, the eighteenth chief priest of Enryaku-ji. Later these two schools each split into four branches.

In 993 a schism finally occurred in the school between priests who followed the lineage of Jikaku and those of Chishō's lineage. Ryōgen from Jikaku's line had occupied the post of chief priest of Enryaku-ji for twenty years and then his disciple Jinzen succeeded him. When Yokei from Chishō's lineage was appointed chief priest, following Jinzen, those of the rival faction fiercely opposed him. Yokei was forced to resign from the post. Thus the disciples in Chishō's line left Mount Hiei and based themselves at Onjō-ji temple. The Onjō-ji branch became known as the Temple (Jimon) school, while the group at Mount Hiei was called the Mountain (Sammon) school. Along with the True Word school, the Tendai school was one of the dominant Buddhist schools of the Heian period (794–1185). *See also* Dengyō; Ryōgen; T'ien-t'ai school; Yokei.

ten demon daughters [十羅刹女] (Jpn *jū-rasetsu-nyo*): Also, ten *rā-*

kshasa daughters, ten *rākshasīs,* or ten demonesses. The Sanskrit word *rākshasa* means demon, and *rākshasī,* female demon. The ten demon daughters appear in the "Dhāranī" (twenty-sixth) chapter of the Lotus Sutra and are described as protectors of those who uphold the sutra. They are Lambā, Vilambā, Kūtadantī (Crooked Teeth), Pushpadantī (Flowery Teeth), Makutadantī (Black Teeth), Keshinī (Much Hair), Achalā (Insatiable), Mālādhārī (Necklace Bearer), Kuntī, and Sarvasattvojohārī (Stealer of the Vital Spirit of All Living Beings). (Note: In his translation of the Lotus Sutra, Kumārajīva rendered into Chinese the meanings of the Sanskrit names of seven demon daughters, but transliterated the remaining three.) In the "Dhāranī" chapter, these ten demon daughters, along with the Mother of Demon Children, vow to shield and guard the sutra's votaries. They speak to the Buddha in unison, saying, "If there are those who fail to heed our spells and trouble and disrupt the preachers of the Law, their heads will split into seven pieces like the branches of the *arjaka* tree."

ten directions [十方] (Jpn *jippō*): The entire universe, all physical space. Specifically, the ten directions are the eight directions of the compass—north, south, east, west, northwest, northeast, southeast, and southwest—plus up and down. Buddhist scriptures refer to the existence of Buddha lands in all directions throughout the universe, each with its own Buddha. The expression "the Buddhas of the ten directions" in the sutras indicates these Buddhas. The phrase *ten directions* often appears with the phrase *three existences,* meaning past, present, and future existences. "The Buddhas of the ten directions and three existences" thus means all Buddhas throughout space and time.

Ten Divisions of Monastic Rules, The [十誦律] (Chin *Shih-sung-lü;* Jpn *Jūju-ritsu*): The text of the *vinaya,* rules of monastic discipline, of the Sarvāstivāda school; Punyatāra and Kumārajīva translated it from Sanskrit into Chinese in the early fifth century. Punyatāra died before completing the translation, and Kumārajīva finished translating the remaining portion with Dharmaruchi. The text consists of ten sections enumerating and explaining monastic regulations, hence the title *The Ten Divisions of Monastic Rules.* The Sanskrit work is not extant in its entirety, but many fragments have been discovered. In China, the study of *The Fourfold Rules of Discipline,* a more concise text, took precedence over that of *The Ten Divisions of Monastic Rules.*

ten doctrines [十宗] (Jpn *jisshū*): *See* five teachings and ten doctrines.

ten evil acts [十悪] (Jpn *jū-aku*): Evils enumerated in the Buddhist scriptures. They are the three physical evils of killing, stealing, and sexual misconduct; the four verbal evils of lying, flattery or indiscriminate and irresponsible speech, defamation, and duplicity; and the three mental evils of greed, anger, and foolishness or the holding of mistaken views. From the viewpoint of the precepts, the ten evil acts constitute violations of the ten good precepts, which proscribe those acts; they are the opposite of the ten good acts, which are to refrain from the ten evil acts.

ten factors of life [十如是] (Jpn *jū-nyoze*): Also, ten suchnesses. Ten factors common to all life in any of the Ten Worlds. They are listed in the "Expedient Means" (second) chapter of the Lotus Sutra, which reads: "The true aspect of all phenomena can only be understood and shared between Buddhas. This reality consists of the appearance, nature, entity, power, influence, internal cause, relation, latent effect, manifest effect, and their consistency from beginning to end." This passage provides a theoretical basis for the principle of the replacement of the three vehicles with the one vehicle taught in the theoretical teaching (first half) of the Lotus Sutra. Since the ten factors are common to all life and phenomena, there can be no fundamental distinction between a Buddha and an ordinary person. On this basis, T'ien-t'ai (538–597) established the philosophical system of three thousand realms in a single moment of life, of which the principle of the ten factors is a component. While the Ten Worlds express differences among phenomena, the ten factors describe the pattern of existence common to all phenomena. For example, both the state of hell and the state of Buddhahood, different as they are, have the ten factors in common.

Briefly, the ten factors are as follows: (1) Appearance: attributes of things discernible from the outside, such as color, form, shape, and behavior. (2) Nature: the inherent disposition or quality of a thing or being that cannot be discerned from the outside. T'ien-t'ai characterizes it as unchanging and irreplaceable. The nature of fire, for instance, is unchanging and cannot be replaced by that of water. He also refers to the "true nature," which he regards as the ultimate truth, or Buddha nature. (3) Entity: the essence of life that permeates and integrates appearance and nature. These first three factors describe the reality of life itself.

The next six factors, from the fourth, power, through the ninth, manifest effect, explain the functions and workings of life. (4) Power: life's potential energy. (5) Influence: the action or movement produced when life's inherent power is activated. (6) Internal cause: the cause latent in life that produces an effect of the same quality as itself, i.e., good, evil, or neutral. (7) Relation: the relationship of indirect causes to the internal cause. Indirect causes are various conditions, both internal and external, that help the internal cause produce an effect. (8) Latent effect: the effect produced in life when an internal cause is activated through its relationship with various conditions. (9) Manifest effect: the tangible, perceivable result that emerges in time as an expression of a latent effect and therefore of an internal cause, again through its relationship with various conditions. Miao-lo (711–782) regarded the Buddhist law of causality described by the four factors from internal cause to manifest effect as the distinctive characteristic of the ten factors. It concerns the cause and effect for attaining Buddhahood. (10) Consistency from beginning to end: the unifying factor among the ten factors. It indicates that all of the other nine factors from the beginning (appearance) to the end (manifest effect) are consistently and harmoniously interrelated. All nine factors thus consistently and harmoniously express the same condition of existence at any given moment.

ten good acts [十善] (Jpn *jū-zen*): The acts of refraining from committing the ten evil acts: (1) killing, (2) stealing, (3) sexual misconduct, (4) lying, (5) flattery or indiscriminate and irresponsible speech, (6) defamation, (7) duplicity, (8) greed, (9) anger, and (10) foolishness or the holding of mistaken views. Thus, the ten good acts are (1) not to kill, (2) not to steal, (3) not to engage in sexual misconduct, (4) not to lie, (5) not to flatter or use indiscriminate and irresponsible speech, (6) not to defame, (7) not to be duplicitous, (8) not to be greedy, (9) not to be angry, and (10) not to be foolish or hold mistaken views. The rules of monastic discipline that call for upholding the ten good acts are called the ten good precepts, which are at the same time an injunction against the ten evil acts.

ten good precepts [十善戒] (Jpn *jū-zen-kai*): The precepts prohibiting commission of the ten evil acts, which are (1) killing, (2) stealing, (3) sexual misconduct, (4) lying, (5) flattery or indiscriminate and irresponsible speech, (6) defamation, (7) duplicity, (8) greed, (9) anger, and (10) foolishness or the holding of mistaken views. According to Buddhist scriptures, if one abides by the ten good precepts, one will be reborn a king; also, those who have become kings are viewed as having been able to do so due to their observance of the ten good precepts in a previous lifetime.

ten great scholars of the Consciousness-Only school [唯識十大論師] (Jpn *yuishiki-jūdai-ronji*): Ten Indian scholars who wrote commentaries on Vasubandhu's *Thirty-Stanza Treatise on the Consciousness-Only Doctrine.* They are Dharmapāla, Gunamati, Sthiramati, Bandhushrī, Nanda, Shuddhachandra, Chitrabhāna, Visheshamitra, Jinaputra, and Jnānachandra. *The Treatise on the Establishment of the Consciousness-Only Doctrine,* the Chinese version of Dharmapāla's commentary on the above treatise, also introduces interpretations on the same work by the other nine scholars.

ten honorable titles [十号] (Jpn *jū-gō*): Ten epithets for a Buddha, expressing such qualities as power, wisdom, virtue, and compassion. Among the several versions of the ten honorable titles, one lists them as follows: (1) Thus Come One (Skt *tathāgata*). One who has come from the world of truth. A Buddha embodies the fundamental truth of all phenomena and grasps the law of causality that permeates past, present, and future. (2) Worthy of Offerings *(arhat)*. One who is qualified to receive offerings from human and heavenly beings. (3) Right and Universal Knowledge *(samyak-sambuddha)*. One with a correct and perfect understanding of all phenomena. (4) Perfect Clarity and Conduct *(vidyā-charana-sampanna)*. One who understands eternity, or the past, present, and future existences, and who is a perfect performer of good deeds. (5) Well Attained *(sugata)*, also Well Gone. One who has gone over to the world of enlightenment. (6) Understanding the World *(lokavid)*. One who understands all secular and religious affairs by grasping the law of causality. (7) Unexcelled Worthy *(anuttara)*. One who stands supreme among all living beings. (8) Trainer of People *(purusha-damya-sārathi)*. One who trains and leads all people to enlightenment. (9) Teacher of Heavenly and Human Beings *(shāstā-deva-manushyānām)*. One who can teach and educate all human and heavenly beings. (10) Buddha, the World-Honored One *(Buddha-bhagavat)*. An awakened one, endowed with perfect wisdom and virtue, who wins the respect of all people. Other versions list Buddha and World-Honored One as two separate titles, in which cases either Understanding the World and Unexcelled Worthy, or Unexcelled Worthy and Trainer of People, are combined as one title, or Thus Come One is excluded.

ten kinds of offerings [十種供養] (Jpn *jisshu-kuyō*): Offerings described in the "Teacher of the Law" (tenth) chapter of the Lotus Sutra. They are offerings of flowers, incense, necklaces, powdered incense, paste incense, incense for burning, silken canopies, streamers and banners, clothing, and music. Another interpretation regards "silken canopies" and "streamers and banners" as one offering, and instead adds the act of pressing one's palms together, mentioned immediately after "music" in the sutra text, as the tenth offering.

ten kings [十王] (Jpn *jū-ō*): Ten kings of the world of the dead described in the Ten Kings Sutra, popularly believed to take turns judging the dead from the seventh day after a person's death until the second anniversary. These judgments occur once every seven days for the first forty-nine days (seven weeks), on the one-hundredth day, on the first anniversary, and on the second anniversary of the person's death. Their true identities are said to be those of Buddhas and bodhisattvas; hence, though outwardly forbidding, they are actually compassionate. They are (1) King Ch'in-kuang (Chin), who judges the dead on the seventh day after their death; (2) King First Creek of the River, who judges the dead on the fourteenth day; (3) King Sung-ti (Chin), who judges the dead on the twenty-first day; (4) King Controller of the Five Sense Organs, who judges the dead on the twenty-eighth day; (5) King Yama, who judges the dead on the thirty-fifth day; (6) King Transformation, who judges the dead on the forty-second day; (7) King T'ai-shan (Chin: named after Mount T'ai), who judges the dead on the forty-ninth day; (8) King Impartial Judge, who judges the dead on the hundredth day; (9) King Imperial City, who judges the dead on the first anniversary; and (10) King Wheel-Turner of the Five Paths, who judges the dead on the second anniversary. The concept of the ten kings is Chinese in origin; the Ten Kings Sutra is regarded as having been written in China.

ten major disciples [十大弟子] (Jpn *jūdai-deshi*): Shakyamuni Buddha's ten principal disciples: Shāriputra, Mahākāshyapa, Ānanda, Subhūti, Pūrna, Maudgalyāyana, Kātyāyana, Aniruddha, Upāli, and Rāhula. Each was known as being foremost among all the Buddha's disciples in a specific quality or area. Shāriputra was known as foremost in wisdom; Mahākāshyapa, in ascetic practices; Ānanda, in hearing the Buddha's teachings; Subhūti, in understanding the doctrine of non-substantiality; Pūrna, in preaching the Law; Maudgalyāyana, in transcendental powers; Kātyāyana, in debate; Aniruddha, in divine insight; Upāli, in observing the precepts; and Rāhula, in inconspicuous practice.

ten major precepts [十重禁戒] (Jpn *jū-jūkinkai*): The ten most important among the fifty-eight rules of discipline for Mahayana bodhisattvas set forth in the Brahmā Net Sutra. (The others are called the forty-eight minor precepts.) The ten major precepts are (1) not to kill, (2) not to steal, (3) not to engage in any sexual relations, (4) not to lie, (5) not to sell liquor, (6) not to speak ill of the past misdeeds of other Buddhists, (7) not to praise oneself or disparage others, (8) not to begrudge offerings or spare one's efforts for the sake of Buddhism, (9) not to give way to anger, and (10) not to speak ill of the three treasures (the Buddha, his teachings, and the Buddhist Order).

ten major writings [十大部] (Jpn *jūdai-bu*): Ten treatises written by Nichiren and later designated by Nikkō (1246–1333), Nichiren's disciple and successor, as his most important writings. In chronological order of writing, they are: (1) *On Chanting the Daimoku of the Lotus Sutra (Shō-*

hokke-daimoku-shō), written at Nagoe in Kamakura and dated the twenty-eighth day of the fifth month, 1260. In a series of fifteen questions and answers, it establishes the supremacy of the Lotus Sutra over the provisional teachings and describes the benefits of chanting the daimoku of the Lotus Sutra, or Nam-myoho-renge-kyo. It explains that this is the teaching and practice for attaining Buddhahood in the Latter Day of the Law. The addressee of the treatise is unknown.

(2) *On Establishing the Correct Teaching for the Peace of the Land (Rissho-ankoku-ron),* submitted in remonstration to the retired but virtual regent, Hōjō Tokiyori, on the sixteenth day of the seventh month, 1260. Written in the form of a dialogue between a host and a visitor, it attributes the disasters befalling the nation to slander of the Lotus Sutra and belief in false forms of Buddhism, particularly the Pure Land (Jōdo) school. It predicts that two further disasters, internal strife and foreign invasion, will occur if the country continues its support of mistaken teachings and priests.

(3) *The Opening of the Eyes (Kaimoku-shō),* written at Tsukahara on Sado Island, where Nichiren was in exile, and completed in the second month of 1272. Nichiren wrote this treatise for all his followers and entrusted it to Shijō Kingo. Using the three virtues of sovereign, teacher, and parent as a standard, it first compares Confucianism, Brahmanism, and Buddhism, and then the various levels of Buddhist teachings, finally revealing the three virtues of the Buddhism of sowing. It also reveals that the teaching that enables all people in the Latter Day of the Law to attain Buddhahood is found in the depths of the "Life Span" (sixteenth) chapter of the Lotus Sutra. It concludes that Nichiren is perfectly endowed with the three virtues of the Buddha in the Latter Day of the Law. Therefore, it is known as the work that defines the object of devotion in Nichiren's teaching in terms of the Person (in contrast with the Law).

(4) *The Object of Devotion for Observing the Mind (Kanjin-no-honzon-shō),* written at Ichinosawa on Sado Island and dated the twenty-fifth day of the fourth month, 1273. It was entrusted to Toki Jōnin. It is known as the work that defines the object of devotion in Nichiren's teaching in terms of the Law (in contrast with the Person), because it sets forth the theoretical basis for the Gohonzon, or the mandala that Nichiren inscribed as the object of devotion for attaining Buddhahood in the Latter Day. It teaches the principle that embracing the Gohonzon is in itself observing one's mind, or attaining enlightenment.

(5) *On Taking the Essence of the Lotus Sutra (Hokke-shuyō-shō),* dated the fifth month of 1274 at Minobu and given to Toki Jōnin. It defines Nam-myoho-renge-kyo of the Three Great Secret Laws, which is the

essence of the Lotus Sutra, as the object of devotion for all people in the Latter Day of the Law.

(6) *The Selection of the Time (Senji-shō),* written at Minobu in 1275 and given to Yui of Nishiyama in Suruga Province. It explains that there is a correct teaching for each of the three periods of the Former Day, Middle Day, and Latter Day of the Law, and that, in the Latter Day, the great pure Law implicit in the "Life Span" (sixteenth) chapter of the Lotus Sutra should and will be propagated.

(7) *On Repaying Debts of Gratitude (Hō'on-shō),* written at Minobu and dated the twenty-first day of the seventh month, 1276. Nichiren wrote this treatise in appreciation for his late teacher Dōzen-bō and sent it to the priests Jōken-bō and Gijō-bō, his former seniors at Seichō-ji temple in Awa Province when he studied there as a youth. It discusses the meaning of repaying debts of gratitude in the light of Buddhism, especially to one's teacher, and concludes that the way to requite such obligations fully is to embrace and propagate the Three Great Secret Laws.

(8) *On the Four Stages of Faith and the Five Stages of Practice (Shishin-gohon-shō),* dated the tenth day of the fourth month, 1277, at Minobu and sent to Toki Jōnin. It discusses the four stages of faith and the five stages of practice formulated by T'ien-t'ai based on the "Distinctions in Benefits" (seventeenth) chapter of the Lotus Sutra, and defines the chanting of Nam-myoho-renge-kyo as the direct way to enlightenment in the Latter Day of the Law.

(9) *Letter to Shimoyama (Shimoyama-goshōsoku),* written at Minobu in the sixth month of 1277 and addressed to Shimoyama Hyōgo Gorō Mitsumoto, the steward of Shimoyama in Kai Province. Inaba-bō Nichiei, one of Nichiren's disciples in Shimoyama, had tried to convert Mitsumoto, his father (his lord, according to another account), and met with extreme opposition. Nichiren wrote this treatise to the steward under Inaba-bō's name and on his behalf. It points out the errors of the various schools and their deleterious effect upon the nation, outlines Nichiren's teachings and the rationale for his activities, and urges Mitsumoto to abandon the Pure Land teachings and take faith in the Lotus Sutra.

(10) *Questions and Answers on the Object of Devotion (Honzon-mondō-shō),* written at Minobu in the ninth month of 1278 and sent to Jōken-bō at Seichō-ji temple. It refutes the objects of devotion of the various schools, particularly those of the True Word (Shingon) school, and establishes in the light of the sutras that the daimoku of the Lotus Sutra, Nam-myoho-renge-kyo, should be the object of devotion in the Latter Day of the Law.

ten meditations [十乗観法] (Jpn *jūjō-kampō*): Ten kinds of meditation set forth by T'ien-t'ai (538–597) in his *Great Concentration and Insight* as a way to observe the truth of life he defined as three thousand realms in a single moment of life. They are as follows: (1) The meditation on the region of the unfathomable. "The region of the unfathomable" means the truth of three thousand realms in a single moment of life, and this meditation is defined as the threefold contemplation in a single mind. This is the principal, self-fulfilling practice, while the other nine are for those who cannot accomplish this meditation. (2) The meditation to arouse compassion. (3) The meditation to enjoy security in the realm of truth. (4) The meditation to eliminate attachments. (5) The meditation to discern what leads to the realization of the true aspect of life and what prevents it. (6) The meditation to make proper use of the thirty-seven aids to the way, or enlightenment. (7) The meditation to remove obstacles to enlightenment while practicing the six *pāramitās*. (8) The meditation to recognize the stages of one's progress. (9) The meditation to stabilize one's mind. (10) The meditation to remove attachment to what is not true enlightenment.

The system of practices formulated in *Great Concentration and Insight* may be broadly divided into two categories. One is a group of preliminary practices comprising twenty-five preparatory exercises. The other is a group of practices for realizing the truth of life directly. The ten meditations constitute this second group. As mentioned above, particular importance is attached to the first of the ten meditations, the meditation on the region of the unfathomable. Miao-lo categorized the ten meditations according to the capacity of the practitioner. Practitioners of superior capacity, he stated, can realize the true aspect of life directly through the meditation on the region of the unfathomable alone; those of intermediate capacity can attain the goal by practicing the first through seventh meditations; and those of lesser capacity must practice all ten meditations.

ten mysteries [十玄門] (Jpn *jū-gemmon*): Ten aspects of the interrelationship of all phenomena as seen from the standpoint of the Buddha's enlightenment. A doctrine of the Flower Garland (Chin Hua-yen; Jpn Kegon) school formulated by Chih-yen (602–668), the second patriarch of the school, and revised by the third patriarch, Fa-tsang. Fa-tsang's version lists the ten mysteries as follows: (1) All phenomena are mutually related and give rise to one another simultaneously. (2) The broad and the narrow are mutually inclusive without impediment; and one action, however small, includes all actions. (3) The many are included in the one and the one in the many, without losing their respective characteristics as "one" and "many." (4) All phenomena are interpenetrated in their essence; one is equal to all and all is equal to one. (5) The hidden and the manifest complement each other and together form one entity. (6) Things that are inconceivably minute also obey the principle of many in one and one in many. (7) All phenomena ceaselessly permeate and reflect one another, like the reflections in the jewels of Indra's net (a net said to hang on a wall in the palace of the god Indra, or Shakra; at each link of the net is a reflective jewel that mirrors the adjacent jewels and the multiple images reflected in them). (8) All phenomena manifest the truth, and the truth is to be found in all phenomena; anything can serve as an example of the truth of the interdependence of all things. (9) The three periods of past, present, and future each have past, present, and future within themselves. This defines nine periods, which together form one period, making ten in all. These ten periods are distinct yet mutually pervasive. This mystery expresses the "one is all, all is one" principle of the Flower Garland school in terms of time. (10) At any time, one phenomenon acts as principal and many phenomena as secondary, thus completing the whole.

In the earlier version, the ten mysteries are given in a different order and with slightly different terminology and two are altogether different. These two are the mystery that all phenomena are manifestations of the mind and none can exist outside the mind; and the mystery that the mind is single and all phenomena diverse, the diverse and the single interacting without obstruction. They are replaced with the above items (2) and (10) respectively in Fa-tsang's revised version. The "ten mysteries" are often mentioned in conjunction with the "six forms." The two concepts explain the same principle from different perspectives.

ten mystic principles [十妙] (Jpn *jū-myō*): Ten principles set forth by T'ien-t'ai (538–597) in *The Profound Meaning of the Lotus Sutra* interpreting the word *myō* of *Myoho-renge-kyo,* the title of the Lotus Sutra. According to T'ien-t'ai, the ten mystic principles are all implicit in the single word *myō.* There are two categories of ten mystic principles: the ten mystic principles of the theoretical teaching (first half) of the Lotus Sutra, and the ten mystic principles of the essential teaching (latter half) of the sutra. In the descriptions below, the word *mystic* is a translation of *myō.*

The ten mystic principles of the theoretical teaching are based on the concepts of the true aspect of all phenomena and the replacement of the three vehicles with the one vehicle. They are (1) the mystic principle of reality, meaning that the objective reality observed and illuminated by wisdom is mystic; (2) the mystic principle of wisdom, that the wisdom with which one understands this reality is mystic; (3) the mystic principle of practice, that practice based on mystic wisdom is mystic; (4) the mystic principle of stages (which are attained through practice), that the stages leading to enlightenment are mystic; (5) the mystic principle of the three elements, that objective reality or truth, subjective wisdom, and the behavior arising from the fusion of these two, are mystic; (6) the mystic principle of responsive communion, meaning that the Buddha appearing in order to respond to the people's desire to seek him is mystic; (7) the mystic principle of transcendental power, that the supernatural powers the Buddha uses to reveal the truth are mystic; (8) the mystic principle of preaching, that the Buddha's preaching what is verbally inexpressible is mystic; (9) the mystic principle of relationship, that all people are related to the Buddha is mystic; and (10) the mystic principle of merit and benefit, that people who received the seeds of Buddhahood major world system dust particle *kalpas* ago finally attain the truth through the process of maturing is mystic.

The ten mystic principles of the essential teaching are based on the revelation of the Buddha's original enlightenment countless *kalpas* in the past as expounded in the "Life Span" (sixteenth) chapter. The ten mystic principles of the theoretical teaching are preparatory to the ten mystic principles of the essential teaching. Because the Buddha who revealed his original enlightenment in the remote past is called the true Buddha, each of the mystic principles of the essential teaching are modified by the word "true." They are the mystic principles of (1) true cause, meaning that the practices of the true Buddha are mystic; (2) true effect, that the merits and virtues attained by the true Buddha are mystic; (3) true land, that the land where the true Buddha dwells is mystic; (4) true responsive communion, that the true Buddha appearing in response to the people's desire to seek him is mystic; (5) true transcendental power, that the supernatural powers the true Buddha displays when he preaches are mystic; (6) true preaching, that the true Buddha's preaching in the remote past is mystic; (7) true relationship, that the people who formed connections to the true Buddha in the remote past are mystic; (8) true nirvana, that the true Buddha's nirvana is not an expedient means but eternal and inherent, and therefore is mystic; (9) true life span, meaning that, though the true Buddha's life span is eternal, his repeatedly being reborn as an ordinary mortal with a life span he desires is mystic; and (10) true benefit, that the benefit the true Buddha bestows upon the people in the Land of Eternally Tranquil Light is mystic.

ten objects [十境] (Jpn *jikkyō*): Also, ten objects of meditation. Objects of meditation set forth by T'ien-t'ai (538–597) in his *Great Concentration and Insight* as part of a comprehensive system of meditation to perceive the truth of life and all phenomena. One begins meditation on the ten objects after completing twenty-five preparatory exercises. The ten objects are (1) the phenomenal world that exists by virtue of the five components (form, perception, conception, volition, and consciousness), the interactions between the six sense organs and their corresponding six objects, and the six consciousnesses arising from those interactions, (2) earthly desires, (3) sickness, (4) karmic effect, (5) diabolical functions, (6) attachment to a certain level of meditation, (7) distorted views, (8) arrogance, (9) attachment to the two vehicles, and (10) attachment to the state of the bodhisattva. Meditation on the first of the ten objects is the basis for meditations on all the other nine. Among the constituents of the first object, particular importance is attached to the fifth of the five components: consciousness, or mind. Through meditation on the component of consciousness, one tries to perceive the truth of three thousand realms in a single moment of life.

ten onenesses [十不二門] (Jpn *jippunimon*): Also, ten non-dualities. Ten principles set forth by Miao-lo (711–782) in *The Annotations on "The Profound Meaning of the Lotus Sutra."* In this work, Miao-lo discusses the ten mystic principles of the theoretical teaching (first half) of the Lotus Sutra and the ten mystic principles of the essential teaching (latter half) of the sutra, which T'ien-t'ai expounded in *The Profound Meaning of the Lotus Sutra,* and reveals the ten onenesses. The section of Miao-lo's work that explains this principle later became an independent work called *The Ten Onenesses.* In it, Miao-lo states that the concept of ten onenesses includes the ten mystic principles of both the theoretical and the essential teachings. The ten onenesses are as follows: (1) The oneness of body and mind. What one observes in meditation is one mind or one thought (Jpn *ichinen*), which is an indivisible whole of body and mind. (2) The oneness of the internal and the external. Though the object of meditation is divided into two—the internal object, or the realm of one mind, a psychosomatic entity; and the external object, or the external world of physical and spiritual phenomena—these two are non-dual because one mind embodies the three truths and includes all three thousand realms. (3) The oneness of the result of practice and the true nature of life. This means that the true nature of life, or the true aspect of all phenomena, is no different from what one ultimately attains through Buddhist practice. The true nature moves one to practice, and practice enables one to manifest the true nature. (4) The oneness of cause and effect. "Cause" here means ordinary people, and "effect," Buddhahood. The oneness of cause and effect means that the Buddha nature inherent in the ordinary person is the same as the Buddha nature that the Buddha has manifested.

(5) The oneness of the impure and the pure. Because ignorance or delusion and enlightenment are two expressions of the same mind and essentially one, the impure mind shrouded in ignorance is itself the pure mind that is enlightened. (6) The oneness of life and its environment. Both the Buddha as a living being and the Buddha land as the environment exist in one mind and are therefore non-dual. (7) The oneness of self and others. "Self" means the Buddha, who teaches, and "others" means ordinary people, who are taught and enlightened. But they are non-dual because both the Buddha and ordinary people embody the three truths and are endowed with all three thousand realms. In other words, both self (Buddhahood) and others (the nine worlds) are inherent in one mind. (8) The oneness of thought, word, and deed. The Buddha saves people through his three categories of action—thought, speech, and behavior. These three categories of the Buddha are no different from those of ordinary people because they arise from the three thousand realms inherent in both. Moreover, these three exist in one mind as a psychosomatic whole and therefore are one. (9) The oneness of the provisional and true teachings. The Buddha preaches the provisional teachings (the three vehicles) and the true teaching (the one vehicle) according to the people's capacity. Because they both spring from the Buddha's enlightened mind, however, they are non-dual. (10) The oneness of benefits. Though people receive different benefits according to the level of the Buddha's teaching that they practice (such as provisional and true), both the Buddha and the people ultimately enjoy the same benefit, just as plants in a field are all nourished equally by the rain.

Ten Onenesses, The [十不二門] (Chin *Shih-pu-erh-men;* Jpn *Jippunimon*): A one-volume work by Miao-lo (711–782) that sets forth the ten onenesses, which include such concepts as the oneness of body and mind, and the oneness of life and its environment. Based on the ten mystic principles T'ien-t'ai expounded in *The Profound Meaning of the Lotus Sutra,* Miao-lo established the ten onenesses in *The Annotations on "The Profound Meaning of the Lotus Sutra."* The part of this work dealing with the ten onenesses was later circulated as an independent text titled *The Ten Onenesses. See also* ten onenesses.

ten pāramitās [十波羅蜜] (Jpn *jū-haramitsu* or *jipparamitsu*): Ten kinds of practice carried out by bodhisattvas for their own enlightenment as well as for the enlightenment of other people. The ten *pāramitās* are the six *pāramitās* (almsgiving, keeping the precepts, forbearance, assiduousness, meditation, and the obtaining of wisdom)—plus the *pāramitās* of expedient means, the vow, power, and knowledge. The *pāramitā* of expedient means is to make full use of skillful means to benefit other people, and the *pāramitā* of the vow is to pledge to lead other people to enlightenment. The *pāramitā* of power is the power of practice, and the *pāramitā* of knowledge, the perfection of knowledge for the purpose of leading other people to enlightenment. These four practices are regarded as auxiliary to the six *pāramitās*. *See also* six *pāramitās*.

ten peerlessnesses [十無上] (Jpn *jū-mujō*): A concept set forth in Vasubandhu's *Treatise on the Lotus Sutra*. The ten peerlessnesses are ten statements asserting the supremacy of different aspects or attributes of the Lotus Sutra. They are as follows: (1) The seeds of enlightenment imparted by the Lotus Sutra are without peer. (2) The practice of the sutra is without peer because it contains supreme virtues and benefits. (3) The sutra is without peer in embracing and enhancing the teachings of all the other sutras, and therefore the power of the sutra is peerless. (4) The sutra's power to enable all people to understand the supreme truth is without peer. (5) The sutra is without peer in transforming all lands into pure lands. (6) The sutra's teaching is foremost among the Buddha's teachings; it is the most profound and without peer. (7) The sutra is without peer in instructing and converting all people. (8) The sutra is without peer in revealing the supreme enlightenment of the Buddha. (9) The aspect of nirvana as expounded in the sutra is without peer. The Buddha enters nirvana to instruct and convert people, though his life is eternal. (10) The wonderful power of the sutra is without peer because of the emergence of the treasure tower of Many Treasures Thus Come One and other unprecedented occurrences.

ten powers [十力] (Jpn *jū-riki*): Ten powers that a Buddha possesses described in *The Great Commentary on the Abhidharma* and other treatises. They are (1) the power of knowing what is true and what is not; (2) the power of knowing karmic causality at work in the lives of all beings throughout past, present, and future; (3) the power of knowing all stages of concentration, emancipation, and meditation; (4) the power of knowing the conditions of life of all people; (5) the power of judging all people's levels of understanding; (6) the power of discerning the superiority or inferiority of all people's capacity; (7) the power of knowing the effects of all people's actions; (8) the power of remembering past lifetimes; (9) the power of knowing when each person will be born and will die, and in what realm that person will be reborn; and (10) the power of eradicating all illusions. Some explanations of the ten powers give a different order or differ slightly in content.

ten precepts [十戒] (Jpn *jikkai*): Ten precepts for male and female novices of the Buddhist Order. They are (1) not to kill, (2) not to steal, (3) to refrain from all sexual activity, (4) not to lie, (5) not to drink intoxicants, (6) not to wear ornaments or perfume, (7) not to listen to singing or watch dancing, (8) not to sleep on an elevated or broad bed, (9) not to eat at an improper hour, i.e., after noon, and (10) not to own valuables such as gold and silver. The term *ten precepts* can also refer to the ten good precepts and the ten major precepts of the Brahmā Net Sutra.

ten rākshasa daughters [十羅刹女] (Jpn *jū-rasetsu-nyo*): The ten demon daughters described in the "Dhāranī" (twenty-sixth) chapter of the Lotus Sutra as protectors of the upholders of the sutra. *See* ten demon daughters.

ten schools [十宗] (Jpn *jisshū*): The ten Buddhist schools of Japan often referred to collectively in Japanese Buddhist works. They are the Dharma Analysis Treasury (Kusha), Establishment of Truth (Jōjitsu), Precepts (Ritsu), Dharma Characteristics (Hossō), Three Treatises (Sanron), Flower Garland (Kegon), Tendai, True Word (Shingon), Zen, and Pure Land (Jōdo) schools. All except the Zen school appeared in Japan before the Kamakura period (1185–1333), while the Zen school emerged early in that period. When Gyōnen (1240–1321), a priest of the Flower Garland school, wrote *The Essentials of the Eight Schools*, he also referred to two newer schools, Zen and Pure Land, thereby covering the ten schools of his day.

Tenshō Daijin [天照大神] (Jpn): The Sun Goddess. A deity in Japanese mythology, later adopted as a protective deity in Japanese Buddhism. *See* Sun Goddess.

ten similes [十喩] (Jpn *jū-yu*): Also, ten analogies or ten comparisons. Ten comparisons set forth in the "Medicine King" (twenty-third) chapter of the Lotus Sutra to illustrate the superiority of the Lotus Sutra over all other sutras and the greatness of its beneficent power. They are as follows: (1) The simile of water; just as the ocean is foremost among all bodies of water, so the Lotus Sutra is the most profound of all the sutras. (2) The simile of mountains; just as Mount Sumeru is highest among all the mountains, so the Lotus Sutra holds the highest place among all the sutras. (3) The simile of the heavenly bodies; just as the moon is foremost among the stars and planets in the night sky, so the Lotus Sutra is likewise among sutras. (4) The simile of the sun; just as the sun can banish all darkness, so the Lotus Sutra can destroy all darkness and that which is not good. (5) The simile of a wheel-turning king; just as the wheel-turning king is foremost among kings, so the Lotus Sutra is the most honored among sutras. (6) The simile of the god Shakra; just as Shakra is king among the thirty-three heavenly gods, so the Lotus Sutra is king among all the sutras. (7) The simile of the great heavenly king Brahmā; just as Brahmā is the father of all living beings, so the Lotus

Sutra is father to all sages and those who seek various levels of awakening. (8) The simile of voice-hearers at the four stages of enlightenment and cause-awakened ones; just as voice-hearers at the four stages of enlightenment (the stages of stream-winner, once-returner, non-returner, and arhat) and cause-awakened ones are foremost among all ordinary beings, so the Lotus Sutra is foremost among all the sutra teachings. This simile also states that one who can uphold the sutra is likewise foremost among all living beings. (9) The simile of bodhisattvas; just as bodhisattvas are foremost among all voice-hearers and cause-awakened ones, so the Lotus Sutra is foremost among all the sutra teachings. (10) The simile of the Buddha; just as the Buddha is king of the doctrines, so the Lotus Sutra is king of the sutras.

ten stages of development [十地] (Skt *dashabhūmi;* Jpn *jū-ji*): Also, simply ten stages. Ten stages through which the practitioner conquers progressively deeper levels of darkness and advances in Buddhist practice. In the system of the fifty-two stages of bodhisattva practice set forth in the Jeweled Necklace Sutra, they are viewed as the forty-first through the fiftieth stages. There are several different sets of "ten stages" listed in different scriptures. The Ten Stages Sutra lists them as follows: (1) the stage of joy, in which one rejoices at realizing a partial aspect of the truth; (2) the stage of freedom from defilement, in which one is free from all defilement; (3) the stage of the emission of light, in which one radiates the light of wisdom; (4) the stage of glowing wisdom, in which the flame of wisdom burns away earthly desires; (5) the stage of overcoming final illusions, in which one surmounts the illusions of darkness, or ignorance of the Middle Way; (6) the stage of the sign of supreme wisdom, in which the supreme wisdom begins to appear; (7) the stage of progression, in which one rises above the paths of the two vehicles; (8) the stage of immobility, in which one dwells firmly in the truth of the Middle Way and cannot be perturbed by anything; (9) the stage of the all-penetrating wisdom, in which one preaches the Law freely and without restriction; and (10) the stage of the Dharma cloud, in which one benefits all sentient beings with the Dharma or Law, just as a cloud sends down rain impartially upon all things.

ten stages of devotion [十廻向] (Jpn *jū-ekō*): The ten stages from the thirty-first through the fortieth of the fifty-two stages of bodhisattva practice according to the Jeweled Necklace Sutra. Preceding the ten stages of devotion are the ten stages of faith, the ten stages of security, and the ten stages of practice. In the ten stages of devotion, one directs one's blessings toward other people. Described in the Jeweled Necklace Sutra and the Flower Garland Sutra, they are as follows: (1) The stage of saving all people and freeing oneself from the characteristics of a common mortal. In this stage, while practicing the six *pāramitās* among the beings of the six paths, one makes efforts to save all of them and at the same time liberates oneself from the characteristics of a common mortal. (2) The stage of indestructibility, in which, with indestructible faith in the three treasures of Buddhism, one penetrates the true nature of all phenomena, realizing their non-substantiality. (3) The stage of impartial devotion to all Buddhas, in which one practices, in successive lifetimes, under all the Buddhas of the three existences. In this stage, one increases all kinds of good roots and transfers their benefit to all beings impartially. (4) The stage of transferring one's benefits to all lands. In this stage, one transfers one's benefits to the Buddhas in all lands, serving and making offerings to them and to all other beings. (5) The stage of obtaining limitless blessings, in which one directs all one's good fortune to the practice of Buddhism, thereby obtaining limitless good fortune and benefit. (6) The stage of impartial benefit, in which one benefits all beings equally. (7) The stage of observing the nature of all people, in which one perceives the coexistence of good and evil inherent in people's lives. (8) The stage of realizing the true aspect of all phenomena. In this stage, one transfers the benefits one obtains through this realization to others. (9) The stage of freedom from all attachments. Here, one perceives all phenomena from the standpoints of both difference and equality and frees oneself from all attachments, thereafter leading others to emancipation. (10) The stage of perceiving all phenomena with infinite wisdom. At this level, one regards all phenomena as manifestations of the Middle Way and, while performing a variety of meritorious acts, uses the resultant benefits for the sake of others.

ten stages of faith [十信] (Jpn *jisshin*): The first ten of the fifty-two stages of bodhisattva practice described in the Jeweled Necklace Sutra. They are (1) arousing pure faith, (2) ever-mindfulness, (3) assiduousness, (4) concentration, (5) wisdom, or perceiving the non-substantiality of all things, (6) keeping the precepts, (7) directing previously acquired good fortune toward attaining enlightenment, (8) guarding the mind against earthly desires, (9) discarding attachments, and (10) making efforts to fulfill one's vows. There are differing descriptions of the content and order of the ten stages of faith.

ten stages of practice [十行] (Jpn *jū-gyō*): The ten stages from the twenty-first through the thirtieth of the fifty-two stages of bodhisattva practice, according to the Jeweled Necklace Sutra. These ten stages follow the ten stages of faith and ten stages of security. In the ten stages of faith and ten stages of security one aims at personal development. In the ten stages of practice, one devotes oneself to altruistic deeds. The sutra lists them as follows: (1) The stage of joyful service, in which one awakens to the non-substantiality of all things and phenomena, and causes others to rejoice by offering them all one's possessions. (2) The stage of beneficial practice, in which one always instructs and benefits others. (3) The stage of never offending, in which one engages in the practice of forbearance and frees oneself from anger, not offending others. It is also called the practice of never resenting. (4) The stage of limitless assiduousness, in which one continues earnest practice in order to lead others to enlightenment, whatever the hardships involved. (5) The stage of non-confusion, in which one is not hindered by illusions or ignorance. (6) The stage of appearance in the Buddha land, in which one is always born in a Buddha land. (7) The stage of non-attachment, in which one perceives all things and phenomena as non-substantial and frees oneself from attachment to them. (8) The stage of attaining the difficult, in which one perfects the practice for cultivating virtues, which is difficult to accomplish. It is also called the stage of praising, in which one praises and promotes the *pāramitās,* or bodhisattva practices for perfection, among the people. (9) The stage of being a model in the preaching of the Law, in which one's practice of preaching and protecting the Law becomes a model for all others. (10) The stage of realizing the truth, in which one is awakened to the truth of the Middle Way.

ten stages of security [十住] (Jpn *jū-jū*): The ten stages from the eleventh through the twentieth of the fifty-two stages of bodhisattva practice. Described in the Jeweled Necklace Sutra, they are (1) arousing the aspiration for Buddhahood, (2) contemplating the non-substantiality of things, (3) performing all possible good deeds, (4) clearly understanding that, because phenomena exist only in relationship to other phenomena, they have no permanent and unchangeable substance of their own, (5) applying all good deeds as a means to developing one's perception of the non-substantiality of things, (6) perfecting the wisdom to perceive the non-substantiality of things, (7) never retrogressing from the realization of the truth of the non-substantiality of things, (8) never harboring false views or losing the aspiration for enlightenment, (9) deeply understanding the Buddha's teachings to the point where one is assured of attaining Buddhahood in the future, and (10) obtaining the wisdom to perceive that, because all things are without substance, there is nothing that is actually born or dies.

ten stages of the mind [十住心] (Jpn *jū-jūshin*): A system of comparative classification formulated by Kōbō (774–835), the founder of the

Japanese True Word (Shingon) school. He explained it fully in *The Treatise on the Ten Stages of the Mind* and summarized it in *The Precious Key to the Secret Treasury*. On the basis of the "Stage of the Mind" chapter of the Mahāvairochana Sutra and *The Treatise on the Mind Aspiring for Enlightenment* by Nāgārjuna, he classified Buddhist and non-Buddhist teachings according to ten stages in the development of religious consciousness. He then placed practitioners of the esoteric teachings of the True Word school in the highest, or tenth, stage. Kōbō described the ten stages as follows: (1) The stage of the human animal, in which one is governed, like an animal, by instincts and passions. This first stage he termed the "mind of lowly man, goatish in its desire." (2) The stage of moral awareness, in which one practices secular virtues. This stage corresponds to Confucianism with its emphasis on moral order, which makes self-control possible but nevertheless is limited to this world. (3) The stage of dawning religious aspiration, in which one relies on supernatural beings and practices in expectation of a heaven beyond this world, thus gaining temporary respite from worldly anxieties. This stage corresponds to Brahmanism and Taoism. (4) The stage of the denial of the ego, in which one sees that only the five components of life are real and that there is no permanent self, thus divesting oneself of the concept of an unchanging ego such as the *ātman* of Brahmanism. Voice-hearers are in this stage. (5) The stage in which one strives to rid oneself of illusions and evil karma by perceiving the twelve-linked chain of causation. Cause-awakened ones belong to this stage. Stages four and five correspond to Hinayana Buddhism. (6) The stage of the bodhisattva mind, in which one arouses non-discriminating compassion for all beings and realizes that the mind alone exists. This stage corresponds to the Dharma Characteristics (Jpn Hossō) school, which is regarded as an early stage of the Mahayana teachings. (7) The stage in which one understands the eight negations and is enlightened to the non-substantiality of both mind and material objects. This stage corresponds to the teachings of the Three Treatises (Sanron) school. (8) The stage in which one realizes the essential oneness of the phenomenal world and the ultimate reality and embraces the one Buddha vehicle. This stage corresponds to the Tendai school. (9) The stage in which one realizes that there is no fixed identity or self-nature within the ultimate truth. This stage corresponds to the Flower Garland (Kegon) school. Stages six, seven, eight, and nine indicate the realm of the Mahayana bodhisattva. (10) The stage of realization of the esoteric truth, i.e., Buddhahood. Kōbō equated this last stage, which he termed the "glorious mind, the most secret and sacred," with Buddhahood, and he correlated it with the True Word school. With these ten stages, Kōbō ranked the teachings of the Flower Garland and True Word schools above the Tendai school, which is based on the Lotus Sutra.

Ten Stages Sutra [十地経] (Skt *Dashabhūmika-sūtra;* Chin *Shih-ti-ching;* Jpn *Jūji-kyō*): A sutra that deals with the ten stages of development. In the system of the fifty-two stages of bodhisattva practice enumerated in the Jeweled Necklace Sutra, the ten stages of development correspond to the forty-first through the fiftieth stages. The Ten Stages Sutra corresponds to the "Ten Stages" chapter of the Flower Garland Sutra. It is generally thought that in India the Ten Stages Sutra was first produced and later included in the voluminous Flower Garland Sutra when the latter was compiled. The Sanskrit text, a Tibetan translation, and several Chinese translations of the Ten Stages Sutra are extant.

ten supernatural powers [十神力] (Jpn *jū-jinriki*): The supernatural powers that Shakyamuni Buddha displays in the "Supernatural Powers" (twenty-first) chapter of the Lotus Sutra, before transferring the essence of the sutra to the Bodhisattvas of the Earth. T'ien-t'ai (538–597) outlines and interprets them in *The Words and Phrases of the Lotus Sutra* as follows: (1) The Buddha extends his long broad tongue until it reaches the Brahma Heaven. This indicates the truth of his words. (2) He emits light of an infinite variety of colors from every pore of his body, illuminating all the worlds in the ten directions. This means that the Buddha's wisdom penetrates everything. (3) He clears his throat, causing the sound to reach the worlds in the ten directions. This indicates that he reveals the truth completely. (4) He snaps his fingers, causing the sound to reach the worlds in the ten directions. This indicates that he rejoices. (5) All the lands in the ten directions tremble in six different ways. (a) This represents the elimination of illusions about the true nature of existence through six levels of practice. Earlier in the same work T'ien-t'ai defined these six levels in terms of the fifty-two stages of bodhisattva practice: the first four levels comprise the ten stages of security, the ten stages of practice, the ten stages of devotion, and the ten stages of development, respectively; the fifth level corresponds to the stage of near-perfect enlightenment, and the sixth level to the stage of perfect enlightenment. (b) "Tremble in six different ways" also represents the purification of the six sense organs. (6) All beings in the worlds of the ten directions behold the Ceremony in the Air and rejoice. This indicates that all Buddhas preach in the same way. (7) Heavenly gods proclaim with loud voices to the beings in these worlds that the Buddha is now expounding a great vehicle sutra called the Lotus Sutra of the Wonderful Law, and that they should therefore rejoice and make offerings to him. This indicates that in the future only this sutra will spread widely. (8) On hearing this proclamation, all the beings in the worlds of the ten directions convert to the Buddha's teaching and become his disciples. This indicates that in the future only those who embrace this sutra will fill the land. (9) The beings scatter offerings of various treasures over the *sahā* world, and these gather together like a cloud and form a jeweled curtain over the Buddhas assembled there. This means that in the future only this sutra will be practiced. (10) Passage between all worlds in the ten directions becomes unobstructed, as though they were one Buddha land. This means that in the future, through the practice of this teaching, all people will open and reveal their innate Buddha wisdom and only the truth will prevail throughout the world.

The Annotations on "The Words and Phrases of the Lotus Sutra" says that the first five of the ten supernatural powers were displayed for the benefit of people in Shakyamuni's time, and the latter five, for the sake of those who would come after his death. In his 1273 work *The Object of Devotion for Observing the Mind,* however, Nichiren interprets all ten as being displayed for the benefit of those who would appear in the future, because the "Supernatural Powers" chapter introduces the transfer of the essence of the Lotus Sutra to be propagated in the Latter Day of the Law.

ten unlawful revisions [十事の非法] (Jpn *jūji-no-hihō*): Also, ten unlawful things. Ten modifications of the rules of monastic discipline practiced by a group of monks in Vaishālī, India, about one hundred years after Shakyamuni Buddha's death. An assembly, headed by Yasa, was convened in Vaishālī to discuss whether those modifications were deviations from the established rules of discipline, with the majority ruling that they were unlawful. This assembly is known as the Second Buddhist Council. Division over the matter resulted in a schism in the Buddhist Order, with the monks of Vaishālī, who had adopted these less rigid rules, forming the Mahāsamghika school, and the majority of the assembly, who had declared them unlawful, forming the Sthaviravāda (Pali Theravāda) school. While the list of these ten practices differs among Buddhist traditions, one describes the ten as stating that monks should be allowed (1) to store salt; (2) to eat after the noon hour; (3) even after having eaten in a village, to take a second meal in another village; (4) to hold the meeting for self-examination and confession of faults and errors at locations other than those prescribed; (5) to conduct a ceremony even if the prescribed number of attendants is not reached; (6) to follow a precedent set by their teacher, even if that precedent departs from monastic rules; (7) to drink a dairy beverage after a meal; (8) to drink unfermented palm juice; (9) to use bedding and mats other than those of the prescribed size; and (10) to accept monetary alms, as well as gifts of gold and silver, and store them.

Ten Worlds [十界] (Jpn *jikkai*): Ten distinct realms or categories of beings referred to in Buddhist scriptures. From the lowest to the highest, the realms of (1) hell, (2) hungry spirits, (3) animals, (4) *asuras,* (5) human beings, (6) heavenly beings, (7) voice-hearers, (8) cause-awakened ones, (9) bodhisattvas, and (10) Buddhas. The Ten Worlds were viewed originally as distinct physical locations, each with its own particular inhabitants. The Lotus Sutra, however, teaches that each of the Ten Worlds contains all ten within it, making it possible to interpret them as potential states of life inherent in each individual being. In other words, from the standpoint of the Lotus Sutra, the Ten Worlds indicates ten potential states or conditions that a person can manifest or experience. The mutual possession of the Ten Worlds is a component principle of three thousand realms in a single moment of life, which T'ien-t'ai (538–597) set forth in *Great Concentration and Insight.*

The Ten Worlds may be described as follows: (1) The world of hell. Nichiren's 1273 treatise *The Object of Devotion for Observing the Mind* states, "Rage is the world of hell" (358). Hell indicates a condition in which living itself is misery and suffering, and in which, devoid of all freedom, one's anger and rage become a source of further self-destruction. (2) The world of hungry spirits. Also called the world of hunger. A condition governed by endless desire for such things as food, profit, pleasure, power, recognition, or fame, in which one is never truly satisfied. The above work reads, "Greed is the world of hungry spirits" (358). (3) The world of animals. Also called the world of animality. It is a condition driven by instinct and lacking in reason, morality, or wisdom with which to control oneself. In this condition, one is ruled by the "law of the jungle," standing in fear of the strong, but despising and preying upon those weaker than oneself. The same work states, "Foolishness is the world of animals" (358). The worlds of hell, hungry spirits, and animals are collectively known as the three evil paths. (4) The world of *asuras.* Also called the world of animosity or the world of anger. In Indian mythology, *asuras* are arrogant and belligerent demons. This condition is called the world of animosity because it is characterized by persistent, though not necessarily overt, aggressiveness. *The Object of Devotion for Observing the Mind* states, "Perversity is the world of *asuras*" (358). It is a condition dominated by ego, in which excessive pride prevents one from revealing one's true self or seeing others as they really are. Compelled by the need to be superior to others or surpass them at any cost, one may feign politeness and even flatter others while inwardly despising them. The worlds of hell, hungry spirits, animals, and *asuras* are collectively called the four evil paths. (5) The world of human beings. Also called the world of humanity. The same work reads, "Calmness is the world of human beings" (358). In this state, one tries to control one's desires and impulses with reason and act in harmony with one's surroundings and other people, while also aspiring for a higher state of life. (6) The world of heavenly beings. Also called the world of heaven. The same work states, "Joy is the world of heaven" (358). This is a condition of contentment and joy that one feels when released from suffering or upon satisfaction of some desire. It is a temporary joy that is dependent upon and may easily change with circumstances. The six worlds from hell through the world of heavenly beings are called the six paths. Beings in the six paths, or those who tend toward these states of life, are largely controlled by the restrictions of their surroundings and are therefore extremely vulnerable to changing circumstances.

The remaining states, in which one transcends the uncertainty of the six paths, are called the four noble worlds: (7) The world of voice-hearers, a condition in which one awakens to the impermanence of all things and the instability of the six paths. Also called the world of learning. In this state, one dedicates oneself to creating a better life through self-reformation and self-development by learning from the ideas, knowledge, and experience of one's predecessors and contemporaries. "Voice-hearers" (Skt *shrāvaka*) originally meant those who listen to the Buddha preach the four noble truths and practice the eightfold path in order to acquire emancipation from earthly desires. (8) The world of cause-awakened ones, a condition in which one perceives the impermanence of all phenomena and strives to free oneself from the sufferings of the six paths by seeing some lasting truth through one's own observations and effort. Also called the world of realization. "Cause-awakened ones," also known as "self-awakened ones" *(pratyekabuddha)*, originally meant those who attain a form of emancipation by perceiving the twelve-linked chain of causation or by observing natural phenomena. Persons in the worlds of voice-hearers and cause-awakened ones, which are together called persons of the two vehicles, are given more to the pursuit of self-perfection than to altruism. They are also willing to look squarely at the reality of death and seek the eternal, in contrast to those in the world of heaven, who are distracted from life's harsh realities. (9) The world of bodhisattvas, a state of compassion in which one thinks of and works for others' happiness even before becoming happy oneself. Bodhisattva, which consists of *bodhi* (enlightenment) and *sattva* (beings), means a person who seeks enlightenment while leading others to enlightenment.

Bodhisattvas find that the way to self-perfection lies only in altruism, working for the enlightenment of others even before their own enlightenment. Nichiren states in *The Object of Devotion for Observing the Mind:* "Even a heartless villain loves his wife and children. He too has a portion of the bodhisattva world within him" (358). (10) The world of Buddhas, or Buddhahood. This is a state of perfect and absolute freedom in which one realizes the true aspect of all phenomena or the true nature of life. One can achieve this state by manifesting the Buddha nature inherent in one's life. From the standpoint of the philosophy of the mutual possession of the Ten Worlds, Buddhahood should not be viewed as a state removed from the sufferings and imperfections of ordinary persons. Attaining Buddhahood does not mean becoming a special being. In this state, one still continues to work against and defeat the negative functions of life and transform any and all difficulty into causes for further development. It is a state of complete access to the boundless wisdom, compassion, courage, and other qualities inherent in life; with these one can create harmony with and among others and between human life and nature. In the above work, Nichiren states, "Buddhahood is the most difficult to demonstrate" (358), but he also says, "That ordinary people born in the latter age can believe in the Lotus Sutra is due to the fact that the world of Buddhahood is present in the human world" (358).

theoretical teaching [迹門] (Jpn *shakumon*): Also, trace teaching. The first half of the twenty-eight-chapter Lotus Sutra, from the "Introduction" (first) chapter through the "Peaceful Practices" (fourteenth) chapter. In *The Words and Phrases of the Lotus Sutra,* T'ien-t'ai (538–597) classifies the Lotus Sutra into two parts: the first fourteen chapters, or the theoretical teaching, and the latter fourteen chapters, or the essential teaching. The theoretical teaching takes the form of preaching by a "provisional Buddha," the historical Shakyamuni Buddha depicted as having first attained enlightenment during his lifetime in India. The essential teaching takes the form of preaching by the Buddha who has discarded this provisional status and revealed his true identity as the Buddha who attained enlightenment in the unimaginably remote past. T'ien-t'ai compared the relationship between the Buddha in his true identity and his provisional manifestation, or between their respective teachings, to that of the moon in the sky and its reflection on the surface of a pond.

The core of the theoretical teaching is the "Expedient Means" (second) chapter, which reveals the true aspect of all phenomena and that the ten factors endow all life. The "Expedient Means" chapter also states that the Buddha's sole purpose is to lead all people to Buddhahood, and that the three vehicles of voice-hearers, cause-awakened ones, and bodhisattvas are no more than expedient means to lead people to the one Buddha vehicle. Though the attainment of Buddhahood by voice-hearers and cause-awakened ones was deemed impossible in the earlier teachings, the theoretical teaching of the Lotus Sutra states that they will attain Buddhahood in the future. Also in this part of the sutra, at the urging of the Buddha, countless bodhisattvas vow to propagate the Lotus Sutra after Shakyamuni Buddha's death. They make this vow in the presence of Many Treasures Buddha and all the other Buddhas assembled from throughout the universe. *See also* essential teaching.

Theravāda school [上座部] (Pali; Skt Sthaviravāda; Jpn Jōza-bu): "Teaching of the Elders." One of the two schools formed by the first schism in the Buddhist Order that took place about one hundred years after Shakyamuni's death in India. The other is the Mahāsamghika school. According to *The Great Commentary on the Abhidharma*, a dispute arose within the Buddhist Order over a five-point modification of doctrine advanced by a monk called Mahādeva. As a result, the Order split into the Theravāda school, which rejected the new interpretations, and the Mahāsamghika school, which accepted them. (Another account, however, attributes the schism to controversy over a more flexible interpretation of the precepts advocated by the monks of the Vriji tribe in Vaishālī.) Of the two schools, the Theravāda school claimed a greater percentage of the elder monks and was more conservative, emphasizing strict adherence to the established precepts and a literal interpretation of doctrine. According to *The Doctrines of the Different Schools*, the Sarvāstivāda school, which developed the *abhidharma*, or exegetical commentary section of the canon, later broke away from Theravāda; under pressure from the Sarvāstivādins, the Theravāda school moved to the Himalayan region where it was thereafter called the Haimavata (Himalaya) school. The Haimavata school later declined.

The Theravāda teaching was also introduced to Sri Lanka by King Ashoka's son Mahendra, where it developed and eventually spread to other parts of South and Southeast Asia. What is called Theravāda, or Southern, Buddhism, can be traced to these teachings introduced to Sri Lanka. *See also* five teachings of Mahādeva; ten unlawful revisions.

third doctrine [第三の法門] (Jpn *daisan-no-hōmon*): The doctrine revealed by the third part of the threefold comparison known as the threefold secret teaching, i.e., the comparison of the "surface" (text) and the "depths" (implicit principle) of the "Life Span" (sixteenth) chapter of the Lotus Sutra. It is Nam-myoho-renge-kyo. In his writing *The Third Doctrine*, Nichiren states: "Nichiren's teaching represents the third doctrine. Though the first and second doctrines have been spoken of in the world rather vaguely, like a dream, the third has never been spoken of at all. Though T'ien-t'ai and Dengyō explained it to some extent, they did not clarify it fully. In the end, they left it for now, the Latter Day of the Law" (855).

In explaining this, Nichikan (1665–1726), the twenty-sixth chief priest of Taiseki-ji temple, cites the three standards of comparison of T'ien-t'ai from his *Profound Meaning of the Lotus Sutra:*

The first standard is whether people of all capacities can attain Buddhahood through a particular sutra. The sutras other than the Lotus Sutra do not reveal that all people have the potential for enlightenment, because, according to the sutras, people's individual capacities are fixed. In contrast, the Lotus Sutra clarifies that all people are capable of attaining enlightenment because all of the Ten Worlds, including Buddhahood, are mutually inclusive and inherent in their lives. This is explained in the "Expedient Means" (second) and "Simile and Parable" (third) chapters of the theoretical teaching (first half) of the Lotus Sutra.

The second standard is whether the process of teaching, i.e., the process of planting the seed of Buddhahood in people's lives and finally harvesting its fruit by leading them to Buddhahood, is revealed in full. In contrast to the Lotus Sutra, which makes clear when Shakyamuni's instruction of the people began and ended, other sutras do not reveal this. This is explained in the "Parable of the Phantom City" (seventh) chapter in the theoretical teaching of the Lotus Sutra.

The above two standards show the superiority of the Lotus Sutra over the other sutras.

The third standard is whether the original relationship between teacher and disciple is revealed. "Teacher" refers to the Buddha. The "Life Span" chapter of the essential teaching (latter half) of the Lotus Sutra reveals that Shakyamuni originally attained enlightenment numberless major world system dust particle *kalpas* in the past, and that ever since then he has been teaching his disciples. The other sutras say that Shakyamuni attained enlightenment in this life in India, and that his disciples first became his followers in this life.

This third standard is used to demonstrate the superiority of the essential teaching of the Lotus Sutra over the theoretical teaching.

T'ien-t'ai's first and second standards, Nichikan says, correspond to the first part of the threefold secret teaching, or the theoretical teaching of the Lotus Sutra. T'ien-t'ai's third standard corresponds to the second part of the threefold secret teaching, or the essential teaching of the sutra. When compared with the threefold secret teaching, T'ien-t'ai's three standards of comparison fall into two categories. Thus Nichikan concludes that the third part of the threefold secret teaching; Nam-myoho-renge-kyo hidden in the depths of the "Life Span" chapter, is the third teaching, or third doctrine.

third group of the listeners of Great Universal Wisdom Excellence Buddha's teaching [大通結縁の第三類] (Jpn *Daitsū-kechien-no-daisan-rui*): The third of three categories of persons who heard the Lotus Sutra of Great Universal Wisdom Excellence Buddha from Shakyamuni when he was the sixteenth son of that Buddha in the remote past. They are described in the "Parable of the Phantom City" (seventh) chapter of the Lotus Sutra. The three categories are (1) those who took faith, embraced the sutra without faltering, and attained Buddhahood; (2) those who at first took faith in the sutra, but later abandoned it and accepted lower Buddhist teachings; and (3) those who heard the sutra, but did not take faith in it. *See also* "Parable of the Phantom City" chapter.

thirteen major prohibitions [十三僧残] (Jpn *jūsan-sōzan*): The second of the eight groups of precepts that constitute the two hundred and fifty precepts for fully ordained monks of the Hinayana teaching. This second group is called in Sanskrit *samghāvashesha* (temporary expulsion from the Buddhist Order). The first group consists of the four unpardonable offenses of killing, theft, having sexual relations, and lying, particularly claiming to have attained insight or understanding that one does not in fact possess. The thirteen major prohibitions are second to the first group in the gravity of the offenses they prohibit, and monks who violate one or another of these prohibitions are divested of membership in the Buddhist Order for a certain period. They are relieved from this punishment by repenting of their offense and confessing it before the other monks.

The thirteen major prohibitions are (1) ejaculating; (2) touching a woman's body; (3) indecent talk with a woman; (4) pretending to be a monk of virtue in order to seduce a woman; (5) matchmaking or acting as an intermediary of adultery; (6) constructing a large dwelling without receiving approval from the Order concerning the size of the dwelling and the site of construction; (7) constructing a dwelling with funds donated by one's patron without receiving approval from the Order concerning the site of construction; (8) groundlessly condemning another monk for having committed one of the four unpardonable offenses; (9) doing the same by skillful use of analogy; (10) attempting to cause disunity in the Order after being warned about it three times by other monks; (11) assisting a disrupter of the Order after being warned about it three times by other monks; (12) complaining about the Order and other monks when ordered by them to leave a particular region because of one's evil deeds; and (13) rejecting other monks' admonitions out of arrogance. The content of the thirteen major prohibitions differs according to the source.

thirteen schools of China [中国十三宗] (Jpn *Chūgoku-jūsan-shū*): The major Buddhist schools that are said to have flourished in China. This enumeration is found in *A History of the Transmission and Propagation of Buddhism in Three Countries* written in 1311 by Gyōnen, a priest of the Japanese Flower Garland (Kegon) school. The "three countries" are India, China, and Japan. In this work, Gyōnen mentions thirteen schools that existed in China from the fifth through the ninth century. The thirteen schools are the Abhidharma (Chin P'i-t'an), Establishment of Truth (Ch'eng-shih), Precepts (Lü), Three Treatises (San-lun), Nirvana (Nieh-p'an), Treatise on the Ten Stages Sutra (Ti-lun), Pure Land (Ching-t'u), Zen (Ch'an), Summary of the Mahayana (She-lun), T'ien-t'ai, Flower Garland (Hua-yen), Dharma Characteristics (Fa-hsiang), and True Word (Chen-yen) schools.

thirty-four forms [三十四身] (Jpn *sanjūshi-shin*): Forms assumed by Bodhisattva Wonderful Sound to save living beings. According to the "Wonderful Sound" (twenty-fourth) chapter of the Lotus Sutra, Bodhisattva Wonderful Sound appears in various forms to instruct and convert living beings. The chapter lists thirty-four forms: King Brahmā, the god Shakra, the heavenly being Freedom, the heavenly being Great Freedom, a great general of heaven, the god Vaishravana, a wheel-turning king, a petty king, a rich man, a householder, a chief minister, a Brahman, a monk, a nun, a layman, a laywoman, the wife of a rich man, the wife of a householder, the wife of a chief minister, the wife of a Brahman, a young boy, a young girl, a heavenly being, a dragon, a *yaksha*, a *gandharva*, an *asura*, a *garuda*, a *kimnara*, a *mahoraga*, a hell dweller, a hungry spirit, a beast, and a woman in the women's quarters of the royal palace.

thirty-seven aids to the way [三十七道品] (Jpn *sanjūshichi-dōhon*): Also, thirty-seven aids to enlightenment or thirty-seven elements of the way. Thirty-seven practices conducive to enlightenment. (The "way" here is synonymous with enlightenment or perfect wisdom.) They are grouped into seven categories: four meditations (meditations on body, sensation, mind, and phenomena), four right efforts (to put an end to existing evil, prevent evil from arising, bring good into existence, and encourage existing good), four steps to attaining transcendental powers (zeal, exertion, memory, and meditative insight), five roots (faith, exertion, memory, meditation, and wisdom), five powers (powers of faith, exertion, memory, meditation, and wisdom), seven aids to enlightenment (memory, discrimination, exertion, joy, lightness and ease, meditation, and impartiality), and eightfold path (right views, right thinking, right speech, right action, right way of life, right endeavor, right mindfulness, and right meditation). Each of these seven categories of practice appears separately in early Buddhist scriptures, and they are thought to have been brought together later to form the thirty-seven aids to the way.

Thirty-Stanza Treatise on the Consciousness-Only Doctrine, The [唯識三十論頌] (Skt *Trimshikā-vijnaptimātratā-siddhi;* Chin *Wei-shih-san-shih-lun-sung;* Jpn *Yuishiki-sanjū-ron-ju*): A short work by Vasubandhu (thought to have lived in the fourth or fifth century) setting forth the essentials of the Consciousness-Only doctrine and translated into Chinese in the mid-seventh century by Hsüan-tsang. It is thought to be the last of Vasubandhu's writings and is one of the principal texts of the Dharma Characteristics (Chin Fa-hsiang; Jpn Hossō) school. Dharmapāla and nine other scholars of the Consciousness-Only school wrote commentaries on this work, which were later compiled as *The Treatise on the Establishment of the Consciousness-Only Doctrine.*

thirty-three forms [三十三身] (Jpn *sanjūsan-shin*): Different forms that Bodhisattva Perceiver of the World's Sounds assumes in order to save living beings. Bodhisattva Perceiver of the World's Sounds appears in these various forms in accordance with the capacity of living beings, for the purpose of instructing and converting them. His thirty-three forms are described in the "Perceiver of the World's Sounds" (twenty-fifth) chapter of the Lotus Sutra, which lists them as a Buddha, a *pratyekabuddha,* a voice-hearer, King Brahmā, the god Shakra, the heavenly being Freedom, the heavenly being Great Freedom, a great general of heaven, the god Vaishravana, a petty king, a rich man, a householder, a chief minister, a Brahman, a monk, a nun, a layman, a laywoman, the wife of a rich man, the wife of a householder, the wife of a chief minister, the wife of a Brahman, a young boy, a young girl, a heavenly being, a dragon, a *yaksha,* a *gandharva,* an *asura,* a *garuda,* a *kimnara,* a *mahoraga,* and a *vajra*-bearing god.

thirty-three gods [三十三天] (Jpn *sanjūsan-ten*): Also, thirty-three heavenly gods. The gods said to live on a plateau at the top of Mount Sumeru. Shakra rules from his palace in the center, and the other thirty-two gods live on four peaks, eight gods to a peak, at each of the plateau's four corners. The abode of these thirty-three gods is the heaven called Trāyastrimsha in Sanskrit (Jpn Tōri-ten), rendered as the Heaven of the Thirty-three Gods in China. The beings in this heaven are said to live one thousand years, though each day of life in that heaven is equal to a hundred years in the human world. Their life span in human terms is therefore one hundred thousand years.

thirty-two features [三十二相] (Jpn *sanjūni-sō*): Remarkable physical characteristics attributed to Buddhas, bodhisattvas, Brahmā, Shakra, and wheel-turning kings, symbolizing their superiority over ordinary people. They are (1) flat soles, (2) markings of a thousand-spoked wheel on the soles, (3) long, slender fingers, (4) broad, flat heels, (5) webbed feet and hands, (6) extremely flexible limbs, (7) protuberant insteps, (8) slender legs like those of a deer, (9) hands that extend past the knees even in a standing position, (10) concealed genitals, (11) body height equal to arm span, (12) body hair that turns upward, (13) one hair growing from each pore, (14) golden skin, (15) light radiating from the body, (16) thin pliant skin, (17) well-developed muscles of the hands, feet, shoulders, and nape of neck, (18) well-developed muscles below the armpits, (19) a dignified torso like that of a lion, (20) a large and straight body, (21) substantial shoulders, (22) forty teeth, (23) even teeth, (24) four white fangs, (25) full cheeks like those of a lion, (26) an unexcelled sense of taste, (27) a long broad tongue, (28) a pure and far-reaching voice, (29) eyes the color of blue lotus blossoms, (30) long eyelashes like those of a cow, (31) a knot of flesh on the head like a topknot, and (32) a tuft of white hair between the eyebrows, curling to the right. The descriptions and order of these features differ slightly among the Buddhist scriptures. According to *The Treatise on the Great Perfection of Wisdom,* they are acquired one by one as a result of good causes made over a total of three *asamkhya kalpas* and one hundred major *kalpas. Great Perfection of Wisdom* also says that in the case of a wheel-turning king these marks are somewhat vague and unstable, while in the case of a Buddha they are obvious and stable. The Buddha is often referred to as possessing the "thirty-two features and eighty characteristics," the eighty characteristics being another set of remarkable qualities possessed by Buddhas and bodhisattvas.

thirty-two features and eighty characteristics [三十二相八十種好] (Jpn *sanjūni-sō-hachijisshugō*): Extraordinary features attributed to Buddhas and bodhisattvas. In most cases, the term "thirty-two features and eighty characteristics" refers to the distinguishing qualities of a Buddha. *See also* eighty characteristics; thirty-two features.

"This is what I heard" [如是我聞] (Skt *evam mayā shrutam;* Jpn *nyoze-gamon*): Also, "Thus have I heard." A phrase that begins many sutras. The sutras are records of Shakyamuni Buddha's teachings that were committed first to memory and passed down orally, and later put into writing. This phrase represents a testimony to the validity and accuracy of what was about to be set down in writing in the form of a sutra. According to tradition, this practice began with the Buddha's disciple Ānanda. In the first compilation of Shakyamuni Buddha's teachings, Ānanda uttered the words "This is what I heard," and then began to recite from memory what he had heard the Buddha preach. Ānanda accompanied Shakyamuni as his personal attendant for many years, hearing and memorizing more of the Buddha's teachings than any other disciple.

Thousand-armed Perceiver of the World's Sounds [千手観音] (Skt Sahasrabhuja; Jpn Senju-kannon): Also, Thousand-armed and Thousand-eyed Perceiver of the World's Sounds. One of the many forms in which Bodhisattva Perceiver of the World's Sounds is depicted in painting and sculpture. In this form he is described as having a thousand arms, each of which has a hand with one eye in the center of the palm. This form of Perceiver of the World's Sounds is usually depicted in images with only forty arms representing the thousand, although some images with a full thousand have been crafted. Thousand-armed Perceiver of the World's Sounds was believed to possess great compassion and the power to prolong life, eradicate evil karma, and cure illness.

thousand-millionfold world [三千大千世界] (Jpn *sanzen-daisen-sekai*): Also, major world system. One of the world systems described in ancient Indian cosmology. *See* major world system.

thousand-spoked wheel [千輻輪相] (Jpn *sempukurin-sō*): Also, thousand-spoked wheel or the markings of the thousand-spoked wheel. One of the thirty-two features that a Buddha is said to possess, appearing on the sole of each foot. According to one account, markings of a thousand-spoked wheel on the sole of each foot represent a Buddha's untiring efforts to turn the wheel of the Law, i.e., to expound his teaching, traveling far and wide on foot to remove people's afflictions. According to several Buddhist scriptures, the markings appear on a Buddha's palms as well as on his feet.

three asamkhya kalpas and a hundred major kalpas [三祇百大劫] (Jpn *sangi-hyakudai-kō*): The period necessary for a bodhisattva to become a Buddha according to the Hinayana *abhidharma* works (doctrinal treatises and commentaries). For three *asamkhya kalpas,* a bodhisattva practices the six *pāramitās.* He serves seventy-five thousand Buddhas for one *asamkhya kalpa,* seventy-six thousand Buddhas for another *asamkhya kalpa,* and seventy-seven thousand Buddhas for a third *asamkhya kalpa.* The Sanskrit word *asamkhya* means innumerable, or according to one account, it represents 10^{59}. After completing the six *pāramitās* for three *asamkhya kalpas,* he still continues to practice for a hundred major *kalpas* in order to obtain the thirty-two features of a Buddha. The period required for a bodhisattva to become a Buddha is variously described as "three *asamkhya kalpas* and a hundred major *kalpas*," "three *asamkhya kalpas*," "three great *asamkhya kalpas*," and "three *asamkhya kalpas* and a hundred *kalpas*."

three ascetics [三仙] (Jpn *san-sen*): Kapila, Ulūka, and Rishabha. Kapila was the founder of the Sāmkhya school, one of the six schools of Vedic philosophy in ancient India. Ulūka, also known as Kanāda, founded the Vaisheshika school, another of the six Vedic schools. Rishabha is said to have maintained the importance of asceticism, and his teachings to have prepared the way for Jainism.

three assemblies in two places [二処三会] (Jpn *nisho-sanne*): The settings in which Shakyamuni preached the Lotus Sutra. *See* two places and three assemblies.

three benefits [三益] (Jpn *san-yaku*): The benefits of sowing, maturing, and harvesting. Sowing, maturing, and harvesting are the three phases of the process by which a Buddha leads people to Buddhahood. These three actions correspond to the growth and development of a plant. First the Buddha plants the seed of Buddhahood in people's lives, then he nurtures it by helping them practice the teaching, and finally he enables them to reap the fruit of Buddhahood.

three bodies [三身] (Skt *trikāya;* Jpn *san-jin*): Three kinds of body a Buddha may possess. A concept set forth in Mahayana Buddhism to organize different views of the Buddha appearing in the sutras. The three bodies are as follows: (1) The Dharma body, or body of the Law (Skt *dharma-kāya*). This is the fundamental truth, or Law, to which a Buddha is enlightened. (2) The reward body *(sambhoga-kāya),* obtained as the reward of completing bodhisattva practices and acquiring the Buddha wisdom. Unlike the Dharma body, which is immaterial, the reward body is thought of as an actual body, although one that is transcendent and imperceptible to ordinary people. (3) The manifested body *(nirmāna-kāya),* or the physical form that a Buddha assumes in this world in order to save the people. Generally, a Buddha was held to possess one of the three bodies. In other words, the three bodies represented three different types of Buddhas—the Buddha of the Dharma body, the Buddha of the reward body, and the Buddha of the manifested body.

On the basis of the Lotus Sutra and the principle of three thousand realms in a single moment of life derived from it, T'ien-t'ai (538–597) maintained that the three bodies are not separate entities but three integral aspects of a single Buddha. From this point of view, the Dharma body indicates the essential property of a Buddha, which is the truth or

Law to which the Buddha is enlightened. The reward body indicates the wisdom, or the spiritual property of a Buddha, which enables the Buddha to perceive the truth. It is called reward body because a Buddha's wisdom is considered the reward derived from ceaseless effort and discipline. The manifested body indicates compassionate actions, or the physical property of a Buddha. It is the body with which a Buddha carries out compassionate actions to lead people to enlightenment, or those actions themselves. In discussing the passage in the "Life Span" (sixteenth) chapter of the Lotus Sutra that reads, "You must listen carefully and hear of the Thus Come One's secret and his transcendental powers," T'ien-t'ai, in *The Words and Phrases of the Lotus Sutra,* interpreted "secret" to mean that a single Buddha possesses all three bodies and that all three bodies are found within a single Buddha.

three calamities [三災] (Jpn *san-sai*): Disasters said to occur at the end of a *kalpa.* There are two sets of three calamities, lesser and greater. (1) The three lesser calamities are warfare, pestilence, and famine. The calamity of famine is also called the calamity of high grain prices or inflation, because inflation was caused by a shortage of grain. These calamities are said to occur at the end of each *kalpa* of decrease in the *kalpa* of continuance. According to one explanation, all three occur at the end of each *kalpa* of decrease; first, war rages for seven days, then epidemics prevail for seven months, and finally famine lasts for seven years. According to another, they occur alternately, pestilence at the end of the first *kalpa* of decrease, war at the end of the second, famine at the end of the third, and so on, each calamity lasting for seven days. In a 1279 letter titled *King Rinda,* Nichiren described the cause of the three lesser calamities as the three poisons of greed, anger, and foolishness, the fundamental evils inherent in life, stating that greed brings about famine, anger incites war, and foolishness leads to pestilence.

(2) The three greater calamities are fire, water, and wind. These are said to occur at the end of the *kalpa* of decline following the *kalpa* of continuance and to destroy the world. In the calamity of fire, seven suns appear at the same time and burn up the world. The flames reach from the hell of incessant suffering to the first meditation heaven in the world of form. In the calamity of water, flood sweeps away everything from the hell of incessant suffering up through the second meditation heaven. In the calamity of wind, a great storm demolishes everything from the hell of incessant suffering up through the third meditation heaven.

three calamities and seven disasters [三災七難] (Jpn *sansai-shichinan*): Catastrophes described in various sutras. The three calamities occur at the end of a *kalpa.* There are two types: the three greater calamities of fire, water, and wind, which destroy the world, and the three lesser calamities of high grain prices or inflation (especially that caused by famine), warfare, and pestilence, from which human society perishes. The seven disasters include war and natural disasters and are generally held to result from slander of the correct teaching. They are mentioned in the Medicine Master, Benevolent Kings, and other sutras. They differ slightly according to the source. Nichiren combined these two different types of calamities in a single phrase to explain the disasters besetting Japan in his time. In his 1260 treatise *On Establishing the Correct Teaching for the Peace of the Land,* he states, based on the sutras, that they occur because both the rulers and the populace turn against the correct teaching. *See also* seven disasters; three calamities.

three cardinal sins [三逆・三逆罪] (Jpn *san-gyaku* or *san-gyakuzai*): Three grave offenses committed by Devadatta. Constituting three of the five cardinal sins, or the five most serious offenses in Buddhism, they are (1) killing an arhat, (2) injuring the Buddha, and (3) causing disunity in the Buddhist Order. The other two of the five cardinal sins are killing one's father and killing one's mother. *See also* Devadatta.

three categories of action [三業] (Jpn *san-gō*): Also, three types of action. Activities carried out with one's body, mouth, and mind, i.e., deeds, words, and thoughts. Buddhism holds that karma, good or evil, is created by these three types of action—mental, verbal, and physical. Here "action" is the translation of the Sanskrit *karman.*

three categories of illusion [三惑] (Jpn *san-waku*): Also, three illusions. A classification of illusions, established by T'ien-t'ai (538–597): (1) illusions of thought and desire, (2) illusions innumerable as particles of dust and sand, and (3) illusions about the true nature of existence. The illusions of thought and desire are illusions to be eradicated by persons of the two vehicles (voice-hearers and cause-awakened ones) and bodhisattvas. The other two categories of illusions are those that bodhisattvas alone go on to eliminate.

Illusions of thought and desire cause people to suffer in the six paths and the threefold world. Illusions of thought are distorted perceptions of the truth and are primarily mental and learned. They consist of the five false views and the five delusive inclinations. The five false views are as follows: (1) Though the body is nothing but a temporary union of the five components, one mistakenly thinks of the self as a separate or independent entity, and though nothing in the universe can belong to an individual, one mistakenly views that which surrounds one as one's own possession. (2) One erroneously believes either that life is totally annihilated at death without continuance in any form, or that life persists after death in some eternally unchanged form such as a soul. (3) One does not recognize the law of cause and effect. (4) One adheres to misconceptions such as regarding inferior things as superior. (5) One views erroneous precepts or practices as the true way to enlightenment. The five delusive inclinations are greed, anger, foolishness, arrogance, and doubt; they arise in relation to the five false views. Hence in the category of illusions of thought, the five false views are regarded as primary and the five delusive inclinations as secondary. In contrast to the chiefly mental illusions of thought, the illusions of desire are emotional and inborn. These include greed, anger, foolishness, and arrogance and arise in connection with the various affairs and phenomena of the threefold world, not because of distorted perceptions of the truth.

Illusions innumerable as particles of dust and sand are illusions that prevent bodhisattvas from saving others. To save others, bodhisattvas must be well versed in innumerable teachings, both religious and secular. This second category of illusions arises when the bodhisattvas try to master these teachings.

Illusions about the true nature of existence are illusions that prevent bodhisattvas from attaining enlightenment, or from awakening to the truth of the Middle Way. In the specific teaching, these illusions are divided into twelve. In the perfect teaching, they are divided into forty-two, the last and most deeply rooted of which is called fundamental darkness. By eliminating fundamental darkness, one attains Buddhahood. In *Great Concentration and Insight,* T'ien-t'ai states that the three categories of illusion are eliminated through meditation aimed at perceiving the unification of the three truths in a single mind. Specifically, the illusions of thought and desire are eliminated by perception of the truth of non-substantiality; illusions innumerable as particles of dust and sand are eliminated by perception of the truth of temporary existence; and illusions about the true nature of existence are eliminated by perception of the truth of the Middle Way.

three categories of preaching [已今当・三説] (Jpn *i-kon-tō* or *san-setsu*): The sutras that Shakyamuni Buddha has preached, now preaches, and will preach. A reference to a passage from the "Teacher of the Law" (tenth) chapter of the Lotus Sutra, where Shakyamuni says, "The sutras I have preached number immeasurable thousands, ten thousands, millions. Among the sutras I have preached, now preach, and will preach, this Lotus Sutra is the most difficult to believe and the most difficult to understand." Regarding this passage, T'ien-t'ai (538–597) defines these three groups of sutras in *The Words and Phrases of the Lotus Sutra* as follows: "The sutras I have preached" refers to all sutras expounded before the

Lotus Sutra; "the sutra I now preach" refers to the Immeasurable Meanings Sutra, the prologue to the Lotus Sutra; and "the sutras I will preach" refers to the Nirvana Sutra. According to T'ien-t'ai, the earlier sutras (the first group of sutras in the above) are provisional teachings and expounded as expedient means to lead to the truth and therefore are easy to believe. The Immeasurable Meanings Sutra says that immeasurable meanings originate from the one Law, but does not refer to the other half of the principle—that immeasurable meanings return to the one Law. Therefore, T'ien-t'ai says, it is easy to believe. He goes on to assert that the Lotus Sutra reveals the one Law and unifies all meanings with it.

The Lotus Sutra also reveals the relationship between the Buddha and disciples in the remote past. Both the theoretical and the essential teachings (respectively the first half and the latter half) of the Lotus Sutra contradict all the earlier sutras and are therefore extremely difficult to believe and difficult to understand. The Nirvana Sutra is easy to believe because it was expounded after the Lotus Sutra; that is, the teachings it contains accord with those of the Lotus Sutra, which by this time are already known. Miao-lo (711–782) states in *The Annotations on "The Words and Phrases of the Lotus Sutra,"* "Though other sutras may call themselves the king among sutras, there is none that announces itself as foremost among all the sutras preached in the past, now being preached, or to be preached in the future." Dengyō (767–822) says in *The Outstanding Principles of the Lotus Sutra:* "All the sutras of the first four periods preached in the past, the Immeasurable Meanings Sutra now being preached, and the Nirvana Sutra to be preached in the future are easy to believe and easy to understand. This is because the Buddha taught these sutras in accordance with the capacity of his listeners. The Lotus Sutra is the most difficult to believe and to understand because in it the Buddha directly revealed what he had attained."

three circles [三輪] (Jpn *san-rin*): The windy circle, watery circle, and gold circle said to lie at the base of the Sumeru world and support it, according to the ancient Indian worldview. They are cylindrical in form and lie one upon another. The windy circle is located at the bottom and rests on space. Upon the windy circle is the watery circle, and upon the watery circle is the gold circle, on which the earth rests with its Mount Sumeru, seas, mountains, and four continents.

three comprehensive precepts [三聚浄戒] (Jpn *sanju-jō-kai*): Also, three comprehensive pure precepts or threefold pure precept. A set of precepts for Mahayana bodhisattvas, whether laity or clergy, expounded in the Brahmā Net Sutra and the Jeweled Necklace Sutra. The first two are for one's own benefit and the last for the benefit of others. They are

(1) the precept that encompasses all the rules and standards of behavior set forth by the Buddha for Mahayana bodhisattvas, i.e., to observe all those precepts and prevent evil; (2) the precept that encompasses all good deeds, i.e., to strive to perform good deeds; and (3) the precept that encompasses all living beings, i.e., to instruct and benefit all living beings. The third is also called the precept for benefiting sentient beings.

three cycles of preaching [三周の説法] (Jpn *sanshū-no-seppō*): Three cycles of preaching described in the Lotus Sutra, in which Shakyamuni Buddha's voice-hearer disciples grasp the doctrine of the "replacement of the three vehicles with the one vehicle." The doctrine reveals that the three vehicles—the teachings for voice-hearers, cause-awakened ones, and bodhisattvas—are not ends in themselves, as the Buddha had taught in sutras other than the Lotus, but expedient means by which he leads people to the one vehicle of Buddhahood. Each of the three cycles consists of Shakyamuni's preaching, his disciples' understanding what he has preached, and his bestowal of a prediction of future enlightenment upon his disciples. The three cycles of preaching occur in the eight chapters of the Lotus Sutra from "Expedient Means" (second) through "Prophecies" (ninth), and the three correspond respectively to three groups of disciples Shakyamuni teaches: those of superior, intermediate, and inferior capacity.

First, in the "Expedient Means" chapter, Shakyamuni preaches the doctrine of the true aspect of all phenomena and replaces the three vehicles with the one vehicle, i.e., that his disciples must abandon the three vehicles and accept the one vehicle. Shāriputra, who is of superior capacity, understands Shakyamuni's preaching, and his enlightenment is then predicted in the "Simile and Parable" (third) chapter.

Second, in the "Simile and Parable" chapter, Shakyamuni relates the parable of the three carts and the burning house for those who have failed to understand the principle. Maudgalyāyana, Mahākāshyapa, Kātyāyana, and Subhūti, who are of intermediate capacity, understand the Buddha's intention through this parable, and their enlightenment is predicted in the "Bestowal of Prophecy" (sixth) chapter.

Third, in the "Parable of the Phantom City" (seventh) chapter, Shakyamuni reveals the relationship between himself and his disciples since the remote past, in order to enlighten those who have failed to understand the meaning of the parable. Pūrna, Ānanda, Rāhula, and many others of inferior capacity, upon hearing about that relationship with Shakyamuni, understand the Buddha's intention and thereby awaken to the one Buddha vehicle. Their enlightenment is predicted in the "Five Hundred Disciples" (eighth) and "Prophecies" chapters.

three Dharma seals [三法印] (Jpn *sambōin*): Also, three seals of Dharma. Three identifying principles of Buddhism: impermanence, non-self, and nirvana. Suffering is added to the above three to form the four Dharma seals. Impermanence means that nothing is lasting or fixed—all is temporary and changing. Non-self means that all things and phenomena are without self-nature, that they have no independent existence of their own. Nirvana is the highest state of calm and serenity, in which one is released from suffering. Suffering means that all existence is suffering. Dharma seals signify a guarantee of the authenticity of doctrines. The three Dharma seals were used as standards to determine whether or not a sutra or a doctrine was valid; if it met these three standards, it was determined to be a valid Buddhist teaching. Chinese Mahayana Buddhism regarded the three or four Dharma seals as a Hinayana concept; it established instead the one Dharma seal, which was the principle of the ultimate reality, or the true aspect of all phenomena. The Dharma seal of the ultimate reality is based on the Lotus Sutra, which sets forth the true aspect of all phenomena.

three divisions of a sutra [三分科経] (Jpn *sambunka-kyō*): Preparation, revelation, and transmission. A three-part format used in interpreting sutras, thought to have been formulated by Tao-an (312–385) of China. Preparation indicates the introductory portion of a sutra in which its purpose is clarified. Revelation, the main portion, contains the sutra's central theme or teaching. Transmission is the concluding portion, which explains the benefit of the sutra and urges that the truth it contains be transmitted to the future.

three divisions of the canon [三蔵] (Skt *tripitaka;* Pali *tipitaka;* Jpn *sanzō*): Three sections or categories into which the Buddhist teachings are divided. They are the sutras, or the Buddha's doctrinal teachings; the *vinaya,* or rules of monastic discipline; and the *abhidharma,* or commentaries on the sutras and the *vinaya. Tri* of the Sanskrit *tripitaka* means three, and *pitaka,* literally a box or basket, indicates a canonical collection. After Shakyamuni Buddha's death, the Buddha's teachings were compiled at the First Buddhist Council, held under the supervision of Mahākāshyapa at the Cave of the Seven Leaves near Rājagriha in Magadha, India. It is said that at that time Ānanda recited the sutras and Upāli recited the *vinaya.* The *abhidharma* section was added later, when various schools began to produce commentaries.

three equalities [三平等] (Jpn *san-byōdō*): A concept set forth by Vasubandhu (fourth or fifth century) in *The Treatise on the Lotus Sutra.* The three equalities are the equality of the vehicle, the equality of the world and nirvana, and the equality of the body. When Vasubandhu explained "the great wisdom of equality" mentioned in the "Treasure Tower" (eleventh) chapter of the Lotus Sutra, he established these three viewpoints to show that the Lotus Sutra represents the Law of absolute equality. The equality of the vehicle means that the one supreme vehicle is given equally to all people, and that the three vehicles (the teachings for voice-hearers, cause-awakened ones, and bodhisattvas) are united by the Lotus Sutra into the one supreme vehicle. The equality of the world and nirvana indicates that there is no fundamental distinction between the world of delusion and nirvana, or enlightenment. The equality of the body, or the equality of the Buddha's body, means that, although the Buddha assumes various forms to save people, the state of Buddhahood equally pervades them all.

three evil paths [三悪道・三悪趣] (Jpn *san-akudō* or *san-akushu*): Also, three evil paths of existence. The realms of hell, hungry spirits, and animals, the lowest three of the six paths. The three evil paths are the realms of suffering into which one falls as a result of evil deeds. "Path" here means state or realm of existence. *See also* six paths; Ten Worlds.

three exhortations and four entreaties [三誡四請] (Jpn *sankai-shishō*): A ritual that takes place at the beginning of the "Life Span" (sixteenth) chapter of the Lotus Sutra before Shakyamuni Buddha reveals his original enlightenment in the remote past. Three times the Buddha exhorts the assembly: "You must believe and understand the truthful words of the Thus Come One," and the assembly, led by Bodhisattva Maitreya, each time replies: "World-Honored One, we beg you to explain. We will believe and accept the Buddha's words." In the style of the sutras, three rounds of exhortation and entreaty in this fashion indicate that an important teaching is about to be revealed. The assembly then entreats the Buddha to preach yet a fourth time. This extraordinary exchange highlights the importance of the teaching to be revealed. These exchanges constitute the three exhortations and four entreaties. Shakyamuni then says, "You must listen carefully and hear of the Thus Come One's secret and his transcendental powers," and proceeds to reveal his original attainment of enlightenment numberless major world system dust particle *kalpas* in the past.

three existences [三世] (Jpn *san-ze*): Past existence, present existence, and future existence. Used to indicate all of time, from the eternal past, through the present, through the eternal future. In Buddhism, they are the three aspects of the eternity of life, linked inseparably by the law of cause and effect. In the sutras, expressions such as "the Buddhas of the three existences" and "the Buddhas of the three existences and ten directions" indicate all Buddhas throughout eternity and boundless space.

three expedient means [三方便] (Jpn *san-hōben*): Also, three types of expedient means. A classification of Shakyamuni's teachings into three categories, set forth by T'ien-t'ai (538–597) in *The Words and Phrases of the Lotus Sutra.* In that work, T'ien-t'ai interprets the title of the second chapter of the Lotus Sutra, "Expedient Means," with his three types of expedient means. Expedient means indicates the teachings the Buddha expounds in order to lead people to the true and supreme teaching. The first category is known as "adaptations of the Law expedient means" (Jpn *hōyū-hōben*), the teachings that were preached in accordance with the people's capacities. The second is called "expedient means that can lead one in" *(nōtsū-hōben),* indicating the teachings the Buddha preached as a gateway to the true teaching. These first two expedient means correspond to the pre-Lotus Sutra teachings and constitute provisional teachings. They are what the Buddha refers to in the "Expedient Means" chapter where he says, "Honestly discarding expedient means, I will preach only the unsurpassed way." The third category, or "secret and wonderful expedient means" *(himyō-hōben),* is the teaching that contains the truth. This expedient means indicates that the Buddha concealed, or kept secret, the truth for the first forty-two years of his preaching life, expounding it only in the Lotus Sutra. When viewed from the standpoint of the Lotus Sutra, however, all the provisional teachings are included in the sutra as partial explanations of the truth. This inclusion is termed "wonderful" *(myō).* Unlike the first two expedient means, the third category is not only a means that leads people to the truth, but also the truth itself.

Nichiren (1222–1282) explains "secret and wonderful expedient means" with the parable of the jewel in the robe from the "Five Hundred Disciples" (eighth) chapter of the Lotus Sutra, in which a poor man has a precious jewel sewn inside his robe but is unaware of it. Because he is unaware, the jewel is "secret," but because he owns it, it is "wonderful." The jewel sewn in the robe indicates that Buddhahood is inherent in all people (wonderful), and the poor man's ignorance of it, that ordinary people are unaware of their own Buddha nature (secret).

threefold contemplation in a single mind [一心三観] (Jpn *isshin-sangan*): Also, threefold contemplation. A method of meditation formulated by T'ien-t'ai (538–597) in *Great Concentration and Insight,* intended to enable one to perceive the unification of the three truths of non-substantiality, temporary existence, and the Middle Way.

While the concept of the unification of the three truths constitutes the doctrinal core of T'ien-t'ai teachings, threefold contemplation in a single mind constitutes the core of T'ien-t'ai practice. T'ien-t'ai doctrine regards each phenomenon as a perfect unity of the three truths and sets forth the threefold contemplation in a single mind as the practice by which one attains insight into this perfect unity. This contemplation involves perceiving the three truths as simultaneously and perfectly integrated and interfused in each phenomenon. By doing so, one is said to rid oneself of the three categories of illusion and acquire at once the three kinds of wisdom—the wisdom of the two vehicles, the wisdom of bodhisattvas, and the Buddha wisdom. T'ien-t'ai also describes a single mind as comprising the three thousand realms. In this sense, threefold contemplation in a single mind is equal to observing a single moment of life and seeing the three thousand realms within it. At the same time, one perceives that all phenomena consist of the three thousand realms.

threefold Lotus Sutra [法華三部経] (Jpn *Hokke-sambu-kyō*): The Immeasurable Meanings Sutra, the Lotus Sutra, and the Universal Worthy Sutra. The Immeasurable Meanings and Universal Worthy sutras serve respectively as the prologue and epilogue to the Lotus Sutra. In the Immeasurable Meanings Sutra, Shakyamuni states, "In these more than forty years, I have not yet revealed the truth," thus making clear that his teachings up until this point are provisional. In this context, the Lotus Sutra says, "The World-Honored One has long expounded his doctrines and now must reveal the truth." The Immeasurable Meanings Sutra also states that all principles and meanings are born from a single Law, thus preparing the way for the Lotus Sutra to reveal that Law. The Lotus Sutra expounds the one Buddha vehicle that enables all people to attain Buddhahood, as well as the Buddha's original enlightenment in the remote past. The Universal Worthy Sutra emphasizes the necessity of propagating the Lotus Sutra.

threefold refuge [三帰・三帰依・三帰戒] (Jpn *san-ki, san-kie,* or *sankikai*): Also, three refuges or triple refuge. To take refuge in the three treasures, i.e., to believe in and give allegiance to the Buddha, the Law (the Buddha's teaching), and the Buddhist Order (community of believers). The threefold refuge can also mean the three treasures themselves. Fidelity to the three treasures is an essential for all Buddhists. The formula "I take refuge in the Buddha, I take refuge in the Law, I take refuge in the Order" was recited as a profession of faith by monks and laypersons from very early times during initiation and other ceremonies. *See also* threefold refuge and observance of the five precepts.

threefold refuge and observance of the five precepts [三帰五戒] (Jpn *sanki-gokai*): To be faithful to the three treasures of the Buddha, the Law (the teaching), and the Buddhist Order (community of believers), and observe the five precepts of not killing, not stealing, not committing sexual misconduct, not lying, and not drinking intoxicants. The threefold refuge and observance of the five precepts were essential to admission to the Order as a lay believer. In the ceremony of admission, a candidate for the Order recited the formula "I take refuge in the Buddha, I take refuge in the Law, I take refuge in the Order," and took a vow to observe the five precepts. Thus the candidate was received into the Order as a lay practitioner.

threefold secret teaching [三重秘伝] (Jpn *sanjū-hiden*): A doctrine Nichikan (1665–1726), the twenty-sixth chief priest of Taiseki-ji temple, established based on the passage in Nichiren's treatise *The Opening of the Eyes* that reads: "The doctrine of three thousand realms in a single moment of life is found in only one place, hidden in the depths of the 'Life Span' chapter of the essential teaching of the Lotus Sutra. Nāgārjuna and Vasubandhu were aware of it but did not bring it forth into the light. T'ien-t'ai Chih-che alone embraced it and kept it ever in mind" (224). Nichikan interpreted this sentence to mean that the doctrine of three thousand realms in a single moment of life is found (1) only in the Lotus Sutra, not in any other sutra; (2) only in the "Life Span" (sixteenth) chapter of the essential teaching (latter half), not in the theoretical teaching (first half) of the Lotus Sutra; and (3) only in the "depths," not on the "surface," of the "Life Span" chapter. The first point corresponds to the comparison of the true teaching (the Lotus Sutra) and the provisional teachings (all the other sutras). The second point corresponds to the comparison of the essential teaching and the theoretical teaching of the Lotus Sutra. The third point corresponds to the comparison of the "depths" and the "surface" of the "Life Span" chapter of the sutra, the former indicating the Buddhism of sowing, and the latter, the Buddhism of the harvest. These three levels of comparison reveal the ultimate teaching of Nichiren, or the Buddhism of sowing, as being Nam-myoho-renge-kyo of the Three Great Secret Laws. Nichikan used the term "threefold secret teaching" because the Buddhism of sowing, hidden threefold in the depths of the "Life Span" chapter, was unknown to the other Nichiren schools.

threefold world [三界] (Jpn *san-gai*): The world of unenlightened beings who transmigrate within the six paths (from hell through the realm of heavenly beings). The threefold world consists of, in ascending order, the world of desire, the world of form, and the world of formlessness: (1) The world of desire comprises the four evil paths (the realms of hell, hungry spirits, animals, and *asuras*), the four continents surrounding Mount Sumeru (that contain the realm of human beings), and the first six divisions of heaven (the lowest part of the realm of heavenly beings).

The beings in this world are ruled by various cravings, such as those for food, drink, and sex. (2) The world of form consists of the four meditation heavens, which are further divided into eighteen heavens (sixteen or seventeen according to other explanations). The beings here are free from desires, cravings, and appetites, but still have physical form and thus are subject to certain material restrictions. (3) The world of formlessness comprises the four realms of Boundless Empty Space, Boundless Consciousness, Nothingness, and Neither Thought Nor No Thought. Here beings are free from desires and from physical form with its material restrictions.

three gates to emancipation [三解脱門] (Jpn *san-gedatsu-mon*): *See* three meditations for emancipation.

three good paths [三善道] (Jpn *san-zendō*): The three realms of *asuras,* human beings, and heavenly beings, as contrasted with the three evil paths of hell, hungry spirits, and animals. They are called "good" because rebirth in these three paths of existence is held to result from one's good deeds in a previous existence. In contrast, the three evil paths are so called because rebirth in these paths is due to one's evil deeds in a former life.

Three Great Secret Laws [三大秘法] (Jpn *sandai-hihō*): The core principles of Nichiren's teaching. They are the object of devotion of the essential teaching, the daimoku of the essential teaching, and the sanctuary of the essential teaching. Here, "essential teaching" refers to the teaching of Nam-myoho-renge-kyo and not to the essential teaching, or the latter fourteen chapters, of the Lotus Sutra. Nichiren (1222–1282) established these three essential principles to enable people in the Latter Day of the Law to attain Buddhahood. They are called secret because they are implicit in the text of the "Life Span" (sixteenth) chapter of the Lotus Sutra and remained hidden or unknown until Nichiren revealed them. Nichiren regarded them as the vital teaching that Shakyamuni Buddha transferred to Bodhisattva Superior Practices in the "Supernatural Powers" (twenty-first) chapter of the sutra. He regarded his mission as one with that of Bodhisattva Superior Practices.

The Three Great Secret Laws represent Nichiren's embodiment of the Mystic Law, to which he was enlightened, in a form that all people can practice and thereby gain access to that Law within their own lives. He associated the Three Great Secret Laws with the three types of learning set forth in Buddhism—precepts, meditation, and wisdom. Specifically, the object of devotion corresponds to meditation, the sanctuary to precepts, and the daimoku to wisdom. Concerning the three types of learning based on the Lotus Sutra, Dengyō (767–822), in his *Questions and Answers on Regulations for Students of the Tendai Lotus School,* states, "The spacelike immovable precept, the spacelike immovable meditation, and the spacelike immovable wisdom—these three all together are transmitted under the name 'Wonderful Law.'" The three types of learning based on the Lotus Sutra are called "spacelike" and "immovable" because, like space, which represents the ultimate truth, they are immovable, or imperturbable. Nikkō, Nichiren's successor, stated that in Nichiren's teachings the object of devotion corresponds to the spacelike immovable meditation, the sanctuary to the spacelike immovable precept, and the daimoku to the spacelike immovable wisdom.

Nichiren mentions the Three Great Secret Laws in several of his writings (all dated after his near execution at Tatsunokuchi and subsequent exile to Sado Island in 1271), and in a work known as *On the Three Great Secret Laws,* he offers a detailed definition.

At the core of the Three Great Secret Laws is the One Great Secret Law. This is the object of devotion of the essential teaching, or Nichiren's embodiment in the form of a mandala of the eternal Law of Nam-myoho-renge-kyo, which he fully realized and manifested in his life. He writes in *The Person and the Law,* "Deep in this mortal flesh I preserve the ultimate secret Law inherited from Shakyamuni Buddha, the lord of teachings, at Eagle Peak" (1097). Because embracing this object of devotion called the Gohonzon is the only precept in Nichiren's teaching, the place where it is enshrined corresponds to the place where one vows to observe the Buddhist precepts—the ordination platform, or sanctuary, of the essential teaching. The term *precept* in Buddhism implies preventing error and putting an end to evil. The daimoku of the essential teaching indicates the invocation or chanting of Nam-myoho-renge-kyo with faith in the object of devotion; it includes chanting the daimoku for oneself and teaching it to others. Thus, both the sanctuary and the daimoku derive from the object of devotion.

Later Nichikan (1665–1726), the twenty-sixth chief priest of Taiseki-ji temple, classified the Three Great Secret Laws into Six Great Secret Laws. First, the object of devotion is viewed in terms of both Person and Law. The Person indicates Nichiren himself, who achieved the enlightenment and virtues of the eternal Buddha and who established the Buddhism of sowing for all people in the Latter Day of the Law. The object of devotion in terms of the Law is the Gohonzon, which embodies Nam-myoho-renge-kyo. Second, the sanctuary also has two aspects, the specified sanctuary and the general sanctuary. The former is the sanctuary to be built at the time of ***kōsen-rufu,*** or wide propagation, in accordance with Nichiren's instruction. This is the place where the object of devotion Nichiren inscribed for all humanity (commonly known as the Dai-

Gohonzon) is to be enshrined when his teaching has been widely spread and established. The general sanctuary is any place where one enshrines the object of devotion and engages in practice. Third, the daimoku of the essential teaching also has two aspects: the daimoku of faith and the daimoku of practice. The former means to believe in the Gohonzon, and the latter means to chant the daimoku and spread it.

According to Nichikan's "Interpreting the Text Based upon Its Essential Meaning," the Six Great Secret Laws are considered a crystallization of the Buddha's eighty-four thousand teachings, the Three Great Secret Laws a crystallization of the Six Great Secret Laws, and the One Great Secret Law a crystallization of the Three Great Secret Laws.

three groups of voice-hearers [三周の声聞] (Jpn *sanshū-no-shōmon*): Also, three groups of voice-hearer disciples. Shakyamuni's voice-hearer disciples, whose enlightenment is prophesied in the theoretical teaching (first half) of the Lotus Sutra. There, Shakyamuni teaches that the sole purpose of the Buddha's advent is to expound the one Buddha vehicle, or the teaching that leads all people to Buddhahood. He explains that the three vehicles, or the teachings directed at voice-hearers, cause-awakened ones, and bodhisattvas, set forth in earlier sutras, are not ends in themselves but only means to lead people to the supreme vehicle of Buddhahood. This concept is called the "replacement of the three vehicles with the one vehicle." Shakyamuni Buddha's disciples are divided into three groups according to their capacity to understand that teaching: those of superior, intermediate, and inferior capacity. This traditional division of capacity was employed by T'ien-t'ai (538–597) and others in interpreting the Lotus Sutra.

A description of the three groups follows. (1) Voice-hearers of superior capacity: Shāriputra. He alone understands the above concept immediately upon hearing the Buddha preach concerning "the true aspect of all phenomena" in the "Expedient Means" (second) chapter. The "Simile and Parable" (third) chapter predicts his enlightenment. (2) Voice-hearers of intermediate capacity: Maudgalyāyana, Kātyāyana, Mahākāshyapa, and Subhūti. They understand the Buddha's message through the parable of the three carts and the burning house related in the "Simile and Parable" chapter. Their enlightenment is predicted in the "Bestowal of Prophecy" (sixth) chapter. (3) Voice-hearers of inferior capacity: Pūrna, Ānanda, Rāhula, and others. They finally understand the Buddha's message by hearing about their relationship with Shakyamuni beginning major world system dust particle *kalpas* in the past, as explained in the "Parable of the Phantom City" (seventh) chapter. Pūrna's enlightenment and that of twelve hundred arhats are prophesied in the "Five Hundred

Disciples" (eighth) chapter, and the enlightenment of Ānanda and Rāhula and two thousand voice-hearers, in the "Prophecies" (ninth) chapter.

Thus, the cycle of Shakyamuni's preaching, the disciples' understanding, and Shakyamuni's prediction of their enlightenment is repeated three times and is accordingly called the three cycles of preaching. Those who received the prophecy of enlightenment through the three cycles of the Buddha's preaching are called the three groups of voice-hearers.

three heavenly sons of light [三光天子] (Jpn *sankō-tenshi*): Also, three heavenly gods of light. The god of the sun, the god of the moon, and the god of the stars.

three illusions [三惑] (Jpn *san-waku*): *See* three categories of illusion.

three inherent potentials of the Buddha nature [三因仏性] (Jpn *san'in-busshō*): A principle formulated by T'ien-t'ai (538–597) that views the Buddha nature from three perspectives. The three inherent potentials are the innate Buddha nature, the wisdom to perceive it, and the good deeds, or practice, to develop this wisdom and cause the Buddha nature to emerge. Beneficent actions aid the development of wisdom, and developed wisdom realizes the innate Buddha nature. In this way, the three constitute causes that work together to enable one to attain the effect of Buddhahood.

three insights [三明] (Jpn *san-myō*): Also, three understandings. Three powers attributed to Buddhas and arhats. They are (1) the ability to know past lives, (2) the ability to know future lives, and (3) the ability to know the essential nature of sufferings in the present life and to eradicate the illusions and earthly desires that cause sufferings. The three insights are often cited together with the six transcendental powers, which are also qualities of Buddhas and arhats, as "the three insights and the six transcendental powers." *See also* six transcendental powers.

three insights and six transcendental powers [三明六通] (Jpn *sammyō-rokutsū*): Powers attributed to Buddhas and arhats. *See* six transcendental powers; three insights.

three kalpas [三劫] (Jpn *san-kō*): The past Glorious Kalpa, the present Wise Kalpa, and the future Constellation Kalpa. The Names of Three Thousand Buddhas Sutra says that in each of these *kalpas* a thousand Buddhas appear, and lists the names of these three thousand Buddhas. *See also* Constellation Kalpa; Glorious Kalpa; Wise Kalpa.

three Kāshyapa brothers [三迦葉] (Jpn *san-kashō*): Three brothers of the village of Uruvilvā near Gayā, a city of Magadha in India, who converted to Shakyamuni's teachings during his early days of preaching. They are Uruvilvā Kāshyapa, Nadī Kāshyapa, and Gayā Kāshyapa. For twelve years (six years by another account), they practiced fire worship in the forest. When Shakyamuni Buddha came to Uruvilvā to preach shortly after his enlightenment, the three brothers received instruction from him and became his followers. At the same time, Uruvilvā Kāshyapa's five hundred disciples, Nadī Kāshyapa's three hundred disciples, and Gayā Kāshyapa's two hundred disciples—one thousand disciples in all—also converted to the Buddha's teachings. They were the third group of individuals to convert to the Buddha's teachings; the five ascetics who heard Shakyamuni's first sermon at Deer Park following his enlightenment were the first. After the five ascetics, the next to convert was Yashas along with his fifty friends.

three kinds of mind [三心] (Jpn *san-jin*): Three requisites for rebirth in the Pure Land of Perfect Bliss set forth in the Meditation on the Buddha Infinite Life Sutra. They are a sincere mind, a mind of deep faith, and a mind of resolve to be reborn in the Pure Land. In *The Nembutsu Chosen above All,* Hōnen (1133–1212), the founder of the Japanese Pure Land (Jōdo) school, emphasized these three kinds of mind as attitudes Pure Land believers should assume when reciting the name of Amida Buddha.

three kinds of non-regression [三不退] (Jpn *san-futai*): Also, three levels of non-regression. Three points past which someone engaged in bodhisattva practice does not return or regress. The first is non-regression from [one's present] stage, or not receding from the stage of development one has attained. The second is non-regression from action, or not retreating from Buddhist practice. The third is non-regression from thought, or not receding from having one's thoughts fixed on the truth. Each of these three is associated with a different level or stage of bodhisattva practice; in the course of bodhisattva practice, one first attains the non-regression from stage, then non-regression from action, and finally non-regression from thought, in which one's thoughts are unwaveringly fixed on the truth. Various Buddhist teachers and scholars established different systems relating the three kinds of non-regression to the fifty-two stages of bodhisattva practice.

three kinds of offerings [三施] (Jpn *san-se*): A categorization of Buddhist offerings or almsgiving into three types: offerings of goods, offerings of the Law, and offerings of fearlessness. An offering of goods means the donation of material goods and includes monetary donations. An offering of the Law means teaching the Law, or explaining the Buddha's teachings, to others. An offering of fearlessness means giving fearlessness or safety to those in frightening or difficult circumstances. A second set of the three kinds of offerings are offerings of goods, offerings of praise and reverence, and offerings of the Law. A third set comprises offerings of food and drink, offerings of rare treasures, and offerings of one's life.

three kinds of tranquillity [三念住・三念処] (Jpn *san-nenjū* or *san-nenjo*): Three aspects of a Buddha's quality of tranquillity. These are three of the Buddha's eighteen unshared properties. The first kind of tranquillity is that a Buddha's mind remains tranquil and undisturbed by feelings of joy when people listen intently to his preaching. The second is that a Buddha's mind remains peaceful and still, without disappointment, even when people listen unwillingly or are unwilling to listen to his preaching. The third is that a Buddha's mind remains peaceful and at rest, neither rejoicing nor grieving, when preaching in the presence of these two types of people. Thus a Buddha's mind remains tranquil regardless of the approval, disapproval, or mixed reactions of those listening to him. *See also* eighteen unshared properties.

three kinds of wisdom [三智] (Jpn *san-chi*): Three kinds of wisdom explained in *The Treatise on the Great Perfection of Wisdom.* They are as follows: (1) The wisdom to understand the universal aspect of phenomena. This is the wisdom of persons of the two vehicles (voice-hearers and cause-awakened ones) who understand the truth of non-substantiality or the non-substantial nature of existence. (2) The wisdom to understand the various paths to enlightenment. Bodhisattvas possess this wisdom, which enables them to understand the individual aspects of existence, or the truth of temporary existence, as well as the various paths to enlightenment, so that they may save others accordingly. (3) The wisdom to understand both the universal aspect and individual aspects of phenomena. This is the Buddha wisdom, which perceives both the universal aspect and individual aspects of all phenomena, or the Middle Way, as well as the various paths to enlightenment. In T'ien-t'ai's teaching, one can obtain the three kinds of wisdom simultaneously through meditation aimed at perceiving the unification of the three truths in a single mind. Hence it is called the three kinds of wisdom in a single mind. Specifically, through perception of the truth of non-substantiality, one obtains the wisdom of the two vehicles; through perception of the truth of temporary existence, one acquires the wisdom of bodhisattvas; and through perception of the truth of the Middle Way, one gains the Buddha wisdom.

three leaders and seven witnesses [三師七証] (Jpn *sanshi-shichishō*): Also, three teachers and seven witnesses. Ten monks whose attendance is required at the ceremony in which a novice receives the entire set of rules of monastic discipline (250 precepts for a monk) and becomes a fully ordained monk. The three leaders play a central role in this ordination ceremony, and the seven witnesses act as witnesses to the event.

The three leaders are (1) a preceptor (also called teacher of discipline), whose role it is to confer the precepts; (2) a chairman, who recites words that describe the intent, significance, and form of the ceremony; and (3) an instructor, who examines an applicant's qualification for ordination and teaches ceremonial manner to him. At least seven monks are required as witnesses to the ordination, though in distant locations where this is impossible, at least two are necessary. Their role is to attest that the ordination rite was conducted properly and that the novice was ordained as a monk. A novice must meet certain requirements to be ordained as a monk. For example, he cannot have had sexual relations while a novice or committed any of the other grave offenses that warrant expulsion from the Buddhist Order, nor can he have asked for ordination for the purpose of making a living. He must be at least twenty years old, have his parents' permission, be free from debt, disease, etc. Who he practiced under as a novice is also considered. The chairman announces a candidate's petition for ordination and questions the assembly three times as to whether the novice is qualified to be accepted into the monkhood. If there is no objection, the candidate is ordained as a monk.

three major works on the Lotus Sutra [法華三大部] (Jpn *Hokke-sandai-bu*): *See* T'ien-t'ai's three major works.

three major writings of the T'ien-t'ai school [天台三大部] (Jpn *Tendai-sandai-bu*): *See* T'ien-t'ai's three major works.

three martyrs of Atsuhara [熱原の三烈士] (Jpn *Atsuhara-no-sanresshi*): Three followers of Nichiren who were arrested and beheaded during the Atsuhara Persecution. They were brothers named Jinshirō, Yagorō, and Yarokurō, farmers in Atsuhara Village in Fuji District of Suruga Province, Japan. They converted to Nichiren's teachings in 1278, when propagation was advancing rapidly in the Fuji area under the leadership of Nikkō. Many priests and laypersons in the area converted, among them three priests of Ryūsen-ji, a local temple of the Tendai school. Alarmed by this, Gyōchi, the temple's deputy chief priest, began to conspire with the authorities to threaten local believers. On the twenty-first day of the ninth month in 1279, twenty farmers, all followers of Nichiren, were arrested on the false charge of stealing rice from fields belonging to Ryūsen-ji and were taken to Kamakura and imprisoned. They were told that they would be freed if they renounced faith in the Lotus Sutra and agreed to recite the Nembutsu (the name of Amida Buddha). None complied, and the three brothers were beheaded on the fifteenth day of the tenth month as an example. According to another account, their execution took place on the eighth day of the fourth month in 1280. Even after their deaths, however, the others are said to have remained firm in their faith. Eventually they were all banished from Atsuhara. *See also* Atsuhara Persecution.

three meditations for emancipation [三解脱門] (Jpn *san-gedatsu-mon*): Also, three gates to emancipation. Three kinds of meditation to free oneself from the sufferings caused by illusions and attain enlightenment. They are (1) the meditation on non-substantiality, i.e., that all things are without substance or absolute self-nature; (2) the meditation on non-discrimination; because all things are without substance, there are no essential differences among them; and (3) the meditation on non-desire; because there are no essential differences among things, there is nothing that should be desired or aspired to.

three metaphors of the essential teaching [本門の三譬] (Jpn *hommon-no-sampi*): *See* six metaphors of the theoretical and essential teachings.

three metaphors of the theoretical teaching [迹門の三譬] (Jpn *shaku-mon-no-sampi*): *See* six metaphors of the theoretical and essential teachings.

three-month retreat [安居] (Skt *varsha* or *vārshika;* Pali *vassa;* Jpn *ango*): Also, rainy-season retreat, summer retreat, or tranquil dwelling. The period when Buddhist monks stopped their travels and outdoor activities for the duration of the summer rainy season and gathered at some sheltered location to devote themselves to study and discipline. The Sanskrit word *varsha* means "rain" and "raining," and *vārshika* means "belonging to the rainy season" or "rainy." During the rainy season in summer in India, monks traditionally dwelt in a cave or a monastery for three months—from the sixteenth day of the fourth month to the fifteenth day of the seventh month. This was because the heavy rainfall made traveling and outdoor activities impractical, and to avoid trampling to death the small living things that emerged in the rain, such as insects and worms. The tradition is said to have begun during the time of Shakyamuni. During this period the monks learned the Buddha's teachings, engaged in meditation and other practices, and repented their errors. On the last day of the three-month retreat, monks publicly confessed their transgressions of monastic discipline. This custom was brought to China and Japan. In Japan, the three-month retreat was first observed in 683.

three mysteries [三密] (Jpn *san-mitsu*): Also, three secrets. Three mysteries of body, mouth, and mind. A principle of Esoteric Buddhism. According to Esoteric Buddhism, since Mahāvairochana Buddha (the Buddha depicted in esoteric sutras) is omnipresent, all beings are the mystic body of that Buddha, all sounds his mystic mouth (voice), and all thoughts his mystic mind. Yet, because the Buddha's body, mouth, and mind are unimaginably profound and beyond ordinary people's understanding, these aspects are called "mysteries." Moreover, the body, mouth, and mind of ordinary people are not essentially different from those of the Buddha, although their Buddha nature is obscured by illusions. In this sense, the body, mouth, and mind of ordinary people in their essential aspect are also called the three mysteries. In terms of practice, the mystery of the body means the forming of mudras, which are gestures with the hands and fingers; the mystery of the mouth refers to the recitation of mantras, or mystic formulas; and the mystery of the mind indicates meditation on an esoteric mandala or one of the figures appearing in it. Esoteric Buddhism teaches that, through these three practices, the body, mouth, and mind of ordinary people are united with those of Mahāvairochana Buddha, thus enabling them to attain Buddhahood in their present form.

three mystic principles [三妙] (Jpn *san-myō*): The true cause, true effect, and true land, indicated in the "Life Span" (sixteenth) chapter of the Lotus Sutra. The first three of the ten mystic principles of the essential teaching (latter half of the sutra) formulated by T'ien-t'ai (538–597) in the part of *The Profound Meaning of the Lotus Sutra* in which he interprets the word *myō*, meaning wonderful or mystic, of Myoho-renge-kyo, the title of the Lotus Sutra of the Wonderful Law.

The true cause is the practice that Shakyamuni Buddha undertook to reach his original enlightenment. The true effect is the original enlightenment that he attained. The true land is the place where the Buddha has been expounding his teachings since his original attainment of enlightenment. The fact that the "Life Span" chapter teaches these three together is called the integration of the three mystic principles. The mystic principle of the true cause is expressed in the passage of the "Life Span" chapter that reads, "Originally I practiced the bodhisattva way, and the life span that I acquired then has yet to come to an end." The mystic principle of the true effect is shown in the passage, "Since I attained Buddhahood, an extremely long period of time has passed." The passage that indicates the mystic principle of the true land is, "Ever since then I have been constantly in this *sahā* world, preaching the Law, teaching and converting."

In his 1273 treatise *The Object of Devotion for Observing the Mind*, Nichiren explains the significance of the three mystic principles: "He [the Buddha of the theoretical teaching] revealed the hundred worlds and thousand factors inherent in life, but he did not expound their eternal nature. . . . The difference between the theoretical and the essential teachings is as great as that between heaven and earth. The latter reveals the eternity of the Ten Worlds and, further, the realm of the environment"

(368). The true cause signifies the nine worlds eternally inherent in life, and the true effect, the Buddhahood eternally inherent in life. Together they reveal the eternity of the Ten Worlds. The true land signifies the realm of the environment, which is also eternal. These three represent "the actual three thousand realms in a single moment of life."

three obstacles and four devils [三障四魔] (Jpn *sanshō-shima*): Various obstacles and hindrances to the practice of Buddhism. They are listed in the Nirvana Sutra and *The Treatise on the Great Perfection of Wisdom.* The three obstacles are (1) the obstacle of earthly desires, or obstacles arising from the three poisons of greed, anger, and foolishness; (2) the obstacle of karma, obstacles due to bad karma created by committing any of the five cardinal sins or ten evil acts; and (3) the obstacle of retribution, obstacles caused by the negative karmic effects of actions in the three evil paths. In a letter he addressed to the Ikegami brothers in 1275, Nichiren states, "The obstacle of earthly desires is the impediments to one's practice that arise from greed, anger, foolishness, and the like; the obstacle of karma is the hindrances presented by one's wife or children; and the obstacle of retribution is the hindrances caused by one's sovereign or parents" (501).

The four devils are (1) the hindrance of the five components, obstructions caused by one's physical and mental functions; (2) the hindrance of earthly desires, obstructions arising from the three poisons; (3) the hindrance of death, meaning one's own untimely death obstructing one's practice of Buddhism, or the premature death of another practitioner causing one to doubt; and (4) the hindrance of the devil king, who is said to assume various forms or take possession of others in order to cause one to discard one's Buddhist practice. This hindrance is regarded as the most difficult to overcome. T'ien-t'ai (538–597) states in *Great Concentration and Insight:* "As practice progresses and understanding grows, the three obstacles and four devils emerge in confusing form, vying with one another to interfere. . . . One should be neither influenced nor frightened by them. If one falls under their influence, one will be led into the paths of evil. If one is frightened by them, one will be prevented from practicing the correct teaching."

three ordination platforms [三戒壇] (Jpn *san-kaidan*): Ordination platforms established at three places in Japan to confer the Buddhist precepts. They were situated at Tōdai-ji temple in Nara, then Japan's capital, Yakushi-ji temple in Shimotsuke Province to the east of Nara, and Kanzeon-ji temple in Chikuzen Province to the west. The ordination platform at Tōdai-ji was established in 754, and those at Yakushi-ji and Kanzeon-ji in 761. For the ordination of priests, Japan was divided into three districts, and the ordination platforms at the three temples were used as the center for each district. *See also* ordination platform.

three paths (1) [三道] (Jpn *san-dō*): Earthly desires, karma, and suffering. They are called "paths" because one leads to the other. Earthly desires, which include greed, anger, foolishness, arrogance, and doubt, give rise to actions that create evil karma. The effect of this evil karma then manifests itself as suffering. Suffering aggravates earthly desires, leading to further misguided action, which in turn brings on more evil karma and suffering. Trapped in this cycle, people are destined to suffer in the lower states of existence known as the six paths. In this way, maintaining a self-perpetuating causal relationship, the three paths function to prevent a person from attaining Buddhahood.

In *The Profound Meaning of the Lotus Sutra* and *Great Concentration and Insight,* however, T'ien-t'ai (538–597) states that the three paths of earthly desires, karma, and suffering are none other than the three virtues of the Dharma body, wisdom, and emancipation. In *The Entity of the Mystic Law,* Nichiren (1222–1282) states, "Such persons, who honestly discard expedient means, put faith in the Lotus Sutra alone, and chant Nam-myoho-renge-kyo, will transform the three paths of earthly desires, karma, and suffering into the three virtues of the Dharma body, wisdom, and emancipation" (420). The three virtues are inseparable from the three paths. One cannot acquire the three virtues apart from the three paths. Therefore there is no need to eliminate the three paths; all one has to do is to manifest the true nature of the three paths, which is ultimately the three virtues. T'ien-t'ai pointed out that the true nature of the three paths is none other than the three virtues, while Nichiren taught that the three virtues are potential within the three paths, and become manifest from among them.

(2) [三途] (Jpn *san-zu*): The path of fire, the path of swords, and the path of blood. The term is used synonymously with the three evil paths of hell, hungry spirits, and animals, and represents the suffering one must undergo in retribution for evil karma one created in a previous life. The path of fire is identified as the world of hell because raging flames devour one's body; the path of swords is identified as the world of hungry spirits because it is said that in that world one is subject to attack by swords; and the path of blood is identified as the world of animals because beings there kill and devour one another.

(3) [三道] (Jpn *san-dō*): Also, three ways. Three stages of practice in the Hinayana teachings. The way of insight, the way of practice, and the way of the arhat, or one who has no more to learn. *See* three ways.

three periods [三時] (Jpn *san-ji*): (1) The Former Day, Middle Day, and Latter Day of the Law. Three consecutive periods or stages into which the time following a Buddha's death is divided. These are also referred to as the periods of the Correct Law, the Counterfeit Law, and the Decadent Law (or the Final Law). During the Former Day of the Law, the spirit of Buddhism prevails, and people can attain enlightenment through its practice. During the Middle Day of the Law, although Buddhism becomes firmly established in society, it grows increasingly formalized, and fewer people benefit from it. In the Latter Day of the Law, people are tainted by the three poisons of greed, anger, and foolishness, and lose their aspiration for enlightenment; Buddhism itself loses the power to lead them to Buddhahood. There are several explanations of the lengths of the three periods following the death of Shakyamuni Buddha. One describes the Former Day and the Middle Day as each lasting one thousand years, and another, five hundred years. A third account has the Former Day lasting for one thousand years, and the Middle Day for five hundred years; and a fourth states that the Former Day lasts for five hundred years, and the Middle Day for one thousand years. All accounts agree that the Latter Day will continue for ten thousand years. In China, Shakyamuni Buddha's death was placed in the fifty-second year of the reign of King Mu (949 B.C.E.) of the Chou dynasty, and the period of the Former Day was defined as five hundred years and that of the Middle Day as one thousand years. Accordingly, it was believed that the Latter Day had begun in the mid-sixth century. In Japan, Shakyamuni Buddha's death was placed in the same year as in China, but an account that defines each period of the Former Day and the Middle Day as one thousand years was accepted, and it was believed that the Latter Day had begun in 1052. Usually these three periods refer to the time after Shakyamuni Buddha's death, but they also pertain to other Buddhas who appear in the sutras. For example, according to the Lotus Sutra, Bodhisattva Never Disparaging lived toward the end of the Middle Day of the Law of the Buddha Awesome Sound King. *See also* Former Day of the Law; Latter Day of the Law; Middle Day of the Law.

(2) A reference to the teachings of the three periods. *See* three periods, teachings of the.

three periods, teachings of the [三時教] (Jpn *sanji-kyō*): Also, three periods. A classification of Shakyamuni Buddha's teachings developed respectively by the Dharma Characteristics (Chin Fa-hsiang; Jpn Hossō) school and the Three Treatises (San-lun; Sanron) school. This system arranges Shakyamuni's teachings into three categories according to the order in which these schools thought they were preached and their content.

A classification by the Dharma Characteristics school based on the Revelation of the Profound Secrets Sutra explains that the first period corresponds to the Hinayana, or Āgama, sutras. During this period, the Buddha taught the four noble truths to refute attachment to the self, or ego. He explained that, though the dharmas, or elements of existence, are real, the self is without substance. The second period corresponds to the Wisdom sutras, which teach that all things are non-substantial and refute attachment to belief in the reality of the dharmas as taught in the Āgama sutras. The third period corresponds to the Flower Garland Sutra, the Revelation of the Profound Secrets Sutra, and the Lotus Sutra. The teachings of this period refute attachment both to the idea that the dharmas are non-substantial and to the belief that they are real. They teach that the dharmas are neither real nor non-substantial; this is called the Middle Way. The teachings of the first two periods are regarded as temporary and imperfect, while those of the third period are considered to reveal the truth.

According to a classification by the Three Treatises school, the first period is that of the Hinayana teachings, which explain that both the mind and the objects it observes (objective reality) are real. The second and third periods constitute that of the Mahayana teachings; the teachings of the second period state that the mind alone is real, and those of the third period, that both the mind and its objects are without substance. The Three Treatises school asserts that only the teachings of the third period are complete and final in meaning.

three poisons [三毒] (Jpn *san-doku*): Greed, anger, and foolishness. The fundamental evils inherent in life that give rise to human suffering. In *The Treatise on the Great Perfection of Wisdom,* the three poisons are regarded as the source of all illusions and earthly desires. The three poisons are so called because they pollute people's lives and work to prevent them from turning their hearts and minds to goodness. *The Words and Phrases of the Lotus Sutra* by T'ien-t'ai speaks of the three poisons as the underlying cause of the three calamities of famine, war, and pestilence, stating: "Because anger increases in intensity, armed strife occurs. Because greed increases in intensity, famine arises. Because foolishness increases in intensity, pestilence breaks out. And because these three calamities occur, earthly desires grow more numerous and powerful than ever, and false views increasingly flourish." In the "Simile and Parable" (third) chapter of the Lotus Sutra, Shakyamuni says to Shāriputra, "He [the Thus Come One] is born into the threefold world, a burning house, rotten and old, in order to save living beings from the fires of birth, aging, sickness, and death, care, suffering, stupidity, misunderstanding, and the three poisons; to teach and convert them and enable them to attain supreme perfect enlightenment."

three powerful enemies [三類の強敵] (Jpn *sanrui-no-gōteki*): Also, three types of enemies. Three types of arrogant people who persecute those who propagate the Lotus Sutra in the evil age after Shakyamuni Buddha's death. Miao-lo (711–782) defines them in his work *The Annotations on "The Words and Phrases of the Lotus Sutra"* on the basis of descriptions in the concluding verse section of the "Encouraging Devotion" (thirteenth) chapter of the Lotus Sutra. In the sutra text, the first type is described as follows: "There will be many ignorant people / who will curse and speak ill of us / and will attack us with swords and staves." The second type: "In that evil age there will be monks / with perverse wisdom and hearts that are fawning and crooked / who will suppose they have attained what they have not attained, / being proud and boastful in heart." And the third type: "Or there will be forest-dwelling monks / wearing clothing of patched rags and living in retirement, / who will claim they are practicing the true way, / despising and looking down on all humankind. / Greedy for profit and support, / they will preach the Law to white-robed laymen / and will be respected and revered by the world / as though they were arhats who possess the six transcendental powers. . . ."

Miao-lo summarizes these three as follows: (1) "The arrogance and presumption of lay people" or arrogant lay people; a reference to those ignorant of Buddhism who curse and speak ill of the practitioners of the Lotus Sutra and attack them with swords and staves. (2) "The arrogance and presumption of members of the Buddhist clergy" or arrogant priests. These are priests with perverse wisdom and hearts that are fawning and crooked who, though failing to understand Buddhism, boast they have attained the Buddhist truth and slander the sutra's practitioners. (3) "The arrogance and presumption of those who pretend to be sages" or arrogant false sages. This third category is described as priests who pretend to be sages and who are revered as such, but when encountering the practitioners of the Lotus Sutra become fearful of losing fame or profit and induce secular authorities to persecute them. In *On "The Words and Phrases,"* Miao-lo sates, "Of these three, the first can be endured. The second exceeds the first, and the third is the most formidable of all. This is because the second and third ones are increasingly harder to recognize for what they really are."

Nichiren (1222–1282) called them the "three powerful enemies" and identified himself as the votary, or true practitioner, of the Lotus Sutra because he was subjected to slander, attacked with swords and staves, and sent into exile twice by the authorities, just as prophesied in the sutra. In his treatise *The Opening of the Eyes,* he says: "At such a time, if the three powerful enemies predicted in the Lotus Sutra did not appear, then who would believe in the words of the Buddha? If it were not for Nichiren, who could fulfill the Buddha's prophecies concerning the votary of the Lotus Sutra?" (243).

three-pronged diamond-pounder [三鈷杵] (Jpn *sanko-sho*): An instrument used in the rituals of Esoteric Buddhism, which has three prongs at either end. The diamond-pounder, *vajra* in Sanskrit, was originally a weapon of ancient India. It was so called because of its hardness, suggesting that, just as a diamond can scratch or break other materials without being damaged, it could prevail over the weapon of any foe. In the rituals of Esoteric Buddhism, the diamond-pounder is symbolic of a firm resolve to attain enlightenment that can destroy any illusion. The ritual implement, usually made of iron or copper, is slender in shape with pointed ends. There is also a five-pronged diamond-pounder and a single-arm diamond-pounder, which has no prongs.

three pronouncements [三箇の勅宣・三箇の鳳詔] (Jpn *sanka-no-chokusen* or *sanka-no-hōshō*): Also, three pronouncements of the Buddha. Exhortations by Shakyamuni Buddha in the "Treasure Tower" (eleventh) chapter of the Lotus Sutra, urging the assembly three times to propagate the Lotus Sutra after his death. These three pronouncements and the two admonitions in the "Devadatta" (twelfth) chapter are collectively called the five proclamations of the Buddha. With the first pronouncement, the Buddha voices his desire to transmit the sutra to someone. The "Treasure Tower" chapter reads: "In a loud voice he [Shakyamuni Buddha] addressed all the four kinds of believers, saying, 'Who is capable of broadly preaching the Lotus Sutra of the Wonderful Law in this *sahā* world? Now is the time to do so, for before long the Thus Come One will enter nirvana. The Buddha wishes to entrust this Lotus Sutra of the Wonderful Law to someone so that it may be preserved.'"

In the second pronouncement, the Buddha expresses his desire to perpetuate the Law for all eternity. The "Treasure Tower" chapter reads: "At that time the World-Honored One, wishing to state his meaning once more, spoke in verse form, saying: '. . . Through this expedient means / they make certain that the Law will long endure. / So I say to the great assembly: / After I have passed into extinction, / who can guard and uphold, / read and recite this sutra? / Now in the presence of the Buddha / let him come forward and speak his vow!'"

In the third pronouncement, the Buddha expounds the difficulty of propagating the sutra after his death by employing the teaching of the six difficult and nine easy acts. This pronouncement reads in part: "The Thus Come One Many Treasures, I myself, / and these emanation Buddhas who have gathered here, / surely know this is our aim. / . . . / All you good men, / each of you must consider carefully! / This is a difficult matter— / it is proper that you should make a great vow. / . . . / if after the Buddha has entered extinction, / in the time of evil, / you can preach this sutra, / that will be difficult indeed! / . . . / All you good men, / after I have entered extinction, / who can accept and uphold, / read and recite this sutra? / Now in the presence of the Buddha / let him come forward and speak his vow!" *See also* six difficult and nine easy acts; two admonitions.

three proofs [三証] (Jpn *san-shō*): Documentary proof, theoretical proof, and actual proof. Three standards set forth by Nichiren (1222–1282) for judging the validity of a given teaching. Documentary proof means that the doctrine of a particular Buddhist school is based upon or in accord with the sutras. Theoretical proof means that a doctrine is compatible with reason and logic. Actual proof means that the content of a doctrine is borne out by actual result when put into practice. Nichiren writes: "In judging the relative merit of Buddhist doctrines, I, Nichiren, believe that the best standards are those of reason and documentary proof. And even more valuable than reason and documentary proof is the proof of actual fact" (599).

three Pure Land sutras [浄土三部経] (Jpn *Jōdo-sambu-kyō*): The three basic sutras of the Pure Land schools in Japan. They are the Buddha Infinite Life Sutra, the Meditation on the Buddha Infinite Life Sutra, and the Amida Sutra. Hōnen (1133–1212), the founder of the Japanese Pure Land school, termed these three sutras the three Pure Land sutras. The three sutras praise the Pure Land of Perfect Bliss, i.e., the Pure Land of Amida Buddha, and exhort people to aspire to rebirth there.

three realms of existence [三世間] (Jpn *san-seken*): The realm of the five components, the realm of living beings, and the realm of the environment. This concept originally appeared in *The Treatise on the Great Perfection of Wisdom,* and T'ien-t'ai (538–597) adopted it as a component of his doctrine of three thousand realms in a single moment of life. The concept of three realms of existence views life from three different standpoints and explains the existence of individual lives in the real world. The five components, a living being as their temporary combination, and that being's environment all manifest the same one of the Ten Worlds at any given point in time.

(1) The realm of the five components: An analysis of the nature of a living entity in terms of how it responds to its surroundings. The five

components are form, perception, conception, volition, and consciousness. Form includes everything that constitutes the body and its sense organs, through which one perceives the outer world. Perception means the function of receiving or apprehending external information through one's sense organs. Conception indicates the function by which one grasps and forms some idea or concept about what has been perceived. Volition means the will to initiate action following the creation of conceptions about what has been perceived. Consciousness is the cognitive function of discernment that integrates the components of perception, conception, and volition. It distinguishes an object from all others, recognizes its characteristics, and exercises value judgments, such as distinguishing between right and wrong. From another viewpoint, while consciousness is regarded as the mind itself, the components of perception, conception, and volition are regarded as mental functions. Form corresponds to the physical aspect of life, and the other four components, to the spiritual aspect. The principle of the five components explains how life expresses each of the Ten Worlds differently. Someone in the world of hell, for example, will perceive, form a conception of, and react to the same object in a completely different manner than someone in the world of bodhisattvas.

(2) The realm of living beings: The individual living being, formed of a temporary union of the five components, who manifests or experiences any of the Ten Worlds. The realm of living beings refers to an individual as an integrated whole, but since no living being exists in perfect isolation, it is also taken to mean the collective body of individuals who interact with one another.

(3) The realm of the environment: The place or land where living beings dwell and carry out life-activities. The state of the land is a reflection of the state of life of the people who live in it. A land manifests any of the Ten Worlds according to which of the Ten Worlds dominate in the lives of its inhabitants. The same land also manifests different worlds for different individuals. Therefore, Nichiren says, "There are not two lands, pure or impure in themselves. The difference lies solely in the good or evil of our minds" (4). In making this statement, Nichiren was countering the popular view that there are separately existing impure lands and pure lands.

In addition, the three realms themselves are not to be viewed separately, but as aspects of an integrated whole, which simultaneously manifests any of the Ten Worlds.

three refuges [三帰・三帰依・三帰戒] (Jpn *san-ki, san-kie,* or *san-kikai*): *See* threefold refuge.

three robes [三衣] (Jpn *sanne*): Three kinds of garments worn by a monk according to the time or the occasion. Together with a mendicant's bowl, or begging bowl, these were the only possessions permitted a monk in India. Originally, the three robes were made only from discarded rags, symbolizing a life of humble asceticism free from secular attachments. One robe was called *samghātī* in Sanskrit and "great robe" in China. A monk wore this robe when visiting a royal palace, going out to beg for alms, or conferring precepts. Made from nine to twenty-five pieces of cloth, it was also called the nine-patch robe. Another was called *uttarāsanga* and "outer robe." An ordinary robe worn by monks when attending Buddhist lectures or performing rites and practices such as reciting a sutra, it was also called the seven-patch robe because it was made from seven pieces of cloth. A third robe was called *antarvāsa* and "inner robe." It was a working garment or undergarment worn by monks while engaged in daily duties or while resting. It was also called the five-patch robe because it was made from five pieces of cloth. In India these three robes were the only garments considered proper for monks, while in China and Japan the concept and significance of the three robes gradually changed. The priests of some schools even came to wear robes of silk, brocade, or other fine fabrics, with priests of higher ranks wearing more expensive or elaborate robes. At present, Buddhist schools have their own rules concerning priestly dress.

three robes and one begging bowl [三衣一鉢] (Jpn *sanne-ippatsu*): The only belongings that the precepts of early Indian Buddhism allow a monk to possess. They exemplify the austere lifestyle of a monk and the determination to divest oneself of worldly attachments in order to seek the way. Monks wore one or another of the three kinds of robes according to the occasion or activity. Monks used their bowls as receptacles for food when eating a meal or when begging.

three rules of preaching [三軌・弘経の三軌] (Jpn *san-ki* or *gukyō-no-sanki*): Also, three rules of the robe, seat, and room. The three rules of preaching represented by the robe, seat, and room of the Thus Come One, or the Buddha. Three essentials for propagating the Lotus Sutra after Shakyamuni Buddha's death mentioned in the "Teacher of the Law" (tenth) chapter of the sutra. That chapter says that one who desires to teach the Lotus Sutra after the Buddha's death should "enter the Thus Come One's room, put on the Thus Come One's robe, and sit in the Thus Come One's seat." It then explains that the room of the Thus Come One means great compassion for all living beings, the robe of the Thus Come One means a gentle and forbearing heart, and the seat of the Thus Come One means the realization that all phenomena are without substance or empty. In effect, this means that in propagating the Lotus Sutra one should have a mind of great compassion, abide in the truth of the non-substantiality of all phenomena, and bear all hardships with patience.

three schools of the south and seven schools of the north [南三北七] (Jpn *nansan-hokushichi*): Also, three schools of southern China and seven schools of northern China. Though generally referred to as "schools," they are actually the ten principal systems of classification of the Buddhist sutras set forth by various Buddhist teachers in China, during the Northern and Southern Dynasties period (439–589). Hence there are no specific names for the respective schools. T'ien-t'ai (538–597) employed this generic designation and outlined these systems in his *Profound Meaning of the Lotus Sutra.*

All three southern schools classified the Buddhist sutras into three categories—the sudden teaching, the gradual teaching, and the indeterminate teaching. The sudden teaching as defined by these schools corresponds to the Flower Garland Sutra; the gradual teaching, to the Āgama sutras, Correct and Equal sutras, Wisdom sutras, Lotus Sutra, and Nirvana Sutra; and the indeterminate teaching, to the Shrīmālā and Golden Light sutras. The difference among the three southern schools lies in their arrangement of the sutras included in the gradual teaching. One school subdivides the gradual teaching into three divisions: the teaching of the reality of things (Āgama sutras), the teaching of the non-substantiality of things (Correct and Equal sutras, Wisdom sutras, and Lotus Sutra), and the teaching of the eternity of the Buddha nature (Nirvana Sutra). Another of the three schools places the Lotus Sutra in an additional category by itself called the teaching uniting all teachings in the one vehicle, thus making four divisions within the gradual teaching. A third school adds a fifth division to the gradual teaching, establishing a separate category for the Vimalakīrti Sutra, the Brahmā Excellent Thought Sutra, and other sutras. This is called the division of the teaching extolling the bodhisattva practice.

The classifications by the seven northern schools are as follows: (1) A division of the Buddhist sutras into five categories called the teaching of human and heavenly beings (ethical teachings), the teaching of the reality of things, the teaching of the non-substantiality of things, the teaching uniting all teachings in the one vehicle, and the teaching of the eternity of the Buddha nature. (2) A twofold classification established by Bodhiruchi dividing Buddhism into the incomplete word teaching (Hinayana or Āgama sutras) and the complete word teaching (Mahayana). (3) A classification established by Hui-kuang, arranging the Buddhist teachings into four doctrines: causes and conditions (the doctrine of *abhidharma* works), temporary name (the doctrine of *The Treatise on the Establishment of Truth*), denial of the reality of things (the doctrine of the Great Perfection of Wisdom Sutra and of the three treatises—*The Treatise on the Middle Way, The Treatise on the Twelve Gates,* and *The One-Hundred-Verse Treatise*), and the eternity of the Buddha nature (the doctrine of the Nirvana Sutra and the Flower Garland Sutra). (4) A five-division system, identical to Hui-kuang's, except that the Flower Garland Sutra occupies an additional category of its own called the doctrine of the phenomenal world. (5) A classification into six doctrines, which adds to Hui-kuang's four-division system the two categories of the true teaching (Lotus Sutra) and the perfect teaching (Great Collection Sutra). (6) A division of Mahayana into two types: one that holds phenomena to be real, and the other that views them as non-substantial. (7) The one voice teaching, which maintains that the Buddha expounds only the one Buddha vehicle and there is no other teaching but this one Buddha vehicle that represents all his lifetime teachings.

T'ien-t'ai refuted these systems of classification and, refining and integrating all existing systems, formulated the classification of the "five periods and eight teachings" to assert the superiority of the Lotus Sutra over all other sutras. *See also* five periods and eight teachings.

three seals of Dharma [三法印] (Jpn *sambōin*): *See* three Dharma seals.

three stages of worthiness [三賢・三賢位] (Jpn *san-gen* or *san-gen-i*): Also, three worthies or three grades of worthiness. Stages of practice in the Hinayana teachings. The first of the three stages of worthiness is the stage of five meditations—the five meditative practices for eliminating greed, anger, foolishness, attachment to the idea of a permanent self, and distractedness of the mind. The second is the stage of observing the objects of meditation respectively. This means to meditate on each of the four objects of meditation—body, sensation, mind, and things—and to perceive body as impure, sensation as marked by suffering, mind as impermanent, and things as without self. The third is the stage of observing all the objects of meditation, i.e., the above four objects, as a whole. Along with the four good roots, the three stages of worthiness constitute the seven expedient means. One who has attained the seven expedient means enters the way of insight, or the first of the three ways, the second being the way of practice, and the third, the way of the arhat. The seven expedient means are preparatory practices leading to the way of insight. The concept of three stages of worthiness also appears in Mahayana Buddhism, in which it refers to stages of bodhisattva practice.

Three Stages school [三階教] (Chin San-chieh-chiao; Jpn Sangai-kyō):

A school founded in China by Hsin-hsing (540–594) based on the idea that the development of Buddhism after Shakyamuni's death is divided into three periods—the Former Day, Middle Day, and Latter Day of the Law. In China, an account defining the duration of the Former Day as five hundred years and the Middle Day as one thousand years was widely accepted, and therefore it was believed that the Latter Day began around 550. (*See* three periods.)

On the premise that the Latter Day had begun, Hsin-hsing taught that in the first stage, or the Former Day of the Law, the people were of superior religious capacity and therefore the one vehicle teaching was effective; in the second stage, or the Middle Day of the Law, the people were of intermediate capacity and the three vehicle teaching was effective; and in the third stage, or the Latter Day of the Law, the people are of markedly inferior capacity and only his own teaching is effective. He further asserted that to attain salvation the people in the Latter Day should not rely on any one particular sutra, but dedicate themselves to all Buddhas and all teachings, and that they should practice all forms of good and avoid all forms of evil.

Hsin-hsing also maintained that, because all people possess the Buddha nature, they are future Buddhas. Faithful to this belief, his followers prostrated themselves in reverence before everyone they met. After Hsin-hsing's death, the Inexhaustible Treasury, a financial foundation to offer relief to the sick and destitute, was established at Hua-tu-ssu temple in Ch'ang-an, the main temple of the Three Stages school. The school emphasized almsgiving and encouraged followers to donate to the Inexhaustible Treasury. In the late seventh century, the rulers of the T'ang dynasty and the other Buddhist schools condemned the teachings and activities of the Three Stages school; consequently, the Inexhaustible Treasury was abolished and the school banned.

three standards of comparison [三種の教相] (Jpn *sanshu-no-kyōsō*): Three viewpoints from which T'ien-t'ai (538–597), in his *Profound Meaning of the Lotus Sutra*, asserted the superiority of the Lotus Sutra over all other sutras and the superiority of the essential teaching (latter half) of the Lotus Sutra over its theoretical teaching (first half). The first standard is whether people of all capacities can attain Buddhahood through a particular sutra. The sutras other than the Lotus Sutra do not reveal that all people have the potential for enlightenment, because those sutras are based on the premise that people's individual capacities are fixed. In contrast, the Lotus Sutra clarifies that all people are capable of attaining enlightenment because all of the Ten Worlds, including Buddhahood, are mutually inclusive and inherent in their lives.

The second standard is whether the process of teaching, i.e., the process of planting the seed of Buddhahood in people's lives and finally harvesting its fruit by leading them to Buddhahood, is revealed in full. In contrast to the Lotus Sutra, which makes clear when Shakyamuni's instruction of the people began and ended, other sutras do not reveal this. The "Parable of the Phantom City" (seventh) chapter in the theoretical teaching (first half) of the Lotus Sutra explains that Shakyamuni Buddha first planted the seed of Buddhahood in the lives of his disciples at a time major world system dust particle *kalpas* in the past when he expounded the Lotus Sutra of the Buddha Great Universal Wisdom Excellence. At that time, the sutra says, Shakyamuni was a bodhisattva and the sixteenth son of Great Universal Wisdom Excellence. Among those who heard his preaching then, some abandoned their faith in the sutra, and after transmigrating in the evil paths, they were born again in India during the lifetime of Shakyamuni Buddha. These were his voice-hearer disciples, whom he prophesied would attain enlightenment in the future through faith in the one vehicle teaching of the Lotus Sutra. The sutras other than the Lotus do not elucidate this process of sowing and harvesting or the beginning and completion of the Buddha's teaching. The above two standards show the superiority of the Lotus Sutra over the other sutras.

The third standard is whether the original relationship between teacher and disciple is revealed. "Teacher" refers to the Buddha. The "Life Span" (sixteenth) chapter of the essential teaching (latter half) of the Lotus Sutra reveals that Shakyamuni originally attained enlightenment numberless major world system dust particle *kalpas* in the past (a time incomparably more remote than major world system dust particle *kalpas* in the past), and that ever since then he has been teaching his disciples. The other sutras say that Shakyamuni attained enlightenment in this life in India, and that his disciples first became his followers in this life. Though some sutras refer to past relationships of certain individuals with the Buddha, these are described as having been formed while Shakyamuni was still engaged in bodhisattva austerities and had not yet attained Buddhahood; therefore, they are not as profound as the bond he formed with his followers numberless major world system dust particle *kalpas* ago. This third standard demonstrates the superiority of the essential teaching of the Lotus Sutra over the theoretical teaching.

three sufferings [三苦] (Jpn *san-ku*): Also, three types of suffering. The first is suffering that results from undesirable causes and conditions. The second is suffering that results from the loss of something desirable, and the third is suffering that results from the impermanence of all phenomena.

three thousand realms in a single moment of life [一念三千] (Jpn *ichinen-sanzen*): Also, the principle of a single moment of life comprising three thousand realms. "A single moment of life" *(ichinen)* is also translated as one mind, one thought, or one thought-moment. A philosophical system established by T'ien-t'ai (538–597) in his *Great Concentration and Insight* on the basis of the phrase "the true aspect of all phenomena" from the "Expedient Means" (second) chapter of the Lotus Sutra. The three thousand realms, or the entire phenomenal world, exist in a single moment of life. The number three thousand here comes from the following calculation: 10 (Ten Worlds) × 10 (Ten Worlds) × 10 (ten factors) × 3 (three realms of existence). Life at any moment manifests one of the Ten Worlds. Each of these worlds possesses the potential for all ten within itself, and this "mutual possession," or mutual inclusion, of the Ten Worlds is represented as 10^2, or a hundred, possible worlds. Each of these hundred worlds possesses the ten factors, making one thousand factors or potentials, and these operate within each of the three realms of existence, thus making three thousand realms.

The theoretical teaching (first half) of the Lotus Sutra expounds the ten factors of life. It also sets forth the attainment of Buddhahood by persons of the two vehicles (voice-hearers and cause-awakened ones), which signifies the mutual possession of the Ten Worlds. The essential teaching (latter half) of the sutra reveals the true cause (the eternal nine worlds), the true effect (eternal Buddhahood), and the true land (the eternal land or realm of the environment). T'ien-t'ai unified all these concepts in one system, three thousand realms in a single moment of life.

Volume five of *Great Concentration and Insight* reads: "Life at each moment is endowed with the Ten Worlds. At the same time, each of the Ten Worlds is endowed with all Ten Worlds, so that an entity of life actually possesses one hundred worlds. Each of these worlds in turn possesses thirty realms, which means that in the one hundred worlds there are three thousand realms. The three thousand realms of existence are all possessed by life in a single moment. If there is no life, that is the end of the matter. But if there is the slightest bit of life, it contains all the three thousand realms. . . . This is what we mean when we speak of the 'region of the unfathomable.'"

"Life at each moment" means life as an indivisible whole that includes body and mind, cause and effect, and sentient and insentient things. A single moment of life is endowed, as stated above, with the three thousand realms. The relationship of these two elements is not such that one precedes the other, or that they are simultaneous in the sense that one is included in the other. Actually they are non-dual or, as T'ien-t'ai put it, "two [in phenomena] but not two [in essence]." The provisional teachings stated that all phenomena arise from the mind, or that they are subordinate to the mind. The Lotus Sutra clarifies that the true aspect is inseparable from all phenomena, and that all phenomena, just as they are, are in themselves the true aspect. When T'ien-t'ai stated, "The three thousand realms of existence are all possessed by life in a single moment. . . . But if there is the slightest bit of life, it contains all the three thousand realms," he is referring to the non-duality of "a single moment of life" and the "three thousand realms."

"The three thousand realms in a single moment of life" is classified into two as the theoretical principle and the actual embodiment of this principle. These are respectively termed the *theoretical three thousand realms in a single moment of life* and the *actual three thousand realms in a single moment of life.* The theoretical principle is based on the theoretical teaching of the Lotus Sutra, which expounds the equality of Buddhahood and the nine worlds. Both, it points out, are manifestations of the true aspect. The theoretical teaching also reveals the mutual possession of the Ten Worlds based on the principle that persons of the two vehicles, who were denied Buddhahood in the provisional teachings, also possess innate Buddhahood and can attain it. Strictly speaking, however, the theoretical teaching reveals only the hundred worlds and, multiplying by the ten factors of life, the thousand factors, and does not reveal their eternal nature. Only when supported by the essential teaching (the latter half) of the Lotus Sutra, can the theoretical teaching be said to expound theoretically, as a possibility, the three thousand realms in a single moment of life.

On the other hand, the essential teaching reveals Shakyamuni's enlightenment in the remote past (the true effect, eternal Buddhahood), the eternal life of his disciples, the Bodhisattvas of the Earth (the true cause, the eternal nine worlds), and the eternity of the *sahā* world (the true land). These explain the eternal Ten Worlds and the eternal three realms of existence, and thus "the actual three thousand realms in a single moment of life."

Despite its comprehensive view, the essential teaching does not go on to reveal the practice that enables one to embody directly this principle of three thousand realms in a single moment of life. Though the sutra says, "If there are those who hear the Law, then not a one will fail to attain Buddhahood," it does not identify what the Law is. That is why

Nichiren (1222–1282) defined the entire Lotus Sutra—both the theoretical and the essential teachings—as representing "the theoretical three thousand realms in a single moment of life."

In contrast, Nichiren embodied his life embracing the three thousand realms in a single moment, or the life of Nam-myoho-renge-kyo, in the mandala known as the Gohonzon and established the practice for attaining Buddhahood. That practice is to chant Nam-myoho-renge-kyo with faith in the Gohonzon. In Nichiren's teaching, this is the practice for "observing the mind," i.e., observing one's own mind and seeing Buddhahood in it. For this reason, his teaching is summarized in the phrase "embracing the Gohonzon is in itself observing one's mind" or "embracing the Gohonzon is in itself attaining Buddhahood."

He states in a 1273 letter known as *Reply to Kyō'ō,* "I, Nichiren, have inscribed my life in *sumi* ink, so believe in the Gohonzon with your whole heart. The Buddha's will is the Lotus Sutra, but the soul of Nichiren is nothing other than Nam-myoho-renge-kyo" (412), and in his 1273 treatise *The Object of Devotion for Observing the Mind:* "Showing profound compassion for those unable to comprehend the gem of the doctrine of three thousand realms in a single moment of life, the Buddha wrapped it within the five characters [of Myoho-renge-kyo], with which he then adorned the necks of the ignorant people of the latter age" (376).

Nichikan (1665–1726), the twenty-sixth chief priest of Taiseki-ji temple, interpreted the above passage of volume five of *Great Concentration and Insight* from the viewpoint of Nichiren's teaching. Nichikan defined "life at each moment" as the life of the eternal Buddha, or Nam-myoho-renge-kyo, which is inscribed down the center of the Gohonzon; he further interpreted "endowed with the Ten Worlds" as the Buddhas, bodhisattvas, and other figures inscribed on both sides of Nam-myoho-renge-kyo in the Gohonzon. These represent the principles of the mutual possession of the Ten Worlds, the hundred worlds and the thousand factors, and the three thousand realms. According to Nichikan, the sentence "The three thousand realms of existence are all possessed by life in a single moment" refers to the "region of the unfathomable," which he interprets as the object of devotion that embodies the principle of three thousand realms in a single moment of life. This is not to be viewed simply as an external object but as something that exists in the life of a person with faith in the object of devotion. Without faith, the object of devotion endowed with the three thousand realms does not exist within one's life. This, Nichikan stated, is the ultimate meaning of T'ien-t'ai's doctrine.

three thousand rules of conduct [三千威儀] (Jpn *sanzen-igi*): Also, three thousand rules of behavior. Strict rules of discipline for monks in the Hinayana teachings. Accounts of how to arrive at the figure of three thousand differ. According to one, the figure three thousand is arrived at by applying the two hundred and fifty precepts (the Hinayana rules of discipline for fully ordained monks) to each of the four activities of daily life: walking, standing, sitting, and lying. The resulting one thousand is then multiplied by three for past, present, and future to total three thousand rules of conduct. By another account, the figure three thousand is not to be taken literally, but simply indicates a large number.

three-time gaining of distinction [三度の高名] (Jpn *sando-no-kōmyō*): Also, three-time distinction. In his 1275 treatise *The Selection of the Time,* Nichiren declares: "In the secular texts it says, 'A sage is one who fully understands those things that have not yet made their appearance.' And in the Buddhist texts it says, 'A sage is one who knows the three existences of life—past, present, and future.' Three times now I have gained distinction by having such knowledge" (579). Nichiren made predictions on three occasions when he remonstrated with the leaders of the Kamakura shogunate, hoping thereby to bring peace and security to the country and protect its people from disaster.

According to *The Selection of the Time,* the first occasion was the sixteenth day of the seventh month, 1260, when he presented his work *On Establishing the Correct Teaching for the Peace of the Land* to Hōjō Tokiyori, the former regent but effective leader of the Kamakura shogunate. "At that time," he writes: "I said to the lay priest Yadoya, 'Please advise His Lordship that devotion to the Zen school and the Nembutsu school should be abandoned. If this advice is not heeded, trouble will break out within the ruling clan, and the nation will be attacked by another country'" (579).

The second time was the twelfth day of the ninth month in 1271, when Hei no Saemon, deputy chief of the Office of Military and Police Affairs (the chief being the regent), came with his men to arrest Nichiren at Matsubagayatsu. At that time Nichiren stated: "Nichiren is the pillar and beam of Japan. Doing away with me is toppling the pillar of Japan! Immediately you will all face 'the calamity of revolt within one's own domain,' or strife among yourselves, and also 'the calamity of invasion from foreign lands'" (579).

The third time was the eighth day of the fourth month in 1274, on his return to Kamakura from his exile on Sado Island, when he said to Hei no Saemon: "The task of praying for victory over the Mongols should not be entrusted to the True Word (Shingon) priests! If so grave a matter is entrusted to them, then the situation will only worsen rapidly and our country will face destruction" (579). Asked when the Mongols would attack, Nichiren replied, "It will probably occur before this year has ended" (579). The first attack by Mongol forces against Japan did in fact take place in the tenth month of 1274. After taking two small Japanese islands, the Mongols mounted an extensive land invasion at Hakata and Hakozaki, but their fleet was heavily damaged and driven back by severe weather. As for Nichiren's prediction of internal strife within the ruling clan, it was fulfilled in the second month of 1272, when Hōjō Tokisuke, a shogunal deputy stationed in Kyoto, revolted against his younger half brother, the regent Hōjō Tokimune, in an attempt to seize power.

three-time purification of the lands [三変土田] (Jpn *sampen-doden*): Shakyamuni Buddha's act of three times purifying countless lands in preparation for the Ceremony in the Air, described in the "Treasure Tower" (eleventh) chapter of the Lotus Sutra. To make room for the Buddhas who are his emanations and who are about to assemble from throughout the ten directions, Shakyamuni purifies three groups of lands, one at a time. First he purifies the *sahā* world where the assembly is taking place, then he purifies "two hundred ten thousand million *nayutas* of lands in each of the eight directions," and finally he purifies yet another "two hundred ten thousand million *nayutas* of lands in each of the eight directions" in the same manner. After the emanation Buddhas have assembled from their own lands throughout the universe, Shakyamuni opens the treasure tower of the Buddha Many Treasures, who invites him to share his seat therein. With this, the Ceremony in the Air begins. *See also* "Emergence of the Treasure Tower" chapter.

three treasures [三宝] (Skt *triratna* or *ratna-traya;* Jpn *sambō*): The three things that all Buddhists should revere and serve. They are the Buddha, the Law (the Buddha's teachings), and the Buddhist Order (community of believers). In Sanskrit, they are known as Buddha, Dharma, and *Samgha.* The Buddha is one who is awakened to the truth of life and the universe. The Dharma, or Law, means the teachings that the Buddha expounds in order to lead all people to enlightenment. The *Samgha,* or Buddhist Order, is the group of persons who practice the Buddha's teachings, preserve the Law, spread it, and transmit it to future generations. The three treasures are endowed with the power to free people from all sufferings and lead them to enlightenment. Traditionally, upon becoming a Buddhist, one vowed to believe in and devote oneself to the three treasures.

Three Treatises school [三論宗] (Chin San-lun-tsung; Jpn Sanron-shū): A school based on three treatises—Nāgārjuna's *Treatise on the Middle Way* and *Treatise on the Twelve Gates,* and Āryadeva's *One-Hundred-Verse Trea-*

tise. Kumārajīva translated these three treatises into Chinese in the early fifth century. Their doctrines were successively transmitted by Tao-sheng, T'an-chi, Seng-lang, Seng-ch'üan, and Fa-lang, and finally systematized by Chi-tsang (549–623), who is often regarded as the first patriarch of the Chinese Three Treatises, or San-lun, school.

The doctrines of the Three Treatises school were transmitted to Japan by three persons during the seventh and early eighth centuries: First, by the Korean priest Hyekwan, known in Japan as Ekan, who went to Japan in 625. He was a disciple of Chi-tsang. Second, by the Chinese priest Chih-tsang, known in Japan as Chizō, who also went to Japan in the seventh century. He studied the Three Treatises doctrines under Ekan at Gangō-ji temple in Nara and returned to China to further his study under Chi-tsang. On his return to Japan, he taught the Three Treatises doctrines at Hōryū-ji temple. Third, by Chizō's disciple Dōji, who went to China in 702 and returned to Japan in 718 with the Three Treatises doctrines. He lived at Daian-ji temple in Nara. Actually, a priest named Kwallŭk (known in Japan as Kanroku) of the Korean state of Paekche had brought the Three Treatises teachings to Japan in 602, but Ekan established the theoretical foundation of the school. For this reason, Ekan is regarded as the first to formally introduce the Three Treatises doctrine to Japan. The lineage of Chizō's disciples, carried on by Chikō and Raikō, was called the Gangō-ji branch of the Three Treatises school, and that of Dōji, the Daian-ji branch.

The Three Treatises doctrine holds that, because all phenomena appear and disappear solely by virtue of their relationship with other phenomena (dependent origination), they have no existence of their own, or self-nature, and are without substance. The school upholds Nāgārjuna's "middle path of the eight negations" (non-birth, non-extinction, non-cessation, non-permanence, non-uniformity, non-diversity, non-coming, and non-going), and sees refutation of dualistic or one-sided views in itself as revealing the truth of the Middle Way.

three True Word sutras [真言三部経] (Jpn *Shingon-sambu-kyō*): The Mahāvairochana, Diamond Crown, and Susiddhikara sutras. In Japan, these sutras form the doctrinal basis for the True Word (Shingon) school and for the esoteric teachings of the Tendai school (Tendai Esotericism). They were called the three True Word sutras, following the model of the Pure Land (Jōdo) school, which had designated three Pure Land sutras. While the True Word school places greater emphasis on the Mahāvairochana and Diamond Crown sutras, which represent the Womb Realm and the Diamond Realm respectively, Tendai Esotericism accords highest respect to the Susiddhikara Sutra, regarding it as a unification of both realms.

three truths [三諦] (Jpn *san-tai*): Also, threefold truth, triple truth, or three perceptions of the truth. The truth of non-substantiality, the truth of temporary existence, and the truth of the Middle Way. The three integral aspects of the truth, or ultimate reality, formulated by T'ien-t'ai (538–597) in *The Profound Meaning of the Lotus Sutra* and *Great Concentration and Insight*. The truth of non-substantiality means that phenomena have no existence of their own; their true nature is non-substantial, indefinable in terms of existence or nonexistence. The truth of temporary existence means that, although non-substantial, all things possess a temporary reality that is in constant flux. The truth of the Middle Way means that the true nature of phenomena is that they are neither non-substantial nor temporary, though they display attributes of both. The Middle Way is the essence of things that continues either in a manifest or a latent state. According to T'ien-t'ai's explanation, the Tripitaka teaching and the connecting teaching do not reveal the truth of the Middle Way and therefore lack the three truths. The specific teaching reveals the three truths but shows them as being separate from and independent of one another; that is, it does not teach that these three are inseparable aspects of all phenomena. This view is called the separation of the three truths. The perfect teaching views the three as an integral whole, each possessing all three within itself. This is called the unification of the three truths.

three types of action [三業] (Jpn *san-gō*): Deeds, words, and thoughts. *See* three categories of action.

three types of character [三性] (Jpn *san-shō*): Also, three natures. A principle of the Yogāchāra, or Consciousness-Only, school classifying all things into three natures—good, bad, and unlabeled, or neutral. "Unlabeled" indicates that which cannot be defined as either good or bad, or which produces neither good nor bad karmic effect.

three types of enemies [三類の敵人] (Jpn *sanrui-no-tekijin*): *See* three powerful enemies.

three types of expedient means [三方便] (Jpn *san-hōben*): *See* three expedient means.

three types of learning [三学] (Jpn *san-gaku*): Also, three disciplines. Three disciplines that Buddhist practitioners seek to master: precepts (Skt *shīla*), meditation *(dhyāna)*, and wisdom *(prajnā)*. These three are said to encompass all aspects of Buddhist doctrine and practice. Precepts are rules or disciplines intended to prevent error and put an end to evil in thought, word, and deed. Meditation is a practice designed to focus one's mind and cause it to become tranquil. Wisdom rids one of illusions and enables one to realize the truth. *See also* meditation; *prajnā;* precepts.

three types of meditation [三等至・三定・三静慮] (Jpn *san-tōji, san-jō,* or *san-jōryo*): Flavor meditation, pure meditation, and free-of-outflows meditation; three meditative practices explained in *The Dharma Analysis Treasury, The Great Commentary on the Abhidharma,* and other works. Flavor meditation is still bound and encumbered by earthly desires; pure meditation enables practitioners to perceive the nature of earthly desires and delusion and emancipates them from these to some extent; and free-of-outflows meditation enables practitioners to obtain wisdom that is completely free from delusions and earthly desires.

three vehicles [三乗] (Jpn *sanjō*): A classification in Mahayana Buddhism of three kinds of teachings, each tailored to the capacity of a specific set of practitioners and enabling them to attain a state of awakening suited to that capacity. "Vehicle" means that which carries one to a destination or state of awakening. The three vehicles are the teachings expounded for voice-hearers (Skt *shrāvaka*), for cause-awakened ones *(pratyekabuddha),* and for bodhisattvas. The voice-hearer vehicle indicates the teachings that enable voice-hearers to attain the state of arhat by awakening them to the four noble truths. The cause-awakened one vehicle is the teachings that lead practitioners to obtain insight into the causal relationship and impermanence of all phenomena through the doctrine of the twelve-linked chain of causation or by observing the changes in the natural world. The bodhisattva vehicle leads bodhisattvas to near-perfect enlightenment and perfect enlightenment, the fifty-first and fifty-second of the fifty-two stages of bodhisattva practice, through the practice of the six *pāramitās.* Generally speaking, Mahayana Buddhism describes the two vehicles of voice-hearers and cause-awakened ones as "lesser vehicles," or Hinayana, while emphasizing the bodhisattva vehicle.

The Lotus Sutra, however, declares that the sole purpose of a Buddha's advent in the world is to enable all people to become Buddhas, and that the three vehicles are accordingly not ends in themselves but means to lead people to the one Buddha vehicle. It identifies the Buddha vehicle as the supreme vehicle that at once encompasses and transcends those three and leads all people to Buddhahood. The "Expedient Means" (second) chapter of the Lotus Sutra says, "The Buddhas, utilizing the power of expedient means, apply distinctions to the one Buddha vehicle and preach as though it were three." It also says, "In the Buddha lands of the ten directions there is only the Law of the one vehicle, there are not two, there are not three." T'ien-t'ai (538–597) expressed this idea as "the replacement of the three vehicles with the one vehicle," a principle that he further divided into two—concise replacement and expanded replacement. The concise replacement of the three vehicles with the one vehicle is a reference to the short passage in the "Expedient Means" chapter that explains "the true aspect of all phenomena" in terms of the ten factors of life. This suggests that all life is endowed with the potential for Buddhahood. The expanded replacement of the three vehicles with the one vehicle refers to the section where Shakyamuni subsequently elaborates on the supremacy of the one vehicle from a variety of perspectives, using parables and other means to explain his meaning. This elaboration includes the latter half of the "Expedient Means" chapter through the "Prophecies" (ninth) chapter.

three vehicle teachings [三乗法] (Jpn *sanjō-hō*): The teachings expounded for voice-hearers, for cause-awakened ones, and for bodhisattvas. From the standpoint of the Lotus Sutra, they are expedient means to instruct and lead the people to the one vehicle teaching of the Lotus Sutra. *See also* three vehicles.

three virtues [三徳] (Jpn *san-toku*): (1) The benevolent functions of sovereign, teacher, and parent a Buddha is said to possess. The virtue of sovereign is the power to protect all living beings, the virtue of teacher is the wisdom to instruct and lead them to enlightenment, and the virtue of parent is the compassion to nurture and support them. Nichiren (1222–1282) interpreted the following passage of the "Simile and Parable" (third) chapter of the Lotus Sutra as expressing the three virtues: "Now this threefold world is all my domain [the virtue of sovereign], and the living beings in it are all my children [the virtue of parent]. Now this place is beset by many pains and trials. I am the only person who can rescue and protect others [the virtue of teacher]." In several of his writings, Nichiren described his role or mission as the votary of the Lotus Sutra in terms of these three virtues. The first line of his treatise *The Opening of the Eyes* reads, "There are three categories of people that all human beings should respect. They are the sovereign, the teacher, and the parent" (220). Near the conclusion of the same work, he states, "I, Nichiren, am sovereign, teacher, and father and mother to all the people of Japan" (287). Because these three virtues are considered the virtues of a Buddha, the above passages are seen as an indication that Nichiren intended *The Opening of the Eyes* as a declaration of his role as the Buddha of the Latter Day of the Law who expounds and spreads the teaching that can lead all people to Buddhahood.

(2) The Dharma body, wisdom, and emancipation; three attributes of a Buddha. The Dharma body means the truth that the Buddha has real-

ized, or the true aspect of all phenomena; wisdom is the capacity to realize this truth; and emancipation means the state of being free from the sufferings of birth and death. There is a correspondence between the three virtues, the three truths, and the Buddha's three bodies: the Dharma body (of the three virtues) corresponds to the truth of the Middle Way and to the Dharma body (of the three bodies), wisdom to the truth of non-substantiality and to the reward body, and emancipation to the truth of temporary existence and to the manifested body. T'ien-t'ai (538–597) states that the "three paths" of earthly desires, karma, and suffering are in reality none other than the three virtues of the Dharma body, wisdom, and emancipation. For example, T'ien-t'ai states in *The Profound Meaning of the Lotus Sutra,* "Straying from the Dharma body constitutes the path of suffering. There is no Dharma body apart from the path of suffering." The true nature of the three paths is the three virtues, but when one cannot manifest the three virtues, one remains in the three paths.

(3) Besides these two categories, there are several other sets of three virtues attributed to Buddhas, such as, for example, the virtue of wisdom to perceive the nature of all things, the virtue of eradicating earthly desires, and the virtue of benefiting living beings.

three ways [三道] (Jpn *san-dō*): Also, three paths. Three stages of practice in the Hinayana teachings. The way of insight, the way of practice, and the way of the arhat, or one who has no more to learn. The way of insight is the stage at which one beholds the four noble truths; hence it is also called the way of beholding the truth. Those who have attained the three stages of worthiness and the four good roots enter the way of insight, where they dispel the illusions of thought and attain the stage of sagehood. They then proceed to the way of practice, where they sever the illusions of desire. The way of the arhat represents the highest stage of awakening attainable to a practitioner of the Hinayana teachings. At this stage one is free from all illusions. The concept of three ways also applies to stages of Mahayana bodhisattva practice.

three worthies [三賢] (Jpn *san-gen*): Stages of practice in the Hinayana teachings. *See* three stages of worthiness.

thrice turned wheel of the Law [三転法輪] (Jpn *san-tembōrin*): Also, three turnings of the wheel of the Law. A classification of Shakyamuni's lifetime teachings into three categories according to the order of their preaching, set forth by Chi-tsang (549–623), a systematizer of the doctrines of the Three Treatises (San-lun) school in China. The thrice turned wheel of the Law consists of the root teaching, the branch teaching, and the teaching that unites the branch teaching with the root teaching. The root teaching represents the teaching that directly reveals the Buddha's enlightenment to bodhisattvas without employing expedient means. It corresponds to the one vehicle teaching of the Flower Garland Sutra. The branch teaching represents the three vehicle teaching, which the Buddha expounded in accordance with the capacity of his listeners. It corresponds to the teaching of the Āgama, Correct and Equal, and Wisdom sutras. The teaching that unites the branch teaching with the root teaching indicates the teaching that unites the three vehicle teaching with the one vehicle teaching. It corresponds to the Lotus Sutra.

Thus Come One [如来] (Skt, Pali *tathāgata;* Jpn *nyorai*): One of the ten honorable titles of a Buddha, meaning one who has come from the realm of truth. This title indicates that a Buddha embodies the fundamental truth of all phenomena and has grasped the law of causality spanning past, present, and future. There are two opinions about the Sanskrit and Pali word *tathāgata.* One view interprets it as a compound of *tathā* and *āgata,* meaning "thus come one" and indicating one who has arrived from the realm of truth. This is the interpretation generally used in Chinese translations. The other interprets the word *tathāgata* as the compound of *tathā* and *gata,* meaning "thus gone one" and indicating one who has gone to the world of enlightenment.

Thus Come One Zen [如来禅] (Jpn *nyorai-zen*): Also, Tathāgata meditation or Thus Come One meditation. A reference to the type of meditation that Bodhidharma introduced to China in the early sixth century with his founding of the Zen (Chin Ch'an) school. The school maintained that the Buddha's enlightenment was transmitted wordlessly, outside the sutras, from Shakyamuni Buddha to Mahākāshyapa and finally to Bodhidharma in the lineage of Zen masters. Later, however, an opinion arose within the school that the expression Thus Come One Zen connotes meditation based on the sutras. For this reason, Bodhidharma's seated meditation, which aims to perceive the Buddha-mind intuitively and directly, came to be called patriarchal Zen, forming a tradition that regards Bodhidharma as its founding patriarch. The school asserts that patriarchal Zen is the highest form of meditation.

Tibetan Buddhism [チベット仏教] (Jpn Chibetto-bukkyō): A distinctive form of Buddhism that developed in Tibet around the seventh century and later in Mongolia and other regions. It is a tradition that derives from Indian Mahayana Buddhism, especially the doctrine of non-substantiality (Skt *shūnyatā*) of the Mādhyamika school, and incorporates the doctrine of the Yogāchāra (Consciousness-Only) school as well as the esoteric rituals of Vajrayāna (Tantric, or Esoteric, Buddhism). Tibetan Buddhism is also monastic, having adopted the *vinaya,* or monastic rules, of early Buddhism. It has traditionally involved a large number of monks and nuns. Tibetan Buddhism is sometimes (incorrectly) referred to as Lamaism, due to its system of "reincarnating" lamas. The title *lama* means a venerable teacher. Some lamas of certain Tibetan monasteries are believed to be successively reincarnated, each head lama being considered a reincarnation of the last in the lineage. In these traditions, sets of instructions are handed down that lead to the identification of a child believed to be the reincarnation of a previous lama. When signs point to a certain child (always a boy), he is tested, and upon passing the tests, is recognized as the reincarnated lama. He then receives monastic training and education and takes on full responsibilities as a lama at a specified age.

Buddhism evolved in Tibet in the early seventh century during the reign of King Songtsen Gampo (581–649). A series of religious kings contributed to its adoption and eventual institution as a state religion. Songtsen Gampo took as his wives a Nepalese princess and a Chinese princess, both of whom were devout Buddhists. They influenced the king to take faith in Buddhism and build the first Buddhist temples in Tibet. Songtsen Gampo also sent Thonmi Sambhota to study Buddhism in India. When he returned, he developed a Tibetan writing system based upon the Indian scripts he had studied (Tibet until that time had no set writing system). With this Tibetan script, translation of Sanskrit Buddhist texts into Tibetan began.

Later King Thisong Detsen (742–797) further established Buddhism in Tibet against strong opposition from practitioners of the native religion called Bon. He invited Shāntarakshita, a noted Indian monk of the Mādhyamika school, to come to Tibet to teach Buddhism. On Shāntarakshita's advice, the king also invited the Indian Tantric master Padmasambhava. Padmasambhava is credited with "converting" the Bon deities to Buddhism (incorporating them into the Buddhist teachings) and quelling Bon opposition. Shāntarakshita and Padmasambhava together established Tibet's first monastery at Samye in 779. The Nyingma, one of today's four major Tibetan Buddhist schools, claims to preserve the teachings of Padmasambhava. King Thisong Detsen also sponsored a religious debate between Kamalashīla, an Indian monk, and Mo-ho-yen, a Chinese priest of the Zen (Ch'an) school, held at the Samye monastery in 794. The king decided in favor of the Indian teacher and thus officially adopted the teachings of Indian Buddhism, or more specifically, the Mahayana teachings founded on Nāgārjuna's philosophy of the Mādhyamika school and the bodhisattva ideal. He rejected the introspective doctrines of Zen that claimed to ensure sudden enlightenment through meditation.

King Thitsug Detsen (806–841), a grandson of King Thisong Detsen, built temples and monasteries and contributed greatly to the translation of Sanskrit Buddhist scriptures into Tibetan as well as to Buddhist art and culture. According to one account, in 841 Bon followers had him assassinated, and his brother, Langdarma, succeeded him. The new king opposed Buddhism. He destroyed temples and monasteries, oppressed Buddhist monks, and abolished Buddhism as an institution; it was not restored until two centuries later. According to another account, the death of King Langdarma led to a power struggle that resulted in the division of the nation and a collapse of the Buddhist Order. In either case, after a period of political and religious turmoil, the ruler of western Tibet invited Atīsha, an Indian Buddhist teacher of the Mādhyamika school, to the region in 1042 to help restore Buddhism.

Atīsha propagated Buddhist teachings, reformed Tantric practices that had involved overt sexual activity, and brought about a revival of Buddhism. Atīsha's teachings were inherited by his disciple Domton, who founded the Kadam school of Tibetan Buddhism. (Later this school was absorbed by the Gelug school, also known as the Yellow Hat school, which was founded in the late fourteenth century by Tsongkapa, a Buddhist reformer.) In the same century, Marpa returned to Tibet from his journey to India to study Buddhism and, with his disciple Milarepa, founded the Kagyu school. By the fourteenth century, Buddhism was well established in Tibet, and most of the available Indian scriptures had been translated into Tibetan. A number of lost Sanskrit scriptures have been preserved until today through their Tibetan translations.

Tibetan Buddhism also spread outside of Tibet, most notably in Mongolia and the Mongol Empire. In the mid-thirteenth century, Sakya Pandita, an eminent scholar of the Sakya school of Tibetan Buddhism, journeyed to Mongolia with his nephew and student, Phagpa. Deeply impressed by them, Mongol officials converted to Buddhism. Later Phagpa was appointed imperial teacher and became an adviser to Kublai Khan, the ruler of the Mongol Empire. He was also appointed the temporal ruler of Tibet. In 1578 the Mongolian ruler Altan Khan hosted the renowned Sonam Gyatso, the leader of the Gelug school of Tibetan Buddhism, and conferred upon him the honorific title "Dalai Lama." *Dalai* is a Mongolian word for ocean. The title was also applied to his two predecessors.

With the aid of the Mongols, the Gelug school and its lineage of Dalai Lamas became the most prominent and powerful in Tibet. The Dalai Lama came to be regarded as the country's spiritual leader and temporal ruler, and each was believed to be a successive incarnation of the bodhisattva Avalokiteshvara, Perceiver of the World's Sounds. Since the popular uprising against Chinese rule in Tibet in 1959 and the resulting exile of the fourteenth Dalai Lama, Tenzin Gyatso (b. 1935), and his followers, interest in Tibetan Buddhism has grown in the West. The Nyingma, Kagyu, Sakya, and Gelug are the four major schools of Tibetan Buddhism, the Gelug being the most prominent.

T'ien-t'ai [天台] (538–597) (PY Tiantai; Jpn Tendai): Also known as Chih-i. The founder of the T'ien-t'ai school in China, commonly referred to as the Great Teacher T'ien-t'ai or the Great Teacher Chih-che (Chih-che meaning "person of wisdom"). The name T'ien-t'ai was taken from Mount T'ien-t'ai where he lived, and this, too, became the name of the Buddhist school he effectively founded. He was a native of Hua-jung in Ching-chou, China, where his father was a senior official in the Liang dynasty government (502–557). The fall of the Liang dynasty forced his family into exile. He lost both parents soon thereafter and in 555 entered the Buddhist priesthood under Fa-hsü at Kuo-yüan-ssu temple. He then went to Mount Ta-hsien where he studied the Lotus Sutra and its related scriptures. In 560 he visited Nan-yüeh (also known as Hui-ssu) on Mount Ta-su to study under him, and as a result of intense practice, he is said to have attained an awakening through the "Medicine King" (twenty-third) chapter of the Lotus Sutra. This awakening is referred to as the "enlightenment on Mount Ta-su."

After seven years of practice under Nan-yüeh, T'ien-t'ai left the mountain and made his way to Chin-ling, the capital of the Ch'en dynasty, where he lived at the temple Wa-kuan-ssu and lectured for eight years on the Lotus Sutra and other texts. His fame spread, and he attracted many followers. Aware that the number of his disciples who were obtaining insight was decreasing, however, and, in order to further his understanding and practice, he retired to Mount T'ien-t'ai in 575. Thereafter, at the emperor's repeated request, he lectured on *The Treatise on the Great Perfection of Wisdom* and the Benevolent Kings Sutra at the imperial court in Chin-ling. In 587, at Kuang-che-ssu temple in Chin-ling, he gave lectures on the Lotus Sutra that were later compiled as *The Words and Phrases of the Lotus Sutra.* After the downfall of the Ch'en dynasty, he returned to his native Ching-chou and there expounded teachings that were set down as *The Profound Meaning of the Lotus Sutra* in 593 and *Great Concentration and Insight* in 594 at Yü-ch'üan-ssu temple. The three works mentioned above were all compiled by his disciple Chang-an and became the three major texts of the T'ien-t'ai school. He then returned to Mount T'ien-t'ai, where he died. Other lectures of T'ien-t'ai compiled by Chang-an include *The Profound Meaning of the "Perceiver of the World's Sounds"*

Chapter and *The Profound Meaning of the Golden Light Sutra.*

T'ien-t'ai criticized the scriptural classifications formulated by the ten major Buddhist schools of his time, which regarded either the Flower Garland Sutra or the Nirvana Sutra as the highest Buddhist teachings. Instead he classified all of Shakyamuni's sutras into "five periods and eight teachings" and through this classification demonstrated the superiority of the Lotus Sutra. He also established the practice of threefold contemplation in a single mind and the principle of three thousand realms in a single moment of life. Because he systematized the doctrine of what became known as the T'ien-t'ai school, he is revered as its founder, though, according to Chang-an's preface to *Great Concentration and Insight,* the lineage of the teaching itself began with Hui-wen, who based his teaching on Nāgārjuna and transferred it to Nan-yüeh.

T'ien-t'ai, Mount [天台山] (PY Tiantai-shan; Jpn Tendai-san): A mountain in Chekiang Province in China where the Great Teacher T'ien-t'ai lived and where the T'ien-t'ai school was based. Both the name of the school and of its founder derive from this mountain. Mount T'ien-t'ai prospered as a center of Chinese Buddhism, and a number of temples were built there. It also had a significant influence on the development of Buddhism in Japan; the majority of priests from Japan who traveled to China to further their Buddhist learning studied at Mount T'ien-t'ai.

T'ien-t'ai school [天台宗] (PY Tiantaizong; Jpn Tendai-shū): A major school of Buddhism founded by T'ien-t'ai (538–597), also known as Chih-i, in China. The school emphasizes two principal disciplines: doctrinal studies and meditative practices. Concerning the former, it adopted a system of classification that organizes all the Buddhist sutras into five periods and eight teachings to clarify their relative position, and based itself on the Lotus Sutra. It also teaches the doctrine of three thousand realms in a single moment of life, the unification of the three truths, the six stages of practice, and others.

Concerning meditative practices, the school maintains that enlightenment is achieved by meditation or observation of one's mind; through such practices one aims to perceive the three truths within one's own life. This practice, called "the threefold contemplation in a single mind," is said to have been established by Hui-wen based on Nāgārjuna's works *The Treatise on the Great Perfection of Wisdom* and *The Treatise on the Middle Way.* Hui-wen transmitted it to Nan-yüeh, who in turn taught it to T'ien-t'ai. T'ien-t'ai refuted the three schools located to the south of the Yangtze River and the seven schools located to the north, all of which believed in the supremacy of either the Flower Garland Sutra or the Nirvana Sutra. He asserted that Shakyamuni's ultimate teaching is to be found in the Lotus Sutra. His lectures on the Lotus Sutra were recorded and compiled by his immediate successor Chang-an, and they became known as the three major writings of the T'ien-t'ai school: *The Profound Meaning of the Lotus Sutra, The Words and Phrases of the Lotus Sutra,* and *Great Concentration and Insight.*

Because T'ien-t'ai established and systematized both the doctrine and practice of the school, he is regarded as its founder. T'ien-t'ai's teaching was transmitted successively to Chang-an, Chih-wei, Hui-wei, Hsüan-lang, Miao-lo, and others. Miao-lo wrote commentaries on the three major writings and is credited with the restoration of the school. In 804 Miao-lo's disciples Tao-sui and Hsing-man taught the T'ien-t'ai principles to Dengyō (also known as Saichō), who had come from Japan to further his studies. Dengyō later founded the Japanese Tendai school ("Tendai" is the Japanese reading of the Chinese T'ien-t'ai). The T'ien-t'ai school declined in China amid the suppression of Buddhism by Emperor Wu-tsung in 845 and the warfare that broke out toward the end of the T'ang dynasty (618–907); many of its texts were lost. The beginning of the Sung dynasty (960–1279) saw a revival of the school during the time of its eleventh patriarch, Ch'ing-sung. Later, however, it divided into two branches, one from the lineage of I-chi and the other from that of Chih-yin. I-chi collected the texts of the T'ien-t'ai school and devoted himself to its restoration. I-chi was succeeded by I-t'ung and then by Chih-li. Chih-li's group called itself the Mountain (Chin Shan-chia; Jpn Sange) school, emphasizing its conviction that it was within the true lineage of Mount T'ien-t'ai, the original base of the T'ien-t'ai school. They called the other branch the Outside-the-Mountain (Shan-wai; Sangai) school, suggesting deviation from the true lineage.

Along with the wane of Chinese Buddhism in general due to foreign invasions at the end of the Sung dynasty, the T'ien-t'ai school also gradually declined. The texts of the school were first brought to Japan by the Chinese priest Chien-chen (Jpn Ganjin) in the mid-eighth century. It was Dengyō, however, who studied them in earnest, went to China to learn the depths of T'ien-t'ai principles, and established the Tendai school in his homeland based upon those teachings.

T'ien-t'ai's three major works [天台三大部] (Jpn *Tendai-sandai-bu*): Also, three major works on the Lotus Sutra, or three major writings of the T'ien-t'ai school. *The Profound Meaning of the Lotus Sutra, The Words and Phrases of the Lotus Sutra,* and *Great Concentration and Insight.* These three works are T'ien-t'ai's lectures recorded and compiled by his disciple Chang-an (561–632). Miao-lo later wrote the following commentaries on them: *The Annotations on "The Profound Meaning of the Lotus Sutra," The Annotations on "The Words and Phrases of the Lotus Sutra,"* and *The Annotations on "Great Concentration and Insight."* Together, these six works formed the doctrinal basis for the T'ien-t'ai school.

Ti-lun school [地論宗] (PY Dilunzong; Jpn Jiron-shū): *See* Treatise on the Ten Stages Sutra school.

Time school [時宗] (Jpn Ji-shū): A school of the Pure Land teaching in Japan founded by Ippen (1239–1289). Its head temple is Shōjōkō-ji in Fujisawa, Kanagawa Prefecture. "Time" (Ji), the name of this school, mirrors its tenet that one should chant the Nembutsu (an invocation of the name of Amida Buddha) with utmost sincerity and with the belief that this moment in time accords with one's last moment. Among the three Pure Land sutras, the school places special emphasis on the Amida Sutra. Ippen traveled throughout the country, distributing talismans with the inscription that the Nembutsu will ensure rebirth in the Pure Land of Amida Buddha. He spread the practice of "dancing Nembutsu" *(odori-nembutsu),* that of chanting the Nembutsu while dancing in the street to drums and bells. His adherents disseminated the Nembutsu in the same way by traveling throughout the country. After Ippen's death, Shinkyō (1237–1319), also called Ta'amida-butsu, became the second patriarch and worked to build temples. He lived at Muryōkō-ji temple, which he founded. An increasing number of priests of the school followed suit, living in temples and abandoning the practice of wandering throughout the country. The school enjoyed the patronage of secular authorities and flourished from the early fourteenth century through the sixteenth century, but declined thereafter with the rising popularity of the True Pure Land (Jōdo Shin) school.

tipitaka [三蔵] (Pali; Jpn *san-zō*): Tripitaka in Sanskrit. *See* three divisions of the canon.

tōba [塔婆] (Jpn): A shortened form of the term *sotoba,* the Japanese transliteration of the Sanskrit word *stūpa,* a type of shrine originating in India where the relics of Shakyamuni Buddha or other sage monks were housed. In Japan, *tōba* is a flat wooden memorial tablet, long and narrow in shape, bearing inscriptions such as passages from the sutras and the posthumous Buddhist name of the deceased. It is placed upright beside the grave during memorial services and left there. *See also* stupa.

Tōdai-ji [東大寺]: The head temple of the Flower Garland (Kegon) school in Nara, Japan. One of the seven major temples of Nara. It was the headquarters of the official provincial temples established throughout the country by imperial edict in 741. Tōdai-ji was built in the middle of the eighth century to fulfill a vow of Emperor Shōmu and opened by Rōben (689–773), who became its first chief priest. A great image of Vairochana Buddha was erected at this temple by an edict of Emperor Shōmu issued in 743. In 749 the bronze statue was completed, and in 752 a grand ceremony was held to consecrate it. In 754 Chien-chen (Jpn Ganjin), a priest of the Chinese Precepts (Lü; Jpn Ritsu) school who had brought the school's teachings with him to Japan, established an ordination platform at Tōdai-ji. There he conducted ceremonies conferring the precepts on the Retired Emperor Shōmu and some four hundred others. In 1180 almost all of the temple's major buildings were burned down by warriors of the Taira clan in the course of their war with the Minamoto clan. The following year, with the support of the Retired Emperor Go-shirakawa and the shogun Minamoto no Yoritomo, Chōgen (1121–1206) rebuilt the temple. In 1567, however, the fires of war again devastated Tōdai-ji, which was then rebuilt with the sponsorship of the Tokugawa shogunate.

Tōfuku-ji [東福寺]: The head temple of the Tōfuku-ji branch of the Rinzai school of Zen, and one of the Five Temples of Kyoto in Japan. Kujō Michiie (1193–1252), the chief minister of the imperial court, made a vow in 1236 to build Tōfuku-ji and in 1243 asked Enni to become its first chief priest. In 1255, three years after Kujō's death, Enni presided over the temple's completion ceremony.

Tō-ji [東寺]: The head temple of the Tō-ji branch of the True Word (Shingon) school, located in Kyoto, Japan. Its formal name is Konkōmyō Shitennō Kyō'ō Gokoku-ji Himitsu Dembō-in, generally shortened to Kyō'ō Gokoku-ji. Tō-ji, meaning East Temple, was so called because it was located to the east of the gate leading to the imperial palace, while Sai-ji, or West Temple, was located to the west of the gate. Both were charged with the protection of the capital. The capital moved to Kyoto in 794, and Emperor Kammu built Tō-ji in 796; in 823 Emperor Saga granted it to Kōbō, the founder of the Japanese True Word school, which practiced Esoteric Buddhism. Thereafter it became a center for the study and practice of Esoteric Buddhism.

Tōjō Kagenobu [東条景信] (n.d.): A steward of Tōjō Village in Nagasa District of Awa Province in Japan and a passionate believer in the Pure Land teachings. His full name and title were Tōjō Saemon-no-jō Kagenobu. When Nichiren first declared his teaching of Nam-myoho-renge-kyo at Seichō-ji temple in that village in 1253, Tōjō Kagenobu was so infuriated by his severe criticism of the Pure Land (Jōdo) school that he attempted to have Nichiren seized. When Nichiren returned to Awa in 1264, the year after he was pardoned from his exile to Itō on the Izu Peninsula, Tōjō Kagenobu and his men ambushed him at a place called

Komatsubara, wounding Nichiren and killing two of his followers. Though it is not certain when, Kagenobu tried to deprive the proprietary lord of two temples in the lord's manor, but failed because Nichiren helped the lord settle the matter in court. This also contributed to his hostility toward Nichiren. *See also* Komatsubara Persecution.

Toki Jōnin [富木常忍] (1216–1299): A lay follower of Nichiren who lived in Wakamiya, Katsushika District of Shimōsa Province, Japan. Because his ancestors owned a manor in Toki, Inaba Province, he was named Toki Tsunenobu. He assumed the name Jōnin, a different reading of Tsunenobu, when he became a lay priest; later he was renamed Nichijō by his teacher, Nichiren. He was also known as the lay priest Toki. He served as a retainer to Lord Chiba. According to one account, he lost his wife and married Myōjō, adopting her son who in 1267 became a disciple of Nichiren and took the name Nitchō. Nitchō was later designated one of the six senior priests by Nichiren. Toki had a son and a daughter by Myōjō. That son, Nitchō (written with different Chinese characters than the name of the adopted son), was appointed the first chief instructor of Omosu Seminary by Nikkō, Nichiren's successor.

Toki became Nichiren's follower around 1254, the year after Nichiren first declared his teaching at Seichō-ji. He was a man of considerable erudition, and Nichiren entrusted him with a number of his more important works including *The Object of Devotion for Observing the Mind*, one of his five major writings. After the Matsubagayatsu Persecution in the eighth month of 1260, Toki Jōnin invited Nichiren to live at his residence. Nichiren stayed there for nearly half a year, during which time many people in Shimōsa converted to his teaching. In 1268 the first emissary from the Mongol Empire arrived, demanding that Japan become a tributary to the empire. Declaring this a sign that the prophecy of foreign invasion he made in *On Establishing the Correct Teaching for the Peace of the Land* was about to be fulfilled, Nichiren sent eleven letters of remonstration to influential political and religious leaders, including the regent Hōjō Tokimune, and demanded an opportunity to defend his teaching in a public religious debate. The following year, Toki Jōnin was summoned to the Office of Legal Affairs of the Kamakura shogunate for questioning together with Ōta Jōmyō and Shijō Kingo, who were also Nichiren's disciples. Nichiren sent a letter instructing them on how to behave at the place of questioning.

While Nichiren was in exile on Sado from 1271 through 1274, Toki Jōnin, with Shijō Kingo, served as a rallying point for his followers. In 1279, when Nisshū and Nichiben, former Tendai priests who had converted to Nichiren's teaching, had to flee the Fuji area in the aftermath of the Atsuhara Persecution, Toki Jōnin and his wife, Myōjō, also known as the lay nun Toki, protected them. In addition to *The Object of Devotion for Observing the Mind,* Toki Jōnin received many treatises and letters from Nichiren, including *On Taking the Essence of the Lotus Sutra, On the Four Stages of Faith and the Five Stages of Practice, Letter from Sado,* and *A Sage Perceives the Three Existences of Life.*

Tokuichi [徳一] : *See* Tokuitsu.

Tokuitsu [徳一] (n.d.): Also known as Tokuichi. A priest of the Dharma Characteristics (Hossō) school in Japan during the late eighth and early ninth centuries. He is well known for his dispute with Dengyō, the founder of the Japanese Tendai school, concerning Dengyō's espousal of the one vehicle teaching over the three vehicle teaching, which Tokuitsu upheld. Tokuitsu studied the teachings of the Dharma Characteristics school under Shūen at Kōfuku-ji temple in Nara and is said to have lived either at Kōfuku-ji or Tōdai-ji temple. Thereafter he moved to Aizu in Ōshū, in northeastern Japan. According to one account, his desire to leave behind all worldly attachments and concentrate on practice in a remote location prompted this move. Another account has it that he was a son of Fujiwara no Nakamaro, a courtier who led an unsuccessful revolt in 764, and was therefore forced to flee the capital of Nara. In the early ninth century, Tokuitsu wrote *On the Buddha Nature, The Mirror on the Meaning of the Middle and the Extreme,* and other works, in which he asserted that the one vehicle teaching of the Lotus Sutra is a provisional doctrine and that the three vehicle teaching is the Buddha's true teaching. Dengyō countered that the one vehicle teaching of the Lotus Sutra is the true teaching and that the three vehicle teachings are merely expedient means to instruct the people and lead them to the one vehicle. Their debate continued until Dengyō's death. Tokuitsu is credited with founding many temples in northeastern Japan, including Chūzen-ji on Mount Tsukuba and Enichi-ji in Aizu, where he died.

Tōshōdai-ji [唐招提寺] : The head temple of the Precepts (Ritsu) school in Nara, Japan, founded in 759 by Chien-chen, the Chinese priest known as Ganjin in Japan. Ganjin built the temple on land donated by the imperial court. It prospered as the center for the study of the Buddhist precepts in Japan. Its historic buildings, such as the golden hall and the sutra repository, and several Buddhist statues preserved there are national treasures.

transference of benefit [廻向・回向] (Skt *parināma* or *parināmana;* Jpn *ekō*): To transfer to others the benefits or "good roots" one gains through Buddhist practice. Mahayana Buddhism holds that these benefits can be transferred to others and even to the deceased. It emphasizes that bodhisattvas should endeavor to transfer their benefits to others so that all people can attain enlightenment.

transfer of the essence of the Lotus Sutra [結要付嘱] (Jpn *ketchō-fuzoku*): Also, transmission of the essence of the Lotus Sutra. In the "Supernatural Powers" (twenty-first) chapter of the Lotus Sutra, Shakyamuni Buddha's entrusting of the sutra's teaching to Bodhisattva Superior Practices and the other Bodhisattvas of the Earth. The sutra reads: "At that time the Buddha spoke to Superior Practices and the others in the great assembly of bodhisattvas, saying: 'The supernatural powers of the Buddhas, as you have seen, are immeasurable, boundless, inconceivable. If in the process of entrusting this sutra to others I were to employ these supernatural powers for immeasurable, boundless hundreds, thousands, ten thousands, millions of *asamkhya kalpas* to describe the benefits of the sutra, I could never finish doing so. To put it briefly, all the doctrines possessed by the Thus Come One, all the freely exercised supernatural powers of the Thus Come One, the storehouse of all the secret essentials of the Thus Come One, all the most profound matters of the Thus Come One—all these are proclaimed, revealed, and clearly expounded in this sutra. For this reason, after the Thus Come One has entered extinction, you must single-mindedly accept, uphold, read, recite, explain, preach, and transcribe it, and practice it as directed.'"

T'ien-t'ai (538–597), in *The Words and Phrases of the Lotus Sutra,* described the passage "all the doctrines possessed by the Thus Come One, all the freely exercised supernatural powers of the Thus Come One, the storehouse of all the secret essentials of the Thus Come One, all the most profound matters of the Thus Come One" as four essential phrases that summarize the Lotus Sutra, calling it the "four-phrase essence" of the sutra. In *The Profound Meaning of the Lotus Sutra,* based on the same sutra passage, T'ien-t'ai formulated five major principles—name, essence, quality, function, and teaching—that endow the sutra's title, *Myoho-renge-kyo:* "To put it briefly, all the doctrines possessed by the Thus Come One [name], all the freely exercised supernatural powers of the Thus Come One [function], the storehouse of all the secret essentials of the Thus Come One [essence], all the most profound matters of the Thus Come One [quality]—all these are proclaimed, revealed, and clearly expounded in this sutra [teaching]." Nichiren interpreted the same sutra passage as indicating Nam-myoho-renge-kyo of the Three Great Secret Laws. *See also* five major principles; Three Great Secret Laws.

transformation body [変化身・化身] (Jpn *henge-shin* or *keshin*): An alternate form assumed by a Buddha or bodhisattva in order to lead living beings to enlightenment. Buddhas and bodhisattvas are said to take on a form most suitable for instructing those they are trying to lead to enlightenment.

transmigration in the six paths [六道輪廻] (Jpn *rokudō-rinne*): The cycle of birth and death that unenlightened beings undergo in the six paths of hell, hungry spirits, animals, *asuras,* human beings, and heavenly beings. Transmigration in the six paths suggests continual rebirth in the realms of delusion and suffering, where one remains at the mercy of earthly desires. Transmigration is a translation of the Sanskrit word *samsāra,* which also means wandering. See also *samsāra;* six paths.

transmigration with change and advance [変易生死] (Jpn *hen'yaku-shōji* or *hennyaku-shōji*): The transmigration that voice-hearers, cause-awakened ones, and bodhisattvas undergo on the way to emancipation. It is contrasted with "transmigration with differences and limitations." Transmigration with change and advance means that one becomes free from transmigration with differences and limitations, or transmigration in the realm of delusion, and advances to higher stages of practice till one attains emancipation. *See also* transmigration with differences and limitations.

transmigration with differences and limitations [分段生死] (Jpn *bun-dan-shōji*): The transmigration of unenlightened beings among the six paths (the lower six of the Ten Worlds, from hell to the world of heavenly beings). In this repeating cycle of rebirth among the six paths, living beings are said to be born with limited life spans and in different forms according to their karma. This kind of transmigration is contrasted with "transmigration with change and advance," which refers to the transmigration of voice-hearers, cause-awakened ones, and bodhisattvas. *See also* transmigration with change and advance.

transmission from mind to mind [以心伝心] (Jpn *ishin-denshin*): A doctrine of the Zen school asserting that the truth to which Shakyamuni Buddha was enlightened is transmitted from mind to mind, from one patriarch to the next. *See also* separate transmission outside the sutras.

transmission of the essence of the Lotus Sutra [結要付嘱] (Jpn *ketchō-fuzoku*): *See* transfer of the essence of the Lotus Sutra.

Transmission of the Lamp, The [伝灯録] (Chin *Ch'uan-teng-lu;* Jpn *Dentō-roku*): A work compiled in 1004, the first year of the Ching-te era, by Tao-yüan of China, a Zen (Ch'an) priest. The full title is *The Ching-te Era Record of the Transmission of the Lamp.* It details the lineage of Zen Buddhism as having been handed down from the "seven Buddhas of the past" through the Indian and Chinese Zen patriarchs to Fa-yen Wen-i (885–958), founder of the Fa-yen school. It gives accounts of a total of 1,701 Zen patriarchs and masters and is regarded in the Zen school as a historical work.

transmission section [流通分] (Jpn *rutsū-bun*): Also, transmission. One of the three sections or divisions of a sutra employed to interpret the sutra's teachings, the other two being the preparation section and the revelation section. The transmission section is the concluding section, which explains the benefit of the sutra and urges that the core teaching in the revelation section be transmitted to the future. *See also* three divisions of a sutra.

Travels of Fa-hsien, The [法顕伝] (Chin *Fa-hsien-chuan;* Jpn *Hokken-den*): An abbreviation of *The Travels of the Eminent Priest Fa-hsien,* also known as *The Record of the Buddhistic Kingdoms.* An account by Fa-hsien (c. 340–420), a Chinese Buddhist pilgrim, of his journeys in Central Asia and India. In 399, around age sixty, Fa-hsien left Ch'ang-an and journeyed through Central Asia to India. There he visited Buddhist sites and sought out Buddhist scriptures. He proceeded to Sri Lanka and visited a number of countries in Southeast Asia as well, returning to China by sea some fifteen years after his departure from Ch'ang-an. *The Travels of Fa-hsien* is valued for the information it provides on the customs, cultures, and practice of Buddhism in India and other countries in the early fifth century.

Trāyastrimsha Heaven [忉利天] (Skt; Jpn Tōri-ten): The second of the six heavens in the world of desire. *See* Heaven of the Thirty-three Gods.

treasure tower [宝塔] (Jpn *hōtō*): A tower or stupa adorned with treasures or jewels. Any of a variety of jeweled stupas depicted in Buddhist scriptures. The best known is the treasure tower of Many Treasures Buddha that appears in the "Treasure Tower" (eleventh) chapter of the Lotus Sutra. According to the sutra, this massive tower emerges from below the earth and measures 250 *yojanas* wide and 500 *yojanas* high. It is adorned with the seven kinds of treasures: gold, silver, lapis lazuli, seashell, agate, pearl, and carnelian, and seated inside the tower is Many Treasures Buddha. T'ien-t'ai (538–597) gives two reasons for the appearance of the treasure tower in the Lotus Sutra: (1) to substantiate the teaching of replacing the three vehicles with the one vehicle expounded in the theoretical teaching (first half) of the Lotus Sutra, and (2) to prepare for Shakyamuni's revelation, in the "Life Span" (sixteenth) chapter of the essential teaching (the sutra's latter half), of his original attainment of enlightenment numberless major world system dust particle *kalpas* in the past.

Nichiren viewed the treasure tower as an allegory for human life in its enlightened state achieved through the chanting of Nam-myoho-renge-kyo. In a letter Nichiren wrote in 1272 known as *On the Treasure Tower,* he says: "In the Latter Day of the Law, no treasure tower exists other than the figures of the men and women who embrace the Lotus Sutra. It follows, therefore, that whether eminent or humble, high or low, those who chant Nam-myoho-renge-kyo are themselves the treasure tower, and, likewise, are themselves the Thus Come One Many Treasures. No treasure tower exists other than Myoho-renge-kyo. The daimoku of the Lotus Sutra is the treasure tower, and the treasure tower is Nam-myoho-renge-kyo" (299). In the same letter, he also refers to the Gohonzon, the object of devotion in his teaching, as "the treasure tower."

"Treasure Tower" chapter [宝塔品] (Jpn *Hōtō-hon*): The eleventh chapter of the Lotus Sutra describing Many Treasures Buddha and his jeweled tower. *See* "Emergence of the Treasure Tower" chapter.

Treasury of Knowledge of the True Law, The [正法眼蔵] (Jpn *Shōbōgenzō*): A work by Dōgen (1200–1253), founder of the Sōtō school of Japanese Zen, in which he discusses the sole practice of single-minded seated meditation *(zazen),* the daily life of practitioners, the rules and teachings of the school, and other topics. It is esteemed as the most important text of the Sōtō school.

Treatise of Five Hundred Questions, The [五百問論] (Chin *Wu-pai-wen-lun;* Jpn *Gohyaku-mon-ron*): A work by Miao-lo (711–782) in question-and-answer form that refutes *Praising the Profundity of the Lotus Sutra* by Tz'u-en (632–682), the founder of the Chinese Dharma Characteristics (Fa-hsiang) school. In it, Miao-lo poses a question concerning a given subject, presents as an answer Tz'u-en's view on the subject from his *Praising the Profundity of the Lotus Sutra,* and then points out the error of Tz'u-en's view. Thus Miao-lo concludes that, although Tz'u-en praised the Lotus Sutra, he misunderstood its meaning because he interpreted it from the standpoint of the Dharma Characteristics doctrine. The treatise contains some 371 questions and answers, but because some of these contain questions within them, it actually addresses more than five hundred questions in all.

Treatise on Accordance with the Correct Doctrine, The [阿毘達磨順正理論] (Chin *A-p'i-ta-mo-shun-cheng-li-lun;* Jpn *Abidatsuma-junshōri-ron*): An eighty-volume work written by Samghabhadra of the Sarvāstivāda school in India in the fourth or fifth century and translated into Chinese in the mid-seventh century by Hsüan-tsang. It attempts to refute Vasubandhu's *Dharma Analysis Treasury,* which itself is a criticism of Sarvāstivāda doctrine from the standpoint of the Sautrāntika school. Samghabhadra's intention was to defend the Sarvāstivāda position. The term *correct doctrine* in the title refers to the Sarvāstivāda doctrine.

Treatise on Rebirth in the Pure Land, The [往生論] (Jpn *Ōjō-ron*): Another title for *The Treatise on the Pure Land,* a short treatise by Vasubandhu on the Buddha Infinite Life Sutra, which was translated into Chinese by Bodhiruchi in 529. See *Treatise on the Pure Land, The.*

Treatise on the Buddha Nature, The [仏性論] (Chin *Fo-hsing-lun;* Jpn *Busshō-ron*): A work attributed to Vasubandhu and translated into Chinese by Paramārtha in the sixth century. It cites various passages from the Lotus and Shrīmālā sutras as well as from *The Treatise on the Stages of Yoga Practice,* and explains in considerable detail the theory of the Buddha nature. It proclaims the universality of the Buddha nature and refutes contrary views held by non-Buddhist scholars as well as Hinayana and Mahayana Buddhist scholars.

Treatise on the Discipline for Attaining Enlightenment, The [菩提資糧論] (Chin *P'u-t'i-tzu-liang-lun;* Jpn *Bodai-shiryō-ron*): A Chinese translation by Dharmagupta (d. 619), a monk from southern India, of a treatise consisting of original verses attributed to Nāgārjuna (c. 150–250) and a prose commentary added later. It sets forth the six *pāramitās* and other practices for bodhisattvas that are conducive to enlightenment.

Treatise on the Establishment of the Consciousness-Only Doctrine, The [成唯識論] (Chin *Ch'eng-wei-shih-lun;* Jpn *Jō-yuishiki-ron*): A commentary on Vasubandhu's *Thirty-Stanza Treatise on the Consciousness-Only Doctrine* by Dharmapāla (530–561), a prominent scholar of the Consciousness-Only school. Hsüan-tsang translated it into Chinese in 659, including in his version not only Dharmapāla's commentary on the above treatise, but also edited interpretations of the same treatise by the other nine of the so-called ten great scholars of Consciousness-Only. This commentary is the principal text of the Dharma Characteristics (Chin Fa-hsiang; Jpn Hossō) school. It sheds light on the Consciousness-Only doctrine, which teaches that the basis of human existence is the *ālaya*-consciousness and that all phenomena arise through activation of the karmic seeds stored in this consciousness.

Treatise on the Establishment of Truth, The [成実論] (Skt *Satyasiddhi-shāstra;* Chin *Ch'eng-shih-lun;* Jpn *Jōjitsu-ron*): A work by Harivarman of India translated into Chinese by Kumārajīva in the early fifth century. It is the primary text of the Establishment of Truth (Chin Ch'eng-shih; Jpn Jōjitsu) school and contains a detailed discussion of the four noble truths. The work consists of five sections, which respectively cover the following topics: (1) The three treasures of the Buddha, the Law, and the *Samgha,* or Buddhist Order. This section also gives a brief explanation of the four noble truths. (2) The first of the four noble truths, that all existence is suffering. This section regards the five components of life—

form, perception, conception, volition, and consciousness—as suffering. (3) The second of the four noble truths, that suffering is caused by craving. This section regards karma and earthly desires as the causes of suffering. (4) The third of the four noble truths, that suffering can be eliminated. This section asserts that one can attain nirvana by discarding three kinds of attachment: attachment to the self, attachment to the dharmas (elements of existence), and attachment to emptiness. If one abandons attachment to, i.e., recognizes the emptiness of, the self and the dharmas, then one seems to have attained emptiness, but if one has attachment to emptiness, it is not emptiness at all. One must also abandon that attachment, in other words, surrender the awareness of emptiness. This section also explains two levels of truth, worldly truth and supreme truth. Worldly truth acknowledges the temporary existence of things and recognizes eighty-four dharmas, which are divided into five categories. The supreme truth is that all existence is empty and without substance. (5) The fourth of the four noble truths, that there is a way or path to eliminating the cause of suffering. This section explains meditation and the wisdom arising from it and expounds twenty-seven stages of practice that lead one to eliminate suffering and attain nirvana.

Treatise on the Great Perfection of Wisdom, The [大智度論] (Skt *Mahāprajnāpāramitā-shāstra;* Chin *Ta-chih-tu-lun;* Jpn *Daichido-ron*): A comprehensive commentary on the Great Perfection of Wisdom Sutra, traditionally attributed to Nāgārjuna (c. 150–250). The Sanskrit and Tibetan texts do not exist; only the Chinese version translated in 405 by Kumārajīva is extant. This work explains the concepts of *prajnā,* or wisdom, and *shūnya,* non-substantiality. Concerning religious practice, it sets forth the bodhisattva ideal, the six *pāramitās,* and other fundamental Mahayana concepts. *The Treatise on the Great Perfection of Wisdom* is also regarded as a treasury of Buddhist stories, such as those of the ascetic Aspiration for the Law, King Shibi, and King Universal Brightness. Primarily a commentary on the Great Perfection of Wisdom Sutra, it also incorporates concepts from the Lotus Sutra and other Mahayana sutras. It is highly valued as a reference in the general study of Mahayana thought.

Treatise on the Lamp for the Latter Day of the Law, The [末法燈明記] (Jpn *Mappō-tōmyō-ki*): A work traditionally attributed to Dengyō (767–822), the founder of the Japanese Tendai school, though his authorship is doubtful. It is dated 801. First it clarifies the three periods of the Former Day, Middle Day, and Latter Day of the Law based on the Wise Kalpa Sutra, the Nirvana Sutra, and the Great Collection Sutra. It asserts that, at the time of its composition, the Middle Day is nearing an end. Also, in the ensuing Latter Day, though Shakyamuni's Buddhism will remain, there will be neither practice of its teachings nor proof (enlightenment) accruing from it. Moreover, it states that in the Latter Day no one will observe the precepts. Therefore, even a priest who does not observe precepts should be revered as a teacher of the people. This writing greatly influenced the Japanese Buddhist teachers of the Kamakura period (1185–1333).

Treatise on the Lamp of Wisdom, The [般若灯論・般若灯論釈] (Skt *Prajnā-pradīpa;* Chin *Pan-jo-teng-lun* or *Pan-jo-teng-lun-shih;* Jpn *Hannya-tōron* or *Hannya-tōron-shaku*): A commentary on Nāgārjuna's *Verses on the Middle Way* (Skt *Madhyamaka-kārikā*) by Bhāvaviveka (c. 490–570), a scholar of the Mādhyamika, or Middle Way, school. The Sanskrit original is no longer extant, but Chinese and Tibetan translations exist. Prabhākaramitra translated the work into Chinese in the early seventh century. In it, Bhāvaviveka set forth his own method of demonstrating the truth of non-substantiality and criticized the method employed by his contemporary Mādhyamika scholar Buddhapālita. As a result, the Mādhyamika school was divided into two—the Svātantrika school, headed by Bhāvaviveka, and the Prāsangika school, led by Buddhapālita. Bhāvaviveka applied Dignāga's system of Buddhist logic to demonstrate the truth of non-substantiality, that all things are without substance. In contrast, Buddhapālita, rather than employing a formal system of logic, used the approach of pointing out contradictions in an opponent's arguments.

Treatise on the Lotus Sutra, The [法華論・法華経論] (Skt *Saddharma-pundarīka-upadesha;* Chin *Fa-hua-lun* or *Fa-hua-ching-lun;* Jpn *Hokke-ron* or *Hokekyō-ron*): A Chinese translation of Vasubandhu's commentary on the Sanskrit Lotus Sutra, *Saddharma-pundarīka-sūtra.* The full title is *The Treatise on the Lotus Sutra of the Wonderful Law.* The Sanskrit text of Vasubandhu's treatise no longer exists, but two Chinese versions are extant, one by Bodhiruchi and T'an-lin, and the other by Ratnamati and Seng-lang. Both were produced in the sixth century. According to tradition, Ratnamati, who was from central India, went to Lo-yang, China, in 508 and translated the *Saddharma-pundarīka-upadesha* with the assistance of Seng-lang. Bodhiruchi, a native of northern India, went to Lo-yang in the same year and produced another Chinese version at Yung-ning-ssu temple with the assistance of T'an-lin.

In this work, Vasubandhu asserts the superiority of the Lotus Sutra over all the other sutras based on three aspects of its content, which he terms the seven parables, the three equalities, and the ten peerlessnesses. The seven parables are the parables related in the Lotus Sutra to illustrate the superiority of the sutra's teaching. The three equalities are:

(1) The equality of the vehicle. The one supreme vehicle is given equally to all people, and the Lotus Sutra unites the three vehicles into the one supreme vehicle. (2) The equality of the world and nirvana. There is no fundamental distinction between the world of delusion and nirvana, or enlightenment. (3) The equality of the body. "Body" here refers to the body of the Buddha. Although the Buddha assumes various forms (or bodies) to lead people to enlightenment, the state of Buddhahood equally pervades them all. Vasubandhu established these three viewpoints to show that the Lotus Sutra is a teaching of absolute equality. The ten peerlessnesses are ten viewpoints from which Vasubandhu asserted the superiority of the Lotus Sutra over all other sutras. One of them, for example, is that the seeds of enlightenment imparted by the Lotus Sutra are without peer. Chi-tsang, Dengyō, and Chishō wrote commentaries on this work. According to Paramārtha's account, more than fifty scholars wrote commentaries on the Lotus Sutra in India, but only Vasubandhu's was brought to China and translated into Chinese. For this reason, *The Treatise on the Lotus Sutra* was regarded in China as the primary text for the study of the Lotus Sutra. Some scholars today maintain that the Lotus Sutra referred to in the Chinese versions of Vasubandhu's work is different in many respects from the sutra that Kumārajīva translated under the title Lotus Sutra of the Wonderful Law, and bears similarity to a Sanskrit text of the Lotus Sutra found in Nepal. *See also* seven parables; ten peerlessnesses.

Treatise on the Lotus Sutra of the Wonderful Law, The [妙法蓮華経憂波提舎] (Jpn *Myoho-renge-kyo-upadaisha*): Vasubandhu's commentary on the Lotus Sutra. See *Treatise on the Lotus Sutra, The.*

Treatise on the Middle Way, The [中論] (Skt *Mādhyamika-shāstra;* Chin *Chung-lun;* Jpn *Chū-ron*): One of Nāgārjuna's (c. 150–250) principal works, translated into Chinese by Kumārajīva in 409. This Chinese translation consists of verses by Nāgārjuna and prose commentary on these verses by Pingala, who lived from the late third through the early fourth century. The Sanskrit text of Nāgārjuna's verses, which is no longer extant, was titled the *Madhyamaka-kārikā,* or *Verses on the Middle Way,* and consisted of some 450 verses in 27 sections. It was regarded as the primary text of the Mādhyamika (Middle Way) school, one of the two main traditions of Mahayana Buddhism in India, the other being the Vijnānavāda (Consciousness-Only) school.

The Treatise on the Middle Way criticizes the assertion of the Sarvāstivāda school that the dharmas, or elements of existence, are real; based on the Wisdom sutras, it expounds the concept of non-substantiality and the practice of the Middle Way. It opens with the eight negations: neither birth nor extinction, neither cessation nor permanence, neither uniformity nor diversity, neither coming nor going. Through the process of negating established ideas of extremes, it leads one to the idea of emptiness, or non-substantiality, which is the core of Buddhist philosophy. *The Treatise on the Middle Way* explains that phenomena have no self-nature and are empty, or without substance, because they arise and disappear only by virtue of their relationship with other phenomena (dependent origination). This non-substantiality, definable neither as existence nor nonexistence, is termed the Middle Way.

Nāgārjuna's conception of non-substantiality formed the theoretical basis of Mahayana Buddhism and exerted an inestimable influence on its later development. In China and Japan, *The Treatise on the Middle Way* became one of the three principal texts of the Three Treatises (Chin San-lun; Jpn Sanron) school, the other two being *The Treatise on the Twelve Gates* also by Nāgārjuna and *The One-Hundred-Verse Treatise* by his disciple Āryadeva.

Treatise on the Mind Aspiring for Enlightenment, The [菩提心論] (Chin *P'u-t'i-hsin-lun;* Jpn *Bodaishin-ron*): A work attributed to Nāgārjuna (c. 150–250) and translated into Chinese in the eighth century by Pu-k'ung (Skt Amoghavajra). Another account attributes the work itself to Pu-k'ung. No Sanskrit version is extant. *The Treatise on the Mind Aspiring for Enlightenment* teaches the important Buddhist concept of aspiration for enlightenment and encourages the development of a mind that seeks Buddhahood. It defines three aspects of a mind that aspires for enlightenment, from the standpoint of Esoteric Buddhism: (1) great compassion to save all living beings, (2) great wisdom to know what sutra is supreme, and (3) meditation. The work also explains various kinds of contemplation put forth in Esoteric Buddhism. Kōbō, the founder of the Japanese True Word (Shingon) school, valued this work, and it was widely studied in his school.

Treatise on the Observation of the Mind, The [観心論] (Chin *Kuan-hsin-lun;* Jpn *Kanjin-ron*): A work by T'ien-t'ai (538–597) that encourages practice of the four forms of meditation, with emphasis on the observation of the mind. This work is said to have been compiled from an oral teaching T'ien-t'ai gave immediately before his death and which he described as his will. T'ien-t'ai's successor, Chang-an, wrote a commentary on the work titled *The Annotations on "The Treatise on the Observation of the Mind."* While *The Treatise on the Observation of the Mind* is considered an important text of the T'ien-t'ai school, Miao-lo pointed out that it limits itself to the four forms of meditation and does not touch on other important principles such as the three thousand realms in a single moment of life, which T'ien-t'ai expounded in *Great Concentration and Insight*. *See also* four forms of meditation.

Treatise on the Profundity of the Lotus Sutra, The [法華玄論] (Chin *Fa-hua-hsüan-lun;* Jpn *Hokke-genron*): A commentary on the Lotus Sutra by Chi-tsang (549–623), a systematizer of the doctrines of the Three Treatises (San-lun) school in China, written from the viewpoint of that school. In this work, Chi-tsang draws on many sutras and treatises, such as the Flower Garland Sutra, the Nirvana Sutra, and *The Treatise on the Great Perfection of Wisdom,* and introduces the content of these texts as well as his and other scholars' views on the Lotus Sutra. The work is regarded as an important reference on interpretations of the Lotus Sutra and other works by Chinese scholars.

Treatise on the Pure Land, The [浄土論] (Chin *Ching-t'u-lun;* Jpn *Jōdo-ron*): (1) Also known as *The Treatise on Rebirth in the Pure Land.* A short treatise by Vasubandhu on the Buddha Infinite Life Sutra. Translated into Chinese in 529 by Bodhiruchi, the work consists of a verse section and a prose section explaining it. It praises the Pure Land of the Buddha Infinite Life, or Amida Buddha, and encourages aspiration for rebirth in that Pure Land. It is valued by the Pure Land (Jōdo) school in addition to the three Pure Land sutras (the Buddha Infinite Life Sutra, the Meditation on the Buddha Infinite Life Sutra, and the Amida Sutra). T'an-luan, the founder of the Chinese Pure Land school, interpreted the work in *The Commentary on "The Treatise on the Pure Land."*

(2) A seventh-century work by Chia-ts'ai, a priest of the Chinese Pure Land school. It clarifies the teachings set forth in *The Collected Essays on the World of Peace and Delight* by Tao-ch'o, the second patriarch of the Chinese Pure Land school. The World of Peace and Delight is another name for Amida Buddha's Pure Land of Perfect Bliss. In this treatise, Chia-ts'ai describes that pure land and the cause for rebirth there, which it exhorts people to seek.

Treatise on the Source of Wisdom, The [阿毘達磨発智論] (Skt *Abhidharma-jnānaprasthāna-shāstra;* Chin *A-p'i-ta-mo-fa-chih-lun;* Jpn *Abidatsuma-hotchi-ron*): A principal *abhidharma,* or doctrinal text, of the Sarvāstivāda school, translated into Chinese by Hsüan-tsang between 657 and 660. Kātyāyanīputra authored this treatise in the second century B.C.E. Around that time, the Sarvāstivāda school had seven doctrinal texts, among which *The Treatise on the Source of Wisdom* was primary. The treatise contributed greatly to the development of Sarvāstivāda thought, and was the focus of many doctrinal studies, which in turn produced other important *abhidharma* works such as *The Great Commentary on the Abhidharma* and *The Dharma Analysis Treasury.* In addition to Hsüan-tsang's translation, there exists one other Chinese version of this work, titled *The Eight-part Treatise*, translated in 383 by Samghadeva and Chu Fo-nien.

Treatise on the Stages of Yoga Practice, The [瑜伽師地論] (Skt *Yogāchārabhūmi;* Chin *Yü-ch'ieh-shih-ti-lun;* Jpn *Yugashiji-ron*): A work attributed to either Maitreya or Asanga and translated into Chinese in the mid-seventh century by Hsüan-tsang. One of the principal treatises of the Dharma Characteristics (Chin Fa-hsiang; Jpn Hossō) school, it consists of one hundred volumes and elucidates the seventeen stages through which the practitioners of the Consciousness-Only doctrine advance toward enlightenment. The work quotes the Revelation of the Profound Secrets Sutra and explains the Consciousness-Only doctrine, particularly with respect to the *ālaya*-consciousness. Yogic practice was the chief discipline of the Consciousness-Only school, hence the title of this work.

Treatise on the Ten Stages of the Mind, The [十住心論] (Jpn *Jūjū-shin-ron*): A work written around 830 by Kōbō (also known as Kūkai), founder of the Japanese True Word (Shingon) school, in response to a decree by Emperor Junna that all Buddhist schools must present a written statement of their doctrine. In this work, based on the "Stage of the Mind" chapter of the Mahāvairochana Sutra and *The Treatise on the Mind Aspiring for Enlightenment,* Kōbō formulates ten stages in the development of religious consciousness that correspond respectively to ten different levels of teachings. He places the mind of a believer in the Lotus Sutra and that of a believer in the Flower Garland Sutra in the eighth and the ninth stages, respectively. He places the mind of a follower of the True Word teaching in the tenth or highest stage, because he says that such a person has comprehended Esoteric Buddhism. See also *Precious Key to the Secret Treasury, The;* ten stages of the mind.

Treatise on the Ten Stages Sutra, The [十地経論] (Chin *Shih-ti-ching-lun;* Jpn *Jūji-kyō-ron*): A work by Vasubandhu, translated into Chinese in the sixth century by Bodhiruchi and Ratnamati. It is a commentary on the Ten Stages Sutra, which is identical with the "Ten Stages" chapter of the Flower Garland Sutra. The ten stages are the stages of the bodhisattva practice leading to enlightenment. The Treatise on the Ten Stages Sutra (Ti-lun) school in China was based on this work. The work was also valued by the Flower Garland (Hua-yen) school.

Treatise on the Ten Stages Sutra school [地論宗] (Chin Ti-lun-tsung; Jpn Jiron-shū): Also known as the Ti-lun school or the Treatise on the Stages school. A school based on Vasubandhu's *Treatise on the Ten Stages Sutra.* One of the thirteen major Buddhist schools said to have flourished in China from the fifth through the ninth century. In the early sixth century Bodhiruchi and Ratnamati translated the Sanskrit text of *The Treatise on the Ten Stages Sutra* into Chinese. Hui-kuang (468–537) studied this treatise and disseminated its teaching and is therefore regarded as a founder of the Treatise on the Ten Stages Sutra school, or the Ti-lun school. The school's masters also studied the Flower Garland Sutra, for the Ten Stages Sutra is identical with the "Ten Stages" chapter of the Flower Garland Sutra. This school divided into the Southern Way (Chin Nan-tao) branch, in the lineage of Ratnamati's disciple Hui-kuang, and the Northern Way (Pei-tao) branch, in the lineage of Bodhiruchi's disciple Tao-ch'ung. The Northern Way school did not develop, while the Southern Way school prospered for a time. Both schools disappeared in the seventh century.

Treatise on the Treasure Vehicle of Buddhahood, The [究竟一乘宝性論] (Skt *Ratnagotravibhāga-mahāyānottaratantra-shāstra;* Chin *Chiu-ching-i-ch'eng-pao-hsing-lun;* Jpn *Kukyō-ichijō-hōshō-ron*): A work by Sāramati, a Mahayana scholar of India, translated into Chinese in the sixth century by Ratnamati. It asserts that all beings possess the "matrix of the Thus Come One" (Skt *tathāgata-garbha,* also called the matrix of the Tathāgata) or the Buddha nature, and that even *icchantikas,* persons of incorrigible disbelief, can attain Buddhahood eventually. This treatise is generally thought to have been written sometime around the end of the fourth or the beginning of the fifth century. Tibetan tradition attributes the verses of this work to Maitreya and commentaries on them to Asanga. Maitreya and Asanga were also Mahayana scholars.

Treatise on the Twelve Gates, The [十二門論] (Chin *Shih-erh-men-lun;* Jpn *Jūni-mon-ron*): A work attributed to Nāgārjuna (c. 150–250) and translated into Chinese in 409 by Kumārajīva. Only the Chinese version is extant. *The Treatise on the Twelve Gates* is one of the three treatises of the Three Treatises (Chin San-lun; Jpn Sanron) school, the other two being *The Treatise on the Middle Way* and *The One-Hundred-Verse Treatise,* and was widely studied in China and Japan. This work consists of twelve sections, each addressing a different subject. It explains the Mahayana doctrine of non-substantiality, concluding that all phenomena are non-substantial in nature.

Treatise Resolving Numerous Doubts about the Pure Land Teachings, The [釈浄土群疑論] (Chin *Shih-ching-t'u-ch'ün-i-lun;* Jpn *Shaku-jōdo-gungi-ron*): Also known as *The Treatise Resolving Numerous Doubts.* A work by Huai-kan, a priest of the Chinese Pure Land school, written in the seventh century. Huai-kan had been a priest of the Dharma Characteristics (Fa-hsiang) school, but later studied under the Pure Land teacher Shan-tao. He died before finishing the work, and Huai-yün, another of

Shan-tao's disciples, completed it. Written in question-and-answer format, this treatise addresses questions about the Pure Land teachings from the standpoint of the Consciousness-Only doctrine of the Dharma Characteristics school.

Treatises of Seng-chao, The [肇論] (Chin *Chao-lun;* Jpn *Jō-ron*): A collection of four treatises by the Chinese priest Seng-chao (384–414), a disciple of Kumārajīva. The first, titled "The Treatise on the Immutability of Essence," states that the true aspect of all phenomena is unchanging. The second, "The Treatise on Non-substantiality," states that all phenomena are without substance because they arise through a combination of causes and conditions. The third, "The Treatise on Incomprehensible Wisdom," states that wisdom (Skt *prajnā*) is beyond ordinary people's understanding. The fourth, "The Treatise on the Inexpressible State of Nirvana," states that nirvana, or enlightenment, is indescribable, and that it neither appears nor disappears.

trikāya [三身] (Skt; Jpn *san-jin*): Three kinds of body a Buddha may possess: the Dharma body, the reward body, and the manifested body. *See* three bodies.

Tripitaka [三蔵] (Skt; Jpn *san-zō*): Three divisions of the Buddhist canon: the sutras (the Buddha's doctrinal teachings), *vinaya* (rules of monastic discipline), and *abhidharma* (commentaries on the sutras and *vinaya*). *See* three divisions of the canon.

Tripitaka master [三蔵] (Skt; Jpn *san-zō*): An honorific title given to those who were well versed in the three divisions of the Buddhist canon, i.e., the sutras, the *vinaya* (rules of monastic discipline), and the *abhidharma* (commentaries on the sutras and *vinaya*). The honorific title "Tripitaka master" was also used in reference to eminent translators of Buddhist scriptures such as Kumārajīva.

Tripitaka teaching [蔵教] (Skt; Jpn *zō-kyō*): One of the four teachings of doctrine formulated by T'ien-t'ai (538–597). The teachings of this category are Hinayana and aim at awakening people to the sufferings of birth and death in the threefold world. They urge the practitioners to rid themselves of earthly desires and attachments in order to escape the cycle of rebirths, or transmigration in the six paths.

triratna [三宝] (Skt; Jpn *sambō*): The three treasures of Buddhism: the Buddha, his teachings, and the Buddhist Order. *See* three treasures.

true aspect of all phenomena [諸法実相] (Jpn *shohō-jissō*): The ultimate truth or reality that permeates all phenomena and is in no way separate from them. A principle expressed in the "Expedient Means" (second) chapter of the Lotus Sutra. The chapter states: "The true aspect of all phenomena can only be understood and shared between Buddhas. This reality consists of the appearance, nature, entity, power, influence, internal cause, relation, latent effect, manifest effect, and their consistency from beginning to end." The "Expedient Means" chapter defines the true aspect of all phenomena as the ten factors of life from "appearance" through "their consistency from beginning to end," which describe the unchanging aspect of life common to all phenomena. Since the ten factors exist in any being of the Ten Worlds, there can be no fundamental distinction between a Buddha and an ordinary person. This revelation of the ten factors of life thus establishes a theoretical basis for the universal attainment of Buddhahood. Based on this passage of the "Expedient Means" chapter, T'ien-t'ai (538–597) established the philosophical system of three thousand realms in a single moment of life. In his 1273 work titled *The True Aspect of All Phenomena,* Nichiren defined "all phenomena" as all living beings and their environments in the Ten Worlds, and "the true aspect" as the Law of Myoho-renge-kyo, the ultimate reality permeating all living beings and their environments in any of the Ten Worlds. All phenomena, he stated, are manifestations of this universal Law; phenomena and the ultimate truth are inseparable and non-dual.

true Buddha [本仏] (Jpn *hombutsu*): A Buddha in his true identity, in contrast to his transient or provisional identity. This term is applied in two specific ways:

(1) To Shakyamuni Buddha as he describes himself in the "Life Span" (sixteenth) chapter of the Lotus Sutra; that is, as having attained Buddhahood in the remote past, countless *kalpas* ago. In that chapter, Shakyamuni states: "In all the worlds the heavenly and human beings and *asuras* all believe that the present Shakyamuni Buddha, after leaving the palace of the Shākyas, seated himself in the place of meditation not far from the city of Gayā and there attained supreme perfect enlightenment. But good men, it has been immeasurable, boundless hundreds, thousands, ten thousands, millions of *nayutas* of *kalpas* since I in fact attained Buddhahood." With this statement, Shakyamuni redefines his identity as a Buddha who originally attained his enlightenment in the remarkably remote past. From the standpoint of the philosophy of the Lotus Sutra, the Shakyamuni who is thought to have attained enlightenment in the current life under the *bodhi* tree in India is a "provisional Buddha," or a Buddha in his transient identity. In this provisional identity, Shakyamuni is seen as a temporary manifestation of the true Buddha who employed various temporary, expedient teachings to prepare people to understand his true identity and true teaching and thereby lead them to enlightenment.

From the perspective of the content of the Lotus Sutra, the true Buddha corresponds to the Shakyamuni depicted in the essential teaching (latter half) of the Lotus Sutra, while the Buddha in his transient identity is the Shakyamuni of the theoretical teaching (first half) of the sutra.

(2) As a reference to Nichiren (1222–1282), applied to him traditionally by those in the lineage of his disciple Nikkō. In *The Profound Meaning of the Lotus Sutra,* T'ien-t'ai (538–597) refers to the true cause and the true effect as the first two of the ten mystic principles of the essential teaching of the Lotus Sutra based on the revelation of Shakyamuni's original attainment of enlightenment in the remote past. He associates the true cause with the sentence in the "Life Span" chapter, "Originally I practiced the bodhisattva way, and the life that I acquired then has yet to come to an end," and the true effect with the sentence "Since I attained Buddhahood, an extremely long period of time has passed." In the remote past, Shakyamuni practiced the bodhisattva way (the true cause) and attained Buddhahood (the true effect). Shakyamuni never specifically reveals, however, what teaching he originally practiced, the original cause or seed of his Buddhahood.

Regarding this, Nichiren states: "The doctrine of the sowing of the seed and its maturing and harvesting is the very heart and core of the Lotus Sutra. All the Buddhas of the three existences and the ten directions have invariably attained Buddhahood through the seeds represented by the five characters of Myoho-renge-kyo" (1015). From this perspective, Nichiren is regarded as the teacher of the true cause, and Shakyamuni as the teacher of the true effect. This is because in the Lotus Sutra Shakyamuni revealed his eternal Buddhahood, the effect of his original bodhisattva practice. He did not, however, reveal the true cause or the nature of the specific practice by which he attained it. Nichiren, on the other hand, revealed the teaching and practice of Nam-myoho-renge-kyo, which he identified as the true cause that enables all people to attain Buddhahood. This viewpoint identifies Nichiren as the true Buddha.

Nichiren explains the passage of the Lotus Sutra cited above, "It has been immeasurable, boundless hundreds, thousands, ten thousands, millions of *nayutas* of *kalpas* since I in fact attained Buddhahood," in *The Record of the Orally Transmitted Teachings.* He says, "'I in fact' is explaining that Shakyamuni in fact attained Buddhahood in the inconceivably remote past. The meaning of this chapter, however, is that 'I' represents the living beings of the phenomenal world. 'I' here refers to each and every being in the Ten Worlds. 'In fact' establishes that 'I' is a Buddha eternally endowed with the three bodies. This is what is being called a 'fact.' 'Attained' refers both to the one who attains and to what is attained. 'Attain' means to open or reveal. It is to reveal that the beings of the phenomenal world are Buddhas eternally endowed with the three bodies. 'Buddhahood' means being enlightened to this." Here Nichiren is saying that every being is essentially "a Buddha eternally endowed with the three bodies," a true Buddha. In this sense, "true Buddha" refers to the Buddha nature eternally inherent in the lives of all living beings. In *The True Aspect of All Phenomena,* Nichiren states, "A common mortal is an entity of the three bodies, and a true Buddha. A Buddha is a function of the three bodies, and a provisional Buddha" (384). *See also* Buddha of beginningless time; Buddha of limitless joy; true cause.

true cause [本因妙] (Jpn *honnin-myō*): Also, the mystic principle of the true cause. One of the ten mystic principles of the essential teaching (latter half) of the Lotus Sutra formulated by T'ien-t'ai (538–597) in *The Profound Meaning of the Lotus Sutra.* It refers to the practice that Shakyamuni carried out countless *kalpas* in the past in order to attain his original enlightenment. The term contrasts with the true effect, or the original enlightenment Shakyamuni achieved countless *kalpas* before his enlightenment in India. The true cause is indicated by the phrase in the "Life Span" (sixteenth) chapter of the Lotus Sutra, "Originally I practiced the bodhisattva way . . ." *Profound Meaning* defines "bodhisattva way" as the true cause of Shakyamuni's original enlightenment. Shakyamuni did not clarify, however, what the bodhisattva way was. T'ien-t'ai interpreted it as a reference to the first stage of security, or the eleventh of the fifty-two stages of bodhisattva practice, i.e., the stage of non-regression, the attainment of which he defined as the true cause for Shakyamuni's original enlightenment. However, what teaching or Law Shakyamuni had practiced to attain the stage of non-regression remained unclear. Nichiren (1222–1282) identified the true cause, or fundamental Law, that enables all Buddhas to attain their enlightenment, as the Law of Nam-myoho-renge-kyo. Because he fully revealed the true cause for attaining Buddhahood and established a universal way of practice, in his lineage Nichiren is called the teacher of the true cause, while Shakyamuni is called the teacher of the true effect.

true effect [本果妙] (Jpn *honga-myō*): Also, the mystic principle of the true effect. The original enlightenment that Shakyamuni attained countless *kalpas* before his enlightenment in India. One of the ten mystic principles of the essential teaching (latter half) of the Lotus Sutra formulated by T'ien-t'ai (538–597) in *The Profound Meaning of the Lotus Sutra.* In contrast, the term "true cause" means the cause for that enlightenment. The true effect is indicated in the passage of the "Life Span" (sixteenth) chapter of the Lotus Sutra that reads, "Since I attained Buddhahood, an extremely long period of time has passed." In *Profound Meaning,* T'ien-t'ai states that, because the true cause leads to the true effect, he expounds the true cause first. In terms of Nichiren's (1222–1282) teaching, however, due to the simultaneity of cause and effect, both the true cause and the true effect are present together in one's life. In his treatise *The Entity of the Mystic Law,* Nichiren states: "When the sage was observing the principle . . . , he perceived that there is this wonderful single Law *[myōhō]* that simultaneously possesses both cause and effect *[renge],* and he named it Myoho-renge. This single Law that is Myoho-renge encompasses within it all the phenomena comprising the Ten Worlds and the three thousand realms, and is lacking in none of them. Anyone who practices this Law will obtain both the cause and the effect of Buddhahood simultaneously" (421). Hence Nichiren is called the teacher of the true cause and the true effect.

true land [本国土妙] (Jpn *honkokudo-myō*): Also, the mystic principle of the true land. One of the ten mystic principles of the essential teaching (latter half) of the Lotus Sutra formulated by T'ien-t'ai (538–597) in *The Profound Meaning of the Lotus Sutra.* It refers to the land where Shakyamuni has always been teaching the Law since the time of his original attainment of enlightenment in the inconceivably distant past. It is indicated in the passage of the "Life Span" (sixteenth) chapter of the Lotus Sutra that reads, "Ever since then I have been constantly in this *sahā* world, preaching the Law, teaching and converting." In many of the pre-Lotus Sutra teachings, the Buddha land is viewed as a realm far apart from this *sahā* world, and Shakyamuni Buddha is said to have appeared in this world only temporarily to expound the Law and lead people to enlightenment. In contrast, the "Life Span" chapter makes it clear that this *sahā* world is itself the true land where the Buddha has always dwelt since his original enlightenment.

true Mahayana teaching [実大乗教] (Jpn *jitsu-daijō-kyō*): A reference to the Lotus Sutra. Contrasted with "provisional Mahayana," indicating the pre-Lotus Sutra teachings according to T'ien-t'ai's classification. T'ien-t'ai (538–597) classified Shakyamuni Buddha's teachings into five periods—the Flower Garland, Āgama, Correct and Equal, Wisdom, and Lotus and Nirvana periods. He defined the teachings of the Flower Garland, Correct and Equal, and Wisdom periods as provisional Mahayana, describing them as teachings meant as temporary means to instruct people and elevate their understanding. In contrast, he described true Mahayana as a full and direct statement of Shakyamuni Buddha's enlightenment that the Buddha revealed irrespective of people's capacity. T'ien-t'ai identified it as the Lotus Sutra, the one vehicle teaching that expounds the possibility of the attainment of Buddhahood by all people.

True Pure Land school [浄土真宗] (Jpn Jōdo Shin-shū): Also known as the Single-minded Practice (Ikkō) school. A school of the Pure Land teaching in Japan founded by Shinran (1173–1262), who outlines its doctrines in his work *The Teaching, Practice, Faith, and Proof.* Based on belief in total reliance on Amida Buddha's power instead of one's own power for achieving salvation, the True Pure Land school rejects the monastic rules of the traditional Pure Land school, permitting its priests to eat meat, marry, and live as laymen. Shinran stressed faith in Amida Buddha and emphasized the power of the Nembutsu, or the recitation of Amida's name; but he held that too much emphasis on repeated recitation implies a tendency to rely on one's own power rather than Amida's grace. He held that even the practitioner's longing for salvation is given by Amida. This view contrasted clearly with that of Hōnen's Pure Land (Jōdo) school, which taught that a believing mind is, strictly speaking, a function of one's own effort. Shinran propagated his teachings in Kyoto and in the Kanto area of central Japan, but the school gained little influence during his lifetime. After his death, his daughter, the nun Kakushin, and his disciples built a mausoleum in Higashiyama in Kyoto, which later became the head temple of the school and was named Hongan-ji. In the fifteenth century, the True Pure Land school spread widely because of the efforts of Ren'nyo, the eighth chief priest of Hongan-ji. Because of pressure from the Pure Land school and other related schools, however, the school refrained from publicly declaring itself the True Pure Land school. Instead it used the name Single-minded Practice (Ikkō) school until 1872 when the name True Pure Land school was officially adopted. *See also* Shinran; *Teaching, Practice, Faith, and Proof, The.*

true teaching [実教] (Jpn *jikkyō*): The teaching in which Shakyamuni Buddha directly revealed his enlightenment. The term is used in contrast with "provisional teachings," or those teachings the Buddha expounded as temporary expedients to lead people to the true teaching. T'ien-t'ai (538–597) defined the true teaching as the Lotus Sutra, which regards the one Buddha vehicle as true and the three vehicles as expedient. Classifying all the Buddhist sutras into five periods and eight teachings, he declared the first four of the five periods and the first three of the four teachings of doctrine to be "provisional," and the last (Lotus and Nirvana period) of the five periods and the last (perfect teaching) of the four teachings of doctrine to be "true."

The Immeasurable Meanings Sutra, considered a prologue to the Lotus Sutra, reads: "In the past I sat upright in the place of meditation for six years under the *bodhi* tree and was able to gain supreme perfect enlightenment. With the Buddha eye I observed all phenomena and knew that this enlightenment could not be explained or described. Why? Because I knew that living beings are not alike in their natures and their desires. And because their natures and desires are not alike, I preached the Law in various different ways. Preaching the Law in various different ways, I made use of the power of expedient means. But in these more than forty years, I have not yet revealed the truth." And the "Expedient Means" (second) chapter of the Lotus Sutra reads, "Honestly discarding expedient means, I will preach only the unsurpassed way." In the first quote, "preaching the Law in various different ways" indicates those teachings expounded prior to the Lotus Sutra, which were expedient or provisional teachings adapted to the capacities of the listeners, and "the truth" means the Lotus Sutra, the "true teaching" that is to be revealed irrespective of people's capacities to understand it. In the next quote, "honestly discarding" indicates the temporary or provisional nature of the pre-Lotus Sutra teachings, and "I will preach only" indicates the permanent or true nature of the "unsurpassed way," the one vehicle teaching of the Lotus Sutra. *See also* eight teachings; five periods.

True Word Precepts school [真言律宗] (Jpn Shingon Risshū): A school of Buddhism in Japan that is based on the doctrines of the True Word (Shingon) school and also observes the Mahayana and Hinayana precepts. Eizon (1201–1290) is regarded as the founder of the True Word Precepts school. In the Kamakura period (1185–1333), Eizon of Saidai-ji temple in Nara traveled widely to expound the benefit of observing the precepts and gained many disciples and converts. While dedicating himself to upholding the precepts and restoring the Precepts (Ritsu) school, Eizon also practiced the teachings of the True Word school. This dual orientation led to his founding of the True Word Precepts school, based at Saidai-ji temple. Ninshō (1217–1303), a disciple of Eizon also known as Ryōkan, lived at Gokuraku-ji temple in Kamakura and disseminated his teacher's doctrine widely in the Kanto region of central Japan. In 1872 the True Word Precepts school became affiliated with the True Word school, but in 1895 it became independent again. The head temple of the school is Saidai-ji.

True Word school [真言宗] (Jpn Shingon-shū): A Buddhist school in Japan established by Kōbō (774–835), also known as Kūkai, that follows the esoteric doctrines and practices found in the Mahāvairochana and Diamond Crown sutras. The name *true word* is the rendering in Chinese of the Sanskrit *mantra* (meaning secret word or mystic formula). In the True Word school, this indicates the words that Mahāvairochana Buddha is said to have uttered. The chanting of these secret words is one of the school's basic esoteric rituals for the attainment of enlightenment.

The True Word school maintains that Esoteric Buddhism was transmitted from Mahāvairochana Buddha to Vajrasattva, and then down through Nāgārjuna, Nāgabodhi, Chin-kang-chih (Skt Vajrabodhi), Pu-k'ung (Amoghavajra), Hui-kuo, and finally to Kōbō. The school also lists eight patriarchs who upheld Esoteric Buddhism: Nāgārjuna and Nāgabodhi who spread it in India; Chin-kang-chih, Pu-k'ung, and Shan-wu-wei (Shubhakarasimha) who introduced and established it in China; I-hsing and Hui-kuo who propagated it in China; and Kōbō who brought it to Japan and founded the True Word school there.

In 716 the monk Shubhakarasimha brought Esoteric Buddhism from India to Ch'ang-an in China, where he became known as Shan-wu-wei. Hsüan-tsung, the sixth emperor of the T'ang dynasty, honored and supported Shan-wu-wei, and his teachings spread widely in China. In 720 Vajrabodhi (Chin-kang-chih) and Amoghavajra (Pu-k'ung) also came from India to Lo-yang in China and introduced more of Esoteric Buddhism.

In 804 Kōbō traveled from Japan to Ch'ang-an, where he studied Esoteric Buddhism under Hui-kuo. During his stay there he received the teachings of the Diamond Realm and Womb Realm mandalas. In 806 he returned to Japan with numerous Buddhist scriptures, esoteric mandalas, and ritual implements, and in 809 entered the capital, Kyoto, where he advocated the supremacy of Esoteric Buddhism. In 816 he was granted a tract of land on Mount Kōya on which to found a monastery. In 823 Kōbō was also given another temple, Tō-ji, in Kyoto, which became the center of esoteric practice in Japan. In the late thirteenth century, differences in doctrinal interpretation resulted in the formation of the New Doctrine (Shingi) school, a branch of the True Word school based at Mount Negoro, and the teachings and traditions of Mount Kōya and Tō-ji came to be called the Old Doctrine (Kogi) school. *See also* Kakuban; Raiyu; Yakushin.

Truth-Revealed Lotus school [顕本法華宗] (Jpn Kempon Hokke-shū): One of the Nichiren schools in Japan. *See* Nichijū.

Ts'ai Yin [蔡愔] (n.d.) (PY Cai Yin; Jpn Saiin): An official who served Emperor Ming (r. 57–75), the second emperor of the Later Han dynasty in China. Dispatched by Emperor Ming to India to seek out the Buddha's teachings, he brought Buddhism to China. Tradition regards this as the first introduction of Buddhism to China. According to *The Liang Dynasty Biographies of Eminent Priests,* Emperor Ming dreamed of a golden man levitating. He asked his ministers and other officials about the dream. One of them said that he had once heard of a god called Buddha, and that the golden man in the emperor's dream must be this Buddha. The emperor sent Ts'ai Yin and the others to India to obtain the Buddha's teachings. At the request of Ts'ai Yin, two Indian Buddhist monks, Kāshyapa Mātanga and Chu Fa-lan (Sanskrit name unknown), came to Lo-yang in China with Buddhist scriptures and images. One account describes the year of this introduction of Buddhism as 67.

Tsukahara Debate [塚原問答] (Jpn Tsukahara-mondō): A debate between Nichiren and priests of several other schools that took place at Tsukahara during his exile on Sado, an island in the Sea of Japan, on the sixteenth day of the first month in 1272. It is described in detail in Nichiren's writing *The Actions of the Votary of the Lotus Sutra.* According to this document, the priests of Sado went in a group to Homma Rokurō Saemon, the deputy constable of Sado Island who had custody of Nichiren, and asked to have Nichiren killed. Homma refused, explaining that Nichiren was under his charge, and suggested that they instead confront him in religious debate. Following Homma's suggestion, several hundred priests of the Pure Land (Jpn Jōdo), True Word (Shingon), and other schools from both Sado and Japan's mainland gathered in the snow in front of Nichiren's lodging. Nichiren, after quelling some initial disorder and name-calling, refuted their statements, pointing out the contradictory assertions and scriptural incompatibilities contained in their doctrines. Several of them, along with their lay followers, renounced their former beliefs on the spot and converted to Nichiren's teachings.

Tsukimaro [月満] (b. 1271): A daughter of Shijō Kingo and his wife, Nichigen-nyo, both of whom were Nichiren's followers. They had two children, a younger daughter named Kyo'ō (literally, Sutra King) born in 1272, and Tsukimaro (Full Moon), who was born on the eighth day of the fifth month, 1271. Nichiren wrote a letter in the fifth month of 1271 in reply to a report from Kingo concerning the birth of the couple's first child and their request that Nichiren name the baby. In it, Nichiren states: "Great Bodhisattva Hachiman, the sovereign deity of this country, was born on the eighth day of the fourth month. Shakyamuni Buddha, the lord of teachings in this *sahā* world, was also born on the eighth day of the fourth month. Though the month is different, your baby girl was also born on the eighth day. She could well be the reincarnation of Shakyamuni Buddha or Hachiman" (188).

Ts'ung-i [従義] (1042–1091) (PY Congyi; Jpn Jūgi): A priest of the T'ien-t'ai school in China. He entered the priesthood at age eight and later studied the T'ien-t'ai teachings under Chi-chung. Ts'ung-i produced many works, including *The Supplement to the Three Major Works on the*

Lotus Sutra. He asserted the supremacy of the T'ien-t'ai doctrine over the doctrines of the Zen (Ch'an), Flower Garland (Hua-yen), and Dharma Characteristics (Fa-hsiang) schools.

Tsung-mi [宗密] (780–841) (PY Zongmi; Jpn Shūmitsu): Also known as the Meditation Master Kuei-feng. The fifth patriarch of the Flower Garland (Hua-yen) school in China. He first studied Confucianism, and then the Zen (Ch'an) doctrine under Tao-yüan. Later he became interested in *The Annotations on the Flower Garland Sutra* by Ch'eng-kuan, the fourth patriarch of the Chinese Flower Garland school, and studied the Flower Garland teachings under his guidance. Tsung-mi authored a number of works, including commentaries on the Flower Garland and Perfect Enlightenment sutras.

Tsun-shih [遵式] (964–1032) (PY Zunshi; Jpn Junshiki): A priest of the T'ien-t'ai school in China. At first he studied the teachings of Zen (Ch'an), but later turned to the T'ien-t'ai doctrine, which he studied under I-t'ung. In 991 he lectured on the Lotus, Vimalakīrti, Nirvana, and Golden Light sutras. In 1022 he was given the name Tz'u-yün (Merciful Cloud) by Emperor Chen-tsung and was thereafter called the Venerable Tz'u-yün. He enhanced the fame of the T'ien-t'ai school, and in 1024 successfully petitioned the throne to have the school's texts and commentaries included in the official Chinese Buddhist canon. He left behind a number of commentaries on both T'ien-t'ai and Pure Land doctrines. When Jakushō, a priest of the Japanese Tendai school, traveled to China in 1003 to study the T'ien-t'ai doctrine, he brought with him a copy of Nan-yüeh's work *The Mahayana Method of Concentration and Insight*, which had been lost for centuries in China. Tsun-shih was so delighted that he wrote an introduction to this work in which he stated: "It [Buddhism] came first from the west, like the moon appearing. Now it is returning from the east, like the sun rising."

tuft of white hair [白毫相・眉間白毫相] (Skt *ūrnā-kesha* or *ūrnā-kosha;* Jpn *byakugō-sō* or *miken-byakugō-sō*): A tuft of white hair between the eyebrows, one of a Buddha's thirty-two features. This tuft of white hair is said to emit a beam of light. *See also* thirty-two features.

Tung-ch'un [東春] (PY *Dongchun;* Jpn *Tōshun*): Another title for *The Supplement to the Meanings of the Commentaries on the Lotus Sutra,* named after the place where the author, Chih-tu, lived. See *Supplement to the Meanings of the Commentaries on the Lotus Sutra, The.*

Tun-huang [敦煌] (PY Dunhuang; Jpn Tonkō): An oasis town located in the western end of the so-called Kansu Corridor, in the present-day northwestern Kansu Province, China; formerly called Kua-chou or Sha-chou. It was a meeting point of two branches of the Silk Road running north and south around the Tarim Basin, and a place of entry into China as well as the starting point from China toward the "western regions." Today it is particularly well known for the religious, cultural, and artistic treasures preserved there in the form of painting and sculpture in its Mo-kao Caves (also known as the Cave of the Thousand Buddhas). Buddhist artwork found therein dates back to the fourth century.

In ancient times, Tun-huang was ruled by a tribal confederation called the Yüeh-chih and then by the Hsiung-nu, known to Europeans as the Huns. During the reign of Emperor Wu (r. 141–87 B.C.E.) of the Former Han dynasty, Tun-huang was brought under Chinese rule. From early on, Tun-huang was an important center for trade between East and West. In the first and second centuries, Buddhism was transmitted to China from India and Central Asia. By the third century, Tun-huang was not only a route of this transmission, but was itself a great center of Buddhism. Buddhist monks from India and Central Asia made sojourns to Tun-huang. The monk Dharmaraksha, who lived in the third and fourth centuries and translated the Lotus and other sutras into Chinese, came from this area and was called the Bodhisattva of Tun-huang. In the fifth century, the Indian monks Dharmaraksha (385–433) and Dharmamitra (356–442) came to this area and stayed for some time to preach. Many priests who traveled from China seeking Buddhist teachings also stopped in Tun-huang en route to India and Central Asia.

Tun-huang, for the most part, remained under the rule of the various Chinese dynasties. In the 780s, however, it fell under Tibetan dominance, which lasted for approximately sixty years. As a result, in Tun-huang, Tibetan Buddhism and Chinese Buddhism encountered and influenced each other. Thereafter Tun-huang was at different times placed under the rule of the Chinese, the Tangut (the people of the Hsi-hsia kingdom, which existed in northwestern China from the early eleventh through the early thirteenth century), and the Mongols. The Mo-kao Caves, southeast of Tun-huang, number about five hundred and are located at the base of the eastern side of a hill called Ming-sha-shan. In 366 the first cave was carved from the cliff side and the construction of others continued thereafter. These caves preserve wall paintings that portray events in Shakyamuni Buddha's life and also the *Jātaka,* stories of the previous lives of the Buddha.

Early in the twentieth century, a large number of ancient manuscripts and documents as well as paintings and other pieces of artwork were found in one of the caves. Among them were numerous manuscripts of Buddhist scriptures, dating from the fifth to the eleventh century. Other items included Taoist, Confucian, Manichaean, and Nestorian scriptures.

In addition to these religious documents, there were many ancient secular documents concerning government, economics, and literature. These records have been important to the study of Chinese social history during that period. The scriptures and documents were written in Chinese, Brāhmī script, Tibetan, Khotanese, Kuchean, Sogdian, Turkish, Uighur, and the writing system of the kingdom of Hsi-hsia. *See also* Mo-kao Caves.

Turfan [トルファン] (Jpn Torufan): A city in the eastern Sinkiang Uighur Autonomous Region of China. It lies on a fertile oasis at the foot of the southern slope of the Tien Shan range and on the northern side of the Turfan Depression, about 110 kilometers southeast of Urumchi, the capital of the Sinkiang Uighur Autonomous Region. The present-day inhabitants of Turfan are mostly Uighur Muslims. Many archaeological and religious relics can be found in the vicinity of Turfan, such as the ruins of ancient capital cities and Buddhist caves. Buddhism once flourished in Turfan, which was home to many monks who engaged in the translation of Buddhist scriptures from Sanskrit into Chinese. In the early seventh century, the Chinese priest and pilgrim Hsüan-tsang, who chronicled his travels through Central Asia and India in *The Record of the Western Regions,* stayed for about a month at a Buddhist monastery in Karakhoja, capital of the Kao-ch'ang kingdom of the Turfan region. There he received support from the Ch'ü, the ruling clan of the kingdom. The Uighurs migrated to the Turfan region in the latter half of the ninth century and built their kingdom there. Though largely adherents of Manichaeanism, they came into contact with the Buddhists in the region and took faith in Buddhism. They translated Buddhist scriptures into the Uighur language and developed a unique Buddhist culture. Later the region became primarily Islamic, but many of the cultural and religious treasures of Buddhism were preserved. Toward the close of the nineteenth century, archaeological exploration began in Central Asia and, from the early twentieth century, was carried out in full scale. Buddhist images and paintings, as well as Buddhist scriptures written in Sanskrit, the Uighur language, and other Central Asian languages, were discovered near Turfan.

turning of the wheel of the Law [転法輪] (Jpn *tembō-rin*): The preaching of a Buddha. The "wheel" (Skt *chakra*) in this expression derives from that possessed by a wheel-turning king, the symbol of an ideal ruler in Indian mythology. The wheel, or *chakra,* was employed to symbolize *dharma-chakra,* or the Buddha's teachings. Just as the wheel-turning king turned his *chakra* to defeat enemies, the Buddha "turned the wheel" of his teachings to subdue people's illusions and earthly desires.

The turning of the wheel of the Law is one of the eight phases of the Buddha's existence—eight successive phases the Buddha is said to have displayed upon descending from the Tushita Heaven into the world. After his attainment of enlightenment, Shakyamuni Buddha gave his first sermon in Deer Park before the five ascetics, with whom he had formerly practiced austerities. On that occasion, he is said to have preached the doctrines of the four noble truths and the eightfold path. This sermon at Deer Park is known as the first turning of the wheel of the Law. *See also* eight phases of a Buddha's existence.

Tushita Heaven [兜率天・覩史多天] (Skt; Jpn Tosotsu-ten or Toshita-ten): "Heaven of Satisfaction." In ancient Indian and Buddhist cosmology, the fourth of the six heavens in the world of desire. The beings in this heaven are said to know satisfaction in the pursuit of pleasure, having transcended insatiable desire. They have a life span of four thousand years, each day of which is equal to four hundred years in the human world. It is said that bodhisattvas are reborn in this heaven just before their rebirth in the world where they will attain Buddhahood. Shakyamuni is said to have descended from this heaven and entered the womb of his mother, Māyā. Tushita consists of an inner court and an outer court. The inner court is the abode of Bodhisattva Maitreya, who is constantly preaching until his future rebirth in the human world as a Buddha. Belief in Maitreya along with aspiration for rebirth in the Tushita Heaven was popular in China in the fifth century and in Japan in the seventh century.

Tu-shun [杜順] (557–640) (PY Dushun; Jpn Tojun): Also known as Fa-shun. The founder of the Flower Garland (Hua-yen) school in China. In 574 he entered the priesthood and studied under a priest named Seng-chen at Yin-sheng-ssu temple. Later he lived on a mountain called Chung-nan-shan and propagated the Flower Garland teaching, receiving support from Emperor T'ai-tsung of the T'ang dynasty. His successor was Chih-yen.

twelve bases [十二入・十二処] (Jpn *jūni-nyū* or *jūni-sho*): *See* twelve sense fields.

twelve divisions of the scriptures [十二部経] (Jpn *jūnibu-kyō*): Also, twelve divisions of the teachings. A classification of Shakyamuni Buddha's teachings according to their content and style of presentation. The term "twelve divisions of the scriptures" is often used in the same sense as "the eighty thousand teachings," indicating the entire body of the Buddha's teachings. The twelve divisions of the scriptures are as follows: (1) *sūtra,* teachings in prose; (2) *geya,* restatements of *sūtra* in verse; (3) *vyākarana,* the Buddha's predictions of the enlightenment of disciples; (4) *gāthā*, teachings set forth by the Buddha in verse; (5) *udāna*, teachings preached by the Buddha spontaneously without request or query from his disciples; (6) *nidāna*, descriptions of the purpose, cause, and occasion of propounding teachings and rules of monastic discipline; (7) *avadāna*, tales of previous lives of persons other than the Buddha; (8) *itivrittaka*, discourses beginning with the words "Thus the World-Honored One said" (according to another definition, stories that describe previous lives of the Buddha's disciples and bodhisattvas); (9) *jātaka*, stories of the Buddha's previous lives; (10) *vaipulya*, expansion of doctrine; (11) *adbhutadharma*, descriptions of marvelous events that concern the Buddha or his disciples (also applied to descriptions that praise the great merit and power of the Buddha and his disciples); and (12) *upadesha*, discourses on the Buddha's teachings. There are also various lists of nine divisions from among these twelve.

twelve divisions of the teachings [十二分教] (Jpn *jūnibun-kyō*): *See* twelve divisions of the scriptures.

twelvefold dhūta practice [十二頭陀行] (Jpn *jūni-zuda-gyō*): Also, twelve *dhūtas*. Twelve disciplines set forth in *The Commentary on the Ten Stages Sutra*, the Twelvefold Dhūta Practice Sutra, and other Buddhist texts. The Sanskrit word *dhūta* means "shaken off," "removed," or "abandoned." In Buddhism, it indicates shaking off or removing oneself from the dust and defilement of earthly desires. Accordingly, *dhūta* practice means practice to purify the body and mind, and to remove the desire for food, clothing, and shelter. The twelvefold *dhūta* practice is (1) to live in a quiet place remote from human habitation, such as a forest, (2) to seek food only by begging for alms, (3) to beg for alms from poor and rich households alike, (4) to eat only once a day, (5) to refrain from overeating, (6) to drink neither fruit juice nor the sap of trees after the noon meal, (7) to wear only robes made of cast-off rags, (8) to possess only three robes, (9) to live in graveyards, (10) to live under a tree, (11) to live in the open air, and (12) to sit and not to lie down. Variations of this list exist.

twelve gods [十二天] (Jpn *jūni-ten*): Twelve kinds of gods said to protect the world. They are the god of earth; the god of water; the god of fire; the god of wind; Īshāna; Shakra; Yama; Brahmā; Vaishravana; the *rākshasa* demon; the god of the sun; and the god of the moon.

twelve great vows [十二大願] (Jpn *jūni-daigan*): Also, twelve vows. The vows Medicine Master Buddha made while engaged in bodhisattva practice to be fulfilled upon his attaining enlightenment, according to the Medicine Master Sutra. They are (1) to emit light that will illuminate innumerable worlds and make all persons equal to him, without any distinction between them; (2) that his light will penetrate and illuminate the darkness inherent in the minds of people, causing them to accomplish whatever they want at will; (3) to cause people to gain whatever they need; (4) to preach the great vehicle teaching and cause people to dwell in the way of enlightenment; (5) to enable people to keep precepts and prevent them from falling into the evil paths of existence; (6) for those whose sense organs are lacking or defective, to mend them or provide new ones; (7) to heal all ills and provide peace and joy to those who are suffering from illness; (8) to enable those women who wish to change into men to fulfill their wish so that they may attain enlightenment; (9) to free people from erroneous views and lead them to correct views and enlightenment; (10) if there are those who are imprisoned and tortured by the authorities, to release them from suffering; (11) if there are those who are tormented by hunger and thirst, to satisfy them with fine food and drink so that they can taste his profound teaching; and (12) to give fine robes to those who have no clothing so that they may protect themselves from the cold and heat. Among these twelve vows, the Medicine Master Sutra accords the highest regard to the seventh, the vow to heal all ills.

twelve-linked chain of causation [十二因縁・十二縁起] (Jpn *jūni-innen* or *jūni-engi*): Also, twelve *nidānas* or twelve-linked chain of dependent origination. An early doctrine of Buddhism showing the causal relationship between ignorance and suffering. The Sanskrit word *nidāna* means cause or cause of existence. Shakyamuni is said to have taught the twelve-linked chain of causation in answer to the question of why people have to experience the sufferings of aging and death. Each link in the chain is a cause that leads to the next. The first link in the chain is ignorance (Skt *avidyā*), which gives rise to (2) action *(samskāra)* (also, volition or karmic action); (3) action causes consciousness *(vijnāna)*, or the function to discern; (4) consciousness causes name and form *(nāma-rūpa)*, or spiritual and material objects of discernment; (5) name and form cause the six sense organs *(shad-āyatana)*; (6) the six sense organs cause contact *(sparsha)*; (7) contact causes sensation *(vedanā)*; (8) sensation causes desire *(trishnā)*; (9) desire causes attachment *(upādāna)*; (10) attachment causes existence *(bhava)*; (11) existence causes birth *(jāti)*; and (12) birth causes aging and death *(jarā-marana)*.

The twelve-linked chain of causation is seen in two ways: the way of transmigration and the way of emancipation. From the viewpoint of the way of transmigration, ignorance gives rise to action, action causes consciousness, etc.; finally, birth causes aging and death as explained above. Thus one is caught in the cycle of delusion and suffering. On the other hand, from the viewpoint of the way of emancipation, if ignorance is wiped out, so is action; if action is wiped out, so is consciousness, etc.; finally, if birth is wiped out, so are aging and suffering. In short, if one eliminates ignorance, which is the source of suffering, one becomes free from the cycle of delusion and suffering, or attains nirvana.

The Great Commentary on the Abhidharma, a text of the Sarvāstivāda school, views the twelve-linked chain of causation as operating over the three existences of life, meaning one's past, present, and future existences. (1) Ignorance and (2) action are together interpreted as the causes created in a past life; (3) consciousness through (7) sensation, as the effects manifest in the present life; (8) desire through (10) existence, as the causes created in the present life; and (11) birth and (12) aging and death, as the effects manifest in the next life. Aging and death in this life are thus the results of causes formed in a previous life.

twelve sense fields [十二入・十二処] (Jpn *jūni-nyū* or *jūni-sho*): Also, twelve bases or twelve sense-media. The six sense organs (eyes, ears, nose, tongue, body, and mind) and their corresponding six objects (color and form, sound, odor, taste, texture, and phenomena). The contact of the six sense organs with the six objects gives rise to the six consciousnesses of sight, hearing, smell, taste, touch, and thought.

twelve sense-media [十二入・十二処] (Jpn *jūni-nyū* or *jūni-sho*): *See* twelve sense fields.

twelve vows [十二願] (Jpn *jūni-gan*): *See* twelve great vows.

twenty-eight heavens [二十八天] (Jpn *nijūhatten* or *nijūhachi-ten*): Subdivisions of the world of heaven—the six heavens in the world of desire, the eighteen heavens (subdivisions of the four meditation heavens in the world of form), and the four immaterial realms in the world of formlessness. The six heavens in the world of desire are the Heaven of the Four Heavenly Kings (Skt Chātur-mahārāja-kāyika), the Heaven of the Thirty-three Gods (Trāyastrimsha), the Yāma Heaven, the Heaven of Satisfaction (Tushita), the Heaven of Enjoying the Conjured (Nirmānarati), and the Heaven of Freely Enjoying Things Conjured by Others (Paranirmita-vasha-vartin). The eighteen heavens in the world of form are the Heaven of Brahmā's Retinue (Brahmakāyika), the Heaven of Brahmā's Aide (Brahmapurohita), and the Heaven of Great Brahmā (Mahābrahman) in the first meditation heaven; the Minor Light Heaven (Parīttābha), the Infinite Light Heaven (Apramānābha), and the Light Sound Heaven (Ābhāsvara, also known as the Utmost Light and Purity Heaven) in the second meditation heaven; the Minor Purity Heaven (Parīttashubha), the Boundless Purity Heaven (Apramānashubha), and the All Pure Heaven (Shubhakritsna) in the third meditation heaven; and the Cloudless Heaven (Anabhraka), the Merit Increasing Heaven (Punyaprasava), the Large Fruitage Heaven (Brihatphala), the Heaven of No Thought (Asamjnin), the Heaven of No Vexations (Avriha), the Heaven of No Heat (Atapa), the Reward Appearing Heaven (Sudrisha), the Heaven of Clear Perception (Sudarshana), and the Akanishtha Heaven in the fourth meditation heaven. The four realms in the world of formlessness are the Realm of Boundless Empty Space (Ākāshānantyāyatana), the Realm of Boundless Consciousness (Vijnānānantyāyatana), the Realm of Nothingness (Ākimchanyāyatana), and the Realm of Neither Thought Nor No Thought (Naivasamjnānāsamjnāyatana).

twenty-eight Indian patriarchs [天竺二十八祖・西天二十八祖・二十八祖] (Jpn *Tenjiku-nijūhasso, Saiten-nijūhasso,* or *nijūhasso*): Also, twenty-eight patriarchs. In the doctrine of the Zen (Chin Ch'an) school in China and Japan, the patriarchs of the Zen teaching in India who inherited and successively transmitted Shakyamuni Buddha's enlightenment, down through Bodhidharma, the founder of the Chinese Zen school. Zen traditionally holds that the content of that transmission is a teaching that Shakyamuni Buddha communicated from "mind to mind" to Mahākāshyapa and did not expound orally. The twenty-eight are (1) Mahākāshyapa, (2) Ānanda, (3) Shānavāsa, (4) Upagupta, (5) Dhritaka, (6) Mikkaka, (7) Vasumitra, (8) Buddhananda, (9) Buddhamitra, (10) Pārshva, (11) Punyayashas, (12) Ashvaghosha, (13) Kapimala, (14) Nāgārjuna, (15) Āryadeva, (16) Rāhulabhadra (also Rāhulatā or Rāhulata), (17) Samghanandi, (18) Samghayashas, (19) Kumārata, (20) Jayata, (21) Vasubandhu, (22) Manorhita, (23) Haklenayashas, (24) Āryasimha, (25) Vāsiasita, (26) Punyamitra, (27) Punyatāra, and (28) Bodhidharma. *See also* Zen school.

twenty-five preparatory exercises [二十五方便] (Jpn *nijūgo-hōben*): Practices undertaken in preparation for entering meditation on the truth of life. They are set forth in T'ien-t'ai's works *Great Concentration and Insight, The Essentials of Concentration and Insight,* and *The Teaching of the Practice of Meditation.* There are five groups of five practices. The first group is (1) observing precepts and purifying one's life, (2) securing appropriate food and clothing, (3) maintaining quiet surroundings, (4) freeing oneself from miscellaneous concerns or distractions, and (5) acquiring a good teacher. The second group involves restraining the five desires, which are the desires for (6) things seen, (7) things heard, (8) things smelled, (9) things tasted, and (10) things touched (restraining each desire constitutes one exercise). The third group comprises exercises to overcome the five obstacles of (11) greed, (12) anger, (13) drowsiness and languor, (14) excitement and depression, and (15) doubt. The fourth group includes practices to regulate (16) eating, (17) sleeping, (18) posture, (19) breathing, and (20) mental state; and the fifth group consists of exercises to develop the qualities of (21) aspiration for enlightenment, (22) assiduousness, (23) concentration, (24) skillful use of wisdom, and (25) single-mindedness.

twenty-five realms of existence [二十五有] (Jpn *nijūgo-u*): Also, twenty-five realms. Subdivisions of the threefold world in which living beings repeat the cycle of birth and death. They consist of fourteen realms in the world of desire, seven in the world of form, and four in the world of formlessness. The realms in the world of desire comprise the four lower worlds (the four evil paths of hell, hungry spirits, animals, and *asuras*); the four continents surrounding Mount Sumeru, which include Jambudvīpa; and the six heavens of desire. The seven realms in the world of form are the Mahābrahman Heaven (here counted as distinct from the first meditation heaven), the four meditation heavens, the Heaven of No Thought, and the realm of the five heavens of purity (taken as one realm). The world of formlessness has four immaterial realms: the Realm of Boundless Empty Space, the Realm of Boundless Consciousness, the Realm of Nothingness, and the Realm of Neither Thought Nor No Thought.

twenty-four-character Lotus Sutra [二十四文字の法華経] (Jpn *nijūyo-moji-no-hokekyō*): Also, twenty-four-character teaching. Words with which Bodhisattva Never Disparaging praised the people he encountered. According to the "Never Disparaging" (twentieth) chapter of the Lotus Sutra, whenever this bodhisattva saw monks, nuns, laymen, or laywomen, he would bow to them in reverence, saying: "I have profound reverence for you, I would never dare treat you with disparagement or arrogance. Why? Because you are all practicing the bodhisattva way and are certain to attain Buddhahood." In Kumārajīva's Chinese translation of the sutra, this passage consists of twenty-four characters.

Although the people cursed and attacked Bodhisattva Never Disparaging with staves and stones, he continued to bow in reverence to them while uttering these words of praise and was eventually able to attain Buddhahood. Meanwhile, those who harassed him converted in the end, but because of their offense of persecuting him they fell into hell and stayed there for a thousand *kalpas* before once more encountering him and attaining Buddhahood. Nichiren, in a letter addressed to his followers in 1273 called *On the Buddha's Prophecy,* writes: "The twenty-four characters of Never Disparaging and the five characters of Nichiren are different in wording, but accord with the same principle. The end of the Buddha Awesome Sound King's Middle Day and the beginning of this Latter Day of the Law are exactly the same in method of conversion" (400). "Five characters" here refers to the phrase Myoho-renge-kyo, or Nam-myoho-renge-kyo, which Nichiren taught as the essence of the Lotus Sutra. Never Disparaging tried to awaken people to their own Buddha nature, but they rejected and attacked him on that account.

Nichiren saw a parallel between his own circumstances and those of Never Disparaging: In trying to awaken people to their inherent Buddhahood by teaching them the essence of the Lotus Sutra, or Nam-myoho-renge-kyo, Nichiren, too, was scorned and attacked. Nevertheless, he was convinced that even those who attacked him would eventually attain Buddhahood through having formed a "reverse relationship" with the teaching he was spreading. According to the "Never Disparaging" chapter, even those who oppose the Lotus Sutra, though suffering due to their opposition, can eventually attain Buddhahood by virtue of the reverse relationship they have formed with that teaching. Elsewhere, Nichiren cited Never Disparaging's behavior as an example of the spirit with which one should practice the Lotus Sutra. In another letter written in 1277 he states: "The heart of the Buddha's lifetime of teachings is the Lotus Sutra, and the heart of the practice of the Lotus Sutra is found in the 'Never Disparaging' chapter. What does Bodhisattva Never Disparaging's profound respect for people signify? The purpose of the appearance in this world of Shakyamuni Buddha, the lord of teachings, lies in his behavior as a human being" (851–52). Because Never Disparaging's behavior toward others was crystallized in the teaching he shared and epitomizes the practice of the Lotus Sutra, it is called the "twenty-four-character Lotus Sutra."

twenty-four successors [付法蔵の二十四人] (Jpn *fuhōzō-no-nijūyo-nin*): Also, twenty-four patriarchs. Those who, after Shakyamuni Buddha's death, successively inherited the lineage of his teachings and propagated them in India. According to *A History of the Buddha's Successors*, there are twenty-three successors of the Buddha. They are (1) Mahākāshyapa, (2) Ānanda, (3) Shānavāsa, (4) Upagupta, (5) Dhritaka, (6) Mikkaka, (7) Buddhananda, (8) Buddhamitra, (9) Pārshva, (10) Punyayashas, (11) Ashvaghosha, (12) Kapimala, (13) Nāgārjuna, (14) Āryadeva, (15) Rāhulabhadra (also Rāhulatā), (16) Samghanandi, (17) Samghayashas, (18) Kumārata, (19) Jayata, (20) Vasubandhu, (21) Manorhita, (22) Haklenayashas, and (23) Āryasimha. The above work states that Ānanda transferred the Buddha's teachings to both Madhyāntika and Shānavāsa. Madhyāntika propagated them in Kashmir but had no known successor.

Shānavāsa transferred the Buddha's teachings to Upagupta, from whom the Buddha's teaching was finally passed on to Āryasimha without intermittence.

Based on this view, the Chinese priest Chang-an (561–632), T'ien-t'ai's successor, while listing the twenty-three successors in his preface to T'ien-t'ai's *Great Concentration and Insight,* went on to state that Madhyāntika and Shānavāsa were contemporaries who both inherited the Buddha's teachings from Ānanda. Therefore, if both are included among the Buddha's successors, he pointed out, there are twenty-four. Among the twenty-four successors, Madhyāntika is regarded as the third and Shānavāsa as the fourth. Chang-an's statement led the T'ien-t'ai school to adopt this view of twenty-four successors, in addition to the traditional view of twenty-three.

twenty Hinayana schools [二十部 · 小乗二十部] (Jpn *nijū-bu* or *shōjō-nijū-bu*): Also, twenty schools. A term applied in the Mahayana tradition to the schools formed by schisms in the Buddhist Order in India resulting from divergent interpretations of Shakyamuni Buddha's teachings after his death. According to *The Doctrines of the Different Schools,* the first schism occurred about one hundred years after Shakyamuni's death in the wake of controversy over five modifications advanced by a monk named Mahādeva. At that point, the Buddhist community split into two schools: the Sthaviravāda (Pali Theravāda) school, which rejected Mahādeva's views, and the Mahāsamghika school, which supported them. *A Correct Commentary on the Rules of Discipline* does not attribute this first schism to Mahādeva's five modifications, however. Instead, it ascribes the division to a dispute over the "ten unlawful revisions"—ten new interpretations of monastic discipline set forth by the monks of the Vriji tribe in Vaishālī.

According to *The Doctrines of the Different Schools,* a split within the Mahāsamghika occurred in the second one-hundred-year period after the Buddha's death. Eventually eight schools derived from the Mahāsamghika, forming nine Mahāsamghika schools: Ekavyāvahārika, Lokottaravāda, Kaukkutika, Bahushrutīya, Prajnāptivādin (also Prajnaptivādin), Chaityavādin, Aparashaila, Uttarashaila, and Mahāsamghika. The Sthaviravāda school divided during the third one-hundred-year period after the Buddha's death; first the Sarvāstivāda school broke away, while the original Sthaviravāda school called itself the Haimavata school. Thereafter the Sarvāstivāda school gave rise to four more schools: Vātsīputrīya, Mahīshāsaka, Kāshyapīya, and Sautrāntika. The Vātsīputrīya school further divided into the Dharmottara, Bhadrayānīya, Sammatīya, and Shannāgarika schools, and the Mahīshāsaka split to form the Dharmagupta school. Thus there were a total of eleven Sthaviravāda schools. Along with the nine Mahāsamghika schools, they form the twenty Hinayana schools. The schools arising from these schisms are sometimes referred to as the eighteen Hinayana schools, a designation that does not include the two original schools, Sthaviravāda and Mahāsamghika.

twenty-line verse [二十行の偈] (Jpn *nijūgyō-no-ge*): Also, twenty lines of verse or twenty-line verse of the "Encouraging Devotion" chapter. The concluding verse section of the "Encouraging Devotion" (thirteenth) chapter of the Lotus Sutra, in which countless multitudes of bodhisattvas vow to Shakyamuni to propagate the sutra in the evil age after his death. This section is called the twenty-line verse because the Chinese translation consists of twenty lines. The verse section begins with the passage: "We beg you not to worry. After the Buddha has passed into extinction, in an age of fear and evil we will preach far and wide." These verses enumerate the persecutions that will occur in the evil age designated in the sutra. Based on these lines from the "Encouraging Devotion" chapter, Miao-lo (711–782) classified those who persecute practitioners of the Lotus Sutra into three types of enemies. Nichiren (1222–1282) called them the three powerful enemies and often pointed out that no one other than himself had ever experienced all the persecutions predicted in the twenty-line verse of the "Encouraging Devotion" chapter on account of the Lotus Sutra. On that basis, he declared himself to be the votary of the Lotus Sutra. *See also* three powerful enemies.

twenty schools [二十部] (Jpn *nijū-bu*): Schools formed by schisms in the Buddhist Order in India after Shakyamuni Buddha's death. *See* twenty Hinayana schools.

Twenty-six Admonitions of Nikkō, The [日興遺誡置文] (Jpn *Nikkō-yuikai-okibumi*): Also known as *The Twenty-six Warning Articles*. A document that Nikkō, Nichiren's designated successor, wrote on the thirteenth day of the first month, 1333, less than a month before his death. This document, written at Omosu Seminary in Fuji District of Suruga Province, Japan, exhorts both priests and laity of future generations to maintain the purity of Nichiren's teachings, and outlines the fundamental spirit of faith, practice, and study. The articles warn against the violation of Nichiren's teachings and the failure to admonish it, prohibit worship at the shrines and temples of erroneous schools, and clarify the difference between the Fuji (Nikkō's) school and the teachings and actions of the five senior priests who were Nichiren's disciples. *The Twenty-six Admonitions of Nikkō* also touches on the correct way of study, the proper conduct of priests, the correct attitude of practitioners in general, and respect for those who propagate the teaching. Article Thirteen, for example, states: "Until *kōsen-rufu* (wide dissemination of the Law) is achieved, propagate the Law to the full extent of your ability without begrudging your life."

Twenty-six Warning Articles, The [日興遺誡置文] (Jpn *Nikkō-yuikai-okibumi*): See *Twenty-six Admonitions of Nikkō, The.*

Twenty-Stanza Treatise on the Consciousness-Only Doctrine, The [唯識二十論] (Skt *Vimshatikā-vijnaptimātratā-siddhi;* Chin *Wei-shih-erh-shih-lun;* Jpn *Yuishiki-nijū-ron*): A short work by Vasubandhu, translated into Chinese in 661 by Hsüan-tsang. It criticizes the erroneous views of non-Buddhist and Hinayana teachings and asserts the validity of the Consciousness-Only doctrine. Two other Chinese translations under different titles were produced in the sixth century by Paramārtha and by Prajnāruchi. *The Twenty-Stanza Treatise on the Consciousness-Only Doctrine* is one of the principal texts of the Dharma Characteristics (Chin Fa-hsiang; Jpn Hossō) school.

twenty-three successors [付法蔵の二十三人・二十三祖] (Jpn *fuhōzō-no-nijūsan-nin* or *nijūsan-so*): Also, twenty-three patriarchs. Those who, after Shakyamuni Buddha's death, successively inherited the lineage of his teachings and propagated them in India. According to *A History of the Buddha's Successors,* they are (1) Mahākāshyapa, (2) Ānanda, (3) Shānavāsa, (4) Upagupta, (5) Dhritaka, (6) Mikkaka, (7) Buddhananda, (8) Buddhamitra, (9) Pārshva, (10) Punyayashas, (11) Ashvaghosha, (12) Kapimala, (13) Nāgārjuna, (14) Āryadeva, (15) Rāhulabhadra (also Rāhulatā), (16) Samghanandi, (17) Samghayashas, (18) Kumārata, (19) Jayata, (20) Vasubandhu, (21) Manorhita, (22) Haklenayashas, and (23) Āryasimha. *See also* twenty-four successors.

two admonitions [二箇の諫暁] (Jpn *nika-no-kangyō*): Also, two enlightening admonitions or two admonitions of the Buddha. In the "Devadatta" (twelfth) chapter of the Lotus Sutra, references to the enlightenment of two kinds of persons for whom enlightenment had theretofore been thought impossible. One is Shakyamuni's prophecy of enlightenment for Devadatta, and the other is the attainment of Buddhahood by the dragon king's daughter. The former demonstrates that evil persons, represented by Devadatta, can become Buddhas, and the latter, that women can become Buddhas. The enlightenment of Devadatta and that of the dragon king's daughter are called "admonitions" because, by revealing the great power of the Lotus Sutra, Shakyamuni admonishes the assembly to embrace and propagate it. These two admonitions, together with the "three pronouncements" in the "Treasure Tower" (eleventh) chapter of the sutra, are called the five proclamations of the Buddha. *See also* three pronouncements.

two hundred and fifty precepts [二百五十戒] (Jpn *nihyaku-gojikkai*): Rules of discipline to be observed by fully ordained monks of Hinayana Buddhism. They are set forth in *The Fourfold Rules of Discipline* and consist of eight groups: (1) Four prohibitions. The prohibition of the four major, or unpardonable, offenses: killing, theft, sexual relations, and lying. Lying refers particularly to claiming a level of insight or understanding that one has not in fact attained. A monk who commits any one of these offenses can be automatically expelled from the Buddhist Order. (2) Thirteen major prohibitions. Monks who violate these may be divested of membership in the Buddhist Order for a certain period. (3) Two indeterminate prohibitions. The prohibition of two kinds of offenses by monks: being alone with a woman in the open and being alone with a woman in seclusion. They are called indeterminate because the punishment for violating them varies according to the nature of, or circumstances surrounding, the act. (4) Thirty standards that prohibit monks from storing things they are not allowed to possess or storing things they are allowed to possess either beyond the prescribed amount or by prohibited means. These offenses are considered light and can be pardoned if the violators confess their offense and relinquish their improper possessions to the Order. Refusal to confess is regarded as a cause for falling into the three evil paths. (5) Ninety standards, the violation of which requires confession to other monks. They deal with light offenses, such as lying about an insignificant matter, killing an insect, and duplicity with the intention of causing discord between two monks. (6) Four standards that concern the receiving of donated meals. For example, a monk is prohibited from receiving an offering of a meal from a nun who is not his relative. The breaking of these rules requires that one confess to another monk. (7) One hundred standards, which concern such matters as meals, dress, preaching, and daily behavior. Violations of these constitute light offenses. Those who commit such offenses unconsciously are required to repent in their hearts, and those who have done so consciously are required to confess to another monk. (8) Seven rules for settling disputes within the Buddhist Order. As an example, when monks are involved in a dispute, both parties must appear before the other monks, who arbitrate the disagreement.

two places and three assemblies [二処三会] (Jpn *nisho-san'e*): Also, three assemblies in two places. The settings in which Shakyamuni preaches the Lotus Sutra, as described in the sutra. The sutra begins with Shakyamuni preaching on Eagle Peak. Then, invoking supernatural powers, he raises the assembly into midair, where he continues to preach. Finally he returns the assembly to Eagle Peak, where the sutra concludes.

The three assemblies are the first assembly, which takes place on Eagle Peak; the Ceremony in the Air, in which the assembly is convened in midair; and the assembly that begins with everyone's return to Eagle Peak. The "two places" are atop Eagle Peak and in the air. The first assembly on Eagle Peak begins with the "Introduction" (first) chapter and continues through the first half of the "Treasure Tower" (eleventh) chapter. The Ceremony in the Air begins in the latter half of the "Treasure Tower" chapter and ends with the "Entrustment" (twenty-second) chapter. The final assembly on Eagle Peak begins with the "Medicine King" (twenty-third) chapter and lasts through the "Universal Worthy" (twenty-eighth) chapter, or until the end of the sutra.

two storehouses [二蔵] (Jpn *nizō*): Also, two storehouses of teachings. A classification of Shakyamuni's lifetime teachings into two categories, set forth by Chi-tsang (549–623), a systematizer of the doctrines of the Three Treatises (San-lun) school in China. The two storehouses are (1) the teachings expounded for persons of the two vehicles (voice-hearers and cause-awakened ones) and (2) the teachings for bodhisattvas. The former corresponds to the Hinayana teachings, and the latter to the Mahayana teachings.

two transfer documents [二箇相承書] (Jpn *nika-sōjō-sho*): Two documents written by Nichiren (1222–1282) naming Nikkō as his legitimate successor: (1) *The Minobu Transfer Document,* also known as *The Document for Entrusting the Law that Nichiren Propagated throughout His Life,* written at Minobu in the ninth month of 1282. In this document, Nichiren transfers the entirety of his teachings to Nikkō and entrusts him with leadership in propagating them. (2) *The Ikegami Transfer Document,* also known as *The Document for Entrusting Minobu-san,* written at the residence of Ikegami Munenaka on the thirteenth day of the tenth month, 1282, the day Nichiren died. It appoints Nikkō as the chief priest of Minobu-san Kuon-ji temple and states that all Nichiren's disciples should follow Nikkō. See also *Ikegami Transfer Document; Minobu Transfer Document.*

two vehicles [二乗] (Jpn *nijō*): The vehicles or teachings that lead voice-hearers (Skt *shrāvaka*) and cause-awakened ones *(pratyekabuddha)* to their respective levels of enlightenment. The vehicle of voice-hearers was intended to lead persons of that capacity to the state of arhat via the teaching of the four noble truths; the vehicle of cause-awakened ones leads those individuals to the awakening to the truths of impermanence and of causal relationship via the teaching of the twelve-linked chain of causation. In early Buddhism, *pratyekabuddhas,* or cause-awakened ones, referred to those who lived apart from human habitation; with no chance to hear the Buddha's teachings, they nevertheless realized the impermanence of all things by observing changes in nature such as the scattering of blossoms or the falling of leaves. Hence they were also called self-awakened ones.

Buddhist texts describe two kinds of self-awakened ones: The first are those who were originally the Buddha's voice-hearer disciples but who, on reaching the stage just below arhatship, chose to practice alone toward the goal of becoming arhats. The second are those who practiced alone in an age without a Buddha and without learning from anyone and achieved a level of enlightenment. Mahayana Buddhism describes the two vehicle teachings as "lesser vehicles," or Hinayana teachings. The provisional Mahayana teachings condemn persons of the two vehicles for seeking their own enlightenment without working for the enlightenment of others, and assert that they can never attain Buddhahood. The Lotus Sutra reveals the one vehicle of Buddhahood and identifies all three vehicles—those of voice-hearers, cause-awakened ones, and bodhisattvas—as expedient means that lead people to the one Buddha vehicle. According to the Lotus Sutra, therefore, even those of the two vehicles can become Buddhas. This is substantiated in the sutra by Shakyamuni's prophecy that all of his voice-hearer disciples will in the future become Buddhas, specifying when and where this will take place and what names they will assume at that time.

Two-Volumed Sutra [双巻経・双観経] (Jpn *Sōkan-gyō*): An alternate title for the Buddha Infinite Life Sutra, a core text of the Pure Land teachings. This name derives from the fact that it consists of two volumes, while the Meditation on the Buddha Infinite Life Sutra, another key Pure Land sutra, consists of one volume. *See* Buddha Infinite Life Sutra.

Tz'u-en [慈恩] (632–682) (PY Cien; Jpn Jion): Also known as K'uei-chi. The founder of the Dharma Characteristics (Fa-hsiang) school in China. Because he lived at Tz'u-en-ssu temple, he was given the title Great Teacher Tz'u-en. Born in Ch'ang-an, he became a student of Hsüan-tsang in 648 and later one of his most outstanding disciples. Tz'u-en collaborated with Hsüan-tsang in translating Buddhist texts, including *The Treatise on the Establishment of the Consciousness-Only Doctrine.* Based on the Consciousness-Only doctrine that Hsüan-tsang had brought from India, Tz'u-en established the Dharma Characteristics school. His works include *The Commentary on "The Treatise on the Establishment of the Consciousness-Only Doctrine," Praising the Profundity of the Lotus Sutra, The Forest of Meanings in the Mahayana Garden of the Law,* and commentaries on the Consciousness-Only doctrine.

Tz'u-en-ssu [慈恩寺] (PY Ciensi; Jpn Jion-ji): Also known as Ta-tz'u-en-ssu. A temple built in Ch'ang-an, China, in 648 by Emperor Kao-tsung of the T'ang dynasty when he was crown prince, as an expression of compassion and gratitude to his mother. Hence the temple name Tz'u-en, or "compassion and debt of gratitude." A building for translation was erected in the temple compound for Hsüan-tsang, who had left Ch'ang-an for India in 629 and returned there with Buddhist scriptures in 645. Hsüan-tsang spent eleven years at the temple, where he translated many scriptures into Chinese. Hence he was given the title Tripitaka Master of Ta-tz'u-en-ssu. After Hsüan-tsang moved to Hsi-ming-ssu temple in 658, his disciple K'uei-chi lived at Tz'u-en-ssu and engaged in translation there; therefore, K'uei-chi was given the title Great Teacher Tz'u-en. The temple compound is said to have been vast, with eighteen hundred rooms. The temple was razed, however, in a nationwide drive to destroy Buddhism initiated by Emperor Wu-tsung of the T'ang dynasty in the mid-ninth century, and today only a seven-story pagoda remains at the site.

U

Udayana [優塡王] (Skt; Pali Udena; Jpn Uden-ō): A king of the city of Kaushāmbī in north-central India and a patron of Shakyamuni Buddha. He converted to the Buddha's teaching at the urging of his wife. Udayana is mentioned in a number of Buddhist sutras. According to the King Udayana Sutra, Udayana, influenced by one of his consorts, attempted to shoot his wife with an arrow. The arrow circled his wife three times, however, and came back to him. Thereupon, she revealed to him that she was a follower of Shakyamuni Buddha and urged him to follow the Buddha as well. Udayana went to see the Buddha, who was then staying in Kaushāmbī, and received instruction from him. According to the Increasing by One Āgama Sutra, when Shakyamuni ascended to the Heaven of the Thirty-three Gods for a considerable time to preach to his mother, Māyā, King Udayana lamented that he could no longer see the Buddha and fell ill. Concerned for their king, his retainers expressed their desire to make an image of the Buddha. Udayana, moved by their resolve, had a five-foot image of the Buddha fashioned out of ox-head sandalwood, and this contributed to his recovery. The sutra regards this as the first image of the Buddha ever made.

Uddaka Rāmaputta [鬱頭藍弗・優陀羅羅摩子] (Pali; Skt Udraka Rāmaputra; Jpn Uzuranhotsu, Utsuzuranfutsu, or Udararamashi): A hermit and master of yogic meditation who lived in a forest near Rājagriha, the capital of Magadha, India. After Shakyamuni renounced the world to lead a religious life, Uddaka Rāmaputta became his second teacher. He had seven hundred disciples and was said to have attained, through meditation, the Realm of Neither Thought Nor No Thought. Shakyamuni quickly mastered this meditation but, finding no fundamental answer to his questions therein, left Uddaka Rāmaputta and turned to the practice of austerities.

Uddiyāna [烏仗那国] (Skt; Jpn Ujōna-koku): Also known as Udyāna. An ancient kingdom to the north of Gandhara in India. *See* Udyāna.

Udraka Rāmaputra [鬱頭藍弗・優陀羅羅摩子] (Skt; Jpn Uzuranhotsu, Utsuzuranfutsu, or Udararamashi): *See* Uddaka Rāmaputta.

udumbara [優曇華] (Skt, Pali; Jpn *udonge*): A plant described in Buddhist scriptures as blooming only once every three thousand years to herald the advent of a wheel-turning king or a Buddha. The *udumbara* is often employed as a symbol for the rarity of encountering a Buddha or hearing a Buddha's teaching. The "King Wonderful Adornment" (twenty-seventh) chapter of the Lotus Sutra says, "Encountering the Buddha is as difficult as encountering the *udumbara* flower."

Udyāna [烏仗那国] (Skt; Jpn Ujōna-koku): Also known as Uddiyāna. A kingdom to the north of Gandhara in ancient India. It is thought to have been located in the region today known as Swat, the area of the Swat River valley in northwestern Pakistan. The capital of Udyāna was at the site of present-day Mingaora, a town just east of the Swat River. In the fourth century B.C.E., Alexander the Great invaded and conquered the Swat and Gandhara regions as he advanced on India, and in the third century B.C.E., King Ashoka is said to have introduced Buddhism to Udyāna. According to the record of Hsüan-tsang, a Chinese priest who traveled in India in the seventh century, Mahayana Buddhism prospered there at the time, with 1,400 monastic buildings on both sides of the Swat River.

Ueno, the lay nun [上野尼] (d. 1284) (Jpn Ueno-ama): A lay follower of Nichiren. She was a daughter of Matsuno Rokurō Saemon and the wife of Nanjō Hyōe Shichirō, the steward of Ueno Village in Suruga Province in Japan. The name Ueno comes from Ueno Village, where her husband was steward. The couple had nine children, including Nanjō Tokimitsu. Sometime between 1260 and 1264, while on an official tour of duty in Kamakura, her husband met Nichiren and converted to his teachings. He died of illness in 1265, while she was pregnant with their last son. She went on to raise her children alone while maintaining faith in Nichiren's teachings.

Ujjayinī [烏闍衍那国] (Skt; Pali Ujjenī; Jpn Ujaenna-koku): Also known as Ujjayanī or Ujjainī. The capital of Avanti, one of the sixteen great states in India in Shakyamuni Buddha's time. Ujjayinī corresponds to present-day Ujjain in Madhya Pradesh state, noted as one of the seven sacred cities of the Hindus. According to tradition, Ashoka was governor of this region when he was a prince. Kātyāyana, one of Shakyamuni Buddha's ten major disciples, was a native of Ujjayinī.

Ulūka [優楼迦・漚楼僧佉] (Skt; Jpn Uruka or Urusōgya): Also known as Kanāda. Regarded as the founder of the Vaisheshika school, one of the six major schools of Brahmanism in ancient India, which was established sometime after the second century. The Vaisheshika Sutra, the basic text of the school, is attributed to Ulūka. The Vaisheshika school analyzes phenomena according to the six principles of entity, attribute, motion, universality, particularity, and unity. Buddhist writings refer to Ulūka as one of the three ascetics of Brahmanism, the other two being Kapila and Rishabha.

Umegiku-nyo [梅菊女] (d. 1267): Nichiren's mother. According to *The Transmission on the First Cleaning Bath* written by Nikkō, Nichiren's immediate disciple and successor. When Nichiren publicly proclaimed his teaching in 1253, she and her husband, Mikuni no Taifu (also Tayū), converted and Nichiren gave her the Buddhist name Myōren (Wonderful Lotus). Her husband died in 1258. In 1263 Nichiren was pardoned from his exile in Itō on the Izu Peninsula and returned to Kamakura. The following year he visited his mother, who was gravely ill, in his home province of Awa and prayed for her recovery. According to Nichiren's letter titled *On Prolonging One's Life Span,* she recovered as a result of his prayers and lived for four more years.

Unborn Enemy [未生怨] (Jpn Mishō'on): Another name for Ajātashatru, a king of Magadha in India in the time of Shakyamuni. *See* Enemy before Birth.

unconditioned, the [無為] (Skt *asamskrita;* Jpn *mui*): Also, realm of the unconditioned. That which does not arise through dependent origination or causation, i.e., which neither depends on nor is subject to any cause or condition. "The unconditioned" often indicates nirvana, enlightenment, or the unchanging Dharma or Law. It contrasts with the conditioned, which comprises all things and phenomena that arise through causation; i.e., that which is changeable and impermanent. Later this term came to mean an unattached or unrestricted state of life, or more broadly the life of a Buddhist. Interpretations of this concept varied among Buddhist schools. The Sarvāstivāda school, for instance, enumerates three categories of the unconditioned: space, the cessation of earthly desires, and the non-appearance of things and phenomena for lack of their causes. The cessation of earthly desires can be attained through Buddhist practice, while the non-appearance of things and phenomena is independent of human intervention, simply because by definition it lacks any cause.

Unequalled One [阿娑摩] (Skt, Pali *asama;* Jpn *ashama*): Also, Unparalleled One. An honorable title of a Buddha. A Buddha is also called "Equal with the Unequalled One" (Skt *asamasama*), which means that, while bodhisattvas and other beings cannot equal Buddhas, Buddhas equal one another.

Unexcelled Worthy [無上士] (Skt, Pali *anuttara;* Jpn *mujōshi*): One of the ten honorable titles of a Buddha, signifying that a Buddha is peerless and stands supreme among all living beings. The Sanskrit word *anuttara* means unsurpassed, unexcelled, supreme, or peerless.

unfixed karma [不定業] (Jpn *fujō-gō*): Also, mutable karma. The opposite of fixed karma. Karma that does not necessarily produce a specific kind of result or reward, or yields an effect that is not destined to appear at or within a certain fixed time. It is regarded as lighter and easier to change than fixed karma. *See also* fixed karma.

unhindered wisdom [無礙智] (Jpn *muge-chi*): The wisdom of a Buddha. Wisdom that penetrates without hindrance all things and phenomena throughout time and space. The "Parable of the Phantom City" (seventh) chapter of the Lotus Sutra reads, "The Buddha wisdom is pure, subtle, wonderful, without outflows, without hindrance, reaching to and penetrating immeasurable *kalpas.*"

unification of the three truths [円融の三諦] (Jpn *en'yū-no-santai*): A principle set forth by T'ien-t'ai (538–597) based on the Lotus Sutra. It explains the three truths of non-substantiality, temporary existence, and the Middle Way as an integrated whole, each of the three containing all three within itself. T'ien-t'ai identified this as the view of the three truths revealed in the perfect teaching, or the Lotus Sutra, in contrast to the separation of the three truths, the view espoused in the specific teaching.

Separation of the three truths is the view of the three truths as separate and independent of one another. The truth of non-substantiality means that phenomena have no existence of their own; their true nature is non-substantial. The truth of temporary existence means that, although non-substantial in nature, all phenomena possess a temporary reality that is in constant flux. The truth of the Middle Way means that all phenomena are characterized by both non-substantiality and temporary existence, yet are in essence neither.

The unification of the three truths means that the truths of non-substantiality, temporary existence, and the Middle Way are inherent in all phenomena. T'ien-t'ai taught a form of meditation called the threefold contemplation in a single mind, aimed at grasping the unification of the three truths, eradicating the three categories of illusion, and acquiring the three kinds of wisdom (the wisdom of the two vehicles, the bodhisattva wisdom, and the Buddha wisdom), all at the same time.

Universal Brightness (1) [普明王] (Skt Shrutasoma; Pali Sutasoma; Jpn Fumyō-ō): The name of Shakyamuni Buddha in a past existence, when he was a king engaged in the *pāramitā,* or practice, of observing precepts. The story of this king, either under the name Universal Brightness (a translation of his Chinese name) or the Sanskrit name Shrutasoma, is related in the Sutra on the Wise and the Foolish, the Benevolent Kings Sutra, *The Treatise on the Great Perfection of Wisdom,* and elsewhere. These sources give slightly different accounts.

According to *The Treatise on the Great Perfection of Wisdom,* King Universal Brightness and 99 other kings (999 by another account) were captured by King Deer Feet (Spotted Feet by another account). King Universal Brightness asked Deer Feet that, before killing him, he first let him carry out a promise he had made to give offerings to a certain Brahman (or monk by another account) in his country. He told Deer Feet that he had no fear of losing his life, but that failing to keep his promise would amount to lying and was hard to bear. King Deer Feet granted him seven days' grace to fulfill his promise. King Universal Brightness returned to his country, where he gave the Brahman offerings and transferred the throne to his son. After proclaiming to his people that speaking only truthful words, or never speaking falsely, is the most important precept, he returned to Deer Feet as he had sworn to do. King Deer Feet was very impressed by the sincerity of Universal Brightness and praised him as a great man of truthful words. King Universal Brightness then explained to Deer Feet from various standpoints the importance of truthful speech. Deer Feet listened to Universal Brightness, put faith in his words, and thereupon released not only Universal Brightness but the other 99 kings as well. *See also* Spotted Feet.

(2) [普明如来] (Skt Samantaprabhāsa; Jpn Fumyō-nyorai): The Thus Come One Universal Brightness. The name that Kaundinya and others of Shakyamuni's voice-hearer disciples will assume when they attain Buddhahood in the future, according to the "Five Hundred Disciples" (eighth) chapter of the Lotus Sutra. In this chapter, Shakyamuni predicts that a group of five hundred arhats and another group of seven hundred will in the future all become Buddhas of the same name, Universal Brightness. *Samanta* of the Sanskrit name Samantaprabhāsa means universal, and *prabhāsa* means brightness.

"Universal Gateway" chapter [普門品] (Jpn *Fumon-bon*): The twenty-fifth chapter of the Lotus Sutra. *See* "Universal Gateway of the Bodhisattva Perceiver of the World's Sounds" chapter.

"Universal Gateway of the Bodhisattva Perceiver of the World's Sounds" chapter [観世音菩薩普門品] (Jpn *Kanzeon-bosatsu-fumon-bon*): The twenty-fifth chapter of the Lotus Sutra, which describes the blessings of Bodhisattva Perceiver of the World's Sounds. Abbreviated as the "Universal Gateway" chapter, the "Perceiver of the World's Sounds" chapter, or the "Bodhisattva Perceiver of the World's Sounds" chapter. At the beginning of the chapter, Bodhisattva Inexhaustible Intent asks Shakyamuni Buddha to explain why Bodhisattva Perceiver of the World's Sounds is so called. Shakyamuni replies that it is because this bodhisattva perceives the troubles of all those who single-mindedly call upon his name and delivers them from danger or harm, anytime and anywhere. He further cites examples of seven disasters from which one can be saved by calling the name of Bodhisattva Perceiver of the World's Sounds: fire, flood, attack by *rākshasa* demons, attack by swords and staves, attack by *yaksha* and other demons, imprisonment, and attack by bandits. Bodhisattva Perceiver of the World's Sounds, he says, also frees people from the three poisons of greed, anger, and foolishness, and grants people's prayers to have children. Shakyamuni then enumerates thirty-three forms that Perceiver of the World's Sounds assumes in order to save the people. He asserts that Bodhisattva Perceiver of the World's Sounds can assume any shape at will, becoming a god, a Brahman, a nonhuman being such as a dragon, or any other appropriate form in order to preach the Buddha's teaching. Moreover, he says, Bodhisattva Perceiver of the World's Sounds is given the epithet Bestower of Fearlessness because he confers the benefit of fearlessness in times of trouble or danger. In China and Japan, this chapter was circulated as an independent sutra titled Perceiver of the World's Sounds, and worship of Bodhisattva Perceiver of the World's Sounds became highly popular in both countries. In Chinese, this bodhisattva is called Kuan-shih-yin or Kuan-yin, and in Japanese, Kanzeon or Kannon.

Universal Practice [普事比丘] (Jpn Fuji-biku): A monk depicted in the Buddha Treasury Sutra as appearing after the death of Great Adornment Buddha of the remote past and striving to lead people to that Buddha's teachings. According to this sutra, one hundred years after the death of the Buddha Great Adornment, that Buddha's followers split into five schools led by the monks Universal Practice, Shore of Suffering, Sawata, Shōko, and Batsunanda respectively, and only Universal Practice upheld the principle of non-substantiality that the Buddha had taught. The leaders of the four other schools, such as the monk Shore of Suffering, held erroneous views, rejecting the concept of non-substantiality and asserting that "self" truly exists. These four leading monks and their followers despised and reviled Universal Practice. For this reason, according to the Buddha Treasury Sutra, these four monks and their followers all fell into hell. (The names Sawata, Shōko, and Batsunanda are Japanese reading of the Chinese names that appear in the sutra, which themselves are phonetic transliterations of the Sanskrit names from the lost Sanskrit text. As transliterations, they carry no particular meaning and cannot be translated into English. The original Sanskrit names are unknown.)

Universal Worthy [普賢菩薩] (Skt Samantabhadra; Jpn Fugen-bosatsu): A bodhisattva who is regarded as symbolic of the virtues of truth and practice. In various sutras, he is depicted as one of the two leading bodhisattvas who attend Shakyamuni Buddha, the other being Manjushrī. He is usually shown on the Buddha's right, riding a white elephant with six tusks. In the "Universal Worthy" (twenty-eighth) chapter of the Lotus Sutra, he vows to protect the Lotus Sutra and its votaries, saying to the Buddha, "In the evil and corrupt age of the last five-hundred-year period, if there is someone who accepts and upholds this sutra, I will guard and protect him, free him from decline and harm, see that he attains peace and tranquillity, and make certain that no one can spy out and take advantage of his shortcomings." In this chapter, he also takes a vow before the Buddha, saying: "I now therefore employ my transcendental powers to guard and protect this sutra. And after the Thus Come One has entered extinction, I will cause it to be widely propagated throughout Jambudvīpa and will see that it never comes to an end."

Bodhisattva Universal Worthy is also the protagonist of the Universal Worthy Sutra, which describes his beneficent power, how to meditate on him, and the benefit accruing from doing so. In the Flower Garland Sutra, Bodhisattva Universal Worthy makes ten great vows concerning his Buddhist practice, such as a vow to bestow all blessings upon all living beings and lead them to Buddhahood. This sutra relates the story of the boy Good Treasures who visits fifty-three teachers in search of the Law. Good Treasures finally meets the fifty-third teacher, Bodhisattva Universal Worthy, and on hearing his ten great vows attains enlightenment. A number of murals from Central Asia and images from China and Japan depicting this bodhisattva are extant.

"Universal Worthy" chapter [普賢品] (Jpn *Fugen-bon*): The twenty-eighth and last chapter of the Lotus Sutra. *See* "Encouragements of the Bodhisattva Universal Worthy" chapter.

Universal Worthy Sutra [普賢経] (Chin *P'u-hsien-ching;* Jpn *Fugen-kyō*):

The abbreviated title of the Sutra on How to Practice Meditation on the Bodhisattva Universal Worthy. Also abbreviated as the Meditation on Universal Worthy Sutra. A one-volume sutra that describes the beneficent power of Bodhisattva Universal Worthy and how to meditate on this bodhisattva. It was translated into Chinese in the early fifth century by Dharmamitra, a monk from Kashmir. Regarded as an epilogue to the Lotus Sutra, it contains a reference to the Lotus Sutra and Shakyamuni's preaching of that sutra. According to the Universal Worthy Sutra's description, Shakyamuni Buddha preached this sutra at Great Forest Monastery in Vaishālī three months before his death. In the beginning of the sutra, Shakyamuni announces to the monks in the assembly, "Three months from now I will enter nirvana." After this announcement, Ānanda, Mahākāshyapa, and Bodhisattva Maitreya question the Buddha about how those who will appear after the Buddha's death can purify all their senses and wipe away all their offenses without either cutting off earthly desires or separating themselves from the five desires. In reply, Shakyamuni says that, by practicing meditation on Bodhisattva Universal Worthy, carrying out repentance, and embracing the great vehicle teaching, they can attain Buddhahood.

unlabeled, the [無記] (Skt *avyākrita;* Jpn *muki*): That which is morally neutral. One of the three types of character, a classification of all things into the three conditions: good, bad, and neutral. "The unlabeled" indicates the neutral, all that is neither good nor bad, or that cannot be categorized as either good or evil.

Unparalleled One [阿娑摩] (Jpn *ashama*): An honorable title of a Buddha. *See* Unequalled One.

unseen crown of the head [無見頂相] (Jpn *mukenchō-sō*): The top of a Buddha's head, which no one can see. One of a Buddha's eighty characteristics. It is said that the crown of a Buddha's head cannot be seen by humans or heavenly beings. This feature is generally identified with a protuberant knot of flesh on the crown of a Buddha's head, one of a Buddha's thirty-two features. For this reason, the unseen crown of the head is also counted as one of the thirty-two features.

unsurpassed enlightenment [無上菩提] (Skt *anuttara-sambodhi;* Jpn *mujō-bodai*): Also, supreme enlightenment or supreme perfect enlightenment. The enlightenment of a Buddha. The Sanskrit *anuttara* means "unsurpassed." A Buddha's enlightenment is so called because it is the highest and supreme among all levels of awakening gained through Buddhist practice. Bodhisattvas make four vows when they first resolve to embark upon the Buddhist practice. These four vows are known as the four universal vows, one of which is to attain unsurpassed enlightenment.

unsurpassed way [無上道] (Jpn *mujō-dō*): The supreme teaching of the Buddha, which leads people to Buddhahood. The term *unsurpassed way* also refers to supreme enlightenment, or the state of Buddhahood. Shakyamuni Buddha says in the "Expedient Means" (second) chapter of the Lotus Sutra, "Honestly discarding expedient means, I will preach only the unsurpassed way." In the "Life Span" (sixteenth) chapter of the sutra, he speaks of his aim and wish as follows: "At all times I think to myself: How can I cause living beings to gain entry into the unsurpassed way and quickly acquire the body of a Buddha?"

upadesha [優婆提舍] (Skt; Jpn *ubadaisha*): Discourses on the Buddha's teachings. One of the twelve divisions of the Buddha's teachings. *Upadesha* refers to Shakyamuni Buddha's discourses on doctrine to his disciples, which took the form of questions and answers. The term also refers to discourses on the Buddha's teachings by his disciples, including doctrinal treatises and commentaries on the sutras.

Upagupta [優婆毱多] (Skt; Jpn Ubakikuta): A native of Mathura in India in the third century B.C.E. He is regarded as the fourth of Shakyamuni Buddha's twenty-three, or the fifth of his twenty-four, successors. Upagupta studied under Shānavāsa and received the transmission of the Buddha's teachings from him. Once when Upagupta was preaching on Mount Urumanda, King Ashoka expressed a desire to go and hear him. Upon learning of this, Upagupta went to Pātaliputra and preached the Buddha's teachings for Ashoka. Out of gratitude, King Ashoka erected stupas at various sites associated with Shakyamuni Buddha.

Upāli [優婆離] (Skt, Pali; Jpn Ubari): One of Shakyamuni's ten major disciples, known as foremost in observing the precepts. He was a barber at the court of Kapilavastu, a small state near the present-day Indian–Nepalese border. When Shakyamuni Buddha returned home to Kapilavastu several years after his enlightenment, Upāli was among the many people there who converted to his teachings. Other converts included Shakyamuni's cousin Ānanda, his half brother Nanda, and his son Rāhula. According to tradition, Upāli was well versed in the causes and circumstances that had brought about the prescription of the *vinaya,* or rules of monastic discipline. At the First Buddhist Council held to compile the Buddha's teachings, Upāli is said to have recited the *vinaya,* while Ānanda recited the sutras.

upāsaka [優婆塞] (Skt, Pali; Jpn *ubasoku*): Buddhist laymen. Those who have faith in Buddhism, revere and serve the three treasures of the Buddha, his teachings, and the Buddhist Order, and observe the five precepts that forbid killing, stealing, sexual misconduct, lying, and drinking intoxicants, yet who do not renounce secular or family ties to live as monks. *Upāsaka* originally meant to serve or one who serves. Buddhist laywomen who, like *upāsaka,* acknowledge allegiance to the three treasures and observe the five precepts are called *upāsikā* in Sanskrit. These terms were used outside of Buddhism as well to refer to lay practitioners of other Indian religious traditions. *Bhikshu* (monks) and *bhikshunī* (nuns), *upāsaka* and *upāsikā,* constitute what are known as the four kinds of believers within the Order. In Chinese translations of the sutras, *upāsaka* and *upāsikā* were interpreted as "men of pure faith" and "women of pure faith" respectively.

upāsikā [優婆夷] (Skt, Pali; Jpn *ubai*): Buddhist laywomen. See *upāsaka.*

Upholder of the Nation [持国天] (Skt Dhritarāshtra; Jpn Jikoku-ten): One of the four heavenly kings of Buddhist mythology. This god is said to live halfway up the eastern side of Mount Sumeru and protect the eastern quarter. In Buddhist scriptures, Upholder of the Nation often appears as a guardian of the Buddha's teachings and a protector of the world along with the other three heavenly kings, Wide-Eyed, Hearer of Many Teachings (also known as Vaishravana), and Increase and Growth. *See also* four heavenly kings.

uposhadha [布薩] (Skt; Pali *uposatha;* Jpn *fusatsu*): Also, *poshadha, upavāsa,* or *upavasatha.* A semimonthly meeting of self-examination and public confession held in Buddhist monasteries in India. At the *uposhadha,* monks recited the precepts for the Buddhist Order, and those who had violated them confessed their offenses. The *uposhadha* was held at the time of the new and full moons.

urabon [盂蘭盆] (Jpn): A Buddhist service in which offerings are made to the three treasures of Buddhism for the benefit of the deceased. In Japan today, it is an annual Buddhist observance honoring the spirits of deceased ancestors and held July 13–15 (August in some areas). *See* service for deceased ancestors.

Urumanda, Mount [優留曼荼山] (Skt; Jpn Urumanda-sen): Also known as Mount Urumunda. A mountain in Mathurā in ancient India. It is said that Shānavāsa, the third of Shakyamuni's twenty-three successors, built a great temple on this mountain and many came there to learn from him.

Uruvilvā [優楼頻螺] (Skt; Pali Uruvelā; Jpn Urubinra): A village near Gayā, a city in the ancient Indian state of Magadha. Shakyamuni engaged in ascetic practice for twelve years (six years according to another view) in a forest near Uruvilvā before he attained enlightenment. After his enlightenment, Shakyamuni Buddha again visited Uruvilvā where he instructed and converted the three Brahman brothers Uruvilvā Kāshyapa,

Nadī Kāshyapa, and Gayā Kāshyapa. These three brothers had five hundred disciples, three hundred disciples, and two hundred disciples respectively, all of whom also converted to the Buddha's teachings. Consequently, Shakyamuni's group suddenly grew to a community of more than a thousand members. Thereafter Shakyamuni left Uruvilvā and proceeded to Rājagriha, the capital of Magadha, to continue teaching.

Uruvilvā Kāshyapa [優楼頻螺迦葉] (Skt; Pali Uruvelā Kassapa; Jpn Urubinra-kashō): One of Shakyamuni Buddha's early converts. Before conversion, he is said to have practiced fire worship. When the Buddha went to Uruvilvā to preach, Uruvilvā Kāshyapa, together with his two brothers, Nadī Kāshyapa and Gayā Kāshyapa, became his follower. All three brothers were leaders among Brahman ascetics, and when Uruvilvā Kāshyapa converted, his five hundred disciples followed suit.

Utmost Light and Purity Heaven [極光浄天] (Jpn Gokukōjō-ten): One of the eighteen heavens in the world of form. *See* Light Sound Heaven.

Utpalavarnā [蓮華色比丘尼] (Skt; Pali Uppalavannā; Jpn Rengeshiki-bikuni): A nun of Shakyamuni Buddha's Order. *The Fourfold Rules of Discipline* tells how she came to renounce the secular world. Just at the time she gave birth to a daughter, she discovered that her husband was having an illicit relationship with her mother and she ran away from home, leaving her baby. Later she became the wife of a rich man in Vārānasī. When her new husband brought home a second wife, however, Utpalavarnā realized that the woman was her daughter. Sorrowing over her destiny, she renounced secular life and became a disciple of the Buddha. Thereafter she engaged in Buddhist practice under the guidance of Mahāprajāpatī and attained the state of arhat. According to *The Treatise on the Great Perfection of Wisdom,* when Devadatta rolled a huge rock down on the Buddha in an attempt to kill him, she reproached Devadatta for his evil act, whereupon Devadatta beat her to death.

Utsubusa, the lady of [内房女房] (n.d.) (Jpn Utsubusa-nyōbō): A follower of Nichiren who lived at Utsubusa in Ihara District of Suruga Province, Japan. Judging from the content of an extant letter Nichiren sent to her in 1280 called *White Horses and White Swans,* she seems to have been a woman of considerable erudition and affluence. Marking the hundredth-day anniversary of her father's death, she made an offering of ten thousand coins to Nichiren and declared that she had read and recited the entire Lotus Sutra once, the "Expedient Means" (second) and "Life Span" (sixteenth) chapters of the sutra three hundred times each, and the verse section of the "Life Span" chapter three hundred times. In addition, she said that she had chanted the daimoku fifty thousand times.

Views differ as to whether she is the same person as the lay nun of Utsubusa, whom Nichiren mentions in his *Letter to Misawa;* one account holds that she is, and another regards her as the lay nun's daughter or daughter-in-law. The latter is most probably the case, however, because Nichiren wrote in *Letter to Misawa,* "[The lay nun of] Utsubusa is the same age that my parents would be" (896).

Utsubusa, the lay nun of [内房の尼] (n.d.) (Jpn Utsubusa-no-ama): A follower of Nichiren who lived at Utsubusa in Ihara District of Suruga Province, Japan. In his *Letter to Misawa,* Nichiren says that she was "the same age that my parents would be" (896). This letter also says that she made a casual visit to Nichiren at Minobu on her way back from visiting the shrine to the god of her ancestors. Although reluctantly, he refused to see her on that occasion, so that she would understand her error in putting the gods before the Lotus Sutra. While one view regards her as the same person as the lady of Utsubusa, to whom Nichiren addressed a 1280 letter called *White Horses and White Swans,* Nichiren's above reference to her age makes this seem unlikely. In *White Horses and White Swans,* Nichiren acknowledges the lady of Utsubusa's offering marking the hundredth day after her father's death, making it likely she was much younger than Nichiren's parents. *See also* Utsubusa, the lady of.

Uttarakuru [鬱単越・倶盧洲] (Skt, Pali; Jpn Uttan'otsu or Kuru-shū): Also known as Kuru. One of the four continents surrounding Mount Sumeru in the ancient Indian worldview. Uttarakuru is situated to the north of Mount Sumeru. The Sanskrit *uttara* means north. *The Dharma Analysis Treasury* says that this continent is square and each side measures two thousand *yojanas.* According to the Rise of the World Sutra, rice grows in this continent without cultivation, and no evil persons are found there. Without being instructed, the people in this land perform the ten good acts, which are to refrain from committing any of the ten evils, which include killing, stealing, and lying. The people there live for one thousand years and after their death are reborn in the heavenly realms; after their span of life expires there, they are reborn in Jambudvīpa.

V

Vaidehī [韋提希] (Skt; Pali Vedehī; Jpn Idaike): The consort of Bimbisāra, king of Magadha in ancient India, and the mother of Ajātashatru. She is said to have been the sister of King Prasenajit of Kosala. When Ajātashatru killed his father Bimbisāra to usurp the throne, he also attempted to kill his mother, Vaidehī. His ministers admonished him against this evil act, and she escaped death. According to the Buddha Infinite Life Sutra, one of the principal texts of the Pure Land (Jōdo) school, Ajātashatru imprisoned his father, King Bimbisāra, and attempted to starve him to death. Vaidehī secretly covered her body with a mixture of honey and flour, and went regularly to visit the king in prison, enabling him to nourish himself and survive. When Ajātashatru discovered this, he was enraged and attempted to kill his mother, but was restrained by his ministers Jīvaka and Chandraprabha. Instead, Ajātashatru had her confined to the palace. She faced Eagle Peak where Shakyamuni Buddha was preaching and prayed to him. Out of pity for her, the Buddha interrupted his preaching and appeared in her chamber with Ānanda and Maudgalyāyana. At her request, he instructed her how to reach the Pure Land of Amida Buddha, or the Buddha Infinite Life.

vaipulya [方等] (Skt; Jpn *hōdō*): Great extension, development, largeness, or thickness, indicating a sutra of great breadth or scope. In Chinese translations of Buddhist scriptures, *vaipulya* was rendered as "correct and equal" or "correct and vast." In his classification of Shakyamuni Buddha's teachings, T'ien-t'ai (538–597) defined the third of the five periods of the Buddha's teachings as Correct and Equal. *Vaipulya* is also a component of the nine divisions or twelve divisions of the scriptures, meaning that part of a sutra that concerns the expansion of doctrine.

Vairochana [毘盧遮那仏] (Skt; Jpn Birushana-butsu): A Buddha who appears in the Flower Garland, Brahmā Net, and Mahāvairochana sutras. The name Vairochana was rendered in Chinese as Light Shining Universally. The Flower Garland Sutra describes his pure land called Lotus Treasury World. A great image of Vairochana Buddha, erected at Tōdai-ji temple in Nara, Japan, by a 743 edict of Emperor Shōmu, was consecrated in 752. The True Word (Jpn Shingon) school equates Vairochana with its central deity, Mahāvairochana. The True Word teachings regard the entire universe as a manifestation of that Buddha.

Vaishālī [毘舎離] (Skt; Pali Vesālī; Jpn Bishari): The capital city of the Licchavi tribe, a tribe belonging to the Vriji confederacy, one of the sixteen great states of ancient India. Vaishālī was one of the six major cities among the sixteen great states and prospered as a center of commerce. Shakyamuni Buddha visited the city on many occasions to preach, staying at Great Forest Monastery and elsewhere. Among the Buddha's followers in Vaishālī was Ambapālī, a courtesan who donated a forest of mango trees to the Buddha. The lay believer Vimalakīrti also lived there. Toward the end of his life, Shakyamuni visited Vaishālī and spent his last rainy season nearby. The Second Buddhist Council was held in Vaishālī about a century after the Buddha's death, and tradition has it that King Ashoka erected a stone pillar in Vaishālī in memory of the Buddha's visit there. Vaishālī is also known as the birthplace of Mahāvīra, the founder of Jainism. Vaishālī is thought to have been located at present-day Basarh in northwestern Bihar state.

Vaishravana [毘沙門天・多聞天] (Skt; Jpn Bishamon-ten or Tamon-ten): Also known as Hearer of Many Teachings. One of the four heavenly kings of Buddhist mythology, this god is said to live halfway up the northern side of Mount Sumeru and protect the northern quarter, accompanied by the two classes of demons called *yaksha* and *rākshasa*. Among the four heavenly kings, he is often regarded as foremost. Vaishravana's name was rendered in Chinese as "Hearer of Many Teachings." This god is said always to protect the place where the Buddha preaches. In the "Dhāranī" (twenty-sixth) chapter of the Lotus Sutra, he pledges to protect the votaries of the sutra. In Japan, as one of the seven beneficent deities, he is called Bishamon-ten. Vaishravana is known as Kubera in Hindu mythology, the king of *yakshas* and the god of wealth.

Vajji [跋耆・跋祇] (Pali; Jpn Baggi): Vriji in Sanskrit. One of the sixteen great states of ancient India. *See* Vriji.

vajra-bearing god [執金剛神] (Skt *vajrapāni* or *vajradhara;* Jpn *shū-kongō-shin*): Also, *vajra*-holding god. A generic term for any deity who wields a *vajra,* a kind of weapon, and protects Buddhism. The Sanskrit word *vajra* was rendered in Chinese as "diamond-pounder." *Pāni* of *vajrapāni* means hand, and *dhara* of *vajradhara* means bearing or holding. The Lotus Sutra lists the thirty-three different forms that Bodhisattva Perceiver of the World's Sounds assumes in order to save people from danger or suffering, the thirty-third of which is a *vajra*-bearing god.

Vajrabodhi [金剛智] (Skt; Jpn Kongōchi): An Indian monk who went to China to disseminate Esoteric Buddhism and became known in China as Chin-kang-chih. *See* Chin-kang-chih.

Vajracchedikā Sutra [金剛般若波羅蜜経] (Skt; Jpn *Kongō-hannya-haramitsu-kyō*): *See* Diamond-like Perfection of Wisdom Sutra.

vajradhātu [金剛界] (Skt; Jpn *kongō-kai*): The Diamond Realm, a realm that represents the wisdom of Mahāvairochana Buddha. *See* Diamond Realm.

Vajrasattva [金剛薩埵] (Skt; Jpn Kongōsatta): The first patriarch in the lineage of transmission of Esoteric Buddhism according to the True Word (Jpn Shingon) school. In that school's tradition, he is said to have received the teachings of Esoteric Buddhism directly from Mahāvairochana Buddha. Vajrasattva is often called "Master of Secrets" in Chinese Buddhist scriptures. The Mahāvairochana Sutra takes the form of questions and answers between Vajrasattva, an aspirant to wisdom, and Mahāvairochana Buddha. According to the esoteric tradition, Vajrasattva heard Mahāvairochana Buddha expound the esoteric teachings, which he then compiled in the form of scripture and sealed in an iron tower in southern India. This tower, it is said, was opened several centuries later by Nāgārjuna (c. 150–250), at which time Vajrasattva appeared and transferred Esoteric Buddhism to him.

Vajrashekhara Sutra [金剛頂経] (Skt; Jpn *Kongōchō-kyō*): Also known as the Diamond Crown Sutra. One of the three basic scriptures of Esoteric Buddhism. *See* Diamond Crown Sutra.

Vajrayāna [金剛乗] (Skt; Jpn Kongō-jō): The Diamond Vehicle. *See* Tantric Buddhism.

vana [林・園林] (Skt, Pali; Jpn *rin* or *onrin*): A grove, forest, or wood. Certain wealthy lay believers offered groves, with monasteries built in them, to Shakyamuni Buddha and his Order. The wealthy merchant Sudatta built Jetavana Monastery as an offering in a grove donated by Jetri, a son of King Prasenajit of Kosala, in the city Shrāvastī. *Jetavana* means Jetri's Grove. Venuvana Monastery, or Bamboo Grove Monastery, was built in a grove offered by Kalandaka, a wealthy patron of the Buddha, in the city Rājagriha. Āmrapālīvana, or Āmrapālī's Grove, was a grove of mango trees offered to the Buddha by Āmrapālī, a courtesan in Vaishālī. Mahāvana Monastery, or Great Forest Monastery, in Vaishālī is also known as a place frequented by the Buddha for preaching.

Varanasi [波羅奈国] (Skt Vārānasī; Pali Bārānasī; Jpn Harana-koku): Also known as Benares. A city on the left bank of the Ganges River in northern India. It was the capital of the Kāshī kingdom, one of the sixteen great states in India in the sixth and fifth centuries B.C.E. Centuries before Shakyamuni Buddha, Varanasi was already a great center of religion and culture. When Shakyamuni visited Varanasi to preach, it was still prominent in those areas and was a commercial center engaged in trade with Shrāvastī and other cities. Deer Park, where the Buddha first preached, corresponds to present-day Sarnath, a few miles north of Varanasi. Later the Kāshī kingdom became a dependency of the Kosala kingdom and was eventually annexed by the kingdom of Magadha. When the Chinese priest Hsüan-tsang visited Varanasi in the seventh century, the city was prosperous; three thousand Buddhist monks living at more than thirty monasteries studied the doctrines of the Sammatīya school of Hinayana Buddhism there. The majority of the inhabitants, however, were non-Buddhists. In the eleventh century, Varanasi fell under the rule of the Muslims. Varanasi is now known as a sacred Hindu city.

varsha [安居] (Skt; Jpn *ango*): The period when Buddhist monks gathered at some sheltered location to devote themselves to study and discipline during the summer rainy season. *See* three-month retreat.

Varshakāra [雨行大臣] (Skt; Jpn Ugyō-daijin): A minister who served King Ajātashatru in the kingdom of Magadha in ancient India in the time of Shakyamuni Buddha. When Ajātashatru was still a prince, Varshakāra conspired with Devadatta and instigated the prince to kill King Bimbisāra, his father and a lay supporter of Shakyamuni. Varshakāra also encouraged King Ajātashatru to harass Shakyamuni Buddha. Later, however, he repented and converted to Buddhism along with Ajātashatru and assisted him in administering the kingdom.

vassa [安居] (Pali; Jpn *ango*): *See* three-month retreat.

Vasubandhu [世親・天親] (n.d.) (Skt; Jpn Seshin or Tenjin): A Buddhist scholar in India thought to have lived around the fourth or fifth century. He is known as the author of *The Dharma Analysis Treasury*. Vasubandhu was born to a Brahman family in Purushapura of Gandhara in northern India. He had an older brother, Asanga. In the central Indian city of Ayodhyā, he studied the doctrine of the Sarvāstivāda school and lectured on *The Great Commentary on the Abhidharma*, the primary text of that school. He compiled these lectures as *The Dharma Analysis Treasury*, which presents a comprehensive discussion of the Sarvāstivāda thought. Thus he became the undisputed master of Hinayana philosophy in India at the time. Vasubandhu at first criticized Mahayana, but later converted to it through the influence of his brother Asanga, whom he assisted thereafter in promoting the Yogāchāra, or Consciousness-Only, school of Mahayana. Vasubandhu is said to have written a thousand works, five hundred related to Hinayana and five hundred to Mahayana. Among those that have survived are *The Twenty-Stanza Treatise on the Consciousness-Only Doctrine*, *The Treatise on the Ten Stages Sutra*, *The Treatise on the Lotus Sutra*, *The Commentary on "The Summary of the Mahayana,"* and *The Treatise on the Buddha Nature*. He is counted as the twentieth of Shakyamuni's twenty-three, or the twenty-first of his twenty-four, successors.

Vasumitra [世友] (n.d.) (Skt; Jpn Seu or Seyū): The monk who led the Fourth Buddhist Council in Kashmir around the second century and helped compile *The Great Commentary on the Abhidharma*. A monk named Vasumitra is also known as the author of *The Doctrines of the Different Schools*, but it is unclear whether this is the same person.

Vatsa [跋蹉] (Skt; Jpn Bassa): One of the sixteen great states in ancient India. Vatsa was located south of the Ganges River in what is today the Indian state of Uttar Pradesh. Its capital was Kaushāmbī. In Shakyamuni Buddha's time, Udayana was king of Vatsa and a follower of the Buddha.

At that time, the three powerful countries of the Ganges Valley—Magadha, Kosala, and Vatsa—were in conflict with one another. Magadha was located to the east of Vatsa, and Kosala, to the north of Vatsa across the Ganges River.

Vātsīputrīya school [犢子部] (Skt; Jpn Tokushi-bu): One of the twenty Hinayana schools. The Vātsīputrīya school broke away from the Sarvāstivāda school and advocated a view of the existence of the self as a separate entity. Later the Vātsīputrīya school split into four—the Dharmottara, Bhadrayānīya, Sammatīya, and Shannāgarika schools.

Vedehī [韋提希] (Pali; Jpn Idaike): Vaidehī in Sanskrit. The consort of Bimbisāra, king of Magadha in ancient India, and the mother of Ajātashatru. *See* Vaidehī.

Venuvana Monastery [竹林精舎] (Skt; Jpn Chikurin-shōja): Bamboo Grove Monastery. A monastery situated in the northern part of Rājagriha in Magadha, India. *See* Bamboo Grove Monastery.

verse [偈] (Skt, Pali *gāthā;* Jpn *ge*): A mode of exposition in Buddhist scriptures. Buddhist teachings and praise of the virtues of Buddhas and bodhisattvas expressed in verse form. Some sutras are written entirely in verse, while others are written in prose interposed with sections of verse. The Sanskrit word *gāthā* means verse, but in the system of the nine divisions or twelve divisions of the teachings, it is used in a narrow sense and contrasted with *geya,* which is also one of the nine or twelve divisions of the teachings. In this classification, while *gāthā* refers to a metered section independent of a preceding prose section, or a metered section that is not preceded by a prose section, *geya* restates in verse form the meaning of a preceding prose section. In Chinese translations of Buddhist scriptures, any phrase of a verse section contains four, five, or seven characters; a number of four-line verses constitute a complete verse section. *See also* four-line verse.

verse section of the "Life Span" chapter [自我偈] (Jpn *Jiga-ge*): The verse section that concludes the "Life Span" (sixteenth) chapter of the Lotus Sutra. It is called *Jiga-ge* in Japanese because it is the verse (Jpn *ge*) that begins with the phrase *"Ji ga toku butsu rai"* (Since I attained Buddhahood). This section reiterates the essence of the chapter in verse form. It restates the teaching of the eternity of the Buddha's enlightened life and explains that, though the Buddha is always in the world, he uses his death as a means to cause people to thirst for the Law. If they are so eager to see him that they would willingly give their lives to do so, he immediately appears and teaches them. He employs such means with the constant thought, expressed in the last of the verse: "How can I cause living beings / to gain entry into the unsurpassed way / and quickly acquire the body of a Buddha?"

Verses on the Middle Way [中頌・中論頌・中論] (Skt *Madhyamaka-kārikā* or *Mādhyamika-kārikā;* Jpn *Chūju, Chūron-ju,* or *Chū-ron*): Also known as *Mūla-madhyamaka-kārikā* ("Verses on the Fundamentals of the Middle Way"). A work by Nāgārjuna (c. 150–250) that became the principal text of the Mādhyamika (Middle Way) school in India. *The Treatise on the Middle Way,* translated by Kumārajīva in 409, consists of *Verses on the Middle Way* by Nāgārjuna and a prose commentary on it by Pingala who lived from the late third through the early fourth century. *Verses on the Middle Way* consists of some 450 verses in 27 sections.

Verses on the Middle Way opens with a passage known as the eight negations, which reads, "Neither birth nor extinction, neither cessation nor permanence, neither uniformity nor diversity, neither coming nor going." It maintains that all phenomena arise by virtue of dependent origination, i.e., their relationship with other phenomena, and therefore that they have no independent existence of their own and are non-substantial in nature. It sets forth the principle and practice of the Middle Way, which transcends and is free from attachment to conceptual polarities such as existence and nonexistence.

The ideas in *Verses on the Middle Way* later gave rise to the Mādhyamika school, one of the two major Mahayana schools in India, the other being the Vijnānavāda, or Consciousness-Only, school, and greatly influenced the theoretical formation and development of Mahayana Buddhism. Commentaries on *Verses on the Middle Way* were written by Pingala, Buddhapālita, Bhāvaviveka, Chandrakīrti, and other scholars. The *Akutobhayā* ("Fearlessness") is a commentary on the same work attributed to Nāgārjuna himself extant only in its Tibetan translation. Among the several existing commentaries, the *Prasannapadā* ("The Clear Worded") by Chandrakīrti, is the only one extant in its original Sanskrit. It is regarded as particularly important because it is only through this commentary that much of the content of the Sanskrit original of *Verses on the Middle Way,* which is no longer extant, is knowable. In China and Japan, Kumārajīva's *Treatise on the Middle Way* became one of the three central texts of the Three Treatises (Chin San-lun; Jpn Sanron) school.

Verses Praising Rebirth in the Pure Land, The [往生礼讃偈] (Jpn *Ōjō-raisan-ge*): See *Praising Rebirth in the Pure Land.*

Vesālī [毘舎離] (Pali; Jpn Bishari): Vaishālī in Sanskrit. One of the sixteen great states of ancient India. *See* Vaishālī.

vetāda [毘陀羅] (Skt; Jpn *bidara*): Also, *vetāla.* An evil spirit said to kill its enemies by setting corpses it has raised from the dead against them. In China, *vetāda* was translated as "corpse-raising demon." In the "Universal Worthy" (twenty-eighth) chapter of the Lotus Sutra, Bodhisattva Universal Worthy tells Shakyamuni Buddha: "If there is someone who accepts and upholds this sutra, I will guard and protect him . . . No devil, devil's son, devil's daughter, devil's minion, or one possessed by the devil, no *yaksha, rākshasa, kumbhānda, pishācha, kritya, pūtana, vetāda,* or other being that torments humans will be able to take advantage of him."

vetāla [毘陀羅] (Skt; Jpn *bidara*): See *vetāda.*

vibhāshā [毘婆沙] (Skt; Jpn *bibasha*): A commentary, specifically, on the *vinaya,* or the rules of monastic discipline and, generally, on a doctrinal treatise. *Upadesha,* in contrast, is a commentary on a sutra.

Vidūdabha [波瑠璃王] (Pali; Jpn Haruri-ō): Virūdhaka in Sanskrit. A king of the state of Kosala in ancient India of Shakyamuni's time. *See* Virūdhaka.

vihāra [精舎] (Skt, Pali; Jpn *shōja*): A Buddhist monastery. The well-known monasteries in Shakyamuni Buddha's time were Jetavana-vihāra, or Jetavana Monastery, located in Shrāvastī, the capital of the Kosala kingdom, and Venuvana-vihāra, or Bamboo Grove Monastery, in Rājagriha, the capital of the Magadha kingdom. These two *vihāras* became the major centers of the Buddha's activities. He also frequented Mahāvana-vihāra, or Great Forest Monastery, in Vaishālī to preach. As Shakyamuni spread his teachings and his followers rapidly increased in number, monasteries were built in many locations of India, especially in the Ganges Valley. Lay patrons of the Buddha built those monasteries and they were donated along with the groves they stood in to the Buddha and his Order. For example, Ghoshila, a wealthy man in Kaushāmbī, built a monastery called Ghoshila-vihāra in a grove that he owned and offered both to the Buddha. During the rainy season in summer, Shakyamuni and his disciples stayed at these monasteries. In the center of the grounds of each was an open court surrounded by small dwellings. After Shakyamuni's death, *vihāras* continued to be built and donated to the Buddhist Order. Noteworthy among them were Kukkutārāma Monastery built by King Ashoka in the third century B.C.E., Nālandā Monastery in the fifth century, and Vikramashilā Monastery around 800.

Vijnānānantya Realm [識無辺処] (Skt; Jpn Shikimuhen-jo): The second lowest of the four realms of the world of formlessness. *See* Realm of Boundless Consciousness.

Vijnānavāda school [唯識派] (Skt; Jpn Yuishiki-ha): Also known as the Consciousness-Only school, one of the two major Mahayana schools in India. *See* Consciousness-Only school.

Vikramashilā Monastery [ヴィクラマシラー寺] (Skt; Jpn Bikuramashirā-ji): A Buddhist monastery built in the Ganges Valley, in what is today Bihar State, India, around 800 by Dharmapāla, the second ruler of the Pāla dynasty. This dynasty ruled eastern India from the mid-eighth to the late twelfth century. Along with Nālandā Monastery, Vikramashilā Monastery prospered as a center for the study of Buddhist doctrines, particularly the esoteric teachings referred to as Tantric Buddhism. On the grounds of the monastery were more than one hundred buildings. Its complete destruction in 1203 by the Muslims, however, is regarded as symbolic of the ultimate decline of Buddhism in India.

Vimalakīrti [維摩詰] (Skt; Jpn Yuimakitsu): A wealthy Buddhist layman of the city of Vaishālī at the time of Shakyamuni. He is the protagonist of the Vimalakīrti Sutra, in which he represents the ideal Mahayana lay believer. According to the sutra, he had mastered the profound doctrines of Mahayana and instructed the people with various skillful means. The sutra depicts him as refuting the Hinayana views held by Shakyamuni's voice-hearer disciples such as Shāriputra with devastating eloquence and preaching Mahayana doctrines to them based on his understanding of non-substantiality and non-duality. *See also* Vimalakīrti Sutra.

Vimalakīrti Sutra [維摩経] (Skt *Vimalakīrti-nirdesha;* Chin *Wei-mo-ching;* Jpn *Yuima-kyō*): A Mahayana sutra about the wealthy layman Vimalakīrti in Vaishālī, translated into Chinese in 406 by Kumārajīva. The full title of Kumārajīva's version is the Sutra on the Expositions of Vimalakīrti. The Sanskrit original is not extant. There are a Tibetan translation and two other Chinese translations: one produced by Chih-ch'ien somewhere between 222 and 229 and the other by Hsüan-tsang in 650. Among the three Chinese translations, Kumārajīva's has been the most popular, and the title "Vimalakīrti Sutra" generally indicates this version.

Vimalakīrti, the protagonist of the sutra, is a wealthy and prominent citizen of the city of Vaishālī at the time of Shakyamuni. In the sutra, he represents the ideal lay believer. He is sick in bed and wonders why the compassionate Buddha fails to show some concern for him. Shakyamuni, aware of his thought, desires to send someone to inquire after his illness. One after the other, he designates each of his ten major disciples, including Shāriputra and Maudgalyāyana, and each of the bodhisattvas, including Maitreya, but each pleads unworthiness, relating a story of how at one time or another he was bested in understanding by Vimalakīrti. At length Bodhisattva Manjushrī agrees to go.

Vimalakīrti, questioned by Manjushrī about the nature of his illness, replies that, because all living beings are ill, he is ill; if all living beings are relieved of sickness, then his sickness will likewise be relieved. He further explains that, because bodhisattvas regard all living beings as their children, it is natural that they will be ill so long as living beings are ill. The sutra thus sets forth the ideal of the Mahayana bodhisattva, which is to draw no distinction between self and others. The dialogue between Vimalakīrti and Bodhisattva Manjushrī continues, and the doctrines of Hinayana are sharply criticized based on the teaching of non-substantiality, which this sutra refers to as non-duality.

Asked point-blank to define non-duality, Vimalakīrti replies with silence, showing that the true nature of things is beyond the limiting concepts imposed by words. Several commentaries on the Vimalakīrti Sutra exist, among them *The Annotations on the Profound Meaning of the Vimalakīrti Sutra* by T'ien-t'ai (538–579) and *The Annotations on the Meaning of the Vimalakīrti Sutra* attributed to Prince Shōtoku (574–622) of Japan.

Vimalamitra [無垢論師・無垢友] (n.d.) (Skt; Jpn Muku-ronji or Mukuyū): A monk of the Sarvāstivāda school, one of the major early Hinayana schools of India, and a native of Kashmir. According to Hsüan-tsang's *Record of the Western Regions,* Vimalamitra traveled throughout India to learn the Buddhist sutras, treatises, and rules of monastic discipline, and became renowned for his vast knowledge of the Buddhist canon. He vowed to validate the teachings of Samghabhadra, a Sarvāstivāda scholar, which had been refuted by Vasubandhu. In addition, he decided to destroy the reputation of the deceased Vasubandhu and ruin the credibility of Mahayana Buddhism. According to the above work, however, before he reached his aim, he went mad; his tongue split in five pieces, and, tormented by remorse, he fell into the hell of incessant suffering.

vimoksha [解脱] (Skt; Jpn *gedatsu*): Emancipation, release, or liberation. The Sanskrit words *vimukti, mukti,* and *moksha* also have the same meaning. *Vimoksha* means release from the bonds of earthly desires, delusion, suffering, and transmigration. While Buddhism sets forth various kinds and stages of emancipation, or enlightenment, the supreme emancipation is nirvana, a state of perfect quietude, freedom, and deliverance.

vimukti [解脱] (Skt; Jpn *gedatsu*): *See* emancipation; *vimoksha.*

vinaya [律] (Skt, Pali; Jpn *ritsu*): The rules of discipline for monks and nuns. One of the three divisions of the Buddhist canon. The original meaning of the word *vinaya* is "to remove [one's evil conduct]" or "to instruct." *Vinaya* is said to be a systematization of the prohibitions and admonishments given by Shakyamuni to his disciples. Each of the early

Buddhist schools had its own collection of the monastic regulations. Extant texts include the *vinaya* of the so-called Pali canon, which belongs to the Theravāda school, and the *vinaya* texts of the Dharmagupta, Sarvāstivāda, Mahīshāsaka, and Mahāsamghika schools, which exist in Chinese translation. These last four are *The Fourfold Rules of Discipline, The Ten Divisions of Monastic Rules, The Fivefold Rules of Discipline,* and *The Great Canon of Monastic Rules,* respectively. In China, several Precepts, or Lü *(vinaya),* schools emerged, using *The Fourfold Rules of Discipline* as their primary text. The most notable of these was the Nan-shan school, founded by Tao-hsüan (596–667). In the eighth century, the Chinese priest Chien-chen (known in Japan as Ganjin) brought the teachings of that school to Japan, where it became the independent Precepts (Ritsu) school.

Vinaya school [律宗] (Skt; Jpn Risshū): *See* Precepts school.

vinayas of the five schools [五部律] (Jpn *gobu-ritsu*): Texts on monastic rules produced by five of the twenty Hinayana schools in India. They are *The Fourfold Rules of Discipline* of the Dharmagupta school, *The Ten Divisions of Monastic Rules* of the Sarvāstivāda school, *The Fivefold Rules of Discipline* of the Mahīshāsaka school, *The Great Canon of Monastic Rules* of the Mahāsamghika school, and *The Monastic Rules for Emancipation* of the Kāshyapīya school. Four of the above five texts are extant in Chinese translation. The text of the Kāshyapīya school is not extant either in Sanskrit or Chinese, though its Chinese title is recorded as *The Monastic Rules for Emancipation.* In China and Japan, *The Fourfold Rules of Discipline* was regarded as the most important of these texts and was used most widely. The Precepts (Chin Lü; Jpn Ritsu) school based itself upon this work.

Virtue Victorious [徳勝童子] (Jpn Tokushō-dōji): A boy who is said to have offered a mud pie to Shakyamuni Buddha. According to *The Story of King Ashoka,* a work translated into Chinese by An Fa-ch'in in the early fourth century, one day when the Buddha was begging for alms in Rājagriha, he came upon two boys, Virtue Victorious and Invincible, while they were playing. The two boys wished to present an offering to the Buddha but had nothing to give, so Virtue Victorious hastily fashioned a mud pie and placed it in the Buddha's begging bowl, while Invincible pressed his palms together in reverence. Because of the blessings from this offering, a hundred years after the Buddha's death, Virtue Victorious was reborn as King Ashoka and Invincible as his consort. In the King Ashoka Sutra, translated by Samghavarman in 512, the boy Virtue Victorious appears with the Sanskrit name Jaya (Victorious), and the boy Invincible, with the name Vijaya, also meaning victorious.

Virūdhaka (Skt) (1) [波瑠璃王] (Pali Vidūdabha; Jpn Haruri-ō): A king of the state of Kosala in India during Shakyamuni's lifetime. His father was Prasenajit. According to the Increasing by One Āgama Sutra, when Prasenajit ascended the throne, he wanted to take a consort from the Shākya tribe and had his wish conveyed to the Shākyas in Kapilavastu. The Shākyas were held to be of noble lineage. A Shākya named Mahānāma conceived a plan to offer his maidservant's daughter, a beautiful woman, to the king in marriage, claiming that the daughter was his own. Prasenajit accepted, and together they had a son, Virūdhaka. When Virūdhaka was eight years old, Prasenajit sent him to Kapilavastu to have him learn archery from the Shākyas. While there, Virūdhaka was ridiculed as the son of a maidservant; thus learning of his lowly birth and that his father had been deceived, he vowed to take revenge on the Shākyas. Later, upon succeeding to the throne after Prasenajit's death, he immediately led an army against Kapilavastu, destroying the Shākya kingdom. According to the sutra, seven days later, as the Buddha had predicted, a violent storm with heavy rain came up suddenly during the night, and Virūdhaka and his warriors, who had been staying by the riverside, drowned, falling into the hell of incessant suffering. According to *The Monastic Rules on Various Matters,* while Prasenajit was away from the capital, Shrāvastī, Virūdhaka usurped the throne. Informed of this, Prasenajit made his way to Rājagriha, the capital of Magadha under Ajātashatru's rule. After he arrived there, however, he became seriously ill and died. Soon after, Virūdhaka massacred the majority of the Shākya tribe, taking revenge for the humiliation he had suffered as a youth.

(2) [増長天] (Jpn Zōjō-ten or Zōchō-ten): The heavenly king Increase and Growth. One of the four heavenly kings. *See* Increase and Growth.

Virūpāksha [広目天] (Skt; Jpn Kōmoku-ten): The heavenly king Wide-Eyed. One of the four heavenly kings. *See* Wide-Eyed.

vīrya [毘梨耶・精進] (Skt; Jpn *biriya* or *shōjin*): Assiduousness or diligence. The fourth of the six *pāramitās,* six practices for Mahayana bodhisattvas. *Vīrya* means untiring zeal and exertion in pursuit of the Buddha way. From very early in the history of Buddhism, *vīrya* has been regarded as an important ethic, and Buddhist scriptures emphasize it repeatedly as an attitude essential to practitioners of Buddhism.

Vishvakarman [毘首羯磨天] (Skt; Jpn Bishukatsuma-ten): A god said to live in the Heaven of the Thirty-three Gods on the summit of Mount Sumeru and who serves Shakra. According to *The Treatise on the Great Perfection of Wisdom,* when Shakyamuni was practicing the *pāramitā* of almsgiving as King Shibi in a past existence, the god Shakra assumed the form of a hawk, and Vishvakarman, that of a dove, to test the king's sincerity. Vishvakarman is regarded as the god of sculpture and architecture and the patron of artisans. *See also* Shibi.

voice-hearer [声聞] (Skt *shrāvaka;* Jpn *shōmon*): Also, voice-hearer disciples. Shakyamuni Buddha's disciples who heard his preaching and strove to attain enlightenment. *Shrāvaka,* or "one who hears the voice," in Shakyamuni's time referred to his disciples, both monks and laymen. Later Mahayana Buddhists applied the term to those Hinayana monks who "heard" the teachings of the four noble truths and aimed at attaining the state of arhat, and eventually, the nirvana of no remainder. The nirvana of no remainder refers to a state in which both body and mind—the sources of suffering—are extinguished. Mahayana sutras criticize voice-hearers as seeking only their own enlightenment and exerting no effort to save others. As a result, many of these sutras characterize them as being unable to attain Buddhahood. The Lotus Sutra, however, defines voice-hearers as those who "take the voice of the Buddha way and cause it to be heard by all." Voice-hearers and cause-awakened ones are called persons of the two vehicles. While most Mahayana sutras deny that such individuals can attain enlightenment, the Lotus Sutra teaches that they can and predicts that they will. The realm of voice-hearers constitutes the seventh of the Ten Worlds and is sometimes referred to as the world of learning.

votary of the Lotus Sutra [法華経の行者] (Jpn *Hokekyō-no-gyōja*): One who practices and propagates the Lotus Sutra in exact accordance with its teachings. Nichiren (1222–1282), in his writings, often identifies himself as the votary of the Lotus Sutra. From Nichiren's perspective, with regard to the propagation of the Lotus Sutra in the time periods following Shakyamuni Buddha's death, T'ien-t'ai in China and Dengyō in Japan were the votaries of the Lotus Sutra in the Middle Day of the Law. In the Latter Day of the Law, the term *votary of the Lotus Sutra* is applied specifically to Nichiren. Nichiren taught the essence of the sutra, or Nam-myoho-renge-kyo, and fulfilled the sutra's prophecies concerning what sort of persecutions a genuine practitioner, or votary, of the Lotus Sutra would face in the turbulent age after the death of Shakyamuni. For this reason, in *The Selection of the Time,* Nichiren declares, "There can be no room to doubt that I, Nichiren, am the foremost votary of the Lotus Sutra in all of Japan" (575). Because he fulfilled the mission the sutra says the votaries of the Lotus Sutra would, never once succumbing to any persecution, he wrote, "Nichiren has now read [and lived] the entirety of the Lotus Sutra" (200), meaning that he lived the sutra exactly as it teaches, or "read" the sutra with his life and actions.

vow [誓願] (Skt *pranidhāna;* Jpn *seigan*): In Buddhism, vows that Buddhas and bodhisattvas take to lead living beings to enlightenment. There are two kinds of vows: universal and individual. The bodhisattvas make four universal vows when they embark on Buddhist practice: (1) to save innumerable living beings, (2) to eradicate unlimited earthly desires, (3) to master inexhaustible doctrines, and (4) to attain unsurpassed enlightenment. Among individual vows, the forty-eight vows of Amida Buddha and the twelve vows of Medicine Master Buddha are well known. These Buddhas made their respective vows in a previous existence before attaining Buddhahood. Such vows made by Buddhas while engaged in bodhisattva practice in previous lives are called "original vows," or *pūrva-pranidhāna* (*pūrva* meaning former or previous) in Sanskrit.

Vriji [跋耆・跋祇] (Skt; Pali Vajji; Jpn Baggi): Also known as Vrijji. One of the sixteen great states of India in Shakyamuni's time. Well known for its republican form of government, Vriji was located north of the Ganges River in northeastern India, straddling the present-day India–Nepal border. Vriji was a confederacy of the Licchavi, Videha, and other tribes, and Vaishālī was one of its major cities. Representatives of the confederacy met to discuss and decide affairs of state by consensus. Vriji was a rival of the Magadha kingdom to its south. It is thought that King Ajātashatru of Magadha conquered it after a protracted war, and that he managed to create dissension within the Vriji confederacy, finally overthrowing it. According to the Long Āgama Sutra, Shakyamuni tried to dissuade Ajātashatru from his attempts to conquer Vriji.

vyākarana [授記・記別・和伽羅那] (Skt; Jpn *juki, kibetsu,* or *wagarana*): A Buddha's prediction that a disciple will attain enlightenment. *See* prophecy of future enlightenment.

W

Wa-kuan-ssu [瓦官寺] (PY Waguansi; Jpn Gakan-ji): A temple built in 364 by Hui-li in Chien-k'ang, China. Many eminent priests delivered lectures on Buddhist doctrines and scriptures there, among them, T'ien-t'ai. After practicing for seven years under Nan-yüeh on Mount Ta-su, T'ien-t'ai (also known as Chih-i) lived in this temple for eight years until he moved to Mount T'ien-t'ai in 575. While at Wa-kuan-ssu temple, he lectured on *The Treatise on the Great Perfection of Wisdom* and the Lotus Sutra, and also wrote *The Teaching of the Practice of Meditation,* which reflects his later ideas in their early stages of development.

Water Carrier [流水] (Skt Jalavāhana; Jpn Rusui): A physician described in the Golden Light Sutra as being a previous incarnation of Shakyamuni Buddha. According to that sutra, Water Carrier lived countless *kalpas* ago in the Middle Day of the Law of a Buddha called Treasure Excellence. Water Carrier's handsome and dignified appearance distinguished him, and he possessed wisdom and expertise in a number of areas and skills, including his knowledge of Buddhist teachings, writing, and mathematics. According to the sutra, an epidemic broke out and spread throughout his country. To save the people, he asked his father, Water Holder, also a skilled physician but too old to provide treatment, to teach him his secret medical practices. After receiving instruction from his father, Water Carrier visited the towns and villages, saving all the people from the ravages of the epidemic. *See also* Water Holder.

Water Holder [持水] (Skt Jatimdhara; Jpn Jisui): A physician mentioned in the Golden Light Sutra. According to that sutra, he lived countless *kalpas* ago in the Middle Day of the Law of a Buddha named Treasure Excellence, during the reign of King Heavenly Unhindered Light who was a believer in the Buddha's teaching. Water Holder was well versed in medicine and healed various kinds of illnesses. When an epidemic swept the country, Water Holder was by then too old to provide treatment. Nevertheless, he taught his secret medical arts to his son, Water Carrier, who then used them to save the people in Water Holder's stead. *See also* Water Carrier.

water of wisdom [智水] (Jpn *chisui*): A metaphor for the power of wisdom to wash away earthly desires and delusions. "Water of wisdom" most often refers to the wisdom of a Buddha.

watery circle [水輪] (Skt *jala-mandala;* Jpn *suirin*): Also, water circle. In the ancient Indian worldview, one of the three circles located under the earth that support the world. When a world is formed, a windy circle first takes shape, and upon this a watery circle develops. Next, on the watery circle a gold circle forms, and upon this forms the land itself with its Mount Sumeru, seas, and mountains. According to *The Dharma Analysis Treasury,* after the windy circle forms, dense clouds rise above it, and rain falls in torrents to form a watery circle 1,120,000 *yojanas* in depth and 1,203,450 *yojanas* in diameter. Gradually the upper layer of the watery circle congeals and finally changes into a layer of gold 320,000 *yojanas* thick, forming the gold circle. The remaining watery circle is thus 800,000 *yojanas* deep. Both the watery circle and the gold circle are the same size in diameter. The Sanskrit word *jala* of *jala-mandala* means water, and *mandala,* disk or circle.

way [道] (Skt *bodhi;* Chin *tao;* Jpn *dō*): The Chinese *tao* (PY *dao*) means road, way, method, reason, a moral principle, a doctrine, the source of all things, etc. Lao Tzu, who is said to have lived in the sixth through the fifth century B.C.E., used it to indicate the fundamental principle or the source of the universe. The religious philosophy he helped establish, known in the West as Taoism, emphasizes "nonaction" (Chin *wu-wei;* Jpn *mui*), which implies letting things take their natural course. When Buddhism was introduced to China, it was first interpreted and translated using Taoist concepts and terminology. This method of interpretation is known as "matching the meaning" *(ke-yi; kakugi).* For example, the Sanskrit *bodhi,* or enlightenment, was rendered as "the way" *(tao)* and nirvana, as "nonaction." Use of "the way" or "attaining the way" to mean enlightenment became well established in Buddhist literature.

way of insight [見道] (Skt *darshana-mārga;* Jpn *ken-dō*): Also, path of insight, way of beholding the truth, or stage of seeing the way. In the Hinayana teachings, the stage of practice at which one beholds the four noble truths. In the way of insight, one is liberated from the characteristics and limitations of ordinary persons and ascends to the stage of sagehood. One who has attained the three stages of worthiness and the four good roots enters the way of insight. This is the first of the "three ways," the other two being the way of practice and the way of the arhat, or one who has no more to learn. In this stage, one obtains wisdom untainted by outflows, or earthly desires, and clearly perceives each of the four noble truths: suffering, the cause of suffering, the cessation of suffering, and the path to the cessation of suffering. The way of insight is also recognized in the Mahayana teachings as a stage of bodhisattva practice.

Wei-chüan [維蠲] (n.d.) (PY Weijuan; Jpn Iken or Yuiken): A priest of the T'ien-t'ai school in China in the ninth century. When Ensai, a priest of the Japanese Tendai school, went to China in 839 (or 838), he brought with him a list of thirty questions (fifty according to another account) about the T'ien-t'ai teachings. Wei-chüan, along with his teacher Kuang-hsiu, answered these questions.

Wei Yüan-sung [衛元嵩] (n.d.) (PY Wei Yuansong; Jpn Ei-gensū): A Buddhist priest who returned to lay life and exhorted Emperor Wu of the Northern Chou dynasty in China to abolish Buddhism. In 567 he submitted a memorial to Emperor Wu stating to the effect that, because Buddhist temples were contrary to the interests of the nation, they should be abolished and Buddhist priests and nuns required to return to lay life. This document was instrumental in influencing Emperor Wu to outlaw Buddhism. In 574 Emperor Wu had Buddhist scriptures and images destroyed and Buddhist priests and nuns returned to lay life. This is counted as one of the four wholesale imperial persecutions of Buddhism in China. *See also* four imperial persecutions of Buddhism in China.

Well Attained [善逝] (Skt, Pali *sugata;* Jpn *zenzei*): Also, Well Gone or Well Departed. Having gone to the world of enlightenment. One of the ten honorable titles of a Buddha. "Well Attained" means that one has eliminated earthly desires with power of wisdom and attained the stage of Buddhahood, never again having to undergo the sufferings of birth and death. *Su* of the Sanskrit and Pali word *sugata* means well or gracefully, and *gata* means gone, departed, or deceased.

Well Gone [善逝] (Jpn *zenzei*): One of the ten honorable titles of a Buddha. *See* Well Attained.

Western Pure Land [西方浄土] (Jpn Saihō-jōdo): Also, Western Paradise. Another name for Amida Buddha's Pure Land of Perfect Bliss, said to be located in the west. According to the Amida Sutra, Amida Buddha dwells in the Land of Perfect Bliss "a hundred thousand million Buddha lands to the west" of this *sahā* world. *See also* Perfect Bliss.

wheel of the Law [法輪] (Skt *dharma-chakra;* Jpn *hōrin*): Also, Dharma-wheel. A term for the Buddha's teachings. The preaching of a Buddha is often expressed in Buddhist scriptures as "turning the wheel of the Law." "Wheel" here is a translation of the Sanskrit *chakra,* the wheel possessed by wheel-turning kings, or ideal rulers in Indian mythology. The *chakra* of a wheel-turning king was a weapon with which he would advance without obstruction and use to subdue enemies of goodness or justice. The Buddha's teachings are compared to the *chakra* because he uses them to defeat or subdue people's earthly desires and illusions and lead them to enlightenment.

wheel treasure [輪宝] (Jpn *rimbō*): One of the seven treasures that a wheel-turning king is said to possess. See *chakra.*

wheel-turning king [転輪聖王・転輪王・輪王] (Skt *chakravarti-rāja, chakravarti-rājan,* or *chakravartin;* Jpn *tenrin-jō'ō, tenrin-ō,* or *rin-ō*): Also, wheel-turning sage king, or wheel-king. An ideal ruler in ancient Indian mythology who governs with justice rather than force and brings tranquillity and comfort to the people. He possesses seven treasures: a wheel, elephants, horses, jewels, jewel-like women, excellent ministers of financial affairs, and generals. He also possesses the thirty-two features as a Buddha does, as well as the four virtues of great wealth, admirable features and form, freedom from worries, and long life. According to some scriptures, when Shakyamuni was born, a hermit-sage named Asita foretold that, if the boy remained in the secular world, he would become a wheel-turning king, but if he renounced secular life, he would become a Buddha.

While turning the wheel he was given by heaven, a wheel-turning king advances everywhere at will and establishes peace. These wheels are of four kinds: gold, silver, copper, and iron, the type of wheel indicating a wheel-turning king's rank, or the extent of his realm and power. A gold-wheel-turning king rules all the four continents surrounding Mount Sumeru; a silver-wheel-turning king, the eastern, western, and southern continents; a copper-wheel-turning king, the eastern and southern continents; and an iron-wheel-turning king, the southern continent, or Jambudvīpa. Buddhist scriptures contain stories of Shakyamuni Buddha's previous incarnations as a wheel-turning king.

White Lotus Society [白蓮社] (Jpn Byakuren-sha): Pai-lien-she, a Chinese religious group that practiced meditation on the Buddha Amida. *See* Pai-lien-she.

white-robed laymen [白衣] (Skt *avadāta-vasana;* Jpn *byakue*): Ordinary persons, Buddhist practitioners who did not take the vows of monks. Laypersons. Since ordinary people wore white robes in Shakyamuni's time in India, the term *white robe* came to indicate laypersons in the Buddhist sutras. In contrast, the term *black robe* indicated Buddhist monks, who usually wore dark robes.

Wide-Eyed [広目天] (Skt Virūpāksha; Jpn Kōmoku-ten): One of the four heavenly kings of Buddhist mythology. This god is said to live halfway up the western side of Mount Sumeru and protect the western quarter. With his divine eyesight, he discerns evil, punishes evildoers, and causes them to aspire for Buddhahood. Wide-Eyed is also known as the lord of *nāga* (dragons) and spirits called *pūtana.* Though the Sanskrit name Virūpāksha was rendered in Chinese as "wide-eyed," it more literally means irregular-, abnormal-, or many-eyed. In Hindu mythology, Virūpāksha is an epithet for the three-eyed god, Shiva.

windy circle [風輪] (Skt *vāyu-mandala;* Jpn *fūrin*): Also, wind circle or circle of wind. According to ancient Indian cosmology, the lowest of the three circles located under the earth that support the world. When a world is formed, the first to appear is the windy circle. According to *The Dharma Analysis Treasury,* a small wind first arises in space. This wind grows and forms the windy circle, a layer of air that is cylindrical in shape and harder than diamond. Upon this circle a watery circle develops, and then a gold circle on top of that. Upon the gold circle, the land is formed with its Mount Sumeru, seas, and mountains. The windy circle is said to be 1,600,000 *yojanas* thick and immeasurable in diameter. The Sanskrit word *vāyu* of *vāyu-mandala* means wind, and *mandala* means disk or circle.

Wisdom Accumulated [智積] (Jpn Chishaku): (1) (Skt Jnānākara) The eldest of the sixteen sons of Great Universal Wisdom Excellence Buddha referred to in the "Parable of the Phantom City" (seventh) chapter of the Lotus Sutra. Hearing his father, the Buddha, preach, he and his brothers renounced secular life and sought instruction in the Law of supreme enlightenment. When the Buddha expounded the Lotus Sutra, they accepted and upheld it. Later they preached the sutra on their father's behalf and thus enabled many people to gain enlightenment. The chapter states that Wisdom Accumulated is now a Buddha named Akshobhya who lives and preaches the Law in the Land of Joy in the east.

(2) (Skt Prajnākūta) A bodhisattva mentioned in the "Devadatta" (twelfth) chapter of the Lotus Sutra. In this chapter, Bodhisattva Manjushrī relates how he has preached the Lotus Sutra in the palace of the dragon king and converted innumerable beings. Bodhisattva Wisdom Accumulated, a follower of the Buddha Many Treasures, wishes to know if there is anyone who applies the sutra in practice and gains Buddhahood quickly. Manjushrī replies that the eight-year-old daughter of the dragon king has attained the stage of non-regression and is capable of readily achieving the Buddha wisdom. Wisdom Accumulated challenges him on the grounds that Buddhahood requires the practice of austerities over a period of countless *kalpas*. At that time, the dragon king's daughter appears, and Wisdom Accumulated and the other members of the assembly see the dragon girl become a Buddha in the space of an instant. Wisdom Accumulated silently believes and accepts what he has witnessed.

wisdom kings [明王] (Skt *vidyā-rāja;* Jpn *myō'ō*): A group of deities said to be capable of destroying all obstacles. Esoteric Buddhism gives them special reverence, depicting them as angry, powerful figures. There are several sets of wisdom kings mentioned in the Buddhist scriptures; these include the five great wisdom kings and the eight great wisdom kings, among others. The five great wisdom kings are Immovable, Conqueror of the Threefold World, Kundalī, Great Awesome Virtue, and Diamond Yaksha. The eight great wisdom kings are the five mentioned above plus Ucchushma, Unconquerable, and Horse-Headed. There is also a wisdom king known as Craving-Filled.

wisdom mudra [智拳印] (Jpn *chiken-in*): The mudra, or sign made with the hands and fingers, of the Thus Come One Mahāvairochana of the Diamond Realm. The wisdom mudra is a form in which the first finger of the left hand, held erect, is grasped with the closed right hand. In Esoteric Buddhism, this mudra is believed to enable one to eradicate illusions and gain the Buddha wisdom.

Wisdom period [般若時] (Jpn Hannya-ji): The period of the Wisdom sutras. The fourth of the five periods, a classification of Shakyamuni's teachings by T'ien-t'ai. *See* five periods.

Wisdom sutras [般若経] (Jpn *Hannya-kyō*): Also known as the Perfection of Wisdom sutras or the Prajnāpāramitā sutras. A generic term for sutras that deal with the teaching of *prajnā-pāramitā,* or the perfection of wisdom, and expound the principle of non-substantiality. Major among the many Wisdom sutras are the Larger Wisdom Sutra, the Smaller Wisdom Sutra, the Benevolent Kings Wisdom Sutra, the Diamond Wisdom Sutra, the Heart Sutra, and the Great Wisdom Sutra, the last being a compilation of a number of Wisdom sutras. Nāgārjuna (c. 150–250) systematized the teachings of the Wisdom sutras in his *Treatise on the Middle Way.* In addition, the Larger Wisdom Sutra formed the basis for *The Treatise on the Great Perfection of Wisdom* attributed to Nāgārjuna, which expounds the doctrine of the Middle Way.

Wise Kalpa [賢劫] (Skt *bhadra-kalpa;* Jpn Ken-gō): Also, Good Kalpa. One of the three *kalpas,* the other two being the past Glorious Kalpa and the future Constellation Kalpa. It refers to the present major *kalpa,* or four-stage cycle of formation, continuance, decline, and disintegration. According to another account, the Wise Kalpa is the name of the *kalpa* of continuance in the present major *kalpa.* According to the Long Āgama Sutra, the last four of the seven Buddhas of the past—Krakucchanda, Kanakamuni, Kāshyapa, and Shakyamuni—appeared in the Wise Kalpa. They made their advent respectively when the human life span was forty thousand years, thirty thousand years, twenty thousand years, and a hundred years. The Wise Kalpa Sutra, translated into Chinese by Dharmaraksha in the late third century, describes the appearance of a thousand Buddhas in the present Wise Kalpa and lists their names. After the above four Buddhas appear, the other 996 Buddhas will make their advent successively, beginning with Maitreya and ending with Ruchika.

wish-granting jewel [如意宝珠] (Skt, Pali *chintāmani;* Jpn *nyoi-hōju*): A jewel said to have the power to produce whatever one desires. It symbolizes the virtue and power of the Buddha and the Buddhist scriptures. *The Treatise on the Great Perfection of Wisdom* states that this jewel can be obtained from the head of a dragon king, and another reference in the same work describes it as a transmutation of the Buddha's relics. According to the Ocean of Meditation on the Buddha Sutra, it is a transmutation of the heart of the giant *garuda* bird, while the Storehouse of Various Treasures Sutra says it is found in the head of the great fish called *makara.*

woman of pure faith [清信女] (Skt, Pali *upāsikā;* Jpn *shōshin-nyo*): A Buddhist laywoman who reveres the three treasures of Buddhism—the Buddha, his teachings, and the Buddhist Order—and has received the five precepts. "Woman of pure faith" is a Chinese translation of the Sanskrit word *upāsikā,* meaning a Buddhist laywoman. Her male counterpart is a "man of pure faith" *(upāsaka).*

Womb Realm [胎蔵界] (Skt *garbhadhātu;* Jpn *taizō-kai*): Also, Womb World. A realm depicted in the Mahāvairochana Sutra, a principal scripture of Esoteric Buddhism. In this realm, all compassionate actions leading to salvation are depicted as being born of and sustained by the fundamental principle of the universe, just as life is nurtured by and born from the womb. The Womb Realm thus represents the "repository of truth," or Dharma body of Mahāvairochana Buddha, that is considered the source of all compassion. This term contrasts with the Diamond Realm, which represents the wisdom of Mahāvairochana. The Womb Realm is represented graphically in Esoteric Buddhism by the Womb Realm mandala. *Garbha* of the Sanskrit name *garbhadhātu* means womb, embryo, or fetus, and *dhātu* means realm, world, or layer.

Womb Realm mandala [胎蔵界曼荼羅] (Jpn *taizōkai-mandara*): Also, Womb World mandala. One of the two mandalas of Esoteric Buddhism, the other being the Diamond Realm mandala. Derived from the Mahāvairochana Sutra, it represents the fundamental principle of the universe, the Dharma body of Mahāvairochana Buddha. In contrast, the Diamond Realm mandala, based on the Diamond Crown Sutra, depicts the Diamond Realm, which represents Mahāvairochana Buddha's wisdom. The version of the Womb Realm mandala, prevalent in Japan, was introduced from China by Kōbō (774–835), the founder of the True Word (Shingon) school. This mandala depicts twelve great halls or courts, with the court of the eight-petaled lotus at its center. Mahāvairochana Buddha is seated in the center of the lotus, while four Buddhas and four bodhisattvas sit on the surrounding petals. The four Buddhas are Jeweled Banner in the east, Florescence King in the south, Infinite Life in the west, and Heavenly Drum Thunder in the north. The four bodhisattvas are Universal Worthy in the southeast, Manjushrī in the southwest, Perceiver of the World's Sounds in the northwest, and Maitreya in the northeast. These eight Buddhas and bodhisattvas represent the virtues of Mahāvairochana Buddha. Mahāvairochana and the other Buddhas and bodhisattvas in this central court are together called the "nine honored ones on the eight-petaled lotus."

Womb World [胎蔵界] (Jpn *taizō-kai*): *See* Womb Realm.

Womb World mandala [胎蔵界曼荼羅] (Jpn *taizōkai-mandara*): *See* Womb Realm mandala.

Wonderful Adornment [妙荘厳王] (Skt Shubhavyūha; Jpn Myōshōgon-nō): A king who appears in the "King Wonderful Adornment" (twenty-seventh) chapter of the Lotus Sutra. According to that chapter, Wonderful

Adornment lived in the age of a Buddha named Cloud Thunder Sound Constellation King Flower Wisdom. Though a believer in Brahmanism, he went to see the Buddha at the urging of his wife Pure Virtue and his two sons Pure Storehouse and Pure Eye, and made various offerings to him. The Buddha prophesied that the king would become a monk, attain enlightenment, and become a Buddha named Sal Tree King. Wonderful Adornment then abdicated the throne in favor of his brother, joined the Buddhist Order with his wife, two sons, and his former subjects, and devoted himself to the practice of the Lotus Sutra. In the final part of the chapter, Shakyamuni identifies King Wonderful Adornment with Bodhisattva Flower Virtue who is present in the assembly on Eagle Peak listening to the preaching of the Lotus Sutra.

Wonderful Bright, Mount [妙光山] (Jpn Myōkō-sen): Another name for Mount Sumeru. *See* Sumeru, Mount.

Wonderful High, Mount [妙高山] (Jpn Myōkō-sen): Another name for Mount Sumeru. *See* Sumeru, Mount.

Wonderfully Bright [妙光菩薩] (Skt Varaprabha; Jpn Myōkō-bosatsu): A bodhisattva described in the "Introduction" (first) chapter of the Lotus Sutra as a previous incarnation of Bodhisattva Manjushrī. According to this chapter, in the remote past, a Buddha named Sun Moon Bright preached the Lotus Sutra to Bodhisattva Wonderfully Bright, who propagated it after that Buddha's death and led Sun Moon Bright's eight sons to enlightenment. Wonderfully Bright had eight hundred disciples, including Bodhisattva Seeker of Fame, who is identified in the chapter as a previous incarnation of Bodhisattva Maitreya.

Wonderful Sound [妙音菩薩] (Skt Gadgadasvara, Gangadasvara, or Gamgadasvara; Jpn Myō'on-bosatsu): A bodhisattva described in the "Wonderful Sound" (twenty-fourth) chapter of the Lotus Sutra. According to this chapter, Wonderful Sound lives in a land called Adorned with Pure Light and serves a Buddha named Pure Flower Constellation King Wisdom. He manifests himself as Brahmā, Shakra, a wheel-turning king, a monk, nun, layman, laywoman, dragon, demon, or any other form to which those he hopes to convert will be receptive, and expounds the Lotus Sutra to them. The "Wonderful Sound" chapter lists thirty-four forms that this bodhisattva assumes in order to save the people. It also says that in the remote past, for a space of twelve thousand years, he employed a hundred thousand types of musical instruments to provide offerings of sound to the Buddha Cloud Thunder Sound King and presented to him eighty-four thousand alms bowls made of the seven kinds of treasures. As a result, Wonderful Sound was reborn in the land called Adorned with Pure Light and acquired supernatural powers. Bodhisattva

Wonderful Sound is present at Eagle Peak with eighty-four thousand bodhisattvas to listen to Shakyamuni Buddha preach the Lotus Sutra and make offerings to him. According to T'ien-t'ai's *Words and Phrases of the Lotus Sutra,* this bodhisattva is called Wonderful Sound because he propagates the Lotus Sutra throughout the ten directions with his wondrous voice. Among the many sutras, Bodhisattva Wonderful Sound appears only in the "Wonderful Sound" chapter of the Lotus Sutra.

"Wonderful Sound" chapter [妙音品] (Jpn *Myō'on-bon*): The twenty-fourth chapter of the Lotus Sutra. *See* "Bodhisattva Wonderful Sound" chapter.

Words and Phrases of the Lotus Sutra, The [法華文句] (Chin *Fa-hua-wen-chü;* Jpn *Hokke-mongu*): One of T'ien-t'ai's three major works, the others being *The Profound Meaning of the Lotus Sutra* and *Great Concentration and Insight.* A ten-volume commentary on the Lotus Sutra, presented originally as a lecture in 587 by T'ien-t'ai, and recorded and compiled by his disciple Chang-an. Each volume consists of two parts. In the section of this work dealing with the "Introduction" (first) chapter of the sutra, T'ien-t'ai divides the Lotus Sutra into three parts: preparation, revelation, and transmission. The teaching of preparation readies people to receive the truth, revelation is the truth that the Buddha imparts, and transmission urges that the truth revealed be handed down for the future. T'ien-t'ai defines the "Introduction" chapter as preparation, the fifteen and a half chapters from the "Expedient Means" (second) chapter through the first half of the "Distinctions in Benefits" (seventeenth) chapter as revelation, and the eleven and a half chapters from the latter half of the "Distinctions in Benefits" chapter through the "Universal Worthy" (twenty-eighth) chapter as transmission. T'ien-t'ai also divides the Lotus Sutra into two parts—the theoretical teaching (first fourteen chapters) and the essential teaching (latter fourteen chapters), and applies the three divisions of preparation, revelation, and transmission to each of these. Within the theoretical teaching, he defines the "Introduction" chapter as preparation, the eight chapters from the "Expedient Means" chapter through the "Prophecies" (ninth) chapter as revelation, and the five chapters from the "Teacher of the Law" (tenth) chapter through the "Peaceful Practices" (fourteenth) chapter as transmission. Concerning the essential teaching, he defines the first half of the "Emerging from the Earth" (fifteenth) chapter as preparation; the one chapter and two halves comprising the latter half of the "Emerging from the Earth" chapter, the entire "Life Span" (sixteenth) chapter, and the first half of the "Distinctions in Benefits" chapter as revelation; and the eleven and a half chapters from the latter half of the "Distinctions in Benefits" chapter through the "Universal Worthy" chapter as transmission.

Subsequently T'ien-t'ai sets forth four guidelines for interpreting the words and phrases of the Lotus Sutra: (1) Causes and conditions; to interpret the words and phrases of the sutra in terms of the causes and conditions that prompted the Buddha to expound them, and to grasp them in terms of the four ways of preaching, or the four ways in which Buddhas expound their teachings. (2) Correlated teachings; to interpret the sutra's words and phrases in correlation with the four teachings of doctrine and the five periods. (3) The theoretical and essential teachings; to interpret the sutra's words and phrases in light of the theoretical and essential teachings of the Lotus Sutra. (4) The observation of the mind; to perceive the truth within one's own mind through the practice of meditation and also to interpret the words and phrases of the sutra from the standpoint of this perception of the truth. Using these four guidelines, T'ien-t'ai explains passages from each chapter of the Lotus Sutra to elucidate profound doctrines of the sutra such as the "replacement of the three vehicles with the one vehicle" and the "revelation of the Buddha's original enlightenment in the remote past."

Words of Truth Sutra [法句経] (Pali *Dhammapada;* Chin *Fa-chü-ching;* Jpn *Hokku-kyō*): Also known as the Sutra on the Words of Truth. A collection of short, practical teachings by Shakyamuni Buddha on topics related to Buddhist practice and daily living. It is often used as an introduction to Buddhism or cited to exemplify basic Buddhist ideas, and was extremely popular in Asian countries. There are both a Pali and a Sanskrit text, each of which has two Chinese translations. One of the two Chinese translations from Pali was produced by Vighna (Chin Wei-ch'i-nan) and others in 224, and the other by Fa-chü and Fa-li between 290 and 306. One of the translations from Sanskrit was produced by Chu Fo-nien toward the end of the fourth century and the other by T'ien-hsi-tsai sometime between 990 and 1000. The Pali text *Dhammapada* was also translated into Latin in 1855 and later into English and other European languages. The *Dhammapada* is said to have been one of the first Buddhist texts introduced to the West.

Work of the Ignorant Shavepate, The [愚禿鈔] (Jpn *Gutoku-shō*): A 1255 writing by Shinran, the founder of the True Pure Land (Jōdo Shin) school in Japan. Shinran had adopted the name Gutoku, meaning "ignorant shavepate," after his exile to Echigo in 1207. This work consists of two volumes. The first volume concerns the classification of the Buddhist teachings and asserts that all teachings other than those pertaining to Amida Buddha's original vows are provisional. The second volume discusses the three kinds of mind (a sincere mind, a mind of deep faith, and a mind resolved to attain rebirth in the Pure Land), the necessity of relying solely upon Amida's mercy, and other topics.

World Freedom King [世自在王仏] (Skt Lokeshvararāja; Jpn Sejizaiō-butsu): A Buddha described in the Buddha Infinite Life Sutra, one of the primary texts of the Pure Land teachings. According to that sutra, Amida Buddha, taking the name Dharma Treasury, carried out Buddhist practice in a previous existence under the Buddha World Freedom King. At that time, in the presence of the Buddha World Freedom King, Dharma Treasury made forty-eight vows concerning the characteristics his Buddha land would embody when he attained supreme enlightenment.

world hero [世雄] (Jpn *seō*): Also, hero of the world or supreme leader of the world. Another name or honorific title of a Buddha. A reference to a Buddha's heroism in conquering all people's earthly desires and sufferings and leading them to enlightenment with supreme wisdom and deep compassion.

World-Honored One [世尊] (Skt, Pali *bhagavat;* Jpn *seson*): One of the ten honorable titles of a Buddha. The Sanskrit *bhagavat* is usually translated into English as "blessed one." In the Chinese Buddhist scriptures, *bhagavat* was rendered as World-Honored One. A Buddha is so called because he is widely revered in the world.

World-Honored One of Great Enlightenment [大覚世尊] (Jpn Daikaku-seson): Also, Greatly Enlightened World-Honored One. An honorific title of a Buddha, usually applied to Shakyamuni Buddha. "Great Enlightenment" indicates the Buddha's enlightenment. "World-Honored One" is one of the Buddha's ten honorific titles, meaning one who is revered by the people of the world.

world of animals [畜生界] (Jpn *chikushō-kai*): Also, realm of animals or world of animality. The third of the Ten Worlds and one of the three, and the four, evil paths. When viewed as a state of life, the world of animals is a condition governed by instinct, in which one has no sense of reason or morality. Beings or persons in this world stand in fear of the strong but despise and prey upon those weaker than themselves. In *The Object of Devotion for Observing the Mind,* Nichiren defines the characteristic of this world as "foolishness," which is one of the three poisons.

world of asuras [修羅界] (Jpn *shura-kai*): Also, realm of *asuras,* world of animosity, or world of anger. The fourth of the Ten Worlds and one of the four evil paths. When viewed as a state of life, the world of *asuras* is a condition dominated by egoistic pride. Persons in this state are compelled by the need to be superior to others in all things, valuing themselves and devaluing others. *Asuras,* belligerent spirits or demons in Indian mythology, were regarded as typifying this condition of life. In *The Object of Devotion for Observing the Mind,* Nichiren defines the characteristic of this world as "perverse," or more literally, "fawning and crooked." Out of extreme pride or a sense of superiority, people in this condition tend to conceal their real motives and flatter others to win praise. While outwardly courteous, however, they inwardly look down on others. Such a person's self-image is distorted and unbalanced, colored by extreme pride or a sense of superiority; the self is perceived as extremely large and important, and others as small and unimportant. Those who remain in this state ultimately do harm to themselves through their own conceit. *See also* four evil paths; three good paths.

world of bodhisattvas [菩薩界] (Jpn *bosatsu-kai*): Also, realm of bodhisattvas. The world of bodhisattvas indicates the state of being a bodhisattva. The ninth of the Ten Worlds and one of the four noble worlds. When viewed as a state of life, the world of bodhisattvas is a condition of compassion in which one not only aspires for enlightenment oneself, but also works for the enlightenment of others even if doing so requires personal sacrifice. Altruism characterizes this world. It is a condition in which self-centeredness is dormant, and an awareness of one's deep connection with others informs one's actions. In *The Object of Devotion for Observing the Mind,* Nichiren states: "Even a heartless villain loves his wife and children. He too has a portion of the bodhisattva world within him" (358), indicating that the world of bodhisattvas is innate in all people.

world of Buddhahood [仏界] (Jpn *bukkai*): Also, realm of Buddhas. The highest of the Ten Worlds. When viewed as a state of life, the world of Buddhahood is a condition of absolute happiness, attained upon gaining the wisdom to realize the ultimate reality of one's own life and the compassion to direct one's activities constantly toward benevolent goals. A person in this state has access to boundless wisdom and compassion, as well as the courage and power to overcome any obstacle. In Mahayana Buddhism, acquiring this state of life is the goal of Buddhist practice. In teachings based on the Lotus Sutra, in particular, the realm of Buddhahood is not viewed as a realm apart from the nine worlds, or from the desires and sufferings of life in the real world. In this sense, it is different from the Hinayana view of nirvana, which is a complete annihilation of desire and suffering that can only be achieved fully upon annihilation of the physical body. Rather, in the world of Buddhahood, one is able to keep constantly in check life's innate "fundamental darkness," the source of destructive impulses and delusion, and function based on an inexhaustible supply of supreme wisdom. In *The Object of Devo-*

tion for Observing the Mind, Nichiren states: "That ordinary people born in the latter age can believe in the Lotus Sutra is due to the fact that the world of Buddhahood is present in the human world" (358).

world of cause-awakened ones [縁覚界] (Jpn *engaku-kai*): Also, realm of cause-awakened ones or world of realization. The eighth of the Ten Worlds and one of the four noble worlds. Cause-awakened ones (Skt *pratyekabuddha*) are those who awaken to the impermanence of all phenomena by perceiving the twelve-linked chain of causation or by observing natural phenomena. While they seek personal emancipation, they tend not to share it with others. For this reason, various sutras describe them as being reprimanded by Shakyamuni Buddha. When viewed as a state of life, the world of cause-awakened ones is a condition in which one perceives the transience of all things and strives to free oneself from the sufferings of the six paths, seeking to learn the way to self-improvement through personal effort and direct observation of the world. In this world, a sense of the impermanence of all things causes one to aspire for something eternal and unchanging. The world of cause-awakened ones and that of voice-hearers constitute the two vehicles. In *The Object of Devotion for Observing the Mind,* Nichiren states: "The fact that all things in this world are transient is perfectly clear to us. Is this not because the worlds of the two vehicles are present in the human world?" (358).

world of desire [欲界] (Skt, Pali *kāma-dhātu;* Jpn *yokkai* or *yoku-kai*): The lowest division of the threefold world. The world of desire is so called because its inhabitants are ruled by desires such as hunger and sexual craving. It comprises the four evil paths (the realms of hell, hungry spirits, animals, and *asuras*), the four continents surrounding Mount Sumeru that human beings inhabit, and the first six divisions of heaven, known as the six heavens of the world of desire. Said to dwell in the sixth, or highest, of the six heavens of the world of desire is the devil king of the sixth heaven, who has a strong desire to control others and prevent them from attaining enlightenment. The Sanskrit and Pali word *kāma* means desire, love, or pleasure, and *dhātu* means world or realm. *See also* four continents; four evil paths; six heavens of the world of desire.

world of endurance [忍土・忍界・堪忍世界] (Jpn *nindo, nin-kai,* or *kan-nin-sekai*): Also, land of forbearance. The *sahā* world, or this world, which is full of sufferings that must be endured. The Sanskrit word *sahā* means earth, but its root, *sah,* means to bear or endure. For this reason, in Chinese *sahā* was rendered as endurance. In Chinese translations of Buddhist scriptures, the word *sahā* was at times left in its Sanskrit form and rendered "*sahā* world," and at times translated to mean the "world of endurance." See also *sahā* world.

world of form [色界] (Skt, Pali *rūpa-dhātu;* Jpn *shiki-kai*): Also, world of matter. The middle division of the threefold world, located above the world of desire. Beings in this realm have physical bodies and are subject to certain material restrictions, but are free of desire and feed on light. The world of form consists of the four meditation heavens and is further subdivided into eighteen heavens (sixteen or seventeen according to other explanations). The highest is the Akanishtha Heaven, or Summit of Being Heaven. The Sanskrit word *rūpa* means form, outward appearance, color, phenomenon, or thing, and *dhātu* means world or realm. *See also* eighteen heavens; four meditation heavens.

world of formlessness [無色界] (Skt *ārūpya-dhātu;* Jpn *mushiki-kai*): Also, realm of formlessness or world of spirit. The highest division of the threefold world. The world of formlessness lies above the world of form and the world of desire. It is the immaterial realm of the spirit, which is said to be free from the limitations of matter and from all thought of matter. This world comprises four realms, which are, in ascending order of quality, the Realm of Boundless Empty Space, the Realm of Boundless Consciousness, the Realm of Nothingness, and the Realm of Neither Thought Nor No Thought. The Realm of Neither Thought Nor No Thought is also called the Summit of Being Heaven because it is the highest heaven (summit) in the world of being, i.e., in the threefold world, or the entire realm of existence. The life spans of beings in these four realms are 20,000 *kalpas* in the first realm, 40,000 *kalpas* in the second realm, 60,000 *kalpas* in the third realm, and 80,000 *kalpas* in the fourth realm. There are four successive levels of meditations called the four meditations on formlessness that respectively lead to rebirth in a successively higher one of these four realms. These realms are also described as states of mind in which one can dwell by achieving the corresponding meditation. The Sanskrit word *ārūpya* means formless, and *dhātu* means world or realm.

world of heavenly beings [天界] (Jpn *ten-kai*): Also, world of heaven, world of rapture, or realm of heavenly beings. The sixth of the Ten Worlds and the highest of the six paths. When viewed as a state of life, the world of heavenly beings is a condition of joy achieved upon the fulfillment of desire or release from suffering. According to the Buddhist scriptures, the world of heavenly beings has twenty-eight subdivisions in the threefold world: six heavens in the world of desire, eighteen (some sources say sixteen or seventeen) in the world of form, and four in the world of formlessness. From a philosophical standpoint, these divisions of the threefold world can be said to represent various kinds of joy. The world of desire symbolizes the desire for existence, instinctive desires, materialistic desires, social desires, etc. When such desires are satisfied, one feels the joy of the world of desire. The joy of the world of form and the joy of the world of formlessness may be equated with the satisfaction of higher desires such as intellectual, artistic, and spiritual desires. Any of the joys of the world of heavenly beings, however, are transient and vulnerable to external circumstances. While those in the world of heaven regard such joys as the ultimate, those in the worlds of the two vehicles (voice-hearers and cause-awakened ones) do not regard even the joy of the world of formlessness as the ultimate but as a process to emancipation.

world of hell [地獄界] (Jpn *jigoku-kai*): The lowest of the Ten Worlds. Buddhist scriptures describe various kinds of hells such as the eight hot hells and the eight cold hells. Viewed as a state of life, it is a condition of extreme suffering in which one is crushed by agony and unable to do anything about it. Unable to move or act freely, one feels violent rage against one's own powerlessness. While the fight to continue living is natural, the agony of hell saps one's vital energy and brings death closer. Hence in *The Object of Devotion for Observing the Mind,* Nichiren describes "rage" as characterizing the world of hell. *See also* hell.

world of human beings [人界] (Jpn *nin-kai*): Also, realm of human beings or world of humanity. The fifth of the Ten Worlds. When viewed as a state of life, the world of human beings indicates a condition in which one can control one's instinctive desires with reason and act in a humane fashion. In *The Object of Devotion for Observing the Mind,* Nichiren describes "calmness" as characterizing the world of human beings. Maintaining calmness, however, is not easy; it requires self-control. This is why, among the Ten Worlds, the world of humanity is considered the first step toward acquiring self-control. Also characteristic of this condition is the desire for self-improvement, the will to seek a higher state of life. Without constant effort, however, one in this world will regress and fall into the lower of the Ten Worlds.

world of hungry spirits [餓鬼界] (Jpn *gaki-kai*): Also, realm of hungry spirits or world of hunger. The second of the Ten Worlds and one of the three, and the four, evil paths. When viewed as a state of life, the world of hungry spirits is a condition ruled by insatiable selfish desire for food, profit, fame, or pleasure. In *The Object of Devotion for Observing the Mind,* Nichiren characterizes the world of hungry spirits as "greed." One in this state is tormented physically and spiritually by relentless craving. The causes for falling into this state are such tendencies as greed, miserliness, and jealousy. Both the Sanskrit word *preta* and the Chinese word *kuei,* whose Japanese reading is *ki* (of *gaki*), literally mean "the deceased" or "spirits of the deceased." The world of hungry spirits is described in the sutras as an underground realm five hundred *yojanas* beneath the surface of the earth located just above hell. *The Treatise on Accordance with the Correct Doctrine* describes three kinds of hungry spirits, each of which is further subdivided into three, and the Meditation on the Correct Teaching Sutra lists thirty-six kinds.

world of voice-hearers [声聞界] (Jpn *shōmon-kai*): Also, realm of voice-hearers or world of learning. The seventh of the Ten Worlds and one of the four noble worlds. The world of voice-hearers and that of cause-awakened ones constitute the two vehicles. Voice-hearers (Skt *shrāvaka*) mean those who listen to the Buddha preach the four noble truths and seek to attain emancipation by eradicating earthly desires. While they seek personal emancipation, they do not share it with others. For this reason, various sutras describe them as being reprimanded by Shakyamuni Buddha. When viewed as a state of life, the world of voice-hearers is a condition in which one perceives the impermanence of all things and the instability of the six paths, and strives toward a lasting state of contentment and stability through self-improvement and self-development.

worms within the lion's body [師子身中の虫] (Jpn *shishi-shinchū-no-mushi*): An analogy for those who, despite being followers of Buddhism, destroy its teachings, just as worms born from the carcass of the lion devour the lion. This analogy appears in the Benevolent Kings Sutra, the Brahmā's Net Sutra, the Lotus-like Face Sutra, and elsewhere. It is intended to point out that members of the Buddhist Order, rather than non-Buddhists, are capable of destroying Buddhism. For example, the Benevolent Kings Sutra says that the upholders of the three treasures of Buddhism, and not non-Buddhists, will become the destroyers of the three treasures, just as worms within the lion's body devour the lion. The Lotus-like Face Sutra tells that, though no other creature ventures to eat the flesh of a dead lion, the worms born from the lion's body devour it; likewise, though the Buddha's teachings cannot be destroyed by outside forces, evil monks who exist within "the body" of the Buddha's teachings can destroy them.

Worthy of Offerings [応供] (Skt *arhat;* Jpn *ōgu*): Also, Worthy of Alms. One of the ten honorable titles of a Buddha. A Buddha is so called because he is qualified to receive offerings from human and heavenly beings. "Worthy of Offerings" also refers to an arhat, or one who has attained the highest stage of Hinayana enlightenment.

Wu-hsüeh Tsu-yüan [無学祖元] (PY Wuxue Zuyuan; Jpn Mugaku Sogen): A priest of the Rinzai (Chin Lin-chi) school of Zen from China who went to Japan, where he is known as Mugaku Sogen. *See* Mugaku Sogen.

Wu-lung [烏竜] (n.d.) (PY Wulong; Jpn Oryō): A skilled calligrapher mentioned in Chinese Buddhist texts. His son I-lung was also an outstanding calligrapher. According to *The Lotus Sutra and Its Traditions,* an eighth-century work by the Chinese priest Seng-hsiang, Wu-lung lived in Ping-chou in northern China and was a believer in Taoism. He hated Buddhism and refused to transcribe Buddhist texts. On his deathbed, he enjoined his son never to transcribe any Buddhist scriptures, especially the Lotus Sutra. After his death, according to this work, Wu-lung fell into the hell of incessant suffering. Unaware of this, I-lung, in obedience to his father's will, vowed not to transcribe any of the Buddhist scriptures. At the command of the lord of Ping-chou, however, much against his will, he transcribed only the sixty-four Chinese characters that constitute the titles of the eight volumes of the Lotus Sutra, though he refused to copy the entire sutra. In a dream he had that night, the sixty-four characters turned into sixty-four Buddhas and saved his father, Wu-lung, from the agonies of hell.

Wu-t'ai, Mount [五台山] (PY Wutai-shan; Jpn Godai-san): Also known as Mount Ch'ing-liang. A mountain located in the Wu-t'ai mountain range in Shansi Province in China. This mountain has long been identified with Mount Clear and Cool (Ch'ing-liang) where, according to the Flower Garland Sutra, Bodhisattva Manjushrī dwells. It was counted as foremost of the four sacred mountains related to Buddhism in China, the other three being Mount P'u-t'o, which is associated with Bodhisattva Perceiver of the World's Sounds; Mount Chiu-hua, with Bodhisattva Earth Repository; and Mount E-mei, with Bodhisattva Universal Worthy. Mount Wu-t'ai prospered as a center of Chinese Buddhism where eminent priests from throughout the country as well as from Central Asia, Korea, and Japan studied, practiced, and lectured. In 766 Pu-k'ung and Han-kuang made it a center of Esoteric Buddhism, building two temples there. In 770 Fa-chao, a noted priest of the Pure Land teachings, engaged there in the practice of reciting the name of Amida Buddha. Ch'eng-kuan (738–839), the fourth patriarch of the Flower Garland (Hua-yen) school, stayed at Ta-hua-yen-ssu temple on Mount Wu-tai and lectured on the Flower Garland Sutra. The mountain was a center of the Flower Garland school and also a center of the Chinese Zen (Ch'an) school. Among the Japanese priests who made a pilgrimage there were Gembō (d. 746), Jikaku (794–864), Chōnen (d. 1016), and Jōjin (1011–1081). Over the centuries, more than one hundred temples are said to have been built on the flat summit of this mountain. Beginning in the Yuan dynasty (1271–1368), lamaseries, or temples of Tibetan Buddhism, were also built there.

Y

Yadoya Mitsunori [宿屋光則] (n.d.): Also known as Yadoya Saemon, Yadoya Saemon Mitsunori, or the lay priest Yadoya. An official of the Kamakura shogunate through whose offices Nichiren in 1260 submitted his treatise *On Establishing the Correct Teaching for the Peace of the Land* to Hōjō Tokiyori, the retired regent but effective ruler of Japan. He served the regents Hōjō Tokiyori and Hōjō Tokimune. In *The Mirror of Eastern Japan,* a historical account of the Kamakura shogunate, he is mentioned as one of the seven persons permitted access to Hōjō Tokiyori when this former regent was on his deathbed in 1263. When the first emissary from the Mongols arrived in Japan in 1268 with a letter demanding tribute, Nichiren sent a letter to Yadoya Mitsunori on the twenty-first day of the eighth month restating the message of *On Establishing the Correct Teaching* and asking him to inform the regent Hōjō Tokimune of it. There was no reply, and on the eleventh day of the tenth month, Nichiren sent eleven letters of remonstration to leading priests and officials, including Hōjō Tokimune and Yadoya Mitsunori. Yadoya Mitsunori was an adherent of Ryōkan of Gokuraku-ji temple, who espoused the True Word Precepts (Shingon-Ritsu) teachings. In 1271, however, when five of Nichiren's disciples, including the priest Nichirō, were imprisoned in a hillside dungeon at Mitsunori's residence, it is said that he became a disciple of Nichiren.

yaksha [夜叉] (Skt; Jpn *yasha*): One of the eight kinds of nonhuman beings mentioned in Buddhist literature. In Hindu mythology, *yakshas* were benevolent spirits and followers of Kubera, the god of wealth, who is also referred to as Vaishravana. Buddhism later included them as one of the eight kinds of nonhuman beings who work to protect Buddhism. *Yakshas* are regarded as followers of the heavenly king Vaishravana who is said to dwell halfway up the northern slope of Mount Sumeru, and also as guardians of the northern quarter. In some sutras, however, they are depicted as ugly, fierce demons that torment or harm human beings. *See also* Vaishravana.

Yakushi [薬師] (Jpn): The Thus Come One Medicine Master (Yakushi-nyorai). Yakushi means Medicine Master. *See* Medicine Master.

Yakushi-ji [薬師寺]: (1) One of the two head temples of the Dharma Characteristics (Hossō) school in Nara, Japan, the other being Kōfuku-ji temple. Both were counted among the seven major temples of Nara. Emperor Temmu (r. 673–686) vowed to build the temple in 680 to house an image of the Buddha Medicine Master (Jpn Yakushi) for the recovery of his ailing consort. Subsequent to his making this vow, her illness was cured. Construction of the temple did not substantially progress, however, until after the emperor's death in 686. His consort, who succeeded him as Empress Jitō, continued the project, and the temple was completed in 698 during the reign of Emperor Mommu. Originally located in the capital of that time, Fujiwara-kyō, the temple was newly built in Nara in 718 after that city became the capital. (Thereafter the original temple in Fujiwara-kyō was called Moto Yakushi-ji, or the original Yakushi-ji.) The structures of Yakushi-ji in Nara were eventually destroyed by fire, earthquakes, and wind storms, but were rebuilt in later centuries. The statue of the Buddha Medicine Master is thought to date to the late seventh or the early eighth century.

(2) A temple that existed in Shimotsuke Province in Japan; today only its ruins remain. It had one of three Buddhist ordination platforms in the country in the mid-eighth century, the other two being at Tōdai-ji temple in Nara and at Kanzeon-ji temple in Chikuzen Province. Yakushi-ji temple was built somewhere between the late seventh and the early eighth centuries. The ordination platform was erected at the temple in 761 to conduct ceremonies conferring the Buddhist precepts upon priests and nuns living in the eastern part of Japan.

Yakushin [益信] (827–906): A priest regarded as a precursor of the Hirosawa branch of the True Word (Shingon) school in Japan. Yakushin entered the priesthood at Daian-ji temple in Nara. He studied the doctrine of the Dharma Characteristics (Hossō) school under Myōsen, a priest of Gangō-ji temple in Nara, and the esoteric teachings under Shūei, a priest of Tō-ji, a head temple of the True Word school in Kyoto. In 887 he advanced to the position of *ajari* (Skt *āchārya*), which in that esoteric tradition qualifies one to receive and transmit the secret doctrines. In 891 he became chief priest of Tō-ji. Kanchō (916–998), a later teacher of Yakushin's doctrines, built Henshō-ji temple at Hirosawa in Kyoto. This became the center of Yakushin's lineage within the True Word school, which thus came to be called the Hirosawa branch.

Yama [閻魔] (Skt, Pali; Jpn Emma): Also known as King Yama. The Vedas describe Yama as the first man to enter the world of the dead and who became the king there. That world was considered a paradise and the king not a punisher of sinners. Later Brahmanic mythology regarded him as one of the guardians (Skt *lokapāla*) of the four cardinal directions, the regent of the south dwelling in a heaven above the world. Finally Yama became known as the just judge *(dharma-rāja)* of the underworld who confronts the dead with a record of their actions while alive and determines their retributions. Though Buddhism originally had no such belief in judgment, Yama was incorporated into Buddhist mythology in China, Tibet, and Japan as the lord of the underworld. In China, under Taoist influence, Yama became one of the ten kings of purgatory and ruled the fifth court, which the dead are said to reach on the thirty-fifth day after death. This image of Yama was introduced to Japan, but Japanese folk belief came to regard Yama both as the judge of the dead and as their guardian deity. In Chinese and Japanese Buddhism, Yama is regarded as the king of hell who judges and determines the rewards and punishments of the dead.

Yāma Heaven [夜摩天] (Skt; Jpn Yama-ten): In Hindu and Buddhist cosmology, the third of the six heavens in the world of desire. This heaven is always illuminated, and its inhabitants enjoy satisfaction of the five desires, which arise in relation to the five sense organs (eyes, ears, nose, tongue, and body). It is located eighty thousand *yojanas* above the Heaven of the Thirty-three Gods, which is on the summit of Mount Sumeru. Yāma Heaven measures eighty thousand *yojanas* on each side. The life span of beings in this heaven is said to be two thousand years, each day of which corresponds to two hundred years in the human world. This means that their life span is equal to 400,000 human years.

Yamashina-dera [山階寺]: The original name of Kōfuku-ji, the head temple of the Dharma Characteristics (Hossō) school in Nara, Japan. It was built in 669 by the wife of Fujiwara no Kamatari, founder of the Fujiwara clan, to memorialize her husband upon his death. Originally located in Yamashina Village in Kyoto, from which it took its name, the temple later moved to Umayasaka in Nara. When it moved again to its present site in Nara, it was renamed Kōfuku-ji. Yamashina-dera was the family temple of the Fujiwaras, who held great political power during much of the Heian period (794–1185).

yāna [乗] (Skt, Pali; Jpn *jō*): A vehicle. In general, any kind of vehicle, such as a boat, cart, or carriage. In Buddhism, *yāna* indicates a Buddhist teaching that "carries" or "transports" people to a particular level of enlightenment. It is a component of a number of Buddhist terms, such as *mahāyāna* (great vehicle), *hīnayāna* (lesser vehicle), *ekayāna* (one vehicle, or supreme vehicle), *buddha-yāna* (Buddha vehicle), *bodhisattva-yāna* (bodhisattva vehicle), *pratyekabuddha-yāna* (cause-awakened one vehicle), and *shrāvaka-yāna* (voice-hearer vehicle). *Shrāvaka-yāna, pratyekabuddha-yāna,* and *bodhisattva-yāna* are collectively called *tri-yāna,* or the three vehicles.

Yasa [耶舍] (Pali; Jpn Yasha): A monk who lived in India about one hundred years after Shakyamuni's death and who headed the Second Buddhist Council in Vaishālī. His full name was Yasa Kākandakaputta. When Yasa went to Vaishālī, he observed monks of the Vriji tribe receiving offerings of gold and silver from lay believers and condemned them for doing so. At that time, accepting monetary alms was forbidden by the monastic rules of the Buddhist Order. The Vriji monks argued that changing conditions in their city demanded a more flexible application of the monastic rules. Yasa assembled seven hundred monks from throughout India to consider the matter. This gathering is known as the Second Buddhist Council. The demands of the Vaishālī monks were rejected by the Council's majority as violating the precepts. Dissension over the issue helped precipitate the first schism in the Order, which resulted in the formation of the Sthaviravāda (Pali Theravāda) and Mahāsamghika schools.

Yashas [耶舍 · 耶輸陀 · 夜輸] (Skt; Pali Yasa; Jpn Yasha, Yashuda, or Yashu): Also known as Yasha or Yashoda. The son of a wealthy merchant in Vārānasī, India. Yashas was Shakyamuni Buddha's sixth convert, and the first after Shakyamuni's conversion of the five ascetics. Yashas became disenchanted with his life of luxury and left home, renouncing secular life to seek religious truth; it was then that he met the Buddha and became his disciple. Yashas' parents and wife subsequently converted as well and are said to have been the Buddha's first lay disciples. At that time, more than fifty of Yashas' friends also renounced secular life to become the Buddha's disciples.

Yashodharā [耶輸陀羅 · 耶輸多羅] (Skt; Pali Yasodharā; Jpn Yashudara or Yashutara): The wife of Shakyamuni before he renounced secular life; mother of Rāhula. According to the Buddhist scriptures, she was a very beautiful woman, and Shuddhodana, Shakyamuni's father, wished for her to be his son's wife. Yashodharā's father offered his daughter to the man who could prove himself most worthy through various feats of intellect and strength, and Shakyamuni easily surpassed all rivals, including his cousin Devadatta. After the birth of their son Rāhula, Shakyamuni renounced secular life and eventually attained enlightenment. Yashodharā converted to his teachings and became a Buddhist nun.

Yin-yüan [隠元] (PY Yinyuan; Jpn Ingen): A Chinese priest who founded the Obaku school of Zen in Japan. He became known as Ingen in Japan. *See* Ingen.

yoga [瑜伽] (Skt, Pali; Jpn *yuga*): A system of meditation with roots in Hindu and Vedic tradition that developed in ancient India. It is aimed at stilling the body and mind, and thus liberating one from their limitations. In this way, the yoga practitioner aims to transcend desire and suffering, achieve concentration, and attain unity with the supreme spirit or truth. Meditation, an essential aspect of yoga, also became a core practice in Buddhism. While forms of yoga have been introduced in the West primarily as a system of physical exercise, the main focus of yoga is meditation, which can include contemplation on Hindu deities and principles. *Āsana,* or physical postures, are intended to support the primary meditative and religious practices of yoga. There are a number of schools of yoga, which employ a variety of disciplines, including breath control, *āsana,* and meditation. Today some of the physical yogic disciplines are practiced widely for health and stress relief without any particular religious motivation.

Yogāchāra school [瑜伽行派] (Skt; Jpn Yugagyō-ha): Also known as the Way of Yoga school, the Yoga Practice school, or the Yoga school. Another name for the Consciousness-Only school of Buddhism. This name derives from the fact that the chief discipline of the Consciousness-Only school was yogic practice. *See also* Consciousness-Only school.

yojana [由旬] (Skt, Pali; Jpn *yujun*): A unit of measurement used in ancient India, said to equal the distance that the royal army was thought able to march in a day. One *yojana* is considered to be about 7 kilometers, although there are several other approximations, such as 9.6, 18, and 24 kilometers. The Sanskrit word *yojana* implies "yoking," indicating the distance that oxen yoked to royal carts traverse in a day.

Yōkan [永観] (1033–1111): Also known as Eikan. A priest of the Three Treatises (Sanron) school and a precursor of the Pure Land (Jōdo) school in Japan. He was born in Kyoto, where he entered the priesthood in 1043 and studied Esoteric Buddhism as a disciple of Jinkan of Zenrin-ji temple. In the following year he went to Tōdai-ji temple and studied the doctrines of the Three Treatises, Dharma Characteristics (Hossō), and Flower Garland (Kegon) schools. He then practiced the Nembutsu, or the recitation of Amida Buddha's name. Later he retired to Kōmyōzan-ji temple in Yamashiro Province where he devoted himself to practicing the Nembutsu. After a decade of such practice, he returned to Tōdai-ji temple and in 1100 was appointed its superintendent. He again left the temple, however, to practice and disseminate the Nembutsu. Yōkan wrote

The Ten Conditions for Rebirth in the Pure Land and *The Rituals of the Assembly for Rebirth in the Pure Land.*

Yokei [余慶] (919–991): A priest of the Tendai school in Japan. He studied the Tendai doctrine under Myōsen and Esoteric Buddhism under Gyōyo. In 989 he was appointed chief priest of Enryaku-ji, the head temple of the Tendai school at Mount Hiei. Because he was from the group of followers of Chishō, the fifth chief priest, he faced strong opposition from a rival group, the followers of Jikaku, the third chief priest. Finally Yokei resigned his post, and in 993, two years after his death, the priests of Chishō's line moved to Onjō-ji temple. This led to a decisive schism between the two groups of the Tendai school.

Yü-ch'üan-ssu [玉泉寺] (PY Yuquansi; Jpn Gyokusen-ji): A temple founded in 592 by T'ien-t'ai in his home region of Ching-chou, China. At this temple, T'ien-t'ai delivered lectures that were later compiled as *The Profound Meaning of the Lotus Sutra* and *Great Concentration and Insight* by his disciple Chang-an.

Yüeh-chih [月氏] (PY Yuezhi; Jpn Gesshi): A people who inhabited Central Asia from the third century B.C.E. through the third century C.E. They were nomads of Iranian origin (Tibetan or Turkish according to another account). The Yüeh-chih lived in the region that includes present-day Kansu Province in China and its surrounding areas for several centuries up through the third century B.C.E. In the second century B.C.E., however, the Yüeh-chih were defeated by the Hsiung-nu, who were expanding their base of power in the Mongolian Plateau. The majority of the Yüeh-chih moved westward into Sogdiana (the present-day Samarkand region of Uzbekistan) and then across the river Amu Darya (formerly, the Oxus) into Bactria, an ancient kingdom roughly in the region of present-day Afghanistan. Conquering Bactria, they settled there and established a kingdom, which the Chinese referred to as the Great Yüeh-chih (Ta-yüeh-chih). The Yüeh-chih who remained in the Kansu and surrounding regions were called the Little Yüeh-chih (Hsiao-yüeh-chih). The Yüeh-chih in Bactria then divided the country into five chiefdoms, whose chieftains are thought to have been from among the conquered inhabitants. Around 139 B.C.E., Chang Ch'ien, an imperial emissary of the Former Han dynasty, visited the Great Yüeh-chih kingdom and brought back to China new information about the world to the west. Later, in the mid-first century, the Kushans, whose chieftains had successively ruled one of the five chiefdoms of Bactria, defeated the other four chieftains and assumed power in the region. They established the Kushan dynasty, which displaced the Yüeh-chih kingdom. Nevertheless, the Chinese still called the Kushan kingdom the Great Yüeh-chih, as is evidenced in Chinese Buddhist texts and other literature. The Kushan kingdom extended its power into India and Central Asia. Lokakshema, who brought Buddhism to Later Han China in the mid-second century, belonged to the so-called Great Yüeh-chih. In China, he translated numerous Mahayana Buddhist scriptures. Chih-ch'ien and Dharmaraksha, who produced many Chinese translations of Sanskrit Buddhist scriptures in the third century, were also from the Great Yüeh-chih.

Yün-kang caves [雲岡石窟] (PY Yungang; Jpn Unkō-sekkutsu): Large-scale Buddhist cave-temples located sixteen kilometers west of the city of Ta-t'ung (PY Datong) in Shansi Province, China. The Yün-kang caves cover an area measuring about one kilometer from east to west. The construction of these cave-temples, which were cut from the rock faces of cliffs, began in the fifth century. Carved from the cave walls inside these temples are statues of the Buddha, bodhisattvas, and other figures. Among the rock-cut Buddhist sculptures found in the Yün-kang caves are images of the Buddha standing sixteen meters in height. The rock walls and ceilings are decorated in relief. The early works at the Yün-kang caves are regarded as representing the culmination of early Buddhist sculpture in China. Around 460 T'an-yao, who was appointed national director of the Buddhist clergy by Emperor Wen-ch'eng of the Northern Wei dynasty, began construction of the Yün-kang cave-temples. The emperor supported his construction because he wanted to ensure the salvation of the emperors before him and tried to restore Buddhism, which had been suppressed by the late Emperor T'ai-wu, his grandfather. T'an-yao built the first five of the Yün-kang cave-temples. The construction continued under dynastic support over thirty years until 494, when Emperor Hsiao-wen transferred the capital from P'ing-ch'eng (present-day Ta-t'ung) to Lo-yang. Later smaller cave-temples were added to the complex.

Yūzū Nembutsu school [融通念仏宗] (Jpn Yūzū Nembutsu-shū): A school of the Pure Land teachings in Japan. *See* Interfusing Nembutsu school.

Z

zazen [坐禅] (Jpn): Seated meditation. The term *zazen* specifically indicates the form of seated meditation practiced in the Zen school of Buddhism. The practice of *zazen* is emphasized especially in the Sōtō school of Zen in Japan. Seated meditation was widely practiced in ancient India. Shakyamuni Buddha sat in meditation when he attained enlightenment under the *bodhi* tree, and incorporated the practice into his teachings. Seated meditation was introduced with Buddhism to China, where various Buddhist schools employed it. T'ien-t'ai (538–597) taught it as core to the integrated system of disciplines he prescribed for observing the true nature of one's mind.

Zengi [善議] (729–812): A priest of the Three Treatises (Sanron) school in Japan. He studied the Three Treatises doctrine under Dōji of Daian-ji temple in Nara and later went to China to further his studies. After returning to Japan, he lived at Daian-ji and preached the Three Treatises doctrine, gaining renown for his learning. Anchō and Gonsō were his disciples. Zengi was among the more than ten eminent priests of the six schools of Nara who assembled to listen to Dengyō lecture on the Tendai doctrine at Takao-dera temple in 802.

Zenkō-ji [善光寺]: A temple in Nagano Prefecture, Japan, affiliated with the Tendai and the Pure Land (Jōdo) schools. Built in the seventh century, it enshrines a statue of Amida Buddha flanked by those of the bodhisattvas Perceiver of the World's Sounds and Great Power. According to this temple's tradition, the statue was Japan's first Buddhist image, sent by King Syŏngmyŏng of the Korean kingdom of Paekche to the Japanese emperor Kimmei in 552 (the traditionally accepted date for the formal introduction of Buddhism to Japan). The Mononobe clan, who opposed Buddhism and claimed it to be the cause of epidemics, repeatedly discarded the statue. According to tradition, however, it was retrieved each time by the Soga clan, the pro-Buddhist faction. In 602 the statue was transported to Shinano Province (present-day Nagano Prefecture) and enshrined in 642 at Zenkō-ji temple, which was built that year.

Zen school [禅宗] (Jpn Zen-shū): A Buddhist school that teaches that enlightenment is to be gained not through doctrinal studies, but rather through direct perception of one's mind through the practice of meditation. Known in China as the Ch'an school, its founder is regarded as Bodhidharma (sixth century). The Zen teaching was summarized in these phrases attributed to Bodhidharma: "A separate transmission outside the sutras," "independent of words or writing," "directly pointing to the human mind," and "perceiving one's true nature and attaining Buddhahood." According to this school, the Buddha's supreme enlightenment has been transmitted wordlessly through the ages from mind to mind through the lineage of its patriarchs. This process began when Shakyamuni Buddha transferred his enlightenment to his disciple Mahākāshyapa, who is regarded as the first patriarch of Zen. According to Zen tradition, one day when Shakyamuni was with his disciples on Eagle Peak, he silently picked a flower and held it up in his hand. At that time only Mahākāshyapa grasped the Buddha's meaning, and smiled. Thus, it is said, the Zen teaching was transferred to Mahākāshyapa with a smile. The lineage is said to have passed to the second patriarch, Ānanda, the third, Shānavāsa, and finally to the twenty-eighth patriarch, Bodhidharma, who brought the "wordless tradition" to China. Thereafter the teaching of Zen was transmitted to the second Chinese patriarch, Hui-k'o, the third, Seng-ts'an, the fourth, Tao-hsin, the fifth, Hung-jen, and the sixth, Hui-neng.

In the time of Hui-neng (638–713), the school split into the Southern school of Zen, which Hui-neng led, and the Northern school, led by Shen-hsiu. The Northern school rapidly declined, and the Southern school became the mainstream of Chinese Zen. Hui-neng's major disciples were Hsing-ssu, Huai-jang, and Shen-hui. Liang-chieh, in the lineage of Hsing-ssu, founded the Ts'ao-tung (Jpn Sōtō) school, and Pen-chi became its second patriarch. Two other schools, the Yün-men (Ummon) and Fa-yen (Hōgen), were founded in the same lineage by Wen-yen and Wen-i, respectively. In the lineage of Huai-jang, Ling-yu founded the Kuei-yang (Igyō) school and his disciple Hui-chi further solidified it, while Lin-chi I-hsüan founded the Lin-chi (Rinzai) school. Among these five schools, the Lin-chi school enjoyed the greatest prosperity, and two branches emerged from it—the Yang-ch'i (Yōgi) school, established by Fang-hui, and the Huang-lung (Ōryū) school, founded by Hui-nan. Together, these schools constitute the so-called "five schools and seven schools" of Southern Zen.

Noted among the first Zen masters in Japan is Dainichi Nōnin, who introduced the Zen teaching to that country in the twelfth century; he called his school the Nihon Daruma, or the Japanese Bodhidharma, school. After his death, his disciples became followers of Dōgen (1200–1253), the founder of the Sōtō school of Japanese Zen, and Nōnin's school perished. In 1187 Eisai brought the teachings of the Lin-chi school of Zen from China after his second visit there, and founded the Japanese Rinzai school. In 1223 Dōgen also went to China and brought back the teachings of the Ts'ao-tung school, based upon which he established the Sōtō school. During the Kamakura (1185–1333) and Muromachi (1336–1573) periods, the Zen teachings became popular among the samurai class and prospered greatly. In 1654 the Chinese priest Yin-yüan, known in Japan as Ingen, came to Japan and later founded the Ōbaku school of Zen.

Zōga [増賀] (917–1003): A priest of the Tendai school in Japan. Born to the distinguished Tachibana family, he renounced secular life to devote himself as a priest to the Tendai practice. In 963 he retired to Tōnomine hill in Yamato Province, where he diligently practiced Tendai meditation and lectured on the Lotus Sutra, *Great Concentration and Insight, The Words and Phrases of the Lotus Sutra,* and other basic texts of the school. With these lectures, he won many disciples.

Zōjō-ten [増長天] (Jpn): The heavenly king Increase and Growth. One of the four heavenly kings. *See* Increase and Growth.

Zōmyō [増命] (843–927): Also known as Jōkan. The tenth chief priest of Enryaku-ji, the head temple of the Tendai school on Mount Hiei in Japan. In 855 he went to Enryaku-ji and studied there. In 867 Zōmyō received the bodhisattva precepts and furthered his study of the Tendai doctrines under Jikaku and Chishō, respectively the third and fifth chief priests of Enryaku-ji. In 899 he became superintendent of Onjō-ji, another main temple of the Tendai school, and in 906 he became the chief priest of Enryaku-ji temple. He gained renown for the apparent effectiveness of his prayers in curing the illnesses of the emperor and retired emperors. In 925 he was appointed to the nationwide position of administrator of priests.

APPENDIX A

Sanskrit and Pali Words

In the left column are Sanskrit and Pali words romanized according to pronunciation as they appear in the dictionary and in the right column are the romanized forms with full diacritical marks. Words that require only macrons are not included in this appendix.

abhayam-dada	abhayaṃ-dada
Abhidharma-hridaya-shāstra	Abhidharma-hṛdaya-śāstra
Abhidharma-jnānaprasthāna-shāstra	Abhidharma-jñānaprasthāna-śāstra
Abhidharmakosha	Abhidharmakośa
Abhidharmakosha-bhāshya	Abhidharmakośa-bhāṣya
Abhidharmakosha-shāstra	Abhidharmakośa-śāstra
Abhidharma-mahāvibhāshā-shāstra	Abhidharma-mahāvibhāṣā-śāstra
abhisheka	abhiṣeka
Achala	Acala
Achalā	Acalā
Achalanātha	Acalanātha
āchārya	ācārya
Achiravatī	Aciravatī
ādāna-vijnāna	ādāna-vijñāna
ahimsā	ahiṃsā
Ajātashatru	Ajātaśatru
Ajita Keshakambala	Ajita Keśakambala
Ajita Keshakambalin	Ajita Keśakambalin
Ājnāta Kaundinya	Ājñāta Kauṇḍinya
Akanishtha	Akaniṣṭha
ākāsha	ākāśa
Ākāshagarbha	Ākāśagarbha
Ākāshānantya	Ākāśānantya
Ākāshānantyāyatana	Ākāśānantyāyatana
Ākimchanya	Ākiṃcanya
Ākimchanyāyatana	Ākiṃcanyāyatana
Akshobhya	Akṣobhya
Ālāra Kālāma	Āḷāra Kālāma
ālaya-vijnāna	ālaya-vijñāna
amala-vijnāna	amala-vijñāna
amrita	amṛta
Amrita	Amṛta

Amritodana	Amṛtodana
Anantachāritra	Anantacāritra
ananta-nirdesha-pratishthāna	ananta-nirdeśa-pratiṣṭhāna
ananta-nirdesha-pratishthāna-samādhi	ananta-nirdeśa-pratiṣṭhāna-samādhi
ānāpāna-smriti	ānāpāna-smṛti
Anāthapindada	Anāthapiṇḍada
Anāthapindika	Anāthapiṇḍika
Anga	Aṅga
Angaja	Aṅgaja
Angulimāla	Aṅgulimāla
Angulimālya	Aṅgulimālya
Anguttara-nikāya	Aṅguttara-nikāya
Anumodanā-punya-nirdesha	Anumodanā-puṇya-nirdeśa
anuttara-dharma-chakra	anuttara-dharma-cakra
anuttara-sambodhi	anuttara-saṃbodhi
anuttara-samyak-sambodhi	anuttara-samyak-saṃbodhi
anuttara-samyak-sambodhi-chitta	anuttara-samyak-saṃbodhi-citta
Aparashaila	Aparaśaila
Apramānābha	Apramāṇābha
Apramānashubha	Apramāṇaśubha
Ārāda Kālāma	Ārāḍa Kālāma
aranya	araṇya
ariya-atthangika-magga	ariya-aṭṭhaṅgika-magga
ārya-ashtānga-mārga	ārya-aṣṭāṅga-mārga
Ārya-prajnāpāramitā-naya-shatapanchashatikā	Ārya-prajñāpāramitā-naya-śatapañcaśatikā
Āryasimha	Āryasiṃha
Asamjnin	Asaṃjñin
asamkhya	asaṃkhya
asamkhyeya	asaṃkhyeya
asamskrita	asaṃskṛta
Asanga	Asaṅga
ashoka	aśoka
Ashoka	Aśoka
ashtānga-mārga	aṣṭāṅga-mārga
ashtāngika-mārga	aṣṭāṅgika-mārga
Ashtasāhasrikā-prajnāpāramitā	Aṣṭasāhasrikā-prajñāpāramitā
ashva	aśva
Ashvaghosha	Aśvaghoṣa
Ashvajit	Aśvajit
Ashvaka	Aśvaka
Ashvakarna	Aśvakarṇa
ashvashīrsha	aśvaśīrṣa
ashvattha	aśvattha
Atata	Aṭaṭa
Ātavaka	Āṭavaka

Atīsha	Atīśa
atthangika-magga	aṭṭhaṅgika-magga
Avalokiteshvara	Avalokiteśvara
Avatamsaka	Avataṃsaka
Avīchi	Avīci
Avriha	Avṛha
avyākrita	avyākṛta
Bahushrutīya	Bahuśrutīya
Bāna	Bāṇa
Bandhushrī	Bandhuśrī
Bārānasī	Bārāṇasī
Bhadraruchi	Bhadraruci
bhaishajya	bhaiṣajya
Bhaishajyaguru	Bhaiṣajyaguru
Bhaishajyaguru-vaidūryaprabharāja-sūtra	Bhaiṣajyaguru-vaiḍūryaprabharāja-sūtra
Bhaishajyarāja	Bhaiṣajyarāja
Bhaishajyarājasamudgata	Bhaiṣajyarājasamudgata
Bhaishajyasamudgata	Bhaiṣajyasamudgata
bhikshu	bhikṣu
bhikshunī	bhikṣuṇī
Bhīshma-garjita-svara-rāja	Bhīṣma-garjita-svara-rāja
bodhi-chitta	bodhi-citta
bodhimanda	bodhimaṇḍa
Bodhiruchi	Bodhiruci
bodhyanga	bodhyaṅga
brahma-charya	brahma-carya
brahma-charyā	brahma-caryā
brāhmana	brāhmaṇa
Brihadratha	Bṛhadratha
Brihatphala	Bṛhatphala
Buddha-avatamsaka-nāma-mahāvaipulya-sūtra	Buddha-avataṃsaka-nāma-mahāvaipulya-sūtra
Buddhacharita	Buddhacarita
buddha-kshetra	buddha-kṣetra
Buddhalochanā	Buddhalocanā
Buddhashānta	Buddhaśānta
Buddha-shāsana	Buddha-śāsana
Buddhasimha	Buddhasiṃha
Buddhayashas	Buddhayaśas
Chaityavādin	Caityavādin
chakkavattin	cakkavattin
chakra	cakra
Chakravāda	Cakravāḍa
Chakravāda-parvata	Cakravāḍa-parvata
chakravartin	cakravartin

chakravarti-rāja	cakravarti-rāja
chakravarti-rājan	cakravarti-rājan
chakshur-vijnāna	cakṣur-vijñāna
Champā	Campā
champaka	campaka
chandāla	caṇḍāla
chandana	candana
chandra	candra
Chandra	Candra
Chandragupta	Candragupta
Chandrakīrti	Candrakīrti
Chandraprabha	Candraprabha
Chandra-sūrya-pradīpa	Candra-sūrya-pradīpa
Chandra-sūrya-vimala-prabhāsa-shrī	Candra-sūrya-vimala-prabhāsa-śrī
Chandrayashas	Candrayaśas
Charaka	Caraka
Charaka-samhitā	Caraka-saṃhitā
chāritra	cāritra
Chārvāka	Cārvāka
Charyā-tantra	Caryā-tantra
chatur-ārya-satya	catur-ārya-satya
chatur-dhyāna	catur-dhyāna
Chātur-mahārāja-kāyika	Cātur-mahārāja-kāyika
Chedi	Ceḍi
Cheka	Ceka
Chinchā	Ciñcā
Chinchāmānavikā	Ciñcāmāṇavikā
chintāmani	cintāmaṇi
Chitrabhāna	Citrabhāna
chitta	citta
chūda	cūḍa
Chūdapanthaka	Cūḍapanthaka
Chūlapanthaka	Cūḷapanthaka
Chūlavamsa	Cūḷavaṃsa
Chunda	Cunda
Dandaka	Daṇḍaka
Dandaloka	Daṇḍaloka
darshana-mārga	darśana-mārga
Dashabala Kāshyapa	Daśabala Kāśyapa
dasha-bhūmi	daśa-bhūmi
Dashabhūmika-sūtra	Daśabhūmika-sūtra
deshanā	deśanā
dhāranī	dhāraṇī
dharma-chakra	dharma-cakra
Dharmagathayashas	Dharmagathayaśas
Dharmaraksha	Dharmarakṣa

Dharmāranya	Dharmāraṇya
Dharmaruchi	Dharmaruci
Dharmashreshthin	Dharmaśreṣṭhin
Dharmashrī	Dharmaśrī
Dharmayashas	Dharmayaśas
dhri	dhṛ
Dhritaka	Dhṛtaka
Dhritarāshtra	Dhṛtarāṣṭra
Dīpamkara	Dīpaṃkara
Dīpavamsa	Dīpavaṃsa
Dona	Doṇa
Drona	Droṇa
Dronodana	Droṇodana
duhukha	duḥkha
dvesha	dveṣa
Ekādasha-mukha	Ekādaśa-mukha
eranda	eraṇḍa
evam mayā shrutam	evaṃ mayā śrutam
Gamgadasvara	Gaṃgadasvara
gandhakutī	gandhakuṭī
Gangā	Gaṅgā
Gangadasvara	Gaṅgadasvara
Gangā-nadī-vālikā	Gaṅgā-naḍī-vālikā
Gangā-nadī-vālukā	Gaṅgā-naḍī-vālukā
garuda	garuḍa
Gayā Kāshyapa	Gayā Kāśyapa
Gayāshīrsha	Gayāśīrṣa
ghosha	ghoṣa
Ghoshila	Ghoṣila
Ghoshila-vihāra	Ghoṣila-vihāra
ghrāna-vijnāna	ghrāṇa-vijñāna
Gijjhakūta	Gijjhakūṭa
goshīrsha	gośīrṣa
goshīrsha-chandana	gośīrṣa-candana
gridhra	gṛdhra
Gridhrakūta	Gṛdhrakūṭa
griha	gṛha
griha-pati	gṛha-pati
guna	guṇa
Gunabhadra	Guṇabhadra
Gunamati	Guṇamati
Gunaprabha	Guṇaprabha
Gunavarman	Guṇavarman
Haklenayasha	Haklenayaśa
Haklenayashas	Haklenayaśas
Harsha	Harṣa

Harsha-charita	Harṣa-carita
Harshavardhana	Harṣavardhana
himsā	hiṃsā
Hiranyavatī	Hiraṇyavatī
Īshādhāra	Īśādhāra
Īshāna	Īśāna
īshvara	īśvara
itivrittaka	itivṛttaka
Jaladhara-garjita-ghosha-susvara-nakshatra-rāja-samkusumitābhijnā	Jaladhara-garjita-ghoṣa-susvara-nakṣatra-rāja-saṃkusumitābhijñā
jala-mandala	jala-maṇḍala
jarā-marana	jarā-maraṇa
Jatimdhara	Jaṭiṃdhara
Jetri	Jetṛ
jihvā-vijnāna	jihvā-vijñāna
jīvamjīva	jīvaṃjīva
jīvamjīvaka	jīvaṃjīvaka
Jnānabhadra	Jñānabhadra
Jnānachandra	Jñānacandra
Jnānagupta	Jñānagupta
Jnānākara	Jñānākara
Jnānaprabha	Jñānaprabha
Jnānayasha	Jñānayaśa
Kacchāna	Kaccāna
Kacchāyana	Kaccāyana
kalavinka	kalaviṅka
Kālayashas	Kālayaśas
Kāli	Kāḷi
Kalinga	Kaliṅga
Kalmāshapāda	Kalmāṣapāda
Kalpanā-manditikā	Kalpanā-maṇḍitikā
kalyāna-mitra	kalyāṇa-mitra
Kamalashīla	Kamalaśīla
kāna	kāṇa
Kanāda	Kaṇāda
Kānadeva	Kāṇadeva
kānchana	kāñcana
kānchana-mandala	kāñcana-maṇḍala
Kanishka	Kaniṣka
Kanthaka	Kaṇṭhaka
Kapisha	Kapiśa
karunā	karuṇā
Karunā-pundarīka-sūtra	Karuṇā-puṇḍarīka-sūtra
Kāshī	Kāśī
Kashmīra	Kaśmīra
Kāshmīra	Kāśmīra

Kāshyapa	Kāśyapa
Kāshyapa Mātanga	Kāśyapa Mātaṅga
Kāshyapīya	Kāśyapīya
Kaukkutika	Kaukkuṭika
Kaundinya	Kauṇḍinya
Kaushāmbī	Kauśāmbī
Kaushika	Kauśika
kāya-vijnāna	kāya-vijñāna
Keshinī	Keśinī
Kharoshthī	Kharoṣṭhī
kimnara	kiṃnara
Kinkara	Kiṅkara
klesha	kleśa
klesha-māra	kleśa-māra
Koshala	Kośala
koti	koṭi
Kriki	Kṛki
Krishna	Kṛṣṇa
Krita	Kṛta
krosha	krośa
kritya	kṛtya
kshama	kṣama
kshana	kṣaṇa
kshānti	kṣānti
Kshāntivādin	Kṣāntivādin
Kshatriya	Kṣatriya
kshetra	kṣetra
kshiti	kṣiti
Kshitigarbha	Kṣitigarbha
Kukkutapada	Kukkuṭapada
Kukkutapāda	Kukkuṭapāda
Kukkutārāma	Kukkuṭārāma
kula-duhitri	kula-duhitṛ
Kumārayāna	Kumārayāṇa
kumbhānda	kumbhāṇḍa
Kundalī	Kuṇḍalī
kunkuma	kuṅkuma
Kurkutārāma	Kurkuṭārāma
kusha	kuśa
kushala-mūla	kuśala-mūla
Kushāna	Kuṣāṇa
Kushinagara	Kuśinagara
Kusuma-tala-garbha-vyūhālamkāra-loka-dhātu-samudra	Kusuma-tala-garbha-vyūhālaṃkāra-loka-dhātu-samudra
kūta	kūṭa
Kūtadantī	Kūṭadantī

Lakshmī	Lakṣmī
Lankā	Laṅkā
Lankāvatāra-sūtra	Laṅkāvatāra-sūtra
Lokakshema	Lokakṣema
Lokeshvararāja	Lokeśvararāja
Madhyamaka-hridaya	Madhyamaka-hṛdaya
Mādhyamika-shāstra	Mādhyamika-śāstra
Mahābhijnā-jnānābhibhū	Mahābhijñā-jñānābhibhū
Mahākacchāna	Mahākaccāna
Mahākacchāyana	Mahākaccāyana
Mahākāshyapa	Mahākāśyapa
mahāparinirvāna	mahāparinirvāṇa
mahāprajnā	mahāprajñā
Mahāprajnāpāramitā-shāstra	Mahāprajñāpāramitā-śāstra
Mahāprajnāpāramitā-sūtra	Mahāprajñāpāramitā-sūtra
Mahāpranāda	Mahāpraṇāda
Mahāsamghika	Mahāsaṃghika
Mahāsāmghika	Mahāsāṃghika
Mahāsammata	Mahāsaṃmata
Mahāsanghika	Mahāsaṅghika
Mahāsānghika	Mahāsāṅghika
Mahāshrī	Mahāśrī
Mahāvairochana	Mahāvairocana
Mahāvamsa	Mahāvaṃsa
Mahayana	Mahāyāna
Mahāyāna-samgraha	Mahāyāna-saṃgraha
Mahāyāna-sūtrālamkāra	Mahāyāna-sūtrālaṃkāra
Maheshvara	Maheśvara
Mahīshāsaka	Mahīśāsaka
Makutadantī	Makuṭadantī
Mānava	Māṇava
Mānavaka	Māṇavaka
mānavikā	māṇavikā
mandala	maṇḍala
Māndhātri	Māndhātṛ
mani	maṇi
manjūshaka	mañjūṣaka
Manjushrī	Mañjuśrī
mano-vijnāna	mano-vijñāna
Marīchi	Marīci
Maskarin Goshālin	Maskarin Gośālin
Maskarin Goshālīputra	Maskarin Gośālīputra
Mātanga	Mātaṅga
Micchaca	Miccaca
Milindapanha	Milindapañha
Mitrayashas	Mitrayaśas

moksha	mokṣa
mriga	mṛga
Mrigadāva	Mṛgadāva
mrityu-māra	mṛtyu-māra
Munishrī	Muniśrī
Nadī Kāshyapa	Nadī Kāśyapa
Nairanjanā	Nairañjanā
Naivasamjnānāsamjnā	Naivasaṃjñānāsaṃjñā
Naivasamjnānāsamjnāyatana	Naivasaṃjñānāsaṃjñāyatana
Nakshatra-rāja-samkusumitābhijna	Nakṣatra-rāja-saṃkusumitābhijña
Nārāyana	Nārāyaṇa
Narendrayashas	Narendrayaśas
Neranjarā	Nerañjarā
Nigantha Nātaputta	Nigaṇṭha Nātaputta
Nimimdhara	Nimiṃdhara
nirdesha	nirdeśa
Nirgrantha Jnātiputra	Nirgrantha Jñātiputra
nirmāna-kāya	nirmāṇa-kāya
Nirmānarati	Nirmāṇarati
nirvāna	nirvāṇa
om	oṃ
Padmasambhava	Padmasaṃbhava
Pakudha Kacchāyana	Pakudha Kaccāyana
pāmsu-kūla	pāṃsu-kūla
pancha-indriya	pañca-indriya
Panchāla	Pañcāla
pancha-skandha	pañca-skandha
Panchavimshatisāhasrikā-prajnāpāramitā	Pañcaviṃśatisāhasrikā-prajñāpāramitā
pāni	pāṇi
Paranirmita-vasha-vartin	Paranirmita-vaśa-vartin
parināma	pariṇāma
parināmana	pariṇāmana
parinirvāna	parinirvāṇa
Parīttashubha	Parīttaśubha
Pārshva	Pārśva
pātala	pāṭala
Pātaliputra	Pāṭaliputra
paticcha-samuppāda	paṭicca-samuppāda
pavāranā	pavāraṇā
Pindola	Piṇḍola
Pindolabhāradvāja	Piṇḍolabhāradvāja
Pingala	Piṅgala
pishacha	piśāca
pitaka	piṭaka
Piyankara	Piyaṅkara

poshadha	poṣadha
prajnā	prajñā
Prajnā	Prajñā
Prajnākūta	Prajñākūṭa
prajnā-pāramitā	prajñā-pāramitā
Prajnāpāramitā-hridaya-sūtra	Prajñāpāramitā-hṛdaya-sūtra
Prajnā-pradīpa	Prajñā-pradīpa
Prajnaptivādin	Prajñaptivādin
Prajnāptivādin	Prajñāptivādin
Prajnāruchi	Prajñāruci
pranidhāna	praṇidhāna
Prāsangika	Prāsaṅgika
pratishthāna	pratiṣṭhāna
Pratyutpanna-buddha-sammukhāvasthita-samādhi-sūtra	Pratyutpanna-buddha-saṃmukhāvasthita-samādhi-sūtra
pravārana	pravāraṇa
pravāranā	pravāraṇā
prithag-jana	pṛthag-jana
Priyankara	Priyaṅkara
pundarīka	puṇḍarīka
Punna	Puṇṇa
punya	puṇya
punya-kshetra	puṇya-kṣetra
Punyamitra	Puṇyamitra
punya-paryāya	puṇya-paryāya
Punyaprasava	Puṇyaprasava
Punyatāra	Puṇyatāra
Punyayashas	Puṇyayaśas
Pūrana	Pūraṇa
Pūrana Kāshyapa	Pūraṇa Kāśyapa
Pūrana Kassapa	Pūraṇa Kassapa
Pūrna	Pūrṇa
Pūrna Maitrāyanīputra	Pūrṇa Maitrāyaṇīputra
purusha-damya-sārathi	puruṣa-damya-sārathi
Purushapura	Puruṣapura
pūrvapranidhāna	pūrvapraṇidhāna
pushpa	puṣpa
Pushpadantī	Puṣpadantī
Pushyamitra	Puṣyamitra
Rājagriha	Rājagṛha
rākshasa	rākṣasa
rākshasī	rākṣasī
rashmi	raśmi
Rashmiprabhāsa	Raśmiprabhāsa
Rashmi-shatasahasra-paripūrna-dhvaja	Raśmi-śatasahasra-paripūrṇa-dhvaja

Rāshtrapāla	Rāṣṭrapāla
Ratnagotravibhāga-mahāyānottaratantra-shāstra	Ratnagotravibhāga-mahāyānottaratantra-śāstra
riddhi	ṛddhi
riddhi-pāda	ṛddhi-pāda
Rigveda	Ṛgveda
Rishabha	Ṛṣabha
rishi	ṛṣi
Rishipatana	Ṛṣipatana
Rohana	Rohaṇa
Ruchi	Ruci
Saddharma-pundarīka-sūtra	Saddharma-puṇḍarīka-sūtra
Saddharma-pundarīka-upadesha	Saddharma-puṇḍarīka-upadeśa
shad-gati	ṣaḍ-gati
Sāgara-vara-dhara-buddhi-vikrīditābhijna	Sāgara-vara-dhara-buddhi-vikrīḍitābhijña
sakridāgāmin	sakṛdāgāmin
samana	samaṇa
sāmanera	sāmaṇera
sāmanerī	sāmaṇerī
Samaya-bhedoparachana-chakra	Samaya-bhedoparacana-cakra
sambhoga-kāya	saṃbhoga-kāya
sambodhi	saṃbodhi
Samdhinirmochana-sūtra	Saṃdhinirmocana-sūtra
samgha	saṃgha
Samghabhadra	Saṃghabhadra
Samghabhūti	Saṃghabhūti
Samghadeva	Saṃghadeva
Samghamitrā	Saṃghamitrā
Samghanandi	Saṃghanandi
Samgharakshita	Saṃgharakṣita
samghātī	saṃghāṭī
Samghavarman	Saṃghavarman
samghāvashesha	saṃghāvaśeṣa
Samghayashas	Saṃghayaśas
samgīti	saṃgīti
Samjayin Vairatīputra	Saṃjayin Vairaṭīputra
Samjīva	Saṃjīva
Sāmkhya	Sāṃkhya
Sammatīya	Saṃmatīya
samsāra	saṃsāra
samskāra	saṃskāra
samyak-sambodhi	samyak-saṃbodhi
samyak-sambuddha	samyak-saṃbuddha
samyojana	saṃyojana
Samyutta-nikāya	Saṃyutta-nikāya

sangha	saṅgha
Sanjaya	Sañjaya
Sanjaya Belatthiputta	Sañjaya Belaṭṭhiputta
Saptaparna	Saptaparṇa
Saptaparnaguhā	Saptaparṇaguhā
Sarva-sattva-priyadarshana	Sarva-sattva-priyadarśana
Sarvatathāgata-tattvasamgraha	Sarvatathāgata-tattvasaṃgraha
Satyasiddhi-shāstra	Satyasiddhi-śāstra
shad-āyatana	ṣaḍ-āyatana
shad-gati	ṣaḍ-gati
shad-indriya	ṣaḍ-indriya
Shāketa	Śāketa
shakra	śakra
Shakra	Śakra
Shakra Devānām Indra	Śakra Devānām Indra
Shakrāditya	Śakrāditya
Shākya	Śākya
Shakyamuni	Śākyamuni
shāla	śāla
Shānakavāsa	Śāṇakavāsa
Shānakavāsin	Śāṇakavāsin
Shānavāsa	Śāṇavāsa
Shāṇavāsin	Śāṇavāsin
Shankhāchārya	Śaṅkhācārya
Shannāgarika	Ṣaṇṇāgarika
Shāntarakshita	Śāntarakṣita
Shārī	Śārī
Shāriputra	Śāriputra
sharīra	śarīra
shāsana	śāsana
Shashiketu	Śaśiketu
shāstā-deva-manushyānām	śāstā-deva-manuṣyānāṃ
shatru	śatru
Shibi	Śibi
Shikhin	Śikhin
shikshamānā	śikṣamāṇā
Shikshānanda	Śikṣānanda
shīla	śīla
Shīlabhadra	Śīlabhadra
Shīlāditya	Śīlāditya
shīrsha	śīrṣa
Shītā	Śītā
Shītavana	Śītavana
Shiva	Śiva
shloka	śloka
shraddhā	śraddhā

shramana	śramaṇa
shrāmanera	śrāmaṇera
shrāmanerī	śrāmaṇerī
shrāmanerikā	śrāmaṇerikā
shrāvaka	śrāvaka
shrāvaka-yāna	śrāvaka-yāna
Shrāvastī	Śrāvastī
Shrīmahādevī	Śrīmahādevī
Shrīmālā	Śrīmālā
Shrīmālādevī-simhanāda-sūtra	Śrīmālādevī-siṃhanāda-sūtra
Shrīvijaya	Śrīvijaya
shrota-vijnāna	śrota-vijñāna
Shrutasoma	Śrutasoma
Shubhakarasimha	Śubhakarasiṃha
Shubhakritsna	Śubhakṛtsna
Shubhavyūha	Śubhavyūha
Shuddhachandra	Śuddhacandra
shuddhāvāsa	śuddhāvāsa
Shuddhodana	Śuddhodana
Shūdra	Śūdra
Shuklodana	Śuklodana
Shunga	Śuṅga
shūnya	śūnya
shūnyatā	śūnyatā
shūramgama	śūraṃgama
Shūramgama	Śūraṃgama
shūramgama-samādhi	śūraṃgama-samādhi
Shūrasena	Śūrasena
Shūryasoma	Śūryasoma
Siddham	Siddhaṃ
simha	siṃha
Simhahanu	Siṃhahanu
simhanāda	siṃhanāda
Simhanādarāja	Siṃhanādarāja
simhāsana	siṃhāsana
smriti	smṛti
sparsha	sparśa
Sudarshana	Sudarśana
Sudhana-shreshthi-dāraka	Sudhana-śreṣṭhi-dāraka
Sudrisha	Sudṛśa
Sunakshatra	Sunakṣatra
Supratishthitachāritra	Supratiṣṭhitacāritra
Sutta Pitaka	Sutta Piṭaka
Suvarnaprabhāsa-sūtra	Suvarṇaprabhāsa-sūtra
Suvarnaprabhāsottama-sūtra	Suvarṇaprabhāsottama-sūtra
Takshaka	Takṣaka

Takshashilā	Takṣaśilā
Tamālapatra-chandana-gandha	Tamālapatra-candana-gandha
Tamālapattra-chandana-gandha	Tamālapattra-candana-gandha
tipitaka	tipiṭaka
Trāyastrimsha	Trāyastriṃśa
Trimshikā-vijnaptimātratā-siddhi	Triṃśikā-vijñaptimātratā-siddhi
tripitaka	tripiṭaka
Tushita	Tuṣita
Tvashtri	Tvaṣṭṛ
Ucchushma	Ucchuṣma
Uddiyāna	Uḍḍiyāna
Udra	Uḍra
upadesha	upadeśa
upasampadā	upasaṃpadā
Upatishya	Upatiṣya
upekshā	upekṣā
uposhadha	upoṣadha
Uppalavannā	Uppalavaṇṇā
Urumanda	Urumaṇḍa
Urumunda	Urumuṇḍa
ūrnā-kesha	ūrṇā-keśa
ūrnā-kosha	ūrṇā-kośa
Uruvilvā Kāshyapa	Uruvilvā Kāśyapa
ushnīsha-shiraskatā	uṣnīṣa-śiraskatā
Utpalavarnā	Utpalavarṇā
uttarāsanga	uttarāsaṅga
Uttarashaila	Uttaraśaila
Vairanjā	Vairañjā
Vairochana	Vairocana
Vaishālī	Vaiśālī
vaishāradya	vaiśāradya
Vaisheshika	Vaiśeṣika
Vaishravana	Vaiśravaṇa
Vaishya	Vaiśya
Vajracchedikā-prajnāpāramitā	Vajracchedikā-prajñāpāramitā
vajrapāni	vajrapāṇi
Vajrashekhara	Vajraśekhara
Vakshu	Vakṣu
vamsa	vaṃsa
Vārānasī	Vārāṇasī
varsha	varṣa
Varshakāra	Varṣakāra
vārshika	vārṣika
Vāshpa	Vāṣpa
vāyu-mandala	vāyu-maṇḍala
Vemachitrin	Vemacitrin

venu	veṇu
Venuvana	Veṇuvana
Venuvana-vihāra	Veṇuvana-vihāra
vetāda	vetāḍa
veyyākarana	veyyākaraṇa
vibhāshā	vibhāṣā
Vidūdabha	Viḍūḍabha
vidyā-charana-sampanna	vidyā-caraṇa-saṃpanna
vijnāna	vijñāna
Vijnānānantya	Vijñānānantya
Vijnānānantyāyatana	Vijñānānantyāyatana
Vijnānavāda	Vijñānavāda
Vikramashilā	Vikramaśilā
Vimalakīrti-nirdesha	Vimalakīrti-nirdeśa
vimoksha	vimokṣa
Vimshatikā-vijnaptimātratā-siddhi	Viṃśatikā-vijñaptimātratā-siddhi
Vimuktichandra	Vimukticandra
Vipashyin	Vipaśyin
Virūdhaka	Virūḍhaka
Virūpāksha	Virūpākṣa
Visheshamitra	Viśeṣamitra
Vishishtachāritra	Viśiṣṭacāritra
Vishnu	Viṣṇu
Vishuddhachāritra	Viśuddhacāritra
Vishvabhū	Viśvabhū
Vishvakarman	Viśvakarman
Vriji	Vṛji
Vritra	Vṛtra
vyākarana	vyākaraṇa
yaksha	yakṣa
Yasa Kākandakaputta	Yasa Kākaṇḍakaputta
Yasha	Yaśa
Yashas	Yaśas
Yashasketu	Yaśasketu
Yashoda	Yaśoda
Yashodharā	Yaśodharā
Yashomitra	Yaśomitra
Yogāchāra	Yogācāra
Yogāchārabhūmi	Yogācārabhūmi
Yugamdhara	Yugaṃdhara

APPENDIX B

Chinese Proper Names

Each column lists in alphabetical order the Chinese proper names appearing in this dictionary with their corresponding Chinese characters in parentheses. Immediately following are the pinyin equivalents. With a very few exceptions, the Chinese words found in the body of the dictionary have been romanized according to the Wade-Giles system.

An Fa-ch'in (安法欽) — An Faqin
An-hsi (安息) — Anxi
An Hsüan (安玄) — An Xuan
An Shih-kao (安世高) — An Shigao
Ch'an (禅) — Chan
Chang-an (章安) — Zhang'an
Ch'ang-an (長安) — Chang'an
Chang Ch'ien (張騫) — Zhang Qian
Chang Fu (張輔) — Zhang Fu
Chang-kuo (張果) — Zhangguo
Ch'ang-ting-ssu (昌定寺) — Changdingsi
Chan-jan (湛然) — Zhanran
Ch'an-lin-ssu (禅林寺) — Chanlinsi
Chao, King (昭王) — Zhao, King
Chao Kuei-chen (趙帰真) — Zhao Guizhen
Ch'en (dynasty) (陳) — Chen
Ch'en Chen (陳鍼) — Chen Zhen
Ch'eng-kuan (澄觀) — Chengguan
Ch'eng-shih (school) (成実) — Chengshi
Ch'eng-shih-tsung (成実宗) — Chengshizong
Chen-kuan (era) (貞観) — Zhenguan
Chen-tsung, Emperor (真宗) — Zhenzong, Emperor
Chen-yen (school) (真言) — Zhenyan
Chen-yüan (era) (貞元) — Zhenyuan
Ch'i (dynasty) (斉) — Qi
Chia-hsiang (嘉祥) — Jiaxiang
Chia-hsiang-ssu (嘉祥寺) — Jiaxiangsi
Chia-ts'ai (迦才) — Jiacai
Chi-ch'ieh-yeh (吉伽夜) — Jiqieye
Chi-chung (継忠) — Jizhong
Chien-chen (鑑真) — Jianzhen
Chien-chih (鑑智) — Jianzhi
Chien-ch'u-ssu (建初寺) — Jianchusi
Ch'ien-fu-ssu (千福寺) — Qianfusi
Chien-k'ang (建康) — Jiankang
Ch'ien-t'ang (銭塘) — Qiantang
Chien-yeh (建業) — Jianye
Chien-yüan (鑑源) — Jianyuan
Chih-chi (智寂) — Zhiji
Chih-ch'ien (支謙) — Zhiqian
Chih-chou (智周) — Zhizhou
Chih-i (智顗) — Zhiyi
Chih-kuan-ssu (止観寺) — Zhiguansi
Chih-li (知礼) — Zhili
Chih-liang (支亮) — Zhiliang
Chih-p'an (志磐) — Zhipan
Chih-pien (智弁) — Zhibian
Chih-sheng (智昇) — Zhisheng
Chih-shou (智首) — Zhishou
Chih-tsang (智蔵) — Zhizang
Chih-tu (智度) — Zhidu
Chih-wei (智威) — Zhiwei
Chih-yen (智厳・智儼) — Zhiyan

Chih-yin（志因）— Zhiyin
Chih-yüan（志遠）— Zhiyuan
Chih-yüan（智円）— Zhiyuan
Ch'in-chou（秦州）— Qinzhou
Ch'ing (dynasty)（清）— Qing
Ch'ing-chao（慶昭）— Qingzhao
Ching-chou（荊州）— Jingzhou
Ching-hsi（荊渓）— Jingxi
Ch'ing-liang（清涼）— Qingliang
Ch'ing-liang, Mt.（清涼山）— Qingliang, Mt.
Ch'ing-lung-ssu（青竜寺）— Qinglongsi
Ch'ing-sung（清竦）— Qingsong
Ching-te (era)（景徳）— Jingde
Ching-t'u (school)（浄土）— Jingtu
Ching-t'u-ssu（浄土寺）— Jingtusi
Ching-tz'u-ssu（浄慈寺）— Jingcisi
Ching-yeh-ssu（浄業寺）— Jingyesi
Ching-ying-ssu（浄影寺）— Jingyingsi
Chin-hua-ssu（金華寺）— Jinhuasi
Chin-kang-chih（金剛智）— Jingangzhi
Chin-ko-ssu（金閣寺）— Jingesi
Ch'in-kuang（秦広）— Qinguang
Chin-ling（金陵）— Jinling
Ch'in-tsung, Emperor（欽宗）— Qinzong, Emperor
Chi-tsang（吉蔵）— Jizang
Chiu-hua, Mt.（九華山）— Jiuhua, Mt.
Cho-an Te-kuang（拙庵徳光）— Zhouan Deguang
Chou (dynasty)（周）— Zhou
Ch'ü (clan)（麴〔氏〕）— Qu
Chuang Tzu（荘子）— Zhuangzi
Chuang-yen-ssu（荘厳寺）— Zhuangyansi
Ch'üan-ya（全雅）— Quanya
Chu Chiang-yen（竺将炎）— Zhu Jiangyan
Chü-ch'ü Meng-hsün（沮渠蒙遜）— Juqu Mengxun
Chu Fa-lan（竺法蘭）— Zhu Falan
Chu Fo-nien（竺仏念）— Zhu Fonian
Chün-cheng（均正）— Junzheng
Chung-nan-shan（終南山）— Zhongnanshan
Chü-she (school)（倶舎）— Jushe
Chü-she-tsung（倶舎宗）— Jushezong
Chu Tao-sheng（竺道生）— Zhu Daosheng
Ch'u-yüan（楚円）— Chuyuan
E-mei, Mt.（峨眉山）— Emei, Mt.
Fa-chao（法照）— Fazhao
Fa-chin（法進）— Fajin
Fa-chü（法炬）— Faju
Fa-ch'üan（法全）— Faquan
Fa-hsiang (school)（法相）— Faxiang
Fa-hsiang-tsung（法相宗）— Faxiang-zong
Fa-hsien（法顕・法賢）— Faxian
Fa-hsü（法緒）— Faxu
Fa-hua-tsung（法華宗）— Fahuazong
Fa-lang（法朗）— Falang
Fa-li（法立）— Fali
Fa-liang（法良）— Faliang
Fang-hui（方会）— Fanghui
Fa-pao（法宝）— Fabao
Fa-shun（法順）— Fashun
Fa-t'ai（法汰）— Fatai
Fa-tao（法道）— Fadao
Fa-t'i-mo-to（筏提摩多）— Fatimoduo
Fa-tsang（法蔵）— Fazang
Fa-tsu（法祖）— Fazu
Fa-yen (school)（法眼）— Fayan
Fa-yen Wen-i（法眼文益）— Fayan Wenyi
Fa-yün（法雲）— Fayun
Fa-yün-ssu（法雲寺）— Fayunsi
Fo-kung-ssu（仏宮寺）— Fogongsi
Fo-lung (Monastery)（仏隴）— Folong
Fo-lung-ssu（仏隴寺）— Folongsi
Fo-shou-chi-ssu（仏授記寺）— Foshoujisi
Fo-t'u-teng（仏図澄）— Fotudeng
Fu Chien（符堅）— Fu Jian

Fu Hsi (傅翕・伏羲) — Fu Xi
Fu Ta-shih (傅大士) — Fu Dashi
Hang-chou (杭州) — Hangzhou
Han-kuang (含光) — Hanguang
Hsiang, Mt. (香山) — Xiang, Mt.
Hsiang-yang (襄陽) — Xiangyang
Hsiao-jan (翛然) — Xiaoran
Hsiao-wen, Emperor (孝文帝) — Xiaowen, Emperor
Hsiao-yüeh-chih (小月支) — Xiaoyuezhi
Hsieh Ling-yün (謝霊運) — Xie Lingyun
Hsieh-ssu (謝寺) — Xiesi
Hsien-shou (賢首) — Xianshou
Hsi-hsia (西夏) — Xixia
Hsi-ming-ssu (西明寺) — Ximingsi
Hsing-huang (興皇) — Xinghuang
Hsing-huang-ssu (興皇寺) — Xinghuangsi
Hsing-man (行満) — Xingman
Hsing-shan-ssu (興善寺) — Xingshansi
Hsing-ssu (行思) — Xingsi
Hsin-hsing (信行) — Xinxing
Hsiu-ch'an-ssu (修禅寺) — Xiuchansi
Hsiung-nu (匈奴) — Xiongnu
Hsüan, Emperor (宣帝) — Xuan, Emperor
Hsüan-chung-ssu (玄中寺) — Xuanzhongsi
Hsüan-lang (玄朗) — Xuanlang
Hsüan-tsang (玄奘) — Xuanzang
Hsüan-tsung, Emperor (玄宗) — Xuanzong, Emperor
Hsüan-ying (玄応) — Xuanying
Huai-jang (懐譲) — Huairang
Huai-kan (懐感) — Huaigan
Huai-yün (懐惲) — Huaiyun
Hua-jung (華容) — Huarong
Huang-lung (school) (黄竜) — Huanglong
Huang-po, Mt. (黄檗山) — Huangbo, Mt.
Huan Hsüan (桓玄) — Huan Xuan
Hua-tu-ssu (化度寺) — Huadusi
Hua-yen (school) (華厳) — Huayan
Hua-yen-tsung (華厳宗) — Huayanzong
Hui-ch'ang (era) (会昌) — Huichang
Hui-chao (慧沼) — Huizhao
Hui-chi (慧寂) — Huiji
Hui-chiao (慧皎) — Huijiao
Hui-chüeh (慧覚) — Huijue
Hui-chün (慧均) — Huijun
Hui-k'o (慧可) — Huike
Hui-kuan (慧観) — Huiguan
Hui-kuang (慧光) — Huiguang
Hui-kuo (恵果) — Huiguo
Hui-li (慧立・慧力) — Huili
Hui-lin (慧琳) — Huilin
Hui-man (慧満) — Huiman
Hui-nan (慧南) — Huinan
Hui-neng (慧能) — Huineng
Hui-ning (会寧) — Huining
Hui-pu (慧布) — Huibu
Hui-ssu (慧思) — Huisi
Hui-tsung, Emperor (徽宗) — Huizong, Emperor
Hui-tz'u (慧次) — Huici
Hui-wei (慧威) — Huiwei
Hui-wen (慧文) — Huiwen
Hui-yen (慧厳) — Huiyan
Hui-yüan (慧遠・慧苑) — Huiyuan
Hui-yung (慧勇) — Huiyong
Hung-ch'eng (弘称) — Hongcheng
Hung-fu-ssu (弘福寺) — Hongfusi
Hung-jen (弘忍) — Hongren
I-chen (義真) — Yizhen
I-chi (義寂) — Yiji
I-ching (義浄) — Yijing
I-hsing (一行) — Yixing
I-hsüan (義玄) — Yixuan
I-jan (逸然) — Yiran
I-lin (義林) — Yilin
I-lung (遺竜) — Yilong
I-shan I-ning (一山一寧) — Yishan Yining
I-t'ung (義通) — Yitong
Jih-chao (日照) — Rizhao
Ju-ching (如浄) — Rujing

Ju-pao (如宝) — Rubao
K'ai-pao-ssu (開宝寺) — Kaibaosi
K'ai-shan (開善) — Kaishan
K'ai-shan-ssu (開善寺) — Kaishansi
K'ai-yüan (era) (開元) — Kaiyuan
K'ai-yüan-ssu (開元寺) — Kaiyuansi
K'ai-yüeh-ssu (開岳寺) — Kaiyuesi
K'ang-chü (康居) — Kangju
K'ang-seng-hui (康僧会) — Kangsenghui
K'ang-seng-k'ai (康僧鎧) — Kangsengkai
Kansu (甘粛) — Gansu
Kao-ch'ang (高昌) — Gaochang
Kao-tsung, Emperor (高宗) — Gaozong, Emperor
Kua-chou (瓜州) — Guazhou
Kuang (広) — Guang
Kuang-che-ssu (光宅寺) — Guangzhesi
Kuang-chou (光州・広州) — Guangzhou
Kuang-hsiu (広脩) — Guangxiu
Kuan-shih-yin (観世音) — Guanshiyin
Kuan-ting (灌頂) — Guanding
Kuan-yin (観音) — Guanyin
K'uei-chi (窺基) — Kuiji
Kuei-feng (圭峰) — Guifeng
Kuei-yang (school) (潙仰) — Guiyang
Kuo-ch'ing-ssu (国清寺) — Guoqingsi
Kuo-yüan-ssu (果願寺) — Guoyuansi
Ku-tsang (姑蔵) — Guzang
Lan-ch'i (蘭渓) — Lanqi
Lan-ch'i Tao-lung (蘭渓道隆) — Lanqi Daolong
Lao Tzu (老子) — Laozi
Le-tsun (楽僔) — Lezun
Liang (dynasty) (梁) — Liang
Liang-chieh (良价) — Liangjie
Liang-chou (涼州) — Liangzhou
Liang-hsü (良諝) — Liangxu
Liang-pi (良賁) — Liangbi
Lien-tan, Mt. (錬丹山) — Liandan, Mt.
Lin-chi (school) (臨済) — Linji
Lin-chi I-hsüan (臨済義玄) — Linji Yixuan
Lin-chi-ssu (臨済寺) — Linjisi
Ling-chiu-shan (霊鷲山) — Lingjiushan
Lin-chi-yüan (臨済院) — Linjiyuan
Ling-kan-ssu (霊感寺) — Linggansi
Ling-yen-ssu (霊巌寺) — Lingyansi
Ling-yu (霊祐) — Lingyou
Liu Sung (dynasty) (劉宋) — Liu Song
Lou-lan (楼蘭) — Loulan
Lo-yang (洛陽) — Luoyang
Lu, Mt. (廬山) — Lu, Mt.
Lü (school) (律) — Lü
Lü Kuang (呂光) — Lü Guang
Lung-an (era) (隆安) — Longan
Lung-hsing-ssu (竜興寺) — Longxingsi
Lung-kuang-ssu (竜光寺) — Longguangsi
Lung-men (caves) (竜門石窟) — Longmen
Lung-yu (隴右) — Longyou
Lü-tsung (律宗) — Lüzong
Meng-hsün (蒙遜) — Mengxun
Miao-lo (妙楽) — Miaole
Miao-lo-ssu (妙楽寺) — Miaolesi
Ming (dynasty) (明) — Ming
Ming, Emperor (明帝) — Ming, Emperor
Ming-sha-shan (鳴沙山) — Mingshashan
Ming-sheng (明勝) — Mingsheng
Mo-ho-yen (摩訶衍) — Moheyan
Mo-kao (Caves) (莫高窟) — Mogao
Mu, King (穆王) — Mu, King
Nan-lin-ssu (南林寺) — Nanlinsi
Nan-shan (school) (南山) — Nanshan
Nan-tao (school) (南道) — Nandao
Nan-yü-chou (南予州) — Nanyuzhou
Nan-yüeh (南岳) — Nanyue

Nieh Ch'eng-yüan (聶承遠) — Nie Chengyuan
Nieh-p'an (school) (涅槃) — Niepan
Nieh-p'an-tsung (涅槃宗) — Niepanzong
Nieh Tao-chen (聶道真) — Nie Daozhen
Pai-lien-she (白蓮社) — Bailianshe
Pai-ma-ssu (白馬寺) — Baimasi
Pan-la-mi-ti (般刺蜜帝) — Banlamidi
Pao-ch'ang (宝唱) — Baochang
Pao-ch'eng-ssu (報城寺) — Baochengsi
Pao-chih (宝誌) — Baozhi
Pao-ching (宝静) — Baojing
Pao-kuei (宝貴) — Baogui
Pao-lin-ssu (宝林寺) — Baolinsi
Pao-shou-ssu (保寿寺) — Baoshousi
Pei-tao (school) (北道) — Beidao
Pen-chi (本寂) — Benji
Pien-ching (汴京) — Bianjing
P'ing-ch'eng (平城) — Pingcheng
Ping-chou (并州) — Bingzhou
P'i-t'an (school) (毘曇) — Pitan
P'i-t'an-tsung (毘曇宗) — Pitanzong
Po Fa-tsu (帛法祖) — Bo Fazu
Po-yüan (帛遠) — Boyuan
P'u-kuang (普光) — Puguang
Pu-k'ung (不空) — Bukong
Pu-tai (布袋) — Budai
P'u-t'o, Mt. (普陀山) — Putuo, Mt.
P'u-yang (濮陽) — Puyang
San-chieh (三階) — Sanjie
San-chieh-chiao (三階教) — Sanjiejiao
San-lun (school) (三論) — Sanlun
San-lun-tsung (三論宗) — Sanlunzong
Seng-chao (僧肇) — Sengzhao
Seng-chen (僧珍) — Sengzhen
Seng-chiu (僧就) — Sengjiu
Seng-ch'üan (僧詮) — Sengquan
Seng-hsiang (僧祥) — Sengxiang
Seng-hsien (僧賢) — Sengxian
Seng-jou (僧柔) — Sengrou
Seng-jui (僧叡) — Sengrui
Seng-lang (僧朗) — Senglang
Seng-min (僧旻) — Sengmin
Seng-sung (僧嵩) — Sengsong
Seng-tao (僧導) — Sengdao
Seng-ts'an (僧璨) — Sengcan
Seng-yin (僧印) — Sengyin
Seng-yu (僧祐) — Sengyou
Sha-chou (沙州) — Shazhou
Shan-chia (school) (山家) — Shanjia
Shan-chia-p'ai (山家派) — Shanjiapai
Shan-shan (鄯善) — Shanshan
Shan-tao (善導) — Shandao
Shan-wai (school) (山外) — Shanwai
Shan-wai-p'ai (山外派) — Shanwaipai
Shan-wu-wei (善無畏) — Shanwuwei
Shao-k'ang (少康) — Shaokang
Shao-lin-ssu (少林寺) — Shaolinsi
She-lun (school) (摂論) — Shelun
She-lun-tsung (摂論宗) — Shelunzong
Shen-hsiu (神秀) — Shenxiu
Shen-hui (神会) — Shenhui
Shen Nung (神農) — Shen Nong
Shen-t'ai (神泰) — Shentai
Shen-tsung, Emperor (神宗) — Shenzong, Emperor
Shen-t'ung-ssu (神通寺) — Shentongsi
Shih-tsung, Emperor (世宗) — Shizong, Emperor
Shuang-lin-ssu (双林寺) — Shuanglinsi
Shun-hsiao (順暁) — Shunxiao
Ssu-lun (school) (四論) — Silun
Ssu-ma (司馬) — Sima
Ssu-ma Ta-teng (司馬達等) — Sima Dadeng
Ssu-ming (四明) — Siming
Ssu-ming Chih-li (四明知礼) — Siming Zhili
Su-chou (蘇州) — Suzhou
Sui (dynasty) (隋) — Sui
Sun Ch'üan (孫権) — Sun Quan
Sung (dynasty) (宋) — Song
Sung, Mt. (嵩山) — Song, Mt.

Sung-ti (宋帝) — Songdi
Sung-yüeh-ssu (嵩岳寺) — Songyuesi
Ta-chin (大津) — Dajin
Ta-hsien, Mt. (大賢山) — Daxian, Mt.
Ta-hsing-shan-ssu (大興善寺) — Daxingshansi
Ta-hua-yen-ssu (大華厳寺) — Dahuayansi
T'ai-chou (台州) — Taizhou
T'ai-po, Mt. (太白山) — Taibo, Mt.
T'ai-shan (太山) — Taishan
T'ai-tsung, Emperor (太宗) — Taizong, Emperor
T'ai-wu, Emperor (太武帝) — Taiwu, Emperor
T'ai-yüan-ssu (太原寺) — Taiyuansi
Ta-li (era) (大暦) — Dali
Ta-ming-ssu (大明寺) — Damingsi
T'an-chi (曇済) — Tanji
T'an-ching (曇景) — Tanjing
T'ang (dynasty) (唐) — Tang
T'an-hsüeh (曇学) — Tanxue
T'an-lin (曇林) — Tanlin
T'an-luan (曇鸞) — Tanluan
T'an-yao (曇曜) — Tanyao
Tao-an (道安) — Daoan
Tao-ch'ang-ssu (道場寺) — Daochangsi
Tao-ch'o (道綽) — Daochuo
Tao-chou (道州) — Daozhou
Tao-ch'ung (道寵) — Daochong
Tao-hsien (道暹) — Daoxian
Tao-hsin (道信) — Daoxin
Tao-hsüan (道宣・道璿) — Daoxuan
T'ao Hung-ching (陶弘景) — Tao Hongjing
Tao-lung (道隆) — Daolong
Tao-sheng (道生) — Daosheng
Tao-shih (道世) — Daoshi
Tao-sui (道邃) — Daosui
Tao-t'ai (道泰) — Daotai
Tao-yüan (道円・道原) — Daoyuan
Ta-su, Mt. (大蘇山) — Dasu, Mt.
Ta-t'ung (大同) — Datong
Ta-tz'u-en-ssu (大慈恩寺) — Daciensi
Ta-yüeh-chih (大月支) — Dayuezhi
Ta-yün-ssu (大雲寺) — Dayunsi
Te-tsung, Emperor (徳宗) — Dezong, Emperor
T'ien-hsi-tsai (天息災) — Tianxizai
T'ien-kung-ssu (天宮寺) — Tiangongsi
T'ien-p'ing-ssu (天平寺) — Tianpingsi
T'ien-t'ai (天台) — Tiantai
T'ien-t'ai, Mt. (天台山) — Tiantai, Mt.
T'ien-t'ung, Mt. (天童山) — Tiantong, Mt.
Ti-lun (school) (地論) — Dilun
Ti-lun-tsung (地論宗) — Dilunzong
Ting-lin-ssu (定林寺) — Dinglinsi
Ting-lin-shang-ssu (定林上寺) — Dinglinshangsi
Ting Wei (丁謂) — Ding Wei
Ti-tsang (地蔵) — Dizang
Ts'ai Yin (蔡愔) — Cai Yin
Tsan-ning (賛寧) — Zanning
Ts'ao-ch'i (曹渓) — Caoqi
Ts'ao-tung (school) (曹洞) — Caodong
Tso-hsi, Mt. (左渓山) — Zuoxi, Mt.
Ts'ung-i (従義) — Congyi
Tsung-mi (宗密) — Zongmi
Tsung-ying (宗穎) — Zongying
Tsun-shih (遵式) — Zunshi
Tung-ch'un (東春) — Dongchun
Tung-lin-ssu (東林寺) — Donglinsi
Tung-yang (東陽) — Dongyang
Tun-huang (敦煌) — Dunhuang
Tu-shun (杜順) — Dushun
Tz'u-en (慈恩) — Cien
Tz'u-en-ssu (慈恩寺) — Ciensi
Tz'u-yün (慈雲) — Ciyun
Wa-kuan-ssu (瓦官寺) — Waguansi
Wang Fu (王浮) — Wang Fu
Wan-kung, Mt. (皖公山) — Wangong, Mt.
Wei-ch'i-nan (維祇難) — Weiqinan
Wei-chüan (維蠲) — Weijuan

Wei-te (威德) — Weide
Wei Yüan-sung (衛元嵩) — Wei Yuansong
Wen, Emperor (文帝) — Wen, Emperor
Wen-ch'eng, Emperor (文成帝) — Wencheng, Emperor
Wen Hsüan (文宣) — Wen Xuan
Wen-i (文益) — Wenyi
Wen-ku (温古) — Wengu
Wen-yen (文偃) — Wenyan
Wu (呉) — Wu
Wu, Emperor (武帝) — Wu, Emperor
Wu, Empress (武后) — Wu, Empress
Wu-chung-ssu (五重寺) — Wuzhongsi
Wu-chun Shih-fan (無準師範) — Wuzhun Shifan
Wu-hsüeh Tsu-yüan (無学祖元) — Wuxue Zuyuan
Wu-lung (烏竜) — Wulong
Wu-men-ssu (呉門寺) — Wumensi
Wu-t'ai, Mt. (五台山) — Wutai, Mt.
Wu-tsung, Emperor (武宗) — Wuzong, Emperor
Wu-wai (物外) — Wuwai
Yang, Emperor (煬帝) — Yang, Emperor
Yang-ch'i (school) (楊岐) — Yangqi
Yang-chou (揚州) — Yangzhou
Yang-ti (煬帝) — Yangdi
Yao Hsing (姚興) — Yao Xing
Yeh (鄴) — Ye
Yen-ts'ung (彦悰) — Yancong
Yin-sheng-ssu (因聖寺) — Yinshengsi
Yin-yüan (隠元) — Yinyuan
Yüan-chao (円照) — Yuanzhao
Yüan-cheng (元政) — Yuanzheng
Yüan-k'ang (元康) — Yuankang
Yüan-t'ung (円通) — Yuantong
Yü-ch'üan-ssu (玉泉寺) — Yuquansi
Yüeh-chih (月支) — Yuezhi
Yung-ning-ssu (永寧寺) — Yongningsi
Yung-p'ing (era) (永平) — Yongping
Yün-hua-ssu (雲華寺) — Yunhuasi
Yün-kang (caves) (雲岡) — Yungang
Yün-men (school) (雲門) — Yunmen
Yü-t'ien (于闐) — Yutian

APPENDIX C

The Documents Referred to in the Dictionary and Their Japanese Titles

Accordance with "The Treatise on the Middle Way," The: *Jun-chū-ron* (順中論)
Accumulated Great Treasures Sutra: *Daihōshaku-kyō* (大宝積経)
Accumulated Treasures Sutra: *Hōshaku-kyō* (宝積経)
Advent of Maitreya Sutra: *Miroku-geshō-kyō* (弥勒下生経)
Afterword to the Lotus Sutra Translation, The: *Hokke-hongyō-kōki* (法華翻経後記)
Analects: *Rongo* (論語)
Annotations on "Great Concentration and Insight," The: *Shikan-bugyōden-guketsu* (止観輔行伝弘決)
Annotations on the Benevolent Kings Sutra, The: *Ninnōkyō-sho* (仁王経疏)
Annotations on "The Dharma Analysis Treasury," The: *Kusharon-sho* (倶舎論疏)
Annotations on the Flower Garland Sutra, The: *Kegongyō-sho* (華厳経疏)
Annotations on "The Fourfold Rules of Discipline," The: *Shibun-ritsu-sho* (四分律疏)
Annotations on the Mahāvairochana Sutra, The: *Dainichikyō-sho* (大日経疏)
Annotations on the Meaning of the Lotus Sutra, The: *Hokke-gisho* (法華義疏)
Annotations on the Meaning of the Vimalakīrti Sutra, The: *Yuimakyō-gisho* (維摩経義疏)
Annotations on the Nirvana Sutra, The: *Nehangyō-sho* (涅槃経疏)
Annotations on "The Profound Meaning of the Lotus Sutra," The: *Hokke-gengi-shakusen* (法華玄義釈籤)
Annotations on "The Profound Meaning of the Perceiver of the World's Sounds Chapter," The: *Kannon-gengi-ki* (観音玄義記)
Annotations on the Profound Meaning of the Vimalakīrti Sutra, The: *Yuimakyō-gensho* (維摩経玄疏)
Annotations on "The Summary of the Mahayana," The: *Shō-daijō-ron-sho* (摂大乗論疏)
Annotations on "The Treatise on the Middle Way," The: Chūganron-sho (中観論疏)
Annotations on "The Treatise on the Observation of the Mind," The: *Kanjin-ron-sho* (観心論疏)
Annotations on "The Words and Phrases of the Lotus Sutra," The: *Hokke-mongu-ki* (法華文句記)
Anthology of the Propagation of Light, The: *Gumyō-shū* (弘明集)
Awakening of Faith. *Kishin-ron* (起信論)

Awakening of Faith in the Mahayana, The: *Daijō-kishin-ron* (大乗起信論)
Basic Rules of Discipline, The: *Sōgi-ritsu-kaihon* (僧祇律戒本)
Basic Treatise for the Explanation of Buddhist Concepts, A: *Honrui-sokuron* (品類足論)
Benevolent Kings Perfection of Wisdom Sutra: *Ninnō-hannya-haramitsu-kyō* (仁王般若波羅蜜経)
Benevolent Kings Sutra: *Ninnō-kyō* (仁王経)
Benevolent Kings Wisdom Sutra: *Ninnō-hannya-kyō* (仁王般若経)
Biographies of Eminent Priests, The: *Kōsō-den* (高僧伝)
Biographies of Eminent Priests of the Great T'ang Dynasty Who Sought the Law in the Western Regions, The: *Daitō-saiiki-guhō-kōsō-den* (大唐西域求法高僧伝)
Biographies of Eminent Priests Who Sought the Law, The: *Guhō-kōsō-den* (求法高僧伝)
Biographies of Eminent Priests Who Sought the Law in the Western Regions, The: *Saiiki-guhō-kōsō-den* (西域求法高僧伝)
Biographies of the Nine Patriarchs of the T'ien-t'ai School, The: *Tendai-kuso-den* (天台九祖伝)
Biography of Āryadeva, The: *Daiba-bosatsu-den* (提婆菩薩伝)
Biography of Bodhisattva Nāgārjuna, The: *Ryūju-bosatsu-den* (竜樹菩薩伝)
Biography of the Dharma Teacher Vasubandhu, The: *Basubanzu-hosshi-den* (婆藪槃豆法師伝)
Biography of the Great Teacher of Mount Hiei, The: *Eizan-daishi-den* (叡山大師伝)
Biography of the Great Teacher T'ien-t'ai Chih-che of the Sui Dynasty, The: *Zui-tendai-chisha-daishi-betsuden* (隋天台智者大師別伝)
Biography of the Tripitaka Master of Ta-tz'u-en-ssu Temple, The: *Daijionji-sanzō-hosshi-den* (大慈恩寺三蔵法師伝)
Biography of the Tripitaka Master of Ta-tz'u-en-ssu Temple of the Great T'ang Dynasty, The: *Daitō-daijionji-sanzō-hosshi-den* (大唐大慈恩寺三蔵法師伝)
Bodhisattva Practice Jeweled Necklace Sutra: *Bosatsu-yōraku-hongō-kyō* (菩薩瓔珞本業経)
Bodhisattva Precepts Sutra: *Bosatsu-kai-kyō* (菩薩戒経)
Brahmā Excellent Thought Sutra: *Shiyaku-kyō* (思益経)
Brahmā Net Sutra: *Bommō-kyō* (梵網経)
Brief History of Japan, A: *Fusō-ryakki* (扶桑略記)
Buddha Infinite Life Sutra: *Muryōju-kyō* (無量寿経)
Buddha's Legacy Teachings Sutra: *Butsu-yuikyō-gyō* (仏遺教経)
Buddhas' Names Sutra: *Butsumyō-kyō* (仏名経)
Buddha's Preaching Life Sutra: *Chūhongi-kyō* (中本起経)
Buddha's Successors Sutra: *Fuhōzō-kyō* (付法蔵経)
Buddha Treasury Sutra: *Butsuzō-kyō* (仏蔵経)
Catalog of Buddhist Scriptures, The: *Naiten-roku* (内典録)
Causality of Past and Present Sutra: *Kako-genzai-inga-kyō* (過去現在因果経)
Causality Sutra: *Inga-kyō* (因果経)
Chen-yüan Era Catalog of the Buddhist Canon, The: *Jōgen-shakkyō-roku* or

Jōgen-nyūzō-roku (貞元釈教録・貞元入蔵録)
Ching-te Era Record of the Transmission of the Lamp, The: *Keitoku-dentō-roku* (景徳伝灯録)
Chronicles of Japan, The: *Nihon-shoki* (日本書紀)
Clarification of Consciousness Sutra: *Kenshiki-kyō* (顕識経)
Clarification of Doctrine, A: *Kenshū-ron* (顕宗論)
Clarification of the Meaning of the Lotus Sutra, A: *Ken-hokke-gi-shō* (顕法華義抄)
Clarification of "The Nembutsu Chosen above All," A: *Ken-senchaku* (顕選択)
Clarification of the Precepts, A: *Kenkai-ron* (顕戒論)
Clarification of the Schools Based on T'ien-t'ai's Doctrine, A: *Ehyō-tendai-shū* or *Ebyō-tendai-shū* (依憑天台集)
Collected Essays on the World of Peace and Delight, The: *Anraku-shū* (安楽集)
Collected Works of the Universally Illuminating Soul-Inspiring One, The: *Henjō-hokki-shōryō-shū* or *Shōryō-shū* (遍照発揮性霊集・性霊集)
Collection of Mahayana Treatises, A: *Daijō-abidatsuma-jūron* (大乗阿毘達磨集論)
Collection of Orally Transmitted Teachings, A: *Juketsu-shū* (授決集)
Collection of Records concerning the Tripitaka, A: *Shutsu-sanzōki-shū* (出三蔵記集)
Commentary on "The Dharma Analysis Treasury," The: *Kusharon-ki* (倶舎論記)
Commentary on the Mahayana Treatise, The: *Shaku-makaen-ron* (釈摩訶衍論)
Commentary on the Meaning of the Mahāvairochana Sutra, The: *Dainichi-kyō-gishaku* (大日経義釈)
Commentary on the Meditation on the Buddha Infinite Life Sutra, The: *Kammryōjukyō-sho* (観無量寿経疏)
Commentary on "The Summary of the Mahayana," The: *Shō-daijōron-shaku* (摂大乗論釈)
Commentary on the Ten Stages Sutra, The: *Jūjū-bibasha-ron* (十住毘婆沙論)
Commentary on "The Thirty-Stanza Treatise on the Consciousness-Only Doctrine," The: *Yuishiki-sanjū-ju-shaku* (唯識三十頌釈)
Commentary on "The Treatise on Rebirth in the Pure Land," The: *Ōjōron-chū* (往生論註)
Commentary on "The Treatise on the Establishment of the Consciousness-Only Doctrine," The: *Jō-yuishikiron-jukki* (成唯識論述記)
Commentary on "The Treatise on the Lotus Sutra," The: *Hokkeron-ki* (法華論記)
Commentary on "The Treatise on the Pure Land," The: *Jōdoron-chū* (浄土論註)
Commitment of Previous Deeds Sutra: *Kōkigyō-kyō* (興起行経)
Comparison of Exoteric and Esoteric Buddhism, A: *Ben-kemmitsu-nikyō-ron* or *Nikyō-ron* (弁顕密二教論・二教論)
Comparison of One-time Recitation and Many-time Recitation, A: *Ichinen-tanen-fumbetsu-ji* (一念多念分別事)

Compassionate White Lotus Flower Sutra: *Hike-kyō* (悲華経)
Complete and Final Teaching on Perfect Enlightenment Sutra: *Daiengaku-shutara-ryōgi-kyō* (大円覚修多羅了義経)
Complete Works of the Fuji School, The: *Fuji-shūgaku-zenshū* (富士宗学全集)
Comprehensive Catalog of Sutras, The: *Sōrishukyō-mokuroku* (綜理衆経目録)
Contemplation on the Mind-Ground Sutra: *Shinjikan-gyō* (心地観経)
Continued Biographies of Eminent Priests, The: *Zoku-kōsō-den* (続高僧伝)
Correct and Vast Great Adornment Sutra: *Hōkō-daishōgon-kyō* (方広大荘厳経)
Correct Commentary on the Rules of Discipline, A: *Zenkenritsu-bibasha* (善見律毘婆沙)
Decline of the Law Sutra: *Hōmetsujin-kyō* (法滅尽経)
Deeds of Harsha, The: *Harusha-charita* (ハルシャ・チャリタ)
Delving into the Profundity of the Flower Garland Sutra: *Kegongyō-tangen-ki* (華厳経探玄記)
Description of the World Sutra: *Seiki-kyō* (世記経)
Dhāranī for the Protection of the Sovereign of the Nation Sutra: *Shugo-kokkaishu-darani-kyō* (守護国界主陀羅尼経)
Dharma Analysis Treasury, The: *Abidatsuma-kusha-ron* or *Kusha-ron* (阿毘達磨倶舎論・倶舎論)
Diamond Crown Sutra: *Kongōchō-kyō* (金剛頂経)
Diamond-like Perfection of Wisdom Sutra: *Kongō-hannya-haramitsu-kyō* (金剛般若波羅蜜経)
Diamond Scalpel, The: *Kongōbei* or *Kongōbei-ron* (金剛錍・金剛錍論)
Diamond Sutra: *Kongō-kyō* (金剛経)
Diamond Wisdom Sutra: *Kongō-hannya-kyō* (金剛般若経)
Dictionary of the Pronunciation and Meaning of Buddhist Terms, A: *Hon'yaku-myōgi-shū* (翻訳名義集)
Different Tenets of the Schools, The: *Bushūi-ron* (部執異論)
Different Views on the Teaching and the Time: *Kyōji-jōron* (教時諍論)
Discrimination of Teachings, The: *Benshū-ron* (弁宗論)
Divergent Concepts in the Sutras and Vinaya Texts: *Kyōritsu-isō* (経律異相)
Doctrine of Attaining Buddhahood in One's Present Form, The: *Sokushin-jōbutsu-gi* (即身成仏義)
Doctrine of "The Nembutsu Chosen above All," The: *Tetsu-senchaku-shū* (徹選択集)
Doctrine of the Original Vow in the Nembutsu, The: *Nembutsu-hongan-gi* (念仏本願義)
Doctrines of the Different Schools, The: *Ibushūrin-ron* (異部宗輪論)
Dragon King of the Sea Sutra: *Kairyūō-kyō* (海竜王経)
Drinking Tea to Improve Health and Prolong Life: *Kissa-yōjō-ki* (喫茶養生記)
Eighteen Schools, The: *Jūhachibu-ron* (十八部論)
Eight-part Treatise, The: *Hakkendo-ron* (八犍度論)
Entering the Middle Way: *Nyū-chū-ron* (入中論)
Epilogue to the Mahāparinirvāna Sutra, The: *Daihatsu-nehangyō-gobun* (大般涅槃経後分)

Essay on the Grand Meaning of the Mahayana, The: *Daijō-daigi-shō* (大乘大義章)
Essay on the Protection of the Nation, An: *Shugo-kokkai-shō* (守護国界章)
Essentials of Concentration and Insight, The: *Shō-shikan* (小止観)
Essentials of Rebirth in the Pure Land, The: *Ōjō-yōshū* (往生要集)
Essentials of the Eight Schools, The: *Hasshū-kōyō* (八宗綱要)
Essentials of "The Fourfold Rules of Discipline," The: *Shibun-ritsu-gyōji-shō* (四分律行事鈔)
Essentials of the Mahāvairochana Sutra, The: *Dainichikyō-shiki* (大日経指帰)
Essentials of the One Vehicle Teaching, The: *Ichijō-yōketsu* (一乗要決)
Essentials of the Pure Land Doctrine, The: *Jōdo-shūyō-shū* (浄土宗要集)
Essentials of "The Ten Onenesses," The: *Jippunimon-shiyō-shō* (十不二門指要抄)
Essentials of the Three Teachings, The: *Sangō-shiiki* (三教指帰)
Essential Works of the Fuji School, The: *Fuji-shūgaku-yōshū* (富士宗学要集)
Extensive Commentary on the Universally Bestowed Bodhisattva Precepts, An: *Futsū-jubosatsukai-kōshaku* (普通授菩薩戒広釈)
Fivefold Rules of Discipline, The: *Gobun-ritsu* (五分律)
Flower Garland Sutra: *Kegon-gyō* (華厳経)
Forest of Gems in the Garden of the Law, The: *Hō'on-jurin* (法苑珠林)
Forest of Meanings in the Garden of the Law, The: *Hō'on-girin-jō* (法苑義林章)
Forest of Meanings in the Mahayana Garden of the Law, The: *Daijō-hō'on-girin-jō* (大乗法苑義林章)
Fourfold Rules of Discipline, The: *Shibun-ritsu* (四分律)
Four Heavenly Kings Sutra: *Shitennō-kyō* (四天王経)
Four-Hundred-Verse Treatise, The: *Shihyaku-ron* (四百論)
Four Peaceful Practices, The: *Shi-anraku-gyō* (四安楽行)
Further Anthology of the Propagation of Light, The: *Kō-gumyō-shū* (広弘明集)
Garland of Birth Stories, The: *Bosatsu-honjō-manron* (菩薩本生鬘論)
Gathering of Jewels, The: *Shūgyoku-shū* (拾玉集)
General Teaching for the Promotion of Seated Meditation, The: *Fukan-zazen-gi* (普勧坐禅儀)
Genkō Era Biographies of Eminent Priests, The: *Genkō-shakusho* (元亨釈書)
Golden Light Sutra: *Konkōmyō-kyō* (金光明経)
Great and Vast Buddha Flower Garland Sutra: *Daihōkō-butsu-kegon-gyō* (大方広仏華厳経)
Great Canon of Monastic Rules, The: *Maka-sōgi-ritsu* (摩訶僧祇律)
Great Cloud Sutra: *Daiun-gyō* (大雲経)
Great Collection Sutra: *Daijikkyō* (大集経)
Great Commentary on the Abhidharma, The: *Abidatsuma-daibibasha-ron* or *Daibibasha-ron* (阿毘達磨大毘婆沙論・大毘婆沙論)
Great Compassion Sutra: *Daihi-kyō* (大悲経)
Great Complete Nirvana Sutra: *Daihatsu-nehan-gyō* (大般涅槃経)
Great Concentration and Insight: *Maka-shikan* (摩訶止観)
Great Correct and Equal Dhāranī Sutra: *Daihōdō-darani-kyō* (大方等陀羅尼経)

Great Crown of the Buddha's Head Shūramgama Meditation Sutra: *Daibutchō-shuryōgon-kyō*（大仏頂首楞厳経）
Great Crown of the Buddha's Head Sutra: *Daibutchō-kyō*（大仏頂経）
Great Ming Dynasty Biographies of Eminent Priests, The: *Daimin-kōsō-den*（大明高僧伝）
Great Ornament of Tales, The: *Daishōgon-rongyō*（大荘厳論経）
Great Perfection of Wisdom Sutra: *Makahannya-haramitsu-kyō* or *Daihannya-haramitta-kyō*（摩訶般若波羅蜜経・大般若波羅蜜多経）
Great T'ang Dynasty Catalog of Buddhist Scriptures, The: *Daitō-naiten-roku*（大唐内典録）
Great Wisdom Sutra: *Daihannya-kyō*（大般若経）
Heart of the Abhidharma, The: *Abidon-shin-ron*（阿毘曇心論）
Heart of the Middle Way, The: *Chūgan-shin-ron*（中観心論）
Heart of the Perfection of Wisdom Sutra: *Hannya-haramitta-shingyō*（般若波羅蜜多心経）
Heart of Wisdom Sutra: *Hannya-shingyō*（般若心経）
Heart Sutra: *Hannya-shingyō*（般若心経）
History of the Buddha's Successors, A: *Fuhōzō-innen-den*（付法蔵因縁伝）
History of the Transmission and Propagation of Buddhism in Three Countries, A: *Sangoku-buppō-dentsū-engi*（三国仏法伝通縁起）
Hymn in Verse to Amida Buddha, The: *San-amidabutsu-ge*（讃阿弥陀仏偈）
Immeasurable Meanings Sutra: *Muryōgi-kyō*（無量義経）
Increasing by One Āgama Sutra: *Zōichi-agon-gyō*（増一阿含経）
Introduction to the Essentials of the Lotus Sutra, An: *Hokke-shūyō-jo*（法華宗要序）
Jātaka: *Honjō-wa*（本生話）
Jeweled Necklace Sutra: *Yōraku-kyō*（瓔珞経）
K'ai-yüan Era Catalog of the Buddhist Canon, The: *Kaigen-shakkyō-roku*（開元釈教録）
King Ashoka Sutra: *Aikuō-kyō*（阿育王経）
King Golden Color Sutra: *Konjikiō-kyō*（金色王経）
King Udayana Sutra: *Uden'ō-kyō*（優填王経）
Lamenting Heresy: *Tan'ni-shō*（歎異抄）
Land of Akshobhya Buddha Sutra: *Ashuku-bukkoku-kyō*（阿閦仏国経）
Larger Wisdom Sutra: *Daibon-hannya-kyō*（大品般若経）
Legacy Teachings Sutra: *Yuikyō-gyō*（遺教経）
Liang Dynasty Biographies of Eminent Priests, The: *Ryō-kōsō-den*（梁高僧伝）
Life of the Great Priest of T'ang China Who Journeyed to the East, The: *Tō-dai-wajō-tōsei-den*（唐大和上東征伝）
Life of the Supervisor of Priests Kūkai, The: *Kūkai-sōzu-den*（空海僧都伝）
Lion Roar of the Thus Come One Sutra: *Nyorai-shishiku-kyō*（如来師子吼経）
Lion's Roar of Queen Shrīmālā Sutra: *Shōman-shishiku-kyō*（勝鬘師子吼経）
Long Āgama Sutra: *Jō-agon-gyō*（長阿含経）
Lotus-like Face Sutra: *Rengemen-kyō*（蓮華面経）
Lotus Sutra: *Hoke-kyō*（法華経）
Lotus Sutra and Its Traditions, The: *Hokke-denki*（法華伝記）

Lotus Sutra of the Correct Law: *Shō-hoke-kyō* (正法華経)
Lotus Sutra of the Wonderful Law: *Myoho-renge-kyo* (妙法蓮華経)
Mahayana Method of Concentration and Insight, The: *Daijō-shikan-hōmon* (大乗止観法門)
Mahayana Secret Solemnity Sutra: *Daijō-mitsugon-kyō* (大乗密厳経)
Matrix of the Thus Come One Sutra: *Nyoraizō-kyō* (如来蔵経)
Meaning of the Flower Garland Sutra Based on an Earlier Commentary, The: *Kegongyō-zuisho-engi-shō* (華厳経随疏演義鈔)
Meaning of the Four Teachings, The: *Shikyō-gi* (四教義)
Meaning of the Lotus Sutra, The: *Hokekyō-giki* or *Hokke-giki* (法華経義記・法華義記)
Meaning of the Six Stages of Practice, The: *Rokusoku-gi* (六即儀)
Medicine Master Sutra: *Yakushi-kyō* (薬師経)
Meditation on Bodhisattva Space Treasury Sutra: *Kan-kokūzō-bosatsu-kyō* (観虚空蔵菩薩経)
Meditation on the Buddha Infinite Life Sutra: *Kammuryōju-kyō* (観無量寿経)
Meditation on the Buddha Sutra: *Kambutsu-sammai-kyō* (観仏三昧経)
Meditation on the Correct Teaching Sutra: *Shōbōnenjo-kyō* (正法念処経)
Meditation on the Two Bodhisattvas Medicine King and Medicine Superior Sutra: *Kan-yakuō-yakujō-nibosatsu-kyō* (観薬王薬上二菩薩経)
Meditation on Universal Worthy Sutra: *Fugen-kan-gyō* (普賢観経)
Meditation Sutra: *Kan-gyō* (観経)
Medium-Length Āgama Sutra: *Chū-agon-gyō* (中阿含経)
Mirror of Eastern Japan, The: *Azuma-kagami* (吾妻鏡)
Mirror on the Meaning of the Middle and the Extreme, The: *Chūhen-gikyō* (中辺義鏡)
Miscellaneous Āgama Sutra: *Zō-agon-gyō* (雑阿含経)
Monastic Rules for Emancipation, The: *Gedatsu-ritsu* (解脱律)
Monastic Rules of the Sarvāstivāda School, The: *Kompon-setsu-issaiubu-binaya* (根本説一切有部毘奈耶)
Monastic Rules of the Sarvāstivāda School on Various Matters, The: *Kompon-setsu-issaiubu-binaya-zoji* (根本説一切有部毘奈耶雑事)
Monastic Rules on Various Matters, The: *Binaya-zōji* (毘奈耶雑事)
Monk Nāgasena Sutra: *Nasen-biku-kyō* (那先比丘経)
Mother of Demon Children Sutra: *Kishimo-kyō* (鬼子母経)
Multitudinous Graceful Actions Sutra: *Fuyō-kyō* (普曜経)
Mysterious Spells for Eliminating the Illnesses of the Five Components Sutra: *Kyakuon'ō-jinju-kyō* (却温黄神呪経)
Mysterious Spells of the Eleven-faced Perceiver of the World's Sounds Sutra: *Jūichimen-kannon-jinju-kyō* (十一面観音神呪経)
Names of Three Thousand Buddhas Sutra: *Sanzen-butsumyō-kyō* (三千仏名経)
Nembutsu Chosen above All, The: *Senchaku-shū* (選択集)
Nembutsu of the Original Vow Chosen above All, The: *Senchaku-hongan-nembutsu-shū* (選択本願念仏集)
New Collection of Ancient and Modern Poetry, A: *Shin-kokin-shū* (新古今集)
Nirvana Sutra: *Nehan-gyō* (涅槃経)

Non-Substantiality of All Phenomena Sutra: *Shohō-mugyō-kyō* (諸法無行経)
Object of Devotion for Observing the Mind, The: *Kanjin-no-honzon-shō* (観心本尊抄)
Ocean of Meditation on the Buddha Sutra: *Kambutsu-sammai-kai-kyō* (観仏三昧海経)
One Hundred Records of the Great Teacher T'ien-t'ai, The: *Kokusei-hyakuroku* (国清百録)
One-Hundred-Verse Treatise, The: *Hyaku-ron* (百論)
One-Hundred-Word Treatise, The: *Hyakuji-ron* (百字論)
On Establishing the Correct Teaching for the Peace of the Land: *Risshō-ankoku-ron* (立正安国論)
On Repaying Debts of Gratitude: *Hō'on-shō* (報恩抄)
On the Buddha Nature: *Busshō-shō* (仏性抄)
On the Destruction of the Order: *Hasō-ji* (破僧事)
On the Peaceful Practices of the Lotus Sutra: *Hokekyō-anrakugyō-gi* (法華経安楽行義)
On Trust in the Heart: *Shinjin-mei* (信心銘)
Opening of the Eyes, The: *Kaimoku-shō* (開目抄)
Orally Transmitted Teachings on Meditation on the Character अ, The: *Ajikan-yōjin-kuketsu* (阿字観用心口決)
Origin of the World Sutra: *Kise-kyō* (起世経)
Ornament of Mahayana Sutras, The: *Daijō-shōgonkyō-ron* (大乗荘厳経論)
Outstanding Principles of the Lotus Sutra, The: *Hokke-shūku* (法華秀句)
Perceiver of the World's Sounds Sutra: *Kannon-gyō* (観音経)
Perfect Enlightenment Sutra: *Engaku-kyō* (円覚経)
Perfection of Wisdom sutras: *Hannya-haramitsu-kyō* (般若波羅蜜経)
Personal Commentary on "The Annotations on the Mahāparinirvāna Sutra": *Daihatsu-nehangyō-sho-shiki* (大般涅槃経疏私記)
Personal Commentary on "The Annotations on the Nirvana Sutra," A: *Nehan-gyo-sho-shiki* (涅槃経疏私記)
Personal Commentary on "The Annotations on the Vimalakīrti Sutra," A: *Yuimakyō-sho-shiki* (維摩経疏私記)
Personal View, A: *Gukan-shō* (愚管抄)
Platform Sutra, The: *Dan-kyō* (壇経)
Platform Sutra of the Sixth Patriarch, The: *Rokuso-dan-kyō* (六祖壇経)
Practice of Wisdom Sutra: *Dōgyō-hannya-kyō* (道行般若経)
Praising Rebirth in the Pure Land: *Ōjō-raisan* (往生礼讃)
Praising the Buddha's Deeds: *Busshogyō-san* (仏所行讃)
Praising the Profundity of the Lotus Sutra: *Hokke-genzan* (法華玄賛)
Prayer for Rain Sutra: *Shōu-kyō* (請雨経)
Precepts for Laymen Sutra: *Ubasoku-kai-kyō* (優婆塞戒経)
Precious Key to the Secret Treasury, The: *Hizō-hōyaku* (秘蔵宝鑰)
Priest Does Not Bow before a King, A: *Shamon-fukyō-ōja-ron* (沙門不敬王者論)
Principle of Wisdom Sutra: *Rishu-kyō* (理趣経)
Profound Meaning of the Four Mahayana Treatises, The: *Daijō-shiron-gengi* (大乗四論玄義)

Profound Meaning of the Golden Light Sutra, The: *Konkōmyō-gengi* (金光明玄義)
Profound Meaning of the Lotus Sutra, The: *Hokke-gengi* (法華玄義)
Profound Meaning of the Nirvana Sutra, The: *Nehangyō-gengi* (涅槃経玄義)
Profound Meaning of the "Perceiver of the World's Sounds" Chapter, The: *Kannon-gengi* (観音玄義)
Profound Meaning of the Three Treatises, The: *Sanron-gengi* (三論玄義)
Profound Meaning of the Vimalakīrti Sutra: *Yuimakyō-gengi* (維摩経玄義)
Profound Secrets Sutra: *Jimmitsu-kyō* (深密経)
Pronunciation and Meaning in the Buddhist Scriptures: *Issaikyō-ongi* (一切経音義)
Propagation of Zen for the Protection of the Country, The: *Kōzen-gokoku-ron* (興禅護国論)
Prophecy of Buddhahood for King Ajātashatru Sutra: *Ajaseō-juketsu-kyō* (阿闍世王授決経)
Protection of the Sovereign of the Nation Sutra: *Shugo-kokkai-kyō* (守護国界経)
Protection Sutra: *Shugo-kyō* (守護経)
Questions and Answers about the Teaching and the Time: *Kyōji-mondō* (教時問答)
Questions and Answers on Regulations for Students of the Tendai Lotus School: *Tendai-hokkeshū-gakushō-shiki-mondō* (天台法華宗学生式問答)
Questions of Brahmā Excellent Thought Sutra: *Shiyaku-bonten-shomon-gyō* (思益梵天所問経)
Questions of King Milinda, The: *Mirindaō-monkyō* (ミリンダ王問経)
Record of a Pilgrimage to China in Search of the Law, The: *Nittō-guhō-junrei-kōki* (入唐求法巡礼行記)
Record of Ensuring the Abiding of the Law, The: *Hōjū-ki* (法住記)
Record of Southern Countries, The: *Nankai-kiki-naihō-den* (南海寄帰内法伝)
Record of the Buddha and the Patriarchs of Various Dynasties, The: *Busso-rekidai-tsūsai* (仏祖歴代通載)
Record of the Buddhistic Kingdoms, The: *Bukkoku-ki* (仏国記)
Record of the Lineage of the Buddha and the Patriarchs, The: *Busso-tōki* (仏祖統紀)
Record of the Orally Transmitted Teachings, The: *Ongi-kuden* (御義口伝)
Record of the Pilgrimage to Mount T'ien-t'ai and Mount Wu-t'ai, The: *San-tendai-godaisan-ki* (参天台五台山記)
Record of the Precepts of the One Mind, The: *Isshin-kaimon* (一心戒文)
Record of the Three Thousand Buddhas of the Three Kalpas, The: *Sankō-sanzembutsu-engi* (三劫三千仏縁起)
Record of the Western Regions, The: *Saiiki-ki* (西域記)
Record of the Western Regions of the Great T'ang Dynasty, The: *Daitō-saiiki-ki* (大唐西域記)
Record of Wonders in the Book of Chou, The: *Shūsho-iki* (周書異記)
Refutation of Erroneous Doctrines, A: *Sai-jarin* (摧邪輪)
Refutation of Objections, The: *Ejō-ron* (廻諍論)

Refutation of "The Nembutsu Chosen above All," A: *Dan-senchaku* (弾選択)
Regulations for Students, The: *Gakushō-shiki* (学生式)
Regulations for Students of the Mountain School, The: *Sange-gakushō-shiki* (山家学生式)
Repaying Debts of Gratitude Sutra: *Hō'on-kyō* (報恩経)
Revelation of the Profound Secrets Sutra: *Gejimmitsu-kyō* (解深密経)
Reverend Nichiu's Teachings on the Formalities: *Ushi-kegi-shō* (有師化儀抄)
Rise of the World Sutra: *Dai-rōtan-kyō* (大楼炭経)
Rituals of the Assembly for Rebirth in the Pure Land, The: *Ōjō-kōshiki* (往生講式)
Secret Commentary on the Aspect of the Diamond Precept, The: *Kongō-kai-tai-hiketsu* (金剛戒体秘決)
Secret Essentials of Meditation, The: *Zenhiyō* (禅秘要)
Secret Solemnity Sutra: *Mitsugon-gyō* (密厳経)
Selection of the Time, The: *Senji-shō* (撰時抄)
Service for the Deceased Sutra: *Urabon-kyō* (盂蘭盆経)
Seven Buddhas Sutra: *Shichibutsu-kyō* (七仏経)
Shūramgama Meditation Sutra: *Shuryōgon-sammai-kyō* (首楞厳三昧経)
Silver-Colored Woman Sutra: *Gonjikinyo-kyō* (銀色女経)
Six Pāramitās Sutra: *Roku-haramitsu-kyō* or *Ropparamitsu-kyo* (六波羅蜜経)
Six-Volume Writings, The: *Rokkan-shō* (六巻抄)
Smaller Wisdom Sutra: *Shōbon-hannya-kyō* (小品般若経)
Sovereign Kings of the Golden Light Sutra: *Konkōmyō-saishō'ō-kyō* (金光明最勝王経)
Sovereign Kings Sutra: *Saishō'ō-kyō* (最勝王経)
Space Treasury Sutra: *Kokūzō-kyō* (虚空蔵経)
Storehouse of Siddham, The: *Shittanzō* (悉曇蔵)
Storehouse of Various Treasures Sutra: *Zōhōzō-kyō* (雑宝蔵経)
Stories of the Words of Truth Sutra: *Hokku-hiyu-kyō* (法句譬喩経)
Story of King Ashoka, The: *Aikuō-den* (阿育王伝)
Summary of the Mahayana, The: *Shō-daijō-ron* (摂大乗論)
Sung Dynasty Biographies of Eminent Priests, The: *Sō-kōsō-den* (宋高僧伝)
Supplemented Lotus Sutra of the Wonderful Law: *Tembon-hoke-kyō* (添品法華経)
Supplement to "The Heart of the Abhidharma," The: *Zo-abidon-shin-ron* (雑阿毘曇心論)
Supplement to the Meanings of the Commentaries on the Lotus Sutra, The: *Hokekyō-shogisan* (法華経疏義纘)
Supplement to the Three Major Works on the Lotus Sutra, The: *Hokke-sandaibu-fuchū* (法華三大部補註)
Supplement to "The Words and Phrases of the Lotus Sutra," The: *Hokke-mongu-fushō-ki* (法華文句輔正記)
Supplement to T'ien-t'ai's Three Major Works, The: *Tendai-sandaibu-fuchū* (天台三大部補註)
Sutra of Collected Birth Stories concerning the Practice of the Six Pāramitās: *Rokudo-jikkyō* (六度集経)

Sutra of Forty-two Sections: *Shijūni-shō-kyō* (四十二章経)
Sutra of Preaching Travels: *Yugyō-kyō* (遊行経)
Sutra of the Buddha Answering the Great Heavenly King Brahmā's Questions: *Daibontennō-mombutsu-ketsugi-kyō* (大梵天王問仏決疑経)
Sutra of the Buddha's Marvelous Deeds in Previous Lifetimes: *Taishi-zuiō-hongi-kyō* (太子瑞応本起経)
Sutra of the Collected Stories of the Buddha's Deeds in Past Lives: *Butsu-hongyō-jikkyō* (仏本行集経)
Sutra of the Lotus Blossom of the Fine Dharma: *Myoho-renge-kyo* (妙法蓮華経)
Sutra of the Lotus of the Wonderful Law: *Myoho-renge-kyo* (妙法蓮華経)
Sutra of the Meditation to Behold the Buddhas: *Hanju-zammai-kyō* (般舟三昧経)
Sutra of Verses: *Shutsuyō-kyō* (出曜経)
Sutra on How to Practice Meditation on the Bodhisattva Universal Worthy: *Kan-fugen-bosatsu-gyōhō-kyō* (観普賢菩薩行法経)
Sutra on Resolving Doubts about the Middle Day of the Law: *Zōbō-ketsugi-kyō* (像法決疑経)
Sutra on the Conversion of Barbarians by Lao Tzu: *Rōshi-keko-kyō* (老子化胡経)
Sutra on the Expositions of Vimalakīrti: *Yuimakitsu-shosetsu-kyō* (維摩詰所説経)
Sutra on the Wise and the Foolish: *Kengu-kyō* (賢愚経)
Tales of Times Now Past: *Konjaku-monogatari* (今昔物語)
T'ang Dynasty Biographies of Eminent Priests, The: *Tō-kōsō-den* (唐高僧伝)
Teaching of the Practice of Meditation, The: *Shidai-zemmon* (次第禅門)
Teaching, Practice, Faith, and Proof, The: *Kyō-gyō-shin-shō* (教行信証)
Teachings Orally Transmitted to Hino'o, The: *Hino'o-kuketsu* (檜尾口訣)
Ten Conditions for Rebirth in the Pure Land: *Ōjō-jūin* (往生拾因)
Ten Divisions of Monastic Rules, The: *Jūju-ritsu* (十誦律)
Ten Kings Sutra: *Jūō-kyō* (十王経)
Ten Onenesses, The: *Jippunimon* (十不二門)
Ten Stages Sutra: *Jūji-kyō* (十地経)
Thirty-Stanza Treatise on the Consciousness-Only Doctrine, The: *Yuishiki-sanjū-ron-ju* (唯識三十論頌)
Transmission of the Lamp, The: *Dentō-roku* (伝灯録)
Travels of Fa-hsien, The: *Hokken-den* (法顕伝)
Travels of the Eminent Priest Fa-hsien, The: *Kōsō-hokken-den* (高僧法顕伝)
Treasury of Knowledge of the True Law, The: *Shōbō-genzō* (正法眼蔵)
Treatise of Five Hundred Questions, The: *Gohyaku-mon-ron* (五百問論)
Treatise on Accordance with the Correct Doctrine, The: *Abidatsuma-junshōri-ron* (阿毘達磨順正理論)
Treatise on Rebirth in the Pure Land, The: *Ōjō-ron* (往生論)
Treatise on Shāriputra's Abhidharma, The: *Sharihotsu-abidon-ron* (舎利弗阿毘曇論)
Treatise on Systems of Cognition, The: *Juryō-ron* (集量論)
Treatise on the Buddha Nature, The: *Busshō-ron* (仏性論)

Treatise on the Correct Principles of Logic, The: *Immyō-shōrimon-ron* (因明正理門論)
Treatise on the Diamond Realm, The: *Kongōkai-shidai* (金剛界次第)
Treatise on the Diamond Wisdom Sutra, The: *Kongō-hannyakyō-ron* (金剛般若経論)
Treatise on the Discipline for Attaining Enlightenment, The: *Bodai-shiryō-ron* (菩提資糧論)
Treatise on the Discrimination of the Middle and the Extreme, The: *Chūhen-fumbetsu-ron* (中辺分別論)
Treatise on the Doctrines of Immediate Attainment of Enlightenment and Gradual Attainment of Enlightenment, The: *Ron-tongo-zengo-gi* (論頓悟漸悟義)
Treatise on the Enlightenment of Plants, The: *Sōmoku-jōbutsu-ron* (草木成仏論)
Treatise on the Establishment of the Consciousness-Only Doctrine, The: *Jō-yuishiki-ron* (成唯識論)
Treatise on the Establishment of Truth, The: *Jōjitsu-ron* (成実論)
Treatise on the Great Perfection of Wisdom, The: *Daichido-ron* (大智度論)
Treatise on the Lamp for the Latter Day of the Law, The: *Mappō-tōmyō-ki* (末法燈明記)
Treatise on the Lamp of Wisdom, The: *Hannya-tōron* or *Hannya-tōron-shaku* (般若灯論・般若灯論釈)
Treatise on the Lotus Sutra, The: *Hokke-ron* or *Hokekyō-ron* (法華論・法華経論)
Treatise on the Lotus Sutra of the Wonderful Law, The: *Myoho-renge-kyo-upadaisha* (妙法蓮華経憂波提舎)
Treatise on the Meaning of the Mahayana, The: *Daijō-gisho* (大乗義章)
Treatise on the Meaning of the Mind Aspiring for Enlightenment, The: *Bodai-shingi-shō* (菩提心義鈔)
Treatise on the Middle Way, The: *Chū-ron* (中論)
Treatise on the Mind Aspiring for Enlightenment, The: *Bodaishin-ron* (菩提心論)
Treatise on the Objects of Cognition, The: *Kan-shoen-ron* (観所縁論)
Treatise on the Observation of the Mind, The: *Kanjin-ron* (観心論)
Treatise on the Profundity of the Lotus Sutra, The: *Hokke-genron* (法華玄論)
Treatise on the Profundity of the Mahayana, The: *Daijō-genron* (大乗玄論)
Treatise on the Pure Land, The: *Jōdo-ron* (浄土論)
Treatise on the Rise of the World, The: *Risse-abidon-ron* (立世阿毘曇論)
Treatise on the Source of Wisdom, The: *Abidatsuma-hotchi-ron* (阿毘達磨発智論)
Treatise on the Stage of Buddhahood Sutra, The: *Butsujikyō-ron* (仏地経論)
Treatise on the Stages of Yoga Practice, The: *Yugashiji-ron* (瑜伽師地論)
Treatise on the Ten Stages of the Mind, The: *Jūjū-shin-ron* (十住心論)
Treatise on the Ten Stages Sutra, The: *Jūjikyō-ron* (十地経論)
Treatise on the Treasure Vehicle of Buddhahood, The: *Kukyō-ichijō-hōshō-ron* (究竟一乗宝性論)

Treatise on the Twelve Gates, The: *Jūni-mon-ron* (十二門論)
Treatise on the Two Teachings, The: *Nikyō-ron* (二教論)
Treatise on the Womb Realm, The: *Taizō-shidai* (胎蔵次第)
Treatise Resolving Numerous Doubts, The: *Gungi-ron* (群疑論)
Treatise Resolving Numerous Doubts about the Pure Land Teachings, The: *Shaku-jōdo-gungi-ron* (釈浄土群疑論)
Treatises of Seng-chao, The: *Jō-ron* (肇論)
Twelvefold Dhūta Practice Sutra: *Jūni-zuda-kyō* (十二頭陀経)
Twelve-year Journey Sutra: *Jūniyū-kyō* (十二遊経)
Twenty-Stanza Treatise on the Consciousness-Only Doctrine, The: *Yuishiki-nijū-ron* (唯識二十論)
Two-Volumed Sutra: *Sōkan-gyō* (双巻経・双観経)
Universal Worthy Sutra: *Fugen-kyō* (普賢経)
Upholder of the Age Sutra: *Jise-kyō* (持世経)
Upholding the Bodhisattva Stage Sutra: *Bosatsu-jiji-kyō* (菩薩地持経)
Verses on the Middle Way: *Chūju, Chūron-ju,* or *Chū-ron* (中頌・中論頌・中論)
Verses Praising Rebirth in the Pure Land, The: *Ōjō-raisan-ge* (往生礼讃偈)
Wisdom sutras: *Hannya-kyō* (般若経)
Wise Kalpa Sutra: *Kengō-kyō* (賢劫経)
Words and Phrases of the Lotus Sutra, The: *Hokke-mongu* (法華文句)
Words of Truth Sutra: *Hokku-kyō* (法句経)
Work of the Ignorant Shavepate, The: *Gutoku-shō* (愚禿鈔)

APPENDIX D

The Sanskrit and Pali Titles of Documents Referred to in the Dictionary

The descriptions of the Sanskrit and Pali titles listed below are found under their corresponding English translations.

Abhidharma-hṛdaya-śāstra (阿毘曇心論): Heart of the Abhidharma, The
Abhidharma-jñānaprasthāna-śāstra (阿毘達磨発智論): Treatise on the Source of Wisdom, The
Abhidharmakośa-bhāṣya (阿毘達磨俱舍論): Dharma Analysis Treasury, The
Abhidharmakośa (阿毘達磨俱舍論): Dharma Analysis Treasury, The
Abhidharma-mahāvibhāṣā-śāstra (阿毘達磨大毘婆沙論): Great Commentary on the Abhidharma, The
Ārya-prajñāpāramitā-naya-śatapañcaśatikā (理趣経): Principle of Wisdom Sutra
Aṣṭasāhasrikā-prajñāpāramitā (摩訶般若波羅蜜経): Great Perfection of Wisdom Sutra
Avataṃsaka-sūtra (華厳経): Flower Garland Sutra
Bhaiṣajyaguru-vaiḍūryaprabharāja-sūtra (薬師経): Medicine Master Sutra
Buddha-avataṃsaka-nāma-mahāvaipulya-sūtra (華厳経): Flower Garland Sutra
Buddhacarita (仏所行讃): Praising the Buddha's Deeds
Daśabhūmika-sūtra (十地経): Ten Stages Sutra
Dhammapada (法句経): Dhammapada
Dīpavaṃsa (島史): Dīpavamsa
Kalpanā-maṇḍitikā (大荘厳論経): Great Ornament of Tales, The
Karuṇā-puṇḍarīka-sūtra (悲華経): Compassionate White Lotus Flower Sutra
Lalitavistara (普曜経): Multitudinous Graceful Actions Sutra
Madhyamaka-kārikā (中頌): Verses on the Middle Way
Mādhyamika-śāstra (中論): Treatise on the Middle Way, The
Mahāprajñāpāramitā-śāstra (大智度論): Treatise on the Great Perfection of Wisdom, The
Mahāprajñāpāramitā-sūtra (大般若経): Great Wisdom Sutra
Mahāvairocana-sūtra (大日経): Mahāvairochana Sutra
Mahāvaṃsa (大史・大王統史): Mahāvamsa
Mahāvastu (大事): Mahāvastu
Mahāyāna-saṃgraha (摂大乗論): Summary of the Mahayana, The
Mahāyāna-sūtrālaṃkāra (大乗荘厳経論): Ornament of Mahayana Sutras, The
Milindapañha (ミリンダ王問経): Milindapanha

Pañcaviṃśatisāhasrikā-prajñāpāramitā (摩訶般若波羅蜜経): Great Perfection of Wisdom Sutra
Prajñāpāramitā-hṛdaya-sūtra (般若心経): Heart Sutra
Prajñā-pradīpa (般若灯論・般若灯論釈): Treatise on the Lamp of Wisdom, The
Pratyutpanna-buddha-saṃmukhāvasthita-samādhi-sūtra (般舟三昧経): Sutra of the Meditation to Behold the Buddhas
Ratnagotravibhāga-mahāyānottaratantra-śāstra (究竟一乗宝性論): Treatise on the Treasure Vehicle of Buddhahood, The
Saddharma-puṇḍarīka-sūtra (法華経): Lotus Sutra
Saddharma-puṇḍarīka-upadeśa (法華論): Treatise on the Lotus Sutra, The
Samaya-bhedoparacana-cakra (異部宗輪論): Doctrines of the Different Schools, The
Saṃdhinirmocana-sūtra (解深密経): Revelation of the Profound Secrets Sutra
Sarvatathāgata-tattvasaṃgraha (金剛頂経): Diamond Crown Sutra
Satyasiddhi-śāstra (成実論): Treatise on the Establishment of Truth, The
Śrīmālādevī-siṃhanāda-sūtra (勝鬘経): Shrīmālā Sutra
Sukhāvatīvyūha (阿弥陀経・無量寿経): Amida Sutra; Buddha Infinite Life Sutra
Susiddhikara-sūtra (蘇悉地経): Susiddhikara Sutra
Suvarṇaprabhāsa-sūtra (金光明経・金光明最勝王経): Golden Light Sutra; Sovereign Kings of the Golden Light Sutra
Tathāgatagarbha-sūtra (如来蔵経): Matrix of the Thus Come One Sutra
Triṃśikā-vijñaptimātratā-siddhi (唯識三十論頌): Thirty-Stanza Treatise on the Consciousness-Only Doctrine, The
Vajracchedikā-prajñāpāramitā (金剛般若波羅蜜経): Diamond-like Perfection of Wisdom Sutra
Vimalakīrti-nirdeśa (維摩経): Vimalakīrti Sutra
Viṃśatikā-vijñaptimātratā-siddhi (唯識二十論): Twenty-Stanza Treatise on the Consciousness-Only Doctrine, The
Yogācārabhūmi (瑜伽師地論): Treatise on the Stages of Yoga Practice, The

APPENDIX E

The Chinese Titles of Documents Referred to in the Dictionary

The descriptions of the Chinese titles listed below are found under their corresponding English translations.

An-lo-chi (安楽集): Collected Essays on the World of Peace and Delight, The
A-p'i-ta-mo-chü-she-lun (阿毘達磨俱舎論): Dharma Analysis Treasury, The
A-p'i-ta-mo-fa-chih-lun (阿毘達磨発智論): Treatise on the Source of Wisdom, The
A-p'i-ta-mo-shun-cheng-li-lun (阿毘達磨順正理論): Treatise on Accordance with the Correct Doctrine, The
A-p'i-ta-mo-ta-p'i-p'o-sha-lun (阿毘達磨大毘婆沙論): Great Commentary on the Abhidharma, The
A-p'i-t'an-hsin-lun (阿毘曇心論): Heart of the Abhidharma, The
Ch'ang-a-han-ching (長阿含経): Long Āgama Sutra
Chao-lun (肇論): Treatises of Seng-chao, The
Cheng-fa-hua-ching (正法華経): Lotus Sutra of the Correct Law
Cheng-fa-nien-ch'u-ching (正法念処経): Meditation on the Correct Teaching Sutra
Ch'eng-shih-lun (成実論): Treatise on the Establishment of Truth, The
Ch'eng-wei-shih-lun (成唯識論): Treatise on the Establishment of the Consciousness-Only Doctrine, The
Chen-yüan-ju-tsang-lu (貞元入蔵録): Chen-yüan Era Catalog of the Buddhist Canon, The
Chen-yüan-shih-chiao-lu (貞元釈教録): Chen-yüan Era Catalog of the Buddhist Canon, The
Chieh-shen-mi-ching (解深密経): Revelation of the Profound Secrets Sutra
Chih-kuan-fu-hsing-chuan-hung-chüeh (止観輔行伝弘決): Annotations on "Great Concentration and Insight," The
Ching-lü-i-hsiang (経律異相): Divergent Concepts in the Sutras and Vinaya Texts
Ching-t'u-lun (浄土論): Treatise on the Pure Land, The
Ching-t'u-lun-chu (浄土論註): Commentary on "The Treatise on the Pure Land," The
Ch'ing-yü-ching (請雨経): Prayer for Rain Sutra
Chin-kang-pan-jo-po-lo-mi-ching (金剛般若波羅蜜経): Diamond-like Perfection of Wisdom Sutra
Chin-kang-pei (金剛錍): Diamond Scalpel, The

Chin-kang-ting-ching (金剛頂経): Diamond Crown Sutra
Chin-kuang-ming-ching (金光明経): Golden Light Sutra
Chin-kuang-ming-tsui-sheng-wang-ching (金光明最勝王経): Sovereign Kings of the Golden Light Sutra
Chiu-ching-i-ch'eng-pao-hsing-lun (究竟一乗宝性論): Treatise on the Treasure Vehicle of Buddhahood, The
Chou-shu-i-chi (周書異記): Record of Wonders in the Book of Chou, The
Ch'uan-teng-lu (伝灯録): Transmission of the Lamp, The
Chung-a-han-ching (中阿含経): Medium-Length Āgama Sutra
Chung-kuan-lun-shu (中観論疏): Annotations on "The Treatise on the Middle Way," The
Chung-lun (中論): Treatise on the Middle Way, The
Ch'u-san-tsang-chi-chi (出三蔵記集): Collection of Records concerning the Tripitaka, A
Ch'u-yao-ching (出曜経): Sutra of Verses
Fa-chü-ching (法句経): Words of Truth Sutra
Fa-hsien-chuan (法顕伝): Travels of Fa-hsien, The
Fa-hua-ching (法華経): Lotus Sutra
Fa-hua-ching-an-lo-hsing-i (法華経安楽行義): On the Peaceful Practices of the Lotus Sutra
Fa-hua-ching-i-chi (法華経義記): Meaning of the Lotus Sutra, The
Fa-hua-ching-lun (法華経論): Treatise on the Lotus Sutra, The
Fa-hua-ching-shu-i-tsuan (法華経疏義纉): Supplement to the Meanings of the Commentaries on the Lotus Sutra, The
Fa-hua-chuan-chi (法華伝記): Lotus Sutra and Its Traditions, The
Fa-hua-fan-ching-hou-chi (法華翻経後記): Afterword to the Lotus Sutra Translation, The
Fa-hua-hsüan-i (法華玄義): Profound Meaning of the Lotus Sutra, The
Fa-hua-hsüan-i-shih-ch'ien (法華玄義釈籤): Annotations on "The Profound Meaning of the Lotus Sutra," The
Fa-hua-hsüan-lun (法華玄論): Treatise on the Profundity of the Lotus Sutra, The
Fa-hua-hsüan-tsan (法華玄賛): Praising the Profundity of the Lotus Sutra
Fa-hua-i-chi (法華義記): Meaning of the Lotus Sutra, The
Fa-hua-i-shu (法華義疏): Annotations on the Meaning of the Lotus Sutra, The
Fa-hua-lun (法華論): Treatise on the Lotus Sutra, The
Fa-hua-san-ta-pu-pu-chu (法華三大部補註): Supplement to the Three Major Works on the Lotus Sutra, The
Fa-hua-wen-chü (法華文句): Words and Phrases of the Lotus Sutra, The
Fa-hua-wen-chü-chi (法華文句記): Annotations on "The Words and Phrases of the Lotus Sutra," The
Fa-hua-wen-chü-fu-cheng-chi (法華文句輔正記): Supplement to "The Words and Phrases of the Lotus Sutra," The
Fa-mieh-chin-ching (法滅尽経): Decline of the Law Sutra
Fan-i-ming-i-chi (翻訳名義集): Dictionary of the Pronunciation and Meaning of Buddhist Terms, A

Fan-wang-ching（梵網経）: Brahmā Net Sutra
Fa-yüan-chu-lin（法苑珠林）: Forest of Gems in the Garden of the Law, The
Fo-hsing-lun（仏性論）: Treatise on the Buddha Nature, The
Fo-ming-ching（仏名経）: Buddhas' Names Sutra
Fo-pen-hsing-chi-ching（仏本行集経）: Sutra of the Collected Stories of the Buddha's Deeds in Past Lives
Fo-so-hsing-tsan（仏所行讃）: Praising the Buddha's Deeds
Fo-tsang-ching（仏蔵経）: Buddha Treasury Sutra
Fo-tsu-t'ung-chi（仏祖統紀）: Record of the Lineage of the Buddha and the Patriarchs, The
Fu-fa-tsang-yin-yüan-chuan（付法蔵因縁伝）: History of the Buddha's Successors, A
Hai-lung-wang-ching（海竜王経）: Dragon King of the Sea Sutra
Hsiang-fa-chüeh-i-ching（像法決疑経）: Sutra on Resolving Doubts about the Middle Day of the Law
Hsiao-p'in-pan-jo-ching（小品般若経）: Smaller Wisdom Sutra
Hsien-tsung-lun（顕宗論）: Clarification of Doctrine, A
Hsien-yü-ching（賢愚経）: Sutra on the Wise and the Foolish
Hsin-ti-kuan-ching（心地観経）: Contemplation on the Mind-Ground Sutra
Hsü-kao-seng-chuan（続高僧伝）: Continued Biographies of Eminent Priests, The
Hua-yen-ching（華厳経）: Flower Garland Sutra
Hua-yen-ching-shu（華厳経疏）: Annotations on the Flower Garland Sutra, The
Hua-yen-ching-t'an-hsüan-chi（華厳経探玄記）: Delving into the Profundity of the Flower Garland Sutra
Hung-ming-chi（弘明集）: Anthology of the Propagation of Light, The
I-chiao-ching（遺教経）: Legacy Teachings Sutra
I-ch'ieh-ching-yin-i（一切経音義）: Pronunciation and Meaning in the Buddhist Scriptures
I-pu-tsung-lun-lun（異部宗輪論）: Doctrines of the Different Schools, The
Jen-wang-ching（仁王経）: Benevolent Kings Sutra
Ju-lai-tsang-ching（如来蔵経）: Matrix of the Thus Come One Sutra
K'ai-yüan-shih-chiao-lu（開元釈教録）: K'ai-yüan Era Catalog of the Buddhist Canon, The
Kuan-fo-san-mei-hai-ching（観仏三昧海経）: Ocean of Meditation on the Buddha Sutra
Kuang-hung-ming-chi（広弘明集）: Further Anthology of the Propagation of Light, The
Kuan-hsin-lun（観心論）: Treatise on the Observation of the Mind, The
Kuan-wu-liang-shou-ching（観無量寿経）: Meditation on the Buddha Infinite Life Sutra
Kuan-wu-liang-shou-ching-shu（観無量寿経疏）: Commentary on the Meditation on the Buddha Infinite Life Sutra, The
Kuan-yin-ching（観音経）: Perceiver of the World's Sounds Sutra
Kuan-yin-hsüan-i（観音玄義）: Profound Meaning of the "Perceiver of the World's Sounds" Chapter, The

Kuo-ch'ing-pai-lu (国清百録): One Hundred Records of the Great Teacher T'ien-t'ai, The
Kuo-ch'ü-hsien-tsai-yin-kuo-ching (過去現在因果経): Causality of Past and Present Sutra
Lao-tzu-hua-hu-ching (老子化胡経): Sutra on the Conversion of Barbarians by Lao Tzu
Leng-ch'ieh-ching (楞伽経): Lankāvatāra Sutra
Liang-kao-seng-chuan (梁高僧伝): Liang Dynasty Biographies of Eminent Priests, The
Li-ch'ü-ching (理趣経): Principle of Wisdom Sutra
Liu-po-lo-mi-ching (六波羅蜜経): Six Pāramitās Sutra
Liu-tsu-t'an-ching (六祖壇経): Platform Sutra of the Sixth Patriarch, The
Miao-fa-lien-hua-ching (妙法蓮華経): Lotus Sutra of the Wonderful Law
Mi-yen-ching (密厳経): Secret Solemnity Sutra
Mo-ho-chih-kuan (摩訶止観): Great Concentration and Insight
Mo-ho-pan-jo-po-lo-mi-ching (摩訶般若波羅蜜経): Great Perfection of Wisdom Sutra
Mo-ho-seng-chih-lü (摩訶僧祇律): Great Canon of Monastic Rules, The
Mo-ya-ching (摩耶経): Māyā Sutra
Nan-hai-chi-kuei-nei-fa-chuan (南海寄帰内法伝): Record of Southern Countries, The
Nieh-p'an-ching (涅槃経): Nirvana Sutra
O-mi-t'o-ching (阿弥陀経): Amida Sutra
Pai-lun (百論): One-Hundred-Verse Treatise, The
Pan-chou-san-mei-ching (般舟三昧経): Sutra of the Meditation to Behold the Buddhas
Pan-jo-hsin-ching (般若心経): Heart Sutra
Pan-jo-teng-lun (般若灯論): Treatise on the Lamp of Wisdom, The
Pao-en-ching (報恩経): Repaying Debts of Gratitude Sutra
Pei-hua-ching (悲華経): Compassionate White Lotus Flower Sutra
P'u-hsien-ching (普賢経): Universal Worthy Sutra
P'u-sa-ying-lo-pen-yeh-ching (菩薩瓔珞本業経): Bodhisattva Practice Jeweled Necklace Sutra
P'u-t'i-hsin-lun (菩提心論): Treatise on the Mind Aspiring for Enlightenment, The
P'u-t'i-tzu-liang-lun (菩提資糧論): Treatise on the Discipline for Attaining Enlightenment, The
P'u-yao-ching (普曜経): Multitudinous Graceful Actions Sutra
San-lun-hsüan-i (三論玄義): Profound Meaning of the Three Treatises, The
Sheng-man-ching (勝鬘経): Shrīmālā Sutra
She-ta-ch'eng-lun (摂大乗論): Summary of the Mahayana, The
Shih-ching-t'u-ch'ün-i-lun (釈浄土群疑論): Treatise Resolving Numerous Doubts about the Pure Land Teachings, The
Shih-chu-p'i-p'o-sha-lun (十住毘婆沙論): Commentary on the Ten Stages Sutra, The
Shih-erh-men-lun (十二門論): Treatise on the Twelve Gates, The

Shih-mo-ho-yen-lun (釈摩訶衍論): Commentary on the Mahayana Treatise, The
Shih-pu-erh-men (十不二門): Ten Onenesses, The
Shih-sung-lü (十誦律): Ten Divisions of Monastic Rules, The
Shih-ti-ching (十地経): Ten Stages Sutra
Shih-ti-ching-lun (十地経論): Treatise on the Ten Stages Sutra, The
Shou-hu-kuo-chieh-ching (守護国界経): Protection of the Sovereign of the Nation Sutra
Shou-leng-yen-ching (首楞厳経): Shūramgama Sutra
Ssu-chiao-i (四教義): Meaning of the Four Teachings, The
Ssu-fen-lü (四分律): Fourfold Rules of Discipline, The
Ssu-fen-lü-hsing-shih-ch'ao (四分律行事鈔): Essentials of "The Fourfold Rules of Discipline," The
Ssu-i-ching (思益経): Brahmā Excellent Thought Sutra
Ssu-i-fan-t'ien-so-wen-ching (思益梵天所問経): Questions of Brahmā Excellent Thought Sutra
Ssu-shih-erh-chang-ching (四十二章経): Sutra of Forty-two Sections
Su-hsi-ti-ching (蘇悉地経): Susiddhikara Sutra
Sung-kao-seng-chuan (宋高僧伝): Sung Dynasty Biographies of Eminent Priests, The
Ta-ch'eng-chih-kuan-fa-men (大乗止観法門): Mahayana Method of Concentration and Insight, The
Ta-ch'eng-ch'i-hsin-lun (大乗起信論): Awakening of Faith in the Mahayana, The
Ta-ch'eng-chuang-yen-ching-lun (大乗荘厳経論): Ornament of Mahayana Sutras, The
Ta-ch'eng-fa-yüan-i-lin-chang (大乗法苑義林章): Forest of Meanings in the Mahayana Garden of the Law, The
Ta-ch'eng-ssu-lun-hsüan-i (大乗四論玄義): Profound Meaning of the Four Mahayana Treatises, The
Ta-chi-ching (大集経): Great Collection Sutra
Ta-chih-tu-lun (大智度論): Treatise on the Great Perfection of Wisdom, The
Ta-chuang-yen-lun-ching (大荘厳論経): Great Ornament of Tales, The
Ta-fan-t'ien-wang-wen-fo-chüeh-i-ching (大梵天王問仏決疑経): Sutra of the Buddha Answering the Great Heavenly King Brahmā's Questions
Ta-jih-ching (大日経): Mahāvairochana Sutra
Ta-jih-ching-i-shih (大日経義釈): Commentary on the Meaning of the Mahāvairochana Sutra, The
Ta-jih-ching-shu (大日経疏): Annotations on the Mahāvairochana Sutra, The
Ta-pan-jo-ching (大般若経): Great Wisdom Sutra
Ta-pan-jo-po-lo-mi-to-ching (大般若波羅蜜多経): Great Perfection of Wisdom Sutra
Ta-pan-nieh-p'an-ching (大般涅槃経): Mahāparinirvāna Sutra
Ta-pan-ni-yüan-ching (大般泥洹経): Mahāparinirvāna Sutra
Ta-pao-chi-ching (大宝積経): Accumulated Great Treasures Sutra
Ta-pei-ching (大悲経): Great Compassion Sutra

Ta-p'in-pan-jo-ching (大品般若経): Larger Wisdom Sutra
Ta-t'ang-hsi-yü-chi (大唐西域記): Record of the Western Regions of the Great T'ang Dynasty, The
Ta-t'ang-hsi-yü-ch'iu-fa-kao-seng-chuan (大唐西域求法高僧伝): Biographies of Eminent Priests of the Great T'ang Dynasty Who Sought the Law in the Western Regions, The
Ta-t'ang-nei-tien-lu (大唐内典録): Great T'ang Dynasty Catalog of Buddhist Scriptures, The
Ta-tz'u-en-ssu-san-tsang-fa-shih-chuan (大慈恩寺三蔵法師伝): Biography of the Tripitaka Master of Ta-tz'u-en-ssu Temple, The
T'ien-p'in-fa-hua-ching (添品法華経): Supplemented Lotus Sutra of the Wonderful Law
Tsa-a-han-ching (雑阿含経): Miscellaneous Āgama Sutra
Tseng-i-a-han-ching (増一阿含経): Increasing by One Āgama Sutra
Tung-ch'un (東春): Supplement to the Meanings of the Commentaries on the Lotus Sutra, The
Wang-sheng-li-tsan (往生礼讃): Praising Rebirth in the Pure Land
Wei-mo-ching (維摩経): Vimalakīrti Sutra
Wei-shih-erh-shih-lun (唯識二十論): Twenty-Stanza Treatise on the Consciousness-Only Doctrine, The
Wei-shih-san-shih-lun-sung (唯識三十論頌): Thirty-Stanza Treatise on the Consciousness-Only Doctrine, The
Wu-fen-lü (五分律): Fivefold Rules of Discipline, The
Wu-liang-i-ching (無量義経): Immeasurable Meanings Sutra
Wu-liang-shou-ching (無量寿経): Buddha Infinite Life Sutra
Wu-pai-wen-lun (五百問論): Treatise of Five Hundred Questions, The
Yao-shih-ching (薬師経): Medicine Master Sutra
Yin-se-nü-ching (銀色女経): Silver-Colored Woman Sutra
Yüan-chüeh-ching (円覚経): Perfect Enlightenment Sutra
Yü-ch'ieh-shih-ti-lun (瑜伽師地論): Treatise on the Stages of Yoga Practice, The
Yü-lan-p'en-ching (盂蘭盆経): Service for the Deceased Sutra

APPENDIX F

Sanskrit and Pali Terms and Names

The explanations of the Sanskrit and Pali terms and names in the left column are found under their corresponding English translations in the right column.

Ābhāsvara	Light Sound Heaven（光音天）
abhayaṃ-dada	Bestower of Fearlessness（施無畏者）
abhidhamma	abhidharma（阿毘達磨）
Abhirati	Abhirati（阿比羅提）
abhiṣeka	ceremony of anointment（灌頂）
Acala	Immovable（不動明王）
Acalanātha	Immovable（不動明王）
ācārya	āchārya（阿闍梨）
ādāna-vijñāna	ādāna-consciousness（阿陀那識）
agada	agada（阿伽陀）
Āgama	Āgama（阿含）
Agastya	Agastya（阿竭多仙）
Agnidatta	Agnidatta（阿耆達多）
Agramati	Superior Intent（勝意比丘）
Ahiṃsā	Ahimsā（アヒンサー）
Ajātaśatru	Ajātashatru（阿闍世王）
Ajita	Ajita（阿逸多）
Ajita Kesakambala	Ajita Kesakambala（阿耆多翅舎欽婆羅）
Ajitavatī	Ajitavatī（阿恃多伐底河）
Ājīvika	Ājīvika school（アージービカ派）
Ājñāta Kauṇḍinya	Ājnāta Kaundinya（阿若憍陳如）
Akaniṣṭha	Akanishtha Heaven（阿迦尼吒天）
ākāśa	ākāsha（虚空）
Ākāśagarbha	Ākāshagarbha（虚空蔵菩薩）
Ākāśānantyāyatana	Realm of Boundless Empty Space（空無辺処）
Ākiṃcanyāyatana	Realm of Nothingness（無所有処）
Akṣobhya	Akshobhya（阿閦仏）
Āḷāra Kālāma	Ālāra Kālāma（阿羅邏迦藍）
ālaya-vijñāna	ālaya-consciousness（阿頼耶識）
amala-vijñāna	amala-consciousness（阿摩羅識）
Ambapālī	Ambapālī（菴婆羅女）
Amitābha	Amida（阿弥陀）
Amitāyus	Amida（阿弥陀）
Amitodana	Amritodana（甘露飯王）

Amoghavajra	Pu-k'ung (不空)
Āmrapālī	Ambapālī (菴婆羅女)
amṛta	amrita (甘露)
Amṛtodana	Amritodana (甘露飯王)
anāgāmin	non-returner (阿那含)
Ānanda	Ānanda (阿難)
ananta	ananta (無辺・無量)
Anantacāritra	Boundless Practices (無辺行菩薩)
ananta-nirdeśa-pratiṣṭhāna-samādhi	samādhi of the origin of immeasurable meanings (無量義処三昧)
ānāpāna-smṛti	breath-counting meditation (数息観)
Anāthapiṇḍada	Sudatta (須達)
Anāthapiṇḍika	Sudatta (須達)
Anavatapta	Anavatapta (阿耨達竜王)
Aṅga	Anga (鴦伽国)
Aṅgulimāla	Angulimāla (央掘摩羅)
Aṅguttara-nikāya	Anguttara-nikāya (増支部)
Aniruddha	Aniruddha (阿那律)
Anuruddha	Aniruddha (阿那律)
anuttara	anuttara (阿耨多羅)
anuttara-saṃbodhi	unsurpassed enlightenment (無上菩提)
anuttara-samyak-saṃbodhi	anuttara-samyak-sambodhi (阿耨多羅三藐三菩提)
Aparagodānīya	Aparagodānīya (瞿耶尼)
araṇya	aranya (阿蘭若)
arhat	arhat (阿羅漢)
ariya-aṭṭhaṅgika-magga	eightfold path (八正道)
arjaka	arjaka (阿梨樹)
ārūpya-dhātu	world of formlessness (無色界)
ārya-aṣṭāṅga-mārga	eightfold path (八正道)
Āryadeva	Āryadeva (提婆)
Āryasiṃha	Āryasimha (師子尊者)
asama	Unequalled One (阿娑摩)
asaṃkhya	asamkhya (阿僧祇)
asaṃskṛta	unconditioned, the (無為)
Asaṅga	Asanga (無著)
Asita	Asita (阿私仙人・阿私陀)
aśoka	ashoka tree (阿輸迦樹)
Aśoka	Ashoka (阿育王)
āsrava	outflows (漏)
Assaji	Ashvajit (阿説示)
aṣṭāṅga-mārga	eightfold path (八正道)
asura	asura (阿修羅)
Aśvaghoṣa	Ashvaghosha (馬鳴)
Aśvajit	Ashvajit (阿説示)
aśvaśīrṣa	horse-headed demons (馬頭)

Āṭavaka	Great Commander（太元帥明王）
atimuktaka	atimuktaka（阿提目多伽）
aṭṭhaṅgika-magga	eightfold path（八正道）
avadāna	avadāna（阿波陀那）
avadāta-vasana	white-robed laymen（白衣）
avaivartika	avaivartika（阿毘跋致）
Avalokitasvara	Perceiver of the World's Sounds（觀世音菩薩）
Avalokiteśvara	Perceiver of the World's Sounds（觀世音菩薩）
Avanti	Avanti（阿槃提国）
Avīci	Avīchi hell（阿鼻地獄）
avidyā	ignorance（無明）
avivartika	avivartika（阿毘跋致）
avyākṛta	unlabeled, the（無記）
Ayodhyā	Ayodhyā（阿踰闍）
bāla	ordinary person（凡夫）
Bālāditya	Bālāditya（幻日王）
Balin	Balin（婆稚阿修羅王）
Bārāṇasī	Varanasi（波羅奈国）
bhadra-kalpa	Wise Kalpa（賢劫）
Bhadrapāla	Bhadrapāla（跋陀婆羅）
Bhadraruci	Bhadraruchi（賢愛論師）
Bhadrika	Bhadrika（跋提）
bhagavat	bhagavat（世尊）
bhaiṣajya	bhaishajya（薬）
Bhaiṣajyaguru	Medicine Master（薬師如来）
Bhaiṣajyarāja	Medicine King（薬王菩薩）
Bhaiṣajyarājasamudgata	Medicine Superior（薬上菩薩）
Bhava-agra	Summit of Being Heaven（有頂天）
Bhāvaviveka	Bhāvaviveka（清弁）
bhikkhu	bhikshu（比丘）
bhikkhunī	bhikshunī（比丘尼）
bhikṣu	bhikshu（比丘）
bhikṣuṇī	bhikshunī（比丘尼）
Bhīṣma-garjita-svara-rāja	Awesome Sound King（威音王仏）
Bimbisāra	Bimbisāra（頻婆娑羅王）
bodhi	bodhi（菩提）
bodhi-citta	aspiration for enlightenment（菩提心）
Bodhidharma	Bodhidharma（菩提達磨）
Bodhiruci	Bodhiruchi（菩提流支・菩提流志）
bodhisattva	bodhisattva（菩薩）
Brahmā	Brahmā（梵天）
brahma-caryā	brahma practice（梵行）
brāhmaṇa	Brahman（婆羅門）
brahma-svara	pure and far-reaching voice（梵音声）
Buddha	Buddha（仏）
Buddhabhadra	Buddhabhadra（仏陀跋陀羅）

buddha-dhātu	Buddha nature（仏性）
Buddhagayā	Buddhagayā（仏陀伽耶）
Buddhaghosa	Buddhaghosa（仏音）
buddha-gotra	Buddha nature（仏性）
Buddhajīva	Buddhajīva（仏陀什）
buddha-kṣetra	Buddha land（仏国土）
Buddhalocanā	Buddha Eye（仏眼）
Buddhamitra	Buddhamitra（仏陀密多）
Buddhananda	Buddhananda（仏陀難提）
Buddhapālita	Buddhapālita（仏護）
Buddhaśānta	Buddhashānta（仏陀扇多）
Buddha-sāsana	Buddha-shāsana（仏教）
Buddha-śāsana	Buddha-shāsana（仏教）
Buddhasiṃha	Buddhasimha（師子覚）
Buddhayaśas	Buddhayashas（仏陀耶舍）
cakra	chakra（輪宝）
Cakravāḍa	Chakravāda（鉄囲山）
cakravartin	chakravartin（転輪聖王）
cakravarti-rāja	wheel-turning king（転輪聖王）
Campā	Champā（瞻波）
campaka	champaka tree（瞻蔔樹）
caṇḍāla	chandāla（旃陀羅）
candana	sandalwood tree（栴檀）
Candra	moon, god of the（月天）
Candrakīrti	Chandrakīrti（月称・月称大臣）
Candraprabha	Chandraprabha（月光大臣）
Candraprabha	Moonlight（月光菩薩）
Candra-sūrya-pradīpa	Sun Moon Bright（日月燈明仏）
Candra-sūrya-vimala-prabhāsa-śrī	Sun Moon Pure Bright Virtue（日月浄明徳仏）
catur-ārya-satya	four noble truths（四諦）
catur-dhyāna	four stages of meditation（四禅定）
Cātur-mahārāja-kāyika	Heaven of the Four Heavenly Kings（四王天）
Chandaka	Chandaka（車匿）
Channa	Chandaka（車匿）
Ciñcā	Chinchā（旃遮）
Ciñcāmāṇavikā	Chinchā（旃遮）
cintāmaṇi	wish-granting jewel（如意宝珠）
Cūḍapanthaka	Chūdapanthaka（周利槃特）
Cūḷapanthaka	Chūdapanthaka（周利槃特）
Cunda	Chunda（純陀）
dāna	almsgiving（布施）
dāna-pati	dāna-pati（檀那）
Daṇḍaka	Dandaka, Mount（檀特山）
darśana-mārga	way of insight（見道）
Dasabala Kassapa	Dashabala Kāshyapa（十力迦葉）

Daśabala Kāśyapa	Dashabala Kāshyapa（十力迦葉）
daśa-bhūmi	ten stages of development（十地）
deśanā	repentance（懺悔）
deva	deva（天）
Devadatta	Devadatta（提婆達多）
deva-loka	heaven（天）
Devarāja	Heavenly King（天王如来）
devātideva	heavenly being among heavenly beings（天中天）
dhamma	dharma（法）
dhāraṇī	dhāranī（陀羅尼）
dharma	dharma（法）
dharma-cakra	wheel of the Law（法輪）
Dharmagupta	Dharmagupta（達摩笈多・達摩掬多）
Dharmagupta	Dharmagupta school（法蔵部）
Dharmakāla	Dharmakāla（曇摩迦羅）
Dharmākara	Dharma Treasury（法蔵比丘）
dharma-kāya	Dharma body（法身）
Dharmamitra	Dharmamitra（曇摩蜜多）
Dharmapāla	Dharmapāla（護法）
Dharmaprabhāsa	Law Bright（法明如来）
dharma-rāja	Dharma King（法王）
Dharmarakṣa	Dharmaraksha（竺法護・曇無讖）
Dharmaruci	Dharmaruchi（曇摩流支）
dharmatā	essential nature of phenomena（法性）
dharma-uddāna	Dharma seal（法印）
Dharmayaśas	Dharmayashas（曇摩耶舍）
Dharmodgata	Dharmodgata（曇無竭菩薩）
dhātu	dhātu（界）
Dhotodana	Dronodana（斛飯王）
Dhṛtaka	Dhritaka（提多迦）
Dhṛtarāṣṭra	Upholder of the Nation（持国天）
dhūta	dhūta practice（頭陀）
dhyāna	meditation（禅定）
Dīgha-nikāya	Dīgha-nikāya（長部）
Dignāga	Dignāga（陳那）
dīpa	dīpa（灯明）
Dīpaṃkara	Burning Torch（燃燈仏）
Dīpavaṃsa	Dīpavamsa（島史）
Divākara	Divākara（地婆訶羅）
Doṇa	Drona（香姓婆羅門）
dosa	anger（瞋恚）
Droṇa	Drona（香姓婆羅門）
Droṇodana	Dronodana（斛飯王）
duḥkha	suffering（苦）
dukkha	suffering（苦）

durgati	evil path（悪道）
dveṣa	anger（瞋恚）
dvīpa	dvīpa（洲）
Ekādaśa-mukha	Eleven-faced Perceiver of the World's Sounds（十一面観音）
eka-yāna	one vehicle（一乗）
eraṇḍa	eranda（伊蘭）
evaṃ mayā śrutam	"This is what I heard"（如是我聞）
Gadgadasvara	Wonderful Sound（妙音菩薩）
gaha-pati	householder（居士）
gandha	gandha（香）
Gandhamādana	Fragrant, Mount（香酔山）
Gandhāra	Gandhara（ガンダーラ）
gandharva	gandharva（乾闥婆）
Gandhavatī	City of Fragrances（衆香城）
Gaṅgā	Ganges River（恒河）
Gaṅgā-naḍī-vālukā	sands of the Ganges（恒河沙）
garbhadhātu	Womb Realm（胎蔵界）
garuḍa	garuda（迦楼羅）
gāthā	verse（偈）
gati	path（趣）
Gautama	Gautama（瞿曇）
Gautamī	Mahāprajāpatī（摩訶波闍波提）
Gayā	Gayā（伽耶城）
Gayā Kāśyapa	Gayā Kāshyapa（伽耶迦葉）
Gayāśīrṣa	Gayāshīrsha, Mount（伽耶山）
Ghoṣila	Ghoshila（瞿師羅）
Gijjhakūṭa	Eagle Peak（霊鷲山）
Girika	Girika（耆利柯）
Godānīya	Aparagodānīya（瞿耶尼）
Gopikā	Gopikā（瞿夷）
gośīrṣa	ox-headed demons（牛頭）
gośīrṣa-candana	ox-head sandalwood（牛頭栴檀）
Gotama	Gautama（瞿曇）
Gotamī	Mahāprajāpatī（摩訶波闍波提）
Gṛdhrakūṭa	Eagle Peak（霊鷲山）
gṛha-pati	householder（居士）
guṇa	benefit（功徳）
Guṇabhadra	Gunabhadra（求那跋陀羅）
Guṇamati	Gunamati（徳慧）
Guṇaprabha	Gunaprabha（徳光）
Guṇavarman	Gunavarman（求那跋摩）
Gurupādaka	Kukkutapāda, Mount（鶏足山）
Haklenayaśas	Haklenayashas（鶴勒夜那）
Hārītī	Mother of Demon Children（鬼子母神）
Harivarman	Harivarman（訶梨跋摩）

Harṣa	Harsha（戒日王）
Himālaya	Snow Mountains（雪山）
Himatala	Himatala（雪山下王）
Himavat	Snow Mountains（雪山）
Hīnayāna	Hinayana Buddhism（小乘仏教）
Hiraṇyavatī	Ajitavatī（阿恃多伐底河）
icchantika	icchantika（一闡提）
Indra	Indra（因陀羅）
indra-jāla	Indra's net（因陀羅網）
indriya	indriya（根）
Īśāna	Ishāna（伊舎那天）
Jaladhara-garjita-ghoṣa-susvara-nakṣatra-rāja-saṃkusumitābhijñā	Cloud Thunder Sound Constellation King Flower Wisdom（雲雷音宿王華智仏）
jala-maṇḍala	watery circle（水輪）
Jalavāhana	Water Carrier（流水）
jambu	jambu tree（閻浮樹）
Jambudīpa	Jambudvīpa（閻浮提）
Jambudvīpa	Jambudvīpa（閻浮提）
Jambūnada	Jambūnada gold（閻浮檀金）
Jāmbūnadaprabhāsa	Jāmbūnada Gold Light（閻浮那提金光如来）
Jātaka	Jātaka（本生話）
Jaṭiṃdhara	Water Holder（持水）
Jayata	Jayata（闍夜多）
Jeta	Jeta（祇陀太子）
Jetavana-vihāra	Jetavana Monastery（祇園精舎）
Jetṛ	Jetri（祇陀太子）
jhāna	meditation（禅定）
Jīvaka	Jīvaka（耆婆）
jīvaṃjīvaka	jīvamjīvaka（命命鳥）
Jñānagupta	Jnānagupta（闍那崛多）
Jñānākara	Wisdom Accumulated（智積）
Jñānaprabha	Jnānaprabha（智光）
Kaccāyana	Kātyāyana（迦旃延）
kālakula	kālakula（迦羅求羅）
Kalandaka	Kalandaka（迦蘭陀）
Kālasūtra	hell of black cords（黒縄地獄）
kalaviṅka	kalavinka（迦陵頻伽）
Kālayaśas	Kālayashas（畺良耶舎）
Kāḷi	Kāli（迦利王）
Kalmāṣapāda	Spotted Feet（斑足王）
Kālodāyin	Kālodāyin（迦留陀夷）
kalpa	kalpa（劫）
kalyāṇa-mitra	good friend（善知識）
kāma-dhātu	world of desire（欲界）
Kammāsapāda	Spotted Feet（斑足王）

Kaṇāda	Ulūka (優楼迦)
Kāṇadeva	Āryadeva (提婆)
Kanakamuni	Kanakamuni (倶那含仏)
kāñcana-maṇḍala	gold circle (金輪)
Kaniṣka	Kanishka (迦弐色迦王)
Kapila	Kapila (迦毘羅)
Kapilavastu	Kapilavastu (迦毘羅衛国)
Kapimala	Kapimala (迦毘摩羅)
karma	karma (業)
karuṇā	compassion (悲)
Kāśī	Kāshī (迦尸国)
Kaśmīra	Kashmir (迦湿弥羅国)
Kāśyapa	Kāshyapa (迦葉菩薩・迦葉仏)
Kāśyapa Mātaṅga	Kāshyapa Mātanga (迦葉摩騰)
Kāśyapīya	Kāshyapīya school (飲光部)
Kātyāyana	Kātyāyana (迦旃延)
Kātyāyanīputra	Kātyāyanīputra (迦多衍尼子)
Kauṇḍinya	Ājnāta Kaundinya (阿若憍陳如)
Kauśāmbī	Kaushāmbī (憍賞弥国)
Kauśika	Kaushika (憍尸迦)
Kharadīya	Kharadīya, Mount (伽羅陀山)
Khuddaka-nikāya	Khuddaka-nikāya (小部)
kilesa	earthly desires (煩悩)
kiṃnara	kimnara (緊那羅)
Kiṅkara	Kinkara (吉迦夜)
kleśa	earthly desires (煩悩)
Kokālika	Kokālika (瞿伽利)
Kosala	Kosala (憍薩羅国)
Kosambī	Kaushāmbī (憍賞弥国)
koṭi	koti (倶胝)
Krakucchanda	Krakucchanda (拘留孫仏)
Kṛki	Kriki (訖哩枳王)
krośa	krosha (倶盧舎)
Kṛta	Krita (訖利多王)
kṣama	repentance (懺悔)
kṣānti	forbearance (忍)
Kṣāntivādin	Forbearance (忍辱仙人)
Kṣatriya	Kshatriya (刹帝利)
kṣetra	kshetra (国土)
Kṣitigarbha	Kshitigarbha (地蔵菩薩)
Kukkuṭapāda	Kukkutapāda, Mount (鶏足山)
Kukkuṭārāma	Kukkutārāma Monastery (鶏頭摩寺)
kula-duhitṛ	good woman (善女人)
kula-putra	good man (善男子)
Kumārajīva	Kumārajīva (鳩摩羅什)
Kumārata	Kumārata (鳩摩羅駄)

Kumārayāṇa	Kumārayāna（鳩摩羅炎）
kumbhāṇḍa	kumbhānda（鳩槃荼）
Kuṇḍalī	Kundalī（軍荼利明王）
Kuntī	Kuntī（皐諦）
Kuru	Uttarakuru（鬱単越）
kuśa	kusha grass（吉祥草）
kuśala-mūla	good root（善根）
Kuśinagara	Kushinagara（拘尸那掲羅）
Kusuma-tala-garbha-vyūhālaṃkāra-loka-dhātu-samudra	Lotus Treasury World（蓮華蔵世界）
Licchavi	Licchavi（離車）
lobha	lobha（貪）
Lokakṣema	Lokakshema（支婁迦讖）
Lokāyata	Lokāyata（順世外道）
Lokeśvararāja	World Freedom King（世自在王仏）
Lumbinī	Lumbinī（藍毘尼）
madhya	madhya（末陀・中）
madhyamā-pratipad	Middle Way（中道）
Mādhyamika	Mādhyamika school（中観派）
Madhyāntika	Madhyāntika（末田提）
Magadha	Magadha（摩掲陀国）
mahā	mahā（摩訶）
Mahābhijñā-jñānābhibhū	Great Universal Wisdom Excellence（大通智勝仏）
Mahābrahmā	Mahābrahmā（大梵天）
Mahādāna	Earnest Donor（能施太子）
Mahādeva	Mahādeva（摩訶提婆）
Mahākaccāyana	Kātyāyana（迦旃延）
Mahākāla	Daikoku（大黒）
Mahākassapa	Mahākāshyapa（摩訶迦葉）
Mahākāśyapa	Mahākāshyapa（摩訶迦葉）
Mahākātyāyana	Kātyāyana（迦旃延）
Mahāmaudgalyāyana	Maudgalyāyana（目連）
Mahāmāyā	Māyā（摩耶）
Mahānāma	Mahānāma（摩訶男）
Mahāpajāpatī	Mahāprajāpatī（摩訶波闍波提）
Mahāpanthaka	Mahāpanthaka（摩訶槃特）
Mahāprajāpatī	Mahāprajāpatī（摩訶波闍波提）
Mahāsaṃghika	Mahāsamghika school（大衆部）
mahāsattva	mahāsattva（摩訶薩）
Mahāsattva	Mahāsattva（摩訶薩埵）
Mahāśrī	Auspicious（吉祥天）
Mahāsthāmaprāpta	Great Power（勢至菩薩）
Mahāvairocana	Mahāvairochana（大日如来）
Mahāvana-vihāra	Great Forest Monastery（大林精舎）

Mahāyāna	Mahayana Buddhism（大乘仏教）
Mahendra	Mahendra（摩呬陀）
Maheśvara	Maheshvara（摩醯首羅天）
Mahinda	Mahendra（摩呬陀）
Mahīśāsaka	Mahīshāsaka school（化地部）
mahoraga	mahoraga（摩睺羅伽）
Maitreya	Maitreya（弥勒）
maitrī	maitrī（慈）
makara	makara（摩竭）
Makkhali Gosāla	Makkhali Gosāla（末伽梨拘舍梨）
Malaya	Malaya, Mount（摩黎山）
Malla	Malla（末羅）
Mallikā	Mallikā（末利）
māna	arrogance（慢）
Māṇava	Learned Youth（儒童）
maṇḍala	mandala（曼荼羅）
māndāra	māndāra flower（曼陀羅華）
Māndhātṛ	Born from the Crown of the Head（頂生王）
maṇi	mani（摩尼）
mañjūṣaka	manjūshaka flower（曼殊沙華）
Mañjuśrī	Manjushrī（文殊師利菩薩）
Manoratha	Manoratha（摩㝹羅他）
Manorhita	Manorhita（摩奴羅）
mano-vijñāna	mano-consciousness（末那識）
mantra	mantra（真言）
māra	devil（魔）
Marīci	Marīchi（摩利支天）
Mātaṅga	Kāshyapa Mātanga（迦葉摩騰）
Mathurā	Mathura（摩突羅国）
Maudgalyāyana	Maudgalyāyana（目連）
Māyā	Māyā（摩耶）
Megha-dundubhi-svara-rāja	Cloud Thunder Sound King（雲雷音王仏）
Meru	Sumeru, Mount（須弥山）
Migadāya	Deer Park（鹿野苑）
Mihirakula	Mihirakula（大族王）
Mikkaka	Mikkaka（弥遮迦）
Milinda	Milinda（弥蘭陀王）
mitra	mitra（知識）
Moggallāna	Maudgalyāyana（目連）
moha	moha（愚癡）
mokṣa	emancipation（解脱）
Mṛgadāva	Deer Park（鹿野苑）
mudrā	mudra（印契）
mukti	emancipation（解脱）
muni	muni（聖者）
Mūrdhagata	Born from the Crown of the Head（頂生王）

Nadī Kāśyapa	Nadī Kāshyapa（那提迦葉）
nāga	dragon deity（竜神）
Nāgabodhi	Nāgabodhi（竜智）
nāga-rāja	dragon kings（竜王）
Nāgārjuna	Nāgārjuna（竜樹）
Nāgasena	Nāgasena（那先比丘）
Nairañjanā	Nairanjanā River（尼連禅河）
Naivasaṃjñānāsaṃjñāyatana	Realm of Neither Thought Nor No Thought（非想非非想処）
Nakṣatra-rāja-saṃkusumitābhijña	Constellation King Flower（宿王華）
Nālandā	Nālandā Monastery（那爛陀寺）
namas	namu（南無）
Nanda	Nanda（難陀）
naraka	hell（地獄）
Nārāyaṇa	Nārāyana（那羅延）
Narendrayaśas	Narendrayashas（那連提耶舎）
nayuta	nayuta（那由他）
Nerañjarā	Nairanjanā River（尼連禅河）
nibbāna	nirvana（涅槃）
Nigaṇṭha Nātaputta	Nigantha Nātaputta（尼乾陀若提子）
niraya	hell（地獄）
nirmāṇa-kāya	manifested body（応身）
Nirmāṇarati	Heaven of Enjoying the Conjured（化楽天）
nirvāṇa	nirvana（涅槃）
nyagrodha	nyagrodha tree（尼拘律樹）
Nyagrodha	Nyagrodha（尼倶律陀）
oṃ	om（唵）
Padma	hell of the crimson lotus（紅蓮地獄）
Padma-garbha-loka-dhātu	Lotus Treasury World（蓮華蔵世界）
Padmaprabha	Flower Glow（華光如来）
Pakudha Kaccāyana	Pakudha Kacchāyana（迦羅鳩駄迦旃延）
pāṃsu-kūla	clothes of patched rags（糞掃衣）
pañca-indriya	five sense organs（五根）
pañca-skandha	five components（五陰）
pāpīyas	pāpīyas（波旬）
pārājika	pārājika（波羅夷）
Paramārtha	Paramārtha（真諦）
pāramitā	pāramitā（波羅蜜）
Paranirmita-vaśa-vartin	Heaven of Freely Enjoying Things Conjured by Others（他化自在天）
pariṇāma	transference of benefit（廻向）
parinirvāṇa	parinirvāna（般涅槃）
Pārśva	Pārshva（脇比丘）
Pasenadi	Prasenajit（波斯匿王）
Pāṭaliputra	Pātaliputra（華氏城）

paṭicca-samuppāda	dependent origination (縁起)
pātra	alms bowl (鉢)
patta	alms bowl (鉢)
pattra	pattra (貝多羅)
pavāraṇā	pravārana (自恣)
Pilindavatsa	Pilindavatsa (畢陵伽婆蹉)
Piṇḍolabhāradvāja	Pindolabhāradvāja (賓頭盧)
Piṅgala	Pingala (青目)
pippala	pippala tree (畢鉢羅樹)
Pippalī	Pippalī Cave (畢鉢羅窟)
piśāca	pishācha (毘舎闍)
poṣadha	uposhadha (布薩)
Potalaka	Potalaka, Mount (補陀落山)
Prabhūtaratna	Many Treasures (多宝如来)
prajñā	prajnā (般若)
Prajñā	Prajnā (般若)
Prajñākūṭa	Wisdom Accumulated (智積)
prajñā-pāramitā	prajnā-pāramitā (般若波羅蜜)
Prajñāruci	Prajnāruchi (般若流支)
praṇidhāna	vow (誓願)
Prāsaṅgika	Prāsangika school (帰謬論証派)
Prasannendriya	Root of Joy (喜根比丘)
Prasenajit	Prasenajit (波斯匿王)
pratigha	pratigha (瞋恚)
pratītya-samutpāda	dependent origination (縁起)
pratyekabuddha	cause-awakened one (縁覚)
pratyutpanna-samādhi	meditation to behold the Buddhas (般舟三昧)
pravāraṇa	pravārana (自恣)
preta	preta (餓鬼)
pṛthag-jana	ordinary person (凡夫)
Puṇṇa	Pūrna (富楼那)
puṇya	punya (功徳)
puṇya-kṣetra	field of good fortune (福田)
Puṇyatāra	Punyatāra (弗若多羅)
Puṇyayaśas	Punyayashas (富那奢)
Pūraṇa Kassapa	Pūrana Kassapa (富蘭那迦葉)
Pūrṇa	Pūrna (富楼那)
pūrvapraṇidhāna	original vows (本願)
Pūrvavideha	Pūrvavideha (弗婆提)
Puṣyamitra	Pushyamitra (弗沙弥多羅王)
pūtana	pūtana (富単那)
rāga	rāga (貪)
Rāgarāja	Craving-Filled (愛染明王)
Rāhula	Rāhula (羅睺羅)
Rāhulabhadra	Rāhulabhadra (羅睺羅跋陀羅)
Rājagṛha	Rājagriha (王舎城)

rākṣasa	rākshasa（羅刹）
Raśmiprabhāsa	Light Bright（光明如来）
Raśmi-śatasahasra-paripūrṇa-dhvaja	Endowed with a Thousand Ten Thousand Glowing Marks（具足千万光相如来）
ratna	ratna（宝）
Ratnaketu	Jewel Sign（宝相如来）
Ratnamati	Ratnamati（勒那摩提）
Ratnatejobhyudgatarāja	King Above Jeweled Dignity and Virtue（宝威徳上王仏）
ratna-traya	three treasures（三宝）
Revata	Revata（離婆多）
Ṛṣipatana	Rishipatana（仙人堕処）
rūpa-dhātu	world of form（色界）
Sadāparibhūta	Never Disparaging（常不軽菩薩）
Sadāprarudita	Ever Wailing（常啼菩薩）
saddhā	faith（信）
ṣaḍ-gati	six paths（六道）
sādhu	sādhu（善哉）
ṣaḍ-indriya	six sense organs（六根）
Sāgara	Sāgara（沙竭羅竜王）
Sāgara-vara-dhara-buddhi-vikrīḍitābhijña	Mountain Sea Wisdom Unrestricted Power King（山海慧自在通王如来）
sahā	sahā world（娑婆世界）
Sahasrabhuja	Thousand-armed Perceiver of the World's Sounds（千手観音）
Śāketa	Shāketa（娑祇多）
Śakra	Shakra（帝釈）
Śakra Devānām Indra	Shakra（帝釈）
sakṛdāgāmin	once-returner（斯陀含）
Śākya	Shākya（釈迦族）
Śākyamuni	Shakyamuni（釈尊）
śāla	sal tree（沙羅樹）
samādhi	samādhi（三昧）
samaṇa	shramana（沙門）
sāmaṇera	shrāmanera（沙弥）
sāmaṇerī	shrāmanerī（沙弥尼）
Samantabhadra	Universal Worthy（普賢菩薩）
Samantaprabhāsa	Universal Brightness（普明如来）
samaya	samaya（三昧耶形）
saṃbhoga-kāya	reward body（報身）
saṃgha	samgha（僧伽）
Saṃghabhadra	Samghabhadra（僧伽跋陀羅）
Saṃghadeva	Samghadeva（僧伽提婆）
Saṃghanandi	Samghanandi（僧伽難提）
Saṃghavarman	Samghavarman（康僧鎧・僧伽跋摩）
Saṃghayaśas	Samghayashas（僧伽耶舎）

saṃgīti	Buddhist Councils（結集）
Saṃjīva	hell of repeated rebirth for torture（等活地獄）
saṃsāra	samsāra（輪廻）
Saṃyutta-nikāya	Samyutta-nikāya（相応部）
Śāṇavāsa	Shānavāsa（商那和修）
saṅgha	samgha（僧伽）
Sañjaya Belaṭṭhiputta	Sanjaya Belatthiputta（刪闍耶毘羅胝子）
Saptaparṇa	Cave of the Seven Leaves（七葉窟）
Saptaratnapadma-vikrāntagāmin	Stepping on Seven Treasure Flowers（蹈七宝華如来）
Sāramati	Sāramati（堅慧）
Sarasvatī	Eloquence（弁才天）
Śāriputra	Shāriputra（舎利弗）
Sarva-sattva-priyadarśana	Gladly Seen by All Living Beings（一切衆生喜見如来・一切衆生喜見菩薩）
Sarvāstivāda	Sarvāstivāda school（説一切有部）
śāsana	shāsana（教）
Śaśiketu	Rare Form（名相）
śāstā-deva-manuṣyānāṃ	Teacher of Heavenly and Human Beings（天人師）
sattva	sattva（薩埵）
Sattva	Sattva（薩埵王子）
Sautrāntika	Sautrāntika school（経量部）
Sāvatthī	Shrāvastī（舎衛城）
Śibi	Shibi（尸毘王）
Siddhārtha	Siddhārtha（悉達多）
Sīhahanu	Simhahanu（師子頬王）
śikṣamāṇā	shikshamānā（式叉摩那）
Śikṣānanda	Shikshānanda（実叉難陀）
śīla	precepts（戒）
Śīlabhadra	Shīlabhadra（戒賢）
Śīlāditya	Shīlāditya（戒日王）
Siṃhahanu	Simhahanu（師子頬王）
siṃhanāda	lion's roar（師子吼）
Siṃhanādarāja	Lion Sound King（師子音王仏）
siṃhāsana	lion seat（師子座）
Śītavana	Shītavana（尸陀林）
śloka	shloka（首盧迦）
soma	soma（蘇摩）
sota-āpanna	stream-winner（須陀洹）
śraddhā	faith（信）
śramaṇa	shramana（沙門）
śrāmaṇera	shrāmanera（沙弥）
śrāmaṇerī	shrāmanerī（沙弥尼）
śrāvaka	voice-hearer（声聞）
Śrāvastī	Shrāvastī（舎衛城）

Śrīmahādevī	Auspicious（吉祥天）
Śrīmālā	Shrīmālā（勝鬘夫人）
srota-āpanna	stream-winner（須陀洹）
Śrutasoma	Universal Brightness（普明王）
Sthaviravāda	Sthaviravāda school（上座部）
Sthiramati	Sthiramati（安慧）
stūpa	stupa（塔）
Subhadra	Subhadra（須跋陀羅）
Śubhakarasiṃha	Shan-wu-wei（善無畏）
Śubhavyūha	Wonderful Adornment（妙荘厳王）
Subhūti	Subhūti（須菩提）
Sudāna	Sudāna（須大拏太子）
Sudarśana	Correct Views（善見城）
Sudatta	Sudatta（須達）
śuddhāvāsa	five heavens of purity（五浄居天）
Śuddhodana	Shuddhodana（浄飯王）
Sudhana-śreṣṭhi-dāraka	Good Treasures（善財童子）
Sudharman	Hall of the Good Law（善法堂）
sugata	Well Attained（善逝）
Sujātā	Sujātā（須闍多）
Sukhāvatī	Perfect Bliss（極楽）
Śuklodana	Shuklodana（白飯王）
sumanā	sumanā（須摩那）
Sumeru	Sumeru, Mount（須弥山）
Sunakṣatra	Sunakshatra（善星比丘）
Sundarananda	Nanda（難陀）
Sundarī	Sundarī（孫陀利）
śūnya	non-substantiality（空）
Suprabuddha	Suprabuddha（善覚）
Supratiṣṭhitacāritra	Firmly Established Practices（安立行菩薩）
śūraṃgama-samādhi	shūramgama meditation（首楞厳三昧）
Sūrya	sun, god of the（日天）
Sūryaprabha	Sunlight（日光菩薩）
Śūryasoma	Shūryasoma（須利耶蘇摩）
Sutasoma	Universal Brightness（普明王）
svabhāva	self-nature（自性）
Svātantrika	Svātantrika school（自立論証派）
Takṣaśilā	Takshashilā（徳叉尸羅）
tāla	tāla tree（多羅樹）
Tamālapattra-candana-gandha	Tamālapattra Sandalwood Fragrance（多摩羅跋栴檀香如来）
Tapana	hell of burning heat（焦熱地獄）
tathāgata	Thus Come One（如来）
tathāgata-dūta	envoy of the Thus Come One（如来の使）
tathāgata-garbha	matrix of the Thus Come One（如来蔵）
tathatā	tathatā（真如）

Theravāda	Theravāda school（上座部）
tipiṭaka	three divisions of the canon（三蔵）
Trailokyavijaya	Conqueror of the Threefold World（降三世明王）
Trāyastriṃśa	Heaven of the Thirty-three Gods（三十三天）
trikāya	three bodies（三身）
tripiṭaka	three divisions of the canon（三蔵）
triratna	three treasures（三宝）
trisāhasra-mahāsāhasraloka-dhātu	major world system（三千大千世界）
Tuṣita	Tushita Heaven（兜率天）
Udayana	Udayana（優塡王）
Uddaka Rāmaputta	Uddaka Rāmaputta（鬱頭藍弗）
Uḍḍiyāna	Uddiyāna（烏仗那国）
Udena	Udayana（優塡王）
Udraka Rāmaputra	Udraka Rāmaputra（鬱頭藍弗）
udumbara	udumbara（優曇華）
Udyāna	Udyāna（烏仗那国）
Ujjayinī	Ujjayinī（烏闍衍那国）
ullambana	service for deceased ancestors（盂蘭盆）
Ulūka	Ulūka（優楼迦）
upadeśa	upadesha（優婆提舎）
Upagupta	Upagupta（優婆毱多）
Upāli	Upāli（優婆離）
upāsaka	man of pure faith（清信士）
upāsikā	woman of pure faith（清信女）
upāya	expedient means（方便）
upoṣadha	uposhadha（布薩）
Uppalavaṇṇā	Utpalavarnā（蓮華色比丘尼）
ūrṇā-keśa	tuft of white hair（白毫相）
Urumaṇḍa	Urumanda, Mount（優留曼荼山）
Uruvelā	Uruvilvā（優楼頻螺）
Uruvelā Kassapa	Uruvilvā Kāshyapa（優楼頻螺迦葉）
Uruvilvā	Uruvilvā（優楼頻螺）
Uruvilvā Kāśyapa	Uruvilvā Kāshyapa（優楼頻螺迦葉）
uṣṇīṣa-śiraskatā	knot of flesh on the head（肉髻相）
Utpalavarṇā	Utpalavarnā（蓮華色比丘尼）
Uttarakuru	Uttarakuru（鬱単越）
Vaidehī	Vaidehī（韋提希）
vaipulya	vaipulya（方等）
Vairocana	Vairochana（毘盧遮那仏）
Vaiśālī	Vaishālī（毘舎離）
vaiśāradya	fearlessness（無畏）
Vaiśravaṇa	Vaishravana（毘沙門天）
Vajji	Vajji（跋耆）
vajra	diamond-pounder（金剛杵）

Vajrabodhi	Chin-kang-chih（金剛智）
vajradhara	vajra-bearing god（執金剛神）
vajradhātu	Diamond Realm（金剛界）
Vajragarbha	Diamond Storehouse（金剛蔵菩薩）
vajrapāṇi	vajra-bearing god（執金剛神）
Vajrasattva	Vajrasattva（金剛薩埵）
Vajrayāna	Tantric Buddhism（タントラ仏教）
vana	vana（園林）
Vārāṇasī	Varanasi（波羅奈国）
Varaprabha	Wonderfully Bright（妙光菩薩）
varṣa	three-month retreat（安居）
Varṣakāra	Varshakāra（雨行大臣）
vārṣika	three-month retreat（安居）
vassa	three-month retreat（安居）
Vasubandhu	Vasubandhu（世親）
Vasumitra	Vasumitra（世友）
Vatsa	Vatsa（跋蹉）
Vātsīputrīya	Vātsīputrīya school（犢子部）
vāyu-maṇḍala	windy circle（風輪）
Vedehī	Vaidehī（韋提希）
Veṇuvana-vihāra	Bamboo Grove Monastery（竹林精舎）
Vesālī	Vaishālī（毘舎離）
vetāḍa	vetāda（毘陀羅）
vetāla	vetāda（毘陀羅）
vibhāṣā	vibhāshā（毘婆沙）
Viḍūḍabha	Virūdhaka（波瑠璃王）
vidyā-rāja	wisdom kings（明王）
vihāra	vihāra（精舎）
Vijñānānantyāyatana	Realm of Boundless Consciousness（識無辺処）
Vijñānavāda	Consciousness-Only school（唯識派）
Vikramaśilā	Vikramashilā Monastery（ビクラマシラー寺）
Vimaladattā	Pure Virtue（浄徳）
Vimalagarbha	Pure Storehouse（浄蔵）
Vimalakīrti	Vimalakīrti（維摩詰）
Vimalamitra	Vimalamitra（無垢論師）
Vimalanetra	Pure Eye（浄眼）
vimokṣa	vimoksha（解脱）
vimukti	emancipation（解脱）
Vimukticandra	Moon of Deliverance（解脱月菩薩）
vinaya	vinaya（律）
Virūḍhaka	Increase and Growth（増長天）
Virūḍhaka	Virūdhaka（波瑠璃王）
Virūpākṣa	Wide-Eyed（広目天）
vīrya	vīrya（精進）
Viśiṣṭacāritra	Superior Practices（上行菩薩）

Viśuddhacāritra	Pure Practices（浄行菩薩）
Viśvakarman	Vishvakarman（毘首羯磨天）
Vṛji	Vriji（跋耆）
vyākaraṇa	prophecy of future enlightenment（授記）
yakṣa	yaksha（夜叉）
Yama	Yama（閻魔）
Yāma	Yāma Heaven（夜摩天）
Yamāntaka	Great Awesome Virtue（大威徳明王）
yāna	yāna（乗）
Yasa	Yasa（耶舎）
Yaśas	Yashas（耶舎）
Yaśodharā	Yashodharā（耶輸陀羅）
yoga	yoga（瑜伽）
Yogācāra	Yogāchāra school（瑜伽行派）
yojana	yojana（由旬）

APPENDIX G: Hinayana Schools

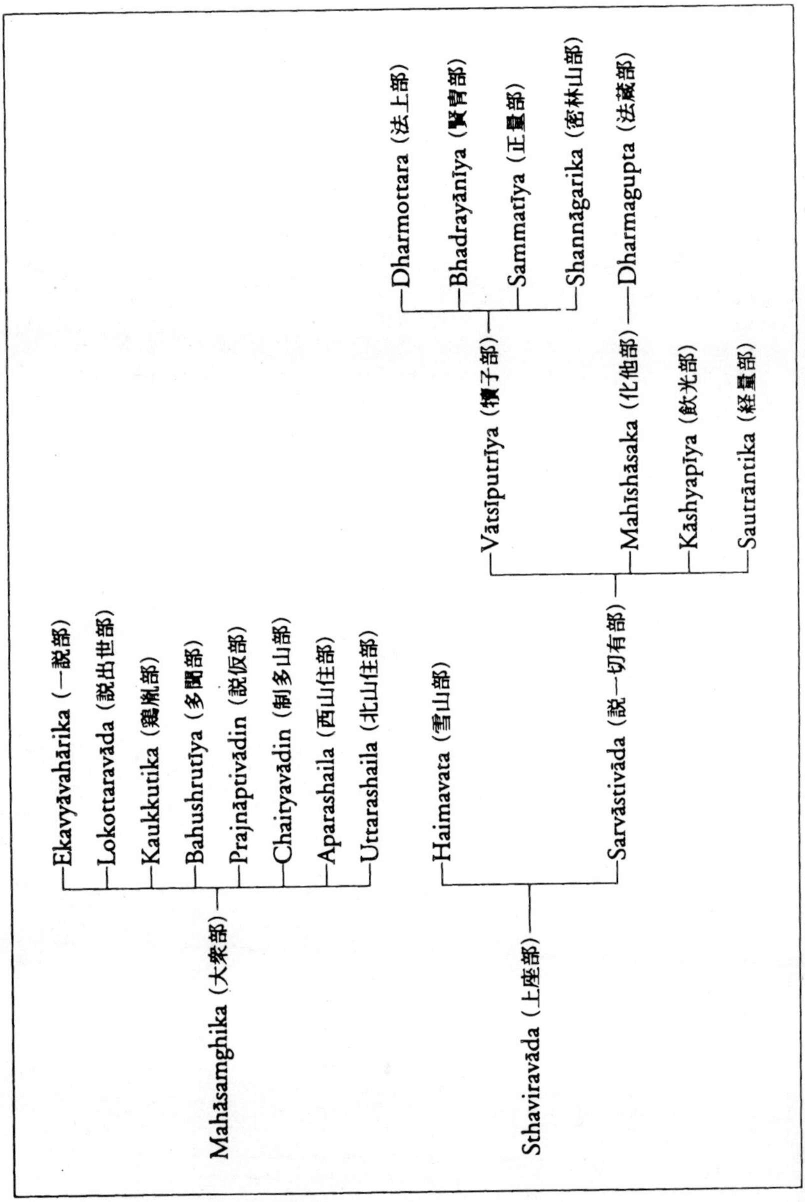

APPENDIX H: Maps

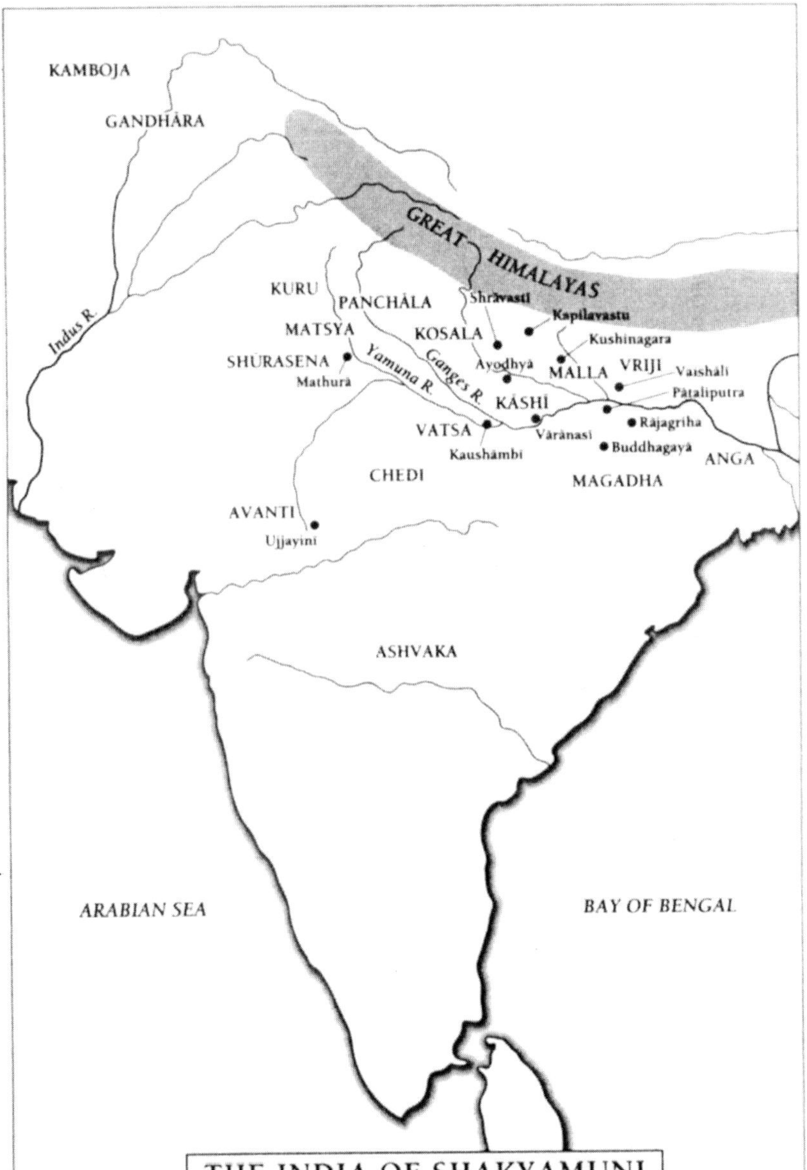

THE INDIA OF SHAKYAMUNI

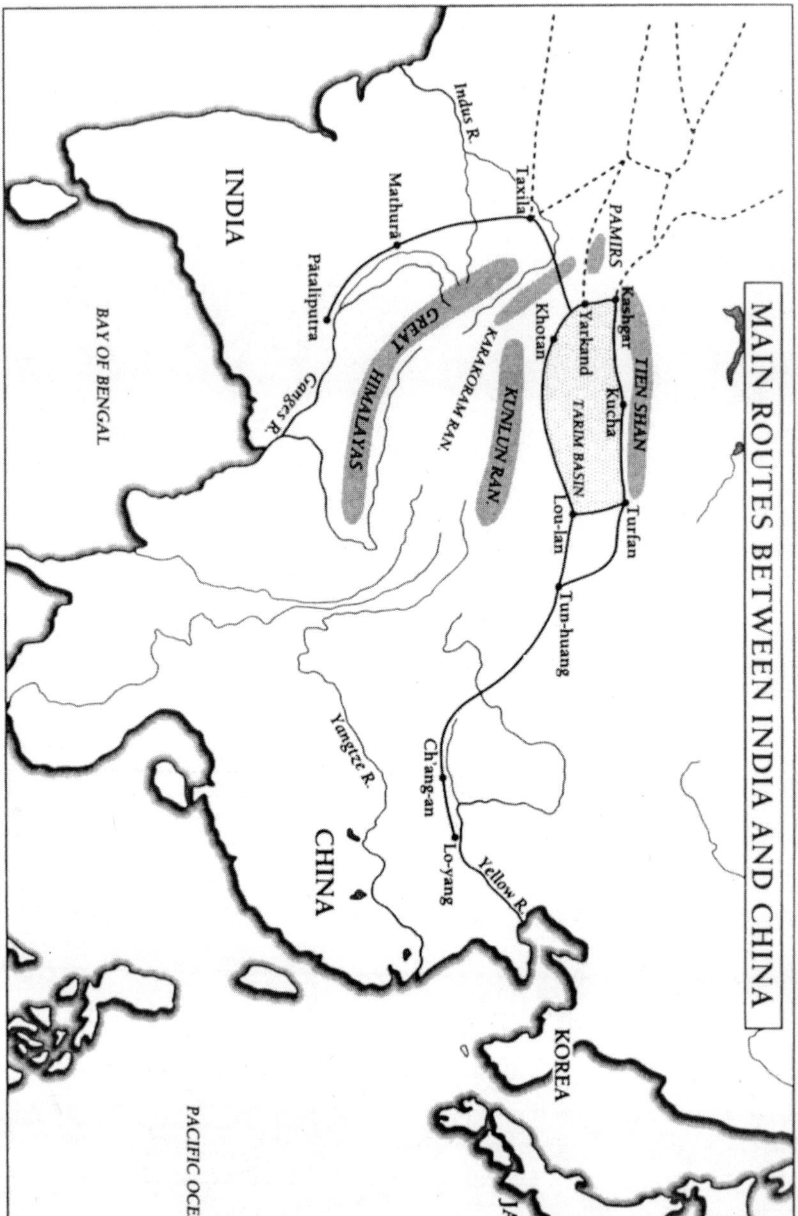
MAIN ROUTES BETWEEN INDIA AND CHINA
INDIA
BAY OF BENGAL
Indus R.
Ganges R.
Taxila
Mathurā
Pātaliputra
GREAT HIMALAYAS
KARAKORAM RAN.
KUNLUN RAN.
PAMIRS
TIEN SHAN
TARIM BASIN
Kashgar
Yarkand
Khotan
Kucha
Turfan
Lou-lan
Tun-huang
Ch'ang-an
Lo-yang
Yellow R.
Yangtze R.
CHINA
KOREA
JAPAN
PACIFIC OCEAN

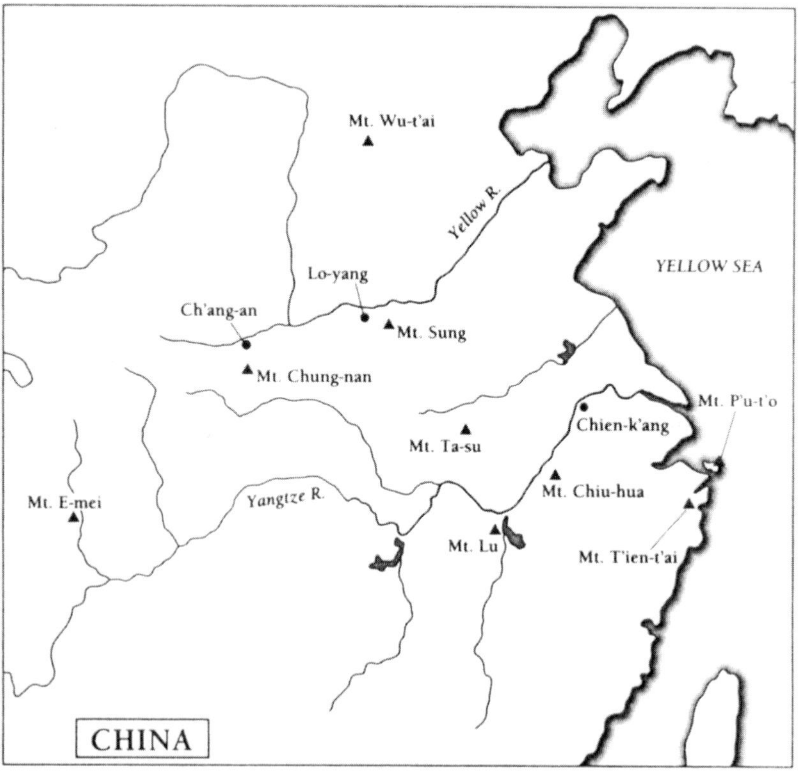
Mt. Wu-t'ai
Yellow R.
YELLOW SEA
Lo-yang
Ch'ang-an
Mt. Sung
Mt. Chung-nan
Mt. P'u-t'o
Chien-k'ang
Mt. Ta-su
Mt. Chiu-hua
Mt. E-mei
Yangtze R.
Mt. Lu
Mt. T'ien-t'ai
CHINA

KOREA AROUND C.E. 550
CHINA
KOGURYŎ
SEA OF JAPAN
SILLA
PAEKCHE
YELLOW SEA
JAPAN

Aki	50
Awa	9
Awa	55
Awaji	53
Bingo	46
Bitchû	45
Bizen	41
Bungo	60
Buzen	58
Chikugo	65
Chikuzen	59
Dewa	2
Echigo	3
Echizen	25
Etchû	22
Harima	40
Hida	21
Higo	64
Hitachi	6
Hizen	66
Hôki	44
Hyûga	61
Iga	28
Iki	67
Inaba	43
Ise	29
Iwami	49
Iyo	57
Izu	10
Izumi	35
Izumo	47
Kaga	24
Kai	15
Kawachi	34

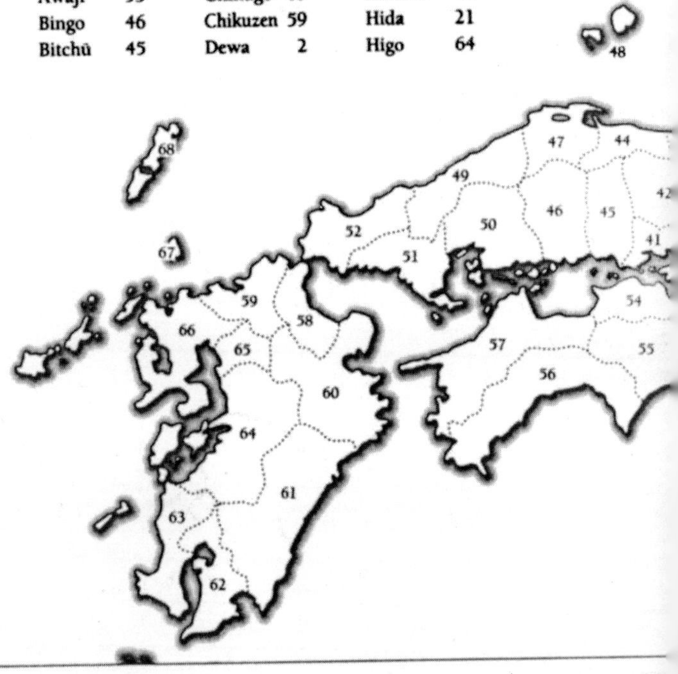

OLD PROVINCES OF JAPAN

rovince names are in alphabetical order. Numbers following
rovince names correspond to those on the map, which show
ie location of each province.

azusa	8	Musashi	12	Ōsumi	62
ii	31	Mutsu	1	Owari	19
ōzuke	13	Nagato	52	Sado	4
ikawa	18	Noto	23	Sagami	11
imasaka	42	Oki	48	Sanuki	54
ino	20	Ōmi	27		

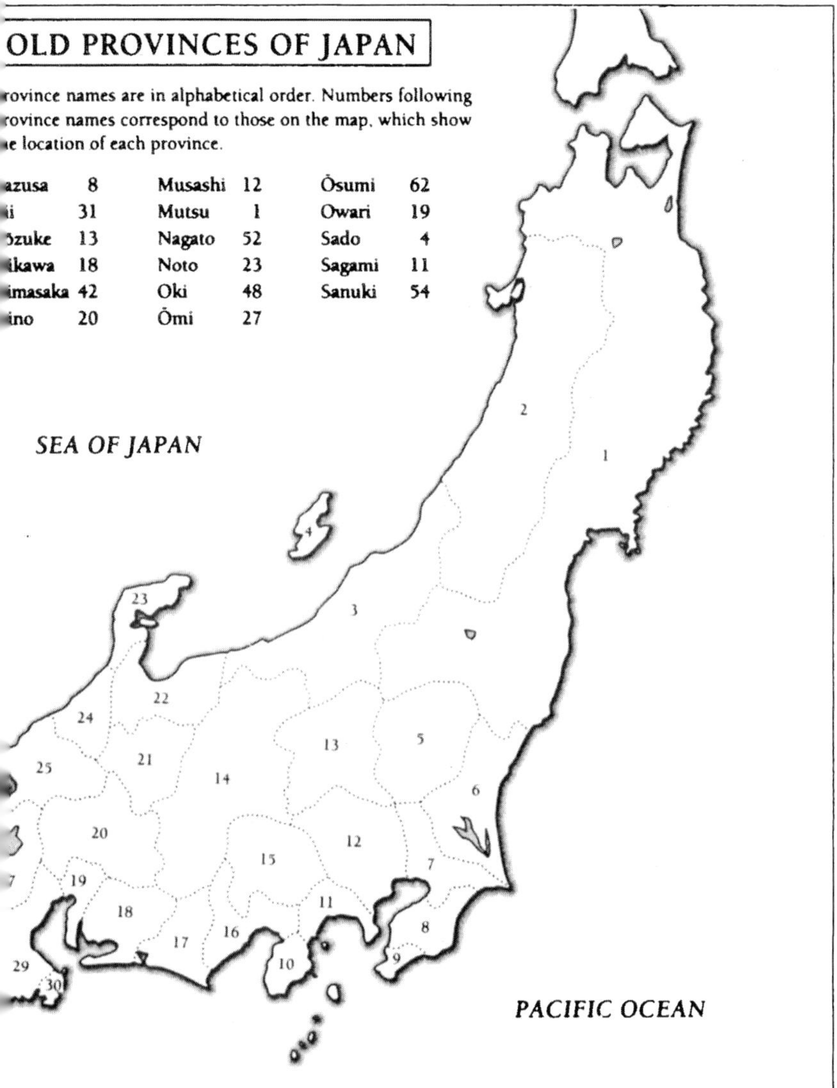

Satsuma	63	Suō	51	Tōtōmi	17
Settsu	36	Suruga	16	Tsushima	68
Shima	30	Tajima	39	Wakasa	26
Shimōsa	7	Tamba	37	Yamashiro	33
Shimotsuke	5	Tango	38	Yamato	32
Shinano	14	Tosa	56		

APPENDIX I

Chinese Dynasties

Hsia	c. 21st–c. 16th century B.C.E.		
Yin (Shang)	c. 16th–c. 11th century B.C.E.		
Chou	c. 1100–256 B.C.E.		
Western Chou	c. 1100–770 B.C.E.		
Eastern Chou	770–256 B.C.E.		
Spring and Autumn period	770–403 B.C.E.		
Warring States period	403–221 B.C.E.		
Ch'in	221–206 B.C.E.		
Han	202 B.C.E.– C.E. 220		
Former Han	202 B.C.E.– C.E. 8		
Later Han	25–220		
Period of the Three Kingdoms	220–280		
Wu 222–280	Wei 220–265	Shu	221–263
Chin	265–420		
Western Chin	265–316		
Eastern Chin	317–420	Later Chao	319–351
		Former Liang	301–376
		Former Ch'in	351–394
		Later Ch'in	384–417
		Northern Liang	397–439
Northern and Southern Dynasties	439–589		
Liu Sung	420–479	Northern Wei	386–534
Ch'i	479–502		
Liang	502–557	Northern Ch'i	550–577
Ch'en	557–589	Norhtern Chou	557–581
Sui	581–618		
T'ang	618–907		
Five Dynasties	907–960		
Sung	960–1279		
Northern Sung	960–1127		
Southern Sung	1127–1279	Liao	916–1125
		Chin	1115–1234
Yüan	1271–1368		
Ming	1368–1644		
Ch'ing	1644–1912		

APPENDIX J

Terms and Names in Japanese

Romanized Japanese terms and names are arranged in alphabetical order and followed by Chinese characters or Japanese syllabary in parentheses. Following next are the corresponding dictionary entries. For example, the Japanese name Aiku-ō is followed by the Chinese characters for the name, and then by Ashoka, which is the corresponding entry. But in cases where there are no corresponding entries, the equivalents of the Japanese terms or names are given and the entries under which you can find their definitions are shown in parentheses. For example, the Japanese term *bosatsu-jō* is followed by its English equivalent *bodhisattva vehicle* and (*See* three vehicles). In this case, you would look for the entry *three vehicles* where you would find *bodhisattva vehicle* in the body of the definition.

Ababa-jigoku（阿婆婆地獄）: Ababa hell (*See* eight cold hells)

abadana（阿波陀那）: *avadāna*

abibatchi（阿毘跋致）: *avaivartika;* stage of non-regression

Abi-daijō（阿鼻大城）: great citadel of the Avīchi hell

abidatsuma（阿毘達磨）: *abhidharma*

Abidatsuma-daibibasha-ron（阿毘達磨大毘婆沙論）: *Great Commentary on the Abhidharma, The*

Abidatsuma-hotchi-ron（阿毘達磨発智論）: *Treatise on the Source of Wisdom, The*

Abidatsuma-junshōri-ron（阿毘達磨順正理論）: *Treatise on Accordance with the Correct Doctrine, The*

Abidatsuma-kusha-ron（阿毘達磨倶舎論）: *Dharma Analysis Treasury, The*

Abidon-shin-ron（阿毘曇心論）: *Heart of the Abhidharma, The*

Abi-jigoku（阿鼻地獄）: Avīchi hell

Abutsu-bō（阿仏房）

adaimokutaka（阿提目多伽）: *atimuktaka*

adana-shiki（阿陀那識）: *ādāna*-consciousness

Agidatta（阿耆達多）: Agnidatta

Agita（阿耆多）: Agnidatta

Agita-shishakimbara（阿耆多翅舎欽婆羅）: Ajita Kesakambala

Agitatsu（阿耆達）: Agnidatta

Agon（阿含）: Āgama

Agon-gyō（阿含経）: Āgama sutras

Agon-ji（阿含時）: Āgama period

Ahaha-jigoku（阿波波地獄）: Hahava hell (*See* eight cold hells)

Ahandai-koku（阿槃提国）: Avanti

ahinsā（アヒンサー）: *ahimsā*

Ahiradai（阿比羅提）: Abhirati

aibetsuri-ku（愛別離苦）: suffering of having to part from those whom one loves (*See* eight sufferings)

Aiku-ō（阿育王）: Ashoka

Aikuō-den（阿育王伝）: *The Story of King Ashoka* (*See* Virtue Victorious)

Aitta（阿逸多）: Ajita

Aizen-myō'ō（愛染明王）: Craving-Filled

ajari（阿闍梨）: *āchārya*
Ajase-ō（阿闍世王）: Ajātashatru
Ājībika-ha（アージービカ派）: Ājīvika school
Ajitabattei-ga（阿恃多伐底河）: Ajitavatī
akada（阿伽陀）: *agada*
Akada-sen（阿竭多仙）: Agastya
Akanita-ten（阿迦尼吒天）: Akanishtha Heaven
Akimoto Tarō Hyōe-no-jō（秋元太郎兵衛尉）
akki（悪鬼）: demon
aku-chishiki（悪知識）: evil friend
akudō（悪道）: evil path
akugō（悪業）: evil deed (*See* three evil paths)
akunin-jōbutsu（悪人成仏）: attainment of Buddhahood by evil persons
akushu（悪趣）: evil path
ama（尼・尼御前）: lay nun
amara-shiki（阿摩羅識）: *amala*-consciousness
Amaterasu Ōmikami（天照大神）: Sun Goddess
Ambara-nyo（菴婆羅女）: Ambapālī
Ambuda-jigoku（頞部陀地獄）: Arbuda hell (*See* eight cold hells)
Amida（阿弥陀）
Amida-kyō（阿弥陀経）: Amida Sutra
Ammora-on（菴没羅園）: Ambapālī Garden
Ammyō（安明）: Calm and Bright
anagon（阿那含）: non-returner
anagon-ka（阿那含果）: stage of the non-returner (*See* four stages of Hinayana enlightenment)
Anan（阿難）: Ānanda
Anaritsu（阿那律）: Aniruddha
andae（安陀会）: *antarvāsa* (*See* three robes)
Angen（安玄）: An Hsüan (*See* Parthia)
ango（安居）: three-month retreat
An-hōkin（安法欽）: An Fa-ch'in
An'ne（安慧）
An'ne（安慧）: Sthiramati
Annen（安然）
Anokuchi（阿耨池）: Anavatapta Lake
Anokudatsu-ryūō（阿耨達竜王）: Anavatapta
anokutara（阿耨多羅）: *anuttara*
anokutara-sammyaku-sambodai（阿耨多羅三藐三菩提）: *anuttara-samyak-sambodhi*
Anraku（安楽）
Anraku-gyō-hon（安楽行品）: "Peaceful Practices" chapter
Anraku-sekai（安楽世界）: Peace and Delight
Anraku-shū（安楽集）: *Collected Essays on the World of Peace and Delight, The*
Anra-on（菴羅園）: Ambapālī Garden
Anryūgyō-bosatsu（安立行菩薩）: Firmly Established Practices
An-seikō（安世高）: An Shih-kao
Ansoku-koku（安息国）: Parthia
Anya-kyōjinnyo（阿若憍陳如）: Ājnāta Kaundinya
An'yō-koku（安養国）: Peace and Sustenance
arakan（阿羅漢）: arhat
arakan-ka（阿羅漢果）: stage of arhat (*See* four stages of Hinayana enlightenment)
arannya（阿蘭若）: *aranya*
Arara-jigoku（阿羅羅地獄）: Alalā hell (*See* eight cold hells)
Arara-karan（阿羅邏迦藍）: Ālāra Kālāma
araya-shiki（阿頼耶識）: *ālaya*-consciousness
arennya（阿練若）: *aranya*
Arida（阿利吒）
ari-ju（阿梨樹）: *arjaka*
Asetsuji（阿説示）: Ashvajit
Asetta-jigoku（頞哳吒地獄）: Atata hell (*See* eight cold hells)

ashama (阿娑摩): Unequalled One
ashamashama (阿娑摩娑摩): Equal with the Unequalled One (*See* Unequalled One)
Ashida (阿私陀): Asita (2)
Ashippa-koku (阿湿波国): Ashvaka (*See* sixteen great states)
Ashi-sennin (阿私仙人): Asita (1)
ashuka-ju (阿輸迦樹): *ashoka* tree
Ashuku-bukkoku-kyō (阿閦仏国経): Land of Akshobhya Buddha Sutra (*See* Akshobhya)
Ashuku-butsu (阿閦仏): Akshobhya
ashura (阿修羅): *asura*
asōgi (阿僧祇): *asamkhya*
Asuka-dera (飛鳥寺)
Atata-jigoku (阿吒吒地獄): Atata hell (*See* eight cold hells)
Atīsha (アティーシャ): Atīsha (*See* Tibetan Buddhism)
Atsuhara-no-hōnan (熱原の法難): Atsuhara Persecution
Atsuhara-no-sanresshi (熱原の三烈士): three martyrs of Atsuhara
Awa-no-kuni (安房国): Awa Province
Ayuja (阿踰闍): Ayodhyā

Bachiashura-ō (婆稚阿修羅王): Balin
Baddabara (跋陀婆羅): Bhadrapāla
Baggi (跋祇): Vriji
baitara (貝多羅): *pattra*
baiyō-kyō (貝葉経): palm-leaf scripture (See *pattra*)
Bakkō-kutsu (莫高窟): Mo-kao Caves
bakku-yoraku (抜苦与楽): removing suffering and giving joy
Bakushu-ga (縛芻河): Vakshu River (*See* four rivers)
banjaku-gō (磐石劫): rock *kalpa*
Banramitai (般刺蜜帝): Pan-la-mi-ti (*See* Shūramgama Sutra)
baramon (婆羅門): Brahman
Basa-koku (婆蹉国): Matsya (*See* sixteen great states)
Bashaha (婆沙波): Vāshpa (*See* five ascetics)
Bassa (跋蹉): Vatsa
Basubanzu-hosshi-den (婆藪槃豆法師伝): *The Biography of the Dharma Teacher Vasubandhu* (*See* Asanga)
Batsudai (跋提): Bhadrika
Batsudaimata (筏提摩多): Fa-t'i-mo-to (See *Commentary on the Mahayana Treatise, The*)
Batsudairika (跋提梨迦): Bhadrika
Batsunanda (跋難陀): *See* Universal Practice
Batsunanda-ryūō (跋難陀竜王): Upananda (*See* eight great dragon kings)
bekkyō (別教): specific teaching
bekkyō-ichijō (別教一乗): one vehicle of the distinct doctrine (*See* five teachings and ten doctrines)
Benchō (弁長)
Ben-kemmitsu-nikyō-ron (弁顕密二教論): *Comparison of Exoteric and Esoteric Buddhism, A*
Bennen (弁円)
bentai (弁体): "Clarification of the Essence" section (*See* five major principles)
Benzai-ten (弁才天): Eloquence
bessō-nenjo (別相念処): specific meditation (*See* four meditations)
betsu-fuzoku (別付嘱): specific transfer
bibasha (毘婆沙): *vibhāshā*
Bibashi-butsu (毘婆尸仏): Vipashyin (*See* seven Buddhas of the past)
bidara (毘陀羅): *vetāda*
Bidon-shū (毘曇宗): Abhidharma school
biku (比丘): *bhikshu*
bikuni (比丘尼): *bhikshunī*
Bikuramashirā-ji (ヴィクラマシラー寺): Vikramashilā Monastery
Bimbashara-ō (頻婆娑羅王): Bimbisāra

Bingara (賓伽羅): Pingala
binnin-keiju-no-tatoe (貧人繋珠の譬): parable of the jewel sewn in the poor man's robe (*See* parable of the jewel in the robe)
Binzuru (賓頭盧): Pindolabhāra-dvāja
Bira-sonja (毘羅尊者): Kapimala
biriya (毘梨耶): *vīrya*
biriya-haramitsu (毘梨耶波羅密): *pāramitā* of assiduousness (*See* six *pāramitās*)
Birushana-butsu (毘盧遮那仏): Vairochana
Bishabu-butsu (毘舎浮仏): Vishvabhū (*See* seven Buddhas of the past)
bishaja (毘舎闍): *pishācha*
Bishamon-ten (毘沙門天): Vaishravana
Bishari (毘舎離): Vaishālī
Bishukatsuma-ten (毘首羯磨天): Vishvakarman
bodai (菩提): *bodhi*
Bodaidaruma (菩提達磨): Bodhidharma
bodai-ju (菩提樹): *bodhi* tree
Bodairushi (菩提流支): Bodhiruchi (1)
Bodairushi (菩提流志): Bodhiruchi (2)
bodai-shin (菩提心): aspiration for enlightenment
Bodaishin-ron (菩提心論): *Treatise on the Mind Aspiring for Enlightenment, The*
Bodai-shiryō-ron (菩提資糧論): *Treatise on the Discipline for Attaining Enlightenment, The*
bōhi-shiaku (防非止悪): preventing error and putting an end to evil
Bommō-kyō (梵網経): Brahmā Net Sutra
bompu (凡夫): ordinary person
bompu-i (凡夫位): stage of ordinary people (*See* four good roots)
bompu-soku-goku (凡夫即極): attaining Buddhahood as a common mortal (*See* attainment of Buddhahood)
bongyō (梵行): brahma practice
Bonho-ten (梵輔天): Heaven of Brahmā's Aide (*See* Brahma Heaven)
bonnō (煩悩): earthly desires
bonnō-joku (煩悩濁): impurity of desire (*See* five impurities)
bonnō-ma (煩悩魔): devil of earthly desires; hindrance of earthly desires (*See* four devils; three obstacles and four devils)
bonnō-muhen-seigandan (煩悩無辺誓願断): vow to eradicate countless earthly desires (*See* four universal vows)
bonnonjō (梵音声): pure and far-reaching voice
bonnō-shō (煩悩障): obstacle of earthly desires (*See* three obstacles and four devils)
bonnō-soku-bodai (煩悩即菩提): earthly desires are enlightenment
bonshō-dōgo-do (凡聖同居土): Land of Sages and Common Mortals
Bonshu-ten (梵衆天): Heaven of Brahmā's Retinue (*See* Brahma Heaven)
Bonsō-butsu (梵相仏): Brahmā Appearance (*See* sixteen princes)
Bonten (梵天): Brahmā
Bon-ten (梵天): Brahma Heaven
bosatsu (菩薩): bodhisattva
bosatsu-dō (菩薩道): bodhisattva way (*See* sowing, maturing, and harvesting)
bosatsu-gyō (菩薩行): bodhisattva practice (*See* Mahayana Buddhism)
Bosatsu-honjō-manron (菩薩本生鬘論): *The Garland of Birth Stories* (*See* Shibi)
bosatsu-jō (菩薩乗): bodhisattva vehicle (*See* three vehicles)

bosatsu-jōshō (菩薩定性): those predestined to be bodhisattvas (*See* five natures)
bosatsu-kai (菩薩戒): bodhisattva precepts (*See* Bodhisattva Practice Jeweled Necklace Sutra)
bosatsu-kai (菩薩界): world of bodhisattvas
Bosatsu-kai-kyō (菩薩戒経): Bodhisattva Precepts Sutra (*See* Brahmā Net Sutra)
bosatsu-makasatsu (菩薩摩訶薩): bodhisattva-mahāsattva
Bosatsu-yōraku-hongō-kyō (菩薩瓔珞本業経): Bodhisattva Practice Jeweled Necklace Sutra
bosatsu-yu (菩薩喩): simile of bodhisattvas (*See* ten similes)
Buddabaddara (仏陀跋陀羅): Buddhabhadra
Buddagaya (仏陀伽耶): Buddhagayā
Buddajū (仏陀什): Buddhajīva
Buddamitta (仏陀密多): Buddhamitra
Buddanandai (仏陀難提): Buddhananda
Buddasenta (仏陀扇多): Buddhashānta
Buddayasha (仏陀耶舎): Buddhayashas
bukkai (仏界): Buddhahood; world of Buddhahood
bukkai-shogu-no-kukai (仏界所具の九界): inclusion of the nine worlds in Buddhahood
bukkai-soku-kukai (仏界即九界): inclusion of the nine worlds in Buddhahood
bukkoku-do (仏国土): Buddha land
Bukkoku-ki (仏国記): *Record of the Buddhistic Kingdoms, The*
bundan-shōji (分段生死): transmigration with differences and limitations
bunshin-soku (分真即): stage of progressive awakening
buppōsō (仏法僧): the Buddha, the Law, and the Buddhist Order (*See* three treasures)
busshari (仏舎利): Buddha's relics
busshi (仏子): children of the Buddha
busshō (仏性): Buddha nature
Busshogyō-san (仏所行讃): *Praising the Buddha's Deeds*
Busshō-ron (仏性論): *Treatise on the Buddha Nature, The*
busshu (仏種): seed of Buddhahood
bussoku-seki (仏足石): stone footprints of the Buddha
Busso-tōki (仏祖統紀): *Record of the Lineage of the Buddha and the Patriarchs, The*
butchi (仏智): Buddha wisdom
butsu (仏): Buddha
butsudō-mujō-seiganjō (仏道無上誓願成): vow to attain supreme enlightenment (*See* four universal vows)
butsu-gen (仏眼): Buddha eye
Butsugen (仏眼): Buddha Eye
Butsugen-butsumo (仏眼仏母): Buddha Eye Buddha Mother (*See* Buddha Eye)
Butsugen-hō (仏眼法): ceremony of Buddha Eye (*See* Buddha Eye)
Butsugen-son (仏眼尊): Honored One Buddha Eye (*See* Buddha Eye)
Butsugo (仏護): Buddhapālita
Butsugū-ji (仏宮寺): Fo-kung-ssu temple (*See* pagoda)
Butsu-hongyō-jikkyō (仏本行集経): Sutra of the Collected Stories of the Buddha's Deeds in Past Lives
butsujō (仏乗): Buddha vehicle
Butsumo (仏母): Buddha Mother
butsumyō-e (仏名会): ceremony of reciting the Buddhas' names
Butsumyō-kyō (仏名経): Buddhas' Names Sutra

butsu-riki (仏力): power of the Buddha (*See* four powers [1])
Butsurō-ji (仏隴寺): Fo-lung-ssu
Butsuryū-shū (仏立宗): Buddha-Founded school (*See* Nichiren school)
butsu-yu (仏喩): simile of the Buddha (*See* ten similes)
Butsu-yuikyō-gyō (仏遺教経): Buddha's Legacy Teachings Sutra
Butsuzō-kyō (仏蔵経): Buddha Treasury Sutra
Buttochō (仏図澄): Fo-t'u-teng
Button (仏音): Buddhaghosa
buttō-sūhai (仏塔崇拝): stupa worship (*See* stupa)
Byakubonnō (白飯王): Shuklodana
byakue (白衣): white-robed laymen
byakugō-sō (白毫相): tuft of white hair
byakuhō (白法): pure Law
byakuhō-ommotsu (白法隠没): The pure Law will become obscured and lost. (*See* five five-hundred-year periods)
byakurenge (白蓮華): white lotus flower (See *renge*)
Byakuren-sha (白蓮社): Pai-lien-she
byakushibutsu (辟支仏): *pratyekabuddha*
byōdō-daie (平等大慧): great wisdom of equality
Byōdō-ō (平等王): King Impartial Judge (*See* ten kings)
byōdō-shō-chi (平等性智): non-discriminating wisdom (*See* five kinds of wisdom)

Charaka (チャラカ): Charaka (*See* Kanishka)
chi (癡): foolishness; *moha*
Chibetto-bukkyō (チベット仏教): Tibetan Buddhism
Chido (智度): Chih-tu
chie-daiichi (智慧第一): foremost in wisdom (*See* Shāriputra)
chie-haramitsu (智慧波羅蜜): *pāramitā* of the obtaining of wisdom (*See* six *pāramitās*)
Chien (智円): Chih-yüan (*See* Outside-the-Mountain School)
Chigi (智顗): Chih-i
Chigon (智儼): Chih-yen (1)
Chigon (智儼): Chih-yen (2)
chi-haramitsu (智波羅蜜): *pāramitā* of knowledge (*See* ten *pāramitās*)
Chihō (智鳳)
Chii (智威): Chih-wei
Chijaku (智寂): Chih-chi (See *One Hundred Records of the Great Teacher T'ien-t'ai, The*)
chiken-in (智拳印): wisdom mudra
Chikō (智光): Jnānaprabha
Chikugo-bō (筑後房): *See* Nichirō
Chikujō-gedō (竹杖外道): Bamboo Staff school
Chikurin-shōja (竹林精舎): Bamboo Grove Monastery
chikushō-kai (畜生界): world of animals
chimpō-se (珍宝施): offerings of rare treasures (*See* three kinds of offerings)
chi-myō (智妙): mystic principle of wisdom (*See* ten mystic principles)
Chinshin (陳鍼): Ch'en Chen
Chirei (知礼): Chih-li
Chisha (智者): Chih-che
Chisha-daishi (智者大師): Great Teacher Chih-che (*See* T'ien-t'ai)
Chishaku (智積): Wisdom Accumulated
chishiki (知識): *mitra*
Chishō (智証)
Chishō (智昇): Chih-sheng (See *K'ai-yüan Era Catalog of the Buddhist Canon, The*)
Chishū (智周): Chih-chou
Chisoku-ten (知足天): Heaven of Satisfaction (*See* Tushita Heaven)
chisui (智水): water of wisdom
Chitatsu (智達)

Chitsū (智通)
Chizō (智蔵)
Chizō (智蔵): Chih-tsang
Chō-bu (長部): *Dīgha-nikāya*
Chōgen (重源)
chō-hō (頂法): peak stage
chōja-gūji-no-tatoe (長者窮子の譬): parable of the wealthy man and his poor son
chōju-ten (長寿天): heaven of long life (*See* eight difficulties)
Chōka (張果): Chang-kuo (*See* Ch'en Chen)
Chōkan (澄観): Ch'eng-kuan
Chōken (張騫): Chang Ch'ien (*See* Yüeh-chih)
Chō-kishin (趙帰真): Chao Kuei-chen (*See* Hui-ch'ang Persecution)
Chōnen (奝然)
Chōsai (長西)
Chōshō-ō (頂生王): Born from the Crown of the Head
chū (中): *madhya* (2)
Chū-agon-gyō (中阿含経): Medium-Length Āgama Sutra
Chū-bu (中部): *Majjhima-nikāya*
chūdai-hachiyō-in (中台八葉院): central court of the eight-petaled lotus (*See* Womb Realm mandala)
chūdō (中道): Middle Way
Chūgan-ha (中観派): Mādhyamika school
Chūgan-ron-sho (中観論疏): *Annotations on "The Treatise on the Middle Way," The*
Chūgan-shin-ron (中観心論): *The Heart of the Middle Way* (*See* Bhāvaviveka)
Chūgoku-jūsan-shū (中国十三宗): thirteen schools of China
Chūju (中頌): *Verses on the Middle Way*
chū-kō (中劫): medium *kalpa*
chū-kon (中根): intermediate capacity (*See* three groups of voice-hearers)
Chū-ron (中論): *Treatise on the Middle Way, The*
Chūron-ju (中論頌): *Verses on the Middle Way*
chūsen-sekai (中千世界): intermediate world system (*See* major world system)
chū-tai (中諦): truth of the Middle Way (*See* three truths)
Chūzan (仲算)

Daian-ji (大安寺)
Daiba (提婆): Āryadeva
Daiba-bosatsu-den (提婆菩薩伝): *The Biography of Āryadeva* (*See* Āryadeva)
Daibadatta (提婆達多): Devadatta
Daibadatta-hon (提婆達多品): "Devadatta" chapter
Daibibasha-ron (大毘婆沙論): *Great Commentary on the Abhidharma, The*
Dai-bō (大坊): Grand Lodging (*See* Nikkō)
Daibodai-ji (大菩提寺): Mahābodhi temple (*See* Buddhagayā)
Daibon-hannya-kyō (大品般若経): Larger Wisdom Sutra
Daibonnō-yu (大梵王喩): simile of the great heavenly king Brahmā (*See* ten similes)
Daibon-ten (大梵天): Heaven of Great Brahmā
Daibon-ten (大梵天): Mahābrahmā
Daibontennō-mombutsu-ketsugi-kyō (大梵天王問仏決疑経): Sutra of the Buddha Answering the Great Heavenly King Brahmā's Questions
Daibutchō-shuryōgon-kyō (大仏頂首楞厳経): Great Crown of the Buddha's Head Shūramgama Meditation Sutra (*See* Shūramgama Sutra [2])
daibyaku-gosha (大白牛車): great white ox cart

daibyakuhō (大白法): great pure Law
Daichido-ron (大智度論): *Treatise on the Great Perfection of Wisdom, The*
daichi-mijin (大地微塵): dust particles of the land
daie (大衣): great robe (*See* three robes)
daienkyō-chi (大円鏡智): great round mirror wisdom (*See* five kinds of wisdom)
dai-fukuden (大福田): great field of good fortune (*See* field of good fortune)
Daigaku Saburō (大学三郎)
Dai-gesshi (大月氏): Great Yüeh-chih
Dai-Gohonzon (大御本尊)
daigo-mi (醍醐味): ghee
Daiguren-jigoku (大紅蓮地獄): hell of the great crimson lotus (*See* hell of the crimson lotus)
Daigyōsetsu-bosatsu (大楽説菩薩): Great Joy of Preaching (*See* "Emergence of the Treasure Tower" chapter)
Daihannya-haramitta-kyō (大般若波羅蜜多経): Great Perfection of Wisdom Sutra (3)
Daihannya-kyō (大般若経): Great Wisdom Sutra
Daihatsu-naion-gyō (大般泥洹経): Mahāparinirvāna Sutra (2)
Daihatsu-nehan-gyō (大般涅槃経): Mahāparinirvāna Sutra (1)(3)
Daihatsu-nehangyō-gobun (大般涅槃経後分): Epilogue to the Mahāparinirvāna Sutra, The (*See* Nirvana Sutra)
Daihi-kyō (大悲経): Great Compassion Sutra
Daihō-bō (大宝坊): Great Treasure Chamber
Daihōkō-butsu-kegon-gyō (大方広仏華厳経): Great and Vast Buddha Flower Garland Sutra (*See* Flower Garland Sutra)
Daihōshaku-kyō (大宝積経): Accumulated Great Treasures Sutra
daiichigi-shitsudan (第一義悉檀): to reveal the ultimate truth directly (*See* four ways of preaching)
Daiitoku-myō'ō (大威徳明王): Great Awesome Virtue
Daiji (大事): *Mahāvastu*
Daiji-ha (大寺派): Mahāvihāra school (*See* Southern Buddhism)
daijikidō (大直道): great direct way (*See* countless *kalpas* of practice)
Daijikkyō (大集経): Great Collection Sutra
Daijion-ji (大慈恩寺): Ta-tz'u-en-ssu
Daijionji-sanzō-hosshi-den (大慈恩寺三蔵法師伝): *Biography of the Tripitaka Master of Ta-tz'u-en-ssu Temple, The*
Daijizai-ten (大自在天): God of Great Freedom (*See* Maheshvara)
daijō (大乗): great vehicle
daijō-bosatsu-kai (大乗菩薩戒): Mahayana bodhisattva precepts; precepts for Mahayana bodhisattvas (*See* Brahmā Net Sutra)
Daijō-bukkyō (大乗仏教): Mahayana Buddhism
daijō-endon-kai (大乗円頓戒): Mahayana precepts of perfect and immediate enlightenment (See *Clarification of the Precepts, A*)
daijō-hōdō-kyō (大乗方等経): correct and equal sutras of the great vehicle (*See* correct and equal sutras)
Daijō-hō'on-girin-jō (大乗法苑義林章): *Forest of Meanings in the Mahayana Garden of the Law, The*
daijō-kai (大乗戒): Mahayana precepts (*See* Brahmā Net Sutra)
daijō-kaidan (大乗戒壇): Mahayana ordination platform
Daijō-kishin-ron (大乗起信論):

Awakening of Faith in the Mahayana, The
Daijō-shikan-hōmon（大乗止観法門）: *Mahayana Method of Concentration and Insight, The*
daijō-shikyō（大乗始教）: elementary Mahayana teaching (*See* five teachings and ten doctrines)
Daijō-shiron-gengi（大乗四論玄義）: *Profound Meaning of the Four Mahayana Treatises, The*
Daijō-shōgonkyō-ron（大乗荘厳経論）: *Ornament of Mahayana Sutras, The*
daijō-shūkyō（大乗終教）: final Mahayana teaching (*See* five teachings and ten doctrines)
dai-jūhachi-gan（第十八願）: eighteenth vow
Daikaku-seson（大覚世尊）: World-Honored One of Great Enlightenment
dai-kō（大劫）: major *kalpa*
Daikoku（大黒）
Daikōzen-ji（大興善寺）: Ta-hsing-shan-ssu
Daikyōkan-jigoku（大叫喚地獄）: hell of great wailing (*See* eight hot hells)
Daiman-baramon（大慢婆羅門）: Great Arrogant Brahman
Daimokkenren（大目犍連）: Mahāmaudgalyāyana
daimoku（題目）
Daimoku-nyorai（大目如来）: Large Eyes (*See* Akshobhya)
Dainembutsu-ji（大念仏寺）: *See* Interfusing Nembutsu school
Dainichi-kyō（大日経）: Mahāvairochana Sutra
Dainichikyō-gishaku（大日経義釈）: *Commentary on the Meaning of the Mahāvairochana Sutra, The*
Dainichikyō-sho（大日経疏）: *Annotations on the Mahāvairochana Sutra, The*
Dainichi Nōnin（大日能忍）
Dainichi-nyorai（大日如来）: Mahāvairochana
dai-no-sansai（大の三災）: three greater calamities (*See* three calamities)
Dai-ōtōshi（大王統史）: *Mahāvamsa*
Dairin-shōja（大林精舎）: Great Forest Monastery
dairoku-ten（第六天）: sixth heaven
dairokuten-no-maō（第六天の魔王）: devil king of the sixth heaven
daisan-no-hōmon（第三の法門）: third doctrine
dai-sensekai（大千世界）: major world system
Daise-taishi（大施太子）: Great Donor (*See* Earnest Donor)
daishi（大師）: great teacher
daishi（大士）: mahāsattva
Daishi（大史）: *Mahāvamsa*
Daishin-ajari（大進阿闍梨）: Daishin
Daishin-bō（大進房）
Daishōgon-bosatsu（大荘厳菩薩）: Great Adornment (2)
Daishōgon-butsu（大荘厳仏）: Great Adornment (1)
Daishōgon-rongyō（大荘厳論経）: *Great Ornament of Tales, The*
Daishōnetsu-jigoku（大焦熱地獄）: hell of great burning heat (*See* eight hot hells)
Daishonin（大聖人）
Daishu-bu（大衆部）: Mahāsamghika school
daisōjō（大僧正）: general administrator of priests (*See* Fa-yün)
Daiso-kaigo（大蘇開悟）: enlightenment on Mount Ta-su (*See* T'ien-t'ai)
Daiso-zan（大蘇山）: Mount Ta-su (*See* Nan-yüeh)
daisōzu（大僧都）: general supervisor of priests (*See* Dōshō)
Daitaka（提多迦）: Dhritaka
Daiten（大天）: Mahādeva

Daiten-no-goji (大天の五事): five teachings of Mahādeva
Daitō-daijionji-sanzō-hosshi-den (大唐大慈恩寺三蔵法師伝): *The Biography of the Tripitaka Master of Ta-tz'u-en-ssu Temple of the Great T'ang Dynasty* (See *Biography of the Tripitaka Master of Ta-tz'u-en-ssu Temple, The*)
Daitō-naiten-roku (大唐内典録): *Great T'ang Dynasty Catalog of Buddhist Scriptures, The*
Daitō-saiiki-guhō-kōsō-den (大唐西域求法高僧伝): *Biographies of Eminent Priests of the Great T'ang Dynasty Who Sought the Law in the Western Regions, The*
Daitō-saiiki-ki (大唐西域記): *Record of the Western Regions of the Great T'ang Dynasty, The*
Daitsūchishō-butsu (大通智勝仏): Great Universal Wisdom Excellence
Daitsū-fukkō (大通覆講): restatement of Great Universal Wisdom Excellence Buddha's teaching
Daitsū-kechien-no-daisanrui (大通結縁の第三類): third group of the listeners of Great Universal Wisdom Excellence Buddha's teaching
Daizoku-ō (大族王): Mihirakula
Dammira-ō (檀弥羅王): Dammira
Dammiri-ō (檀弥利王): Dammiri
Dandoku-sen (檀特山): Dandaka, Mount
dan-haramitsu (檀波羅密): *pāramitā* of almsgiving (*See* six *pāramitās*)
danka (檀家): donating family (See *dāna-pati*)
Dan-kyō (壇経): *Platform Sutra, The*
danna (檀那): *dāna-pati*
Danna (檀那)
Danna-ryū (檀那流): Danna school
dan'otsu (檀越): *dāna-pati*
Dan-senchaku (弾選択): *Refutation of "The Nembutsu Chosen above All," A*
Darai Rama (ダライ・ラマ): Dalai Lama (*See* Tibetan Buddhism)
darani (陀羅尼): *dhāranī*
Darani-hon (陀羅尼品): "Dhāranī" chapter
Daruma (達磨): Bodhidharma
Darumagyūta (達摩笈多): Dharmagupta (1)
Darumakikuta (達摩掬多): Dharmagupta (2)
Darumarājika-tō (ダルマラージカ塔): Dharmarājika stupa (*See* Takshashilā)
datchaku-buppō (脱益仏法): Buddhism of the harvest
datsueba (奪衣婆): garment-snatching demoness
datsumyō-sha (奪命者): robber of life (*See* devil)
dembō-kanjō (伝法灌頂): anointment ceremony to invest a person with the rank of *āchārya* (*See* ceremony of anointment)
Dengyō (伝教)
Dentō-roku (伝灯録): *Transmission of the Lamp, The*
dō (道): path; way
Dōan (道安): Tao-an
Dōgen (道元)
Dōgen (道原): Tao-yüan (See *Transmission of the Lamp, The*)
dōgo-do (同居土): land of co-dwelling (*See* Land of Sages and Common Mortals)
dōgo-edo (同居穢土): impure land of co-dwelling (*See* Land of Sages and Common Mortals)
dōgo-jōdo (同居浄土): pure land of co-dwelling (*See* Land of Sages and Common Mortals)
Do-issai-seken-kunō-butsu (度一切世間苦悩仏): Saving All from Worldly Suffering (*See* sixteen princes)

Dōji (道慈)
dōjō (道場): place of practice
dokkaku (独覚): self-awakened one
dokko-sho (独鈷杵): single-armed diamond-pounder (*See* diamond-pounder)
dokku-no-en (毒鼓の縁): poison-drum relationship
dokuichi-hommon (独一本門): unique essential teaching (*See* essential teaching)
dokuju-hon (読誦品): stage of reading and reciting the Lotus Sutra (*See* five stages of practice)
dokuju-tamon-kengo (読誦多聞堅固): age of reading, reciting, and listening (*See* five five-hundred-year periods)
Dōkyō (道鏡)
dōkyō-ichijō (同教一乗): one vehicle of the identical doctrine (*See* five teachings and ten doctrines)
Dommakara (曇摩迦羅): Dharmakāla
Dommamitta (曇摩蜜多): Dharmamitra
Dommanandai (曇摩難提): Dharmanandi (*See* Chu Fo-nien)
Dommarushi (曇摩流支): Dharmaruchi
Dommayasha (曇摩耶舎): Dharmayashas
Dommukatsu-bosatsu (曇無竭菩薩): Dharmodgata
Dommumitta (曇無蜜多): Dharmamitra
Dommushin (曇無讖): Dharmaraksha (2)
Dommutoku-bu (曇無徳部): Dharmagupta school
dōmon-zōjōman (道門増上慢): arrogance and presumption of members of the Buddhist clergy (*See* three powerful enemies)
Dōmyō-ten (同名天): Same Name (*See* Same Birth and Same Name)
Dongaku (曇学): T'an-hsüeh (*See* Sutra on the Wise and the Foolish)
Donkakara (曇柯迦羅): Dharmakāla
Donran (曇鸞): T'an-luan
Donrin (曇林): T'an-lin (See *Treatise on the Lotus Sutra, The*)
Don'yō (曇曜): T'an-yao
dōrin-ō (銅輪王): copper-wheel-turning king (*See* four wheel-turning kings)
Dōryū (道隆)
Dōsen (道璿)
Dōsen (道暹): Tao-hsien
Dōsen (道宣): Tao-hsüan (1)
Dōshaku (道綽): Tao-ch'o
dōshin (道心): aspiration for the way (*See* aspiration for enlightenment)
Dōshin (道信): Tao-hsin
Dōshō (道昭)
Dōshō (道生): Tao-sheng
Dōshō Dōmyō (同生同名): Same Birth and Same Name
Dōshō-ten (同生天): Same Birth (*See* Same Birth and Same Name)
dōshu-chi (道種智): wisdom to understand the various paths to enlightenment (*See* three kinds of wisdom)
Dōsui (道邃): Tao-sui
dō-tai (道諦): truth of the path to the cessation of suffering (*See* four noble truths)
dōtai-ishin (同体異心): one in body but different in mind (*See* many in body, one in mind)
Dōzen-bō (道善房)
Dōzui (道邃): Tao-sui

Eben (恵便)
Ebisu (恵比須): *See* seven beneficent deities
Echi (依智)
edo (穢土): impure land
e-gen (慧眼): wisdom eye (*See* five types of vision)

Egi-hammon-shō (依義判文抄): "The Interpreting the Text Based upon Its Essential Meaning" (See *Six-Volume Writings, The*)
Egon (慧厳): Hui-yen
ehō-fuenin (依法不依人): to rely on the Law and not upon persons (*See* four standards)
Ehyō-tendai-shū (依憑天台集): *Clarification of the Schools Based on T'ien-t'ai's Doctrine, A*
Ei-gensū (衛元嵩): Wei Yüan-sung
Eihei-ji (永平寺): *See* Sōtō school
Eikan (永観)
Eisai (栄西)
E-issai-seken-fui-butsu (壊一切世間怖畏仏): Destroying All Worldly Fears (*See* sixteen princes)
Eizon (叡尊)
Eji (慧次): Hui-tz'u
Ejō (懐譲): Huai-jang (*See* Zen school)
Eka (慧可): Hui-k'o
Ekaku (慧覚): Hui-chüeh (*See* Sutra on the Wise and the Foolish)
Ekan (慧灌)
Ekan (懐感): Huai-kan
Ekan (慧観): Hui-kuan
Ekin (慧均): Hui-chün (See *Profound Meaning of the Four Mahayana Treatises, The*)
ekō (廻向): transference of benefit
e-kō (壊劫): *kalpa* of decline
Ekō (慧皎): Hui-chiao (See *Liang Dynasty Biographies of Eminent Priests, The*)
Ekō (慧光): Hui-kuang
ekō-hotsugan-shin (廻向発願心): mind of resolve to be reborn in the Pure Land (*See* three kinds of mind)
Ema Mitsutoki (江間光時)
Embudai (閻浮提): Jambudvīpa
embudan-gon (閻浮檀金): Jambūnada gold
embu-ju (閻浮樹): *jambu* tree
Embunadai-konkō-nyorai (閻浮那提金光如来): Jāmbūnada Gold Light
Emma (閻魔): Yama
Emon (慧文): Hui-wen
Enan (慧南): Hui-nan (*See* Lin-chi school)
Enchin (円珍)
Enchō (円澄)
endon-kai (円頓戒): precepts of perfect and immediate enlightenment
Endō Saemon-no-jō (遠藤左衛門尉)
engaku (縁覚): cause-awakened one
engaku (円覚): perfect enlightenment
Engaku-ji (円覚寺)
engaku-jō (縁覚乗): cause-awakened one vehicle (*See* three vehicles)
engaku-jōshō (縁覚定性): those predestined to be cause-awakened ones (*See* five natures)
engaku-kai (縁覚界): world of cause-awakened ones
Engaku-kyō (円覚経): Perfect Enlightenment Sutra
engi (縁起): dependent origination
en-gyō (円教): perfect teaching
enichi (慧日): sun of wisdom
en-kai (円戒): perfect precepts
Enni (円爾)
Ennin (円仁)
En no Ozunu (役小角)
En no Ubasoku (役の優婆塞): *See* En no Ozunu
Enō (慧能): Hui-neng
Enryaku-ji (延暦寺)
Ensai (円載)
Enshō (円照): Yüan-chao (See *Chen-yüan Era Catalog of the Buddhist Canon, The*)
en'yū-no-santai (円融の三諦): unification of the three truths
Eon (慧遠): Hui-yüan (1)(2)
Eon (慧苑): Hui-yüan (3)
eriju-no-tatoe (衣裏珠の譬): parable of the jewel in the robe

Erin (慧琳): Hui-lin (See *Pronunciation and Meaning in the Buddhist Scriptures* [2])
Eryō (慧亮)
Eryū (慧立): Hui-li (See *Biography of the Tripitaka Master of Ta-tz'u-en-ssu Temple, The*)
Eshi (慧思): Hui-ssu
Eshin (恵心)
Eshin-ryū (恵心流): Eshin school
eshō-funi (依正不二): oneness of life and its environment
Eun (懐惲): Huai-yün (See *Treatise Resolving Numerous Doubts about the Pure Land Teachings, The*)
e-za-shitsu (衣座室): robe, seat, and room

fuchūtō-kai (不偸盗戒): not to steal (*See* five precepts)
Fu-daishi (傅大士): Fu Ta-shih
Fudaraku-sen (補陀落山): Potalaka, Mount
Fudō-butsu (不動仏): Immovable (2)
Fudōchi-butsu (不動智仏): Immovable Wisdom
Fudō-myō'ō (不動明王): Immovable (1)
fugen (不還): non-returner
Fugen-bon (普賢品): "Universal Worthy" chapter
Fugen-bosatsu (普賢菩薩): Universal Worthy
Fugen-bosatsu-hon (普賢菩薩品): "Bodhisattva Universal Worthy" chapter
Fugen-bosatsu-kambotsu-hon (普賢菩薩勧発品): "Encouragements of the Bodhisattva Universal Worthy" chapter
Fugen-kyō (普賢経): Universal Worthy Sutra
fuhen-shinnyo-no-ri (不変真如の理): eternal and unchanging truth (*See* Nam-myoho-renge-kyo)
Fuhōzō-innen-den (付法蔵因縁伝): *History of the Buddha's Successors, A*
Fuhōzō-kyō (付法蔵経): Buddha's Successors Sutra
fuhōzō-no-nijūsan-nin (付法蔵の二十三人): twenty-three successors
fuhōzō-no-nijūyo-nin (付法蔵の二十四人): twenty-four successors
fujain-kai (不邪婬戒): not to engage in sexual misconduct (*See* five precepts)
Fuji-biku (普事比丘): Universal Practice
Fuji-isseki-monto-zonchi-no-koto (富士一跡門徒存知の事): *Guidelines for Believers of the Fuji School, The*
Fuji-monryū (富士門流): Fuji school
Fuji-shūgaku-yōshū (富士宗学要集): *Essential Works of the Fuji School, The*
Fuji-shūgaku-zenshū (富士宗学全集): *Complete Works of the Fuji School, The*
fujō-gō (不定業): unfixed karma
fujō-kan (不浄観): meditation on the vileness of the body
fujō-kyō (不定教): indeterminate teaching (*See* four teachings of method)
fujō-seppō (不浄説法): to preach from an impure motive (*See* Buddha Treasury Sutra)
fujō-shō (不定性): indeterminate group (*See* five natures)
fuju-fuse (不受不施): non-acceptance of alms and non-giving of alms (*See* Nichikō)
Fuju Fuse-ha (不受不施派): No Alms Accepting or Giving school
Fuju Fuse Kōmon-ha (不受不施講門派): No Alms Accepting or Giving Nichikō school
fukashigi-kyō (不可思議境): region of the unfathomable (*See* observa-

tion of the mind)
Fuken (符堅): Fu Chien (*See* Kumārajīva)
Fukō (普光): P'u-kuang
Fukū (不空): Pu-k'ung
fukuden (福田): field of good fortune
Fukūjōju-nyorai (不空成就如来): Infallible Realization (*See* five Buddhas)
Fukurokuju (福禄寿): *See* seven beneficent deities
Fukushō-ten (福生天): Merit Increasing Heaven (*See* eighteen heavens)
fukutoku (福徳): *punya*
Fukyō-bon (不軽品): "Never Disparaging" chapter
Fukyō-bosatsu (不軽菩薩): Never Disparaging
Fumbetsu-kudoku-hon (分別功徳品): "Distinctions in Benefits" chapter
fumen-zetsu (覆面舌): face-covering tongue
fumōgo-kai (不妄語戒): not to lie (*See* five precepts)
Fumon-bon (普門品): "Universal Gateway" chapter
Fumyō-nyorai (普明如来): Universal Brightness (2)
Fumyō-ō (普明王): Universal Brightness (1)
Funamori Yasaburō (船守弥三郎)
Funasha (富那奢): Punyayashas
Fundari-jigoku (芬陀利地獄): Pundarīka hell (*See* eight cold hells)
funjin (分身): emanations of the Buddha
funzōe (糞掃衣): clothes of patched rags
fuonju-kai (不飲酒戒): not to consume intoxicants (*See* five precepts)
Furanna-kashō (富蘭那迦葉): Pūrana Kassapa
fūrin (風輪): windy circle
Furuna (富楼那): Pūrna
furyū-monji (不立文字): independent of words or writing
fusatsu (布薩): *uposhadha*
fuse (布施): almsgiving
fuse-haramitsu (布施波羅蜜): *pāramitā* of almsgiving (*See* six *pāramitās*)
fusesshō-kai (不殺生戒): not to kill (*See* five precepts)
fushō (不生): person of no rebirth (*See* arhat)
fushō-fumetsu (不生不滅): non-birth and non-extinction (*See* realization of the non-birth and non-extinction of all phenomena)
Fusō-ryakki (扶桑略記): *Brief History of Japan, A*
fusshaku-kō (払石劫): rock-rubbing kalpa (*See* rock *kapla*)
futai-i (不退位): stage of non-regression
futanna (富単那): *pūtana*
Futsunyatara (弗若多羅): Punyatāra
Fuyō-kyō (普曜経): Multitudinous Graceful Actions Sutra

Gakan-ji (瓦官寺): Wa-kuan-ssu
gaki (餓鬼): hungry spirits; *preta*
gaki-kai (餓鬼界): world of hungry spirits
Gakkō-bosatsu (月光菩薩): Moonlight
Gakkō-daijin (月光大臣): Chandraprabha
gakuhō-kanjō (学法灌頂): anointment ceremony to confer the status of practitioner of Esoteric Buddhism (*See* ceremony of anointment)
Gakushō-shiki (学生式): *Regulations for Students, The* (See *Regulations for Students of the Mountain School, The*)
gampon-no-hosshō (元品の法性): fundamental nature of enlightenment

gampon-no-mumyō（元品の無明）: fundamental darkness
Gandāra（ガンダーラ）: Gandhara
Gangō-ji（元興寺）
gan-haramitsu（願波羅蜜）: *pāramitā* of the vow (*See* ten *pāramitās*)
Ganjin（鑑真）
Ganjisu-gawa（ガンジス河）: Ganges River
Gankō（含光）: Han-kuang
Gasshō-daijin（月称大臣）: Chandrakīrti (2)
gatsuai-zammai（月愛三昧）: moon-loving meditation
Gatsuzō-bosatsu（月蔵菩薩）: Moon Storehouse (*See* age of quarrels and disputes)
Gatten（月天）: moon, god of the
Gaya-jō（伽耶城）: Gayā
Gaya-kashō（伽耶迦葉）: Gayā Kāshyapa
Gaya-sen（伽耶山）: Gayāshīrsha, Mount
ge（偈）: verse
gebon（外凡）: outer rank of ordinary people; the lower rank of ordinary practitioners (*See* four good roots)
gedatsu（解脱）: emancipation; *vimoksha*
Gedatsugatsu-bosatsu（解脱月菩薩）: Moon of Deliverance
gedatsu-kengo（解脱堅固）: age of attaining liberation (*See* five five-hundred-year periods)
Gejimmitsu-kyō（解深密経）: Revelation of the Profound Secrets Sutra
ge-kon（下根）: inferior capacity (*See* three groups of voice-hearers)
gekū-daiichi（解空第一）: foremost in understanding the doctrine of non-substantiality (*See* Subhūti)
Gembō（玄昉）
gemmetsu-mon（還滅門）: way of emancipation (*See* twelve-linked chain of causation)
Gengu-kyō（賢愚経）: Sutra on the Wise and the Foolish
Genjō（玄奘）: Hsüan-tsang
Genju（賢首）: Hsien-shou
Genju-bosatsu（賢首菩薩）: Chief Wise
gen-kō（減劫）: *kalpa* of decrease
Genkō-shakusho（元亨釈書）: *Genkō Era Biographies of Eminent Priests, The*
Genkū（源空）
Gennichi-ō（幻日王）: Bālāditya
Gennin（源仁）
Gen'o（玄応）: Hsüan-ying (See *Pronunciation and Meaning in the Buddhist Scriptures* [1])
Genrō（玄朗）: Hsüan-lang
gen-se（現世）: present existence (*See* three existences)
Genshin（源信）
gen-shō（現証）: actual proof (*See* three proofs)
Gensō（彦悰）: Yen-ts'ung (See *Biography of the Tripitaka Master of Ta-tz'u-en-ssu Temple, The*)
genzai-se（現在世）: present existence (*See* three existences)
Gerugu-ha（ゲルグ派）: Gelug school (*See* Tibetan Buddhism)
geshu（下種）: planting the seeds of Buddhahood
geshu-buppō（下種仏法）: Buddhism of sowing
Gesshi（月氏）: Yüeh-chih
Gesshi-bosatsu（月氏菩薩）: Bodhisattva of Yüeh-chih (*See* Dharmaraksha)
Gesshō（月称）: Chandrakīrti (1)
geyū（外用）: outward behavior (*See* Superior Practices)
Giba（耆婆）: Jīvaka
Gida-taishi（祇陀太子）: Jetri
Gien（義淵）
Gien-no-shichi-jōsoku（義淵の七上足）: seven superior disciples of Gien (*See* Gien)

Gigen (義玄): I-hsüan (*See* Lin-chi school)
Gijaku (義寂): I-chi (*See* T'ien-t'ai school)
Gijō (義浄): I-ching
Gijō-bō (義浄房)
Gikkodoku (給孤独): Anāthapindada
gi-no-kaidan (義の戒壇): general sanctuary (*See* Three Great Secret Laws)
ginrin-ō (銀輪王): silver-wheel-turning king (*See* four wheel-turning kings)
Gion-shōja (祇園精舎): Jetavana Monastery
Girika (耆利柯): Girika
Gishakussen (耆闍崛山): Gridhrakūta
Gishin (義真)
Gitsū (義通): I-t'ung (*See* T'ien-t'ai school)
giya (祇夜): *geya* (*See* verse)
gō (業): karma
go-biku (五比丘): five ascetics
go-bu (五部): five Āgamas
gōbuku (降伏): subjugation of evil (*See* Susiddhikara Sutra)
gobun-hosshin (五分法身): fivefold bodies of the Law
Gobun-ritsu (五分律): *Fivefold Rules of Discipline, The*
gobu-ritsu (五部律): *vinayas* of the five schools
go-butsu (五仏): five Buddhas
go-butsu (五仏): five categories of Buddhas
gobutsu-dōdō (五仏道同): the five categories of Buddhas all employ a similar process (*See* five categories of Buddhas)
go-chi (五智): five kinds of wisdom
gochi-nyorai (五智如来): five wisdom Buddhas
go-dai (五大): five elements
godai-bu (五大部): five major writings
godai-myō'ō (五大明王): five great wisdom kings
godairiki-bosatsu (五大力菩薩): five mighty bodhisattvas
Godai-san (五台山): Wu-t'ai, Mount
godaison (五大尊): five honored ones
godan-hō (五壇法): ceremony of the five altars (*See* five great wisdom kings)
go-dō (五道): five paths
go-donshi (五鈍使): five delusive inclinations
Godō-tenrin-ō (五道転輪王): King Wheel-Turner of the Five Paths (*See* ten kings)
Gōga (恒河): Ganges River
go-gai (五蓋): five obscurations
gōga-sha (恒河沙): sands of the Ganges
go-gen (五眼): five types of vision
go-gohyakusai (後五百歳): fifth five-hundred-year period
go-gyakuzai (五逆罪): five cardinal sins
go-haramitsu (五波羅蜜): five *pāramitās*
gohō (五法): five ascetic practices
Gohō (護法): Dharmapāla
go-hon (五品): five stages of practice
Gohonzon (御本尊)
Gohonzon-shichika-no-sōjō (御本尊七箇の相承): *Transmission of Seven Teachings on the Gohonzon, The* (*See* Myōjō Pond)
Gohyaku-deshi-hon (五百弟子品): "Five Hundred Disciples" chapter
Gohyaku-deshi-juki-hon (五百弟子受記品): "Prophecy of Enlightenment for Five Hundred Disciples" chapter
gohyaku-jintengō (五百塵点劫): numberless major world system dust particle *kalpas*
gohyaku-kai (五百戒): five hundred precepts

Gohyaku-mon-ron (五百問論): *Treatise of Five Hundred Questions, The*
go-ja (五邪): five improper ways of livelihood
go-ji (五時): five periods
goji-hakkyō (五時八教): five periods and eight teachings
go-jinzū (五神通): five transcendental powers
goji-shichiji (五字七字): five or seven characters
go-jō (五乗): five vehicles
go-jōgo-ten (五浄居天): five heavens of purity
go-joku (五濁): five impurities
gojō'on-ku (五盛陰苦): suffering arising from the five components of life (*See* eight sufferings)
gojōshin-kan (五停心観): five meditations
gojū-gen (五重玄): five major principles
gojūni-i (五十二位): fifty-two stages of bodhisattva practice
gojū-no-sōtai (五重の相対): fivefold comparison
gojū-no-tō (五重の塔): five-storied pagoda (*See* pagoda)
gojū-sandan (五重三段): fivefold view of revelation
gojū-tenden (五十展転): continual propagation to the fiftieth person
go-kai (五戒): five precepts
Gokan-ō (五官王): King Controller of the Five Sense Organs (*See* ten kings)
goka-no-gohyakusai (五箇の五百歳): five five-hundred-year periods
goka-no-hōshō (五箇の鳳詔): five proclamations of the Buddha
go-ke (五家): five schools of Zen
goke-shichishū (五家七宗): five schools and seven schools (*See* Zen school)
Goke-shū (牛貨洲): Aparagodānīya
go-kō (五綱): five guides for propagation
gokoku-sambukyō (護国三部経): three sutras for the protection of the nation (*See* Golden Light Sutra)
go-kon (五根): five roots
go-kon (五根): five sense organs
gokō-shiyui (五劫思惟): pondering for five *kalpas* (*See* Amida)
goko-sho (五鈷杵): five-pronged diamond-pounder (*See* diamond-pounder)
Gokukōjō-ten (極光浄天): Utmost Light and Purity Heaven
Gokuraku (極楽): Perfect Bliss
Gokuraku-ji (極楽寺)
Gokuraku-jōdo (極楽浄土): Pure Land of Perfect Bliss
gokyō-jisshū (五教十宗): five teachings and ten doctrines
gōma (降魔): conquering devils (*See* eight phases of a Buddha's existence)
go-mi (五味): five flavors
Gomyō (護命)
gon-daijō-kyō (権大乗教): provisional Mahayana teachings
gonge (権化): provisional manifestation
gongyō (勤行)
Gonin-shoha-shō (五人所破抄): *On Refuting the Five Priests*
Gonjikinyo-kyō (銀色女経): Silver-Colored Woman Sutra
gonjitsu-funimon (権実不二門): oneness of the provisional and true teachings (*See* ten onenesses)
gon-kyō (権経): provisional sutras
gon-kyō (権教): provisional teachings
Gonsō (勤操)
Gon'yo (厳誉)
go-on (五陰): five components
go'on-kewagō (五陰仮和合): temporary union of the five components

(*See* five false views)
go'on-seken (五陰世間): realm of the five components (*See* three realms of existence)
go-riki (五力): five powers
gorin-kan (五輪観): meditation on the five elements
go-rishi (五利使): five false views
go-rōsō (五老僧): five senior priests
Gōsanze-myō'ō (降三世明王): Conqueror of the Threefold World
gosen-kiko (五千起去): the rising from the seats and withdrawal of the five thousand persons (*See* five thousand arrogant persons)
gosen-no-jōman (五千の上慢): five thousand arrogant persons
gosen-shichisen-no-kyōgyō (五千七千の経教): five thousand or seven thousand volumes of Buddhist scriptures (*See* five thousand and forty-eight volumes)
gosen-shijūhachi-kan (五千四十八巻): five thousand and forty-eight volumes
go-shin (五辛): five strong-flavored foods
go-shō (五性): five natures
go-shō (五障): five obstacles
gō-shō (業障): obstacle of karma (*See* three obstacles and four devils)
Gosho (御書)
go-shōgyō (五正行): five correct practices
goshō-sanjū (五障三従): five obstacles and three obediences
go-shu (五趣): five paths
goshu-jamyō (五種邪命): five improper ways of livelihood
goshu-no-shōgyō (五種の正行): five correct practices
goshu-no-shugyō (五種の修行): five practices
goshu-no-zōgyō (五種の雑行): five sundry practices
gosō-jōshin-kan (五相成身観): five-fold meditation
go-sui (五衰): five signs of decay
go-tenjiku (五天竺): five regions of India
go-tsū (五通): five transcendental powers
go-un (五蘊): five components
go-yoku (五欲): five desires
Gozan (五山): Five Temples
gozu (牛頭): ox-headed demons
gozu-sendan (牛頭栴檀): ox-head sandalwood
guchi (愚癡): foolishness; *moha*
gufutokku (求不得苦): suffering of being unable to obtain what one desires (*See* eight sufferings)
Guhō-kōsō-den (求法高僧伝): *Biographies of Eminent Priests Who Sought the Law, The*
gukyō-no-sanki (弘経の三軌): three rules of preaching
gummō-hyōzō-no-tatoe (群盲評象の譬): parable of the blind men and the elephant
Gumyō-bosatsu (求名菩薩): Seeker of Fame (*See* "Introduction" chapter)
gumyō-chō (共命鳥): *jīvamjīvaka*
Gumyō-shū (弘明集): *Anthology of the Propagation of Light, The*
Gunabaddara (求那跋陀羅): Gunabhadra
Gunabatsuma (求那跋摩): Gunavarman
Gundari-myō'ō (軍荼利明王): Kundalī
Gungi-ron (群疑論): *The Treatise Resolving Numerous Doubts* (See *Treatise Resolving Numerous Doubts about the Pure Land Teachings, The*)
Guren-jigoku (紅蓮地獄): hell of the crimson lotus
gusoku-kai (具足戒): complete precepts

Gusoku-semmankōsō-nyorai (具足千万光相如来): Endowed with a Thousand Ten Thousand Glowing Marks
Gutoku-shō (愚禿鈔): *Work of the Ignorant Shavepate, The*
guzai-furi (求財不利): to seek wealth in vain (*See* eight kinds of sufferings)
gyaku-en (逆縁): reverse relationship
Gyakurokayada (逆路伽耶陀): Anti-Lokāyata school
Gyōbō-bonji (楽法梵志): Aspiration for the Law
Gyōchi (行智)
gyō-futai (行不退): non-regression from action (*See* three kinds of non-regression)
Gyōhyō (行表)
gyō-jū-za-ga (行住坐臥): walking, standing, sitting, and lying down (*See* four activities of daily life)
Gyōki (行基)
Gyokusen-ji (玉泉寺): Yü-ch'üan-ssu
Gyōman (行滿): Hsing-man
gyō-myō (行妙): mystic principle of practice (*See* ten mystic principles)
Gyōnen (凝然)
gyō-no-daimoku (行の題目): daimoku of practice (*See* Three Great Secret Laws)
gyō-riki (行力): power of practice (*See* four powers [1])
Gyōshi (行思): Hsing-ssu (*See* Zen school)

hachi (鉢): alms bowl
hachibu-shu (八部衆): eight kinds of nonhuman beings
hachidai-jigoku (八大地獄): eight great hells
hachidai-myō'ō (八大明王): eight great wisdom kings (*See* wisdom kings)
hachidai-ryūō (八大竜王): eight great dragon kings
hachi-gedatsu (八解脱): eight emancipations
hachi-harai (八波羅夷): eight *pārājika* offenses
hachi-ja (八邪): eight errors
hachijisshugō (八十種好): eighty characteristics
hachijū (八重): eight major offenses
hachikyōkai (八敬戒): eight precepts of reverence
hachi-man (八慢): eight types of arrogance
Hachiman (八幡)
hachiman-hōzō (八万法蔵): eighty thousand teachings
hachiman-shisen (八万四千): eighty-four thousand
hachiman-shisen-hōzō (八万四千法蔵): eighty-four thousand teachings
hachi-nan (八難): eight difficulties
hachinetsu-jigoku (八熱地獄): eight hot hells
hachi-ryūō (八竜王): eight dragon kings
hachi-tendō (八顚倒): eight inverted views (*See* four inverted views)
hachiyō-kuson (八葉九尊): nine honored ones on the eight-petaled lotus
Hadoma-jigoku (鉢特摩地獄): Padma hell (*See* eight cold hells)
haishu (敗種): rotten seeds
hajun (波旬): *pāpīyas*
Hakiri Sanenaga (波木井実長)
hakkan-jigoku (八寒地獄): eight cold hells
Hakkendo-ron (八犍度論): *Eight-part Treatise* (See *Treatise on the Source of Wisdom, The*)
hakku (八苦): eight sufferings
hakkyō (八教): eight teachings
Hakuba-ji (白馬寺): Pai-ma-ssu
hakuba-no-kyō (白馬の教): teaching brought by white horses (*See* Chu Fa-lan)

Haku-hōso (帛法祖): Po Fa-tsu
Hakuon (帛遠): Po-yüan
hangyō (判教): "Evaluation of the Teaching" section (*See* five major principles)
hangyō-hanza-zammai (半行半坐三昧): half-active and half-sitting meditation (*See* four forms of meditation)
Hanjara-koku (般闍羅国): Panchāla (*See* sixteen great states)
hanju-zammai (般舟三昧): meditation to behold the Buddhas
Hanju-zammai-kyō (般舟三昧経): Sutra of the Meditation to Behold the Buddhas
hannya (般若): *prajnā*
Hannya (般若): Prajnā
hannya-haramitsu (般若波羅蜜): *prajnā-pāramitā*
Hannya-haramitsu-kyō (般若波羅蜜経): Perfection of Wisdom sutras
Hannya-ji (般若時): Wisdom period
Hannya-kyō (般若経): Wisdom sutras
Hannyarushi (般若流支): Prajnāruchi
Hannya-shingyō (般若心経): Heart Sutra
Hannya-tōron (般若灯論): *Treatise on the Lamp of Wisdom, The*
Hanramittei (般刺蜜帝): Pan-la-mi-ti (*See* Shūramgama Sutra)
Hansoku-ō (斑足王): Spotted Feet
Happon-ha (八品派): Eight Chapters school (*See* Nichiren school)
happu (八不): eight negations
happū (八風): eight winds
happu-chūdō (八不中道): middle path of the eight negations
harai (波羅夷): *pārājika*
haramitsu (波羅蜜): *pāramitā*
Harana-koku (波羅奈国): Varanasi
Haruri-ō (波瑠璃王): Virūdhaka (1)
Harusha-charita (ハルシャ・チャリタ): *Harsha-charita* (*See* Shīlāditya)
Hashinoku-ō (波斯匿王): Prasenajit
hassaikai (八斎戒): eight precepts
Hassen (法全): Fa-ch'üan
hasshiki (八識): eight consciousnesses
hasshō-dō (八正道): eightfold path
hasshū (八宗): eight schools
Hasshū-kōyō (八宗綱要): *Essentials of the Eight Schools, The*
hasshu-no-dainan (八種の大難): eight kinds of sufferings
hasshū-no-so (八宗の祖): founder of the eight schools (*See* Nāgārjuna)
hassō-sabutsu (八相作仏): eight phases of a Buddha's existence
Hatsu-naion-gyō (般泥洹経): Parinirvāna Sutra
hatsu-nehan (般涅槃): *parinirvāna*
ha-wagōsō (破和合僧): causing disunity in the Buddhist Order (*See* five cardinal sins)
Hazuma-jigoku (波頭摩地獄): Padma hell (*See* eight cold hells)
Hei no Saemon (平左衛門)
heireita (薜荔多): *preta*
hendoku-iyaku (変毒為薬): changing poison into medicine
henge-shin (変化身): transformation body
Henjō-hokki-shōryō-shū (遍照発揮性霊集): *The Collected Works of the Universally Illuminating Soul-Inspiring One* (*See* Shinzei)
Henjō-kongō (遍照金剛): Universal Illumination and Diamond (*See* Kōbō)
Henjō-ō (変成王): King Transformation (*See* ten kings)
Henjō-ten (遍浄天): All Pure Heaven (*See* eighteen heavens)
hen'yaku-shōji (変易生死): transmigration with change and advance
hi (悲): compassion
Hiei-zan (比叡山): Hiei, Mount
higan (彼岸): other shore

Higashi Hongan-ji (東本願寺): *See* Hongan-ji
higyō-hiza-zammai (非行非坐三昧): meditation in an unspecified posture for an unspecified period (*See* four forms of meditation)
hiji-fūu-nan (非時風雨難): calamity of unseasonable storms (*See* seven disasters)
hijō (非情): insentient beings
hijō-no-jōbutsu (非情の成仏): enlightenment of insentient beings (*See* enlightenment of plants)
Hike-kyō (悲華経): Compassionate White Lotus Flower Sutra
Hiki Yoshimoto (比企能本)
himitsu-fujō-kyō (秘密不定教): secret indeterminate teaching (*See* four teachings of methods)
himitsu-kyō (秘密教): secret teaching (*See* four teachings of methods)
himitsu-shu (秘密主): Master of Secrets (*See* Vajrasattva)
himyō-hōben (秘妙方便): secret and wonderful expedient means (*See* three expedient means)
hinnyo-no-ittō (貧女の一灯): "The Poor Woman's Lamp" (See *dīpa*)
hippara-ju (畢鉢羅樹): *pippala* tree
Hippara-kutsu (畢鉢羅窟): Pippalī Cave
Hirosawa-ryū (広沢流): Hirosawa branch (*See* Yakushin)
Hisō-hihisō-sho (非想非非想処): Realm of Neither Thought Nor No Thought
Hisō-hihisō-sho-jō (非想非非想処定): meditation on the Realm of Neither Thought Nor No Thought (*See* Realm of Neither Thought Nor No Thought)
Hisō-hihisō-ten (非想非非想天): Heaven of Neither Thought Nor No Thought
Hitsuryōgabasha (畢陵伽婆蹉): Pilindavatsa
Hiyu-hon (譬喩品): "Simile and Parable" chapter
hiyu-renge (譬喩蓮華): figurative lotus
Hizō-hōyaku (秘蔵宝鑰): *Precious Key to the Secret Treasury, The*
hō (法): *dharma;* Law
hō (宝): *ratna*
hōben (方便): expedient means
Hōben-bon (方便品): "Expedient Means" chapter
hōben-do (方便土): Land of Transition
hōben-haramitsu (方便波羅蜜): *pāramitā* of expedient means (*See* ten *pāramitās*)
Hōben-shō (方便章): "Preparatory Practices" chapter (See *Great Concentration and Insight*)
hōbō (謗法): slander
Hōbō (法宝): Fa-pao
hōdō (方等): *vaipulya*
Hōdō (法道): Fa-tao
Hōdō-ji (方等時): Correct and Equal period
hōdō-kyō (方等経): correct and equal sutras
Hōdō-kyō (方等経): Correct and Equal sutras
Hōdō-nyorai (宝幢如来): Jeweled Banner (*See* five Buddhas)
Hōe (方会): Fang-hui (*See* Lin-chi school)
Hōe-bosatsu (法慧菩薩): Dharma Wisdom
hōgen (法眼): Dharma eye
Hōgen-shū (法眼宗): Fa-yen school (*See* Zen school)
hō-honzon (法本尊): object of devotion in terms of the Law (*See* Gohonzon)
Hōi-butsu (宝威仏): Jeweled Dignity
hōin (法印): Dharma seal
Hōitokujō'ō-butsu (宝威徳上王仏):

King Above Jeweled Dignity and Virtue
hōjin (報身): reward body
hōjin-butsu (報身仏): Buddha of the reward body (*See* three bodies)
Hōjō-bosatsu (法上菩薩): Dharma Arisen (*See* Dharmodgata)
Hōjō-bu (法上部): Dharmottara school (*See* eighteen Hinayana schools)
hōjō-e (放生会): life-liberating practice
Hōjō Yagenta (北条弥源太)
Hōjū-ki (法住記): *The Record of Ensuring the Abiding of the Law* (*See* sixteen arhats)
Hōjun (法順): Fa-shun
hōkai-taishō-chi (法界体性智): wisdom of the essence of the phenomenal world (*See* five kinds of wisdom)
Hoke-kyō (法華経): Lotus Sutra
Hokekyō-anrakugyō-gi (法華経安楽行義): *On the Peaceful Practices of the Lotus Sutra*
Hokekyō-daigo-no-maki (法華経第五の巻): fifth scroll of the Lotus Sutra
Hokekyō-giki (法華経義記): *Meaning of the Lotus Sutra, The*
Hokekyō-no-gyōja (法華経の行者): votary of the Lotus Sutra
Hokekyō-ron (法華経論): *Treatise on the Lotus Sutra, The*
Hokekyō-shogisan (法華経疏義纘): *Supplement to the Meanings of the Commentaries on the Lotus Sutra, The*
Hōken (法賢): Fa-hsien (2)
Hōki-bō (伯耆房)
Hokke-denki (法華伝記): *Lotus Sutra and Its Traditions, The*
Hokke-gengi (法華玄義): *Profound Meaning of the Lotus Sutra, The*
Hokke-gengi-shakusen (法華玄義釈籤): *Annotations on "The Profound Meaning of the Lotus Sutra," The*
Hokke-genron (法華玄論): *Treatise on the Profundity of the Lotus Sutra, The*
Hokke-genzan (法華玄賛): *Praising the Profundity of the Lotus Sutra*
Hokke-giki (法華義記): *Meaning of the Lotus Sutra, The*
Hokke-gisho (法華義疏): *Annotations on the Meaning of the Lotus Sutra, The*
Hokke-hongyō-kōki (法華翻経後記): *Afterword to the Lotus Sutra Translation, The*
Hokke-jisshō (法華十勝): ten superior characteristics of the Lotus Sutra (See *Outstanding Principles of the Lotus Sutra, The*)
Hokke-metuzai-no-tera (法華滅罪之寺): temples for the eradication of past offenses by the power of the Lotus Sutra (*See* provincial temples)
Hokke-mongu (法華文句): *Words and Phrases of the Lotus Sutra, The*
Hokke-mongu-fushō-ki (法華文句輔正記): *Supplement to "The Words and Phrases of the Lotus Sutra," The*
Hokke-mongu-ki (法華文句記): *Annotations on "The Words and Phrases of the Lotus Sutra," The*
Hokken (法顕): Fa-hsien (1)
Hokken-den (法顕伝): *Travels of Fa-hsien, The*
Hokke-nehan-ji (法華涅槃時): Lotus and Nirvana period
Hokke-no-en (法華の円): perfect teaching of the Lotus Sutra (*See* four teachings of doctrine)
Hokke-ron (法華論): *Treatise on the Lotus Sutra, The*
Hokke-sambu-kyō (法華三部経): threefold Lotus Sutra
Hokke-sammai (法華三昧): Lotus meditation

Hokke-sandai-bu (法華三大部): three major works on the Lotus Sutra
Hokke-sandaibu-fuchū (法華三大部補註): *Supplement to the Three Major Works on the Lotus Sutra, The*
Hokke-shū (法華宗): Lotus school
Hokke-shūku (法華秀句): *Outstanding Principles of the Lotus Sutra, The*
Hokke-shū Shimmon-ryū (法華宗真門流): Nisshin branch of the Lotus school (*See* Nichiren school)
Hokke-shuyō-shō (法華取要抄): *On Taking the Essence of the Lotus Sutra*
Hokke-zammai (法華三昧): Lotus meditation
Hokku-kyō (法句経): *Dhammapada;* Words of Truth Sutra
hokkyō (法橋): Dharma bridge (*See* Dharma seal)
Hokkyō-ritsu (北京律): Precepts school of the Northern Capital (*See* Precepts school)
Hōkō-daishōgon-kyō (方広大荘厳経): Correct and Vast Great Adornment Sutra (*See* Multitudinous Graceful Actions Sutra)
Hokuden-bukkyō (北伝仏教): Northern Buddhism
Hokudō-ha (北道派): Northern Way school (*See* Treatise on the Ten Stages school)
hokuji-den (北寺伝): transmission of the Northern Temple (*See* Dharma Characteristics school)
Hokusanjū-bu (北山住部): Uttarashaila school (*See* eighteen Hinayana schools)
Hokushū Zen (北宗禅): Northern school of Zen
hō-kuyō (法供養): offering of the Law (*See* offering)
hombutsu (本仏): true Buddha
Hōmetsujin-kyō (法滅尽経): Decline of the Law Sutra
Homma Rokurō Saemon (本間六郎左衛門)
hommon (本門): essential teaching
Hommon Hokke-shū (本門法華宗): Essential Teaching Lotus school (*See* Nichiren school)
hommon-no-daimoku (本門の題目): daimoku of the essential teaching
hommon-no-honzon (本門の本尊): object of devotion of the essential teaching
hommon-no-jūmyō (本門の十妙): ten mystic principles of the essential teaching (*See* ten mystic principles)
hommon-no-kaidan (本門の戒壇): sanctuary of the essential teaching
hommon-no-sampi (本門の三譬): three metaphors of the essential teaching
Hommon-shū (本門宗): Essential Teaching school (*See* Nichiren Shōshū)
hōmon-mujin-seiganchi (法門無尽誓願知): vow to master immeasurable Buddhist teachings (*See* four universal vows)
Hōmyō-nyorai (法明如来): Law Bright
honchi (本地): true identity (*See* true Buddha)
hon-dō (本堂): main hall (*See* seven-halled temple)
Hōnen (法然)
hongaku (本覚): inherent enlightenment; original enlightenment (1)
honga-myō (本果妙): true effect
honga-myō-no-kyōshu (本果妙の教主): teacher of the true effect
hongan (本願): original vows
Hongan-ji (本願寺)
honge-no-bosatsu (本化の菩薩): bodhisattvas of the essential teaching

honjaku-no-roppi（本迹の六譬）: six metaphors of the theoretical and essential teachings
honjintsū-myō（本神通妙）: mystic principle of true transcendental power (*See* ten mystic principles)
Honjō-wa（本生話）: *Jātaka*
honjumyō-myō（本寿命妙）: mystic principle of true life span (*See* ten mystic principles)
honkannō-myō（本感応妙）: mystic principle of true responsive communion (*See* ten mystic principles)
honkenzoku-myō（本眷属妙）: mystic principle of true relationship (*See* ten mystic principles)
honkokudo-myō（本国土妙）: true land
honnehan-myō（本涅槃妙）: mystic principle of true nirvana (*See* ten mystic principles)
honnin-honga-no-shu（本因本果の主）: teacher of the true cause and the true effect (*See* true effect)
honnin-myō（本因妙）: true cause
honnin-myō-no-kyōshu（本因妙の教主）: teacher of the true cause
honriyaku-myō（本利益妙）: mystic principle of true benefit (*See* ten mystic principles)
hon-roku（本六）: six elder disciples of Nikkō
honseppō-myō（本説法妙）: mystic principle of true preaching (*See* ten mystic principles)
Hon'yaku-myōgi-shū（翻訳名義集）: *Dictionary of the Pronunciation and Meaning of Buddhist Terms, A*
Honzon-mondō-shō（本尊問答抄）: *Questions and Answers on the Object of Devotion*
hō'ō（法王）: Dharma King
Hō'on-jurin（法苑珠林）: *Forest of Gems in the Garden of the Law, The*
Hō'on-kyō（報恩経）: Repaying Debts of Gratitude Sutra
Hō'on-shō（報恩抄）: *On Repaying Debts of Gratitude*
Hoppō-bukkyō（北方仏教）: Northern Buddhism
Hōren（法蓮）
hō-riki（法力）: power of the Law (*See* four powers [1])
hōrin（法輪）: wheel of the Law
Hōrō（法朗）: Fa-lang
Hōryū-ji（法隆寺）
hō-se（法施）: offering of the Law (*See* almsgiving)
Hōshaku-kyō（宝積経）: Accumulated Treasures Sutra
hōshin（報身）: reward body
Hoshina Gorō Tarō（星名五郎太郎）
hōshin-butsu（報身仏）: Buddha of the reward body
hō-shō（報障）: obstacle of retribution (*See* three obstacles and four devils)
Hōshō（法照）: Fa-chao
Hōshō（宝唱）: Pao-ch'ang (See *Divergent Concepts in the Sutras and Vinaya Texts*)
Hōshō-nyorai（宝生如来）: Jewel Born (*See* five Buddhas)
Hōshō-nyorai（宝勝如来）: Treasure Excellence (*See* Water Holder)
Hōso（法祖）: Fa-tsu
Hosokusa-danrin（細草檀林）: Hosokusa Seminary (*See* Nichikan)
Hōsō-nyorai（宝相如来）: Jewel Sign
hosshaku-kempon（発迹顕本）: casting off the transient and revealing the true
Hosshamittara-ō（弗沙弥多羅王）: Pushyamitra
hosshi（法師）: Dharma teacher
Hosshi-hon（法師品）: "Teacher of the Law" chapter
Hosshi-kudoku-hon（法師功徳品）: "Benefits of the Teacher of the Law" chapter
hosshin（法身）: Dharma body

hosshin-butsu（法身仏）: Buddha of the Dharma body
hosshin-geshu（発心下種）: sowing the seeds by leading one to arouse faith in the teaching (*See* planting the seeds of Buddhahood)
hosshin-no-shari（法身の舎利）: relics of the Dharma body (*See* Buddha's relics)
hosshō（法性）: essential nature of phenomena
Hosshō（法勝）: Dharmashrī (See *Heart of the Abhidharma, The*)
Hosshō（法照）: Fa-chao
Hossō-shū（法相宗）: Dharma Characteristics school
hossū（法数）: doctrines with numerical themes; numerical doctrines (*See* four Āgama sutras)
Hōtan（和田）: Khotan
Hotchi-ron（発智論）: *Treatise on the Source of Wisdom, The*
Hotei（布袋）: *See* seven beneficent deities
hōtō（法灯）: lamp of Dharma (See *dīpa*)
hōtō（宝塔）: treasure tower
Hōtō-hon（宝塔品）: "Treasure Tower" chapter
hotoke（仏）: Buddha
Hotsubadai（弗婆提）: Pūrvavideha
Hōun（法雲）: Fa-yün
hōun-ji（法雲地）: stage of the Dharma cloud (*See* ten stages of development)
Hōyu-bosatsu（法涌菩薩）: Dharma Emerged (*See* Dharmodgata)
hōyū-hōben（法用方便）: adaptations of the Law expedient means (*See* three expedient means)
Hōzō（法蔵）: Fa-tsang
Hōzō-biku（法蔵比丘）: Dharma Treasury
Hōzō-bu（法蔵部）: Dharmagupta school
hōzu（法頭）: Dharma magistrate
(*See* discipline master)
hyakkai-sennyo（百界千如）: hundred worlds and thousand factors
hyaku-fuku（百福）: hundred blessings
Hyaku-ron（百論）: *One-Hundred-Verse Treatise, The*
hyakushibutsu（辟支仏）: *pratyekabuddha*
Hyōe no Saemon（兵衛の左衛門）: *See* Sajiki, the lady of

i-anraku-gyō（意安楽行）: peaceful practice of the mind (*See* four peaceful practices)
Ibushūrin-ron（異部宗輪論）: *Doctrines of the Different Schools, The*
ichi-butsujō（一仏乗）: one Buddha vehicle
ichidai-hihō（一大秘法）: One Great Secret Law
ichidaiji（一大事）: one great reason
ichigen-no-kame（一眼の亀）: one-eyed turtle
Ichigyō（一行）: I-hsing
ichi-hijiri（市聖）: Sage of the Streets (*See* Kūya)
ichijō（一乗）: one vehicle
ichijō-hō（一乗法）: one vehicle teaching
Ichijō-yōketsu（一乗要決）: *Essentials of the One Vehicle Teaching, The*
ichinen（一念）
ichinen-gi（一念義）: doctrine of one-time recitation
ichinen-sanzen（一念三千）: three thousand realms in a single moment of life
ichinen-shinge（一念信解）: to believe in and understand the Lotus Sutra even for a moment (*See* four stages of faith)
Ichinosawa-nyūdō（一谷入道）: Ichinosawa, the lay priest
ichirai（一来）: once-returner
Idaike（韋提希）: Vaidehī

i-futai (位不退): non-regression from stage (*See* three kinds of non-regression)
Igyō-bon (易行品): "Easy Practice" chapter
igyō-dō (易行道): easy-to-practice way
Igyō-shū (潙仰宗): Kuei-yang school (*See* Zen school)
Ikaruga-dera (斑鳩寺): *See* Hōryū-ji
Ikegami Munenaga (池上宗長)
Ikegami Munenaka (池上宗仲)
Ikegami-sōjō-sho (池上相承書): *Ikegami Transfer Document, The*
Ikegami Yasumitsu (池上康光): *See* Ikegami Munenaga; Ikegami Munenaka
Iken (維蠲): Wei-chüan
Ikkō-shū (一向宗): Single-minded Practice school
i-kon-tō (已今当): three categories of preaching
i-mitsu (意密): mystery of the mind (*See* three mysteries)
i-myō (位妙): mystic principle of stages (*See* ten mystic principles)
Inaba-bō (因幡房)
Indara (因陀羅): Indra
Indara-mō (因陀羅網): Indra's net
Indo-bodaiju (インドボダイジュ): pipal tree
inga (因果): cause and effect
inga-funimon (因果不二門): oneness of cause and effect (*See* ten onenesses)
inga-guji (因果倶時): simultaneity of cause and effect
inga-iji (因果異時): non-simultaneity of cause and effect (*See* simultaneity of cause and effect)
Inga-kyō (因果経): Causality Sutra (*See* Causality of Past and Present Sutra)
ingei (印契): mudra
Ingen (隠元)
i'nin-shitsudan (為人悉檀): to teach according to people's respective capacities (*See* four ways of preaching)
innen (因縁): dependent origination
innen-kan (因縁観): meditation on dependent origination (*See* five meditations)
Ionnō-butsu (威音王仏): Awesome Sound King
Ippen (一遍)
ippōin (一法印): one Dharma seal (*See* Dharma seal)
ippon-nihan (一品二半): one chapter and two halves
iran (伊蘭): *eranda*
Iryō (遺竜): I-lung
Ishana-ten (伊舎那天): Īshāna
Ishikawa no Hyōe-nyūdō (石河の兵衛入道): Ishikawa no Hyōe, the lay priest
Ishikawa-shōja (石川精舎): Ishikawa Monastery
ishin-daie (以信代慧): substituting faith for wisdom
ishin-denshin (以心伝心): transmission from mind to mind
ishin-tokunyū (以信得入): gaining entrance through faith alone (*See* "Simile and Parable" chapter)
issai-chi (一切智): wisdom to understand the universal aspect of phenomena (*See* three kinds of wisdom)
issai-kaiku (一切皆苦): All existence is suffering. (*See* Dharma seal)
issaikyō (一切経): entire body of Buddhist scriptures (*See* five thousand and forty-eight volumes)
Issaikyō-ongi (一切経音義): *Pronunciation and Meaning in the Buddhist Scriptures*
issai-shu-chi (一切種智): wisdom to understand both the universal aspect and individual aspects of phenomena (*See* three kinds of wisdom)

Issai-shujō-kiken-bosatsu (一切衆生喜見菩薩): Gladly Seen by All Living Beings (2)
Issai-shujō-kiken-nyorai (一切衆生喜見如来): Gladly Seen by All Living Beings (1)
issai-shujō-shitsu'u-busshō (一切衆生悉有仏性): All living beings alike possess the Buddha nature. (*See* Buddha nature)
Issan Ichinei (一山一寧): I-shan I-ning (*See* Kokan Shiren)
issendai (一闡提): *icchantika*
Issetsu-bu (一説部): Ekavyāvahārika school (*See* eighteen Hinayana schools)
Isshin-kaimon (一心戒文): *The Record of the Precepts of the One Mind* (*See* Kōjō)
isshin-sanchi (一心三智): three kinds of wisdom in a single mind (*See* three kinds of wisdom)
isshin-sangan (一心三観): threefold contemplation in a single mind
isshin-soku-sanjin (一身即三身): A single Buddha possesses all three bodies. (*See* three bodies)
isshō-jōbutsu (一生成仏): attaining Buddhahood in this lifetime
itai-dōshin (異体同心): many in body, one in mind
itton-kyō (一音教): one voice teaching (*See* three schools of the south and seven schools of the north)
Izu-ruzai (伊豆流罪): Izu Exile

jakkō-do (寂光土): Land of Tranquil Light
Jakunichi-bō (寂日房)
Jakunichi-bō Nikke (寂日房日家) (1)
Jakunichi-bō Nikke (寂日房日華) (2)
Jakushō (寂照)
Jamyō-gedō (邪命外道): Ājīvika school
Janakutta (闍那崛多): Jnānagupta
Jayana (闍夜那): Jayata
Jayata (闍夜多): Jayata
ji (慈): *maitrī*
Jibakara (地婆訶羅): Divākara
Jibu-bō (治部房)
Jie (慈慧)
Jien (慈円)
Jiga-ge (自我偈): verse section of the "Life Span" chapter
jigoku (地獄): hell
jigoku-kai (地獄界): world of hell
jigyō-keta (自行化他): benefiting oneself and benefiting others; practice for oneself and others
jihi (慈悲): compassion
jihi-kan (慈悲観): meditation on compassion (*See* five meditations)
jijuyūshin (自受用身): Buddha of limitless joy; Buddha of self-enjoyment
jikai-haramitsu (持戒波羅蜜): *pāramitā* of keeping the precepts (*See* six *pāramitās*)
jikai-hongyaku-nan (自界叛逆難): calamity of revolt within one's own domain
Jikaku (慈覚)
jiki-dō (食堂): dining hall (*See* seven-halled temple)
jikihō-gaki (食法餓鬼): Law-devouring hungry spirit
jikishi-ninshin (直指人心): direct pointing to the human mind
jikkai (十戒): ten precepts
jikkai (十界): Ten Worlds
jikkai-gogu (十界互具): mutual possession of the Ten Worlds
jikkyō (十境): ten objects
jikkyō (実経): true sutra (*See* provisional sutras)
jikkyō (実教): true teaching
Jikoku-ten (持国天): Upholder of the Nation
Jiku-butsunen (竺仏念): Chu Fo-nien

Jiku-dōshō (竺道生): Chu Tao-sheng
Jiku-hōgo (竺法護): Dharmaraksha (1)
Jiku-hōran (竺法蘭): Chu Fa-lan
Jimmitsu-kyō (深密経): Profound Secrets Sutra
Jimon-ha (寺門派): Temple school
jinja-waku (塵沙惑): illusions innumerable as particles of dust and sand (*See* three categories of illusion)
jinkyō-tsū (神境通): power to be anywhere at will (*See* six transcendental powers)
Jinna (陳那): Dignāga
ji-no-ichinen-sanzen (事の一念三千): actual three thousand realms in a single moment of life (*See* three thousand realms in a single moment of life)
ji-no-kaidan (事の戒壇): specified sanctuary (*See* Three Great Secret Laws)
Jinriki-hon (神力品): "Supernatural Powers" chapter
jinshin-kanjō (深信観成): to realize with deep faith the truth expounded by the Buddha (*See* four stages of faith)
Jinshirō (神四郎): *See* three martyrs of Atsuhara
Jinshū (神秀): Shen-hsiu
jinsoku-tsū (神足通): power to be anywhere at will (*See* six transcendental powers)
Jintai (神泰): Shen-t'ai
jintsū-daiichi (神通第一): foremost in transcendental powers (*See* Maudgalyāyana)
Jintsū-ji (神通寺): Shen-t'ung-ssu temple (*See* pagoda)
jintsū-myō (神通妙): mystic principle of transcendental power (*See* ten mystic principles)
jintsū-riki (神通力): supernatural power; transcendental power (*See* six transcendental powers)
Jion (慈恩): Tz'u-en
Jion-ji (慈恩寺): Tz'u-en-ssu
jipparamitsu (十波羅蜜): ten *pāramitās*
jippō (十方): ten directions
jippō-bunshin-no-shobutsu (十方分身の諸仏): emanation Buddhas of the ten directions (*See* emanations of the Buddha)
jippō-do (実報土): Land of Actual Reward
jippō-no-shobutsu (十方の諸仏): Buddhas of the ten directions (*See* ten directions)
jippunimon (十不二門): ten onenesses
Jippunimon (十不二門): *Ten Onenesses, The*
jiri (自利): benefiting oneself (*See* benefiting oneself and benefiting others)
jiriki (自力): power of self
jiri-kumitsu (事理倶密): esoteric teachings in both theory and practice
jiri-rita (自利利他): benefiting oneself and benefiting others
jiritsu-daiichi (持律第一): foremost in observing the precepts (*See* Upāli)
Jiritsuronshō-ha (自立論証派): Svātantrika school
Jiron-shū (地論宗): Treatise on the Ten Stages Sutra school
jishi (自恣): *pravārana*
Jishi (慈氏): Compassionate One
jishō (自性): self-nature
jishō-shin (自性身): self-nature body (*See* Buddha of self-enjoyment)
Ji-shū (時宗): Time school
Jison (慈尊): Compassionate Honored One
Jisshananda (実叉難陀): Shikshānanda

jisshin (十信): ten stages of faith
jisshū (十宗): ten doctrines
jisshū (十宗): ten schools
jisshu-kuyō (十種供養): ten kinds of offerings
jissō (実相): true aspect (*See* true aspect of all phenomena)
jissō-in (実相印): Dharma seal of the ultimate reality (*See* Dharma seal)
Jissō-ji (実相寺)
Jisui (持水): Water Holder
jita-funi-mon (自他不二門): oneness of self and others (*See* ten onenesses)
jitsu-daijō-kyo (実大乗教): true Mahayana teaching
Jitsue (実慧)
jittai (集諦): truth of the origin of suffering (*See* four noble truths)
Jittoku (実得): Truly Attaining (*See* six ministers)
jiyu-no-bosatsu (地涌の菩薩): Bodhisattvas of the Earth
Jizō-bosatsu (地蔵菩薩): Earth Repository
Jizō-shinkō (地蔵信仰): belief in Bodhisattva Earth Repository (*See* Earth Repository)
jō (乗): *yāna*
Jō-agon-gyō (長阿含経): Long Āgama Sutra
Jōbonnō (浄飯王): Shuddhodana
jo-bun (序分): preparation section
jōbutsu (成仏): attainment of Buddhahood
Jōchi-ji (浄智寺): *See* Five Temples
jōdo (浄土): pure land
jōdō (成道): attaining the way (*See* way)
Jōdo-goso (浄土五祖): five patriarchs of the Chinese Pure Land school
Jōdo-kyō (浄土教): Pure Land school (1)
Jōdo-ron (浄土論): *Treatise on the Pure Land, The*
Jōdoron-chū (浄土論註): *Commentary on "The Treatise on the Pure Land," The*
Jōdo-sambu-kyō (浄土三部経): three Pure Land sutras
Jōdo Shin-shū (浄土真宗): True Pure Land school
Jōdo-shū (浄土宗): Pure Land school
jōe (上衣): outer robe (*See* three robes)
Jōfukyō-bosatsu (常不軽菩薩): Never Disparaging
Jōfukyō-bosatsu-hon (常不軽菩薩品): "Bodhisattva Never Disparaging" chapter
Jōgen (浄眼): Pure Eye
Jōgen-roku (貞元録): Chen-yüan era catalog (See *Chen-yüan Era Catalog of the Buddhist Canon, The*)
Jōgen-shakkyō-roku (貞元釈教録): *Chen-yüan Era Catalog of the Buddhist Canon, The*
jōgō (定業): fixed karma
jōgo-jōbu (調御丈夫): Trainer of People (*See* ten honorable titles)
jōgo-ten (浄居天): heavens of purity
Jōgū-taishi (上宮太子): Prince Jōgū (*See* Shōtoku, Prince)
jo-gyō (助行): supporting practice (See *Six-Volume Writings, The*)
Jōgyō-bosatsu (浄行菩薩): Pure Practices
Jōgyō-bosatsu (上行菩薩): Superior Practices
Jōgyō-bosatsu-no-saitan (上行菩薩の再誕): reincarnation of Bodhisattva Superior Practices (*See* Superior Practices)
jōgyō-zammai (常行三昧): constant active meditation (*See* four forms of meditation)
Jo-hon (序品): "Introduction" chapter
jōjakkō-do (常寂光土): Land of Eternally Tranquil Light

Jōjin (成尋)
Jōjitsu-ron (成実論): *Treatise on the Establishment of Truth, The*
Jōjitsu-shū (成実宗): Establishment of Truth school
jō-jū-e-kū (成住壊空): formation, continuance, decline, and disintegration (*See* four *kalpas*)
jōjū-kyō (常住教): teaching of the eternity of the Buddha nature (*See* three schools of the south and seven schools of the north)
Jōkaku-bō (成覚房)
Jōkan (静観)
Jōken-bō (浄顕房)
Jōkeshukuōchi-butsu (浄華宿王智仏): Pure Flower Constellation King Wisdom (*See* "Bodhisattva Wonderful Sound" chapter)
jō-kō (成劫): *kalpa* of formation
Jōkō-butsu (錠光仏): Fixed Light
Jōkōmyō-ji (浄光明寺)
jō-kon (上根): superior capacity (*See* three groups of voice-hearers)
Jōkōshōgon-koku (浄光荘厳国): Adorned with Pure Light (*See* "Bodhisattva Wonderful Sound" chapter)
Jōmetsu-butsu (常滅仏): Ever Extinguished (*See* sixteen princes)
Jōmyō-ji (浄妙寺): *See* Five Temples
Jōmyōku-ron (浄明句論): *Prasannapadā* (*See* Chandrakīrti [1])
jō-raku-ga-jō (常楽我浄): eternity, happiness, true self, and purity (*See* four virtues)
Jō-ron (肇論): *Treatises of Seng-chao, The*
Jōruri-sekai (浄瑠璃世界): Pure Emerald World
Jōse-bosatsu (常施菩薩): Constant Donations (*See* Sutra on Resolving Doubts about the Middle Day of the Law)
Jōshō (定照): See *Refutation of "The Nembutsu Chosen above All," A*
jōshō-bosatsu (定性菩薩): those predestined to be bodhisattvas (*See* five natures)
jōshō-engaku (定性縁覚): those predestined to be cause-awakened ones (*See* five natures)
Jōshōjin-bosatsu (常精進菩薩): Constant Exertion (*See* "Benefits of the Teacher of the Law" chapter)
jo-shō-rutsū (序正流通): preparation, revelation, and transmission (See *Words and Phrases of the Lotus Sutra, The*)
jōshosa-chi (成所作智): wisdom of perfect practice (*See* five kinds of wisdom)
jōshō-shōmon (定性声聞): those predestined to be voice-hearers (*See* five natures)
Jōtai-bosatsu (常啼菩薩): Ever Wailing
Jōtoku-bunin (浄徳夫人): Pure Virtue
Jō-yuishiki-ron (成唯識論): *Treatise on the Establishment of the Consciousness-Only Doctrine, The*
Jōza-bu (上座部): Theravāda school
jōza-zammai (常坐三昧): constant sitting meditation (*See* four forms of meditation)
Jōzō (浄蔵): Pure Storehouse
jū-aku (十悪): ten evil acts
jū-chōyō (十長養): ten steps in the nourishment of perfection (*See* Brahmā Net Sutra)
jūdai-bu (十大部): ten major writings
jūdai-deshi (十大弟子): ten major disciples
Judō (儒童): Learned Youth
jū-ekō (十廻向): ten stages of devotion
Jufuku-ji (寿福寺)
Jugaku-mugaku-ninki-hon (授学無学人記品): "Prophecies Conferred on Learners and Adepts" chapter

jū-gemmon (十玄門): ten mysteries
Jūgi (従義): Ts'ung-i
jū-gō (十号): ten honorable titles
jū-gyō (十行): ten stages of practice
jūhachi-bu (十八部): eighteen Hinayana schools
jūhachi-fugūhō (十八不共法): eighteen unshared properties
jūhachi-hen (十八変): eighteen miraculous powers
jūhachi-kai (十八界): eighteen elements
jūhachi-ten (十八天): eighteen heavens
jū-haramitsu (十波羅蜜): ten *pāramitās*
jū-hosshu (十発趣): ten initial stages (*See* Brahmā Net Sutra)
Jūichimen-kannon (十一面観音): Eleven-faced Perceiver of the World's Sounds
Jūichimen-kannon-jinju-kyō (十一面観音神呪経): Mysterious Spells of the Eleven-faced Perceiver of the World's Sounds Sutra (*See* Eleven-faced Perceiver of the World's Sounds)
jūin-shika (従因至果): cause to effect (*See* cause and effect)
jūittsū-gosho (十一通御書): eleven letters of remonstration (*See* Toki Jōnin)
jū-ji (十地): ten stages of development
Jūji-kyō (十地経): Ten Stages Sutra
Jūjikyō-ron (十地経論): *Treatise on the Ten Stages Sutra, The*
jūji-no-hihō (十事の非法): ten unlawful revisions
jū-jinriki (十神力): ten supernatural powers
juji-soku-kanjin (受持即観心): Embracing the Gohonzon is in itself observing one's own mind. (*See* observation of the mind)
Jūji-yujuppon (従地涌出品): "Emerging from the Earth" chapter
jūjō-kampō (十乗観法): ten meditations
jūju (重頌): *geya*
jū-jū (十住): ten stages of security
Jūjū-bibasha-ron (十住毘婆沙論): *Commentary on the Ten Stages Sutra, The*
jū-jūkinkai (十重禁戒): ten major precepts
Jūju-ritsu (十誦律): *Ten Divisions of Monastic Rules, The*
jū-jūshin (十住心): ten stages of the mind
Jūjū-shin-ron (十住心論): *Treatise on the Ten Stages of the Mind, The*
jūka-kōin (従果向因): effect to cause (*See* cause and effect)
Juketsu-shū (授決集): *Collection of Orally Transmitted Teachings, A*
juki (授記): prophecy of future enlightenment
Juki-hon (授記品): "Bestowal of Prophecy" chapter
jū-kō (住劫): *kalpa* of continuance
jūkō-daiku-no-gen (住劫第九の減): ninth period of decrease in the *kalpa* of continuance
jū-kongō (十金剛): ten diamond steps of firmness (*See* Brahmā Net Sutra)
Jūkudoku-bon (十功徳品): "Ten Benefits" chapter (*See* Immeasurable Meanings Sutra)
jumon (呪文): magic spells (*See* Shugendō school)
jū-mujō (十無上): ten peerlessnesses
jū-myō (十妙): ten mystic principles
Junda (純陀): Chunda
jun'en (純円): pure and perfect teaching (*See* combining, excluding, corresponding, and including)
jun'en (順縁): relationship of acceptance (*See* reverse relationship)

jungen-gō (順現業): karma whose effects are destined to appear in the same lifetime (*See* fixed karma)
jungo-gō (順後業): karma whose effects are destined to appear in a third or even later lifetime (*See* fixed karma)
Jungyō (順暁): Shun-hsiao
jūnibu-kyō (十二部経): twelve divisions of the scriptures
jūnibun-kyō (十二分教): twelve divisions of the teachings
jūni-daigan (十二大願): twelve great vows
jūni-gan (十二願): twelve vows
jūni-innen (十二因縁): twelve-linked chain of causation
Jūni-mon-ron (十二門論): *Treatise on the Twelve Gates, The*
junin-funi-mon (受潤不二門): oneness of benefits (*See* ten onenesses)
jūni-nyū (十二入): twelve sense fields
jūni-sho (十二処): twelve sense fields
jūni-ten (十二天): twelve gods
jūni-zuda-gyō (十二頭陀行): twelvefold *dhūta* practice
Junsai (遵西)
Junse-gedō (順世外道): Lokāyata
Junshiki (遵式): Tsun-shih
junshō-gō (順生業): karma whose effects are destined to appear in the next lifetime (*See* fixed karma)
Junshōri-ron (順正理論): *Treatise on Accordance with the Correct Doctrine, The*
jū-nyoze (十如是): ten factors of life
jū-ō (十王): ten kings
jū-rasetsu-nyo (十羅刹女): ten demon daughters
Jūren (住蓮)
jū-riki (十力): ten powers
Jūriki-kashō (十力迦葉): Dashabala Kāshyapa
Jurōjin (寿老人): *See* seven beneficent deities
jūroku-daikoku (十六大国): sixteen great states
jūroku-kan (十六観): sixteen types of meditation
jūroku-ōji (十六王子): sixteen princes
jūroku-rakan (十六羅漢): sixteen arhats
Juryō-hon (寿量品): "Life Span" chapter
jūshi-hibō (十四誹謗): fourteen slanders
Jūshin-bon (住心品): "Stage of the Mind" chapter (*See* ten stages of the mind)
jū-yu (十喩): ten similes
jū-zen (十善): ten good acts
jū-zen-kai (十善戒): ten good precepts
juzu (数珠): prayer beads

Kabimara (迦毘摩羅): Kapimala
Kabira (迦毘羅): Kapila
Kabirae-koku (迦毘羅衛国): Kapilavastu
Kadamu-ha (カダム派): Kadam school (*See* Tibetan Buddhism)
Kagyū-ha (カギュー派): Kagyu school (*See* Tibetan Buddhism)
kai (界): *dhātu*
kai (戒): precepts
kai-butchiken (開仏知見): to open the door of Buddha wisdom to all living beings (*See* "Expedient Means" chapter)
kaidan (戒壇): ordination platform
Kaifukeō-nyorai (開敷華王如来): Florescence King (*See* five Buddhas)
kaifumbetsu-kan (界分別観): meditation on the correct discernment of the phenomenal world (*See* five meditations)
Kaigen (戒賢): Shīlabhadra
Kaigen-ji (開元寺): K'ai-yüan-ssu

kaigen-kuyō (開眼供養): eye-opening ceremony
Kaigen-shakkyō-roku (開元釈教録): *K'ai-yüan Era Catalog of the Buddhist Canon, The*
kaigon-kenjitsu (開権顕実): opening the provisional and revealing the true
kaigon-kennon (開近顕遠): opening the near and revealing the distant
kaihō-gyō (回峰行): making a round on the mountain (*See* Sō'ō)
kaiin-zammai (海印三昧): ocean-imprint meditation
kai-ji-go-nyū (開示悟入): to open the door of Buddha wisdom to all living beings, to show the Buddha wisdom to living beings, to cause living beings to awaken to the Buddha wisdom, and induce living beings to enter the path of Buddha wisdom (*See* "Expedient Means" chapter)
kai-jō-e (戒定慧): precepts, meditation, and wisdom
Kai-kō (甲斐公): *See* Nichiji
Kaimoku-shō (開目抄): *Opening of the Eyes, The*
Kainichi-ō (戒日王): Shīlāditya
Kairyūō-kyō (海竜王経): Dragon King of the Sea Sutra
kaisan-ken'ichi (開三顕一): replacement of the three vehicles with the one vehicle
Kaishō-no-haibutsu (会昌の廃仏): Hui-ch'ang Persecution
kaiten-no-jōbutsu (改転の成仏): attaining Buddhahood through transformation (*See* attainment of Buddhahood)
kaji-fuu-nan (過時不雨難): calamity of drought (*See* seven disasters)
Kajō (嘉祥): Chia-hsiang
Kakaba-jigoku (臛臛婆地獄): Hahava hell (*See* eight cold hells)
kakō (火坑): fiery pit
Kako-genzai-inga-kyō (過去現在因果経): Causality of Past and Present Sutra
kakō-sammai (火坑三昧): fire-pit meditation
kako-se (過去世): past existence (*See* three existences)
kako-shichi-butsu (過去七仏): seven Buddhas of the past
Kakuban (覚鑁)
kakugi (格義): matching the meaning (*See* way)
Kakumyō (覚明)
Kakunyo (覚如): *See* Hongan-ji
kakurin (鶴林): crane grove (*See* sal tree)
Kakurokuyana (鶴勒夜那): Haklenayashas
kakusha (覚者): Enlightened One
Kakushin-ni (覚信尼): *See* Hongan-ji
Kakutoku-biku (覚徳比丘): Realization of Virtue
Kakuun (覚運)
kakyō (火坑): fiery pit
kakyō-zammai (火坑三昧): fire-pit meditation
Kamakura-gozan (鎌倉五山): Five Temples of Kamakura (*See* Five Temples)
Kamarashīra (カマラシーラ): Kamalashīla (*See* Tibetan Buddhism)
Kambosha-koku (甘菩遮国): Kamboja (*See* sixteen great states)
Kambotsu-hon (勧発品): "Encouragements" chapter
kambutsu-sammai (観仏三昧): meditation to behold the Buddhas (*See* Sutra of the Meditation to Behold the Buddhas)
Kambutsu-sammai-kai-kyō (観仏三昧海経): Ocean of Meditation on the Buddha Sutra
Kambutsu-sammai-kyō (観仏三昧経): Meditation on the Buddha Sutra
Kammuryōju-kyō (観無量寿経):

Meditation on the Buddha Infinite Life Sutra
Kammuryōjukyō-sho (観無量寿経疏): *Commentary on the Meditation on the Buddha Infinite Life Sutra, The*
Kanāda (カナーダ): Kanāda
Kanadaiba (迦那提婆): Kānadeva
Kanahara-hokkō (金原法橋): *See* Kimbara
Kanchi-zenji (鑑智禅師): Meditation Master Chien-chih (*See* Seng-ts'an)
Kanchō (寛朝): *See* Yakushin
Kan-fugen-bosatsu-gyōhō-kyō (観普賢菩薩行法経): Sutra on How to Practice Meditation on the Bodhisattva Universal Worthy
kan-fukashigi-kyō (観不可思議境): meditation on the region of the unfathomable (*See* ten meditations)
kan-fushigi-kyō (観不思議境): meditation on the region of the unfathomable (*See* ten meditations)
kangi-ji (歓喜地): stage of joy (*See* ten stages of development)
Kangi-koku (歓喜国): Land of Joy
Kan-gyō (観経): Meditation Sutra
kangyō-soku (観行即): stage of perception and action
Kanishika-ō (迦弐色迦王): Kanishka
Kanji-hon (勧持品): "Encouraging Devotion" chapter
Kanjihon-no-nijūgyō-no-ge (観持品の二十行の偈): twenty-line verse of the "Encouraging Devotion" chapter (*See* "Encouraging Devotion" chapter)
kanjin (観心): observation of the mind
Kanjin-no-honzon-shō (観心本尊抄): *Object of Devotion for Observing the Mind, The*
Kanjin-ron (観心論): *Treatise on the Observation of the Mind, The*
Kanjizai-bosatsu (観自在菩薩): Freely Perceiving
kanjō (灌頂): ceremony of anointment
Kanjō (灌頂): Kuan-ting
Kanki-zōyaku-nyorai (歓喜増益如来): Joy Increasing (*See* Possessor of Virtue)
kanku-chō (寒苦鳥): cold-suffering bird
kannin-sekai (堪忍世界): world of endurance
kannō-myō (感応妙): mystic principle of responsive communion (*See* ten mystic principles)
Kannon-bon (観音品): "Perceiver of the World's Sounds" chapter
Kannon-bosatsu (観音菩薩): Perceiver of Sounds
Kannon-gengi (観音玄義): *Profound Meaning of the "Perceiver of the World's Sounds" Chapter, The*
Kannon-gyō (観音経): Perceiver of the World's Sounds Sutra
Kanrin (寒林): Shītavana
kanro (甘露): *amrita*
Kanrobonnō (甘露飯王): Amritodana
Kanroku (観勒)
kan'yaku-butten (漢訳仏典): Chinese versions of Buddhist scriptures (*See* five thousand and forty-eight volumes)
Kan-yakuō-yakujō-nibosatsu-kyō (観薬王薬上二菩薩経): Meditation on the Two Bodhisattvas Medicine King and Medicine Superior Sutra (*See* Medicine King)
Kanzeon-bosatsu (観世音菩薩): Perceiver of the World's Sounds
Kanzeon-bosatsu-bon (観世音菩薩品): "Bodhisattva Perceiver of the World's Sounds" chapter
Kanzeon-bosatsu-fumon-bon (観世音菩薩普門品): "Universal Gateway

of the Bodhisattva Perceiver of the World's Sounds" chapter
Kanzeon-ji (観世音寺)
Karada-sen (伽羅陀山): Kharadīya, Mount
karagura (迦羅求羅): *kālakula*
Karakuda-kasennen (迦羅鳩駄迦旃延): Pakudha Kacchāyana
karakura (迦羅求羅): *kālakula*
Karanda (迦蘭陀): Kalandaka
Karibatsuma (訶梨跋摩): Harivarman
Kari-ō (迦利王): Kāli
Karudai (迦留陀夷): Kālodāyin
karura (迦楼羅): *garuda*
karyōbinga (迦陵頻伽): *kalavinka*
Kasai (迦才): Chia-ts'ai (See *Treatise on the Pure Land, The* [2])
Kasei-kairō (河西回廊): Kansu Corridor (*See* Tun-huang)
Kasennen (迦旃延): Kātyāyana
Kashi-koku (迦尸国): Kāshī
Kashō-bosatsu (迦葉菩薩): Kāshyapa (1)
Kashō-butsu (迦葉仏): Kāshyapa (2)
Kashōi-bu (迦葉遺部): Kāshyapīya school
Kashō-matō (迦葉摩騰): Kāshyapa Mātanga
kashō-zammai (火生三昧): flame-emitting meditation
Kashumira-koku (迦湿弥羅国): Kashmir
Kataennishi (迦多衍尼子): Kātyāyanīputra
kataku (火宅): burning house
kataku-no-tatoe (火宅の譬): parable of the burning house
Kataumi (片海)
katsuma-mandara (羯磨曼荼羅): karma mandala
Katsuron-ha (勝論派): Vaisheshika school (*See* Ulūka)
Katsuryōga-koku (羯陵伽国): Kalinga (*See* Ashoka)
Kawanobe-no-nyūdō (河野辺の入道): Kawanobe, the lay priest of
kazu (火途): path of fire (*See* three paths [2])
kechien-kanjō (結縁灌頂): anointment ceremony to establish a relationship between the individual and the Buddha (*See* ceremony of anointment)
kechimyaku (血脈): heritage of the Law
Kedo-ji (化度寺): Hua-tu-ssu temple (*See* Three Stages school)
kegi-no-shikyō (化儀の四教): four teachings of method
Kegi-shō (化儀抄): *On the Formalities*
Kegon-gyō (華厳経): Flower Garland Sutra
Kegongyō-sho (華厳経疏): *Annotations on the Flower Garland Sutra, The*
Kegongyō-tangen-ki (華厳経探玄記): *Delving into the Profundity of the Flower Garland Sutra*
Kegon-ji (華厳時): Flower Garland period
Kegon-shū (華厳宗): Flower Garland school
kehō-no-shikyō (化法の四教): four teachings of doctrine
keichū-myōju-no-tatoe (髻中明珠の譬): parable of the bright jewel in the topknot
Keihin-koku (罽賓国): Kashmir
Keihō-zenji (圭峰禅師): Meditation Master Kuei-feng (*See* Tsung-mi)
Keiin-bu (鶏胤部): Kaukkutika school (*See* eighteen Hinayana schools)
Keika (恵果): Hui-kuo
Keikei (荊渓): Ching-hsi
Keishō (慶昭): Ch'ing-chao (*See* Outside-the-Mountain school)
Keisoku-sen (鶏足山): Kukkutapāda, Mount
Keitoku-dentō-roku (景徳伝灯録):

Ching-te Era Record of the Transmission of the Lamp, The
Keizuma-ji (鶏頭摩寺): Kukkutārāma Monastery
Keji-bu (化地部): Mahīshāsaka school
kejō (化城): phantom city
kejō-hōsho-no-tatoe (化城宝処の譬): parable of the phantom city and the treasure land
kejō-yu (化城喩): parable of the phantom city
Kejō-yu-hon (化城喩品): "Parable of the Phantom City" chapter
Kekō-nyorai (華光如来): Flower Glow
Kempon Hokke-shū (顕本法華宗): Truth-Revealed Lotus school
Ken'ai-ronji (賢愛論師): Bhadraruchi
Kenchō-ji (建長寺)
Kenchoku (犍陟): Kanthaka (*See* Chandaka)
Kenchū-bu (賢胄部): Bhadrayānīya school (*See* eighteen Hinayana schools)
kenda (乾陀): *gandha*
Kendara-koku (健駄羅国): Gandhara
kendatsuba (乾闥婆): *gandharva*
ken-dō (見道): way of insight
kendon (慳貪): greed and stinginess
Ken'e (堅慧): Sāramati
Ken-gō (賢劫): Wise Kalpa
Kengu-kyō (賢愚経): Sutra on the Wise and the Foolish
kengyō-rokudo-hon (兼行六度品): stage of embracing the Lotus Sutra and practicing the six *pāramitās* (*See* five stages of practice)
Ken-hōtō-hon (見宝塔品): "Emergence of the Treasure Tower" chapter
kenji-waku (見思惑): illusions of thought and desire
ken-joku (見濁): impurity of thought (*See* five impurities)
Kenkai-ron (顕戒論): *Clarification of the Precepts, A*
kenkyō (顕教): exoteric teachings
Kenne (堅慧): Sāramati
kenneō (懸衣翁): garment-suspending demon
Kennin-ji (建仁寺)
kenro-fujō-kyō (顕露不定教): explicit indeterminate teaching (*See* four teachings of method)
Ken-senchaku (顕選択): *Clarification of "The Nembutsu Chosen above All," A* (*See* Ryūkan)
Kenshin (顕真)
Kensho-ji (建初寺): Chien-ch'u-ssu temple (*See* K'ang-seng-hui)
kenshō-jōbutsu (見性成仏): perceiving one's true nature and attaining Buddhahood (*See* Zen school)
Kenshū-ron (顕宗論): *Clarification of Doctrine, A*
kentai (顕体): "Clarification of the Essence" section (*See* five major principles)
ken-tan-tai-tai (兼但対帯): combining, excluding, corresponding, and including
ken-waku (見惑): illusions of thought (*See* illusions of thought and desire)
ken'yaku (顕益): conspicuous benefit
kenzoku-myō (眷属妙): mystic principle of relationship (*See* ten mystic principles)
Keraku-ten (化楽天): Heaven of Enjoying the Conjured
Keshi-jō (華氏城): Pātaliputra
keshi-kō (芥子劫): mustard-seed *kalpa*
keshin (化身): transformation body
keshin-metchi (灰身滅智): reducing the body to ashes and annihilating consciousness
ke-shō (化生): birth by transformation (*See* four forms of birth)

ke-tai (仮諦): truth of temporary existence (*See* three truths)
ketchō-fuzoku (結要付嘱): transfer of the essence of the Lotus Sutra
Ketoku-bosatsu (華徳菩薩): Flower Virtue (*See* "Bodhisattva Wonderful Sound" chapter)
ketsujō-shō (決定性): determinate groups
ketsujū (結集): Buddhist Councils
ketsumyaku (血脈): heritage of the Law
ketsuzu (血途): path of blood (*See* three paths [2])
Kezō-sekai (華蔵世界): Lotus Treasury World
ki (鬼): demon
Kiben-baramon (鬼弁婆羅門): Demon Eloquence
kibetsu (記別): prophecy of future enlightenment
Kibyūronshō-ha (帰謬論証派): Prāsangika school
kichijō-sō (吉祥草): *kusha* grass
Kichijō-ten (吉祥天): Auspicious
Kichizō (吉蔵): Chi-tsang
Kiji (亀茲): Kucha
kijin (鬼神): spirits
Kijiru-sekkutsu (キジル石窟): Kizil caves
Kiken-bosatsu (喜見菩薩): Gladly Seen
Kiken-jō (喜見城): Joyful to See
Kiki (窺基): K'uei-chi
Kikkaya (吉迦夜): Kinkara
Kikon-biku (喜根比丘): Root of Joy
Kimbara-hokkyō (金原法橋): Kimbara
kimon (鬼門): demon gate (*See* Enryaku-ji)
kimyō (帰命): devotion; dedicating one's life (*See* Nam-myoho-renge-kyo)
Kinkaku-ji (金閣寺): Chin-ko-ssu temple (*See* Han-kuang)
kinnara (緊那羅): *kimnara*
Kiren-ga (熙連河): Hiranyavatī
Kiriki-ō (訖哩枳王): Kriki
Kirita-ō (訖利多王): Krita
kishi-ki (起屍鬼): corpse-raising demon (See *vetāda*)
Kishimojin (鬼子母神): Mother of Demon Children
Kishimo-kyō (鬼子母経): Mother of Demon Children Sutra (*See* Mother of Demon Children)
Kishin-ron (起信論): *Awakening of Faith*
Kissa-yōjō-ki (喫茶養生記): *Drinking Tea to Improve Health and Prolong Life* (*See* Eisai)
Kittoku (吉徳): Auspicious Virtue (*See* six ministers)
Kiyomizu-dera (清水寺)
kō (香): *gandha*
kō (劫): *kalpa*
Kō-ama (国府尼): Kō, the lay nun of
kōan (公案)
Kōben (高弁)
Kōbō (弘法)
Kōchi (広智)
kōchō-zetsu (広長舌): long broad tongue
Kōdai-nyo (皐諦女): Kuntī
kōdō (講堂): lecture hall
Kōen (皇円): See *Brief History of Japan, A*
Kōfuku-ji (興福寺)
Kogi-ha (古義派・古義真言宗): Old Doctrine school (*See* True Word school)
Kō-gumyō-shū (広弘明集): *Further Anthology of the Propagation of Light, The*
kōi-tasetsu (広為他説): to expound the teaching of the Lotus Sutra widely for others (*See* four stages of faith)
koji (居士): householder
kōjin (香神): god of fragrance
Kōjō (光定)

Kō-jō (香城): City of Fragrances
kō-joku (劫濁): impurity of the age (*See* five impurities)
kōkaigon-kennon (広開近顕遠): opening the near and revealing the distant in expanded form (*See* opening the near and revealing the distant)
kōkaisan-ken'ichi (広開三顕一): expanded replacement of the three vehicles with the one vehicle
Kokan Shiren (虎関師錬)
Kōka-ten (広果天): Large Fruitage Heaven (*See* eighteen heavens)
kokki (穀貴): high grain prices
Kōkō (興皇): Hsing-huang
Kokoba-jigoku (虎虎婆地獄): Huhuva hell (*See* eight cold hells)
kokū (虚空): *ākāsha*
Kokubonnō (斛飯王): Dronodana
kokubun-ji (国分寺): provincial temples
kokubun-niji (国分尼寺): provincial temples for nuns
kokudo (国土): *kshetra*
kokudo-seken (国土世間): realm of the environment (*See* three realms of existence)
kokū-e (虚空会): Ceremony in the Air
kokū-fudō-e (虚空不動慧): spacelike immovable wisdom (*See* Three Great Secret Laws)
kokū-fudō-jō (虚空不動定): spacelike immovable meditation (*See* Three Great Secret Laws)
kokū-fudō-kai (虚空不動戒): spacelike immovable precept (*See* Three Great Secret Laws)
Kokujō-jigoku (黒縄地獄): hell of black cords
Kokūjū-butsu (虚空住仏): Void-Dwelling (*See* sixteen princes)
Kokusei-hyakuroku (国清百録): *One Hundred Records of the Great Teacher T'ien-t'ai, The*
Kokusei-ji (国清寺): Kuo-ch'ing-ssu
kokushi (国師): teacher of the nation
Kokūzō-bosatsu (虚空蔵菩薩): Space Treasury
Komatsubara-no-hōnan (小松原の法難): Komatsubara Persecution
Kōmoku-ten (広目天): Wide-Eyed
kompon-bonnō (根本煩悩): fundamental earthly desires (*See* earthly desires)
kompon-hōrin (根本法輪): root teaching
Kōmyō-nyorai (光明如来): Light Bright
kon (根): *indriya*
kon-dō (金堂): golden hall (*See* seven-halled temple)
Kongōbei (金剛錍): *Diamond Scalpel, The*
Kongōbu-ji (金剛峯寺)
Kongōchi (金剛智): Chin-kang-chih
Kongōchō-kyō (金剛頂経): Diamond Crown Sutra
Kongōdō-bosatsu (金剛幢菩薩): Diamond Banner
Kongō-hannya-haramitsu-kyō (金剛般若波羅蜜経): Diamond-like Perfection of Wisdom Sutra
Kongō-hannya-kyō (金剛般若経): Diamond Wisdom Sutra
Kongōharamitta-bosatsu (金剛波羅蜜多菩薩): Diamond Pāramitā (*See* five mighty bodhisattvas)
Kongōhō-bosatsu (金剛宝菩薩): Diamond Treasure (*See* five mighty bodhisattvas)
kongō-hōki-kai (金剛宝器戒): precept of the diamond chalice
Kongō-jō (金剛乗): Vajrayāna
kongō-kai (金剛界): Diamond Realm
Kongōkai-dainichi (金剛界大日): Mahāvairochana of the Diamond Realm (*See* Mahāvairochana)
kongōkai-mandara (金剛界曼荼羅): Diamond Realm mandala

Kongōku-bosatsu (金剛吼菩薩): Diamond Roar (*See* five mighty bodhisattvas)
Kongō-kyō (金剛経): Diamond Sutra
Kongōri-bosatsu (金剛利菩薩): Diamond Benefit (*See* five mighty bodhisattvas)
Kongōsatta (金剛薩埵): Vajrasattva
kongō-sho (金剛杵): diamond-pounder
Kongōshu-bosatsu (金剛手菩薩): Diamond Hand (*See* five mighty bodhisattvas)
Kongōyasha-bosatsu (金剛薬叉菩薩): Diamond Yaksha (*See* five mighty bodhisattvas)
Kongōyasha-myō'ō (金剛夜叉明王): Diamond Yaksha (*See* five great wisdom kings)
Kongōzō-bosatsu (金剛蔵菩薩): Diamond Storehouse
Kōnichi-ama (光日尼): Kōnichi, the lay nun
Kōnichi-bō (光日房)
Kōnin (弘忍): Hung-jen
konji-chō (金翅鳥): golden-winged bird
Konjiki-ō (金色王): Golden Color
Konjikiō-kyō (金色王経): King Golden Color Sutra (*See* Golden Color)
Konkōmyō-kyō (金光明経): Golden Light Sutra
Konkōmyō-saishō'ō-kyō (金光明最勝王経): Sovereign Kings of the Golden Light Sutra
Konkōmyō-shitennō-gokoku-no-tera (金光明四天王護国之寺): temples for the protection of the nation by the power of the Golden Light Sutra and the four heavenly kings (*See* provincial temples)
Kō-no-ama (国府尼): Kō, the lay nun of
konrin (金輪): gold circle
konrin-hō (金輪宝): gold-wheel treasure
konrin-ō (金輪王): gold-wheel-turning king
Konron-sammyaku (崑崙山脈): Kunlun Mountains (*See* Silk Road)
Kō-nyūdō (国府入道): Kō, the lay priest of
Kō'on-ten (光音天): Light Sound Heaven
Kōsai (幸西)
Kō-sen (香山): Fragrant, Mount
kōsen-rufu (広宣流布)
kō-shitsu (香室): hall of fragrance (See *gandha*)
Kōshō-baramon (香姓婆羅門): Drona
Kōshō-koku (高昌国): Kao-ch'ang
Kōshū (広脩): Kuang-hsiu
Kōsō-den (高僧伝): *Biographies of Eminent Priests, The*
Kōsōe (康僧会): K'ang-seng-hui
Kōsōgai (康僧鎧): Samghavarman (1)
Kōsui-sen (香酔山): Fragrant, Mount
Kōtaku-ji (光宅寺): Kuang-che-ssu
kotsugen-no-baramon (乞眼の婆羅門): eye-begging Brahman
kotsujiki-gyō (乞食行): practice of alms-begging (See *bhikshu*)
Kōya-san (高野山): Kōya, Mount
Kōzen-gokoku-ron (興禅護国論): *Propagation of Zen for the Protection of the Country, The*
ku (苦): suffering
kū (空): *ākāsha*
kū (空): non-substantiality
ku-anraku-gyō (口安楽行): peaceful practice of the mouth (*See* four peaceful practices)
Kubo-no-ama (窪尼): Kubo, the lay nun of
kubun-kyō (九分経): nine divisions of the scriptures

kubun-kyō（九分教）: nine divisions of the teachings
kudoku（功徳）: benefit; *punya*
kudoku-ju（功徳聚）: cluster of blessings (*See* mandala)
Kudokurin-bosatsu（功徳林菩薩）: Forest of Merits
kudoku-riyaku-myō（功徳利益妙）: mystic principle of merit and benefit (*See* ten mystic principles)
Kudon（瞿曇）: Gautama
Kudō Yoshitaka（工藤吉隆）
Kugan-biku（苦岸比丘）: Shore of Suffering
kū-gedatsumon（空解脱門）: meditation on non-substantiality (*See* three meditations for emancipation)
kūgen（空閑）: deserted and quiet place (See *aranya*)
Kugyari（瞿伽利）: Kokālika
kugyō（苦行）: ascetic practice; austere practice (*See* five ascetics)
kuhanda（鳩槃荼）: *kumbhānda*
Kui（瞿夷）: Gopikā
Kujaku-myō'ō（孔雀明王）: Peacock King (*See* En no Ozunu)
kujūgoshu-no-gedō（九十五種の外道）: ninety-five non-Buddhist schools
kukai（苦海）: sea of suffering (*See* sea of the sufferings of birth and death)
ku-kai（九界）: nine worlds
Kūkai（空海）
kukai-shogu-no-bukkai（九界所具の仏界）: inclusion of Buddhahood in the nine worlds
kukai-soku-bukkai（九界即仏界）: inclusion of Buddhahood in the nine worlds
Kukari（瞿伽利）: Kokālika
kū-kō（空劫）: *kalpa* of disintegration
Kukyō-ichijō-hōshō-ron（究竟一乗宝性論）: *Treatise on the Treasure Vehicle of Buddhahood, The*
kukyō-soku（究竟即）: stage of ultimate enlightenment
ku-man（九慢）: nine types of arrogance
Kumarada（鳩摩羅駄）: Kumārata
Kumaraen（鳩摩羅炎）: Kumārayāna
Kumarajū（鳩摩羅什）: Kumārajīva
ku-mitsu（口密）: mystery of the mouth (*See* three mysteries)
Kumotsuzu-jigoku（拘物頭地獄）: Kumuda hell (*See* eight cold hells)
Kūmuhen-jo（空無辺処）: Realm of Boundless Empty Space
Kūmuhenjo-jō（空無辺処定）: meditation on the Realm of Boundless Empty Space (*See* Realm of Boundless Empty Space)
Kūmuhenjo-ten（空無辺処天）: Heaven of Boundless Empty Space
Kumutora-sekkutsu（クムトラ石窟）: Kumtura caves (*See* Kucha)
Kunagon-butsu（倶那含仏）: Kanakamuni
kunjū-kyō（捃拾教）: teaching of gleaning
kuon-ganjo（久遠元初）
kuonganjo-no-jijuyūshin（久遠元初の自受用身）: Buddha of beginningless time
Kuon-ji（久遠寺）
kuon-jitujō（久遠実成）: attainment of Buddhahood in the remote past
kuō-no-dainan（九横の大難）: nine great ordeals
Kuratsukuri no Tori（鞍作止利）: *See* Shiba Tatsuto
Kurō-koku（拘楼国）: Kuru (*See* sixteen great states)
kurosha（倶盧舎）: *krosha*
Kuru-shū（倶盧洲）: Uttarakuru
Kuruson-butsu（拘留孫仏）: Krakucchanda
kusen-hakkai（九山八海）: nine mountains and eight seas
Kushāna-chō（クシャーナ朝）: Kushan

Kusha-ron (倶舎論): *Dharma Analysis Treasury, The*
Kusharon-sho (倶舎論疏): *The Annotations on "The Dharma Analysis Treasury"* (*See* Fa-pao)
Kusha-shū (倶舎宗): Dharma Analysis Treasury school
ku-shiki (九識): nine consciousnesses
Kushinagara (拘尸那掲羅): Kushinagara
Kushira (瞿師羅): Ghoshila
Kushira-on (瞿師羅園): Ghoshila Grove (*See* Ghoshila)
Kushira-shōja (瞿師羅精舎): Ghoshila Monastery (*See* Ghoshila)
ku-shū (九宗): nine schools
kusuri (薬): *bhaishajya*
ku-tai (苦諦): truth of suffering (*See* four noble truths)
kū-tai (空諦): truth of non-substantiality (*See* three truths)
kutei (倶胝): *koti*
Kutoku (苦得): Painfully Acquired
Kuwagayatsu-mondō (桑が谷問答): Kuwagayatsu Debate (*See* Ryūzō-bō)
Kūya (空也)
kuyaku (旧訳): old translations
Kuyani (瞿耶尼): Aparagodānīya
kuyō (供養): offering
kuyō-kugyō-se (供養恭敬施): offerings of praise and reverence (*See* three kinds of offerings)
kyakuryaku-no-santai (隔歴の三諦): separation of the three truths
Kyō-biku (脇比丘): Pārshva
kyōchi-myōgō (境智冥合): fusion of reality and wisdom
Kyōdommi (憍曇弥): Gautamī
kyōge-betsuden (教外別伝): separate transmission outside the sutras
Kyō-gyō-shin-shō (教行信証): *Teaching, Practice, Faith, and Proof, The*
kyō-gyō-shō (教行証): teaching, practice, and proof
kyōhan (教判): comparative classification
Kyōjinnyo (憍陳如): Kaundinya
kyōkan (経巻). sutra scroll (See *dīpa*)
Kyōkan-jigoku (叫喚地獄): hell of wailing (*See* eight hot hells)
kyō-myō (境妙): mystic principle of reality (*See* ten mystic principles)
Kyōnin-bō (鏡忍房)
Kyō'ō (経王)
Kyō'ō Gokoku-ji (教王護国寺)
Kyōritsu-isō (経律異相): *Divergent Concepts in the Sutras and Vinaya Texts*
kyō-ritsu-ron (経律論): sutras, texts of the rules of monastic discipline, and doctrinal treatises (*See* Jōjin)
kyōroku (経録): catalog of the Buddhist canon (*See* Seng-yu)
Kyōryō-bu (経量部): Sautrāntika school
Kyōryōyasha (畺良耶舎): Kālayashas
Kyōsara-koku (憍薩羅国): Kosala
Kyōshika (憍尸迦): Kaushika
kyōshō (経証): scriptural reference (See *On Establishing the Correct Teaching for the Peace of the Land*)
Kyōshōmi-koku (憍賞弥国): Kaushāmbī
kyōshu (教主): lord of teachings
Kyōshū (経集): *Suttanipāta*
kyōsō-hanjaku (教相判釈): comparative classification
Kyō-sonja (脇尊者): Pārshva
Kyoto-gozan (京都五山): Five Temples of Kyoto (*See* Five Temples)
kyōzō (経蔵): sutra repository
kyū-kai (九界): nine worlds
kyūkai-soku-bukkai (九界即仏界): inclusion of Buddhahood in the nine worlds

ma (魔): devil
mada (末陀): *madhya* (1)

Madendai (末田提): Madhyāntika
magoraga (摩睺羅伽): mahoraga
Mahābihāra (マハービハーラ): Mahāvihāra (*See* Southern Buddhism)
Mahinda (摩呬陀): Mahendra
maka (摩訶): *mahā*
Makadaiba (摩訶提婆): Mahādeva
Makada-koku (摩掲陀国): Magadha
Makaen (摩訶衍): Mo-ho-yen (*See* Tibetan Buddhism)
Makahadoma-jigoku (摩訶鉢特摩地獄): Mahāpadma hell (*See* eight cold hells)
Makahajahadai (摩訶波闍波提): Mahāprajāpatī
Makahandoku (摩訶槃特): Mahāpanthaka
Makahannya-haramitsu-kyō (摩訶般若波羅蜜経): Great Perfection of Wisdom Sutra (1)(2)
Makakara-ten (摩訶迦羅天): Mahākāla
Makakasennen (摩訶迦旃延): Mahākātyāyana
Makakashō (摩訶迦葉): Mahākāshyapa
Makamaya (摩訶摩耶): Mahāmāyā
Makamokkenren (摩訶目犍連): Mahāmaudgalyāyana
Makanan (摩訶男): Mahānāma
makasatsu (摩訶薩): mahāsattva
Makasatta (摩訶薩埵): Mahāsattva
Maka-shikan (摩訶止観): *Great Concentration and Insight*
Maka-sōgi-ritsu (摩訶僧祇律): *Great Canon of Monastic Rules, The*
makatsu (摩竭): *makara*
Makeishura-ten (摩醯首羅天): Maheshvara
Makiguchi Tsunesaburō (牧口常三郎): *See* Soka Gakkai
Makkari-kushari (末伽梨拘舎梨): Makkhali Gosāla
Mampuku-ji (万福寺): *See* Ōbaku school
man (慢): arrogance
mana-shiki (末那識): *mano*-consciousness
Manashi-ryūō (摩那斯竜王): Manasvin (*See* eight great dragon kings)
mandara (曼荼羅): mandala
mandara-ke (曼陀羅華): *māndāra* flower
Mandata-ō (曼陀多王): Born from the Crown of the Head
mandō (慢幢): banner of arrogance (*See* arrogance)
mani (摩尼): *mani*
Manju-ji (万寿寺): *See* Five Temples
manjusha-ge (曼殊沙華): *manjūshaka* flower
Manura (摩奴羅): Manorhita
Manurata (摩菟羅他): Manoratha
maō (魔王): devil king
mappō (末法): Latter Day of the Law
Mappō-sō'ō-shō (末法相応抄): "The Teaching for the Latter Day" (See *Six-Volume Writings, The*)
Mappō-tōmyō-ki (末法燈明記): *Treatise on the Lamp for the Latter Day of the Law, The*
Māra (マーラ): Māra (*See* devil)
Marei-sen (摩黎山): Malaya, Mount
Mari (末利): Mallikā
Mari-sen (摩黎山): Malaya, Mount
Marishi-ten (摩利支天): Marīchi
Marupa (マルパ): Marpa (*See* Tibetan Buddhism)
Ma-ten (魔天): Heaven of Māra
Matōba (摩沓婆): Mādhava (*See* Gunamati)
Matōga (摩騰迦): Mātanga
Matora-koku (摩突羅国): Mathura
Matsubagayatsu (松葉ケ谷)
Matsubagayatsu-no-hōnan (松葉ケ谷の法難): Matsubagayatsu Persecution
Matsuno Rokurō Saemon (松野六郎左衛門)

Matsura (末羅): Malla
Maya (摩耶): Māyā
Maya-kyō (摩耶経): Māyā Sutra
meigo-funi (迷悟不二): oneness of delusion and enlightenment
Mei-tei (明帝): Emperor Ming (*See* Pai-ma-ssu)
Memyō (馬鳴): Ashvaghosha
mettai (滅諦): truth of the cessation of suffering (*See* four noble truths)
mezu (馬頭): horse-headed demons
Mii-dera (三井寺)
miken-byakugō-sō (眉間白毫相): tuft of white hair between the eyebrows
mikkyō (密教): Esoteric Buddhism
Mikuni no Taifu (三国太夫)
Minobu-san (身延山): Minobu, Mount
Minobu-san-fuzoku-sho (身延山付嘱書): *Document for Entrusting Minobu-san, The*
Minobu-sōjō-sho (身延相承書): *Minobu Transfer Document, The*
mirai-se (未来世): future existence (*See* three existences)
Mirakutsu (弥羅掘)
Mīrān (ミーラーン): Miran
Miranda-ō (弥蘭陀王): Milinda
Mirarēpa (ミラレーパ): Milarepa (*See* Tibetan Buddhism)
Mirindaō-monkyō (ミリンダ王問経): *Milindapanha*
Miroku (弥勒): Maitreya (2)
Miroku-bosatsu (弥勒菩薩): Maitreya (1)
Miroku-geshō-kyō (弥勒下生経): Advent of Maitreya Sutra (*See* Earth Repository)
Miroku-shinkō (弥勒信仰): belief in Maitreya (*See* Maitreya [1])
Misawa Kojirō (三沢小次郎)
Mishaka (弥遮迦): Mikkaka
Mishasoku-bu (弥沙塞部): Mahīshāsaka school
Mishō'on (未生怨): Enemy before Birth
Mitsugon (密厳): Secret Solemnity
Mitsugon-gyō (密厳経): Secret Solemnity Sutra
Mitsugon-jōdo (密厳浄土): Pure Land of Secret Solemnity
mitsugyō-daiichi (密行第一): foremost in inconspicuous practice (*See* Rāhula)
Mitsurinsen-bu (密林山部): Shannāgarika school (*See* eighteen Hinayana schools)
mōki-no-tatoe (盲亀の譬): parable of the blind turtle (*See* one-eyed turtle)
Mokkenren (目犍連): Maudgalyāyana
Mokkenrenshi-teishu (目犍連子帝須): Moggaliputta Tissa (*See* Buddhist Councils)
Mokuren (目連): Maudgalyāyana
mompō-geshu (聞法下種): sowing the seeds by letting one hear the teaching (*See* planting the seeds of Buddhahood)
Mongaku (文覚)
Monjushiri-bosatsu (文殊師利菩薩): Manjushrī
mon-shō (文証): documentary proof (*See* three proofs)
Montei-hichin-shō (文底秘沈抄): "The Meanings Hidden in the Depths" (See *Six-Volume Writings, The*)
Mubon-ten (無煩天): Heaven of No Vexations (*See* eighteen heavens)
mubotsu-shiki (無没識): never-perishing consciousness (See *ālaya*-consciousness)
mugaku (無学): one who has nothing more to learn (*See* arhat)
mugaku-dō (無学道): way of the arhat (*See* three ways)
Mugaku Sogen (無学祖元)
mugan-gedatsumon (無願解脱門):

meditation on non-desire (*See* three meditations for emancipation)
muge-chi (無礙智): unhindered wisdom
muhen (無辺): *ananta*
Muhengyō-bosatsu (無辺行菩薩): Boundless Practices
mui (無畏): fearlessness
mui (無為): nonaction (*See* way)
mui (無為): unconditioned, the
Muijūrikiku-bosatsu (無畏十力吼菩薩): Roar of Fearlessness and Ten Powers (*See* five mighty bodhisattvas)
mui-se (無畏施): offering of fearlessness (*See* almsgiving)
Muisen-ji (無畏山寺): Abhayagiri monastery (*See* Southern Buddhism)
Muisenji-ha (無畏山寺派): Abhayagiri school (*See* Southern Buddhism)
Mujaku (無著): Asanga
mujin-engi (無尽縁起): interrelation of all phenomena; mutual inclusiveness of all phenomena (*See* Indra's net)
Mujinni-bosatsu (無尽意菩薩): Inexhaustible Intent (*See* "Universal Gateway of the Bodhisattva Perceiver of the World's Sounds" chapter)
Mujin-zō (無尽蔵): Inexhaustible Treasury (*See* Three Stages school)
mu-jisho (無自性): nonexistence of self-nature (*See* non-substantiality)
mujō (無上): *anuttara*
mujō-bodai (無上菩提): unsurpassed enlightenment
mujō-dō (無上道): unsurpassed way
mujō-hōju (無上宝聚): cluster of unsurpassed jewels (*See* four great voice-hearers)
mujōshi (無上士): Unexcelled Worthy
mujō-shōtō-shōgaku (無上正等正覚): *anuttara-samyak-sambodhi*
mukenchō-sō (無見頂相): unseen crown of the head
Muken-daijō (無間大城): great citadel of the hell of incessant suffering
Muken-jigoku (無間地獄): hell of incessant suffering
muki (無記): unlabeled, the
Muku-ronji (無垢論師): Vimalamitra
Muku-sekai (無垢世界): Spotless World (*See* dragon king's daughter)
muku-shiki (無垢識): free-of-defilement consciousness (See *amala*-consciousness)
Mukuyū (無垢友): Vimalamitra
mumyō (無明): ignorance; *moha*
mumyō-waku (無明惑): illusions about the true nature of existence (*See* three categories of illusion)
Munetchi (無熱池): Heat-Free Lake
Munetsu-ten (無熱天): Heaven of No Heat (*See* eighteen heavens)
muni (牟尼): *muni*
muro (無漏): freedom from outflows (*See* outflows)
muro-chi (無漏智): wisdom without outflows (*See* four good roots)
muro-jō (無漏定): meditation without outflows (*See* outflows)
muro-shin (無漏身): body without outflows (*See* outflows)
muryō (無量): *ananta*
Muryōgi-kyō (無量義経): Immeasurable Meanings Sutra
muryōgisho-sammai (無量義処三昧): *samādhi* of the origin of immeasurable meanings
Muryōi (無量意): Immeasurable Intention (See *ananta*)
Muryōjō-ten (無量浄天): Boundless Purity Heaven (*See* twenty-eight heavens)

Muryōju-butsu (無量寿仏): Amitāyus; Infinite Life
Muryōju-kyō (無量寿経): Buddha Infinite Life Sutra
Muryōkō-butsu (無量光仏): Amitābha; Infinite Light
Muryōkō-ten (無量光天): Infinite Light Heaven (*See* eighteen heavens)
Muryōrikiku-bosatsu (無量力吼菩薩): Infinitely Powerful Roar (*See* five mighty bodhisattvas)
musa-no-sanjin (無作の三身): Buddha eternally endowed with the three bodies (*See* true Buddha)
mushi-chi (無師智): teacherless wisdom
mushiki-kai (無色界): world of formlessness
mushō-bōnin (無生法忍): realization of the non-birth and non-extinction of all phenomena
Mushō-dōji (無勝童子): Invincible
Mushoi (無所畏): Fearlessness (*See* six ministers)
mushō-ujō (無性有情): those without the nature of enlightenment (*See* five natures)
Mushou-sho (無所有処): Realm of Nothingness
Mushousho-jō (無所有処定): meditation on the Realm of Nothingness (*See* Realm of Nothingness)
Mushousho-ten (無所有処天): Heaven of Nothingness
mu-shushō (無種性): those without the nature of enlightenment (*See* five natures)
musō-gedatsumon (無相解脱門): meditation on non-discrimination (*See* three meditations for emancipation)
Musō-ten (無想天): Heaven of No Thought (*See* eighteen heavens)
muu-ju (無憂樹): *ashoka* tree
Muun-ten (無雲天): Cloudless Heaven (*See* eighteen heavens)
muyo-nehan (無余涅槃): nirvana of no remainder
myō (妙)
Myōe (明恵)
myōgaku (妙覚): perfect enlightenment
myōgyōsoku (明行足): Perfect Clarity and Conduct (*See* ten honorable titles)
myōhō (妙法): Mystic Law
Myōhō-ama (妙法尼): Myōhō, the lay nun
Myoho-renge-kyo (妙法蓮華経)
Myoho-renge-kyo (妙法蓮華経): Lotus Sutra of the Wonderful Law
Myōhō-renge-kyō-upadaisha (妙法蓮華経憂波提舎): *Treatise on the Lotus Sutra of the Wonderful Law, The*
Myōichi-ama (妙一尼): Myōichi, the lay nun
Myōichi-nyo (妙一女)
myōji-soku (名字即): stage of hearing the name and words of the truth
Myōjō-ga-ike (明星が池): Myōjō Pond
myō-joku (命濁): impurity of life span (*See* five impurities)
myōjō-ten (明星天): god of the stars (*See* three heavenly sons of light)
myō-kansatsu-chi (妙観察智): wisdom of insight into the particulars (*See* five kinds of wisdom)
Myōki-koku (妙喜国): Land of Wonderful Joy
Myōkō-bosatsu (妙光菩薩): Wonderfully Bright
Myōkō-sen (妙光山): Wonderful Bright, Mount
Myōkō-sen (妙高山): Wonderful High, Mount
Myōmitsu (妙密)
myōmyō-chō (命命鳥): *jīvamjīvaka*
myō'ō (明王): wisdom kings

Myō'on-bon (妙音品): "Wonderful Sound" chapter
Myō'on-bosatsu (妙音菩薩): Wonderful Sound
Myō'on-bosatsu-hon (妙音菩薩品): "Bodhisattva Wonderful Sound" chapter
Myōraku (妙楽): Miao-lo
Myōren (妙蓮)
Myōshin-ama (妙心尼): Myōshin, the lay nun
Myōshō (明勝): Ming-sheng
Myōshōgonnō (妙荘厳王): Wonderful Adornment
Myōshōgonnō-hon (妙荘厳王品): "King Wonderful Adornment" chapter
Myōshōgonnō-honji-hon (妙荘厳王本事品): "Former Affairs of King Wonderful Adornment" chapter
myōshū (明宗): "Elucidation of Quality" section (*See* five major principles)
Myōsō-nyorai (名相如来): Rare Form
myō-tai-shū-yū-kyō (名体宗用教): name, essence, quality, function, and teaching (*See* five major principles)
Myōun (明雲)
myōyaku (冥益): inconspicuous benefit

Nadai-kashō (那提迦葉): Nadī Kāshyapa
Nagoe-no-ama (名越の尼): Nagoe, the lay nun of
naibon (内凡): inner rank of ordinary people; the higher rank of ordinary practitioners (*See* four good roots)
naie (内衣): inner robe (*See* three robes)
naige-funi-mon (内外不二門): oneness of the internal and the external (*See* ten onenesses)
naishō (内証): inner enlightenment (*See* Superior Practices)
Naiten-roku (内典録): *Catalog of Buddhist Scriptures, The*
Nakaoki-nyūdō (中興入道): Nakaoki, the lay priest of
Nambu Rokurō Sanenaga (南部六郎実長)
Nam-myoho-renge-kyo (南無妙法蓮華経)
nampō (煖法): heat stage
Nampō-bukkyō (南方仏教): Southern Buddhism
namu (南無)
Namu Amida Butsu (南無阿弥陀仏)
Nanda (難陀): Nanda
nandaimon (南大門): great south gate
Nanda-ryūō (難陀竜王): Nanda (*See* eight great dragon kings)
Nanden-bukkyō (南伝仏教): Southern Buddhism
Nandō-ha (南道派): Southern Way school (*See* Treatise on the Ten Stages school)
Nan-embudai (南閻浮提): southern continent (*See* Jambudvīpa)
Nangaku (南岳): Nan-yüeh
nangyō-dō (難行道): difficult-to-practice way
nan-i (煖位): heat stage
nanji-den (南寺伝): transmission of the Southern Temple (*See* Dharma Characteristics school)
Nanjō Hyōe Shichirō (南条兵衛七郎)
Nanjō Shichirō Gorō (南条七郎五郎)
Nanjō Tokimitsu (南条時光)
Nankai-kiki-naihō-den (南海寄帰内法伝): *Record of Southern Countries, The*
Nankyō-ritsu (南京律): Precepts school of the Southern Capital (*See* Precepts school)
nansan-hokushichi (南三北七): three schools of the south and seven schools of the north

Nanshū Zen (南宗禅): Southern school of Zen
nanto-rokushū (南都六宗): six schools of Nara
nanto-shichidaiji (南都七大寺): seven major temples of Nara
Nanzan Risshū (南山律宗): Nan-shan branch of the Precepts school (*See* Tao-hsüan)
Nanzen-ji (南禅寺): *See* Five Temples
Naraen (那羅延): Nārāyana
naraku (奈落): *naraka*
Naranda-ji (那爛陀寺): Nālandā Monastery
Narendaiyasha (那連提耶舎): Narendrayashas
Nasen-biku (那先比丘): Nāgasena
nayuta (那由多): *nayuta*
nehan (涅槃): nirvana
Nehan-gyō (涅槃経): Nirvana Sutra
nehan-jakujō (涅槃寂静): Nirvana is tranquil and quiet. (*See* Dharma seal)
Nehan-shū (涅槃宗): Nirvana school
Nembutsu (念仏)
Nembutsu-shū (念仏宗): Nembutsu school
Nen'a (然阿)
nen-futai (念不退): non-regression from thought (*See* three kinds of non-regression)
Nentō-butsu (燃燈仏): Burning Torch
Nichiben (日弁)
Nichidai (日代)
nichigatsu-hakushoku-nan (日月薄蝕難): calamity of solar and lunar eclipses (*See* seven disasters)
Nichigatsu-jōmyōtoku-butsu (日月浄明徳仏): Sun Moon Pure Bright Virtue
Nichigatsu-tōmyō-butsu (日月燈明仏): Sun Moon Bright
Nichigen-nyo (日眼女)
Nichigō (日郷)
Nichiji (日持)
Nichijū (日什)
Nichijun (日順)
Nichikan (日寛)
Nichikō (日講)
Nichimoku (日目)
Nichimyō (日妙)
Nichinyo (日女)
Nichiō (日奥)
Nichiren (日蓮)
Nichiren-ichigo-guhō-fuzoku-sho (日蓮一期弘法付嘱書): *Document for Entrusting the Law that Nichiren Propagated throughout His Life, The*
Nichiren Shōshū (日蓮正宗)
Nichiren-shū (日蓮宗): Nichiren school
Nichirō (日朗)
Nichiu (日有)
Nichizen (日禅)
Nichizō (日像): *See* Nichiren school
Nichizō-biku (日蔵比丘): Sun Repository (*See* Medicine King)
Nichizon (日尊)
Nihon Daruma-shū (日本達磨宗): Japanese Bodhidharma school (*See* Nōnin)
nihyaku-gojikkai (二百五十戒): two hundred and fifty precepts
Niiama (新尼)
Niida Shirō Nobutsuna (新田四郎信綱)
Niike Saemon-no-jō (新池左衛門尉)
nijō (二乗): two vehicles
nijō-sabutsu (二乗作仏): attainment of Buddhahood by persons of the two vehicles
nijū-bu (二十部): twenty Hinayana schools
nijūgo-hōben (二十五方便): twenty-five preparatory exercises
nijūgo-u (二十五有): twenty-five realms of existence
nijūgyō-no-ge (二十行の偈): twenty-line verse

nijūhasso (二十八祖): twenty-eight Indian patriarchs
nijūhatten (二十八天): twenty-eight heavens
nijūsan-so (二十三祖): twenty-three successors
nijūyo-moji-no-hokekyō (二十四文字の法華経): twenty-four-character Lotus Sutra
nikai-hachiban (二界八番): beings of the two worlds and the eight groups
nika-no-kangyō (二箇の諫暁): two admonitions
nika-sōjō-sho (二箇相承書): two transfer documents
nikāya (ニカーヤ): *nikāya* (*See* Āgama sutras)
Nikenda-nyakudaishi (尼乾陀若提子): Nigantha Nātaputta
Nikke (日華)
nikkei-sō (肉髻相): knot of flesh on the head
Nikkō (日興)
Nikkō-ato-jōjō-no-koto (日興跡条条の事): *Matters to Be Observed after Nikkō's Death* (*See* Nikkō)
Nikkō-bosatsu (日光菩薩): Sunlight
Nikkō-butsu (日光仏): Sunlight (*See* Constellation Kalpa)
nikkō-yu (日光喩): simile of the sun (*See* ten similes)
Nikkō-yuikai-okibumi (日興遺誡置文): *Twenty-six Admonitions of Nikkō, The*
Nikō (日向)
Nikō-ki (日向記): *Nikō's Records*
niku-gen (肉眼): eye of ordinary people (*See* five types of vision)
Nikurida (尼倶律陀): Nyagrodha
nikurui-ju (尼倶類樹): *nyagrodha* tree
Nikyō-ron (二教論): *Comparison of Exoteric and Esoteric Buddhism, A*
Nikyō-ron (二教論): *Treatise on the Two Teachings, The* (*See* Tao-an [2])
Nimindara-sen (尼民達羅山): Nimimdhara (*See* four seas)
Nimma-ha (ニンマ派): Nyingma school (*See* Tibetan Buddhism)
nimpō-ikka (人法一箇): oneness of the Person and the Law
nin (忍): forbearance
nindo (忍土): world of endurance
Ningai (仁海): *See* Shōbō
nin-honzon (人本尊): object of devotion in terms of the Person (*See* Gohonzon)
nin-i (忍位): perception stage
nini-funi (而二不二): two but not two (*See* oneness of body and mind)
nin-jō (人乗): vehicle of ordinary people (*See* five vehicles)
nin-kai (忍界): world of endurance
nin-kai (人界): world of human beings
Ninki-hon (人記品): "Prophecies" chapter
ninniku (忍辱): forbearance
ninniku-haramitsu (忍辱波羅蜜): *pāramitā* of forbearance (*See* six *pāramitās*)
ninniku-no-koromo (忍辱の衣): robe of forbearance
ninniku-no-yoroi (忍辱の鎧): armor of perseverance
Ninniku-sennin (忍辱仙人): Forbearance
Ninnō-kyō (仁王経): Benevolent Kings Sutra
nin-pō (忍法): perception stage
Ninshō (忍性)
ninshū-shitsueki-nan (人衆疾疫難): calamity of pestilence (*See* seven disasters)
Nirabuda-jigoku (尼剌部陀地獄): Nirarbuda hell (*See* eight cold hells)

Nirenzen-ga（尼連禅河）: Nairanjanā River
Nishi Hongan-ji（西本願寺）: *See* Hongan-ji
Nishiyama-nyūdō（西山入道）: Nishiyama, the lay priest of
nisho-san'e（二処三会）: two places and three assemblies
nishu-kuyō（二種供養）: two kinds of offerings (*See* offering)
nisoku-son（二足尊）: most honored of two-legged beings
Nissen（日仙）
Nisshō（日昭）
Nisshō（日照）: Jih-chao
Nisshū（日秀）
Nitchō（日頂）
Nitchō（日澄）
Nitten（日天）: sun, god of the
Nittō-guhō-junrei-kōki（入唐求法巡礼行記）: *Record of a Pilgrimage to China in Search of the Law, The*
nizen-kyō（爾前教）: pre-Lotus Sutra teachings
nizen-no-en（爾前の円）: perfect teaching expounded in the pre-Lotus Sutra teachings (*See* perfect teaching)
nizō（二蔵）: two storehouses
nōe（納衣）: clothes of patched rags
nōnin（能忍）: One Who Can Endure
Nōnin（能忍）
Nōse-taishi（能施太子）: Earnest Donor
nōtsū-hōben（能通方便）: expedient means that can lead one in (*See* three expedient means)
Nyohō（如宝）
Nyoi（如意）: Manoratha
nyoi-hōju（如意宝珠）: wish-granting jewel
Nyojaku Nichiman（如寂日満）: *See* Abutsu-bō
nyonin-jōbutsu（女人成仏）: attainment of Buddhahood by women
nyorai（如来）: Thus Come One
Nyorai-jinriki-hon（如来神力品）: "Supernatural Powers of the Thus Come One" chapter
Nyorai-juryō-hon（如来寿量品）: "Life Span of the Thus Come One" chapter
nyorai-no-ji（如来の事）: Thus Come One's work (*See* envoy of the Thus Come One)
nyorai-no-koromo（如来の衣）: Thus Come One's robe (*See* robe, seat, and room)
nyorai-no-shitsu（如来の室）: Thus Come One's room (*See* robe, seat, and room)
nyorai-no-tsukai（如来の使）: envoy of the Thus Come One
nyorai-no-za（如来の座）: Thus Come One's seat (*See* robe, seat, and room)
nyorai-zen（如来禅）: Thus Come One Zen
nyorai-zō（如来蔵）: matrix of the Thus Come One
Nyoraizō-kyō（如来蔵経）: Matrix of the Thus Come One Sutra
nyōyaku-ujō-kai（饒益有情戒）: precept for benefiting sentient beings
nyoze-gamon（如是我聞）: "This is what I heard"
nyūdō（入道）: lay priest
nyūwa-ninniku-no-koromo（柔和忍辱の衣）: robe of gentleness and patience (*See* robe of forbearance)

Ōama（大尼）
oashisu-toshi-kokka（オアシス都市国家）: oasis city-states (*See* Silk Road)
Ōbaku-shū（黄檗宗）: Ōbaku school
odori-nembutsu（踊念仏）: dancing Nembutsu (*See* Ippen)
Ō Fu（王浮）: Wang Fu (*See* Sutra on the Conversion of Barbarians by Lao Tzu)

Ōga-koku (鴦伽国): Anga
ōgu (応供): Worthy of Offerings
Ōhara-mondō (大原問答): Ōhara Discourse
ōjin (応身): manifested body
ōjin-butsu (応身仏): Buddha of the manifested body
Ōjō-raisan (往生礼讃): *Praising Rebirth in the Pure Land*
Ōjō-raisan-ge (往生礼讃偈): *Verses Praising Rebirth in the Pure Land, The*
Ōjō-ron (往生論): *Treatise on Rebirth in the Pure Land, The*
Ōjōron-chū (往生論註): *Commentary on "The Treatise on Rebirth in the Pure Land," The*
Ōjō-yōshū (往生要集): *Essentials of Rebirth in the Pure Land, The*
Okō-kikigaki (御講聞書): *Recorded Lectures, The*
Ōkutsumara (央掘摩羅): Angulimāla
Omosu-dansho (重須談所): Omosu Seminary
on (唵): *om*
Ongi-kuden (御義口伝): *Record of the Orally Transmitted Teachings, The*
Ōnichi-nyo (王日女)
onjiki-se (飲食施): offerings of food and drink (*See* three kinds of offerings)
Onjō-ji (園城寺)
Onkō-bu (飲光部): Kāshyapīya school
on-ma (陰魔): devil of the five components; hindrance of the five components (*See* four devils; three obstacles and four devils)
Ono-ryū (小野流): Ono branch (*See* Shōbō)
onrin (園林): *vana*
onzōe-ku (怨憎会苦): suffering of having to meet with those whom one hates (*See* eight sufferings)
Oryō (烏竜): Wu-lung
Ōryū-ha (黄竜派): Huang-lung school (*See* Zen school)
Ōsha-jō (王舎城): Rājagriha
Ōta Jōmyō (大田乗明)
Oto-gozen (乙御前): Oto
Ōwa-no-shūron (応和の宗論): Ōwa Debate

Padomasambaba (パドマサンババ): Padmasambhava (*See* Tibetan Buddhism)
Pakupa (パクパ): Phagpa (*See* Tibetan Buddhism)

Ragora (羅睺羅): Rāhula; Rāhulabhadra
Ragorabaddara (羅睺羅跋陀羅): Rāhulabhadra
Raidenku-bosatsu (雷電吼菩薩): Thunderbolt Roar (*See* five mighty bodhisattvas)
Raikōmyō (雷光明): Lightning Glow (*See* Medicine King)
Raitawara (頼吒和羅): *Rāshtrapāla* (*See* Ashvaghosha)
Raiyu (頼瑜)
Rakuhenge-ten (楽変化天): Heaven of Enjoying the Conjured
Rakuson (楽僔): Le-tsun (*See* Mo-kao Caves)
Rambini (藍毘尼): Lumbinī
Rambini-en (藍毘尼園): Lumbinī Gardens (*See* Lumbinī)
Rankei Dōryū (蘭渓道隆)
ran-shō (卵生): birth from eggs (*See* four forms of birth)
rasetsu (羅刹): *rākshasa*
rasetsu-nyo (羅刹女): *rākshasī*
Reiyū (霊祐): Ling-yu (*See* Zen school)
Reiyūkai (霊友会)
Renchō (蓮長): *See* Nichiren
renge (蓮華)
Rengeshiki-bikuni (蓮華色比丘尼): Utpalavarnā

Rengezō-sekai（蓮華蔵世界）: Lotus Treasury World
retsu-ōjin（劣応身）: inferior manifested body
Ribata（離婆多）: Revata
Rida（利吒）
ridō-jishō（理同事勝）: equal in principle but superior in practice
ri-himitsu（理秘密）: esoteric teachings in theory
riki-haramitsu（力波羅蜜）: *pāramitā* of power (*See* ten *pāramitās*)
rimbō（輪宝）: *chakra*
rin（林）: *vana*
Rinda-ō（輪陀王）: Rinda
rin'en-gusoku（輪円具足）: perfectly endowed (*See* mandala)
rinne（輪廻）: *samsāra*
rinne-shōji（輪廻生死）: repeated cycle of birth and death (See *samsāra*)
rinnō-yu（輪王喩）: simile of a wheel-turning king (*See* ten similes)
rin-ō（輪王）: wheel-turning king
ri-no-ichinen-sanzen（理の一念三千）: theoretical three thousand realms in a single moment of life (*See* three thousand realms in a single moment of life)
Rinzai Gigen（臨済義玄）: Lin-chi I-hsüan (*See* Zen school)
Rinzai-shū（臨済宗）: Lin-chi school; Rinzai school
Risha（離車）: Licchavi
ri-shō（理証）: theoretical proof (*See* three proofs)
Rishu-kyō（理趣経）: Principle of Wisdom Sutra
ri-soku（理即）: stage of being a Buddha in theory
risshi（律師）: discipline master
Risshō-ankoku-ron（立正安国論）: *On Establishing the Correct Teaching for the Peace of the Land*
Risshō Kōseikai（立正佼成会）
Risshū（律宗）: Precepts school
rita（利他）: benefiting others (*See* benefiting oneself and benefiting others)
rita-gyō（利他行）: altruistic practice (*See* Mahayana Buddhism)
ritsu（律）: *vinaya*
ro（漏）: outflows
Rōben（良弁）
rōi-byōshi-no-tatoe（良医病子の譬）: parable of the skilled physician and his sick children
rojin-tsū（漏尽通）: power to eradicate illusions and earthly desires (*See* six transcendental powers)
Rokkan-naion-kyō（六巻泥洹経）: six-volume Nirvana Sutra (*See* Mahāparinirvāna Sutra [2])
Rokkan-shō（六巻抄）: *Six-Volume Writings, The*
rokkon（六根）: six sense organs
rokkon-shōjō（六根清浄）: purification of the six sense organs
rokkyō（六境）: six objects
roku-dai（六大）: six elements
rokudai-hihō（六大秘法）: Six Great Secret Laws (*See* Three Great Secret Laws)
roku-daijin（六大臣）: six ministers
roku-dō（六道）: six paths
rokudō-rinne（六道輪廻）: transmigration in the six paths
rokudō-shishō（六道四生）: six paths and the four forms of birth (*See* four forms of birth)
rokugun-biku（六群比丘）: six monks, group of
roku-haramitsu（六波羅蜜）: six *pāramitās*
Rokuharamitsu-kyō（六波羅蜜経）: Six Pāramitās Sutra
roku-jinzū（六神通）: six transcendental powers
rokuji-raisan（六時礼讃）: reciting verses of praise six times a day (See *Praising Rebirth in the Pure Land*)
rokujū-kai（六重戒）: six precepts (2)

roku-jūzai (六重罪): six major offenses
rokuman-gōgasha (六万恒河沙): sands of sixty thousand Ganges Rivers (*See* "Emerging from the Earth" chapter)
Rokunamadai (勒那摩提): Ratnamati
rokunan-kui (六難九易): six difficult and nine easy acts
roku-nen (六念): six kinds of contemplation
Rokuon-ji (鹿苑時): Deer Park period
roku-rōsō (六老僧): six senior priests
roku-sainichi (六斎日): six days of purification
rokushi-gedō (六師外道): six non-Buddhist teachers
roku-shiki (六識): six consciousnesses
roku-shin (六臣): six ministers
roku-sō (六相): six forms
Rokuso-dan-kyō (六祖壇経): *Platform Sutra of the Sixth Patriarch, The*
roku-soku (六即): six stages of practice
Rokusoku-ō (鹿足王): Deer Feet
roku-tsū (六通): six transcendental powers
roku-wakyō (六和敬): six types of harmony and reverence
Rokuya-on (鹿野苑): Deer Park
roku-yoku (六欲): six desires
rokuyoku-ten (六欲天): six heavens of the world of desire
roku-zui (六瑞): six auspicious happenings
rongi-daiichi (論議第一): foremost in debate (*See* Kātyāyana)
ron'yū (論用): "Discussion of Function" section (*See* five major principles)
ropparamitsu (六波羅蜜): six *pāramitās*
Ropparamitsu-kyō (六波羅蜜経): Six Pāramitās Sutra
roppō-kai (六法戒): six precepts (1)
Ropunōru (ロプ・ノール): Lop Nor (*See* Lou-lan)
Rōran (楼蘭): Lou-lan
Rōshi-keko-kyō (老子化胡経): Sutra on the Conversion of Barbarians by Lao Tzu
Ro-zan (廬山): Mount Lu (*See* Hui-yüan)
Rurikōshō-nyorai (瑠璃光照如来): Lapis Lazuli Brightness (*See* Medicine King)
Rusui (流水): Water Carrier
ruten-mon (流転門): way of transmigration (*See* twelve-linked chain of causation)
rutsū-bun (流通分): transmission section
ryakkaisan-ken'ichi (略開三顕一): concise replacement of the three vehicles with the one vehicle
ryakkō-shugyō (歴劫修行): countless *kalpas* of practice
ryakuge-gonshu (略解言趣): to generally understand the import of the words of the Lotus Sutra (*See* four stages of faith)
ryaku-kaigon-kennon (略開近顕遠): opening the near and revealing the distant in concise form (*See* opening the near and revealing the distant)
Ryōchū (良忠)
Ryōga-kyō (楞伽経): Lankāvatāra Sutra
Ryōgen (良源)
Ryōhi (良賁): Liang-pi
Ryōjo (良諝): Liang-hsü
Ryōju-sen (霊鷲山): Eagle Peak
Ryōkai (良价): Liang-chieh (*See* Zen school)
Ryōkan (良観)
Ryokō (呂光): Lü Kuang (*See* Kumārajīva)

Ryō-kōsō-den (梁高僧伝): *Liang Dynasty Biographies of Eminent Priests, The*
Ryōnin (良忍)
Ryō-no-sandai-hosshi (梁の三大法師): three great Dharma teachers of the Liang dynasty (*See* Fa-yün)
ryōsoku-son (両足尊): most honored of two-legged beings
Ryōzen-e (霊山会): assembly on Eagle Peak (*See* two places and three assemblies)
Ryōzen-jōdo (霊山浄土): pure land of Eagle Peak (*See* Eagle Peak)
Ryūchi (竜智): Nāgabodhi
ryūgū (竜宮): dragon palace (*See* Sāgara)
ryūjin (竜神): dragon deity
Ryūju (竜樹): Nāgārjuna
Ryūju-bosatsu-den (竜樹菩薩伝): *The Biography of Bodhisattva Nāgārjuna* (*See* Nāgārjuna)
Ryūkan (隆寛)
Ryūmon-sekkutsu (竜門石窟): Lung-men caves
ryūnyo (竜女): dragon king's daughter
ryūō (竜王): dragon kings
Ryūōku-bosatsu (竜王吼菩薩): Dragon King's Roar (*See* five mighty bodhisattvas)
Ryūsen-ji (滝泉寺)
Ryūshin (隆真)
Ryūzō-bō (竜象房)

Sado-bō (佐渡房)
Sado-ruzai (佐渡流罪): Sado Exile
Saichō (最澄)
Saidai-ji (西大寺)
Sai-goke-shū (西牛貨洲): Apara-godānīya
Saihō-jōdo (西方浄土): Western Pure Land
saihō-jūman-okudo (西方十万億土): a hundred thousand million Buddha lands to the west (*See* Western Pure Land)
Saiiki-ki (西域記): *Record of the Western Regions, The*
Saiin (蔡愔): Ts'ai Yin
Sai-jarin (摧邪輪): *Refutation of Erroneous Doctrines, A*
Saimyō-ji (西明寺): Hsi-ming-ssu
Saimyō-ji (最明寺)
Saimyō-ji-nyūdō (最明寺入道): lay priest of Saimyō-ji (*See* Saimyō-ji)
Sairen-bō (最蓮房)
Saishō'ō-kyō (最勝王経): Sovereign Kings Sutra
Saiten-nijūhasso (西天二十八祖): twenty-eight Indian patriarchs
Sajiki-nyōbō (桟敷女房): Sajiki, the lady of
Sakya-ha (サキャ派): Sakya school (*See* Tibetan Buddhism)
sambō (三宝): three treasures
samböin (三法印): three Dharma seals
Sambu-issō-no-hōnan (三武一宗の法難): four imperial persecutions of Buddhism in China
sambunka-kyō (三分科経): three divisions of a sutra
sammai (三昧): *samādhi*
sammaya-gyō (三昧耶形): *samaya*
Sammi-bō (三位房)
Sammon-ha (山門派): Mountain school (1)
sammui (三無為): three categories of the unconditioned (*See* unconditioned, the)
sammyō-gōron (三妙合論): integration of the three mystic principles
sammyō-rokutsū (三明六通): three insights and six transcendental powers
sampen-doden (三変土田): three-time purification of the lands
Samuiē-ji (サムイェー寺): Samye monastery (*See* Tibetan Buddhism)
san-akudō (三悪道): three evil paths

san-akushu（三悪趣）: three evil paths
san-byōdō（三平等）: three equalities
san-chi（三智）: three kinds of wisdom
sandai-hihō（三大秘法）: Three Great Secret Laws
san-dō（三道）: three paths (1)
san-dō（三道）: three ways
san-doku（三毒）: three poisons
sando-no-kōmyō（三度の高名）: three-time gaining of distinction
san-futai（三不退）: three kinds of non-regression
san-fuzengon（三不善根）: three bad roots (*See* good roots)
san-gai（三界）: threefold world
Sangai-ha（山外派）: Outside-the-Mountain school
Sangai-kyō（三階教）: Three Stages school
Sangai-zenji（三階禅師）: San-chieh, the Meditation Master
san-gaku（三学）: three types of learning
sangaku-shinkō（山岳信仰）: mountain worship (*See* Shugendō school)
sange（懺悔）: repentance
san-gedatsu-mon（三解脱門）: three meditations for emancipation
Sange-gakushō-shiki（山家学生式）: *Regulations for Students of the Mountain School, The*
Sange-ha（山家派）: Mountain school (2)
san-gen（三賢）: three stages of worthiness
sangi-hyakudai-kō（三祇百大劫）: three *asamkhya kalpas* and a hundred major *kalpas*
san-gō（三業）: three categories of action
sangō-funi-mon（三業不二門）: oneness of thought, word, and deed (*See* ten onenesses)
Sangoku-buppō-dentsū-engi（三国仏法伝通縁起）: *A History of the Transmission and Propagation of Buddhism in Three Countries* (*See* Gyōnen)
sangoku-shishi（三国四師）: four teachers of the three countries
san-gyakuzai（三逆罪）: three cardinal sins
san-hōben（三方便）: three expedient means
sanhō-myō（三法妙）: mystic principle of three elements (*See* ten mystic principles)
san'in-busshō（三因仏性）: three inherent potentials of the Buddha nature
Sanjaya-birateishi（刪闍耶毘羅胝子）: Sanjaya Belatthiputta
san-ji（三時）: three periods (1)
sanji-kyō（三時教）: three periods, teachings of the
san-jin（三身）: three bodies
san-jin（三心）: three kinds of mind
sanjin-soku-isshin（三身即一身）: All three bodies are found within a single Buddha. (*See* three bodies)
sanjō（三乗）: three vehicles
san-jō（三定）: three types of meditation
sanjō-hō（三乗法）: three vehicle teachings
san-jōryo（三静慮）: three types of meditation
sanjū（三従）: three obediences (*See* five obstacles)
sanjū-hiden（三重秘伝）: threefold secret teaching
Sanjū-hiden-shō（三重秘伝抄）: "The Threefold Secret Teaching" (See *Six-Volume Writings, The*)
sanju-jō-kai（三聚浄戒）: three comprehensive precepts
sanjūni-sō（三十二相）: thirty-two features
sanjūni-sō-hachijisshugō（三十二相八

十種好): thirty-two features and eighty characteristics
sanjūsan-shin (三十三身): thirty-three forms
sanjūsan-ten (三十三天): Heaven of the Thirty-three Gods
sanjūsan-ten (三十三天): thirty-three gods
sanjūshichi-dōhon (三十七道品): thirty-seven aids to the way
sanjūshi-shin (三十四身): thirty-four forms
san-kaidan (三戒壇): three ordination platforms
sankai-shishō (三誡四請): three exhortations and four entreaties
sanka-no-chokusen (三箇の勅宣): three pronouncements
sanka-no-hōshō (三箇の鳳詔): three pronouncements
san-kashō (三迦葉): three Kāshyapa brothers
san-ki (三帰): threefold refuge
san-ki (三軌): three rules of preaching
san-kie (三帰依): threefold refuge
sanki-gokai (三帰五戒): threefold refuge and observance of the five precepts
Sānkiya-gakuha (サーンキヤ学派): Sāmkhya school (*See* Kapila)
san-kō (三劫): three *kalpas*
sanko-sho (三鈷杵): three-pronged diamond-pounder
sankō-tenshi (三光天子): three heavenly sons of light
san-ku (三苦): three sufferings
san-mitsu (三密): three mysteries
san-myō (三明): three insights
san-myō (三妙): three mystic principles
sanne (三衣): three robes
Sannei (賛寧): Tsan-ning (See *Sung Dynasty Biographies of Eminent Priests, The*)
sanne-ippatsu (三衣一鉢): three robes and one begging bowl
san-nenjū (三念住): three kinds of tranquillity
Sannō (山王): Mountain King
san-rin (三輪): three circles
Sanron-gengi (三論玄義): *Profound Meaning of the Three Treatises, The*
Sanron-shū (三論宗): Three Treatises school
sanrui-no-gōteki (三類の強敵): three powerful enemies
sanrui-no-tekijin (三類の敵人): three types of enemies
san-sai (三災): three calamities
sansai-shichinan (三災七難): three calamities and seven disasters
san-se (三施): three kinds of offerings
san-seken (三世間): three realms of existence
san-sen (三仙): three ascetics
san-setsu (三説): three categories of preaching
sansha-kataku-no-tatoe (三車火宅の譬): parable of the three carts and the burning house
sanshi-shichishō (三師七証): three leaders and seven witnesses
san-shō (三証): three proofs
san-shō (三性): three types of character
sanshō-shima (三障四魔): three obstacles and four devils
sanshu-no-kyōsō (三種の教相): three standards of comparison
sanshū-no-seppō (三周の説法): three cycles of preaching
sanshū-no-shōmon (三周の声聞): three groups of voice-hearers
sansō-nimoku-no-tatoe (三草二木の譬): parable of the three kinds of medicinal herbs and two kinds of trees
san-tai (三諦): three truths
san-tembōrin (三転法輪): thrice

turned wheel of the Law
San-tendai-godaisan-ki（参天台五台山記）: *The Record of the Pilgrimage to Mount T'ien-t'ai and Mount Wu-t'ai* (*See* Jōjin)
san-tōji（三等至）: three types of meditation
san-toku（三徳）: three virtues
san-waku（三惑）: three categories of illusion
san-yaku（三益）: three benefits
san-yu（山喩）: simile of mountains (*See* ten similes)
san-ze（三世）: three existences
sanze-jippō-no-shobutsu（三世十方の諸仏）: Buddhas of the ten directions and three existences (*See* ten directions)
sanzen-daisen-sekai（三千大千世界）: major world system
san-zendō（三善道）: three good paths
san-zengon（三善根）: three good roots (*See* good root)
sanzen-igi（三千威儀）: three thousand rules of conduct
sanzen-jintengō（三千塵点劫）: major world system dust particle *kalpas*
san-zenkon（三善根）: three good roots (*See* good root)
sanze-no-shobutsu（三世の諸仏）: Buddhas of the three existences (*See* three existences)
san-zō（三蔵）: three divisions of the canon
san-zō（三蔵）: Tripitaka master
san-zu（三途）: three paths (2)
sanzu-no-kawa（三途の河）: river of three crossings
sarai-niko（作礼而去）: "bowed in obeisance and departed"
Sasshō（薩生）
satori（悟）: enlightenment
satta（薩埵）: *sattva*
Satta-ōji（薩埵王子）: Mahāsattva
Saundara-nanda（サウンダラ・ナンダ）: *Saundarananda* (*See* Ashvaghosha)
Sawata（薩和多）: *See* Universal Practice
sazen-sago（佐前佐後）: before and after Sado
sedaiippō（世第一法）: foremost worldly stage
Seichō-ji（清澄寺）
seigan（誓願）: vow
seigan-anrakugyō（誓願安楽行）: peaceful practice of vows (*See* four peaceful practices)
Seiryō-ji（清凉寺）
Seiryū-ji（青竜寺）: Ch'ing-lung-ssu
Seishi-bosatsu（勢至菩薩）: Great Power
seishuku-henge-nan（星宿変怪難）: calamity of extraordinary changes in the heavens (*See* seven disasters)
Seishukukō-chōja（星宿光長者）: Constellation Light (*See* Medicine King)
Seitasan-bu（制多山部）: Chaityavādin school (*See* eighteen Hinayana schools)
Seizanjū-bu（西山住部）: Aparashaila school (*See* eighteen Hinayana schools)
Sejizaiō-butsu（世自在王仏）: World Freedom King
sekenge（世間解）: Understanding the World (*See* ten honorable titles)
seken-shitsudan（世間悉檀）: to teach Buddhism in secular terms (*See* four ways of preaching)
Sembu-shū（贍部洲）: Jambudvīpa
Sembutsu-dō（千仏洞）: Cave of the Thousand Buddhas
Sempa（瞻波）: Champā
sempuku-ju（瞻蔔樹）: *champaka* tree
sempukurin-sō（千輻輪相）: thousand-spoked wheel
semui-sha（施無畏者）: Bestower of Fearlessness

Senchaku-shū（選択集）: *Nembutsu Chosen above All, The*
sendai-haramitsu（羼提波羅蜜）: *pāramitā* of forbearance (*See* six *pāramitās*)
sendan（栴檀）: sandalwood tree
sendan-no-ukigi（栴檀の浮木）: floating sandalwood log (*See* one-eyed turtle)
sendara（旃陀羅）: *chandāla*
Sengaie-jizaitsūō-nyorai（山海慧自在通王如来）: Mountain Sea Wisdom Unrestricted Power King
Senji-shō（撰時抄）: *Selection of the Time, The*
senjō-funimon（染浄不二門）: oneness of the impure and the pure (*See* ten onenesses)
Senju-kannon（千手観音）: Thousand-armed Perceiver of the World's Sounds
senju-nembutsu（専修念仏）: exclusive practice of the Nembutsu
Senkan（千観）
Sennichi-ama（千日尼）: Sennichi, the lay nun
Sennin-dasho（仙人堕処）: Rishipatana; Sage Ascetics-Gathering
Sennyū-ji（泉涌寺）: *See* Shunjō
Sensha-nyo（旃遮女）: Chinchā
senshō-zōjōman（僭聖増上慢）: arrogance and presumption of those who pretend to be sages (*See* three powerful enemies)
Sen'yo-kokuō（仙予国王）: Sen'yo
seō（世雄）: world hero
seppō-daiichi（説法第一）: foremost in preaching the Law (*See* Pūrna)
seppō-hon（説法品）: stage of expounding the Lotus Sutra to others (*See* five stages of practice)
Seppō-hon（説法品）: "Preaching the Law" chapter (*See* Immeasurable Meanings Sutra)
seppō-myō（説法妙）: mystic principle of preaching (*See* ten mystic principles)
Seshin（世親）: Vasubandhu
seson（世尊）: *bhagavat;* World-Honored One
Sessen（雪山）: Snow Mountains
Sessen-bu（雪山部）: Haimavata school (*See* Theravāda school)
Sessen-dōji（雪山童子）: Snow Mountains, the boy
Sessenge-ō（雪山下王）: Himatala
setsudo（刹土）: *kshetra*
Setsu-issaiu-bu（説一切有部）: Sarvāstivāda school
Setsuke-bu（説仮部）: Prajnāptivādin school (*See* eighteen Hinayana schools)
setsuna（刹那）: *kshana* (See *ichinen*)
Setsushusse-bu（説出世部）: Lokottarabvāda school (*See* eighteen Hinayana schools)
setsuteiri（刹帝利）: Kshatriya
setsu-zoku（殺賊）: destroyer of bandits (*See* arhat)
Seu（世友）: Vasumitra
sha（捨）: impartiality; *upekshā* (*See* four infinite virtues)
shaba-sekai（娑婆世界）: *sahā* world
shaba-soku-jakkō（娑婆即寂光）: The sahā world is in itself the Land of Eternally Tranquil Light. (See *sahā* world)
Shae-jō（舎衛城）: Shrāvastī
shae-no-san'oku（舎衛の三億）: three hundred thousand families of Shrāvastī (*See* Shrāvastī)
Shagita（娑祇多）: Shāketa
sha-hei-kaku-hō（捨閉閣抛）: "discard, close, ignore, and abandon"
Shakamuni（釈迦牟尼）: Shakyamuni
Shakara-ryūō（沙竭羅竜王）: Sāgara
Shaka-zoku（釈迦族）: Shākya
shakke-no-bosatsu（迹化の菩薩）: bodhisattvas of the theoretical teaching
shaku（迹）: provisional identity; transient identity (*See* casting off

the transient and revealing the true)
shakubuku (折伏)
shakubutsu (迹仏): provisional Buddha
Shakudai-kan'in (釈提桓因): Shakra Devānām Indra
Shaku-jōdo-gungi-ron (釈浄土群疑論): *Treatise Resolving Numerous Doubts about the Pure Land Teachings, The*
Shaku-makaen-ron (釈摩訶衍論): *Commentary on the Mahayana Treatise, The*
shakumon (迹門): theoretical teaching
shakumon-no-jūmyō (迹門の十妙): ten mystic principles of the theoretical teaching (*See* ten mystic principles)
shakumon-no-sampi (迹門の三譬): three metaphors of the theoretical teaching
shakumyō (釈名): "Interpretation of the Name" section (*See* five major principles)
shakushi (折指): Broken Finger (*See* Ajātashatru)
Shakuson (釈尊): Shakyamuni
shami (沙弥): *shrāmanera*
shamini (沙弥尼): *shrāmanerī*
shamon (沙門): *shramana*
Shamon-fukyō-ōja-ron (沙門不敬王者論): *A Priest Does Not Bow before a King* (*See* Hui-yüan [1])
shana-gō (遮那業): Vairochana discipline (See *Regulations for Students of the Mountain School, The*)
Shanoku (車匿): Chandaka
Shāntarakushita (シャーンタラクシタ): Shāntarakshita (*See* Tibetan Buddhism)
shara-ju (沙羅樹): sal tree
Sharajuō-butsu (沙羅樹王仏): Sal Tree King (*See* Wonderful Adornment)
shara-no-shiken (沙羅の四見): four views of the sal grove
shara-rin (沙羅林): sal grove (*See* four views of the sal grove)
Sha-reiun (謝霊運): Hsieh Ling-yün (*See* Mahāparinirvāna Sutra)
Sharihotsu (舎利弗): Shāriputra
shi-agon-gyō (四阿含経): four Āgama sutras
shi-akudō (四悪道): four evil paths
shi-akushu (四悪趣): four evil paths
shi-anraku-gyō (四安楽行): four peaceful practices
Shi-anraku-gyō (四安楽行): *Four Peaceful Practices, The*
Shiba (シヴァ): Shiva (*See* Maheshvara)
Shiban (志磐): Chih-p'an (See *Record of the Lineage of the Buddha and the Patriarchs, The*)
Shiba Tatsuto (司馬達等)
Shibi-ō (尸毘王): Shibi
shi-bosatsu (四菩薩): four bodhisattvas
Shibun-ritsu (四分律): *Fourfold Rules of Discipline, The*
Shibun-ritsu-gyōji-shō (四分律行事鈔): *Essentials of "The Fourfold Rules of Discipline," The*
shichi-bodaibun (七菩提分): seven aids to enlightenment
shichidō-garan (七堂伽藍): seven-halled temple
shichi-fukujin (七福神): seven beneficent deities
shichi-gyaku (七逆): seven cardinal sins
shichi-hi (七譬): seven parables
shichi-hō (七宝): seven kinds of treasures (1)
shichi-hō (七宝): seven treasures
shichi-hōben (七方便): seven expedient means
shichihyaku-ketsujū (七百結集): Gathering of Seven Hundred Monks (*See* Buddhist Councils)

shichi-kakushi (七覚支): seven aids to enlightenment
shichi-ken (七賢): seven stages of worthiness; seven worthies
shichi-kijin (七鬼神): seven guardian spirits
shichi-man (七慢): seven types of arrogance
shichi-nan (七難): seven disasters
shichisho-hachie (七処八会): eight successive assemblies in seven different locations (*See* Dharma Wisdom)
shichi-shōzai (七聖財): seven kinds of treasures (2)
shichi-shu (七衆): seven kinds of believers
shichi-shū (七宗): seven schools
Shichiyō-kutsu (七葉窟): Cave of the Seven Leaves
shichi-zai (七財): seven kinds of treasures (2)
Shida-ga (私陀河): Shītā River (*See* four rivers)
shidagon (斯陀含): once-returner
shidagon-ka (斯陀含果): stage of the once-returner (*See* four stages of Hinayana enlightenment)
shi-dai (四大): four elements
shidai-deshi (四大弟子): four major disciples
shidai-ga (四大河): four great rivers
shidai-kai (四大海): four great seas
Shidai-koku (支提国): Chedi (*See* sixteen great states)
shidai-shōmon (四大声聞): four great voice-hearers
shidai-shū (四大洲): four great continents
shidai-tennō (四大天王): four great heavenly kings
Shidarin (尸陀林): Shītavana
Shiddatta (悉達多): Siddhārtha
shi-do (四土): four kinds of lands
shido-no-rokuzui (此土の六瑞): six auspicious happenings in this world (*See* six auspicious happenings)
shie (四依): four ranks of sages
shie (四依): four standards
Shien (思円)
shie-no-bosatsu (四依の菩薩): four ranks of bodhisattvas
shi-fujōjiki (四不浄食): four improper ways of livelihood
shi-ga (四河): four rivers
shigan (此岸): this shore (*See* other shore)
shigu-seigan (四弘誓願): four universal vows
shi-haraizai (四波羅夷罪): four *pārājika* offenses
shi-hōin (四法印): four Dharma seals
shi-i (四違): four dislikes (*See* eight winds)
shi-igi (四威儀): four activities of daily life
Shiiji Shirō (椎地四郎)
Shiin (志因): Chih-yin (*See* T'ien-t'ai school)
shi-jamyōjiki (四邪命食): four improper ways of livelihood
shiji-kuyō (四事供養): four kinds of offerings
shi-jinsoku (四神足): four steps to transcendental powers
Shijō Kingo (四条金吾)
shijō-shōkaku-no-hotoke (始成正覚の仏): the Buddha who attained enlightenment for the first time in his present lifetime (*See* attainment of Buddhahood in the remote past)
shijū (四重): four grave prohibitions
shijūhachi-gan (四十八願): forty-eight vows
shijūhachi-kyōkai (四十八軽戒): forty-eight minor precepts
shijūkin (四重禁): four grave prohibitions
Shijūku-in (四十九院)

shi-jun (四順): four favorites (*See* eight winds)
shijūnihon-no-mumyō (四十二品の無明): forty-two levels of ignorance
Shijūni-shō-kyō (四十二章経): Sutra of Forty-two Sections
shijū-no-kōhai (四重の興廃): fourfold rise and fall
shi-jūzai (四重罪): four major offenses
shi-ka (四果): four stages of Hinayana enlightenment
shika-byakushi-butsu-yu (四果辟支仏喩): simile of voice-hearers at the four stages of enlightenment and cause-awakened ones (*See* ten similes)
shi-kai (四海): four seas
shikaku (始覚): acquired enlightenment
shikan (止観): concentration and insight
Shikan-bugyōden-guketsu (止観輔行伝弘決): *Annotations on "Great Concentration and Insight," The*
shika-no-kakugen (四箇の格言): four dictums
shi-ke (四華): four kinds of flowers
Shiken (支謙): Chih-ch'ien
Shiki-butsu (尸棄仏): Shikhin (*See* seven Buddhas of the past)
shiki-ju-sō-gyō-shiki (色受想行識): form, perception, conception, volition, and consciousness (*See* five components)
shiki-kai (色界): world of form
Shikikukyō-ten (色究竟天): Akanishtha Heaven
Shikimuhen-jo (識無辺処): Realm of Boundless Consciousness
Shikimuhenjo-jō (識無辺処定): meditation on the Realm of Boundless Consciousness (*See* Realm of Boundless Consciousness)
Shikimuhenjo-ten (識無辺処天): Heaven of Boundless Consciousness
shikishamana (式叉摩那): *shikshamānā*
shikishin-funi (色心不二): oneness of body and mind
shi-kō (四劫): four *kalpas*
shi-ku (四苦): four sufferings
shiku-ge (四句偈): four-line verse
shi-kū-jō (四空定): four meditations on formlessness
shiku-no-yōbō (四句の要法): four-phrase essence of the Lotus Sutra
shi-kū-sho (四空処): four realms of the world of formlessness
Shikyō-gi (四教義): *Meaning of the Four Teachings, The*
shi-ma (死魔): devil of death; hindrance of death (*See* four devils; three obstacles and four devils)
shi-ma (四魔): four devils
shimatsu-hōrin (枝末法輪): branch teaching
shimatsu-kyō (枝末教): branch teaching
Shimei Chirei (四明知礼): Ssu-ming Chih-li (*See* Chih-li)
shimi (四味): first four flavors
shimi-sankyō (四味三教): four flavors and three teachings
shimmyō-se (身命施): offerings of one's life (*See* three kinds of offerings)
shimon-yūkan (四門遊観): four meetings
Shimoyama-goshōsoku (下山御消息): *Letter to Shimoyama*
shi-muge-ben (四無礙弁): four unlimited kinds of eloquence (*See* four unlimited kinds of knowledge)
shi-muge-chi (四無礙智): four unlimited kinds of knowledge
shi-mui (四無畏): four fearlessnesses
shi-muryōshin (四無量心): four infinite virtues

shi-mushiki-jō (四無色定): four meditations on formlessness
shi-mushiki-kai (四無色界): four realms of the world of formlessness
shi-mushoi (四無所畏): four fearlessnesses
shin (瞋): anger
shin (信): faith
shin-anraku-gyō (身安楽行): peaceful practice of the body (*See* four peaceful practices)
Shindai (真諦): Paramārtha
Shindo-ga (信度河): Sindhu River (*See* four rivers)
shi-nenjū (四念住): four meditations
Shinga (真雅)
shinge (信解): belief and understanding (*See* faith)
Shinge-hon (信解品): "Belief and Understanding" chapter
Shingi-ha (新義派・新義真言宗): New Doctrine school (*See* True Word school)
shingon (真言): mantra
Shingon Risshū (真言律宗): True Word Precepts school
Shingon-sambu-kyō (真言三部経): three True Word sutras
Shingon-shū (真言宗): True Word school
Shingyō (信行): Hsin-hsing
shin-gyō-gaku (信行学): faith, practice, and study
Shinjikan-gyō (心地観経): Contemplation on the Mind-Ground Sutra
Shinjō (審祥)
Shinkō-ō (秦広王): King Ch'in-kuang (*See* ten kings)
Shinkyō (真教): *See* Time school
shin-mitsu (身密): mystery of the body (*See* three mysteries)
shinni (瞋恚): anger
shin-no-daimoku (信の題目): daimoku of faith (*See* Three Great Secret Laws)
shinnyo (真如): *tathatā*
Shinran (親鸞)
shin-riki (信力): power of faith (*See* four powers [1]; five powers)
shin-roku (新六): six new disciples of Nikkō
Shinsen-en (神泉苑): Shinsen-en garden
shintai (真諦): supreme truth (*See* Establishment of Truth school)
shin'yaku (新訳): new translations
shi-nyoisoku (四如意足): four steps to transcendental powers
Shinzei (真済)
shi-on (四恩): four debts of gratitude
Shi'on (志遠): Chih-yüan
Shiō-ten (四王天): Heaven of the Four Heavenly Kings
shippō (七宝): seven kinds of treasures (1)
shippō (七宝): seven treasures
shira-haramitsu (尸羅波羅蜜): *pāramitā* of keeping the precepts (*See* six *pāramitās*)
Shiren (師錬)
shi-riki (四力): four powers
shi-rinnō (四輪王): four wheel-turning kings
shi-ron (四論): four treatises
Shiron-shū (四論宗): Four Treatises school
Shirukasen (支婁迦讖): Lokakshema
Shiruku-rōdo (シルクロード): Silk Road
shi-sei (四聖): four noble worlds
shi-shaku (四釈): four guidelines
Shishikaku (師子覚): Buddhasimha
shishi-ku (師子吼): lion's roar
Shishikyō-ō (師子頰王): Simhahanu
shi-shin (四身): four bodies (*See* Buddha of self-enjoyment)
shi-shin (四信): four objects of faith
shi-shin (四信): four stages of faith
shishin-gohon (四信五品): four

stages of faith and five stages of practice
Shishin-gohon-shō (四信五品抄): *On the Four Stages of Faith and the Five Stages of Practice*
Shishion-butsu (師子音仏): Lion Voice (*See* sixteen princes)
Shishionnō-butsu (師子音王仏): Lion Sound King
shishi-shinchū-no-mushi (師子身中の虫): worms within the lion's body
Shishisō-butsu (師子相仏): Lion Appearance (*See* sixteen princes)
shishi-sōjō (師資相承): transmission of the Law from teacher to disciple (*See* heritage of the Law)
Shishi-sonja (師子尊者): Āryasimha
shi-shitsudan (四悉檀): four ways of preaching
shishi-za (師子座): lion seat
shi-shō (四生): four forms of birth
shi-shō (四聖): four noble worlds
shi-shōbō (四摂法): four methods of winning people
shi-shōdan (四正断): four right efforts
shi-shōgon (四正勤): four right efforts
shi-shōtai (四聖諦): four noble truths
shi-shu (四衆): four kinds of believers
shi-shū (四洲): four continents
shishu-mandara (四種曼荼羅): four types of mandalas
shishu-sammai (四種三昧): four forms of meditation
shishu-shaku (四種釈): four guidelines
shisshō (湿生): birth from dampness (*See* four forms of birth)
shi-tai (四諦): four noble truths
Shitchigi (悉知義): Complete Understanding of Meanings (*See* six ministers)
shi-tendō (四顛倒): four inverted views
shi-tenge (四天下): four-continent world
shi-tennō (四天王): four heavenly kings
Shitennō-ji (四天王寺)
shi-toku (四徳): four virtues
Shittan (悉曇): Siddham (*See* Annen)
shi-waku (思惑): illusions of desire (*See* illusions of thought and desire)
Shiyaku-bonten (思益梵天): Brahmā Excellent Thought (*See* Questions of Brahmā Excellent Thought Sutra)
Shiyaku-bonten-shomon-gyō (思益梵天所問経): Questions of Brahmā Excellent Thought Sutra
Shiyaku-kyō (思益経): Brahmā Excellent Thought Sutra
shi-zengon (四善根): four good roots
shi-zenjō (四禅定): four stages of meditation
shizenten (四禅天): four meditation heavens
Shōan (章安): Chang-an
Shōben (清弁): Bhāvaviveka
shōbō (正法): Former Day of the Law
Shōbō (聖宝)
Shō-bō (少輔房)
Shōbō-genzō (正法眼蔵): *Treasury of Knowledge of the True Law, The*
Shōbōnenjo-kyō (正法念処経): Meditation on the Correct Teaching Sutra
Shōbon-hannya-kyō (小品般若経): Smaller Wisdom Sutra
Shō-bu (小部): *Khuddaka-nikāya*
shōbutsu-funi (生仏不二): oneness of living beings and Buddhas
Shōdaiba (聖提婆): Āryadeva
Shō-daijō-ron (摂大乗論): *Summary of the Mahayana, The*

Shōdō-mon (聖道門): Sacred Way teachings
shōgakunyo (正学女): *shikshamānā*
shōgo (正語): right speech (*See* eightfold path)
shōgō (正業): right action (*See* eightfold path)
Shōgon-kō (荘厳劫): Glorious Kalpa
shō-gyō (正行): correct practices (*See* sundry practices)
shō-gyō (正行): primary practice (See *Six-Volume Writings, The*)
shogyō-mujō (諸行無常): All things are impermanent. (*See* Dharma seal)
shōgyō-rokudo-hon (正行六度品): stage of perfecting one's practice of the six *pāramitās* (*See* five stages of practice)
shōhenchi (正遍知): Right and Universal Knowledge (*See* ten honorable titles)
shohō-jissō (諸法実相): true aspect of all phenomena
Shō-hoke-kyō (正法華経): Lotus Sutra of the Correct Law
Shōhokke-daimoku-shō (唱法華題目抄): *On Chanting the Daimoku of the Lotus Sutra*
shohō-muga (諸法無我): Nothing has an independent existence of its own. (*See* Dharma seal)
Shō-Hondō (正本堂): Grand Main Temple (*See* Soka Gakkai)
shō-i (聖位): stage of sages (*See* four good roots)
Shōi-biku (勝意比丘): Superior Intent
Shōichi (聖一)
shōja (精舎): *vihāra*
Shōjari-sennin (尚闍梨仙人): Shōjari
shoji (初地): first stage of development
shōjin (精進): *vīrya*
shōjin-haramitsu (精進波羅蜜): *pāramitā* of assiduousness (*See* six *pāramitās*)
shōji-no-kukai (生死の苦海): sea of the sufferings of birth and death
shōji-soku-nehan (生死即涅槃): sufferings of birth and death are nirvana
shōjō (小乗): lesser vehicle
shōjō (正定): right meditation (*See* eightfold path)
Shōjō-bukkyō (小乗仏教): Hinayana Buddhism
shōjō-jūhachi-bu (小乗十八部): eighteen Hinayana schools
shōjō-kai (小乗戒): Hinayana precepts (*See* Brahmā Net Sutra)
shōjō-kyō (小乗教): Hinayana teaching (*See* five teachings and ten doctrines)
shōjō-nijū-bu (小乗二十部): twenty Hinayana schools
shōjō-shiki (清浄識): pure consciousness (See *amala*-consciousness)
Shōjō-ten (少浄天): Minor Purity Heaven (*See* eighteen heavens)
shojū (初住): first stage of security
shōju (摂受)
Shōkaku-bō (正覚房)
shōken (正見): right views (*See* eightfold path)
shō-kō (小劫): small *kalpa*
Shōko (将去): *See* Universal Practice
Shōkō (聖光)
Shōkoku-ji (相国寺): *See* Five Temples
Shokō-ō (初江王): King First Creek of the River (*See* ten kings)
Shōkō-ten (少光天): Minor Light Heaven (*See* eighteen heavens)
Shōkū (証空)
Shōman-bunin (勝鬘夫人): Shrīmālā
Shōman-gyō (勝鬘経): Shrīmālā Sutra
Shōman-shishiku-kyō (勝鬘師子吼

経): Lion's Roar of Queen Shrīmālā Sutra
shōmatsu-kihon-hōrin (摂末帰本法輪): teaching that unites the branch teaching with the root teaching
Shōmoku (青目): Pingala
shōmon (声聞): voice-hearer
shōmon-jō (声聞乗): voice-hearer vehicle (*See* three vehicles)
shōmon-jōshō (声聞定性): those predestined to be voice-hearers (*See* five natures)
shōmon-kai (声聞界): world of voice-hearers
Shōmu-tennō (聖武天皇): Shōmu, Emperor
shōmyō (声明): musical recitation of sutras (*See* Ryōnin)
shōmyō (正命): right way of life (*See* eightfold path)
Shōnawashu (商那和修): Shānavāsa
shōnen (正念): right mindfulness (*See* eightfold path)
Shōnetsu-jigoku (焦熱地獄): hell of burning heat
shōnin (聖人): *muni*
shō-no-sansai (小の三災): three lesser calamities (*See* three calamities)
shō-ōjin (勝応身): superior manifested body
Shō-ōtōshi (小王統史): *Chūlavamsa* (See *Mahāvamsa*)
Shōrin-ji (少林寺): Shao-lin-ssu temple (*See* Bodhidharma)
shō-ritsugi-kai (摂律儀戒): precept that encompasses all the rules and standards (*See* three comprehensive precepts)
shōrō (鐘楼): bell tower (*See* seven-halled temple)
shō-rō-byō-shi (生老病死): birth, aging, sickness, and death (*See* four sufferings)
Shōron-shū (摂論宗): Summary of the Mahayana school
Shōryō-bu (正量部): Sammatīya school (*See* eighteen Hinayana schools)
shōryō-chi (清涼池): clear cool pond
Shōryō-kokushi (清涼国師): Teacher of the Nation Ch'ing-liang (*See* Ch'eng-kuan)
Shōryō-zan (清涼山): Ch'ing-liang, Mount
Shōryō-zan (清涼山): Clear and Cool, Mount
shō-sensekai (小千世界): minor world system (*See* major world system)
shōshi (正思): right thinking (*See* eightfold path)
Shōshi (小史): *Chūlavamsa* (See *Mahāvamsa*)
shōshin-ji (清信士): man of pure faith
shōshin-no-shari (生身の舎利): relics of the physical body (*See* Buddha's relics)
shōshin-nyo (清信女): woman of pure faith
Shōshin-shū (勝身洲): Pūrvavideha
Shōshō (清竦): Ch'ing-sung (*See* T'ien-t'ai school)
shōshōjin (正精進): right endeavor (*See* eightfold path)
shōshu (焦種): scorched seeds
shōshū-bun (正宗分): revelation section
shō-shujō-kai (摂衆生戒): precept that encompasses all living beings
Shōshuku-kō (星宿劫): Constellation Kalpa
Shōshū-shō (正修章): "Correct Practice" chapter (See *Great Concentration and Insight*)
sho-tembōrin (初転法輪): first turning of the wheel of the Law (*See* turning of the wheel of the Law)
shoten-zenjin (諸天善神): heavenly gods and benevolent deities

Shōtoku-taishi (聖徳太子): Shōtoku, Prince
Shōu-kyō (請雨経): Prayer for Rain Sutra
shōyoku-chisoku (少欲知足): little desire and contentment with a little gain
shō-zembō-kai (摂善法戒): precept that encompasses all good deeds (*See* three comprehensive precepts)
shozuiki-hon (初随喜品): initial stage of rejoicing
shu (趣): path
shū (洲): *dvīpa*
Shubaddara (須跋陀羅): Subhadra
Shubin (守敏)
Shubodai (須菩提): Subhūti
Shudaina-taishi (須大拏太子): Sudāna
shudaon (須陀洹): stream-winner
shudaon-ka (須陀洹果): stage of the stream-winner (*See* four stages of Hinayana enlightenment)
Shudara (首陀羅): Shūdra (*See* Brahman)
Shudasuma-ō (須陀須摩王): Shrutasoma
Shudatsu (須達): Sudatta
shu-dō (修道): way of practice (*See* three ways)
Shūei (宗叡)
Shūen (修円)
Shugen (衆賢): Samghabhadra
Shugendō (修験道): Shugendō school
Shugō-jigoku (衆合地獄): hell of crushing (*See* eight hot hells)
Shugo-kokkai-kyō (守護国界経): Protection of the Sovereign of the Nation Sutra
Shugo-kokkai-shō (守護国界章): *Essay on the Protection of the Nation, An*
Shugo-kyō (守護経): Protection Sutra
Shujata (須闍多): Sujātā
shūji (種子): karmic seeds (See *ālaya*-consciousness)
shūji-shiki (執持識): maintaining-consciousness
shujō-joku (衆生濁): impurity of living beings (*See* five impurities)
shujō-muhen-seigando (衆生無辺誓願度): vow to save innumerable living beings (*See* four universal vows)
shujō-seken (衆生世間): realm of living beings (*See* three realms of existence)
shu-juku-datsu (種熟脱): sowing, maturing, and harvesting
shū-ki (臭鬼): stinking spirits; stinking demons (See *pūtana*)
Shukō-jō (衆香城): City of Fragrances
shū-kongō-shin (執金剛神): *vajra*-bearing god
shukumyō-tsū (宿命通): power to know past lives (*See* six transcendental powers)
Shukuōke (宿王華): Constellation King Flower
shumana (須摩那): *sumanā*
Shumichō-butsu (須弥頂仏): Sumeru Peak (*See* sixteen princes)
Shumi-sen (須弥山): Sumeru, Mount
Shumisen-sekai (須弥山世界): Sumeru world
Shumisō-butsu (須弥相仏): Sumeru Appearance (*See* Constellation Kalpa)
Shūmitsu (宗密): Tsung-mi
Shunjō (俊芿)
shura-kai (修羅界): world of *asuras*
Shurihandoku (周利槃特): Chūdapanthaka
Shuriyasoma (須利耶蘇摩): Shūryasoma
shuroka (首盧迦): *shloka*
Shuryōgon-kyō (首楞厳経): Shūramgama Sutra

shuryōgon-zammai（首楞厳三昧）: *shūramgama* meditation
shu-shi-shin（主師親）: sovereign, teacher, and parent
shu-shi-shin-no-santoku（主師親の三徳）: three virtues of sovereign, teacher, and parent (See *Opening of the Eyes, The*)
Shushō-den（殊勝殿）: Superior Palace (*See* Correct Views)
shushō-funimon（修性不二門）: oneness of the result of practice and the true nature of life (*See* ten onenesses)
Shūsho-iki（周書異記）: *Record of Wonders in the Book of Chou, The*
shushō-yu（衆星喩）: simile of the heavenly bodies (*See* ten similes)
shusse-no-honkai（出世の本懐）: purpose of one's advent (*See* Dai-Gohonzon)
Shutsu-sanzō-kishū（出三蔵記集）: *Collection of Records concerning the Tripitaka, A*
shutsu-songyō-butsu（出尊形仏）: Buddha who has forsaken august appearances (*See* Gohonzon)
Shutsuyō-kyō（出曜経）: Sutra of Verses
Shuzen-ji（修禅寺）
Shuzen-ji（修禅寺）: Hsiu-ch'an-ssu
sōbetsu-no-nigi（総別の二義）: general and specific viewpoints
Sōbin（僧旻）: Seng-min
sō-bō（僧房）: dormitory for priests (*See* seven-halled temple)
sōdai-myō（相待妙）: comparative *myō*; relative *myō*
Sōdō（僧導）: Seng-tao (*See* Establishment of Truth school)
Sōei（僧叡）: Seng-jui
sō-fuzoku（総付嘱）: general transfer
Soga no Umako（蘇我馬子）: *See* Eben
Sōgi-ritsu-kaihon（僧祇律戒本）: *The Basic Rules of Discipline* (*See* Dharmakāla)
sōgya（僧伽）: *samgha*
Sōgyabaddara（僧伽跋陀羅）: Samghabhadra
Sōgyabatsuma（僧伽跋摩）: Samghavarman (2)
Sōgyadaiba（僧伽提婆）: Samghadeva
Sōgyamitta（僧伽蜜多）: Samghamitrā (*See* Ashoka)
Sōgyanandai（僧伽難提）: Samghanandi
sōgyari（僧伽梨）: *samghātī* (*See* three robes)
Sōgyayasha（僧伽耶舎）: Samghayashas
sōhei（僧兵）: warrior-monks (*See* Myōun)
Sōji-ji（総持寺）: *See* Sōtō school
sōji-soku（相似即）: stage of resemblance to enlightenment
sōjō（僧正）: administrator of priests
Sōjō（僧肇）: Seng-chao
sōjō-no-do（爪上の土）: specks of dirt on a fingernail
Soka Gakkai（創価学会）
Soka Kyōiku Gakkai（創価教育学会）: *See* Soka Gakkai
Sōkan-gyō（双巻経）: Two-Volumed Sutra
Sō-kōsō-den（宋高僧伝）: *Sung Dynasty Biographies of Eminent Priests, The*
sokushin-jōbutsu（即身成仏）: attaining Buddhahood in one's present form
soma（蘇摩）: *soma*
somana（蘇摩那）: *sumanā*
Sōmin（僧旻）: Seng-min
sōmoku-jōbutsu（草木成仏）: enlightenment of plants
Sondara-nanda（孫陀羅難陀）: Sundarananda
Sondari（孫陀利）: Sundarī
Sonsoku-sen（尊足山）: Gurupādaka, Mount
Sontsengampo（ソンツェンガンポ）:

Songtsen Gampo (*See* Tibetan Buddhism)
Sōnyū (僧柔): Seng-jou
Sō'ō (相応)
Sō'ō-bu (相応部): *Samyutta-nikāya*
Soraba-koku (蘇羅婆国): Shūrasena (*See* sixteen great states)
Sōrishukyō-mokuroku (綜理衆経目録): *The Comprehensive Catalog of Sutras* (*See* Tao-an)
Sōrō (僧朗): Seng-lang
Soroku-koku (疏勒国): Kashgar
Sōsan (僧璨): Seng-ts'an
Sōsen (僧詮): Seng-ch'üan
Soshitsuji-kyō (蘇悉地経): Susiddhikara Sutra
soshi-zen (祖師禅): patriarchal Zen
Sōshō (僧祥): Seng-hsiang (See *Lotus Sutra and Its Traditions, The*)
sōsō-nenjo (総相念処): general meditation (*See* four meditations)
Sōtei-ō (宋帝王): King Sung-ti (*See* ten kings)
sotoba (率塔婆)
Sōtō-shū (曹洞宗): Sōtō school
Sōtō-shū (曹洞宗): Ts'ao-tung school (*See* Zen school)
Soya Dōsō (曾谷道宗)
Soya-nyūdō (曾谷入道): Soya, the lay priest
Soya Kyōshin (曾谷教信)
Sōyū (僧祐): Seng-yu
sōzu (僧都): supervisor of priests
Sūgaku-ji (嵩岳寺): Sung-yüeh-ssu (*See* pagoda)
suijaku (垂迹): provisional identity; transient identity (*See* true Buddha)
suirin (水輪): watery circle
sui-yu (水喩): simile of water (*See* ten similes)
Sukābatībyūha (スカーヴァティーヴューハ): *Sukhāvatīvyūha*
Suriyasoma (須利耶蘇摩): Shūryasoma
susoku-kan (数息観): breath-counting meditation
Suzudannō (須頭檀王): Suzudan

tado-no-rokuzui (他土の六瑞): six auspicious happenings in other worlds (*See* six auspicious happenings)
Tahō-nyorai (多宝如来): Many Treasures
Taigen-hō (太元帥法): ceremony of Great Commander (*See* Great Commander)
Taigen-myō'ō (太元帥明王): Great Commander
taiji-shitsudan (対治悉檀): to help people abandon their illusions and free themselves from the three poisons (*See* four ways of preaching)
Taimitsu (台密): Tendai Esotericism
Tai-mō (帝網): Indra's net
Taiseki-ji (大石寺)
Taishaku (帝釈): Shakra
Taishaku-yu (帝釈喩): simile of the god Shakra (*See* ten similes)
tai-shō (胎生): birth from the womb (*See* four forms of birth)
Taisō-butsu (帝相仏): Emperor Appearance (*See* sixteen princes)
Taizan-ō (太山王): King T'ai-shan (*See* ten kings)
taizō-kai (胎蔵界): Womb Realm
Taizōkai-dainichi (胎蔵界大日): Mahāvairochana of the Womb Realm (*See* Mahāvairochana)
taizōkai-mandara (胎蔵界曼荼羅): Womb Realm mandala
tajuyūshin (他受用身): Buddha of beneficence
Takahashi Rokurō Hyōe-nyūdō (高橋六郎兵衛入道): Takahashi Rokurō Hyōe, the lay priest
takara (宝): *ratna*
Takejizai-ten (他化自在天): Freely Enjoying Things Conjured by Others

Takejizai-ten (他化自在天): Heaven of Freely Enjoying Things Conjured by Others
takoku-shimpitsu-nan (他国侵逼難): calamity of invasion from foreign lands
Takushira (タクシラ): Taxila
Tamarabatsu-sendankō-jintsū-butsu (多摩羅跋栴檀香神通仏): Tamālapattra Sandalwood Fragrance Transcendental Power (*See* sixteen princes)
Tamarabatsu-sendankō-nyorai (多摩羅跋栴檀香如来): Tamālapattra Sandalwood Fragrance
Tamon-bu (多聞部): Bahushrutīya school (*See* eighteen Hinayana schools)
tamon-daiichi (多聞第一): foremost in hearing the Buddha's teachings (*See* Ānanda)
Tamon-ten (多聞天): Hearer of Many Teachings
tandai (探題): discussion supervisor (*See* Ryūshin)
tanen-gi (多念義): doctrine of many-time recitation
Tannen (湛然): Chan-jan
Tan'ni-shō (歎異抄): *Lamenting Heresy*
Tantora-bukkyō (タントラ仏教): Tantric Buddhism
tara-ju (多羅樹): *tāla* tree
tariki (他力): power of another
Tarimu-bonchi (タリム盆地): Tarim Basin
tashin-tsū (他心通): power to know the thoughts of all other minds (*See* six transcendental powers)
Tatsunokuchi-no-hōnan (竜の口の法難): Tatsunokuchi Persecution
tazō-tōji-kengo (多造塔寺堅固): age of building temples and stupas (*See* five five-hundred-year periods)
Tembon-hoke-kyō (添品法華経): Supplemented Lotus Sutra of the Wonderful Law
tembō-rin (転法輪): turning of the wheel of the Law
temma (天魔): heavenly devil
ten (天): *deva*
ten (天): heaven
tenchū-ten (天中天): heavenly being among heavenly beings
Tendai (天台): T'ien-t'ai
Tendai Hokke-shū (天台法華宗): Tendai Lotus school
Tendai-hokkeshū-gakushō-shiki-mondō (天台法華宗学生式問答): *Questions and Answers on Regulations for Students of the Tendai Lotus School* (*See* Three Great Secret Laws)
Tendai-san (天台山): T'ien-t'ai, Mount
Tendai-sandai-bu (天台三大部): T'ien-t'ai's three major works
Tendai-sandaibu-fuchū (天台三大部補註): *Supplement to T'ien-t'ai's Three Major Works, The*
Tendai-shamon (天台沙門): priests of the Tendai school (*See* five senior priests)
Tendai-shū (天台宗): Tendai school
Tendai-shū (天台宗): T'ien-t'ai school
ten-gen (天眼): heavenly eye (*See* five types of vision)
tengen-daiichi (天眼第一): foremost in divine insight (*See* Aniruddha)
tengen-tsū (天眼通): power to see anything anywhere (*See* six transcendental powers)
Tenjiku-nijūhasso (天竺二十八祖): twenty-eight Indian patriarchs
Tenjin (天親): Vasubandhu
ten-jō (天乗): vehicle of heavenly beings (*See* five vehicles)
tenjū-kyōju (転重軽受): lessening one's karmic retribution
ten-kai (天界): world of heavenly beings

Tenkuraion-nyorai（天鼓雷音如来）: Heavenly Drum Thunder (*See* five Buddhas)
tennin-shi（天人師）: Teacher of Heavenly and Human Beings
tennin-son（天人尊）: most honored of heavenly and human beings (*See* heavenly being among heavenly beings)
tenni-tsū（天耳通）: power to hear any sound anywhere (*See* six transcendental powers)
Tennō-nyorai（天王如来）: Heavenly King
tenrin-jō'ō（転輪聖王）: *chakravartin;* wheel-turning king
Tenryū-ji（天竜寺）: *See* Five Temples
tenshi-ma（天子魔）: heavenly devil; hindrance of the devil king (*See* four devils; three obstacles and four devils)
Tenshō Daijin（天照大神）: Sun Goddess
Tensokusai（天息災）: T'ien-hsi-tsai (*See* Words of Truth Sutra)
Tenzan-sammyaku（天山山脈）: Tien Shan range (*See* Silk Road)
Tetchi-sen（鉄囲山）: Iron Encircling Mountains
tetsurin-ō（鉄輪王）: iron-wheel-turning king (*See* four wheel-turning kings)
Tisondetsen（ティソンデツェン）: Thisong Detsen (*See* Tibetan Buddhism)
Titsukudetsen（ティツクデツェン）: Thitsug Detsen (*See* Tibetan Buddhism)
tō（塔）: pagoda; stupa
tōba（塔婆）
Tōdai-ji（東大寺）
Tō-daiwajō-tōsei-den（唐大和上東征伝）: *The Life of the Great Priest of T'ang China Who Journeyed to the East* (*See* Ganjin)
Toda Jōsei（戸田城聖）: *See* Soka Gakkai
Tōfuku-ji（東福寺）
tōgaku（等覚）: near-perfect enlightenment
tō-higan（到彼岸）: reaching the other shore (*See* sea of the sufferings of birth and death)
Tō-ji（東寺）
Tōjō Kagenobu（東条景信）
tōjō-kengo（闘諍堅固）: age of quarrels and disputes
Tojun（杜順）: Tu-shun
Tōkatsu-jigoku（等活地獄）: hell of repeated rebirth for torture
Tōke-sanne-shō（当家三衣抄）: "The Three Robes of This School" (See *Six-Volume Writings, The*)
Toki Jōnin（富木常忍）
Tō-kōsō-den（唐高僧伝）: *T'ang Dynasty Biographies of Eminent Priests, The*
Tokudaisei-bosatsu（得大勢菩薩）: Gainer of Great Authority
Tokue（徳慧）: Gunamati
Tokugyō-bon（徳行品）: "Virtuous Practices" chapter (*See* Immeasurable Meanings Sutra)
Tokuitsu（徳一）
Tokukō（徳光）: Gunaprabha
Tōkurō Moritsuna（藤九郎守綱）: *See* Abutsu-bō
Tokushaka-ryūō（徳叉迦竜王）: Takshaka (*See* eight great dragon kings)
Tokushashira（徳叉尸羅）: Takshashilā
Tokushi-bu（犢子部）: Vātsīputrīya school
Tokushō-dōji（徳勝童子）: Virtue Victorious
tōmyō（灯明）: *dīpa*
ton（貪）: greed
ton-go（頓悟）: sudden enlightenment (*See* Northern school of Zen)
ton-jin-chi（貪瞋癡）: greed, anger,

and foolishness (*See* three poisons)
Tonkō（敦煌）: Tun-huang
Tonkō-bosatsu（敦煌菩薩）: Bodhisattva of Tun-huang (*See* Dharmaraksha)
ton-kyō（頓教）: sudden teaching
ton'yoku（貪欲）: greed
Tōrin-ji（東林寺）: Tung-lin-ssu temple (*See* Pai-lien-she)
Tōri-ten（忉利天）: Trāyastrimsha Heaven
Torufan（トルファン）: Turfan
Tōryū-gyōji-shō（当流行事抄）: "The Practices of This School" (See *Six-Volume Writings, The*)
Tōshi（島史）: *Dīpavamsa*
Toshi-ō（都市王）: King Imperial City (*See* ten kings)
Tōshippōke-nyorai（蹈七宝華如来）: Stepping on Seven Treasure Flowers
Tōshōdai-ji（唐招提寺）
Tōshun（東春）: *Tung-ch'un*
Tosotsu-ten（兜率天）: Tushita Heaven
tōtai-renge（当体蓮華）: lotus of the entity
tōzu（刀途）: path of swords (*See* three paths [2])
tsū-gyō（通教）: connecting teaching
Tsukahara-mondō（塚原問答）: Tsukahara Debate
Tsukimaro（月満）
Tsuonkapa（ツォンカパ）: Tsongkapa (*See* Tibetan Buddhism)

ubadaisha（優婆提舎）: *upadesha*
ubai（優婆夷）: *upāsikā*
Ubakikuta（優婆毱多）: Upagupta
Ubari（優婆離）: Upāli
ubasoku（優婆塞）: *upāsaka*
Ubuyu-sōjō-no-koto（産湯相承事）: *The Transmission on the First Cleaning Bath* (*See* Umegiku-nyo)
Uchō-ten（有頂天）: Summit of Being Heaven
Udararamashi（優陀羅羅摩子）: Uddaka Rāmaputta
Udayabadda（優陀耶跋陀）: Udāyibhadra (*See* Pātaliputra)
Uden-ō（優塡王）: Udayana
Uden'ō-kyō（優塡王経）: King Udayana Sutra (*See* Udayana)
udonge（優曇華）: udumbara
Ueno-ama（上野尼）: Ueno, the lay nun
Ueno-kenjin（上野賢人）: Ueno the Worthy (*See* Nanjō Tokimitsu)
Ugyō-daijin（雨行大臣）: Varshakāra
Uhara-jigoku（優鉢羅地獄）: Utpala hell (*See* eight cold hells)
Uhara-ryūō（優鉢羅竜王）: Utpalaka (*See* eight great dragon kings)
ui（有為）: the conditioned (*See* unconditioned, the)
Ujaenna-koku（烏闍衍那国）: Ujjayinī
ujō（有情）: sentient beings
Ujōna-koku（烏仗那国）: Udyāna
Umegiku-nyo（梅菊女）
Ummon-shū（雲門宗）: Yün-men school (*See* Zen school)
Unjizai-butsu（雲自在仏）: Cloud Freedom (*See* sixteen princes)
Unjizaiō-butsu（雲自在王仏）: Cloud Freedom King (*See* sixteen princes)
Unkō-sekkutsu（雲岡石窟）: Yün-kang caves
Unraionnō-butsu（雲雷音王仏）: Cloud Thunder Sound King
Unraion-shukuōkechi-butsu（雲雷音宿王華智仏）: Cloud Thunder Sound Constellation King Flower Wisdom
urabon（盂蘭盆）: service for deceased ancestors
Urabon-kyō（盂蘭盆経）: Service for the Deceased Sutra
uro（有漏）: presence of outflows (*See* outflows)
uro-chi（有漏智）: wisdom that retains outflows (*See* outflows)

uro-jō (有漏定): meditation accompanied by outflows (*See* outflows)
uro-shin (有漏身): body with outflows (*See* outflows)
Urubinra (優楼頻螺): Uruvilvā
Urubinra-kashō (優楼頻螺迦葉): Uruvilvā Kāshyapa
Uruka (優楼迦): Ulūka
Urumanda-sen (優留曼荼山): Urumanda, Mount
Ushi-kegi-shō (有師化儀抄): *Reverend Nichiu's Teachings on the Formalities*
usō-kyō (有相教): teaching of the reality of things (*See* three schools of the south and seven schools of the north)
Uten (于闐): Khotan
Utoku-ō (有徳王): Possessor of Virtue
Utsubusa-no-ama (内房の尼): Utsubusa, the lay nun of
Utsubusa-nyōbō (内房女房): Utsubusa, the lady of
Uttan'otsu (鬱単越): Uttarakuru
uttarasō (鬱多羅僧): *uttarāsanga* (*See* three robes)
uyo-nehan (有余涅槃): nirvana of remainder
Uzuranhotsu (鬱頭藍弗): Uddaka Rāmaputta

Washukitsu-ryūō (和修吉竜王): Vāsuki (*See* eight great dragon kings)

Yadoya Mitsunori (宿屋光則)
Yagorō (弥五郎): *See* three martyrs of Atsuhara
yaku (薬): *bhaishajya*
Yakujō-bosatsu (薬上菩薩): Medicine Superior
Yakuō-bosatsu (薬王菩薩): Medicine King
Yakuō-bosatsu-honji-hon (薬王菩薩本事品): "Former Affairs of the Bodhisattva Medicine King" chapter
Yakuō-hon (薬王品): "Medicine King" chapter
Yakushi-ji (薬師寺)
Yakushi-kyō (薬師経): Medicine Master Sutra
Yakushin (益信)
Yakushi-nyorai (薬師如来): Medicine Master
yakusō-yu (薬草喩): parable of the medicinal herbs
Yakusōyu-hon (薬草喩品): "Parable of the Medicinal Herbs" chapter
Yamashina-dera (山階寺)
Yama-ten (夜摩天): Yāma Heaven
Yarokurō (弥六郎): *See* three martyrs of Atsuhara
yasha (夜叉): *yaksha*
Yasha (耶舎): Yasa
Yasha (耶舎): Yashas
Yashudara (耶輸陀羅): Yashodharā
Yōgi-ha (楊岐派): Yang-ch'i school (*See* Zen school)
Yōkan (永観)
Yokei (余慶)
yokkai (欲界): world of desire
Yōkō (姚興): Yao Hsing (*See* Kumārajīva)
Yōraku-kyō (瓔珞経): Jeweled Necklace Sutra
yoru (預流): stream-winner
yuga (瑜伽): yoga
Yugagyō-chūgan-ha (瑜伽行中観派): Yogāchāra-Mādhyamika school (*See* Mādhyamika school)
Yugagyō-ha (瑜伽行派): Yogāchāra school
Yugashiji-ron (瑜伽師地論): *Treatise on the Stages of Yoga Practice, The*
Yugyō-kyō (遊行経): Sutra of Preaching Travels (*See* Long Āgama Sutra)
Yugyō Shōnin (遊行上人): Wandering Sage (*See* Ippen)
Yuien (唯円): See *Lamenting Heresy*

Yuiken (維蠲): Wei-chüan
Yuikyō-gyō (遺教経): Legacy Teachings Sutra
Yuimakitsu (維摩詰): Vimalakīrti
Yuima-kyō (維摩経): Vimalakīrti Sutra
Yuishiki-ha (唯識派): Consciousness-Only school
yuishiki-jūdai-ronji (唯識十大論師): ten great scholars of the Consciousness-Only school
Yuishiki-nijū-ron (唯識二十論): *Twenty-Stanza Treatise on the Consciousness-Only Doctrine, The*
Yuishiki-sanjū-ron-ju (唯識三十論頌): *Thirty-Stanza Treatise on the Consciousness-Only Doctrine, The*
yujun (由旬): *yojana*
Yujuppon (涌出品): "Emerging from the Earth" chapter
Yūshō-ō (友称王): Mitrayashas (*See* Shrīmālā)
Yuze-bosatsu (勇施菩薩): Brave Donor (*See* "Dhāranī" chapter)
Yūzū Nembutsu-shū (融通念仏宗): Interfusing Nembutsu school

zai-se (財施): offering of goods (*See* almsgiving)
zazen (坐禅): seated meditation
Zembō-dō (善法堂): Hall of the Good Law
Zemmui (善無畏): Shan-wu-wei
zen (禅): meditation
zen'aku-funi (善悪不二): oneness of good and evil
zen-chishiki (善知識): good friend
Zendō (善導): Shan-tao
Zen'e-sen'nin (善慧仙人): Good Wisdom (*See* Causality of Past and Present Sutra)
Zengen-ten (善現天): Reward Appearing Heaven (*See* eighteen heavens)
Zengi (善議)
zen-go (漸悟): gradual enlightenment (*See* Northern school of Zen)
zengon (善根): good root
zenji (禅師): meditation master
zenjin (善神): benevolent gods
zenjō (禅定): meditation
zen-haramitsu (禅波羅蜜): *pāramitā* of meditation (*See* six *pāramitās*)
zenjō-kengo (禅定堅固): age of meditation (*See* five five-hundred-year periods)
Zenkaku (善覚): Suprabuddha
Zenken-jō (善見城): Correct Views
Zenken-ten (善見天): Heaven of Clear Perception (*See* eighteen heavens)
zenki (善鬼): good spirits (*See* spirits)
Zen-kō (善劫): Good Kalpa
Zenkō-ji (善光寺)
zenkon (善根): good root
zen-kyō (漸教): gradual teaching
zen-nanshi (善男子): good man
Zennichi-maro (善日丸): *See* Nichiren
zen-nyonin (善女人): good woman
zen-shimi (前四味): first four flavors
Zenshin (善信): See *bhikshunī*
Zenshō-biku (善星比丘): Sunakshatra
Zen-shū (禅宗): Zen school
zenzai (善哉): *sādhu*
Zenzai-dōji (善財童子): Good Treasures
zenzei (善逝): Well Attained
Zenzen (鄯善): Shan-shan kingdom (*See* Lou-lan)
Zeshō-bō (是聖房): *See* Nichiren
zetsudai-myō (絶待妙): absolute *myō*
Zō-agon-gyō (雑阿含経): Miscellaneous Āgama Sutra
zōbō (像法): Middle Day of the Law
Zōbō-ketsugi-kyō (像法決疑経): Sutra on Resolving Doubts about the Middle Day of the Law

Zōchō-ten (増長天): Increase and Growth
Zōga (増賀)
zō-gyō (雑行): sundry practices
Zōichi-agon-gyō (増一阿含経): Increasing by One Āgama Sutra
Zōjō-ten (増長天): Increase and Growth
zō-kō (増劫): *kalpa* of increase
Zoku-kōsō-den (続高僧伝): *Continued Biographies of Eminent Priests, The*
Zokurui-hon (嘱累品): "Entrustment" chapter
zokushū-zōjōman (俗衆増上慢): arrogance and presumption of lay people (*See* three powerful enemies)
zokutai (俗諦): worldly truth (*See* Establishment of Truth school)
zō-kyō (蔵教): Tripitaka teaching
Zōmyō (増命)
Zōshi-bu (増支部): *Anguttara-nikāya*
zō-shiki (蔵識): storehouse consciousness
Zōtoku (蔵徳): Virtue Contained (*See* six ministers)
Zōzu-sen (象頭山): Gayāshīrsha, Mount
zuda (頭陀): *dhūta* practice
zuda-daiichi (頭陀第一): foremost in the ascetic practices (*See* Mahākāshyapa)
zuda-gyō (頭陀行): *dhūta* practice
zuhasa-shichibun (頭破作七分): Their heads will split into seven pieces. (*See* ten demon daughters)
zui-bonnō (随煩悩): derivative earthly desires (*See* earthly desires)
zuien-shinnyo-no-chi (随縁真如の智): wisdom that functions in accordance with changing circumstances (*See* Nam-myoho-renge-kyo)
zuihō-bini (随方毘尼): precept of adapting to local customs
zuijii (随自意): preaching in accordance with one's own mind
zuiki-hon (随喜品): stage of rejoicing on hearing the Lotus Sutra (*See* five stages of practice)
Zuiki-hon (随喜品): "Responding with Joy" chapter
Zuiki-kudoku-hon (随喜功徳品): "Benefits of Responding with Joy" chapter
zuitai (随他意): preaching in accordance with the minds of others
Zui-tendai-chisha-daishi-betsuden (隋天台智者大師別伝): *The Biography of the Great Teacher T'ien-t'ai Chih-che of the Sui Dynasty* (*See* Chang-an)